AMERICAN
DECADES
1990-1999

AMERICAN DECADES
1990 - 1999

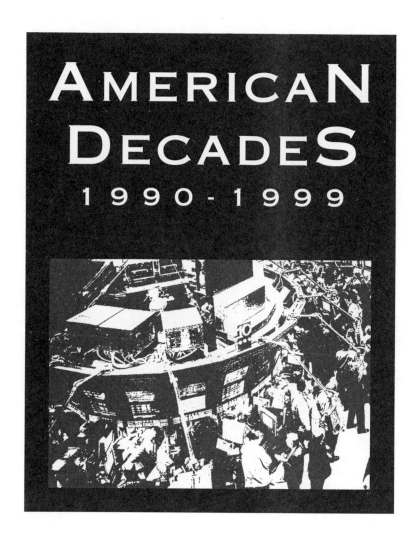

EDITED BY

TANDY McCONNELL

REF E 169.12 .A419 1994 v.10

American decades

A MANLY, INC. BOOK

GALE GROUP

Detroit
New York
San Francisco
London
Boston
Woodbridge, CT

AMERICAN DECADES
1990-1999

Matthew J. Bruccoli and Richard Layman, *Editorial Directors*

Library of Congress Catalog Card Number 93-040732

ISBN 0-7876-4030-1

Printed in the United States of America

10 9 8 7 6 5 4 3

CONTENTS

INTRODUCTION

The Short Century. The decade of the 1990s ended with a party. As the clock struck midnight on 31 December 1999 people around the world welcomed a new millennium that only the dreariest of pedants noted would not really begin for another twelve months. That issue was beside the point. The millennial celebration might have been manufactured and ill-timed, but it was fun. However, did it really mark the end of an era? Only rarely have the pivotal events of human history happened when the years end in zeros. For that reason, historians of the modern world look to the French Revolution in 1789 to mark the end of the ancien régime, the beginning of the nineteenth century, and the start of the modern world. Similarly, the outbreak of World War I in 1914 serves to close the chronological brackets on the nineteenth century. There are good reasons for this demarcation. The optimism that had marked America's colonial and westward expansion and industrial development suffered a rude shock in the trenches of the Great War. Also, though the United States emerged from the war relatively unscathed, American poets, preachers, and philosophers were no longer confident in the triumph of their civilization. Yet, neither was there any possibility of turning back from America's new status as a global power in the century that lie ahead. In war, commerce, culture, and virtually every sphere of human endeavor, the decades after 1914 made up America's century. However, if the nineteenth century was long, America's century started late and ended unexpectedly. The Berlin Wall, symbol of the Cold War, fell in November 1989; a year earlier, no one could have predicted such an event. The Soviet Union abandoned one-party rule in 1990 and ceased to exist the next year. The United States entered the 1990s as the world's only remaining superpower. At the same time, digital technology was transforming the way people communicated, did business, even the way they thought. New technologies, especially the manipulation of the genetic code, promised to cure and prevent genetic malfunctions from cancer to birth defects. Meanwhile, old diseases such as tuberculosis, thought defeated in the age of antibiotics, as well as newly emerging diseases such as the hantavirus, threatened to reverse the twentieth century's revolution in health care. The relative affluence of the United States and much of the West—unimaginable a century earlier—contributed inadvertently to the strains on the global ecosystem in the form of global warming, acid rain, and a rapid depletion of the planet's biodiversity. Overall the 1990s began as a decade full of promises that were not fulfilled when it ended.

End of the Cold War. Though the dissolution of the Soviet Union was greeted enthusiastically in America, it was a mixed blessing. Though President George Bush was able to use the new post–Cold War global dynamic to build a temporary coalition that defeated Iraq in the 1990 Gulf War, his "new world order" proved to be exceedingly disorderly. In the former communist state of Yugoslavia, national and religious rivalries that had been suppressed under communism re-emerged with a level of carnage not seen in Europe since World War II. Similar conflicts in Africa and elsewhere, and America's frustration in coping effectively with them, suggested that though the United States had in some ways "won" the Cold War, it had by no means won the peace. In the Caribbean, Fidel Castro continued to thumb his nose at American foreign policy as he had done for forty years. In Iraq, Saddam Hussein, though defeated militarily, still clung defiantly to power. The blunt tools of the Cold War era proved valueless in dealing with local and regional conflicts. The fear grew that though the end of the Cold War made global thermonuclear war with Russia less likely, the risk of a regional nuclear war involving India, Pakistan, Israel, North Korea, or some other well-armed power increased dramatically.

Brave New World. *Time* justified its choice of Albert Einstein as "Person of the Century" with a quotation from Einstein himself, "Politics is for the moment. An equation is for eternity." However, the technological innovations that bore fruit in the 1990s, such as the Internet, the proliferation of personal computers, and genetic engineering, were all the products of long, painstaking work on the part of thousands of scientists and engineers who measured progress in the smallest of increments and who built on ground broken decades earlier. The changes were, nonetheless, momentous. At the beginning of the Gulf War, reporters for the Cable News Network (CNN) reported live from Baghdad. That reporters could cover the action live already seemed to be taken for granted, but never before had virtually instant coverage of developing events become so crucial and even so expected. Also, though the Internet had existed for decades as a way for computers to communicate with each other, the development of the World Wide Web and easy to use operating systems and programs as well as substantially cheaper, faster, and more powerful computers, gave millions of Americans a way to send e-mail, download music, and buy books "on-line." The purpose and function of computers had changed: no longer were they used just to compute, but to communicate, advertise, and sell things. People could stay in touch more readily—e-mail seemed less intrusive than a phone call, and neither as formal nor as much trouble as writing a letter—but in so doing, they became increasingly isolated from their real neighbors. Computers became more powerful, not just in what they enabled people to do, but in the ways their use shaped human behavior and made people dependent on them. The Y2K Bug demonstrated the power and the vulnerability of a digital society. The programming glitch that threatened to crash computers worldwide as their internal clocks turned from "99" to "00" caused doomsday scenarios to seem realistic and even sober people bought electric generators and stored away a few weeks of groceries just in case the electrical and commercial infrastructures failed at the stroke of midnight.

Communications Revolution. Computers started to displace typewriters in American offices during the 1980s. By 1999, the once-familiar clickety-clack of typing had been silenced, replaced by the plastic sounds of computer keyboards. E-mail replaced pen-and-paper correspondence. Cellular phones and pagers intruded into restaurants, trains, and other public venues. Technology stocks skyrocketed in value, dominating the financial news. Because the World Wide Web had no central structure and few rules, people could promote any cause and sell any product on it as long as they found an audience. Hate groups could target young people with seductive messages of racial pride, but so too could the government, churches, community organizations, and schools use the medium to promote their concerns and keep in touch with people. It also offered extraordinary opportunities for entrepreneurs with an idea and a modicum of funding. America Online, Netscape, Amazon.com, and others offered services no one had imagined a need for in the 1980s. They grew exponentially to keep up with demand. The rapid and unforeseen expansion of the technology and Internet sector, reflected in the Nasdaq stock index, made millionaires out of thousands of small investors in start-up companies that had brought little more to the table than an idea, a business plan, and a commitment to hard work. Among the most successful, Amazon.com, sold books over the Internet. Turning a profit from the first month of its existence, eBay.com simply provided an electronic infrastructure for customers to bid on each other's possessions. For a while in the late 1990s, investors ignored such traditional indications of stock worth as earnings—or even potential earnings—and poured millions of dollars into dot com companies. The market corrections of early 2000 shook out some of these companies, but in the last half of the 1990s, the American economy had entered a new era whose rules had not yet been discovered and in which everything seemed possible. Yet, in spite of the glamour of the new economy, Americans worked harder and longer to stay ahead. Industrial workers found themselves competing with laborers in Asia and Latin America whose standards of living and low pay made them inviting to American manufacturers. Other employers, desiring "flexibility" in the workforce and needing to lower expenses to maintain earnings, depended increasingly on part-time and temporary workers who received no health care or retirement benefits. At the same time, cost-cutting executives received large salary packages. Many workers unprepared for the high-tech work environment worried about their future.

Moderation and Extremism. For most Americans, the decade of the 1990s was a time of plentiful employment opportunities. In his 1992 presidential campaign, Bill Clinton hammered again and again on the Bush administration's seeming lack of interest in domestic issues. His campaign staff members repeatedly proclaimed "It's the economy stupid!" as they marketed the Baby Boomer governor from Arkansas to voters accustomed to presidents who had been born in the Depression. Clinton won the elections of 1992 because he was a master of television campaigning. His two-term presidency succeeded because the economy prospered, inflation stayed in check, and virtually anyone who wanted a job could find one. He defined himself as a New Democrat, which meant that on occasion his fiscal and trade policies had more in common with Republicans than New Dealers. Such moderation played well in the 1990s. In spite of several manifest political and personal blunders, voters approved of the job he was doing. Strident voices on the right, such as that of perennial presidential candidate Pat Buchannan, complained that the administration was selling out the country while advocates of traditionally Democratic agendas, such as labor and the environment, feared that their values were being ignored in the rush to the center. Real extremists, from anarchists to neofascists, were largely ignored by the majority unless they turned, like the Unabomber, to violence as a means of communication.

Focus for Discontent. Schools have long served American communities as a locus of community identity. High-school and college sports teams provided something around which people could rally. Learning was pretty much taken for granted, as was inequality. Even after the integration of most schools in America, there were rich school districts and poor ones. Some teachers were effective; some were not. By the 1990s, schools were being expected to do more and more, providing social and psychiatric services for communities and families while preparing young people for successful, productive lives in a rapidly changing economy. Education was a high-stakes, competitive game in which the losers faced a lifetime of low-paying and low-status jobs. Thus, it mattered that the Constitutional demand for "equal protection" came to be applied to schools where the opportunities were anything but equal. Not only were well-heeled private schools able to offer the children of well-to-do parents a superior education, but also public schools in suburban districts benefitted from a strong tax base and voters willing to put tax money into school facilities and teacher salaries. Students at inner city and rural schools made do with fewer resources. Some succeeded in spite of the uneven playing field, but many more did not. The problem was addressed in the 1990s, but was far from solved. Some parents took the education of their children into their own hands through home schooling, often for religious reasons, but sometimes because they felt they could do a better job than the public schools. In addition, as schools reflected the violence of the broader community, parents worried about their children's safety in the classroom. In brief, school became politicized more than at any time in the history of public education. Taxpayers and parents demanded results, but there were no quick fixes to be had. President Clinton's goal of making the Internet available in every classroom largely missed the point. The Internet served as a vast, randomly organized library, as a place to chat and look for ideas, but was it an educational tool? Millions of dollars were spent rather uncritically on computers for classrooms that might have been better spent on books or painting or dance classes.

Superstars and Consumers. Sports, music, and movies in the 1990s were dominated by superstars. It was easier to market stars than teams, and big-time sports, more than ever before, were packaged to sell. The difference between the rock concert and the playoff game was a matter of content, not organization. Often enough, the lines between sports and other amusements blurred into a homogenized entertainment package that catered to spectators who watched on TV and to advertisers who watched the spectators. The advertisements aired during the Super Bowl were regularly more interesting than the plays. However, though sports were increasingly commodified, they never quite lost their purity. Records were made and broken as women and men pushed themselves to the limits of muscle and mind, and the unexpected happened just often enough to make watching interesting. Among the millions of people who still played sports for fun, a gradual transition seemed to be taking place. Americans still went bowling, but not often in leagues. They ran, they swam laps, they played raquetball with a friend, but teams and leagues, except among the young, foundered in the growing fragmentation of American culture. Even in religion Americans reflected their pervasive individualism. From New Age Spirituality to mainstream churches, Americans turned to religion more often to "meet their spiritual needs" than out of a sense that worship and service was something they ought to do. Traditional Protestant—and some Catholic and Jewish—congregations became increasingly entertainment oriented. Worship became more lively and less tied to traditional ways of doing things, but the ease with which Americans moved from denomination to denomination—

looking for comfort, not theological resonance—suggested that few bothered themselves much with the theological content of their purported belief. Moreover, the emphasis on family values often served effectively to exclude gays and lesbians and others who were not part of traditional family structures.

Style. If the 1980s was the decade to dress for success, the 1990s was a time for going casually to work and scruffily just about everywhere else. It all started—like so much else in the decade—with the computer and Internet industry where the highly skilled and creative designers, programmers, and engineers at Microsoft, Apple, and Adobe as well as hundreds of start-up companies had never bothered to learn to wear a tie. When IBM, the traditional domain of the starched white shirt and striped tie started to follow the trend in casual attire, it was only a matter of time before "white-collar" workers around the country started wearing golf shirts to work. Traditionalists grumbled about the loss of dignity, and a great many company men and women kept on their business suits, but in fundamental ways, the meaning of what one wore had changed dramatically. The stiff and starchy business suit, whether worn by women or men, had for decades denoted the power and status of the wearer. Business executives, doctors, and bankers wore suits. Salespeople did too, but mostly so that they could fit in with and look like the executives. Golf shirts were normally worn at the golf course. However, in the technological revolutions of the 1990s, engineers and programmers, not white-collar workers, dominated the economy, and their value was in what they knew how to do, not in the aura of respectability they exuded. Thus, the most highly valued workers in America started showing up for work wearing pretty much what they pleased. Women who in the 1980s might have worn dark-colored "power suits" with heavily padded shoulders, could dress in feminine pinks, or even blue jeans and hiking boots. Male or female, the higher their status, the less their employers cared what they wore. Yet Americans, especially the young, always cared about such things. In high school fashions pushed toward extremes the Baby Boomer parents of the so-called Generation X could not have imagined in their own youth. Early in the decade, when the Seattle "grunge" band Nirvana exploded onto the nation's musical scene, white youth gleefully embraced the band's thrift-store look. The ever-obliging American fashion industry moved quickly to supply over-the-counter fashions, including stack-heel combat boots and other paraphernalia of alienation. The "Goth" look, with white face makeup and black trench coats, was made infamous—and thus attractive—by its association with the 1999 school shooting at Columbine High School in Colorado. Black youth responded more readily to the "hip-hop" look of rap musicians, wearing hooded sweatshirts, expensive sneakers, and ballooning pants hung so low around the hips that the designer-underwear label showed. Even the most utilitarian things people used, from toothbrushes to automobiles, came to be expressions of individualism.

Law and Justice. For Americans whose exposure to the courtroom had been largely limited to episodes of *L.A. Law* and *Ally McBeal*, the real-life courtroom dramas of the 1990s were both revelatory and disturbing. The trial of O. J. Simpson, played out live for over a year ended with most whites in America persuaded of his guilt and most blacks believing in his innocence. The only opinions that mattered, those of the jury, found him not guilty, but Americans of every race believed that, had the former football star and actor not been able to match the legal talent and financial resources of the Los Angeles prosecutor's office, his conviction would have been a foregone conclusion. Almost equally disturbing was evidence, presented by the defense, of misconduct, incompetence, and racist attitudes on the part of police officers charged with investigating the murders of Ron Goldman and Nicole Brown Simpson. That situation, combined with the memory of the videotaped police beating of black motorist Rodney King and the subsequent failure of a jury to convict the officers involved, left millions of black Americans feeling that equal justice was still a distant dream. Indeed, the emphasis on law and order of the 1980s and 1990s had its drawbacks. State and federal prosecutors succeeded in convicting and imprisoning record numbers of criminals during the 1980s. Perhaps because people convicted of violent crimes or serious drug offences could count on serving long prison sentences—often automatically extended to life on the third felony conviction—the violent crime rate fell during the 1990s as prison populations skyrocketed. Yet, the criminals that most concerned Americans seemed disturbingly immune to threats of prosecution and punishment. When a young woman named Susan Smith strapped her two young sons into their car seats and sent the car rolling into a South Carolina lake, she initially reported that a black man had taken her car and children and tearfully appeared on national television to beg for their safe return. When she confessed to the crime, most people just felt sick at heart. Likewise, the rash of school shootings, culminating in 1999 at Columbine High School in Littleton, Colorado, left law enforcement and school officials scrambling to make children and parents feel safer by installing metal detectors and monitoring behavior, but no one knew how to predict or prevent such random violence. For only the second time in American history, a president of the United States was impeached by the House of Representatives and tried by the Senate. President Bill Clinton stood accused of lying to a grand jury and using his position to obstruct justice. Few people doubted that he had done precisely that, but a majority of Americans refused to accept the Republican contention that his actions constituted "high crimes and misdemeanors." Americans seemed to have become tired of scandal mongers, and Clinton agreed. Clinton was acquited and the Independent Prosecution Law, enacted in the wake of the Watergate Scandal (1972), was allowed to lapse. Clinton continued in office, acquitted, if not entirely vindicated in the eyes of the American people.

Uncertainty. At the end of the century, Americans were better connected, wealthier, and more diverse than ever before. Yet, it was neither the prosperity nor the technology that made the 1990s remarkable. Americans sensed that they were entering into a new era in world history, radically different from even the recent past. The "greatest generation" that had weathered the Depression and fought World War II was entering into its twilight years. The oldest members of the postwar Baby Boomer generation were nearing retirement. The future for their children seemed to harbor the brightest of possibilities, but in a rapidly evolving world, no one felt particularly secure. Retirees feared that the younger generation would not remember or respect the sacrifices they had made. Young people feared that the Baby Boomers would bankrupt Social Security. Black people struggled for economic parity, and whites feared that parity would come at their expense. Even the decade's most pervasive innovations, the Internet and the World Wide Web, were fraught with uncertainty. The pervasive image of the Internet, as an infinitely expandable and evermore complex web of interconnected points, was threatening in a world where personal responsibility, the concomitant of power and freedom, was not a widely cherished value. Diversity, the mantra of both major political parties and the password of the Internet, demanded of many Americans a degree of tolerance they were not prepared to grant. Like Prospero, the rightful duke of Milan in William Shakespeare's *The Tempest,* America in the 1990s wielded enormous power but, confronted with new and dangerous opportunities, was as yet unsure what to do with it.

—Tandy McConnell,
Columbia College,
Columbia, South Carolina

ACKNOWLEDGMENTS

This book was produced by Manly, Inc. Karen L. Rood is senior editor and Anthony J. Scotti Jr. is series editor. James F. Tidd Jr. was the in-house editor.

Production manager is Philip B. Dematteis.

Administrative support was provided by Ann M. Cheschi, Dawnca T. Williams, and Mary A. Womble.

Accountant is Kathy Weston. Accounting assistant is Amber L. Coker.

Copyediting supervisor is Phyllis A. Avant. The copyediting staff includes Brenda Carol Blanton, Allen E. Friend Jr., Melissa D. Hinton, William Tobias Mathes, Jennifer S. Reid, Nancy E. Smith, and Elizabeth Jo Ann Sumner. Freelance copyeditor is Rebecca Mayo.

Editorial associates are Michael S. Allen and Michael S. Martin.

Layout and graphics supervisor is Janet E. Hill. The graphics staff includes Karla Corley Brown and Zoe R. Cook.

Office manager is Kathy Lawler Merlette.

Permissions editor is Jeff Miller.

Photography editors are Charles Mims, Scott Nemzek, and Paul Talbot.

Digital photographic copy work was performed by Joseph M. Bruccoli.

SGML supervisor is Cory McNair. The SGML staff includes Frank Graham, Linda Dalton Mullinax, Jason Paddock, and Alex Snead.

Systems manager is Marie L. Parker.

Typesetting supervisor is Kathleen M. Flanagan. The typesetting staff includes Mark J. McEwan, Patricia Flanagan Salisbury, and Alison Smith. Freelance typesetters are Wanda Adams and Vicki Grivetti.

Walter W. Ross did library research. He was assisted by Steven Gross and the following librarians at the Thomas Cooper Library of the University of South Carolina: circulation department head Tucker Taylor; reference department head Virginia W. Weathers; Brette Barclay, Marilee Birchfield, Paul Cammarata, Gary Geer, Michael Macan, Tom Marcil, Rose Marshall, and Sharon Verba; interlibrary loan department head John Brunswick; and Robert Arndt, Hayden Battle, Barry Bull, Jo Cottingham, Marna Hostetler, Marieum McClary, Erika Peake, and Nelson Rivera, interlibrary loan staff.

Dr. McConnell also would like to thank Amy Sellers and Catherine Harm, students at Columbia College, who served as editorial assistants, tracking down obscure but vital facts and keeping things in reasonable order. The following people contributed entries for the Arts chapter: Jason Paddock of Manly (Music: Hip-Hop Trends), Burt Pardue of Columbia (Music: Jazz), and Dr. James Patterson of the USC Theater Department (Theater). In the Law and Justice chapter, Peter Mayes of Columbia wrote the Headline Maker on O. J. Simpson. The reference librarians at the J. Drake Edens Library of Columbia College, Amy Fordham, Sandy Leach, and Jane Tuttle answered many questions and found information in the most unlikely places. In addition, the Department of History and Political Science at Columbia College offered the editor the time and encouragement to bring this project to fruition. Dr. McConnell dedicates this book to all his students.

AMERICAN DECADES

1990 - 1999

WORLD EVENTS: SELECTED OCCURRENCES OUTSIDE THE UNITED STATES

1990

- The world population is 5.3 billion.
- *The Cambridge Social History of Britain 1750–1950,* edited by F. M. L. Thompson, is published.
- Antonia Susan Byatt's novel *Possession* is published.
- Ian McEwan's novel *The Innocent* is published.
- Damian Hirst sculpts *My Way.*
- Brian Ferneyhough composes String Quartet No. 4.
- Xavier Koller's film *Journey of Hope* premieres.
- Alexander Solzhenitsyn receives the Russia State Literature Prize for *The Gulag Archipelago* (1974–1978).
- Canadian scientists discover fossils of the oldest known multicellular animals, dating from six hundred million years ago.
- Pope John Paul II consecrates the largest cathedral in the world in Yamoussoukro, Ivory Coast.

1 Jan.	Vaclav Havel, playwright and former dissident and prisoner of conscience, is sworn in as president of Czechoslovakia. After Slovakia secedes from the union, he remains president of the Czech Republic.
3 Jan.	Panamanian president Manuel Noriega surrenders to American authorities and is extradited to the United States to face charges of drug smuggling.
24 Jan.	Japan launches the first probe sent to the Moon since 1976. In March the probe places a small satellite in lunar orbit.
2 Feb.	President F. W. de Klerk of South Africa ends the thirty-year ban on the African National Congress (ANC).
7 Feb.	The Central Committee of the Communist Party in the Soviet Union votes to end the Party's monopoly on political power.
11 Feb.	Nelson Mandela is released after serving twenty-seven years in prison in South Africa.
21 Feb.	The Republic of Namibia becomes an independent, sovereign state.
25 Feb.	A U.S.-backed coalition under Violeta Chamorro wins the elections in Nicaragua, defeating Daniel Ortega's Sandinista government.
26 Feb.	The Soviet Union agrees to a phased withdrawal of its troops from Czechoslovakia, to be completed in sixteen months.
11 Mar.	Lithuania declares its independence from the Union of Soviet Socialist Republics (U.S.S.R.).

11 Mar.	Soviet troops begin to withdraw from Hungary.
15 Mar.	Mikhail Gorbachev is sworn in as the first executive president of the U.S.S.R.
24 Mar.	In the Australian general elections, the ruling Labour Party is returned to office for a fourth time.
31 Mar.	After the police disperse an antipoll tax demonstration in Trafalgar Square, London, riots and looting occur in the West End.
1 Apr.	One thousand inmates riot in Strangeways Prison, Manchester, Britain. Later in the month, specially trained police officers storm the facilities.
1 Apr.	Robert Mugabe wins the presidential elections in Zimbabwe.
13 Apr.	The Soviet government admits responsibility and expresses regret for the 1940 massacre of Polish army officers in the Katyn Forest near Moscow.
1 May	Protesters jeer Mikhail Gorbachev at the May Day parade in Red Square, Moscow.
3 May	The North Atlantic Treaty Organization (NATO) agrees to grant full membership to Germany after its reunification.
4 May	Latvia declares itself an independent, sovereign state; Estonia follows suit four days later.
15 May	As a result of concern over "mad-cow disease" (bovine spongiform encephalopathy, or BSE), schools and hospitals in the United Kingdom ban home-produced beef.
20 May	In the first free elections in Romania since 1937, the National Salvation Front wins a majority of the votes, and Ion Iliescu is elected president.
22 May	North and South Yemen merge to form the Yemen Republic.
29 May	Boris Yeltsin is elected president of the Russian Federation.
12 June	The Russian Federation declares itself a sovereign state.
12 June	The fundamentalist Islamic Salvation Front wins a majority of votes in the Algerian local elections.
20 June	Uzbekistan declares itself an independent, sovereign state.
22 June	The Canadian provinces of Manitoba and Newfoundland refuse to ratify the Meech Lake Accord recognizing Quebec as a "distinct society."
1 July	East Germany agrees to cede sovereignty over economic, monetary, and social polity to the West German government.
8 July	Indian military forces seize control of Kashmir following separatist violence.
12 July	Boris Yeltsin and other reformers in the U.S.S.R. renounce their Communist Party membership.
16 July	The Ukrainian Parliament votes for sovereignty.
Aug.	Iraqi forces invade Kuwait and the Emir flees to Saudi Arabia.
6 Aug.	The United Nations (U.N.) Security Council imposes sanctions (including an oil embargo) against Iraq.
7 Aug.	President George Bush begins to send American troops to Saudi Arabia to prevent an Iraqi invasion.
9 Aug.	Iraq officially announces the annexation of Kuwait.
31 Aug.	East and West Germany sign a reunification treaty.

12 Sept.	The Soviet Union agrees to set 1994 as the date of withdrawal of its troops from East Germany.
2 Oct.	The German Democratic Republic ceases to exist at midnight, and East and West Germany unite as the Federal Republic of Germany.
27 Oct.	The Labour Party of New Zealand loses the elections to the National Party led by James Bolgar.
27 Oct.	The European Community (EC) Summit opens in Rome to discuss economic and monetary union by 1994. With the exception of Britain, all the members agree to achieve a single currency by the year 2000.
28 Oct.	Elections in Georgia, U.S.S.R., result in a victory for non-Communist parties, which call for independence and a market economy.
7 Nov.	Mary Robinson becomes the first woman president of the Republic of Ireland.
20 Nov.	Prime Minister Margaret Thatcher fails to secure the margin needed to win reelection as leader of the British Conservative Party.
25 Nov.	Lebanese and Syrian troops assume policing responsibilities from Christian militiamen in East Beirut.
26 Nov.	After thirty-one years as prime minister of Singapore, Lee Kuan Yew resigns.
27 Nov.	John Major wins enough ballots to become leader of the British Conservative Party; the next day Thatcher resigns and Major becomes prime minister.
9 Dec.	In the Polish presidential election, Lech Walesa achieves a landslide victory.
9 Dec.	Slobodan Milošović of the Serbian Socialist Party is elected president of Serbia in the first free elections in fifty years.
16 Dec.	Father Jean-Bertrand Aristide wins the first presidential election in Haiti.
23 Dec.	More than 90 percent of the voters in Slovenia endorse independence from Yugoslavia.

1991

- Architects Robert Venturi and Denise Scott Brown complete their work on the Sainsbury Wing, National Gallery, London.
- Michael Dummett's *The Logical Basis of Metaphysics* is published.
- Angela Carter's novel *Wise Children* is published.
- Ben Okri's novel *The Famished Road* is published.
- Jung Chang's novel *Wild Swans* is published.
- Harrison Birtwistle's opera *Sir Gawain and the Green Knight* premieres.
- Alan Bennett's play *The Madness of George III* premieres.
- Krzysztof Kieślowski's film *The Double Life of Veronique* premieres.
- Gabriele Salvatores' film *Mediterraneo* premieres.
- Researchers announce the discovery of a gene responsible for mental retardation.
- The preserved remains of a man from approximately 3,300 B.C.E. is discovered in the Italian Alps.

16 Jan.	A U.S.-led coalition begins an air offensive (Operation Desert Storm) to liberate Kuwait from Iraqi occupation.
18 Jan.	Iraq launches Scud missiles at targets in Israel.
24 Feb.	Coalition troops in the Persian Gulf launch a ground offensive against Iraqi forces; three days later Kuwait City is liberated.
1 Mar.	Popular revolts begin in Basra and other Shi'ite cities of Iraq; most are crushed by government troops before the end of the month.
14 Mar.	The "Birmingham Six" are released after a British appeals court finds their 1974 conviction for the Irish Republican Army (IRA) pub bombings to be "unsatisfactory."
27 Mar.	The United States begins to withdraw its medium-range missiles from Europe.
31 Mar.	The military structure of the Warsaw Pact is dissolved.
9 Apr.	The Georgian parliament votes to assert independence from the Soviet Union.
30 Apr.	Kurdish refugees in Iraq begin to move into Western-protected havens.
15 May	Edith Cresson becomes the first woman prime minister of France.
18 May	Chemist Helen Sharman is the first Briton to go into space, as a participant in a Soviet space mission.
21 May	A Tamil extremist assassinates former Indian prime minister Rajiv Gandhi.
31 May	President Dos Santos and Jonas Savimbi, leader of União Nacional para a Independência Total de Angola (UNITA), sign a peace agreement in Lisbon, Portugal, ending the Angolan civil war.
June	The Land Acts, Group Areas Act, and 1950 Population Registration Act are rescinded, thus destroying the legal framework for apartheid in South Africa.
25 June	The republics of Croatia and Slovenia declare their independence from Yugoslavia.
July	The discovery of massive fraud and involvement in organized crime, arms dealing, and the drug trade leads to the collapse of the Bank of Credit and Commerce International.
1 July	The Warsaw Pact is formally dissolved.
31 July	President George Bush and President Mikhail Gorbachev sign the Strategic Arms Reduction Treaty (START) to reduce arsenals of long-range nuclear weapons by one-third.
8 Aug.	The British journalist John McCarthy is released after 1,943 days of captivity in Lebanon.
19 Aug.	Gennady Yanayev leads Communist hardliners in a coup against President Gorbachev, who is placed under house arrest in the Crimea. Military rule is imposed in many U.S.S.R. cities.
20 Aug.	Estonia declares its independence from the Soviet Union, followed by Latvia the next day.
21 Aug.	The coup in the U.S.S.R. collapses following widespread resistance led by Boris Yeltsin.
24 Aug.	Mikhail Gorbachev resigns as First Secretary of the Communist Party of the Soviet Union (CPSU). Five days later the Parliament suspends the Communist Party and seizes its assets.
27 Aug.	Serbian forces take the Croatian city of Vukovar after an eighty-six-day siege.

30 Aug.	Azerbaijan declares its independence from the Soviet Union.
6 Sept.	The Soviet Union officially recognizes the independence of Latvia, Lithuania, and Estonia.
8 Sept.	Macedonia votes to declare independence from Yugoslavia.
22 Sept.	Armenia declares its independence from the Soviet Union.
25 Sept.	The eleven-year civil war in El Salvador ends with the signing of a peace accord.
19 Oct.	Albanian legislators declare Kosovo independent from Yugoslavia.
24 Nov.	The Green Party and Flemish extremists make considerable gains in the Belgian elections.
5 Dec.	The business empire of Robert Maxwell collapses with huge debts and rumors of misappropriated pension funds.
8 Dec.	The leaders of Russia, Belarus, and the Ukraine agree to form the Common-wealth of Independent States (CIS); eight of the nine other republics join on 21 December.
9-10 Dec.	At a summit in Maastricht, Holland, European Community leaders agree on a closer economic and political union (the Maastricht Treaty or the Treaty on European Union).
20 Dec.	Ante Markovic resigns as the prime minister of Yugoslavia.
25 Dec.	Mikhail Gorbachev resigns as president of the Soviet Union, and the U.S.S.R. officially ceases to exist.

1992

- J. K. Galbraith's *The Culture of Contentment* is published.
- The first volume of *The Letters of Samuel Johnson*, edited by Bruce Redford, is published.
- Michael Ondaatje's novel *The English Patient* is published.
- Ana Teresa Torres' novel *Dona Ines vs. Oblivion* is published.
- Damian Hirst sculpts *The Physical Impossibility of Death in the Mind of Some-one Living.*
- Regis Wargnier's film *Indochine* premieres.
- Fernando Trueba's film *Belle Epoque* premieres.
- The Lloyds insurance market in London announces losses of £2 billion.
- Despite a ruling by a court of appeals, ten Australian women are ordained to the Anglican priesthood.

1 Jan.	Boutros Boutros-Ghali becomes U.N. Secretary-General.
15 Jan.	The EC recognizes Croatia and Slovenia as independent republics.
6 Feb.	Barbara Mills becomes the first woman Director of Public Prosecutions in England and Wales.
13 Feb.	The Swedish government announces an end to its policy of neutrality.
1 Mar.	Although Bosnian Serbs boycott the proceedings, a referendum in Bos-nia-Herzegovina decides in favor of becoming an independent, sovereign state.
2 Mar.	Militant Serbs, Croats, and Muslims clash in Sarajevo.

5 Mar.	The Council of Baltic Sea States is established to foster economic development and strengthen links with the EC.
19 Mar.	Buckingham Palace announces the separation of the Duke and Duchess of York, who were married in 1986.
6 Apr.	The Lombard League, the Greens, and the anti-Mafia La Rete Party win substantial victories in the Italian general elections.
7 Apr.	The EC officially recognizes the independence of Bosnia-Herzegovina.
8 Apr.	Serb and federal (Yugoslav) army forces begin to bombard Sarajevo.
9 Apr.	A British general election returns the Conservatives for a fourth term.
27 Apr.	Betty Boothroyd is elected the first woman speaker of the British House of Commons.
2 June	A Danish referendum votes against ratifying the Maastricht Treaty signed by EC leaders the previous December.
3-14 June	Delegates from 178 countries attend the U.N.-sponsored Conference on Environment and Development in Rio de Janeiro, Brazil.
18 June	The Republic of Ireland endorses the Maastricht Treaty.
3 Aug.	The ANC begins a massive protest campaign in South Africa.
13 Aug.	The U.N. condemns the Serbs' "ethnic cleansing" (forced removal) program.
22-26 Aug.	In Rostock, Germany, antiforeigner riots occur at a reception center for refugees.
16 Sept.	British Chancellor of the Exchequer, Norman Lamont, increases the base rate of the pound to forestall speculative selling on the stock market.
20 Sept.	The French people vote narrowly in favor of the Maastricht Treaty.
12 Oct.	Demonstrations occur in many Latin American countries in protest of the five-hundredth anniversary of Christopher Columbus's discovery of America.
13 Oct.	Despite a huge public outcry, the British government announces that coal production will cease at thirty-one of the country's fifty coal mines.
26 Oct.	Canadians, in a referendum, reject the Charlottetown agreement which would grant concessions to French-speaking Quebec.
31 Oct.	The Vatican formally rehabilitates the astronomer and physicist Galileo Galilei, who was condemned by the Inquisition in 1633 for advocating heliocentricity.
11 Nov.	The Church of England General Synod approves women's being ordained to the priesthood.
16 Nov.	The Goldstone Commission in South Africa exposes a state-operated campaign to discredit the ANC.
6 Dec.	Hindu extremists destroy the sixteenth-century mosque at Ayodhya, and 1,200 Indians are killed in the resulting violence.
9 Dec.	Operation Restore Hope begins with the arrival of U.S. troops in Mogadishu, Somalia, to supervise the delivery of international food aid.
16 Dec.	The Czech National Council adopts a constitution that will come into effect on 1 January 1993.
29 Dec.	Brazilian President Fernando Collor de Mello resigns one day before he is found guilty of corruption and official misconduct; he is banned from public office for eight years.

1993

- Margaret Thatcher's *The Downing Street Years* is published.
- Sculptor Rachel Whiteread receives the Turner Prize for *House*, the plaster cast of the inside of a house in the East End of London.
- Isabel Allende's novel *The Infinite Plain* is published.
- Roddy Doyle's novel *Paddy Clarke Ha Ha Ha* is published.
- Dacia Maraini's novel *The Silent Duchess* is published.
- Harold Pinter's play *Moonlight* premieres.
- British mathematician Andrew Wiles solves "Fermat's Last Theorem," a mathematical problem first posed by the Frenchman Pierre de Fermat in the seventeenth century.
- Russian authorities announce that they possess the Schliemann Gold, objects found by Heinrich Schliemann at the ancient city of Troy in 1873 and which disappeared from Berlin at the end of World War II.
- Samples of deoxyribonucleic acid (DNA) from the Duke of Edinburgh and other relatives of the Romanov royal family prove that recently discovered remains are indeed those of Czar Nicholas II and his family, who were executed by the Bolsheviks in 1918.

1 Jan.	The single market of the EC comes into force.
1 Jan.	The Czech and Slovak republics become separate sovereign countries.
10 Feb.	A corruption scandal rocks the Italian government and leads to a series of resignations.
11 Feb.	Both Queen Elizabeth II of Britain and the Prince of Wales volunteer to pay income tax and capital gains tax on their private incomes.
22 Feb.	The U.N. Security Council creates a tribunal relating to war crimes in the former Yugoslavia; it is the first such tribunal since the Nuremberg trials of 1945–1946.
25 Feb.	In Cuba the first direct elections to the national assembly occur, with an official turnout of 99.6 percent.
12 Mar.	In an emergency session, the Russian Congress votes to restrict the powers of Boris Yeltsin and rejects his proposed constitutional amendments.
12 Mar.	North Korea withdraws from the Treaty on Nuclear Non-Proliferation of Nuclear Weapons.
16 Mar.	The British government imposes a value-added tax on domestic fuel.
27 Mar.	Jiang Zemin becomes state president of China.
29 Mar.	Edouard Balladur becomes the prime minister of France, and the Socialist Party loses many seats in the national legislature.
4 May	The Scott inquiry begins to examine the involvement of the British government in the export of arms to Iraq.
6 May	The U.N. Security Council declares "safe areas" in Sarajevo, Tuzla, Zepa, Goradze, Bihac, and Srebrenica in Bosnia-Herzegovina.
18 May	Denmark approves the Maastricht Treaty.
29 May	A Neo-Nazi arson attack in Solingen, Germany, results in the death of five Turkish women.
30 May	Bosnian Serb forces attack Goradze and Srebrenica.

13 June	Kim Campbell of the Progressive Conservative Party becomes the first woman prime minister of Canada.
23 June	International sanctions are imposed on Haiti.
18 July	The Liberal Democrats, in power since 1955, lose the Japanese general elections.
22 July	In Britain the House of Commons votes to reject the Maastricht Treaty; the next day it is approved by a vote of confidence proposed by Prime Minister John Major.
2 Aug.	The European Exchange Rate Mechanism collapses, and currencies are allowed to fluctuate within 15 percent of the central rates.
6 Aug.	Buckingham Palace in London is opened to the general public.
13 Sept.	Yassir Arafat of the Palestine Liberation Organization (PLO) and Yitzhak Rabin of Israel sign a peace accord in Washington, D.C. Under the agreement, the Israelis pledge to withdraw from the Gaza Strip and Jericho.
21 Sept.	Boris Yeltsin suspends the Russian parliament and calls for elections, but the Supreme Soviet ignores his order and swears in Alexandr Rutskoi as president.
27 Sept.	Troops seal off the White House in Moscow, the seat of the Russian parliament.
3 Oct.	U.S. Special Forces, on a mission to capture two Habr Gidr clan leaders, followers of the warlord Mohamed Farrah Aidid, are ambushed in Mogadishu, Somalia. Eighteen American soldiers are killed and dozens more wounded. Somali losses amount to approximately five hundred dead and one thousand wounded.
4 Oct.	The rebels holding out in the Moscow parliament building surrender; a state of emergency remains in effect until 18 October.
5 Oct.	The Papal encyclical *Veritatis splendor* (The Splendour of Truth), affirming Catholic moral teachings, is published.
25 Oct.	In the Canadian general elections, the Liberal Party wins a decisive victory. Ten days later Jean Chrétien is sworn in as prime minister.
1 Nov.	The Maastricht Treaty comes into force, and the European Community becomes the European Union (EU).
12 Dec.	Liberal Democrats, led by nationalist Vladimir Zhirinovsky, win a large share of seats in the Russian legislature. Meanwhile, voters approve Yeltsin's constitution.
18 Nov.	South Africa adopts a new constitution allowing majority rule.
14 Dec.	The British prime minister issues the guidelines for peace talks on Northern Ireland.
15 Dec.	John Major and Albert Reynolds, the prime ministers of Britain and the Republic of Ireland, respectively, make the Downing Street Declaration, stating the basis for a peace agreement in Northern Ireland.
15 Dec.	In Geneva, Switzerland, 117 nations sign the General Agreement on Tariffs and Trade (GATT) Final Act.

1994

* The world population is 5.5 billion.
* V. S. Naipaul's novel *A Way in the World* is published.
* Barbara Trapido's novel *Juggling* is published.
* Peter Maxwell Davies composes Symphony No. 5.

- Nikita Mikhalkov's film *Burnt by the Sun* premieres.

- The cleaning of Michelangelo's paintings in the Sistine Chapel in the Vatican is completed.

1 Jan.	The Zapatista National Liberation Army leads a revolt in the state of Chiapas, Mexico.
1 Jan.	The North American Free Trade Agreement (NAFTA) between the United States, Mexico, and Canada comes into effect.
1 Jan.	The European Economic Area is established in preparation for economic and monetary union in Europe.
30 Jan.	Peter Leko becomes the youngest grand master in the history of chess.
31 Jan.	Gerry Adams, president of Sinn Féin, the political wing of the IRA, is granted a visa to visit the United States.
18 Mar.	Bosnia-Herzegovina and Croatia sign an accord to create a federation of Bosnian Muslims and Croats.
12 Mar.	The first women priests in the Church of England are ordained at Bristol Cathedral.
24 Mar.	The factions in Somalia sign a peace agreement, and U.S. troops withdraw the next day.
26-27 Mar.	The Freedom Alliance wins parliamentary elections in Italy.
Apr.	The presidents of Rwanda and Burundi are killed in an airplane crash; a massive wave of rioting occurs and hundreds are killed in the Rwandan capital of Kigali.
26-29 Apr.	The ANC wins an overwhelming victory in the first nonracial general election in South African history.
6 May	The Channel Tunnel between Britain and France is officially opened.
10 May	Nelson Mandela is sworn in as president of South Africa.
12 May	John Smith, the leader of the British Labour Party, dies; he is replaced by Tony Blair on 21 July.
13 May	The Palestinian National Authority assumes control of the Jericho area of the occupied West Bank after Israeli military forces withdraw. Five days later Israeli troops withdraw from the Gaza Strip.
27 May	The writer Alexander Solzhenitsyn returns to Russia after twenty years in exile.
1 June	South Africa rejoins the British Commonwealth.
5 June	Former U.S. president Jimmy Carter visits North Korea to help diffuse a crisis over nuclear inspections.
1 July	Yassir Arafat, chairman of the PLO, enters Gaza for the first time in twenty-five years; on the 5th he visits Jericho.
2 July	Colombian soccer player Andrés Escobar is killed in Medellin. Escobar had inadvertently scored a goal against his own team in the game that eliminated Colombia from the World Cup.
8 July	Kim Il Sung, leader of North Korea, dies at the age of eighty-two.
9 July	The Chinese government announces that the legislative council in Hong Kong will be terminated once China resumes control of the city in 1997.
12 July	The high court in Germany approves the use of German armed forces outside the NATO area in collective security operations.

15 July	Jacques Santer, prime minister of Luxembourg, is chosen as president of the European Commission of the EU.
16-22 July	Fragments of the comet Shoemaker-Levy 9 collide with the planet Jupiter.
18 July	The Rwandan Patriotic Front claims a victory in the Rwandan civil war and Pasteur Bizimungu assumes the presidency. Later in the month over two million Rwandans are reported to have fled the country. International relief efforts airlift foodstuffs and medical supplies to the refugee camps on the borders.
25 July	In a ceremony in Washington, D.C., King Hussein of Jordan and Yitzhak Rabin, prime minister of Israel, sign a joint declaration formally ending the conflict between their countries.
31 July	The U.N. Security Council authorizes "all necessary means" to remove the military regime in Haiti.
1 Aug.	A U.N. commission is established to investigate human rights violations in Rwanda.
14 Aug.	The infamous terrorist "Carlos the Jackal" is apprehended in Khartoum, Sudan.
31 Aug.	The IRA announces a complete cessation of violence in Northern Ireland.
19 Sept.	American troops invade Haiti; seven days later the U.S. government lifts the sanctions imposed on the island country.
28 Sept.	An estimated nine hundred people die when the car ferry *Estonia* sinks in the Baltic Sea off Finland.
30 Sept.	After landing at Shannon airport, Russian president Boris Yeltsin refuses to leave his plane and meet with the Irish prime minister.
15 Oct.	President Aristide returns to Haiti after a three-year exile.
22 Nov.	An investigation begins after Italian prime minister Silvio Berlusconi is accused of bribery. He resigns one month later.
25-26 Nov.	Opposition forces launch an unsuccessful attack on the Chechen capital of Grozny.
28 Nov.	Norway rejects EU membership.
11 Dec.	Russian troops invade the breakaway republic of Chechnya.
15 Dec.	John Bruton of Fine Gael forms a new coalition and becomes prime minister of the Republic of Ireland.
17 Dec.	The presidents of Argentina, Brazil, Paraguay, and Uruguay sign a pact creating the Southern Common Market (Mercosur), the second-largest customs union in the world.
31 Dec.	Russian troops attack Grozny.

1995

- Salman Rushdie's novel *The Moor's Last Sigh* is published.
- Umberto Eco's novel *The Island of the Day Before* is published.
- *The Stories of Vladimir Nabokov* is published.
- David Hare's play *Racing Demon* premieres.
- Marleen Gorris's film *Antonia's Line* premieres.

1 Jan.	Sweden, Finland, and Austria join the EU, bringing its total membership to fifteen.

1 Jan.	The World Trade Organization (WTO), the successor to GATT, comes into existence with eighty-one member countries.
11 Jan.	Pope John Paul II begins an eleven-day tour of Asia and Australia. An estimated four million people attend his open-air mass in Manila on the 15th.
15 Jan.	In Northern Ireland troops end daytime patrols in Belfast in response to the ceasefire.
17 Jan.	In Kobe, Japan, more than five thousand people are killed in an earthquake.
19 Jan.	Russian troops take the presidential palace in Grozny.
31 Jan.	Severe flooding affects large areas of northern Europe, and in the Netherlands alone two hundred thousand people evacuate their homes.
26 Feb.	The oldest merchant bank in Britain, Baring's, collapses following £600 million in losses.
28 Feb.	U.S. and Italian marines begin to evacuate 1,500 U.N. troops from Somalia after warring factions refuse to abide to a ceasefire.
10 Mar.	Kostas Stephanopoulos is sworn in as president of Greece.
19 Mar.	The Social Democratic Party wins in the Finnish general elections.
20 Mar.	Terrorists release the nerve gas sarin in a Tokyo subway, killing twelve and injuring five thousand.
27 Mar.	South African president Nelson Mandela dismisses his estranged wife, Winnie, from government service.
28 Mar.	The U.N. World Climate Conference opens in Berlin with delegates from more than 130 nations in attendance.
4 Apr.	Approximately four hundred Hutu women and children are reported dead following a massacre by Burundi soldiers and Tutsi gunmen.
16 Apr.	Spain and Canada resolve their dispute over fishing rights off the coast of Newfoundland.
22 Apr.	The Tutsi-led Rwanda Patriotic Army kills two thousand Hutu refugees at a camp in southern Rwanda.
1 May	A four-month ceasefire sponsored by the U.N. ends in Bosnia-Herzegovina, and heavy fighting occurs in Croatia.
10 May	In Zaire, health officials report that an outbreak of the deadly Ebola virus has claimed many lives.
15 May	Aum Shinrikyo cult leader Shoko Asahara is arrested in connection with the March gas attack in Tokyo.
16 May	Serb artillery begins to bombard Sarajevo again after a year's respite.
19 May	The government coalition in Thailand, led by Chuan Leekpai, resigns over a land reform scandal.
21 May	Jean-Luc Dehaene retains control of the Belgian government following the general elections.
25 May	NATO warplanes bomb Bosnian Serb targets after the Serbs refuse to relinquish control of their heavy weapons to peacekeeping forces. The next day the Bosnian Serbs seize U.N. soldiers as hostages.
30-31 May	In the first royal visit since 1911, the Prince of Wales tours the Republic of Ireland.

2 June	The Bosnian Serbs start to release their U.N. hostages; by the 18th, all have been freed.
15 June	An earthquake in Egion, Greece, kills at least twenty-two people and leaves thousands homeless.
19 June	Chechen gunmen release Russian hostages, in anticipation of resuming negotiations with Moscow to end the six-month conflict in Chechnya.
26 June	In Addis Ababa, Ethiopia, President Hosni Mubarak of Egypt narrowly escapes an assassination attempt.
29 June	Approximately five hundred people die when a department store collapses in Seoul, South Korea.
9 July	French naval commandos storm *Rainbow Warrior II,* flagship of the environmental group Greenpeace, near Mururoa Atoll in the South Pacific, where France planned nuclear testing.
11 July	The Bosnian Serbs overrun the U.N. safe area of Srebrenica.
25 July	The U.N. safe area of Zepa falls to the Bosnian Serbs. Meanwhile, a war crimes tribunal at The Hague indicts Bosnian Serb leader Radovan Karadžić and General Ratko Mladić for crimes against humanity.
26 July	The U.S. Senate votes to lift the arms embargo against Bosnia.
3 Aug.	In an effort to end the twelve-year civil war in Sri Lanka, sweeping constitutional changes are announced, giving the Tamils regional self-rule.
Aug.	Croat troops expel rebellious Serbs from the Croatian enclave of Krajina.
10 Aug.	The U.N. Security Council receives a special report detailing the massacre of 2,700 Bosnian Muslim men and boys, following the fall of Srebrenica in July.
15 Aug.	On the fiftieth anniversary of the end of World War II, the Japanese prime minister offers a "heartfelt apology" for the suffering that his country caused.
24 Aug.	In China, U.S. human rights activist Harry Wu is sentenced to fifteen years in jail for spying but is deported, instead, to the United States.
30 Aug.	NATO planes and U.N. artillery begin to bomb Serb military positions in retaliation for attacks on Sarajevo.
1 Sept.	Warring factions in Liberia sign a peace agreement to end the six-year civil war.
4 Sept.	More than five thousand delegates attend the fourth U.N. World Conference on Women in Beijing.
5 Sept.	Amid widespread international protest, France carries out an underground nuclear test at Mururoa Atoll.
28 Sept.	Israeli prime minister Yitzhak Rabin and PLO chairman Yāsir Arafat sign an accord in Washington, D.C., transferring control of much of the West Bank to Palestinian control.
12 Oct.	A sixty-day ceasefire takes effect in Bosnia.
21 Oct.	In New York, leaders of more than 140 countries gather to celebrate the fiftieth anniversary of the U.N.
25 Oct.	Israeli troops commence an evacuation from the West Bank towns, to be completed in six months. This event marks the beginning of the end of nearly thirty years of Israeli military rule.
30 Oct.	In a Quebec referendum, voters narrowly reject independence from Canada.

4 Nov.	A Jewish extremist assassinates Israeli prime minister Yitzhak Rabin at a peace rally in Tel Aviv.
5 Nov.	In a landslide victory, Eduard Shevardnadze is returned as president of the former Soviet republic of Georgia.
19 Nov.	Socialist Aleksander Kwasniewski wins the Polish presidential election.
21 Nov.	In Dayton, Ohio, warring parties sign an agreement to end the four-year-old conflict in Bosnia-Herzegovina. A NATO ground force will be deployed to implement the agreement.
24 Nov.	French public workers begin a series of strikes to protest the government's planned welfare reforms. The three weeks of unrest are the worst disruption to transport and public services in France since 1968.
2 Dec.	Nick Leeson is imprisoned in Singapore for six years after pleading guilty to fraud charges relating to the collapse of Baring's Bank in February.
14 Dec.	At a ceremony in Paris the presidents of Bosnia, Serbia, and Croatia formally sign a peace accord, ending a conflict which had claimed an estimated two hundred thousand lives and left three million homeless.
15-16 Dec.	At an EU summit in Madrid, European leaders agree to name the proposed single currency the "euro."
20 Dec.	In Bosnia sixty thousand NATO peacekeeping troops begin Operation Joint Endeavor.
20 Dec.	Thousands are reported dead after two months of fighting around Kabul, Afghanistan, as radical Islamic Taleban militia seek to overthrow the government.

1996

- *After Rain,* a collection of stories by William Trevor, is published.
- Patrick O'Brian's novel *The Yellow Admiral* is published.
- Mario Vargas Llosa's novel *Death in the Andes* is published.
- Kobo Abe's novel *Kangaroo Notebook* is published.
- Jan Sverak's film *Kolya* premieres.

15 Jan.	Russian troops storm the village of Pervomaiskoye, where Chechen rebels had held more than one hundred hostages for a week.
16 Jan.	Captain Julius Maado Bio stages a military coup and seizes control of the government in Sierra Leone.
21 Jan.	PLO chairman Yassir Arafat is elected the first president of Palestine in history.
29 Jan.	The two-hundred-year-old La Fenice opera house in Venice is destroyed by fire.
31 Jan.	Tamil Tiger terrorists detonate a truck bomb in central Colombo, Sri Lanka, killing 55 and wounding 1,500.
7 Feb.	One hundred and eighty-nine people die when a Boeing 757 crashes off the coast of the Dominican Republic.
9 Feb.	An IRA bomb kills two in London, signaling an end to the seventeen-month ceasefire.
24 Feb.	Cuba shoots down two unarmed Cessna planes flown by Cuban-Americans, with the loss of four lives. The U.S. government protests this act as a blatant violation of international law.

25 Feb.	Two suicide bombers of Hamas, an Islamic extremist movement, kill twenty-five Israelis in Jerusalem and Ashkelon. Thirty-four more die in further attacks on 3 and 4 March.
8 Mar.	China test fires three M9 ballistic missiles into the sea off Taiwan, and the U.S. responds by sending two aircraft carriers into the area.
25 Mar.	The EU imposes a worldwide ban on exports of British beef out of concern over possible transmission to humans of BSE in the form of Creutzfeldt-Jakob disease.
31 Mar.	President Yeltsin announces a ceasefire and partial withdrawal of Russian troops from Chechnya.
2 Apr.	Britain proposes the slaughter of 4.6 million cattle in an attempt to end the spread of BSE.
6 Apr.	Government troops in Liberia launch an assault on rebel leader General Roosevelt Johnson's compound.
11 Apr.	In their first attack on the city in fourteen years, Israeli gunships fire rockets into the southern suburbs of Beirut in retaliation for Hizbullah attacks on northern Israel.
21 May	Six hundred people die when an overloaded Tanzanian ferry sinks on Lake Victoria.
29 May	The right-wing Likud Party wins the general elections in Israel, and Binyamin Netanyahu becomes prime minister on 18 June.
4 June	The *Ariane 5,* an European Space Agency rocket, explodes on liftoff in French Guiana.
9 June	King Bhumibol of Thailand, the longest-serving monarch in the world, celebrates his fifty years on the throne by granting amnesty to 26,000 prisoners.
15 June	An IRA bomb, one of the largest devices ever exploded in Britain, injures about 220 people in Manchester.
18 June	President Yeltsin of Russia dismisses Defense Minister General Pavel Grachev and other hardliners.
21-23 June	The Arab League meets to discuss the election of a right-wing government in Israel.
25 June	Nineteen U.S. servicemen are killed in a terrorist bombing near Dhahran, Saudi Arabia. The previously unknown Islamic group Hizbullah-Gulf claims responsibility.
10 July	One thousand British troops are sent to Northern Ireland in response to renewed violence.
19 July	Bosnian Serb leader Radovan Karadžić, indicted for war crimes, resigns as president of the Bosnian Serb Republic and head of the ruling Serb Democratic Party.
20 July	Hutu rebels kill three hundred Tutsis in Burundi.
4 July	A bomb explodes on a crowded commuter train in Colombo, Sri Lanka; 70 people are killed and 450 injured.
25 July	In a military coup in Burundi, Tutsi opposition leader Pierre Buyoya is installed as head of state.
25 July	Israeli prime minister Netanyahu offers to withdraw troops from southern Lebanon if Syria promises to disarm Hizbullah.

21 Aug.	Former president F. W. de Klerk publicly apologizes for the suffering caused by five decades of apartheid in South Africa.
26 Aug.	In South Korea, former President Chun Doo Hwan is sentenced to death and former President Roh Tae Woo receives twenty-two years in jail for their roles in the 1979 military coup; their sentences are later reduced.
28 Aug.	In the United Kingdom, a high court grants a divorce to the Prince and Princess of Wales, ending their fifteen-year marriage.
29 Aug.	Russian government officials and Chechen rebel leaders sign a peace treaty, thus ending the nearly two years of fighting which resulted in ninety thousand deaths. A decision on the sovereignty of Chechnya is delayed until 2001.
4 Sept.	Israeli prime minister Benjamin Netanyahu and PLO leader Yāsir Arafat hold peace talks for the first time in the Gaza Strip.
5 Sept.	Turkish war planes attack suspected rebel Turkish Kurd bases in northern Iraq.
26 Sept.	Israel declares a state of emergency after the worst fighting in thirty years occurs in the West Bank and Gaza Strip.
27 Sept.	Rebel Taleban militia overrun Kabul, depose the government, and impose strict Islamic law in Afghanistan.
17 Oct.	President Boris Yeltsin of Russia dismisses security chief Aleksandr Lebed amid allegations that he was plotting a revolt.
23 Oct.	Hutu refugees begin to flee from Zaire to escape the escalating fighting between the army and Tutsi tribesmen.
11 Nov.	Near Delhi, India, a Saudi Arabian Boeing 747 and Kazakh Airways Ilyushin-76 collide in midair, and 350 people are killed.
18-29 Nov.	French truck drivers blockade roads across France until the government accedes to their demands for higher wages and shorter hours.
28 Nov.	General Ratko Mladić, indicted by a war crimes tribunal, resigns as commander of the Bosnian Serb Army.
11 Dec.	The shipping tycoon Tung Chee-hwa is named to be the chief executive of Hong Kong after China reclaims the city from Britain in 1997.
13 Dec.	Delegates at the EU summit in Dublin revise the Maastricht Treaty; new banknotes of euro currency in denominations of five, ten, twenty, fifty, one hundred, two hundred, and five hundred euros are unveiled.
17 Dec.	President Mobutu Sese Seko, who had been receiving cancer treatment in Europe, returns to Zaire in order to quell the insurgency.
17 Dec.	Leftist guerrillas of the Tupac Amarú Revolutionary Movement, demanding the release of their jailed comrades, seize nearly five hundred guests at the Japanese embassy in Lima, Peru.
26 Dec.	Five thousand riot police break up a massive antigovernment demonstration in Belgrade, Serbia.
27 Dec.	The Chinese and Russians sign bilateral agreements in Moscow, reducing military forces along the Sino-Russian border.
29 Dec.	The last Russian troops leave Chechnya.
29 Dec.	At a ceremony in Guatemala City, the Guatemalan National Revolutionary Unity (URNG) Movement and the government sign a peace agreement ending thirty-six years of civil war.

1997

- J. K. Rowling's *Harry Potter and the Philosopher's Stone* is published in Britain. It comes to the United States in 1998 as *Harry Potter and the Sorcerer's Stone.*
- Peter Ackroyd's novel *Milton in America* is published.
- Amos Oz's novel *Panther in the Basement* is published.
- Francisco Goldman's novel *The Ordinary Seaman* is published.
- *Romans-fleuves,* a book of poetry by Pierre Nepveu, is published.
- Roberto Benigni's film *La Vita e Bella* premieres.
- Scientists at the Roslin Institute in Scotland report that they have cloned a sheep named Dolly.

1 Jan.	As Israeli troops prepare to withdraw from the West Bank town of Hebron, a lone Israeli gunman injures six Arabs.
1 Jan.	Kofi Annan of Ghana becomes the seventh Secretary-General of the U.N., replacing Boutros Boutros-Ghali.
5 Jan.	More than one hundred thousand people protest against the government in Belgrade, Serbia. A larger demonstration with four hundred thousand occurs on 13 January.
15 Jan.	Israeli and Palestinian cabinets approve a new peace arrangement concerning Hebron, in which 80 percent of the West Bank town will be turned over to Palestinian control.
4 Feb.	Seventy-three Israeli servicemen are killed when two helicopters crash near the border of southern Lebanon.
5 Feb.	The Swiss government approves the establishment of bank funds to compensate Holocaust victims and their heirs.
12 Feb.	An Iranian-sponsored foundation increases the bounty for killing Salman Rushdie, author of *The Satanic Verses* (1989), to $2.5 million.
19 Feb.	Chinese leader Deng Xiaoping dies at the age of ninety-two.
2 Mar.	Albanian leaders declare a state of emergency as antigovernment protests increase.
6 Mar.	The Polish shipyard Gdansk, the birthplace of the Solidarity Movement, closes with the loss of 3,800 jobs.
11 Mar.	Russian president Boris Yeltsin dismisses most of his cabinet.
13 Mar.	A Jordanian soldier shoots and kills seven Israeli schoolgirls at the Hill of Peace in the Jordan Valley.
19 Mar.	Italy declares a state of emergency because of an influx of ten thousand Albanian refugees.
30 Mar.	Dozens are injured in riots in the West Bank following the Israeli decision to build 32,000 Jewish homes in east Jerusalem.
22 Apr.	Peruvian commandos storm the residence of the Japanese ambassador in Lima and rescue the remaining seventy-one hostages held by leftist guerrillas for the past 126 days. All the terrorists are killed in the assault.
2 May	After a landslide victory by the Labour Party on the previous day, Tony Blair is appointed the youngest prime minister in Britain since 1812 (he is only forty-three years old).
7 May	A U.S. government special report accuses Switzerland of accepting gold looted by the Nazis from occupied countries during World War II.

10 May	An earthquake in Iran, near the Afghan border, results in the death of 1,600 people.
17 May	After thirty-two years in power, President Mobutu of Zaire flees to Morocco. Rebel leader Laurent Kabila proclaims himself head of state and renames the country the Democratic Republic of Congo.
23 May	Prime Minister Tony Blair announces that Britain will accede to the EU Social Chapter.
30 May	Four hundred Westerners evacuate from Sierra Leone as fighting intensifies between rebel forces and Nigerian-backed government troops.
23-27 June	Eighty-five heads of state attend Earth Summit II at the United Nations in New York to discuss environmental issues.
30 June	At midnight the city of Hong Kong returns to Chinese sovereignty after 156 years as a British colony.
6 July	A coup topples from power Cambodian prime minister Prince Norodom Ranariddh.
8 July	NATO invites Poland, Hungary, and the Czech Republic to join the alliance in time for its fiftieth anniversary in 1999.
10 July	In Bosnia, British soldiers shoot an indicted war criminal and arrest another.
15 July	The Serbian leader Slobodan Milosević is elected unopposed as president of the Federal Republic of Yugoslavia for a four-year term.
16 July	President Jacques Santer of the EU Commission presents a plan for an expanded twenty-one-member EU to include five former communist states and Cyprus.
20 July	The IRA announces the restoration of the 1994 ceasefire broken last February.
25 July	A Khmer Rouge people's tribunal sentences guerrilla leader Pol Pot to life imprisonment for his 1970s government policies that led to the death of two million Cambodians.
5 Aug.	A Korean Air Boeing 747 crashes on the U.S. protectorate of Guam with the loss of 220 lives.
31 Aug.	Diana, Princess of Wales, dies in a car crash in Paris. An estimated two billion television viewers worldwide watch her funeral in London on 6 September.
13 Sept.	The state funeral in Calcutta of Mother Teresa (who died on 5 September) is attended by dignitaries from around the world.
25 Sept.	Briton Andy Green sets a new world land-speed record of 714 mph when he drives the jet-powered car *Thrust SSC* across the Nevada desert. On 17 October he becomes the first person to break the sound barrier on land, reaching a speed of 764.18 mph.
26 Sept.	In Italy an earthquake kills eleven people, leaves thousands homeless, and seriously damages the thirteenth-century Basilica of St. Francis.
1 Oct.	In Israel the ailing Shaikh Ahmad Yasin, founder of the Islamic resistance movement Hamas, is released from jail in order to secure the freedom of Israeli agents arrested in Jordan.
8 Oct.	Kim Jong Il, son of the late Kim Il Sung, becomes the general secretary of the ruling Workers' Party in North Korea.
9 Oct.	Four hundred Mexicans die when hurricane *Pauline* strikes the Pacific resort of Acapulco.

13 Oct.	Tony Blair meets with Sinn Féin leader Gerry Adams, becoming the first British prime minister to meet with an IRA leader in seventy-six years.
22 Oct.	President Nelson Mandela of South Africa travels to Tripoli to mediate in Libya's dispute with the U.S. and British governments over extradition of two men suspected of the 1988 Lockerbie bombing.
8 Nov.	Chinese leaders attend the completion of the damming of the River Yangtse, one of the largest hydroelectric projects in the world. The dam created a four-hundred-mile-long mile long lake and resulted in the displacement of 1.2 million people.
9 Nov.	Russian and Chinese officials sign a declaration defining their joint 2,800-mile disputed border.
24 Nov.	Yamaichi Securities collapses with losses of 3.2 billion yen, the biggest financial failure in Japan since 1945.
4 Dec.	At a U.N. conference in Ottawa, Canada, delegates from 125 nations sign an agreement banning the use, production, transfer, and stockpiling of antipersonnel landmines. The United States, China, and Russia refuse to sign the convention.
10 Dec.	At the U.N. Conference on Climate Control in Kyoto, Japan, representatives of industrial nations pledge to reduce greenhouse gas emissions by the early twenty-first century in an effort to slow global warming.
11 Dec.	In a ceremony at Portsmouth, England, the royal yacht *Britannica* is decommissioned after forty-five years of service.
22 Dec.	Paramilitary gunmen kill forty-five peasants in southern Mexico.
30 Dec.	Islamic militants massacre 412 people in the Algerian province of Relizan.

1998

- Mario Vargas Llosa's novel *The Notebooks of Don Rigoberto* is published.
- Dorit Rabinyan's novel *Persian Brides* is published.
- Ying Chen's novel *Ingratitude* is published.
- Seamus Heaney's *Opened Ground: Selected Poems 1966–1996* is published.

5 Jan.	Amnesty International reports that more than eighty thousand people had died as a result of fighting in Algeria since 1992.
25 Jan.	Tamil Tigers bomb Sri Lanka'a holiest shrine, the Temple of the Tooth in Kandy, killing eleven.
28 Jan.	Twenty-six people are sentenced to death in India for their involvement in the 1991 assassination of Rajiv Gandhi.
3 Feb.	A U.S. military aircraft accidentally cuts a wire supporting a cable car at an Italian ski resort; twenty people are killed.
4 Feb.	Four thousand people are reported killed after an earthquake strikes northern Afghanistan.
13 Feb.	In Australia a constitutional convention votes in favor of holding a referendum on ending links with the British Commonwealth.
16 Feb.	A Taiwanese A-300 Airbus crashes on approach to Taipei and 260 people are killed.
23 Feb.	U.N. Secretary-General Kofi Annan and Iraqi leaders reach an agreement to give U.N. weapons inspectors unrestricted access to all sites in Iraq.

25 Feb.	Kim Dae Jung is inaugurated as president of South Korea.
1 Mar.	In the United Kingdom, the "Countryside Alliance" arranges a march on London by 250,000 people to highlight the perceived government threat to the traditional rural way of life.
2 Mar.	Serb riot police disperse a demonstration of fifty thousand Albanians seeking autonomy in Pristina, the capital of Kosovo.
25 Mar.	The European Commission declares that eleven states would join the monetary union and that it would start to issue the euro single currency in January 1999.
1 Apr.	The Israeli security cabinet votes to withdraw troops from southern Lebanon.
2 Apr.	Former French cabinet minister Maurice Papon receives a ten-year jail sentence for his role in deporting Jews to Nazi concentration camps in World War II.
15 Apr.	Pol Pot, the former Khmer Rouge dictator of Cambodia, dies.
24 Apr.	Twenty-two men and women are publicly executed in Rwanda for their part in the 1994 massacres.
27 Apr.	Serb police and the Yugoslav army pour into the province of Kosovo to suppress the separatist Kosovo Liberation Army.
11 May	Despite Western threats of international sanctions, India conducts three underground nuclear weapons tests in the Rajasthan desert.
14 May	Israeli security forces shoot and kill eight Palestinians during attacks on isolated Jewish settlements in the Gaza Strip.
21 May	Following nationwide protests, General Suharto resigns as President of Indonesia after thirty-two years in power.
22 May	Referendums in Northern Ireland and the Republic of Ireland produce votes in favor of the multiparty peace accord signed on 10 April, the so-called Good Friday Agreement.
30 May	Three thousand people die following the second earthquake to strike remote northern Afghanistan.
12 June	World stock markets slump in response to news that Japan is officially in recession.
12 June	Queen Margrethe of Denmark opens the four-mile-long Storebaelt Bridge, linking eastern and western Denmark. It is the second-longest suspension bridge in the world.
15 June	NATO aircraft stage Operation Falcon through Albania and Macedonia as a warning to Serbia to stop its oppression of Kosovo.
16 June	The World Bank warns that Asia is on the brink of a deep recession.
16 June	After a cyclone hits northern India, 1,300 are dead and 10,000 reported missing.
2 July	The largest terminal in the world opens at the Chek Lap Kok Airport in Hong Kong.
10 July	Six hundred people are reported dead in severe flooding in the Chinese province of Sichuan.
17 July	A massive tidal wave hits the northwestern coast of Papua New Guinea, killing three thousand people.
17 July	A state funeral is held in St. Petersburg, Russia, for the internment of the remains of Czar Nicholas II, his family, and servants, who were executed by the Bolsheviks in 1918.

3 Aug.   Serbian security forces burn Albanian towns in Kosovo. An estimated 180,000 people have been displaced since the conflict started in March.

5 Aug.   The Iraqi parliament calls for an end to the oil embargo and an immediate freeze on the activities of U.N. weapons inspectors.

7 Aug.   A car bomb explodes outside the U.S. embassy in Nairobi, Kenya. At least 240 are killed and 5,000 injured. Another terrorist bomb kills 10 at the U.S. embassy in Dar es Salaam, Tanzania.

11 Aug.   In the biggest industrial merger in history, British Petroleum announces the takeover of U.S. oil company Amoco.

12 Aug.   King Hussein of Jordan, in an American hospital for cancer treatment, delegates domestic powers to his brother, Crown Prince Hasan.

13 Aug.   Swiss banks agree to pay £767 million ($1.25 billion) to victims of the Holocaust, whose assets had been plundered by the Nazis.

15 Aug.   An IRA car bomb kills twenty-eight and injures two hundred in Omagh, County Tyrone in Northern Ireland.

20 Aug.   The United States launches cruise missiles on suspected terrorist bases in Afghanistan and on a chemical weapons facility in Sudan in retaliation for the 7 August attacks on its embassies in East Africa.

24 Aug.   The British and American governments offer to hold a trial in the Netherlands for the two Libyans accused of bombing a Pan Am airplane over Lockerbie, Scotland, in 1988; however, the men must be tried under Scottish law.

4 Sept.   An U.N. International Criminal Tribunal sentences former Rwandan Prime minister Jean Kambanda to life in jail for genocide.

14 Sept.   More than fifty thousand Albanians have fled Kosovo in the past week.

24 Sept.   The British and Iranian governments come to an agreement over the safety of author Salman Rushdie, who has been under a threat of death since 1989.

18 Oct.   Former Chilean leader Augusto Pinochet is arrested at a London hospital. A Spanish judge had requested his extradition for human rights violations during his tenure in office (1973-1990).

26 Oct.   Ecuador and Peru sign a treaty ending their one-hundred-year-old border dispute.

30 Oct.   Hurricane Mitch causes flash flooding and mudslides in Central America; ten thousand people are reported dead in Honduras and Nicaragua.

15 Nov.   The United States calls off cruise missile attacks against Iraq when, at the last minute, the latter agrees to let the U.N. continue weapons inspections.

24 Nov.   The Yassir Arafat International Airport opens in the Gaza Strip.

25 Nov.   A special panel in the British House of Lords votes in favor of extraditing Ugarte Pinochet.

26 Nov.   A Tokyo court refuses to compensate former British prisoners of war for Japanese mistreatment during World War II.

28 Nov.   Israeli forces bombard Hizballuh positions in southern Lebanon following the death of seven Israeli soldiers in an ambush.

9 Dec.   Ruth Dreifuss is elected the first woman president of Switzerland.

16-20 Dec.   U.S. and British forces conduct Operation Desert Fox, a series of massive bombing raids against Iraq following that country's continued refusal to cooperate with U.N. weapons inspectors.

1999

17 Dec.	A high court in Britain rescinds the 25 November ruling enabling extradition of Pinochet because of a judge's links to Amnesty International.

- Patrick O'Brian's novel *Blue at the Mizzen* is published.
- Aleksandr Solzhenitsyn's novel *November 1916* is published.
- Pedro Almodovar's film *All About My Mother* premieres.
- One-half of the planet's population is under the age of twenty-five years, with 95 percent of the growth occurring in the Third World.
- As the year 2000 approaches, the nations of the world prepare for the potential computer problems of Y2K.

Jan.	North and South Korea hold talks on a peace settlement.
Jan.	The European Union issues the first euro.
25 Jan.	At least 1,170 people die in Colombia following an earthquake measuring 6.3 on the Richter scale.
7 Feb.	King Hussein of Jordan dies of cancer after a forty-six-year reign; he is succeeded by his son, King Abdullah.
9 Feb.	The trial of three former government ministers begins in Paris, France. The officials are charged with manslaughter for delaying HIV-testing of the national blood supply, which led to HIV infections for hundreds of people.
Mar.	Government and rebel forces clash in the northern region of Chad.
Mar.	The Czech Republic ratifies the invitation to join NATO.
Mar.	Iraq accuses the United States of spying and continues to confront Allied forces in the "no-fly zones."
Mar.	The Icelandic legislature calls for a resumption of whaling.
1 Mar.	The international treaty banning land mines goes into effect. All signers of the treaty must destroy their stockpiles of mines within four years and clear all mines on their territory within ten years.
21 Mar.	Swiss psychiatrist Bertrand Piccard and British pilot Brian Jones become the first men to successfully fly around the world in a balloon. Their balloon, *Breitling Orbiter 3,* lands in the Egyptian desert after a journey of 25,362 miles in twenty-one days.
24 Mar.	NATO begins Operation Allied Force, a massive bombing campaign against Yugoslav targets in order to protect the Albanian majority in the province of Kosovo.
Apr.	Both India and Pakistan conduct ballistic missile tests.
Apr.	Bosnian indictments are passed against Radovan Karadžić and Ratko Mladić.
1 Apr.	Canada designates a 770,000-square-mile area as the Arctic Territory, or Nunavut. The region is one-fifth the size of Canada's total land mass but has only 25,000 inhabitants, most of whom are Inuit.
17 Apr.	The first in a series of mail bombings occurs in London. Three people are killed before the perpetrator is apprehended.
May	India launches air strikes against the bases of Pakistani-backed guerrillas in Kashmir.

May	The Belgian government outlaws the Hell's Angels motorcycle gang.
May	France confirms that nuclear tests had damaged the coral beds of French Polynesia.
May	Archaeologists discover a Mayan city in a dense forest on the Yucatán Peninsula, Mexico.
8 May	China calls for an emergency session of the U.N. Security Council, following the U.S. bombing of the Chinese embassy in Belgrade.
17 May	Ehud Barak, a decorated soldier, is elected Israeli prime minister and replaces Benjamin Netanyahu, who had been accused of corruption and delaying the Middle East peace process.
28 May	The annual conference of the International Whaling Commission ends at St. George's, Grenada; the thirteen-year-old ban on commercial whaling remains in effect.
29 May	A civilian government under President Olusegun Obasanjo assumes power in Nigeria.
June	Russian officials decide to abandon the Mir space station.
June	Indian and Pakistani ground forces clash in Kashmir.
10 June	NATO suspends its air raids as Serb forces begin to withdraw from Kosovo.
20 June	Serb forces complete their withdrawal from Kosovo, and NATO announces the conclusion of Operation Allied Force.
24 June	In Brussels, Belgium, Red Cross officials state that the preceding year's natural disasters were the most devastating on record and predict that catastrophes would become more widespread as the climate changes.
29 June	Israeli lawyers announce the application process for Holocaust survivors to receive compensation from two Swiss banks.
23 July	King Hassan II of Morocco dies at the age of seventy; he is succeeded by his son, Crown Prince Sidi Mohamed.
27 July	The United States places a trade ban on Afghanistan. Meanwhile, the ruling Taliban militia launches major attacks against opposition forces loyal to ousted President Burhanuddin Rabbani.
12 Aug.	A North Korean government official states that his country reserves the right to test a new long-range missile capable of reaching U.S. territory. This announcement follows a naval confrontation with South Korean vessels in which thirty North Korean sailors were killed.
17 Aug.	Turkey is hit by its worst natural disaster in sixty years. A devastating earthquake measuring 7.4 on the Richter scale kills approximately 17,000 people.
Sept.	In a U.N.-sponsored referendum, East Timor votes to be independent from Indonesia, and violence ensues as pro-Indonesian forces protest the decision.
Sept.	Russia decides to resume whaling operations.
21 Sept.	The island of Taiwan suffers from a massive earthquake that measures 7.6 on the Richter scale. More than two thousand people die and twelve thousand buildings are destroyed.
21 Sept.	Anthropologists declare that a woman's skull found in Brazil is the oldest human fossil in the Americas. The skull, first discovered in 1975, is approximately 11,500 years old.
Oct.	Scientists in Siberia exhume an intact mammoth.

2 Oct.	For the second time in a decade, Russia launches a ground offensive against the breakaway republic of Chechnya.
4 Oct.	Palestinian and Israeli negotiators agree on opening a "safe passage" route linking the West Bank and Gaza Strip.
12 Oct.	The world population reaches six billion people.
27 Oct.	Gunmen storm the Armenian parliament, killing Prime Minister Vazgen Sarkisian and several others.
29 Oct.	A cyclone strikes the east coast of India, killing approximately 10,000 people and leaving 2.5 million homeless.
29 Oct.	An EU panel declares British beef to be safe for human consumption, rejecting the French argument to continue an exportation ban because of fears of bovine spongiform encephalopathy, better known as Creutzfeldt-Jakob, or "mad cow" disease.
Nov.	Most hereditary peers are stripped of their right to sit and vote in the House of Lords, the unelected upper chamber of the British Parliament.
Nov.	Hong Kong officials approve the construction of a Disney theme park.
17 Nov.	Scientists report that the Arctic Ocean's ice cap has shrunk more dramatically than previously believed. The cap is 4.3 feet thinner than the last time measurements were taken in 1976.
21 Nov.	China announces the launch of a space vehicle capable of carrying astronauts.
2 Dec.	Britain hands over power in Northern Ireland to a twelve-member cabinet of Protestants and Catholics.
3 Dec.	The World Trade Organization (WTO) meeting ends in Seattle, Washington, following a week of violent protests by environmentalists and anarchists.
17 Dec.	Flooding in Venezuela causes mudslides that eventually kill an estimated ten thousand people.
17 Dec.	Germany establishes a fund of $5.2 billion in order to compensate slave laborers and other victims of the Third Reich.
19 Dec.	China takes back possession of Macau after 442 years of Portuguese rule.
24 Dec.	Kashmiri separatists hijack an Indian Airlines jet.
31 Dec.	After eighty-five years of control, the United States officially relinquishes the Panama Canal to the country of Panama.
31 Dec.	Boris Yeltsin resigns and is replaced by Vladimir Putin as president of Russia.

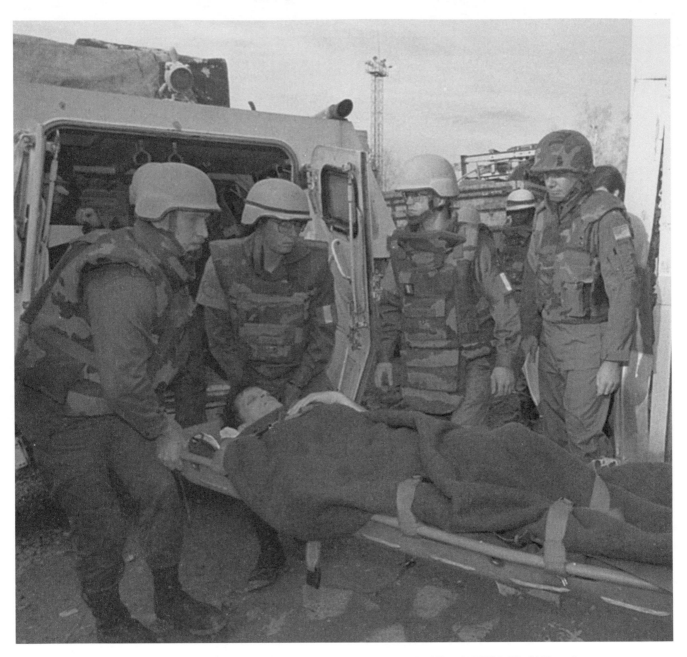

U.S. troops, under U.N. command in Bosnia, transferring wounded soldiers (AP/Wide World Photos)

CHAPTER TWO

THE ARTS

by VERONICA BRUCE MCCONNELL, ROBERT MCCONNELL,
MARK G. MALVASI, and MEG GREENE

CONTENTS

1990

Movies

Another 48 Hours, directed by Walter Hill and starring Eddie Murphy and Nick Nolte; *Awakenings,* directed by Penny Marshall and starring Robert De Niro and Robin Williams; *Bird on a Wire,* directed by John Badham and starring Mel Gibson, Goldie Hawn, and David Carradine; *Dances with Wolves,* directed by and starring Kevin Costner; *Days of Thunder,* directed by Tony Scott and starring Tom Cruise, Robert Duvall, Nicole Kidman, and Randy Quaid; *Dick Tracy,* directed by Warren Beatty and starring Beatty, Al Pacino, and Madonna; *Die Hard 2,* directed by Renny Harlin and starring Bruce Willis and Bonnie Bedelia; *Flatliners,* directed by Joel Schumacher and starring Kiefer Sutherland, Julia Roberts, and Kevin Bacon; *Ghost,* directed by Jerry Zucker and starring Patrick Swayze, Demi Moore, and Whoopi Goldberg; *The Godfather Part III,* directed by Francis Ford Coppola and starring Al Pacino, Diane Keaton, and Andy Garcia; *GoodFellas,* directed by Martin Scorsese and starring Robert De Niro, Ray Liotta, and Joe Pesci; *The Grifters,* directed by Stephen Frears and starring Anjelica Huston, John Cusack, and Annette Bening; *Henry and June,* directed by Philip Kaufman and starring Fred Ward, Uma Thurman, and Maria de Medeiros; *Home Alone,* directed by Chris Columbus and starring Macaulay Culkin, Joe Pesci, and Daniel Stern; *The Hunt for Red October,* directed by John McTiernan and starring Sean Connery, Alec Baldwin, Sam Neill, and James Earl Jones; *Presumed Innocent,* directed by Alan J. Pakula and starring Harrison Ford and Bonnie Bedelia; *Pretty Woman,* directed by Garry Marshall and starring Richard Gere and Julia Roberts; *Reversal of Fortune,* directed by Barbet Schroeder and starring Glenn Close, Jeremy Irons, and Ron Silver; *Teenage Mutant Ninja Turtles,* directed by Steve Barron and starring Michelan Sisti, Leif Tilden, and Dave Forman; *Total Recall,* directed by Paul Verhoeven and starring Arnold Schwarzenegger and Sharon Stone.

Novels

Nicholson Baker, *Room Temperature;* Frederick Barthelme, *Natural Selection;* Vance Bourjaily, *Old Soldier;* T. Coraghessan Boyle, *East is East;* Frederick Busch, *Harry and Catherine;* Tom Clancy, *Clear and Present Danger;* Patricia Cornwell, *Post Mortem;* Michael Crichton, *Jurassic Park;* Clive Cussler, *Dragon;* Ivan Doig, *Ride with Me, Mariah Montana;* Dominick Dunne, *An Inconvenient Woman;* Richard Ford, *Wildlife;* George Garrett, *Entered from the Sun;* George V. Higgins, *Victories;* Tony Hillerman, *Coyote Waits;* Alice Hoffman, *Seventh Heaven;* Charles Johnson, *Middle Passage;* Barbara Kingsolver, *Animal Dreams;* Elmore Leonard, *Get Shorty;* Robert Ludlum, *The Bourne Ultimatum;* Peter Matthiessen, *Killing Mr. Watson;* Jill McCorkle, *Ferris Beach;* Larry McMurtry, *Buffalo Girls;* Sue Miller, *Family Pictures;* Joyce Carol Oates, *Because It Is Bitter, And Because It Is My Heart;* Tim O'Brien, *The Things They Carried;* Reynolds Price, *The Tongues of Angels;* Thomas Pynchon, *Vineland;* Anne Rice, *The Witching Hour;* Philip Roth, *Deception;* Dori Sanders, *Clover;* Danielle Steel, *Message from Nam;* Scott Turow, *The Burden of Proof;* John Updike, *Rabbit at Rest;* Kurt Vonnegut, *Hocus Pocus;* Joseph Wambaugh, *The Golden Orange;* John Edgar Wideman, *Philadelphia Fire.*

Popular Songs

Wilson Phillips, "Hold On"; Roxette, "It Must Have Been Love"; Sinead O'Connor, "Nothing Compares 2 U"; Bell Biv Devoe, "Poison"; Madonna, "Vogue"; Mariah Carey, "Vision of Love"; Phil Collins, "Another Day In Paradise"; En Vogue, "Hold On"; Billy Idol, "Cradle of Love"; Jon Bon Jovi, "Blaze of Glory."

Feb.

The New York Public Library launches a major retrospective of the work of Berenice Abbott, the largest exhibit ever accorded a living photographer.

18 Mar.	The largest art theft since 1911 occurs at the Gardner Museum in Boston. Among the stolen paintings, which are valued at $200 million, are five by Edgar Degas and *Storm on the Sea of Galilee,* the only known landscape by Rembrandt. The museum is uninsured.
Sept.	President George Bush presents artist Jasper Johns a silver National Medal of Arts for helping to make the United States a "cultural giant."
27 Sept.	The Motion Picture Association of America drops its X rating and begins using an NC-17 rating for movies to which no one under seventeen can be admitted.
Oct.	President Bush awards artist Andrew Wyeth a Congressional Gold Medal, making him the first artist to receive the award.
5 Oct.	The Contemporary Arts Center in Cincinnati and its director, Dennis Barrie, are acquitted of obscenity charges stemming from exhibition of *The Perfect Moment,* a controversial group of homoerotic photographs by Robert Mapplethorpe.
Nov.	The Armand Hammer Museum of Art and Cultural Center opens in Los Angeles after Hammer, president of Occidental Petroleum, wins a stockholders' suit challenging his right to use company funds to build the museum.
14 Nov.	Pop-music group Milli Vanilli admits to lip-synching hits such as "Girl You Know It's True." Its Grammy Award for Best New Artist of 1989 is revoked.
Dec.	Congress requires that artists funded by the National Endowment for the Arts (NEA) must return grant money if their works are judged obscene.

1991

Movies	*The Addams Family,* directed by Barry Sonnenfeld and starring Anjelica Huston and Raul Julia; *Backdraft,* directed by Ron Howard and starring Kurt Russell, William Baldwin, Robert De Niro, and Donald Sutherland; *Beauty and the Beast,* animated feature, directed by Barry Trousdale and Kirk Wise; *City Slickers,* directed by Ron Underwood and starring Billy Crystal and Jack Palance; *Dying Young,* directed by Joel Schumacher and starring Julia Roberts, Colleen Dewhurst, and Ellen Burstyn; *Father of the Bride,* directed by Charles Shyer and starring Steve Martin and Diane Keaton; *Fried Green Tomatoes,* directed by Jon Avnet and starring Kathy Bates and Jessica Tandy; *Grand Canyon,* directed by Lawrence Kasdan and starring Danny Glover, Kevin Kline, and Steve Martin; *JFK,* directed by Oliver Stone and starring Kevin Costner, Sissy Spacek, Kevin Bacon, and Tommy Lee Jones; *The Naked Gun 2 ½: The Smell of Fear,* directed by David Zucker and starring Leslie Nielsen, Priscilla Presley, George Kennedy, and O. J. Simpson; *New Jack City,* directed by Mario Van Peebles and starring Wesley Snipes and Ice T; *Point Break,* directed by Kathryn Bigelow and starring Patrick Swayze and Keanu Reeves; *Robin Hood: Prince of Thieves,* directed by Kevin Reynolds and starring Kevin Costner and Morgan Freeman; *The Silence of the Lambs,* directed by Jonathan Demme and starring Jodie Foster and Anthony Hopkins; *Sleeping With the Enemy,* directed by Joseph Ruben and starring Julia Roberts; *Thelma & Louise,* directed by Ridley Scott and starring Susan Sarandon and Geena Davis; *Terminator 2: Judgment Day,* directed by James Cameron and starring Arnold Schwarzenegger; *What About Bob?,* directed by Frank Oz and starring Bill Murray and Richard Dreyfuss; *White Fang,* directed by Randal Kleiser and starring Ethan Hawke.

Novels	Julia Alvarez, *How the Garcia Girls Lost Their Accents;* Nicholson Baker, *U&I;* Russell Banks, *The Sweet Hereafter;* John Barth, *The Last Voyage of Somebody the Sailor;* Madison Smartt Bell, *Doctor Sleep;* Harold Brodkey, *Runaway Soul;* Frederick Buechner, *Telling Secrets;* Frederick Busch, *Closing Arguments;* Robert Coover, *Pinocchio in Venice;* Don DeLillo, *Mao II;* Pete Dexter, *Brotherly Love;* Stephen Dixon, *Frog;* Bret Easton Ellis, *American Psycho;* Gail Godwin, *Father Melancholy's Daughter;* John Grisham, *The Firm;* Norman Mailer, *Harlot's Ghost;* Richard Moore, *The Investigator;* Walter Mosley, *Devil in a Blue Dress;* Marge Piercy, *He, She, and It;* Philip Roth, *Patrimony: A True Story;* Norman Rush, *Mating;* Sandra Scofield, *Beyond Deserving;* Issac Bashevis Singer, *Scum;* Jane Smiley, *A Thousand Acres;* Danielle Steel, *Heartbeat;* Amy Tan, *The Kitchen God's Wife;* Anne Tyler, *Saint Maybe.*
Popular Songs	Bryan Adams, "(Everything I Do) I Do It For You"; Color Me Badd, "I Wanna Sex You Up"; C & C Music Factory, "Gonna Make You Sweat"; Paula Abdul, "Hush, Hush"; Timothy T., "One More Try"; EMF, "Unbelievable"; Extreme, "More Than Words"; Hi-Five, "I Like The Way" (The Kissing Game); Surface, "The First Time"; Amy Grant, "Baby, Baby."
11 Mar.	Walter Annenberg announces that on his death his collection of more than fifty Impressionist and Postimpressionist European paintings, watercolors, and drawings—valued at $1 billion—will be donated to the Metropolitan Museum of Art in New York City.
15 Mar.	*The West as America: Reinterpreting Images of the Frontier* opens at the National Museum of American Art in Washington, D.C. The controversial exhibit includes works that depict white violence and racism in American history, provoking questions over public funding for such shows. The show goes on to the Denver Museum in August and the St. Louis Art Museum in November.
24 Sept.	The Seattle grunge band Nirvana releases *Nevermind.* By 11 January a song from the album, "Smells Like Teen Spirit," has reached number one on the *Billboard* singles charts and has become an alternative rock anthem for "Generation X."

1992

Movies	*Aladdin,* animated feature, directed by John Musker and Ron Clements; *Basic Instinct,* directed by Paul Verhoeven and starring Michael Douglas and Sharon Stone; *Batman Returns,* directed by Tim Burton and starring Michael Keaton, Danny DeVito, and Michelle Pfeiffer; *The Bodyguard,* directed by Mick Jackson and starring Kevin Costner and Whitney Houston; *Bram Stoker's Dracula,* directed by Francis Ford Coppola and starring Garry Oldman, Winona Ryder, Anthony Hopkins, and Keanu Reeves; *The Crying Game,* directed by Neil Jordan and starring Stephen Rea, Miranda Richardson, and Forrest Whittaker; *Death Becomes Her,* directed by Robert Zemeckis and starring Meryl Streep, Bruce Willis, Goldie Hawn, and Isabella Rossellini; *Far and Away,* directed by Ron Howard and starring Tom Cruise and Nicole Kidman; *A Few Good Men,* directed by Rob Reiner and starring Kevin Bacon, Kiefer Sutherland, Jack Nicholson, Tom Cruise, and Demi Moore; *Glengarry Glen Ross,* directed by James Foley and starring Al Pacino, Jack Lemmon, Kevin Spacey, Alec Baldwin, Alan Arkin, and Ed Harris; *The Hand that Rocks the Cradle,* directed by Curtis Hanson and starring Annabella Sciorra and Rebecca De Mornay; *Home Alone 2: Lost in New York,* directed by Chris Columbus and starring Macaulay Culkin, Joe Pesci, and Daniel Stern; *Honeymoon in Vegas,* directed by Andrew Bergman and starring James Caan, Nicolas Cage, Sarah Jessica Parker, and Pat Morita; *Housesitter,* directed by Frank Oz and starring Steve Martin and Goldie Hawn; *Howards End,*

directed by James Ivory and starring Anthony Hopkins, Emma Thompson, Vanessa Redgrave, and Helena Bonham Carter; *The Last of the Mohicans,* directed by Michael Mann and starring Daniel Day-Lewis and Madeleine Stowe; *A League of Their Own,* directed by Penny Marshall and starring Tom Hanks, Madonna, Geena Davis, and Rosie O'Donnell; *Lethal Weapon 3,* directed by Richard Donner and starring Mel Gibson, Danny Glover, Joe Pesci and Rene Russo; *Malcolm X,* directed by Spike Lee and starring Denzel Washington and Angela Bassett; *My Cousin Vinny,* directed by Jonathan Lynn and starring Joe Pesci and Marisa Tomei; *Passenger 57,* directed by Kevin Hooks and starring Wesley Snipes; *Patriot Games,* directed by Phillip Noyce and starring Harrison Ford and Anne Archer; *The Player,* directed by Robert Altman and starring Tim Robbins and Whoopi Goldberg; *A River Runs Through It,* directed by Robert Redford and starring Brad Pitt, Craig Sheffer, and Tom Skerritt; *Scent of a Woman,* directed by Martin Brest and starring Al Pacino and Chris O'Donnell; *Sister Act,* directed by Emile Ardolino and starring Whoopi Goldberg, Maggie Smith, and Kathy Najimy; *Sneakers,* directed by Phil Alden Robinson and starring Robert Redford, Sidney Poitier, Dan Aykroyd, Ben Kingsley, and River Phoenix; *Under Siege,* directed by Andrew Davis and starring Steven Seagal; *Unforgiven,* directed by Clint Eastwood and starring Eastwood, Gene Hackman, Morgan Freeman, and Richard Harris; *Wayne's World,* directed by Penelope Spheeris and starring Mike Myers and Dana Carvey; *White Men Can't Jump,* directed by Ron Shelton and starring Woody Harrelson and Wesley Snipes.

Novels

Dorothy Allison, *Bastard out of Carolina;* Paul Auster, *Leviathan;* Nicholson Baker, *Vox;* Richard Bausch, *Violence;* Robert Olen Butler, *A Good Scent from a Strange Mountain;* Joan Didion, *After Henry;* David James Duncan, *The Brothers K;* Ellen Gilchrist, *Net of Jewels;* John Grisham, *The Pelican Brief;* George V. Higgins, *Defending Billy Ryan;* Alice Hoffman, *Turtle Moon;* William Kennedy, *Very Old Bones;* Ken Kesey, *Sailor Song;* Stephen King, *Dolores Claiborne;* W. P. Kinsella, *Box Socials;* Dean Koontz, *Hideaway;* Elmore Leonard, *Rum Punch;* Cormac McCarthy, *All the Pretty Horses;* Jill McCorkle, *Carolina Moon;* Alice McDermott, *At Weddings and Wakes;* Thomas McGuane, *Nothing But Blue Skies;* Jay McInerney, *Brightness Falls;* Terry McMillan, *Waiting to Exhale;* Larry McMurtry, *The Evening Star;* James Michener, *Mexico;* Toni Morrison, *Jazz;* Gloria Naylor, *Bailey's Cafe;* Joyce Carol Oates, *Black Water;* Chaim Potok, *I Am the Clay;* Reynolds Price, *Blue Calhoun;* Richard Price, *Clockers;* E. Annie Proulx, *Postcards;* Anne Rice, *The Tale of the Body Thief;* Leslie Silko, *Almanac of the Dead;* Lee Smith, *The Devil's Dream;* Susan Sontag, *The Volcano Lover;* Danielle Steel, *Mixed Blessings;* Donna Tartt, *The Secret History;* John Updike, *Memoirs of the Ford Administration;* Gore Vidal, *Live from Golgotha;* Alice Walker, *Possessing the Secret of Joy;* Robert James Waller, *The Bridges of Madison County;* Joseph Wambaugh, *Fugitive Nights;* Larry Woiwode, *Indian Affairs.*

Popular Songs

Sir Mix-A-Lot, "Baby Got Back"; Kris Kross, "Jump"; Boyz II Men, "End Of The Road"; Billy Ray Cyrus, "Achy Breaky Heart"; Eric Clapton, "Tears In Heaven"; Right Said Fred, "I'm Too Sexy"; House of Pain, "Jump Around"; Red Hot Chili Peppers, "Under The Bridge"; Nirvana, "Smells Like Teen Spirit"; Guns N' Roses, "November Rain."

• Compact discs surpass cassette tapes as the preferred medium for recorded music.

21 Feb.

In the continuing controversy over NEA funding for controversial artists, Republican presidential hopeful Patrick Buchanan accuses the Bush administration of supporting "filthy and blasphemous art," and President Bush responds by firing NEA chairman John E. Frohnmayer.

1993

Movies

Demolition Man, directed by Marco Brambilla and starring Sylvester Stallone and Wesley Snipes; *Dennis the Menace*, directed by Nick Castle and starring Walter Matthau; *Falling Down*, directed by Joel Schumacher and starring Michael Douglas and Robert Duvall; *The Firm*, directed by Sydney Pollack and starring Tom Cruise and Gene Hackman; *The Fugitive*, directed by Andrew Davis and starring Harrison Ford and Tommy Lee Jones; *Groundhog Day*, directed by Harold Ramis and starring Bill Murray and Andie MacDowell; *In the Line of Fire*, directed by Wolfgang Petersen and starring Clint Eastwood, John Malkovich, and Rene Russo; *In the Name of the Father*, directed by Jim Sheridan and starring Daniel Day-Lewis and Emma Thompson; *Indecent Proposal*, directed by Adrian Lyne and starring Robert Redford, Demi Moore, and Woody Harrelson; *Jurassic Park*, directed by Steven Spielberg and starring Sam Neill, Laura Dern, and Jeff Goldblum; *Last Action Hero*, directed by John McTiernan and starring Arnold Schwarzenegger and F. Murray Abraham; *Lost in Yonkers*, directed by Martha Coolidge and starring Richard Dreyfuss; *Philadelphia*, directed by Jonathan Demme and starring Tom Hanks and Denzel Washington; *The Piano*, directed by Jane Campion and starring Holly Hunter, Harvey Keitel, and Sam Neill; *Rising Sun*, directed by Philip Kaufman and starring Sean Connery, Wesley Snipes, and Harvey Keitel; *Schindler's List*, directed by Steven Spielberg and starring Liam Neeson, Ben Kingsley, and Ralph Fiennes; *Six Degrees of Separation*, directed by Fred Schepisi and starring Stockard Channing, Will Smith, and Donald Sutherland; *Sleepless in Seattle*, directed by Nora Ephron and starring Tom Hanks and Meg Ryan; *Sommersby*, directed by Jon Amiel and starring Richard Gere and Jodie Foster; *Tombstone*, directed by George P. Cosmatos and starring Kurt Russell and Val Kilmer.

Novels

Walter Abish, *Eclipse Fever;* Alice Adams, *Almost Perfect;* William Baldwin, *The Hard to Catch Mercy;* Frederick Barthelme, *Brothers;* Richard Bausch, *Rebel Powers;* Madison Smartt Bell, *Save Me, Joe Louis;* T. Coraghessan Boyle, *The Road to Wellville;* Frederick Buechner, *The Son of Laughter;* James Lee Burke, *In the Electric Mist with Confederate Dead;* Frederick Busch, *Long Way from Home;* Frank Conroy, *Body & Soul;* James Dickey, *To the White Sea;* Ivan Doig, *Heart Earth;* Ken Follett, *A Dangerous Fortune;* Ernest J. Gaines, *A Lesson Before Dying;* David Guterson, *Snow Falling on Cedars;* John Grisham, *The Client* and *A Time to Kill;* Kathryn Harrison, *Exposure;* Ernest Hebert, *Mad Boys;* George V. Higgins, *Bomber's Law;* Oscar Hijuelos, *The Fourteen Sisters of Emilio Montez O'Brien;* Tony Hillerman, *Sacred Clowns;* William Kennedy, *Riding the Yellow Trolley Car;* Barbara Kingsolver, *Pigs in Heaven;* Dean Koontz, *Mr. Murder;* Alan Lightman, *Einstein's Dreams;* Elmore Leonard, *Pronto;* Bobbie Ann Mason, *Feather Crowns;* Larry McMurtry, *Streets of Laredo;* Joyce Carol Oates, *Foxfire;* E. Annie Proulx, *The Shipping News;* Ishmael Reed, *Japanese by Spring;* Anne Rice, *Lasher;* Philip Roth, *Operation Shylock;* Dori Sanders, *Her Own Place;* Joseph Wambaugh, *Finnegan's Week.*

Popular Songs

Whitney Houston, "I Will Always Love You"; Tag Team, "Whoomp! (There It Is)"; Wreck-N-Effect, "Rump Shaker"; Silk, "Freak Me"; Dr. Dre, "Nuthin' But A G Thang"; UB40, "Can't Help Falling In Love"; Snow, "Informer"; Shai, "If I Ever Fall In Love"; Duice, "Dazzey Duks"; H-Town, "Knockin' Da Boots."

- The movie *Lost in Yonkers* is edited on an Avid Media Composer system, the first nonlinear editing system to allow viewing at the "real-time" rate of twenty-four frames per second. It converts film images into digital bits that can be manipulated on a computer.

1994

Movies

Ace Ventura: Pet Detective, directed by Tom Shadyac and starring Jim Carrey and Courteney Cox; *Clear and Present Danger*, directed by Phillip Noyce and starring Harrison Ford, Willem Dafoe, Anne Archer, and James Earl Jones; *Disclosure*, directed by Barry Levinson and starring Michael Douglas, Demi Moore, and Donald Sutherland; *Dumb & Dumber*, directed by Peter Farrelly and starring Jim Carrey and Jeff Daniels; *The Flintstones*, directed by Brian Levant and starring John Goodman, Elizabeth Perkins, Rick Moranis, and Rosie O'Donnell; *Forrest Gump*, directed by Robert Zemeckis and starring Tom Hanks; *Guarding Tess*, directed by Hugh Wilson and starring Shirley MacLaine and Nicolas Cage; *Interview with the Vampire: The Vampire Chronicles*, directed by Neil Jordan and starring Tom Cruise, Brad Pitt, and Antonio Banderas; *The Lion King*, animated feature, directed by Roger Allers and Rob Minkoff; *The Mask*, directed by Charles Russell and starring Jim Carrey and Cameron Diaz; *Maverick*, directed by Richard Donner and starring Mel Gibson, Jodie Foster, and James Garner; *Mrs. Doubtfire*, directed by Chris Columbus and starring Robin Williams and Sally Field; *Natural Born Killers*, directed by Oliver Stone and starring Woody Harrelson and Juliette Lewis; *Nobody's Fool*, directed by Robert Benton and starring Paul Newman, Jessica Tandy, Bruce Willis, and Melanie Griffith; *The Paper*, directed by Ron Howard and starring Michael Keaton, Glenn Close, Robert Duvall, Marisa Tomei, and Randy Quaid; *The Pelican Brief*, directed by Alan J. Pakula and starring Julia Roberts and Denzel Washington; *Pulp Fiction*, directed by Quentin Tarantino and starring John Travolta, Samuel L. Jackson, and Uma Thurman; *Quiz Show*, directed by Robert Redford and starring John Tuturro, Rob Morrow, and Ralph Fiennes; *The River Wild*, directed by Curtis Hanson and starring Meryl Streep and Kevin Bacon; *The Shawshank Redemption*, directed by Frank Darabont and starring Tim Robbins and Morgan Freeman; *Speed*, directed by Jan de Bont and starring Keanu Reeves, Dennis Hopper, and Sandra Bullock; *Star Trek Generations*, directed by David Carson and starring Patrick Stewart and William Shatner; *True Lies*, directed by James Cameron and starring Arnold Schwarzenegger, Jamie Lee Curtis, and Tom Arnold.

Novels

Paul Auster, *Mr. Vertigo*; John Barth, *Once Upon a Time*; Louis Begley, *As Max Saw It*; Thomas Berger, *Robert Crews*; Doris Betts, *Souls Raised From the Dead*; Harold Brodkey, *Profane Friendship*; Charles Bukowski, *Pulp*; James Lee Burke, *Dixie City Jam*; Robert Olen Butler, *They Whisper*; Caleb Carr, *The Alienist*; Carolyn Chute, *Merry Men*; Tom Clancy, *Debt of Honor*; Mary Higgins Clark, *Remember Me*; Michael Crichton, *Disclosure*; E. L. Doctorow, *The Waterworks*; John Gregory Dunne, *Playland*; Bret Easton Ellis, *The Informers*; Louise Erdrich, *The Bingo Palace*; Irvin Faust, *Jim Dandy*; William Gaddis, *A Frolic of His Own*; Gail Godwin, *The Good Husband*; Ellen Gilchrist, *Anabasis*; William Goyen, *Half a Look of Cain*; Shirley Ann Grau, *Roadwalkers*; John Grisham, *The Chamber*; Jane Hamilton, *A Map of the World*; Mark Harris, *The Tale Maker*; Joseph Heller, *Closing Time*; Alice Hoffman, *Second Nature*; John Irving, *A Son of the Circus*; Stephen King, *Insomnia*; David Mamet, *The Village*; Cormac McCarthy, *The Crossing*; Larry McMurtry, *Pretty Boy Floyd*; Walter Mosley, *Black Betty*; Joyce Carol Oates, *What I Lived For*; Tim O'Brien, *In the Lake of the Woods*; Robert B. Parker, *All Our Yesterdays*; Jayne Anne Phillips, *Shelter*; Marge Piercy, *The Longings of Women*; Anne Rice, *Taltos*; Danielle Steel, *The Gift*; Peter Taylor, *In the Tennessee Country*; John Updike, *Brazil*.

Popular Songs

All-4-One, "I Swear"; Boyz II Men, "I'll Make Love To You"; R. Kelly, "Bump N' Grind"; Bryan Adams, Rod Stewart, and Sting, "All For Love"; Ace of Base, "The Sign"; Celine Dion, "The Power of Love"; Warren G & Nate Dogg, "Regulate"; Coolio, "Fantastic Voyage."

1995

12–14 Aug. Woodstock '94 commemorates the twenty-fifth anniversary of the original week-end-long concert held near Woodstock, New York. Performers include Bob Dylan and the Allman Brothers, who performed at the 1969 concert, as well as the groups Green Day and Nine Inch Nails.

Movies *The American President*, directed by Rob Reiner and starring Michael Douglas, Annette Bening, and Martin Sheen; *Apollo 13*, directed by Ron Howard and starring Tom Hanks, Bill Paxton, and Kevin Bacon; *Babe*, directed by Chris Noonan; *Braveheart*, directed by and starring Mel Gibson; *The Bridges of Madison County*, directed by Clint Eastwood and starring Eastwood and Meryl Streep; *Clueless*, directed by Amy Heckerling and starring Alicia Silverstone; *Crimson Tide*, directed by Tony Scott and starring Gene Hackman and Denzel Washington; *Dead Man Walking*, directed by Tim Robbins and starring Susan Sarandon and Sean Penn; *Devil in a Blue Dress*, directed by Carl Franklin and starring Denzel Washington; *First Knight*, directed by Jerry Zucker and starring Sean Connery and Richard Gere; *Get Shorty*, directed by Barry Sonnenfeld and starring John Travolta, Gene Hackman, Rene Russo, and Danny DeVito; *Golden-Eye*, directed by Martin Campbell and starring Pierce Brosnan; *Grumpier Old Men*, directed by Howard Deutch and starring Walter Matthau, Jack Lemmon, Ann-Margret, and Sophia Loren; *Leaving Las Vegas*, directed by Mike Figgis and starring Nicolas Cage and Elizabeth Shue; *Nixon*, directed by Oliver Stone and starring Anthony Hopkins; *Pocahontas*, animated feature, directed by Mike Gabriel and Eric Goldberg; *Sense and Sensibility*, directed by Ang Lee and starring Kate Winslet, Emma Thompson, and Hugh Grant; *Toy Story*, animated feature, directed by John Lasseter; *The Usual Suspects*, directed by Bryan Singer and starring Stephen Baldwin and Kevin Spacey; *Waiting to Exhale*, directed by Forrest Whittaker and starring Whitney Houston and Angela Bassett; *While You Were Sleeping*, directed by John Turteltaub and starring Sandra Bullock.

Novels Alice Adams, *A Southern Exposure*; Julia Alvarez, *In the Time of the Butterflies*; Frederick Barthelme, *Painted Desert*; Rick Bass, *In the Loyal Mountains*; Ann Beattie, *Another You*; Madison Smartt Bell, *All Souls' Rising*; T. Coraghessan Boyle, *The Tortilla Curtain*; Nicholas Delbanco, *In the Name of Mercy*; Pete Dexter, *The Paperboy*; Stanley Elkin, *Mrs. Ted Bliss*; Richard Ford, *Independence Day*; William H. Gass, *The Tunnel*; John Grisham, *The Rainmaker*; John Herman, *The Weight of Love*; George V. Higgins, *Swan Boats at Four*; Alice Hoffman, *Practical Magic*; Mary Hood, *Familiar Heat*; John Keene, *Annotations*; David Long, *Blue Spruce*; Sue Miller, *The Distinguished Guest*; Joyce Carol Oates, *Zombie*; Robert B. Parker, *Thin Air*; Richard Powers, *Galatea 2.2*; Reynolds Price, *The Promise of Rest*; Philip Roth, *Sabbath's Theater*; Mary Lee Settle, *Choices*; Jane Smiley, *Moo*; Lee Smith, *Saving Grace*; Amy Tan, *The Hundred Secret Senses*; Anne Tyler, *Ladder of Years*.

Popular Songs Coolio featuring L.V., "Gangsta's Paradise"; TLC, "Creep"; Mariah Carey, "Fantasy"; TLC, "Waterfalls"; Monica, "Don't Take It Personal"; Shaggy, "Boombastic/In The Summertime"; The Notorious B.I.G., "One More Chance/

Stay With Me"; Adina Howard, "Freak Like Me"; Montell Jordan, "This Is How We Do It"; Michael Jackson, "You Are Not Alone."

1 June In a speech delivered in Los Angeles, Republican presidential candidate Robert Dole denounces the American entertainment industry for "debasing U.S. culture with movies, music and television programs that had produced 'nightmares of depravity' drenched in sex and violence."

1 Sept. The Rock and Roll Hall of Fame and Museum, designed by architect I. M. Pei, opens in Cleveland.

2 Oct. At a performance of *Otello* the Metropolitan Opera in New York unveils Met Titles, providing simultaneous translations on screens mounted on audience seats.

21 Nov. Capitol Records releases the much-anticipated *Beatles Anthology I*, which includes the previously unreleased recording of "Free as a Bird."

1996

Movies *The Cable Guy*, directed by Ben Stiller and starring Jim Carrey and Matthew Broderick; *Courage Under Fire*, directed by Edward Zwick and starring Denzel Washington, Meg Ryan, and Lou Diamond Phillips; *The English Patient*, directed by Anthony Minghella and starring Ralph Fiennes and Juliette Binoche; *Evita*, directed by Alan Parker and starring Madonna and Antonio Banderas; *Executive Decision*, directed by Stuart Baird and starring Kurt Russell, Steven Seagal, and Halle Berry; *Fargo*, directed by Joel Coen and starring Frances McDormand; *First Wives Club*, directed by Hugh Wilson and starring Goldie Hawn, Bette Midler, Diane Keaton; *Hunchback of Notre Dame*, animated feature, directed by Gary Trousdale and Kirk Wise; *Independence Day*, directed by Roland Emmerich and starring Will Smith, Robert Duvall, Dennis Quaid, and Jeff Goldblum; *Jack*, directed by Francis Ford Coppola and starring Robin Williams, Diane Lane, Bill Cosby, and Jennifer Lopez; *Jerry Maguire*, directed by Cameron Crowe and starring Tom Cruise and Cuba Gooding Jr.; *Mission, Impossible*, directed by Brian de Palma and starring Tom Cruise; *The Nutty Professor*, directed by Tom Shadyac and starring Eddie Murphy and Jada Pinkett; *101 Dalmations*, directed by Stephen Herek and starring Glenn Close and Jeff Daniels; *The People vs. Larry Flynt*, directed by Milos Forman and starring Woody Harrelson and Courtney Love; *Primal Fear*, directed by Gregory Hoblit and starring Richard Gere and Frances McDormand; *Ransom*, directed by Ron Howard and starring Mel Gibson and Rene Russo; *The Rock*, directed by Michael Bay and starring Sean Connery and Nicolas Cage; *Shine*, directed by Scott Hicks and starring Geoffrey Rush; *Sling Blade*, directed by Billy Bob Thornton and starring Thornton, John Ritter, and J. T. Walsh; *Tin Cup*, directed by Ron Shelton and starring Kevin Costner and Rene Russo; *Twister*, directed by Jan de Bont and starring Helen Hunt and Bill Paxton.

Novels Anonymous [Joe Klein], *Primary Colors;* Richard Bausch, *Good Evening Mr. & Mrs. America, and All the Ships at Sea;* Madison Smartt Bell, *Ten Indians;* Thomas Berger, *Suspects;* Wendell Berry, *A World Lost;* Harold Brodkey, *This Wild Darkness;* Larry Brown, *Father and Son;* James Lee Burke, *Cadillac Jukebox;* Fred Chappell, *Farewell, I'm Bound to Leave You;* Mary Higgins Clark, *Moonlight Becomes You;* Robert Coover, *John's Wife;* Michael Crichton, *Airframe;* Joan Didion, *The Last Thing He Wanted;* Nicholas Evans, *The Horse Whisperer;* John Grisham, *The Runaway Jury;* George V. Higgins, *Sandra Nichols Found Dead;* Tony Hillerman, *The Fallen Man;* William Kennedy, *The Flaming Corsage;*

Jamaica Kincaid, *Autobiography of My Mother;* William Kotzwinkle, *The Bear Went Over the Mountain;* Elmore Leonard, *Out of Sight;* Clarence Major, *Dirty Bird Blues;* Ed McBain, *Gladly the Cross-Eyed Bear;* Jill McCorkle, *Carolina Moon;* Terry McMillan, *How Stella Got Her Groove Back;* Steven Millhauser, *Martin Dressler;* Jacquelyn Mitchard, *The Deep End of the Ocean;* Walter Mosley, *A Little Yellow Dog;* Joyce Carol Oates, *We Were the Mulvaneys;* James Patterson, *Jack & Jill;* Janet Peery, *The River Beyond the World;* E. Annie Proulx, *Accordion Crimes;* Anne Rice, *The Servant of the Bones;* John Updike, *In the Beauty of the Lilies;* Joseph Wambaugh, *Floaters;* John Edgar Wideman, *The Cattle Killing.*

Popular Songs

Los Del Rio, "Macarena (Bayside Boys Mix)"; Mariah Carey & Boyz II Men, "One Sweet Day"; Bone Thugs-N-Harmony, "Tha Crossroads"; 2Pac (Featuring K-Ci & JoJo), "How Do U Want It/California Love"; Keith Sweat, "Twisted"; Toni Braxton, "You're Makin' Me High/Let It Flow"; Whitney Houson, "Exhale (Shoop Shoop)"; Quad City D.J's, "C'Mon N' Ride It (The Train)"; Celine Dion, "Because You Loved Me"; LL Cool J, "Hey Lover."

13 Feb.

The musical *Rent* opens to rave reviews on Broadway.

Mar.

Legal thriller writer John Grisham charges that director Oliver Stone is responsible for the death of Grisham's friend William Savage, because the two teenagers who committed the crime claim to have been inspired by Stone's 1994 movie, *Natural Born Killers.*

Nov.

Marc Chagall 1907–1917 at the Los Angeles County Museum includes early Chagall paintings never before exhibited in the United States.

1997

Movies

Absolute Power, directed by Clint Eastwood and starring Eastwood, Gene Hackman, and Ed Harris; *Air Force One,* directed by Wolfgang Peterson and starring Harrison Ford and Glenn Close; *Anastasia,* animated feature, directed by Don Bluth and Gary Goldmanstarring; *As Good as It Gets,* directed by James L. Brooks and starring Helen Hunt and Jack Nicholson; *Austin Powers: International Man of Mystery,* directed by Jay Roach and starring Mike Myers and Elizabeth Hurley; *Batman and Robin,* directed by Joel Schumacher and starring George Clooney, Chris O'Donnell, and Uma Thurman; *Con Air,* directed by Simon West and starring Nicolas Cage and John Cusack; *Conspiracy Theory,* directed by Richard Donner and starring Mel Gibson and Julia Roberts; *Contact,* directed by Robert Zemeckis and starring Jodie Foster and Matthew McConaughey; *Devil's Advocate,* directed by Taylor Hackford and starring Al Pacino, Keanu Reeves, and Charlize Theron; *Face/Off,* directed by John Woo and starring John Travolta and Nicolas Cage; *The Full Monty,* directed by Peter Cantanneo and starring Robert Carlyle, Tom Wilkinson, and Mark Addy; *Good Will Hunting,* directed by Gus Van Sant and starring Matt Damon and Robin Williams; *The Ice Storm,* directed by Ang Lee and starring Kevin Kline and Sigourney Weaver; *In & Out,* directed by Frank Oz and starring Kevin Kline, John Cusack, Tom Selleck, and Matt Dillon; *The Jackal,* directed by Michael Caton-Jones and starring Bruce Willis, Richard Gere, and Sidney Poitier; *John Grisham's The Rainmaker,* directed by Francis Ford Coppola and starring Danny DeVito and Matt Damon; *L.A. Confidential,* directed by Curtis Hanson and starring Kevin Spacey, Russell Crowe, Danny DeVito, and Kim Basinger; *Lolita,* directed by Adrian Lyne and starring Jeremy Irons and Melanie Griffith; *The Lost World: Jurassic Park,* directed by Steven Spielberg and starring Jeff Goldblum and Julianne Moore; *Men in Black,* directed by Barry Sonnenfeld and starring Tommy Lee Jones and Will Smith; *Soul Food*, directed by George Tillman and starring Vivica A. Fox, Vanessa Williams, and Nia Long; *Titanic*, directed by James Cameron and starring Kate Winslet and Leonardo DiCaprio; *Tomorrow Never Dies*, directed by Roger Spottiswoode and starring Pierce Brosnan.

Novels

Alice Adams, *Medicine Men;* Julia Alvarez, *Yo;* Frederick Barthelme, *Bob the Gambler;* Doris Betts, *The Sharp Teeth of Love;* Frederick Buechner, *On the Road with the Archangel;* James Lee Burke, *Cimarron Rose;* Frederick Busch, *Girls;* Robert Olen Butler, *The Deep Green Sea;* Caleb Carr, *The Angel of Darkness;* Mary Higgins Clark, *Pretend You Don't See Her;* Nicholas Delbanco, *Old Scores;* Don DeLillo, *Underworld;* Stephen Dobyns, *The Church of the Dead Girls;* Dominick Dunne, *Another City, Not My Own;* Charles Frazier, *Cold Mountain;* Ellen Gilchrist, *Sarah Conley;* Arthur Golden, *Memoirs of a Geisha;* John Grisham, *The Partner;* Allan Gurganus, *Plays Well with Others;* John Hawkes, *An Irish Eye;* George V. Higgins, *A Change of Gravity;* Alice Hoffman, *Here on Earth;* Madison Jones, *Nashville 1864;* Stephen King, *Wizard* and *Glass;* Robert Ludlum, *Matarese Countdown;* Peter Matthiessen, *Lost Man's River;* Jay McInerney, *The Last of the Savages;* Larry McMurtry, *Comanche Moon;* Walter Mosley, *Blue Light;* Joyce Carol Oates, *Man Crazy;* Cynthia Ozick, *Puttermesser Papers;* Thomas Pynchon, *Mason & Dixon;* Philip Roth, *American Pastoral;* John Updike, *Toward the End of Time;* Kurt Vonnegut, *Timequake;* Edmund White, *The Farewell Symphony;* Tom Wolfe, *Ambush at Fort Bragg.*

Popular Songs

Elton John, "Candle In The Wind/Something About The Way You Look Tonight"; Puff Daddy and Faith Evans, "I'll Be Missing You"; Puff Daddy (Featuring Mase), "Can't Nobody Hold Me Down"; LeAnn Rimes, "How Do I Live"; Usher, "You Make Me Wanna"; Spice Girls, "Wannabe"; Hanson, "MMMBop"; Mark Morrison, "Return Of The Mack"; Tim McGraw With Faith Hill, "It's Your Love"; The Notorious B.I.G. (Featuring Puff Daddy & Mase), "Mo Money Mo Problems."

19 June

Cats stages its 6,138th performance, moving ahead of *A Chorus Line* as the longest running Broadway show in history.

19 Dec.

Titanic opens in American movie theaters. The most expensive movie of all time, it has cost nearly $300 million to produce and market.

1998

Movies

Affliction, directed by Paul Schrader and starring Sissy Spacek, Nick Nolte, James Coburn, and Willem Dafoe; *American History X*, directed by Tony Kaye and starring Edward Norton and Edward Furlong; and *The Apostle*, directed by Robert Duvall and starring Duvall, Farrah Fawcett, Billy Bob Thornton, and June Carter Cash; *Beloved*, directed by Jonathan Demme and starring Oprah Winfrey and Danny Glover; *A Bug's Life*, animated feature, directed by John Lasseter and Andrew Stanton; *Bulworth*, directed by Warren Beatty and starring Beatty and Halle Berry; *City of Angels*, directed by Brad Silberling and starring Nicolas Cage and Meg Ryan; *A Civil Action*, directed by Steven Zaillian and starring John Travolta and Robert Duvall; *Dancing at Lughnasa*, directed by Pat O'Connor and starring Meryl Streep and Michael Gambon; *Deep Impact*, directed by Mimi Leder and starring Robert Duvall, Tea Leoni, and Morgan Freeman; *Dr. Dolittle*, directed by Betty Thomas and starring Eddie Murphy and Ossie Davis; *Elizabeth*, directed by Shekhar Kapur and starring Cate Blanchett and Geoffrey

Rush; *Enemy of the State,* directed by Tony Scott and starring Will Smith, Gene Hackman, and Lisa Bonet; *Fallen,* directed by Gregory Hoblit and starring Denzel Washington, John Goodman, and Donald Sutherland; *Fear and Loathing in Las Vegas,* directed by Terry Gilliam and starring Johnny Depp and Benicio Del Toro; *Great Expectations,* directed by Stuart Walker and starring Ethan Hawke and Gwyneth Paltrow; *He Got Game,* directed by Spike Lee and starring Denzel Washington, Ray Allen, and Ned Beatty; *Hope Floats,* directed by Forrest Whittaker and starring Sandra Bullock and Harry Connick Jr.; *The Horse Whisperer,* directed by Robert Redford and starring Redford and Kristin Scott Thomas; *How Stella Got Her Groove Back,* directed by Kevin Rodney Sullivan and starring Angela Bassett; *Les Miserables,* directed by Bille August and starring Liam Neeson, Uma Thurman, and Claire Danes; *Meet Joe Black,* directed by Martin Brest and starring Anthony Hopkins and Brad Pitt; *Mulan,* animated feature, directed by Barry Cook and Tony Bancroft; *One True Thing,* directed by Carl Franklin and starring Meryl Streep, Renee Zellweger, and William Hurt; *Out of Sight,* directed by Steven Soderbergh and starring George Clooney and Jennifer Lopez; *Patch Adams,* directed by Tom Shadyac and starring Robin Williams; *Pleasantville,* directed by Gary Ross and starring Tobey Maguire, Jeff Daniels, and Joan Allen; *Primary Colors,* directed by Mike Nichols and starring John Travolta, Emma Thompson, Kathy Bates, and Billy Bob Thornton; *The Prince of Egypt,* animated feature, directed by Brenda Chapman and Steve Hickner; *Saving Private Ryan,* directed by Steven Spielberg and starring Tom Hanks; *Shakespeare in Love,* directed by John Madden and starring Joseph Fiennes and Gwyneth Paltrow; *There's Something About Mary,* directed by Bobby Farrelly and Peter Farrelly and starring Cameron Diaz, Matt Dillon, and Ben Stiller; *The Thin Red Line,* directed by Terrence Malick and starring Sean Penn and Nick Nolte; *The Truman Show,* directed by Peter Weir and starring Jim Carrey, Ed Harris, and Laura Linney; *The Waterboy,* directed by Frank Coraci and starring Adam Sandler, Kathy Bates, and Henry Winkler; *You've Got Mail,* directed by Nora Ephron and starring Tom Hanks and Meg Ryan.

Novels
Nicholson Baker, *The Everlasting Story of Nory;* Russell Banks, *Cloudsplitter;* Andrea Barrett, *The Voyage of the Narwhal;* Richard Bausch, *In the Night Season;* Louis Begley, *Mistler's Exit;* T. Coraghessan Boyle, *Riven Rock;* Frederick Buechner, *The Storm;* Robert Coover, *Ghost Town;* Louise Erdrich, *Antelope Wife;* John Grisham, *The Street Lawyer;* George V. Higgins, *The Agent;* Tony Hillerman, *The First Eagle;* John Irving, *A Widow for One Year;* Gayl Jones, *The Healing;* Barbara Kingsolver, *The Poisonwood Bible;* Stephen King, *Bag of Bones;* Wally Lamb, *I Know This Much Is True;* Elmore Leonard, *Cuba Libre;* Cormac McCarthy, *Cities of the Plain;* Jill McCorkle, *Final Vinyl Days;* Alice McDermott, *Charming Billy;* Toni Morrison, *Paradise;* Gloria Naylor, *The Men of Brewster Place;* Joyce Carol Oates, *My Heart Laid Bare;* Reynolds Price, *Roxanne Slade;* Richard Price, *Freedomland;* Anne Rice, *The Vampire Armand;* Philip Roth, *I Married a Communist;* Jane Smiley, *The All-True Travels and Adventures of Lidie Newton;* Nicholas Sparks, *Message in a Bottle;* Anne Tyler, *A Patchwork Planet;* John Updike, *Bech at Bay;* Alice Walker, *By the Light of My Father's Smile;* Bailey White, *Quite a Year for Plums;* John Edgar Wideman, *Two Cities;* Tom Wolfe, *A Man in Full.*

Popular Songs
Brandy & Monica, "The Boy Is Mine"; Next, "Too Close"; Shania Twain, "You're Still The One"; Elton John, "Something About The Way You Look Tonight/Candle In The Wind 1997"; Puff Daddy & The Family, "Been Around The World"; LeAnn Rimes, "How Do I Live"; Usher, "Nice & Slow"; Destiny's Child, "No, No, No"; Usher, "My Way"; Mariah Carey, "My All."

- *Titanic* becomes the highest-grossing movie of all time, earning more than $580 million in the United States and winning a record-tying eleven Academy Awards, including those for Best Picture and Best Director (James Cameron).

- Movie-theater owners agree to require teenagers to show photo IDs to get in to see R rated movies.

16 June The American Film Institute announces its list of the top one hundred motion pictures of all time. *Citizen Kane* is number one, sparking a 1,600 percent increase in video rentals of the movie.

26 June *The Art of the Motorcycle* opens at the Guggenheim Museum in New York City; critics charge that industrial design has no place in an art museum, but attendance breaks museum records.

Nov. Volume 200 of the *Dictionary of Literary Biography* is published.

1999

Movies *American Beauty,* directed by Sam Mendes and starring Kevin Spacey; *American Pie,* directed by Paul Weitz and starring Jason Biggs and Shannon Elizabeth; *Analyze This,* directed by Harold Ramis and starring Billy Crystal and Robert De Niro; *Angela's Ashes,* directed by Alan Parker and starring Emily Watson and Robert Carlyle; *Anna and the King,* directed by Andy Tennant and starring Jodie Foster and Chow Yun-Fat; *Any Given Sunday,* directed by Oliver Stone and starring Al Pacino, Cameron Diaz, Dennis Quaid, and James Woods; *Anywhere but Here,* directed by Wayne Wang and starring Susan Sarandon and Natalie Portman; *Being John Malkovich,* directed by Spike Jonze and starring John Cusack, John Malkovich, and Cameron Diaz; *The Blair Witch Project,* directed by Daniel Myrick and Eduardo Sanchez and starring Heather Donahue and Michael Williams; *The Bone Collector,* directed by Phillip Noyce and starring Denzel Washington and Angelina Jolie; *Buena Vista Social Club,* documentary, directed by Wim Wenders; *The Cider House Rules,* directed by Lasse Hallström and starring Tobey Maguire, Charlize Theron, and Michael Caine; *Double Jeopardy,* directed by Bruce Beresford and starring Tommy Lee Jones and Ashley Judd; *EdTV,* directed by Ron Howard and starring Matthew McConaughey, Jenna Elfman, and Woody Harrelson; *Election,* directed by Alexander Payne and starring Matthew Broderick and Reese Witherspoon; *End of the Affair,* directed by Neil Jordan and starring Ralph Fiennes, Julianne Moore, and Stephen Rea; *The General's Daughter,* directed by Simon West and starring John Travolta and Madeleine Stowe; *Girl, Interrupted,* directed by James Mangold and starring Winona Ryder, Angelina Jolie, and Whoopi Goldberg; *The Green Mile,* directed by Frank Darabont and starring Tom Hanks; *The Hurricane,* directed by Norman Jewison and starring Denzel Washington; *The Insider,* directed by Michael Mann and starring Al Pacino and Russell Crowe; *The Iron Giant,* animated feature, directed by Brad Bird; *Magnolia,* directed by Thomas Anderson and starring Tom Cruise and Julianne Moore; *Man on the Moon,* directed by Milos Forman and starring Jim Carrey, Danny DeVito, and Courtney Love; *The Matrix,* directed by the Wachowski Brothers, and starring Keanu Reeves and Laurence Fishburne; *Music of the Heart,* directed by Wes Craven and starring Meryl Streep, Aidan Quinn, and Angela Bassett; *Notting Hill,* directed by Roger Michell and starring Julia Roberts and Hugh Grant; *October Sky,* directed by Joe Johnston and starring Jake Gyllenhaal, Chris Cooper, and Laura Dern; *South Park: Bigger, Longer & Uncut,* animated feature, directed by Trey Parker; *Star Wars: Episode I: The Phantom Menace,* directed by George Lucas and starring Liam Neeson; *Stuart Little,* directed by Rob Minkoff and starring Geena Davis, Michael J. Fox, and Gwyneth Paltrow; *Summer of Sam*, directed by Spike Lee and starring John Leguizamo; *Tarzan*, animated feature, directed by Kevin Lima and Chris Buck; *Three Kings*, directed by David O'Russell and starring George Clooney, Mark Wahlberg, and Ice Cube; *Toy Story 2*, animated feature, directed by John Lasseter; *Walk on the Moon*, directed by Tony Goldwyn and starring Diane Lane, Liev Schreiber, and Anna Paquin.

Novels   Paul Auster, *Timbuktu*; Thomas Berger, *The Return of Little Big Man*; Frederick Busch, *The Night Inspector*; Carolyn Chute, *Snow Man*; Stephen Dobyns, *Boy in the Water*; Ivan Doig, *Mountain Time*; Ralph Ellison, *Juneteenth*; Janet Fitch, *White Oleander*; John Grisham, *The Testament*; Oscar Hijuelos, *Empress of the Splendid Season*; Tama Janowitz, *A Certain Age*; Stephen King, *The Girl Who Loved Tom Gordon*; Peter Matthiessen, *Bone by Bone*; Thomas McGuane, *Some Horses*; Larry McMurtry, *Duane's Depressed*; Sue Miller, *While I Was Gone*; Walter Mosley, *Walkin' the Dog*; Joyce Carol Oates, *Broke Heart Blues*; Anne Rice, *Vittorio*.

Popular Songs   Cher, "Believe"; Deborah Cox, "Nobody's Supposed To be Here"; R. Kelly & Celine Dion, "I'm Your Angel"; Britney Spears, ". . . Baby One More Time"; Christina Aguiliera, "Genie In A Bottle"; Whitney Houston (featuring Faith Evans and Kelly Price), "Heartbreak Hotel"; LFO, "Summer Girls"; Jennifer Lopez, "If You Had My Love"; Ricky Martin, "Livin' La Vida Loca"; Monica, "Angel of Mine."

17 Apr.   As NATO forces bomb Belgrade, the Yugoslav movie academy awards top honors to *Wag the Dog*, about White House aides who stage a phony crisis in the Balkans to draw attention away from a presidential sex scandal.

19 May   *Star Wars: Episode I: The Phantom Menace* is released and breaks a string of box-office records. The movie grosses $102.7 million in five days.

14 July   *The Blair Witch Project* is released, becoming a cult-movie classic and grossing more than $140 million. Because the production cost of the movie was only $30,000, it is the most profitable motion picture of all time.

23–25 July   Woodstock '99 is held in Rome, New York. Concertgoers complain that the spirit of the original Woodstock has been compromised and commercialized. The crowd sets fires and destroys property during the finale, and several sexual assaults are reported.

Sept.   Mayor Rudolph W. Giuliani of New York City threatens to cut off funding and cancel the lease for the Brooklyn Museum of Art if it continues with plans to show *Sensation*, an exhibit of works by contemporary British artists that he labels profane and blasphemous.

OVERVIEW

Hype, Hope, and Decline. Despite some notable achievements, the American arts of the 1990s seemed to be gripped by an end-of-the-century cynicism, with profit governing product. Giving people want they wanted (or what marketing experts thought they wanted) seemed the primary motive in the entertainment and publishing industries. Movies were more violent and more dependent on new computer-generated effects than in earlier decades. The popular-music industry was dominated by grunge rock, rap, and teen pop. Broadway producers tended to play it safe with moneymaking musicals, including revivals of past hits, and they continued the 1980s trend of hoping that big Hollywood stars would find their theatrical roots and bring audiences with them.

Art. The art world was shaken in 1989, when conservatives in Congress attacked the NEA for funding institutions that had provided grants to photographers Andres Serrano and Robert Mapplethorpe to create works that Senators Jesse Helms (R-N.C.) and Alphonse D'Amato (R-N.Y.), among others, considered morally offensive. In 1989 and 1990, in the midst of calls for the outright abolition of the NEA, Congress cut the NEA budget and required that works by funded artists must adhere to community standards of decency. Artists countered that such conditions discouraged creativity. Karen Finley, one of the artists who lost NEA funding because of the provocative nature of her work, warned: "We have lost our inventiveness for the sake of appearances." Despite such gloomy conclusions artists continued to offer overtly social and political commentary in disturbing works that managed to offend some members of the public. The installation and performance art of critically acclaimed artists such as Matthew Barney and Cindy Sherman took on taboo subjects and employed visually repellant materials and animalistic images, prompting one critic to suggest that the lure of such art was the "weird pleasure" of watching "whatever improbable carnival comes next." Mayor Rudolph Giuliani of New York City took on the art world in 1999, when he tried to close down an exhibit of modern British art at the Brooklyn Museum, which included a painting that he and members of the local Catholic hierarchy considered offensive and sacrilegious. The definition of art became increasingly blurred in the 1990s, as some artists began to employ computer terminals and internet modems to create original art works. Despite confusion and controversy the art world witnessed a boom in art collecting, with purchasers paying record prices, not only for paintings by the great Impressionists but also for works by contemporary avant-garde artists.

Motion Pictures. Movie makers also experimented with previously taboo subjects. Raw sex, vulgarity, and violence appeared in movies designed to shock and excite. Even critically praised movies such as *Pulp Fiction* (1994), *Sling Blade* (1996), and *Saving Private Ryan* (1998) were violent. Pointed political satire in movies such as *Wag the Dog* (1997) and *Bulworth* (1998) gave voice to Americans' disenchantment with their political leaders. As movies seemed to substitute special effects for plot development, moviegoers came to expect mind boggling visual effects, especially from such masters of movie technology as George Lucas and James Cameron. The Star Wars trilogy was re-released with souped up visual images and added material in order to take advantage of advances made in computer technology. Cameron's *Titanic* allowed viewers to relive the sinking of that superliner on its maiden voyage.

Music. The popular-music industry was dominated by the teen market, with grunge rock and gangsta rap in the early 1990s and teen pop and other forms of rap and "alternative" music later in the decade. Musicians, more than ever, engaged in brazen self-promotion to sell their works. Raucous (even anarchistic) bands such as Nirvana, Rage Against the Machine, 2 Live Crew, and NWA dominated the music market. The group called Marilyn Manson spoke to discontented young people through music described as "death metal": heavy-metal rock with an occult message. Pop singer-songwriter Mariah Carey had more number-one hits than any other female vocalist, and only eight fewer than Elvis Presley.

Writers and Readers. New technology revolutionized how books were published and marketed. By the end of the decade innovative internet booksellers such as Amazon.com helped to revitalize book sales even as they threatened traditional book retailers. Thousands of local bookstores disappeared, crushed in an increasingly competitive industry dominated by warehouse-size stores that marketed books more profitably, if not always elegantly. Though a lot of people talked about electronic publishing as a way to replace paper and cloth books, e-books were still a commodity of the future and had little influence on the trade-book market though electronic data base publishing enhanced the utility of standard reference works for specialized markets. Readers still bought traditional books, paying for the privilege of entering alone into lives and situations another's imagination had created for them. Yet, the literary situation of the 1990s was not rosy. Though President William Jefferson Clinton invited poet Maya Angelou to read at his first inauguration, poetry was virtually ignored by readers and publishers for much of the decade. With publishers eyeing the bottom line, it also became difficult for promising young fiction writers to find outlets for their work.

Theater. The trends that began in earlier decades still dominated theater in the 1990s. Broadway continued to be the proving ground that established brand names that could be marketed across America by touring companies.

Important not-for-profit regional theaters continued to develop new plays that later moved to Broadway or off-Broadway. Megamusicals continued to move from London to New York and from there across America. In fact, few productions that opened on Broadway had not first proved successful somewhere else. Finally, theater of special interest to minority groups continued to thrive and to develop.

Technology. Digital technology and the Internet changed the way music was made, bought, and sold (and eased the way for millions of fans to help themselves illegally to the music they wanted without paying for it). The Internet offered many aspiring artists the opportunities to express their creativity to an audience previously unreachable by nonmainstream performers. Some music websites began to promote individuals not backed by music companies. Other artists bypassed the role traditionally played by entertainment corporations and released their music, books, and art works on inexpensive websites or home pages.

TOPICS IN THE NEWS

ART AND POLITICS

NEA Restrictions. The National Endowment for the Arts (NEA) was established by Congress in 1965 to serve "the public good by nurturing human creativity, supporting community spirit, and fostering appreciation of the excellence and diversity of our nation's artistic accomplishments." Since then it has provided grants to artists, museums, and galleries to encourage artists whose work shows promise but is unlikely to attract large audiences or private funding. In May and June 1989 controversy erupted in Congress over NEA support for Andres Serrano, whose *Piss Christ* is a photograph of a crucifix immersed in Serrano's urine, and Robert Mapplethorpe, whose photographs included homoerotic and sadomasochistic images. On 12 June, fearful of a political battle over its federal funding, the Corcoran Museum in Washington, D.C., canceled Mapplethorpe's controversial show, *The Perfect Moment,* which had already been exhibited in Philadelphia and Chicago and later went on to other cities. For months Senator Jesse Helms (R-N.C.) and others excoriated the NEA for subsidizing "disgusting" and "blasphemous" art with taxpayers' money. The annual NEA appropriations bill, passed on 28 October 1989, imposed conditions on future funds for the two institutions that had given grants

to Serrano and Mapplethorpe, and it specified that no NEA funding could be used "to promote, disseminate, or produce materials which . . . may be considered obscene, including but not limited to, depictions of sadomasochism, homoeroticism, the sexual exploitation of children, or individuals engaged in sex acts and which, when taken as a whole, do not have serious literary, artistic, political, or scientific value." The next annual funding bill, passed in December 1990, specified that obscenity should be defined in accordance with community standards of decency and that artists whose work was judged obscene must return their NEA grant money.

Fallout. In the midst of the continuing debate, the Mapplethorpe exhibit went on to several cities, where it was shown without incident. When it reached the Contemporary Arts Center (CAC) in Cincinnati on 7 April 1990, however, the Hamilton County sheriff's department shut down the museum. The CAC and its director, Dennis Barrie, were subsequently indicted on obscenity charges, and on 5 October they were found not guilty.

The NEA Four. While arts supporters were applauding the acquittal in Cincinnati as a victory for freedom of expression, a long battle over NEA funding was brewing.

Members of the Association of Art Museum Directors protesting cuts in federal funding for the arts during their 1990 annual meeting at the Art Institute of Chicago (photograph by Thomas Cinoman; © 1993 the Art Institute of Chicago)

When the controversial performance artists Holly Hughes, John Fleck, Tim Miller, and Karen Finley—all of whom had previously received small NEA grants—applied for new NEA funding, they were recommended for grants by an initial screening panel, but on 29 June 1990 John Frohnmayer, director of the NEA, vetoed funding for the four artists because of the nature of their work. Arguing that the new NEA standards violated the initial intent of the 1965 law creating the NEA and represented an effort to limit freedom of expression, these artists sued the NEA. Finley's suit went all the way to the Supreme Court, which ruled on 25 June 1998 that the NEA could consider general standards of decency when making grants; in other words, that refusal to fund Finley's artist expressions did not limit her freedom to perform them. Finley profited from her newfound notoriety, but other artists who were denied funds were not as lucky.

Fellowship Cuts. The NEA suffered from funding cuts throughout the 1990s. In 1996 Congress not only slashed appropriations for the NEA but also eliminated fellowships for individual artists except for folk artists, jazz musicians, and writers. It also cut off operating subsidies to theaters and museums, making it necessary, for example, for a the-

ater to fill its seats with paying customers, discouraging experimental and challenging performances that are not popular with general audiences. As Norman Frisch, consultant for Arts International, observed, "There's not going to be such a thing as a professional non-commercial artist anymore. We're moving back towards a giant chasm between commercial artists and amateur artists." Hardest hit were artists who relied on high-tech video equipment and postmodern dance troupes whose performance pieces are hard to create and generate little revenue. Frisch concluded that the NEA was "now merely a facade" and that "we have lost our inventiveness for the sake of appearances." Furthermore, corporations have been unwilling to fill the gaps left by the cuts in NEA funding. Many had relied on the NEA to indicate artists worthy of financing, and without that guidance many companies were not willing to take chances.

The Brooklyn Museum Controversy. In late September 1999 New York City mayor Rudolph W. Giuliani threatened to cut off city subsidies and revoke the lease for the Brooklyn Museum of Art if the museum board did not cancel *Sensation*, an exhibit of works by contemporary British artists scheduled to open in October. He was responding to complaints from the Roman Catholic Bishop of Brooklyn and the Catholic League for Religion and Civil Rights, who called the show profane and "disgusting" and objected to the use of tax dollars to support a show that they saw as an attack on Catholicism. Arguing "You don't have a right to government subsidy for desecrating somebody's else's religion," Giuliani singled out as especially blasphemous Chris Ofili's *Holy Virgin Mary* (1996), a portrait of a black Madonna to which the artist stuck cutouts of vaginas and buttocks from pornographic magazines and shellacked clumps of elephant dung. Defenders of the work said it explored ideas of blasphemy and worship, race and religion. Supporters of the museum and the artists defended the exhibit on grounds of freedom of expression and artistic integrity, arguing that the museum was clearly protected under the First Amendment. Many critics noted that the works on display were not great art but asserted that the museum should remain open and the public should be given a chance to view them. They accused Giuliani, who was then campaigning to become the Republican nominee in the 2000 New York senatorial race, of pandering to conservative voters. The museum sued the city in district court, and on 2 November 1999 federal judge Nina Gershon ruled in favor of the museum, forcing restoration of its city subsidy (about one-third of its total budget). Museum chairman Arnold Lehman called the ruling a victory for the citizens of New York and for freedom of expression.

Sources:

Michael Kimmelman, "Cutting Through the Cynicism in Art Furor," *New York Times,* 24 September 1999, pp. B1, B6.

Kimmelman, "A Madonna's Many Meanings in the Art World," *New York Times,* 5 October 1999, pp. E1, E3.

Joseph Wesley Zeigler, *Arts in Crisis: The National Endowment for the Arts versus America* (Chicago: A Capella Books, 1994).

THE ART MARKET

Price Inflation. "Millennium fever" gripped the art market in the 1990s. The London-based *Daily Telegraph Art 100 Index,* which traces prices of works by the one hundred top artists in the world, reported a price rise of 26 percent from January through November 1998, double the increase for 1997. "The market is extremely strong," said New York dealer David Nash. "There's a lot of money around, most of it in the hands of Americans and Europeans." Like stock in Internet companies, art works sold for higher and higher prices throughout the 1990s but—as was also the case with internet stocks—prices did not always equate with value. In the early 1990s prices paid for modern masterpieces were already setting records. Constantin Brancusi's 1919 *Golden Bird* sold for $12 million; Vincent van Gogh's *Portrait of Dr. Gachet* was bought for $82.5 million; and Pierre Renoir's *Au Moulin de la Galette* went for $78.1 million. With the art market so overheated, even prices for artists whose works were traditionally widely available were high—for example, Edgar Degas's *Racehorses* brought $9.98 million, and Henri Matisse's *The Persian Robe* sold for $4.5 million. By the late 1990s, however, the market

seemed to have passed its peak. Van Gogh's *Portrait of Dr. Gachet* was offered for sale privately in 1998 at an asking price of $80 million.

New Collectors. Many art buyers were new to the business of collecting. Often they were looking for ways to invest money they made in the booming stock market of the 1990s. The new collectors included Japanese businessmen such as Ryoei Saito, who saw art works by established artists as good long-term investments. Another new collector was Las Vegas impresario Steve Wynn, who spent in the neighborhood of $300 million in 1997 and 1998 on Impressionist art to display at his casinos.

The Market for Contemporary Art. American contemporary art sold well in the late 1990s. Art from the 1980s and 1990s had substantial resale value at auction. In 1997 the Museum of Modern Art in New York purchased a complete set of Cindy Sherman's *Untitled Film Stills* (1977–1980)—sixty-nine photographs—for $1 million. At the fall 1999 auction of contemporary art in New York City, Sherman pieces sold for as much as $96,000, and Christie's in London sold a Sherman piece for a record $144,045. Artists considered controversial in the 1980s made comebacks in the late 1990s. Prices rose for works by Jeff Koons, who outraged the art world in the 1980s and early 1990s by appropriating the works of others in his pieces. He was even convicted of copyright infringement in 1992, after he used a greeting-card photograph in one of his sculptures. Also in the late 1990s a self-portrait by 1980s phenomenon Jean-Michel Basquiat, who died of a heroin overdose in 1988, sold for $3.3 million.

Source:

Thane Peterson, "These Prices Are Surreal," *Business Week,* no. 3610 (28 December 1998 – 4 January 1999): 170–173.

ART THEFT

Tracking Nazi and Soviet Art Thefts. During World War II the Nazis stole large numbers of art works from Jews who either fled Europe or were sent to concentration camps, and the German army looted works from museums and private collections in occupied countries. Then, as the Third Reich collapsed, the Soviet army sent special brigades to find art treasures in Soviet-occupied Germany. According to one estimate, the Soviets took 2.5 million art works and 10 million books and manuscripts back to Russia. About 1.5 million items were returned to East Germany in the 1950s. In the 1990s several new organizations—the Holocaust Art Restitution Project (HARP), the Commission for Art Recovery, and the Art and Archive Foundation—were founded to help survivors and descendants locate missing family heirlooms. As John Marks has pointed out, many survivors and descendants of victims of the Holocaust "see this art not only as a commodity but also as one of their last links to a vanished past. For them, memory and identity are on the line." After a half century, however, efforts to recover missing art works have proved difficult, often because documentation has been lost or destroyed. Some of the lost pieces have found their way into American museums and private collections, and in June 1998 Philippe de Montebello, director of the Metropolitan Museum of Art in New York City, joined with a group of other American museum directors in an agreement to create a central database of all works with suspicious pasts.

Returned Paintings. Some looted paintings have been discovered. In August 1998 the relatives of two Holocaust victims who had owned Edgar Degas's *Landscape with Smokestacks* agreed to let the Art Institute of Chicago keep the painting, donated to the museum by a member of its board of trustees, in exchange for a payment of roughly $500,000. Often stolen works are located by chance. In 1998 Henri Matisse's *Odalisque,* left behind by Paul Rosenberg, a Jewish art dealer, when he fled Europe in 1940, turned up at the Seattle Art Museum. The daughter of the art collector who had bought the painting in good faith and donated it to the museum saw the work in a book about looted art and notified Rosenberg's heirs. In June 1999, faced with legal proceedings to recover the work, the board of the Seattle Art Museum voted unanimously to return it to the heirs.

The Wadsworth Atheneum Case. In another case, a visitor to the Wadsworth Atheneum in Hartford, Connecticut, recognized Jacopo Zucchi's *The Bath of Bathsheba,* which had been on display there since 1965, as the same painting he had seen in a Berlin museum in the 1920s, when it had been on loan from the Italian government. The subsequent inquiry discovered that the Soviets had confiscated the work at the end of World War II. It later surfaced in Paris, where the Wadsworth Atheneum bought it during the 1960s.

Seizure of Paintings in Manhattan. In July 1998 it was returned to the Italian government. In January of the same year, Manhattan district attorney Robert Morgenthau seized two paintings by Egon Schiele that were on loan to the Museum of Modern Art from the Leopold Foundation in Vienna, preventing their return to Austria until legal proceedings could determine their rightful owners. They were claimed by relatives of the original owners. One of the paintings had been confiscated from a man who perished at Dachau while the other was seized from a woman who fled to London in 1938. In this case, however, a New York judge ruled that the paintings should be sent back to Austria.

Van Gogh's *Wheat Field with Cypresses.* In at least one case a painting believed to have been stolen by the Nazis turned out to come from a legitimate source. In 1993 the Metropolitan Museum bought Vincent van Gogh's *Wheat Field with Cypresses* from the son of a Swiss businessman known to have bought looted Nazi art, though its provenance, or ownership history, for the years 1939–1951 was uncertain. A *New York Times* reporter discovered, however, that a grandchild of the Jewish art collector who was the original owner had sold the painting to the businessman in 1951, thus legitimizing the museum's ownership of the painting.

Sources:
William Glaberson, Hazy Legal Terrain," *New York Times,* 30 September 1999, p. B12;

Robert Hughes, "Hold those Paintings!" *Time,* 151 (19 January 1998): 70;

John Marks, "How Did All that Art End Up in Museums?" *U.S. News & World Report,* 124 (8 June 1998): 38–40;

Nomi Morris and Karen Nickel Anhalt, "Plundered as Germany Fell," *Maclean's,* 111 (27 July 1998): 51.

ART TRENDS

New Attempts to Define "Art." In the 1990s even the most knowledgeable and sophisticated critics were sometimes hard-pressed to distinguish brilliance from schlock, with conservative critics bemoaning the depths to which so-called artists had fallen. For example, Roger Kimball, managing editor of the conservative art journal *The New Criterion,* bemoaned the pervasiveness of performance art, "that euphemism for politicized psycho-drama." One of the most controversial works at the 1993 biennial exhibition of new art at the Whitney Museum of American Art in New York City was *Gnaw,* an installation created by Janine Antoni to express her opinions on love, beauty, and artifice. Using a large block of chocolate, a block of lard, and a polished metal-and-glass display case, she chewed and spat out some of the chocolate and lard and shaped the pieces into hearts and lipsticks, which she displayed in the case as if they were the work of a fashion designer. According to critic Arthur C. Danto, *Gnaw* represented "the bulimic's fantasies of beauty and of love, for the sake of which she forces herself to throw up." While some critics, including Danto, praised the work as brilliant and effective, culture

---

THE TOP TEN LIVING ARTISTS

In 1999 *ARTnews* asked museum directors, curators, and art critics around the world to name "the top ten artists working today." The ten artists mentioned most often, whom the magazine listed in alphabetical order, were:

Matthew Barney

Louise Bourgeois

Jasper Johns

Ilya Kabakov

Agnes Martin

Bruce Nauman

Sigmar Polke

Gerhard Richter

Cindy Sherman

Jeff Wall

Source: "The Ten Best Living Artists," *ARTnews,* 98 (December 1999): 137–147.

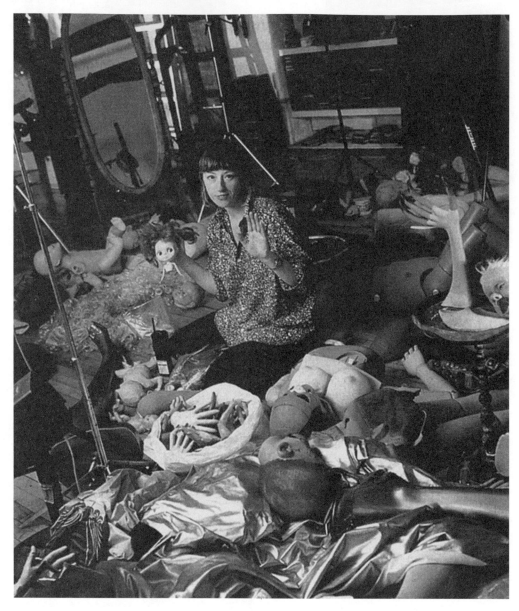

Cindy Sherman amid props in her studio (© Michel Arnaud; Bettmann/Corbis)

conservatives called it an example of the unintelligent, uncreative "display of psycho-pathology and radical slogan-eering" that passes for art in contemporary America. Kimball, in fact, wrote of his "bitter disillusionment" that Charles Ray's forty-five-foot fire-truck sculpture, displayed outside the museum, was not a real fire truck signaling "the ultimate act of performance art": a fire destroying the Whitney and all the works in the 1993 biennial.

A Major Postmodernist. In the 1990s performance artist Cindy Sherman was recognized by many critics and museum directors as a major American artist. In fact, as Barbara Pollack of *ARTnews* has commented, Sherman "put a face on postmodernism." She first gained critical acclaim with her *Untitled Film Stills* (1977–1980), in which she satirized stereotypical images of women in Hollywood movies. Since then Sherman has become well known for her studies of identity and gender stereotypes in works that combine portraiture and photography. For the controversial 1993 Whitney biennial, Sherman photographed man-

nequins with simulated genitalia to create what Ralph Rugoff called "sexual scenarios rife with overtones of viola-tion and brutality." Her contribution to the 1995 biennial was more surreal and Dadaesque and less sexually charged that her 1993 work. Explaining her intentions, she noted, "I was sort of playing with the idea of violence. And I think that, as with some dadaist photography, people might see a misogynist streak." In 1997 Sherman directed *Office Killer*, a horror movie in which an unhappy female office worker works off her sexual frustration by going on a killing spree. The movie, which starred Carol Kane and Molly Ring-wald, failed to gain Sherman much attention outside art circles. Sherman's 1999 show at the Metro Picture Gallery in New York City used Barbie dolls and toy action figures in scenes of horror and brutality. By then some critics were charging that her new work lacked originality. According to Vince Aletti of the *Village Voice*, she was caught up in her own obsessions, "stalled in the grotesque—a rut where disgust, outrage, and pain are mitigated only by humor at

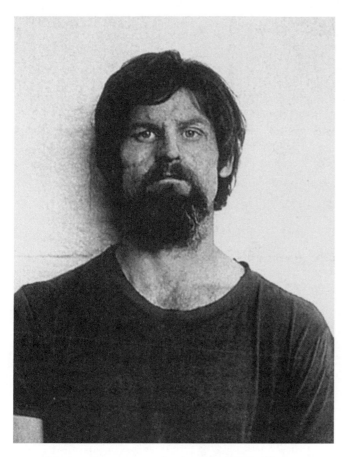

Matthew Barney as convicted murderer Gary Gilmore
in *Cremaster 2* (1999)

question the boundaries separating sculpture, installation, body art, and video art. Barney has often blurred the distinction between masculine and feminine as well, assuming personae that defied gender stereotypes. Some critics have described his works as "posthuman," rather than "postmodern."

Cremaster. Barney's most influential body of work in the 1990s was *Cremaster,* a projected five-part series he began showing in 1994. (The title refers to the muscle that causes the testicles to retract into the body when they are exposed to cold.) By 1999 he had created three parts as videos and then made a fourth part, which he labeled *Cremaster 2,* using 35mm film. Pollack has described the characters in *Cremaster,* including those played by Barney, as "oddly formed creatures with equally bewildering genitals," and she commented that the movies are "filled with vivid images difficult to shake from memory." Shown at the Walker Art Center in Minneapolis in September and October 1999, *Cremaster 2* is ostensibly about murderer Gary Gilmore, who was executed by firing squad at his own request in 1977. The most ambitious part of the series *Cremaster 2* includes an installation of objects and movie stills in addition to the movie, with a cast that includes Barney as Gilmore, novelist Norman Mailer as Houdini, a Brahma bull, and the Mormon Tabernacle Choir. Always changing, always questioning, and always fascinating, Barney has challenged viewers to interpret his complex works, but as Madoff has commented, "If you're willing to spend the time to untie his Gordian knot of symbolic acts and images . . . you'll find a maniacal, systematic and deeply imagined vision of a world as strangely alternate as Lewis Carroll's in *Through the Looking Glass.*"

Dial-up Art. Performance art brings the audience and its reactions into the artwork. In 1998 Karen Finley, one of the most controversial performance artists of the 1980s and 1990s, began a daily telephone conversation with anyone who wanted to dial 1-900-ALL-KAREN and pay to take part in the "performance." Finley became well known in the 1980s for performance pieces in which she smeared her naked body with yams or chocolate, and in 1990 she was denied NEA funding because of the sexual and political content of such works. According to Finley, "they had to make me out to be a pervert, deviant, a wild animal, which is how women's sexuality is seen. In reality I embodied this psychological fear of women's sexuality that's projected onto all women. That's what the myth is about." She responded to the 1998 Supreme Court ruling against her suit to regain NEA funding by launching *The Return of the Chocolate-Smeared Woman,* a sequel to the controversial performance piece that led to the loss of her grant money. "I'm going to enjoy my status as a loser," she told an interviewer. In fact, the publicity surrounding her battle with the NEA made Finley a celebrity, attracting large audiences to her performances, and in 1993 she was awarded a Guggenheim Fellowship. During the 1990s Finley adopted a performance style in which she interrupted her monologues to berate people who laughed when she thought they

its blackest." Yet, Pollack disagreed, writing that "Sherman subordinates herself as a work of eternal fiction—unknowable and ultimately absent from the artwork." Sherman's works sold for record high prices in the late 1990s, and *ARTnews* magazine included her on its list of the ten best living artists.

Bizarre Fantasies. Another artist on the *ARTnews* top-ten list was Matthew Barney, who started out as a "bad-boy" artist in the early 1990s but by 1997 had become the first recipient of the $50,000 Hugo Boss Award from the Guggenheim Museum in New York City for his contributions to contemporary art. Barney had his first solo show in 1991 at the Barbara Gladstone Gallery in New York City just two years after graduating from Yale University, and he has since had shows in other major U.S. cities as well as in London and Tokyo. Some viewers have been observed to shudder at Barney's works, in which he generally combines the media of performance, sculpture, and film to create outrageous spectacles that combine what Pollack has called "the brawny esthetics of athleticism with a masochistic attraction to physical extremes." Barney has appeared in his works playing such diverse roles as a ram wearing a morning coat, a satyr in the backseat of a stretch limousine, and Harry Houdini throwing himself naked and chained into the Danube under the eyes of a weeping Ursula Andress. He has also been videotaped using rock-climbing equipment of his own design to scale the walls and ceiling of a gallery, his body smeared with Vaseline—forcing viewers to

Fred Tomaselli's *Brain with Flowers* (1990–1997), blotter acid, pills, leaves, photocollage, acrylic, and resin on a wood panel (Collection of the artist)

should not or tried to leave early. *The American Chestnut* (1998) included a series of vignettes "to demonstrate the struggle that people go through when they are humiliated. How people try and be reasonable and even think they deserve it when they're put down or something bad happens when they're trying to grow." As an example of female narrative, she used a script that she rummaged through occasionally. As she explained, "Women haven't been allowed to express their opinions, so when they do, in recipes or journals or in literature like Barbara Pym or Jane Austen, they tend to be overloaded with observations. It's an interior world with interior dialogue."

Other Performance Artists. Also during the 1990s, Vanessa Beecroft's *Show* featured a two-and-a-half hour spectacle of "languorous immobility" and "reciprocal staring" that some critics admired for its "unsettling beauty and a passive-aggressive quality." Jason Sprinkle's performance art drew attention in 1996, when he left a large "heart-shaped sculpture in a pickup truck whose fender bore the word 'bomb'" on a street in his native Seattle. This "performance" resulted in a five-hour evacuation of downtown Seattle. Sprinkle explained that he was protesting plans to allow motor traffic on a pedestrians-only street through the center of the city.

Abstract Art. Described by Danto to be "one of the best American painters today," David Reed attempts to create "a sense of absence" in his paintings, because "absence makes you want to fill it in and participate." While Danto characterizes Reed's style as "Manhattan Baroque," another critic, Dave Hickey, says that Reed, who was born in San Diego and has worked in Manhat-

tan since 1971, is a "California" painter because his works have "a kind of decorum . . . that relates to a cool abstraction and a cool, relaxed sensibility." Reed has incorporated his paintings in installations and video projects, as well as in the "Collector's Bedroom" he designed in 1998 for the architectural firm OpenOffice. In all Reed's work, says critic Barbara A. MacAdam, he embraces "nothing less than the conscious and unconscious, time and space, the real and imagined, the intellect and emotion, life and death, landscape and interior, ocean and prairie, and so on ad infinitum in such a way that we sense it all but can never actually see it." His paintings—including 1999 works such as *#446* and *#449*—almost seem to escape the margins of the canvas with undulating swirls if paint interrupted by other patterns and clashing colors—all suggesting what MacAdam calls "the unexpected rhythms of nature and life." For a 1999 traveling exhibit he digitally inserted some of his paintings into a video of the Alfred Hitchcock movie *Vertigo* (1958).

Drug Collages. During the 1990s another New York–based artist, Fred Tomaselli, became well-known for making collages in which he imbedded various kinds of over-the-counter, prescription drugs, as well as various hallucinogens and psychedelics, in tamper-proof resin panels. In an interview with Fred Bendheim, Tomaselli explained that he was inspired by the experiences of friends with AIDS and his own "pretty colorful drug past" to think about "this conundrum. Drugs have a conflicting nature: the were saving life, but also destroying life." In discussing the goal of such works, he stated: "I'm not out to correct any societal ills, but I do have a belief in beauty, the sublime, and the transcendental, even in an age so brutalized, ugly, and cynical."

Digital Art. Computer technology in the 1990s provided artists a new medium for self-expression, as well as a new means of marketing and displaying art. For example, Maciej Wisniewski, a New York–based artist who also worked as software developer for IBM, invented Netomat, which "cuts through the flow of information and gets a snapshot of the Internet from several different sources," creating a new artistic medium with unlimited potential. Another new digital advance for artists, Icontext, is built around the commonly used 128-character computer code known as ASCII (American Standard Code for Information Interchange) and combines word-processor programs, paint programs, and chat software. Artists such as Andy C. Deck used computer and interactive technology to "explore the intersection of text and image." Using such new technology is expensive, and internet artists have often sought corporate sponsors, who pay to use web artists' works in online promotional campaigns. Corporations like to sponsor web art because they view it as "cutting edge" and believe it appeals to sophisticated, affluent consumers. Digital artists are happy to participate in advertising campaigns while they wait for a market for their art to develop within the traditional museum and gallery community. The 1997 biennial at the Whitney Museum gave digital art the sort of exposure it needed to attract collectors, by including several works that used and addressed the new technology, most notably Doug Aitken's website *Loaded* and "a massive technological fantasy" by Jason Rhoades. In November 1999 the Whitney announced plans to feature digital art prominently at its 2000 biennial, from interactive websites to multimedia narratives. Among the nine websites that were included were Mark Amerika's *Grammatron,* a work of hypertext fiction; Ben Benjamin's *superbad.com* website; John F. Simon Jr.'s *Every Icon* software; Darcey Steinke's *Blindspot,* an interactive, multimedia narrative; and *Fakeshop,* a New York-based group project that combines live performance with video conferencing, chat, and graphics.

Graffiti Art. Graffiti art, which emerged in the late 1970s as part of the "hip-hop" culture of the South Bronx, began to achieve recognition as a respectable art form in the 1980s, with graffiti artists such as Jean-Michel Basquiat, Futura 2000, Fab Five Freddy, and the United Artists group achieving success in the booming art market. In the 1990s, however, other graffiti artists were still struggling to make the art establishment recognize them as fine artists and to convince galleries to display their work. James "James-TOP" Cade said, "We want to educate people of color about this urban art form, hoping that our people will become consumers of our art." When Dondi-TOP, one of the graffiti artists who achieved mainstream recognition, died in 1998, fellow graffiti artists mounted a retrospective exhibit of his work to educate the public about graffiti as an art form. In 1999 San Francisco graffiti artist Barry McGee had one of his works placed in the permanent collection of the San Francisco Museum of Modern Art collection, but many street artists maintain their radical independence, insisting that there is no need to pay money to visit a gallery when one can see art on any city street.

Subway Art. Typically, graffiti artists have started out by using subway stations and trains as canvases; by "tagging" or signing their work they became known to regular subway passengers. From the beginning of the graffiti-art movement, not everyone has been impressed. While some viewers have called it a form of folk art, others have labeled it "vandalism," and various urban governments have attempted to curb what they consider defacement of public property. In May 1995, for example, Philadelphia mayor Ed Rendell announced a major campaign of "zero tolerance" for graffiti in that city. Arguing that graffiti destroyed the morale of the city, he justified the crackdown by alleging that graffiti artists were connection with gangs, drugs, and violence. African American leaders became angry because most of the arrested graffiti "taggers" were black, while, in fact, graffiti artists came from other races as well.

Sources:

Vince Aletti, "Doll Parts," *Village Voice,* 26 May – 1 June 1999, pp. 131–136.

Fred Bendheim, "Drugs and the Art of Fred Tomaselli," *Lancet,* 354 (28 August 1999): 781.

Arthur C. Danto, "The 1993 Whitney Biennial," *Nation,* 256 (19 April 1993): 533–536.

Jonathan Gregg, "Framing Technology," *Time Digital Daily,* 19 March 1997, Time.com, Internet website.

Peter Hay Halpert, Untitled note on Cindy Sherman's photographs, *American Photo,* 10 (March/April 1999): 50.

Anita Hamilton, "Clicking on the Canvas, *Time,* 155 (10 April 2000): 129.

Roger Kimball, "Of Chocolate, Lard, and Politics," *National Review,* 45 (26 April 1993): 54–56.

Barbara A. MacAdam, "A Minimalist in Barque Trappings," *ARTnews,* 98 (December 1999): 158–162.

Steven Henry Madoff, "Hallucinatory Acts," *Time,* 154 (30 August 1999): 67, 70.

Matthew Mirapaul, "Whitney Biennial May Include Digital Art Works," *New York Times,* 25 November 1999, p. E5.

Barbara Pollack, "Self-Denial," *ARTnews,* 98 (December 1999): 146.

Pollack, "The Wizard of Odd," *ARTnews,* 98 (December 1999): 138.

Ralph Rugoff, "The Show of Shows,"*Harper's Bazaar,* no. 3400 (March 1995): 332–337.

Melanie Wise, "Graffiti: 'Writing in the City," *San Francisco Urban Institute Quarterly,* 1 (Winter 1996–1997).

LITERATURE: FICTION TRENDS

The Decline of Minimalism. Among the most important literary trends of the 1980s was minimalism, which can in fact be traced back to the spare prose of Ernest Hemingway. Among the best minimalist works are startlingly original, insightful, well-crafted, and moving works such as Ann Beattie's novel *Chilly Scenes in Winter* (1976) and Raymond Carver's short-story collection *Cathedral* (1981). By the 1990s, however, minimalism seemed to have exhausted its creative possibilities. Minimalist writers of the 1990s wrote fiction that seemed too restricted, not only in time, place, and plot, but also in the emotional

E. ANNIE PROULX

The SHIP-PING NEWS

A NOVEL

Dust jacket for the novel that won the 1993 National Book Award and the 1994 Pulitzer Prize for fiction. The setting is a Newfoundland village where the traditional lifestyle is being destroyed by the decline of the Canadian fishing industry.

range of the characters—who all too predictably were members of the lower class. Critics began to complain about novels featuring inarticulate truck drivers, unskilled laborers, waitresses, hairdressers, convenience store clerks, and mechanics, all of whom seemed to live in trailer parks. Not only were they listless, passionless, and intellectually, morally, emotionally, and spiritually exhausted, but such characters seemed totally unaware of what they thought about any aspect of their lives. Strictly speaking, critics charged, the average piece of 1990s minimalist fiction was not really a story at all. There was often no plot to speak of and change, if it occurred at all, was random and, therefore, insignificant. Novelist Madison Smartt Bell charged that minimalism offered an "anorexic aesthetic" in which less really was less, and in a 1999 interview novelist Tom Wolfe echoed Bell's assessment: "The novel in this country is being starved to death by the novelists. . . . It now suffers from advanced anorexia nervosa." Wolfe blamed the decline on the vogue during the second half of the century for novels as "psychological studies rather than big social studies" and complained, "When the novelists said we can't embrace life any more, . . . the novel began to die." Earlier in the decade, editor David Jauss had already come to the

conclusion that "what we need, and deserve is an approach to fiction that is less homogeneous. . . . But even more than a more heterogenous approach to fiction, we need more writers . . . who will rediscover fiction's primary subject—the effect of time and experience on people—and its primary hope—the possibility of change."

The New Regionalism. One hopeful sign that the novel might still be revived was the favorable reception of works by writers who might be grouped as new regionalists. Like other trends of the 1990s, the so-called new regionalists had been achieving recognition since at least the 1980s, when, for example, Carolyn Chute's novel *The Beans of Egypt, Maine* (1985) and John Casey's *Spartina* (1988), set in coastal Rhode Island, were surprise best-sellers. The new regionalists drew on the lessons of the great modernist and a variety of other sources, including in some cases the Latin American magical realists, to create technically polished works that depict rural life without the sentimentality and condescension that marred so much regionalist fiction of the nineteenth century. While such fiction might have appealed to Americans' end-of-the-century urge to rediscover their roots, it often included harsh messages about alarming discrepancies between the American dream and the American reality, past and present. One novelist who had been writing since the mid 1960s, Cormac McCarthy, achieved public recognition in the 1990s when his *All the Pretty Horses* (1992), the first volume of his Border Trilogy, won both a National Book Award and a National Book Critics' Award, and he went on to attract readers with the next two volumes, *The Crossing* (1994), and *Cities of the Plain* (1998). Often criticized for the violence of his fiction and praised for its lyricism, McCarthy set his trilogy on both sides of the Mexican border early in the twentieth century, focusing on characters caught between the traditional lifestyle of the nineteenth century and the inexorable "progress" of modernization. A similar theme is apparent in the novels of Carolyn Chute, whose *Merry Men* (1994) and *Snow Man* (1999) are set among the rural poor of New England. Unlike most of these writers, Annie Proulx (pronounced Pru), has never restricted herself to one region. Her critically acclaimed first novel, *Postcards* (1992) is set in rural New England, while her second novel, *The Shipping News* (1993), which earned her a Pulitzer Prize and a National Book Award, is set in Newfoundland, and her third, *Accordion Crimes* (1996) is set in various regions of the United States over a period of about a century. *Close Range* (1999), a collection of short stories, is set in Wyoming. Often praised for her lyrical prose style, Proulx has been unafraid to tackle the big social themes that the minimalists eschew, taking on Americans' most treasured myths about the nation's history. Two other writers who have never limited themselves to particular regions or themes also contributed to regional fiction in the 1990s. Peter Matthiessen's trilogy *Killing Mr. Watson* (1990), *Lost Man's River* (1997), and *Bone by Bone* (1999) depicts life in Florida as it was before the arrival of resort hotels and Disney World, while Jane Smiley's *A Thousand Acres* (1991) follows the decline of a farm family in Iowa. Other notable regional novels of the decade were David Guterson's *Snow Falling on Cedars* (1993), set in the Pacific Northwest, and Kent Haruf's *Plainsong* (1999), which immersed readers in the life of a small community in Colorado. One indication of the growing popularity and importance of regional literature was the founding of Storylines America in October 1997. A cooperative venture between public libraries and public radio stations, Storylines America is a series of broadcast book discussions designed to promote the reading and discussion of regional literature.

Southern Fiction. Regionalism never died in the South, and Southern writers contributed to the national resurgence of its popularity during the 1990s. Authors with established reputations continued to publish critically acclaimed novels. Novels by women writers with established followings included Anne Tyler's *Saint Maybe* (1991), *Ladder of Years* (1995), and *A Patchwork Planet* (1998); Lee Smith's *The Devil's Dream* (1992) and *Saving Grace* (1995); Doris Betts's *Souls Raised From the Dead* (1994) and *The Sharp Teeth of Love* (1997); Mary Lee Settle's *Choices* (1995); Bobbie Ann Mason's *Feather Crowns* (1993); and Jill McCorkle's *Carolina Moon* (1992). Among the elder statesmen of Southern fiction were Reynolds Price with *The Tongues of Angels* (1990), *Blue Calhoun* (1992), and *The Promise of Rest* (1995); Peter Taylor with *In the Tennessee Country* (1994), and Texan Larry McMurtry with *The Evening Star* (1992), *Streets of Laredo* (1993), *Pretty Boy Floyd* (1994); *Comanche Moon* (1997), and *Duane's Depressed* (1999). Dorothy Allison's *Bastard out of Carolina* (1992) and Charles Frazier's *Cold Mountain* (1997) were among the critically acclaimed first novels of the decade. Writing of the "blithely and gracefully eclectic" nature of Southern fiction in the 1990s novelist George Garrett singled out a long list of novels as proof that there is "much more to living Southern literature than meets the eye." His list included Madison Smartt Bell's *Barking Man* (1990), *Doctor Sleep* (1992), and *All Souls' Rising* (1996); Kelly Cherry's *The Society of Friends* (1999); R. H. W. Dillard's *Omniphobia* (1995); Judith Hawkes's *Julian's House* (1991), *My Soul to Keep* (1996), and *The Heart of a Witch* (1999); and Dale Phillips's *My People's Waltz* (1999).

African American Fiction. Several important African American novels appeared during the 1990s, including Ralph Ellison's long-awaited *Juneteenth* (1999). Unfinished at the time of his death in 1994, the published version of the novel is only part of a long work-in-progress, assembled and edited by Ellison's friend and literary executor John F. Callahan. Toni Morrison, who won the 1993 Nobel Prize in Literature, produced *Jazz* (1992) and *Paradise* (1998). New books by other African American novelists with established reputations were also published during the decade, including Ernest J. Gaines's *A Lesson Before Dying* (1993), Gloria Naylor's *Bailey's Cafe* (1992) and *The Men of Brewster Place* (1998), Ishmael Reed's *Japanese by Spring* (1993), Alice Walker's *Possessing the Secret of Joy* (1992), and John Edgar Wideman's *Philadelphia Fire*

Dust jacket for one of the best-selling legal thrillers of the 1990s

(1990), *The Cattle Killing* (1996), and *Two Cities* (1998). At the same time a new generation of African American novelists began to make its presence felt. These writers included Dori Sanders with *Clover* (1990) and *Her Own Place* (1993), Fred D'Aguiar with *Dear Future* (1996) and *Feeding the Ghosts* (1999), John Keene with *Annotations* (1995), Danzy Senna with *Caucasia* (1998), Margaret Cezair Thompson with *The True History of Paradise* (1999), and Colson Whitehead with *The Intuitionist* (1998). Terry McMillan had two popular successes with *Waiting to Exhale* (1992) and *How Stella Got Her Groove Back* (1996), both adapted as motion pictures, and Tina McElroy Ansa's *Ugly Ways*, Bebe Moore Campbell's *Brothers and Sisters*, and Connie Briscoe's *Sisters and Lovers* all sold well in 1995.

Mystery and Crime Fiction. A perennial favorite among readers, mystery and crime novel soared in popularity during the 1990s. In each year of the decade more than 1,500 new mysteries appeared. Following the success of Scott Turow's *Presumed Innocent* (1987), lawyer-turned-novelist John Grisham transformed the legal thriller into a best-selling genre. In many ways Robert B. Parker remained the dean of detective writers, at least among those in the hard-boiled tradition of Dashiell Hammett and Raymond Chandler. Parker's Spenser, the protagonist of novels such as *Double Deuce* (1992) and *Paper Doll* (1993), is a prototypical hard-boiled hero patterned after Hammett's Sam Spade and Chandler's Philip Marlowe. Robert Crais's Elvis

THE WRITER'S SHRINKING MARKET

Despite a booming economy during the second half of the 1990s, many American publishers cut their fiction lists and tended to be unwilling to take chances on new authors, relying instead on novels by authors whose earlier books had sold successfully. The prospect of high volume sales rather than literary merit often determined which books got published and which did not. "As the marketable chances of 'serious' and 'literary' fiction continue to dwindled and diminish," complained novelist George Garrett in 1992, "it is the publishers alone who are empowered to turn their particular picture of reality, no matter how distorted or illusory, into a self-fulfilling prophecy. . . . Did you seriously imagine that readers have anything to do with the process?" Another novelist, Lance Olsen, complained that publishing in the 1990s produced "the literary equivalent of all those seemingly mass-produced abstract paintings, themselves the artistic equivalent of wallpaper for the wealthy, . . . that litter lots of galleries these days: decorative arts, art as space-filler or time-passer. Sitcom art. CNN art. Waldenbooks, it turns out, is the literary analog for K-Mart and Pizza Hut." Olsen and others also objected to the proliferation of creative-writing programs, of which there were more than 330 in the United States and Canada by the end of the decade. Since the 1960s, these programs have gradually become "word factories" destined to produce prose that Olsen calls "glossy," "emotionless," "unremarkable," and "tame," and writers who are "mildly talented in a technical sort of way."

Sources: George Garrett, "Soil of Hope: New and Other Voices in Southern Fiction for the Nineties," *ANQ*, 5 (October 1992): 193-195.

Lance Olsen, "The Michael Jacksonization of American Fiction," *ANQ*, 5 (October 1992): 171–179.

Cole is a sort of Philip Marlowe for the 1990s. While Spencer is a veteran of the Korean War, Cole fought in the Vietnam War and occasionally talks to his cat. During the nineties two female writers, Sue Grafton and Sara Peretsky, continued the sagas of their hard-boiled women detectives: Grafton's Kinsey Millhone and Peretsky's V. I. Warshawski. Walter Mosley and James Lee Burke may be the most literary detective writers of the decade. Moseley's Ezekiel "Easy" Rollins and Burke's Dave Robicheaux are two of the most complex and intriguing characters to grace the mystery fiction of the 1990s. James Ellroy transcended the genre of mystery fiction with his crime novels rooted in social history. *L.A. Confidential* (1990), the third novel in his L.A. Quartet, was filmed and won an Academy Award for Best Screenplay in 1997, Ellroy's place as a leading crime writer of the decade was reinforced. Tony Hillerman continued his excellent detective series set in the midst of

Native American life in the Southwest. There were also mysteries for animal lovers, such as Rita Mae Brown's Sneaky Pie Brown mysteries. High-tech thrillers involving the Internet began to appear at the end of the decade, as well as science-fiction mysteries such as Philip Finch's *f2f* (1997) and Philip Kerr's *Grid* (1997). Historical mysteries, including Margaret Frazer's *Novice's Tale* (1992), Candace Robb's *Apothecary Rose* (1994), and Margaret Lawrence's *Hearts and Bones* (1996) were increasingly in demand. The most popular mystery novels of the 1990s were realistic and believable. Mystery and detective fiction reflects the condition of society at the time in which its is written. If the majority of such fiction written during the 1990s was any indication, gang leaders, drug lords, crime bosses, corrupt police officers, and venal public officials dominated the world, seeping into and destroying the lives of ordinary men and women. Detectives took it upon themselves to grapple with this evil and to restore, at least temporarily, a sense of rationality and virtue.

Cyberpunk. Another trend that surfaced during the mid 1980s and continued into the 1990s became known as "cyberpunk." Particularly attractive to young science-fiction fans, cyperpunk is situated in a futuristic world ruled by technology. Typically a host of lowlifes operating on the fringes of society try to overcome, or escape, domination by powerful computers and sinister multinational corporations. Examples of the genre in the 1990s were Mark Leyner's hallucinatory *My Cousin, My Gastroenterologist* (1990) and Richard Power's complex *The Gold Bug Variations* (1991). By the early 1990s cyberpunk had splintered into subgenres, most notably steam punk and splatterpunk. Steam-punk fiction presents alternate versions of history. For example, *Difference Engine* (1991), by Bruce Sterling and William Gibson, offers a picture of what might have happened if Charles Babbage had built the computer he imagined in the 1830s, ushering in the Information Age some 160 years before the fact. Splatterpunk presents an often gruesome vision of the present as populated by the morally bankrupt and the outright psychotic. Perhaps the best-known splatterpunk novel is Bret Easton Ellis's controversial *American Psycho* (1991).

Graphic Fiction. Described as contemporary analogue to medieval illuminated manuscripts, graphic fiction combines skillful comic-book art with elements of the novel. The best example of graphic fiction to appear during the 1990s was the second volume of Art Spiegelman's *Maus*, published in 1992. (The first volume came out in 1986.) Together these somber books tell the story of Spiegelman's father, a Holocaust survivor, in the form of black-and-white cartoon drawings that depict the Poles as pigs, the Jews as mice, and the Nazis as cats.

Sources:
Frederick Barthelme, "On Being Wrong: Convicted Minimalist Spills Bean," *New York Times Book Review*, 3 April 1988), pp. 1, 25–27.

Madison Smartt Bell, "Less is Less: The Dwindling American Short Story," *Harpers*, 272 (April 1986): 64–69.

George Garrett, "Soil of Hope: New and Other Voices in Southern Fiction for the Nineties," *ANQ,* 5 (October 1992): 193-195.

Rick Henderson, "Looking for Clues," *Reason,* 26 (December 1994): 52–58.

David Jauss, "Literature at the End of the Century: An Editorial Perspective," *Literary Review,* 33 (Winter 1990): 164–171.

Georgia Lomax and Susan Brandehoff, "Storylines America Joins Libraries and Public Radio in Smash Kick-Off," *American Libraries,* 29 (January 1998): 88–90.

Lance Olsen, "The Michael Jacksonization of American Fiction," *ANQ,* 5 (October 1992): 171–179.

Michele Ross, "Mystery Book Trends," *Christian Science Monitor,* 30 September 1996, p. 10.

Pete Vilbig, "E. Annie Proulx," *Literary Cavalcade,* 52 (November/December 1999): 11.

Paul West, *Sheer Fiction* (New Paltz, N.Y.: McPherson, 1987).

Ed Williams, "Is The Novel Still Withering on the Vine? Tom Wolfe Thinks So," *Charlotte Observer,* 24 November 1999.

LITERATURE: READING GROUPS

Readers Unite. Though critics were bemoaning the decline in quality of the books on bookstore shelves, reading became more popular in the 1990s than it had been in decades. By 1999 there were approximately five-hundred thousand readers' book clubs in the United States, nearly double the number that existed in 1994. Even before the formation of Oprah Winfrey's Book Club in 1997, the popularity of book clubs had begun to soar. Winfrey's promotion of books and reading on her television show had a major impact on the trend. As Shelly Minton Bostwick, a member of two book-discussion groups in Madison, Wisconsin, explained, "Until Oprah Winfrey's focus, book discussion clubs and groups had always been there, but in a quieter way. Now, thanks in huge part to the power and publicity she commands, everyone has learned about us. Many new people have discovered the joys of reading, sharing and expressing opinions about a selected book." Meeting in libraries, bookstores, and private homes, book clubs attracted readers of all ages and in all regions of the country, appealing to a wide variety of literary tastes. Some were devoted only to mysteries or romances; others focused on classic or contemporary fiction, biography, science fiction, history, or books dealing with social issues. Children's reading groups became especially popular. A survey conducted by *Publishers Weekly* in 1998 indicated that 78 percent of teenagers thought reading was a "cool thing to do," while 86 percent said that they read "for fun." Sixty percent of teenagers who read on a regular basis believed that they were smarter than their peers who did not. People also joined reading clubs for reasons other than their love of books. For many, membership in a reading club provided an opportunity to discuss something besides work and family and to express their ideas to others. In *The Reading Group Handbook* (1998) Rachel W. Jacobsohn wrote, "Book groups are the evolutionary advancement of sewing bees, 'meetings' at the corner tavern, or neighborhood gatherings on the front stoop." Bostwick echoed Jacobsohn's views, noting the exhilaration that book-club members feel when they realize they "really do have opinions to express and intelligent thoughts to share with others. You know, this experience can even change one's life."

Oprah Winfrey's Book Club. When popular daytime talk-show host Oprah Winfrey started a book club, no one, perhaps not even Winfrey, expected her choices of books to carry much weight with book buyers. But her viewers trusted her choices, and becoming an Oprah Book Club selection virtually guaranteed increased publicity, sales, and critical attention. In December 1996, when Winfrey selected Toni Morrison's 1977 novel *Song of Solomon* as the second book-club offering, Morrison recalled, "I'd never heard of such a thing, and when someone called, all excited, with the news, all I could think was, 'Who's going to buy a book because of Oprah?'" Then, however, Morrison was astonished to discover that one million copies of the novel were sold, "And sales of my other books in paperback jumped about 25%." In fact, Morrison experienced more commercial success as a result of Winfrey's selection than she had after she won the Nobel Prize in Literature in 1993. Winfrey was credited with bringing new readers to bookstores. In choosing books by new writers as well as established authors, Winfrey was guided by her own concerns and tastes. Her eclectic selections include novels that deal with living with a disabled child (*Jewel* by Bret Lott); responsibility in the death of a child (*Midwives* by Chris Bohjalian); the ties that bind in a black community (*Paradise* by Toni Morrison); and a study of the foster-care system (*White Oleander* by Janet Fitch). Other choices deal with missing persons, bitter partings, and acrimonious divorces. Some religious commentators have noted a consistent rejection of God in Winfrey's selections, and critics have criticized the selections as sentimental, unnecessarily graphic, or sexist. For members of the book club, however, Winfrey's taste in reading matter resembled their own.

Sources:

Susan Wise Bauer, "Oprah's Misery Index," *Christianity Today,* 7 December 1998, pp. 70–74.

Carol Bryan, "Oprah, Just Look What You've Done!" *Library Imagination Paper,* 21 (Spring 1999): 4.

Paul Gray, "Paradise Found," *Time,* 151 (19 January 1998): 62–68.

Rachel W. Jacobsohn, *The Reading Group Handbook* (New York: Hyperion Press, 1998).

LITERATURE: SUPERSTARS

Updike's Farewell to Rabbit. During the 1990s several writers who came of age at midcentury published new and often provocative works. *Rabbit at Rest* (1996), John Updike's fourth and final installment in the saga of Harry "Rabbit" Angstrom—which began with *Rabbit Run* (1961) and continued with *Rabbit Redux* (1971) and *Rabbit is Rich* (1981)—completes the story of the former high-school basketball star who has enjoyed the benefits and endured the emptiness of the middle-class American Dream.

The Wolfe Controversy. Updike was also involved in literary controversy with his criticism of *A Man in Full* (1998), a novel by Tom Wolfe, who became well-known in the 1960s for journalistic nonfiction such as *The Kandy-*

In an interview conducted in 1998, John Updike described Harry "Rabbit" Angstrom, the protagonist of *Rabbit Run* (1961), *Rabbit Redux* (1971), *Rabbit is Rich* (1981), and *Rabbit at Rest* (1996):

I wanted to describe American life as it's seen by one of its losers, a man who, in the American style, peaked quite early. Who has made a fetish of youth because his own youth was his best period. Who has been looking for feel-good sensations ever since. Who mixes religion and sex shamelessly and helplessly, because these are the two areas in which there's some kind of transcendence. . . . His good qualities to me were that he was lively and innocent enough to be interested. Things dawned on him somewhat slowly. He wasn't a New Yorker who was ahead of the trends. . . . He's a Wordsworthian observer, constantly surprised.

Source: Will Hochman and Ellen Spiegel, "An Interview with John Updike," *Missouri Review*, 23, no. 2 (2000): 81–95.

Kolored Tangerine-Flake Streamline Baby (1965) and *The Electric Kool-Aid Acid Test* (1968). His second novel, *A Man in Full*, continued the satire of the American middle and upper classes that he had begun in his first, the best-selling *Bonfire of the Vanities* (1981), turning his story of an Atlanta businessman into a commentary on American life at the end of the century and the millennium. While some reviewers applauded Wolfe's attempt to work with such a large canvas, Updike in his review for *The New Yorker* characterized Wolfe's novel as "entertainment, not literature, even literature in a modest aspirant form." Norman Mailer joined Updike in criticizing Wolfe, writing in *The New York Review of Books* that Wolfe had failed ignominiously because he had written a sprawling book designed to appeal to the masses. "At certain points," Mailer declared, "reading the work can even be said to resemble the act of making love to a three-hundred-pound woman. Once she gets on top, it's over. Fall in love, or be asphyxiated." In *The New York Observer* academic Harold Bloom relegated Wolfe to the level of a failed Honoré Balzac. Despite such criticism Wolfe's novel became a best-seller. "Why are these old men rising off their pallets to condemn my book?," Wolfe asked. Answering his own question, he replied: "Because my book has cast a very big shadow, and people like Mailer and Updike find themselves in the dark. And what do you

President John Palms of the University of South Carolina greeting novelist John Updike, the keynote speaker at the conference on literary biography celebrating the publication of the two hundredth volume of the *Dictionary of Literary Biography*, 13 November 1998 (courtesy of Thomas Cooper Library, University of South Carolina)

do when you find yourself in the dark? You whistle. They're whistling in the dark."

Social Epics and Family Sagas. Another social epic of the 1990s was Don DeLillo's *Underworld* (1997), which depicts the United States as "a place where paranoia has replaced religion as an organizing principle." Meanwhile, Alice McDermott won a National Book Award for the elegiac *Charming Billy* (1998), in which she gathered the family and friends of deceased alcoholic Billy Lynch to hoist a few glasses in his memory at a Bronx bar, providing a moving but unsentimental portrait of Irish American life. Philip Roth's *I Married a Communist* (1998) details the downfall of a prominent radio actor during the McCarthy Era of the 1950s, while the reclusive Thomas Pynchon offered his own idiosyncratic views on the fate of the American Dream in *Vineland* (1990) and *Mason & Dixon* (1997), and E. L. Doctorow continued his look at the American past in *The Waterworks* (1994).

Sources:

Harold Bloom, "Tom Wolfe, Entertaining Pop Writer, Doesn't Pass the Balzac Acid Test," *New York Observer*, 9 November 1998, p. 19.

Malcolm Jones Jr. and Ray Sawhill, "Mr. Wolfe Bites Back," *Newsweek*, 133 (28 December 1998 – 4 January 1999): 82–83.

Norman Mailer, "A Man Half Full," *New York Review of Books*, 54 (17 December 1998): 18–22.

John Updike, "Awriiiiighhhhhhhhht," *New Yorker*, 74 (9 November 1998): 99–102.

MARKETING MINORITY LITERATURE

The African American Market. Publishers and booksellers discovered a large African American market during the 1980s. African American women in particular swarmed bookstores in search of contemporary fiction such as Tina McElroy Ansa's *Ugly Ways*, Bebe Moore Campbell's *Brothers and Sisters*, and Connie Briscoe's *Sisters and Lovers*—all published in 1995. "Although women read more in general, there's a higher proportion of female readers in the African-American community," Clara Villarosa, owner of the Hue Man Experience bookstore in Denver, Colorado, said in 1995. "Black women want to pick up a book, sit down and forget about their troubles for the day." A frequent lament among critics, however, was that, as all American readers, African Americans tended to buy popular fiction rather than serious literary works. According to literary agent Denise Stinson, "consumers are continuing to read lighter fare; and not just African Americans, either. People like their literature like TV: entertaining. They don't want to have to think about it when it's over. They don't want to read books like [Toni Morrison's] *Beloved*. . . ." During the 1990s publishers tended to neglect serious writers of color, complained Martha Southgate, book editor of *Essence* magazine. "I've read too many books that are thin retreads of [Terry McMillan's] *Waiting to Exhale*."

The Hispanic Market. In the early 1990s American publishers became aware of the growing middle-class Hispanic market in the United States and began expanding their Spanish-language offerings, creating new series aimed at the more than 26 million Hispanics in the country.

"Almost everyone in publishing has been on the verge of doing this," explained Kay Barrett of Vintage Books, a paperback division of Random House Inc., in 1995. "If you carve the numbers and look at purchasing power," said Shelly Lipton, president of Lipton Communications Group, "it suggests that there is certainly a multi-million-dollar business potential." Two volumes in the Alfaguara-Vintage Espanol series, Sandra Cisneros's *House on Mango Street* (1991) and Esmeralda Santiago's *When I Was Puerto-Rican* (1994), sold about fifteen thousand copies, and Loida Martiza Perez's *Geographies of Home* (1997) garnered critical acclaim. Despite these successes, some in the publishing industry remained skeptical that the bump in the sale of Hispanic books represented a long-term trend. Martha Levin of Anchor Books said in 1995: "I'm not convinced that we can make a go of it, which is why I'm doing it title by title."

Sources:

Kim Campbell, "Book Publishers Say 'Hola' to U.S. Hispanic Market," *Christian Science Monitor*, 20 April 1995, p. 9.

"Craft Versus Commerce," *Black Issues Book Review*, 2 (January/February 2000): 45–46.

"The Year of the Black Author," *Black Enterprise*, 25 (February 1995): 116.

MOTION PICTURES: POLITICS AND HISTORY

Life Imitating Art? Movies of the 1990s expressed Americans' cynicism about politicians and the political process. In *Wag the Dog*, released in late 1997, presidential advisers create a nonexistent international crisis to divert attention from a breaking story that accuses the president of fondling a young girl. The president's advisers and aides, experts at letting the tail wag the dog, hire a Hollywood producer to give the illusory incident a sense of reality. With his help they create footage of bombed-out villages and manufacture a true-blue American "hero" for public consumption. The following year, during revelations about President William J. Clinton's sexual relationship with Monica Lewinsky, pundits frequently accused the president of trying to "wag the dog" to divert attention from the scandal—particularly in December 1998, when he ordered the bombing of Baghdad just as the House of Representatives began debate on whether he should be impeached.

Art Imitating Life? The *Time* magazine cover for 16 March 1998 featured a photograph of John Travolta and the words "Lights! Camera! Clinton!" to spotlight coverage of the new political movie *Primary Colors*, adapted from Washington columnist Joe Klein's anonymous 1996 novel, which was based loosely on President Clinton's successful 1992 presidential campaign. Released in the midst of the Lewinsky scandal, the movie focuses on a young campaign aide whose idealism is destroyed by the pragmatic, no-holds-barred attitude of the candidate and his staff. Though Klein claimed that his characters were not exact matches to real people, critics and viewers easily identified Jack and Susan Stanton as the Clintons, Lawrence Harris as Clinton primary rival Paul Tsongas, Fred Picker as third-party candidate H. Ross Perot, campaign operative

Richard Jemmons as James Carville, and Henry Burton, the idealistic young aide, as George Stephanopoulos.

Truth versus Fiction. *Primary Colors* and *Wag the Dog* depict politics as unconcerned with truth and fairness. Another movie of the late 1990s, Warren Beatty's *Bulworth* (1998), contends that, despite its avowals to the contrary, the American public does not really want politicians to tell them the truth. Beatty, who also wrote and directed his movie, plays Jay Bulworth, a middle-aged, liberal California senator who is sick of the state of American politics and culture. After putting out a contract on his own life, he begins to state publicly what he really thinks. Charging that there is no fundamental difference between the two political parties because special interests rule both, he asserts that politicians will never say Hollywood produces "mostly crap" because they are too dependent on the money and publicity clout of movie-star backers. Conversely, he says politicians will never do anything about black issues until blacks have enough money to buy power within the political establishment. By the end of the movie he has offended nearly everyone, making the point that the public prefers pleasant lies to uncomfortable truths.

Rewriting History. Cynicism about government was also apparent in movies about earlier events in the twentieth century. Director Oliver Stone, who revisited recent American history in the 1980s with *Platoon* (1986) and *Born on the Fourth of July* (1989), began the 1990s with *JFK* (1991), a $40-million movie that revived conspiracy theories about the 1963 assassination of President John F. Kennedy. Stone began with a theory advanced by New Orleans district attorney Jim Garrison, played by Kevin Costner in the movie, selected some of his ideas, omitted others, and then added new information and conjecture to create his own theory of why President Kennedy was assassinated: "the Beast" (a conspiracy of Wall Street, the CIA, the military, and the FBI) killed him because he was planning to pull U.S. troops out of Vietnam. Stone also combined computer animation with real news footage, prompting some journalists and historians to express the concern that viewers might confuse fact and fiction. Unlike traditional historical dramas, *JFK* showed moviegoers what no one could have seen in the same frame with what everyone remembered seeing. One critic commented that nobody "can cook up imagery as arrestingly oddball as Stone." In response to such criticism Stone defended his movie "as something between entertainment and fact," and he implied that he had "angered the powers that be" because he had hit on the truth. One of the most judicious views of the movie was expressed by Thomas Reeves: "*JFK* is an entertaining and at times moving film. But it is not to be confused with history. . . . Oliver Stone is waging war against America, which he sees as ultraconservative, repressive, imperialistic, greedy, immoral, and homicidal. There is a case for polemicism, of course, as long as it is accurately labeled."

Revising Nixon. Another Stone project was *Nixon* (1995), which one critic described as "Hollywood's con-

Director Barry Levinson with Dustin Hoffman and Robert De Niro on the set of *Wag the Dog* (AP/Wide World Photos)

troversial director meets America's most controversial president." Critics and historians noted that Stone's Richard Nixon, played by Anthony Hopkins, was a creation that neither Nixon loyalists nor Nixon haters could easily recognize. This Nixon claimed that liberals hated him because he "fixed" the "tear gassing, the riots, [and] burning draft cards." Continuing his obsession with conspiracy, Stone suggested the same "Beast" that killed Kennedy targeted Nixon because he pursued, and achieved, détente with China. As in *JFK,* Stone mixed historical news footage with new docudrama-style footage to reenact Nixon's best-known moments. He portrayed Nixon in an enigmatic, yet surprisingly sympathetic, light, humanizing an unpopular leader.

History According to Gump. Not all movies of the 1990s were cynical about American politics. Starring Tom Hanks in the title role, *Forrest Gump,* one of the most popular movies of 1994, is the story of a man with an IQ of 75 who takes part in every major event in American history since World War II. Among other things, Forrest wins the Medal of Honor for heroism in the Vietnam War and helps President Richard M. Nixon bring détente to China. Critic Roger Ebert characterized the movie as "a medita-

Steven Spielberg and Liam Neeson on the set of *Schindler's List* (Star Stills, © Universal Studios and Amblin Entertainment)

tion on our times, as seen through the eyes of a man who lacks cynicism and takes things for exactly what they are" and noted that Forrest survives these turbulent decades "with only honesty and niceness as his shield." *Time* magazine critic Richard Corliss commented that Forrest is "an innocent on loan to a cynical world" and said the movie "wants to find an optimism in survival."

The Movie of the Decade. Steven Spielberg's *Schindler's List* (1993), a motion picture about the Nazi Holocaust, has been widely acclaimed as the best movie of the 1990s. Adapted from a 1982 novel by Thomas Keneally, the movie depicts the conversion of Oskar Schindler (played by Liam Neeson), a businessman who belongs to the Nazi Party but is less interested in politics than in profiting from the German occupation of Poland by using Jewish laborers to make cooking utensils for the German army in his factory. Yet, he becomes increasingly affected by the plight of his workers and ends up spending his fortune to create a safe haven for 1,200 of them, a munitions factory that never produces a usable shell. Filmed on location in Krakow and Auschwitz, Poland, the movie was shot in grainy black-and-white creating the effect of old newsreel footage and intensifying the horror of Nazi atrocities. Commenting about filming the movie on location, Spielberg said, "This has been the best experience I've had making a movie. I feel more connected with the material than I've ever felt before." The movie won seven Academy Awards including best picture, best director, best cinematography, and best screen adaptation. When he accepted the Best Picture Oscar for *Schindler's List*, Spielberg thanked "the six million who can't be watching this, among the one bil-

lion watching this telecast tonight" and called the movie the "culmination of a long personal struggle with my Jewish identity." After the success of the movie Spielberg founded the Survivors of the Shoah Visual History Foundation, which records the testimonies of Holocaust survivors.

World War II in the Movies. Later in the decade Spielberg returned to his examination of the war era with *Saving Private Ryan* (1998), a tribute to the American soldiers who fought and died in the D-Day invasion of Europe. The movie starred Tom Hanks and earned Spielberg another Oscar for directing. Critics, including Leonard Maltin, faulted conventional plotting in the script but were impressed with its "complex examination of heroism" and its Oscar-winning cinematography, which Maltin called "the most realistic, relentlessly harrowing battle footage ever committed to a fiction film . . . [creating] the ultimate vision of war as hell on earth." Critics also praised *The Thin Red Line* (1998), directed by Terrence Malick, best known for two critically acclaimed movies of the 1970s: *Badlands* (1973) and *Days of Heaven* (1978). Focusing on the Pacific campaign to retake Guadalcanal from the Japanese, the movie is a remake of the 1964 movie of the same name, both of which are adaptations of James Jones's 1962 novel. Contrasting Edenic scenery of the Pacific islands with the horrors of battle, the 1998 movie, whose stars include Sean Penn and Nick Nolte, is Malick's meditation about moral chaos. It does not really address (or intend to address) what happened at the real battle of Guadalcanal. Viewers are deliberately left confused about the plot, which is subordinated to a larger existential theme. The movie opens with a question—"Why does nature contend with itself?"—and focuses on the ways "in which all living beings are founded on the necessity of killing one another."

The Gulf War in the Movies. Edward Zwick, director of the Civil War drama *Glory* (1989), returned to historical filmmaking with *Courage Under Fire* (1996), the first attempt to depict the 1991 Gulf War in a Hollywood movie. Starring Denzel Washington and Meg Ryan, the movie examines what it takes to be an officer, a leader, and a hero. Another noteworthy Gulf War movie was the gritty action-adventure drama *Three Kings* (1999)—directed by David O. Russell and starring George Clooney, Mark Wahlberg, Ice Cube, and Spike Jonze—about four renegades who try to pull off a big gold heist. The movie tells a good story and includes some perceptive digs at Bush administration policies. Critics compared the movie favorably to the motion pictures of Martin Scorsese, Oliver Stone, Robert Altman, and Quentin Tarantino.

Sources:

Margaret Carlson, "A Terminal Case Of Telling The Truth," *Time,* 151 (11 May 1998): 78.

Tom Carson, "Stone Alone: Kicking Nixon Around," *Village Voice,* 2 January 1996, p. 17.

Richard Corliss, "Death of a Salesman," *Time,* 146 (18 December 1995): 74.

Corliss, "Hollywood's Last Decent Man," *Time,* 144 (11 July 1994): 58.

Corliss, "True Colors," *Time,* 151 (16 March 1998): 64.

Pat Dowell, Dan Georgakas, and Herb Boyd,. "Warren Beatty's Bulworth: Will the Real Bulworth Please Stand Up?" *Cineaste,* 24 (15 December 1998): 6–11.

Roger Ebert, Review of *Forrest Gump, Chicago Sun-Times,* 6 July 1994.

Ebert, Review of *JFK, Chicago Sun-Times,* 20 December 1990.

Ebert, Review of *Nixon, Chicago Sun-Times,* 20 December 1995.

Ebert, Review of *Schindler's List, Chicago Sun-Times,* 15 December 1993.

Leonard Maltin, ed., *Leonard Maltin's Movie & Video Guide, 2001 Edition* (New York: Signet, 2000).

Joseph McBride, *Steven Spielberg: A Biography* (New York: Simon & Schuster, 1997).

Marita Sturken, "Reenactment, Fantasy, and the Paranoia of History: Oliver Stone's Docudramas," *History and Theory,* 36 (1997): 64–79.

Steve Vineburg, "Wag the Dog," *Boston Phoenix,* 5 January 1998.

MOTION PICTURES: SCREEN VIOLENCE

Teen Violence and the Movies. In the movies of the 1990s violence was more prevalent and more graphic than ever before, even as many educators and politicians—as well as some moviemakers—expressed concerns about the connection between violence on the screen and the increasing levels of violence on the streets and in schools. After the release of Oliver Stone's *Natural Born Killers* (1994), in which a pair of hedonistic sociopaths played by Woody Harrelson and Juliette Lewis go on a senseless killing spree, teenaged murderers around the world claimed to have been inspired by the movie. The staging of the shootings at Columbine High School in April 1999 was similar to those in *The Basketball Diaries* (1995), in which a trench-coat-clad young man with a machine gun attacks people who had mocked him. This sort of violence is different from that in the popular action movies of the 1980s, where heroes such

---

GUTSY WOMEN IN THE MOVIES

Some of the movie roles for women in the 1990s were more complex and grittier than those of earlier decades. In *The Grifters* (1990) Annette Bening and Anjelica Huston played tough con artists at odds with one another. Jodie Foster had a major hit with *The Silence of the Lambs* (1991), in which she played an FBI trainee who convinces a savage mass murderer (played by Anthony Hopkins) to help her solve a grisly crime, proving her toughness in a traditionally masculine job.

Susan Sarandon and Geena Davis starred as the female equivalents of Butch Cassidy and Sundance in *Thelma & Louise* (1991), a dark comedy about two women on the run from meaningless relationships who end up as murderers on the run from the law. Pop-music star Madonna played another sort of tough woman in *Evita* (1996), director Alan Parker's screen version of Andrew Lloyd Webber's hit musical about Eva Peron, who clawed her way from poverty to become first lady and then president of Argentina. Some reviewers noted that Madonna had an almost mystical identification with Eva Peron. As Madonna explained, "Its comforting to know that I'm not the only person the press picks on or tries to turn into a monster or dehumanize in some way . . . I feel like I understand where she came from. And I love her." Despite the increase in strong roles for women, however, Foster complained that women's parts were still all too often "written as plot adjuncts: sister of, daughter of. The hero has to save someone so they wrap that someone in cord and put her on a railroad track."

Sources: Richard Corliss, "Women on the Verge of a Nervy Breakthrough," *Time,* 137 (18 February 1991): 58–60.

Alice Hoffman, "Thelma & Louise," *Premiere,* 11 (October 1997): 69.

Susan Isaacs, *Brave Dames and Wimpettes* (New York: Ballentine, 1999).

---

as Rambo sprayed bullets in defense of the American way of life. Rather, movies such as *Natural Born Killers* and *The Basketball Diaries* —as well as *Kalifornia* (1993), in which Lewis and Brad Pitt play serial killers—seem to celebrate purposeless violence in a deliberately provocative manner. Psychologists, politicians, educators, and concerned citizens in general began to discuss what levels of violence were acceptable in motion pictures and when graphic depictions of violence might be justified in moral and artistic terms—say, for example, in *Saving Private Ryan,* which attempts to educate the public about the D-Day invasion was really like.

Raising the Bar. One of the most critically acclaimed movies of 1994—a year that critics consider to be the best of the decade for movies—seemed to raise the level of acceptable violence. Quentin Tarantino's *Pulp Fiction* is an outrageous comedy filled with profanity, senseless shoot-

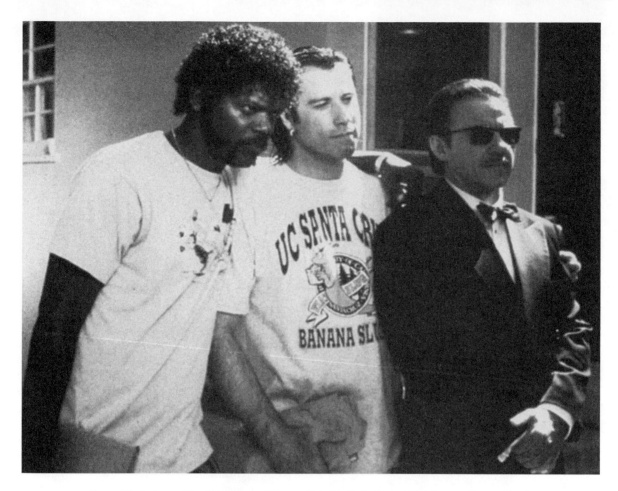

Samuel L. Jackson, John Travolta, and Harvey Keitel in *Pulp Fiction* (© Miramax Buena Vista)

ings and stabbings, sadomasochism, a homosexual rape, and drug overdoses—all designed to have audiences reeling from one experience to the next. Tarantino intended the movie as a tribute to old pulp-magazine stories about hard-boiled detectives who survive in an amoral world of crime and violence by being as tough and ruthless as the criminals they are trying to defeat. Tarantino's tough-guy heroes, however, are not detectives but hit men, played by John Travolta and Samuel L. Jackson, who blunder through a bizarre sequence of events played out on-screen in a non-linear fashion. Critics praised Travolta's acting and acknowledged the artistry of the movie, for which Tarantino and Roger Avary won the Best Original Screenplay Oscar. Yet, some commentators also took Tarantino to task for the violence in the movie. According to Tom Whalen, the movie lacked "moral clarity," but other critics took exception to that characterization, pointing out that there are far fewer dead people in *Pulp Fiction* than there are in movies such as *Rambo: First Blood Part II* (1985), *Cyborg* (1989), or *Marked for Death* (1990).

Violence and Redemption. Another of the top-rated movies of 1994 was *The Shawshank Redemption*, a movie about hope, friendship, love, and survival, that is also a riveting prison drama filled with violence. Directed by Frank Darabont and adapted from a novella by Stephen King, the movie stars Tim Robbins as Andy Dufresne, a banker con-demned to life imprisonment in a maximum security prison for the double murder of his wife and her lover. Insisting on his innocence, he endures beatings, taunts, baiting, and sexual propositions. Gradually, with the help of another lifer, played by Morgan Freeman, he learns to survive by putting his intelligence and savvy to work, and he continues to hold out hope for freedom because: "Fear can hold you prisoner. Hope can set you free." As Roger Ebert pointed out, *The Shawshank Redemption* "is not about violence, riots or melodrama. The word 'redemption' is in the title for a reason." Andy's final redemption is both physical and spiritual.

Grisham's Crusade. Some critics also found redeeming qualities in *Natural Born Killers*. Ebert, for example, pointed out that the movie is not so much about the two murders as it is "about the way they electrify the media and exhilarate the public." While Stone may have intended the movie as an exposé of American society's morally bankrupt obsession with violence and celebrity, many critics blasted Stone for glorifying murder and exploiting the obsession he had set out to expose. As teenage murderers began to pro-claim their kinship to Mickey and Mallory, the two killers in Stone's movie, one case in particular made headlines. In 1995 a couple in their late teens shot two people, killing one and paralyzing the other. The young woman later told investigators that they had been taking LSD and her boyfriend had begun fantasizing about reenacting a scene from *Natural Born Killers*. The man who was murdered, William Savage, was a friend of author-lawyer John Grisham, who wrote an article in his magazine, *The Oxford American* (Spring 1996), charging that Stone should be held responsible under product-liability laws for the copycat murders inspired by his movie. According to Grisham, *Natural Born Killers* "catered to unbalanced people," while Stone thinks that because "he's an artist" he does not have to be concerned "with the effects of what he produces." If, however, Stone loses a $1 million product-liability lawsuit, said Grisham, "the party will be over." Stone's legal representative called the charges "ridiculously bizarre" and said Grisham should focus his anger on the "gun toting crazies." A noted First Amendment attorney, Martin Garbus, characterized Grisham's legal thinking as "preposterous" and no such suit was ever filed against Stone, but in 1997 an attorney for Patsy Byers, the woman who was paralyzed, filed a civil suit on other grounds against Stone and Time Warner, the studio that produced the movie, charging that they "knew . . . or should have known" that the movie would inspire violent behavior. The suit was still unsettled in autumn 2000.

Regulating the Movies. In 1990 the Motion Picture Association of America replaced the old X rating with an NC-17 rating for movies that included excessive violence or overt sexuality and instructed theater owners that anyone under seventeen should not be admitted to such movies. Because newspapers often refused to advertise NC-17 movies, and theaters frequently refused to show them, directors whose movies earned NC-17 ratings began cutting or reshooting scenes to earn the less-restrictive R rating. The first big commercial movie rated NC-17, *Showgirls* (1995), bombed with critics and moviegoers, less for its rating than for its hackneyed script and amateurish acting. By the mid 1990s politicians had begun to target movie violence and to accuse the entertainment industry of creating what Republican presidential candidate Robert Dole called "nightmares of depravity." Congressman Henry Hyde (R-Ill.) proposed legislation to ban sales of violent materials to minors. Senator John McCain (R-Ariz.) proposed a bill to require the entertainment industry to label violent products with government-approved warnings. Another proposed bill would keep movie directors from using federal property as a setting for violent pictures. Critics of such legislation called them "hand-wringing" measures that might appeal to voters but would have little impact on the movie and recording industries.

Sources:

Todd and Kenneth Womack Davis, "Shepherding the Weak: The Ethics of Redemption in Quentin Tarantino's Pulp Fiction," *Literature Film Quarterly*, 26, no. 1 (1998): 60–66.

Tim Dirks, "The Shawshank Redemption," *The Greatest Films*, online at <www.filmsite.org> or <www.greatestfilms.org>.

Susan J. Douglas, "The Devil Made Me Do It: Is Natural Born Killers the Ford Pinto of Movies," *Nation*, 268 (5 April 1999): 50.

Martha Duffy, "Grisham's Law," *Time*, 145 (8 May 1995): 87–88.

Roger Ebert, Review of *Natural Born Killers*, *Chicago Sun-Times*, 26 August 1994.

Ebert, Review of *Pulp Fiction*, *Chicago Sun-Times*, 10 October 1994.

Ebert, Review of *The Shawshank Redemption*, *Chicago Sun-Times*, 17 October 1999.

Elizabeth Gleick, "A Time to Sue," *Time*, 147 (17 June 1996): 90.

Michael Schnayerson, "Natural Born Opponents," *Vanity Fair*, no. 431 (July 1996): 98–105, 141–144.

Tom Whalen, "Film Noir: Killer Style," *Literature Film Quarterly*, 23, no. 1 (1995): 2–5.

MOTION PICTURES: SPECIAL EFFECTS

Digital technology. During the 1990s, digital sound, editing, photography, and special effects revolutionized movie making, creating the biggest change in how movies are made since the introduction of synchronized sound in 1927. The use of digital editing in *Forrest Gump* (1994) demonstrates the enormous strides made in motion-picture technology during the 1990s. Gary Sinise plays a character whose legs are blown off in battle. While in earlier movies an actor would have played his scenes with his lower legs taped behind his thighs, digital technology could remove Sinise's legs after the footage was shot. Moviemakers used a blue screen and 3-D digital technology—developed by George Lucas's Industrial Light and Magic, the special-effects division of LucasFilm—to create the illusion of a legless actor so successfully that viewers could not tell the scene was digitally enhanced. Also in *Forrest Gump*, director Robert Zemeckis, who was already well known for his successful blending of live action and animation in *Who Framed Roger Rabbit* (1988), used computer graphics to put Forrest Gump, played by Tom Hanks, in scenes with presidents John F. Kennedy and Lyndon B. Johnson, as well as George Wallace and John Lennon.

Blending Science and Fantasy. In 1977 the first *Star Wars* movie amazed moviegoers with heretofore unimagined special effects, but by the 1990s technology had advanced so rapidly that the movie seemed dated and amateurish. When Lucas re-released *Star Wars*, *The Empire Strikes Back* (1980), and *Return of the Jedi* (1983) in 1997 he not only added new scenes to the trilogy but also re-created many of the special effects using technology that was not available in the 1970s and 1980s. Steven Spielberg used digital imaging in *Jurassic Park* (1993) and *The Lost World: Jurassic Park* (1997) to create amazingly realistic dinosaurs, while director Ron Howard used it successfully in *Apollo 13* (1995) to re-create the liftoff of a Saturn V rocket, adding ice, vapor, fire, and burnout. The critical failure of *Star Wars: Episode One: The Phantom Menace* (1999) illustrated an unbending rule of storytelling: special effects are nice, but they can never substitute for interesting characters and compelling story lines. Still, the new technology has major implications for moviemaking. As French movie maker Jean-Jacques Annaud put it, "The cinema was built around an animated picture. It has the option of becoming an animated painting."

Blockbuster. In 1997 James Cameron, director of the action hits *The Terminator* (1984), *Terminator 2: Judgment Day* (1991), and *True Lies* (1994), released the

The scene in *Forrest Gump* for which director Robert Zemeckis used computer graphics to insert actor Tom Hanks (left) into existing news footage of President John F. Kennedy (AP/Wide World Photos)

technological blockbuster of the decade, his version of the 1912 sinking of the *Titanic*. The movie opens with filmed underwater footage of the wreck, filmed by a camera unit that operated outside a submarine, capturing images of corroded woodwork, wall paneling, ornately carved doors, and the grand staircase. For scenes of the *Titanic* before its fateful collision with an iceberg in the North Atlantic, Cameron used computer imaging to capture the ship leaving port, as smoke coiled around hundreds of people moving on deck. Then he employed what he called "reconstructed realism" to simulate the ship listing, splitting in two, and sinking while her doomed passengers rolled down the decks and into their watery graves. At Fox Studios Baja, Cameron built a seventeen-million-gallon oceanfront tank in which an almost full-size exterior model of the ship was erected against a 270-degree background of uninterrupted ocean horizon. For ship interiors every detail was meticulously researched and re-created. Yet, technology was not an end in itself for Cameron. He wanted to "use hard-core technological means to explore emotions" and spent more than $200 million in the attempt. As *Titanic* neared, and missed, its deadline, rumors circulated that the movie was in trouble. In December 1997, however, it had a triumphant world premiere in Tokyo, and one critic called it a "marriage of imagination and technology in the Hollywood tradition of well crafted epics." *Titanic* went on to overtake *Star Wars* as the top-grossing movie of all time, reaching a domestic gross of more than $500 million in only fourteen weeks, where *Star Wars* had grossed $461 million in 1977 and 1997 together. *Newsweek* researchers discovered that 60 percent of the tickets sold were

bought by women, many of whom saw the movie several times. After years of male-oriented action movies, *Titanic* was a big-budget action movie that attracted female moviegoers with a tender love story. *Titanic* won eleven Oscars, including best director and best picture, but many critics were not enthralled with the movie. *The Village Voice* complained that it mixed "hokiness and hokum" and argued that the story line relied on a cliché-ridden love story. Other critics were kinder, and a few saw *Titanic* as the *Gone With The Wind* (1939) of the 1990s.

Sources:

Gina Hahn, "Menace to Society," *Atlantic Unbound,* 19 May 1999, online at <www.theatlantic.com/unbound>.

J. Hoberman, "The Iceberg Cometh," *Village Voice,* 23 December 1997, p. 79.

Peter Kramer, "Women First: 'Titanic' (1997), Action-Adventure Films and Hollywood's Female Audience," *Historical Journal of Film, Radio & Television,* 18 (October 1998): 599–619.

Ed Marsh, *James Cameron's Titanic* (New York: Harper Perennial, 1997).

Scott McQuire, "Digital Dialectics: The Paradox of Cinema in a Studio without Walls," *Historical Journal of Film, Radio & Television,* 19 (August 1999): 379–397.

MOTION PICTURES: THE INDEPENDENTS

"Indie" pictures. By the final decades of the twentieth century, independent, or "indie," movies were no longer just low-budget pictures with unusual subject matter that were usually shown in small, so-called art-house theaters because of their lack of appeal to the general public. Instead, an "indie" picture became defined as any movie that was funded by sources other than a major studio, and some of them cost just as much to make as movies made by the studios. Some critics have pointed out that this trend

Frances McDormand in *Fargo* (AP/Wide World Photos)

tends to discourage experimentation and risk taking among movie makers. Faced with high production costs, they need to attract wider audiences or risk losing money.

Award Winners. Two of the best independent movies of the 1990s were *Sling Blade* (1996), written and directed by Billy Bob Thornton, who also starred in his movie, and *Fargo* (1996), written by Joel and Ethan Coen and directed by Joel Coen. In *Sling Blade* Thornton plays a mentally deficient man who murders out of good intentions. Roger Ebert commented that "if *Forrest Gump* had been written by William Faulkner the result might have been something like *Sling Blade*." The movie was nominated for a Best Picture Oscar and earned Billy Bob Thornton an Academy Award for best screen adaptation and a nomination for best actor. *Fargo,* a darkly comic movie about midwinter kidnapping and murder in a small Minnesota town, earned Frances McDormand an Oscar for Best Actress and a Best Screenplay Oscar for the Coens.

Reynolds's Comeback. Directed by twenty-seven-year-old Paul Thomas Anderson, *Boogie Nights* (1997) was praised by critics and billed as a comeback for actor Burt Reynolds. A detached, unprovocative study of the adult-movie industry, *Boogie Nights* had little to do with sex or pornography and a great deal to say about how makers of porn movies create and promote them as consumer products.

40 Acres and a Mule. Spike Lee, whose independent production company, 40 Acres and a Mule Filmworks, had two big hits in the 1980s with *She's Gotta Have It* (1986)

and *Do the Right Thing* (1989), made news in the 1990s with three thought-provoking movies that examine how Americans look at race issues. *Jungle Fever* (1991), starring Wesley Snipes and Annabella Sciorra, is about the consequences of a love affair between a happily married, successful black man and his white secretary, and it includes a subplot that deals realistically with the destructive nature of the urban crack-cocaine culture. Lee's biggest movie of the decade was *Malcolm X* (1992), starring Denzel Washington with a script by Lee and Arnold Perl based on *Autobiography of Malcolm X* (1965). Because Warner Bros. was distributing the movie, radical black activists feared that Lee would cave in to the Hollywood establishment and make a "safe" movie that would ease the fears of middle-class blacks and whites, but Lee declared, "This is going to be *my* vision of Malcolm X." Lee was also criticized for allowing the movie to be promoted with merchandise such as Malcolm X hats and T-shirts. In the end the movie offered a balanced and intelligent portrait of the black separatist leader—including his inflammatory speeches on race separatism, the divisive in-fighting among black nationalists, and his later transcendent experience in Mecca. Lee hoped that the movie would help to establish a dialogue between the races that would enable them to move beyond stereotyping and race baiting to get to the truth of Malcolm X's message. Another Lee movie, *Get on the Bus* (1996), starring Ossie Davis, focuses on a group of twenty black men taking a cross-country bus trip to attend the 1995 Million Man March in Washington, D.C. The movie does not avoid the anti–Semitism and white racism of march organizer Louis Farrakhan, but presents the Million Man

THE TOP "INDIE" MOVIES

When the Internet Movie Database asked its users to rank the top fifty independent motion pictures of all time, thirty-seven of the fifty were movies released in the 1990s. (Number one was *Dr. Strangelove or: How I Learned to Stop Worrying and Love the Bomb* [1964]). As of 11 September 2000, the 1990s movies on the list included: no. 2, *The Usual Suspects* (1995); no. 4, *Pulp Fiction* (1994), no. 5, *Being John Malkovich* (1999); no. 7, *The Silence of the Lambs* (1991); no. 8, *American History X* (1998); no. 15, *Reservoir Dogs* (1992); no. 19, *Sling Blade* (1996); no. 24, *Fargo* (1996); no. 34, *Good Will Hunting* (1997); no. 37, *Secrets & Lies* (1996); and no. 47, *The Cider House Rules* (1999).

Source: "Top 50 Independent Movies, *Internet Movie Database*, 11 September 2000, online at <us.imbd.com>.

March as being about family and mutual understanding, not about Farrakhan and his views.

The Most Profitable Movie Ever Made. In 1999 a low-budget independent movie, *The Blair Witch Project,* surprised everyone by becoming a cult phenomenon and then a box-office success. Owing in large measure to innovative on-line internet advertising and promotion, it grossed $140 million, far less than big-budget blockbusters such as *Star Wars* and *Titanic,* but since University of Central Florida film students Daniel Myrick and Eduardo Sanchez spent only $30,000 to make the movie, its net earnings made it the most profitable movie of all time. The movie was shot in eight days with a script that changed daily; it featured unknown actors; its "special effects" were created by people talking to each other; and it was shot entirely with hand-held film and video cameras, resulting in such shaky images that some moviegoers complained of dizziness and nausea. The movie took advantage of the late 1990s obsession with "reality programming," videotapes, and the internet. Millions of people logged on to *The Blair Witch Project* website, which included details left out of the movie. As one fan put it "Netizens have finally seen their own image on the big screen, and are ready for more." The movie was picked up by the independent distributor Artisan Entertainment and released nationwide in summer 1999, possibly creating a trend for marketing such low-budget movies to national audiences. The success of *The Blair Witch Project* led to predictions that mainstream moviemakers might begin using video cameras to reduce production costs.

Attacking White Supremacy. Another independent movie that received critical acclaim was conceptual artist Tony Kaye's directorial debut, *American History X* (1998). Edward Norton plays a skinhead who has served a prison sentence for the murders of two young black men and has renounced his white supremacist views. When he returns home to Venice, California, he discovers that his younger brother, who idolizes him, has adopted the same extremist views. According to screenwriter David McKenna, "The point I tried to make in the script is that a person is not born a racist. It is learned through environment and the people that surround you." McKenna interviewed several "skinheads" and said he "wanted to write an accurate portrayal of how good kids from good families can get so terribly lost" and to examine the "possibility for redemption."

Sources:

Harry Allen, "Can You Digit?" *Premiere,* 13 (November 1999): 93–103.

Douglas Brode, *Denzel Washington: His Films and Career* (New York: Carol, 1996).

Roger Ebert, Review of *Sling Blade, Chicago Sun-Times,* 1996, online at <www.suntimes.com/ebert>.

John Horn, "Trading Places," *Premiere,* 12 (October 1998): 57–61.

Janet Maslin, "Vanished in the Woods, Where Panic Meets Imagination," review of *The Blair Witch Project, New York Times,* 14 July 1999, pp. E1, E5.

Josh Ozersky, "The Blair Witch Project," *Atlantic Unbound,* 11 August 1999, online at <www.theatlantic.com/unbound>.

Peter Travers, "Fargo," *Rolling Stone,* no. 730 (21 March 1996): 104.

MUSIC: CLASSICAL TRENDS

Music and Money. Attendance at symphony concerts rose from 24.7 million to 30.8 million between 1989 and 1999, suggesting a modest resurgence of interest in classical music. During the same period, however, the number of classical radio stations declined to fewer than 160. Labor disputes also plagued several major orchestras, including the San Francisco Opera Orchestra, the New Orleans Symphony, the Atlanta Symphony, the Oregon Symphony, and the Philadelphia Orchestra. In addition, nineteen of the largest symphony orchestras in the United States had deficits averaging approximately $750,000 per orchestra. These financial woes arose in part because of a congressional reorganization of the National Endowment for the Arts (NEA) that effectively prohibited the NEA from awarding grants to defray operating costs. A decrease in the total appropriations for the NEA since 1996 led to an additional decline of nearly 40 percent in direct federal grants to symphony orchestras. As a result, tax-funded state arts agencies became important sources of income for symphony orchestras throughout the United States. By the 1998–1999 season, more than 44 percent of orchestra revenue came from such organizations.

The Changing Symphony Orchestra. The Wolf Report (1992), published by the American Symphony Orchestra League (ASOL), a national organization serving 850 U.S. orchestras, warned that symphony orchestras in the United States were "economically fragile" and in danger of becoming "both culturally and socially irrelevant." The next year the ASOL followed up with "Americanization of the American Orchestra," offering suggestions about how to popularize orchestras so that they would "reflect the cultural and ethnic world around them." Many people affiliated with orchestras throughout the country responded to the report with disdain, charging that the ASOL was opting for political correctness and attempting to subvert the traditional mission of the symphony orchestra. By 1996, however, it had become apparent that the directors of many orchestras had applied the ASOL report as a model to revitalize their organizations, instituting cultural, community outreach, and educational programs that had been outlined in the "Americanization of the American Orchestra." They staged free concerts, theme concerts, and multimedia presentations and established informational web sites and telephone hotlines. Some even linked concert series to sporting events. To cultivate a new generation of young listeners, orchestra directors established educational programs such as the Los Angeles Philharmonic "Composer in the Classroom" series and the Baltimore Symphony series of casual concerts that featured talks, interviews, and skits. The St. Louis Symphony began efforts to reach the African American community through black churches. The Detroit Symphony and the Detroit public-school system built a performing-arts high school on the grounds of its new Orchestra Place. "It's a new world out there," declared Catherine French. "We've got to prepare musicians not just to play the notes, but to be musical resources for their communities, to be complete musical citizens. And musicians around the country now are starting to reevaluate what it means to be a symphony musician. But when you see the energy and enthusiasm coming out of some of these conservatories now, you have to believe that the future is very, very bright."

Women in Classical Music. In September 1998 JoAnn Falletta became the first female conductor of a major U.S. symphony orchestra when she took over as conductor of the Buffalo Philharmonic Orchestra. Her new job was perhaps the most significant American orchestra post ever entrusted to a woman. After Falletta had penetrated this formerly all-male bastion, other women followed. In 1999 Anne Manson began her tenure as conductor of the Kansas City Symphony. Before Falletta took over the Buffalo Philharmonic, women had been the principal conductors at several smaller symphonies. Gisele Ben-Dor has led the Santa Barbara Symphony since 1994 and Catherine Comet directed the Grand Rapids Symphony for eleven years before stepping down in 1998.

Female Musicians. During the 1990s promoters of classical music came to recognize that even serious musicians could use all their assets to attract audiences. "Let's face it," said violinist Maria Bachmann, "people go into record stores and a lot of times buy recordings on the basis of what they see on the cover." On the back cover of her album *Kiss on Wood* (1995) she included a photograph of herself that, at least by the standards of classical musicians, displayed a generous amount of cleavage. Thai-Chinese-British violinist Vanessa-Mae (born Vanessa-Mae Vanakorn Nicholson) appeared on the cover of the single from her first album *The Violin Player* (1995) wearing a soaking wet see-through white shift and made a video in which she strolled seductively on the beach wearing tight hot pants. *The Violin Player* sold 300,000 copies in the United States and 3.2 million copies internationally, and within two weeks of its release in 1996, her *Classical Album 1* sold 500,000 copies worldwide, becoming the fastest-selling classical solo album of all time. The intent of such marketing was clearly to make classical music more appealing to a wider audience. Performers who marketed their talents by using their sexuality, however, ran the risk of being taken less seriously as artists.

Blacks in Symphony Orchestras. African Americans are still underrepresented in major symphony orchestras. As of 1997, for example, the Detroit Symphony had but three black members; the New York Philharmonic Orchestra had only one; and the Chicago Symphony had none. In 1994, however, Andre Raphel Smith, then only thirty-one years old, became assistant conductor for the Philadelphia Orchestra. Smith came to Philadelphia from the St. Louis Symphony, where he had been heavily involved in its community outreach program. Smith takes seriously his responsibility "to make the orchestra more accessible to the African-American community. Traditionally, African-Americans have not felt welcome in concert halls. Orchestras haven't done enough to address those needs."

Black Opera Singers. By the 1990s black female opera singers such as Kathleen Battle, Grace Bumbry, Barbara Hendricks, Jessye Norman, Leontyne Price, and Shirley Verrett had become household names among opera aficionados. By contrast, however, Simon Estes is the only black male opera singer with an international reputation. During the 1990s, Estes publicly and repeatedly alleged that he could not sing in the United States because American producers refused to hire black male vocalists for leading roles, because, he asserted, "There's been a perception that African American males can't kiss or embrace white women onstage." Vinson Cole, a respected African American lyric tenor, echoed Estes's sentiments, saying that two opera companies "told my management that they couldn't hire a black singer with a [white] female partner." Michael Morgan, African American music director of the Oakland East Bay Symphony, disagreed. Morgan argued that the problem with blacks entering the world of classical music was not primarily racism. It was, rather, that there were too few black classical musicians and opera singers. A spokesman for the Metropolitan Opera of New York stated that casting at the Met was completely color blind. Speight Jenkins, director of the Seattle Opera, countered that there was racism in opera but not because company directors themselves were racists. Instead, they worried needlessly about how their predominately white audiences would react to black male singers in leading roles. Still, the feeling that opera producers and the directors of opera companies discriminated against blacks ran deep among African Americans in classical music. George Shirley, an African American lyric tenor who sang leading roles at the Met during the 1960s, summed up the feelings of many black performers in the 1990s when he said, "it was my experience that the darker the skin color of a singer, the less likely the singer was to have a successful operatic career."

Composition and Performance. Throughout the 1990s symphony orchestras and opera companies showed increased interest in the work of contemporary American composers. Especially enthusiastic in this regard were the Tanglewood Festival in Lenox, Massachusetts, and Spoleto USA in Charleston, South Carolina. Dubbed "America's most-performed composer," John Adams was also in constant demand as a conductor. Symphonies and ensembles premiered one of his new compositions virtually every year, and orchestras around the world regularly performed his older works. Minimalist pioneer Philip Glass continued to be prolific during the 1990s, composing works for opera, orchestra, ensemble, keyboard, voice, and dance. Another minimalist composer, Steve Reich, won praise for works that were characterized as "absolutely spellbinding. . . , intensely visceral and frequently almost hallucinogenic in impact." Several young classical composers earned Pulitzer Prizes during the 1990s. Shulamit Ran, who won in 1991 for her *Symphony*, was only the second female composer to earn the prize. Melinda Wagner followed her in 1999, winning the award for her *Concerto for Flute, Strings, and Percussion*. George Walker, who won in 1996 for *Lilacs*, was the first African American winner. Aaron Jay Kernis received the prize in 1998 for his *String Quartet No. 2, Musica Instrumentalis*.

Crossover. The sales of classical recordings plummeted during the 1990s. One attempt to save the classical-music recording business was to create a classical-pop crossover, with classical musicians recording popular music and popular musicians going classical. In 1992 cellist Yo-Yo Ma teamed with improvisational vocalist Bobby McFerrin to create a blend of jazz and classical music. Ma also produced several crossover albums during the 1990s, including *Appalachia Waltz* (1996), which included Celtic, bluegrass, classical, and world music, and the playful *Soul of the Tango* (1997). He also made videos that showcase his collaborations with artists such as choreographer Mark Morris, moviemaker Atom Egoyan, and ice dancers Torvil and Dean. In 1998 pop singer Michael Bolton released a CD of classical and operatic selections that was number one on the *Billboard* classical charts for six weeks. Paul McCartney's symphonic efforts, *The Liverpool Oratorio* (1991) and *Standing Stone* (1997), topped the classical charts and played to sold-out audiences at Carnegie Hall in New York City. Among the most intelligent and successful crossover projects was Joe Jackson's *Heaven and Hell* (1997), a classically influenced cycle of songs about the seven deadly sins. By the end to the 1990s, crossover albums accounted for nearly all the best-selling classical recordings. Modestly successful crossover albums sold between 150,000 and 200,000 copies while the most successful classical albums sold 50,000 to 75,000 copies. "As a musician, you may want to put your imagination 300 years back," said Yo-Yo Ma, "but you have to understand today in order to renew the older tradition." The risk, of course, is that the crossover mix of pop and classical will distort classical music rather than revitalize it. Yet, at the end of the 1990s, crossover seemed to be the future for classical music.

Classical Radio. Classical-music radio stations also sought new ways to combat loss of audience in the 1990s. While in years past many cities had six or seven classical stations, during the 1990s the number of classical stations shrank to fewer than 160 nationwide, and their listeners were mostly aging Americans, while they needed to attract a "money demographic" audience of thirty-five- to forty-four-year-olds. Audience research revealed that this demographic group, "harried by rush hour or by boisterous kids" was most likely to stay tuned to music in the pastoral mode–light, airy, and melodic. Stations began to modify their playlists accordingly, angering some critics, who called what they heard "Air pudding" and "Muzak" and charged that the stations did not "create an appreciation for the art form" by directing "programming toward the most unintrusive, unobjectionable kind of music." Radio station owners acknowledged the purists' objections but countered that new listeners must be found if classical stations were going to survive.

Sources:

Karen Campbell, "The Future of American Orchestras May Be Bright After All," *Christian Science Monitor*, 16 July 1996, p. 10.

Yahlin Chang, "Cross Over, Beethoven," *Newsweek*, 131 (20 April 1998): 60–62.

"Classics Go Pop," *Economist*, 327 (3 April 1993): 82–84.

Thomas Grose, "The Lieder of the Pack," *U.S. News & World Report*, 9 February 1998, p. 71.

Brendan Koerner, "Eine kleine NachtMuzaz," *U.S. News & World Report*, 6 April 1998, p. 57.

John Marks, "Selling 'jailbait' Bach," *U.S. News & World Report*, 121 (11 November 1996): 58–59.

Charles Rosen, "Classical Music in Twilight," *Harper's* (March 1998): 52–56.

Greg Sandow, "The Classical Color Line," *Village Voice*, 8 April 1997, pp. 71–72.

Charlene Marmer Solomon, "Passing the Baton," *Black Enterprise*, 25 (October 1994): 62.

Herman Trotter, "Buffalo's New Conductor," *American Record Guide*, 62 (January/February 1999): 16–18.

Vroon, "Two Strikes For American Orchestras," *American Record Guide*, 60 (January/February 1997): 49–50.

Michael Walsh and David S. Levy, "Seductive Strings," *Time*, 146 (11 December 1995): 78–80.

"Whither Classical Music?" *American Record Guide*, 62 (November/December 1999): 6–9.

MUSIC: COUNTRY TRENDS

A New Generation. As country music moved closer to mainstream popular music in the 1990s new female vocalists such as Shania Twain, Faith Hill, LeAnn Rimes, and the Dixie Chicks came to the fore. Male country artists such as Garth Brooks, Steve Earle, Alan Jackson, Marty Stuart, and Tim McGraw were also popular, but many of the top country stars of the 1970s and 1980s disappeared from the charts. Many traditionalists charged that country music was losing its sense of history, but "New Country" star Alison Krauss and mainstream country artist Alan Jackson, among others, continued to highlight their links to classic country.

New Country Women. The big news in country music during the 1990s was the emergence of new female stars. With her supermodel looks and a sultry, beguiling voice, Canadian Shania Twain would have been called a pop-country crossover singer in the 1980s, but in the 1990s she was considered New Country. In 1995, her second album, *The Woman in Me,* sold more than 11 million copies in the United States; four singles from the album hit the top of the country charts; and the album crossed over to the top pop charts. By the end of the decade the album had sold 11 million copies, and her next album, *Come On Over* (1997) had sold 16 million. After the success of her debut album, *Blue* (1996), thirteen-year-old LeAnn Rimes became the youngest singer ever nominated for a Country Music Award and the following year she won Grammy Awards for Best New Artist and Best Country Performance. Often compared to Tanya Tucker, who was fourteen when she released "Delta Dawn" in the 1970s, Rimes had a much smoother voice than Tucker. Alison Krauss's sensitive, deeply felt awareness of lyrics and music is apparent in all her recordings, earning her a loyal following. In 1993, at twenty-one, she became the youngest member of the Grand Ole Opry. Her 1995 album *Now That I've Found You: A Collection* sold 2 million copies. Two other albums, *Every Time You Say Goodbye* (1992) and *So Long So Wrong* (1997) won Grammys for Best Bluegrass Album. By the end of the decade she had won ten Grammys and four Country Music Association Awards, securing her reputation as one of the best performers of bluegrass and country music.

Sources:
"Alison Krauss," online at <www.country.com>.

"LeAnn Rimes," online at <www.rockonthenet.com>.

"Shania Twain," online at <www.rockonthenet.com>.

MUSIC: GRUNGE ROCK

Born in Seattle. Characterized by distorted guitar sounds and dispirited vocals, the grunge sound emerged in 1991–1992 from the Seattle music scene, where it had been popular for most of the 1980s. As Clark Humphrey has written, it was an "angry, disheveled" version of rock, "stories complete with misconceptions and more than a few downright lies." The grunge movement was supposedly authentic street rock—not a bunch of packaged bands hyped by major music record producers. The bands that succeeded, however, did so because they signed with major record labels, leaving behind other local talent. As Hum-

phrey insisted, "There is no singular 'Seattle Sound,' but there is a common Seattle attitude. We believe in making great music and art, not in the trappings of celebrity."

National Celebrity. The record company most responsible for introducing grunge to a national audience was Seattle-based Sub Pop Records, which signed bands such as Green River, Soundgarden, Blood Circus, Swallow, Nirvana, and TAD. As a means of marketing the sound, the company promoted the bands' anti-yuppie message by distributing T-shirts emblazoned with the word *Loser* to mock the yuppie obsession with success.

Nirvana. The best-known of the grunge bands was Nirvana, formed in 1986 in Olympia, Washington, by Kurt Cobain and Krist Novoselic, who had played together in other groups. In 1988 they signed a record deal with Sub Pop Records, released the single "Love Buzz," and were discovered by Everett True, a writer for the British *New Musical Express.* His positive review of the band and its Seattle area cohort created interest in grunge in general and particularly Nirvana, which often smashed musical equipment and was known for sound-system feedback and musical distortion. The band's first album, *Bleach,* released in June 1989, was unpolished, but Cobain was already demonstrating his melodic and lyrical creativity. By 1991 Nirvana had parted company with Sub Pop and signed with David Geffen's DGC Records, with which the band recorded its second album, *Nevermind.* By October the

NET AID

On 9 October 1999 three all-star concerts were staged as a sequel to the 1985 Live Aid famine relief concert. This time however the concerts were broadcasts on the internet, on the Net Aid website www.netaid.org, marking the first time a benefit concert was aired in this way. Held at Giants Stadium in East Rutherford, New Jersey, Wembley Stadium in London, and the Palais de Nations in Geneva, the three overlapping concerts were primarily to promote the website of the United Nations Development Program, a clearinghouse for world volunteer efforts, fund-raising, agricultural information, business development, and internet organizing. Net Aid sent out 125,000 simultaneous video streams to 132 countries—ten times more than any previous online video casts.

The U.S. concert took lasted eight hours and featured acts such as Wyclef Jean with Bono, Puff Daddy, Sting, Jewel, Mary J. Blige, Busta Rhymes, Sheryl Crow, the Black Crowes, Counting Crows, Jimmy Page, Cheb Mami, and Zucchero.

Source: Jon Pareles, "Net Aid: The Stars Give a Party for a Global Web Site," *New York Times,* 11 October 1999.

Kurt Cobain (right) and Nirvana taping an MTV special, 10 January 1992 (photograph by Mark Kates)

album had gone gold, and it is now listed at number one on the *Spin* magazine internet ranking of the ninety top albums of the 1990s. According to Humphrey, *Nevermind* "was a bracing jolt of post-adolescent energy and attitude that managed to unite metalheads and alternative music types alike, while roping in those curious listeners attracted by the subversive single 'Smells Like Teen Spirit.'" Soon the band was performing on *Saturday Night Live* and recorded an acoustic session for the MTV *Unplugged* series. In 1993 they released *In Utero.* Despite such success, Kurt Cobain was consumed by an addiction to heroin. He nearly overdosed on a sedative in Rome in early 1994 and in April he shot and killed himself. His death ended the life of Nirvana as well. The band members dissolved Nirvana and later formed their own musical groups.

Hole. Cobain left behind a daughter and his wife, Courtney Love, who had founded the grunge band Hole in 1989. With guitarist Eric Erlandson, bassist Jill Emery, and drummer Caroline Rue, Love recorded Hole's first album, *Rat Bastard,* in 1990. By 1992 Hole had signed with DGC. After Cobain committed suicide in 1994, Hole released a new album, *Live Through This,* and two months after its release, the group's bass guitarist, Kristen Pfaff, died of a heroin overdose. *Live Through This* was a platinum album, and Love became notorious for her onstage behavior, cutting herself, verbally abusing her audience, performing simulated fellatio, attacking fans, and diving into the audience, where she frequently had her clothes torn off. In the late 1990s Love embarked on a movie career and cleaned up her image. One persistent rumor was that Cobain was the creative force behind *Live Through This.* Smashing Pumpkins musician Billy Corgan told *Select* magazine that there would have been no new Hole album without Cobain, implying that Cobain had written the songs. Corgan had songwriting credits on five of the twelve songs on the 1999 Hole album *Celebrity Skin.*

Source:
Clark Humphrey, *Loser: The Real Seattle Music Story* (Portland, Ore.: Feral House, 1995).

MUSIC: HEAVY METAL AND ALTERNATIVE ROCK

Metal Revival. After a lull in the middle of the decade heavy metal had a revival toward the end of the 1990s. In 1997 the first Ozzfest, featuring Marilyn Manson, grossed almost as much money as the highest grossing tour package of the women's rock tour Lilith Fair. The metal bands of the 1990s had disparate sounds, but the general approach was aggressive and disturbing lyrics and guitar music with a hint of hip-hop and electrical wizardry. Some bands were classed as "death metal," a reference to their macabre outlook, which seems to appeal mostly to male college students.

Satanism. The band called Marilyn Manson used neo-Satanism as its gimmick to attract audiences. Their four million fans loved their heavy-metal rock with an occult mystique. The band traces its origins to 1989 when Brian Warner met guitarist Scott Putesky, and the two decided to form a band. Warner assumed the name Marilyn Manson (blending the names of movie star Marilyn Monroe and convicted murderer Charles Manson), and Putesky became Daisy Berkowitz (heiress Daisy Duke and serial killer David Berkowitz). Eventually they added new band members to form Marilyn Manson and the Spooky Kids, but around 1992 the whole group became known as just Marilyn Manson. The following year they were noticed by Trent Reznor of Nine Inch Nails, signed a recording contract to his Nothing Records label, and began appearing as the opening act for Nine Inch Nails. Marilyn Manson's first album, *Portrait of an American Family,* was released in July 1994 and the subsequent exposure during Nine Inch Nails concerts helped to publicize the band to heavy-metal fans. Marilyn Manson has not been reluctant to offend religious organizations. Warner even arranged to become an honorary minister in the Church of Satan, and during a show in Utah, he tore up a copy of the Book of Mormon. The group's 1996 album, *Antichrist Superstar,* did nothing to calm worries about its Satanism, but it appealed to a wide group of fans. In October 1996 it reached number three on the *Billboard* albums chart. It sold 1.4 million copies, and radio airplay of the single "The Beautiful People" was widespread. Pat Robertson's *700 Club* began protesting Marilyn Manson concerts and managed to have them canceled in some cases, but religious protest had little effect. The band appeared on the 1997 MTV Video Music Awards show, where Warner sang "The Beautiful People" while displaying his naked buttocks to the audience. In the late 1990s Manson embraced the "glam rock" style, which includes elaborate costumes and stage set, as well as sexually provocative album jackets.

Negative Lyrics. Other 1990s heavy-metal performers were known for disturbing lyrics. Trent Reznor of Nine Inch Nails defended his group's lyrics by saying, "When I'm on stage singing—screaming this primal scream—I look at the audience, and everyone else is screaming the lyrics back at me. Even though what I'm saying appears negative, the release of it becomes a positive kind of experience, I think, and provides some catharsis to other people." Alanis Morissette, who broke into the music business performing in Canadian Tulip Festivals and then became a teen dance-party star, was far removed from those roots by 1994, when her album *Jagged Little Pill* revealed her deepest, most tortured thoughts and emotions. Her songs explored her sexuality, failed relationships, feelings about the Catholic Church, and other aspects of her identity crises. Within six weeks the album had reached number ten on the *Billboard* albums chart, mostly on the strength of "You Oughta Know," described as an "anthem of angry neo-feminists everywhere." Morissette's album remained on the chart for a solid year, won six Grammy Awards, and became the all-time best-selling U.S. debut album by a female solo artist.

Sources:
"Alanis Morissette," 1 October 1999, online at <www.wallofsound.go.com>.

Mikal Gilmore, "The Lost Boys," *Rolling Stone,* no. 755 (6 March 1997): 36–46.

Ben Ratliff, "Rock & Roll," *Rolling Stone,* no. 755 (4 February 1999): 19–21.

During the 1990s massive changes took place in hip-hop culture. Hip-hop started out in the South Bronx as a street-born cultural movement grounded by what have become known as the four pillars of hip-hop: DJ-ing, MC-ing (later known as rapping), breakdancing, and graffiti art. By the 1990s many of the original elements of hip-hop music had been stripped away, and rap music had emerged. Rap was a force in the 1980s, with Run-DMC and LL Cool J spreading the Bronx-born sound from Brooklyn to Beverly Hills, but few would have expected performers such as MC Hammer and Vanilla Ice to make rap music a central force in pop radio. By the 1990s the authentic voice of ghetto youth had become mindless jingles with polished beats that suburban teenagers nationwide could dance to at school dances. Rap made its way into movies and television commercials. Rapping had left the ghetto, and lost touch with its roots.

West Coast Gangsta Rap. At the beginning of the 1990s some performers decided to take rap back to the impoverished streets from which it emerged. Street credibility became an essential part of rap music. Taking their cues from early hard-core artists such as Public Enemy and Boogie Down Productions, West Coast artists such as former N.W.A. members Dr. Dre and Ice Cube tried to convey the violence of living in the ghetto through a new style called gangsta rap, which— unlike earlier hard-core rap—had massive cross-over appeal. Tracks such as Ice Cube's "It Was a Good Day" (1992) and Snoop Doggy Dogg's "Who I Am (What's My Name)" (1993) were MTV and pop-radio mainstays. Snoop Doggy Dogg's *Doggystyle* (1993) became the first debut album ever to make its entry on the pop-albums chart at number one. Gangsta rap became the predominant sound of the early 1990s, and the more menacing it sounded, the more references it made to guns and illegal substances, the better it was received by a naive, largely white, suburban teenage audience. The lyrics sparked heated controversy with interest groups lobbying for tighter restrictions on explicit content.

The East Coast Sound. At the same time gangsta-rap arose in the West, another hip-hop sound was emerging on the East Coast. New, positive-minded, Afrocentric groups started to bring a jazzier, more intellectual style to rap music. Groups such as the Jungle Brothers, A Tribe Called Quest, De La Soul, and Leaders of the New School formed a new alliance called the Native Tongues, which focused on black thought and black history. Alongside other influential groups, such as EPMD and Gang Starr, their soulful sounds and creative rhymes brought the hip-hop culture back to the music. Despite crossover tracks such as De La Soul's "Me, Myself, and I," East Coast rap remained mostly underground while West Coast gangsta rap was commercialized.

Return of the East Coast Sound. Many rap fans disliked the misogynistic, gun-waving attitude of the West Coast movement. In 1993–1994 two critical releases that com-

Jazz musician Donald Byrd playing with Gang Starr member Guru (photograph by Tracy Funches)

Conflicts between the two groups were even suggested as motives for the murders of two superstars, Tupac Shakur in 1996 and Notorious B.I.G. "Biggie Smalls" in 1997. By the end of the 1990s hip-hop had splintered further into southern rap led by No Limit Records, a new romantic pseudo gangsta rap led by DMX and the Ruff Ryders, underground hip-hop on labels such as Rawkus and Stones Throw, and a myriad of other crews. "Turntablism," an new evolution in DJ-ing, in which DJs use turntables like musical instruments, gained a huge following thanks to albums by the Invisbl Skratch Picklz and the X-cutioners.

Source:
Sacha Jenkins, Elliott Wilson, Chairman Mao, Gariel Alvarez, and Brent Rollins, *Ego Trip's Book of Rap Lists* (New York: St. Martin's Griffin, 1999).

MUSIC: JAZZ

The Death of Jazz? Jazz is rumored to have died in the 1990s, but in fact, jazz earned wider recognition, attained greater respectability, and attracted larger audiences than ever before. The iconography of jazz was more fashionable and more prevalent than when jazz was new, vigorous, and innovative. Glossy magazine advertisements for liquor, cigars, luxury automobiles, and other amenities of the "good life" often depicted a soulful saxophonist, trumpeter, or vocalist. With eyes shut tight and perspiration glistening on their foreheads, these jazz performers offered representations of the intensity, pleasure, and sophistication with which companies wished to associate their products. Yet, palpable feelings of unease counterbalanced the popularity of jazz. Throughout the 1990s, jazz aficionados found ample reason to sit on the ground and tell sad stories about the death of kings (and queens). The passing of Art Blakey, Miles Davis, Ella Fitzgerald, Stan Getz, Dizzy Gillespie, Carmen McRae, Gerry Mulligan, Frank Sinatra, Mel Torme, and Sarah Vaughan marked the end of an era on the American jazz scene. Of those giants who remained, vibraphonist Lionel Hampton and trumpeter Harry "Sweets" Edison, formerly a member of the Basie Orchestra, were in their eighties. Pianist Oscar Peterson was in his seventies and still performing despite the effects of a stroke. Critics began to wonder aloud whether the rising generation of jazz artists, however talented, could fill the void, though Sonny Rollins remained a towering presence, and Jackie McLean served as an apostle of modern jazz for a new generation of listeners.

Out with the Old, In with the Old. Who was the new Miles or Monk, the new Bird or 'Trane of the 1990s? What recording of the decade was the equivalent of Miles Davis's 1959 masterpiece "Kind of Blue?" Reissues of classic recordings, such as Davis's collaborations with Canadian arranger Gil Evans, and a tribute to John Coltrane, were popular. According to one line of criticism, however, these collections were little more than splendid museum pieces that revealed the arid banality of much contemporary jazz. Even those who abhorred Coltrane's

pletely changed hip-hop shifted rap fans' attention back to the East. The first was the group Wu Tang Clan's debut album, *Enter the Wu Tang (36 Chambers)* (1993). Led by rapper-producer RZA, the Wu Tang Clan had a hard, but comical edge, and with the RZA's production and creative lyrics, the Wu Tang far surpassed everyone in terms of originality. A year later Nas's debut album, *Illmatic,* displayed a more realistic picture of life on the streets. Both albums were huge commercial successes.

Divisions. During the last half of the decade people who were concerned with holding to the roots of hip-hop culture began to call themselves hip-hop artists to distinguish themselves from commercially exploitive "rappers." Hip-hop performers concerned with artistic skill were harshly critical of new rap superstars such as Master P and his No Limit Records cohorts and Sean "Puffy" Combs and his Bad Boy Entertainment group. New hip-hop artists such as Black Star, the Jurassic 5, and the Black Eyed Peas, gained audiences because of their talent and innovations, giving back to hip-hop the original soul that made it such a powerful movement in the late 1970s. A stronger divide also developed between East and West Coast artists.

Second Line paying tribute to Al Hirt and other recently deceased jazz and blues musicians at the thirtieth Jazz and Heritage Festival in New Orleans, May 1999 (AP/Wide World Photos)

"sheets-of-sound" solos (frenzied, improvisational epics that could last for thirty minutes or longer) agreed that, more than thirty years after his death, Coltrane's stylistic innovations were unmatched. Jazz critic Francis Davis summarized these concerns in a provocative essay published in 1996. Writing in *The Atlantic Monthly,* Davis complained that among the new generation of jazz musicians "there are no Thelonious Monks or Ornette Colemans. . . , no innovators or woolly eccentrics among those we've heard from so far. In setting craftsmanship as their highest goal these neophytes remind me of such second-tier stars of the Fifties and Sixties as Blue Mitchell and Wynton Kelly—players whose modesty and good taste made them ideal sidemen but whose own record dates invariably lacked the dark corners and disfigurements of character that separate great music from merely good." Davis then made the arresting observation that whereas critics were formerly the guardians of the musical canon, measuring the value of each new contribution against the standards of the past, now musicians themselves embraced tradition while critics fretted and fumed at the apparent scarcity of the fresh, the adventurous, and the spontaneous—characteristics that Whitney Balliett, jazz critic for *The New Yorker,* once identified as "the sound of surprise."

The Rise of Neoclassicism. Following World War II, the bebop sound of trumpeter Dizzy Gillespie, alto saxophonist Charlie Parker, and others began to supplant the big-band music of the Swing Era. Wearied by the predictable harmonic structure of bebop, Ornette Coleman and John Coltrane pioneered the avant-garde atonal free jazz of the 1960s; another faction, most effectively represented by the group Spyro Gyra and Chick Corea, was influential in the mid 1970s, embracing the fusion of jazz and rock. During the 1980s, the advocates of the so-called neoclassical movement sought to reverse the lowering of musical standards that had resulted from the self-indulgence of the avant-garde and the commercial success of the jazz-rock fusion. Trumpeter Wynton Marsalis emerged as the leader of this austere, patrician band of musical traditionalists. More than two decades earlier, James Lincoln Collier, who ironically became one of Marsalis's principal antagonists during the 1990s, reached similar conclusions. In the epilogue to *The Making of Jazz* (1978) Collier wrote: "We have to divest ourselves of the idea that the history of jazz has always been toward better and better. In no art has this ever been the case. . . . Jazz has always been obsessed with the new, with experimentation, and the result has been that it has rarely paused to exploit its discoveries before leaping out to make fresh ones. . . . Jazz needs, at the moment, a respite from experiments. It needs time to consolidate gains, to go back and re-examine what is there. There is enough work left undone to last many lifetimes."

An Ambiguous Future. Efforts to revitalize the tradition, of course, carried inherent risks. Too much solemnity and too much reverence for old standards might alienate new audiences and inhibit artistic creativity. Yet, neotraditionalists argued, in view of the damage that the worst excesses of avant-garde and fusion wrought during the 1970s and 1980s, the gamble was worth taking, even if the neoclassical reaction produced an over-emphasis on technique as an end in itself. Besides, many emerging jazz artists of the 1990s, including Terrence Blanchard, James Carter, Kenny Garrett, Roy Hargrove, Donald Harrison, Nicholas Payton, Joshua Redman, and Marcus Roberts, although superb technicians, restored vitality and emotion to their music. Equally encouraging was the appearance of a coterie of young vocalists, chief among them singer-pianist Diana Krall, who revived the beauties of melody and brought new life to classic jazz tunes. Despite these promising developments, jazz at the end of the 1990s remained in something of a crisis. Exiled to the periphery, jazz simply could not compete with the pervasive music-video culture of MTV. In that circumstance, jazz faced a predicament similar to those of classical music, poetry, fiction, and the visual arts in the age of postmodernism.

Sources:
James Lincoln Collier, *Jazz: The American Theme Song* (New York: Oxford University Press, 1993).

Collier, *The Making of Jazz* (Boston: Houghton Mifflin, 1978).

Clive Davis, "Has Jazz Gone Classical?" *Wilson Quarterly*, 21 (Spring 1997): 56–63.

Francis Davis, "Like Young," *Atlantic Monthly*, 278 (July 1996): 92–97.

MUSIC: LATINO RESURGENCE

Latin-Pop Crossover. One big reason for the renewed popularity of the Latin sound in music during the 1990s was Ricky Martin, who impressed even jaded Hollywood attendees at the 1999 Grammy Awards with his hip-hop rendition of "The Cup of Life." Formerly one of the teen vocalists in 1980s group Menudo, Martin made the most of his handsome Latin looks and his considerable vocal prowess during the late 1990s. His album *Ricky Martin* hit number one on the album charts in May 1999. In an August 1999 *Rolling Stone* interview, he explained the basis for his musical sound: "I said, 'Wait a minute. Keep it simple. You were born in Puerto Rico, and you're a Latin—even though the first stuff you listened to was Journey, Foreigner, Cheap Trick, Boston—so let's play with it a little, not be stereotypical." Another Latin artist with broad demographic appeal is Jennifer Lopez, who got her start as the star of *Selena* (1997), a movie about a young Taguan singer. Lopez's sex appeal, dance moves, and singing ability served her well in the recording business. Her single "If You Had My Love" made the Billboard Hot 100.

Audience. Martin and Lopez are only two of the new Latin artists with broad demographic appeal. As choreographer Chitons Rivera said, "This is an amazing thing that's happening now. . . . Everybody wants to live the la Veda local [life on the move]." Part of the explanation for the trend may be the growing Hispanic population of the United States. Latinos will soon be the largest minority group in America. Another popular Latino was twenty-four-year-old Lou Bega, an Afro-Cuban singer whose brassy rendition of "Mambo No. 5" hit the top of the Spanish, Austrian, Swiss, Dutch, and German music charts after selling 13 million copies and stayed at number one for ten straight weeks. Four weeks after it was released in the United States, it reached number eleven on the Billboard Hot 100.

Sources:
Debra Birnbaum, "Jennifer Lopez," *Redbook*, 193 (September 1999): 59.

Nancy Collins, "Ricky Martin, The Rolling Stone Interview," *Rolling Stone*, no. 818 (5 August 1999): 48–55.

MUSIC: POP TRENDS

Woman Power. *The Rolling Stone Illustrated History of Rock & Roll* noted in 1992 that "As more women plug in electric guitars and bash away at drum kits, they are empowered, articulating a voice that before had gone unheard. And what they have to say might just make a difference—and make it to Number One." While Madonna's notoriety may have waned by the end of the 1990s, by then her fifteen-year career as "pop music chameleon" and sometime movie star had made her a household word. Madonna managed to stay on top by beating the system at its own game. In 1990 she beat MTV by turning its rejection of a Madonna video into big bucks for herself. In 1992 her book *Sex*, which showed her in various states of undress with members of both sexes, grossed more than $25 million the first week it was in bookstores but also earned her a lot of negative publicity. Madonna explained, "If you read the text, it was completely tongue in cheek. Unfortunately, my sense of humor was not something that a mainstream audience picks up. For me all it did was expose our society's hangups about sexuality. Yes I took a beating, and yes, a lot of the things that were said were hurtful and unfair. . . . But there are no mistakes. It was a great learning experience." The book was intended to advertise her seventh album, *Erotica*, which sold more than two million copies. That same year she signed a deal with Time Warner for $60 million. Madonna's next two projects, *Bedtime Stories* (1994) and *Ray of Light* (1998), also spent time at number one on the *Billboard* albums chart.

A Diva for the 1990s. Mariah Carey rose to the heights of the music world after handing a demo tape of her songs to Tommy Mottola, president of Columbia Records (later Sony Music Entertainment) at a party. (The two were married in 1993 and divorced in 1998.) Her debut album, *Mariah Carey*, was released by Columbia Records in 1990. Despite its saccharin lyrics, the album sold six million copies, and two songs from the album reached number one. She won two Grammy awards in 1991, one for Best Pop Vocal Performance and another for Best New Artist. Unlike Carey's later albums, this one was written by music-business songwriters. Carey, who had been writing songs by the time she was in high school, soon became involved in the entire process of creating her albums, from writing, or helping to write, the songs, to arranging and coproducing her subsequent albums. She was one of the most prolific singer-songwriters of the 1990s, and only five of the singles she released during the decade failed to reach number one on the pop charts. She had more number-one hits than any other female soloist, and only eight fewer number-one hits than Elvis Presley, the all-time leader. Some of these hits include "Vision of Love," "I Don't Wanna Cry," "Hero," "Dreamlover," "Fantasy," "Always Be My Baby," and "Heartbreaker." Carey has a well-deserved reputation as a perfectionist. She once recorded one hundred versions of the same song ("Honey").

Whitney Houston. Columbia signed Carey with the hope that she would challenge Whitney Houston, the reigning pop diva with a five-octave vocal range and a melodic and smooth delivery. Houston's success continued in the 1990s with record sales topping 100 million. She also branched out into acting, making what Leonard Maltin called a "solid film debut" in *The Bodyguard* (1992) opposite Kevin Costner and earning Grammys for the soundtrack album and the single "I Will Always Love You."

Other Divas. In 1996 Janet Jackson signed a contract with Virgin Records for an estimated $80 million but *Design of a Decade,* her subsequent CD set of greatest hits from 1986 to 1996, had sluggish sales. (Her brother Michael, the reigning pop star of the 1980s, also declined in popularity.)

Teen Pop. "Blissfully nonjudgmental" was one description of the teen music audience in the 1990s. If a single was up-tempo and easy to dance to, teens bought it—especially if the recording artist was good looking. That was the case with Britney Spears, who landed a part in an off-Broadway production of *Ruthless* in 1991, at age ten, and the following year joined the cast of the Mickey Mouse Club on the Disney Channel. By the time the show was canceled in 1993, she had signed a recording contract with Jive Records. By 1999, at seventeen, Spears had become a major pop idol and her hit single ". . . Baby One More Time" and topped the charts.

The Backstreet Boys. An ultra-cool sophisticated harmony and pleasant melodies characterized the songs of the Backstreet Boys, one of the most popular teen pop all-male vocal ensembles of the late 1990s. They had seven platinum singles from their album *Millenium* (1999), and tickets for their fall 1999 concert tour sold out in one hour on 17 August, for a gross profit of $30 million.

Kids' Buying Power. The success of such teen-pop idols demonstrates the irresistible power of the $50 billion a year in household spending influenced by children. Children in the 1990s had more disposable income than ever before, and Hollywood and the record industry soon realized this fact. "Kids are a little bit more mature at a younger age today," said Nickelodeon network vice president of talent relations Paula Kaplan. Parents became more aware than ever of their children's material needs and "more involved in what their kids are doing. I think parents and kids alike listen to pop music groups like Hanson, Spice Girls, and the Backstreet Boys." After Hanson, which had a major hit

single with "MMMBop" in 1997, appeared on the Nickelodeon Kids' Choice Awards (which has a viewing audience of six- to twelve-year-olds), their album *In the Middle of Nowhere* (1997) moved from sixty-three to thirty-six on the Billboard albums chart.

Sources:

Anthony DeCurtis and James Henke, eds., *The Rolling Stone Illustrated History of Rock & Roll* (New York: Random House, 1992).

Christopher John Farley, "Are they worth all that cash? (lucrative contracts for J. Jackson and others)," *Time,* 147 (29 January 1996): 545.

Chris Nickson, *Mariah Carey Revisited* (New York: St. Martin's Griffin, 1998).

Craig Rosen, "Labels Tap Into Kid Power," *Billboard,* 110 (30 May 1998): 5-6.

"Royal budget cuts for the king of pop (M. Jackson)," *People Weekly,* 49 (4 May 1998), pp. 6–7.

David Thigpen, "A Sweet Sensation," *Time,* 153 (1 March 1999): 71.

Richard Zoglin, "Mad for Evita," *Time,* 148 (30 December 1996–6 January 1997): 134–137.

MUSIC: RHYTHM & BLUES

R & B Balladeer. Producer, songwriter, and performer Babyface (Kenneth Edmonds) was the R & B success story of the 1990s. He and Antonio "L.A" Reid, his partner in LaFace Records, won the 1992 Grammy for Producer of the Year, and they shared the Best R & B Song Grammy with Daryl Simmons for the Boyz II Men single "End of the Road" (1992). Later that year they produced Whitney Houston's soundtrack album for *The Bodyguard,* which won the Grammy for the Album of the Year. In 1994 Babyface wrote the Boyz II Men single "I'll Make Love to You," which won the Grammy for Best R & B Song, and recorded "When Can I See You," which earned him a Grammy for Best Male R & B Vocal Performance. Three more Grammys for Producer of the Year followed (1995, 1996, and 1997). In 1996 Houston's "Exhale (Shoop Shoop)," written by Babyface, won the Grammy for Best R & B Song, and the following year Eric Clapton's single "Change the World," produced by Babyface, won Record of the Year.

R & B for Women. During the same decade Babyface also wrote songs for Madonna, Toni Braxton, Mariah Carey, Aretha Franklin, Celine Dion, TLC, Tevin Campbell, Gladys Knight, Bobby Brown, and Bell Biv Devoe—and recorded four albums of his own. Perhaps best known for his movie soundtrack for *Waiting to Exhale* (1995), he was particularly appealing to women. Whitney Houston was quoted as saying, "He's the only guy I know who can write about how a woman feels."

Source:

"Voices of Change," *New York,* 32 (6 September 1999): 28–32.

THEATER: COMMERCIALIZING BROADWAY

The Disney Invasion. Two of the biggest musicals on Broadway during the 1990s were *Beauty and the Beast* and *The Lion King,* adaptations of Disney animated motion pictures, prompting some theater lovers to predict the beginning of the end for the Great White Way. To market the shows Disney employed the same techniques it used to

Jason Raize as Simba in the Broadway production of
The Lion King

promote any of its entertainment products: massive advertising campaigns, fast-food tie-ins, and even coloring books. "We traded on the shows' powerful association with hit movies that families watch on video," said Peter Schneider, president of Walt Disney Studios. The publicity and marketing campaigns made the shows virtually critic proof. Disney chairman Michael Eisner created Disney Theatrical Productions, renovated the New Amsterdam Theater at a cost of more than $30 million, and declared Disney to be a force to be reckoned with on Broadway.

Broadway Success. Following the success of *Beauty and the Beast,* which opened in 1994 and succeeded despite tepid reviews, Disney launched *The Lion King* in 1997, and even skeptics took notice. Disney had come to Broadway to stay, and the product, critics grudgingly admitted, was not bad. As director and designer, Disney executives chose gifted artistic designer Julie Taymor, who transformed Disney's animated tale of a young lion cub's coming of age into a magical, mystical, and haunting theatrical experience. For her work in *The*

Lion King Taymor won three Tonys: Outstanding Director of a Musical, Costume Design, and Puppet Design.

Hard-Sell Marketing. The arrival on Broadway of entertainment giant Disney Studios—a company that generated more than $4.6 billion in cash flow in 1998 alone—only escalated a trend toward hard-sell marketing of performances. Disney followed on the heels of the successful British entrepreneurial team of Andrew Lloyd Webber and Cameron Mackintosh, who made Webber's musicals the most popular hits of the 1990s. Commercial survival has always depended on ticket sales, and without sophisticated new marketing techniques heralded by Disney and other corporate backers, many shows of the late 1990s would have closed early and unprofitably. Yet, in one respect, the rules of Broadway had changed. No longer did a bad review in *The New York Times* spell the death of a production.

A Rock Marshmallow. One example of how bad reviews could be counteracted by good publicity was the rock musical *Footloose.* When it opened in 1998, reviewers dismissed it as a "flavorless marshmallow" from "theatrical nowheresville." Yet, MTV advertising spots featuring glittering musical numbers drew young people to the theaters in record numbers. Savvy marketing seemed to have turned *Footloose* into runaway hit, but by the end of the decade the musical had yet to break even.

Sources:

Sylviane Gold, "The Disney Difference," *American Theatre,* 14 (December 1997): 14–18.

William A. Henry III, "Glimpses of Looniness," *Time,* 137 (4 February 1991): 62.

Larry Light, "The Great Hyped Way," *Business Week,* no. 3627 (3 May 1999): 131, 135.

THEATER: DRAMA

Variety. While money continued to be the overriding factor in what constituted Broadway "success," ensuring the domination of musicals, an eclectic mix of notable new dramatic works found their audiences. John Guare's *Six Degrees of Separation,* a demonstration of physical closeness and psychological isolation, represented the best Broadway had to offer in the 1990s. Wendy Wasserstein's *An American Daughter* exemplified how a political whispering campaign ruined the chances of a woman from a prominent family awaiting Senate confirmation as surgeon general. August Wilson continued his look at the black experience in America with *Two Trains Running,* set in a Pittsburgh luncheonette in 1969. Winner of the Tony Award for Best Play and the Pulitzer Prize for Drama in 1991, Neil Simon's *Lost in Yonkers* focused on a mildly retarded woman who planned to marry a similarly handicapped usher whom she has met a few times at a local movie theater. One critic responded to the play by commenting, "Simon's terrain is the border country between laughter and tears." *Last Night of Ballyhoo,* a romantic comedy about two women preparing for a major social event, the 1939 premiere of *Gone With the Wind* in Atlanta, earned playwright Alfred Uhry the 1997 Tony for Best Play. The winner of that award in 1998, Yasmina Reza's *Art* was a comedy of manners that took a humorous look at intellectual pretensions and the

Roscoe Lee Browne, Cynthia Martells, and Al White in the Broadway production of August Wilson's *Two Trains Running*

bonds of friendship. Warren Leight's *Side Man,* winner of the 1999 Tony Award for Best Play, dramatized the life of a jazzman who reviewer Brian Adams described as "at once a modern day hollow man and a musician full of life." While in the 1990s it suffered from criticisms that it had sold out to Disney and big-business advertisers, Broadway continued to entertain and captivate audiences with plays that spoke to the human condition.

Broadway and the AIDS Crisis. The 1992 and 1993 Broadway seasons were dominated by Tony Kushner's two-part play *Angels in America: Millennium Approaches* and *Angels in America: Perestroika.* Directed by George C. Wolfe, the two parts totaled seven hours in length. *Angels in America* dealt with AIDS in America and the crisis of conscience it posed for Americans who were unready for its consequences. As Kushner described the play in a 1992 *Vogue* interview, the first part was "about despair," while "Part Two therefore must be about hope, but I think we're in terrible, terrible trouble. Our hope may simply be, as Prior (a character in the play) says, an addiction to being alive." Kushner won a Pulitzer Prize for part one and Tony Awards for both parts of his cycle, which integrated historical figures such as Roy Cohn into an eclectic group of fictitious homosexual and heterosexual characters. He managed to politicize the AIDS crisis in a format that caused people to take notice, giving the gay community a rallying point for action and becoming a new spokesman. Kushner realized he risked alienating not only culture conservatives but mem-

bers of the artistic community, but he said, "You have to be interesting and you have to be daring and you have to be willing to write things that shock. Shock is part of art. Art that's polite is not much fun."

The Last Temptation of Christ Revisited. Another play that capitalized on the shock value of homosexuality in Western society was Terrence McNally's 1998 drama *Corpus Christi.* On the heels of his Tony-winning plays *Love! Valour! Compassion!* (1995) and *Master Class* (1996), McNally presented one of the most controversial plays of the 1990s: *Corpus Christi* featured a Christ-like character who had sexual intercourse with his male disciples. While many theater people called the play an avant-garde triumph, some religious leaders found it blasphemous. Two thousand religious protestors showed up for a rally while a celebrity-studded group of four hundred demonstrated in support of McNally's play and his First Amendment rights. "No one should be protesting to remove something from the stage," said television producer Norman Lear. In October 1999 Islamic fundamentalists in Great Britain issued an edict condemning McNally and *Corpus Christi* for depicting a homosexual Jesus and called for his death. Critics were divided about the artistic merits of the play. Some felt that after an innovative and startling beginning, the play did "not live up to the high expectations the pre-show hype has proffered."

Sources:
Brian Adams, "Side Man," *Theatre Reviews Limited,* 28 April 1999, online at <www.theatrereviews.com>.

Playbills for the Broadway productions of Tony Kushner's two-part play about AIDS

Andrea Bernstein, "Tony Kushner," *Mother Jones*, 20 (July–August 1995): 59, 64.

Ben Brantley, "Sometimes the Eye of the Beholder Sees Too Clearly for Its Own Good," *New York Times*, 2 March 1998, pp. E1, E4.

David Roberts, "Corpus Christi," *Theatre Reviews Limited*, 3 October 1998, online at <www.theatrereviews.com>.

THEATER: MUSICALS

Imports. Musicals dominated Broadway in the 1990s as long-running British imports continued to draw audiences. In 1997 Andrew Lloyd Webber's *Cats,* which opened in 1982 and finally closed in 2000, became the longest running production in Broadway history, breaking the record set by *A Chorus Line.* Webber's *Phantom of the Opera,* which opened in 1988, continued to draw full houses, while his *Les Misérables,* which opened in 1987, closed down for a short time in 1997 for retuning and then reopened. Alain Boublil and Claude-Michel Schonberg's *Miss Saigon* opened in 1991 and was still running in 2000. These imports were all guided by the British whiz-kid producer Cameron Macintosh.

Touring Companies. Musicals that became established as important Broadway "brand names" then toured nationwide. At one time in the 1990s there were at least three national companies of *Cats, Les Misérables,* and *Phantom of the Opera.* While *Phantom of the Opera,* for example, could gross about $700,000 a week on Broadway in the 1,600-seat Imperial Theatre, on the road it could play in much larger theaters, such as those in Buffalo and Tempe, Arizona, and gross more than $1.2 million per week.

Retreads. Revivals of classic American musicals from earlier decades proliferated during the last decade of the century. Frank Loesser's *Guys and Dolls* had a three-year run on Broadway, beginning in 1992, and toured for nearly three more years. There were also profitable revivals of Loesser's *How To Succeed in Business Without Really Trying,* Richard Adler and Ross's *Damn Yankees,* Richard Rodgers and Oscar Hammerstein's *Carousel* and *The Sound of Music,* Cole Porter's *Kiss Me Kate,* George and Ira Gershwin's *Girl Crazy,* and Irving Berlin's *Annie Get Your Gun.* Perhaps the most successful of the revivals was John Fred Kander and Fred Ebb's *Chicago,* directed by Bob Fosse, which opened to rave reviews in 1997 and soon had two companies touring and a British production in the West End of London.

Disney Hits Broadway. With a few notable exceptions, new American musicals were not successful on Broadway. The Disney company turned two of their animated films into worldwide theatrical hits. *Beauty and the Beast* opened in 1994 to decidedly mixed reviews but was still playing at the end of the decade. *The Lion King* won a total of six Tony Awards in 1998 and has played to 100.1

The cast of the Broadway production of *Rent* taking a curtain call, 1996 (AP/Wide World Photos)

percent of capacity since opening in New York in November 1997.

Other New Musicals. *Five Guys Named Moe* celebrated the music of Louis Jordan while *Jelly's Last Jam* told the story of Jelly Roll Morton. One of the most ingenious musical plotlines of the decade appeared in Stephen Sondheim's *Assassins,* which opened off-Broadway. The show is based on the concept that assassins constitute a sort of club, with past and future killers inspiring each other in a grand conspiracy that includes John Wilkes Booth, John W. Hinckley Jr., Leon Czolgosz (assassin of William McKinley), and Giuseppe Zangara (who attempted to kill Franklin D. Roosevelt). All of these assassins show up in Dallas to persuade Lee Harvey Oswald to shoot himself. Peter Stone's Broadway show *Titanic* opened in 1997, before the movie phenomenon, and, although the reviews were mediocre, it made money and was a success at the Tonys.

Social Relevance. Socially relevant musicals failed to generate audience appeal. *Parade,* directed by Hal Prince with book by Alfred Uhry, retold the story of the 1913 murder of young Mary Phagan and the arrest of Leo Frank, manager of the pencil factory where the girl worked. Leo Frank, who was Jewish, was found guilty of the murder. After his death sentence was commuted, he was lynched. Critics called the play a "somber show" that fell "uncomfortably between the stools of history and art." Music legend Paul Simon tried his hand at Broadway composing with *The Capeman,* based on the true story of Puerto Rican immigrant Salvador Agron who in 1959, at age sixteen, killed two teenagers in a New York City playground while wearing a flashy black and red

cape. He was convicted and later pardoned, dying of a heart attack at age forty-three. The play cost a staggering $11 million to produce and was forced to postpone its December 1997 opening for "retuning." Most of the criticism was heaped on Simon, who had full artistic control. After firing two directors because of "artistic differences" Simon asked choreographer Mark Morris to take over the production. Finally opening in February 1998, the show was critically panned as a "popera" and attracted few theatergoers. Relatives of the murder victims complained about what they feared would be the glorification of Agron. Others complained of a white songwriter perpetuating Latino stereotypes. After a run of only sixty-nine days *The Capeman* closed. The show may have been the most notorious "bomb" of the 1990s, but it had an excellent soundtrack and a stellar cast, with Ruben Blades as the older Salvador and Latino heartthrob Marc Anthony as the young Capeman. A more successful Broadway history lesson, *Ragtime: The Musical,* was Garth Drabinsky's adaption of E. L. Doctorow's 1975 novel. The production made a Broadway star out of leading man Brian Stokes Mitchell. Garth Drabinsky, the Canadian producer, has been hailed as the "savior of the American musical theater" for his willingness to mount lavish shows with social themes that restored a "lost grandeur" to Broadway. Drabinsky oversaw every aspect of *Ragtime* and managed to get Doctorow to help with the adaptation to the musical stage. Doctorow credits Drabinsky for understanding the "American allegory implicit in the text," which deals with "American society's coming to terms with the new century's beckoning

Still in her twenties during the 1990s, Audra McDonald captivated audiences at Broadway musicals with her beautiful soprano voice, which various critics characterized as "tangy," "beautifully focused," "warm," and "spellbinding." She earned Tonys for her featured roles in *Carousel* (1994), *Master Class* (1996), and *Ragtime* (1998). In 1999 she created the title role in the world premiere of *Marie Christine*, Michael John LaChiusa's adaptation of the Medea myth. She also performed with several symphony orchestras, and made her first solo album, *Way Back to Paradise* (1998), comprising fourteen songs by five young composers for the musical theater. More than one critic has called McDonald "the best thing that's happened to the theater world in years."

Sources: Jim Brosseau, "The Era of Audra," *Town and Country*, 153, (November 1999): 123+.

Marc Peyser, "Back to Paradise with Audra," *Newsweek*, 134 (13 December 1999): 94.

potential for both good and bad and the spirit driving its citizens to explore their broadened physical and personal horizons." The stage production made good use of period music—ragtime melodies, lullabies, love ballads, and vaudeville tunes—to move the story along, creating what one reviewer called "a kaleidoscope whose brilliant colors glitter against a constantly threatening darkness" of twentieth-century America.

Bohemian Chic. The winner of the 1996 Tony for Best Musical and the Pulitzer Prize in Drama, *Rent* was one of the shows that redefined the Broadway musical for the 1990s. It was loosely based on the opera *La Bohème*, but instead of re-creating Giacomo Puccini's Parisian locale and colorful characters, this hard-edged musical had its base in the street culture of the 1990s. Originally starring Adam Pascal, Anthony Rapp, and Idina Menzel, *Rent* focuses on Roger (or Rodolfo), an "HIV-positive punk-rocker struggling to write one great song before his time is up." Puccini's Mimi was reinvented as a dancer in an S&M club. Their friends include an artist / video geek, a musician / drag queen, and a vixen with a lesbian lover. As one critic observed, "these bracingly unromanticized characters and events are sharply observed—in all

their complex humanity." Jonathan Larson's music and lyrics included hard rock and reggae, "with bits of gospel, grunge and even a tango heard along the way." Larson died of an aortic aneurysm just before *Rent* opened on Broadway in February 1996.

Kinetic Fusion. *Bring in 'da Noise, Bring in 'da Funk*, developed by dancer-rapper Savion Glover and director George C. Wolfe, won four Tony awards in 1996. Another musical for the 1990s, it retold "African-American history through a kinetic fusion of tap and rap." From slave ships to ragtime, from jazz in the cities to caricatures in Hollywood, the show told the story of race in America, ending with a scene in which four well-dressed men cannot attract a New York cabbie's attention because of the color of their skin. Twenty-two-year-old Glover, who was both star and choreographer, had previously performed on Broadway at age twelve in *Tap Dance Kid*, and starred in *Black and Blue* and *Jelly's Last Jam*. *Time* critic Martha Duffy described the "demon drive" of the dancers, all men, and added: "The sounds vary as strains of jazz, blues, hip-hop and gospel interweave. This is a very raucous show, about as far removed from the classic buck-and-wing as tap can get." Marketing the show through nontraditional, as well as traditional, means brought in a more racially and demographically diverse audience than was usual for Broadway shows. As Ben Brantley observed, *Bring in 'da Noise, Bring in 'da Funk* struck chords of concern with which its audience was familiar—fears of urban tension, poverty, and loss.

Opening Doors. Because of their commercial success, *Rent* and *Bring in da Funk* opened up Broadway for other nontraditional musical productions. New groups of musical composers, artists, and performers had improved chances of being heard by producers concerned for the bottom line.

Sources:
Ben Brantley, "Flying Feet Electrify the Sweep of History," *New York Times*, 26 April 1996, pp. C1, C4.

Brantley, "Ragtime: A Diorama With Nostalgia Rampant," *New York Times*, 19 January 1998, pp. E1, E11.

Martha Duffy, "Is It Taps for Broadway?" *Time*, 147 (6 May 1996): 80.

Brian D. Johnson, "Bullish on Broadway," *Maclean's*, 111 (26 January 1998): 72–74.

Patrick Pacheco, "Rhythms of America in Touring Bring in 'da Noise, Bring in 'da Funk," 19 March 1998, online at <www.playbillonline.com>.

Michael Portantiere, "The Backstage Odyssey of Rent," 16 April 1996 online at <www.playbillonline.com>.

Michael Tueth, "The Dreams of an Era," *America*, 178 (28 March 1998): 21–22.

HEADLINE MAKERS

JOHN GRISHAM

1955-
NOVELIST

Publishing Superstar. By far the best-selling author of the 1990s, John Grisham is perhaps, as his former agent Jay Garon declared, "the most successful author in the history of the book-publishing business."

Street Lawyer. Grisham did not set out to become a writer. Born in Jonesboro, Arkansas, he was the son of a construction worker who continually moved his family around the Deep South. Grisham earned a law degree from the University of Mississippi and established a modest practice in Southaven, Mississippi, a town of twenty-five thousand just across the state line from Tennessee. After spending ten years practicing criminal and personal-injury law, Grisham admitted that his career "was not very fulfilling. I was a street lawyer, one of a thousand in a profession that was and is terribly overcrowded. Competition was fierce; ethics [were] often compromised; and I could never bring myself to advertise." His metamorphosis into a best-selling author began unexpectedly as he sat in the De Soto County Court House in Hernando, Mississippi, listening to the testimony of a twelve-year-old rape victim. The girl's poise and courage inspired Grisham, who rose at five o'clock in the morning every day for the next three years to work on his first novel, *A Time to Kill* (1989), the story of a black father who takes revenge on the white men who raped his daughter. Publisher after publisher rejected the book, until Bill Thompson at Wynwood Press, the editor who had discovered Stephen King, decided to take a chance on Grisham's novel. The first printing numbered only five thousand copies, one thousand of which Grisham purchased and resold from the trunk of his Volvo.

Hitting the Jackpot. The publication of *A Time to Kill* did not change Grisham's life. He continued practicing law

and serving in the Mississippi state legislature, to which he had been elected in 1983, while he worked on his second novel, *The Firm.* When Doubleday published the book in 1991, however, Grisham became an overnight sensation. "One day I woke up and realized that I had won the lottery," Grisham recalled in 1997. "I walked out of my law office without turning off the lights, and I have never looked back." Grisham's formula for success has remained constant from the outset of his literary career. A devout Southern Baptist, he has kept his novels free of vulgar language and sex. "I have never been tempted to resort to gratuitous sex, profanity, or violence. I couldn't write a book that I would be embarrassed for my kids to read a few years from now. Plus my mother would kill me." In addition, Grisham creates fairly uncomplicated characters and fashions breathtakingly suspenseful plots. Instead of writing to impress the critics, he has produced novels that he believes people will enjoy reading. "I sometimes sacrifice narrative in a deliberate effort to turn pages," he explained. "You throw an innocent person in there and get 'em caught up in a conspiracy and then you get 'em out." By the end of 1993, *The Firm* had sold more than twelve million copies in the United States alone. After *The Firm*, Grisham produced a best-seller every year: *The Pelican Brief* (1992), *The Client* (1993), *The Chamber* (1994), *The Rainmaker* (1995), *The Runaway Jury* (1996), *The Partner* (1997), *The Street Lawyer* (1998), *The Testament* (1999), and *The Brethren* (2000). Six of his novels were made into motion pictures that grossed millions at the box office, and he wrote the story on which Robert Altman's movie *The Gingerbread Man* (1998) was based.

Reclusive Celebrity. *Forbes* magazine estimated Grisham's 1998 income at more than $30 million. The worldwide gross of his nine novels and the subsequent screen adaptations has exceeded $1 billion. Grisham has indeed become "big business." Yet, he has made a conscious effort to prevent fame and money from ruining his life. To escape the distractions of celebrity, he and his family moved from Oxford, Mississippi, in 1995 for the seclusion of a 204-year-old plantation house surrounded by one hundred acres of land in Albemarle County, Virginia, about twenty-five miles from Charlottesville. "We still think of ourselves as regular people," Grisham insisted at the time. "We want to keep things normal for ourselves and for our kids, so there's a constant undercurrent of trying to maintain a normal lifestyle." Grisham is undaunted by critics who accuse him of writing the same novel again and again. He does not regard his books as literature, characterizing them instead as "high-quality, professional entertainment." Yet, he is widely credited with revitalizing the legal thriller. He has also developed the sense that his popularity is fleeting. "I firmly believe all this is temporary. It will be over one of these days—five years from now, ten years from now. The books will stop selling for whatever reason."

Sources:

Jennifer Ferranti, "Grisham's Law," *Saturday Evening Post,* 269 (March/April 1997): 42–45.

Edwin Howard, "Grisham's Golden Touch Remains Untarnished," *Nashville Business Journal,* 11 (26 June 1995): 13–14.

Howard, "Parallel Elements—Links Between Oxford's Faulkner and Grisham," *Memphis Business Journal,* 18 (12 August 1996): 28–29.

Malcolm Jones, Ray Sawhill, and others, "Grisham's Gospel," *Newsweek,* 133 (15 February 1999): 65–67.

Gene Lyons, "John Grisham," *Entertainment Weekly,* no. 203/204 (31 December 1993 – 1 January 1994): 24–25.

Mary Beth Pringle, *John Grisham: A Critical Companion* (Westport, Conn.: Greenwood Press, 1997).

Jeff Zaleski, "The Grisham Business," *Publishers Weekly* (19 January 1998): 248.

WYNTON MARSALIS

1962-

MUSICIAN, COMPOSER

A Life in Music. The second of six sons born to Ellis and Dolores Marsalis, Wynton Marsalis cannot recall a time when music was unimportant to him. His father is an accomplished jazz pianist, and three of his brothers—saxophonist Branford, trombonist Delfeayo, and drummer Jason—are also jazz musicians. Wynton Marsalis began to play the trumpet seriously in 1974, at the age of twelve. While in high school, he performed with funk, jazz, and marching bands, as well as with symphony orchestras. He later attended the prestigious Juilliard School in New York City, and in 1980 he joined Art Blakey's Jazz Messengers and signed a recording contract with Columbia Records. By 1999 Marsalis had released forty recordings and sold more than eight million records worldwide. He has earned eight Grammy Awards for jazz and classical recordings and a ninth for his contribution to an album of stories for children. In 1997 he won the Pulitzer Prize in Music for his epic jazz oratorio *Blood on the Fields,* a musical exploration of slavery in the United States. The artistic director of the jazz program at the Lincoln Center in New York City, Marsalis has also devoted himself to advancing the musical education of young people around the world.

Musical Education. Marsalis contends that for some time popular music has undergone a process of infantilization. Once American popular music "switched from an adult base to an adolescent base," Marsalis complains, "that was a major step backward. Pop music used to be adult music, with adult sensibilities. But since pop made that switch to an adolescent base, it has never been able to return, as music, to what it was. And I guess it's understandable, because in terms of commerciality, it becomes more successful every year." Serious musicians, he urges, have a responsibility to reverse the erosion of musical standards rather than to contribute to the "dumbing down" of music. He has thus made it his mission to introduce new generations of musicians and audiences to the musical treasures of the past. He calls music "the memory of a people, their history. If you listen to the music of Beethoven or Bach, it projects much of what they thought and understood. When you're playing their music, you're interfacing with not only their great minds but with the memory of a whole group of people for whom they were the conduits." He has likened the benefits of studying music to participation in sports. Both music and sports require hard work, dedication, and discipline. Moreover, he adds, studying music improves students' thinking in other disciplines, because it teaches young people "how to sense form, how to understand things that evolve through time, how to converse—which is certainly one of the most important human skills—and how to interact with other people with style. These are all the same things you'd have to deal with if you were a businessperson." In 1995 Marsalis joined with the American Public Broadcasting System to present *Marsalis on Music,* a four-part series of one-hour programs on rhythm, form, wind ensembles and jazz bands, and practice. The series is an outgrowth of Marsalis's belief that serious education in music ought not to be reserved only for the talented few. Even children of modest ability, he argues, benefit from the exposure to and the study of music.

Controversy. Over the years the jazz community has had its share of internecine squabbles, and Marsalis was no stranger to controversy during the 1990s. He tangled more than once with legendary trumpeter Miles Davis over questions of musical style, emerging from these encounters as the leader of the movement to revive and maintain traditional jazz in the United States and to elevate jazz to the status of American classical music. "I don't mind a battle or a fight," he has acknowledged. "That lets you know you're alive. There's nothing wrong with a good battle." His pronouncements on musical tradition have aroused sharp disagreement and even resentment among other jazz aficionados. Rivals have accused Marsalis and his principal adviser, the outspoken critic Stanley Crouch, of indulging in "Crow Jim," a term that composer Leonard Feather coined in the 1940s to describe reverse racism and discrimination. By 1993, many other musicians and critics were grumbling that Marsalis's jazz programs at the Lincoln Center consistently ignored the contributions of white musicians such as Bill Evans and Benny Goodman. Although Marsalis categorically denied any racial motivations behind these programs, a televised interview in which he referred to those in control of the music industry as "people who read the Torah and stuff" did not enhance his credibility. During the summer of 1994 Marsalis challenged his chief and most persistent antagonist, jazz historian James Lincoln Collier, to a public debate. The catalyst for the debate was a letter Marsalis had written to *The New York Times Book Review* denouncing a positive review of Collier's *Jazz: The American Theme Song* (1993), in which Collier not only included a forceful critique of Stanley Crouch but also reproached Marsalis for turning "to blacks as authorities on . . . music simply because they are black." At the debate, which took place at Lincoln Center, Marsalis promised in his opening remarks to administer a "whipping." By most accounts he did so, pointing out several inaccuracies in Collier's controversial and unflattering biography of Duke Ellington. Yet, observers also agreed that it was Collier rather than Marsalis who came out of the confrontation with his reputation and his dignity intact.

Preserving the Musical Past. Some critics believe that Marsalis will never create a body of work as inspired or enduring as the music he admires. By the end of the decade, sales of his recordings had declined, in part because during the 1990s he released respectable but undistinguished material. Yet, he has nonetheless made a significant contribution to preserving an art form.

Sources:

Laura Andrews, "Wynton Marsalis Awarded Pulitzer Prize Denied Duke Ellington 32 Years Ago," *New York Amsterdam News,* 10 May 1997, pp. 21–22.

Clive Davis, "Has Jazz Gone Classical?," *Wilson Quarterly,* 21 (Spring 1997): 56-63.

John J. Mahlmann, "In the Practice Room with Wynton Marsalis," *Teaching Music,* 4 (February 1997): 64–65.

Ned Martel and Craig Offman, "Wynton's Battle Cry," *George,* 3 (April 1998): 43.

Evonne Nolan, "Wynton Marsalis," *Teaching Music,* 3 (October 1995): 42–43.

Lynn Norment, "Wynton Marsalis: The Private Man Behind the Music," *Ebony,* 54 (August 1999): 84–87.

TONI MORRISON

1931-

NOVELIST

Nobel Prize Winner. When Toni Morrison won the Nobel Prize for Literature in 1993, she became the first American woman to receive the award since Pearl Buck in 1938, and the first African American woman ever to be so honored. In describing her work, the Nobel Committee stated: "She delves into the language itself, a language she wants to free from the fetters of race. And she addresses us with the luster of poetry."

Career. Born Chloe Anthony Wofford in Lorain, Ohio, Morrison graduated from Howard University in 1953 and earned a master's degree in English at Cornell University in 1955. After a series of university teaching jobs, she became the Robert F. Goheen Professor of the Humanities at Princeton University in 1988. Over her long career as a writer Morrison has used poetic language in an unflinching examination of gender conflicts, race relations, and other aspects of American society, winning a National Book Critics Circle Award for *Song of Solomon* in 1977 and a Pulitzer Prize for *Beloved* in 1988. As she explained it, "My work requires me to think about how free I can be as an African American woman writer in my genderized, sexualized, wholly radicalized world." In the novels *The Bluest Eye* (1970), *Sula* (1973), *Song of Solomon,* (1977), *Tar Baby* (1981), *Beloved* (1987), *Jazz* (1992), and *Paradise* (1998) Morrison has demonstrated her mastery of literary technique. When asked for her reaction to winning the Nobel Prize for Literature she responded, "When I heard I'd won you heard no 'Aw, shucks' from me. The prize didn't change my inner assessment of what I'm capable of doing, but I welcomed it as a public, representational affirmation of my work. I was surprised at how patriotic I felt, being the first native-born American winner since John Steinbeck. I felt pride that a black and a woman had been recognized in such an international forum." In her Nobel address in Stockholm, Morrison said, "The vitality of language lies in its ability to limn the actual, imagined and possible lives of its speakers, readers, writers. Although its poise is sometimes in displacing experience, it is not a substitute for it. It arcs toward the place where meaning may lie." Henry Louis Gates, chairman of the African American Studies Department at Harvard University, said: "I think she got the Nobel Prize for two books, essentially, *Beloved* and *Jazz.*" He called *Jazz* a "truly brilliant postmodern book" and said Morrison was "as great and as innovative as Faulkner and García Marquez and Woolf. That's why she deserved the Nobel Prize."

Race matters. *Paradise,* Morrison's first book after winning the Nobel Prize, was conceived as the final installment of a trilogy that examines love in all its forms. In the first installment, *Beloved,* she told the troubling tale of an escaped slave whose love for her daughter was so strong that she would rather kill the child than see her returned to servitude. The second volume, *Jazz,* looks at "elicit" love, telling the story of a married man in Harlem during the 1920s who murders his young girlfriend after she jilts him for a younger man. That story is interwoven with the related story of a wealthy white and her mulatto son during the reconstruction era. Paul Gray described the form of love treated in *Paradise* as "a hunger for security, the desire to create perfection in an imperfect world." In tracing the fates of former slaves who migrated west after the Civil War, Morrison was struck by the admonition that appeared in the ads for black settlers: "Come Prepared or Not at All."

Setting her novel in an all-black town in Oklahoma, she used this aphorism to construct a tale of rejection, isolation, anger, and collective memory. While she is known for her careful dissection of race relations, Morrison deliberately refused to concentrate on race in *Paradise*. As she told Gray, "I wanted the readers to wonder about the race of those girls [in the local convent] until those readers understood that their race didn't matter. I want to dissuade people from reading literature in that way." She added: "Race is the least reliable information you can have about someone. It's real information, but it tells you next to nothing."

Sources:

Douglas Century, *Toni Morrison* (New York: Chelsea House, 1994).

Jan Furman, *Toni Morrison's Fiction* (Columbia: University of South Carolina Press, 1996).

Paul Gray, "Paradise Found," *Time,* 151 (19 January 1998): 62–68.

Trudier Harris, *Fiction and Folklore: The Novels of Toni Morrison* (Knoxville: University of Tennessee Press, 1991).

Wilfred D. Samuels and Clenora Weems, *Toni Morrison* (Boston: Twayne, 1990).

QUENTIN TARANTINO

1963-

MOVIE DIRECTOR, SCREENWRITER

A Scorsese for the 1990s. Quentin Tarantino burst onto the movie scene in 1992 with his shockingly violent, critically acclaimed movie *Reservoir Dogs,* which he directed and played a small role in, as well as writing the screenplay. He did the same for his biggest hit of the decade, *Pulp Fiction* (1994), which prompted some to call him the new Martin Scorsese—a moviemaker who could depict the anxieties of the 1990s as Scorsese had done in the 1970s with movies such as *Mean Streets* (1973) and *Taxi Driver* (1976). A few critics even went so far as to predict that Tarantino would be the "savior of American film making."

High-School Dropout. Born in Knoxville, Tennessee, Tarantino grew up in suburban Los Angeles, where during high school he worked part-time as an usher in a pornographic movie theater. After quitting school before graduation, he worked for about five years at Video Archives, which he calls "the best video store in the Los Angeles area," where he met future director Roger Avary, who later worked with him on the script for *Pulp Fiction*. Unlike most other directors and screenwriters of his generation, Tarantino learned everything he knows about moviemaking from his life-long addiction to movie watching, not from courses in film school.

Career. After two incomplete independent movie projects in the mid 1980s, and a bit part as an Elvis impersonator on an episode of *The Golden Girls* in 1988, Tarantino won critical praise and shocked moviegoers with *Reservoir Dogs*, especially with the now-famous scene in which an ear is sliced off with a razor. His next major project was the screenplay for another violent movie, Oliver Stone's *Natural Born Killers* (1994). Stone's alterations to the script during the filming prompted an angry reaction from Tarantino, bringing out the difference between the two moviemakers' sensibilities. As critic Ron Rosenbaum noted in *Esquire* (December 1997), Stone is the "Mythic Macho Outdoor Man of Nature" while Tarantino is the "Aesthete Analyst of Indoor Intrigue and Internal Self-Consciousness." Stone's movies, Rosenbaum pointed out, are full of action, while Tarantino's, though violent, are filled with dialogue that takes the viewer inside the psyches of his characters, and they are loaded with visual and verbal references to earlier movie and literary genres. These characteristics are clearly apparent in his next project, *Pulp Fiction,* which Roger Ebert called "a comedy about blood, guts, violence, strange sex, drugs, fixed fights, dead body disposal, leather freaks and a wristwatch that makes a dark journey down through the generations." The movie, for which Tarantino and Avary won a Best Original Screenplay Oscar, is an insider's homage to the mobster movies and pulp-fiction detective stories of the 1930s. Tarantino's love of language is apparent in the dialogue, which put his movies on a level above the typical action movies of the 1990s. Tarantino is a self-confessed lover of the movie. Though his other movies of the decade—including *Jackie Brown* (1997), based on a novel by Elmore Leonard—attracted less attention than *Pulp Fiction,* Tarantino seems likely to continue surprising and shocking moviegoers with the products of his idiosyncratic imagination.

Sources:

Jami Bernard, *Quentin Tarantino: The Man and His Movies* (New York: HarperPerennial, 1995).

Wensley Clarkson, *Quentin Tarantino: Shooting from the Hip* (Woodstock, N.Y.: Overlook Press, 1995).

Jeff Dawson, *Quentin Tarantino: The Cinema of Cool* (New York: Applause, 1995).

Roger Ebert, Review of *Pulp Fiction, Chicago Sun-Times,* 10 October 1994.

PEOPLE IN THE NEWS

On 9 May 1996 **Julie Andrews,** star of *Victor/Victoria,* refused to be considered for the Tony Award for Best Actress in a Broadway Musical because the Tony committee had not nominated the other cast members.

On 20 January 1993, poet **Maya Angelou** read "The Pulse of the Morning" at the inauguration of President William Jefferson Clinton.

In July 1998 **Tina Brown** resigned after six years as editor of *The New Yorker.* She was replaced by **David Remnick,** who restored the original literary emphasis of the magazine. Brown and **Ron Galotti** joined with Miramax Films in establishing Talk Media to publish *Talk* magazine (in collaboration with Hearst Magazines), produce television programming, and publish books.

In 1994 dancer and choreographer **Trisha Brown** performed *If You Couldn't See Me* with her back and face turned away from the audience, creating what critic Jack Anderson called "a sculptural object come to life."

In 1998 **Garth Fagan,** whose first job on Broadway was as choreographer for *The Lion King,* won Tony, Drama Desk, Outer Critics Circle, and Astaire Awards for his work on the show.

In 1994 photographer **Felice Frankel** became artist in residence and research scientist at the Massachusetts Institute of Technology, where she has helped scientists explain their work to the public through her visually arresting photographs.

Aaron Lansky, president of the National Yiddish Book Center, dedicated a new home for the institution in Amherst, Massachusetts, in 1997. He was credited with saving more than 1.3 million Yiddish-language books from oblivion.

Ralph Lemon, choreographer, achieved international critical and popular acclaim when his ballet *Bogus Pomp,* set to music by Frank Zappa, had its premiere in Lyons, France, in fall 1990.

After twenty-five years as a documentary photographer whose work was better known than her name, **Mary Ellen Mark** had a retrospective show of her life's work in 1992; it opened at the International Center of Photography in New York City and traveled to fifteen other museums.

Francine Patterson, president of the Gorilla Foundation, revealed in November 1997 that ape art of the 1950s usually resembled that of the Abstract Expressionists then in its ascendence, but that the 1990s gorilla paintings of Koko and Michael "represent things in the real world," such as birds or balls. Koko and Michael have used sign language to explain their paintings, which may be seen at www.gorilla.org.

In 1998 **Martin Puryear,** a sculptor recognized for his skill in transforming wood and steel into innovative works of art, completed his eight-year collaboration with landscape architect **Michael Van Valkenburgh** on the renovation of the 4,500 square-foot Vera List Courtyard at the New School for Social Research in New York City.

In 1999 movie fan **Vance Rigo** quit his job so he could be first in line for tickets to *Star Wars: Episode I: The Phantom Menace,* explaining, "I had to set my priorities straight."

Beginning in 1975 and continuing through the 1980s and 1990s, environmental artist **James Turrell** used earth-moving equipment to transform the Roden Crater, an extinct volcano in northern Arizona, into a work of art, finally announcing his completion date as 2000.

In April 1991 **Mary Verde-Fletcher,** a dancer who had been unable to stand or walk since childhood, performed as a dancer in *Gypsy* and *Above* at the Beck Center in Cleveland.

Video artist **Bill Viola,** whose works *I Do Not Know What It Is I Am Like* (1986) and *The Messenger* (1997) were influenced by his own near-death experience, was the subject of a 1998 survey exhibition at the Whitney Museum in New York City.

AWARDS

PULITZER PRIZES

1990

Fiction: *The Mambo Kings Play Songs of Love*, by **Oscar Hijuelos**

Drama: *The Piano Lesson*, by **August Wilson**

Poetry: *The World Doesn't End*, by **Charles Simic**

Music: *Duplicates: A Concerto for Two Pianos and Orchestra*, by **Mel Powell**

1991

Fiction: *Rabbit at Rest*, by **John Updike**

Drama: *Lost in Yonkers*, by **Neil Simon**

Poetry: *Near Changes*, by **Mona Van Duyn**

Music: *Symphony*, by **Shulamit Ran**

1992

Fiction: *A Thousand Acres*, by **Jane Smiley**

Drama: *The Kentucky Cycle*, by **Robert Schenkkan**

Poetry: *Selected Poems*, by **James Tate**

Music: *The Face of the Night, The Heart of the Dark*, by **Wayne Peterson**

1993

Fiction: *A Good Scent From a Strange Mountain*, by **Robert Olen Butler**

Drama: *Angels In America: Millennium Approaches*, by **Tony Kushner**

Poetry: *The Wild Iris*, by **Louise Gluck**

Music: *Trombone Concerto*, by **Christopher Rouse**

1994

Fiction: *The Shipping News*, by **E. Annie Proulx**

Drama: *Three Tall Women*, by **Edward Albee**

Poetry: *Neon Vernacular*, by **Yusef Komunyakaa**

Music: *Of Reminiscences and Reflections*, by **Gunther Schuller**

1995

Fiction: *The Stone Diaries*, by **Carol Shields**

Drama: *The Young Man from Atlanta*, by **Horton Foote**

Poetry: *The Simple Truth*, by **Philip Levine**

Music: *Stringmusic*, by **Morton Gould**

1996

Fiction: *Independence Day*, by **Richard Ford**

Drama: *Rent*, by **Jonathan Larson**

Poetry: *The Dream of the Unified Field*, by **Jorie Graham**

Music: *Lilacs*, by **George Walker**

1997

Fiction: *Martin Dressler: The Tale of an American Dreamer*, by **Steven Millhauser**

Drama: (No Award)

Poetry: *Alive Together: New and Selected Poems*, by **Lisa Mueller**

Music: *Blood on the Fields*, by **Wynton Marsalis**

1998

Fiction: *American Pastoral*, by **Philip Roth**

Drama: *How I Learned to Drive*, by **Paula Vogel**

Poetry: *Black Zodiac*, by **Charles Wright**

Music: *String Quartet No. 2, Musica Instrumentalis*, by **Aaron Jay Kernis**

1999

Fiction: *The Hours*, by **Michael Cunningham**

Drama: *Wit*, by **Margaret Edison**

Poetry: *Blizzard of One,* by **Mark Strand**

Music: *Concerto for Flute, Strings, and Percussion,* by **Melinda Wagner**

ANTOINETTE PERRY AWARDS (TONYS)

1990

Play: *The Grapes of Wrath,* by **Frank Galati**

Actor: **Robert Morse,** *Tru*

Actress, Dramatic Star: **Maggie Smith,** *Lettice and Lovage*

Musical: *City of Angels,* produced by **Nick Vanoff, Roger Berlind, Jujamcyn Theaters, Suntory International Corp.,** and **The Shubert Organization**

Actor, Musical Star: **James Naughton,** *City of Angels*

Actress, Musical Star: **Tyne Daly,** *Gypsy*

1991

Play: *Lost in Yonkers,* by **Neil Simon**

Actor, Dramatic Star: **Nigel Hawthorne,** *Shadowlands*

Actress, Dramatic Star: **Mercedes Ruehl,** *Lost in Yonkers*

Musical: *The Will Rogers Follies,* produced by **Pierre Cossette, Martin Richards, Sam Crothers, James M. Nederlander, Stewart F. Lane, Max Weitzenhoffer,** and **Japan Satellite Broadcasting, Inc.**

Actor, Musical Star: **Jonathan Pryce,** *Miss Saigon*

Actress, Musical Star: **Lea Salonga,** *Miss Saigon*

1992

Play: *Dancing at Lughnasa,* by **Brian Friel**

Actor, Dramatic Star: **Judd Hirsch,** *Conversations With My Father*

Actress, Dramatic Star: **Glenn Close,** *Death and the Maiden*

Musical: *Crazy for You,* by **George and Ira Gershwin**

Actor, Musical Star: **Gregory Hines,** *Jelly's Last Jam*

Actress, Musical Star: **Faith Prince,** Guys and Dolls)

1993

Play: *Angels in America: Millennium Approaches,* by **Tony Kushner**

Actor, Dramatic Star: **Ron Leibman,** *Angels in America: Millennium Approaches*

Actress, Dramatic Star: **Madeline Kahn,** *The Sisters Rosensweig*

Musical: *Kiss of the Spider Woman: The Musical,* produced by the **Live Entertainment Corp. of Canada/Garth Drabinsky**

Actor, Musical Star: **Brent Carver,** *Kiss of the Spider Woman—The Musical*

Actress, Musical Star: **Chitons Rivera,** *Kiss of the Spider Woman—The Musical*

1994

Play: *Angels in America: Perestroika,* by **Tony Kushner**

Actor, Dramatic Star: **Stephen Spinella,** *Angels in America: Perestroika*

Actress, Dramatic Star: **Diana Rigg,** *Medea*

Musical: *Passion,* produced by **The Shubert Organization, Capital Cities/ABC, Roger Berlind,** and **Scott Rudin**

Actor, Musical Star: **Boyd Gaines,** *She Loves Me*

Actress, Musical Star: **Donna Murphy,** *Passion*

1995

Play: *Love! Valour! Compassion!* by **Terrence McNally**

Actor, Dramatic Star: **Ralph Fiennes,** *Hamlet*

Actress, Dramatic Star: **Cherry Jones,** *The Heiress*

Musical: *Sunset Boulevard,* produced by **The Really Useful Company**

Actor, Musical Star: **Matthew Broderick,** *How to Succeed in Business Without Really Trying!*

Actress, Musical Star: **Glenn Close,** *Sunset Boulevard*

1996

Play: *Master Class,* by **Terrence McNally**

Actor, Dramatic Star: **George Grizzard,** *A Delicate Balance*

Actress, Dramatic Star: **Zoe Caldwell,** *Master Class*

Musical: *Rent,* produced by **Jeffrey Seller, Kevin McCollum, Allan S. Gordon,** and **The New York Theatre Workshop**

Actor, Musical Star: **Nathan Lane,** *A Funny Thing Happened on the Way to the Forum*

Actress, Musical Star: **Donna Murphy,** *The King and I*

1997

Play: *Last Night of Ballyhoo,* by **Alfred Uhry**

Actor, Dramatic Star: **Christopher Plummer,** *Barrymore*

Actress, Dramatic Star: **Janet McTeer,** *A Doll's House*

Musical: *Titanic,* produced by **Dodger Endemol Theatricals, Richard S. Pechter,** and **The John F. Kennedy Center**

Actor, Musical Star: **James Naughton,** *Chicago*

Actress, Musical Star: **Bebe Neuwirth,** *Chicago*

1998

Play: *Art,* by **Yasmina Reza**

Actor, Dramatic Star: **Anthony LaPaglia,** *A View From the Bridge*

Actress, Dramatic Star: **Marie Mullen,** *The Beauty Queen of Leenane*

Musical: *The Lion King,* produced by **Disney**

Actor, Musical Star: **Alan Cumming,** *Cabaret*

Actress, Musical Star: **Natasha Richardson,** *Cabaret*

1999

Play: *Side Man,* by **Warren Leight**

Actor, Dramatic Star: **Brian Dennehy,** *Death of a Salesman*

Actress, Dramatic Star: **Judi Dench,** *Amy's View*

Musical: *Fosse,* produced by **Livent (U.S.) Inc.**

Actor, Musical Star: **Martin Short,** *Little Me*

Actress, Musical Star: **Bernadette Peters,** *Annie Get Your Gun*

ACADEMY OF MOTION PICTURE ARTS AND SCIENCES AWARDS (OSCARS)

1990

Actor: **Jeremy Irons,** *Reversal of Fortune*

Actress: **Kathy Bates,** *Misery*

Director: **Kevin Costner,** *Dances With Wolves*

Picture: *Dances With Wolves*

1991

Actor: **Anthony Hopkins,** *The Silence of the Lambs*

Actress: **Jodie Foster,** *The Silence of the Lambs*

Director: **Jonathan Demme,** *The Silence of the Lambs*

Picture: *The Silence of the Lambs*

1992

Actor: **Al Pacino,** *Scent of a Woman*

Actress: **Emma Thompson,** *Howards End*

Director: **Clint Eastwood,** *Unforgiven*

Picture: *Unforgiven*

1993

Actor: **Tom Hanks,** *Philadelphia*

Actress: **Holly Hunter,** *The Piano*

Director: **Steven Spielberg,** *Schindler's List*

Picture: *Schindler's List*

1994

Actor: **Tom Hanks,** *Forrest Gump*

Actress: **Jessica Lange,** *Blue Sky*

Director: **Robert Zemeckis,** *Forrest Gump*

Picture: *Forrest Gump*

1995

Actor: **Nicolas Cage,** *Leaving Las Vegas*

Actress: **Susan Sarandon,** *Dead Man Walking*

Director: **Mel Gibson,** *Braveheart*

Picture: *Braveheart*

1996

Actor: **Geoffrey Rush,** *Shine*

Actress: **Frances McDormand,** *Fargo*

Director: **Anthony Minghella,** *The English Patient*

Picture: *The English Patient*

1997

Actor: **Jack Nicholson,** *As Good As It Gets*

Actress: **Helen Hunt,** *As Good As It Gets*

Director: **James Cameron,** *Titanic*

Picture: *Titanic*

1998

Actor: **Roberto Benigni,** *Life is Beautiful*

Actress: **Gwyneth Paltrow,** *Shakespeare in Love*

Director: **Steven Spielberg,** *Saving Private Ryan*

Picture: *Shakespeare in Love*

1999

Actor: **Kevin Spacey,** *American Beauty*

Actress: **Hilary Swank,** *Boys Don't Cry*

Director: **Sam Mendes,** *American Beauty*

Picture: *American Beauty*

THE NATIONAL ACADEMY OF RECORDING ARTS & SCIENCES AWARDS (GRAMMY AWARDS)

1990

Record: **Phil Collins,** "Another Day in Paradise"

Album: **Quincy Jones,** *Back on the Block*

1991

Record: **Natalie Cole with Nat King Cole,** "Unforgettable"

Album: **Natalie Cole,** *Unforgettable*

1992

Record: **Eric Clapton,** "Tears in Heaven"

Album: **Eric Clapton,** *Eric Clapton Unplugged*

1993

Record: **Whitney Houston,** "I Will Always Love You"

Album: **Whitney Houston,** *The Bodyguard* (soundtrack)

1994

Record: **Sheryl Crow,** "All I Wanna Do"

Album: **Tony Bennett,** *Tony Bennett MTV Unplugged*

1995

Record: **Seal,** "Kiss From a Rose"

Album: **Alanis Morissette,** *Jagged Little Pill*

1996

Record: **Eric Clapton,** "Change the World"

Album: **Celine Dion,** *Falling Into You*

1997

Record: **Shawn Colvin,** "Sunny Came Home"

Album: **Bob Dylan,** *Time Out of Mind*

1998

Record: **Celine Dion,** "My Heart Will Go On"

Album: **Lauryn Hill,** *The Miseducation of Lauryn Hill*

1999

Record: **Santana featuring Rob Thomas,** "Smooth"

Album: **Santana,** *Supernatural*

DEATHS

Berenice Abbott, 93, photographer, best known for her portraits of American expatriates in Paris during the 1920s and her documentary photographs of New York life during the 1930s and 1940s, 9 December 1991.

Gene Autry, 91, singer and actor, who starred in a series of musical-western movies, including *Singing Cowboy* (1936), *Red River Valley* (1936), and *Rhythm in the Saddle* (1938), 2 October 1998.

Pearl Bailey, 72, recording artist and actress, whose Broadway appearances included a part in *House of Flowers* (1954) and the lead in the all-black production of *Hello, Dolly* (1967) and whose screen credits include *Carmen Jones* (1954), *St. Louis Blues* (1958), and *Porgy and Bess* (1959), 7 August 1990.

Leonard Bernstein, 72, conductor of the New York Philharmonic Orchestra (1957–1969) and composer whose best-known works were the scores for Jerome Robbins's ballet *Fancy Free* (1944) and the Broadway musicals *Candide* (1956) and *West Side Story* (1957), 14 October 1990.

Sonny Bono, 62, singer who was part of the pop-music duo Sonny & Cher during the late 1960s and early 1970s and then went on to become a successful restaurateur and a member of the House of Representatives, 5 January 1998.

George Burns, 100, actor who teamed with his wife, Gracie Allen, on comedy shows on radio in the 1930s and television in the 1950s, and performed in movies such as *Oh, God* (1977), 9 March 1996.

John Cage, 80, avant-garde composer of works such as *Imaginary Landscape #4* (1951) and *4'33* (1952), in which he claimed to have liberated "nonmusical sounds" to demonstrate that "everything we do is music," 12 August 1992.

Cab Calloway, 86, jazz musician best known for the song "Minnie the Moocher," 18 November 1994.

John Candy, 41, comedy actor, best known for his work on the television show *Second City Television*, 4 April 1994.

Frank Capra, 94, movie director who expressed an unshakable belief in the American dream in movies such as *It Happened One Night* (1934), *Mr. Deeds Goes to Town* (1936), and *Mr. Smith Goes to Washington* (1939), 3 September 1991.

James Clavell, 70, popular novelist whose books include *Tai-Pan* (1966) and *Shogun* (1975), 7 September 1994.

Kurt Cobain, 27, founding member of the alternative rock band Nirvana, by suicide, 8 April 1994.

Claudette Colbert, 92, actress who won an Oscar for her performance opposite Clark Gable in *It Happened One Night* (1934), 30 July 1996.

Aaron Copland, 90, classical composer who combined modern tonal music, jazz, and folk tunes in works such as scores for the ballets *Billy the Kid* (1938), *Rodeo* (1942), and *Appalachian Spring* (1944) and the movies *Of Mice and Men* (1939), *Our Town* (1940), *The Red Pony* (1948), and *The Heiress* (1949), 2 December 1990.

Joseph Cotten, 89, actor who started out with Orson Welles's Mercury Theater and later had roles in Welles's movies *Citizen Kane* (1941), *The Magnificent Ambersons* (1942), and *The Third Man* (1949), 6 February 1994.

Miles Davis, 65, jazz trumpeter who played in Charlie Parker's bebop quintet in the late 1940s and later became known for his of cool jazz, hard bop, and fusion, 28 September 1991.

Sammy Davis Jr., 64, singer, dancer, actor, and member of Frank Sinatra's "Rat Pack," whose hit songs include "Hey There" (1954), "What Kind of Fool Am I?" (1962), and "Candy Man" (1972) and whose screen credits include *Porgy and Bess* (1959), *The Threepenny Opera* (1963), *Sweet Charity* (1969), and *Tap* (1989), 16 May 1990.

Willem de Kooning, 92, abstract expressionist artist who helped to put New York City at the center of the international art world after World War II, 1 March 1997.

John Denver, 53, recording artist whose hit singles include "Country Roads," "Thank God I'm a Country Boy," "Rocky Mountain High," and "Annie's Song," 12 October 1997.

James Dickey, 74, poet and novelist, who won a National Book Award for his verse collection *Buckdancer's Choice* (1965) and earned popular and critical acclaim for his novel *Deliverance* (1970), 19 January 1997.

Allen Drury, 80, author and journalist, who won a Pulitzer Prize for his novel *Advise and Consent* (1959), 2 September 1998.

Ralph Ellison, 80, author of the groundbreaking *Invisible Man* (1952), and the posthumously published *Juneteenth* (1999), novels about the African American experience in the United States, 16 April 1994.

Tom Ewell, 85, character actor who had supporting roles in movies such as *Adam's Rib* (1949) and *The Seven Year Itch* (1955), 12 September 1994.

Ella Fitzgerald, 78, jazz singer known for her ability sing in scat, swing, bebop, and improvisational styles and whose first and best-known hit was "A-Tisket, A-Tasket" (1938), 14 June 1996.

Jerry Garcia, 54, founding member and lead guitarist in the Grateful Dead, who helped create the psychedelic-rock sound of the 1960s and later pioneered "country rock," 9 August 1995.

Greer Garson, 91, actress whose screen credits include *Pride and Prejudice* (1940), *Mrs. Miniver* (1942), and *Madame Curie* (1943), 6 April 1996.

John Birks "Dizzy" Gillespie, 76, jazz trumpeter and composer who created the bebop sound with Charlie "Bird" Parker, 6 January 1993.

Allen Ginsberg, 70, poet, whose long poem *Howl* (1956) is one of the most notable works by a member of the Beat Generation, 5 April 1997.

Martha Graham, 96, pioneering modern dancer best known for her choreography of *Letter to the World* (1940), *Appalachian Spring* (1944), *Clytemnestra* (1958), and *Circe* (1963), 1 April 1991.

Alex Haley, 70, coauthor of *Autobiography of Malcolm X* (1965) and author of *Roots: The Saga of an American Family* (1976), the best-selling chronicle of seven generations of his family, going back to their ancestors in Africa, 10 February 1992.

Armand Hammer, 92, industrialist and art patron who left his private collection, valued at $250 million, to the new Armand Hammer Museum of Art and Cultural Center in Los Angeles, 10 December 1990.

Keith Haring, 31, artist who turned grafitti into fine art, of an AIDS-related illness, 16 February 1990.

Joseph Heller, 76, novelist whose World War II *Catch-22* (1961) became a favorite of antiwar activists during the Vietnam War, 10 December 1999.

Jim Henson, 54, creator of the puppet characters featured on the educational television series *Sesame Street* and *The Muppet Show*, as well as in the movies *The Muppet Movie* (1979), *The Great Muppet Caper* (1981), and *The Muppets Take Manhattan* (1984), 16 May 1990.

Audrey Hepburn, 63, actress who won an Academy Award for her role in *Roman Holiday* (1953) and received Oscar nominations for *Sabrina* (1954), *The Nun's Story* (1959), *Breakfast at Tiffany's* (1961), and *Wait Until Dark* (1967), 20 January 1993.

John Hersey, 78, journalist and fiction writer who won a Pulitzer Prize for his first novel, *A Bell for Adano* (1944), which portrays a megalomaniacal American general during the Allied occupation of Italy; he went on to write two more World War II novels, *Hiroshima* (1946) and *The Wall* (1950), before he was forty, 24 March 1993.

Al Hirt, 76, jazz trumpeter who won a 1963 Grammy for *Java* and played at the inauguration of President John F. Kennedy in 1961, 27 April 1999.

Burl Ives, 85, folk singer and actor who won an Academy Award for his performance in *The Big Country* (1958), 14 April 1995.

Raul Julia, 54, versatile actor whose screen credits include *Kiss of the Spider Woman* (1985) and *The Addams Family* (1991), 24 October 1994.

Madeline Kahn, 57, actress and comedienne, whose screen credits include Mel Brooks's *Young Frankenstein* (1974), 3 December 1999.

Garson Kanin, 86, playwright, screenwriter, and director, who wrote the Broadway hit *Born Yesterday* (1946), and joined with his wife, Ruth Gordon, to write screenplays for successful movies such as *A Double Life* (1947), *Adam's Rib* (1949), *Pat and Mike* (1952), and *It Should Happen to You* (1954), 13 March 1999.

Gene Kelly, 83, dancer and actor who starred in, choreographed, and codirected movies such as *On the Town* (1949), *An American in Paris* (1951), and *Singin' in the Rain* (1952), 2 February 1996.

Richard Kiley, 76, actor who won a Tony for his portrayal of Don Quixote in the Broadway production of *Man of La Mancha*, 5 March 1999.

Howard Koch, 92, Hollywood screenwriter, who helped to write movies such as *Sergeant York* (1941), *Casablanca* (1943), and *Rhapsody in Blue* (1945) and was blacklisted during the 1950s for alleged communist leanings, 17 August 1995.

Stanley Kubrick, 70, director, screenwriter, and producer, whose screen credits include *Paths of Glory* (1957), *Spartacus* (1960), *Dr. Strangelove* (1964), *2001: A Space Odyssey* (1968), *A Clockwork Orange* (1971), *Full Metal Jacket* (1987), and *Eyes Wide Shut* (1999), 7 March 1999.

Burt Lancaster, 81, Hollywood actor who won an Oscar for his lead role in *Elmer Gantry* (1960), 20 October 1994.

Jonathan Larson, 35, composer who won a posthumous Pulitzer Prize for *Rent*, which opened on Broadway to rave reviews a few weeks after his death on 25 January 1996.

Ida Lupino, 77, actress who starred in movies such as *High Sierra* (1941), *On Dangerous Ground* (1952), and *The Big Knife* (1955) and became the first successful woman movie director during the 1950s, 3 August 1995.

Andrew Lytle, 92, the last of the Vanderbilt Agrarian writers, best known for his biography of Confederate General Nathan Bedford Forrest (1931) and his novels *The Long Night* (1936), *At the Moon's Inn* (1941), *A Name for Evil* (1947), and *The Velvet Horn* (1957), 12 December 1995.

Fred MacMurray, 83, actor who appeared in the movies *Double Indemnity* (1944), *The Caine Mutiny* (1954), *The Shaggy Dog* (1959), and *The Absent Minded Professor* (1961), as well as the 1960s television series *My Three Sons*, 5 November 1991.

Dean Martin, 78, singer, movie actor, and member of Frank Sinatra's "Rat Pack," who teamed with Jerry Lewis for screwball comedies from 1949 into the early 1950s and then went on to play straight roles in movies such as *The Young Lions* (1958), 25 December 1995.

Mary Martin, 76, actress and singer well known for her acting in Broadway musicals such as *South Pacific* (1949), *Peter Pan* (1954), and *The Sound of Music* (1959), 3 November 1990.

Victor Mature, 86, actor whose screen credits include *My Darling Clementine* (1946), *Samson and Delilah* (1949), and *After the Fox* (1966), 4 August 1999.

Butterfly McQueen, 84, who played Prissy in *Gone with the Wind* (1939), 22 December 1995.

James Michener, 90, novelist who won a Pulitzer Prize for his first book, *Tales of the South Pacific* (1947) and wrote best-selling novels such as *The Bridge at Toko-Ri* (1953), *Hawaii* (1959), *Centennial* (1974), and *Caribbean* (1989), 16 October 1997.

Robert Mitchum, 79, actor who played tough guys in nearly one hundred movies, most notably *The Night of the Hunter* (1955) and *Cape Fear* (1962), 1 July 1997.

Robert Motherwell, 76, Abstract Expressionist artist known for his *Spanish Elegies* series, 16 July 1991.

Maureen O'Sullivan, 87, actress who starred as Jane in the Tarzan movies of the 1930s, 22 June 1998.

Alan J. Pakula, 70, director of movies such as *All the President's Men* (1976) and *Sophie's Choice* (1982) and producer of *To Kill a Mockingbird* (1962), 19 November 1998.

George Peppard, 65, actor who starred opposite Audrey Hepburn in *Breakfast at Tiffany's* (1961), 8 May 1994.

Anthony Perkins, 60, who started out as a juvenile actor in Broadway plays such as in *Tea and Sympathy* (1953) and as an adult became famous for his portrayal of the psychotic Norman Bates in Alfred Hitchcock's *Psycho* (1960), 21 September 1992.

River Phoenix, 23, actor whose screen credits include *Stand by Me* (1985), *The Mosquito Coast* (1986), *Indiana Jones and the Last Crusade* (1989), and *My Own Private Idaho* (1991), of a heart attack induced by a drug overdose, 31 October 1993.

Walker Percy, 73, Southern writer whose first novel, *The Moviegoer* (1961), earned him a National Book Award and established his reputation as an important philosophical fiction writer, 10 May 1990.

Selena Quintanilla Perez, 24, Latin-American Taguan singer shot to death by her fan-club president, 31 March 1995.

Mario Puzo, 78, novelist and screenwriter, best known for his novel *The Godfather* (1969) and the screenplays he wrote with Francis Ford Coppola for *The Godfather* (1972) and *The Godfather Part II* (1974), 2 July 1999.

Jose Quintero, 75, notable stage director and founder of the Circle in the Square acting company, 26 February 1999.

Jerome Robbins, 79, choreographer best known for his work on musicals such as *The King and I* (1951), *Peter Pan* (1954), *West Side Story* (1957), *Gypsy* (1959), and *Fiddler on the Roof* (1964), 29 July 1998.

Ginger Rogers, 83, actress who danced with Fred Astaire in movies such as *Top Hat* (1935) and *Shall We Dance?* (1937) and won an Academy Award for *Kitty Foyle* (1940), 25 April 1995.

Miklos Rozsa, 88, composer who won Oscars for his movie scores for *Spellbound* (1945), *A Double Life* (1947), and *Ben-Hur* (1959), 27 July 1995.

George C. Scott, 71, actor who won an Oscar for his leading role in *Patton* (1970) and was praised for his powerful performances in movies such as *Anatomy of a Murder* (1959), *The Hustler* (1961), and *Dr. Strangelove* (1964), 22 September 1999.

Dr. Seuss (Theodor Seuss Geisel), 87, writer and illustrator of popular children's books such as *Horton Hatches the Egg* (1940), *The Cat in the Hat* (1957), *Green Eggs and Ham* (1960), and *The Lorax* (1971), 24 September 1991.

Tupac Shakur, 25, gangsta rapper, 13 September 1996, six days after he was shot four times in a drive-by shooting.

Frank Sinatra, 83, popular singer and actor, whose best-selling songs included "Dream" (1945), "Strangers in the Night" (1966), and "My Way" (1969) and whose movie credits include parts in *The Man with the Golden Arm* (1955), *Guys and Dolls* (1956), and *The Manchurian Candidate* (1962), and an Oscar-winning supporting role in *From Here to Eternity* (1953), 14 May 1998.

Gene Siskel, 53, movie critic for the *Chicago Tribune*, who appeared with Roger Ebert on the influential television show *Siskel & Ebert At the Movies*, 20 February 1999.

The Notorious B.I.G. "Biggie Smalls," 24, the *Billboard* magazine Rapper of the Year for 1995, killed in a drive-by shooting, 9 March 1997.

Barbara Stanwyck, 82, actress best known for her roles in the movies *Stella Dallas* (1937), *The Lady Eve* (1941), and *Double Indemnity* (1944), 20 January 1990.

James Stewart, 89, actor, who won an Academy Award for his performance in *The Philadelphia Story* (1940) and starred in movie classics such as *Mr. Smith Goes to Washington* (1939), *It's A Wonderful Life* (1946), *Harvey* (1950), *Rear Window* (1954), and *Vertigo* (1958), 2 July 1997.

Jessica Tandy, 85, actress who won Tony Awards for her stage performances in *A Streetcar Named Desire* (1948), *The Gin Game* (1978), and *Foxfire* (1987), and an Academy Award for her lead role in the movie version of *Driving Miss Daisy* (1989), 11 September 1994.

Mel Torme, 73, singer known as the "Velvet Fog" and composer of "The Christmas Song," 5 June 1999.

Lana Turner, 75, actress whose screen credits include *The Postman Always Rings Twice* (1946) and *Peyton Place* (1957), 29 June 1995.

Sarah Vaughan, 66, jazz vocalist nicknamed the "Divine One" who was credited with popularizing the bebop sound, 4 April 1990.

Tammy Wynette, 55, country singer best known for her ballad "Stand By Your Man," 5 March 1998.

Frank Zappa, 52, rock musician-composer and founder of the Mothers of Invention, 14 December 1993.

PUBLICATIONS

Russell Baker, and others, *Inventing The Truth: The Art and Craft of Memoir,* revised edition, edited by William Zinsser (New York: Houghton Mifflin, 1998).

David Bayles and Ted Orland, *Art & Fear: Observations on the Perils (And Rewards) of Artmaking* (Santa Barbara, Cal.: Capra Press, 1994).

Harold Bloom, *The Western Canon: The Books and School of the Ages* (New York: Harcourt Brace, 1994).

James Lincoln Collier, *Jazz: The American Theme Song* (New York: Oxford University Press, 1993).

Louise Cowan and Os Guinness, eds., *Invitation to the Classics* (Grand Rapids, Mich.: Baker Book House, 1998).

Anthony DeCurtis and James Henke, eds., *The Rolling Stone Illustrated History of Rock & Roll* (New York: Random House, 1992).

Clifton Fadiman and John F. Majors, *The New Lifetime Reading Plan* (New York: HarperCollins, 1997).

Barbara Haskell, *The American Century: Art & Culture, 1900–1950* (New York: Whitney Museum of American Art in association with Norton, 1999).

Dave Hickey, *Air Guitar: Essays on Art & Democracy* (Los Angeles: Art Issues; New York: Distributed Art Publishers, 1997).

Steven D. Kendall, *New Jack Cinema: Hollywood's African-American Directors* (Silver Spring, Md.: J. L. Denser, 1994).

Michael Korda, *Another Life: A Memoir of Other People* (New York: Random House, 1999).

James Miller, *Flowers In The Dustbin: The Rise of Rock and Roll, 1947–1977* (New York: Simon & Schuster, 1999).

Henry Petroski, *The Book on the Bookshelf* (New York: Knopf, 1999).

Craig Werner, *A Change Is Gonna Come: Music, Race & The Soul of America* (New York: Plume, 1998).

Joseph Wesley Zeigler, *Arts in Crisis: The National Endowment for the Arts Versus America* (Pennington, N.J.: A Cappella Books, 1994).

CHAPTER THREE

BUSINESS AND THE ECONOMY

by MARK G. MALVASI and MEG GREENE

CONTENTS

Sidebars and tables are listed in italics.

1990

2 Jan.	Dow Jones reaches a record high, closing at 2800.15.
10 Jan.	Warner Communications and Time Inc. complete a $14.1 billion merger, establishing the largest media conglomerate in the world.
31 Jan.	McDonald's Corporation opens the first fast-food restaurant in Pushkin Square in Moscow.
13 Feb.	Drexel Burnham Lambert declares bankruptcy in the largest securities company failure ever.
Apr.	The minimum wage in the United States is raised to $3.80 per hour.
12 Apr.	Under pressure from environmental groups, three top U.S. tuna canneries, H. J. Heinz, Van de Camp, and Bumblebee, implement "dolphin-safe" tuna-catching practices.
18 Apr.	Bankruptcy court forces Frank Lorenzo to leave Eastern Airlines.
23 May	Reports indicate that the cost of rescuing the savings and loan industry may be as high as $130 billion.
1 June	The Dow Jones hits a record high, closing at 2900.97.
4 June	Greyhound Lines Inc., the bus company, files for bankruptcy.
21 Nov.	Junk-bond king Michael R. Milken is sentenced to ten years in jail for securities violations.
26 Nov.	Japanese business giant Matsushita Electric Industrial Company agrees to acquire MCA Inc. for $6.6 billion. The deal is sealed on 3 January 1991, for $6.9 billion.
28 Dec.	The U.S. government reports that its chief economic forecasting gauge, the Index of Leading Indicators, plunged 1.2 percent the previous month, the fifth consecutive monthly drop.

1991

8 Jan.	Pan American World Airways (Pan Am) files for bankruptcy.
17 Jan.	The Dow Jones index rises 114.60 points, the second highest one-day point gain ever.
Apr.	The minimum wage is raised to $4.25 per hour.
7 Apr.	The Dow Jones index closes above 3,000 for the first time.
3 July	Apple Computer and IBM publicly join together in an effort to exchange technologies and develop new equipment.

1992

3 Jan.	The Dow Jones index closes above 3,200 for the first time, ending the day at 3201.48.
7 Jan.	President George Bush arrives in Japan for talks on trade, saying he is determined to "increase access for American goods and services."

1993

24 Feb.	General Motors Corporation announces a record $4.5 billion loss in 1991 and says it will close twenty-one plants and lay off some 74,000 workers in the next four years.
13 Apr.	American Airlines reduces its first-class fares ranging from 20 percent to 50 percent.
23 Apr.	McDonald's opens its first fast-food restaurant in Beijing, China.
5 June	The government announces that the unemployment rate has jumped to 7.5 percent, the highest level in nearly eight years.
2 July	Braniff Airlines goes out of business.
5 Sept.	A strike that had idled nearly 43,000 General Motors workers ends as members of United Auto Workers (UAW) in Lordstown, Ohio, approve a new agreement.

4 Feb.	General Motors is held negligent in a jury decision; the company knew of a faulty fuel-tank design that caused the death of a teenager but did nothing about it. The jury awards $105.2 million to the parents.
9 Apr.	General Motors is asked to recall millions of trucks that are regarded as hazardous.
8 June	The Equal Employment Opportunity Commission (EEOC) rules that employers cannot refuse to hire disabled employees because of high insurance costs.
25 June	The Supreme Court rules that employees must prove discrimination in bias cases.
27 July	IBM announces an $8.9 million program that will revive the company; plans include the elimination of sixty thousand jobs and a reduction in factories.
2 Nov.	The Dow Jones index hits a record high of 3,697.64.
9 Nov.	Vice President Al Gore and businessman H. Ross Perot debate the North American Free Trade Agreement (NAFTA) on the CNN television program "Larry King Live."
14 Dec.	The United Mine Workers (UMW) approve a five-year contract, ending a strike that had affected seven states and some of the biggest coal operators in the nation.
28 Dec.	The Dow Jones index hits a record high of 3,793.49.

1994

•	Viacom Inc. announces a merger with Blockbuster Entertainment Corporation in an $8.4 billion deal.
1 Jan.	NAFTA goes into effect.
7 Jan.	The government reports that the unemployment rate fell to a three-year low of 6.4 percent in December 1993.
24 Jan.	The Dow Jones index closes above 3,900 for the first time, ending the day at 3,914.48.

4 Feb.   The Federal Reserve increases interest rates for the first time in five years in a surprise announcement; the announcement triggers a large sell-off on Wall Street.

1 Apr.   The government reports the unemployment rate for March remained unchanged from February, at 6.5 percent.

4 Apr.   Netscape Communications is founded.

24 May   The United States and Japan agree to revive efforts that would open Japanese markets to U.S. goods.

15 July   In a settlement with the Justice Department, Microsoft promises to end practices used to corner the personal computer software program market.

Nov.   A flaw discovered by a math professor in Intel's new Pentium processor ends up costing the company more than $475 million; Intel vows to replace all faulty processors.

1995

14 Feb.   A federal judge rejects the Justice Department's proposed antitrust settlement with Microsoft Corporation; the decision is later overturned on appeal.

23 Feb.   The Dow Jones industrial average closes above the 4,000 mark for the first time, ending the day at 4,003.33.

26 Feb.   The United States and China avert a trade war by signing an agreement.

10 Mar.   The Labor Department reports the unemployment rate for February dropped to 5.4 percent, down 0.3 percent from the previous month.

12 Apr.   Billionaire Kirk Kerkorian and former Chrysler chairman Lido Anthony "Lee" Iacocca make an unsolicited $22.8 billion bid to buy the third largest U.S. automaker; Chrysler says "no sale."

15 May   Dow Corning Corporation files for Chapter 11 bankruptcy protection; it cites large expenses from liability lawsuits as a factor.

26 May   In the largest recall ever in tobacco-industry history, Philip Morris stops sales of several cigarette brands, including the top-selling Marlboro, because some filters are reported to be contaminated.

18 June   The Dow Jones industrial average closes above 4,500 for the first time, ending the day at 4,510.79.

19 July   In the busiest trading day in its history, the Dow Jones ends at 4,628.87, after plunging more than 130 points earlier in the session.

21 Aug.   The Philip Morris and R. J. Reynolds tobacco companies agree to drop libel suits against ABC News; the network apologizes for an earlier report stating that cigarette companies added nicotine in order to addict smokers.

14 Sept.   The Dow Jones index closes above 4,800, ending the trading day at 4,801.80, a new record.

20 Sept.   In a move that stuns Wall Street, AT&T announces its intentions to split into three companies: a long distance carrier, an Internet service provider, and a telephone equipment company.

22 Sept. Time Warner Inc. announces a $7.5 billion deal to buy Turner Broadcasting System Inc. The deal is completed on 11 October.

21 Nov. The Dow Jones industrial average closes above the 5,000 mark for the first time, rising 40.46 points to 5,023.55.

24 Nov. Westinghouse Electric Corporation buys CBS Inc. for $5.4 billion.

18 Dec. The Dow drops 101.52 points, its biggest one-day loss in four years.

1996

• For the first time, personal-computer sales exceed the sale of television sets.

4 Jan. Retailers report that the 1995 Christmas retail season was the worst on record since 1990.

1 Apr. SBC Communications buys Pacific Telesis for $17 billion; this merger of these two Bell companies will serve more than thirty million telephone lines in seven states.

22 Apr. Bell Atlantic and NYNEX agree on one of the largest corporate mergers in U.S. history, making the new company the second largest telephone company in the country after AT&T.

2 May In a move guaranteed to hurt cigarette manufacturers, 3M Media announces it will no longer accept tobacco contracts for its billboards after 1996.

17 July The Federal Trade Commission (FTC) approves the Time-Warner merger with Turner Broadcasting System, creating the largest media company in the world.

6 Sept. The jobless rate is reported at 5.1 percent, the lowest figure in seven years.

7 Oct. The Dow Jones index breaks the 6,000 mark.

Nov. Archer Daniels Midland (ADM) announces it will pay a record $100 million fine for price fixing.

15 Nov. Texaco settles a racial discrimination lawsuit, agreeing to pay more than $140 million, a record for racial discrimination cases, in light of reports that tapes existed in which executives were caught making disparaging remarks about minorities and were planning to destroy incriminating documents.

15 Dec. Boeing Company announces plans to acquire McDonnell-Douglas Corporation for $13.3 billion, making it the largest business deal in the aerospace industry.

1997

9 Jan. Volkswagen agrees to pay $100 million to General Motors to settle an espionage lawsuit in which the former was accused of stealing trade secrets.

23 Jan. Some of the worst freezing conditions in more than seven years damage more than $250 million worth of Florida crops.

24 Jan. Supermarket chain Publix agrees to pay $81.5 million to settle a lawsuit accusing the chain of discrimination against one hundred thousand female employees.

31 Jan.	The government reports that the economy is strong and that the rate of inflation is at its lowest level in thirty years.
5 Feb.	Morgan Stanley and Dean Witter Discover agree to merge; the $8.8 billion stock transaction creates the largest securities firm in the country, with a market value of $20 billion. The merger takes place in May.
13 Feb.	The Dow Jones index breaks 7,000 points.
20 May	General Motors announces it will begin making cars in China.
6 June	The unemployment rate is reported at 4.8 percent, the lowest since 1973.
28 July	According to *Forbes*, the three richest people or families in the world are William Henry "Bill" Gates III of Microsoft ($36.4 billion); the Walton family of Wal-Mart retailers ($27.6 billion); and Warren Buffett, financier ($25.2 billion).
3 Aug.	A strike by 185,000 United Parcel Service (UPS) workers severely inconveniences many businesses.
6 Aug.	Microsoft and Apple form a partnership; the two once-bitter rivals agree on a financial and business plan in which Microsoft will pay Apple $150 million.
30 Aug.	NationsBank announces its acquisition of Florida franchise Barnett Banks for $15.5 billion in stock, a new record.
1 Sept.	The minimum wage is raised from $4.75 to $5.15 an hour.
2 Sept.	In the largest single-day rise ever, the Dow Jones index gains 257.35 points.
24 Sept.	Travelers Group announces a merger with Wall Street powerhouse Salomon Brothers for $9 billion.
7 Nov.	The Department of Labor reports that the U.S. jobless rate stands at 4.7 percent, the lowest since 1973.
10 Nov.	MCI Communications, the second largest long-distance U.S. phone company, is bought by Worldcom Inc. for $43 billion, making it the largest merger in U.S. business history.
11 Nov.	The Eastman Kodak Company announces it will lay off ten thousand workers, almost 10 percent of its entire workforce, making it the largest such action of 1997.
25 Nov.	Federal investigators say that they have uncovered a scheme devised by organized crime to infiltrate Wall Street. Nineteen men are charged with duping investors in nineteen states.
5 Dec.	The U.S. government reports that the economy produced more than four hundred thousand new jobs in November, that the unemployment rate is now 4.8 percent, and that hourly wages have increased by seven cents.
13 Dec.	The United States and 101 other countries, meeting in Geneva, Switzerland, sign a global trade agreement that will open financial markets by dismantling barriers to foreign ownership of such institutions as banks and investment firms.
24 Dec.	Thirty brokerage firms, including some of the most respected and well-known names on Wall Street, agree to pay $900 million to end a civil suit in which they had been accused of conspiring to fix prices on the Nasdaq stock exchange for many years.

1998

- With a market value of $262 million, software maker Microsoft passes former manufacturing giant General Electric as the biggest company in the United States.

9 Jan. The stock market declines by nearly 3 percent (222 points) with news that the financial crisis in Asia could hurt the U.S. economy.

19 Jan. *The New York Times* reports that Compaq, Intel, and Microsoft, the big three of the computer industry, will announce a joint venture with the largest local telephone companies to provide improved Internet service over regular phone lines.

4 Mar. The U.S. Supreme Court rules unanimously that federal law protects employees from sexual harassment in the workplace by people of the same sex.

6 Apr. Citicorp and Travelers Group Inc. disclose that they have agreed to a merger, valued at more than $70 billion, that will create the largest financial services business in the world. Reacting to the news, the Dow Jones average breaks the 9,000 mark.

13 Apr. Two huge banking mergers are announced: NationsBank with Bank America, and Banc One with First Chicago.

6 May The German industrial giant Daimler-Benz A.G., manufacturer of the Mercedes-Benz automobile, reveals that it will purchase the U.S. car manufacturer Chrysler Corporation for $36 billion, making it the largest industrial takeover in history, and the largest acquisition of a U.S. company by a foreign company.

8 May The Department of Labor reports that the unemployment rate for April was 4.3 percent, the lowest since 1970.

11 May SBC Communications announces that it will acquire Ameritech Corporation for $62 billion, creating the largest telephone company in the nation.

14 May Just hours before state and federal governments are set to file extensive antitrust lawsuits against Microsoft Corporation, the company agrees to postpone the launch of its newest operating system, Windows '98, for three days.

8 June The FTC files an antitrust lawsuit against Intel, the largest computer chip maker in the world, alleging that the company had attempted to coerce three computer manufacturers to turn over patented technology rights.

10 June Alan Greenspan, Chairman of the Federal Reserve, pronounces that the U.S. economy is in good shape and that interest rates will not be raised.

15 June The Wall Street indexes plunge by 207 points over continued fears that Asian financial instability will stall U.S. business growth.

24 June AT&T announces that it will purchase Tele-Communications Inc., the second-largest U.S. cable TV company, for $31.8 billion.

26 June The Supreme Court clarifies the law on sexual harassment in the workplace with two decisions.

26 July AT&T and British Telecom announce that they will merge most of their international operations into a jointly owned company.

28 July Bell Atlantic announces that it has agreed to buy GTE for $52.8 billion in stock.

31 July The Commerce Department reports that the U.S. economy experienced slow growth during the second quarter; Wall Street responds with a 143-point drop in the market.

9 Aug.   Almost 73,000 telephone workers go on strike against Bell Atlantic because the company also uses nonunion workers.

11 Aug.   British Petroleum (BP) announces that it will buy U.S. oil company giant Amoco for $48.2 billion, making it the largest oil industry merger ever.

27 Aug.   The worst trading day of 1998 occurs as the Dow plunges 4.19 percent, or more than 357 points, causing international markets to fall as well.

28 Aug.   The Dow falls another 114 points, making this week the worst week since 1989; overall, the market is down almost 14 percent.

31 Aug.   The Dow falls yet again; this time plunging 512 points, or almost 6.4 percent, as both large and small investors sell.

1 Sept.   The stock market regains almost half of what it had lost as the Dow records a record 1.21 billion shares being bought and sold.

29 Sept.   In response to the turmoil in the stock market, the Federal Reserve agrees to cut interest rates 1/4 of 1 percent.

15 Oct.   The Federal Reserve again cuts interest rates by another 1/4 percentage point.

24 Nov.   America Online announces its plans to buy Netscape Communications Corporation.

1 Dec.   The largest U.S. oil company, Exxon, announces it will buy the second largest oil company, Mobil, for $80 billion, forming the largest corporation in the world.

1999

8 Mar.   Faced with ongoing lawsuits, RJR Nabisco announces it will split its food and tobacco businesses.

29 Mar.   The Dow closes above 10,000 for the first time.

13 Apr.   After meeting with twenty business executives, the White House announces it will resume trade negotiations with China.

3 May   The Dow closes above 11,000 only twenty-four trading days after breaking the 10,000 mark, making it the fastest rise in history.

7 Sept.   Viacom Inc. announces it will buy the CBS Corporation for $37.3 billion, making it the largest media merger ever and creating the second-largest media company after Time-Warner.

4 Oct.   MCI Worldcom Inc., the second-largest long-distance U.S. phone carrier, agrees to purchase Sprint Corporation for $108 billion in stock; if approved, the deal would be the largest in corporate history.

15 Oct.   The stock market plunges almost 267 points (2.59 percent), ending one of the worst weeks ever since October of 1989.

Dec.   The Dow again reaches 10,000 points.

OVERVIEW

Introduction. "The business of America is business," quipped President Calvin Coolidge in the 1920s. Not even "Silent Cal," however, could have predicted what happened to business at the end of the twentieth century, when the remarkable performance of the U.S. economy called into question assumptions, methods, practices, values, and truths of long standing. Suddenly, and in many instances quite unexpectedly, the old rules governing business no longer applied and no one knew for sure what the new rules were going to be. A volatile and unpredictable decade for business, the 1990s was as full of opportunity and promise as it was peril and apprehension.

The Internet. This upheaval resulted primarily from the advent of the Internet, which transformed life for most Americans. Suddenly the whole world was more accessible as an unprecedented quantity and variety of information enabled companies and individuals to function more efficiently and profitably. The Internet fundamentally changed business as brash, computer-savvy entrepreneurs eclipsed many of their more venerable, and now vulnerable, counterparts, who found themselves struggling to make sense of the new cyberworld. Observers differed, however, on how the Internet was altering the world; when the World Wide Web made the Internet more accessible, starting in 1994, the traditional understanding of how business operated came into question. Possibilities for this new technology seemed endless: online companies overshadowed legendary corporations; financing and marketing became more accessible and efficient; bureaucracies broke down; business, government, and intellectual orthodoxies came under attack; and, as proponents had contended, a new sense of democracy and community developed.

"New Economy." Internet technology may also have permanently enhanced the productive capacity of the economy and accelerated its rate of growth, while keeping at bay the inflation of prices and wages that in the past had undermined prosperity. As a consequence, the integration of the international economy proceeded apace: the Dow Jones Industrial Average soared; companies merged to form bigger, richer, and more powerful entities; and experts speculated about how long the boom would last and what, if anything, might finally bring it to an end. No one, though, could deny that a new economy began to take shape—one that differed from what economists had expected. The most startling aspect of this new economy was that it challenged the view that inflation would result from a growth rate higher than 2.5 percent coupled with an unemployment rate below 5 percent. After 1993, as the U.S. economy exceeded these rates for the first time since the 1970s, there still were no inflationary pressures retarding economic advances.

Impact on Workers. The "New Economy" affected different sectors of the workforce in various ways. The top percentile of workers received high salaries, in part because often there were not enough individuals with the specialized skills needed to fill these positions. Blue- and white-collar workers often fared less well, as the strikes and increasing labor friction in many industrial firms indicated. This second tier of workers at best saw small economic gains, but they often had to labor longer hours and take second jobs, or send spouses or even teenage children into the workplace. Unskilled workers often suffered the most from economic changes as many companies closed facilities to relocate to areas with cheaper labor.

Globalization. At the other extreme, multinational corporations increasingly dominated the world economy, pushing forward economic globalization. As the decade drew to a close, eight of the top twenty-five economic entities in the world, measured in terms of market value, were corporations. In addition, international institutions gained substantial control over the economies of sovereign states. Critics of this development raised the specter of world government, while defenders of globalization argued that it was an inevitable transformation. Already enmeshed in the digital economy, Americans prepared to enter an economic future of mammoth corporations and banks, electronic money, and individual wealth accounts—a future that appeared as unsettling as it did radiant.

Business Management and Practice. In response to these rapid and far-reaching economic changes, companies altered their management styles and strategies, as well as their business methods and practices. One popular managerial fad was known as "reengineering," the idea that companies could identify their essential activities and processes and then make them as efficient as possible. Peripheral operations and employees therefore had to be eliminated, and reengineering thus led to corporate downsizing. An alternative to the inflexibility inherent within this model was "liberation management," which emphasized a lack of structure and favored corporate organizations that were continually changing. From these new theories of management there emerged a distinctly new breed of corporation, such as Asea Brown Boveri (ABB) and Dell Computer.

Corporate Welfare and Crime. In the midst of extraordinary affluence, large corporations continued to benefit from government largess in the form of "corporate welfare," defined as "any action by local, state or federal government that gives a corporation or an entire industry a benefit not offered to others." Governments regularly extended tax breaks; offered low-interest loans; discounted utility bills; paid for infrastructure development; and provided funds to advertise products, build facilities, sponsor research, and train employees. Proponents argued that corporate welfare created jobs; critics charged, however, that the positions were seldom substantial, and that deceit and corruption in both business and government often resulted from these policies. Corporate crime often flourished, as criminals employed computer technology to revive classic money-laundering schemes, funneling billions in illegal funds through legitimate businesses.

Small Business. Despite the multibillion-dollar corporate mergers that dominated the economy, many small companies flourished. Although approximately three out of five small businesses failed, while more successful ones were often targets of corporate takeovers, they accounted for 99 percent of the 23.3 million nonfarm businesses in the United States at the end of the decade. Small businesses employed 53 percent of private-sector employees, constituted 47 percent of sales, and accounted for 51 percent of output. Frequently they performed better than their bigger counterparts and remained attractive to potential investors.

Labor. Workers, by contrast, especially those lacking education and skills, were often left behind in the new knowledge- and information-based economy. To remain competitive many companies had trimmed their workforce. Still, an expanding economy actually created more jobs than it lost. Workers forced new demands, though, as even corporate employees had to acquire new skills that made them move marketable to other industries. Blue-collar workers, on the contrary, had fewer opportunities as industrial and manufacturing jobs evaporated. For workers who lacked the education and skills to enter the new job market, wages rose only slightly and opportunities emerged only in the low-paying service industry. Economic prosperity did little to ease the widening gap in income distribution between white- and blue-collar workers. In addition, management continued to confront questions of discrimination and harassment toward women, minorities, and seniors.

Workplace Spirituality. Unsatisfied with the fruits of prosperity, increasing numbers of workers and executives turned to spirituality and religion in their quest to find meaning and purpose in work and life. A spiritual revival swept corporate America as executives of all faiths mixed religion and management, transferring into offices, shops, and factories the lessons formerly confined to churches, temples, synagogues, and mosques. Workplace Bible study and prayer groups formed and met regularly. There were also many conferences on spirituality in the workplace and three separate research centers devoted to the investigation and analysis of corporate spirituality. Spending more time than ever before on the job, Americans started bringing their faith to work in an effort to find a deeper sense of meaning and fulfillment. That quest was one of the motives behind the new spirituality. Perhaps the most important impetus, however, was mounting evidence that workplace programs emphasizing spirituality eased employees' psyches, increased their productivity, and diminished turnover.

TOPICS IN THE NEWS

THE AMERICAN ECONOMY

"New Economy." The second half of the 1990s marked the longest sustained stretch of economic growth in U.S. history. Unlike other periods of long-term economic expansion reversed by rising inflation, growth continued and even accelerated as inflation declined. The combination of rapid technological change, rise of the services sector, and emergence of the global marketplace had experts convinced that the United States was in the midst of "a second industrial revolution." Despite the historical inaccuracy of the label (the second industrial revolution took place during the latter half of the nineteenth century), there can be no denying that a new U.S. economy began to take shape—one that defied many long-standing economic axioms. Since 1980, for example, the economy lost approximately 43 million jobs through restructuring and downsizing. Economists called them "sunset jobs." In their place, as analyst Horace W. Brock pointed out, that same economy created seventy-one million new jobs, a net gain of twenty-eight million positions. More important, economists regarded these slots as "sunrise jobs" in industries that had a future. The majority of economists attributed these developments to a restructuring of companies and an economy abetted by such governmental policies as the North American Free Trade Agreement (NAFTA), enacted in 1994. NAFTA created a continental economy, so the argument ran, that helped initiate and sustain growth and development. In addition, many economists pointed to the breakup of AT&T (1995) and the deregulation of the telecommunications industry as enhancing opportunities for competition, innovation, and growth. Most surprising was that this expansion occurred without the traditional stimulus of increased deficit spending. On the contrary, deficit spending decreased from $290 billion in 1992 to $67 billion by 1997. At the same time, a decline in the influence of organized labor, for better or worse, enabled firms to exercise greater flexibility. Companies also began with increasing ease and frequency to relocate facilities and jobs to locations inside and outside the United States where wages were lower than those paid to unionized workers. In addition, they hired growing numbers of temporary workers to whom they often provided no health or retirement benefits. Finally, they began to "outsource" many opera-

---

"TWO COMMAS"

Living through one of the biggest economic booms in U.S. history provided many Americans with the opportunity to amass great personal fortunes. Whether by getting lucky in the stock market, making the most of stock options, or being on the ground floor of an Internet start-up, many Americans struck it rich in the 1990s. So many, in fact, that the old tried-and-true ways of getting rich—perseverance and perspiration—seemed destined to fall by the wayside. Between 1995 and 1998 about one million new millionaires appeared. The term "having two commas" signified that someone had achieved his or her first million. The number of Americans enjoying "three commas," or their first billion, went up, too. *Forbes* magazine reported in 1999 that on its list of the 400 richest Americans, 250 were billionaires, up 60 from the previous year.

---

tions such as bookkeeping. Taken together, these procedures helped to lower costs and elevate profit margins. The most unexpected aspect of this boom was that it challenged two basic assumptions: that a growth rate of more than 2.5 percent and an unemployment rate below 5 percent, however desirable in theory, were unrealistic because they generated inflation. After 1993 the U.S. economy grew at an annual rate of about 4 percent, and by the second half of the decade unemployment fell below 5 percent for the first time since the 1970s. Yet, no inflationary pressures appeared to retard or reverse these economic advances.

The Federal Reserve. For years the Federal Reserve struggled to fit what happened to the U.S. economy into a traditional framework. Growth was robust, stocks soared, unemployment declined, and yet inflation was virtually nonexistent. Eventually, chairman Alan Greenspan admitted that he could not explain these extraordinary developments according to the old rules and simply gave up trying to do so. By mid 1999 officials at the Federal Reserve agreed that the country was in the midst of a "productivity boom" fueled by technological innovation that enabled the economy to expand faster than anyone had once thought

Federal Reserve chairman Alan Greenspan and U.S. Treasury secretary Robert E. Rubin unveiling a blow-up of the newly designed $20 bill on 20 May 1998 (AP/Wide World Photos)

possible, without initiating the price and wage increases that ordinarily extinguished such growth. By the late 1990s Greenspan's task became adjusting policy to this new reality. "The Fed is moving in a very different direction," acknowledged former vice-chairman Manuel H. Johnson in 1999. "You'll probably see less tightening in the future." Without convincing evidence that the economy was expanding too rapidly, or increasing prices and wages, Greenspan became more inclined to wait before raising interest rates. He also made sure that the information found its way to the financial community well in advance of any adjustments, hoping that businesses would slow economic growth and thereby make a hike in rates unnecessary. Central to Greenspan's thinking was his belief, which eventually gained a consensus among other officials at the Federal Reserve, that productivity growth, which had languished at about 1 percent a year throughout the 1970s and 1980s, had made a long-term and perhaps permanent increase to 2 percent or higher, as companies began utilizing information technology to become more efficient and productive. Even skeptics such as Roger W. Ferguson, governor of the Federal Reserve, became convinced. "Is this rise in productivity cyclical because the economy is strong, or is this a change in the trend?," asked Ferguson. "The evidence is mounting that it's a change in the trend." Wil-

liam Poole, president of the Federal Reserve Bank in St. Louis, initially echoed Ferguson's conclusions. "My earlier position was that the evidence for a convincing breakout of productivity wasn't there." In a speech delivered on 16 April 1999, however, Poole conceded that "it is increasingly reasonable to believe that the U.S. has indeed turned the corner on productivity growth." To be sure, Greenspan and his colleagues maintained a healthy degree of skepticism about the duration of the "productivity boom." By the end of the decade, however, they had come to see it as the only explanation for sustained economic growth without the specter of inflation. Even officials who accepted that the "productivity boom" permitted the economy to grow faster without inflation, nevertheless recognized that there were limits to its performance. "The old rules about overtaxing productive capacity still apply to new limits," insisted Fed governor Laurence Meyer.

Uneven Impact. Conventional wisdom among economists long suggested that if the U.S. economy expanded at a rate faster than 2.5 percent, it would eventually strain productive resources beyond their capacity and prices would rise as the supply of commodities on the market decreased. Similarly, if the unemployment rate fell below 5 percent it would increase competition for jobs and force companies to pay higher wages to attract employees. Although neither of these developments took place, their failure to appear masked the uneven impact of the new economy on different sectors of the workforce. Among the top 20 or 30 percent of the U.S. workforce, salaries were high in part because there were often not enough persons with the specialized education, training, and skills to fill the jobs. For example, the technology sector grew at an overall annual rate of 40 percent. By the end of the decade, the Information Technology Association of America estimated that the high-tech industry faced a shortage of approximately 190,000 workers. Although this labor shortage kept wages and salaries high, the falling costs of computer technology and software enabled corporations to prosper. Both blue- and white-collar workers in other industries did not fare so well, as the rash of strikes and increasing labor friction at such firms as General Motors, Chrysler, Goodyear, and Caterpillar indicated. Workers complained that companies were forcing them to work overtime rather than hiring additional employees. To save money, companies also began to outsource production to nonunion shops. This second tier of the workforce at best managed to make small economic gains, but only by working longer hours, sending additional members of the household into the workplace, and laboring at second or temporary jobs without benefits. At the bottom of the economy, unskilled workers benefited least and suffered most from the economic changes that took place. As companies closed expensive, inefficient, and aging facilities to relocate to cheaper areas inside the United States and around the world (primarily in Mexico and Asia), hundreds of thousands of unskilled U.S. workers lost their jobs. The textile industry in the Carolinas—along with the steel, auto, and machine-tool industries in the Midwest—was especially hard hit. Wage pressures at the top of the workforce did not translate into higher prices, in part because employers compensated by driving wages lower at other levels. If it demonstrated anything, the economic transformation revealed that unskilled workers were being left behind and left out, and that there were no longer common interests uniting different segments of the working class. Previous assumptions and concerns about working-class consciousness and solidarity, therefore, no longer applied.

The Future. As the decade drew to a close, predictions abounded about the course the U.S. economy would take in the twenty-first century. Would it continue to expand or would the inflation of wages and prices eventually bring its achievements to an end? Economists pointed with optimism to small, efficient high-tech companies such as the Transarc Corporation in Pittsburgh, Pennsylvania. Many economists maintained that companies such as Transarc, which IBM purchased in 1994, fueled the economic boom. The financial sector was another major source of growth, which most economists saw continuing into the new millennium. If the Federal Reserve raised interest rates aggressively, of course, it could slow economic growth, but new, high-tech companies are not as sensitive to the adjustment

of interest rates as are construction, housing, and retail businesses. The adverse affects of higher interest rates would thus fall disproportionately on the lowest tier of the workforce, particularly on those with few or no skills seeking entry-level positions. "For the first time in 20 years, we have people saying 'If I play by the rules, maybe I can get a job'," stated Tom Murphy, mayor of Pittsburgh, in 1997. To continue that trend, however, Murphy noted that "we need sustained growth to get them back into the marketplace." At the same time, economists worried that the greatest challenge to sustained growth might not be traditional concerns about inflation and the business cycle at all, but instead the vast and growing disparity in worker education and skills, as well as what potential employees have to offer. Cities, counties, and states struggled as never before to train or retrain workers and get them into the job market before the shortage of labor became acute. These efforts notwithstanding, experts generally agreed that labor shortages would grow worse in coming decades. According to Timothy Parks, president of the Pittsburgh Regional Alliance, 60 percent of all jobs in the United States in 1950 required unskilled labor. That figure contracted to 25 percent by 1997 and shrank to an estimated 15 percent by 2000. Meanwhile, the quest to find "knowledge workers" went on unabated and was frequently unfulfilled. In such cities as Atlanta, Dallas, and Phoenix, companies eased their shortage of "human capital" by luring workers with requisite skills from other parts of the country or by hiring immigrants, mostly from Asia. If the benefits of the "new economy" are ever to be more widely distributed among all segments of the population, schools—along with job training, social service, and economic development agencies—have to do a better job of preparing men and women to meet the requirements of employment. It became painfully evident that the old rules governing the economy no longer applied, and equally obvious that no one knew what the new rules would be. Inflation, monetary policy, or interest rates may not determine future economic growth; rather, a lack of preparation, planning, education, and skills may prevent U.S. business from taking full advantage of the opportunities that the dynamic "new economy" created.

Sources:

Karl A. Albrecht and Ron Zemke, *Service America!: Doing Business in the New Economy* (Homewood, Ill.: Dow Jones-Irwin, 1985).

Robert D. Atkinson and Randolph H. Court, "Nine Myths About the New Economy," *The New Economy Index*, Progressive Policy Institute, Internet website.

Jeffrey E. Garten, *World View: Global Strategies for the New Economy* (Cambridge, Mass.: Harvard Business School Publishing, 2000).

William J. Holstein, "The New Economy," *U. S. News and World Report*, 122 (26 May 1997): 42–48.

Kevin Kelly, *New Rules for the New Economy: 10 Radical Strategies for a Connected World* (New York: Viking, 1998).

Joan Magretta, ed., *Managing in the New Economy* (Cambridge, Mass.: Harvard Business School Publishing, 1999).

Lester C. Thurow, *Building Wealth: The New Rules for Individuals, Companies, and Nations in a Knowledge-Based Economy* (New York: HarperCollins, 1999).

Owen Ullmann, Laura Cohn, and Michael J. Mandel, "The Fed's New Rule Book," *Business Week* (3 May 1999): 46–48.

Seven Days That Shook the World. One week in April 1998 rocked the financial world. On 6 April the huge insurance and brokerage firm Travelers Group announced plans to merge with Citicorp, then the second largest bank in the United States. The new company was capitalized with assets of $76 billion and immediately became the largest financial-services company in the world. By including nonbank assets, Citicorp-Travelers was valued at $697.5 billion. One week later, on 13 April, the chairman of Banc One, John B. McCoy, announced the merger of his company, valued at $116 billion, with First Chicago NBD Corporation, valued at $115 billion. On the same day, Hugh McColl Jr. of NationsBank engineered a merger with BankAmerica, creating a new conglomerate with deposits of $346 billion, the second largest bank in the United States and the fifth largest in the world. These mergers were part of a complex, ongoing revolution that by the 1990s had already begun to transform banking, finance, and investment. At the center of this revolution was a conflict between what bankers call "consolidation" and "disintermediation," the latter meaning the removal of intermediaries, for example banks, from financial transactions. The advocates of "disintermediation," such as computer-software giants Microsoft and Intuit, believe that the future belongs to companies that can master new technology and give customers and investors almost total control over their finances. Investment banker David Shaw stated in 1998 that "the whole financial industry will likely be turned upside down, with shrinkage in some areas and perhaps some outright failures among those firms that are unable to use technology effectively." McColl disagreed; the future, he argued, belongs to the mammoth financial institutions that can package investments and provide customers with a myriad of services from insurance to investments, from car loans to airline tickets. Of course, he acknowledged that size alone will not be enough to ensure success. Financial institutions, large and small, must stay informed about technological innovations that now govern the industry, and be nimble and smart enough to take advantage of them. Those that will not, cannot, or do not shall be among the casualties. McColl realized that one day banking would become like war. During the 1990s that day arrived. "We have a lot of competition these days," he said just after completing the merger with BankAmerica, "even from people like Microsoft. . . . Software is becoming everything."

Big Banks. McCoy mused that in the future there would be only five or six banking conglomerates in the world. Financial analysts attributed the record profits generated to these massive consolidations and to the application of new technologies. In 1997 the income of the banking industry was $59.2 billion, an increase of 13 percent ($51.5 billion) over 1996. According to statistics compiled by the Federal Deposit Insurance Corporation (FDIC) 599 bank mergers took place in 1997 alone, reducing the number of banks in the United States from nearly

A VISA electronic cash card terminal in use in the company cafeteria in Foster City, California, on 10 April 1996 (AP/Wide World Photos)

14,000 to 9,143. Consolidation sent bank stocks soaring. From their low point in 1990, bank stocks rose nearly twice as fast as average stocks, which themselves increased in value at a rate nearly twice as fast as the historical standard. Consolidation also saved money for the banks. Several studies showed, however, that despite increased profits banks imposed higher costs on consumers, with the institutions themselves being the chief beneficiaries of these transactions. In 1998, for instance, non-interest service fees accounted for 33 percent of profits, totaling $18.5 billion. A report issued by the U.S. Public Interest Group disclosed that consumers paid 15 percent more to maintain regular checking accounts at a big rather than a small bank. The report of the Federal Reserve to Congress in June 1997 contained similar findings. "Merger mania is making the fee-gouging big banks even bigger," complained Ed Mierzwinski, consumer-program director for the Public Interest Group. "Fewer and bigger banks mean consumers face fewer choices, less competition and . . . higher fees." In a study of 470 banks, released in April 1998, the Public Interest Group reported a rapid increase in the number of banks that imposed a surcharge on noncustomers for using their Automatic Teller Machines (ATMs). Some, like Banc One, charged account holders for using its own Rapid Cash Machines. Bigger banks had more surcharges and fees, which were, on average, $1.35 higher than those of smaller banks. The banks "say these mergers create efficiencies," explained Mary Griffin of the Consumers Union in 1998. "But with the efficiencies there is a dis-econony of scale, which costs consumers more." In other words, it cost more for customers to save. "Over 12 million families already can't afford to bank," Mierzwinski pointed out in 1998. "Mergers just exacerbate that problem."

Does Money Have a Future? By the 1990s Americans were already becoming immersed in the technology of the digital economy. "The distinction between software and money is disappearing," declared William Niskanen, chairman of the CATO Institute. If cyberspace really is "the final frontier of finance," then cash began to go where no money had gone before. MasterCard, for example, invested millions to develop an e-cash system called Mondex; its cards are embedded with a microchip that can store not only electronic dollars but also five other types of currency, an abbreviated medical history, and a personalized electronic key that can unlock the doors of the cardholder's apartment, house, and office. "The chip that we are putting on the card now will form the platform for the ultimate in remote access for consumers to their funds, anytime, anywhere," said Henry Mundt, MasterCard executive vice president for global access. "What we really see happening in the future," Mundt continued, "is consumers being able to design their cards to meet their individual needs. We refer to that as moving more toward life-style cards." The idea of digital money, e-cash, is simple. Instead of storing value in paper, e-cash saves it in a series of digits and codes that are as portable and exchangeable as paper, but more secure and even "smarter." If e-cash is lost or stolen, its proponents maintain, the card can easily be canceled via computer and its value transferred to another card. E-cash is also more mutable and controllable than paper money. It enables individuals to send funds over the Internet, encoded in an e-mail message rather than sending cash, checks, money orders, or wire transfers. Digital currency can also be programmed so that it can be spent only in specific ways; money budgeted for food cannot be used to go to the movies or visit the local pub. Finally, e-cash, unlike paper money when withdrawn from an account, continues to earn interest until it is withdrawn. This characteristic of e-cash gave rise to another extraordinary aspect of the digital financial revolution: the dissolution of the government monopoly on money. Cardholders are free to acquire e-cash from worldwide lenders willing to pay higher interest rates than U.S. banks. As long as e-cash is easily convertible and widely accepted, customers will find that there is no reason to limit themselves to the currency of a single government. Government-issued money will not cease to exist, but it will have to compete with dozens of other currencies, each tailored to meet the specific needs of customers. "Digital cash has no boundaries," explained Richard W. Rahn, president of Novecon Ltd., a technology consulting firm. "The more such innovations succeed," Professor George A. Selgin of the University of Georgia suggested, "the less the public will have to rely on central banks as direct sources of exchange media. This seems to me to be particularly obvious in the case of E-money." The best money will likely be the most flexible and versatile. "In the electronic city, the final step in the evolution of money is being taken," declared Howard M. Greenspan, president of Heraclitus Corporation, a management consulting firm located in Toronto. "Money is being demonetized. Money is being eliminated."

Risk Management. Two variables characterize investments: risk and reward, which tend to be proportional. The greater the reward sought, the greater the risk usually involved. It was the idea of Charles Sanford Jr., CEO of Bankers Trust, to break all sorts of investments into small clusters of risk, enter them into a computer, and auction them on a global network. Sanford reasoned that investors with different assets and needs would purchase the various sorts of risks. Because "risk bundles" were derived from an array of investments, Sanford called them "derivatives." To explain this new investment strategy, Sanford embraced the theory of "particle finance." He proposed to look deep inside every investment in an effort to understand how markets worked at any given time. Sanford's innovation proved hugely popular. By enabling financial institutions to manage their finances more thoroughly and carefully, derivatives offered the possibility of increased rewards with decreased risks. Suddenly what had seemed to be an immutable law of finance—that risk and reward were proportional, that an investor could not get a bigger reward without taking a bigger risk—no longer applied. This investment strategy, of course, was not foolproof. Nor did it guarantee automatic success, as the citizens of Orange County, California, discovered in 1994 when their local government lost millions of taxpayer dollars in a failed derivatives transaction. The advent of derivatives, however, fundamentally altered the rules of finance and investment. For individual investors derivatives created hundreds of investment options besides stocks, such as Japanese real estate or Russian oil futures, all packaged and marketed by giant banks and investment firms. "This is like the automobile's coming," proclaimed Sanford in 1998, "We'd always had transportation—people walked, eventually they rode donkeys—but the automobile was a break from everything that came before it. Risk management will do that to finance. It's a total break." In Sanford's vision, every asset, large and small, will become part of a giant, interconnected financial network. Everyone will have an electronic "wealth account" that will automatically match financial needs with available options. If, for example, a real estate developer anywhere in the world needs a short-term loan and is willing to pay for the privilege of using other people's money, an individual, computerized wealth account will decide if the potential risk is worth the potential return and, if it is, will lock in the deal without any prompting from the account holder. These integrated accounts, Sanford asserted, will make such older transactions as getting a loan or trading in stocks obsolete. Computerized wealth accounts, according to Sanford, will consider every factor in

RAILROAD RESURGENCE

During the 1990s the United States experience a reemergence of the railroad industry as an important mode of transportation. After decades of decline, train travel and use surged; by 1997, railroads were transporting almost 84 percent more freight than they did during their peak during World War II. Part of the boom can be traced to decreased shipping costs, which fell 62 percent between 1985 and 1996. Still, while the resurgence revitalized train transportation, it has come at a cost. Increasingly, railroad companies came under fire for market abuses and their failure to keep up with demand. There was even talk about deregulation or perhaps a restructuring of the entire industry. Critics pointed to problems such as those of Union Pacific (UP), considered one of the best in railroad transportation, in handling traffic from Southern Pacific, which UP bought in 1999. Shippers were unhappy with the overall quality of service they were receiving. Frequent disruptions caused costly delays, such as when Nebraska farmers waited for molasses used in cattle feed. Other companies pointed to shipments sitting at railroad docks, waiting for late trains to pick up and deliver. Employees were unhappy as well, often working under increasingly stressful and fatiguing conditions. As train use moved into the next century, many people took a wait-and-see attitude before deciding whether railroads were up to the challenge.

planning the financial needs of investors. In a speech titled "Financial Markets in 2020," delivered in 1993, Sanford concluded that: "Yesterday's income and today's wealth will always be known with a high degree of confidence. Wealth accounts will be instantly tapped via 'wealth cards.' For example, you will be able to pay for your sports car by instantly drawing on part of the wealth inherent in your vacation house." Sanford has never resisted the implications of his own logic. Derivatives and individual wealth accounts, he argued, will eventually make banks and similar financial institutions irrelevant.

Problems and Prospects. These changes in finance are the ones to which bankers such as McColl responded when they created the "superbanks" in the hope of offering an almost infinite variety of wealth accounts to individual investors. Yet, taking complex financial transactions out of the hands of knowledgeable and experienced bankers and brokers, and putting them into the hands of consumers, carries inherent risks. "Banks have been making less and less money from traditional lines of business," pointed out Douglas Gale, a professor of economics at New York University. "What they have found lucrative is designing derivatives. But if you're using derivatives and you don't understand the technology or you don't know what you're doing, there is a real danger here. It's like letting a child

play with a nuclear reactor." Critics also wondered what would happen if this interconnected computer network crashed or hackers broke into it, or if a banking house or financial institution collapsed, as did Barings PLC in 1995 when trader Nicholas Leeson gambled and lost assets of £850m. "There is no chance that a money market will fail and threaten the underpinnings of the system," counseled Steve Cone, an executive at Fidelity Investments. Such reassurances, however, have not quieted all the skeptics. Some question whether the new, interconnected global market will mean that a bad year for one economy might unintentionally but unavoidably precipitate a worldwide recession or depression. Furthermore, governmental regulation of the emerging system of banking and finance had already become virtually impossible by the end of the decade. Alan Greenspan, chairman of the Federal Reserve Board, announced its abandonment of efforts at regulation. The burden came to rest on the corporations themselves. "To continue to be effective," Greenspan wrote in 1996, "government's regulatory role must increasingly assure the effective risk-management systems are in place in the private sector. As financial systems become more complex, detailed rules and standards have become both burdensome and ineffective." Consumers might find these changes terrifying, but superbankers such as McColl love them. Gigantic banks of the sort he helped to create are "too large to fail." In the end, they may or may not serve customers and investors well, but by offering e-cash, individual-wealth accounts, consumer derivatives, and a host of other services, they intend to make themselves not only rich but indispensable to the operation of the modern economy.

Sources:

"Big, Big Banks," *The Economist*, 354 (18 March 2000): 5.

Valerie Block, "Atlanta Conference Previews Future of Money," *American Banker*, 161 (14 May 1996): 17.

William Davidson, "Does Money Exist?," *Forbes*, 157 (3 June 1996): 26.

"E-Cash," *The Economist*, 354 (19 February 2000): 67.

Carol H. Fancher, "Smart Cards," *Scientific American*, 275 (August 1996): 40–45.

"Invasion of the Superbanks," *Business Week* (1 November 1999): 175.

Daniel Kadlec, "The Banks Vault," *Time*, 151 (27 April 1998): 58.

Jeffery M. Lacker, "Stored Value Cards: Costly Private Substitutes for Government Currency," *Economic Quarterly*, 82 (Summer 1996): 25.

Brian Nixon, "E-Cash," *America's Community Banker*, 5 (June 1996): 34–38.

Joshua Cooper Ramo, "The Big Bank Theory," *Time*, 151 (27 April 1998): 46–58.

Phil Roosevelt, "Hunting Season: Get Ready for Another Round of Bank Mergers," *Barron's*, 79 (6 December 1999): 20–21.

BULL MARKET

Riding the Bull. It is an understatement to say that during the 1990s the stock market was volatile. On 17 April 1991 the Dow Jones Industrial Average closed above three thousand points for the first time in history. By 1995 the Dow had gained 33.5 percent in value and passed the four thousand mark. In 1997 it reached a high of eight thousand, but began to fluctuate wildly and unpredictably. In late October 1997, for instance, the stock market came as close to crashing as it

Stock traders at the New York Stock Exchange cheer a record one-day point gain of 337.17 on 28 October 1997. More than one billion shares were traded on the NYSE that day (AP/Wide World Photos).

had in the decade when the Dow plummeted a record 554 points in a single day, equaling 7.2 percent of its total value, only to rebound with a record 337-point rise the following day. At the end of the week the market ebbed and flowed its way to a mark of 7,442.08, a loss of a mere 4 percent in value. Even as it declined, however, the value of stocks remained far greater than it had been at the beginning of the decade. By 1998 the Dow reached nine thousand; it closed the decade near eleven thousand points, with no apparent limits on its ascent. The problem was that no one really knew how the market would perform over the short or long term. Chairman of the Federal Reserve Board, Alan Greenspan, periodically tried to slow economic growth and bring the soaring stock market back to earth by raising interest rates as a hedge against inflation. Greenspan interpreted the "correction" in 1997 as a "salutary event" for a market driven by what he characterized as "irrational exuberance." Although the market continued to rise steadily, and sometimes dramatically, after 1997, many experts feared that its volatility suggested the bottom could drop out at any moment without giving much advanced warning of trouble. After the decline of 1997, David N. Dreman of Dreman Value Management, a New York investment firm, declared "this was a market waiting for a trigger. When all is said and done, this market is still overvalued."

Market Strength. Even with the market hovering around eleven thousand points, apprehensions remained. Yet, during periods of market volatility and decline, there were consistently more signs of economic strength than weakness, at least insofar as investors were concerned. In the midst of the collapse of stock values in 1997, the federal budget deficit fell to $22.6 billion, the lowest it had been since 1974. At the same time, wages rose only 0.9 percent, relieving fears of inflation. Cheaper imports from Asia helped keep prices low in the United States. Finally, when market values tumbled, many companies invested in their own stock. These transactions helped to stabilize and even rally the market. Bert Whitehead, a financial consultant in Franklin, Michigan, referred to the 1997 downturn as the "Dow October Clearance Sale," and urged clients to buy while the price per share was low. Market analyst James A. Bianco of Arbor Trading in Barrington, Illinois, estimated that the Dow would have had to fall below five thousand points before portfolios began to experience any irrecoverable loss in value. The market rallied in 1998, rising during the spring and summer, but losing nearly 17 percent of its value by the fall. Such analysts as Robert J. Samuelson predicted a recession when the market tumbled on 19 April 1999, with such high-tech stocks as AOL, Microsoft, Cisco, and other companies in the Dow Jones Internet Commerce Index losing a record 17 percent of their value in a single day of trading. Yet, by 21 April 1999, the Dow climbed to a record 10581 points. The rally was driven by investors who abandoned technology stocks and put their money into industrial shares. To experts, this long-awaited shift marked a welcome broadening of the market, which many thought had been too concentrated. "The shift is healthy," said John S. Tilson, managing director at Roger Engermann & Associates Inc., an investment firm in Pasadena, California. "The narrow bias that the market had before could have led to something bad happening." Alfred Goldman, chief market strategist at A. G. Edwards & Sons, Inc., added, that "the bears have had another arrow taken out of their quiver." Suddenly many experts wondered whether the market, despite its volatility, might not after all be entering a stronger phase that might continue for a long time.

Permanent Prosperity? Will the stock market continue to rise, and if so, how far and for how long? Those were questions market analysts asked as the decade drew to a close. Many apparently looked forward to an endlessly prosperous future, believing that the U.S. economy had undergone a fundamental structural change. Edward Yardeni, chief economist for Deutsche Morgan Grenfell, was lyrical in predicting a "new-era economy" driven by information technology, global markets, and world peace that promised to generate unprecedented corporate earnings and continually rising stock prices. Yardeni and others who shared his perspective posited a "long boom," which would carry the economy past all the difficulties and limitations that formerly hampered it. In an essay titled "The Long Boom" published in *Barron's* in 1997, Peter Schwartz and Peter Leyden took readers on a journey through a twenty-first century economy so affluent that the problems of poverty and war simply disappeared. "We are watching the beginnings of a global economic boom on a scale never experienced before," Schwartz and Leyden intoned. Yardeni, Schwartz, and Leyden provided flamboyant visions; more sedate, mainstream economic and market analysts also asked whether the economic successes could be sustained. Everyone agreed that, given previous assumptions, the performance of the economy during the second half of the 1990s was remarkable, unprecedented, and nothing short of incredible. They disagreed, though, about whether these accomplishments were a portent or temporary phase. Crucial questions remained. Can Americans safely assume that stock prices will continue to soar, that unemployment will continue to decline, and that inflation will continue to recede? No one was certain. Those who argued for the "long boom" based their projections on the extraordinary performance of the U.S. economy, which since 1994 exceeded nearly all predictions and expectations. Optimists thus insisted that the economy had at last solved its persistent structural problems. Sustained growth, they insisted, would no longer create shortages in labor and raw materials, would no longer tax the productive capacity of industry, and would therefore not bring the higher wages, costs, and prices that traditionally slowed economic growth.

The Economic Future. Critics of this scenario suggested that changing demographics of the United States would frustrate the "long boom" prosperity. Between 1945 and 1973 the economy grew at a rate of 3.5 percent a year. Much of that growth resulted from an unusual surge in U.S. population: the arrival of the "baby boomer" generation. In 1963 only 38 percent of the population was in the workforce; by 1998, however, more than 50 percent worked. In 2010, when the oldest members of the baby-boomer generation begin to retire, there will be fewer young workers to replace them. Scholars project that the labor force will grow at a rate of about 0.9 percent per year between 1999 and 2010. Projections of the Social Security Administration show the annual growth rate of the labor force falling around 2020 to 0.2 percent because of lower birth rates in the latter decades of the twentieth century. Even if all the other calculations of the "long boom" theorists prove correct, critics maintain that a shortage of workers will eventually reverse the sustained economic-growth model. Proponents of the "long boom" respond that if the United States can no longer count on favorable demographics, it can, because of technological innovations and advancements, still anticipate increased productivity. They point to the success of such companies as General Electric (GE) and Chrysler, both of which increased productivity through the judicious use of new technology. There is little evidence, however, that the economy as a whole is following the example of GE and Chrysler. Since 1975, the productivity growth rate has been slightly more than 1 percent a year, with virtually no upward trend apparent by the end of the 1990s. Incredible as it may seem, considering the massive changes that took place in the U.S. economy, most scholars agreed that the overall rate of productivity growth experienced no substantial transformation. Individual success stories notwithstanding, studies showed that companies that downsized or turned to computer technology often did not realize any lasting increase in productivity. There also seems to be no definitive statistical evidence to suggest an aggregate increase in productivity. The greatest gains in productivity came in the manufacturing sector, but because it became so productive, these firms employed an ever diminishing percentage of the workforce, declining from 31 percent in 1960 to 15.8 percent by 1995. This decline is expected to continue into the twenty-first century. According to statistics compiled by the Bureau of Labor Statistics and the International Monetary Fund, only 10 percent of the U.S. workforce will be employed in manufacturing by 2017. Since the 1960s there has been a continual exodus of U.S. workers from highly productive manufacturing jobs to less productive jobs in the service sector. Given these considerations, many economists believe that it is unwarranted to expect the phenomenal economic growth and prosperity to continue indefinitely.

Sources:

Adam Bryant, "They're Rich (And You're Not)," *Newsweek*, 134 (5 July 1999): 36–43.

Ann Reily Dowd, "The Panic of '98," *Kiplinger's Personal Finance Magazine*, 52 (July 1998): 24–25.

Fred Hirsh and M. J. Rossant, *Social Limits to Growth*, iUniverse.com, 1999, Internet website.

Jeffery M. Laderman, "The Case for Dow 10,000," *Business Week* (7 December 1998): 124–125.

Laderman and Marci Vickers, "A Wiser Bull?," *Business Week* (3 May 1999): 38–41.

Philip J. Longman, "Is Prosperity Permanent?," *U.S. News & World Report*, 123 (10 November 1997): 36–39.

Bill Powell, "The Globe Shutters," *Newsweek*, 130 (10 November 1997): 30–34.

Jane Bryant Quinn, "What Should You Do?," *Newsweek*, 130 (10 November 1997): 36–38.

Robert J. Samuelson, "The Crash of '99?," *Newsweek*, 132 (12 October 1998): 26–31.

Peter Schwartz and Peter Leyden, "The Long Boom," *Barron's*, 77 (September 1997): 17–19.

Allan Sloan, "Reality Bites," *Newsweek*, 130 (10 November 1997): 39–43.

Anne Kates Smith and James M. Pethokoukis, "The Bucking Bull," *U.S. News and World Report*, 123 (10 November 1997): 26–32.

Suzanne Woolley and Jeffery M. Laderman, "How Worried Should You Be?," *Business Week* (17 August 1998): 30–33.

BUSINESS AND CRIME

Corporate Crime Wave. American business, which shattered many records for growth and profits during the 1990s, also made its contribution to the annals of corporate crime. In one of the most publicized corporate crimes of the decade, the Archer Daniels Midland Company (ADM) agreed in 1997 to pay a record fine of $100 million for price fixing on two commodities: lysine, a feed supplement for livestock, and citric acid, an ingredient used in soft drinks and detergent. In exchange for the guilty plea and a promise to aid the Justice Department in its ongoing investigation, the government granted ADM immunity from prosecution on charges of fixing the price of high-fructose corn syrup, one of the two leading products the company manufactures. (Fuel ethanol is the other). The insurance industry also provided ample opportunity for criminal activity. In 1994 Metropolitan Life was fined $20 million for cheating its customers and Mutual of New York paid $12.5 million to policyholders in Alabama whom the company had bilked in what *The Wall Street Journal* characterized as only "the latest in a series involving deceptive sale practices of the nation's biggest insurers." In 1996 Prudential, the largest insurance company in the United States, was fined $35 million and ordered to pay an additional $1 billion in restitution to policyholders it had defrauded. "Churning" was the name given to the racket whereby as many as ten million customers were persuaded to use the cash value of old policies to pay the premiums on new, more expensive policies. Prudential agents did not inform them that upgrading their policies would be so costly that it would rapidly erode the equity the old policies had accrued, leaving them with premiums they could not afford and hence effecting a cancellation of their coverage. Arthur F. Ryan, chairman of Prudential since 1994, admitted the allegations were true and fired several agents and managers along with a senior vice president. Some disgruntled former employees, however, cooperated with government investigators, providing the sordid details about business operations at "The Rock." Potentially the most damaging evidence was the sworn testimony of several former employees charging that Prudential executives ordered them to destroy any documents that revealed unsavory or illegal marketing practices.

Medical Fraud. According to the General Accounting Office (GAO), medical supply and service companies cheated the government out of at least $100 billion a year during the decade. In 1997, for example, SmithKline Beecham agreed to pay more than $300 million to the government because it had billed Medicare for unnecessary blood tests. That settlement was still less than the record $379 million that National Medical Enterprises paid in 1994 for alleged fraud in psychiatric services. In February 1996 Corning, Inc. paid $6.8 million to settle allegations that its Bioran Medical Laboratory regularly billed Medicare for blood tests that physicians had not requested. Eight months later, in October 1996, Corning was fined again, this time $119 million, for fraudulent billing by Damon Clinical Laboratories, one of its subsidiaries. By then, however, Corning was an old hand at the game, having paid fines of $39.8 million in 1993 and $8.6 million in 1995 to settle similar charges. SmithKline, National Medical Enterprises, and Corning were hardly the only offenders. Between 1989 and 1994 as many as twenty-five million customers were overcharged $600 million for contact lenses. The attorneys general in twenty-two states filed suit against the largest contact lens manufacturers, Bausch & Lomb, Johnson & Johnson Vision Products, and Ciba Vision Corporation, as well as against several optometry trade organizations for alleged involvement in a price-fixing conspiracy. The suits were still pending as the decade ended. One of the more egregious, although not necessarily criminal, examples of corporate misconduct was the use of homeless, often alcoholic, men as human guinea pigs to test experimental drugs. The Food and Drug Administration (FDA) placed Eli Lilly & Company under criminal investigation for such practices. As the deputy director of the FDA explained, using these individuals in drug testing violated the rule that drugs can be tested only on people who can make "a truly voluntary and uncoerced decision" to participate. As of 1999, though, the government had filed no criminal or civil charges against Eli Lilly.

Fraud and the Defense Industry. Faulty bolts that left missiles dangling perilously from the wings of jet fighters and defective gearboxes that forced emergency landings, caused in-flight fires, and led to at least one plane crash were just two examples of the rampant criminal activity that troubled the defense industry throughout the 1990s. United Telecontrol Electronics (UTE) knowingly used defective bolts to hold missiles in place on military aircraft. Fraudulent computer measurements were used to make it appear as if the bolts had passed inspection. Although the crime cost U.S. taxpayers million of dollars and put the lives of servicemen and others in jeopardy, the most severe penalty imposed was on a former UTE vice president who received twenty-one months in prison and a $40,000 fine. Officials at Lucas Industries admitted to manufacturing defective gearboxes for Navy F-18 fighters and to falsifying records. The government imposed a substantial fine of $106 million, but the company, which generates an estimated $6.7 billion in annual revenue, easily absorbed the penalty. Fraud in the defense industry had become so commonplace that it scarcely elicited comment. In addition to the manufacture of faulty equipment, defense contractors routinely engaged in influence peddling and deceptive bookkeeping. Alliant Techsystems was under investigation for overcharging the Pentagon by "tens of millions of dollars on various missile-production contracts." In the 1980s Litton methodically defrauded the government by inflating prices, charging twice for some raw materials, and failing to disclose rebates received from vendors on dozens of electronics contracts with the U.S. Navy. In the 1990s Litton was again the subject of an investigation for fraud; government agents raided its Los Angeles offices in 1996 in search of evidence proving overcharges dating back at least ten years. When Lockheed merged with the Martin Marietta in 1995, it settled the longest-running influence peddling scandal in U.S. history by paying a fine of $5.3 million. The payment resolved a lawsuit that accused Martin Marietta of making $30 million from overcharges on a contract it had received with the help of a corrupt Navy department official. The project, to build a supersonic low-altitude target to test the Navy's missile-defense system, was eventually abandoned. Cost overruns amounting to nearly 100 percent, due primarily to the fallacious bid by Martin Marietta, were the main reason the project failed. The company, nevertheless, made $192 million in profits. Finally, McDonnell Douglas was fined $500,000 for misleading the Pentagon on a $6.6 billion contract to construct the C-17 cargo jet. The company informed the government that it would break even on the contract, although internal company estimates showed that the government would lose at least $1 billion, which it did. American taxpayers are paying the bills.

Crisis at the American Stock Exchange. In April 1999 Richard A. Grasso, chairman of the Securities and Exchange Commission (SEC), announced that it had launched an investigation of the New York Stock Exchange (NYSE). Central to the inquiry was the question of whether the NYSE adequately policed stockbrokers who executed trades on the exchange floor. The investigation came in the wake of a federal indictment of the NYSE in 1998 alleging illegal trading by floor brokers. The reputation of Nasdaq, the principal rival of the NYSE, was also tarnished during the investigation by scandals and accusations. Lawsuits and an SEC report alleged that Nasdaq conspired to fix stock prices. Only the American Stock Exchange (AMEX) escaped legal difficulties, but it continued to have trouble luring and keeping top equity listings. Yet, AMEX had established and maintained a reputation for integrity that was second to none. AMEX officials noted with justifiable pride that its floor membership had not

been subject to a single criminal indictment or major SEC investigation since the late 1970s. A six-month inquiry conducted by *Business Week,* however, exposed what many regard as the hidden business scandal of the decade since, as *Business Week* reporter Gary Weiss argued, the problems "that have beset the Amex have had absolutely no publicity." There were five significant findings of the *Business Week* probe: AMEX options specialists and traders regularly engaged in price-fixing and other trading improprieties; with the concurrence of the SEC, AMEX officials routinely disciplined, usually mildly, their own members when they discovered wrongdoing; their reputation was a mirage, as AMEX had been rocked by a major trading scandal involving Pascuale Schettino, a top official at its most powerful specialist firm of Spear, Leads & Kellogg; Joseph Giamanco, who headed the specialist firm GHM, Inc., traded for personal profit in the stocks of companies in which his firm specialized, which would not only have violated AMEX rules but also federal securities laws, which prohibit brokers from using information not available to the public; and the AMEX, SEC, and appropriate law enforcement agencies failed to investigate the allegations of options trader Edward R. Manfredonia about the illegal activities taking place on the exchange floor, and that, in short, AMEX failed adequately to govern itself. Outgoing AMEX CEO Richard F. Syron, scheduled to step down on 1 June 1999, vigorously defended the integrity of the AMEX. He dismissed the allegations as unfounded. "I think over the last several years . . . there's always room for improvement, but [we have done] a pretty good job here in the regulatory climate at the Amex." On the exchange floor, however, Weiss found such sentiments "viewed with disdain." Many AMEX brokerage officials and floor personnel wondered what would become of a corporate organization and culture that "turns a blind eye" to improper and illegal conduct, especially when carried on by some of its most illustrious members.

Corporate Crime Goes High-Tech. Insider trading and the selling of junk bonds were two of the more prominent and exotic examples of corporate crime during the 1980s. What a difference a decade makes. In the 1990s corporate criminals went back to basics, reviving classic money laundering schemes, but with a new, high-tech twist. To launder billions in illegal funds through legitimate business and banks, all high-tech criminals had to do was switch on their personal computers. Sitting at their keyboards, they could conceal their ill-gotten gains by mixing it with the trillions of dollars that circulate daily through the international system of banking and finance. Russian gangsters, for example, allegedly laundered as much as $10 billion through various accounts at the Bank of New York. Law enforcement agencies investigating the charge suspect that the Russians used electronic means to divert government and corporate funds, and perhaps even a loan to the Russian government from the International Monetary Fund (IMF). Virtually instantaneous wire transfers became standard practice for businesses, but such electronic transactions also became a potent weapon in the arsenal of money launderers. Computers have made it possible for criminals to execute a vast array of transfers with such speed that authorities simply cannot trace all of them. A report of the Canadian government estimates that a minimum of $1 trillion in illicit proceeds was laundered every year since 1991. Wire transfers are "one of the most used techniques" for laundering money, explains Patrick Moulette, executive secretary of the Financial Action Task Force on Money Laundering, which was created by the leading industrial nations to combat the problem. Technology exists to hamper or even prevent electronic-money laundering, but the inconvenience it causes in the conduct of legitimate business and the costs of implementation have prompted banking officials to reject it. "There is no doubt we could design a system that would be impenetrable to people who want to launder money, but I doubt the banks would stand for it," declared Samuel D. Porteous, director of business intelligence for Kroll Associates Canada, an investigating firm. "It's a question of how much people want to spend." In 1999, as the result of fierce opposition from the banking industry, federal officials abandoned proposed legislation that would have tightened the requirements that banks know the customers with whom they do business and account for the origins and destination of the money transferred to and from various accounts. "We don't need new laws and regulations," protested John J. Byrne, senior counsel at the American Bankers Association. "The easiest thing is to overreact." By the late 1990s, however, representatives of the Financial Action Task Force on Money Laundering warned that in addition to computer transfers, high-tech criminals had begun to use smart cards, which store cash electronically, on-line banking, and electronic cash to launder money. In Moulette's view, by the end of the decade it had become "very easy for the launderer" to make crime pay.

Sources:

Morton Mintz, "Response: What About Corporate Crime?," *Nieman Reports*, 52 (Spring 1998): 28–30.

Robert Sherril, "A Year in Corporate Crime," *Nation*, 246 (7 April 1997): 11–17.

Gary Silverman, Margaret Coker, Laura Cohn, and Carol Matlack, "Dirty Money Goes Digital," *Business Week* (20 September 1999): 128–132.

Gary Weiss, "Scandal on Wall Street," *Business Week* (26 April 1999): 96–112.

BUSINESS MANAGEMENT

Reengineering. The rapidly changing economy of the 1990s demanded that companies large and small alter their modes of operation. The first popular managerial fad of the decade was known as "reengineering." James Champy, cofounder of the consulting firm CSC Index, and Michael Hammer, an electrical engineer and former professor of computer science at the Massachusetts Institute of Technology (MIT), conceived of "reengineering" and brought it to international prominence. Champy and Hammer defined the concept as "the fundamental rethinking and radical redesign of business processes to achieve dramatic improvements in critical measures of performance such as cost, quality, service and speed." Central to reengineering is

PETS AT WORK

One trend that became popular at several companies during the 1990s was the practice of allowing people to bring their pets to work. Netscape Communications began the practice when it introduced an office policy, "Dogs At Work." Eventually not only dogs were invited to visit their master's office, but also cats and even fish were approved. The rules were simple: the pets could stay as long as they behaved themselves and did not break the "two incidents" rules. The animal could then not come back until it graduated from obedience training. Netscape cited that by allowing such a policy, it had an easier time attracting potential employees. Other companies that instituted similar policies found that in some cases worker productivity went up and that people were willing to work longer hours if they did not have to worry about their pets at home. Some companies took note; however, many managers, citing health and safety concerns, refused to change company policy regarding pets at work. Others, such as Ben and Jerry's Ice Cream, offered a compromise. Employees were allowed to bring their pets to work for the annual "Dog Days of Summer" party where the visitors were given a free flea dip and a lunch of hot dogs.

the tenet that companies identify their essential activities and processes, and then make them as efficient as possible. Operations or individuals on the periphery, therefore, had to be discarded. Reengineering thus provided the theoretical rationale for much of the corporate downsizing that took place during the decade. "Don't automate, obliterate," Hammer insisted. In Champy's and Hammer's view, however, reengineering amounted to more than merely altering, refining, and streamlining processes. As they envisioned, it was nothing less than a formula for corporate revolution. If revolution it was, then reengineering failed. There are three basic reasons to explain its breakdown. First, corporations by their very nature are not revolutionary. It is difficult, if not impossible, to change longstanding corporate customs, habits, and practices overnight. Second, reengineering appeared, and often was, inhumane. For reengineering purists, depersonalization became the route to efficiency. Third, reengineering began as an effort to overcome organizational rigidity, but, as many critics pointed out, it replaced one set of organizational strictures with another.

Liberation Management. To correct the inflexibility inherent within the reengineering model, Tom Peters posited "liberation management" in which organizational structures were notable for their lack of structure. Companies such as the Cable News Network (CNN) and Asea Brown Boveri (ABB) became Peters's exemplars, prospering, he argued, because of an organizational imagination and agility that enabled them to meet the needs of the moment in a perpetually changing marketplace. Cru-

Labor activist Cheryl Riggs in the deserted sewing room of the Lee Apparel company in St. Joseph, Missouri, on 30 October 1995, after workers were told of plans to terminate their jobs (AP/Wide World Photos)

cial to the new, free-flowing, amorphous corporate structures that Peters envisioned were mutually beneficial, albeit temporary, networks of customers and suppliers. "Old ideas about size must be scuttled," Peters wrote. "'New big,' which can be very big indeed, is 'network big.' That is, size measured by market power, say, is a function of the firm's extended family of fleeting and semi-permanent cohorts, not so much a matter of what it owns and directly controls." Peters's theory is animated by "fashion." The liberation model of corporate organization was fast moving and continually changing. "Tomorrow's effective 'organization'," Peters concluded, "will be conjured up anew each day." Peters hoped that applying his principles would permit organizations to recombine knowledge and work. In the economy of the twenty-first century, he maintained, everyone will have to be an expert of some sort, and companies will not have the luxury of ignoring the ideas and expertise of their "workers" if they wish to survive. "For the last 100 years or so," Peters asserted, "we've assumed that there is one place where expertise should reside: with 'expert' staffs at division, group, sector, or corporate. And another, very different, place where the (mere) work gets done. The new organization regime puts expertise back, close to the action—as it was in craft-oriented, pre-industrial revolution days. . . . We are not, then, ignoring 'expertise' at all. We are simply shifting its locus, expanding its reach, giving it new respect—and acknowledging that everyone must be an expert in a fast-paced, fashionized world."

The Shamrock, the Federal, and the Triple-I. Among the most extensive and insightful commentaries on liberation management came from British theorist Charles Handy, who saw three interrelated and overlapping types of organizations emerging during the 1990s. The first he called the "shamrock organization"— "a form of organization based around a core of essential executives and workers supported by outside contractors and part-time help." The second was identified as the "federal" model. In federal organizations, management is concerned almost exclusively with developing, coordinating, and implementing long-term planning and strategy. Day-to-day operations, however, are left to regional directors, plant managers, supervisors, and even the workers themselves. The third Handy labeled the "Triple I," for its emphasis on "Information," "Intelligence," and "Ideas." In organizations structured around the "Triple-I," there are, properly speaking, no workers and no managers. There are, instead, individuals who are all, by turns, workers, managers, experts, and executives as need and circumstances dictate. The "wise organization" of the future, Handy wrote, "already knows that their [sic] smart people are not to be easily defined as workers or as managers but as individuals, as specialists, as professionals or executives, or as leader, . . . and that they and it need also to be obsessed with the pursuit of learning if they are going to keep up with the pace of change."

Sources:

Stuart Crainer, *The Management Century: A Critical Review of 20th Century Thought and Practice* (San Francisco: Jossey-Bass, 2000).

Michael Hammer and James Champy, *Reengineering the Corporation: A Manifesto for the Business Revolution* (New York: HarperBusiness, 1993).

Charles Handy, *The Age of Unreason* (Cambridge, Mass.: Harvard Business School Press, 1989).

Tom Peters, *Liberation Management: Necessary Disorganization for the Nanosecond Ninties* (New York: Knopf, 1992).

BUSINESS PRACTICES

Asea Brown Boveri. A distinctly new breed of corporation emerged during the 1990s. The largest engineering firm in the world, employing more than 213,000 persons in fifty countries, Asea Brown Boveri (ABB) was the product of a merger between the Swedish company Asea and the Swiss company Brown Boveri, which was completed in August 1987. To manage such a vast organization with as minimal a bureaucracy as possible, ABB chief executive Percy Barnevik introduced a complex managerial structure. An executive committee supervises all facets of the operation while the company itself is broken into thirty-five business sectors with an additional five thousand profit centers. The objective was to combine the benefits of being a large, international organization with the advantages of a small business. Although it has proven highly effective, the intricate managerial structure and practice of ABB has thus far not provided a model for other companies to imitate. Business experts suggest that few companies can combine the global vision with the local presence that has defined ABB. Analyses indicate that the company is free of pointless and destructive infighting, while constructive criticism and debate is welcomed from any quarter. Managers from different countries communicate with each other and work together. Corporate decisions are thought through, supported by information and analysis, and carried out. As one business expert put it: "ABB is a ringing endorsement for professional management at the end of the twentieth century."

JUNK MAIL

During the 1990s Americans received thirty-four pounds of junk mail a year. Direct mailing was a big business; Americans spent almost $244 million in response to junk mail, with $48 million spent on catalogue merchandise alone. Driving the boom in junk mail was an increasingly sophisticated network of information gathering, which allowed solicitors to "target" customers more effectively. Sales of mailing lists constituted a small cottage industry within the industry, as solicitors, eager to garner names for their products or causes, would buy lists with names and addresses, as well as information such as sex, marital status, and, in some cases, preferences, likes, and dislikes, in order to project the buying potential for each possible customer. Still, the presence of watchdog groups and individuals stopped some companies from selling, renting, or trading their mailing lists. In 1996 alone, more than three million persons took advantage of the Direct Marketing Association's (DMA) Mail Preference Service to have their names removed from lists. The DMA also compiled a list of privacy standards that went into effect by 1999, but that may not be enough. Estimates of junk mail sent in 1997 showed that if anything, direct mailings were projected to triple in volume in the next decade.

General Electric. When, in December 1980, Jack Welch became CEO and chairman of General Electric (GE), the annual net income of the company was $1.7 billion. By most measures, GE was then enjoying an unspectacular, but steady and healthy, average growth rate of about 9 percent a year. A company that traced its pedigree directly to the Edison Electric Light Company, which Thomas Alva Edison founded in 1878, GE was, at the time Welch took the reins, the only original company still listed on the Dow Jones Industrial Index since the latter's inception in 1896. GE had endured the vicissitudes of time and change with an extraordinary resilience. During the 1980s Welch put his stamp on GE, and on corporate America as well, by carrying out a complete overhaul of the various divisions of the company. Welch virtually invented downsizing; during the 1980s he eliminated nearly two hundred thousand jobs and saved more than $6 billion. In 1984 the editors of *Fortune* called him the "toughest boss in America." Perhaps Welch was unnecessarily brutal, but GE was a leaner and stronger organization. Having torn GE apart, Welch set out to rebuild it in the 1990s. Central to this effort was the program "Work-Out," launched in 1989, which was an astonishing success. It helped systematically to break down barriers and rebuild the lines of communication and bonds of trust between workers and management. It provided employees with a forum in which to discuss their concerns and then gave them the power actually to change the way the company operated. As Janet C. Lowe explained in *Jack Welch Speaks* (1998): "The idea was to hold a three-day, informal town meeting with 40 to 100 employees from all ranks of GE. The boss kicked things off by reviewing the business and laying out the agenda, then he or she left. The employees broke into groups, and aided by a facilitator, attacked separate parts of the problem. At the end, the boss returned to hear the proposed solutions. The boss had only three options: The idea could be accepted on the spot; rejected on the spot; or more information could be requested. If the boss asked for more information, he had to name a team and set a deadline for making a decision." Finally, at the end of 1995, Welch initiated a quality-control program called Six Sigma, which spread the responsibility for quality control throughout all divisions and levels. "We blew up the old quality organizations," Welch said, "because they were off to the side. Now, it's the job of the leader, the job of the manager, the job of the employee—everyone's job is quality." Welch's efforts yielded rich dividends. The total assets of GE increased from a respectable $20 billion in 1981 to $304 billion by 1997 to a staggering $498 billion by 1999, making GE the second-largest company and the twelfth-largest economic entity in the world.

Toyota. Since at least the mid 1960s U.S. automakers have lurched from one crisis to another. They have all been trying to catch up with and, if possible, surpass their Japanese rival, Toyota. Founded in 1918 as the Toyoda Spinning & Weaving Company, Toyota came late to the manufacture of automobiles, beginning production only in the early 1950s. The Toyota Production System, which has guided the company from the outset, is based on three principles. The first is "just-in-time" production, that is, making cars in accord with market conditions not in anticipation of fluctuations in demand. The second is that quality is everyone's responsibility and that problems, once identified, must be solved with all possible dispatch. The third is the concept of the "value stream." Instead of regarding the company as a series of unrelated products, procedures, and processes, it must be an integrated entity, a continuous, unbroken "stream" that included suppliers, customers, and everyone in between. The Toyota philosophy reached its apex in 1990 with the introduction of the Lexus. Initially greeted as another triumph of Japanese imitation, this time of the Germans, the Lexus, according to Stuart Crainer, actually "out-engineered Mercedes and BMW." Development of the Lexus took seven years, cost $2 billion, required the development of 450 prototypes, generated 200 patents, and commanded the expertise of 1,400 engineers and 2,300 technicians. In the end, Toyota got the car it wanted. Typical of this company, however, the Lexus was about more than engineering. When problems led to an early recall, Toyota had dealers call customers personally to explain the situation and what was to be done about it. Like every other company, Toyota has made its share of mistakes, but when it has done so it usually solves them in a friendly, humane, and efficient way. This philosophy propelled Toyota to the forefront of the auto industry; and the company is now the third largest automaker in the world, trailing only General Motors and Ford. It sells five million vehicles a year: 1.3 million in North America, 2 million in Japan, and 500,000 in Europe. In Japan, Toyota controls nearly 40 percent of the retail market. Its sales figures for 1998 were $88.5 billion with a net profit of $3.5 billion.

Dell Computer. Michael Dell's moment of inspiration came when he realized that personal computers (PCs) could be built for and sold directly to individual customers. This procedure enabled Dell to eliminate the middlemen and the production costs and price increases that they typically engendered. It also meant that Dell did not have to maintain a large inventory, thus eliminating warehousing costs, taxes paid on stock, and insurance expenses. Low overhead and high-profit margins not only made good business sense, but also they were essential in the rapidly expanding and constantly changing computer industry. "There is a popular idea now that if you reduce your inventory and build to order, you'll be just like Dell. Well, that's one part of the puzzle," Dell says, "but there are other parts, too." Dell explains the success of his company by pointing out that he has taken "a disciplined approach to understanding how we create value in the PC industry, selecting the right markets, staying focused on a clear business model and just executing." Dell has by all accounts delivered both the product and service that customers expect and demand. In so doing, he created brand identification and loyalty as well as consumer rapport and satisfaction. "You actually get to have a relationship with the customer," says Dell. "And that creates valuable information, which in turn allows us to leverage our relationships with both suppliers and customers. Couple that information with technology and you have the

Dell employee Bertha Renteria assembles a computer at the Austin, Texas, plant on 25 October 1999 (AP/Wide World Photos).

infrastructure to revolutionize business models of major global companies." Dell Computer was one of the unexpected business successes of the 1990s. It had the best performing stock of the decade, and *Fortune* ranked Dell fourth among America's Most Admired Companies, behind only General Electric, Coca-Cola, and Microsoft. Many business analysts believe that not the corporate giants, but relatively small Dell Computer will provide the model of business organization, practice, and success for the future.

Sources:

Kevin Barham and Claudia Heimer, *ABB: The Dancing Giant: Creating the Globally Connected Corporation* (London: Financial Times/Pitman, 1998).

John Byrne, "How Jack Welch Runs GE," *Business Week* (8 June 1998): 90–102.

James C. Collins and Jerry I. Porras, *Built to Last: Successful Habits of Visionary Companies* (New York: HarperBusiness, 1994).

Stuart Crainer, *The Management Century: A Critical Review of 20th Century Thought and Practice* (San Francisco: Jossey-Bass, 2000).

Sumantra Ghoshal and Christopher A. Bartlett, *The Individualized Corporation: A Fundamentally New Approach to Management* (New York: HarperBusiness, 1997).

Richard Tanner Pascale, *Managing on the Edge: How the Smartest Companies Use Conflict to Stay Ahead* (New York: Simon & Schuster, 1990).

Emily Thompson, "Mystery At the Top: Toyota's Executive Shuffle Doesn't Clear Up Anything," *Business Week* (26 April 1999): 52.

Jack Welch, *Jack Welch Speaks*, compiled by Janet C. Lowe (New York: Wiley & Sons, 1998).

CHANGING FACE OF BUSINESS

Women. Throughout the 1990s business offered women a mixture of advances and disappointments. Increasing numbers of women entered the workplace and moved into traditionally male-dominated occupations. At the same time, women were paid on average 30 percent less than their male counterparts doing the same job. The National Committee on Pay Equity found that women lost an average $12,573 per year, or as much as $440,047 during the course of a lifetime because of unequal pay practices. Yet, as the decade drew to a close, women themselves noted the positive changes taking place in the office and boardroom. "In the past decade," observed Renee Amoore of Amoore Health Systems Inc. in 1997, "the work place has become more dynamic. Women are now able to compete aggressively at the same level as men. I have found over the years that men are now more receptive to including us at the executive-management level." E. Lee Beard of First Federal Savings Bank of Hazelton, Pennsylvania, added "there are more women in management and executive positions. This has provided more peers with whom to network who have many common bonds in terms of career challenges." Finally, Katherine Bishop of Lebanon [Pa.] Seaboard Corporation noted that "there are more women in responsible positions and therefore greater acceptance of women managers by both men and other women." Although acknowledging how far they had come, women, nevertheless, recognized how far they still had to go. Many complained of the "good old boy network" that serves men in hiring practices, acculturation to the company, and advancement through the corporate hierarchy. Experiencing less overt discrimination, women, however, continued to battle for acceptance and equality. "While we've made tremendous strides," said Amoore, "we need to see more women assuming decision-making positions. There is also a need to acquire capital capabilities to effectively develop and operate these businesses. As women begin to undertake these positions, we can begin to establish a 'good old girl network.'" Many women occupied middle management positions but did not rise to the upper echelons of the corporate world in representative numbers. "Women dominate middle management," asserted Dorrit Bern of Charming Shoppes Inc., "but not CEO and senior-management teams." According to Catalyst, a New York firm that monitors and analyzes trends involving women in the workplace, only 2.4 percent have made it to the "top rungs of the corporate ladder." As a result of such limitations, as well as concerns about having the flexibility to balance home life and career, many women opted out of the corporate world and went into business for themselves. According to a 1998 survey conducted by the Office of Advocacy of the U.S. Small Business Administration, 8.5 million women owned businesses in the United States in 1997. That figure increased to 9.1 million by 1999, and accounted for more than 33 percent of all small businesses. The "1999 Facts on Women-Owned Businesses: Trends in the Top 50 Metropolitan Areas," a National Foundation for Women Business Owners and Wells Fargo report, indicated that between 1992 and 1999 the number of women-owned businesses in each of the top fifty metropolitan areas grew from between 33 and 50 percent, generating a combined $2.1 trillion in annual sales. Witnessing the exodus of women from the traditional corporate workplace, Jan Berninger of CoreStates Bank, since absorbed by First Union, commented that more women "seem to be opting out to smaller businesses or owning their own companies where there is more control over their lives and professional aspirations."

Minorities. Like women, minorities continued to make progress in corporate America during the 1990s. Native Americans, African Americans, Asian Americans, Hispanic Americans, and members of other minority groups advanced to positions of prominence, authority, and high salary with greater frequency than ever before. These gains notwithstanding, business experts agree that minorities were still underrepresented at the highest levels of corporate management. Even Asian Americans who made an impact on business, especially on technology companies, out of proportion to their percentage in the population, continued to lag behind in rising to the level of management, according to a 1997 study conducted by Queens College (NY). Although the U.S. population includes

---

NOSTALGIA BOOM

With the overload of information and the faster-than-the-speed-of-light movement of technology, many Americans were quite simply overwhelmed during the 1990s. One response was a return to many of the products and packaging that the Baby-Boomer generation grew up with from the 1950s to 1970s. The nostalgia craze surfaced everywhere in U.S. culture. Madison Avenue began "recycling" old product logos and even archival footage in many commercials. Grocery stores featured items that bore their original packaging. Television got into the act with the introduction of Nickelodeon's "TV-Land," a sly return to the shows and even commercials that many boomers watched as children. Many radio stations switched to different types of "oldies" formats in an attempt to find new listeners. One of the biggest comebacks was the return of the Volkswagen Beetle, albeit somewhat modified to fit modern standards, but still boasting the trademark lines that make it instantly recognizable. Restaurants such as A&W returned to 1950s ambience with great success. Those who studied the nostalgia phenomenon predicted that as boomers continued to age, the nostalgia for their past, even if it was an idealized one, would only continue to grow. Others saw the embracing of the nostalgia as an even sadder commentary on the culture of the 1990s, which one consultant flatly stated "lack[ed] distinction." In any case, not just baby boomers were drawn to revisiting the sights and sounds of their youth; the younger generation also became intrigued.

Autodesk Inc. CEO Carol Bertz, giving the keynote address
at the Women In Technology International conference
in Santa Clara, California, on 24 June 1998
(AP/Wide World Photos)

approximately 30 percent minorities, statistics for the decade showed fewer minorities entering upper management or sitting on the boards of directors. As of 1999 Bell Atlantic Corporation, a leading telecommunications firm, had 20 percent minority representation on its board. Meanwhile, among Bell Atlantic's leading competitors, AllTel Corporation, based in Little Rock, Arkansas, had 14 percent and Global Crossing Ltd. of Hamilton, Bermuda, only 10 percent. Employers often complained that there simply were not enough minority candidates qualified to fill executive positions. John Lawson, president of the National Association of Minorities in Cable, a watchdog group that monitors minority hiring and promotion in the cable industry, disputed this notion. "There is availability there," Lawson declared in 1999, "I just don't think they're [members of minority groups] being hired." In an address delivered to the National Community Reinvestment Coalition on 22 March 2000, Federal Reserve chairman Alan Greenspan echoed Lawson's views, declaring that discrimination is bad for business. Although a prosperous economy had increased wages and employment opportunities for

nearly all workers, Greenspan pointed out that the benefits of that prosperity have not been shared equitably. "By removing the noneconomic distortions that arise as a result of discrimination," Greenspan asserted, "we can generate higher returns to both human and physical capital." Advocates of the economic advancement of women and minorities, such as Laura Russell of the Women's Educational and Industrial Union, trace the roots of employment discrimination to inadequate school systems in poor neighborhoods where the benefits of the unprecedented 108-month economic boom were barely apparent. Yet, even among minorities who attained a level of education comparable with their white counterparts, wage inequities remained high. Statistics compiled by the federal government in 1997 revealed that a white male college graduate earned median pay of $21.45 per hour. An Asian male with the same degree earned $19.86 per hour. Similarly educated Hispanic and African American males made $17.37 and $16.53, respectively.

Seniors. Executives of more than fifty years of age were an endangered species in the corporate world. Riding the crest of the downsizing wave, companies could not get rid of them quickly enough. Then something curious happened. Companies began to face a crisis that business experts called the "age-related brain drain." Those executives who opted for, or who were compelled to accept, early retirement left many companies facing a shortage of managerial talent. "There's a knowledge problem in organizations," asserted William C. Byham, president and chief executive of Development Dimensions International, a human-resources consultant firm. "All the history is going out the door." As a consequence, corporations such as Chevron, Monsanto, and Prudential were moving decisively to retain their most talented and experienced executives. These companies, for example, are fashioning consulting contracts and part-time assignments to accommodate older workers. They are learning that flexibility pays big dividends, and that to retain their most valued employees they must meet their needs. Some companies went so far as bringing older workers out of retirement to provide stability and experience in critical positions and to pass on their knowledge, wisdom, and skills to younger colleagues. As more and more companies retained or recalled older executives, however, they had to contend with a host of management problems such as lingering ageism and intergenerational conflict. However corporations decide to address these issues, they can no longer avoid them. Declining birthrates in the United States have corresponded to the rise of an information- and knowledge-based economy, which demands greater numbers of white-collar workers. Between 1998 and 2010 estimates compiled by Development Dimensions International suggest that managerial jobs will increase by 21 percent while the number of persons between the ages of thirty-five and fifty will decline by 5 percent. The median age of the U.S. workforce during the 1990s rose to nearly forty, up from 34.9 in 1979. Even with improvements in productivity and continued immigration, some scholars argued that there will not be enough people available to meet the demand for executive positions in future decades. "The pressure is building," says Ken Dychtwald, president and CEO of Age Wave, a business-development firm focusing on workers over fifty. "It's almost like geological plates, but it's demographic plates. The graying of America," Dychtwald concludes, "will alter everything from office furniture to the meaning of work itself." To remain competitive corporations, it seems, have had to learn how to spin silver into gold. As John K. Castle, chairman of the leveraged-buyout firm Castle Harlan Inc., explains, "There's a treasure trove of talent being overlooked."

Sources:

Robert Bellinger, "There's Still Work to be Done," *Electronic Engineering Times*, 973, 29 September 1997: A2–A3.

Patricia Buhler, "The Impact of Women in Business in the '90s," *Supervision*, 52 (November 1991): 21–23.

Ken Dychtwald, *Age Wave: How the Most Important Trend of Our Time Will Change Our Future* (New York: Bantam Doubleday Dell, 1990).

Beverly Goldberg, *Age Works: What Corporate America Must Do to Survive the Graying of the Workforce* (New York: Free Press, 2000).

Diane E. Lewis, "Greenspan Says Discrimination Against Women, Minorities, Hurts Business," *Boston Globe*, 24 March 2000.

Jason P. McKay, "Minority Executives Get Disconnected," *tele.com*, 5 (17 April 2000): 46–47.

"The Next Big Wave," *San Antonio Business Journal*, 12 (18–24 December 1998): 54.

Jennifer Reingold and Diane Brady, "Brain Drain," *Business Week* (20 September 1999): 112–126.

"Women-Owned Businesses Doubled During the 1990s," *Wichita Business Journal*, 14 (2 July 1999): 5.

Ron Zemike, Claire Raines, and Bob Filipczak, *Generations at Work: Managing the Clash of Veterans, Boomers, Xers, and Nexters in Your Workplace* (New York: Amacom, 1999).

CORPORATE WELFARE

What is Corporate Welfare? During the second half of the 1990s, in the midst of one of the most sustained periods of economic growth and prosperity in U.S. history, the federal government paid out approximately $125 billion per year to corporations. Advocates applauded these payments as promoting "economic development" or as evidence of "public-private partnership." Critics denounced them as "corporate welfare." From the debates involving this issue there emerged no consistent definition of "corporate welfare," although a commonly accepted one is "any action by local, state or federal government that gives a corporation or an entire industry a benefit not offered to others." These advantages can come in many forms: governments regularly extended significant tax breaks to corporations, for example, including deals that permitted them to pay only 25 percent of their assessed property taxes, granted them the right to make purchases without paying sales tax, and reduced or eliminated taxes on corporate profits. Governments extended partial tax immunity if companies located in certain areas and allowed executives to write off as business expenses some of their perquisites. Corporate welfare also came in the form of low-interest loans from municipalities and states at interest rates cheaper than banks charged. In addition, government funds were used to advertise products, build new factories, and train employees. Governments also awarded grants to fund research that enabled companies to improve productivity and enhance profits. Finally, corporations received perpetual discounts on utility bills and even had local governments pay to install water and sewer lines, as well as landscape corporate property. The justification for corporate welfare has long been that the government is helping companies create jobs. Between 1992 and 1998, for instance, Congress allocated $5 billion to operate the Export-Import Bank of the United States, which subsidizes U.S. companies that do business overseas. James A. Harmon, president and chairman of the bank, asserted that "American workers . . . have higher-quality, better-paying jobs, thanks to Eximbank's financing."

Downside of Corporate Welfare. Labor statistics, however, suggest more complex and ambiguous results. The five principal beneficiaries of this largess were AT&T, Bechtel, Boeing, General Electric, and McDonnell Douglas (now part of Boeing). Together these companies accounted for approximately 40 percent of all loans, grants, and subsidies from the bank during the 1990s. Yet, throughout the decade, employment at these companies fell by a combined 38 percent. During the same period, in 1996, Congress voted to reduce welfare payments to individuals and families. The rationale to curtail such programs as Aid to Dependent Families (ADF) and to impose a lifetime limit on the amount of aid a person could receive was that the system no longer worked. Welfare was deemed unjust, destroyed the incentive to work, and perpetuated social and economic dependence among recipients. Yet, critics charged, corporate welfare continued with many of the same results. Writing in *Time*, Donald L. Barlett and James B. Steele argued that as corporate welfare continued to expand, penetrating every corner of the economy, it "turned politicians into bribery specialists, and smart business people into con artists. And most surprising of all, it . . . rarely created new jobs. . . . In some ways, it represents pork-barrel legislation of the worst order. The difference, of course, is that instead of rewarding the poor, it rewards the powerful."

Local Cost. At the state and local levels, politicians were just as eager as their federal counterparts to extend generous financial arrangements to corporations. According to Barlett and Steele, though, the courting of corporations, many of which were not serious about relocating, did not so much strengthen state and local economies as it incited "a growing economic war among the states." Like the federal government, state and local governments gave corporations money to relocate, even from one building to another, and offered tax incentives to create jobs and hire new employees. They paid to train these workers, or at the least provided a portion of their wages while they were in training. Existing roads were repaved and widened, and new ones built to accommodate corporate needs. They excused corporations from paying sales and property taxes, and relieved them from taxes on investment income.

Senators Edward Moore Kennedy (D-Mass.) and Sam Dale Brownback (R-Kan.) pledging to eliminate "Corporate Welfare" during a Capitol Hill press conference on 28 January 1997 (AP/Wide World Photos)

States Incentives. In 1991, for example, Indiana gave $451 million in various economic incentives to United Airlines to construct an aircraft maintenance facility that would employ 6,300 workers. The state subsidy amounted to $72,000 per job. In 1993 Alabama gave $253 million ($77.5 million for the construction or improvement of roads, water, and sewer lines; $92.1 million to acquire land, build the factory, and construct a training school; $83.6 million in training funds and tax rebates) to Mercedes-Benz to build an automobile assembly plant in Vance, near Tuscaloosa, which was to employ 1,500 persons. The subsidy amounted to $169,000 per job. That same year New Mexico and the community of Rio Rancho, just north of Albuquerque, lured Intel Corporation to build a fabricating plant in Sandoval County with a $2 billion industrial revenue bond, and a second bond in 1995 worth $8 billion, the largest local government bond offering in history. Sandoval County held title to the land, structure, and equipment, which it then leased to Intel. Since governments cannot be taxed, however, this arrangement enabled Intel to avoid paying property and sales taxes. An additional investment/tax-credit deal permitted Intel to be paid a portion of the state income tax withheld from its employees. These and other benefits added up to $330 billion dollars in aid for Intel. In 1997 Pennsylvania gave $307 million, with an additional $199 million in aid coming from the federal government, to Kvaerner ASA, a Norwegian engineering and construction firm, to open a shipyard at the Philadelphia Naval Yard that would employ 950 per-

sons. The subsidy amounted to $323,000 per job. If each worker made an average annual salary of $50,000 and thus paid approximately $6,700 per year in state and local taxes, it would take more than forty-eight years of tax collections from these shipyard employees to repay the initial costs of creating their jobs. These calculations, of course, assume that the workers relocated to Philadelphia and did not move from other jobs within the city where they were already paying taxes. The Arkansas Economic Development Commission (AEDC) declined a request from the town of Evansville for $750,000 to complete the $1.5 million construction of a new water-treatment system that would provide residents with water that is safe for drinking, bathing, and washing clothes, a luxury they did not enjoy. According to representatives of the AEDC, there was simply no money in the budget to fund such initiatives. At the same time, however, the AEDC granted Frito-Lay a subsidy package worth more than $10 million, in addition to $104.7 million in revenue bonds, to build and equip a potato-chip manufacturing plant in Jonesboro. Other incentives included the 140-acre site on which the plant was to be built, constructing a rail spur, road improvements, extending tax credits for new employees, and offering a 20 percent discount on sewer bills for the next fifteen years. For each worker employed at the plant, the state government invested approximately $61,000. The cost of subsidizing thirteen employees would have provided more than enough money ($793,000) to build the water treatment plant.

Localities. For many counties and municipalities, the consequences of corporate welfare were just as serious and disappointing. In 1991 ABB Instruments Incorporated, a subsidiary of Asea Brown Boveri, a Swiss and Swedish conglomerate, requested tax breaks and other incentives from the County of Monroe (New York) Industrial Development Agency (COMIDA) to move from its old building in downtown Rochester to a new suburban industrial park. Only when the company threatened to relocate operations to Ohio, England, Mexico, or Venezuela did COMIDA issue $21 million in industrial revenue bonds and excuse ABB from paying sales taxes on the materials used to construct its new plant. COMIDA also waived a portion of the real estate taxes for a period of ten years. To secure these incentives, ABB was required to create twenty new jobs; if it failed to do so, it had to repay a portion of the tax reduction. Even before moving into its new building, however, ABB Instruments began eliminating rather than increasing jobs. When ABB representatives initially approached COMIDA, its Rochester employees numbered 723. By December 1996 its Rochester workforce totaled 393. Rather than creating the new positions, it eliminated 330 existing jobs. Yet, the company refused to refund the tax incentives, pleading poverty. "If you rescind the tax exemption," an ABB spokesman told COMIDA, "we'll owe $1.2 million in taxes, which we can't afford." As of 1999 Monroe County had waived collection of this debt. ABB thus received $26 million in tax breaks and economic aid from the county only to cut jobs.

General Motors at the Trough. Industry analysts suggest that if the General Motors Corporation (GMC) is to survive into the twenty-first century, it will have to eliminate fifty thousand jobs. As a consequence the company began auctioning jobs to the highest bidders in the communities where it did business. In 1996 New York State awarded GM $16.9 million in tax exemptions, training grants, and lower utility costs along with an additional $3 million in the reduction of sales tax from local government, so that it could afford to retool its plant in Tonowanda and not move to another city. As a result, between 1996 and 1998, GM eliminated two hundred jobs at its Tonowanda factory. In effect, state and local governments provided $99,000 in incentives for each job that GM abolished. During the summer of 1997 GM announced that it was considering the expansion of an assembly plant located in Moraine, Ohio, at a cost of $355 million. The decision, GM officials declared, would hinge on whether the city was willing to grant tax breaks. After all, officials intimated, it might be cheaper simply to close the plant and build elsewhere, since two other cities, Shreveport, Louisiana, and Linden, New Jersey, both already home to GM truck plants, were competing for the facility. Although executives later apologized for any misconceptions their comments might have caused, the company lied about any intentions of relocating the plant to Shreveport or Linden. The local government of Moraine, taking no chances,

nevertheless agreed to exempt GM from taxes on the $355 million worth of machinery, equipment, and inventory for ten years and from real estate taxes for fifteen years on building construction and renovation, estimated to cost $65 million. GM also received a direct cash subsidy of $1 million. For the fiscal year 1995–1996, when GM extracted these concessions, company profits totalled $11.8 billion. In 1998 the government of Moraine extended an additional $28 million in tax relief to GM in the hope of persuading the company to build another plant in the area.

Why Corporate Welfare? Ten million new jobs were created between 1990 and 1999, mostly in small or medium-sized businesses. Fortune 500 companies, on the contrary, eliminated more jobs than they created, and yet they were the principal beneficiaries of corporate welfare. At what cost? asked Barlett and Steele. "The equivalent of nearly two weekly paychecks from every working man and woman in America—extra money that would stay in their pockets if it didn't go to support some business venture or other." The corporate lobby is rich and powerful, however, sponsoring seminars, publishing journals, and operating trade associations. It has access to city halls, statehouses, Capitol Hill, and the White House. Critics and advocates alike agree that government officials were ultimately responsible for the continuation and expansion of corporate welfare. Charles Horn, an Ohio state senator and a persistent critic of corporate welfare, said in 1998: "We know companies are manipulative, but it's the nature of business to go after every dollar that's legally available. Don't place the blame on the company; place the blame on government. This is government's folly."

Sources:

Donald L. Barlett and James B. Steele, "Corporate Welfare," *Time*, 152 (9 November 1998): 36–54.

Tim W. Ferguson and Josephine Lee, "Corporate Welfare," *Forbes*, 161 (20 April 1998): 42–44.

James K. Glassman, "Corporate Welfare Queens: When It Comes to Subsidies for Companies, Congress Can't Say No," *U.S. News & World Report*, 122 (19 May 1997): 53.

Philip D. Harvey, "Taxpayer-Funded Subsidies Are Robin Hood in Reverse," *Insight on the News*, 14 (16 April 1998): 30.

Thomas A. Hemphill, "Confronting Corporate Welfare," *Business Horizons*, 40 (November-December 1997): 2–8.

Greg LeRoy, "The Terrible Ten Corporate Candy Store Deals of 1998," *Progressive*, 63 (May 1999): 27.

Timothy W. Maies and Sean Paige, "Business Fares Well With Welfare," *Insight on the News*, 13 (29 December 1997): 12–13.

Stephen Moore, "Corporate Welfare Queens," *National Review*, 49 (19 May 1997): 27–28.

Paulette Olson and Dell Champlin, "Ending Corporate Welfare As We Know It: An Institutional Analysis of the Dual Structure of Welfare," *Journal of Economic Issues*, 32 (September 1998): 759–772.

Alan K. Ota, "Criticism of Corporate Welfare Heats Up in Congress," *Congressional Quarterly Weekly Report*, 56 (17 January 1998): 121–122.

T. J. Rodgers, "End Corporate Welfare Now!" *Chief Executive* (December 1998), 42–45.

Allan Sloan, "What Goes Around," *Newsweek*, 132 (12 October 1998): 32–34.

GLOBAL ECONOMY

Implications of Globalization. A small group of countries, principally those whose economic policies were integrated under the auspices of the Group of Seven (G7), played the leading role in the process of economic globalization. The overwhelming majority of nations, meanwhile, had to adapt to economic conditions shaped almost entirely without their participation. At the same time, globalization began to undercut the economic primacy of the nation-state. The power and influence of multinational corporations grew during the 1990s, so much so that they rather than nation-states became the driving force of globalization. Eight of the top twenty-five economic entities in the world, measured in terms of market value, were corporations. According to figures compiled for 1999, the economy of the United States continued to dominate the world, with a market value in U.S. dollars of $15.013 trillion. Japan ($4.244 trillion) was a distant second, followed by the United Kingdom ($2.775 trillion), France ($1.304 trillion), and Germany ($1.229 trillion). Seven U.S. companies and one Japanese company ranked in the top twenty-five. Microsoft occupied tenth place, with a market value of $546 billion. General Electric ($498 billion) was twelfth, ahead of Australia ($424 billion) and Spain ($390 billion). Cisco Systems ($355 billion) was fifteenth, leading Taiwan ($339 billion) and Sweden ($318 billion). Intel ($305 billion), Exxon-Mobil ($295 billion), and Wal-Mart ($289 billion) ranked eighteenth, nineteenth, and twentieth respectively, ahead of South Korea ($285 billion) and Finland ($276 billion). Nippon ($274 billion) ranked twenty-third and AOL Time-Warner ($244 billion) twenty-fourth, ahead of South Africa ($232 billion).

World Government? Much of the economic power formerly vested in nation-states also came to rest with such international institutions as the European Union (EU), World Trade Organization (WTO), and International Monetary Fund (IMF). These entities gained substantial control over the national economies of sovereign states. Critics of this development, such as Ralph Nader and Patrick J. Buchanan, raised the specter of world government, sensing an alarming concentration of power in multinational and international hands. The triumph of the WTO, Nader complained, "means foreign regulation of America. . . . It means secret tribunals can rule against our laws." Defenders of globalization, on the contrary, believed that it was an inevitable change and that the only question remaining was what sort of world economy and government would be established. Nations have always traded with one another for their mutual benefit, argued Robert Wright in *New Republic*. They will doubtless continue to do so. He contended, however, that when leaders at last recognize the advantages to eliminating grievances and animosity they will submit to common governance and adjudication. The benefits of this arrangement, Wright speculated, will far outweigh the costs, preserving economic order, dispensing justice, eliminating inequitable advantages, and inhibiting destructive competition.

Difficult Transition. Globalization, nonetheless, caused serious problems, especially in so-called developing countries with transitional economies. Advocates of globalization, such as Wright, insisted that the environmental problems, exodus of low-skill jobs from high-wage nations, and human-rights violations, which led many to oppose change, "are just about impossible to solve without . . . the power of sanction that the WTO, more than any other world body, has to offer." "Globalization is great," Wright concluded, "on balance, it makes the world's poor people less poor. . . . And it fosters a fine-grained economic interdependence that makes war among nations less thinkable." In an address delivered at the World Economic Forum in Davos, Switzerland (December 1997), Mexican president Ernesto Zedillo Ponce de León expressed similar views. "In order for developing nations to overcome their state of poverty," Zedillo asserted, "they need to open their borders and participate in globalization. Those interested in protecting workers' rights—and in pressuring the World Trade Organization to do so—must realize that this is an honorable but long-term goal that will not be achieved with any immediacy. Commerce is the most powerful tool in ensuring that the international rights of laborers in developing countries are protected."

Globalization in Action. Thanks largely to the North American Free Trade Agreement (NAFTA), many advocates of the global economy cited Mexico as the model to persuade developing countries to pin their markets and their hopes to free trade and economic competition. Since NAFTA went into effect in 1994, proponents of globalization such as President Zedillo point out that impoverished Mexican cities have reaped the benefits. Ciudad Juarez, located directly across the Rio Grande from El Paso, Texas, has gained more than $4 billion in foreign investment and 150,000 manufacturing jobs. Yet, a study conducted by the Labor University of Mexico found that the purchasing power of Mexican workers declined considerably since 1994 and eroded by 86 percent since the 1970s. In 1995, for example, the average daily minimum wage of Mexican workers was enough to purchase 44.9 pounds (20.36 kilograms) of tortillas or 2.24 gallons (8.5 liters) of milk. In 1999, after operating under NAFTA for five years, the same workers could purchase only 16.9 pounds (7.65 kilograms) of tortillas or 1.4 gallons (5.3 liters) of milk. The study also indicated a large increase in unemployment in agriculture and small business, sectors of the economy that could not compete with subsidized U.S. imports entering the country as a result of NAFTA. Many Mexicans, nevertheless, were happy for the opportunity to work in the *maquiladoras*, the foreign-owned factories in which imported parts are assembled for export. Despite low pay and poor working conditions, factory work represents a vast improvement from the sugar cane and corn fields in which they formerly labored. President Zedillo argued that "most people fail to realize . . . that the low salaries and poor conditions to which most workers are subject is their only alternative to extreme rural poverty." Alternately, Bob Jeff-

Mexican assembly line workers in a Samsung Electromagnetics plant in Tijuana, Mexico, on 18 November 1998 (AP/Wide World Photos)

cott of the Maquila Solidarity Network (MSN), located in Toronto, Canada, maintained that "there's always a place that will have lower wages. There's always a place that will have lower economic standards. It's leading to 'de-development.'" Whether in favor of or opposed to globalization, economic and political leaders had to begin paying closer attention not only to the distribution of goods, money, and services in the global marketplace, but also to the costs and benefits among various countries. They could not afford to be unaware of who thrived and who suffered as a result of this monumental economic transformation.

The Perils of Globalization. The advocacy of the international free market favors developed countries and powerful multinational corporations. Already the wealthiest nation, the United States gained the most from economic globalization, the progress of which failed to eliminate, and in some respects even enhanced, the divergence in economic growth and development between rich and poor countries as well as the economic, social, and political inequalities within nations. Nor did the advocates of globalization adequately address the crucial problems of environmental standards and workers' rights. Environmentalists, union organizers, and human-rights activists brought many of these issues and concerns to worldwide attention with the violent demonstrations that disrupted the meeting of the WTO held in Seattle, Washington, in December 1999. Becoming ever more mindful of the problems that globalization created, members of the economic, political, and corporate elite began to speak out against them, even if they had not yet found the means of solving them. Michel Camdessus, managing director of the International Monetary Fund (IMF), declared in the keynote address deliv-

ered at the Tenth United Nations Conference on Trade and Development (UNCTAD) in Bangkok, Thailand (February 2000), that "the greatest concern of our time is poverty. . . . It is the ultimate systematic threat facing humanity. The widening gaps between rich and poor within nations," Camdessus continued, "is morally outrageous, economically wasteful, and potentially socially explosive. If the poor are left hopeless, poverty will undermine the fabric of our societies through confrontation, violence, and civil disorder." Similarly, Klaus Schwab, founder and chairman of the World Economic Forum (WEF), called for "responsible globalization," "leadership based on values," and "common ethical and moral standards" that will include in the movement toward globalization all those currently being left out. To do so, Schwab acknowledged, will require the reform of the leading international economic and financial organizations.

Sources:

Oleg Bogomolov, "A Challenge to the World Order," *Nezavisimaya Gazeta* (27 January 2000), reprinted in *World Press Review,* 47 (April 2000): 7–8.

Martin Carnoy, and others, *The New Global Economy in the Information Age: Reflections on Our Changing World* (University Park: Pennsylvania State University Press, 1993).

Franklin Foer, "Protest Too Much," *New Republic,* 222 (1 May 2000): 21–23.

Jeffrey E. Garten, ed., *World View: Global Strategies for the New Economy* (Cambridge, Mass.: Harvard Business School Press, 2000).

Pierre Haski, "The Bosses Grow Rich on Vocabulary," *Liberation* (31 January 2000), reprinted in *World Press Review,* 47 (April 2000): 9.

William J. Holstein, Steven D. Kaye, and Fred Vogelstein, "One World, One Market," *U.S. News and World Report,* 123 (10 November 1997): 40–43.

"March Madness," *New Republic,* 222 (1 May 2000): 9.

Dani Rodrik, "The Global Fix," *New Republic,* 219 (2 November 1998): 17–19.

Robert Samuelson, "Global Boom or Bust?," *Newsweek,* 130 (10 November 1997): 35.

John Stackhouse, "Happy to Be Exploited," *The Globe and Mail* (2 December 1999), reprinted in *World Press Review,* 47 (April 2000): 10.

Joseph Stiglitz, "The Insider: What I Learned at the World Economic Crisis," *The New Republic,* 222 (17 & 24 April 2000): 56–60.

Robert Wright, "Continental Drift," *The New Republic,* 222 (17 January 2000): 18–23.

THE INTERNET

Dawn of the Internet Age. In October 1969 two teams of computer scientists, one at the University of California, Los Angeles, and the other at the Bell laboratories in Menlo Park, California, linked computers over telephone lines to operate as a single system. The U.S. military had sponsored the research, seeking to establish a national communications network that would continue to operate even if part of the system were disabled or destroyed in a nuclear attack. Such was the genesis of the "Internet Age." During the 1990s the Internet became a force that transformed every aspect of life. Anyone with a computer, telephone, and modem literally had at their fingertips a staggering quantity and variety of information. As the decade drew to a close, the possibilities of the new technology seemed endless. Certainly the initial impact of the Internet has been profound, especially for business. Upstart on-line companies humbled corporations that once seemed unassailable. Financial markets became more accessible and efficient for those who wished to raise or invest money. Accessibility and efficiency, in fact, may be the lodestone and the polestar of the Internet. The Net broke down bureaucracies; challenged corporate, governmental, and intellectual orthodoxies; and, as some argue, encouraged a stronger sense of democracy and community. For good or ill, such developments have led to revolutions in the past.

The Internet Revolution. Out of the primordial ooze of the Internet there evolved a host of new species: new companies, business models, corporate structures, even industries. The 1990s was a time of such tumult and confusion as far as the Internet was concerned that no one could agree on what was happening, let alone about what the future was likely to bring. Since 1994, when the World Wide Web made the Internet more accessible, all the formerly immutable truths about business have been called into question. In 1997, for instance, Yahoo! Inc. was nothing more than a Web search index. By 1999 it had become a major media company commanding a $40 billion market capitalization. How did this transformation take place? Experts scratched their heads and shrugged their shoulders in wonder at advertisers and investors who jumped on the Yahoo! bandwagon, but enough did, making it a multibillion-dollar corporation. Equally astonishing, the staid executives at venerable Hewlett-Packard seriously discussed giving away multimillion-dollar computer systems to Internet startup companies in exchange for a share of the "e-revenues." Finally, and perhaps most fantastic, companies such as Amazon.com and eToys Inc., which, by the end of the decade had yet to turn

THE RETURN OF CUSTOMER SERVICE

In a bid to attract shoppers to their stores, retailers found resuming the notion of "customer service" went a long way. Retailers during the 1990s saw that customers were overwhelmed by the "sameness" in much of the merchandise as well as intimidated by the high-pressure sales environment. Using an idea some called "retail-tainment," stores such as the cosmetics chain Sephora and the famed department store Bloomingdale's switched to more customer-friendly and low-key atmosphere for shoppers. The goal was to make shopping more theatrical and fun. This attitude was reflected in everything from overall store design, installing coffee bars such as those found at the bookstore chains Barnes & Noble and Borders, to having executives, such as the ones at Bloomingdale's, greet customers as they entered the store. Among other innovations being tried: small exhibits; visitor's centers, complete with a concierge; and "business centers" at which customers could watch CNN, send a fax, and even get their shoes shined.

a profit, continued to command multibillion-dollar market capitalizations that attracted untold numbers of investors. The world, at least the world of cyberbusiness, seemed to have gone mad. It certainly perplexed traditional executives who had spent their working lives trying to build companies with real offices, factories, assets, and profits.

Net Impact. The Internet, as everyone knew, was not the work of madmen. The Center for Research in Electronic Commerce at the University of Texas at Austin estimated that as of 1999 the Internet economy totaled $301 billion—if on-line sales of industrial and consumer goods and services were combined with the equipment and software needed to operate and support e-commerce. The U.S. automobile industry, by comparison, was worth $350 billion in 1999. If the level of growth experienced since 1994 continues, commerce on the Internet will be as perilous to some businesses, and perhaps even entire industries, as it will be profitable to others. Hardly a company or industry did not undergo some upheaval that changed the way in which it was organized and defined, because of the Internet. Mark T. Hogan, vice president of the e-GM Internet unit for the General Motors Corporation (GMC), admitted that "we've come to realize that if we don't move with Internet speed, we could become extinct." These consequences were the result of one inescapable fact of doing business in the 1990s: the Internet put customers in charge as never before. In 1999 Gary Hamel, chairman of the management consultancy firm Strategos and a research fellow at the Harvard Business School, explained: "For many companies, customer ignorance was a profit center." With access to the wealth of information that the Internet pro-

Workers at the Amazon.com distribution warehouse in Seattle, Washington, on 15 December 1999 (AP/Wide World Photos)

vided, however, customers pointed and clicked their way to the best goods and services at the lowest prices. The Internet offered new advantages to merchants as well, who could now identify individual customers and collect unprecedented quantities of data about the character and pattern of their purchases. Yet, the rise of the Internet compelled executives to rethink the nature of the companies they managed. Suddenly, factories, stores, trucks, warehouses, and even employees, once regarded as competitive assets, came to be liabilities. Saavy companies began to jettison, or to avoid altogether, building costly facilities or hiring legions of sales representatives. They concentrated instead on expanding their capacity to use the Internet, which even provided opportunities to access resources outside the company. It became common corporate practice, for example, for one company to form a temporary partnership with another—a partnership that coalesced and dissolved with each new project. Forrester Research Inc. labeled this process "dynamic trade." To reinvent themselves, many companies moved from being manufacturers to becoming "service providers." Hewlett-Packard (HP), for example, began using the Internet to remake itself from a manufacturer of computers into an "e-services" company. Instead of making and selling computers, HP marketed computing network services over the Internet for a monthly fee, or in the case of an e-commerce site, for a percentage of the transaction revenues. Ann M. Livermore, CEO of the $14 billion Enterprise Computing Solutions for HP, estimated in 1999 that such fees alone could eventually account for 80 percent of the division's annual revenues. Of course, for every opportunity the Internet created there was

a concurrent fear. As late as 1993, what grocery store owner could have believed his chief competition would come from a virtual superstore called the Webvan Group Inc.? What automobile dealer could have suspected that a software company such as Microsoft Corporation would be one of his biggest rivals? Could bankers and stockbrokers have guessed that the on-line brokerage firm E*Trade Group Inc. would siphon off their customers' accounts with such ease? In industry after industry, interlopers and upstarts swarmed like locusts, creating and exploiting new, efficient, on-line markets, and often devouring the profits of established companies in the process.

The Internet and Economic Growth. Throughout the fifteenth century, estimates economist J. Bradford DeLong of the University of California at Berkeley, global per capita income rose at a rate of 0.1 percent a year. During the next five hundred years the annual rate of growth gradually increased until it reached approximately 3 percent in the second half of the twentieth century. By the 1990s it appeared as if the growth rate of the global economy was poised to expand again, this time exponentially. Experts agreed that the single most important reason for this dramatic worldwide explosion in economic productivity and value was the advent of the Internet. The Internet altered the dynamics of the global economy at least as much as had the introduction of railroads and electricity. Among other considerations, the evolution of the Internet has meant that the traditional requirements of economic growth and development, access to and control of capital and labor, may no longer be the principal determinants of economic strength. Economic power became increasingly and inextricably linked to the control and manipulation of information. The initial manifestation of Internet potential was the performance of the American economy. Since World War II, Western Europe and Japan had gradually eroded U.S. economic supremacy. In 1970 the per capita income in the United States was 31 percent higher than that in other major industrialized countries. By 1991 the difference had narrowed to just 10 percent. With the coming of the Internet, however, the distance widened to 22 percent by 1999. The situation is somewhat analogous to the British domination of the industrial world during the first half of the nineteenth century, before industrialization spread to the Continent. "This is historically unique," declared Luc Soete, an economist at Maastricht University in the Netherlands and the leading European expert on the "new economy": "For the first time in the postwar period, you have growth divergence—the pulling away of the leading technological country."

The Internet and the Global Economy. Many economists, however, believe that the accelerated growth of the U.S. economy was only the first act in the drama of sustained global economic expansion. The international economy, they pointed out, was no longer solely or even primarily dependent on commerce in goods, the mechanism that had propelled all previous surges in economic growth. With the adoption of the Internet it became easier to import and export services as well: banking, education, consulting, retailing, and even gambling. "In the 1990s, the Internet became 'the backbone of greater service trade,'" proclaimed Joseph Quinlan, senior international economist at Morgan Stanley Dean Witter. The rapid diffusion of knowledge and information was the crucial element that the Internet provided. Perhaps never before had Sir Francis Bacon's aphorism "Knowledge is Power" been so apt. "There are lots of reasons to think the Internet will lead to much more rapid diffusion of knowledge," said Jonathan Eaton, an economist at Boston University, in 1999. Eaton and his collaborator, Samuel Kortum, have estimated that global economic growth could increase as much as one full percentage point in the coming decade. Although neither the U.S. nor world economy had attained that level by the end of the century, the United States had come close. By 1999 it dominated the Internet, accounting for more than 50 percent of all individuals on-line and 75 percent of all Internet commerce. Not surprisingly, the United States, the first nation to develop and implement Internet technology, enjoyed the lion's share of the economic benefits the Internet generated. Most observers predict that this advantage will decline over time. A study conducted by Juniper Communications, Inc. anticipated that the number of European households with access to the Internet will triple between 1999 and 2004. In Asia, especially in China and Japan, the study forecast that the number of persons regularly using the Internet will at least double by 2001. As a consequence, by 2003 the United States will account for only 50 percent of Internet commerce. Already, at the end of the decade, Iceland, Finland, and Sweden had more Internet use per capita than the United States.

Impediments to Globalization. Yet, four important impediments remained to the Internet achieving the full global impact many believe to be its destiny. First, the United States had the largest home market. Despite movement toward a more unified Europe, the multitude of languages, cultures, and governments in Europe and Asia slowed the advance of the Internet compared with the large, consolidated, and still relatively homogeneous United States. Second, economists have suggested that the introduction of the euro, the common European currency, also diverted the Internet Revolution. "The Internet is making the world global," Soete stated. "But [with the euro] we made Europe more European." Third, in most European countries local phone calls are still charged by the minute, a practice that discouraged extensive use of the Internet. Fourth, despite the increasing availability of venture capital, Europe still lagged far behind the United States in access to this indispensable component of economic growth and development. Asia was even further behind and having even more difficulty attracting venture capital. With its immense markets, however, Asia may have a better chance of thriving in the Internet Age than Europe. Economists agree that the key to the next stage of Internet development will be whether financial innovation can keep pace with technological change. American financiers were prepared to invest in new Internet companies; Japanese and European investors, by contrast, were not, remaining bound to more traditional corporations. If these differences persist, the locus of technological and economic innovation will likely remain the United States, no matter how many websites and Internet users there are in Europe and Asia.

Regulating the Net. As e-commerce grew into a trillion-dollar business, only one force seemed capable of slowing down or stopping its evolution: politics. Concerned about the potential of the Internet to invade people's privacy, take their money, and generally wreak havoc, politicians around the world began to contemplate new laws to prevent the revolutionary potential of the Internet from being abused. The impulse to regulate the Net, in turn, distressed entrepreneurs, lest their vision of a global-electronic marketplace foundered on the shoals of inconsistent, uncoordinated local and national rules ranging from decency standards to privacy laws to sales taxes. E-businesses pleaded with the U.S. government to allow them to police themselves. The Clinton administration complied. In 1997 President Bill Clinton's longtime aide Ira C. Magaziner, now a private consultant, wrote "Framework for Global Electronic Commerce," a blueprint for the governance of the Internet. Magaziner argued that regulation ought to be kept to a minimum. Over-regulation, he concluded, would inhibit the global reach and evolving technology of the Net. Magaziner went so far as to suggest that governments recuse themselves from making policy for the Internet and turn the process over to such international groups as the World Intellectual Property Organization (WIPO) or the Organization for Economic Cooperation & Development (OECD). The problem with Magaziner's proposal, already apparent by the end of the 1990s, was the lack of accountability. Neither of the regulatory boards of the WIPO nor the OECD are composed of elected officials with responsibility to a constituency. As a consequence, both organizations have operated in relative secrecy, without the obligation even to follow due process. This arrangement made it easier for corporations to dominate regulatory procedures and harder for governments or consumers to protest their decisions. Harvard Law School professor Lawrence Lessing criticized the regulatory process, arguing that: "You've had interested parties in closed meetings for the past three years making this code for Internet commerce tilted in their favor." Similarly, Professor A. Michael Froomkin of the University of Miami Law School complained that "business has figured out that you can get what you want from [private] regulatory processes. Democracy is a messy way of making decisions, but one of the reasons is that we try to ensure that different groups are heard." One organization that made some progress toward regulatory democracy is the Internet Corporation for Assigned Names & Numbers (ICANN), which monitors the Internet address system. Since its inception in the summer of 1998, ICANN has established conflict of interest rules, opened some of its board meetings to the media and general public, and worked to develop a mechanism to elect board members. To many, ICANN has come to represent the most viable alternative to cumbersome government regulation, on the one hand, and self-serving corporate tyranny, on the other.

Sources:

Stephen Baker, "Taming the Wild, Wild Web," *Business Week* (4 October 1999): 154–160.

Martin Carnoy and others, *The New Global Economy in the Information Age: Reflections on Our Changing World* (University Park: Pennsylvania State University Press, 1993).

Christopher Farrell, "All the World's an Auction Now," *Business Week* (4 October 1999): 120–128.

Andrew Ferguson, "Auction Nation," *Time,* 154 (27 December 1999): 80–85.

Mike France, "The Net: How to Head Off Big-Time Regulation," *Business Week* (10 May 1999): 89–90.

Karl Taro Greenfield, "Click and Bricks," *Time,* 154 (27 December 1999): 86–94.

Linda Himelstein, "Yahoo!: The Company, the Strategy, the Stock," *Business Week* (7 September 1999): 66–76.

Robert D. Hof, "The 'Click' Here Economy," *Business Week* (22 June 1998): 122–130.

Hof, "A New Era of Bright Hopes and Terrible Fears," *Business Week* (4 October 1999): 84–98.

Michael Kratz, "Cruising Inside Amazon," *Time,* 154 (27 December 1999): 66–71.

Michael J. Mandel, "The Internet Economy," *Business Week* (22 February 1999): 30–32.

Mandel, "The Internet Economy," *Business Week* (4 October 1999): 72–77.

Otis Port, "Customers Move into the Driver's Seat," *Business Week* (4 October 1999): 103–106.

Joshua Quittner, "An Eye on the Future," *Time,* 154 (27 December 1999): 56–64.

LOVE, BUSINESS, AND THE LAW

The Discovery of Sexual Harassment. During the late 1970s and early 1980s the concept of sexual harassment existed only in the mind of a young legal scholar named Catherine A. MacKinnon. By the 1990s MacKinnon had become a prominent law professor at the University of Michigan and 15,000 sexual harassment complaints were being filed annually with the federal Equal Employment Opportunity Commission (EEOC). Now it is impossible for even the most diligent of executives to stay current with the vast and diverse body of precedent and law that sexual harassment cases have generated. Few, though, can afford to ignore the numbers, such as the record $34 million payment that Mitsubishi Motor Corporation made in 1998 to settle an EEOC investigation of alleged harassment taking place at their plant in Normal, Illinois. The legal system has also disciplined companies for an apparently too rigid enforcement of sexual harassment policies. When the Miller Brewing Company fired a manager for telling his secretary about a lurid and salacious episode of *Seinfeld,* a jury awarded him $26 million in damages and lost wages and ordered the company to give him back his job. To avoid finding themselves, and placing their companies, in similar jeopardy on either side of this inflammatory issue, many executives and managers, such as those at Aerotek, a high-tech temp agency, simply adopted a policy that prohibited employees from dating or even socializing with coworkers. Others, however, turned increasingly to consultants and experts for advice and guidance. Dennis Powers, a law professor at the University of Southern Oregon, warned, "today's fling is tomorrow's filing." Littler Mendelson, the largest U.S. employment law firm, for example, drew up "love contracts" between those engaging in workplace romances, especially if the persons involved happened to be superior and subordinate. Such contracts stipulate that, despite the legal risks, both parties "independently and collectively desire to undertake and pursue a mutually consensual social and amorous relationship." Art Bauer, founder and CEO of American Media, invited corporate executives to view free of charge his videos *Sexual Harassment—Is it or Isn't It?* and *Stopping Sexual Harassment Before It Starts.* Bauer was just one among thousands of lawyers, consultants, and therapists who found it profitable to monitor and interpret the latest judicial rulings and legal precedents with regard to sexual harassment in the workplace. Like many of his counterparts, Bauer tried to calm fearful executives—by promising not only to uncover but also to prevent harassment, and to eliminate the conditions that encourage it.

Regulating Romance. Ricky Silberman, former vice chairman of the EEOC, speculated about the human ability to "fall in love and get married and have children if people are going to be working in areas where we don't allow that to happen, or where it happens only under the threat of litigation." Despite Silberman's concerns, office romances continued to be a prominent issue in the workplace. In 1988 a study conducted by the Bureau of National

NEW EXECUTIVE DIVORCE

During the 1990s many business executives and CEOs learned that marriage, like work, can be one of the most important business ventures they would ever undertake. When marriage goes bad, it can be as costly as the collapse of any other business venture. Increasingly, divorce cases involving wealthy businessmen turned ugly, especially over the issues of alimony and other financial settlements. Executives faced the reality of not only handing over large sums of money to their former spouses, but also hefty stock and pension packages, and, in some cases, even a chair on the company board. To fight back, many executives have resorted to stashing hidden assets away in secret Caribbean trusts. Wives have retaliated by airing the couple's dirty laundry for the court and the public. In any case, lawyers stood to benefit the most, often walking away with seven-figure fees. As a result, the boards of many companies now consider the possibility that their executives may face divorce; and if so, what the company must do to protect itself, its assets, and its future from vindictive spouses.

Affairs found that nearly 33 percent of all romances began at work. Dennis M. Powers, in *The Office Romance: Playing With Fire Without Getting Burned* (1999), calculated that between six and eight million Americans entered into such relationships every year in the 1990s. According to a survey conducted in 1994 by the American Management Association, nearly 50 percent of workplace liaisons resulted in a long-term relationship or marriage, "better odds than for nonworkplace romances," Powers pointed out. Nevertheless, the workplace remained a hazardous place to undertake romance. Corporate America started establishing regulations, procedures, and guidelines to govern workplace dating and relationships in the interest of preventing sexual harassment litigation. The growing body of federal, state, and corporate law forced millions of Americans to struggle to clarify what conduct constituted a legally actionable offense. Experts agreed that the most potentially dangerous relationships were those between superiors and subordinates. In the litigious 1990s the central questions seemed always to be just how welcome and reciprocal were the advances, attention, and affection of the superior. "I can't tell you how many cases we get daily that are like this," explained Garry G. Mathiason, senior partner at Littler Mendelson. Mathiason described the breakup of superior-subordinate relationships as "nothing less than a thermonuclear blast occurring in your workplace." Banning workplace relationships, the preferred method among corporate executives for solving the problem of sexual harassment, was also fraught with surprising perils. "All any good attorney would have to do," according to Powers, "is find one person that had a relationship and wasn't fired, and one

who was, and you're off to the races." Wary of the legal ramifications of prohibiting romance, almost as much as permitting or unwittingly encouraging it, companies began to look for ways to discourage it, or at least to manage and contain its often acrimonious repercussions, especially when superiors and subordinates were involved. One policy that became popular was known as "date-and-tell." Under such a rule the couple must tell a supervisor of their relationship. The supervisor is then responsible for informing a designated person in the corporate hierarchy who advises the couple of their legal rights. At the same time, company officials gained the legal protection of knowing that the relationship was consensual and that they were not exposed to litigation by permitting, either through acts of omission or commission, the creation of a hostile work environment. The other approach was the "love contract," to which Littler Mendelson holds almost exclusive title. At the end of the decade love contracts had yet to gain as widespread an acceptance as the "date-and-tell" policy, although Littler Mendelson had drawn up approximately one thousand by the end of 1999, usually in response to an employer's apprehension about a relationship involving a top executive. The love contract, Mathiason admits, "is a tool for extreme cases and indicative of extreme times."

Sensitivity and Sensibility. The most pervasive method of eliminating sexual harassment from the workplace was sensitivity training, which involved examining case studies and conducting role playing within the larger context of promoting diversity. Trainers, whether special consultants, employment attorneys, or human-resources personnel, familiarized executives and employees with the implications of the latest court decisions while discouraging the speech and behavior that caused offense, especially from men. To companies large and small the cost benefit of sensitivity training was unmistakable. "If you can prevent one lawsuit a year and save a legal bill of $50,000, and if it costs you $25,000 to give a seminar, that's pretty hard to resist," said Jerome B. Kauff, a New York employment lawyer. Critics, though, feared an insidious effect. In sensitivity training sessions, instructors encouraged employees to tailor their remarks and conduct to a legal construct known as the "reasonable woman." With the avoidance of litigation being the utmost concern, charged such scholars as Walter Olson, author of *The Excuse Factory: How Employment Law is Paralyzing the American Workplace* (1997), the "reasonable woman" became "whoever is thinnest-skinned." Yet, if the goal was to get men to think twice about their conduct toward women in the workplace, then it seems to have worked. By the end of the decade the most stringent sexual-harassment policies were usually those that workers imposed upon themselves. Many male executives and workers refrained entirely from telling jokes, hugging, or touching their female associates or clients, or complimenting them on their dress or appearance. Most harassment experts suggested that there was no need for this level of prudence, and even the U.S. Supreme Court rendered a decision in favor of "low-level flirtation." Some experts, though, were not surprised at the extreme measures taken to avoid arousing even the suspicion of intentions or actions considered unsavory and potentially litigious. This development, critics insisted, was the predictable result of perceptions, laws, and litigation that were out of proportion to the problems they intended to address. According to Barbara J. Ledeen, executive director for policy at the Independent Women's Forum, the excesses prove that "you can't legislate how people treat each other. The more the legal code eats up the area that used to be reserved for an informal kind of civil code, the worse things are going to get." Proponents of stricter sexual harassment laws and punishments for those who violate them, or who tolerate their violation, on the contrary, pointed out that for many women the old "civil code" included not only lower-paying jobs but also predatory superiors and pornography as standard office decor, as well as sexual and nonsexual intimidation and hostility. "It's not as though there was a neutral state of affairs in which everyone got along peachy keen before Title VII took effect," suggested Yale University law professor Vicki Schultz. Conservative critics blamed feminism, but as Schultz has argued, the sexual harassment policies became more a corporate than a feminist initiative. The original message of sexual harassment law, she declared, was "don't use sex as a weapon of exclusion and marginalization of women." That ideal was gradually transformed into one more in keeping with the traditional objective of management: to rationalize the workplace. "The goal," explained Schultz, "became 'Let's have people leave sex behind when they come to work—it's too volatile.'" Between 1993 and 1998, however, according to a survey conducted by the Society for Human Resource Management, only 4 percent of companies experienced sexual harassment lawsuits. Although not wishing to deny the reality or trivialize the problem of sexual harassment, many companies, such as AT&T, began to implement principles, guidelines, and regulations grounded in practicality and common sense. This approach, explained company spokesman Burke Stinson, was to respond forcefully and unhesitatingly whenever the company uncovered an obvious or egregious instance. "We've had six-figure people recruited into the company at no small expense, and we've let them go within a few weeks because of sexual-harassment activities," Stinson said. "You get that kind of word of mouth, you know you're in a company that takes the problem seriously." Stinson compared sexual-harassment policies at AT&T and many other companies, large and small, to traffic laws. AT&T had 110,000 employees. "That's a fairly big city, and you need sexual-harassment policies the way a city needs traffic laws. While most people are good drivers, there are some fools out there."

Sources:

James Lardner, "Cupid's Cubicles," *U.S. News and World Report,* 125 (14 December 1998): 44–54.

Catherine A. MacKinnon, *Sexual Harassment of Working Women: A Case of Sex Discrimination* (New Haven: Yale University Press, 1979).

Joann Muller, "Ford: The High Cost of Harassment," *Business Week* (15 November 1999): 94–95.

Walter Olson, *The Excuse Factory: How Employment Law is Paralyzing the American Workplace* (New York: Free Press, 1997).

Dennis M. Powers, *The Office Romance: Playing With Fire Without Getting Burned* (New York: American Management Association, 1999).

Jeffrey Rosen, "Fall of Private Man," *New Republic,* 222 (12 June 2000): 22–29.

William Symonds and others, "Divorce Executive Style," *Business Week* (3 August 1998): 56–62.

MERGERS AND MONOPOLIES

Merger Mania. For three consecutive years, between 1995 and 1997, the value of mergers and acquisitions in the United States increased to record levels. Some 27,600 companies joined forces, more than in the entire decade of the 1980s. In 1999 even more companies hastened to unite into behemoth corporations created by the "merger mania."

Rockefeller's Revenge. When in December 1998 Exxon and Mobil agreed to merge, pundits immediately labeled the $86.355 billion deal "Rockefeller's Revenge." Both companies originated as part of John D. Rockefeller Sr.'s Standard Oil monopoly, together accounting for more than half of the Standard Oil Trust until the Supreme Court disbanded it on 15 May 1911. In 1998 as well, Amoco, also a scion of Standard Oil, agreed to be purchased by British Petroleum (BP) for $55 billion. The following year, BP acquired the Atlantic Richfield Company (ARCO), another successor of Standard Oil, for $33.7 billion. Initially, the U.S. assets of BP derived in large measure from the absorption of another offspring of Standard Oil, Sohio. What the judiciary put asunder at the beginning of the twentieth century, entrepreneurs have been busy putting back together at its end. During the 1990s "Big Oil" got even bigger. Historical analogies, however, only go so far. At the zenith of its power, Standard Oil controlled 84 percent of the petroleum market in the United States. Exxon-Mobil, although the largest oil company in the world, by contrast, controls approximately 22 percent. Yet, the economic conditions that prompted Exxon and Mobil to merge bore a striking resemblance to those that prevailed in the past. Ron Chernow, author of *Titan: The Life of John D. Rockefeller, Sr.* (1998), said in an interview that "the economic environment was absolutely the same in the 1870s, when Rockefeller began the trust, as it is today." When the Exxon-Mobil merger was proposed and completed, there was a worldwide glut in crude oil that kept prices low. Although they rose considerably afterward, in December 1998 gasoline prices hovered around 97 cents per gallon, the equivalent of 23 cents per gallon in 1970 dollars. In addition, the price of crude oil fell from $23 a barrel in 1997 to $11 a barrel in 1998. The reason, of course, was supply. In 1998 the oil industry produced approximately one million more barrels of oil per day than it sold. The surplus, in part triggered by the decrease in the consumption of oil in depressed Asian markets, drove down the price. Throughout its history the oil industry has been plagued by overproduction. "The challenge has always been to control the surplus," explained Leo Drollas, deputy director of the Centre for Global Energy Studies in Lon-

Competing gas stations in Stamford, Connecticut, on 30 November 1999, prior to the announcement of a merger of their companies (AP/Wide World Photos)

don. Excess supply and falling prices created a strong incentive for consolidation. By merging, Exxon and Mobil cut production and distribution costs and maintained their profit margins, as had their common ancestor, Standard Oil. Another factor prompting the union was the increasing supply of capital necessary to develop new sources of oil. Virtually all potential oil fields are in areas that are geographically remote and politically unstable, such as those located in West Africa and along the Caspian Sea. By combining, Exxon and Mobile hoped that they would attain greater leverage in negotiations with foreign governments and thereby enhance their competitive advantage in the global marketplace.

Media Moguls. On 22 April 1999, just six weeks after completing the $69.9 billion acquisition of cable giant Tele-Communications, Inc., Michael Armstrong, CEO of AT&T, announced plans to make a $63.1 billion deal. This time the target was the MediaOne Group. Armstrong's offer trumped an earlier $48 billion bid that Comcast Corporation had made. If approved, the merger will make AT&T the single largest cable operator in the United States, reaching no fewer than 60 percent of households with telephone, cable, and Internet services. Another merger, announced on 28 July 1998 (and approved by the Federal Communications Commission [FCC] in June 2000) brought together two prominent media and telecommunications firms, Bell Atlantic and GTE. The $70.9 billion deal created the largest local telephone company and unleashed a telecommunications colossus in an already rapidly consolidating market. The new company, known as

Verizon Communications, will sell communications packages ranging from long-distance and local telephone service to wireless and high-speed Internet access. Industry analysts also expect Verizon to expand into video entertainment and interactive gaming. "They certainly control a huge, huge, area," commented Meredith Rosenberg, an analyst with the Yankee Group in Boston. "They have the direct pipe line to the consumer, and they can really control the customers. It's just a huge opportunity in terms of selling bundled services. The possibilities are endless." The merger brought sixty-three million local telephone lines, or 33 percent of all lines in the United States, under the control of Verizon. In addition, Verizon has approximately twenty-five million wireless telephone customers, more than twice the number of AT&T, making Verizon the largest wireless operation in the country. Company officials reported that Verizon had a market worth of nearly $150 billion with annual revenues of $60 billion. As such, the deal dwarfs the $15.1 billion merger of Time-Warner in 1990 and even the $18.3 billion acquisition of Capital Cities/ABC by the Walt Disney Corporation in 1996. All, however, may be surpassed by the proposed purchase of Sprint by MCI WorldCom for $129 billion, a merger still pending at the end of 1999.

Breaking Up Is Hard to Do. On 18 May 1998 the Department of Justice and twenty states filed an antitrust suit in U.S. district court in Washington, D.C., against the Microsoft Corporation. The suit alleged that Microsoft illegally manipulated technology to control the software industry and undermine its competition, particularly

Netscape Communications Corporation, the maker of Netscape Navigator, which Microsoft executives feared would marginalize the Microsoft Windows program. At the time the suit was filed, some critics of Microsoft, such as Payam Zamani, cofounder and executive vice president of Autoweb.com, went so far as to claim that "if Microsoft wins this battle, it means the Information Age will be Bill Gates's." For his part, William Henry "Bill" Gates III, the chairman of Microsoft, maintained that his company had done nothing illegal. "All the contracts we did are perfectly normal, legal contracts that have in no way made it impossible for Netscape to market their products," Gates asserted in 1998. The Justice Department won round one. On 7 June 2000 U.S. District Judge Thomas Penfield Jackson ruled that Microsoft was a monopoly. Calling Microsoft "untrustworthy" and characterizing its executives as "unwilling to accept the notion that [they] broke the law," Judge Jackson ordered the company be split in two, one branch controlling the Windows operating system, which runs 90 percent of all personal computers (PCs), and the other incorporating all additional applications, including the Internet Explorer, web-browsing software, Microsoft Office, Microsoft Network, and WebTV. Jackson also imposed stringent restrictions on the conduct of Microsoft in an attempt to remedy its antitrust violations. If the ruling is carried out, Microsoft will have to disclose the inner workings of the Windows program to competitors to make certain it is compatible with their systems; offer the manufacturers of PCs uniform pricing for all Microsoft products; and permit PC manufacturers to customize the main Windows screen and to delete Microsoft browsers, e-mail, and other software from their systems. Jackson's ruling marked the most severe antitrust prescription since the breakup of AT&T in 1984. Gates criticized the decision as "an unwarranted and unjustified intrusion" that in effect meant the "government can take away what you created if it turns out to be too popular." Other Microsoft officials called Jackson's ruling "draconian" and a "corporate death sentence" that will disrupt the computer industry and damage the economy. Although appeals could delay implementation of the decision for years, Justice Department officials remained optimistic that the division of Microsoft will encourage the sort of accelerated technological innovation and development that they believe Microsoft inhibited. The most likely to benefit are such companies as Sun Microsystems and Palm and Psion, which are creating the wireless operating systems of the future. If these companies flourish, bulky PCs will be displaced by an assortment of Internet appliances, such as digital assistants and digital cellular telephones, that run on non-Windows operating systems such as Linux, Macintosh, and Unix. Many within the computer industry, such as Mike Pettit, president of ProComp, an industry trade association that lobbied the government to investigate Microsoft, regarded the decision as ultimately to the benefit of Microsoft. On balance, Pettit concluded, the split "opens up opportunities . . . for them to innovate and market creatively. They no longer can fall back on illegal business practices." Rob Enderle, senior analyst at Giga Information Group in Santa Clara, California, added that "Microsoft is big and unwieldy at a time when they [sic] face more competition than ever. This gives them the ability to focus and shape their company accordingly." Whatever the final outcome of the case, Microsoft is unlikely to lose its customer base. Industry estimates suggest that it will take at least five years for its market share to fall below 50 percent, if it ever does. Tom Kemp, vice president of products at NetIQ, a systems management software firm also located in Santa Clara, pointed out that companies invested a fortune in Windows and other Microsoft products during the 1990s and are not about to "abandon Microsoft overnight."

Sources:

Ron Chernow, *Titan: The Life of John D. Rockefeller, Sr.* (New York: Random House, 1998).

Amy Cortese, "The Battle for the Cyber Future," *Business Week* (1 June 1998): 38–41.

Paul Davidson, "Appeal Could Go Directly to Supreme Court," *USA Today,* 8 June 2000.

Davidson, "Microsoft Awaits a New Hand," *USA Today,* 8 June 2000.

Mike France, "What Penalties for Microsoft?," *Business Week* (22 February 1999): 76, 80.

Steve Hamm, "Microsoft: How Vulnerable?," *Business Week* (22 February 1999): 60–64.

Philip J. Longman and Jack Egan, "Why Big Oil is Getting a Lot Bigger," *U.S. News & World Report,* 125 (14 December 1998): 26–28.

Stacy Perman, "Is Bigger Really Better?," *Time,* 151 (27 April 1998): 56.

Gary Rivlin, *The Plot to Get Bill Gates: An Irreverent Investigation of the World's Richest Man—and the People Who Hate Him* (New York: Times Books, 1999).

Richard Siklos and Amy Barrett, "The Net-Phone-TV-Cable Monster," *Business Week* (10 May 1999): 30–32.

Jon Swartz, "Microsoft Split Ordered," *USA Today,* 8 June 2000.

"Telephone Giants Cleared to Merge," *Richmond Times-Dispatch,* 15 June 2000.

RELIGION IN THE WORKPLACE

Corporate Spirituality. Since 1993 three hundred employees of the Xerox Corporation, from managers to clerks, have participated in "vision quests," a $400 million program designed to revolutionize product development. Alone for twenty-four hours in the New Mexico desert or the Catskill Mountains, workers communed with nature, seeking insights to help the struggling copier company. Many within and outside the company snickered and scoffed, but, says John F. Elter, the Xerox chief engineer who headed the project, "for almost everyone, this was a real spiritual experience." The outcome was one of the most surprising corporate success stories of the 1990s: the production of the 265DC, a 97 percent recyclable copier-fax-printer. Word of this venture attracted senior executives from companies as diverse as Ford Motors, Nike, and Harley-Davidson to Xerox design offices in Rochester, New York, in September 1999, not only to see the machine but also to discuss the program that inspired it. Executives of other companies, such as Taco Bell, Pizza Hut, and Wal-Mart, were also unashamedly bringing spirituality and/or religion into the workplace. If they had attempted to do so during the 1980s, they would have inspired ridicule, ostracism, and perhaps even a lawsuit. By the 1990s, however, a spiritual revival had swept corporate America as executives of all faiths mixed religion and management, transferring into offices, shops, and factories the lessons formerly confined to churches, temples, synagogues, and mosques.

The Corporate "God Squad." Throughout the 1990s such books as *Jesus, CEO : Using Ancient Wisdom for Visionary Leadership* (1995) and *The Seven Habits of Highly Effective People* (1989) became best-sellers among corporate executives interested in developing a spiritual life. Recognizing opportunity when they saw it, such spiritual gurus as Deepak Chopra and M. Scott Peck began to counsel executives about how to solve the problems of their companies and how to enhance the happiness and productivity of their employees. It thus became commonplace for high-level corporate executives regularly to attend prayer breakfasts or luncheons and spiritual conferences. In Minneapolis, for example, executives began gathering monthly to listen to such corporate leaders as William W. George of Medtronic, Inc. or Marilyn Carlson Nelson of Carlson Company expound solutions to the problems of modern business based on scripture. In the Silicon Valley, a group of high-tech Hindus, including Suhas Patil of Cirrus Logic, Gururaj "Desh" Deshpande of Cascade Communications, and Krishan Kalra of BioGenex, attempted to integrate modern technology with ancient spirituality. Kalra turned to the *Bhagavad Gita* (ca. 1st–2nd century A.D.) for spiritual solace and lessons on how to guide his business. In Boston, executives met at invitation-only prayer breakfasts called "First Tuesday," an ecumenical gathering still shrouded in the utmost secrecy. Jeffery B. Swartz, chief executive of Timberland Company and an Orthodox Jew, began to consult both the Torah and his rabbi about business decisions and company policies. Nor were ordinary workers excluded from or immune to this corporate spiritual revival. S. Truett Cathy, an evangelical Christian and the CEO of Chick-fil-A, sponsored a prayer service every Monday morning for all employees who cared to attend. Cathy also closed his restaurants on Sundays to enable his workers to keep the Sabbath and spend time with their families. More than ten thousand workplace Bible study and prayer groups formed and met regularly during the decade, according to statistics compiled by the Fellowship for Companies for Christ International. In 1994 there was only one annual conference on spirituality in the workplace; by 1999 there were thirty. The trend became so pronounced that even the academy could not help but take note of it. The Universities of Denver, New Haven, and St. Thomas (Minnesota) established separate research centers devoted to the investigation and analysis of corporate spirituality, while the number of books published on the subject nearly quadrupled, from twenty in 1990 to seventy-nine in 1999. Laura Nash, a business ethicist at Harvard Divinity School and author of *Believers in Business* (1994), stated that "spirituality in the workplace is exploding."

The Quest for Meaning and Productivity. According to a Gallup research poll conducted in 1999, 95 percent of Americans said they believed in God or a universal spirit, and 51 percent agreed that modern life left them too busy to pray as often or as deeply as they would like. Spending more time than ever before on the job, Americans started bringing their faith to work in an effort to find a deeper sense of meaning and fulfillment. That quest was one of the motives behind the new spirituality. Perhaps the most important impetus, however, was mounting evidence that workplace programs emphasizing spirituality not only eased employees' psyches but also increased their productivity. Data compiled by McKinsey & Company of Australia showed that when corporations engaged in programs that used spiritual techniques, productivity improved and turnover declined. Ian I. Mitroff and Elizabeth A. Denton's *Spiritual Audit of Corporate America: A Hard Look at Spirituality, Religion, and Values in the Workplace* (1999) disclosed that employees who worked for companies they considered to be "spiritual" were less fearful, less likely to compromise their values, and more prepared to devote themselves to their jobs and colleagues. Mitroff, a professor at the Marshall School of Business at the University of Southern California, conjectured that "spirituality could be the ultimate competitive advantage." Sixty percent of those interviewed for the study welcomed the presence of spirituality in the workplace, so long as no proselytizing or indoctrination took place.

Perils of Workplace Spirituality. The impulse to convert the unbeliever, of course, was always a danger. As spirituality penetrated more deeply into the workplace, pointed out Howard A. Simon, a San Francisco employment attorney, "more and more conflicts" erupted. On one side were evangelical Christians who attached a conservative social and political agenda to their spiritual message. On the other were New Agers who advocated self-help and self-realization, as well as a host of individuals who held singular beliefs or engaged in unusual practices. Companies had to deal with employees who believed themselves to be the Messiah, workers who fell to their knees outside colleague's offices or cubicles to pray aloud or speak in tongues, and even a warlock who insisted that he receive Halloween off as a day of religious observance. More serious, the Equal Employment Opportunity Commission (EEOC) reported that since 1992 there was a 29 percent increase in the number of religious-discrimination cases involving the workplace. Meanwhile, skeptics contend that the spiritual revival was merely another management ploy to exploit people's faith and spiritual longing in an effort to enhance profit margins. To circumvent such problems, many companies and executives put forth a pluralist, ecumenical, nondenominational message, which placed a premium on free expression and which pundits labeled "secular spirituality." Still, problems remained. Abuses included management consultants who were allegedly operatives for the Church of Scientology and who used their seminars to recruit new members. Throughout 1998 and

Two employees of the Ventura County district attorney's office, Vinse Gilliam and Mindy Morter, pray on 2 September 1999 during a Christian meeting, which gathers at work once a week (AP/Wide World Photos).

1999 companies worried about employees who were seemingly overwhelmed by a phenomenon dubbed "millennial madness," which often included violent scenarios. One of the most notorious cases of religious harassment in the workplace involved Jennifer Venters, a former radio dispatcher for the Delphi, Indiana, Police Department. Venters alleged that Chief of Police Larry Ives objected to her living with a female roommate, asked if she had entertained male police officers with pornography, accused her of engaging in sexual relations with members of her family, and avowed that she had sacrificed animals as part of a Satanic ceremony. According to court documents, Ives later suggested that if Venters refused to change her sinful ways, she would be "better off just killing herself." The Seventh U.S. Circuit Court of Appeals found merit in Venter's accusations of religious harassment at work and bound the case over for trial. The dispute was later settled out of court for $105,000 without admission of liability either from Ives or the city of Delphi. In general, federal legislation requires companies to make "reasonable accommodations" for employees with religious or spiritual needs, just as they are compelled to do for the disabled. Title VII of the Civil Rights Act of 1964 offers broad protection to religion. The courts, however, have been consistent and exacting about not permitting managers or employees to create a "hostile work environment" for others by harassing employees about their beliefs.

Sources:

Michelle Conlin, "Religion in the Workplace: The Growing Presence of Spirituality in Corporate America," *Business Week* (1 November 1999): 151–158.

Stephen R. Covey, *The Seven Habits of Highly Effective People* (New York: Simon & Schuster, 1989).

George Gallup Jr. and Timothy Jones, *The Next American Spirituality: Finding God in the Twenty-First Century* (Colorado Springs, Colo.: Cook Communications, 2000).

Charles Handy, *The Hungry Spirit: Beyond Capitalism: A Quest for Purpose in the Modern World* (New York: Broadway, 1999).

Laurie Beth Jones, *Jesus, CEO: Using Ancient Wisdom for Visionary Leadership* (New York: Hyperion, 1995).

Ian I. Mitroff and Elizabeth A. Denton, *A Spiritual Audit of Corporate America: A Hard Look at Spirituality, Religion, and Values in the Workplace* (San Francisco: Jossey-Bass, 1999).

Laura L. Nash, *Believers in Business* (Nashville, Tenn.: Nelson, 1994).

SMALL BUSINESS

Does Size Really Matter? With multibillion-dollar corporate mergers dominating the business news throughout the 1990s, it is counterintuitive to think of small companies flourishing and prospering. Most did not; approximately three out of five (60 percent) small businesses begun in the decade failed. Those that did thrive were often the targets of corporate takeovers or buyouts. Yet, by the end of the decade, small businesses accounted for 99 percent of the 23.3 million nonfarm businesses in the United States, according to statistics compiled by the Small Business Administration (SBA). Sole proprietorships made up 16.7 million of these small businesses, while 1.6 million were partnerships and 5 million were corporations. The SBA noted that these figures were based on tax returns, so the number of sole proprietorships may be inflated by artists, freelance writers, and other self-employed persons who were not technically businesses. As of 1996, the last year for which complete statistics are available, small businesses employed 53 percent of the workforce in the private sector, made 47 percent of the sales, and accounted for 51 percent of the total private sector output. According to the Department of Labor, approximately 750,000 small businesses were created each year; about 10 percent, or 75,000, of them failed within the first ten to twelve months of operation. Those that succeed, however, often do better than their bigger counterparts; the most successful far outperformed their larger counterparts, generating an average annual sales growth of 59.8 percent and an average annual earnings growth of 102.8 percent during 1996 and 1997. Companies listed on the Standard & Poor's (S&P) Industrial Index, by contrast, achieved an average annual sales growth of 7.6 percent and average annual earnings growth of 9.8 percent during the same period. The return on capital investment among the best one hundred small businesses averaged 31.1 percent, while the S & P average was only 11.9 percent. Small business, however, did not fare as well on Wall Street. Throughout the 1990s, big caps consistently out-performed small caps in the stock market. When small caps began to make advances in the second half of 1997, the Asian financial crisis killed the rally. While the S & P 500 stock index rose nearly 32 percent in 1997, the Russell 2000, a barometer for small-company stocks, rose only 22 percent. Small businesses, nevertheless, remained an attractive potential investment. Small-cap stocks were considerably and consistently cheaper than the stocks of large corporations, and the price-to-earnings ratio of small-caps, although not as high, was still viable. As of 1998 the price-to-earnings ratio of the S & P 500 was 22.4, based on an earnings growth of 10.2 percent. The price-to-earnings ratio of the Russell 2000 was slightly lower at 20.4, but with a much higher earnings growth of 20.6 percent. Those numbers, especially the high growth rates, kept enough investment and venture capital flowing into small businesses to produce some stunning results.

Three Small Businesses That Succeeded. No single type of small business provided the design for success. Small businesses that hit it big during the 1990s engaged in a wide array of enterprises, from drug testing to software troubling-shooting to motor sports, horse racing, and gaming; they had in common, however, a combination of business savvy, clear focus, and relentless discipline that enabled them to outperform even their larger rivals. Among the most successful and fastest growing small businesses was Kendle International Inc., a drug-testing company located in Cincinnati, Ohio. In 1998 Kendle topped the list of Hot Growth Companies compiled by *Business Week*. Between 1994 and 1997 its revenues expanded at the astounding annual rate of 168.9 percent, to $44.2 million. During that same period, net income grew 158.8 percent

ROLL-UPS

The brainchild of venture-capital investor Steve Harter, "roll-ups" was an unusual and innovative way to bring together small companies engaged in similar businesses. Beginning in the early 1990s, Harter approached several companies and arranged for an IPO to buy the companies and combine them into a single unit. The earnings allowed the entrepreneurs to buy additional companies. In the process, many employees and managers of the small companies became millionaires through the stock options offered to them. Harter's critics, who dubbed the "roll-ups" as "poof IPO's," claimed that it was often difficult to integrate several different companies and that, if the new company grew too quickly, the whole deal could collapse, leaving stocks tumbling, investors out of luck, and companies in ruins.

annually, to $3.7 million. The company also boasted an average annual return on capital investment of 59.3 percent. In the early 1990s, however, Kendle, despite a reputation for integrity and reliability in running clinical drug tests, was losing business to larger and more well-known competitors. The owners, Candace Kendle Bryan and her husband Christopher C. Bergen, began making plans to go public, which the company did in August 1997. Since then the value of Kendle stock has risen steadily and the company began to acquire other laboratories. In 1998 its sales nearly doubled to $84.5 million, with earnings growing 148 percent, to $6.2 million.

Aris Corporation. For Paul Song, chairman and CEO of Aris Corporation, the computer network and software problems that cause expensive headaches for other companies are the stuff profits are made from. The specialty of Song's company is making the latest software easy to use. Although Aris, based in Bellevue, Washington, competes with the giants such as Andersen Consulting, revenues soared at an annual rate of 96.8 percent between 1994 and 1997, reaching a high of $55 million with net earnings of $5.3 million. When Song launched Aris in the early 1990s, he had only $1,000 in a savings account and an answering machine. He won his first big contract to help the Weyerhauser Company implement a computer network that would track information from its lumber mills to its box plants. By the end of the decade Aris had become a six-hundred-person operation serving the likes of Boeing, the Internal Revenue Service (IRS), and Lockheed Martin. Song realized as early as 1993 that in addition to fine-tuning networks and software, there was money to be made in offering technical support and training after the system was up and running. By 1997, 39 percent of company revenue derived from such training classes. Aris even instructs the marketing staff at Microsoft on how to use its own Exchange e-mail program. Aris went public in 1997 and raised sufficient capital from its initial public offering to

Ed Vidler, the owner, helps customers in his 5 & 10 store in East Aurora, New York (AP/Wide World Photos).

acquire four rival companies in the United States and two British consulting firms. In 1998 its revenues rose 64 percent, to $90 million, and profits rose 36 percent, to $7.2 million.

Dover Downs. When Dover Downs Entertainment Inc. opened Dover Downs, a horse-and-motor racetrack, in 1969, the project and the company nearly failed. By the mid 1990s, however, thanks to the booming gaming and motor-sports business, the company racked up an average annual revenue growth of 99.8 percent and an average annual earnings growth of 70.9 percent between 1994 and 1997, to accompany a 31.6 percent return on invested capital. Since going public in October of 1996 the value of its stock had risen 85 percent. "They've evolved from an undervalued little company into a real growth story," said Kevin C. Holt, a research analyst at Strong Capital Management, Inc., which holds nearly 130,000 shares of Dover stock. Dover Downs can thank the state of Delaware for some of its good fortune. In 1994 the state legislature passed a law that permitted horse-racing tracks to install slot machines. The law was a boon to Dover Downs. Gaming revenues increased from less than $1 million in 1994 to $81 million by 1997. In March 1998 the legislature passed an additional law that doubled, to two thousand, the number of slot machines permitted at any one location. The income from gaming funded an aggressive program of expansion. In the fall of 1997 Dover purchased Nashville Speedway USA for $3 million and, in conjunction with Gaylord Entertainment, is building a $40 million racing complex outside of Nashville. In March 1998 Dover struck a deal to merge with the Grand Prix Association of Long Beach, California, which owns tracks in St. Louis and Memphis. Those deals gave Dover Entertainment a coast-to-coast presence and, by the end of the decade, vaulted it into the big leagues of auto racing.

Three Small Businesses That Failed. During the 1990s small businesses also failed for a variety of reasons. Most commonly, however, they ran into serious trouble when they miscalculated the market for their products, misunderstood their competition, or moved into new enterprises without adequate preparation or for which they may have been ill-suited. In 1996 Parlux Fragrances Inc. exuded the aroma of success. The company had enjoyed double digit profit increases under the leadership of Illia Lekach, a Russian immigrant, and garnered $8 million in earnings from $68 million in sales by March 1996. Since then, however, its performance has not smelled as sweet. In both 1997 and 1998 Parlux lost almost as much as it made in 1996, with losses averaging about $6.7 million per year. The value of its stock dropped 81 percent by the end of April 1998, and Lekach admitted that Parlux "suffered from a series of mistakes." The most serious problems seem to have arisen from the introduction of Perry Ellis America in 1996, a fragrance named after the clothing designer who died in 1986, because it was unable to compete with another product that appeared at the same time: Tommy, marketed under the name of the fashionable designer Tommy Hilfiger. The fate of Parlux provides a cautionary tale for other small companies, showing how quickly even successful businesses can falter and fail. If the earnings projections of Wall Street stock analysts are not met, the results can be disastrous.

Other Disasters. Another promising small company, Lafayette Industries Inc., fared even worse than Parlux. Lafayette enjoyed considerable success manufacturing display cabinets for department stores. Buoyed by its achievements, Lafayette took a wrong turn in 1995 into the manufacture of, among other things, debit-card vending machines. The transformation failed and in March 1997 Nasdaq removed Lafayette stock from its small-cap listing; the company continued to flounder. Netmanage Inc., which produced software that enabled desktop computers to access the Internet, also experienced a similar fate. The company found itself awash in a sea of red ink when Microsoft Windows 95, which bundles in the same Internet features, made Netmanage's software package superfluous to PC users and thus captured and dominated the market Netmanage sought to enter. As a result, the stock value of Netmanage plummeted 76.3 percent by 1998.

Sources:

Amy Barrett, "Hot Growth Companies," *Business Week* (1 June 1998): 70–74.

Barrett, "Speed Demon," *Business Week* (1 June 1998): 82, 86.

Seanna Browder, "A Software Tuner and Coach," *Business Week* (1 June 1998): 78, 82.

Peter Galuskza, "The $44 Million Mom-And-Pop," *Business Week* (1 June 1998): 74–76.

WORKERS

Me First! In the wide open, freewheeling job market of the 1990s the mantra became "Me First!" Employers may have welcomed or lamented the newly emboldened U.S. workforce, but they accepted it as a fact of life. As the economy prospered the unemployment rate fell to less than 5 percent. With fewer workers entering the job market and competing for more jobs, prospective employees had greater leverage than they had enjoyed at any time since the 1960s. "In 35 years in the recruiting business I have never seen the equal of these times," said Alan Schonberg, president and CEO of Management Recruiters International in Cleveland, Ohio. "This is the most pervasive, job-candidate-driven market possibly ever." A survey released in April 1997 by the American Management Association found that nearly half of the four hundred human-resources executives polled from medium and large companies said skilled workers were in short supply. Sixty-seven percent of the executives in mining, manufacturing, and construction, as well as business and professional services, predicted that the situation would intensify by the year 2000. Although few experts believed the hiring bonanza would last forever, virtually all agreed that it had already brought revolutionary changes to the workplace that will redefine work, and attitudes toward it, well into the twenty-first century. If the Great Depression of the 1930s produced a cautious and frugal generation, modest in its

desires and expectations, the "long boom" of the 1990s created a demanding and impatient generation, brazen in its pursuit of the main chance. Certainly the job market supported taking bold action. During the second half of the decade, employers worried lest a labor shortage force them to close a division or postpone the launch of a new product. They were thus more likely to accommodate a current or perspective employee who requested a promotion, substantial raise or signing bonus, stock options, flexible work schedule, additional vacation time, or special training at company expense. If one company was unwilling to meet an employee's or candidate's demands, they easily marketed themselves elsewhere. The establishment of such job-finding mechanisms as career databases on the Internet, job fairs, and internships gave those looking for work more ways to access and explore new opportunities. "Job candidates today can afford to be picky and go for what they really want," explained Marilyn Moats Kennedy, managing partner for Career Strategies in Wilmette, Illinois. Former Secretary of Labor Robert B. Reich saw the changing nature of, and attitudes toward, work reflected in the growing numbers of self-employed, which totaled 10.5 million in 1997, compared to 7 million in 1970. In 1997 Reich calculated that the self-employed would soon make up as much as 20 percent of the workforce. The self-employed work first for themselves, Reich declared, and are willing "to hopscotch" among jobs. "Loyalty is dead," he concluded.

Hidden Anxieties. In part fear drove this new audacity. Despite the remarkable prosperity of the 1990s, to remain competitive, companies such as AT&T; Sears, Roebuck; IBM; Boeing; and others faced constant pressure to cut costs. Wall Street analysts punished them for falling short of earning projections, and overseas rivals benefiting from cheaper labor enjoyed a distinct competitive advantage. The easiest, quickest, and surest way to cut costs remained trimming the size of the workforce. In 1996, for example, AT&T announced it would lay off forty thousand workers by 1999. In 1998 alone, in the midst of unprecedented affluence, U.S. corporations laid off 103,000 workers, the most since 1993 according to the outplacement specialist firm Challenger, Gray & Christmas. Between 1980 and 1999 the U.S. economy lost 43,000,000 jobs. Economists at the Federal Reserve Bank of Chicago estimated that in 1995, the most recent year from which complete data existed, workers had a 3.4 percent chance of being laid off. That risk, although comparatively small, increased workers' anxieties and prompted them continually to reevaluate their options. If a worker could not count on his or her present employer to continue providing a paycheck, why not consider an offer from a rival? Increasing numbers of workers opted out entirely and incorporated themselves, selling their services to companies eager to give people work without giving them jobs or paying the costs of insurance and pensions.

Free Agents, Nomads, and Globalists. The good news was that while the U.S. economy had lost 43,000,000 jobs, it had created 71,000,000 new positions, a net gain of 28,000,000. The booming economy, combined with changing ideas of

During the twelfth annual DISCO International Career Resources Inc. job fair in Boston on 23 October 1998, Yuici Ando, representing Morgan Stanley, interviews a prospective employee interested in relocating to Japan (AP/Wide World Photos).

work, made older methods of career planning obsolete. "Free Agents" joined the expanding ranks of the self-employed and tried freelancing their way to professional and, they hoped, financial independence. "Nomads" went to work for one company, but never stopped looking for another job with higher pay, better benefits, and additional perquisites. When they found what they were looking for, they changed jobs and began the process anew. "Globalists," a class of corporate paladins who "have laptop, will travel," also surfaced, vaulting from time zone to time zone in the modern, borderless, international economy. The most arresting, and often most frightening, aspect of the new style of employment was the enormous demands it made on workers. Even those who remained in corporate jobs, the old-fashioned "Organization Man" or "Organization Woman," had to acquire skills and experience that were transferable to other companies and even other industries. Free Agents, Nomads, and Globalists had to stay informed about current developments in an array of fields, from marketing to finance to technology, simply to remain employable. As a consequence, concluded Joanne B. Ciulla, the Coston Family Chair of Leadership and Ethics at the Jepson School of Leadership Studies, University of Richmond, Americans in the 1990s worked too hard and enjoyed life too little. Part of the problem, in Ciulla's view, was that corporations sought to squeeze maximum profits from their employees, whether they worked full-time, part-time, or freelanced. For their part, workers reflected the growing unwillingness to live with less in

the way of material possessions, and so readily acquiesced to company demands as long as the pay and compensation were to their liking. They purchased their "independence" at a high price.

Blue-Collar Workers. Blue-collar workers had a different problem, and the new styles of employment provided them fewer opportunities and little solace. For skilled workers, especially electricians, carpenters, and pipe fitters, there was abundant work. According to the National Center for Construction Education and Research, builders and contractors complained of shortages of skilled workers throughout the decade. Bureau of Labor Statistics projections suggested, however, that between 1996 and 2006 the five fastest growing occupations will be database manager (+118 percent), computer engineer (+109 percent), systems analyst (+103 percent), personal aide (+85 percent), and physical therapy assistant (+79 percent). The growth of such occupations suggested the development of a high-tech and skilled service economy. Those who did not aspire, or who lacked the education and skills, to enter this new job market faced rather bleak prospects. For such workers, wages rose only slightly during the 1990s, an average of approximately 3.8 percent, although complete statistics were unavailable as of 1999. Starting salaries for corporate attorneys, by contrast, rose 12 percent in 1997. Graduates with an MBA who were recruited by major Wall Street investment banks did even better. Their starting salaries, including bonuses, increased 33 percent. There was no evidence that economic prosperity did anything to ease the widening gap in income distribution. In addition, many blue-collar jobs, especially in manufacturing, continued to evaporate. Estimates suggest that by 2006 manufacturing jobs will account for a mere 12 percent of the workforce. Between 1994 and 2005 the Bureau of Labor Statistics estimates that the five fastest growing jobs in real numbers will be cashiers (+562,000), janitors (+559,000), retail sales clerks (+532,000), waiters and waitresses (+479,000), and registered nurses (+473,000). Although all require some skills, only nursing requires a college education. Meanwhile, the five jobs expected to undergo the most severe decline are farmers (-273,000), typists (-212,000), bookkeepers, accountants, and auditors (-178,000), bank tellers (-152,000), and garment workers (-140,000), each the victims not only of a changing economy but, also to some extent, of technological obsolescence. If they did not learn a new set of skills, many unem-

ployed and unskilled workers were virtually unemployable in any but the most low-paying service-sector jobs. The new economy was leaving them behind.

Sources:

Joanne B. Ciulla, *The Working Life: The Promise and Betrayal of Modern Work* (New York: Times Books, 2000).

Kim Clark, "Gimme, Gimme, Gimme," *U.S. News & World Report*, 127 (1 November 1999): 88–92.

Clark, "Why It Pays to Quit," *U.S. News & World Report*, 127 (1 November 1999): 47–86.

Louise Lief, "An End to the Dead-End Job?" *U.S. News & World Report*, 123 (27 October 1997): 86–87.

Daniel McGinn and John McCormick, "Your Next Job," *Newsweek*, 133 (1 February 1999): 43–45.

Amy Saltzman, "Making It in a Sizzling Economy," *U.S. News & World Report*, 122 (23 June 1997): 50–58.

Saltzman, "When Less is More," *U.S. News & World Report*, 123 (27 October 1997): 79–84.

HEADLINE MAKERS

JILL BARAD

1951-
PRESIDENT AND CEO OF MATTEL INC.

No Goals. Jill Elikann Barad's life was not always focused. Born in Queens, New York, Barad grew up in a creative household. Her father was a TV director and her mother, an artist and pianist. By the time she was in her teens, her life appeared dominated by show business and fashion. She tried college for three years, but then decided to take a job selling cosmetics. After a year she returned to school and got her degree in 1973. "I had no clue what I wanted to do. I just saw jobs as fun. I had no goals," she later admitted. She tried her hand at several jobs: modeling, acting, and as a traveling cosmetician-trainer for Coty Cosmetics. In 1979 she married Thomas K. Barad, an aspiring movie producer. The couple moved to Los Angeles. Soon after the birth of her first child, Barad landed a job in Mattel's novelty development unit in 1981. Her first project, "A Bad Case of Worms," flopped, but Barad's enthusiasm and energy got her noticed.

Fight for Your Point of View. Soon Barad pushed for better assignments. Finally she was moved in 1985 to the Barbie Division as one of two product managers. Her job was to "update" the doll, which Mattel had introduced in 1959. Barad developed several new looks and occupations for Barbie. In time, she built up revenues from the doll from a respectable $200 million to an astounding $1.9 billion. In the process, Barad also earned a reputation for being an outspoken and combative maverick both within and outside the company. In 1992 Barad's tenacity paid off. She became president and CEO of Mattel at a time when company fortunes were particularly shaky.

A Living Doll? One of Barad's favorite statistics is that every second three Barbie dolls are sold. Even though Barad flaunts her own kind of flamboyance, she is no Barbie doll herself. Since becoming head of Mattel Inc., Barad has overseen an operation that in 1994 earned more than $2.7 billion in revenues. Of that amount, the Barbie doll, thirty-five years old and still going strong, earned $1 billion. By 1998 revenues soared to more than $4.8 billion. Barad is proud of what the toy has accomplished. "I'm very conscious of showing that Barbie's been an astronaut or that she's a doctor," Barad explained. "It's what we do in the world, not what we look like, that will be remembered." Coming from a woman who first graced the halls of the venerable toy company in short purple skirts, these are words to ponder.

Troubles in Toyland. During her tenure as CEO, Barad restored Mattel to robust financial health and then, in October 1999, watched as revenues began to tumble. Children moved away from playing with traditional toys to hyped interactive gadgetry. Mattel had yet to make many inroads in that market. Barad embarked on cost-cutting measures and tried to make Barbie even "hipper" in an attempt to boost sales. Part of Barad's strategy was to take the company beyond the family-products realm into such areas as educational software, a move that as of 1999 cost Mattel anywhere from $50 to $100 million and substantial losses in fourth-quarter earnings. Some insiders say that Barad had only herself to blame for not paying more attention to the bottom line and chasing away management talent—in seven years, five executives quit because of Barad. Others point to the rigorous and microscopic attention that has been the bane of many leading female executives. The question that remained at the end of the decade was how long Barad could hold on before she was either forced out or chose to leave the company.

Sources:

"Jill Barad," *People*, 41 (9 May 1994): 109.

J. P. Donlon, "A Doll's House," *Chief Executive* (September 1997): 32–36.

Kathleen Morris, "Trouble in Toyland," *Business Week* (15 March 1999): 40.

"Princess on a Steeple," *The Economist*, 353 (9 October 1999): 84.

"The Rise of Jill Barad," *Business Week* (25 May 1998): 112–119.

JEFF BEZOS

1964-

CHAIRMAN OF AMAZON.COM

Pioneering Spirit. The Bezos family can trace its American roots to Colonel Robert Hall, who at the beginning of the nineteenth century moved to San Antonio, Texas, from his home in Tennessee. Bezos's great-great grandfather, Bernhardt Vesper, acquired a 25,000-acre ranch in Cotulla in the southern part of Texas, where young Jeffrey Preston Bezos spent summers with his grandparents. The pioneering spirit seems to be part of the family bloodline, even if the new frontier lies in cyberspace. Born on 12 January 1964, when his mother, Jackie Bezos, was only seventeen years old, Jeff Bezos never knew his father. "I've never been curious about him," he explains. "My real father is the guy who raised me." Yet another pioneer, Mike Bezos, a Cuban refugee who came to the United States by himself at the age of fifteen, married Jeff's mother and raised Jeff as his son.

Biggest Store on Earth. Bezos had a simple ambition. He wanted to own and operate the biggest store on earth, one that sold everything from cars to food, "anything except firearms and certain live animals." "Anything," Bezos proclaimed, "with a capital *A*." Bezos's vision that the Internet would revolutionize commerce was prescient, innovative, and, critics charged, outrageous. Many wondered how long the money would hold out, since Bezos had already spent a bank vault full of cash to finance a company that posted a net loss of $350 million in 1999 alone. "The chance of a painful failure goes up as they increase the chips on the table," explained Scott Sipprelle, founding partner of the investment firm Midtown Research Group. "As the company grows in scale, the absolute dollars it's losing are greater and greater." Bezos remains unfazed by his critics, convinced that as the volume of customers visiting Amazon.com increases he will be able to offer the lowest prices. Bezos may have the last laugh. At the end of 1999 Amazon stock stood at $94 per share, had split three times, and had annual sales approaching $1 billion. Holly Becker of Salomon Smith Barney argued that Wall Street might "look back on these growing pains and realize management's foresight in developing one of the smartest strategies in business history."

Making of a Dotcommunist. Besides his father and mother, Bezos's heroes are Thomas Alva Edison and Walt Disney. Of Disney, Bezos said: "The thing that always amazed me was how powerful his vision was. He knew exactly what he wanted to build and teamed up with a bunch of really smart people and built it. Everyone thought it wouldn't work, and he had to persuade the banks to lend him $400 million. But he did it." Bezos's own moment of insight came in 1994. Sitting in front of his computer in his 39th-floor office in midtown Manhattan, Bezos clicked onto a site that measured Internet use. To his astonishment, Bezos discovered that the Internet was growing at a rate of 2,300 percent a year. "It was a wake-up call," he remembers. "I started thinking, O.K., what kind of business opportunity might be here?" On 16 July 1995 Bezos launched Amazon.com and the rest is history. What follows may be the high-tech version of the Chinese Cultural Revolution, with Chairman Bezos preparing the nation and the world to take the Great Leap Forward into the age of e-commerce.

Sources:

Katrina Booker, "Amazon vs. Everybody," *Fortune*, 140 (8 November 1999): 120–126.

Joshua Quittner, "An Eye on the Future," *Time*, 154 (27 December 1999): 66.

Joshua Cooper Ramo, "Jeff Bezos: King of the Internet," *Time*, 154 (27 December 1999): 54–55.

Chris Taylor, "Totally Mad," *Time*, 154 (11 October 1999): 52–54.

GEOFFREY C. BIBLE

1937-

CHAIRMAN AND CEO OF PHILIP MORRIS

Formative Experiences. Born in Australia in 1937, Geoffrey C. Bible worked his way up the corporate ranks and eventually became CEO of one of the largest U.S. tobacco firms. One of his most formative experiences, however, took place far from corporate headquarters. From 1959 to 1964 he lived among Palestinian refugees while working for a United Nations relief agency, an experience that left a deep and lasting impression. "I've seen a lot of misery in my life," he recalled in an interview with *Business Week* in 1998. "If you see these little toddlers with flies all over their eyes, a rag over them and nothing else in 100-degree heat, you sort of get a real taste of what hunger is." He joined Philip Morris in 1968. In charge of overseas tobacco operations between 1987 and 1990, Bible championed the acquisition of local cigarette companies in former communist countries, a bold but risky venture that paid off, enabling Philip Morris to command the tobacco markets throughout Eastern Europe. Named CEO in 1994, Bible by the end of the decade had spent thirty-one years with the company. He had intended to retire in 1997 but agreed to stay on to guide Philip Morris through the most tumultuous period in its history. Not inclined to respond passively to conflict and controversy, Bible has come out fighting, consistently aggressive not only in his defense of Philip Morris but in his efforts to diversify and strengthen the company.

Under Fire. Probably no head of a major corporation during the 1990s was as embattled as Bible. Critics regarded him as nothing less than a villain, perhaps the devil incarnate. Bible's uncompromising defense of Philip Morris earned him the sobriquet "the Crocodile Dundee of the tobacco industry." When presented with damning documents that spelled out historical industry tactics of targeting young smokers, he said he was embarrassed and claimed that the company under his direction would never engage in such practices. During a deposition in Florida in 1997, he became the first executive of a major tobacco company to admit that cigarettes "might have" contributed to thousands of deaths.

Waging War. Behind the controversial public figure who waged unrelenting war on his critics, filing lawsuits against both the American Broadcasting Corporation (ABC) and the Food and Drug Administration (FDA), is a more complicated private man. When, in 1995, Bible learned that more than one thousand senior citizens in New York City were on a waiting list to participate in the Meals-on-Wheels program, he took immediate action.

Within a few months a $1.3 million check arrived from Philip Morris to eliminate the waiting period. That act of charity, however, did not eliminate the many problems that Philip Morris had to confront. In 1997 Bible joined tobacco industry negotiations to fashion the most contentious peace treaty in business history. To the consternation of many Philip Morris executives, Bible agreed, first, to eradicate the venerable Marlboro Man from advertisements and, second, to have the company pay an estimated $175 billion of the $368.5 billion tobacco settlement. Announced with considerable fanfare, the deal that Bible helped broker collapsed within ten months, the victim of political and public opposition. The failure of the agreement, and the continued vilification of Philip Morris, left Bible bloodied but unbowed. "This company is filled with decent, hard-working people, no different than any other," he repeats. "We go to church. Our children go to school. We need to do more to restore self-pride amongst our employees . . . and to have our place at the table like any other corporation. . . . We are working all over the world in the most genuine, upright, forthright, honest fashion that we possibly can."

The Future at Philip Morris. Bible acknowledges that Philip Morris faces a long and difficult struggle to regain public confidence. Yet, as of 1999, he expressed no plans to transform the basic portfolio of company businesses with acquisitions outside its core interests in tobacco, food, and beer, or to divide the company into separate divisions. Bible's strategy for Philip Morris has not changed since the day he took over as chairman and CEO. He has vowed to fight hard and win in the courts. "We will come out of it," he promised, "about that I have no doubt at all."

Sources:
John A. Byrne, "Philip Morris: Inside America's Most Reviled Company," *Business Week* (29 November 1999): 176–186.

Bill Dedman, "Executive Says He's Uncertain About Tobacco's Harm," *New York Times*, 3 March 1998.

Dedman, "Tobacco Chief 'Horrified' Over Evidence," *New York Times*, 4 March 1998.

Leslie Wines, "Geoffrey C. Bible: Up in Smoke?" *Journal of Business Strategy*, 16 (September/October 1995): 45.

WARREN BUFFETT

1930-

CHAIRMAN AND CEO OF BERKSHIRE HATHAWAY INC.

The Oracle of Omaha. Without a doubt Warren Edward Buffett is the greatest stock investor in modern times, and perhaps the most prescient oracle in the history of the stock market. If an individual had invested $10,000 in Berkshire Hathaway when Buffett purchased a controlling interest in 1965, by 1999 that individual's portfolio would have been worth $51 million. Had that same individual invested $10,000 in the Standard & Poor's 500-stock index, their portfolio would have been worth a mere $497,431. Yet, Buffett has not added a major position to the stock portfolio of Berkshire Hathaway since amassing 4.3 percent of McDonald's Corporation in 1995. During the second half of the 1990s he transformed what had previously been a sideline at Berkshire Hathaway into a main focus: the acquisition of entire companies. Between 1996 and 1999 Berkshire Hathaway, located in Omaha, Nebraska, spent $27.3 billion to purchase seven companies in industries as diverse as aviation, fast food, and home furnishings. The effect was immediate and dramatic. The shift in emphasis transformed Berkshire Hathaway from a closed-end fund to a bona fide operating company. In 1996 the stock portfolio of Berkshire Hathaway accounted for 76 percent of the company's $29.9 billion in assets; only three years later the assets in stocks plummeted to 32 percent while total assets quadrupled to $124 billion.

A Misunderstood Giant. The conventional wisdom is that Berkshire Hathaway stock will bring a premium because of Buffett's reputation as a latter-day King Midas. Certainly there is something to be said for Buffett's reputation. Yet, according to Alice Schroeder, a PaineWebber Insurance analyst who published a comprehensive study of Berkshire Hathaway, it is "possibly the most talked about and the least understood company in the world." Schroeder asserts, for instance, that despite the so-called Buffett premium, Berkshire stock is actually undervalued, trading far below its real value, which she has estimated to be between $91,000 and $97,000 per A share. In 1999 the A shares of Berkshire Hathaway stock traded at about $70,000. Schroeder explains the devaluation of Berkshire Hathaway stock by pointing out that the stock market misperceives the company as little more than the sum of the stocks in its portfolio and so tends to overreact to news about the seven stocks that form the core of Berkshire Hathaway's holdings: Coca-Cola, Gillette, American Express, Freddie Mac, Wells Fargo, Walt Disney, and the Washington Post Company. Despite changes that the company has undergone, Buffet remains true to his conservative precepts of investing. He prefers, as he puts it, a sure thing today to the next big thing, no matter how spectacular its potential might be. He will not, for example, invest in Internet stocks because no one can predict their performance over the next ten years. "I can't do it myself," he says, "and if I don't know, I don't invest."

When I Paint My Masterpiece. Buffett is all business almost all of the time. His tastes are simple, his habits frugal. Unlike the new generation of corporate leaders, such as Bill Gates or Jeff Bezos, Buffett neither spends money nor gives it away. He just makes it. He is an entrepreneur, not a philanthropist. Furthermore, in an era when most CEOs at least pay lip service to shareholder rights, Buffett is a throwback to an age when a corporate mogul was a corporate mogul and did as he pleased with his company. "Berk-

shire is the company I wanted to create," Buffett has said. "It's not the company that Alfred P. Sloan wanted to create. It fits me. I run it with our investors and managers in mind, but it is designed to fit me. . . . The problem I've got with doing anything else except what I'm doing," he admits, "is that there is nothing remotely as fun as running Berkshire. . . . Berkshire is my painting, so it should look the way I want it to when it's done."

Sources:

Anthony Bianco, "The Warren Buffett You Don't Know," *Business Week* (5 July 1999): 55–66.

Robert G. Hagstrom & Peter Lynch, *The Warren Buffett Way: Investment Strategies of the World's Greatest Investor* (New York: John Wiley & Sons, 1997).

Roger Lowenstein, *Buffett: The Making of An American Capitalist* (New York: Doubleday, 1996).

Allan Sloan, "Buffett Takes it All With Him," *Newsweek*, 134 (27 November 1999): 53.

Theodore Spencer, "The Investors of the Century," *Fortune*, 140 (20 December 1999): 154–158.

KEN CHENAULT

1951–

CEO OF AMERICAN EXPRESS

Man of Destiny. Born in 1951 in New York City, Chenault, one of five children, was the second son of Hortenius and Anne Chenault. Coming of age during the Civil Rights era made its mark on the young Chenault. "My father's basic view was that you really needed to concentrate on the things you can control, and what you can control is your own performance." Chenault took his father's advice seriously. In school he demonstrated poise and leadership qualities that would later impress others as he moved through the corporate world. He studied at Bowdoin College and then enrolled in Harvard Law School. Still, Chenault admits that he was a late bloomer in school; the thought of studying business did not occur to him until he was in his twenties, after realizing that he did not want to practice law.

Trying Something New. In 1981 Chenault accepted a job with American Express. Starting in the strategic planning department, Chenault advanced to vice president in charge of marketing, where he convinced company officials that the merchandise-services division, a foundering arm of the AmEx company, was worth saving. They put Chenault in charge; in two years revenues soared from $150 million to more than $500 million. From 1986 to 1989 Chenault found himself on the fast track, being promoted three times. Still, Chenault grew frustrated at the unwillingness of the company to recognize that times were changing and the company also needed to change if it were to survive. Finally, in 1991, the call came.

Room for Improvement. Working with new CEO Harvey Golub, Chenault, now senior card executive, embarked on a cost-cutting overhaul of the company. His measures were so successful that by 1995 Chenault was promoted to vice chairman. Finally, in late 1999, Golub announced that by 2001 Chenault would succeed him as CEO. Although Chenault was not the first African American to become a CEO, he was the first to control a financial-services giant that operates on a global scale. In the meantime, Golub and Chenault developed their three-prong growth strategy for the future. The plan calls for expanding the card network through banks and financial institutions; casting a wider net with its financial and investment services; and increasing the market share in overseas businesses and markets. In creating and overseeing the new corporate agenda, Chenault hopes to make AmEx bigger, stronger, and a greater presence in the marketplace. His advice to other CEOs? "Leaders must focus an organization on facing reality," he says. "Then they give them the confidence and support to inspire them to change that reality."

A True Leader. When Chenault was brought on board American Express, the company was on the brink of collapse, feeling the pinch from other large credit card companies such as Visa and Mastercard. Under his direction as president and chief officer, American Express began to battle back. In the process, Chenault led the company through a painful restructuring process that organized $3 billion in spending and increased the number of credit cards that AmEx offers from four to sixty; in the process, he kept AmEx merchants happy with the company.

Sources:

"Chenault to Head American Express," *Direct Marketing,* 22 (June 1999): 6.

Caroline V. Clarke, "Meeting the Challenge of Corporate Leadership," *Black Enterprise,* 26 (August 1995): 156–158.

Marjorie Whigham Desir, "Leadership Has Its Rewards," *Black Enterprise,* 30 (September 1999): 73–78.

"The Rise of a Star," *Business Week* (21 December 1998): 60–68.

ABBY JOSEPH COHEN

1952-

CHIEF MARKET STRATEGIST, GOLDMAN, SACHS & CO.

Substance Over Style. Born in Queens, New York, in 1952 to a Polish-immigrant mother and a father whose parents had come from Poland in 1913, Abby Joseph Cohen received a B.A. in economics and computer science from Cornell University in 1973 and an M.S. in economics from George Washington University in 1976. In 1973 she married David M. Cohen, director of labor and employee relations at Columbia University. Since 1983, when they moved back to New York from Baltimore, where Cohen had been working for T. Rowe Price Associates Inc., she and her family have lived in the same Queens neighborhood where Cohen grew up. She commutes to work on the bus. "We are not a Wall Street family," she says, "a Wall Street career is not the end-all and be-all for us." Cohen began her career in the mid 1970s as a research assistant at the Federal Reserve Board in Washington, D.C., where she learned "to be flexible in my analysis and to look beneath the usual rules of thumb to the underlying dynamics." It is, indeed, the depth and extent of her research that set Cohen apart from other market analysts. Along with her colleague, Gabrielle U. Napalitano, Cohen rigorously examined every quarterly earnings report of every major company on the Standard & Poor's (S & P) 500 list. This task was labor-intensive and time-consuming, but Cohen believed it necessary in an era in which the frequency of big tax write-offs and changes in accounting procedures complicated the business of earnings forecasting. Although traditional measures were of little use in gauging the progress of a market blessed with robust growth and anemic inflation, Cohen remained steadfast in her conviction that technology-driven prosperity would enable the market to grow without setting off inflationary pressures that in the past had induced recessions. Throughout her career, however, Cohen has been more interested in getting her analysis right than in attracting attention with flamboyant but incorrect predictions. If anything, during the long bull market of the 1990s, she was too conservative, consistently underestimating the pace at which the market rose. To many traders, brokers, and investors, Cohen and her work have long represented the triumph of substance over style.

When Abby Talks, People Listen. On 16 November 1996 the Dow Jones Industrial Average was up sixty-five points and apparently headed for another record close when someone convulsed Wall Street with the rumor that Cohen had altered her market forecast. The Dow fell like a stone—a very heavy stone—surrendering sixty points of its gain in little more than an hour. Meanwhile, Cohen, attending a speech by Jon S. Corzine, CEO of Goldman, Sachs, was blissfully unaware of what was taking place until someone tapped her on the shoulder and said: "There's an emergency. You must call the office." Cohen reached Steven M. Wagshal, who connected her to the intercom system linking Goldman, Sachs offices throughout the world. He also connected her to the trading floor at the New York Stock Exchange. Wagshal then witnessed an extraordinary sequence of events. The sound of Cohen's voice brought the cavernous trading room to a standstill. As soon as she made it clear that she had not altered her optimistic market forecast, hundreds of traders and brokers rushed en masse to the telephones. The market began immediately to rise, ending the day up thirty-five points. Cohen had spoken. "It was as if the world were falling," recalled Wagshal, "and Abby came in and lifted it up again."

No Crystal Ball. With her demur business suits and sensible shoes, Cohen projects a rather unprepossessing figure. According to associates, she would be the first to admit that her reputation is exaggerated. "Abby is a nice person and all," declared Laszlo Birinyi Jr. of Birinyi Associates, "but her reputation for walking on water is overdone." Cohen explains that "it's not like I have a crystal ball sending out signals." She has nevertheless established a reputation for hard work, keen analysis, and professionalism that has distinguished her from many other market sages past and present. "Abby is an incredible professional strategist who enhances our position in the financial marketplace and also gives us a sense of confidence internally about our strategies," says Goldman, Sachs CEO Corzine. Yet, Cohen's performance has not always been flawless. More than once she errantly predicted that small-cap stocks would outperform blue chips, and she has also made poorly timed recommendations to put money into commodities. Even when she is wrong, however, she made her case with insight. "Abby does not have to be right on the market to be of great value to me," says Linda P. Strumpf of the Ford Foundation, a client of Cohen's for more than fifteen years. Apparently, Strumpf is not alone. Cohen's opinions about how the stock market will perform were more influential than anyone else's, with the exception of Warren Buffett. "A year ago, when Abby was inducted into our Hall of Fame, I said she was the most influential woman on Wall Street," remarked Louis Rukeyser, host of *Wall $treet Week* in 1998. "But now I would say that she is the most influential market forecaster, period."

Sources:

Anthony Bianco, "The Prophet of Wall Street," *Business Week* (1 June 1998): 125–134.

"More From Abby Cohen," *Wall Street Journal,* 2 February 1997.

Jospeh Nocera, "Abby Cohen's Awkward Situation," *Fortune,* 138 (7 September 1998): 29–31.

James Pethokouis, "Safer Investing," *U. S. News & World Report,* 125 (19 October 1998): 64–67.

BILL GATES

1955-

CHAIRMAN OF MICROSOFT CORPORATION

Microsoft. Critics' grievances notwithstanding, William Henry "Bill" Gates III has compiled an impressive resume. Born in 1955, Gates and his two sisters grew up in Seattle, the children of William Henry Gates II, an attorney, and Mary Gates, a schoolteacher, regent of the University of Washington, and chairwoman of United Way International. Gates began programming computers at the age of thirteen. In 1973 he entered Harvard University, where he developed the programming language BASIC (Beginner's All-purpose Symbolic Instruction Code) for the first microcomputer, the MITS Altair. In 1975, during his junior year, Gates left Harvard and moved to Albuquerque, New Mexico, to head a company that he called "Micro-soft." In 1978 the company, now spelled minus the hyphen, relocated to Seattle, Washington. As of 1999 the Microsoft Corporation, with a market value of $546 billion, was the wealthiest company and tenth largest economic entity in the world. For the fiscal year ending in June 1999, Microsoft posted revenues of $19.75 billion. Gates credits his own "foresight and vision regarding personal computing" as essential to the success of Microsoft and the entire software industry. Yet, his management and technical expertise have not escaped the scrutiny and fire of critics. In their biography, titled *Gates,* Stephen Manes and Paul Andrews characterize Gates the corporate manager as intolerant, abrasive, and dismissive. He cut corners on labor costs and was "tightfisted beyond the boundaries of the law."

Big Break. Gates's big break came in 1980, when Microsoft acquired the right to license the 86-DOS that Seattle Computer had developed. Gates renamed it MS-DOS and offered a package deal to IBM that included it and all the computer languages that Microsoft had acquired in exchange for advances, royalties, and licensing fees. Executives at IBM agreed; all IBM and IBM-compatible PCs carried Microsoft software. This transaction, asserts cultural historian Jackson Lears, one of Gates's main critics, exemplifies the essence of the man behind Microsoft. For all his technical expertise, Lears wrote, Gates "is more a salesman than an inventor. Nearly all of Gates's major achievements have involved appropriating the innovations of other people, then brilliantly mass-producing and marketing them. The vendor of virtual reality, Gates is the perfect business hero for a postmodern era."

William the Conqueror. Napoleon Bonaparte was among Gates's boyhood idols. Driven by a persistent desire to master the economic world, just as Napoleon was driven to master the military and political worlds, Gates built his own Grand Empire, only to see it assailed from all sides. If the Department of Justice gets its way, he may yet see it dismantled. Like Napoleon, too, critics charge, Gates pretends to be, or perhaps actually thinks of himself as being, egalitarian and democratic. Napoleon codified and extended the liberty, equality, and fraternity of the French Revolution but ruled Europe as a dictator. Gates, apparently filled with an egalitarian and democratic fervor, posits a utopian future in which technology will enrich and empower everyone. Yet, as many critics maintain, Gates yoked this vision to an irresistible and irreversible technological determinism. In Gates's view, the democratization of power is arising from a worldwide network of personal computers that have created what he calls a "digital nervous system." He asserted in *The Road Ahead* and *Business @ The Speed of Thought* that the old, undemocratic, hierarchical social, political, and economic structures cannot withstand the new, democratic, egalitarian force of the digital age. For Gates, the attachment to the past is as unbearable as it is unacceptable; it stands not only in the way of technological, but also social and political, progress. He seems to assume that all Americans are, will be, and want to be connected, trading in Internet stocks, and building McMansions. He does not seem to realize, according to his adversaries, that 67 percent of U.S. household incomes are stagnant or declining, and that 50 percent of Americans have no assets at all. Gates's vision of the future, his critics suggest, may therefore amount to democracy for those who can afford it, actually masking the growing economic, social, and political disparities between the rich and everyone else.

Gates the Philanthropist. As of 1999 Gates was worth at least $87.5 billion. His 18.5 percent stake in Microsoft accounted for $76 billion, while his personal fortune amounted to $11.5 billion and counting. Of that latter figure, $5 billion is in Gates's personal investment portfolio. Gates divided the remaining $6.5 billion between two huge foundations, the William H. Gates Foundation and the Gates Learning Foundation, set up to fund charitable and philanthropic work. In 1999 Gates and his wife, Melinda, also launched the Bill and Melinda Gates Foundation, endowed with more than $17 million, to support philanthropic initiatives in global health, especially in the Third World, and in education, especially in the inner cities and low-income communities of the United States and Canada. By the end of 1999 it had committed more than $300 million to these causes. Gates is also determined that every classroom and public library in the United States be connected to the Internet. There is little doubt that his philanthropy sprung from good intentions and noble motives, and that many benefits will come to those who are the recipients of his largess. Again, however, critics have accused Gates of acting out of self-interest. In giving away computers to schools, libraries, and community centers, they hasten to point out, Gates has ensured that these institutions will be in need of Microsoft technology. Moreover, given the federal antitrust case against Microsoft, which generated months of bad publicity, Gates needed to do something to boost his popularity and revive his reputation. Paying for vaccinations for children in Zimbabwe or scholarships for students in East St. Louis brought him the kind of benign, even generous, recognition that he sought and removed, albeit temporarily, the negative attention from the front page.

The Visionary. Gates likes to talk about the future. As the decade drew to a close, his own future and that of Microsoft remained in doubt. On 7 June 2000, in the most severe antitrust prescription since the breakup of AT&T in 1984, U.S. District Judge Thomas Penfield Jackson ruled that Microsoft was a monopoly and ordered it be split into two companies. What the ruling means for Microsoft is ultimately less interesting than what it means for Gates's vision of the future, as he is not merely marketing an assortment of technologies, but marketing a way of life. Gates advocates what he calls "friction-free capitalism" in which society will achieve commercial harmony and democratic autonomy through the application of technology. The Internet, Gates insisted in *The Road Ahead*, will offer individuals unlimited options and will put them in charge of managing these alternatives. He wants to give "people the power to do what they want, where and when they want, on any device." Gates has an enduring faith that people can systematically and efficiently control their everyday lives with technology. His many critics have declared, however, that for all his talk about choice, democracy, and equality, Gates is an authoritarian who simply cannot admit that there will be winners and losers in his technophilic vision of progress, any more than he can imagine life beyond the Net or fathom that some people might not wish to work, play, and live solely in cyberspace.

Sources:
"Bill Gates," *Microsoft*, Internet website.

Adam Cohen, "'Microsoft Enjoys Monopoly Power,'" *Time*, 154 (15 November 1999): 61–69.

Amy Cortese, "The Battle for the Cyber Future," *Business Week* (1 June 1998): 38–41.

Bill Gates, Nathan Myhrvold, and Peter Rinearson, *The Road Ahead* (New York: Viking, 1995).

Gates and Collins Hemingway, *Business @ the Speed of Thought: Using a Digital Nervous System* (New York: Warner, 1999).

Jackson Lears, "Unsweet Smell of Success," *New Republic* (18 October 1999): 29–38.

Stephen Manes and Paul Andrews, *Gates: How Microsoft's Mogul Reinvented an Industry—And Made Himself the Richest Man in America* (New York: Doubleday, 1993).

Michael Moeller, "Remaking Microsoft," *Business Week* (17 May 1999): 106–114.

Gary Rivlin, *The Plot to Get Bill Gates: An Irreverent Investigation of the World's Richest Man—and the People Who Hate Him* (New York: Times Books, 1999).

Andy Serwer, "One Family's Finances: How Bill Gates Invests His Money," *Fortune*, 139 (15 March 1999): 68–86.

Jon Swartz, "Microsoft Split Ordered," *USA Today*, 8 June 2000.

"Visionary-in-Chief: A Talk with Chairman Bill Gates on the World Beyond Windows," *Business Week* (17 May 1999): 114–115.

Dori Jones Yang, "The Empire Strikes Out," *U.S. News & World Report*, 127 (15 November 1999): 46–53.

ALAN GREENSPAN

1926-

CHAIRMAN OF THE FEDERAL RESERVE BOARD

Eclectic Talents, Diverse Careers. Born in New York City on 6 March 1926, the son of a stockbroker and a retail salesclerk, Alan Greenspan early displayed impressive mathematical skills. In fact, many considered him something of a mathematical prodigy. After finishing high school, however, Greenspan enrolled in The Juilliard School and played saxophone and clarinet with a touring swing band during the 1940s. In

1945 Greenspan's musical career came to an end when he enrolled in New York University to study economics. He completed a B.A. in 1948, graduating summa cum laude, and earned an M.A. in 1950. He then entered the doctoral program at Columbia University. In the early 1950s Greenspan dropped out of Columbia and went to work for the National Industrial Conference Board (NICB). In 1977 NYU conferred his Ph.D. without requiring Greenspan to complete a dissertation. After leaving the NICB in 1954, Greenspan and bond-trader William Townsend founded Townsend-Greenspan & Company, Inc., a consulting firm that offered economic forecasts to corporations and banks. He served as chairman and president of Townsend-Greenspan between 1954 and 1977, and again between 1977 and 1987, before dissolving the partnership upon his appointment as chairman of the Federal Reserve Board (the Fed).

Dollars and Sense. As chairman of the Fed, Greenspan displayed a rare combination of intellectual acumen and political savvy. He is an erudite economist with a remarkable sensitivity to the shifting political currents. Such characteristics enabled him to serve as chairman under three different administrations: those of presidents Ronald Reagan, George Bush, and Bill Clinton. Greenspan got his first taste of public life as director of policy research for Richard M. Nixon's presidential campaign in 1968. President Gerald R. Ford appointed Greenspan chairman of his Council of Economic Advisors, on which he served from 1974 until 1977. Out of politics between 1977 and 1987, Greenspan returned to Washington when Reagan nominated him as the chairman of the Federal Reserve Board, a position he has held ever since.

Greenspan at the Fed. In October 1987, two months after he took office, the stock market crashed. Greenspan took quick and decisive action. A child during the Great Depression, Greenspan got the Fed to pump money into the banking system, thereby avoiding the liquidity trap that magnified the problems of the market in 1929. In so doing, he helped to avert a worse crisis on Wall Street. Given Greenspan's fiscal conservatism and comments about the "irrational exuberance" of the market, it is likely that he interpreted the events of October 1987 as a logical and necessary consequence of a steep and unwarranted rise in stock prices, which took place without due consideration of the true strength of the U.S. economy. Since his earliest days at the Fed, Greenspan has been obsessed with balancing the economy between the cycles of boom and bust. In his first years as chairman, Greenspan raised interest rates with great frequency in an effort to keep inflation to a minimum. He raised rates in 1989 and 1990, easing off slightly during the Gulf War and the recession of 1990–1992. In 1994, the most controversial period of Greenspan's tenure, he raised interest rates six times in order to quell rapid economic growth that he saw as inflationary. Those who were at the Fed remember it as a period of triumph. Alan Blinder, vice chairman of the Federal Reserve Board through 1996, called this period "the most successful episode of monetary policy in the history of the Fed," and other analysts in the financial community were equally free with their accolades. Those in the business community and labor movement, however, saw the increases as reflecting

Greenspan's ideological bias toward low inflation even at the cost of higher unemployment and economic contraction. They maintained that the economy could grow at a faster rate than the Fed allowed without sparking inflationary pressures. Greenspan's tight money policies, his critics argued, kept profits down, wages stagnant, and economic expansion paralyzed.

Pragmatism Triumphs at the Fed. To nearly everyone's surprise, during the second half of the decade, Greenspan showed a remarkable lack of dogmatism in setting policy at the Fed. In 1998 and 1999 he became a great advocate of the so-called New Economy, raising interest rates just once. That increase was almost pro forma, a signal to the markets that he was still watching. In his public speeches, Greenspan has also increasingly suggested that improvements in productivity and technology have made American business more efficient, thus lowering inflationary pressures and enabling the economy to grow without generating higher prices and wages. Uncharacteristically, Greenspan dismissed official productivity figures as too low, insisting that the difficulties of measuring productivity in a service economy concealed the real gains U.S. business has reaped since 1994. As a result, he has proven more willing to allow the economy to grow without raising interest rates as a hedge against inflation. If forced to choose, Greenspan would still prefer lower inflation and higher unemployment. For the moment, he believes that the U.S. economy could have it all: low inflation and low unemployment coupled with a high rate of growth.

Sources:

"Alan Greenspan," *ABCnews.com*, Internet website.

"Members of the Board of Governors: Alan Greenspan, Chairman," *The Federal Reserve Board*, Internet website.

David B. Sicilia and Jeffrey L. Cruikshank, *The Greenspan Effect: Words That Move the World's Markets* (New York: McGraw-Hill, 2000).

John Surowiecki, "What Has Greenspan Done at the Fed?," *The Motley Fool*, Internet website.

Surowiecki, "Who is Alan Greenspan?," *The Motley Fool*, Internet website.

Owen Ullmann, Laura Cohn, and Michael J. Mandel, "The Fed's New Rule Book," *Business Week* (3 May 1999): 46–48.

JACK WELCH

1935-
CHAIRMAN AND CEO OF THE GENERAL ELECTRIC CORPORATION

Shaken, Not Stirred. At forty-five, John Francis "Jack" Welch was the youngest chief executive officer that the General Electric Corporation (GE) had ever had. When Welch took control of the company in December 1980, GE was the model American corporation. It was a juggernaut: conservative, staid, cautious, prudent, unexciting, and reliable. Its net income in 1980 was $1.7 billion, with a steady and healthy growth rate of 9 percent a year. Like most GE executives and CEOs, Welch was a company insider who had risen through the corporate ranks. No other corporation has been as successful at recruiting and nurturing talent from within or has managed to sustain such a consistent performance over such an extended period of time. Everyone anticipated that GE would continue to chart its smooth course once Welch took the helm. They could not have been more wrong. Welch had no plans of settling quietly into the executive suite. Steady but unspectacular progress, he believed, was no longer acceptable in the increasingly competitive economy. To the astonishment of all and the dismay of many, Welch shook up GE as the company had never been shaken before.

"Neutron Jack": Toughest Boss. During the 1980s, Welch completely overhauled the business operations of GE. He eliminated some divisions and subsidiaries and acquired others. In the process, he was among the first to implement the practice of downsizing. So ruthlessly did Welch abolish jobs that in 1984 the editors of *Fortune* ordained him the "toughest boss in America." Welch cut two thousand jobs and saved the company more than $6 million. The mainstream media dubbed him "Neutron Jack," the man who, like the neutron bomb, swept away human beings but left buildings intact. Not surprisingly, many at GE and throughout the corporate world despised Welch, who knew his actions were raising grave concerns among other top executives, to say nothing of the workforce. "I didn't start with a morale problem," he declared with typical candor, "I created it! The leader who tries to move a large organization counter to what his followers perceive to be necessary has a very difficult time. I had never had to do this before. I had always had the luxury of building a business and being the cheerleader. But it was clear that we had to reposition ourselves and put our chips on those businesses that could survive on a global scale." Perhaps Welch was unnecessarily brutal in introducing GE to the new realities of business, but he created a stronger, if leaner, company. In the meantime, whatever the defects of his methods, Welch had utterly changed attitudes at GE, eradicating any sense of complacency about, or contentment with, the status quo. Despite the travail of nearly tearing the company apart, Welch believed that he had prepared GE to compete more effectively in the emerging global marketplace of the following decade and the twenty-first century.

The House That Jack Rebuilt. In the 1990s Welch set out to restore what he had torn asunder. Central to this effort were two programs: "Work-Out," launched in 1989, and "Sigma Six," begun in 1995. Welch called Work-Out "a relentless, end-less company-wide search for a better way to do everything we do." With his usual gusto, he brought twenty business-school professors and consultants to GE to help turn the concept of Work-Out into a reality. Work-Out was a communications instrument that Welch offered to GE employees. It gave them the opportunity dramatically to alter their working lives. "The idea was to hold a three-day, informal town meeting with 40 to 100 employees from all ranks of GE," explained Janet Lowe in her book *Jack Welch Speaks.* The program gave the employees a powerful voice in identifying problems and in offering and implementing solutions. Since its inception, the program has been overwhelmingly successful. Above all, it helped to rebuild the trust between GE employees and management, which Welch's reorganization had all but destroyed. With Work-Out, Welch encouraged and enabled people to talk to one another, work together, and share information and experience. They have reveled in the opportunity. Sigma Six was a company-wide quality-control program that made products and services the responsibility of every division, manager, and employee. "We blew up the old quality organization," Welch said, "because they were off to the side. Now it's the job of the leader, the job of the manager, the job of the employee—everyone's job is quality." Since taking over as CEO and chairman, Welch has torn down, reshaped, and rebuilt GE. Through it all, the company has remained extremely profitable. In 1981 GE had total assets of $20 billion and revenues of $27.24 billion; company earnings were $1.65 billion. With 440,000 employees worldwide, GE had a market value of $12 billion. At the end of 1997, more than sixteen years into Welch's tenure as CEO, total GE assets had grown to $304 billion and revenues to $90.84 billion. With only 270,000 employees in one hundred countries, the company produced earnings of $8.2 billion and had a market value of $300 billion. At the end of the century few had anything but praise for Welch and his vigorous and thoughtful leadership. *Fortune* named Welch, who announced his intention to retire in April 2001, as the "manager of the century"; the editors thus added their voices to the growing chorus that credits Welch not with putting GE on top but with accomplishing something far more difficult: making sure the company stayed there.

Sources:

John Byrne, "How Jack Welch Runs GE," *Business Week* (8 June 1998): 90–102.

Stuart Crainer, *The Management Century: A Critical Review of 20th Century Thought and Practice* (San Francisco: Jossey-Bass, 2000).

Janet Lowe, *Jack Welch Speaks* (New York: Wiley & Sons, 1998).

Richard Pascale, *Managing on the Edge* (New York: Simon & Schuster, 1990).

Jerry Porras and Jim Collins, *Built to Last* (New York: Century, 1997).

PEOPLE IN THE NEWS

On 1 February 1992 **Ron Carey** was sworn in as the first Teamsters (International Brotherhood of Teamsters) president elected by the rank and file of the union.

In 1993 **James Champy's** and **Michael Hammer's** book, *Reengineering the Corporation: A Manifesto for the Business Revolution* was published; it quickly became the "downsizer's bible."

In April 1998 **Robert L. Crandall** retired as president of American Airlines; during his eighteen-year tenure the airlines initiated such innovations as frequent-flyer miles and super-saver fares.

In 1995 **Millard S. Drexler** took over the clothing chain Gap, Inc.; by 1999 he had turned the once-stagnant company around, posting profits around 30 percent above average, at a time when many retail stores were only averaging 5 percent above normal profits.

On 16 March 1992 **Robert J. Eaton,** head of the profitable European operations of General Motors Corporation, joined auto manufacturer Chrysler Corporation as successor to Chairman **Lido Anthony "Lee" Iacocca.**

In 1997 New Jersey businessman **Charles F. Feeney** reportedly had in the last decade given away more than $600 million to charity; another $3.5 billion, almost the entire sum of Feeney's estimated wealth, had also been turned over to his two charitable foundations. Remarkably, Feeney had made the contributions anonymously.

In December 1995, after a fire swept through three factories of Malden Mills Industries, CEO **Aaron Feuerstein**, grandson of the founder, announced that the company would continue to pay employees wages for three months and insurance benefits for nine months, costing the company some $10 million; the facilities returned to full productive capacity within ninety days.

In July 1996 *Forbes* announced that **William Henry "Bill" Gates III** was the richest man in the world with an estimated personal worth of $12.9 billion.

In May 1998 **Andrew S. Grove,** cofounder and CEO of Intel, stepped down; during Grove's tenure Intel emerged as the leading computer-chip maker in the world.

On 15 April 1992 hotel tycoon **Leona Helmsley** began serving a four-year prison sentence for tax evasion; she was released after serving eighteen months.

On 14 May 1992 **Lee Iacocca,** CEO of Chrysler Corporation, announced that he would step down from the post at the end of the year.

Karen L. Katen assumed control of Pfizer Pharmaceuticals in 1995; during her tenure as president, the drug company emerged as one of the leading companies in the United States with the introduction of breakout pharmaceuticals such as the anti-impotence drug Viagra.

In 1994 **Todd Krizelman** and **Stephan Paternot,** both students at Cornell University, created theglobe.com, which would become one of the more successful Internet ventures; when the company went public on 13 November 1998, it was valued at $35 million.

In October 1997 **Robert C. Merton** and **Myron S. Scholes** won the Nobel Prize in economics for their creation of a formula used for the valuation of stock options. [Other American Nobel Prize winners for economics during the decade included **Harry M. Markowitz** (1990), **Merton H. Miller** (1991), **William F. Sharpe** (1991), **Gary S. Becker** (1992), **Robert W. Fogel** (1993), **Douglass C. North** (1993), **John C. Harsanyi** (1994), **John F. Nash Jr.** (1994), **Robert E. Lucas Jr.** (1995), and **William S. Vickrey** (1996).]

On 2 April 1993 U.S. tobacco giant Philip Morris, under the direction of CEO **Michael Miles,** cut the price of its "branded" cigarettes by 25 percent; the move prompted the day to be dubbed as "Marlboro Friday"; Miles resigned a year later.

On 24 April 1990 junk-bond king **Michael R. Milken** avoided trial on insider trading and racketeering charges by pleading guilty to six less serious felony violations and agreeing to pay fines and penalties totaling $600 million.

In March 1998 **Marilyn Carlson Nelson** became CEO of Carlson Companies, a Minneapolis-based leisure travel agency; under her leadership, Carlson became one of the largest travel agencies in the world, increasing its business by 200 percent.

In October 1999 entrepreneur **Martha Stewart's** company, Martha Stewart Living Omnimedia, in an initial public offering (IPO) on Wall Street, surged to a 98 percent gain on the New York Stock Exchange, handily beating the World Wrestling Federation, which gained only 48 percent on the Nasdaq.

On 14 June 1996 **Stephen P. Yokich** was elected president of the United Auto Workers (UAW) at the triennial convention of the union in Anaheim, California.

DEATHS

Carl Ally, 74, advertising executive whose aggressive style included naming rival companies in ads, 15 February 1999.

R. Stanton Avery, 90, businessman and inventor of the self-adhesive label that bear his name, 12 December 1997.

César Estrada Chávez, 66, labor activist, founder of the United Farmworkers of America, 23 April 1993.

Jack Kent Cooke, 84, owner of newspapers, sports teams, and television stations, 6 April 1997.

Max Factor Jr., 91, cosmetics mogul and inventor of the smudge-proof lipstick and waterproof mascara, 7 June 1996.

Avery Fisher, 87, founder of electronics company and philanthropist, 26 February 1994.

Julio R. Gallo, 83, cofounder and president of E & J Gallo Winery, one of the largest wineries in the world, 2 May 1993.

Harold Sydney Geneen, 87, British-born U.S. businessman who transformed ITT from a small company into an international conglomerate, 21 November 1997.

Thomas W. Gleason, 92, labor union official, former president of the International Longshoreman's Association, 24 December 1992.

Robert Klark Graham, 90, developer of plastic shatterproof eyeglasses, 13 February 1997.

Harry Brakmann Helmsley, 87, self-made New York real-estate billionaire, 4 January 1997.

Jay Lovestone, 91, controversial labor figure in the American Federation of Labor-Congress of Industrial Organizations (AFL-CIO), 7 March 1990.

Daniel Keith Ludwig, 95, American shipowner and real-estate tycoon, for years listed as one of the richest men in the world, 27 August 1992.

William G. McGowan, 64, chairman of MCI, which challenged rival AT&T's monopoly as a long-distance service provider, 8 June 1992.

David Packard, 83, cofounder of Hewlett-Packard Company, 26 March 1996.

Lawrence Johnston Peter, 70, author who satirized corporate life and coined the phrase "Peter Principle," 12 January 1990.

Charles G. "Bebe" Rebozo, 85, Florida banker and controversial friend to former president Richard M. Nixon, 8 May 1998.

Jheri (Robert) Redding, 90, founder of a hair-care empire, inventor of creme rinse, pH-balanced shampoo, and the perm product Jheri-Curl, 15 March 1998.

Steven J. Ross, 65, CEO who oversaw the merger that produced Time Warner Inc., 20 December 1992.

Robert W. Sarnoff, 78, former Radio Corporation of America (RCA) chairman and president of National Broadcasting Company (NBC), responsible for turning RCA into a conglomerate through the acquisition of other unrelated businesses, 22 February 1997.

Norton Simon, 86, California industrialist, art collector, and outspoken public figure, 2 June 1993.

Maurice Hubert Stans, 90, businessman who served in the Eisenhower and Nixon administrations and was found guilty of minor violations relating to the 1972 Nixon reelection campaign, 14 April 1998.

William S. Vickrey, 82, economist and winner of the 1996 Nobel Prize for economics, 10 October 1996.

Sam Moore Walton, 74, billionaire and founder of Wal-Mart retail stores, 5 April 1992.

An Wang, 70, founder of Wang Laboratories, creator of early prototype of the microchip, 24 March 1990.

Thomas John Watson Jr., 79, IBM president credited with leading company into the computer era, former ambassador to the U.S.S.R. (1979–1981), 31 December 1993.

Frank G. Wells, 62, president of the Walt Disney Company, 3 April 1994.

Cornelius Vanderbilt Whitney, 93, cofounder of Pan American Airways, movie producer, 13 December 1992.

PUBLICATIONS

David Bach, *Smart Women Finish Rich: 7 Steps to Achieving Financial Security and Funding Your Dreams* (New York: Broadway, 1999).

Marcus Buckingham and Curt Coffman, *First, Break All the Rules: What the World's Greatest Managers Do Differently* (New York: Simon & Schuster, 1999).

James C. Collins and Jerry I. Porris, *Built To Last: Successful Habits of Visionary Companies* (New York: HarperBusiness, 1994).

Stephen R. Covey, *The 7 Habits of Highly Effective People: Restoring the Character Ethic* (New York: Simon & Schuster, 1989).

Diane Coyle, *The Weightless World: Strategies for Managing the Digital Economy* (Cambridge, Mass.: MIT Press, 1998).

Michael A. Cusumano and David B. Yoffie, *Competing On Internet Time: Lessons From Netscape and Its Battle With Microsoft* (New York: Free Press, 1998).

Bob Davis and David Wessel, *Prosperity: The Coming Twenty-Year Boom and What It Means to You* (New York: Times Business, 1998).

Philip Evans and Thomas S. Wurster, *Blown To Bits: How the New Economics of Information Transforms Strategy* (Cambridge, Mass.: Harvard Business School Press, 2000).

Bill Gates and Collins Hemingway, *Business @ the Speed of Thought: Using a Digital Nervous System* (New York: Warner, 1999).

Eliyahu M. Goldratt and Jeff Cox, *The Goal: A Process of Ongoing Improvement,* revised edition (Springfield, Mass.: North River, 1992).

Robert G. Hagstrome Jr., *The Warren Buffett Way: Investment Strategies of the World's Greatest Investor* (New York: Wiley & Sons, 1994).

Charles Handy, *The Age of Unreason* (Cambridge, Mass.: Harvard Business School Press, 1989).

Spencer Johnson, *Who Moved My Cheese?: An Amazing Way to Deal with Change in your Work and in Your Life* (New York: Putnam, 1998).

Paul Krugman, *The Age of Diminished Expectations: U.S. Economic Policy in the 1990s* (Cambridge, Mass.: MIT Press, 1990).

The Dalai Lama, *Ethics for a New Millennium* (New York: Riverhead, 1999).

Peter Lynch and John Rothchild, *Beating the Street* (New York: Simon & Schuster, 1993).

Bob Nelson, *1001 Ways to Reward Employees* (New York: Workman, 1994).

William J. O'Neil, *How To Make Money in Stocks: A Winning System in Good Times or Bad* (New York: McGraw-Hill, 1991).

Suze Orman, *The Courage To Be Rich: Creating a Life of Material and Spiritual Abundance* (New York: Riverhead, 1999).

Orman, *The 9 Steps to Financial Freedom* (New York: Crown, 1997).

Thomas Petzinger Jr., *The New Pioneers: The Men and Women Who Are Transforming the Workplace and the Marketplace* (New York: Simon & Schuster, 1999).

Peter M. Senge, *The Fifth Discipline: The Art and Practice of the Learning Organization* (New York: Doubleday/Currency, 1994).

Thomas J. Stanley and William D. Danko, *The Millionaire Next Door: The Surprising Secrets of America's Wealthy* (Atlanta: Longstreet, 1996).

Kate White, *Why Good Girls Don't Get Ahead—But Gutsy Girls Do: Nine Secrets Every Career Woman Must Know* (New York: Warner, 1995).

Michael Wolff, *Burn Rate: How I Survived the Gold Rush Years on the Internet* (New York: Simon & Schuster, 1998).

Advertizing Age, periodical.

Barron's, periodical.

Best's Review, periodical.

Business Week, periodical.

The Economist, periodical.

Finance & Development, periodical.

Forbes, periodical.

Fortune, periodical.

Harvard Business Review, periodical.

Investor, periodical.

Kiplinger's Personal Finance Magazine, periodical.

Mutual Funds, periodical.

SmartMoney, periodical.

Wall Street Journal, periodical.

Worth, periodical.

The Wal Mart store in North Kingston, Rhode Island. Many businessmen fear that stores such as this threaten local merchants (AP/Wide World Photos).

EDUCATION

by LINDA HUSKEY

CONTENTS

Sidebars and tables are listed in italics.

1990

- The U.S. Department of Education reports that enrollment of black students at private colleges and universities in the United States rose by 7.1 percent between 1986 and 1988, while black enrollment in public universities rose by only 0.2 percent in the same period.

- A release of Scholastic Aptitude Test (SAT) scores for 1990 shows that the national average for mathematics remained constant at 476, while the average score on the verbal section fell from 427 to 424, the lowest level in a decade.

- The College Board, in its annual report on college costs, reports that the average cost of a year of college increased by 5 percent to 8 percent for the 1990-1991 school year. In terms of tuition and room and board, the most expensive colleges are Bennington College in Vermont ($21,550), Sarah Lawrence College in New York ($21,490), and New York University ($21,400).

- According to the *New England Journal of Medicine,* a study conducted at Brown University finds that sexual activity among college women had changed little since 1975, in spite of the threat posed by acquired immuno-deficiency syndrome (AIDS) and other sexually-transmitted diseases.

- The National Assessment of Educational Progress releases a report on the first test of student geography skills. Although most students are able to locate major countries on a map and show knowledge of places and subjects recently in the news, they have problems with other areas such as trade, environment, and population growth. Male students answer an average of 61 percent of the questions correctly, and female students 54 percent. White students score an average of 61 percent, Hispanics 48 percent, and blacks 43 percent. Scores are highest in the central region, lowest in the Southeast.

- The Teach for America program is launched to recruit young liberal-arts graduates to teach for two years.

9 Jan. The U.S. Supreme Court rules unanimously that universities do not hold any special status that would protect them against disclosure of confidential peer review materials.

6 Feb. In an effort to relieve severe overcrowding in the city's public schools, the Los Angeles Board of Education votes to require all schools within the district to convert to a year-round schedule as of July 1991.

23 Feb. Bishop College in Dallas, once the largest black college in the western United States, is sold at a bankruptcy auction, believed to be the first such auction of an entire college in the nation.

5 Mar. "Channel One," a commercially sponsored television news program designed for use in high school classrooms, makes its formal debut in four hundred schools across the country.

7 Mar. Teachers in West Virginia walk off their jobs to demand better pay and an upgrading of the state's education system in the first statewide teachers' strike in state history. Teachers return to classes on 19 March.

30 Apr. The Carnegie Foundation for the Advancement of Teaching releases the report "Campus Life: In Search of Community," which decries administrators' lack of concern over student crime, alcohol abuse, and growing racial and sexual intolerance.

18 May	The trustees of all-women Mills College in Oakland, California, vote to rescind a decision they had made on 3 May to admit men after two weeks of heated student protests and boycotts had shut down the 138-year-old school.
4 June	The Supreme Court upholds a federal law that requires public high schools to give student political and religious groups the same access to facilities that is available for other extracurricular activities.
5 June	The New Jersey Supreme Court rules that the state's system of funding public education with local property taxes is unconstitutional because it benefits wealthy school districts at the expense of poor ones.
12 June	North Dakota voters reject a proposed temporary increase in the state sales tax. The increase, to 6 percent from 5 percent, would have lasted for one year and would have raised an estimated $42 million for public education.
26 July	President George Bush signs into law the Americans with Disabilities Act (ADA), which prohibits discrimination against people with physical or mental disabilities. Employment, transportation, telecommunications, and public accommodations (including school buildings) are some of the key areas affected by the law.
25 Sept.	President Bush signs into law a $1.6 billion bill designed to improve vocational education by calling on states to integrate academic skills into vocational classes, to develop standards for measuring vocational-technical students' competencies in basic and advanced skills, as well as providing funding for "tech-prep" programs linking high schools with local community colleges.
9 Nov.	President Bush signs into law the Student Right-to-Know and Campus Security Act requiring all colleges and universities to publish annual statistics on their graduation rates, crime rates, and security procedures.
7 Dec.	Astronauts onboard the space shuttle Columbia beam a classroom lesson on star formation and celestial radiation from space to forty-one middle-school students gathered at National Aeronautics and Space Administration (NASA) centers in Huntsville, Alabama and Greenbelt, Maryland.

1991

- U.S. Secretary of Education Lauro F. Cavazos Jr. is replaced by Lamar Alexander.

- Yale University's secret society Skull and Bones spends seven months in a battle between alumni directors and students over a decision to admit women to the club for the first time.

- The Centers for Disease Control releases a report based on a 1990 survey, the Youth Risk Behavior Survey, which found that almost one in five American high school students sometimes carried a gun, knife, or other weapon to school.

- A Gallup poll instituted by an insurance network reports that 6 percent of U.S. teenagers said they had tried to commit suicide. Another 15 percent said they had "come very close to trying."

- The U.S. Department of Education releases a study that found that Spanish-speaking students learned English at about the same rate regardless of whether they were taught in bilingual programs or in all-English programs.

- The Senate votes to bar Pell educational grants to prisoners.

- More than one hundred students in Duncan, South Carolina, are suspended for displaying the Confederate battle flag or protesting the school's decision to ban it. The suspensions lead to a debate about racism and freedom of expression at James F. Byrnes High School, where 23 percent of the student body is black.

22 Feb. Johns Hopkins University, which has one of the most prestigious medical schools in the country, announces that it will sell its tobacco company stocks, stating that its holding of such stocks was "incompatible" with its "mission to disseminate information on the treatment and prevention of disease and illness."

28 Mar. A U.S. District Court judge in New York City rules that it was illegal for a company to make photocopies of articles and book excerpts and assemble them into anthologies for sale to college and university students.

22 May The Justice Department signs a consent decree with eight Ivy League colleges and universities in which the schools agree not to share information on student financial aid and tuition or faculty salaries, thereby preventing action on charges of civil antitrust violations.

12 July H. Joachim Maitre resigns as dean of Boston University's College of Communications after it was revealed that he had plagiarized an article by Public Broadcasting Service (PBS) film critic Michael Medved in a commencement address in May.

21 Oct. Trustees of the University of Bridgeport in Connecticut vote unanimously to reject a takeover and aid offer from Reverend Sun Myung Moon's Unification Church. The Moon organization had offered $50 million in aid, plus a guarantee of at least one thousand additional students, in exchange for control over the university.

1 Nov. A physics graduate student who is distraught over his failure to win an academic award shoots and kills five people and critically injures another at the University of Iowa.

13 Nov. Doreen Kimura presents results of a study that found that, like her previous study of the effect of female hormonal cycles, men's standardized test results varied according to their cycle of the male testosterone hormone. In the fall, when men's testosterone levels rose, scores were highest, while in the spring, when levels fell, results were lowest.

26 Nov. The New York City Public School system begins implementing a plan to provide free condoms upon request as part of an AIDS education program. The plan sparks controversy since it does not require students to obtain parental permission in order to receive condoms.

1992

- A judge in California issues an injunction barring state action against a San Jose high school for showing the "Channel One" news program, instead forcing the school to notify parents and teachers in writing that students have the option to participate in a supervised alternative rather than view "Channel One."

- The U.S. Department of Education releases a report on high school-dropout figures that found the rate among sixteen to twenty-four-year-old Hispanics had increased to 35.3 percent in 1991 from 34.3 percent in 1972. For those same years, the rate for blacks ages sixteen to twenty-four had declined to 13.6 percent from 21.3 percent, and the rate for whites in that age group had dropped to 8.9 percent from 12.3 percent.

- The Association for the Evaluation of Educational Achievement tests children ages nine and fourteen. It finds that U.S. students rank second among nine-year-olds and ninth among fourteen-year-olds in a thirty-one nation study.

- A Gallup poll survey of 1,306 adults finds that 68 percent support the distribution of condoms in public schools, with 25 percent stating that prophylactics should be given out only with parental consent.

- Glassboro State College changes its name to Rowan College of New Jersey after businessman Henry M. Rowan donates $100 million, the largest individual gift ever given to a public college or university.

- Rejecting an argument by Educational Testing Service (ETS) that it was impossible to raise an SAT score from 620 to 1,030 in eight months, a New York state judge orders reinstatement of the score earned by Brian Dalton, who claims he was ill during the first examination and had since taken a coaching course.

18 Jan. A seventeen-year-old shoots and kills an English teacher and a janitor and holds classmates hostage at his Grayson, Kentucky, high school.

12 Feb. The report "How Schools Shortchange Women," commissioned by the American Association of University Women Educational Foundation and prepared by the Wellesley College Center for Research on Women, states that girls faced widespread bias in classrooms across the United States.

26 Feb. Two students are shot to death by a classmate in a hallway at Thomas Jefferson High School in Brooklyn, New York, less than two hours before Mayor David Dinkins is scheduled to visit the school to urge pupils to avoid drugs and violence.

26 Feb. The U.S. Supreme Court rules unanimously in the case of *Franklin* v. *Gwinnett County Public Schools* that Title IX of a 1972 education law entitled students at schools receiving federal funds who were the victims of sexual harassment and other forms of sex discrimination to sue for monetary damages.

1 May A twenty-year-old dropout kills four, wounds nine, and holds dozens of other hostages for more than eight hours at Lindhurst High School in Olivehurst, California.

24 June The Supreme Court rules 5–4 that nonsectarian prayers delivered at a public high school graduation violated First Amendment principles separating church and state.

26 June The Supreme Court decides 8–1 that the state of Mississippi has not satisfied its constitutional obligation to eliminate segregation within its public university system by applying "race-neutral" admission policies at its five formerly "whites-only" campuses or its three historically black campuses.

30 July   The U.S. Census Bureau releases data on metropolitan areas from the 1990 census that found that those living in metropolitan areas tended to be more educated than those living elsewhere—the proportion of the population with at least a bachelor's degree was 22.5 percent in metropolitan areas, and 13 percent in other areas.

1 Sept.   According to a survey released by the liberal constitutional rights group, People for the American Way, attempts to censor public-school texts and other educational materials in 1991 had increased 50 percent from the year earlier total to 376 incidents, with 41 percent of those censorship attempts finding success.

11 Sept.   A seventeen-year-old runs through a crowded hallway shooting a revolver and injuring six students in Amarillo, Texas.

28 Sept.   After a two-year investigation, the U.S. Department of Education Office for Civil Rights announces that the University of California at Berkeley's law school had violated federal civil rights laws by giving preferential treatment to minority applicants in an attempt to diversify the student body.

23 Oct.   A student is sentenced to six months in jail for lying under oath about cheating on the SAT, in what was believed to be the first such criminal prosecution related to the college-entrance exam.

6 Nov.   A thirteen-year-old boy shoots into a crowded playground and kills an eighteen-year-old student in Lancaster, Pennsylvania.

1993

- Richard W. Riley replaces Lamar Alexander as U.S. Secretary of Education.

- The American Federation of Teachers (AFT) reports that public school teachers across the nation were paid an average salary of $35,104 during the 1992-1993 school year. The highest state average was Connecticut ($48,918), while South Dakota teachers were paid the lowest on average ($24,291).

- Tensions rise at the University of Pennsylvania when five black sorority sisters charge a white student of racial harassment after he called them "water buffalo."

- South Boston High School remains closed from 6 May to 10 May following a racially-charged brawl outside the school that occurred when white students staged a walkout over safety issues during a visit by Boston mayor Raymond Flynn (D).

3 Jan.   A former drama teacher at the exclusive Phillips Exeter Academy in New Hampshire is sentenced to five years in prison for possession and distribution of child pornography.

21 Jan.   In Los Angeles, California, a fifteen-year-old who took a gun to school because he feared gang members accidentally fires the pistol in the classroom, killing one classmate and wounding another. The school district begins random screening of students by using portable metal detectors.

22 Feb.   A seventeen-year-old is gunned down by a fifteen-year-old in the hallway of his San Fernando Valley, California, high school.

3 Aug. The Senate confirms former University of Pennsylvania president, Sheldon Hackney, as chairman of the National Endowment for the Humanities.

2 Sept. A fifteen-year-old is fatally shot in the hallway of Franklin D. Roosevelt High School in Dallas, Texas, by a sixteen-year-old classmate.

8 Sept. The Boston Teachers Union votes in favor of a new contract that would directly tie teachers' pay to improvements in student performance.

20 Sept. About 90 percent of New York City public schools open after emergency asbestos inspections caused an eleven-day delay. The mayor ordered the new inspections when it was revealed that many inspections were mishandled in the 1980s.

15 Oct. University of Massachusetts chancellor David Scott announces that the school would retain the Minuteman mascot that protestors claimed promoted racism, sexism, and violence in the form of a white man toting a musket.

1 Nov. School officials in Hempstead, Texas, reverse a ban on pregnant girls belonging to the cheerleading squad after a threatened lawsuit from the National Organization for Women (NOW) and the American Civil Liberties Union (ACLU). Four of the fifteen-member squad had been removed under the policy, although one had been reinstated after she had an abortion.

3 Nov. The school board in Minneapolis, Minnesota, votes unanimously to hire a consulting firm to run the city's schools.

1994

- Harvard University announces that it would use the Common Application, a standard college application form used by more than 135 other private colleges and universities nationwide.

- Twenty-four midshipmen are expelled from the U.S. Naval Academy for their part in a cheating scandal involving an electrical engineering exam in December 1992.

- The Supreme Court rules 6-3 that a special school district set up to accommodate disabled children in Kiryas Joel, a town in Upstate New York inhabited entirely by members of an orthodox Jewish enclave, is unconstitutional.

- The annual survey of college freshmen conducted by the American council on Education and the University of California, Los Angeles reveals that only 31.9 percent of freshmen, the lowest percentage in twenty-nine years, reported that "keeping up with political affairs" is an important goal.

- The state with the highest percentage of graduates taking the SAT is Connecticut, with 80 percent; the states with the lowest percentage, 4 percent, are Mississippi and Utah.

21 Jan. A seventeen-year-old Kennard, Texas, student shoots and kills himself during his first-period class.

19 Mar. The Scholastic Assessment Test replaces the Scholastic Aptitude Test as the most widely used college entrance exam. The College Board changes the test in response to criticisms of bias and unreliability.

12 Apr. A ten-year-old shoots and kills an eleven-year-old classmate on their elementary school playground in Butte, Montana.

5 June — Michael Kearney, a ten-year-old, is the youngest American to graduate from college when he receives a bachelor's degree with a major in anthropology from the University of South Alabama in Mobile.

7 Aug. — Harry Kloor, a graduate student at Purdue University, is the first person in the United States ever to be awarded two simultaneous doctorate degrees (Physics and Chemistry).

7 Sept. — A sixteen-year-old student is gunned down in front of his high school in an apparent gang-related incident in Hollywood, California.

1995

- The Education Resources Institute reports that the total value of federal college loans in 1994 reached $23.1 billion, a significant increase over the 1984 figure of $7.9 billion. Analysts attribute the rise to increasing college costs and the failure of federal grant monies to keep pace.

- Scholarships for Jewish female students at the Stern College for Women and Albert Einstein College of Medicine are created by a $22 million bequest to Yeshiva University in New York City from Anne Scheiber, a stockbroker who aggressively invested the $5,000 with which she retired in 1994.

- A study by the Economic Policy Institute reports that increases in school spending during the past twenty-five years went largely to uses other than traditional classrooms. The study shows that 38 percent of new school funding supports the needs of disabled students and 19 percent goes to other types of special education, while 26 percent is used for regular education costs.

- In one of the ten largest private gifts ever made to a U.S. college or university, retired investment banker John L. Loeb and his wife give $70.5 million to Harvard University.

- Results of tests conducted by the National Assessment of Educational Progress in 1994 show that only 34 percent of high school seniors are rated proficient readers, down from 37 percent in 1992. In the test intended to measure how well students understand and analyze what they read, 70 percent of seniors could partially master solid reading skills, compared with 75 percent in 1992. Scores for fourth and eighth graders remain about the same as in 1992.

- In a national study conducted by the Harvard School of Public Health, it is confirmed that the rate of alcohol consumption among college students is far higher for residents of fraternities and sororities than for students who do not belong to such organizations. In a survey of 14,700 students at 115 colleges, 86 percent of fraternity residents and 80 percent of sorority residents report they were binge drinkers (five or more consecutive drinks for men and four for women, on at least one occasion during the previous two weeks) as opposed to 45 percent of male students and 36 percent of female students not associated with fraternities or sororities.

- The AFT reports that public school teachers' salaries in the 1994-1995 school year increased by an average of 2.7 percent nationwide from the previous school year, slightly below the annual rate of inflation of 2.8 percent.

- The Edison Project, a program founded by media entrepreneur Christopher Whittle, is implemented at the beginning of the school year at four public elementary schools across the United States. The new program is guided by the philosophy that public schools would be more effective if they were privately run, cutting down on government bureaucracy.

- The Consortium on Productivity in the Schools, a panel of productivity experts, releases a report stating that U.S. public schools did not use effectively the $285 billion received yearly from the federal government. Among the recommendations are suggestions for more autonomy for schools, teachers, and principals, financial rewards for schools that showed the most progress, and required national examinations for students to earn their diplomas.

3 Mar. The Cleveland, Ohio, public school system, a 74,000-student-district, is put under state control by a federal judge because of its $125 million debt.

5 Apr. An investigative report published in the *Wall Street Journal* reveals that many colleges and universities report false information about test scores and graduation rates to people compiling data for popular published guides that rank schools. In a comparison of those guides with reports sent to debt-ratings agencies and investors, the study found inflated average SAT scores and graduation rates.

26 Apr. The Supreme Court rules 5-4 that the Gun-Free School Zones Act of 1990, making possession of a firearm within one thousand feet of a school a federal offense, is unconstitutional.

5 May University of Washington officials announce a $10 million gift to the school from Microsoft Corporation founder Bill Gates for the Mary Gates Endowment for Students in memory of his late mother. Gates also donated $12 million to the same university in 1991 to set up a molecular biotechnology department.

28 May Ethiopian student Sinedu Tadesse stabs her roommate to death in their dormitory room at Harvard University, wounds an overnight guest, and then hangs herself in one of the dorm's bathrooms in an apparent reaction to a request to change roommates.

26 June The Supreme Court upholds by a 6-3 vote a random drug-testing program for public school student athletes. The case, *Veronia School District* v. *Acton,* provides the first ruling on a school-sponsored program and was the first in which the court upheld a program that tested individuals at random.

29 June The Supreme Court rules 5-4 that the University of Virginia violated a student group's First Amendment rights to publish a student-run Christian journal by denying it the same funding resources that were available to secular student-run magazines. University officials responded by offering a 25 percent refund of annual activity fees to students who disagreed with the political or religious views of campus groups.

31 July U.S. District Judge Frank Mays Hull upholds a Georgia law that required a minute of silent meditation at the beginning of each school day because it does not violate standards set in 1971 by the Supreme Court, which allowed prayer in school if it has a secular purpose, does not advance or promote religion, and does not excessively intertwine the government with religion.

12 Sept. U.S. Justice Richard P. Matsch ends a court-supervised desegregation program dating back to 1969, which included compulsory race-based busing for many students in Denver, Colorado, public schools.

1 Oct.	Michael Bloomberg, the founder and owner of the Bloomberg L.P. news and information service, announces that he will donate $55 million to Johns Hopkins University.
25 Oct.	Seven high school students, ages fourteen to eighteen, are killed and more than two dozen others are injured when a commuter train crashes into a school bus in Fox River Grove, Illinois, a small town located about forty miles northwest of Chicago.
9 Nov.	Gordon Y.S. Wu, a prominent Hong Kong developer, announces a gift of $100 million to Princeton University's School of Engineering and Applied Science, the largest ever cash donation by a foreigner to a university in the United States.
9 Nov.	Courtney and Chris Salthouse, fraternal twins from Chamblee, Georgia, become the first set of twins simultaneously to achieve the highest possible score (1600) on the SAT college entrance examination.
5 Dec.	An Arizona state court judge rules that a public school district had the right to require students to wear school uniforms. The ruling affirms that such a requirement cannot be overruled by parents.

1996

- Funding for the U.S. Department of Education increases to $26.3 billion from $21.5 billion in the previous year.

- The College Board reports that the average cost of attending a U.S. college or university continues to increase at a rate that exceeds the national inflation rate. The average cost of tuition and fees for in-state students attending public four-year colleges and universities increases to $2,966 for the 1996-1997 academic year, up 5.5 percent from the previous year.

- Using figures from the National Assessment of Educational Progress, the Education Trust reports that the gap in achievement between white and minority students has widened in recent years.

- The U.S. Fourth Circuit Court of Appeals upholds a Baltimore, Maryland, law prohibiting billboard advertisements for cigarettes near schools and other areas that minors are likely to frequent.

- A study by the American Council on Education reports that the number of racial and ethnic minorities attending U.S. colleges and universities has increased by 5 percent from 1993 to 1994, an increase that was twice as large as that of the previous year.

- The percentage of student borrowers who defaulted on their federal loans fell to 11.6 percent in the 1993 fiscal year according to a report released by the Department of Education.

- The release of the U.S. Census Bureau report, "Educational Attainment in the United States: March 1995," reveals that for the first time the high school graduation rate for black Americans was roughly equal to the graduation rate for whites, although the rate for Hispanic Americans continued to lag far behind the nation's overall graduation rate. Experts attribute much of the improvement to an increase in high-school equivalency diplomas earned by black adults returning to school.

- A study by the American Association of University Professors reports the average salary of college and university faculty members reached $50,980 per year for the 1995–1996 academic year. The increase of about 3 percent was slightly ahead of the 2.5 percent of inflation for the same period.

- A panel of teachers and historians determine a revised set of national standards for the teaching of history. National standards developed in 1995 were harshly criticized for negative portrayals found in biased wording of sample assignments. The new standards focused on broad guidelines concerning what primary and secondary students should learn about U.S. and world history and omitted sample assignments.

- The National Commission on Teaching & America's Future releases the influential report, "What Matters Most," which argues for policy changes to ensure a caring, competent, and qualified teacher in every classroom.

23 Jan. The board of education in Hartford, Connecticut, votes to cancel a contract that granted a private firm, Educational Alternatives, Inc., management control over the district's thirty-two public schools.

2 Feb. Two students and a teacher are shot in their Frontier Junior High School by a fourteen-year-old student in Moses Lake, Washington.

11 Apr. An eighteen-year old senior is killed by a shotgun blast from a sixteen-year-old classmate in the parking lot of his Talladega High School in Alabama.

8 May A federal judge lifts a desegregation order that required the Cleveland, Ohio, school district to integrate its public schools through busing after the district's recent claim that ending the court-ordered busing would save the schools $10 million.

20 May Three students, one Native American and two African American students, are told they will not receive their high school diplomas from Muskogee High School in Oklahoma because they wore cultural symbols on their clothing at their graduation, violating the graduation dress code. The students are required to attend twenty-five days of summer school as punishment.

15 Aug. Three professors are killed at San Diego State University when a graduate student opens fire with a handgun at the defense of his engineering thesis. The thesis had been previously turned down.

26 Sept. A sixteen-year-old student is charged with killing an English teacher in his Dekalb County, Georgia, alternative school.

30 Sept. The Chicago school board places 109 of the city's 557 public elementary and high schools on academic probation. The move enables the schools to receive expert help in developing improved teaching strategies. If the schools fail to improve, however, the school board has the authority to replace principals and faculty members.

29 Oct. George Kobayashi, the head of a test-preparation school, is arrested for a scam that took advantage of time-zone differences to provide answers to students taking standardized tests in California to determine admission to graduate schools.

31 Oct. A seventeen-year-old student dies after being shot in the hallway of his St. Louis high school by a classmate.

14 Nov. The federally appointed Washington, D.C., financial control board releases a report that says that Washington's public school system is unacceptable "by every important educational and management measure." The board eventually takes over the district's school system, removing the eleven elected school-board members. The superintendent is dismissed and eleven other school employees who dealt with the education budget are also fired.

15 Nov. The public school system in Boston, Massachusetts, announces an end to its use of racial preferences (35 percent of admissions for minorities) in response to a lawsuit from the father of a white girl who was denied admission to the elite Boston Latin School even though her entrance exam scores were higher than 103 black and Hispanic students who were granted admission.

20 Dec. Delegates from the United States and 159 other nations meeting in Geneva, Switzerland, reach two landmark treaties designed to extend international copyright protection to material distributed by way of electronic media, such as the Internet. The treaties uphold the continued practice of "fair use" for copying excerpts for educational purposes.

1997

- Voters in Orange County, California, support a local school board's decision to abandon bilingual education.

- President Bill Clinton chooses the Little Rock campus of the University of Arkansas as the site for his presidential library.

- Yale University rejects an offer from homosexual playwright Larry Kramer to donate several million dollars to fund a permanent gay studies professorship at the school, citing that only the faculty had the power to determine curriculum and establish tenured teaching positions.

- The U.S. Department of Education estimates an increase by 2007–2008 of 2.1 million students from the 52.2 million for the 1997-1998 school year.

- Georgetown University, affiliated with the Roman Catholic Church, accepts the resignation of Dr. Mark R. Hughes after he admitted performing research on human embryos for in vitro fertilization, a practice opposed by the Church.

8 Feb. President Clinton announces the first $14.3 million (out of $200 million) in Department of Education grants to public schools to help them connect to the Internet.

13 Feb. Eighteen of the nineteen trustees of Adelphi University, New York, resign in order to avoid a costly court battle over their dismissal. At issue is their lack of responsibility in allowing the president to receive, without proper evaluations, compensation that was far out of line with similar institutions.

17 Mar. Three Detroit high school students are charged with murder following the shooting death of a sixteen-year-old freshman at Pershing High School.

24 Mar. The Ohio Supreme Court orders the legislature to formulate a more equitable school-funding system. Annual spending per pupil in Ohio ranges from $4,000 to $12,000 in the current property tax-based system.

2 Apr.	An Epitope, Inc. executive resigns after his firm had imported tainted frozen Mexican strawberries that caused an outbreak of Hepatitis A in several Michigan schools. Federal law prohibits the serving of food produced outside the United States in federally-funded school lunch programs.
16 Apr.	The Connecticut Senate and House of Representatives approves a measure transferring control of the Hartford Public School system from local authorities to the state government following allegations of mismanagement and shortcomings in student achievement.
2-4 May	In Boulder, Colorado, a crowd of fifteen hundred youths throw stones and bricks at police when they arrive to put out a bonfire reportedly set by University of Colorado students celebrating the end of their classes. The following night approximately five hundred students gather in the same spot for a second confrontation with police.
6 May	The AFT elects Sandra Feldman, president of New York City's United Federation of Teachers, to succeed the late Albert Shanker as president.
4 June	President Clinton signs a bill revising the 1975 Individuals with Disabilities Education Act. Major provisions are: changes in the funding formulas (relieving some of the local district burdens); a requirement that most federal spending occur in direct benefit of the classroom (not in administrative and attorney costs); and a greater flexibility in disciplining disabled students.
5 June	Two hundred million dollars, the largest gift ever given to a U.S. college or university, is donated by the F. W. Olin Foundation to build the Franklin W. Olin College of Engineering in Needham, Massachusetts.
23 June	The Supreme Court rules 5-4 that the Constitution does not prohibit public school teachers from entering parochial schools to provide remedial education and guidance counseling to poor children who are struggling academically.
7 Aug.	For the third time in four years, school officials in Washington, D.C., report that school openings will be delayed because of uncompleted repairs to buildings.
26 Aug.	Benjamin Wynne, a student at Louisiana State University, dies of alcohol poisoning after downing more than twenty drinks while celebrating his fraternity's pledge week. Three others at the same party are hospitalized.
26 Aug.	The College Board reports the results of the SAT for 1997: the average math score rose to 511 from 508, the highest recorded in twenty-six years, and the average verbal score remained the same at 505.
29 Sept.	Scott Krueger, an eighteen-year old pledge at the Phi Gamma Delta fraternity at the Massachusetts Institute of Technology, dies of alcohol poisoning following a drinking binge.
1 Oct.	A sixteen-year-old student murders his mother and fatally shoots two fellow students in Pearl, Mississippi.
21 Oct.	Results of a nationwide exam conducted by the National Assessment of Education Progress show that two out of three U.S. students have a basic understanding of science.
7 Nov.	A fourteen-year-old student is fatally shot and another is wounded across the street from their Jacksonville, Florida, high school.
1 Dec.	A fourteen-year-old boy opens fire on classmates at Heath High School in West Paducah, Kentucky, killing three girls and injuring five others.

11 Dec. Madlyn Abramson announces a gift from her family to the University of Pennsylvania in the amount of $100 million for a cancer research center. The gift is the largest to a cancer center in the nation and one of the ten largest to a university.

1998

- Republicans block a plan proposed by President Clinton for a tax initiative for states to boost spending on school construction.

- In an initiative called the Children's Scholarship Fund, a group of business leaders pledges to raise $200 million for a program to provide private-school tuition vouchers to impoverished students.

- The College Board commissions a study on grade inflation after a comparison of SAT scores of students with A averages shows an increase in the percentage of students with high grades and lower test scores.

- Results of the Third International Mathematics and Science Study indicate that 55 percent of U.S. twelfth graders—more than any of the other twenty countries in the study—said they work at least three hours a day at a paid job.

- Delegates to the National Education Association's Representative Assembly resoundingly reject guidelines for merging with the AFT.

4 Feb. Mary Kay Letourneau, a former Seattle teacher, is arrested after being discovered by police in a car with the former student whom she had confessed to having sexual relations with since he was thirteen years old.

24 Mar. Two youths, ages thirteen and eleven, carry out a fatal shooting spree at their junior high school in Jonesboro, Arkansas. Five people—four students and a teacher—are killed in the gunfire, and ten others are wounded.

24 Apr. A fourteen-year-old middle-school student shoots and kills a teacher and wounds two students and a second teacher near Edinboro, Pennsylvania.

2 May Nearly three thousand students take part in a protest against Michigan State University's ban on alcohol at a favorite tailgating locale in Lansing.

2 May The *Chronicle of Higher Education* releases a report showing that the number of alcohol-related arrests have risen 10 percent at five hundred major college campuses. Drug-related arrests have risen 5 percent.

19 May An eighteen-year-old honor student opens fire in a parking lot at his Fayetteville, Tennessee, high school, killing a classmate.

21 May A fifteen-year-old high school student in Springfield, Oregon, fatally shoots his parents and then opens fire in his school's crowded cafeteria. One student dies immediately while another dies the next day; twenty-two others are wounded.

15 June A fourteen-year-old boy wounds a teacher and a classroom aide in Richmond, Virginia, when he fires an automatic handgun in the hallway of Armstrong High School.

21 July President Clinton vetoes legislation that would have permitted parents with modest to low income to save up to $2,000 a year per child in tax-free savings accounts.

1 Sept.   The College Board reports in its annual release of national average SAT scores that suburban students scored about thirty points higher than urban ones on each section.

24 Sept.   George Soros, a Hungarian-born financier, announces his donation of $1.2 million over four years to the Maryland State Department of Education's Correctional Educational Program to fund post-secondary courses for the state's inmates as well as provide help to released prisoners in finding jobs.

7 Oct.   President Clinton signs a bill reauthorizing the 1965 Higher Education Act for five years with provisions for lower interest rates for students and an incremental increase in the total amount available through a Pell Grant.

21 Oct.   Two men are charged in the beating death of a twenty-one-year-old homosexual University of Wyoming student.

22 Oct.   President Clinton signs a bill expanding federal aid to charter schools while also setting stricter standards for schools to qualify for federal funding.

31 Oct.   A bill is signed by President Clinton overhauling the federal vocational programs, which, in part, increases the percentage of funds available to local authorities and schools from 75 percent to 85 percent.

30 Nov.   Martha Ingram, chairwoman of Ingram Industries, Inc., a wholesale distributor based in Nashville, Tennessee, donates a gift of stock valued at $300 million to Vanderbilt University in what is perhaps the largest private donation ever made to a college or university.

1999

- In a study released by the Center for Education Information, teacher-candidates tend to be older (around thirty) and are more likely to be male, which is a significant shift from the profile of fifteen years earlier.

- Harvard researchers release a study that says that 3.5 percent of college students have guns other than hunting weapons at school.

- Denver public school teachers begin a pilot study of merit pay increases linked directly to student performance for those students in their classrooms.

- From a survey conducted by the National Center on Addiction and Substance Abuse at Columbia University, a link is discovered between the quality of a father's relationship with his teenage children and the teenagers' likelihood of substance abuse. Poor relationships indicated a 68 percent greater chance of a teen smoking, drinking alcohol, or using drugs.

15 Jan.   The U.S. Department of the Navy, in an effort to reverse a downward trend in recruitment, announces that it would now only require 90 percent as opposed to the previous 95 percent of its recruits to have high school diplomas.

20 Jan.   Sylvan Learning Centers, Inc., a private education company that provides testing and tutoring services, announces its first step in developing a global network of for-profit colleges with the purchase of Universidad Europea de Madrid.

9 Feb.   Dartmouth College president James Wright announces a ban on single-sex fraternities and sororities in an effort to promote healthier relations between men and women and to curb incidences of binge drinking.

3 Mar.	The Supreme Court rules 7-2 that disabled students in public schools may have individuals who are not physicians provide them with special assistance during the school day.
22 Mar.	The Supreme Court rules 8-1 that the state of Ohio does not need to apply a policy on time spent in the classroom during labor negotiations with public university professors.
20 Apr.	Radcliffe College announces it will merge with Harvard University, a neighboring institution with which the school had been affiliated since its inception in 1879.
20 Apr.	At Columbine High School in Littleton, Colorado, two boys, ages seventeen and eighteen, shoot and kill twelve fellow students and a teacher, and wound more than twenty other classmates. Both of the perpetrators commit suicide.
21 Apr.	Metro-Goldwyn-Mayer, Inc. recalls video copies of its 1995 movie, *The Basketball Diaries,* in the wake of the Columbine High School shootings because it depicts a character in a black coat shooting a teacher and students.
29 Apr.	President Clinton signs into law the "Ed-Flex" bill, granting states greater flexibility over federal funds for education.
5 May	Ten state governors announce a cooperative effort in the development of curriculum and standardized tests for middle school mathematics through the nonprofit organization Achieve, Inc.
20 May	A fifteen-year-old boy opens fire on an indoor commons area at Heritage High School in Conyers, Georgia, injuring six students.
5 June	The space shuttle *Discovery* releases a $1 million educational satellite, *Starshine,* into orbit in order for students around the world to track it.
10 Aug.	A thirty-seven-year-old man opens fire in a Jewish day care center in Los Angeles, California, wounding five students and caretakers.
23 Aug.	In response to a student's display of a Star of David pendant at his Gulfport, Mississippi, high school, the Harrison County School Board exempts religious symbols from a general ban aimed at the wearing of gang symbols.
6 Sept.	Gregory Smith, a ten-year-old boy, begins his freshman year at Randolph-Macon College in Ashland, Virginia, after completing his high school curriculum in twenty-two months.
8 Sept.	After a week-long strike, the Detroit Federation of Teachers ratifies a new three-year contract that reduces classroom size in kindergarten through third grade to an optimum of seventeen students. Classes had averaged more than twice that before the negotiations.
16 Sept.	In the largest donation ever in the area of education, Microsoft Corporation Chairman Bill Gates and his wife Melinda announce the creation of a $1 billion college scholarship fund for minority students to be administered through the United Negro College Fund, the Hispanic Scholarship Fund, and the American Indian College Fund.
1 Oct.	A forty-one-year-old white man is arrested on charges that he had planted two bombs on the predominantly black Florida A&M University campus.
8 Nov.	Reverend Jesse Jackson leads a protest march in Decatur, Illinois, after seven students were expelled for two years from the school for their participation in a brawl at the 17 September Eisenhower High School football game. The suspension is later reduced to one year.

OVERVIEW

Money Well Spent. The 1990s, the decade of account-ability in education, forced inordinate attention on the field. Across the nation, parents, business leaders, and politicians demanded higher test scores, responsible fiscal expenditures, guarantees that students were learning, and the removal of ineffective teachers from the classroom. By the end of the 1980s, it was evident that Scholastic Aptitude Test (SAT) scores (the common national examination used for college admissions) were continuing to fall—or at best, not rising. Strong teacher unions were continually fighting issues of merit-pay and the testing of employed teachers. The American public began to demand an accounting for the quality of education students were receiving. Constant comparisons to tested abilities of children in other countries and the rising concern about the skill levels of high school graduates, which usually reflected badly on American youth, prompted many groups to clamor for substantial improvements.

Options. Many reformers turned to alternative modes of teaching the country's youth. If more money and the often contradictory ideas from respected practitioners could not alter the bleak picture of education in the nation, then perhaps reliance on public education was not the best solution. A groundswell of support appeared for increased options outside the domain of local school districts. Of the more than forty million school-aged children in the country in the late 1990s, thirty million were in public schools, but some estimated that more than one-half of the parents of those public school children would have provided a private education for their children if they could have afforded the exorbitant cost of tuition. Even schools costing several thousand dollars a year, such as some of those found in Catholic systems, were out of the price range of many American families. The idea of providing vouchers to families who could use them for not only private schools, but also for tuition at successful public schools outside their district, grew in popularity. As the concept developed supporters, opponents made their views widely known—in courts, the media, and political forums. School choice as an issue was hotly debated throughout the decade.

Other Alternatives. Typically, alternative education was viewed as the province of liberal or humanistic/progressive philosophies. However, the rise of more conservative, reli-gious-based education belied that assumption. Home schooling became much more acceptable as parents increasingly displayed their growing dissatisfaction with public schools. Alternative schools subscribing to a specific educational philosophy, such as the Coalition of Essential Schools, Montessori, and Waldorf, flourished. Books were published to sell parents on the myriad of options. Ronald E. Koetzsch's *The Parents' Guide to Alternatives in Education* (1997) asserts, "Every family can find an educational approach that is appropriate both for its children and for the family as a whole." When quasi-private, but publicly funded, charter school movements gained popularity, parents saw an opportunity to provide an alternative within the public school system. The number of charter schools in the country grew exponentially toward the end of the decade.

Concerns Over Safety. One of the major concerns of parents centered on the issue of their children's well-being while at school. When queried about schools' shortcomings, increasingly parents voiced the safety and welfare of their children as fears. In a 1990 study conducted by the Centers for Disease Control on youth health risks, 31.5 percent of young males reported carrying a weapon to school. (In isolated incidents around the country, the media repeatedly covered incidents of shootings by students in not only high schools, but also in middle schools.) Even day care centers were not immune to the specter of violence. Senseless deaths of students and teachers horrified the nation regularly. Among the victims of the Oklahoma City bombing were children and teachers at a day care. While test scores and improved achievement remained an educational agenda for the country, increasingly schools were forced to wrestle with the social behaviors of its students. Metal detectors, policemen, and routine locker searches became familiar fixtures in schools across the country. Suburban and rural schools soon faced the same issues. Once again, funds were being spent on items that had no direct correlation with learning in the classroom.

Minorities. The issue of funding and pupil expenses found its way to several state and district courts, as school districts grappled with methods of financing the schools. Many states were found to have illegal systems of funding education. Historically, school districts relied solely upon property taxes for income. This approach meant that richer districts spending more monies at the expense of typically black and Hispanic poorer areas were unconstitutional. In some states the differences in annual expenditures ranged from $3,000 to $12,000 per student.

Desegregation. Court-mandated desegregation oversight was lifted during the decade in many large school districts around the country. Although many cities still had predominantly black or predominantly white high schools, the Supreme Court ruled that the racial makeup of schools was often a result of demographic shifts that occurred after redistricting and other methods had been enacted to alleviate forced segregation. Districts had met the requirements of the original mandate and were no longer liable for correcting imbalances.

Affirmative Action. At the level of higher education, affirmative action took a major blow in the 1990s. The policy, which demanded quotas for minorities in hiring and some college admissions practices, came under fire in several states and their university systems. Voters decided to repeal the policies in controversial moves that had major repercussions in the racial makeup of the student bodies of those schools. The courts, however, supported the decision ruling that racial quotas in admissions were not appropriate methods for managing diversity on college campuses. Government figures showed that college enrollment by whites continued to outpace that of minorities, a trend that began in the late 1980s.

The Disabled. The plight of disabled students everywhere was eased when President George Bush signed the Americans with Disabilities Act in 1990. Affecting all walks of life, passage of the bill provided support for the transportation, access, and telecommunication needs of the country's physically or mentally disabled population. Hailed as a major civil-rights coup, the ADA provided guidelines on the level of support schools and other public institutions were expected to provide for the disabled. Although it was generally seen as a positive step forward, schools everywhere had to begin planning for adjustments to facilities and services that had serious impacts on their budgets.

New Programs. Greater focus also was placed on finding solutions for the problems encountered by students with learning disabilities. Programs developed to enable students with different learning styles to cope in mainstream classrooms. At the same time, a heavy reliance on medications to relieve some of the symptoms of Attention Deficit Disorder (ADD) came into favor. The controversial drug Ritalin was used successfully in some cases, but the powerful remedy raised concerns about the effects of long-term use, such as loss of personality.

Computers. Few factors impacted school budgets in quite the same way as the infusion of technology into the schools. As access to computers became one of the measures used to compare schools, administrators found themselves pouring thousands if not millions of dollars into equipping classrooms, networking buildings, and upgrading computer labs. The use of the Internet as a teaching tool became a hot topic in the field. Workshops and publications assisted teachers in integrating the technology into the curriculum. As schools scrambled to find experts to install computer hardware in buildings that were not built to accommodate it, educators combed the literature to find legitimate methods of applying the few educational software products available to their instructional methods. Schools grappled with a student body that was more technically aware than its teaching faculty. Lack of accessibility still hindered many schools. In 1993, just over 65 percent of students reported using a computer at school. Citing the vital importance of connecting the nation's schools to the world, the federal government stepped in with a program known as "e-rate" to provide financial assistance to schools enlarging their technological capabilities. Many other grant-making organizations also supplied schools with the necessary funds to improve their facilities.

Slow Change. Although early successes in the use of technology as a powerful motivating tool for students in all areas was exhibited, broad use still remained elusive. Some schools found themselves unable to justify the large expense in terms of improved student performance. Still others reported the availability of the equipment and software packages, but faculty members were unable or unwilling to shift their teaching methods to utilize the new resources. As businesses and colleges clamored for basic skills in word processing and other computerized routines, schools found themselves addressing changes in curriculum to meet their students' needs. As homes across the country began to report the number of computers the way they reported the number of televisions, the issue of access began to be a dividing line between the "haves" and the "have-nots."

The Internet. Access to the Internet in and of itself also prompted many debates. Without any legal regulation of what was available on the Internet, issues of children's access to pornography and inappropriate literature became a national concern. Who was responsible for limiting what children could and could not see? How could technology itself assist in the restriction of what children could access? Was restriction a matter of censorship or one of protection for children? Although legislation designed to protect children from harmful sites on the Internet failed, many products and policies were developed to address the issue. Overall, it seemed the benefits and convenience of the Internet overshadowed any attempts to regulate it.

Economic Boom. The growth in the American economy over the course of the decade spilled over into gains for education. The amount of philanthropy rose steadily during the nineties. Gifts in the millions of dollars increased endowments of colleges around the country, and interest in donating to precollegiate schools grew as well. The federal government also showed a steady increase in its Department of Education budgets, a far cry from earlier moves to dismantle it. By 1998, 40.9 percent of federal budget funds for education came from the Department of Education, with a total outlay of $75.1 billion in the fiscal year 1998 emanating from the U.S. Government.

Tuition. Despite this economic prosperity, tuition and fees at colleges and universities around the country grew at an unprecedented rate. The costs of higher education skyrocketed well beyond the pace of inflation. In the school year 1991-1992, the costs rose between 7 percent and 14 percent; in the previous year, the rise had been between 5 percent and 8 percent. Unfortunately, salaries for those same institutions did not keep pace.

The Federal Role. Historically and legislatively, education had been the province of the states. The federal government had no authority to dictate policy or program in the nation's schools. That role expanded, however, with various guidelines and funding initiatives. The Goals 2000 Program, initiated originally by a forum of the nation's governors late in the 1980s, supported by President Bush and eventually approved by his successor Bill Clinton, provided for clear educational objectives for the country for the remainder of the 1990s. Yet, testing results continued to show that improved student achievement was elusive. Educational experts and politicians forecasted that the lofty goals were unlikely to be met.

Crisis. National standards became a hot topic during the decade. Many felt that certain requirements should be highlighted for all of the nation's schools. Several states enacted their own standards, and controversy erupted over an attempt by a national group to establish History standards for the country. The use of standards was not questioned, but who should set them became an unresolved issue. Educators argued that politicians had no place in determining curricula, especially given the transient nature of their positions. Legislators displayed no trust in the educators who had not been able to improve student achievement without specific, statewide established standards. Still others argued that national standards were needed, while governors argued vehemently that education was the responsibility of the states. In the meantime, teachers and administrators struggled to adjust curricula and teaching methods so that students would be able to meet the impending, yet in some cases unknown, standards.

Assessment. As standards were debated, so were the methods of assessing student performance in relation to those standards. Defining the necessary skills varied from state to state. Maryland instituted a service learning component. New York focused on a school-to-work initiative. Concerns over the reliability of multiple-choice standardized tests made way for experiments with performance-based testing and essays to measure critical thinking. Researchers like Grant Wiggins urged schools to "measure those skills that have lasting value." Still, standardized tests that gauged progress on basic verbal and mathematics skills continued to be the number one measure of the country's progress toward the Goals 2000 objectives.

TOPICS IN THE NEWS

AFFIRMATIVE ACTION

Rethinking Quotas. Affirmative action, which relies upon race- or gender-based preferences in school admissions, public hiring, and public contracting decisions for an institution, suffered a major defeat in the 1990s. California voters passed Proposition 209 in November 1996, making the state the first in the nation to bar state-sponsored affirmative action programs. After extensive legal battles, the Supreme Court refused to hear an appeal of the case that ruled that the law did not violate the Constitution's Fourteenth Amendment. Also in 1996, the U.S. Fifth Circuit Court of Appeals in New Orleans, Louisiana, struck down an affirmative action admissions policy at the University of Texas School of Law in Austin. That decision effectively banned race-based admissions at state-run schools in Texas, Louisiana, and Mississippi, the three states that came under the jurisdiction of the appeals court.

Resegregation. President Bill Clinton at the commencement address of the University of San Diego in 1997 said, "I know that the people of California voted to repeal affirmative action without any ill motive. The vast majority of them simply did it with a conviction that discrimination and isolation are no longer barriers to achievement. But consider the results. Minority enrollments in law school and other graduate programs are plummeting for the first time in decades. Assuming the same will likely happen in undergraduate education, we must not resegregate higher education or leave it to the private universities to do the public's work. To those who oppose affirmative action, I

EBONICS

Late in December 1996, the local school board in Oakland, California, unanimously decided that the district would recognize "black English" as a separate language as opposed to a dialect of English or a form of slang. As a distinct language, Ebonics (from the words ebony and phonics) could be used to teach students in their primary language with the aim of improving achievement for the city's black children. Proponents of the plan asserted that Ebonics contained linguistic elements from African languages and that many black Americans had retained speaking patterns from their African roots. By allowing teachers to recognize the separate language, supporters argued that more effective teaching could take place.

Critics immediately condemned the move as an abrogation of the need to teach standard English to African American children. Accusations that the move was a ploy to enable the district to access funds aimed at non-English speaking students were denied by the district. African American civil-rights leader, Reverend Jesse Jackson, called for the district to reverse its decision, arguing that black students who could not use standard English would have difficulty finding jobs. A week after the school board announced its decision, Secretary of Education Richard Riley confirmed that the Clinton administration could not accept the concept of Ebonics as a separate language. The following month, the Oakland school board altered its plan in the wake of rising criticisms that they had insulted the learning abilities of black children.

Some linguists supported the notion of recognizing Ebonics in schools and teaching that it was different, not wrong. One teacher in a Los Angeles elementary school shared with children that there was "home language" and "school language." Others asserted that the differences in language were not issues of heritage but of class. In all cases, teachers were encouraged to teach standard English to their students. Al Shanker, former president of the American Federation of Teachers, asked, "How can teachers juggle 'maintaining the legitimacy of Ebonics' with teaching children not to use it?" Several analysts feared that the entire issue had caused a backlash against programs (like Affirmative Action) designed to address the statistically poor academic performance of minorities. Although the issue of Ebonics disappeared from the national scene, the underlying problems the Oakland School Board sought to address continued.

Sources: Karen Hopkins Meyers, "Oakland, California Ebonics Debate," *American Education Annual: Trends and Issues in the Educational Community,* edited by Mary Alampi and Peter M. Comeau (Detroit: Gale, 1999).

Lucille Renwick, *"Ebonics: The Sound and the Fury,"* Family.com, Internet website.

ask you to come up with an alternative. I would embrace it if I could find a better way."

Initiative 200. At the time of the California ruling, twenty-six states had similar initiatives pending. In 1998, 58 percent of the voters in Washington State approved the ban of state and local agencies from granting preferential treatment on the basis of race, ethnicity or gender when admitting students to state schools, hiring for state jobs, or awarding state contracts in a measure known as Initiative 200. The debate raged on across the country.

King. Many representatives of the American Civil Liberties Union (ACLU) and black civil rights organizations decried the move as a step backward. Martin Luther King III, the oldest son of slain civil-rights leader Reverend Martin Luther King Jr., announced that he was forming a new national coalition to fight for affirmative action. The Atlanta-based Americans United for Affirmative Action was developed in response to the vote in California and to the launch of the American Civil Rights Institute, a national anti-affirmative-action group headed by Ward Connerly, a black California businessman who had pushed

THE BELL CURVE

The publication in 1994 of *The Bell Curve: Intelligence and Class Structure,* authored by Richard J. Herrnstein and Charles Murray, sparked major controversy across the nation. Although it echoed many of the ideas of current thinking about intelligence and its link to heredity, many scholars continued to debate the degree to which intelligence is inherited. Chief among the complaints of the book, and why it attracted such widespread attention, were the assertions that "blacks as a group are intellectually inferior to whites and that there is not much that education—or intervention of any sort—can do to close that gap."

The 860-page book, full of statistics and the culmination of an eight-year collaboration, put forth as its central theme the idea that America is increasingly divided by intellectual ability. The authors raised the concern that the leaders of the country, the intellectual elite, were further removed and isolated from the growing underclass. In presenting their arguments, Herrnstein and Murray condemned efforts to solve the nation's problems through attempts at raising intellectual levels as a move that had no chance of success. Although they offered little in the way of remedies, the two did suggest that parents be allowed greater freedom in choosing the schools that their children attend and that more funds be targeted toward the most gifted students.

Source: Debra Viadero, "Education Experts Assail Book on I.Q. and Class," *Education Week,* 26 October 1994.

California State Senator Diane Watson (D-Los Angeles) protests against Proposition 209 on 1 November 1996. The measure was designed to eliminate preferential hiring or college admissions based on race or gender (AP/Wide World Photos).

for Proposition 209, legislation designed to eliminate quotas in higher education.

Test Case. Opponents of affirmative action were frustrated, however, by the settlement in 1997 of a Supreme Court case just weeks before the decision could be rendered relating to the choice of firing a white teacher in New Jersey based on the need to maintain racial balance within her business education department. The case, *Piscataway* v. *Taxman*, was viewed as a good test case for the Supreme Court because the facts of the case–two teachers equally qualified and the school board's preference criterion narrowly defined–were so clearly drawn.

Enrollment Figures. Proponents of affirmative action pointed to enrollment figures at schools affected by the recent measures as justification for the need of affirmative action programs. The law school at the University of California at Los Angeles reported that only twenty-one black students had been admitted for the 1997-1998 school year, the lowest total in nearly thirty years and down 80 percent from the previous year. About one hundred black applicants had gained admission for the 1996-1997 academic

year. The law school at the system's Berkeley campus had admitted fourteen black students for the coming school year, down from seventy-five from the previous year. Both law schools said that similar drops in admissions had occurred among Hispanic applicants.

Sources:

Facts on File, volumes 56, 57, 58 (New York: Facts on File, 1996, 1997, 1998).

ALTERNATIVE EDUCATION

Public Dissatisfaction. As reports of violence and a lack of appreciable rise in achievement scores plagued American schools, parents increasingly looked for options to sending their children to the local public school. School reform advocates, tired of fighting within the system, sought to develop alternatives to the public school system. Still others argued that the best way to hold the public schools accountable for performance was through the tried and true economic method–consumer choice. John Chubb and Terry Moe, in their provocative work, *Politics, Markets, and America's Schools* (1990), argued for a theory once proposed by Nobel prize winning economist, Milton Friedman: that free enterprise was necessary to force failing institutions out of business. While government could establish standards, a free-market system of private institutions providing education would inevitably use market forces to improve performance. Public debate on the options continued throughout the decade, with the various options gaining strength with changes in the ruling parties of the local, state, and federal governments. Although less than one-half of the people in an annual Gallup Poll favored allowing students to choose a private school at public expense, the numbers who agreed with the idea grew steadily during the 1990s, from 26 percent in 1991 to 44 percent in 1998.

Homeschooling. Over the last two decades, homeschooling became a growing popular choice. Chosen primarily by conservative Christian families, nearly 80 percent of homeschooling happened because of a distrust of the public school system and the appearance of emphasis on materialism, sexual promiscuity, and drug use. Lately, however, parents have listened to the cry of educators that parents should be more involved in their children's education. Parents who do get involved sometimes are not happy with what they find. Homeschooled children numbered over a million by the late 1990s. Strengths of homeschooling, in addition to an avoidance of popular, mainstream culture for some, included the prolonged time spent as a family, a higher degree of meaningful interaction between parents and children, an ability to illustrate that education does not end when the bell rings or when vacation arrives, and a more individualized program of study.

Opposition. Critics, on the other hand, argued that homeschooled children do not develop the normal social skills that come with interaction in a school setting. Parents maintained that the typical classroom setting does not resemble a normal social setting and many of the interactions–bullying, elitism, teasing, and conformism

A group of students in a La Marque, Texas, homeschool music class. During the 1990s parents increasingly sought alternatives to traditional methods of schooling (AP/Wide World Photos).

due to peer pressure—are not healthy. Social interactions outside the school such as the Boy Scouts and club sports were frequently used in lieu of ones found in the public school classroom.

The States. Different states had different laws regarding homeschooling, although there were no longer any states that viewed homeschooling as an abetting of truancy. Some states required a great deal of cooperation between homeschool parents and the local school districts. In others, a simple letter to the state department of education was sufficient for approval to educate children in the home. Although homeschooling could cause economic hardships for families whose finances required both parents to work outside the home, it increased in popularity and acceptability during the 1990s.

Charter Schools. Charter schools are public institutions that operate under a charter contract that has been negotiated between the school's organizers (teachers or parents, for example) and a sponsor (such as a local school board, a state board of education, or a university), which oversees the provisions of the charter. The charter describes the school's instructional plan, specific educational outcomes and measures, and its management and financial plan. As public charter institutions, they receive state funding, but are independent legal entities that have the ability to con-

trol their own finances, including hiring and outside contract decisions. Most charters are granted for a specified amount of time. If the schools fail to meet the conditions of their charters, they are closed.

Growth. Minnesota enacted the first charter school law in 1991. By the end of 1998, 1,051 charter schools were in operation in twenty-seven states plus the District of Columbia. From the first opening in 1992, thirty-two charter schools closed their doors. The demand for the schools remained high: 70 percent of the schools reported a waiting list. Each year, more states passed charter legislation, and several amended their laws to increase the numbers of charters that could be granted.

Generalities. In practice, there was wide variability from state to state in charter law and charter mission, which meant that charter schools operated differently depending on the state legislation under which the charter school was approved. The specific schools themselves also varied greatly, where they targeted diverse student populations and instituted vastly different educational philosophies. In effect, there was no typical charter school. Whereas some schools mirrored the ideals of the school reforms of the 1990s, others relied more on conventional, traditional pedagogy and programs. According to the Center for Educational Reform, however, these generalities can be drawn:

SCHOOL UNIFORMS

During the 1990s several school districts attempted to restore order to their classrooms, reduce fighting over gang colors, and decrease the level of theft in their buildings by allowing schools to require students to wear uniforms. Long a practice in private education, especially in Catholic schools, the use of school uniforms was thought to bring a sense of collegiality to students and return the focus to what was happening in the classroom. Proponents of the policy suggested that the use of uniforms allows students to put themselves in a mind-set for school as they dress in the morning. Others thought that it reduces stress levels that accompany adolescents as they become comfortable with their self-image—no need to concern themselves with a "look," because everyone "looks" the same.

In Long Beach, California, where uniforms were made mandatory for all elementary and middle school children in 1984, reports indicated that disciplinary problems declined in a range of categories: school crime by 36 percent, fights by 51 percent, sex offenses by 74 percent, weapons offenses by 50 percent, assault and battery offenses by 34 percent, and vandalism by 18 percent. "We can't attribute the improvement exclusively to school uniforms, but we think it's more than coincidental," said district spokesman Dick Van Der Laan.

A report released in the September/October 1998 issue of *The Journal of Educational Research* disagreed, however. Researchers David L. Brunsma and Kerry A. Rockquemore analyzed data on nearly five thousand sophomores in a federal study begun in 1988. They determined that tenth graders were no less likely to outperform others if they were in uniform. "Requiring school uniforms is like cleaning and painting a deteriorating building," said Brunsma, an associate professor of sociology at the University of Alabama in Huntsville. "It will grab a community's attention and grab students' attention, but that will fade away if the excitement about education isn't followed up by some real reform efforts."

Source: "Research Notes," *Education Week*, 11 November 1998, Family.com Internet website.

---

60 percent of charter schools enroll fewer than two hundred students, whereas only 16 percent of other public schools have such small student bodies; charter schools have, on average, a racial composition similar to statewide averages or have a higher proportion of students of color; charter schools serve a slightly lower proportion of students with disabilities; and charter schools enroll approximately the same proportion of low-income students, on average, as other public schools.

Autonomy. Supporters of the charter school movement, which included both the Democratic White House and the Republican Congress of the late 1990s, found the concept allowed autonomy without sacrificing accountability. Many charter schools remained small entities and could provide more individualized attention that comes with smaller classes. Detractors countered that the emphasis on charter schools took the attention away from reform efforts in public schools. There was also a genuine concern that charter schools were one step away from the approval of vouchers for school choice.

Vouchers. One of the initial ideas for school choice promoted the use of vouchers for parents to choose the school that best fit the needs of their children. Again, based on an idea that the free-market system would then ferret out the inefficient and ineffectual schools in favor of those that parents chose, the concept of vouchers found its way to legislators. Successfully implemented in several states, vouchers continued to come under fire throughout the nation.

Funds. Each state used a different formula for determining eligibility of funds. For instance, in Florida, a student at a school that had received a failing grade on state test results two out of every four years became eligible for a voucher of up to $4,000 to attend a qualified public, private, or religious school. In Milwaukee, a program that began in 1990 and awarded vouchers worth up to $2,446 to 341 students, served 6,194 students in 1999 with a maximum $4,894 voucher. Family income in this case (which must be under 175 percent of the federal poverty level) was the determining factor.

Counterarguments. Two major concerns that critics used focused on the use of public funds for religious schools and the harm done to school systems by the diversion of public funds from public schools. Senator Edward M. Kennedy (D-Massachusetts) was quoted in *The Christian Science Monitor* on 26 June 1992: "It is a serious mistake to use Federal tax dollars to support private schools. . . . Our goal in education reform is to improve the public schools, not abandon them." In a related argument, educator Jonathan Kozol said in *Essence* in August 1992, "I'm bitterly opposed to vouchers. The concept is as sinister as can be. [Education Secretary Lamar] Alexander has a seductive formula for selling vouchers to the public. He says rich people already have the choice to send their child to private schools; why don't poor parents have the same choice? One would think he was ready to send poor black children in Harlem to Exeter [Academy in New Hampshire]. But he's only talking about vouchers of a couple thousand dollars. That might be part of the tuition at the lowest-level private school. Rich people will use it as a subsidy for the best schools. The only way it would be just is if every child in America got an equal voucher pegged for the best private schools in America."

THE EDISON PROJECT

The concept of "for-profit" schools grabbed the attention of the media in 1991 with the announcement by Whittle Communications of the Edison Project. Whittle, the media giant that brought Channel One to high schools across the country, proposed a private business venture that would deliver a first rate education to all students at the same cost per pupil as was being spent by public schools. A core team of developers was assembled, with Benno C. Schmidt Jr., former Yale University president, at its helm as chief executive officer (CEO), to launch the first one hundred schools in 1996. Originally planned as a network of private schools, the focus changed and became a cooperative partnership with school districts around the nation. In 1994 the project began opening its first wave of Edison schools.

The Edison Project remained true to its mission of "offering first-rate education to a cross-section of students at public school costs." Focusing on such basic issues as published academic standards, increased professional development, emphasis on technology, and low overhead (for example, reduced costs for central administration), the Edison Project continued to open schools across the nation. Among the changes implemented by the project, the school year was extended by about a month and at least one extra hour was added to the school day. Students received free computers to use at home and were given along with parents and teachers electronic-mail accounts which were intended to foster better communication between home and school. Students were taught Spanish, art, and music every day, and attended classes on character and ethics. In addition, principals and teachers had complete control over their schools' budget, and parents participated in the hiring of teachers. Critics of the program worried that the need to make a profit could take precedence over the quality of education.

Source: John E. Chubb, "Lessons in School Reform from the Edison Project," *New Schools for a New Century*, edited by Diane Ravitch and Joseph P. Viteretti (New Haven: Yale University Press, 1997), pp. 86-122.

Drucker and Chubb. Proponents, on the other hand, had equally passionate views. Peter F. Drucker, renowned for his advice to the business world on management, said in the *Los Angeles Times* in September 1991, "Since the public schools aren't going to reform, we need a voucher system [to allow students to go to the school of their choice]. . . . There are six schools within biking distance in Claremont. There's no reason for all of them to have the same pedagogical philosophy. [Without vouchers,] you'll never get any competition going." John Chubb, Senior Fellow at the Brookings Institute, proposed a more basic notion in the May-June 1991 issue of *The Sat-*

urday Evening Post: "The unions are opposed [to the idea], not because they are not concerned about the poor, but obviously because they are in business to protect the livelihood of all union members. A choice system is a potential threat to the incompetent or the marginal teacher. People who are doing a poor job, obviously, will not be chosen. And unions cannot support a program that will jeopardize the jobs of some of their teachers."

Legalities. Court battles abounded during the decade to abolish voucher systems across the nation. In June 1998, the Wisconsin Supreme Court upheld that state's program expansion to include religious schools. In April of 1999, the Maine Supreme Court ruled that state-funded school vouchers could not be used to send children to parochial schools. The battle did not end with the decade.

Sources:
Ronald E. Koetzsch, *The Parents' Guide to Alternatives in Education* (Boston: Shambhala, 1997).

Diane Ravitch and Joseph P. Viteritti, eds., *New Schools for a New Century* (New Haven: Yale University Press, 1997).

ASSESSMENT

Reformers. Ever critical of standardized testing as the sole means of measuring ability in students, countless educational reformers continued the mantra that assessments should be performance-based, that authentic methods of assessment were crucial. Noted assessment researcher Grant Wiggins said in his dynamic work, *Understanding by Design* (1998), "If tests determine what teachers actually teach and what students will study for—*and they do*—then test those capacities and habits we think are essential and test them in context." And yet, standardized tests, whether administered on a district or national level, continued to be the norm in terms of not only measuring student abilities, but also in measuring schools. Principals routinely bemoaned the fact that local newspapers published standardized test scores in a format that was designed to "rank" schools according to their average scores. They knew that the picture of a school's success was much richer than could be shown by a single score, and their attitudes mirrored the sentiments of reformers who fought for similar changes in the evaluation of students.

SAT. The Coalition of Essential Schools founder, Ted Sizer, in the article "Telling Silences" from the January 1996 *Education Digest* said, "The measures on which we ultimately depend have to plumb well what we do in fact value. What we care about–the long term intellectual habits and resourcefulness of every citizen–may be difficult to assess, indeed impossible to assess in familiar ways; but to persist with 'high stakes' testing that does not address these areas, while pretending it does, is indefensible." Nonetheless, parents across the country demanded valid assessments that "proved" that the schools were doing the job. The most familiar of those measures were Scholastic Aptitude Test (SAT) scores used for college admissions. Critics claimed the national exam was an unreliable predictor of future college achievement. Others

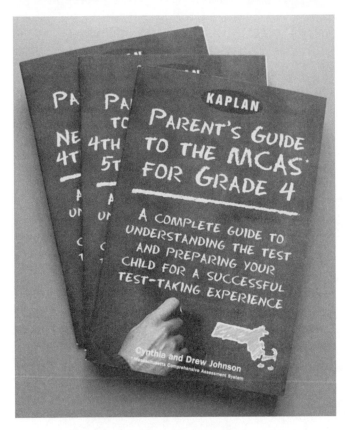

Guidebooks for the parents of students preparing to take the Massachusetts Comprehensive Assessment System tests in 1999 (AP/Wide World Photos)

Instead, the board created a written essay as one of the options in its achievement test series.

4) The SAT was increased to two hours and fifty minutes (up from its former two hours and thirty minutes) and was renamed the Scholastic Assessment Test. It continued to be scored on a scale that ranged from two hundred to eight hundred on each section.

5) The verbal and math changes on the SAT also affected the Preliminary Scholastic Aptitude Test (PSAT) which was given as a prelude to the SAT and was used to award National Merit Scholarships.

Zappardino. Despite the changes, the SAT remained under attack. Pamela Zappardino, the executive director of FairTest, said that even though women tended to perform better than men in high school courses, they scored consistently lower on standardized tests. Research has shown that both the questions and the structure of standardized tests may be biased against women, she said. The Cambridge, Massachusetts-based group advocated

complained that the SAT measured only narrow skills and that it was too easy for commercial "coaching" firms to tutor students for the test.

A New Look. In the wake of those criticisms (and ones charging racial and gender bias), the College Board approved changes to the SAT. After a three-year study by a panel of fifteen educators, the College Board announced in 1990 that these results would take effect in 1994:

1) On the math section of the test, the number of multiple-choice questions was reduced to fifteen, rather than twenty, quantitative comparisons. Some ten open-ended questions were added, to which students were required to provide their own answers. In addition, students were permitted to use calculators on the test for the first time.

2) On the verbal section, a set of twenty-five questions that had required students to identify word opposites, or antonyms, was dropped. More questions on reading comprehension were added, and the reading passages on which those questions were based were longer.

3) The College Board rejected a proposal that would have added a mandatory, twenty-minute essay section to the test. Some critics had argued that a written essay would be unfair to blacks and to Hispanics and Asian Americans who were not native English speakers.

THE UNION NON-MERGER

In 1998 an historic event captured the attention of the educational world. The two largest labor unions in the field, the 2.3 million-member National Education Association (NEA) and the 980,000-member American Federation of Teachers (AFT) considered merging into one solitary union. The merger would have melded two immense national organizations, as well as the state and local groups, into one "unified voice for America's teachers." The proposal, which required a two-thirds majority, was soundly defeated by the NEA Assembly delegates in New Orleans on 4 July 1998 by a 5,624 to 4,091 vote.

Why wouldn't teachers prefer to have a stronger voice in bargaining and lobbying cases? Some analysts suggested that the two groups were too far apart structurally and demographically. Others felt that the affiliation that the AFT had with the strong labor union, the AFL-CIO, was not in keeping with the concept of an education "profession." Still others argued that few teachers would be affected by the merger since the NEA was the dominant factor in most state politics.

The issue, however, stayed alive despite the defeat. The AFT approved the measure by a 97 percent vote, and many state-level organizations planned mergers. The increased emphasis on school choice, privatization, and outsourcing continued to point to a need for a single unified front for the nation's teachers.

Source: Bruce S. Cooper, "Merging America's Teachers Unions," *American Education Annual: Trends and Issues in the Educational Community,* edited by Mary Alampi and Peter M. Comeau (Detroit: Gale, 1999).

"Students are going to be 10 times as diverse as the school faculty in the 21st century. There will be more Hispanic students than black students for the first time in our nation's history. In fact, there are 215 nations in the world, and every one of them has someone living in the United States."

Harold Hodgkinson, Director
Center for Demographic Policy, Institute for Educational Leadership, Washington, D.C.

In 2009, "students of all ages typically have a computer of their own. . . . Intelligent courseware has emerged as a common means of learning. Recent controversial studies have shown that students can learn basic skills such as reading and math just as readily as with human teachers. . . . The traditional mode of a human teacher instructing a group of children is still prevalent, but schools are increasingly relying on software approaches, leaving human teachers to attend primarily to issues of motivation, psychological well-being, and socialization."

Ray Kurzweil, *The Age of Spiritual Machines: When Computers Exceed Human Intelligence* (1999)

"Despite the opposition of those with power and money, there will be greatly expanded public school choice in the coming years. There are now about 1,600 charter schools. By 2005, there will be as many as 5,000."

Joe Nathan, Director
Center for School Change, Humphrey Institute of Public Affairs, Minneapolis

"The future of teaching looks bright. . . . Peter Drucker argues that over the long-term, teachers will be better-compensated as they become more productive, just as other workers have. He predicts that in the future, teaching will be a higher-value, better-paid profession, thanks to technology, and I agree."

Bill Gates, *The Road Ahead* (1995)

"In the 2007-08 school year, the average salary for public school teachers will climb to $38,522–3 percent more than the average in 1996-97."

U.S. Department of Education

"By the year 2025, three-quarters of the state affiliates of the American Federation of Teachers and the National Education Association will have merged. Leaders of the two unions will interpret this as a 'mandate' to go ahead and merge at the national level."

Julia Koppich, *United Mind Workers: Unions and Teaching in the Knowledge Society* (1997)

"Kids are torn in many directions today, and the popular culture is very powerful and deeply anti-intellectual. I don't think that schools are irrelevant; if anything, I think that their saving power is needed more than ever. Their relevance, I suspect, will depend on their capacity to be different from the popular culture, not to imitate it."

Diane Ravitch, Education historian
New York University and the Brookings Institution in Washington, D.C.

"The five states that will see the largest increase in public school enrollment between 1999 and 2009 are: Nevada, Idaho, Arizona, Hawaii, New Mexico."

U.S. Department of Education

"When I am 30, I'll have a computer that has long arms that can clean the house and cook meals. And another computer that has a little slot that money comes out of to pay for groceries and stuff."

A 6th grade girl, to her teacher, from *Visions of Technology*, edited by Richard Rhodes (1999).

Source: "Ten Millennium Predictions," compiled by Karen L. Abercrombie and Drew Lindsay for *Education Week*, 1 November 1999.

---

eliminating standardized tests as a college-entrance requirement–a step 235 four-year colleges and universities have taken. "When you try to reduce a person down to two or three numbers," Ms. Zappardino said, "by necessity you cannot have a fair system."

Student Selectivity. When popular magazines began ranking colleges, such as the ones found in *U.S. News & World Report*, critics again condemned the use of numbers to rank schools. Whereas the magazine staff used a combination of criteria to develop the ranking, SAT scores of incoming freshmen were among those numbers used. High-school counselors complained that some families use the rankings as the only decision-making tool in deciding on college applications. College admission counselors also rebuffed the ratings. Rae Lee Siporin, the director of admissions for the University of California at Los Angeles, bashed the *U.S. News & World Report* ranking system for its use of a "student selectivity" rating. "What does selectivity have to do with the quality of your institution?" she asked. A large applicant pool might say something about a school's immediate popularity, such as whether it won the Rose Bowl or the national basketball championship, she said, "but I'm not sure how that makes you a qualitatively better institution." The magazine rankings grew in popularity, however, prompting versions that dealt with specific types of graduate schools and other programs.

States. As the national educational community tries to align with the growing support for standards and accountability, states across the nation are devising their own standardized tests to measure the degree to which students have met their established standards. As more high-stakes tests are required, and as teacher performance, student graduation or promotion, or even school and district autonomy are determined by these tests, the pressure to "teach to the test" increases. In one specific instance, a group of high-achieving eleventh graders in Chicago's top-ranked Whitney Young High School purposefully failed portions of the Illinois Goal Assessment Program, sending a letter to the principal: "We refuse to feed into this test-taking frenzy." It was the fourth in a battery of standardized tests the students were required to take that school year. The students complained that real learning is being shoved aside while teachers focus on boosting test scores. In polls, however, these tests win wide public support despite a fear that too much time teaching to the test crowds out creative thinking and puts too much emphasis on facts regurgitation.

Rethinking Schools. Some critics argue that standardized tests are attempting to do too much. Defining the purpose of the assessment is critical to determining which assessment should be used and when. "For example, an assessment designed to evaluate how well a school, overall, is teaching its students to read should not be used to decide whether a particular student should or should not be promoted to fourth grade. Furthermore, any assessment should ultimately serve, and not undercut, the primary goal of helping the student," claimed Bob Peterson and Monty Neill in the Spring 1999 issue of *Rethinking Schools*.

Sources:
Jeanne Ponessa, "College Rankings Rankle Counselors, Admissions Offices," *Education Week on the WEB*, 22 November 1995, Internet website.

Ponessa, "Math and Verbal Scores Up on Revamped SAT," *Education Week on the WEB*, 6 September 1995, Internet website.

GOALS 2000: EDUCATE AMERICA ACT

The Proposal. On 25 February 1990, the National Governors' Association adopted a set of six goals designed to boost student achievement in the United States by the year 2000. The goals were developed by the governors in consultation with the White House, and were based on a plan developed at an education summit that President George Bush had held with the nation's governors in September 1989. As the government continued to further define the objectives and budgeting issues that accompanied the bold move, critics and supporters began the debate on the appropriateness of federal intervention in a state mandate–

public education. Key among the questions was how progress on the goals would be determined and whether a clear delineation between church and state was made in light of implied support for vouchers.

A New Law. In March 1994, President Bill Clinton signed the bill into law. In addition to the original six goals, two were added that involved teacher training and the role of parents in a child's education. (The last objective caused great concern among conservative groups and was later amended.) Although considered by some an ineffective compromise, the law encouraged each state to set its own competency standards in lieu of a single set of national standards. The 1996 revision, designed to answer some criticisms about the role of the federal government in the process, managed to placate some critics, but raised other concerns about the original intent of fostering systemic, standards-based school reform. "It started off as a program with its own integrity, and now it's beginning to lose all integrity," said Michael Kirst, a professor of education at Stanford University in California. Deleting federal review of plans guarantees that "the federal government will have no idea what's going on in any state," he said. Scholar and former assistant in the Education Department Diane Ravitch said, "I just don't know what's left except a program in which the money passes from the Education Department to the states and from the states to the districts for whatever good things they want to do and the districts can define as good."

Progress Not Seen. Perhaps the greatest indictment of all came from the assessments of the country's progress. According to the annual reports submitted by the National Education Goals Panel, the independent group created by the Act to monitor the nation's advancement on the goals, it was unlikely that the country would meet most of its objectives by the year 2000. In 1996, after analyzing twenty major indicators of improvements in education, the committee said that American schools had improved in five of the areas, worsened in eight, and remained approximately unchanged in seven. The most progress had reportedly been made on efforts to raise the nation's high-school graduation rate. The previous year, the panel had reported that the strongest signs of progress were related to students' success in math and science classes. The percentage of students in the fourth grade meeting national math achievement standards had risen to 18 percent in 1992, up from 13 percent in 1990. During the same period, math achievement had climbed to 25 percent from 20 percent among eighth graders, and to 16 percent from 13 percent among twelfth graders. Panel members also indicated that increasing numbers of female college students were earning degrees in math and the sciences.

Making a Difference. Nonetheless, supporters of the law pointed to the increasing number of states with competency standards in core subjects and the move toward state-wide assessments of progress on those standards as evidence that the Goals 2000: Educate America Act was making a difference. Although those assessments caused

GOALS 2000: EDUCATE AMERICA ACT

1) All children will start school ready to learn.

2) The nation's high school graduation rate will increase to 90 percent.

3) Students in grades 4, 8, and 12 will demonstrate competency in nine core academic areas.

4) The United States will be first in international comparisons of math and science achievement.

5) Adult literacy will be universal.

6) Schools will be free of drugs and violence.

7) Teachers will have access to continual professional-development opportunities.

8) All schools will increase parental involvement in their children's education.

The 1996 amendment to the act had the following provisions:

1) School districts in states that were not participating in Goals 2000 were allowed to apply for aid on their own if they had the approval of the state education agency.

2) A requirement that states submit school-improvement plans to the U.S. Secretary of Education was removed. States were still to draft plans based on challenging standards and aligned assessments, but could get money by promising that it would be spent properly.

3) Provisions specifying the membership of state and local panels charged with drafting the state and local plans were deleted.

4) The National Education Standards and Improvement Council was formally eliminated.

5) References to "opportunity to learn" standards for measuring school services, including a requirement that states create opportunity-to-learn "standards or strategies," were removed.

6) No district, state, or school "shall be required...to provide outcomes-based education or school-based health clinics."

7) The Goals 2000 law will not "require or permit any state or federal official to inspect a home, judge how parents raise their children, or remove children from their parents."

Source: Mark Pitsch, "To Placate Conservatives, Measure Alters Goals 2000," *Education Week on the Web*, 1 May 1996, Internet website.

---

their own debates, the public attention on the state of education in America could not be denied.

Sources:
Education Week on the WEB, 1996, Internet website.
The U.S. Department of Education, Internet website.

POLITICAL CORRECTNESS

Multiculturalism. The arguments over political correctness were not new to the 1990s, but took on a life of their own when discussions of college and school curricula were hotly debated in the media. On one side stood reformists who wished to see the inclusion of multicultural history and literature, on the other, conservatives who argued for a basic core curriculum that retained much of what had been known as the heart of the western civilization. In an ever-expanding field of knowledge, what was essential and what could be saved for later, more in-depth study? Proponents of the need to expand the concept of history argued that the dominant, "dead white males" of typical Western Civilization courses were but a small fraction of the picture of our past and needed to be expanded to include the contributions of women and those of various ethnic heritages. Critics charged that to forego the study of crucial individuals and facts in order to emphasize contributions by all subgroups of the population failed to provide students with a basic foundation to interpret the events, movements, and eras of history.

NEH. The media's attention was drawn to the debate as it centered on the national history standards proposed by a team of educators and historians supported by the National Endowment for the Humanities (NEH). Eliciting harsh criticisms, the standards first developed in 1995 were finally revised in 1996. Much of the controversy arose from the wording of sample history assignments in the original version of the standards because the negative portrayals of U.S. history and heroes were questioned. Gary Nash, history professor at the University of California, Los Angeles, and codirector of the group that wrote the guidelines, argued that the standards were designed to encourage students to "exercise their own judgment in reading conflicting views of any piece of history and understand that there are multiple perspectives." A vocal opponent of the stan-

Fans waving Confederate flags at a University of Mississippi football game (AP/Wide World Photos)

dards as written, Lynne Cheney, former chair of the NEH, countered that although history should be inclusive, "it's a very great error to quit teaching basic history in the name of political correctness." As an example of some of the problems with the standards, she pointed to the absence of teaching that George Washington was the first president. Lawrence Levine, in a December 1993 article in the *Journal of American History* concluded, "To teach a history that excludes large areas of American culture and ignores the experiences of significant segments of the American people is to teach a history that fails to touch us, that fails to explain America to us or to anyone else. We need, not a new history, but a more profound and indeed more complex understanding of our old history."

Speech Codes. During the late 1980s and early 1990s, several colleges yielded to public concern embodied by racial harassment and instituted so-called speech bans. In an effort to protect the civil rights of frequently "historically underrepresented or disadvantaged" people, schools put into practice rules that prohibited verbal or symbolic behavior that could be construed as derogatory, abusive, or demeaning. Each campus had its own version of the rules, but all came under fire from the academics in the institutions that enacted the policies. Citing a conflict with the entire notion of freedom of speech and with the notion of academic freedom, critics used a 1993 example at the University of Pennsylvania of how the rules could be unfairly applied (black sorority members accused a white student of racial harassment for calling them "water buffalo"). In some cases, the constitutionality of the rules was debated. And yet, universities across the country con-

tinued to try to find a balance between the right of free speech and the "right" to be free from harassment.

Academic Freedom. The political correctness debate continued with charges against faculty members for using sexual examples to explain ideas or demeaning ethnic heritage through the use of offending terms. Shocked academics spent thousands of dollars on legal fees defending themselves from what they considered ludicrous accusations. And yet, the debate continued. In some cases, university administrators viewed the process as one of sensitization to the issues. Racism and sexism would not be tolerated in an arena where academic freedom was paramount.

Battleground. The label "political correctness" itself was hotly debated by academics. Resonating with the history of repressive thought that the Right associated with communism and the Left with McCarthyism, the idea of a campus succumbing to instances of political correctness was repugnant to all. It seemed whenever a school instituted a change that someone did not like, charges of political correctness were lobbed. Ultimately the battle continued, although it confined itself more to the college campuses where it began than in the general media where wide public attention held sway.

Sources:

Alan Charles Kors and Harvey A. Silvergate, *The Shadow University: The Betrayal of Liberty on America's Campuses* (New York: Free Press, 1998).

Louis Menand, ed., *The Future of Academic Freedom* (Chicago: University of Chicago Press, 1996).

"National Standards for History Discussion on H-Net Lists," *H-TEACH*, Internet website.

FREEDOM OF SPEECH?

In 1993, Eden Jacobowitz, a freshman at the University of Pennsylvania, called a group of young black women "water buffalo" and touched off a battle over freedom of speech at the elite Ivy League school. While studying one night, he and several others in the vicinity had yelled out requests for quiet while a group of sorority sisters began a late night celebration under his dormitory window. After about twenty minutes, he returned to the window and hurled, "Shut up, you water buffalo! If you want a party, there's a zoo a mile from here." Investigations followed, and Jacobowitz, the only identifiable participant who confessed to shouting at women he identified as black, was charged with violating the university's racial harassment rules. Jacobowitz and his supporters steadfastly denied that he had used a racial epithet.

After months of hearings and involvement of the American Civil Liberties Union (ACLU) and other outside organizations, the charges were dropped and Jacobowitz expressed his regrets. The scars left on the university community, however, ran deep. The media used the incident to highlight the running debate on college campuses over freedom of speech and the destructive nature of harmful speech.

Source: *Facts on File*, volumes 53 and 54 (New York: Facts on File, 1993, 1994).

SEXUAL HARASSMENT

Beyond Teasing. A study released by the American Association of University Women (AAUW) in 1993 reported that 85 percent of all girls and 76 percent of all boys in grades eight through eleven said that they had been sexually harassed in some manner in school. A survey conducted by Louis Harris & Associates of 1,632 boys and girls in public schools concluded that "sexual harassment in schools is creating a hostile environment that compromises the education of America's children." The survey characterized sexual harassment as "unwanted and unwelcome sexual behavior," ranging from sexual comments, jokes, gestures, or looks to forced physical activity. Critics contended that the report used too broad a definition of sexual harassment.

Statistics. Seventy-six percent of all girls polled and 56 percent of boys said they had been the recipients of unwanted sexual comments or looks. Sixty-five percent of girls and 42 percent of boys said they had been touched, grabbed or pinched in a sexual manner. About 80 percent of such harassment was by other students, while the rest stemmed from teachers and staff, the poll found. Seventy percent of girls who reported being harassed said that they felt "very" or "somewhat upset" when they were subjected to such behavior, compared with 24 percent of boys. About one-third of the girls who reported harass-

ment said that the treatment made them want to avoid going to school or talking in class, compared with a little over 10 percent of the boys.

Stein. As pointed out by Nan D. Stein, in her chapter "It Happens Here, Too: Sexual Harassment and Child Sexual Abuse in Elementary and Secondary Schools" for the 1993 National Study of School Evaluation (NSSE) yearbook, *Gender and Education,* "With children age twelve and older, sexual harassment is all too often dismissed as 'typical adolescent behavior,' and misconstrued as a normal rite of passage, as awkward 'getting-to-know-you' behaviors. Instead of being carefully defined and communicated to students, teachers, and administrators, sexual harassment is trivialized, condoned, or described as 'flirting' or 'initiation rites.'" She cites research that showed that although student-to-student sexual harassment was more prevalent than teacher-to-student sexual harassment, and that female students were more likely to be victims, students also were victimized as employees–either as part of a school-sponsored co-op program or as part of an afterschool job.

Offenders. In 1996, a six-year-old boy in Lexington, North Carolina, was accused of sexual harassment and suspended for a day for kissing a female classmate on the cheek. District spokeswoman Jane Martin reportedly said, "Unwelcome is unwelcome at any age." In an interview on NBC's Today show she defended the action by saying, "Sexual harassment is an issue in the workplace as well as in our schools, and there's a responsibility to educate our children, regardless of how young they are." However, officials later backed off from the charge of sexual harassment, and released a statement saying that the young man had been suspended for violating a rule forbidding "unwarranted and unwelcome touching of one student by another." The story made international headlines and caused great debate over what was being termed by some as political correctness carried to extremes. The school board voted a few weeks later to revise its sexual harassment policy so that it took into account the student's age and maturity and his or her intent.

Overreaction? In the meantime, another young man in New York City was likewise accused of sexual harassment. This time, a seven-year-old had been given a five-day suspension (that was later rescinded) for kissing a female classmate and tearing a button from her skirt. The boy claimed he took the button because his favorite story, Corduroy, was about a teddy bear with a missing button. Critics, including the city's mayor, Rudolph W. Giuliani (R), claimed the school had overreacted.

Source:
Facts on File, volumes 53 and 56 (New York: Facts on File, 1993, 1996).

SINGLE SEX EDUCATION

Benefits. In 1992, a report issued by the American Association of University Women (AAUW) stated that girls faced widespread bias in classrooms across the United States. In the report, "How Schools Shortchange Women," researchers surveyed more than one thousand previous stud-

Jesse Helms greeting Jonathan Prevette (October 6, 1996) in Raleigh, North Carolina (AP/Wide World Photos)

ies and articles on girls and education. Among the key findings cited in the report were the following:

1) Girls continued to score lower than boys on standardized tests in mathematics and science, even though their grades in the classroom tended to be higher.

2) Teachers called on boys more often, gave them more detailed criticism and allowed them to shout out answers while reprimanding girls for doing the same.

3) Few girls chose to pursue careers in math or science, and few teachers encouraged them to do so.

4) Many textbooks continued to stereotype women and failed to address issues of concern to women, such as discrimination and sexual abuse.

Although the report was designed to encourage a change in behavior in the co-ed classroom, the report was read by many as a mandate to pursue single-sex education.

Court Battles. In the following years, the media focused on how several states, specifically New York and California, experimented with gender-segregated public schools. Both the American Civil Liberties Union (ACLU) and the National Organization for Women (NOW) bitterly opposed the concept and began fighting the battle in the courts. Many educators who work in all-girls' schools say that they make a positive difference in the social, intellectual, and academic development of the girls. Studies highlighting the benefits were questioned as to whether the improvement is a result of smaller classes and academic rigor or if the absence of boys truly made a difference.

A New Study. In 1998, the AAUW released another study, "Separated by Sex: A Critical Look at Single-Sex Education for Girls." The report noted that since 1991, the student population of all-girls' schools grew from 29,000 to 38,000. Without conducting new research, but merely reviewing the existing literature, the report essentially concluded that if public schools could become more like private schools, girls would receive a better education without having to be separated from boys.

VMI. Despite the encouraging results, proponents of single sex education found themselves embattled when it came to schools that used public funds. Cries of violations of civil rights in terms of equal protection guaranteed by the Fourteenth Amendment led many arguments to the courts. The issue extended to the level of higher education. In 1996 the Supreme Court ruled that the Virginia Military Institute (VMI) must begin admitting women after 157 years of a male-only student body. The academy was one of the last remaining single-sex colleges in the country that accepted state funds. Private schools, however, continued to find a market for parents who believed that separating the genders allowed students to focus on their academic needs without the constant distractions of their social desires.

Sources:
Facts on File, volumes 52 and 56 (New York: Facts on File, 1992, 1996).

Sarah Barbara Watstein, "Single-Sex Academies," *in American Education Annual: Trends and Issues in the Educational Community,* edited by Mary Alampi and Peter M. Comeau (Detroit: Gale, 1999).

Students in an experimental all-female math class at William Allen Middle School in Moorestown, New Jersey, designed to test whether gender-segregated classes helped children improve academically (AP/Wide World Photos)

TEACHING EVOLUTION

A Contested Theory. In spite of its virtually universal acceptance among biologists as a fundamental scientific principle, evolution remained a point of contention in the 1990s in many classrooms, school boards, and among conservative Christian parents. Although the idea of natural selection occurred to naturalists Alfred Russel Wallace and Charles Robert Darwin at about the same time, Darwin got *On the Origin of Species By Means of Natural Selection; or, The Preservation of Favoured Races in the Struggle for Life* (1859) into print first, and it was his name that became attached to the theory. Both Darwin and Wallace had been looking for a way to explain biological diversity. Briefly put, the theory of evolution by means of natural selection posits that individuals within a population differ in small ways, and these variations can be inherited. Farmers in the nineteenth century knew, for example, that black sheep tended to beget black sheep, and since black wool was less valuable than white, the shepherds prevented sheep with darker coats from breeding. This artificial selection, Darwin believed, had a counterpart in the natural world where some traits— size, coloration, or sense of smell—were desirable in that they made it more likely that an individual would reproduce either by making itself more attractive to the opposite sex (or, in the case of flowers, to pollinating bees) or by being better able to escape predators or find food. Animals and plants with less desirable traits often failed to reproduce and the traits themselves, like black wool, became less common. Over thousands of generations small, inherited advantages accumulated until a recognizably new species emerged, better adapted to its environment than its ancestors had been.

It followed then, Darwin argued in *The Descent of Man, and Selection in Relation to Sex* (1871), that all living things, from people to paramecia, evolved from common ancestors. While evolutionary biology made no specific claims about the role of God, Darwin's theory clearly challenged a literal interpretation of the first three chapters of the biblical book of Genesis. During the early decades of the twentieth century a belief in the literal truth of Holy Scripture came to define the bedrock of Christian doctrine for a substantial number of believers who came to be identified as Fundamentalists. It was this conflict that eventuated in the 1925 trial, often known as the "Monkey Trial," of John T. Scopes in Dayton, Tennessee. Scopes had challenged the state law that forbids the teaching of evolution in the schools.

Scientific Creationism. In the 1970s and 1980s scientific creationism, a belief that the six days of creation described in the Bible could be defended scientifically, became popularized in the religious press, although most biologists, geologists, and cosmologists dismissed it. In 1981, however, lawmakers in Louisiana passed legislation requiring "balanced treatment" of both evolution and Creation Science. In 1987, in *Edwards* v. *Aguillard,* and repeatedly thereafter, the U.S. Supreme Court ruled that such a requirement was invalid because it violated "the Establishment Clause of the First Amendment, because it lacks a clear secular purpose." Creation science, the Court said, was a statement of theology, not biology. This setback did not stop determined members of school boards across the country from trying to sidestep the ruling and effectively delete evolution from the curriculum or make sure that it was countered with a presentation of creation science as an alternative.

A science teacher at Shawnee Mission West High School in Shawnee Mission, Kansas,
where the teaching of evolution is allowed (AP/Wide World Photos)

Kansas Board of Education. In August 1999 the Kansas State Board of Education adopted new standards for the teaching of science and effectively removed any discussion of evolution as an explanatory model for human origins. Although Benchmark Five of the state standards for eighth grade natural sciences said, "Over time, genetic variation acted upon by natural selection has brought variations in populations," the document referred to this widely observed and documented phenomenon as "microevolution." That the same mechanisms of natural selection that can be observed in isolated populations can also explain the emergence of homo sapiens and all other living things was neglected. The decision was widely praised by religious conservatives as an effective way to avoid running afoul of the Supreme Court ban on teaching creation science. Scholars, science educators, and advocates of church-state separation were appalled. Barry W. Lynn, executive director of Americans United for Separation of Church and State, spoke for many opponents of the measure when he said, "This act . . . took us back 100 years in science teaching and education."

Evolving Controversy. Although the decision surprised, bemused, and outraged many scientists, politicians, journalists, and parents, national polls suggested that they ought to have seen it coming. *The Christian Century*, for instance, reported that 40 percent of Americans favored teaching "creation science" instead of evolution. Sixty-eight percent want creationism taught in conjunction with evolution as equally viable theories about the origins and development of life on earth. According to a Gallup Poll, 44 percent of Americans consider themselves to be "creationists," strictly

defined as those who assert that God, within the last ten thousand years, created humans in their present form. Thirty-nine percent described themselves as "theistic evolutionists" who believe that God has guided evolution over millions of years. Only 7 percent, by contrast, thought of themselves as "Darwinists" for whom God played no role in either creation or evolution. The remaining 10 percent are undecided about the issue. Not long before the Kansas School Board took action, similar quarrels had erupted in California, Colorado, Idaho, Illinois, Iowa, Nebraska, Oregon, and Washington. The state textbook committees in Alabama and Oklahoma had already inserted disclaimers into science books stating that evolution was an unproven theory that students were by no means obliged to accept as fact. The attorney general of Oklahoma subsequently ordered the disclaimer removed. The Kansas Board of Education decision thus only intensified an ongoing dispute in which adversaries on both sides would do well to recall God's question to Job: "Where were you when I laid the foundations of the earth?" (Job 38:4).

Sources:
Brian Cabell, "Kansas School Board's Evolution Ruling Angers Science Community," *CNN.com*, 12 August 1999, Internet website.

Colleen Carroll, "Evolution of a Creationist Victory," *National Catholic Reporter*, 35 (8 October 1999): 3–6.

"Creation Mysteries: Kansas Board of Education Downgrades Teaching of Evolution," *The Christian Century*, 116 (25 August 1999): 795.

Kansas State Board of Education, "Curricular Standards for Science Education," adopted 7 December 1999, *Kansas State Board of Education*, Internet website.

Nancy Pearcy, "We're Not in Kansas Anymore," *Christianity Today*, 44 (22 May 2000): 42–51.

TECHNOLOGY

Major Influence. The proliferation of technology during the 1990s obviously affected schools around the country. As Vice President Al Gore said regarding the expansion of technology in schools in remarks to the 1994 National Education Association Higher Education Conference, "the net result will be to elevate our ability to equip the children and adults seeking education in this nation as we have never been able to do before." Computer technology became a necessary addition to the infrastructure of every school in the nation. Indeed, in some ways it redefined the concept of "school" through its ability to allow instruction and interaction to happen in more than one distinct location simultaneously. What once was a luxury became a requirement for schools. As the decade progressed so did expectations of students, parents, and employers about the school's ability to provide the necessary skills to function in an increasingly technical world.

The Internet. As the use of the Internet became more commercialized in the latter part of the 1990s, it is hard to remember it was originally intended to connect university and government researchers across the nation and eventually the world with each other's data. A change in its use occurred when publishers wished to print their materials online. Copyright became an issue and programmers were set to develop methods of limiting access to what had been free information. Copyright infringe-ments and the wide interactive nature (through email and chat rooms) provoked active debates about the regulation of the Internet, often prompted by concerns that since anyone could publish to the World Wide Web, then children could not be protected from harmful materials or people.

Accessibility. Teachers comfortable with the technology lauded the interactivity, the immediacy, and the globalization of the information. The possibilities of discussions with students in foreign countries, the ability for students to publish, and the chance to gain access to a wide range of government information led teachers to encourage students to access materials outside their classrooms in a way that could not have happened before. Consequently, the Internet became a favored tool, and its use as an educational conduit was recognized across the country. Between 1994 and 1998, Internet access in public schools increased from 35 to 89 percent, but the percentage of classrooms with access only went from 3 to 51 percent.

Universal Service. Recognizing that schools with severely limited resources would begin to lag even further behind other schools, the Clinton administration took steps to equalize the ability of schools to provide Internet access to their students. In 1996, as part of the Telecommunications Act, the Universal Service program was born. Commonly known as the "E-rate," the program structured a series of discounts for schools and

Students at Forest Lane Academy in Dallas, Texas, on 29 September 1999 (AP/Wide World Photos)

libraries to help defray the cost of telecommunications and Internet technologies. The details of the controversial program were left to the Federal Communications Commission (FCC), which inaugurated the program in May 1997. The FCC determined several guidelines, including which schools and libraries were eligible to receive discounts, the amount of discounts that schools and libraries could receive, and what services were eligible for discounts.

Funding. Overseen by the Schools and Libraries Division (SLD) of the Universal Service Administrative Company, the program received over 62,000 applications in its first two years of operation. Funding requests topped $2.435 billion by the second year, and far exceeded the first year's requests of over $2 billion. Originally slated to have a budget of $2.25 billion per year, the FCC cut the program's funding for the first year to only $1.2 billion, thereby forcing the SLD to deny or significantly reduce the grant to each school. It was clear, however, that schools and libraries saw an imperative for increasing their accessibility to the Internet and were prepared to present plans that outlined their specific needs.

Criticisms. In spite of the growing popularity of the Internet, some opponents of the E-rate felt that schools should be spending their money in other areas—that the vast, unpredictable, often unreliable, and in some cases unmanageable glut of information available on the Internet was more glitz than substance. Still others objected to the method used to provide the discounts—mandated fees to providers (such as long distance companies) that inevitably were passed on to consumers.

Definition. As rapid as the growth was in terms of the use of the Internet, both socially and as a teaching tool, the use of the computer in other walks of educational life expanded almost as quickly. Schools that originally used their computers to teach computer science were now bombarded with requests to teach computer applications as well, or in some cases, instead. The computers were no longer the province of the "nerds"; their use was a requirement of all students. Schools struggled with issues of how technology fit into the curricula. If teachers were expected to use technology to teach, should students be expected to demonstrate their competence in basic technology? Better yet, what were the basic technology skills? How did research skills fit into that picture? Did schools teach the use of a specific applications product? These questions plagued many schools as they tried to determine not only how to make use of the technology, but how to measure the cost effectiveness of their expenditures.

Growing Technophobia. Whereas most students felt entirely comfortable with computers and accompanying technology, and in many cases, expected its use, teachers required more convincing. Fears of increased plagiarism, dismay at redirected funds, claims of "making life easier," and unwillingness to look foolish in front of students who were obviously better versed in the use of the technology were but a few of the stumbling blocks faced by administrators trying to convince teachers of their technology plans. Others, recognizing the revolutionary changes that technology wrought in the business world, called for an immediate increase in its use.

Sources:

Digest of Education Statistics, 1999 (Washington, D.C.: U.S. Government Printing Office, 1999).

Barbara Means et. al, *Using Technology to Support Education Reform* (Washington, D.C.: U.S. Government Printing Office, 1993).

VIOLENCE IN SCHOOLS

Media Coverage. Perhaps more than any other educational issue in the 1990s, the subject of violence in schools made news. A rash of gun violence in seemingly "safe" suburban schools around the country indicated that violence was not just an urban problem. Lobbyists for and against gun control entered into heated debates about the cause of the problem. Hollywood, video games, parents, schools, and lack of religion all were blamed. In a mad search for the solution, few analysts could agree on the root of the problem. For the first time since the early 1970s, violence was seen as one of the major problems in schools according to the annual Gallup poll taken on public attitudes toward the public schools. It topped the list in 1998.

Recurring Pattern. For years, isolated incidents of killings, shootings, stabbings, and other school violence saddened the country, but were acknowledged more as random acts of evil that were symptomatic of the plight of poor schools or sometimes the result of a single deranged mind. It wasn't until a pattern of mass shootings occurred around the country in the late 1990s that attention was focused on the problem as a national concern. How could these monstrous events happen? Was no one aware of the intentions of these shooters? How could they get their hands on these weapons of destruction? What was their motivation?

Who's to Blame? Robert J. Dole, Republican candidate for the presidency during the 1996 elections, accused the entertainment industry of "bombarding our children with destructive messages of casual violence and even more casual sex." Dole stated in a 1995 speech, "A line has been crossed, not just of taste, but of human dignity and decency . . . every time sexual violence is given a catchy tune, when teen suicide is set to an appealing beat, when Hollywood's dream factories turn out nightmares of depravity." Dole cited two popular films, *Natural Born Killers* (1994) and *True Romance* (1993), that had depicted extreme violence. He also singled out the rappers Ice-T, Geto Boys, and 2 Live Crew as well as the heavy-metal band Cannibal Corpse as contributors to the glorification of violence. In response, Oliver Stone, the director of *Natural Born Killers*, said that it was "the height of hypocrisy for Senator Dole, who wants to repeal the [1994] assault weapons ban, to blame Hollywood for the violence in our

A student being checked for weapons at a St. Clairsville, Ohio, high school on 28 April 1999 as part of measures adopted nationwide to stop violence in schools (AP/Wide World Photos)

society." Michael Fuchs, the chairman of Time Warner Music Group, said that offensive lyrics by his company's recording artists were "the price you pay for freedom of expression." Hilary Rosen, president of the Recording Industry Association of America, claimed that violent messages in recordings weren't the problem. Asserting that millions of people hear a record without committing acts of violence, she claims the issue is "what happens when troubling music connects with troubled minds."

Warped Perceptions. President Bill Clinton in his weekly radio address 23 May 1998 blamed a culture that "desensitizes" children to violence for the recent rash of school shootings. Clinton said that youths' exposure to violence in movies, on television, and in video games warped their perceptions. He called on Congress to pass a proposed juvenile crime bill that would ban juveniles convicted of violent offenses from purchasing firearms for the rest of their lives. Gun-control advocates called for stricter curbs on the sale and use of firearms. One proposed law would require trigger locks to be installed on guns. Opponents of such measures argued that penalties should focus on people who committed crime with guns.

Statistics. According to a study published in the *Journal of the American Medical Association* in 1998, violence among American teenagers declined between 1991 and 1997. The study showed broad declines in several categories of violent activity. Some 18 percent of high school students reported carrying a weapon—defined as a gun, knife or club—within the past thirty days, down from 26 percent in 1991.

Source:

Facts on File, volumes 56, 57, 58 (New York: Facts on File, 1996, 1997, 1998).

HEADLINE MAKERS

WALTER H. ANNENBERG

1908-

PHILANTHROPIST; PUBLISHER; DIPLOMAT

The Key to Leadership. The 1990s provided Walter H. Annenberg the opportunity to contribute to one of the most fundamental causes he supported throughout his life—education. Long a financial supporter of various colleges and universities, Annenberg turned his eye to America's public schools with an unprecedented gift of $500 million. His shift in focus underscored his belief that education is what "holds civilization together," and that kindergarten through twelfth grade is where children grow intellectually and develop character and where our attentions must dwell. His 1993 announcement of matching grants to improve education in public schools was Annenberg's effort in turning attention to what he considered a national security issue: eleven-year-olds shooting each other was a nightmare for this country's future.

Resources. Walter Annenberg spent the better part of his adult life rebuilding the family fortune after his father was sent to jail and charged fines of $9.5 million in the late 1930s for tax evasion. As the sole son in a family of eight, Walter was named heir to the newly named Triangle Corporation, the holding company of the *Philadelphia Inquirer,* the *Daily Racing Form,* and several other publications. After thirty years at its helm, Annenberg sold ownership of the *Philadelphia Inquirer* and continued to divest his holdings in Triangle, which among other assets included television stations and two magazines he founded, *TV Guide* and *Seventeen.* His successes in Great Britain as Richard M. Nixon's ambassador coexisted with his supervision of his interests in the United States. After selling Triangle to Rupert Murdoch in the late 1980s, Annenberg turned his attention to investments and his charitable goals through the Annenberg Foundation.

Essential Projects. In a letter to his descendents, Annenberg advised that when it came to gift giving, "few things are as essential as education." He encouraged them to approach charity with the notion that it should be used as leverage to induce others in the public and private sector to engage in worthwhile projects. For that reason, many of Annenberg's donations took the form of matching funds gifts. Likewise, his first donation, to his alma mater, Peddie School, given upon graduation, was a revenue-producing gift that Annenberg hoped would allow the school through rentals to fund its maintenance costs. Vartan Gregorian, overseer of his $500 million public school grant and longtime friend, pictured Annenberg as one who believed that "success has its price, that there is an obligation to spread wealth, that philanthropy is not charity, but an investment in our future."

Other Institutions. Annenberg gave so handsomely in the 1990s to education that some of his grants of only a few hundred thousand or $1 million are easily overlooked. He began the decade with a $50-million matching grant to the United Negro College Fund. Among other beneficiaries of his generosity were the Archdiocese of Philadelphia schools, a small boarding academy in Mississippi for disadvantaged black youth, presidential libraries, Jewish and Catholic universities, small colleges, Episcopal day schools, and museums. Annenberg once remarked, "I made my money from Catholics, Protestants, Jews, whites, blacks, men and women, and I give it back the same way."

Responsibility. In announcing his $500 million donation to public education, Annnenberg said, "I wanted to elevate precollegiate education to a national priority. I wanted to startle our leaders and public and get their attention. It is my responsibility as a citizen." Annenberg's gift went partially ($50 million) to the newly named Annenberg Institute for School Reform at Brown University under the directorship of Ted Sizer. Another $50 million went to the nonprofit New American Schools Development Corporation, a nonprofit, nonpartisan group that identified visionaries who would design innovative programs in model schools. The Education Commission of the States, a research and policy group, received $6.4 million. The remaining $385 million became known as the Annenberg Challenge and provided matching grants to initiate reform in some of the nation's largest and most troubled school districts, as well as in rural schools. In 1998, more than two thousand schools with nearly 1.5 million students had been involved in the Annenberg Challenge.

Source:
Christopher Ogden, *Legacy: A Biography of Walter and Moses Annenberg* (Boston: Little, Brown, 1999).

LYNNE V. CHENEY

1941-

AUTHOR, CHAIRPERSON OF THE NATIONAL ENDOWMENT FOR THE HUMANITIES

NEH. Lynne Cheney served as head of the National Endowment for the Humanities (NEH) for seven years under Presidents Ronald Reagan and George Bush while facing several highly public and controversial issues, not the least of which was the debate surrounding the National Endowment for the Arts (NEA) support of a controversial exhibit by artist Robert Mapplethorpe. Her background as an avid champion of education at all levels led the NEH, however, to expand its mission beyond that of supporting scholarly research to include supporting excellence in both elementary and secondary schools. Several annual reports generated by the NEH during Cheney's tenure focused on the place of humanities in education.

Early Career. Cheney, who earned a doctorate in nineteenth-century British literature at the University of Wisconsin, began her career as an instructor at the collegiate level. Her marriage to Dick Cheney (Chief of Staff for President Gerald Ford and Secretary of Defense for President Bush) influenced her decision to start freelance writing. The author or coauthor of several political/thriller novels, Cheney also coauthored with her husband a biographical work on several of the Speakers of the House. It was the role of senior editor at the *Washingtonian* magazine that she relinquished to become head of the NEH, however. When asked about the projects at the NEH of which she was proudest, Cheney frequently pointed to a program funded in partnership with *Reader's Digest* that gave outstanding teachers across the nation opportunities to study further the subjects they taught.

Political Correctness. Cheney's concern about the "rewriting of history" first surfaced while she was at the NEH. It was a crusade she continued long after she left. Cheney came under fire from some academics after the publication of her third annual report at the NEH proposing a core curriculum for college students that emphasized Western civilization. Cheney dismissed the comments in light of her ignored recommendation that a full year of study of the cultures of China, Japan, or Islam be included. Nonetheless, as the battle over appropriate core subject matter continued across the country, Cheney became a leader in the media and in the lecture circuit on the potential dangers of multicultural education. Focusing on what separates us rather than what binds people together, Cheney theorized, would tear the country apart. In speaking out against political correctness, Cheney said, "Our colleges and universities should be about pursuing truth, not about pursuing political agendas."

Life After the NEH. Cheney continued to write and speak actively on issues of politics, public policy, and education throughout the 1990s. A cohost on CNN's *Crossfire Sunday*, and Fellow at the American Enterprise Institute, Cheney also frequently appeared on national news broadcasts on ABC and PBS expressing opinions on a variety of public issues. Known as a persuasive advocate for improving American education, she championed school choice for parents, alternative certification for teachers, and national standards to measure student achievement. Her 1995 book, *Telling the Truth: Why Our Culture and Our Country Have Stopped Making Sense, And What We Can Do About It*, forcefully argued for her viewpoint and analysis of the state of American culture.

Source:
Current Biography Yearbook, 1992 (New York: H.W. Wilson, 1992).

MARIAN WRIGHT EDELMAN

1939-

CHILDREN'S ACTIVIST; FOUNDER AND PRESIDENT OF THE CHILDREN'S DEFENSE FUND

Top Priority. Devoting her life to improving the plight of children, Marian Wright Edelman failed to understand the blinders worn by citizens of one of the richest countries in the world when it came to investing in one of its most precious resources. Her ceaseless efforts to focus national attention on issues of child health care, teen pregnancy, children in poverty, child labor laws, and preparing children to learn, earned her well-deserved recognition as an effective lobbyist and consultant. She said, "How sad and unfair that the children who come into the world with the least—whose parents are the least able to provide them with health care, good nutrition, shelter, and stimulation—are also the children who are least likely to have access to quality developmental early childhood education." Edelman's concern for children of all races and classes, and her arguments supported with indisputable facts and statistics, garnered widespread support for issues that she placed before government.

Mississippi. As a civil-rights activist in the 1960s, Edelman was appalled by the feelings of hopelessness among poor black Southern families, especially its children. Her efforts as counsel to the Child Development Group of Mississippi (CDGM) ensured that the 1965 Head Start funds would be available to children of that state. As the first black female lawyer to pass the bar exam in Mississippi, she spent several years working to help the poor receive the attention they needed through legal representation, testimony to Senate subcommittees, and a personal tour given to Senator Robert F. Kennedy of the squalid conditions in the Mississippi Delta.

Efforts in Washington. After marriage, a move to Washington, D.C., and a short stint in Boston as director of Harvard's Center for Law and Education, Edelman returned to her work with the Washington Research Project that she had established in 1968, a group dedicated to research and advocacy. She founded the Children's Defense Fund (CDF) from that group in 1973 to provide support for America's "voiceless and voteless millions." Well-known by all of Congress, she and her organization lobbied on issues that affect children. Believing that prevention is far less expensive than remediation, Edelman continued to fight for "a healthy start, a head start, and a fair start" for America's children. In 1992, advertisements funded by the CDF figured prominently in the media during the national elections.

Stand For Children. On 1 June 1996, the first annual *Stand For Children* rally was held at the Lincoln Memorial in Washington, D.C. More than three-hundred-thousand people attended. Edelman played a major role in the formation and presentation of the event, which was sponsored initially by the CDF. She published a children's book highlighting her words of encouragement shared with the attendees. Continuing in her efforts to promote the welfare of children, Edelman hoped the annual gathering would become the equivalent to the children's movement as Earth Day was to the environmental movement.

Sources:

Marian Wright Edelman, *Lanterns: A Memoir of Mentors* (Boston: Beacon, 1999).

Edelman, *Stand for Children* (New York: Hyperion, 1998).

Wendie C. Old, *Marian Wright Edelman: Fighting for Children's Rights* (Springfield, N.J.: Enslow, 1995).

SHANNON R. FAULKNER

1975-

MILITARY ACADEMY STUDENT

Acceptance. Shannon R. Faulkner wanted to attend the prestigious South Carolina military college, The Citadel. In 1993, when she applied to the 152-year-old institution, she was accepted. The problem was that it was all-male and she was female. Faulkner had deleted all references to her gender in her application, but when the school discovered the error they quickly withdrew their offer of enrollment. Accepted on her qualifications, but denied because of her gender, Faulkner started down the controversial road of changing tradition because she believed it was unconstitutional to discriminate against women by denying them a Citadel education. As one of two all male, publicly funded military academies in the country, The Citadel braced for a long court battle. Armed with attorneys and the support of the National Organization for Women (NOW), Faulkner brought national attention to the issue.

Unpopular Campaign. Unpopular among not only alumni and students of The Citadel, but their mothers and daughters as well, Faulkner's efforts to enroll in the traditional academy were hotly debated in public arenas around the country. The nation's other all-male, state-funded military academy, Virginia Military Institute (VMI), also faced a court battle with the Justice Department. During the two-and-a-half-year legal proceedings, Faulkner, her family, and her lawyers faced threats from angry opponents. The Federal Bureau of Investigation (FBI) was called in to investigate in the wake of the threats, vandalism to the Faulkner home, and other visible violence that the case wrought.

The Courts. Faulkner became the first woman to attend day classes at the Citadel in January 1994 after overcoming obstacles created by The Citadel's defense team. Faulkner was not allowed, however, to join the corps of cadets or participate in any military training. In April 1995, the Fourth U.S. Circuit Court ruled that Faulkner could join the corps unless South Carolina had a court-approved program by August to provide similar leadership education for women. In May, Converse College in Spartanburg agreed to create a $10 million, state-funded South Carolina Women's Leadership Institute as an alternative. Critics immediately responded with cries that there was no way to "equate a modest woman's school with military training." The court agreed that there was not adequate time to assess the efficacy of the parallel program, and the Citadel was ordered to allow Faulkner to enter as a cadet while a trial date was set for the following November. The school asked the U.S. Supreme Court to intervene, but Justices William H. Rehnquist and Antonin Scalia refused to keep Faulkner from becoming the first female cadet at the Citadel.

The New Cadet. After the long battle, Faulkner won her fight against the tradition that prevented women from getting the same military education as men in her state. "That tradition needs to end and it will end on August 12," Faulkner stated as she accepted a 1995 Woman of Courage Award at the NOW National Conference. Accompanied by federal marshals and her parents, Faulkner began her career at The Citadel, only to be in the news again less than a week later when she left the school after spending several days in the infirmary. Physically unprepared for the rigors of "hell week" cadets face upon entering, Faulkner dropped out. Cadets were photographed cheering and celebrating as a tearful Faulkner left the campus.

The Fight Continues. In September 1995, Nancy Melette applied for admission and took Faulkner's place in the court battle. Eyes turned then to the battle being fought by VMI. On 26 June 1996, the Supreme Court ruled that VMI must admit women or give up its state funding because its single-sex admission policy violated the equal protection clause of the Constitution's Fourteenth Amendment. The Citadel, in response, also capitulated and changed its admission policy. Court battles continued, however, as judges tried to ensure that the concept of equality was fairly and reasonably applied to the female cadets. Of the four female cadets who enrolled in The Citadel in the fall of 1996, two quit mid-year amid allegations of harassment and safety issues (ten male cadets faced disciplinary action in connection with those incidents). In the spring of 1999, Nancy Mace became the first female graduate of The Citadel.

Sources:

Lisa Bennett-Haigney, "Faulkner Makes History at the Citadel," *National Times (National Organization for Women)* August 1995, Internet website.

"The Citadel Goes Coed," *Charleston.net*, 1997, Internet website.

WALTER E. MASSEY

1938-

PHYSICIST; PRESIDENT OF MOREHOUSE COLLEGE; CHAIRMAN OF THE NATIONAL SCIENCE FOUNDATION

Scientific Community. Walter Massey, who had majored in physics at Morehouse College, returned as president to his alma mater, a prestigious, historically black college for young men in Atlanta, Georgia, after a long, distinguished career teaching and promoting science around the country in universities and scientific organizations. Beginning his physics work at the Argonne National Laboratory at the University of Chicago, Massey chose education over pure research as a way to become involved with the social issues of the 1960s. His assistant professorship at the University of Illinois led to work at Brown University, and eventually a return to the University of Chicago and Argonne. At that time, he was actively involved with the American Association for the Advancement of Science, becoming the president of its board of directors in 1988 and chairman from 1989 to 1990. He was appointed by President George Bush to chair the National Science Foundation in 1991, and left that position only for a role as senior vice-president and provost at the University of California.

Educational Reform. While at the University of Illinois, Massey began to realize the struggle faced by black students entering college with a poor preparation for studying the sciences. During his tenure at Brown University, Massey founded a program called Inner-City Teachers of Science, whose mission was to train urban public school teachers in science and to help design curricula for their programs. His goal was to influence those schools that frequently had the responsibility for educating young black students. While at the University of Chicago, Massey also helped found the Summer Research Opportunities Program for Minority Students, a program designed to match minority students with a faculty member for an eight to ten week summer research project. Highly successful, the program boasted a 75-80 percent rate of continued graduate or professional education for participants as opposed to the normal 20 percent.

Skilled Administrator. Massey's skills as an administrator were developed at Brown where he served as both full professor and dean of the college. When lured back to the University of Chicago and the Argonne National Laboratory, he oversaw many fascinating experiments and improved the relationships between the Lab and the University. Eventually a position of Vice President of Research at Argonne National Laboratory was created for him. His skills stood him in good stead when he faced an unsettled scientific community as Chairman of the National Science Foundation. Continuing the policies of his controversial predecessor, Massey chose to emphasize the practical applications of science while at the same time recognizing the significant contributions made by individual scientists doing basic research. He continued to influence the scientific world through his supervision of ten campuses and three national laboratories at the University of California.

Continuing Influence. Massey's influence continued at Morehouse. Pledging to promote scientific literacy among all students in humanities and science, he accepted the role of President of Morehouse College after the school faced a financial scandal involving his predecessor. His purposes in returning to his alma mater included a desire to return to a "grassroots level" of involvement with the teaching of science. Plans included linking programs at the school with those of larger research universities. His contacts in the scientific world permitted him to plan on a large scale.

Source:
Current Biography Yearbook, 1997 (New York: H.W. Wilson, 1997).

BILL NYE

1955-
TELEVISION PERSONALITY

Education and Entertainment. *Bill Nye the Science Guy* was one of Vice President Al Gore's favorite TV shows. The zany half-hour program aired on Public Broadcasting System (PBS) channels around the nation and, though it was aimed at fourth graders, it appealed to people of all ages. In a format replete with "cool" music, stunts, and flashy graphics, *Bill Nye the Science Guy* took one important scientific concept with each episode and used it as the learning objective for that show. Interviews with "way cool" scientists and bizarre demonstrations of how science is applied in everyday life were hallmarks of the Emmy-Award winning program.

Beginnings. Bill Nye was raised in Washington, D.C., and studied mechanical engineering under Carl Sagan at Cornell University. After beginning his engineering career at Boeing Corporation in Seattle, Washington, Nye began moonlighting as a stand-up comic after friends dared him to enter a Steve Martin look-alike contest. He premiered the Science Guy as a regular on *Almost Live!,* a local comedy-variety television show. He and several Seattle producers convinced the National Science Foundation (NSF) and the U.S. Department of Energy to fund a pilot which so impressed Disney executives, they offered to jointly produce the show with PBS and the NSF. In 1993 the premiere installment of the show aired to rave reviews.

A Different Approach. Michael Eisner, chairman of Disney, said Nye "makes you understand very sophisticated concepts. I learn all those things I probably should have learned in high school." Focusing on one concept each show, Nye provided real life examples to show children how science touches their lives. For example, in one episode, he stripped to his shorts in a meat locker to show that "temperature doesn't cause colds, germs do." In another, he illustrated the scale of the solar system by using a soccer field and high-speed photography of driving 423 miles away. Providing experiments that children could try at home was another popular facet of his show. Children also liked the fast pace and unpredictability of the program.

Public Response. Hailed by many educators as an example of ways that teaching could be done to hold the attention of children and make it fun, the show was sometimes criticized for presenting an unrealistic picture of the hard work a success-

ful career in science took. Nye, nonetheless took the concept into other forms of media through the publication of books with accessible language such as *Bill Nye the Science Guy's Big Blast of Science* (1993) and *Bill Nye the Science Guy's Big Blue Ocean* (1999), CD-ROM games involving earth science with a meteor headed for Earth, and exhibits at Disney's Epcot Center. Understandable and engaging, Bill Nye made science come alive for children across the country.

Sources:
Peter Carlin, "Force of Nature," *People* (21 October 1996): 69.

Current Biography Yearbook 1998 (New York: H.W. Wilson, 1998), p. 433-435.

RICHARD W. RILEY

1933-
SECRETARY OF EDUCATION; GOVERNOR OF SOUTH CAROLINA

The "Education Governor." Richard W. Riley began his political career as a member of the South Carolina House of Representatives in 1963. After losing the Democratic nomination in 1974, he was elected in 1979 as the governor of South Carolina. Although the South Carolina legislature rejected his first education reform package, he returned with a proposal formulated from ideas proposed by citizens at local forums he had organized. In order to garner widespread support for his plan, he began with convincing local business and educational leaders of its worth. Riley then launched a massive public relations effort to convince voters to fund the plan with a one-cent increase in the sales tax. With the slogan, "A Penny for Their Thoughts," Riley used this statewide support to engage the legislature in a debate that ultimately resulted in passing the Education Improvement Act of 1984. Tougher standards for students, teachers, and administrators proved valuable when, in the next few years, student performance in South Carolina made a marked jump in national comparisons.

President Clinton. In a move that drew bipartisan support, President-elect Bill Clinton nominated Riley as his Secretary of Education. Riley also served as personnel director of the Clinton-Gore transition team, selecting hundreds of subcabinet appointees for positions in the Clinton administration. As governors, both Riley and Clinton had worked together in the National Governors' Association to promote education. Many of their proposals as governors became part of the president's Goals 2000 program. Riley served as chairman of the National Governors' Association's Task Force on Readiness whose 1986 report provided recommendations that found their way into the education summit held in 1990.

Making his Mark. As Education Secretary, Riley began formulating policy for the Clinton administration almost immediately. He rescinded the controversial policy of the former education secretary on race-based scholarships. Riley also worked with Labor Secretary Robert B. Reich in presenting a reform package that would affect workplace readiness skills, as well as national standards for academic competence. Another early accomplishment of Riley's was the streamlining of the college lending program and the decrease in defaults on student loans. He focused on improving public schools and, unlike the previous administration, showed little support for vouchers or other incentives for parents to move toward private education. In an interview with Tamara Henry in *USA Today*, Riley said, "What I would like to do is move this country forward where we have an education system that is universal, cohesive, and driven by high standards."

Second Term. Riley was reconfirmed as Education Secretary when Clinton was re-elected president in 1996. His work on national standards for excellence in school performance continued. Speaking across the country and in national publications, Riley asserted that the improvement of public education was dependent on the elevation of teaching to the status of a first-class profession. This change, he acknowledged, would require an increase in teachers' traditionally low salaries as well as higher standards and more rigorous training for future teachers. His proposals included a three-step system for the preparation of teachers similar to that required of doctors: internship, residency, and certification. Riley also believed that large, impersonal high schools should make way for smaller, more nurturing places that could assist teens through the difficulties of adolescence. In addition to favoring "exit exams" for high school students, Riley urged parents to limit the hours teens worked in after-school jobs to no more than twenty hours per week.

Sources:

Current Biography Yearbook 1993 (New York: H.W. Wilson, 1993).

"Valuable Lesson," *Shoot* (26 February 1999): 4.

THEODORE R. SIZER

1932-

FOUNDER OF THE COALITION OF ESSENTIAL SCHOOLS

Firsthand Experience. Ted Sizer left Harvard University and the position of Dean of the School of Education in the late 1960s to return to "the trenches." He wanted to experience life in a school to better inform his theories of educational reform. As Headmaster of the elite Phillips Academy in Andover, Massachusetts, he found excellent examples of what to do and what not to do. Again in the late 1990s, Sizer ran a school along with his wife, Nancy. This time it was one of his Coalition of Essential

Schools, the Francis W. Parker Charter Essential School in Rhode Island. Sizer was able to see some of his best ideas for student achievement.

Horace as a Trilogy. Perhaps best known for his trilogy of books using a fictional, composite teacher to remark on the state of public education, Sizer made his mark on the educational reform movement over the course of several decades. *Horace's Compromise* (1984), *Horace's School* (1992), and *Horace's Hope* (1996) together form a picture of Sizer's interpretations of what is, should be, and could be in the realm of U.S. education. Reflecting the maturity of Sizer's own involvement with the field, Horace drew an authentic view of the realities and possibilities faced by teachers every day. The ideas proposed in the three books were promoted through the publication of a newsletter aptly named *Horace*.

Achievements. Academics were a part of Sizer's life from the moment he was born. His father was an art history professor at Yale University. As the youngest of six children, Sizer was raised a "faculty brat." After attending college at Yale, Sizer got his first taste of professional education as an artillery training officer in the Army. After his experiences at Harvard and Phillips Andover, Sizer spent many years as a professor at Brown University, retiring in 1996. In 1993 he helped to launch and lead the Annenberg Institute for School Reform, which he left in 1996. While maintaining those two positions, he also served as chair of the Coalition of Essential Schools, a premier school reform organization he founded in 1984. Sizer watched this group of schools grow in fifteen years from twelve schools to over 250 (with another 830 considering membership), evidence that there continued to be widespread support for his ideas. Sizer, a popular speaker, voiced ideas that critics sometimes complained left a vague picture of student abilities. A strong proponent of multiple performance assessments, Sizer acknowledged the current realities of standardized tests, but argued that they showed a limited view of not only a student's competence but of the school's as well.

School Reform. Sizer was described by colleagues as an optimist. Faced with the slow and mostly political barriers to substantive change in schools, he nevertheless maintained his faith that a difference could be made in America's schools. He often voiced his concern about the "factory system" of education—long entrenched in American schools—which forced children into artificial age-based classes. Organized for efficiency rather than effectiveness, such cohorts shuffled along to six to seven classes in succession, where they would be taught isolated subjects. A cautious supporter of the standards movement and of accountability of progress toward identified goals, he questioned who should set those standards given the constantly changing political arena where they seemed to lie. Sizer's voice in moving schools toward reform was heard in all corners of the country during the 1990s.

Sources:

David Ruenzel, "The Essential Ted Sizer," *Education Week* (4 December 1996): 32-37.

Theodore Sizer, "Telling Silences in Education Reform," *The Education Digest* (January 1996): 44-47.

PEOPLE IN THE NEWS

William J. Bennett, former U.S. Secretary of Education, was quoted in *Vanity Fair* in 1994: "The moral education of our children is the first priority of a nation. We're not just talking about learning subjects here, about history or calculus—whatever. In the education of our children, we're involved in nothing less than the architecture of souls."

Derik Bok, Harvard University president reporting in 1990 on the university's divestiture of all stockholdings in tobacco companies, said the decision had been "motivated by a desire not to be associated as a shareholder with companies engaged in significant sales of products that create a substantial and unjustified risk of harm to other human beings."

Ernest L. Boyer, President, Carnegie Foundation for the Advancement of Teaching, commented on the increasing federal role in education, "If I had ever whispered 'national standards', I think I would have lost my job [as Commissioner in the 1970s]. We bent over backwards 15 years ago so that no one would think we were interfering [with state and local control of education]. Within a decade, we have gone from this preoccupation of local control to national standards. There is no turning back."

William E. Brock, former U.S. Secretary of Labor, proclaimed in 1990: "Education is the most backward single institution in all the U.S. Between 38¢ and 41¢ of our education dollar gets to the classroom. That is an act of irrationality. We are not putting our resources where the kids are. In the city of New York there are more school administrators than there are in all of France. In the state of New York there are more administrators than there are in all of the European Community, and the EC has 12 countries and 320 million people."

A group of 150 Wellesley students had presented a petition to university president Nan Keohane in April 1990, protesting the invitation to **Barbara Bush** as commencement speaker, because she was a woman who had "gained recognition through the achievements of her husband, which contravenes what we have been taught over the last four years at Wellesley." Mrs. Bush, who had dropped out of Smith College to marry, said she thought the students were very reasonable, but added, "I don't think they understand where I'm coming from. I chose to live the life I've lived."

In a 1994 issue of *USA Today*, **Michael Casserly**, executive director, Council of the Great City Schools, said: "You've got facilities that most adults would never think of working in themselves, and buildings that send clear signals to kids about how they're valued. Certainly, Congress wouldn't work in facilities like that."

President **Bill Clinton**, during one of his weekly radio addresses in 1996, announced that he would require states to deny welfare benefits to teenage mothers who did not attend school. He said: "We have to make it clear that a baby doesn't give you a right, and won't give you the money to leave home and drop out of school."

Mario M. Cuomo, former governor of New York (D), bemoaned educational critics' viewpoints with, "Why didn't they ever say that about defense? You need money for missiles, but not money for schoolhouses. . . . You need money for Generals, but not money for teachers. I don't understand how, when it's convenient, you can say, 'You can't throw money at a problem,' but if it's defense, you have to throw money at it."

In discussing teacher education, **Linda Darling-Hammond**, professor of Education, Teachers College, Columbia University, voiced: "We've always been able to produce wonderful demonstration schools. You can always get terrific teachers in one school, but we're not doing enough to address the fact that we're not producing enough terrific teachers for all schools."

James J. Davis, interim chairman, Department Of Foreign Languages, Howard University, said: "I advise students to study a foreign language regardless of which one it is, because foreign-language study is not just about learning a second language but about opening your mind to a larger world. Language is really about culture."

Robert J. Dole (R-Kansas), while a frontrunner in the race for the 1996 Republican presidential nomination, attacked multilingual education programs in a speech delivered to the 1995 American Legion national convention: "We need the glue of language to help hold us together."

In 1994 **Ken Ducote**, Director of Facility Planning for the New Orleans Public Schools, voiced his frustrations as, "Imagine if you were on the school board and you were faced with closing schools, increasing teacher-student ratios, cutting athletics or putting off maintenance. Which one of those would you do?"

In 1992 **Joseph Duffey**, President, American University, Washington, D.C., cautioned: "By the year 2000, American higher education will no longer be dominant in the world. Our general belief in education and our ability to finance it are running out."

In 1991 **Jaime Escalante**, profiled in the movie *Stand and Deliver* (1988), left the East Los Angeles high school where he had achieved success with a group of primarily Hispanic students taking the Advanced Placement Examination in Calculus, because he said many members of the local teachers' union were apathetic and allowed too many students to fail.

John E. Frohnmayer, Chairman, National Endowment for the Arts, in 1991 upheld: "I would like to persuade those who really care about education that the arts ought to be central to the curriculum. Arts education is not recreational; it's not secondary; it's not 'nice' if you have a lot of money and a lot of time. It's critical to the process of learning to think, of learning to be a productive citizen, of learning to make connections of disconnected items, which is the real substance of genius."

Midshipman **Juliane Gallina** was appointed by the U.S. Naval Academy as its first female brigade commander, or leader of the 4,300-member corps of midshipmen, in 1991.

Keith Geiger, President of the National Education Association (NEA), said in 1990: "Children don't drop out in high school or middle school. They drop out–in their heads–in elementary school."

In 1991 U.S. Congressman **Richard A. Gephardt** (D-Missouri) bemoaned the nation's graduation rate. "It is natural that war [such as the recent Persian Gulf war] begets metaphors. If we can build 'smart' bombs, surely we can graduate smart kids. If 90 percent of our soldiers have graduated from high school, how can we be satisfied when only 60 percent of our civilian workers have?"

According to **Milton Goldberg**, Executive Director, National Education Commission on Time and Learning, "If reform is to truly take hold, the six-hour, 180-day school year should be relegated to museums–an exhibit from our education past."

U.S. Representative **Fred Grandy** (R-Iowa) pointed out a disturbing statistic: "There is an educational bias in this country toward people who follow an education system from kindergarten through college. Sixty percent of Federal education funds are spent on higher education–but only 30 percent of high-school students go to college. The lack of attention given to the other 70 percent has surfaced in the decline of individual income, lagging productivity and an under-educated and non-competitive workforce."

Kansas Governor **Bill Graves** (R) called the 11 August 1999 decision by the state Board of Education to remove the theory of evolution from its official science curriculum "a terrible, tragic, embarrassing solution to a problem that didn't exist."

Paul Hill, senior researcher at the Rand Corporation, theorized in 1991: "It's a false assumption that because public schools are publicly funded they have to be all things to all people. Public-school authorities should create portfolios of schools, each with a different focus, in math and science, say, or vocational education."

David Honeyman, Associate Professor of Education, University of Florida, proclaimed: "A small town has as much trouble building one new school as an urban community has building 25."

Augusta F. Kappner, Assistant Secretary for Vocational and Adult Education, U.S. Department of Education, said to a reporter from *The New York Times* in April 1994: "The days were when a young person in Pittsburgh could drop out of school, go to a steel mill and get a good job. Those jobs aren't available anymore. Young people don't see the connection between learning in high school and what lies ahead for them in the job market."

Thomas H. Kean, former Governor of New Jersey (R), declared: "The [high school] diploma is more a proof of age than it is any kind of achievement."

Supreme Court Justice **Anthony M. Kennedy**, in a 1992 ruling that opened the door for school districts to be released from court supervised desegregation, said: "Racial balance is not to be achieved for its own sake. Once the racial imbalance due to de jure violation has been remedied, the school district is under no duty to remedy imbalance that is caused by demographic factors."

In response to "No Turning Back," a report released by the Business Roundtable, a group of nearly two hundred chief executive officers of the nation's largest corporations, Maine Governor **Angus King** (Ind.) said: "You did just the right thing by focusing on the states–that's where the action is. You can make a real difference on the state level."

Glen Linden, professor of history, Southern Methodist University, expressed his view: "Some shift of the money is essential [to help students in poor districts get good educations. But] presently there isn't any willingness to share the burden of public education. The people with the money are opting out. We say the future is children, but we're not going to support the black kids, brown kids. We've got to say they're not my kids or your kids but the nation's kids. If not, we're a Third World country down the road."

The University of California at Berkeley expelled junior **Andrew Martinez**, known as the "Naked Guy," in January 1993 for appearing on campus clad only in sandals and a backpack after the school instituted a ban on nudity. Martinez said that his nudity was a form of protest against social mores and sexual repression.

Myriam Met, foreign language coordinator in the Montgomery County, Maryland, public schools, expressed: "Languages will be a survival skill for the 21st century. It's unfortunate that people would think the only reason for learning a language is to sell more widgets abroad. But just because they're doing it for that reason doesn't mean they won't benefit in other ways."

Surgeon General Antonia C. Novello established a task force in 1991 after a detailed survey by the Health and Human Services Department revealed that more than one-half of the 20.7 million students in grades seven through twelve drank alcoholic beverages.

Gregory M. St. L. O'Brien, President, University of New Orleans, theorized in 1991: "Urban universities are doing for the cities in the 1990s what the land-grant colleges did for the rural areas in the 1800s."

Commenting on the evolution of education in America, Leonard Pellicer, professor of education, University of South Carolina, said: "When we started out with education in America, we basically brought kids to school and taught them reading, writing and arithmetic. Now we transport them, we feed them, give them career counseling, personal counseling. We discipline them, and develop them socially. Everything is so much more complicated and it takes a different kind of person [as principal] to maintain a grasp of what's going on."

James J. Renier, chairman, Honeywell, Inc., proclaimed in 1991: "One of the best things you can do to help solve the educational crisis in the United States today is to work on the problems that affect little kids from minus nine months to the time they get to kindergarten."

National Center on Fair & Open Testing, an organization opposed to standardized tests, dismissed the changes announced in 1990 to the Scholastic Aptitude Test (SAT) as insignificant. "FairTest concludes that the new SAT amounts to little more than rearranging the deck chairs on an educational Titanic," said the group's public education director, Robert Schaeffer. "None of these changes address the SAT's real flaws."

Albert Shanker, the President of the American Federation of Teachers, called the proposal endorsed by President George Bush and known as the Education Goals 2000 "pie in the sky."

Baylor University president Robert B. Sloan Jr. affirmed that although the institution had held its first on-campus dance in its 151-year history in 1996, provocative dancing and "lewd gyrations" would continue to be banned at campus dances.

President of the College Board, Donald M. Stewart, in an annual report released in 1991 blamed the highest step increase in average college costs since 1983 on the current recession. Four-year public colleges raised their tuition by an average of 14 percent.

DEATHS

Marguerite Ross Barnett, 49, first black woman to serve as head of a major U.S. university, 26 February 1992.

Daisy Bates, 84, civil rights leader and former president of the Arkansas chapter of the National Association for the Advancement of Colored People (NAACP), who gained national attention when she counteracted the governor's attempt to prevent nine black students from entering Little Rock's Central High School, 4 November 1999.

Terrell H. Bell, 74, top U.S. education official (under three Republican presidents), who commissioned the 1983 report, "A Nation at Risk," which helped draw public attention to declining educational standards, 22 June 1996.

Allan Bloom, 62, professor of political philosophy at the University of Chicago, who gained fame for his 1987 best-selling, yet controversial, book, *The Closing of the American Mind*, 7 October 1992.

Ernest LeRoy Boyer, 67, former U.S. Commissioner of Education under President Jimmy Carter and president of the Carnegie Foundation, who published several books on education, including *Scholarship Reconsidered* (1990) and *The Basic School* (1995), and served as chancellor of the State University of New York, 8 December 1995.

Harvie Branscomb, 103, chancellor of Vanderbilt University, who guided the school to national prominence, 24 July 1998.

Mary Ingraham Bunting-Smith, 87, president of Radcliffe College, who led efforts to allow women to earn Harvard degrees and access to business and graduate courses. She founded the Radcliffe Institute (later renamed the Bunting

Institute), and was the first woman to work for the U.S. Atomic Energy Commission, where she served as commissioner, 21 January 1998.

Mary Steichen Calderone, 94, advocate of sex education in U.S. public schools, who also successfully lobbied the American Medical Association to have it distribute birth control information and prescribe birth control measures. She also coauthored *The Family Book About Sexuality* (1981) and *Talking With Your Child About Sex* (1982), 24 October 1998.

James Samuel Coleman, 68, influential sociologist, whose research on the relationship between education and race shaped the debate on school desegregation and busing efforts in the 1960s and 1970s, 25 March 1995.

Donald Norwood Davies, 91, federal judge, who issued landmark decision in 1957 to integrate white and black students in Little Rock, Arkansas, public schools, 18 April 1996.

Paul Engle, 82, writer and poet, who, together with his wife, Chinese novelist Hua-ling Nieh, founded the international writing program at the University of Iowa in 1967 and developed it into one of the country's most acclaimed programs for creative writers, 22 March 1991.

John King Fairbank, 84, professor, who pioneered the development of modern Chinese studies as an academic discipline, 14 September 1991.

Arthur Sherwood Fleming, 91, former president of Ohio Wesleyan University, the University of Oregon, and Macalester College, served as U.S. Secretary of Health, Education and Welfare under President Dwight D. Eisenhower, 7 September 1996.

Paul A. Freund, 83, Harvard University professor and leading U.S. constitutional scholar whose writings helped shape policies granting Congress greater authority in matters affecting the national economy, 5 February 1992.

James William Fulbright, 89, Democratic senator from Arkansas prominent in the field of U.S. foreign policy, who introduced legislation that laid the groundwork for the United Nations, whose collected speeches opposing U.S. involvement in the Vietnam War became a bestseller (*The Arrogance of Power*, 1966), and who founded the government-sponsored international exchange program known as the Fulbright exchange program, 9 February 1995.

Wendall Arthur Garrity, Jr., 79, federal justice, who mandated busing in Boston in 1974 as a method of desegregating the public schools, 16 September 1999.

Laurence McKinley Gould, 98, former president of Carleton College, who explored Antarctica with Richard E. Byrd and led the United States in an international effort to prevent territorial claims on the continent, 20 June 1995.

John Alfred Hannah, 88, first chairman of the U.S. Commission on Civil Rights, 1957-1969 and president of Michigan State University, 1941-1969, during which time the university grew from a small, agricultural school of 6,000 students to a major university of 45,000, 23 February 1991.

Osborne Bennett Hardison Jr., 61, director of the Folger Shakespeare Library in Washington, D.C. from 1969 to 1983 and a professor of literature at Georgetown University, 5 August 1990.

Harriet L. Hardy, 87, the first female full professor at Harvard University Medical School, whose specialties included occupational sicknesses and the health threats posed by nuclear energy, 13 October 1993.

Charles Johnston Hitch, 85, former president of the University of California during the turbulent 1960s and 1970s and official in the Department of Defense under Presidents John F. Kennedy and Lyndon B. Johnson, 11 September 1995.

Samuel Ichiye Hiyakawa, 85, author, college president, and controversial senator, who became a symbol of adult authority during student protests in 1968 when he ripped wires out of a loudspeaker during a demonstration at San Francisco State University where he was acting president, 27 February 1992.

Hamilton Earl Holmes, 54, one of the first two black students at the University of Georgia and later an orthopedic surgeon and faculty member at Emory University, 26 October 1995.

Leanne Katz, 65, free speech advocate, who served as the executive director of the National Coalition Against Censorship since its founding in 1974, working tirelessly against banning books in school libraries, 2 March 1997.

Francis Keppel, 73, U.S. Commissioner of Education, 1962-1966, who played a major role in the development of the National Assessment of Educational Progress, 19 February 1990.

Grayson Louis Kirk, 94, president of Columbia University, who resigned after summoning police to disband student protests in 1968 when hundreds of students and faculty members were injured. During his term in office he had quadrupled the endowment, doubled the university's library holdings, and instigated several new programs, 21 November 1997.

Joseph Kitagawa, 77, Dean of the University of Chicago School of Divinity, who led in the effort to recognize religion as an independent academic discipline in U.S. colleges. He strove to introduce Japanese religions to the West and founded the international journal *History of Religions*, 7 October 1992.

Christopher Lasch, 61, leftist history professor and author, whose best-known work, *The Culture of Narcissism* (1978), explored the effect of industrial capitalism on American culture, 14 February 1994.

Max Lerner, 89, journalist, *New York Post* columnist, and university educator, who campaigned tirelessly for the improvement of educational standards and who drew national attention in the 1950s and early 1960s for his liberal and often controversial stances when he criticized Western culture for espousing a "fear of ideas," 5 June 1992.

Robert Quarles Marston, 76, president of the University of Florida when it became one of the ten largest schools in the United States and who also served as director of the National Institutes of Health (NIH), but was dismissed in a dispute with the Nixon administration over the distribution of NIH resources, 14 March 1999.

Earl James McGrath, 90, head of the federal Office of Education under Presidents Harry S Truman and Dwight D. Eisenhower, who resigned in protest from his post as Commissioner of Education over federal education budget cuts, 14 January 1993.

Virginia McMartin, 88, founder of a preschool, who was accused (though not convicted) in a famous child molestation case along with members of her family in the 1980s, 17 December 1995.

James Bryan McMillan, 78, judge who helped establish a national standard for school desegregation in the United States with a 1969 decision that ordered extensive busing in Charlotte, North Carolina, 4 March 1995.

Carl J. Megel, 92, past president and former lobbyist of the American Federation of Teachers, 18 September 1992.

James M. Nabrit Jr., 97, president of Howard University in the 1960s, who was also involved in many major civil rights cases including the 1954 *Bolling* v. *Sharpe*, which helped bring about the desegregation of public schools in Washington, D.C., 27 December 1997.

Walter Ridley, 86, the first African American to earn a doctorate degree from a southern university, who served as president of Elizabeth City College as well as president of the American Teachers Association, 26 September 1996.

John Pearson Roche, 70, professor of political science, adviser to Presidents John F. Kennedy and Lyndon B. Johnson, speechwriter for Hubert Humphrey, and syndicated columnist of liberal political viewpoints in "A Word Edgewise," 6 May 1994.

Frank Anthony Rose, 70, president of the University of Alabama, 1958-1969, who helped mediate between Alabama Governor George Wallace (a staunch opponent of desegregation) and the federal government in 1963, when the university admitted its first black students, 1 February 1991.

Abram Leon Sachar, 94, chancellor and founding president of Brandeis University, 24 July 1993.

Terry Sanford, 80, former president of Duke University, who also served as governor and U.S. senator from the state of North Carolina, 18 April 1998.

Mario Savio, 53, mathematics and philosophy teacher at Sonoma State University, who gained fame as a student protest leader in the Free Speech Movement at the University of California at Berkeley in the 1960s, including the historic 1964 sit-in, 6 November 1996.

Reverend Joseph A. Sellinger, 72, president of Loyola College in Baltimore, Maryland, who transformed it from a small commuter school into one of the country's leading Jesuit colleges, 19 April 1993.

Albert Shanker, 68, president of the American Federation of Teachers (AFT) from 1974 to 1997, 22 February 1997.

Howard Robert Swearer, 59, president of Brown University in Providence, Rhode Island, 1977-1988, who was credited with resolving financial and student dissatisfaction issues and renewing Brown's reputation as a major international university, 19 October 1991.

Norman H. Topping, 89, viral researcher and university leader, who in the 1930s developed a typhus vaccine for Allied soldiers in World War II, and who went on to become president and then chancellor of the University of Southern California and is credited with turning the school into a major research institution, 18 November 1997.

William Appleman Williams, 68, historian, who was the author of several revisionist books that challenged traditional interpretations of American history and was often called the founder of the "New Left" school, 5 March 1990.

PUBLICATIONS

Mary Alampi and Peter M. Comeau, eds., *American Education Annual: Trends and Issues in the Educational Community* (Detroit: Gale, 1999).

Regis Bernhardt and others, eds., *Curriculum Leadership: Rethinking Schools for the 21st Century* (Cresskill, N.J.: Hampton Press, 1998).

Sari Knopp Biklen and Diane Pollard, eds., *Gender and Education* (Chicago: National Study of School Evaluation [NSSE], 1993).

Rita Chawla-Duggan and Christopher J. Pole, eds., *Reshaping Education in the 1990s: Perspectives on Primary Schooling* (London & Washington: Falmer Press, 1996).

Lynne V. Cheney, *Telling the Truth: Why Our Culture and Our Country Have Stopped Making Sense, And What We Can Do About It* (New York: Simon & Schuster, 1995).

The College Board, *Higher Education's Landscape: Demographic Issues in the 1990s* (New York: College Board Publications, 1995).

Constance Ewing Cook, *Lobbying for Higher Education: How Colleges and Universities Influence Federal Policy* (Nashville: Vanderbilt University Press, 1998).

Marian Wright Edelman, *Lanterns: A Memoir of Mentors* (Boston: Beacon Press, 1999).

Edelman, *Stand for Children* (New York: Hyperion, 1998).

Samuel M. Ehrenhalt, *Public Education: A Major American Growth Industry in the 1990s* (Albany, N.Y.: Nelson A. Rockefeller Institute of Government, 2000).

Debbie Epstein, ed., *Challenging Lesbian and Gay Inequalities in Education* (Buckingham, U.K. & Philadelphia: Open University Press, 1994).

Roger Geiger, ed., *The American College in the Nineteenth Century* (Nashville: Vanderbilt University Press, 2000).

Clark Kerr, Marian L. Gade, and Maureen Kawaoka, *Troubled Times for American Higher Education: The 1990s and Beyond* (Albany: State University of New York Press, 1994).

Ronald E. Koetzsch, *The Parents' Guide to Alternatives in Education* (Boston: Shambhala, 1997).

Alan Charles Kors and Harvey A. Silvergate, *The Shadow University: The Betrayal of Liberty on America's Campuses* (New York: Free Press, 1998).

Helen F. Ladd, Rosemary Chalk, and Janet S. Hansen, eds., *Equity and Adequacy in Education Finance: Issues and Perspectives* (Washington, D.C.: Committee on Education Finance, Commission on Behavioral and Social Sciences and Education, National Research Council, National Academy Press, 1999).

David Levine and others, eds., *Rethinking Schools: An Agenda for Change* (New York : New Press, 1995).

Robert Lowe and Barbara Miner, eds., *False Choices: Why School Vouchers Threaten Our Children's Future* (Milwaukee, Wis.: Rethinking Schools, 1993).

Barbara Means, ed., *Technology and Education Reform: The Reality Behind the Promise* (San Francisco: Jossey-Bass, 1994).

Louis Menand, ed., *The Future of Academic Freedom* (Chicago: University of Chicago Press, 1996).

Roslyn Arlin Mickelson, ed., *Children on the Streets of the Americas: Homelessness, Education, and Globalization in the United States, Brazil, and Cuba* (London & New York: Routledge, 2000).

Christopher Newfield and Ronald Strickland, eds., *After Political Correctness: The Humanities and Society in the 1990s* (Boulder, Colo.: Westview Press, 1995).

Wendie C. Old, *Marian Wright Edelman: Fighting for Children's Rights* (Springfield, N.J.: Enslow, 1995).

Michael D. Parsons, *Power and Politics: Federal Higher Education Policy Making in the 1990s* (Albany: State University of New York Press, 1997).

Theresa Perry and Lisa Delpit, eds., *The Real Ebonics Debate: Power, Language, and the Education of African-American Children* (Boston: Beacon Press, 1998).

Diane Ravitch and Joseph P. Viteritti, eds., *New Schools for a New Century* (New Haven, Conn.: Yale University Press, 1997).

Dolores A. Stegelin, ed., *Early Childhood Education: Policy Issues for the 1990s* (Norwood, N.J.: Ablex, 1992).

Sally Tomlinson and Maurice Craft, eds., *Ethnic Relations and Schooling: Policy and Practice in the 1990s* (London & Atlantic Highlands, N.J.: Athlone, 1995).

U.S. Department of Education, Office of Educational Research and Improvement, National Center for Education Statistics, *Digest of Education Statistics, 1999* (Washington, D.C.: U.S. Government Printing Office, 1999).

Donovan R. Walling, ed., *At the Threshold of the Millennium* (Bloomington, Ind.: Phi Delta Kappa Educational Foundation, 1995).

Grant Wiggins and Jay McTighe, *Understanding by Design* (Alexandria, Va.: Association for Supervision and Curriculum Development, 1998).

FASHION

by MARY K. PRATT

CONTENTS

Sidebars and tables are listed in italics.

1990

Feb. Men's bolo ties are popular items. Designer Ralph Lauren shows them with his Polo line, while rock star Bruce Springsteen is photographed sporting one. These Western-influenced string-thin ties are fastened at the neck with decorative clasps that come in everything from silver to stone, with costs ranging from $10 to $300.

Mar. *Vogue* declares: "Pretty Makes A Comeback." Designers show softer suits, jackets with softer shoulders, curvy tailoring, and fluid skirts and pants for women. The "power dressing" of the 1980s, with its sharply tailored suits and distinct shoulder pads, is over.

Apr. Real estate tycoon Donald John Trump opens his Taj Mahal in Atlantic City, N.J. Architect Francis Xavier Dumont designed the 420-million-square-foot, $1 billion structure. Not everyone was impressed. Nancy Gibbs writes in *Time* that "the façade looks edible, the work of a candymaker gone mad."

July French designer Claude Montana's fall collection for men features the monochromatic look: black trousers and a black sports coat over a black mock turtleneck.

Aug. French designers such as Hermès, Christian Dior, Ungaro, Yohji Yamamoto, and Pierre Balmain all show generously cut overcoats for men that emphasize a comfortable, relaxed look.

Sept. Men's designers, led by Italian designer Giorgio Armani, abandon the stiff tailoring of 1980s "power dressing" and instead turn out suits with more comfortable cuts. Colors remain traditional, with suits turning up in grays and browns.

1991

- Lingerie becomes outerwear. Singer/actress Cher is featured in a black lace bra paired with a black mesh top and blue jeans. Cindy Crawford dons a black lace bodysuit; singer Barbara Streisand wears a cream-colored bustier under a cream blazer; the fall Paris couture shows by Gianni Versace, Chanel, Christian Dior, Christian Lacroix, and Thierry Mugler feature versions of the corseted evening gown.

Jan. American firm I. M. Pei & Partners' new seventy-story tower for the Bank of China in Hong Kong becomes the tallest building in Asia and fifth-highest structure in the world.

Feb. With a nod to 1960s styles, women part their bobbed tresses on the side. Actress Laura Dern and models Linda Evangelista and Claudia Schiffer sport styles with parts—sometimes on the left, other times on the right.

- Psychedelic prints add a splash of color to the otherwise staid world of men's fashion. These colorful designs show up on shirts, jackets, pants, and accessories—but only among a select, and daring, set of men.

Apr. A sour economy inspires high-end designers to cast a creative eye toward frugality. Michael Kors, for example, shows summer suits from his KORS line that are suitable through the fall, while the design team Alphabeta sells a four-in-one reversible coat in silk taffeta.

- Fitness-inspired clothes such as bodysuits, maillots, unitards, and leggings are used as a base for clothes worn outside the gym; designers, such as Paris-based Karl Lagerfeld, show them as part of their ready-to-wear collections. Unlike the items worn in gyms, however, these body-hugging fashions come in fabrics that shimmer and shine.

June   Sheer tops, worn over bras, are used by women for both day and evening wear. Bras-turned-tops come in everything from leather to lace.

July   Sport sandals, particularly the popular Teva brand, make a splash. These must-have footwear feature sturdy soles with treads that will not slip on the trail, materials that dry quickly, and strong straps that do not give when being used for hiking or biking.

- Anna Sui has her first show with a fall collection that combines hip and classic lines, such as bright peacoat-style jackets over kilts. Nothing in the show costs more than $400.

- Designers abandon the straight and narrow as they show skirts that allow for movement, with features such as pleats, slits, and asymmetric hems. Donna Karan, for example, offers a wool twill sarong for $470.

Aug.   The European men's collections feature relaxed, roomy blazers that blur the line between formal office wear and casual dress. These sport coats come in hues of gray, brown, tan, and green.

Sept.   Long hair makes a comeback, as models Cindy Crawford, Elaine Irwin, and Karen Mulder show off their lengthy locks.

- Donna Karan introduces her first line of men's clothing with a fall collection that includes a navy wool crepe suit, a gray cashmere suit, and a black suit, as well as ties and vests in gold hues.

Oct.   As part of the dressing-down trend, American and European design houses, such as Emporio Armani, Basile, Joseph Abboud, and Hugo Boss, feature sport jackets in chenille—a soft, lush fabric—in colors such as cranberry, brown, and blue.

Nov.   The Guggenheim Museum taps California-based architect Frank O. Gehry to design a museum of modern art in Bilbao, Spain.

- Coach, started in 1941 with six employees working in a New York City loft, celebrates fifty years in business. Coach bags earned a loyal following, among both men and women, because of their classic look, trademark untreated leather, and brass fittings inspired by saddlery from the eighteenth and nineteenth centuries. To mark the occasion, Coach reissues limited-edition originals such as the "dinky shopping bag," releases new designs, and updates traditional bags in colors such as golden yellow and deep pink.

Dec.   Giorgio Armani launches his first A/X: Armani Exchange in New York. The store carries the Armani Jeans label as well as a complete collection of casual clothes.

1992

Jan.   Renovations are under way on the Boston Public Library, a National Landmark designed by McKim, Mead & White and built between 1888 and 1894.

Feb.   Spring runway shows feature classic twin sets—lightweight knit shells worn under matching cardigans. Designer Michael Kors's version is a sleeveless silk turtleneck paired with the cardigan in winter white. TSE Cashmere shows its classic version with a crewneck collar in red, while Isaac Mizrahi unveils similar classic styles in black and purple.

- American and European designers exhibit warm-weather suits for men in less-than-traditional hues. Dolce & Gabbana shows suits in white, Andrew Fezza features a single-breasted linen sports jacket and trousers in burnt orange, and Byblos comes out with a double-breasted silk suit in pale orange.

- Frank O. Gehry unveils his collection of furniture, with four chairs, two tables, and one ottoman.

- Designers feature pantsuits in their spring shows, but they present them in unconventional ways. Vests stand in for jackets, while pants come in all sorts of styles, from pegged to fluid. Bra tops replace blouses—at least on the catwalk.

Mar. Two-tone loafers for women are a hot commodity. Shoemakers turn them out in a variety of color combinations; Gucci, for instance, pairs lemon and white.

- Navy and khaki dominate men's spring fashions.

- Platform shoes, with their inches-high soles and even higher heels, enjoy a revival, particularly among younger women and teenagers. Rhinestone-covered shoes, wedge sandals, and foot-high vinyl sneakers are worn by women.

May Designers take scissors to their creations, adding ragged edges and tattered hems for a "sophisticated destruction," as Paris-based designer Karl Lagerfeld calls it. His designs for Chanel feature a dress with its hem ripped, a taffeta gown that appears to be losing its lining, and a jacket with its collar unraveling. Lagerfeld is not alone; Rei Kawakubo, for her spring line for the French design house of Comme des Garcons, features unfinished clothes and a trench coat hacked off at the waist.

Aug. Camel is the cool color for women. Designers turn out dresses, suits, and coats in the hue, often mixing the shade with cream and brown.

- Boots are back in a variety of shapes and sizes. Among the choices are Nine West's colorful cowboy boots at $125 a pair. The September 1992 issue of *Vogue* calls them "perfect for any up-to-date urban cowgirl."

Sept. Joseph Abboud introduces a lower-priced second line, J.O.E. Calvin Klein also launches a second line, cK.

Oct. The Guggenheim Museum in New York City reopens after a $50 million expansion and renovation.

Nov. Spike Lee's movie *Malcolm X* debuts in theaters, helping to create a market for T-shirts and baseball caps bearing a simple "X" for Malcolm X, the slain 1960s leader of the Nation of Islam.

1993

Feb. In a nod to 1970s nostalgia, designers start piecing patchwork into their collections. Designer Todd Oldham says, "I love patchwork because it's a way to paint with fabric—and one can work in the most obscure colors and patterns."

July Fall collections for women lack a unifying theme. In the *Vogue* "Runway Report," Katherine Betts says, "Rags? Romance? Rubber bands? Religion? Like a broken compass spinning aimlessly, the fall collections failed to indicate one strong direction. Never have fashion's camps been so splintered and the choices so plentiful."

Aug. As part of an overall trend to pare down, designers such as Calvin Klein bring a utilitarian approach to men's fashion, with stark, simple lines that echo Amish values. Suit jackets are single-breasted and worn with white cotton shirts; colors are staid—black, charcoal, and white.

- Native American jewelry enjoys a revival. Earrings, rings, pins, and tie clips feature motifs taken from the Southwest, such as jumping men, running animals, and charging warriors. Pieces come in silver, stone, and bone.

Sept. Peacoats push past the traditional long coat as the hot choice for women. European couture houses such as Chanel and Gianni Versace, as well as American companies such as Guess and Calvin Klein, turn out peacoats, although designers update this classic by using unexpected colors and unusual fabrics, such as leather and cableknit.

- Donna Karan launches a second line for men, DKNY, adopting the same name as her women's second line, which was started in 1989.

- Men return to boots for fashion footwear.

- Vests in fabrics such as knit, leather, suede, and corduroy become a must-have accessory for men.

1994

Jan. Designers point to a new direction in men's suits as they show leaner, longer shapes that create a close-to-the-body silhouette. Some of the American and European designers tapping into this new look are Joseph Abboud, Canali, Ermenegildo Zegna, and Donna Karan.

Mar. American and European designers add bold splashes of color to their collections for men with shirts and ties in vivid colors (yellows, reds, and blues) and patterns (stripes, checks, and plaids).

June *Vogue* declares "the bold red lip" as the cosmetic style for the fall.

- Slick hair slides back into popularity; woman's hair, long or short, is worn off the face.

July Hemlines for skirts become more moderate. Designers tried to push long lines earlier in the decade, but they flopped; so did microminis. The new length is closer to the knee.

- Men turn to authentic, old-style denim jeans, spurred in part by collectors who pay $5,000 for a never-worn Levi's jacket from the 1940s and $15,000 for a Lee cowboy jacket from the 1920s.

Aug. Knitwear becomes a staple in the fall fashion menswear collections. Calvin Klein shows V-neck sweaters with his suits, Giorgio Armani designs three-piece suits in knit fabrics, and Donna Karan turns out a cardigan-style coat.

- The latest in women's hairstyles is the classic, unfussy, above-the-shoulder bob. Famous women sharing the style include actresses Sharon Stone, Jodie Foster, and Jennifer Jason Leigh, as well as models Linda Evangelista and Naomi Campbell.

- Sportswear designer Tommy Hilfiger unveils his first complete line of tailored men's clothing, showing classic styles in suits, sport jackets, and coats.

Dec. The Wonderbra becomes an instant hit in the United States, as women flock to stores to get the latest in push-up bra technology. Some stores even set a one-per-customer limit as Wonderbras fly off the shelves.

- *Time* names the Chrysler Neon as one of the best products of 1994, declaring: "Detroit's new subcompacts are stylish, drivable and affordable, too, none more so than this remarkably popular little Chrysler. Most striking are its aggressive lines, responsive handling and tops-in-class acceleration."

1995

18 Jan.	The San Francisco Museum of Modern Art, designed by Swiss native Mario Botta, opens.
	• Retro influences show up in clothes. British designer Vivienne Westwood shows duchess satin corsets and bustles; Richard Tyler features a white stretch-stain sheath as a nod to the 1930s; Anna Sui touts floral-print dresses reminiscent of the 1940s; and John Galliano, based in France, features 1950s-style peplumed suits.
Feb.	Nude-colored hosiery, for a bare-looking leg, is a key item to be worn with skirts.
Apr.	Nautica, known for its sailing-inspired line of men's sportswear, introduces a complete collection of tailored clothing with items such as navy blazers, silk sport jackets, and seersucker suits.
July	The Korean War Veterans Memorial is unveiled in Washington, D.C.
	• Refinement returns after several seasons of a slumping economy and the accompanying trend toward modest and casual dressing. Women's clothes are elegant and tasteful; suits, sheath dresses, and classic camel coats all make comebacks.
Aug.	Slim-cut pants for women are back in style. Calvin Klein, Anne Klein, Marc Jacobs, DKNY, and Richard Tyler all feature them in their fall runway shows.
	• The Rock and Roll Hall of Fame and Museum, designed by I. M. Pei, opens on the shores of Lake Erie in Cleveland, Ohio.
Oct.	Menswear takes on a slimming effect as designers use strict tailoring to create jackets that are close to the body and trousers that are narrow with plain fronts. While the clothes are far from tight-fitting, designers sometimes use stretch fabrics to ensure a comfortable fit.
Nov.	Men catch up with women this fall and turn to classic camel as the color of choice for jackets, pants, and overcoats.
Dec.	Chanel's Vamp nail polishes, in dark blood-red colors, develop a following after first appearing on the Paris runways a year earlier.

1996

Jan.	The one-button single-breasted suit is the hot look for men, with designers such as Giorgio Armani, Calvin Klein, and Richard Tyler producing such outfits.
Apr.	The Council on Tall Buildings and Urban Habitat, based in Bethlehem, Pennsylvania, names the 1,483-foot-tall Petronas Twin Towers, under construction in Kuala Lampur, Malaysia, as the world's tallest building. The structure, by Cesar Pelli & Associates, supercedes the record held by the Sears Tower in Chicago, which enjoyed a twenty-three-year run at the top spot.
May	The hit Broadway musical *Rent* inspires a line of clothing, as Bloomingdale's opens a *Rent* boutique in Manhattan. The look is colorful and youthful, with spandex pants, miniskirts, and halter tops in prices that range from $30 to $60.
June	Following the comeback of classic-style clothes, the "updo" hairstyle returns. Some of the most stylish looks for summer are the French twist, chignon, and simple ponytail.
	• Donna Karan's company goes public with a stock offering on Wall Street.
Oct.	The period movie *Emma* inspires designers such as Christian Dior, John Galliano, and Chanel, who all show empire-waist dresses as part of their couture collections in Paris.

- The Mary Jane shoe, with schoolgirl styling, a rounded toe, a simple strap across the arch that buckles, and a modest heel that is fat and flared, becomes a hit.

1997

Feb. Simple chic is the key term in fashion. The look is minimal, but not monastic. It's a no-frills, no-ruffles approach to dressing.

Mar. Men's suit jackets get a little longer, completely covering the trouser seat when the arms rest at the sides.

Apr. Slides, a sandal-like shoe that features a simple stretch of material—often leather—across the top of the foot, becomes a popular look for summer.

- Men's footwear for spring features elegant square-toed loafers and lace-up shoes, as well as sturdy sandals and classic desert boots.

June A pair of century-old Levi's found in a mineshaft sell for $25,000.

19 Oct. The $100 million Guggenheim Museum in Bilbao, Spain, designed by Frank O. Gehry, opens.

16 Dec. The J. Paul Getty Center in California, a collection of hilltop buildings on 710 acres, designed by Richard Meier, opens.

1998

Jan. The Spice Girls appear on the cover of *Vogue*. The original five members of this British pop group reflect the teen street style of the 1990s.

- The new length in skirts is just below the knee.

Mar. The minimalism seen in fashion during the early part of the decade slips away, as opulence—diamonds, pearls, designer suits, luxurious fabrics, furs, and ball gowns—becomes more acceptable and visible.

- Popular colors for women's clothing are fire-engine red, canary yellow, and sapphire blue.
- The sheath dress, a fitted A-line-style dress made popular by actress Audrey Hepburn in the 1960s, becomes a key look.

5 May President Bill Clinton dedicates the Ronald Reagan Building and International Trade Center in Washington, D.C.

July Men turn away from the sculpted suit, returning to the more relaxed look of the sack suit. Despite its name, the garment has the classic lines of a formal suit in a more comfortable cut.

- Monona Terrace, a plaza first conceived by Frank Lloyd Wright, opens in Madison, Wisconsin, thirty-eight years after Wright's death.

Oct. In step with a revival of swing and ballroom music, women are wearing pretty, full skirts.

Dec. Khakis are everywhere, seemingly replacing denim jeans as the first choice in casual dressing for both men and women.

1999

17 Feb.	Calvin Klein pulls his ads for children's underwear after critics charge that they are pornographic. The ads feature young boys and girls in their underwear jumping on a sofa.
May	Designers pick up the popularity of khaki for their men's suits. Calvin Klein turns out one in linen and cotton for $1,195.
Nov.	The tankini, a bathing suit with bikini bottoms paired with a tank top, rides a wave of popularity.

Models walking the catwalk for the Ralph Lauren Spring 1996 show in New York (AP/Wide World Photos)

OVERVIEW

Setting a New Direction. Several major trends in style in the 1990s were established almost from the start of the decade. Menswear and women's wear designers created softer, less constructed clothes—and often second lines at lower costs—to match the buyer's needs in the United States. Designers also turned out fashions that were more relaxed and casual than their 1980s counterparts. Building designs also targeted specific demographics, as architects continued to mold modernism, postmodernism, and deconstructivism into forms that matched their clients' needs, the surroundings of the buildings, and the environment. Structures soared to new heights. Frank O. Gehry began work on the $100 million Guggenheim Museum in Bilbao, Spain; construction on Richard Meier's J. Paul Getty Center in California was under way; and Cesar Pelli & Associates was working on the 1,483-foot-tall Petronas Twin Towers in Kuala Lampur, Malaysia, which in April 1996 superceded the Sears Tower in Chicago as the tallest structure in the world.

Backlash Against the Go-go 1980s. Americans in the 1990s did more than just set a new course as they cruised toward the end of the century; they made a clean break from the 1980s. Almost from the start of the new decade, men and women rejected the "power dressing" that dominated the earlier boom years. Men took off the formal, dark suits and red "power" ties long associated with the Republican White House of the 1980s, while women cast off their masculine-style suits with oversized shoulder pads. Instead, both genders adopted a more casual stance, making cotton khaki pants and knit tops staples for both home and office attire. The backlash against the 1980s spilled over into building designs as well; Americans sought out houses and offices that were in balance with community, environmental, and their own needs.

Relaxed Attitudes. As part of this backlash, Americans relaxed their style standards. Offices across the country adopted casual-dress codes. Although employers at first allowed dress-down Fridays or casual days during summers only, many companies adopted casual dress as a full-time policy by the end of the decade. In addition, young people, influenced by a new wave of rock music known as grunge, centered in the Pacific Northwest, started wearing loose-fitting jeans, old flannel shirts, and T-shirts. Haute couture designers brought some of these thriftstore, down-on-your-luck elements into their top lines. Even President Bill Clinton, a Democrat, adopted the new relaxed style, and he was frequently photographed while exercising in casual clothes such as jogging suits and shorts and T-shirts. Grunge music and its accompanying fashion, however, did not last past the middle part of the decade. Nevertheless, styles stayed relaxed for the entire 1990s.

Natural Tendencies. At the end of the twentieth century, Americans showed a renewed interest in their natural surroundings, an emphasis that became evident in architecture, as well as interior design. Architects crafted buildings out of natural materials, sometimes going as far as to specify that wood had to come from sustainable sources; they also designed structures to fit in with their natural surroundings, using colors or materials that mimicked the environment around the building. Structures were built with carefully placed windows that brought in natural light and allowed views of the outdoors. Interior designers also picked up this trend, turning to natural fabrics—from wood to stone—to furnish homes. Professional designers and consumers alike created home interiors painted in natural hues, such as green and blue, to help bridge the natural and artificial worlds.

Looking Backward. Although fashion and design took on new directions in the 1990s, designers of all sorts cast an eye to the past. Clothing manufacturers brought back all sorts of styles seen throughout the twentieth century, including elegant, bias-cut satin gowns (1930s), simple A-line shift dresses (1960s), and bell-bottom jeans (1970s). While the postmodernist school of architecture continued to emphasize that new structures include elements that linked them to the past, architects were also involved in high-profile restoration projects aimed at saving landmark buildings. Architects also designed several memorials honoring individuals such as former President Franklin Delano Roosevelt and slain civil-rights leader Martin Luther King Jr., as well as groups such as veterans and Japanese-Americans. Even automakers did not let this retro trend pass them by. They, too, revived past designs, for example, reintroducing the Volkswagen Beetle.

Innovation Thrives. Despite the retro influences, designers did not lose their innovative touch. As was evident at nearly every fashion show, they pushed boundaries with new fashions, materials, and approaches to standard styles. For instance, Donna Karan produced Nehru jackets for men, Gianni Versace introduced a new material known as chain mail that flowed over the body, and Calvin Klein offered a single fragrance to be worn by both men and women. Architects were no less inventive. Gehry drew on the rich shipbuilding tradition in Bilbao, Spain, to design the Guggenheim Museum, which resembles an abstract ship. He used thin, shimmering titanium panels on its exterior to set the structure off from nineteenth century buildings in the city.

Diversity Reigns. Fashion varied from person to person, and a variety of styles thrived in the 1990s. Calvin Klein produced clean, refined lines; Tommy Hilfiger turned out traditional clothes with urban flair; and Jean-Paul Gaultier often created outlandish fashions better suited for the theater than the street. American consumers were just as diverse in their tastes, wearing everything from pinstripe suits for a high-powered look to matching separates of one

shade for a minimalistic presentation. Khakis and polo shirts for a down-to-earth everyday appearance were also popular. American homes and buildings were equally mixed in their designs. Architects and interior designers created innovative, futuristic buildings and spaces, as well as structures that relied on traditional shapes, such as the New England farmstead.

Dressing Up. Although an undeniable trend toward more-casual styles emerged in nearly every aspect of design in the 1990s, dress-up fashion did not die. Women returned to dresses and romantic fashions as the economy improved. They aspired to classic styles such as those worn by former First Lady Jacqueline Kennedy Onassis and movie star Audrey Hepburn. This movement helped push the A-line shift dress, worn so gracefully by Hepburn three decades earlier, back to the height of fashion. Dresses with romantic empire waists also returned, as did slip dresses and flowing skirts. Men also took time to dress up, even in the age of casual style; they wore modern suits, with sport jackets sometimes made of leather or suede rather than traditional wool.

TOPICS IN THE NEWS

CLOTHING TRENDS

Dressing Down. The phrase "dress-down days" had barely been seen in print at the start of the 1990s, yet within a few years the idea of casual clothing worn at the office took off. Employers and employees called the innovation the casual day, casual Friday, or office casual. By some estimates, loosened dress codes applied to half of all U.S. workers by 1995. A survey published in the May 1996 issue of *McCall's* revealed that 64 percent of all readers who responded worked in an office with a casual-day policy that applied year-round. Although employers often instituted these policies as perks, some workers found them confusing. Traditional offices had definite rules for dress; casual offices did not. A host of seminars, magazine articles, and books tried to fill the void. Levi Strauss, which in 1996 estimated that 90 percent of employers allowed some casual days and 33 percent had full-time casual-dress policies, spent millions on ads, brochures, videos, and training to instruct people about the new corporate climate. Some New York City investment-bank bosses even left voice- mail messages specifying what was acceptable. Employers sometimes

worried about these new policies when they saw workers showing up in bike shorts and sweatshirts. Although each office had different standards, general rules emerged in this new era of office attire. The idea was to look comfortable and casual, but not sloppy and ungroomed. A denim shirt was fine; old T-shirts were not. Khakis, and sometimes jeans, passed muster; sweatpants did not. Women turned up for work in knit tops paired with long, flowing skirts or plain trousers in colors as diverse as red and pink to blue and black. Men went to the office dressed in knit turtleneck tops or button-down shirts, casual trousers, and relaxed sport jackets (which were optional); they picked clothes in neutral hues, such as tan, brown, and black.

Out-of-touch Designs. The designs shown at haute couture shows often had no resemblance to what was sold in stores and worn on the streets. Designers frequently showcased pieces that women and men would not dare to wear out in public. Woody Hochswender asked in the December 1993 issue of *Esquire,* "Why *do* they insist on showing this stuff when they must realize

Versace models practicing for the Fall fashion show in New York in 1998 (AP/Wide World Photos)

that we are never going to wear it? Some things are beyond the pale, and skirts for men are certainly one of them." Some of the strange looks that designers showed for menswear for spring 1993 included John Bartlett's take on Hare Krishna style, as models with shaved heads wore flowing orange robes and drawstring pants. Donna Karan exhibited extra-long black wool suit jackets that reminded some observers of the attire worn by Hasidic Jews. Designers created just as outlandish creations for women. Paris-based Yves Saint Laurent in 1990 featured a black lace evening dress where the edges of the fabric did not meet but were instead held together by two bright-pink satin bows at one side. The same year Chanel offered a mini-skirted wool-tweed suit with thigh-high boots in matching fabric. As critics rightly pointed out, a woman would need to be not only young but also exceptionally trim to wear these fashions. Even the penchant for retro fashions left women unable to wear some of the choices. For instance, in 1991 designers and stores stocked short shifts, often in floral prints in primary colors; they also pushed short dresses with empire waists and bouffant skirts called "baby dolls." Although women enjoyed some of the nostalgic styles, they did not accept the ones that made them look like children. Sales clerks reported that the cutesy styles were

not selling. Some other follies featured in 1990s fashion were a black fur hat in the shape of Mickey Mouse ears from the house of Chanel, the continued use of underwear as outerwear, microminis, and bare midriffs.

Retro influences. As the twentieth century came to a close, fashion did not cast an eye forward, but rather looked backward. Clothes reflected a host of styles that had emerged in earlier decades. Women saw the return of the 1930s slip dress, the 1940s beret, and the flowing layers of the 1970s. Donna Karan, for example, designed a long, flowing floral-patterned dress with thin straps and a halter-style top that would also have been stylish in the 1970s. Love beads returned as accessories to go with bell-bottom pants and crocheted cardigans that created a 1960s image. Miniskirts and headbands echoed the 1960s look. The 1970s inspired a return of the platform shoe, with its high, chunky heels and elevated soles. Nostalgia also sparked the comeback of sky-high heels known as stilettos, strappy high-heeled sandals, and high boots. Men were not immune to the retro influence, either. Wide ties in loud colors also attempted a comeback. Suits, meanwhile, often drew on previous designs, as new styles were merely variations on what had come before. Modern suits resembled the traditional, single-breasted, two-button sack suit of the

CASUAL DRESS

As casual days in corporate America became more common, expectations about what to wear fell. Americans did not dress down only on designated workdays, but seemed to dress casually all the time. Jeans became acceptable attire to wear just about everywhere, as did sneakers. Celebrities went out in bike shorts and baseball caps, and supermodels sported T-shirts and jeans. Movie star Brad Pitt showed up for the premiere of *Legends of the Fall* (1994) not in a tuxedo but in a baggy gray sweater. When movie moguls Jeffrey Katzenberg, Steven Spielberg, and David Geffen held a press conference to announce the formation of their new studio in October 1994, none of them wore a suit; only Katzenberg wore a tie. Rock stars such as Kurt Cobain of the Seattle band Nirvana brought torn jeans, untucked flannel shirts, and ratty T-shirts to the heights of fashion in the early 1990s. They even gave it a name: grunge. Although young people latched onto the grunge look as their own, adults were not immune to its influences. Even President Bill Clinton stopped looking presidential, as photographers snapped photograph after photograph of him jogging in shorts and logo T-shirts. Fashion historian Anne Hollander told *Newsweek* in February 1995 that "we have lost the ideal of adult self-respect, and we're dressing like rebellious children."

Sources: Christopher John Farley, "Rock's Anxious Rebels," *Time*, 142 (25 October 1993): 60–66.

Jerry Adler, "Have We Become a Nation of Slobs?" *Newsweek*, 125 (20 February 1995): 56–62.

Susan Brady Konig, "Dressing Down," *National Review*, 49 (13 October 1997): 51.

Office attire. Men in the 1990s had almost unprecedented freedom when it came to office attire. Dress-down Fridays and casual days loosened dress codes at offices across the United States. Men once accustomed to wearing a dark suit, formal button-down shirt, tie, and wingtips discovered a variety of new styles, both formal and informal. The suit, of course, did not disappear. Men still bought traditional suits, both single- and double-breasted versions, in standard shades of blue, black, and gray. Ties never went out of style, and their widths remained moderate—neither exceedingly narrow nor ostentatiously wide—although their colors and designs became more vibrant. New fashion twists were employed, however. Sport coats came in leather, tailored suits were paired with T-shirts, and denim shirts went with everything.

New options. While the traditional suit never disappeared, it relinquished its role as the only option for the office. American men bought thirteen million suits in 1994, down by 1.6 million since 1989. Neckties became optional on some or even all days, depending on a man's career and his office environment. In its place, jeans, khakis, polo shirts, casual button-down shirts, and even sneakers became acceptable in many offices on designated days. Some compa-

Rapper Pras modeling for the Spring '99 Hilfiger collection (AP/Wide World Photos)

1960s. Pinstripe suits remained popular. Men and women also enjoyed a revival of some sensible fashions, such as ergonomically designed Birkenstock sandals and Hush Puppies loafers.

Sources:
Jerry Adler, "Have We Become a Nation of Slobs?" *Newsweek*, 125 (20 February 1995): 56–62.

Holly Brubach, "A Certain Age," *New Yorker*, 66 (5 November 1990): 122–128.

"Can I Wear This to Work?" *McCall's*, 123 (May 1996): 26.

Nina Darnton, "Not-So-Groovy Threads," *Newsweek*, 117 (25 March 1991): 63.

Ron DiGennaro, "Behind the Seams," *Esquire*, 119 (March 1993): 176–179.

Martha Duffy, "Fashion's Fall," *Time*, 143 (25 April 1994): 76–80.

Woody Hochswender, "Tempest in a B-Cup," *Esquire*, 120 (December 1993): 119–122.

Suzy Menkes, "What's Modern Now?" *Vogue*, 183 (January 1993): 91–101.

William Nabers, "The New Corporate Uniforms," *Fortune*, 132 (13 November 1995): 132–137.

Angela Pattison and Nigel Cawthorne, *A Century of Style: Shoes: Icons of Style in the 20th Century* (Secaucus, N.J.: Chartwell, 1997), pp. 152–153.

Jolie Solomon, "Why Worry About Pleat Pulls and Sloppy Socks?" *Newsweek*, 128 (30 September 1996): 51.

Richard Stengel, "Best of '90," *Time*, 136 (31 December 1990): 40–62.

nies, particularly high-tech operations with plenty of young employees and owners, even allowed workers to wear T-shirts, shorts, and sandals.

Suits. Although suits were not the staple they once had been, designers continued to feature them prominently in their shows. Couture designers, however, often presented new interpretations and nonconforming colors. For example, French designer Claude Montana offered one suit in orange. In 1996 Donna Karan designed jackets with Nehru collars, an Asian-style with no lapels, that came in nontraditional fabrics such as shantung silk and linen.

Sources:

Jerry Adler, "Have We Become a Nation of Slobs?" *Newsweek*, 125 (20 February 1995): 56–62.

"Highly Evolved," *Esquire*, 128 (August 1997): 82–87.

Woody Hochswender, "Updating Male Chic," *Esquire*, 126 (November 1996): 117–118.

William Nabers, "The New Corporate Uniforms," *Fortune*, 132 (13 November 1995): 132–137.

"The Shapes of Things to Come," *Esquire*, 116 (December 1991): 182–185.

CLOTHING TRENDS FOR WOMEN

Minimalism to Millennium. No one particular style defined women's fashions in the 1990s. Skirts were long and short, depending on the season. Blouses were either modestly romantic or daringly sheer. Pants could be wide-legged or tailored. No color seemed to dominate, as designers showed—and women wore—fashions in everything from grays, blacks, and whites to blues, pinks, and reds. *Vogue* took this view on the decade in its July 1998 edition: "In fashion, it's been a dizzying ride. Early on, designers set impossibly strict standards for women, stripping down style to monk-like minimalism. That period was followed by a no-holds-barred revival of all things lavish and ornamental. But now the pendulum has swung toward a less extreme middle ground, a place of understated luxury and a quiet, very modern comfort. The nineties as we see them now are about a less constructed, more personal look—which women, not surprisingly, support."

Classic to Sexy. Despite the nod to individual style, designers still tried to set the standards of each season by introducing fashions that varied from minimalist to extravagant. Jil Sander of Germany won over American women with her spare lines and basic palette. Miuccia Prada for the Milan, Italy-based House of Prada also developed a strong following in the United States with designs that emphasized classic, clean lines with a 1990s flair: neatly fitted coats and dresses, dropped waists, and narrow belts. Italian designer Gianni Versace, on the other hand, used bright colors and sexy styles—he sent models out in leather bondage dresses for his 1992 fall collection—to build his global fashion empire.

Diversity. American designers showed no less diversity. Richard Tyler gained fame for clothes that were near-custom quality. His jackets were known for their graceful cut and perfect tailoring. Donna Karan used luxurious materials to craft well-tailored coats, long and short skirts, blouses

and pants that followed the lines of the body without being overtly sexy. Calvin Klein presented a full wardrobe, everything from office clothes to evening wear, with designs that featured simple, refined lines in natural fibers such as cashmere, linen, silk, leather, and suede; his clothes usually came in earth tones and neutrals. With so many choices and styles from which to choose, women knew they were in control of how they wanted to look. They decided which skirt length worked well for them, which trouser style looked best, and which colors flattered them the most. In the 1990s designers did not dictate style. Instead, women decided what was fashion.

Return to Romance. Women did not take long to distance themselves from the 1980s fashion dictums of "power dressing." They quickly abandoned the strictly tailored suits,

DIANA, PRINCESS OF WALES

One of the most watched personalities in the fashion world was Diana, Princess of Wales. Her seemingly fairy-tale marriage to Prince Charles, on 29 July 1981 focused the attention of the world on her. The 1990s, however, brought a new interest in her fashion decisions as her separation and divorce allowed her both a more personal choice and more mature selection when it came to clothes. Freed from dress codes dictated by Buckingham Palace, Diana showed her own personal glamour. Diana wore clothes from famous European designers such as Valentino, Gianni Versace, Christian Lacroix, Karl Lagerfeld for Chanel, and Emanuel Ungaro. She also patronized the London-based Catherine Walker, as well as John Galliano, who created his first dress for the French couture house of Dior for Diana. Diana also showed her down-to-earth side in her street clothes, which included wearing khakis on her humanitarian trips, as well as gym clothes while heading to and from workouts.

Her penchant for fashion, however, also earned her some criticism. British tabloids in 1994 reported that her fashion and beauty expenses totaled $240,000 a year. Despite the ensuing uproar over the bills, the American as well as the British public were enthralled by her style. Public interest was perhaps most evident in 1997, just months before her death in an automobile crash at the age of thirty-six. Diana had raised $5.7 million for charity with an auction of seventy-nine of her dresses and gowns. The blue velvet dress she wore to a White House dinner, where she danced with American actor John Travolta, was won for $222,500 at the auction, held by Christie's in New York City.

Sources: Ginia Bellafante, "People," *Time*, 143 (30 May 1994): 69.

Hamish Bowles, "A Fashion Tribute," *Vogue*, 187 (November 1997): 290–293.

Belinda Luscombe, "People," *Time*, 149 (7 July 1997): 113.

Fashion photographers at the Spring/Summer 1999 Helmut Lang collection shown in New York on 17 September 1998 (AP/Wide World Photos)

oversized shoulder pads, and over-the-top glamour that dominated the previous decade. Instead, women turned to more feminine styles that added class and grace to both work wardrobes and evening attire. This romantic look evolved over time, but its influence was evident throughout the decade. *Vogue* declared: "This is the era of femininity in dress—of jackets with softer shoulders, of curvy tailoring, of fluidity in skirts. Of dresses that show the body without grabbing it. Of lace and chiffon and untucked shirts over soft shorts." The March 1990 *Vogue* cover announced: "Pretty Makes A Comeback." Even delicate pinks came on strong, appearing in all sorts of shades. Dresses replaced suits. Soft fabrics, such as chiffon, succeeded stiff wool. Carefully coifed hair supplanted severely cropped locks. From the start of the decade, designers favored the classic sheath dress, also known as the Audrey Hepburn dress for the actress who wore it so gracefully during the 1960s, with its simple A-line shape and modest hemline.

Feminine Fashions. The trend toward feminine fashions did not abate later in the decade, as both French couture and American sportswear designers turned out classy and classic creations. Tailored, slim-skirted suits that tapered at the waist reminded women of the enduring elegance of former First Lady Jacqueline Kennedy Onassis, who died in 1994. Hemlines fell modestly at the knee; some women paired the new skirt length with stiletto heels to add a more feminine line. Reds, pinks, and fuchsias further distinguished women

from men. Pastels returned, too. "We are seeing a return to elegance, and it is unquestionably commercial," Saks Fifth Avenue fashion director Nicole Fischelis told *Time* in April 1995. Soft, romantic, and feminine fashions were worn everywhere from daytime offices to nighttime parties. Suits, sheath dresses, and knee-length skirts turned up at businesses. Outside the office, women wore delicate dresses, such as the lingerie-styled slip dress. Jill Stuart in 1997 turned out a slip-style dress in a light-blue crocheted rayon. Daryl K produced a pale peach halter dress made of silk and Lycra. Sheer sweaters, fluid wide-legged pants, fitted trousers, and camisole-style tops also added a delicate flair to women's wardrobes. Colors ranged from soft pastels and neutrals to playful citrus shades, such as lime green, orange, and yellow. Fabrics favored for these feminine looks included lightweight wools, chiffon, crepe de chine, and jersey.

Office Dressing. Women showed their diverse tastes when it came to picking their wardrobes for work. Although they generally selected clothes that were less formal than their 1980s counterparts, women still wore suits. The jacket remained an essential item. The traditional blazer was looser, but not baggy, and longer; it had a natural, comfortable fit. Women chose both double-breasted and single-breasted jackets in every color, from neutrals such as brown and gray to vibrant hues such as yellow and red. They paired jackets with both pants and skirts. Pinstripe suits proved popular as well. Tom Ford, Calvin Klein, and Ralph Lauren were just a few of the designers featuring the formal style in the mid 1990s. Although individual style dominated the decade, women still had rules to contend with. While designers showed lots of pantsuits, some female executives felt uncomfortable wearing pants to the office. Meanwhile, some women working in offices on casual or dress-down days felt confused about the new rules for attire. Fashion experts advised women to wear comfortable clothes, such as denim shirts, knit twin sets, long skirts, and flat-front trousers. They also warned women to keep a professional look, which meant no low-cut or midriff-baring tops, ripped jeans, sweatpants, or dirty sneakers.

Overexposed. Many modern garments showed off the body. Midriff-baring tops and "baby doll" dresses put the woman's body in the spotlight. Tights and leggings were the rage, helping to blur the line between gym gear and street clothes. Leggings, which, as the name suggests, fit the legs like a glove, were often paired with bulky sweaters that came down past the hips and came in everything from Lycra-nylon blends to cashmere to velvet. The legs were not the only body part getting attention; much of the body was overexposed in the 1990s. Bustiers, slips, and bras came out from underneath and were promoted to a new role as outerwear.

Sources:

Ginia Bellafante, "La Dolce Vita," *Time*, 150 (28 July 1997): 36–44.

Bellafante, "Lessons in Lessness," *Time*, 144 (7 November 1994): 70–72.

Bellafante, "Tired of Chic Simple? Welcome to the New Romance," *Time*, 151 (6 April 1998): 66–68.

"Can I Wear This to Work?" *McCall's*, 123 (May 1996): 26.

"Corporate Challenge," *Vogue*, 186 (September 1996): 242.

Martha Duffy, "A New Touch of Class," *Time*, 145 (17 April 1995): 58–63.

Duffy, "Stripping Down to Essentials," *Time*, 135 (14 May 1990): 80–81.

Duffy, "Understated Art," *Time*, 146 (20 November 1995): 112.

Cathy Horyn, "Fashion Taboos at Work," *Vogue*, 183 (August 1993): 218–221.

"The Living Is Breezy," *Time*, 149 (26 May 1997): 90–91.

Kate Mulvey and Melissa Richards, *Decades of Beauty* (London: Hamlyn, 1998), p. 196.

Valerie Burnham Oliver, *Fashion and Costume in American Popular Culture: A Reference Guide* (Westport, Conn.: Greenwood Press, 1996), p. 53.

"Rethinking Pink," *Vogue*, 180 (March 1990): 478–485.

Janet Siroto, "Jackets Required," *Vogue*, 183 (March 1993): 324–333.

Anne Stegemeyer, *Who's Who in Fashion* (New York: Fairchild Publications, 1996), pp. 120–121, 129–130, 240.

"View," *Vogue*, 180 (November 1990): 146.

"Vogue Point of View," *Vogue*, 180 (January 1990): 145–159; 180 (April 1990): 325–357; 188 (July 1998): 85.

CLOTHING TRENDS FOR YOUTH

The Grunge Look. American youth greeted the new decade in ripped-up jeans. The look, a carryover from the 1980s, featured jeans—new and old—with strategically placed horizontal slits, usually across the knee. The trend was just a harbinger of what was ahead. A new fashion scene took shape in 1991, when the Seattle-based alternative rock band Nirvana released its commercial breakthrough album, *Nevermind*. Suddenly, the Seattle music scene—and its image—was the look for Generation X, as teens and young adults in their twenties were sometimes called. The music tapped into the sense of angst shared by many young people as the economy continued to spiral downward early in the decade. Grunge was a response to the power dressing and elitism of the 1980s, as rock bands such as Soundgarden, Pearl Jam, Alice in Chains, and Nirvana led the way. Their look, rooted in urban bohemianism and club comfort, was emulated by youth around the country. The new uniform was not only easy to assemble, it was cheap: thrift-store finds fit in perfectly. Loose-fitting pants—either old jeans or long shorts for both girls and guys—formed the basis of the look. Thrift-store trousers were also acceptable. Ratty flannel, button-down shirts worn over T-shirts, or long-sleeved undershirts defined grunge. Torn corduroy jackets or old cardigans were optional. Converse high-top sneakers, boots, and heavy-soled shoes—particularly ones by Doc Martens—were preferred. Baseball caps topped off the look. Like most trends, grunge eventually gave way to new fads. The rage began to ebb when twenty-seven-year-old Kurt Cobain, lead singer of Nirvana, was found dead from an apparently self-inflicted gunshot wound in April 1994.

Hip-hop Effect. While alternative rock brought grunge to the forefront in the early 1990s, hip-hop music created its own fashion empire throughout the decade. Hip-hop and rap, terms that were almost interchangeable, traced their roots back to black street music of the 1970s. This music, as well as its accompanying culture and fashion, grew throughout the 1980s and exploded in the 1990s. In 1998, for example, rap outsold country music, which was formerly the top-selling format in the United States. Rap sold more than eighty-one million compact discs, tapes, and albums that year. The growth of this musical format brought incredible demand for its fashion counterpart. The hip-hop look was diverse, and evolved over time, as it was adopted by white youth. One of the most enduring images of hip-hop, however, were baggy pants worn around the hip to expose underwear waistbands bearing designer names. Other essentials included pricey sneakers (sometimes worn with laces untied), hooded sweatshirts ("hoodies," with the hoods often covering the head), and flashes of jewelry (preferably gold or platinum). While these items defined hip-hop fashions, the look progressed—jeans that were super-baggy at the start of the decade were merely loose by its end. Baseball caps that used to be worn backward faced front again or at least to the side for some youths, and shared the top spot with ski caps (known as "skullies"). Gold jewelry gave way to ethnic African accoutrements, such as colorful, native batik fabrics. Hoodies made way for loose-fitting hockey jerseys, polo shirts, ski jackets, and varsity jackets. Sneakers paved the way for hiking boots. Brand names also played an important role in hip-hop fashions, as many styles prominently featured logos. Jeans and shirts labeled "Tommy Hilfiger" were hot commodities, as was Ralph Lauren's Polo logo. African-American labels—FUBU (an acronym for the slogan For Us by Us), Naughty Gear, Phat Farm, Pure Playaz, UB Tuff, and Wu-Wear—were particularly important in the hip-hop culture. Musicians and rappers such as LL Cool J, Tupac Shakur, Puff Daddy (who would also introduce his own line of fashions, call Sean John), and Lauryn Hill helped to set style standards.

Mix and Match. Just like their adult counterparts, stylish teens did not follow a singular fashion dictum. Rather, they borrowed from past decades, different cultures, and a variety of styles. Young women were spotted wearing 1960s-type tie-dyes and 1970s-style jeans with flared bottoms. Girls wore miniskirts, knee-length floral skirts, and ankle-grazing A-line cotton skirts. They were just as likely to wear platform shoes, with their high clunky heels and elevated soles, as they were to sport a pair of loafers, updated for the 1990s with thick heels, or

a pair of felt-covered clogs. Young men, on the other hand, borrowed from the 1980s preppy look. Simple long-sleeved button-down shirts were classic yet comfortable enough to make the grade with students. Polo shirts also earned high marks.

Fashion Favorites. Teenagers of both genders shared some fashion favorites, particularly toward the end of the decade. Although jeans—particularly loose-fitting, wide-legged ones—were a fashion staple, khakis nearly overtook them as the essential item to own. These simple cotton pants with their classic cut provided the comfort and easy style students sought. Cargo pants and carpenter pants also became important features in teen fashion; they, like khakis, were usually made of cotton. Cargo pants featured large pockets on the outside of the pant legs, while carpenter pants featured a variety of small pockets and loops (originally designed to hold a carpenter's tools). T-shirts, pullover sweaters, polo shirts, and sweatshirts typically topped the look. Brand names popular at the time include cK by Calvin Klein, Tommy Hilfiger, and Polo. Teens shopped at such stores as The Gap, Abercrombie & Fitch, and Old Navy. Color schemes were usually basic—browns, tans, and

BODY ART

Once only seen on the chests and arms of such individuals as sailors or motorcycle gang members, tattoos, along with body piercing, became a fashionable statement during the 1990s for a wide range of Americans. Tattooing was common historically among many cultures, but gained popularity in the English-speaking world primarily on the bodies of sailors who had traveled to the South Seas as early as the 1700s. Many of these works of skin art featured indecently clad women, which the U.S. Navy at the beginning of the twentieth century attempted to stop their sailors from acquiring, at least the most offensive images.

During the decade more individuals, especially women, started altering their bodies. Tattoos ranged from tiny drawings hidden away from sight, to elaborate masterpieces that covered the arms, neck, and back. Anyone watching professional football, basketball, or wrestling was certain to view several athletes sporting tattoos. These works were no longer restricted to the traditional drawings done primarily in black, but became increasingly colorful and elaborate with new advances in equipment and inks. While the huge baby pins and other elaborate pierced jewelry of the punk period passed, many young men and women pierced other parts of their bodies. Popular locations for body jewelry, outside of the earlobe, included the nose, tongue, and belly button.

One of the more visible athletes so adorned, with his nose ring and ever-changing hair color, was National Basket-

ball Association (NBA) forward Dennis Rodman. In almost any sport one could glimpse tatoos on the players's biceps and feet. Athletes were not alone, however, in coloring their skin, as many actors and musicians, especially rock and rap artists, were adorned with tattoos. The music video channel, Music Television (MTV), is credited by some tatoo artists with popularizing the art form.

Another new wrinkle to skin art was that African Americans in greater numbers began to get tattoos. For decades the only blacks with tattoos tended to be members of black fraternities, but as rap and gang-related materials gained in popularity, the art form spread to a wider audience. Rapper-actor Tupac Shakur's torso, for instance, was covered with tattooed messages.

The first tattoo convention was held in Houston, Texas, in 1976. In the 1990s regular conventions, both national and international, attracted both professional artists and curious onlookers. Tattooing was also being recognized as a legitimate art form. Even museums exhibited tattoo designs, such as the "Pierced Hearts and True Love" show in 1996 at the Williams Art Museum in Williamstown, Massachusetts.

Sources: Don Ed Hardy, "Tattoo History Source Book: Yesterday and Today," transcribed and edited by Steve Gilbert, *Tattoo.Com,* Internet website.

"Sailors Tattoos," *Tattoo Archive,* Internet website.

Students in Albuquerque, New Mexico, wearing loose-fitting clothing (AP/Wide World Photos)

khakis. Jeans almost always were some shade of blue. Tops, when not a basic white T-shirt, came in standard shades such as brown, gray, green, and blue. Hints of color came through with items such as a yellow jacket, red sweater, or orange T-shirt.

Sources:

"17 Most Wanted," *Seventeen*, 58 (August 1999): 230–231.

Bill Barol, "Anatomy of a Fad," *Newsweek*, 115 (Summer/Fall 1990): 40–41.

"Boho Baby," *Seventeen*, 58 (September 1999): 72.

Lloyd Boston, *Men of Color: Fashion History Fundamentals* (New York: Artisan, 1998), p. 46.

Jay Cocks, "Rap Around The Globe," *Time*, 140 (19 October 1992): 70–71.

Denise Cowie, "Cargo Pants, Carpenter Togs, Extra-Wide-Leg Jeans Spell Fashion," *The State* (Columbia, S.C.): 2 August 1998.

Tamala M. Edwards and Joel Stein, "Getting Giggy with A Hoodie," *Time*, 151 (19 January 1998): 71–72.

Christopher John Farley, "Hip-Hop Nation," *Time*, 153 (8 February 1999): 54–64.

Farley, "Rock's Anxious Rebels," *Time*, 142 (25 October 1993): 60–66.

Bruce Handy, "Never Mind," *Time*, 143 (18 April 1994): 70–72.

"Multiple Choice," *Seventeen*, 58 (September 1999): 240–247.

Jonathan Poneman, "Grunge & Glory," *Vogue*, 182 (December 1992): 253–260, 312.

Mary K. Pratt, "Comfort Is Common Thread for Fashions on Campus," *The State* (Columbia, S.C.): Student Life Fall Edition 1999.

"Toggle Switch," *Seventeen*, 58 (September 1999): 82.

"Trends 4 Fall," *Seventeen*, 58 (August 1999): 223–229.

FASHION INDUSTRY

A Designer Murder. Italian designer Gianni Versace had just returned home from getting coffee at a café near his South Beach, Miami, home. As he neared the steps of his house, around 8:30 a.m. on 15 July 1997, he was shot in the back of the head and then once more as he lay on the ground. He was pronounced dead at the hospital. Police announced that they suspected the gunman was Andrew Phillip Cunanan, age twenty-seven, a suspect in several other murders around the United States. Cunanan was found dead on 23 July 1997 in a Miami houseboat after a four-hour standoff with police. The assailant's death brought little relief to a fashion public that had grown quite fond of the slain designer's work.

A Popular Designer. Versace was born on 2 December 1946 in Reggio di Calabria, Italy. His mother, Francesca, was a dressmaker; he fashioned puppets from remnants found on the floor of her workroom. At nine he designed his first dress: a one-shoulder gown made from velvet. Versace learned much in the clothing racks of his mother's shop, including the tailoring and selling techniques that would later help him develop a $1 billion fashion empire.

A mourner placing flowers outside Gianni Versace's Miami Beach house on 16 July 1997, the day after the famous fashion designer was slain (AP/Wide World Photos)

Versace worked for his mother until he was twenty-five. Although he never attended design school, he moved to Milan in 1972 to design for a series of Italian labels. After his brother, Santo, joined him to handle the business side, Versace launched his own collection of men's and women's clothes at the end of 1978. He expanded his design house during the next two decades to include ready-to-wear clothes, leather goods, fragrances, and home furnishings. In 1996 his clothing sales totaled $560 million, with revenue coming from several lines—Gianni Versace, Istante, Versus, Versatile, Versace Jeans Couture, Versace Sport, Versace Classic V2, and Young Versace. Sales from his fragrance line totaled $150 million, housewares brought in another $40 million, and accessories added $250 million. Versace's clothes featured sex and glamour, psychedelic prints, and vivid colors. Reaction to his early shows was cautious, with some critics calling his designs vulgar and lewd. Others considered his designs too flashy. For example, Versace added accoutrements of denim and plastic to couture gowns that cost $20,000 and more. Yet, he was also considered innovative. In 1982 he showed a new fabric, his now-famous chain mail, which flowed over the body. That year he won the first in a series of L'Occhio d'Oro awards, a prestigious Italian fashion honor, for Best Womenswear Designer. His taste for sexy clothes did not wane: in 1992 he presented an array of leather bondage dresses. His creativity and innovation also showed in his marketing skills, which allowed him to move from a single salon in 1978 to more than three hundred boutiques around the world by the late 1990s. Versace was the first designer to use magazine models on the catwalk when showing his clothes. He put celebrities in the front row of his shows. Both moves garnered instant publicity for his collections and helped fuse the worlds of fashion and entertainment. Versace also gained fame for his lavish lifestyle. He owned stately villas and compounds in Milan, Lake Como, Miami Beach, and New York City. He owned an art collection that included works by Pablo Picasso, Roy Lichtenstein, and Julien Schnabel. He had private jets, threw dinner parties for two hundred guests, and held glossy store openings. Among his famous clients and friends were Diana, Princess of Wales, and Madonna. He was also generous. He gave liberally to charities, especially those involved in AIDS. He also supported young designers—attending the debut of Marc Jacobs's line and urging fashion editors to check out the work of Todd Oldham early in his career. His brother along with his sister, Donatella, her husband and their two children, were also important in his life. His siblings took over the business after his death, and as the decade ended, the design house of Versace was still alive.

Model Weight. A big topic in the fashion world had nothing to do with clothes, but rather what was underneath: the bodies. The early part of the decade featured a return to super-skinny supermodels. Kate Moss, who gained fame when she appeared topless in Calvin Klein ads, led the return of the waif-like look; she was five-feet-seven-inches and weighed ninety-eight pounds. This new look was the antithesis of 1980s supermodels, such as Cindy Crawford and Claudia Schiffer, whose bodies were slim yet curved, toned, and muscular. The new supermodels did not share their predecessors' penchant for glamorous makeup, either, as many appeared practically barefaced and pale on countless magazine pages. Elizabeth Tilberis, editor in chief of *Harper's Bazaar*, called them "angelic little boys." While their bodies often lacked womanly curves, many saw their look as simple, yet feminine. "The gamine isn't about shoulder pads, fitted suits, corsets, stretch clothing or false lashes. In a word, the gamine isn't so 'done,'" wrote Jody Shields in the January 1993 issue of *Vogue*. Models who gained fame with this look included Lucie de La Falaise, Shalom, Meghan Douglas, Patricia Hartmann, and Kristen McMenamy.

Diversity in Modeling. The public, however, was not always enamored with this trend toward thin. Some critics charged that admiring girls might become anorexic trying to obtain Moss's slim proportions. Others protested the implication fashions implied that women had to be incredibly thin to be stylish and beautiful. In a letter published in the 22 February 1993 *Newsweek*, a woman asked: "How could you report on the return of the superskinny look to the forefront of fashion and not mention its connection to eating disorders?" Meanwhile, Calista Flockhart, star of the sitcom *Ally McBeal* on the FOX television network, made news in 1999 when some criticized her five-foot-five-inch, one-hundred-pound frame. Despite the controversy about the size of fashion models and Hollywood stars, curvy models found success. Toward the end of the 1990s, sexiness returned to fashion. Leading designers and photographers started to use curvaceous, although still slim, models such as Carmen Kass and Gisele. The back and forth on the topic of model weight yielded some changes in the fashion industry. By the end of the decade, magazines, designers, and photographers featured a wider variety of body shapes—and different racial groups.

Sources:
Ginia Bellafante, "La Dolce Vita," *Time*, 150 (28 July 1997): 36–44.

"The Best of People 1993," *Time*, 143 (3 January 1994): 88.

John Greenwald, "Will His Fashion Empire Survive?" *Time*, 150 (28 July 1997): 42.

J. Leland, "Back to Twiggy," *Newsweek*, 121 (1 February 1993); 64–65.

"Letters," *Newsweek*, 121 (22 February 1993): 16.

Kate Mulvey and Melissa Richards, *Decades of Beauty* (London: Hamlyn, 1998), p.193, 195, 202.

Susan Schindehette, "Going to Extremes," *People Weekly*, 52 (18 October 1999): 110–114.

Jody Shields, "The Return of the Gamine," *Vogue*, 183 (January 1993): 137–141.

Lowri Turner, *Gianni Versace: Fashion's Last Emperor* (London: Essential in association with Chameleon Books, 1997), pp. 18–116.

Philip Weiss, "The Return of the Curve," *Vogue*, 189 (July 1999): 192–195.

Anna Wintour, "Gianni Versace, 1946–1997: A Remembrance," *Vogue*, 187 (September 1997): 628–629.

MODERN ARCHITECTURE: DESIGN

Modernism, Postmodernism, Deconstructivism. No one architectural style defined the 1990s, as several themes played a role in building designs at the end of the century.

Modernism, which came to prominence in the 1960s, featured rectilinear geometry, minimalism, and an ordering of space; its philosophy called for form to follow function. It gave way to postmodernism in the late 1970s and 1980s. Postmodernism linked present and past designs, as well as brought ornamentation and context back to architecture. Deconstructivism followed, although it waned quickly. Deconstructivist architecture was identified by its fragmented forms. A "Deconstructivist Architecture" exhibition at the Museum of Modern Art in New York in June 1988 provided a glimpse of what was ahead. The exhibition featured the works, most yet to be built, of Frank O. Gehry, Daniel Libeskind, Rem Koolhaas, Peter Eisenman, Zaha Hadid, Bernard Tschumi, and Coop Himmelblau. Mark Wigley, associate curator of the MOMA show, wrote: "What is being disturbed is a set of deeply entrenched cultural assumptions which underlie a certain view of architecture, assumptions about order, harmony, stability and unity." Each movement, though, had its share of criticism. Some critics accused modernism in its pure form of ignoring people's emotional needs; others saw postmodernism, particularly with its early reliance on facades, as superficial in its references to the past. Meanwhile, some reviewers charged that deconstructivism was shocking and inappropriate. Despite the fact that each movement had perceived drawbacks, architects continued to build in all three styles. The combination of these prevailing aesthetic directions, however, prompted architects to scrutinize their designs. Stephen A. Kliment wrote, in the November 1990 issue *of Architectural Record*, "In this day and age, when any style goes (Modernism included) and any style is buildable, the architect is forced, every time he/she sits down at the drawing board or CAD terminal, to ask: what *is* good?"

Livable Spaces. One trend that emerged in 1990s architecture was the recognition of a need to create livable spaces. Whether designing private homes, corporate buildings, or public spaces, architects often focused on how the building would fit their clients. "Many people are calling for designs that respond to the individual needs of users and not the generic building formulas of developers or the stylistic prejudices of architects," *Architectural Record* declared in its July 1991 edition. Architects answered the call. Although styles ranged from innovative to traditional, private homes commissioned by architects reflected the occupants and their needs, whether it was for spacious living or smaller quarters. For example, they created great rooms, rather than separate living, dining, and family rooms, to provide the free-flowing space that clients wanted. Architects also considered how their buildings would impact the environment; they spoke about the need to design buildings that would consume less energy, create less pollution, and use fewer natural resources. Gregory Hodkinson told *Architectural Record* in 1991: "The environment is the key issue. The realization that resources are finite and that we are, in fact, permanently affecting the environment will be the overriding concern in the way we produce buildings, the way we organize our industries, and the way we structure our transportation system." William McDonough completed an office complex for Gap Inc. in 1997 in San Bruno, California, that paid careful attention to the environment. Native grasses and wildflowers were planted in six inches of soil on the roofs; the greenery, besides its environmental appeal, served as a thermal and acoustic insulator. Designs also called for wood floors and veneer harvested from managed, sustainable forests. The ventilation system was designed to draw in cool air at night, almost eliminating the need for air conditioning. Meanwhile, light filled the building from windows that allowed views of the outdoors from almost any spot in the building, helping to bring nature inside. Structures were also designed to fit their surroundings. "A building should feel like it belongs where it is—not like an import or something portable that could be taken to another place," Donald J. Canty wrote in the January 1990 issue of *Architectural Record*. Architects often drew their inspiration from the setting. A Connecticut home designed by New York architect Steve Harris, for example, was a twentieth century version of a traditional New England farmstead. Harris used white-cedar shingles and related the twenty-three-foot-high barrel-vaulted living room, pent-roofed kitchen wing, and thirty-two-foot-high tower to a traditional barn, shed, and silo, respectively.

A Drive to Preserve. Although new buildings made headlines most often, there were also several high-profile renovations. The drive to preserve what had already been built traced it roots to the 1960s, when Congress passed the National Historic Preservation Act (1966, revised in 1980). The preservation movement gave architects new opportunities to restore, renovate, and redesign landmark buildings, including everything from theaters to libraries to city halls. The $156 million renovation of Ellis Island, through which millions of immigrants passed as they entered the United States, was a case in point. The firms of Beyer Blinder Belle and Notter Finegold & Alexander provided the designs for renovating the buildings, which reopened to the public in September 1990 after an eight-year restoration. The centerpiece of the project was the Main Building, originally designed in a French Renaissance style by Boring & Tilton at the turn of the nineteenth century. Before starting renovations, the modern architects stabilized the building by drying it out using large heaters outside and pressurized dry air inside. Exterior repairs, such as cleaning the facades and repairing bricks, followed. Rooms inside the building were then converted for use as a library, theaters, and exhibitions areas.

Grand Central. John Belle of Beyer Blinder Belle also spent the decade renovating Grand Central Terminal in New York. The Beaux-Arts train station was designed by Whitney Warren and opened in 1913. Belle first renovated the Main Waiting Room, cleaning the Caen stone (a scored plasterlike material), repairing the Tennessee marble floor with the same stone, and refurbishing the nickel- and gold-plated chandeliers. Renovating the Main Concourse was another significant part of the project.

TRANSPORTATION BY DESIGN

Architectural innovations were evident in new transportation facilities, particularly airports, in the 1990s. The new International Terminal at Chicago O'Hare International Airport, which opened in 1994, is one example. Designed by Perkins & Will Architects, the monumental rooms are framed in lightweight exposed steel and receive plenty of daylight. The ticketing pavilion has a soaring roof that is low at the ends and high in the middle. The ramp-control tower anchors the pavilion at its highest point.

Denver's International Airport, under construction in the early part of the 1990s, also drew considerable attention. Although much scrutiny focused on its $1.9 billion cost, other critics assailed its visual drama. White caps top the 1.3-million-square-foot structure. The tented peak-and-valley profiles come from double layers of less than .28-inch-thick Teflon-coated fiberglass. The roof is supported by two rows of steel masts and reinforced by steel cables to protect against wind and snow loads.

Cesar Pelli's new terminal at the Ronald Reagan Airport in Washington, D.C., also drew attention. The 1997 addition has a simple footprint in the shape of a capital E. The terminal forms the vertical line, while three piers form the horizontal strokes. At the bottom of the vertical stroke, a concourse connects the new terminal to the existing one. The terminal has structural vaults and a one-and-a-half acre glass curtain wall enclosing one side of the concourse. Pelli used these elements to help establish a sense of scale and to orient passengers.

Plans for a new Salt Lake City International Airport also proved to be innovative. The designs, by a joint Gensler/HNTB team, departed from typical airport layouts that called for fingers that extend from a central hub. The plan instead called for a linear spine that would run perpendicular to the terminal and roadways. It also called for the structure to reflect the landscape of Utah, with rust, purple, red, green, and gold used on the base, while a glass skin would allow airport visitors to see spectacular views of the surrounding mountains. The airport was scheduled to be built in two phases over fifteen years.

Sources: Alice Y. Kimm, "Salt Lake City Airport Will Fly in a New Pattern," *Architectural Record*, (December 1998): 38.

Charles Linn, "Cesar Pelli's New Passenger Terminal at National Airport in Washington, D.C., Eases the Life of the World-weary Traveler," *Architectural Record*, 185 (October 1997): 89–95.

Linn, "Form Follows Flight," *Architectural Record*, 182 (June 1994): 116–123.

Karen D. Stein, "'Snow-Capped' Symbol," *Architectural Record*, 181 (June 1993): 106–107.

Geologist Bruce Clark in his Farmington, New Mexico, cave home on 1 May 1997 (AP/Wide World Photos)

Early drawings by the firm Warren and Wetmore showed twin staircases facing each other at either end, but the east staircase was never built. Beyer Blinder Belle designed a new staircase made of the same Bottocino marble to match the existing staircase. The famous Sky Ceiling mural in the Main Concourse was also restored. Other pieces of the restoration included removing the ticket offices, built in 1927, to improve flow, revitalizing the balconies that overlook the Main Concourse, and renovating the Lower Concourse for use as a food court. The project cost $200 million.

American Homes. Like most other aspects of style in the 1990s, Americans showed diverse tastes when it came to the homes they built. A survey for *McCall's* put this question to readers: "If you could have anything you wanted, what would it be?" For many, the answer was a dream house, the top pick being a cozy cottage. Readers also showed a great deal of diversity in their choices, however, with others dreaming of large Victorians or Tudor-style mansions or contemporary Mediterranean homes. Architects designed homes to fit the owners' needs, regional influences, and surrounding environments, further guaranteeing diversity in housing styles. "Houses reveal what clients value, how they live, where they live. In a successful project, the house expresses a resonance between a client and an architect's vision," Karen Stein wrote in *Architectural Record* (April 1997).

Housing Trends. Despite the wide selection of housing styles at the end of the century, some trends emerged. Homes featured open floor plans to accommodate a desire for greater living space and "master suites," instead of simple master bedrooms. These spacious suites frequently featured walk-in closets, sitting areas, and attached spa-style bathrooms. Modern dwellings often showcased natural materials such as stone, wood, and stucco, as well as large windows to let in plenty of natural light. Architects took inspiration from existing regional structures and also designed homes that fit into their natural surroundings. Architect Josh Schweitzer, for example, designed "The Monument" outside of Joshua Tree National Monument in California to blend into its environment; the geometric exterior is painted orange, olive-green, and purple-blue. Schweitzer said "the colors are the colors of the desert" and "the monolithic forms of the buildings echo the forms of the rocks."

Wright. One of most recognized American architects, Frank Lloyd Wright, received considerable attention in the 1990s—even though he had died in 1959. The news focused on two of his designs: the Guggenheim Museum in New York, which opened in 1959, and the Monona Terrace in Madison, Wisconsin. The first received an addition, designed by the firm of Gwathmey Siegel & Associates. The second finally came to fruition, built by Wright's successor firm, Taliesin Architects. Fans and critics alike weighed in with their opinions on modern modifications to an American architectural hero's designs.

The Guggenheim. Wright intended his ziggurat design for the Guggenheim Museum to clash with the city, his structure to be seen as a piece of art as well as a building. The museum became one of Wright's best-known creations; however, it did not provide enough space to display art. The museum trustees decided to expand and tapped Gwathmey Siegel & Associates in 1982 for the project. Charles Gwathmey and Robert Siegel designed the expansion on a thirty-five-foot sliver of land behind the museum. The result was a new $24 million tower behind Wright's masterpiece and a $22 million renovation to the interior of the existing structure. The addition was criticized as bland. Architecture critic Carter Wiseman wrote in *Architectural Record* (October 1992): " 'Plain Vanilla' is too charitable a description for the blandified 10-story 'background' slab." The interior renovation, however, opened up some of Wright's original design. The upper end of the stunning spiral ramp, which had been sealed off for storage, was reopened. Skylights, which had been covered to prevent sunlight from damaging paintings, were retrofitted with protective glass. As a result, curators had use of the roomiest gallery in Wright's building and light again filled the space. The interior renovation seemed to win more fans than the outside addition. Kurt Anderson wrote in *Time* that "Gwathmey's intelligent, intricate, loving work inside is a revelation, making it a far, far better museum than it has ever been."

Wisconsin. A Wright design was also revived in Wisconsin. In 1938 Wright, a Wisconsin native, unveiled his plans for Monona Terrace as a way to tie together the capital area, downtown business district, and Lake Monona of Madison. He had revised his plans, but he died before the project was built. In the early 1990s, however, the city decided to turn Wright's vision into reality. Though not as large and encompassing as Wright had envisioned, Monona Terrace opened in July 1997. The structure as built was a semicircular 250,000-square-foot convention center with five levels of exhibition halls and meeting rooms. It retained Wright's curvilinear form, but the interior spaces are not of his design; its use as a convention center was not his intent either. Although Taliesin Architects was involved, some questioned the accuracy of promotional pamphlets that boasted "A Public Space by Frank Lloyd Wright" and suggested the correct title should say that the design was "inspired by" or "in the style of" Wright. Architect Anthony Puttnam, a Wright apprentice in the 1950s, spoke in support of the project in the 12 June 1995 issue of *Time:* "I don't think we've done anything that Wright wouldn't have done. He was very open to change. He knew the importance of accommodating the client."

Sources:

Sarah Amelar and others, "Record Houses 1999," *Architectural Record,* 187 (April 1999): 97–144.

Kurt Anderson, "Finally Doing Right by Wright," *Time,* 143 (6 July 1992): 64–65.

Andrea Bauman, "How to Get Your Dream House!" *McCall's,* 122 (October 1994): 144–147.

Donald Canty, "An Agenda for the Nineties," *Architectural Record,* 178 (January 1990): 72–73.

David Dillon, "Is this Monona Terrace really Wright?" *Architectural Record,* 186 (March 1998): 94–97.

John Elson, "The Wrong Wright?" *Time,* 145 (12 June 1995): 70.

Nora Richter Greer, "Preserving Preservation," *Architectural Record,* 179 (March 1991): 88–89, 179.

Charles Gwathmey, "On Wright's Foundations," *Architectural Record,* 180 (October 1992): 104–105.

Philip Jodidio, *New Forms: Architecture in the 1990s* (Köln & New York: Taschen, 1997), pp. 163, 166.

Stephen A. Kliment, "Split Personality," *Architectural Record,* 179 (June 1991): 9.

Kliment, "What *Is* Good Design?" *Architectural Record,* 178 (November 1990): 11.

Leslie Lampert, "The New American Home: 1993," *Ladies' Home Journal,* 110 (March 1993): 152–163.

Nancy Levinson, "Renovation Scoreboard," *Architectural Record,* 181 (January 1993): 70–73.

"Madison Votes for Frank Lloyd Wright—50 Years Later," *Architectural Record,* 181 (January 1993): 28.

Clifford A. Pearson, "Future Talk," *Architectural Record,* 179 (July 1991): 176–181.

Pearson, "Project Diary : Beyer Blinder Belle's Makeover of Grand Central Terminal Involved Careful Restoration and Critical Changes," *Architectural Record,* 187 (February 1999): 85–95.

Pearson, "Reopening America's Gates," *Architectural Record,* 178 (July 1990): 46–57.

"Record Houses 1991," *Architectural Record,* 179 (April 1991): 69–133.

"Record Houses 1993," *Architectural Record,* 181 (April 1993): 63–107.

"Record Houses 1997," *Architectural Record,* 185 (April 1997): 61–117.

Roger Rosenblatt, "The Man Who Wants Buildings to Love Kids," *Time,* 153 (22 February 1999): 70–73.

Tamara Schneider, "The New American Home 1992," *Ladies' Home Journal,* 109 (February 1992): 144–149.

Carter Wiseman, "Guggenheim Go-Around," *Architectural Record,* 180 (October 1992): 102–103.

MODERN ARCHITECTURE: MUSEUMS AND MONUMENTS

Monumental museums. Museum construction reached new heights at the end of the twentieth century. These buildings drew on diverse styling elements, ranging from the objects the museums were intended to house to the surrounding environment to history itself. Starting in the 1980s and carrying into the 1990s, Europe, Japan, and, to a lesser extent, the United States commissioned new architectural treasures to house artistic jewels. One of the most significant projects was American architect I. M. Pei's work for the Louvre in Paris, France. In the first phase, completed in 1989, Pei erected the famous modernistic glass pyramid as a new entrance amid the nineteenth-century architecture of the Cour Napoleon. The second phase, completed in 1993, encompassed the Richelieu wing. Pei, who was tapped for the project by French president François-Maurice Mitterrand, doubled the Louvre's exhibition space with his renovation of the three-story Richelieu wing. He also invited criticism by combining the museum with an underground shopping gallery, but the elegant new commercial area features an

The J. Paul Getty Center in Los Angeles, designed by Richard Meier, opened to the public on 16 December 1997 (AP/Wide World Photos)

opened on 18 January 1995, features a textured brick veneer and an almost windowless design, though a central *oculus*, which from the exterior appears in the form of a truncated cylinder, brings a generous amount of light into the structure, particularly the top-lit galleries on the upper floor.

Holocaust Memorial and Museum. The United States Holocaust Memorial and Museum in Washington, D.C., opened in 1993 after more than a dozen years in planning and construction. Architect James Ingo Freed, who grew up in Nazi Germany but fled to the United States in 1939, designed the building. Freed, from Pei Cobb Freed & Partners, sought to use the fabric of the building to convey the frightening nature of Nazi death camps. The bland façade hints at chilling efficiency. The rough brick in the Hall of Witness suggests the walled-in camps, while metal strapping reminds visitors of a crematorium. On the other hand, the Hall of Remembrance, which is almost detached from the main structure, provides a space for contemplation—with cutout glimpses of the Jefferson, Lincoln, and Washington memorials.

American Heritage Center. Architect Antoine Predock drew on local heritage to design the American Heritage Center in Laramie, Wyoming, which was completed in 1993. Reminiscent of American Indian tepees, the axis of the structure is aligned with two summits, Medicine Bow Peak and Pilot's Knob. The cone and its base house the American Heritage Center. A long, terraced structure with a flat roof trails the cone and houses the University of Wyoming Art Museum. Predock said this "consciously monumental landscape abstraction represents a symbol for future campus growth . . . and a statement of the powerful spirit of Wyoming."

Gehry in Spain. The $100 million Guggenheim Museum opened in Bilbao, Spain, on 19 October 1997 and set the architectural world talking. Designed by American architect Frank O. Gehry, the glass and titanium museum rises distinctively from the nineteenth-century buildings that define the rest of Bilbao. The structure covers 250,000 square feet, with 112,000 square feet dedicated to exhibition space. It is twice as big as the Guggenheim museums in New York City. Built over four years and financed by the Basque government, the museum was expected to draw five hundred thousand new visitors to the region annually. The museum won accolades from architects as well as the public. Architect Philip Johnson dubbed the museum "the greatest building of our time." The hulking structure on the bank of the Nervión River is clad in shimmering, but thin, titanium panels that seem to make portions of the museum ripple in the wind. Although its otherworldly appearance seems out of synch with the rest of the old city, Gehry drew on Bilbao's history for his design. Shipbuilding yards, loading docks, cranes, and warehouses line the river, and the museum evokes Bilbao's cityscape and history. The abstract metal "sails" and "hulls" echo local maritime traditions, although some have likened the structure to other objects, including a mermaid, waterfall, or fish. Gehry wrote during the early design stages: "To be at the bend of a working river intersected by a large bridge

inverted Pei pyramid, echoing the one outside and allowing light to bathe the beige limestone walls. Pei arranged the exhibition rooms to allow art to be displayed in a succession of schools and periods, and he provided windows to help orient visitors. Pei also designed the lighting system for the painting departments, which allowed a mixture of natural and electric light.

Rock and Roll Hall of Fame. Pei, who admitted a preference for jazz, also designed the Rock and Roll Hall of Fame and Museum on the shores of Lake Erie in Cleveland, Ohio. His cantilevered, asymmetrical design features distinctive geometric shapes: a pyramid atrium, a concrete rectangular tower, and a trapezoid-shaped structure that juts out over the lake. The main exhibition space is one level below the ground floor, while the Hall of Fame is one level above. A circulation tower connects all levels. The metal and glass exterior mirrors the hard edge of rock music, while the interior white and gray color scheme allows objects in the museum collection to stand out. Pei claimed in *Time* (4 September 1995) that "the music has that youthful energy. It has to come through in this building."

San Francisco MOMA. Meanwhile, on the West Coast the trustees of the San Francisco Museum of Modern Art hired Swiss native Mario Botta to design a new structure to house their collection. The five-story building, which and connecting urban fabric of a fairly dense city to the river's edge with a place for modern art is my idea of heaven." The interior of the museum soars as well. The central atrium is seventeen stories high and features white Sheetrock, plate glass hung on steel, and titanium. Catwalks, open stairs, walkways, and glass-enclosed elevators branch off into galleries that encircle the atrium on three levels. One of these galleries is one-and-a-quarter times larger than a football field, yet is completely free of structural columns; the gallery was built to house a 104-foot-long, 13-foot-tall sculpture titled "snake" by Richard Serra. Gehry designed a variety of exhibition spaces, from classical, square-shaped galleries for modest-scale pieces to free-form areas for larger works of art. The smaller galleries feature limestone blocks, which he said related to the city in both their scale and material; Gehry chose metals for the free-form galleries, which he said relates to the river.

Meier's J. Paul Getty Center. Perched on a 710-acre hilltop above the San Diego Freeway in the Brentwood section of Los Angeles, the J. Paul Getty Center is a modern masterpiece by Richard Meier. After whittling down a list of thirty-three architects to just three finalists, a committee for the Getty Trust hired Meier—one of the chief U.S. exponents of late modernist classicism—in 1984. Meier said, "I think what the Getty selection committee particularly liked were my ideas about opacity and transparency, about the making of space, about the relationship between public space and more quiet space, and about the importance of natural light for more ceremonial spaces and subdued light for gallery spaces." After thirteen years of work, the Getty Center opened on 16 December 1997. The $1 billion project earned the distinction of being one of the most expensive arts complexes ever built; some calculations put it as the most costly structure ever built in the United States. Yet, the Getty Center did not capture headlines for its price tag; its importance both for architecture and for the arts garnered most of the attention. The center, which has nearly one million square feet of space, is a collection of six separate units on a ridge. Terraces and plazas link the structures, helping to create a campus that resembles, in a modernist way, an Italian hill town. The buildings are clad in Italian travertine and porcelain-enameled aluminum. In the 3 November 1997 issue of *Time,* Meier proposed that people "think of it as a small college campus with different departments, some more visible than others—not a museum but an institution in which art predominates." The separate units house art, archival facilities, high-tech conservation and research, and educational programs. When it was completed, Meier said: "As I walk around the Getty now and see the play of light on different surfaces, the way in which the light changes, the way in which the light affects the quality of the architecture, and the way in which the architecture heightens one's awareness of the light, I think, this is phenomenal. This really works."

Memorials. As the century drew to a close, people sought to memorialize some of the important individuals and events of earlier times. They turned to several architects to immortalize the leaders and events that marked past eras. Each

architect brought distinct designs to monuments built or planned in the 1990s. W. Kent Cooper, William P. Lecky, Frank C. Gaylord, and Louis Nelson collaborated on the Korean War Veterans Memorial, which was unveiled in Washington, D.C., in July 1995. The memorial, located south of the reflecting pool and opposite the Vietnam memorial, features a granite wall that runs along the site. The wall has images of doctors, pilots, seamen, and troops sandblasted into the surface. The FDR Memorial, designed by landscape architect Lawrence Halprin, was dedicated in May 1997. An open gallery depicts scenes from the four terms (1933–1945) that Franklin Delano Roosevelt served as president. There are ten sculptures, both freestanding and bas-relief, and twenty-three slabs inscribed with Roosevelt's words. The memorial, however, prompted debate because the three sculptures of FDR did not show the wheelchair, leg braces, canes, and crutches on which he had depended. Disabled Americans protested the omission, while others pointed out that FDR found it necessary to hide these devices in the 1930s and early 1940s. The Women in Military Service to America Memorial was dedicated 18 October 1997 at the Arlington National Cemetery near Washington, D.C. Designed by Weiss/Manfredi Architects of New York City, the structure completed an existing, decorative retaining wall designed in 1927 by McKim, Mead & White at the end of Memorial Bridge. As part of the redesign, the architects had women's names etched onto skylights; shadows of the names were cast on vertical marble panels that line the interior space.

Future Projects. Plans were laid in the 1990s for several other memorials. John R. Collins and Alison J. Towers, husband and wife and principals at Towers Collins Architects, won, in 1997, the national design competition out of 554 entries for an American Indian memorial planned for Little Bighorn Battlefield National Monument in Montana. Their design called for a circular earthen berm with a gathering space in the middle. Meanwhile, the Commission of Fine Arts in 1998 approved the design for a World War II Memorial. Architect Friedrich St. Florian envisioned granite arches and arms of stone and metal that frame an interior plaza. The National Japanese American Memorial Foundation broke ground in October 1999 for a memorial near the U.S. Capitol to honor the patriotism of Japanese Americans and those who were interned during World War II. Architect Davis Buckley, who designed the memorial, called for a granite wall detailing Japanese immigration to the United States and two bronze Japanese cranes entwined in barbed wire. Groundwork for a memorial to slain civil-rights leader Martin Luther King Jr. was well under way in 1999, as the Washington-Alexandria Center for Architecture called for design submissions for a monument under the theme "The Man—the Movement—the Message." Winners were announced in 2000.

Sources:

Christopher John Farley, "Forever Rockin'," *Time,* 146 (4 September 1995): 62–63.

Charles Gandee, "Spanish Conquest," *Vogue,* 187 (October 1997): 370–373, 434.

David Hill, "Husband and Wife Design New Little Bighorn Memorial," *Architectural Record*, 185 (June 1997): 33.

Robert Hughes, "Bravo! Bravo!" *Time*, 150 (3 November 1997): 98–105.

Philip Jodidio, *New Forms: Architecture in the 1990s* (Köln & New York: Taschen, 1997), pp. 163, 166.

"Korean War Remembered," *Architectural Record*, 183 (August 1995): 15.

Lance Morrow, "Never Forget," *Time*, 141 (26 April 1993): 56–57.

"News Briefs," *Architectural Record*, 187 (October 1999): 69.

Clifford A. Pearson, "Rock and Roll Hall of Fame and Museum, Cleveland," *Architectural Record*, 182 (September 1994): 32.

James S. Russell, "Permanent Witness," *Architectural Record*, 181 (July 1993): 59–67.

Thomas A. Sancton, "Pei's Palace of Art," *Time*, 142 (29 November 1993): 68–70.

Ellen Sands, "Commission Holds Its Fire and Approves World War II Memorial," *Architectural Record*, 186 (July 1998): 36.

Sands, "Memorial Uses Glass and Light to Honor Women in the Military," *Architectural Record*, 185 (November 1997): 41.

Sands, "MLK Is Next for D.C.," *Architectural Record*, 187 (April 1999): 53.

Hugh Sidey, "Where's His Wheelchair?" *Time*, 145 (6 March 1995): 105.

"U.S. Holocaust Museum Challenges Literal Architectural Interpretations of History," *Architectural Record*, 181 (May 1993): 27.

MODERN INTERIOR DESIGNS

Diversity in Design. No single look defined interior design in the 1990s. Styles were influenced by everything from minimalism to the Arts-and-Crafts movement; professional interior designers and American consumers alike drew on regional styles, historical trends, and personal tastes to create dwellings that were highly individualistic. Minimalism, as the name suggests, highlighted the absence of decoration. Walls and doors were white, windows were bare, and furnishings were spare. Critics thought it sterile and impersonal; proponents, on the other hand, found the design style calming and said it focused attention on the quality of the few pieces that were visible. A passion for antiques balanced minimalism. Americans gathered all sorts of collectibles at auctions, flea markets, and yard sales to help create homes that looked as if they had been in their family for generations. A renewed interest in art deco and the simple, clean, and almost futuristic lines of the 1950s also helped designers create interiors reminiscent of the past. Meanwhile, the Arts-and-Crafts movement brought to prominence regional furniture makers whose specialty pieces featured fine workmanship and individual designs. Another trend in the 1990s brought the outside indoors: wall colors mirrored natural shades, while large windows and skylights let in natural light. Designers also focused on the environment when choosing materials; they looked for wood that came from renewable sources, such as plantations or natural forests certified as sustainable. Restorers reconstructed antiques without using toxic chemicals. Some manufacturers used recycled plastics or wood to create new home and office items. Still, there was no shortage of materials found in showcase interiors: homes and offices featured every-

DESIGN AND THE ART OF PLACEMENT

Prominent designers and big-time magazines were not the only influences on how people and interiors looked in the 1990s. *Feng shui* shaped design as well. *Feng shui* (pronounced FUNG shway) is the ancient Chinese art of placement that mixes metaphysics, superstition, astrology, and philosophy. Practitioners believed that good fortune and balance depended on factors such as the direction of a building and furnishings in a room. The principles of *feng shui* caught on early in the decade, in part as a backlash against the go-go 1980s. The idea was that by using certain colors and placements, one could create balance and harmony, and in turn affect mood and outcome. Some concepts were simple and easy to follow; others were complex and required charts or professional practitioners to help achieve them.

Interest in *feng shui* started with how items were arranged at home and work. Simple principles used by some practitioners included getting rid of clutter which could disrupt balance, and maintaining healthy, vibrant plants to enhance one's life energy, or "*chi.*" More complex ideas focused on arranging furniture and accessories based on an octagonal chart called the "bagua," with its eight sides corresponding to compass directions, life qualities, colors, and numbers, in addition to animals, seasons, and elements in some cases.

Some people also adapted the principles of *feng shui* to appearance. Articles and books pointed out what clothing colors corresponded to different qualities and how colors affected *chi.* Red, for example, corresponded to luck, rationality, and power; it was also the color of fame. Green related to the hope of extraordinary luck. Lively colors, such as red, green, or any colorful mix, stimulated design creativity. Black represented either wealth and hopelessness, depending on the circumstances. Some women even promoted the use of these principles when applying makeup. Wearing purple, gold and green on the eyes symbolized wealth and power, while wearing red—the color of fame—helped one stand out in a crowd.

Sources: Zan Dubin, "The Cosmos as Fashion Guide," *Los Angeles Times*, 29 June 1995.

Suzanne C. Ryan, "Making a Face with Feng Shui Cosmetic Spirit," *Boston Globe*, 19 October 1999.

Stacey Tiedge, "Workplace Can Benefit from Feng Shui," *Seattle Times*, 2 September 1999.

thing from stainless steel and glass to granite and woods of all sorts.

Trends in the Home. Although interior design was quite diverse, some trends emerged on the home front,

A living room decorated along harmonious *feng shui* lines (The Interior Archive/Simon Brown)

specifically the use of natural tones, classic styles, and comfortable furnishings. Colors and materials in the home drew on the natural world. Earth tones such as yellows, greens, browns, reds, soft blues, and purples gave homes a soothing and relaxing décor. Materials such as wood, ceramics, cotton, and velvets lent a soft, natural feeling to homes. Designers also updated clean, classic looks—oversized upholstered club chairs, leather sofas, traditional chandeliers—for the American families of the 1990s. To give a home a personal and familiar feel, designers showcased items collected by those dwelling inside. Some termed this combination of design styles—the mix of earthy materials and traditional furnishings—"rustic elegance."

Sources:
"'96 Trends," *Better Homes and Gardens,* 74 (January 1996): 19–40.

Vilma Barr, *The Illustrated Room: 20th Century of Interior Design Rendering,* edited by Dani Antman (New York: McGraw-Hill, 1997), pp. 215–217.

Julie V. Iovine, "Minimalism: A whole lot of nothing or a state of grace?" *The New York Times,* 26 September 1996.

Leslie Lampert, "Ladies' Home Journal Decorates the New American Home 1995," *Ladies' Home Journal,* 112 (February 1995): 174–178.

Lampert, "The New American Home 1994," *Ladies' Home Journal,* 111 (February 1994): 116–121; 111 (March 1994): 122–125.

"Record Interiors," *Architectural Record,* 179 (September 1991): 73–133; 180 (September 1992): 77–135.

Tamara Schneider, "The New American Home 1992," *Ladies' Home Journal,* 109 (February 1992): 144–149.

"Trends '97," *Better Homes and Gardens,* 75 (January 1997): 37–42.

"Trends '98," *Better Homes and Gardens,* 76 (January 1998): 19–32.

NEW AUTOMOTIVE DESIGNS

The Look. The family sedan was just one of many popular designs in the 1990s, but Americans also bought everything from bulky sport utility vehicles (SUVs) to the rounded Volkswagen Beetle to sleek, luxury roadsters. Designers throughout most of the decade seemed to base their creations not so much on their imaginations as on the dictates of government rules on safety, fuel economy, and the environment. Some notable designs included the 1994 Chrysler LH sedans, which moved the base of the windshield forward and increased the wheelbase by pushing the rear wheels back to create a new look; the 1998 Mercedes-Benz ML320 SUV combined carlike qualities without sacrificing off-road capability. Another important design was the Ford Taurus. When Ford Motors introduced the 1986 Taurus, its softly rounded contours were a sharp contrast to the

One of the largest SUVs of 1998, the Ford Excursion (AP/Wide World Photos)

boxy-looking cars favored in the early and mid 1980s. The "jelly bean" look came to dominate the shape of the early 1990s, as the Taurus ranked as the best-selling car in the United States for three years running. Automotive designers, however, moved away from that shape later in the decade, as the market for automobiles—the cost of which averaged above $20,000—became increasingly fragmented. Designers pushed for more distinctive looks for the hundreds of models of cars and trucks on the market. Even Ford decided to restyle the Taurus. On 27 September 1995, Ford launched its redesigned model, which when viewed from the side had an elongated oval shape. "We kept trying to make it sleek, sleek and sleeker," designer Doug Gaffka told *Time* in September 1995.

Retro Influences. Automotive designers, like clothing designers, took their cues from the past. Volkswagen reintroduced the Beetle at the January 1998 Detroit auto show, updating the distinctive, rounded shape of the 1960s VW Bug. The new model made driving a small car stylish again. The Beetle, though, was just the start of the retro influence in cars. Ford announced plans for a new version of the T-Bird, General Motors announced plans for its Chevrolet Impala, and Dodge for its Charger—all of which shared the spotlight at the January 1999 Detroit auto show. The names were not the only retro part of these vehicles, however; designers used the original cars for inspiration. For example, the 2001 Ford Thunderbird roadster took its styling cues from the 1955 T-Bird; the updated design retained the portholes, oval grille, and hood scoop of the original, although it dumped the bullet-head lamps, large chrome bumpers, and whitewalls on the tires. Ford expected to sell the 2001 T-Bird in 2000 for between $30,000 and $40,000.

Sport Utility Vehicles. If one had to pick a single vehicle to define the 1990s, the choice would have to be the sport utility vehicle, which picked up where the

minivans left off. Powerful, popular, and pricey, SUVs dominated the market at the end of the millennium. Annual sales in the United States jumped from about 900,000 in 1991 to 3.1 million in 1999. The number of SUVs on the roads climbed from seven million in 1993 to about twenty million in 1998. There were about twenty-five different models on the market in 1999, with another twenty or so expected to reach consumers in 2000 and 2001. The large size and heavy design of SUVs made their drivers feel safer and more confident. Owners also said they liked the space, which was big enough to haul children, pets, and cargo of all sorts. SUVS also became a status symbol, with luxury models such as the 1999 leather-lined Lexus LX470 costing $60,000. Once limited to the boxy Jeep or GMC truck, with stripped-down interiors that could be hosed out, SUVs were spartan fare until families started buying them, and automakers thereafter created sleeker, more luxurious models that still had the power to haul a boat. In addition to the Ford Explorer and Chevy Suburban and Blazer, luxury automakers Mercedes-Benz and BMW added their versions to the U.S. market. Luxury and size became selling points for many SUVs, with Ford winning headlines in 1999 when it introduced the Excursion—larger in all dimensions than any other SUV. Some critics of SUVs, however, noted that these large automobiles harmed the environment, wasted valuable resources, and endangered drivers in smaller cars.

Return of the Roadsters. Despite the popularity of sport utility vehicles, another significant trend in automotive design focused on the small and sportier roadster. The details of these cars varied from company to company, but all roadsters shared a basic design: two seats, a sleek sporty look, and low-to-the-ground styling. The return of the roadster started in 1989, when Mazda launched its $15,000 two-seat convertible, the

Miata. Mazda's success with the classic sports car—more than half a million were sold by 1999—prompted other automakers to follow. BMW introduced its sporty two-seater, the Z3, in 1996 with a price tag of $32,000. Porsche built the Boxster, while Mercedes-Benz presented its SLK. Honda also got into the act with its 2000 Honda S2000, priced at $32,415. Sales of the roadsters were so strong, that in 1999 Mazda offered its Miata Tenth Anniversary model at $26,875. The anniversary model featured an exclusive sapphire-blue paint with matching convertible top, and a two-tone interior in blue suede and black leather.

Sources:

Frank Ahrens, "Suburban Warriors," *Washington Post Magazine* (7 November 1999): 10–15, 25, 27–30.

Brian S. Akre, "Stars of the '99 Auto Show Echo the Past," *Buffalo News*, 29 December 1998.

Frank Gibney Jr., "After the Bug, The Bird: Detroit Goes Retro," *Time*, 153 (18 January 1999): 58.

Bob Golfen, "The True Sports Car; Honda's Roadster Pure, High-Tech Fun," *The Arizona Republic*, 27 November 1999.

Bill Griffith, "Big Wheels 2000 Trucks, Vans & Sport Utility Vehicles; Trucks and SUVs Continue to Dominate Sales and the Roads," *The Boston Globe*, 18 November 1999.

James R. Healey, "Sports Cars Still Speeding into Buyer's Hearts," *USA Today*, 29 September 1999.

Leon Jaroff, "Trying to Top the Taurus," *Time*, 146 (4 September 1995): 58–60.

Dan Jedlicka, "Cult-Status Mazda Miata Rolls Out Special Edition with Style and Exclusivity; Ten Years After," *Chicago Sun-Times*, 19 July 1999.

Michael Lamm, "30 Designs That Changed the Face of the Automobile," *The New York Times*, 21 October 1998.

John O'Dell, "Out With the Old. . .," *Los Angeles Times*, 21 October 1999.

Steve Pasteiner, "Elements of Style: Forty Years of Automotive Design," *AutoWeek*, 46 (13 July 1998): 74.

HEADLINE MAKERS

FRANK O. GEHRY

1929 -

ARCHITECT

Background. Born in Toronto, Canada, Frank O. Gehry came to the forefront of architecture well before the 1990s. He studied at the University of Southern California, Los Angeles (1949–1951) and at Harvard University (1956–1957). The principal of Gehry and Associates, Los Angeles, since 1962, he received the prestigious Pritzker Prize in 1989. When he accepted the award, he spoke about establishing a link between art and architecture that would influence his work for the next decade: "I explored the process of new construction materials to try giving feeling and spirit to form. In trying to find the essence of my own expression, I fantasized that I was an artist standing before a white canvas deciding what the first move should be."

Architecture as Art. Gehry was a pioneer in the movement to return architecture to its standing as fine art. One example of his links to art is the Chiat/Day Main Street building, completed in 1991, in Venice, California. The façade of the building is an enormous pair of black binoculars designed by Gehry's friends Claes Oldenburg and Coosje van Bruggen. Cars enter the structure by driving beneath the binoculars; small offices and conference rooms were built within the cylinders. Gehry's use of sculptural forms was also evident in his designs for the $100 million Guggenheim Museum, which opened in Bilbao, Spain, on 19 October 1997. The glass-and-titanium structure echoed the shipbuilding history of the city with its abstract design resembling a ship.

Museum Pieces. In the late 1990s Gehry undertook another museum project: the Experience Music Project (EMP) in Seattle, Washington. The $60 million complex "will use music to engage people in an entirely new way. The exhibits and building treat music as a living and evolving art form. I wanted the building design to evoke the energy of music," Gehry told *Architectural Record* in January 1997. His designs for the three-story, 110,000-square-foot complex called for an arrangement of six components, whose exterior surfaces and colors (bright orange, blue, and gold) were intended to evoke images of broken pieces of Stratocaster guitars. Looping overhead cables were meant to resemble busted guitar strings. A reporter for the *Seattle Times* wrote that the museum looks like "a space-ship that fell from the sky and got a little roughed up on landing." The museum opened to the public in June 2000.

Future Plans. In 1999 Gehry won an invitation-only competition to design an addition to the Corcoran Gallery of Art and College of Art and Design in Washington, D.C. The $40 million project, which was slated to start in 2001, called for renovating the original Beaux-Arts building designed by Ernest Flagg in 1897.

Sources:

Charles Gandee, "Conquest," *Vogue*, 187 (October 1997): 370–373, 434.

"Gehry Designs 'Far Out' Interactive Music Museum," *Architectural Record*, 185 (January 1997): 45.

Robert Hughes, "Bravo! Bravo!" *Time*, 150 (3 November 1997): 98–105.

Philip Jodidio, *New Forms: Architecture in the 1990s* (Köln & New York: Taschen, 1997), pp. 9, 44, 158–159, 228.

Ellen Palmer Sands, "Gehry Throws Another Curve with Extension to Corcoran Gallery," *Architectural Record*, 187 (August 1999): 60.

TOMMY HILFIGER

1952-
FASHION DESIGNER

Background. Tommy Hilfiger started his fashion career by peddling jeans around New York state and opening a string of small clothing stores. He later worked as a designer for Jordache. In 1984 he teamed up with Hong Kong tycoon Mohan Murjani to set up his own design shop and introduce his first collection. Hilfiger compared himself with established American designers, such as Calvin Klein and Ralph Lauren, in early advertisements. Although the industry scoffed at such boldness, Hilfiger's success in the menswear market came quickly when, in 1992, his preppie-style clothes caught on with black teenagers. In 1995 he was named the Menswear Designer of the Year by the Council of Fashion Designers of America.

Tapping a Market. Hilfiger embraced the inner-city market, adding urban flair to his fairly conservative clothes by emphasizing oversized logos and baggy styles. In the 16 September 1996 issue of *Time*, Russell Simmons, founder of Def Jam Records, contended that "Tommy's clothing represents the American Dream to black kids. They're not interested in buying holey jeans; they want high-quality merchandise." A big boost came in March 1994 when rapper Snoop Doggy Dogg (Cordazer Calvin Broadus) appeared, on the television show *Saturday Night Live*, wearing a jersey with the Hilfiger logo. Sales jumped by $93 million the following year. Hilfiger's connection to the black market was also evident in some of his advertising. He used female rap-per Spinderella (Latoya Silk) and music-industry tycoon Quincy Jones's daughter, Kidada as models in 1996; male rapper Treach (Anthony Criss) appeared on the catwalk during Hilfiger's spring/summer 1997 show.

Popular Logo. Hilfiger made his mark with well-made, casual clothing—with a distinctive red, white, and blue logo that instantly alerted people to one of his designs. He also placed "Tommy" across T-shirts and an oversized "H" on the front of sweaters. These bold logos became an effective form of advertising, as Hilfiger's popularity soared and his clothes reached a variety of markets: young and adult, black and white, men and women.

Branching Out. After the success of his menswear line, Hilfiger launched a collection and a floral fragrance for women in 1996. He named both "Tommy Girl." Like his designs for men, his women's clothes were well-cut, preppie in style, and emblazoned with the easily recognizable Hilfiger logos. The prices were well within the reach of many teens: the Tommy Girl line was all under $200, with many pieces under $50. In September 1996 fashion consultant Tom Logan told *Time* that Hilfiger "knows how to market a concept as very few do. His is a brand kids want to be seen in, and it is presented exactly right." Hilfiger added tailored men's clothing, with clean-cut styles, and full-cut American suits and jackets for business, in 1994. He launched Tommy Jeans, a line specifically for teens, in 1998. Hilfiger also planned a sportswear line for teens, accessories, and a career line for 2000.

Avoiding Negatives. Despite the urban street style of his clothes, Hilfiger did not tap into the more negative side of the image. His ads promote a sense of Americana, with women and men smiling and laughing in hometown settings. His women's line featured bright plaids and smart tops and sweaters; his clothes were comfortable, colorful, and fairly conservative. Richard Martin wrote in *Contemporary Fashion* that "Hilfiger has come closer to Main Street, a colorful Americana that still waves flags, that still loves button-down collars, that appreciates classics, that adores his 'good, clean fun' along with family values and may even abhor pretense or promiscuity, that strives for college and collegiate looks but would never rebel too much even on campus, and that dresses a little more modestly and traditionally than those who prefer his designer-commerce confreres." Hilfiger's clothes and image paid off, as his company was ranked fifth in the Fairchild 100 survey in November 1999, up from the ninth spot in 1997.

Sources:

Martha Duffy, "H Stands for Hilfiger," *Time*, 148 (16 September 1996): 66.

The Fashion Book (London: Phaidon, 1998), p. 211.

Richard Martin, "Hilfiger, Tommy," in *Contemporary Fashion*, edited by Martin (New York: St. James Press, 1995), pp. 228–229.

"The Modern Touch for Banner Brands," *Women's Wear Daily Fairchild 100 Supplement* (Fairchild Publications, November 1999), p. 74.

DONNA KARAN

1948-
FASHION DESIGNER

Beginnings. Donna Karan was literally born into the world of fashion in 1948. Her father was a tailor and her mother a model and showroom representative. She designed her first collection in high school. Karan attended the Parson's School of Design, but dropped out after her second year to join Anne Klein. She was fired nine months later and went to work for another sportswear house. She returned to Klein in 1968, however, and became an associate designer in 1971. When Karan was named head designer in 1973 she asked her school friend Louis Dell'Olio to join her as co-designer. Together, they created a classic, yet stylish, sportswear look. Her early training and connections helped in forming her own company. Karan and her husband, Stephan Weiss, founded Donna Karan New York in 1984; Klein's parent company, Takihyo Corporation, backed the new firm. By the end of the 1990s, Karan was one of the leading designers in the United States.

Clothes that Hug and Hide. Karan's first collection was based on body-conscious wear: a body suit to be worn with long or short skirts, blouses, and pants. Well-tailored coats and bold accessories completed the wardrobe, which from the beginning were made of luxurious materials. Karan, who often wore layers of black cashmere, designed her clothes and accessories based on what she herself would wear. She also created designs that flattered the women, so her clothes worked as well on a size four as they did on a size ten. Her corporate philosophy was that clothes should be designed to hug a woman but also hide her imperfections. Karan believed that clothes should be easily transferred from day to evening and summer to winter. As a result, her trademark items became bodysuits, unitards, black cashmere, and stretch fabric. She also paid particular attention to fabric and cut. The look she created was powerful, urban, and professional with elements of sensuality.

Expanding Business. Donna Karan New York expanded dramatically during the decade, adding in 1991 the DKNY menswear collection, which became known for its comfort and sensuality, as had her women's collections. Karan founded Donna Karan Beauty Company, a fragrance and cosmetic division, in 1992. Also in 1992 Karan established a lingerie line, as well as DKNY Kids. Company revenues, which were $119 million in 1989, reached $268 million in 1992. Karan took the company public in June 1996, where the stock debuted at $26 a share. Karan's divisions also allowed the company to offer several price ranges. Her top-of-the-line selections were pricey, with a woman's pants suit costing $650, a woman's blazer costing $1,100 and a man's wool crepe suit costing $1,350. The DKNY division, however, was priced somewhat lower: a woman's wool blazer cost $450. In October 1999, Donna Karan International Inc. and Liz Claiborne Inc. announced a deal that would allow Liz Claiborne to license Karan's name to make a new line of women's casual clothing at department-store prices. The line was expected to debut in the spring of 2001. Karan said the agreement allowed her company to reach a broader consumer base. Even without the new line, her company by the end of the 1990s was designing a large selection of merchandise, including clothes, lingerie, sleepwear, loungewear, handbags, jewelry, scarves, belts, hosiery, shoes, and sunglasses.

Sources:

Kevin Almond, "Karan, Donna," in *Contemporary Fashion*, edited by Richard Martin (New York: St. James Press, 1995), pp. 267–270.

The Fashion Book (London: Phaidon, 1998), p. 241.

Betsy Israel, "Donna, The Collection," *New York Times*, 13 December 1992.

"Karan and Claiborne Reach Licensing Deal," *New York Times*, 15 October 1999.

Barbara Rudolph, "Donna Inc.," *Time*, 140 (30 November 1992): 54–57.

Anne Stegemeyer, *Who's Who in Fashion* (New York: Fairchild Publications, 1996), pp. 120–121.

CALVIN KLEIN

1942-
FASHION DESIGNER

Early Years. Calvin Klein, in many ways, defined American fashion at the end of the twentieth century. Klein was born in the Bronx, New York, and attended the New York High School of Art and Design. Starting with dresses and coats, he soon branched out into sportswear. In his twenty-five years as a top designer, Klein promoted his vision of minimalism and sophisticated fashions in natural fabrics and colors. Klein formed Calvin Klein Ltd. in 1968 and built his business into a fashion empire over the next three decades, creating women's ready-to-wear and sportswear, menswear, underwear, home furnishings, and fragrances. He once said: "I made a lot of things that go with things."

Form and Function. Klein's modernist style has been defined as spare, an expression of American style. He once pointed out that, "It's important not to confuse simplicity with uninteresting." His clothes, which included both day and evening wear, were simplified and refined with clean lines, and were made of natural and often luxurious fibers such as cashmere, linen, silk, leather, and suede. He generally used earth tones and neutrals to help define his understated elegance. Klein's fashions reflected the idea that form follows function, whether they were his designer-label jeans or bias-cut evening gown. His chaste construction—he avoided linings and complications—allowed mobility and freedom.

Growing Fame. Although Klein was well established in the 1980s, the New York City-based designer continued to gain fame in the 1990s. His lines of jeans, womenswear, and menswear continued to sell, as did his perfumes, home furnishings, and underwear. He also introduced new fragrances, such as his Escape lines in 1991–1992, and then he launched a major campaign for cK One, a single fragrance worn by both men and women. *Time* named Klein one of the twenty-five most influential Americans in 1996 and said: "Each season his models have ambled down the runway in clothes created in quiet protest against fashion's outlandish theatricality." In June 1996, Richard Martin, curator of the Costume Institute at the Metropolitan Museum of Art, told *Time:* "The clothing is extraordinarily important. He is the true American Puritan. Even as his style has evolved over time, it's always about eliminating anything that is not necessary, and always thinking of the garment as being pure as possible."

Criticism. The accolades, however, were tempered by sharp criticism of his advertising campaigns. His ads often pushed boundaries in their use of gender and sex. First came near-naked models, most notably Kate Moss, Marky Mark, and Antonio Sabato Jr. Then, in 1995, a Klein campaign featured models who looked like teenagers in sexually evocative poses. *Seventeen* magazine refused to carry the ads, and President Bill Clinton protested their content. The American Family Association demanded to know the ages of the models (Klein declined to disclose this information) and asked the Justice Department to investigate whether Klein violated child-pornography laws. Then came his 1999 ads featuring young boys and girls in underwear jumping on a sofa. Critics again charged that the ads went too far, with some complaining that they were pornographic. Klein pulled the ads on 17 Febuary 1999, a day before the campaign was to be launched with a billboard in Times Square in New York City. Despite the controversy, Klein remained on top. In November 1999 the Fairchild 100 survey listed Calvin Klein as the top designer brand, noting that industry observers predicted that its sales could generate $1 billion a year.

Sources:

Margaret Carlson, "Where Calvin Crossed the Line," *Time,* 146 (11 September 1995): 64.

The Fashion Book (London: Phaidon, 1998), p. 253.

"Klein Kills Ads Critics Claimed Offensive," *The State* (Columbia, S.C.), 18 February 1999.

Richard Martin, "Klein, Calvin," in *Contemporary Fashion,* edited by Martin (New York: St. James Press, 1995), pp. 283–285.

"The Modern Touch for Banner Brands," *Women's Wear Daily Fairchild 100 Supplement* (Fairchild Publications, November 1999), p. 74.

Anne Stegemeyer, *Who's Who in Fashion* (New York: Fairchild Publications, 1996), pp. 129–130.

"Time's 25 Most Influential Americans," *Time,* 148 (17 June 1996): 56–57.

RICHARD MEIER

1934–
ARCHITECT

Education and Training. A native of Newark, New Jersey, Meier received his architectural training at Cornell University. He worked in the office of Marcel Breuer from 1960 to 1963 and established his own practice in 1963. He received the Pritzker Prize in 1984 and a Royal Gold Medal in 1988.

Getty Center. The 1980s set the stage for how Meier would spend the next decade. Then based in New York City, the architect learned in 1984 that he was chosen to design the J. Paul Getty Center in Los Angeles, California. Built on a 710-acre hilltop, the $1 billion Getty Center opened on 16 December 1997. The collection of six separate units linked by terraces and plazas has nearly one million square feet of space. The campus combines both modern and classic forms. Meier said of his creation: "In my mind I keep returning to the Romans—to Hadrian's Villa, to Caprarola for their sequence of spaces, their thick-walled presence, their sense of order, the way in which building and landscape belong to each other."

Other Projects. Although the Getty Center defined Meier's work in the 1990s, it certainly was not his only project. Meier's Stadthaus civic center in Ulm, Germany, was dedicated on 12 November 1993. The three-story complex was clad in Rosa Dante granite and white stucco. In addition to building a complex of exhibition spaces, an assembly hall, café, and tourist information center, Meier also redesigned its home, the Münsterplatz. Most of the historic city of Ulm was destroyed during World War II, and the reconstruction paid little attention to architectural quality. Meier's improvements, which included a curved wall that leads people into the square, helped redefine the center plaza of Ulm as a place to congregate. He successfully integrated his modern, geometric designs with the historic setting. Other significant projects of Meier's included the Canal Plus headquarters, Paris, France (1988–1991); City Hall and Library, The Hague, The Netherlands (1990–1995); and the Museum of Contemporary Art, Barcelona, Spain (1988–1995).

Sources:

Charles Gandee, "Modern Man," *Vogue,* 187 (December 1997): 284–288, 346.

Robert Hughes, "Bravo! Bravo!" *Time,* 150 (3 November 1997): 98–105.

Philip Jodidio, *New Forms: Architecture in the 1990s* (Köln & New York: Taschen, 1997), pp. 7, 113, 116, 119, 230.

I. M. PEI

1917-
ARCHITECT

Background. A native of China, Ieoh Ming Pei emigrated to the United States in 1935. He earned a bachelor's degree in architecture at the Massachusetts Institute of Technology in 1940 and then attended Harvard University, where he earned a master's in architecture and a doctorate. Pei formed I. M. Pei & Associates in 1955 and has earned several prestigious architectural awards, including the American Institute of Architecture Gold Medal in 1979 and the Pritzker Prize in 1983.

Museum Visions. Pei's work spread across the globe in the 1990s. French president François-Maurice Mitterrand called on Pei to redesign the Louvre. Pei completed the first phase in 1989, which included the construction of a glass pyramid as a new entrance. Although critics charged that the modern design sharply contrasted with the surrounding nineteenth-century architecture, the French public came to accept Pei's design as the newest Parisian attraction. Pei also redesigned the Richelieu wing as part of the second phase of museum renovation, which was completed in 1993. An underground shopping gallery added during the renovation featured an inverted glass pyramid. The bold simplicity of his pyramid instantly made it a landmark in modern architecture. Another project, the Rock and Roll Hall of Fame and Museum, brought Pei back to the United States. Although he preferred jazz, his structure mirrored the energy of rock with a geometric design of glass and metal. The museum, which opened in 1995, is located in Cleveland, Ohio.

Bell Tower. Pei's work was not limited to museums, however. He designed the Bell Tower at Misono, Shiga, for a religious sect, the Worldwide Spiritual Organization. Completed in 1990, Pei based the design on the *bachi*, a traditional Japanese musical instrument. The Bell Tower is pure and simple, with a white tower slightly flared at the top where it encases the bells. He also designed the Miho Museum for the same sect. Most of this building is underground; the structure includes a pedestrian tunnel, bridge, and glass roofs, evoking traditional Japanese forms. Pei donated a collection of papers that documents his work to the Library of Congress in October 1997. Although he was in his seventies and eighties, Pei continued to work. He told *Architectural Record* in August 1998 that, "I am now able to concentrate on what I enjoy doing. I wanted to be able to give the time and thought that certain projects deserve."

Sources:
"I. M. Pei Presents Papers to Library of Congress," *Architectural Record*, 185 (October 1997): 41.

Philip Jodidio, *New Forms: Architecture in the 1990s* (Köln & New York: Taschen, 1997), pp. 83–84, 100, 104, 175, 177, 231.

James S. Russell, "Pei Communes with Nature at Japan's Remote Miho Museum," *Architectural Record*, 186 (August 1998): 43.

Thomas Sancton, "Pei's Palace of Art," *Time*, 142 (29 November 1993): 68–70.

CESAR PELLI

1926 -
ARCHITECT

Recognition. Cesar Pelli was born in Argentina and received a degree in architecture in 1949 from Tucuman University. He emigrated to the United States in 1952 and earned a master's in architecture in 1954 from the University of Illinois. After becoming dean of the School of Architecture at Yale in 1977, he opened his own office, Cesar Pelli and Associates, in New Haven, Connecticut. Pelli won the AIA Gold Medal in 1995. At the time, he was praised for his ability to create commercial buildings "that speak with an urban and civilized voice."

Carnegie Hall Tower. Pelli entered the 1990s triumphantly. He already had a string of recent accomplishments, such as the Pacific Design Center in West Hollywood, California, the World Financial Center on Wall Street in New York City, and the Norwest Center in Minneapolis, Minnesota. In September 1990 his Carnegie Hall Tower brought the architect to new heights. The structure, designed to house both offices and apartments, is a full block deep and sixty stories tall, yet it remains sleek at just fifty feet wide. *Time* correspondent Kurt Andersen wrote in September 1990 that this "slender, elegant slab is like a dancer among thugs." Pelli designed the tower to fit with its partner and next-door neighbor, Carnegie Hall. He echoed the century-old Roman brick and terra cotta in the tower's brick skin, in five shades of brown and amber, and extended Carnegie Hall's Beaux-Arts façade. Pelli reported in September 1990 that "constraints are not necessarily negative. They force you to try avenues you would have ignored."

Worldwide Creations. Like many other prominent architects, Pelli's work took him around the globe. He completed Canary Wharf Tower in London, England, in 1991; NTT Shinjuku Headquarters Building in Tokyo, Japan, in 1995; and a new passenger terminal at Ronald Reagan National Airport in Washington, D.C. His Petronas Towers in Kuala Lampur, Malaysia, were particularly noteworthy. The structure, at 1,483 feet, surpassed the Sears Tower in Chicago, Illinois, as the world's tallest building. Its importance goes much deeper, however. Pelli placed the towers shoulder to shoulder, creating a focal point of the space in between. A bridge linking the towers at the forty-first and forty-second stories draws one's eyes to the void. Pelli's designs echoed Islamic design. The architect used intersecting squares to form an eight-pointed star and then added curved bays between the points to create a unique footprint for the building. Other projects of note include a 3.2 million-square-foot mass transit hub in Hong Kong. Pelli was chosen in the mid 1990s to design the complex to integrate the central subway station with a new air terminal. The first phase called for a 1,312-foot-tall office tower, a 689-foot-tall tower, and a four-story retail podium with a public roof garden. Subsequent phases called for a hotel and apartments. Also at the end of the 1990s, Pelli was chosen to lead a design team for new concert spaces at the Orange County Performing Arts Center in Costa Mesa, California.

Sources:

Kurt Andersen, "Big Yet Still Beautiful," *Time*, 136 (24 September 1990): 98–99.

"Briefs," *Architectural Record*, 183 (January 1995): 15.

Philip Jodidio, *New Forms: Architecture in the 1990s* (Köln & New York: Taschen, 1997), pp. 64, 66, 23.

"New Briefs," *Architectural Record*, 185 (May 1997): 58.

Clifford A. Pearson, "Other Than Their Status as the World's Tallest Buildings, What Else do Cesar Pelli's Petronas Towers Have Going for Them?" *Architectural Record*, 188 (January 1999): 92–101.

"Pelli's New Plan," *Architectural Record*, 187 (January 1999): 55.

PEOPLE IN THE NEWS

Actress **Jennifer Aniston,** who portrayed Rachel on the TV show *Friends* inspired a craze in the mid 1990s for a longer version of the shag haircut. Women across the country demanded that their hairstylists give them the "Rachel" or *Friends* cut, a face-framing, multilayered look. *Friends* debuted in the 1994–1995 television season on the National Broadcasting Company (NBC) network and was still running at the end of the decade.

Carolyn Bessette made headlines, not just for marrying **John F. Kennedy Jr.** (son of President **John F. Kennedy**) on 21 September 1996, but for wearing a simple, yet elegant, white slip dress designed by **Narciso Rodriguez.** Bessette-Kennedy went on to become a symbol of the new American style with its clean, classic lines before she and her husband died in a plane crash on 16 July 1999.

Bill Blass retired at age seventy-seven after sixty years in the fashion business. Blass, an important figure on the American fashion scene for his classic styles, held his last show—his spring 2000 collection—in New York in October 1999.

Newsweek featured **Diane Von Furstenberg** on a cover in 1976 for her wrap dresses. The American designer enjoyed a revival of these 1970-style dresses in the mid 1990s.

Lizzy Gardiner was the perfect golden girl at the Academy Awards in 1995. The Australian designer, who won an Oscar for the costumes she and **Tim Chappel** designed for *The Adventures of Priscilla, Queen of the Desert* (1994), showed up at the ceremony in an evening dress made of 254 American Express Gold Cards.

Architect **Michael Graves** introduced a line of kitchen accessories to be sold through the Target chain of discount stores. The Graves Design Collection, which featured everything from spatulas to a patio set, went on sale in January 1999.

With a grant from the National Endowment for the Arts (NEA), urban architect **John Kaliski's** private firm researched the histories of several Los Angeles neighborhoods in an effort to understand how urban sprawl developed. His idea was to make U.S. cities more livable with parks as well as to save their housing and community gardens.

Tom Kinslow and **Simon Ungers** designed the T-House in Wilton, New York. The structure, built with quarter-inch oxidized nickel chromium steel in a simple geometric form, combined the client's request to have living quarters (in the lower section) and a library (in the top section).

The young rap duo Kriss Kross drew as much attention for their dress as their music. **Daddy Mack (Chris Smith)** and **Mack Daddy (Chris Kelly),** both thirteen, wore their baseball caps, T-shirts, and overalls backward. They called it "the krossed-out look." Most called it short-lived.

Pop singer **Madonna** and **Jean-Paul Gaultier** teamed up for her 1990 "Blond Ambition Tour." Gaultier designed Madonna's provocative outfits, including a cone-shaped bra.

Stella McCartney, daughter of a former Beetle **Paul McCartney** and his American-photographer wife, **Linda Eastman McCartney,** made her Paris runway debut in October 1996 at age twenty-five as the new designer for the House of Chloé.

American designer **Isaac Mizrahi** gave the public an inside look into the world of fashion with his 1995 movie *Unzipped.*

Actress **Gwyneth Paltrow,** with her fresh face, minimal makeup, no fuss hair, and classic styles, set new standards for beauty and fashion in the mid and late 1990s. When she appeared on the August 1996 cover of *Vogue*, the magazine declared her "the nineties It girl."

Designer **Patrick Robinson** made his debut collection for Anne Klein in April 1995. Robinson, twenty-eight at the time, replaced **Richard Tyler** at the helm of Anne Klein, one of the biggest design houses in the United States.

In 1990 New York architect **Robert A. M. Stern** introduced his designs in a line of seating and tables for Hickory Business Furniture. The twenty or so new pieces were all crafted in wood and featured clean lines that blended classic styling with innovation.

The March 1990 issue of *Vogue* listed among its "Designers to watch in the 1990s" **Zang Toi, José Barrera, Mark Badgley, James Mischka, Todd Oldham, Maria Snyder,** and **Christian Francis Roth.**

Architect **Robert Venturi,** who launched postmodernism in the 1960s, had his addition to the National Gallery of Art on Trafalgar Square in London dedicated in 1991; in 1992 Seattle opened the Venturi-designed Seattle Art Museum.

Author **Naomi Wolf,** a graduate of Yale University and a Rhodes Scholar, challenged the marketing of unrealistic beauty standards in her book, *The Beauty Myth: How Images of Beauty Are Used Against Women* (1991).

AWARDS

COUNCIL OF FASHION DESIGNERS OF AMERICA

1990

Womenswear Designer of the Year: Donna Karan

Menswear Designer of the Year: Joseph Abboud

Perry Ellis Award: Christian Francis Roth

1991

Womenswear Designer of the Year: Isaac Mizrahi

Menswear Designer of the Year: Roger Forsythe

Perry Ellis Award: Todd Oldham

1992

Womenswear Designer of the Year: Marc Jacobs

Menswear Designer of the Year: Donna Karan

Perry Ellis Award: Anna Sui

1993

Womenswear Designer of the Year: Calvin Klein

Menswear Designer of the Year: Calvin Klein

Perry Ellis Award for Womenswear: Richard Tyler

Perry Ellis Award for Menswear: John Bartlett

1994

Womenswear Designer of the Year: Richard Tyler

Perry Ellis Award for Womenswear: Victor Alfaro and Cynthia Rowley (tie)

Perry Ellis Award for Menswear: Robert Freda

1995

Womenswear Designer of the Year: Ralph Lauren

Menswear Designer of the Year: Tommy Hilfiger

Perry Ellis Award for Womenswear: Marie-Anne Oudejans for Tocca

Perry Ellis Award for Menswear: Richard Tyler / Richard Bengtsson and Edward Pavlick for Richard Edwards (tie)

1996

Womenswear Designer of the Year: Donna Karan

Menswear Designer of the Year: Ralph Lauren

Perry Ellis Award for Womenswear: Daryl Kerrigan for Daryl K.

Perry Ellis Award for Menswear: Gene Meyer

1997

Womenswear Designer of the Year: Marc Jacobs

Menswear Designer of the Year: John Bartlett

Perry Ellis Award for Womenswear: Narciso Rodriguez

Perry Ellis Menswear Award Nominees: Sandy Dalal

1998/1999

Womenswear Designer of the Year: Michael Kors

Menswear Designer of the Year: Calvin Klein

Perry Ellis Award for Womenswear: Josh Patner and Bryan Bradley for Tuleh

Perry Ellis Award for Menswear: Matt Nye

AMERICAN INSTITUTE OF ARCHITECTS

AIA Gold Medal (The Board of Directors recognizes distinguished service to the architectural profession.)

1990 — E. Fay Jones

1991 — Charles W. Moore

1992 — Benjamin Thompson

1993 — Thomas Jefferson (honored posthumously); Kevin Roche

1994 — Sir Norman Foster

1995 — Cesar Pelli

1996 — No Winner

1997 — Richard Meier

1998 — No Winner

1999 — Frank O. Gehry

AMERICAN SOCIETY OF INTERIOR DESIGNERS

ASID Designer of Distinction Award (Recognizes an ASID interior designer who has made outstanding contributions toward achieving the organization's goal of design excellence.)

1990 — No winner

1991 — No winner

1992 — No winner

1993 — No winner

1994 — Charles D. Gandy

1995 — Andrew Staffelbach

1996 — Joseph Minton

1997 — Phyllis Martin-Vegue

1998 — Janet Schirn

1999 — Gary E. Wheeler

ASID Design for Humanity Award (Bestowed upon an individual or institution that has made a significant contribution toward improving the quality of the human environment through design-related activities.)

1990 — The Scavenger Hotline

1991 — E.I. Du Pont de Nemours & Company

1992 — The Preservation Resource Center

1993 — Neighborhood Design Center

1994 — Elizabeth Paepcke & The International Design Conference in Aspen

1995 — Cranbrook Academy of Art

1996 — Wayne Ruga and the Center for Health Design

1997 — Barbara J. Campbell, Accessibility Guidebook For Washington, D.C.

1998 — Wm. L. Wilkoff, FASID, District Design

1999 — AlliedSignal, Inc.-Polymers Division

MOTOR TREND CAR OF THE YEAR

1990 — Lincoln Town Car

1991 — Chevrolet Caprice Classic LTZ

1992 — Cadillac Seville Touring Sedan

1993 — Ford Probe GT

1994 — Ford Mustang

1995 — Chrysler Cirrus

1996 — Dodge Caravan

1997 — Chevrolet Malibu

1998 — Chevrolet Corvette

1999 — Chrysler 300M

DEATHS

Herbert L. Beckwith, 94, architect, helped design eleven buildings on the campus of the Massachusetts Institute of Technology, where he introduced modern architecture and worked as a professor, 3 June 1997.

Pietro Belluschi, 94, modernist architect, designed the glass and aluminum Commonwealth Building in Portland, Oregon (1947), which is considered the first glass curtain-wall structure in the United States; a former dean at the Massachusetts Institute of Technology School of Architecture and Planning; and recipient of the 1972 AIA Gold Medal, 14 February 1994.

Samuel Brody, 66, designer, partner in Davis, Brody, Chermayeff, Geismar, deHarak Associates; one of the leaders of the team that designed the U.S. Pavilion at Expo 70 in Osaka, Japan, 28 July 1992.

Gordon Miller Buehrig, 85, legendary automobile designer; helped design the Duesenberg Model J and Auburn Boattail Speedster in the 1920s and 1930s; in 1935 designed the Cord, which featured front-wheel drive and flip-top headlights; patented the T-top roof, 22 January 1990.

Gordon Bunshaft, 81, modernist architect; created landmark skyscrapers, museums, and libraries such as the Lever House in New York (1952), the Pepsi Cola Building (1960), and the Hirshhorn Museum in Washington (1974); won the Pritzker Prize in 1988 and was recognized for establishing the international style as the choice for corporate American architecture, 6 August 1990.

Joseph Esherick, 83, architect, designed some of the first Sea Ranch houses, designed the Cannery in San Francisco (1969) and the Monterey Aquarium (1980), taught for decades at the University of California at Berkeley, and won the AIA Gold Medal in 1989, 17 December 1998.

Roger Ferri, 42, architect, known for his theories integrating nature into buildings, 21 November 1991.

Lisa Fonssagrives-Penn, 80, Swedish-born fashion model in the 1940s and 1950s who posed for some of the most famous photographers of the age, including Irving Penn, whom she married in 1950, 4 February 1996.

Abraham W. Geller, 83, architect, designed office buildings and city projects, defended of social mission of modernism, 14 August 1995.

Bertrand Goldberg, 84, architect, in the early 1960s designed a pair of cylindrical apartment towers known as Marina City in Chicago, 8 October 1997.

Myron Goldsmith, 77, architect and engineer, designed the McMath-Pierce Solar Telescope facility at Kitt Peak in Arizona (1962), 15 July 1996.

John Graham, 82, architect, helped design the six-hundred-foot Space Needle in Seattle for the 1962 World's Fair, 29 January 1991.

Halston (Roy Halston Frowick), 57, designer, personified American fashions in the 1970s; dressed stars such as Candice Bergen, Liza Minnelli, and Elizabeth Taylor, as well as first ladies Jacqueline Kennedy and Betty Ford; also credited with introducing women to the pillbox hat, slinky jerseys, tunics, and ultrasuede, 26 March 1990.

Margot Byra "Margaux" Hemingway, 41, model and actress, granddaughter of Ernest Hemingway, 28 June 1996.

Arthur Cort Holden, 103, architect, principal in several firms during his lifetime; focused on housing and house financing, 18 December 1993.

Franklin D. Israel, 50, architect, used bold, colorful designs to embody the vibrancy of Hollywood, 10 June 1996.

A. Edwin Kendrew, 90, architect, former vice president of the Colonial Williamsburg Foundation, involved in restoring the historic site since 1926, 22 August 1993.

William J. Levitt, 86, contractor, changed the American landscape with his moderate-costing suburban housing developments known as Levittown, the first of which was built in 1947 on Long Island, New York; within four years, Levittown had 17,000 identical eight-hundred-square-foot, two-bedroom homes, 28 January 1994.

Jean Louis, 89, Oscar-winning designer, his fluid fashions were worn by Hollywood stars; designed the form-fitting, flesh-colored sequined gown worn by Marilyn Monroe when she sang "Happy Birthday" to President John F. Kennedy, 20 April 1997.

Charles Luckman, 89, architect and industrialist, his firm designed Madison Square Garden (1968); helped create the Prudential Center in Boston, Cape Canaveral Space Center in Florida, Johnson Space Center in Houston, Aloha Stadium in Hawaii, and the Lever House in New York, 25 January 1999.

Vera Maxwell, 93, sportswear designer, created the cotton jumpsuits for women working during World World II, and in 1974 designed the "Speed Suit" that, with no zippers or buttons, could be pulled on by busy women in seconds, 15 January 1995.

Charles Willard Moore, 68, architect, recipient of the AIA Gold Medal in 1991, 16 December 1993.

Lewis Mumford, 94, architectural critic, his articles appeared in *The New Yorker* and *Architectural Record,* author of *The Culture of Cities* (1938), 26 January 1990.

George Nakashima, 85, architect and master woodworker, called a "living national treasure" by the American Crafts Museum in New York, 15 June 1990.

Mollie Parnis (Livingston), 90ish, fashion designer, her dresses were worn by first ladies Mamie Eisenhower and Betty Ford, built a multimillion-dollar fashion business with her husband Leon Livingston, 18 July 1992.

Jay Pritzker, 76, architect and hotelier, founded the Hyatt chain, in 1979 established the Pritzker Architecture Prize (considered the most prestigious honor in the field), 23 January 1999.

Paul Marvin Rudolph, 78, architect, proponent of modernist architecture whose style was severe, monumental, and concrete; works included the Art and Architecture Building at Yale University, where he served as chairman of the architecture department, 8 August 1997.

Adele Simpson, 91, fashion designer, her popularity spanned more than three decades, from the late 1940s through the 1970s; her ladylike pieces were worn by first ladies Lady Bird Johnson, Pat Nixon, and Barbara Bush, as well as many Hollywood stars, 23 August 1995.

Brooks Stevens, 83, industrial designer, designed streamlined Studebakers, Harley-Davidsons, Evinrude outboard motors, and lawn mowers; also designed the fiberglass "Wienermobile" used by Oscar-Mayer to promote its hotdogs, 4 January 1995.

Ted Tingling, 79, British-born sportswear designer whose brightly colored dresses shocked the usually staid world of tennis; his designs were worn by top tennis players such as Billie Jean King, Rosie Casals, and Virginia Wade, 23 May 1990.

William Turnbull Jr., 62, architect, helped define the Northern California style through his buildings, which were often simple wooden structures; was best known for his Sea Ranch condominium project (1964), 26 June 1997.

Gianni Versace, 50, Italian designer who brought sex and glamour to his designs; counted Diana, Princess of Wales, Elizabeth Hurley, and Madonna among his clients, 15 July 1997.

Harry Mohr Weese, 83, Chicago architect who designed the Washington (D.C.) Area Mass Transit Authority subway system (1977), as well as the Time-Life Building in Chicago (1968), 29 October 1998.

PUBLICATIONS

Vilma Barr, *The Illustrated Room: 20th Century of Interior Design Rendering,* edited by Dani Antman (New York: McGraw-Hill, 1997).

The Fashion Book (London: Phaidon, 1998).

Philip Jodidio, *New Forms: Architecture in the 1990s* (Köln & New York: Taschen, 1997).

Richard Martin, ed., *Contemporary Fashion* (New York: St. James Press, 1995).

Kate Mulvey and Melissa Richards, *Decades of Beauty* (London: Hamlyn, 1998).

Anne Stegemeyer, *Who's Who in Fashion* (New York: Fairchild Publications, 1996).

Architectural Digest, periodical.

Architectural Record, periodical.

Architecture, periodical.

The restored Grand Central Station in New York City (AP/Wide World Photos)

GOVERNMENT AND POLITICS

by RICHARD H. FOSTER and ANNE M. MCCULLOCH

CONTENTS

Sidebars and tables are listed in italics.

1990

3 Jan. Manuel Antonio Noriega Moreno, dictator of Panama (1983–1989), is arrested on drug smuggling, racketeering, and money laundering charges.

1 June An agreement on armaments is reached at the U.S.–U.S.S.R. summit (30 May to 3 June) in Washington, D.C.

2 Aug. Saddam Hussein's Iraqi army seizes Kuwait; President George Bush freezes Iraqi and Kuwaiti assets in U.S. financial institutions; the United Nations (U.N.) calls on Iraq to withdraw.

7 Aug. U.S. Secretary of Defense Richard Bruce Cheney visits Saudi Arabia, and the United States sends the 82nd Airborne and several fighter squadrons to the Middle East.

22 Aug. President Bush calls up U.S. military reserves.

8 Nov. President Bush orders further military deployments to the Middle East.

20 Nov. A suit is filed by forty-five liberal Democratic legislators demanding that President Bush seek Congressional approval for military operations, but the suit is thrown out of court.

22 Nov. President Bush, his wife, Barbara Bush, and several cabinet officials visit servicemen in the Middle East for Thanksgiving.

29 Nov. The U.N. Security Council sets midnight Eastern Standard Time, 15 January 1991, as the deadline for Iraqi withdrawal from Kuwait; if that date is not met, force can be used by the allies to oust the invaders.

30 Nov. President Bush offers Iraq a diplomatic exchange to discuss the emergency.

1991

9 Jan. U.S. Secretary of State James Addison Baker III and Iraqi Foreign Minister Tariq Aziz meet in Geneva, Switzerland, with no resolution of the crisis in Kuwait.

12 Jan. The 102nd Congress passes Senate Joint Resolution 2, authorizing the President to use U.S. armed forces against Iraq pursuant to U.N. Security Council Resolution 678.

16 Jan. U.S. warplanes and missiles attack Iraq and occupied Kuwait in Operation Desert Storm.

13 Feb. U.S. bombers destroy a bunker in Baghdad sheltering several hundred Iraqi civilians; at least three hundred people die in the attack.

23 Feb. U.S. and U.N. ground troops invade Iraq.

25 Feb. Twenty-five U.S. servicemen are killed in an Iraqi missile attack on a barracks in Saudi Arabia.

27 Feb. One day after Kuwait is declared free of Hussein's soldiers, President Bush orders a cease-fire, as fleeing Iraqi troops surrender in massive numbers.

3 Mar. Iraq accepts terms and conditions of cease-fire.

1 Oct. The United States suspends assistance to Haiti following a military coup d'état on 30 September against democratically elected leftist Jean-Bertrand Aristide. U.S. officials are forced over the ensuing months to deal with a mass exodus of Haitians fleeing their country in boats.

6 Oct.	Anita Hill accuses Judge Clarence Thomas, who has been nominated to fill a seat on the U.S. Supreme Court, of sexual harassment.
15 Oct.	Thomas is confirmed as an associate justice of the Supreme Court by a Senate vote of fifty-two to forty-eight. He takes the judicial oath on 23 October.
20–23 Oct.	An out-of-control brush fire in the Oakland/Berkeley hills of California destroys more than 3,000 homes, kills 24 people, and leaves more than 150 injured.
18 Nov.	After years as hostages, Terry Waites (English) and Thomas M. Sutherland are freed by their Lebanese captors.
2–4 Dec.	Three remaining American hostages are freed in Lebanon by Syrian intervention. All western hostages will be released by 17 June 1992.

1992

26 Jan.	Arkansas Governor Bill Clinton, a candidate for the Democratic nomination for president, and his wife, Hillary Rodham Clinton, appear on CBS's *60 Minutes* to discuss rumors about their marriage.
1 Feb.	President Bush and Russian President Boris Yeltsin proclaim a formal end to the Cold War.
21 Feb.	The United States lifts trade sanctions against China.
16 June	Former Secretary of Defense Caspar W. Weinberger (1981–1987) is indicted for his actions in the Iran-Contra affair (1985–1986), a scandal that arose out of a secret deal by the Reagan administration to sell $30 million in arms to Iran in order to use the profits to fund covert activities in Nicaragua.
13 July	The Democratic National Convention, meeting in New York City, nominates Governor Clinton for president and Senator Al Gore (D-Tennessee) as vice president.
20 Aug.	The Republican National Convention, meeting in Houston, nominates President Bush for reelection, as well as his vice president, Dan Quayle.
24 Aug.	Hurricane Andrew, packing 150-mph winds, slams into the Florida coast, then hits Louisiana. With damage estimates of between $15 and 20 billion, it is the most costly hurricane in U.S. history.
3 Nov.	The Clinton-Gore ticket defeats the Bush-Quayle ticket.
24 Nov.	U.S. armed forces leave the Philippines after a presence there of nearly one hundred years.
24 Dec.	As his term in office nears an end, President Bush pardons all former Reagan officials who were involved in the Iran-Contra affair.

1993

20 Jan.	Bill Clinton is inaugurated as the forty-second president of the United States.
26 Feb.	A bomb explodes in the basement garage of the World Trade Center in New York City. Six people are killed and more than one thousand injured, many by smoke inhalation during the course of the evacuation.

19 Apr.	A fifty-one-day siege by the Federal Bureau of Investigation (FBI) and Bureau of Alcohol, Tobacco, and Firearms (ATF) of the Branch Davidian compound near Waco, Texas, ends in a fiery inferno, killing approximately eighty men, women, and children. Despite a federal hearing and a criminal trial, the cause of the conflagration is not determined.
June–August	The Mississippi River floods across nine states (North Dakota, South Dakota, Minnesota, Wisconsin, Iowa, Nebraska, Illinois, Kansas, and Missouri), causing fifty deaths and $10 billion in damage.
20 July	White House deputy counsel Vincent W. Foster Jr. is found dead of an apparently self-inflicted gunshot wound, in Fort Marcy Park, Virginia.
10 Aug.	Ruth Bader Ginsburg becomes the second woman to serve on the U.S. Supreme Court. She was nominated for the bench on 14 June.
17 Nov.	The House of Representatives approves the North American Free Trade Agreement (NAFTA). Four days later, the Senate also approves the pact.
30 Nov.	President Clinton signs the Brady Handgun Violence Prevention Act, which regulated firearm sales by requiring background checks for purchasers.

1994

17 Jan.	The Northridge, California, earthquake registers 6.6 on the Richter scale. Sixty-one people are killed and more than eight thousand others are injured.
3 Feb.	President Clinton ends the trade embargo against the Republic of Vietnam, which had been put into effect in 1975.
22 Apr.	Former President Nixon dies in a New York City hospital.
6 May	Paula Corbin Jones files suit in federal court charging President Clinton with having committed sexual harassment against her while he was governor of Arkansas.
6 Nov.	The Republicans sweep the midterm elections; on 4 January they take control of both houses of the U.S. Congress.
5 Dec.	Newton Leroy "Newt" Gingrich (R-Georgia) is chosen as Speaker of the House.

1995

14 Feb.	The alleged mastermind of the World Trade Center bombing, Ramzi Ahmed Yousef, is arrested in Pakistan and returned to the United States for trial.
21 Feb.	The United States approves a $20 billion aid package to help the ailing Mexican economy.
19 Apr.	A bomb hidden in a rental truck explodes outside the Alfred P. Murrah Federal Building in Oklahoma City and kills 168 people, including children at a daycare center in the structure.
Summer	Monica S. Lewinsky serves as an intern at the White House.

1996

8 Sept.	Senator Robert William "Bob" Packwood (R-Oregon) resigns under pressure because of charges of sexual harassment, obstructing an investigation, and conflict of interest for soliciting employment for his wife from influential constituents.
Dec.	The White House and Congressional Republicans joust over the national budget, resulting in the longest federal shutdown in U.S. history, twenty-two days, ending on 6 January 1996.

5 Mar.	Senator Robert Joseph Dole (R-Kansas) wins the Super Tuesday Republican primaries.
3 Apr.	Secretary of Commerce Ronald H. Brown and thirty-four others, including several CEOs of U.S. firms, are killed while on a trade mission when their plane crashes in Croatia.
6 Apr.	Lewinsky obtains a $33,000-a-year job in public relations at the Pentagon.
9 Apr.	President Clinton signs the Line-Item Veto bill.
14 Aug.	The Republican National Convention, meeting in San Diego, nominates Senator Dole for president and Representative Jack French Kemp (R-New York) for vice president.
26 Aug.	The Democratic National Convention, meeting in Chicago, nominates President Clinton and Vice President Gore.
21 Sept.	The Virginia Military Institute (VMI), a state-supported all-male military school, agrees to admit women.
5 Nov.	The Clinton-Gore ticket is reelected, but the Republicans retain control of Congress.
5 Dec.	President Clinton appoints Madeleine Korbel Albright as the first female Secretary of State.

1997

17 Jan.	Gingrich is found guilty of ethics violations ten days after being reelected as House Speaker.
20 Jan.	President Clinton is inaugurated for his second term in office.
4 Mar.	The Senate defeats the balanced-budget amendment.
8 Apr.	The U.S. Court of Appeals upholds a California ban on affirmative action.
28 July	The Clinton administration and Republicans agree on a balanced budget.
29 Oct.	U.S. members of a U.N. weapons-inspection team are expelled from Iraq.
2 Dec.	Attorney General Janet Reno decides that telephone calls made from the White House, allegedly for political purposes, by President Clinton and Vice President Gore do not warrant an independent investigation.

1998

21 Jan.	President Clinton denies an alleged affair with former White House intern Lewinsky.
3 Feb.	President Clinton proposes first balanced budget since 1973.
12 Feb.	The line-item veto is found unconstitutional by the U.S. Supreme Court.
25 June	President Clinton visits China.
25 July	Independent Counsel Kenneth W. Starr subpoenas President Clinton to testify in a grand jury investigation.
6 Aug.	Lewinsky testifies before the grand jury.
7 Aug.	Two bombs, believed to be the work of Muslim militants, explode at U.S. embassies in Kenya and Tanzania.
17 Aug.	President Clinton testifies before the grand jury and admits his affair with Lewinsky.
11 Sept.	Starr submits his report to Congress, outlining the basis for Articles of Impeachment against the president.
3 Nov.	The Democrats unexpectedly gain seats in Congress during the midterm elections.
9 Nov.	Gingrich resigns his office and seat in Congress.
9 Dec.	The House Judiciary Committee begins discussion on four articles of impeachment.
18 Dec.	U.S. planes drop bombs over Baghdad, Iraq in retaliation for violations of the U.N.-sanctioned no-fly zone.
	• The House of Representatives begins debate on the four articles of impeachment.
19 Dec.	The House of Representatives approves two articles of impeachment against President Clinton.
28 Dec.	House Speaker-elect Robert L. Livingston Jr. (R-Louisiana) resigns from Congress after revelations of marital infidelity.

1999

6 Jan.	The House of Representatives elects John Dennis Hastert (R-Illinois) as Speaker of the House.
7 Jan.	The U.S. Senate impeachment trial of President Clinton begins with Chief Justice William Hubbs Rehnquist presiding.
13 Jan.	President Clinton's legal team presents his defense.
12 Feb.	The Senate fails to convict President Clinton on the two articles of impeachment.
24 Mar.	The North Atlantic Treaty Organization (NATO) launches air attacks against Serbian forces occupying Kosovo.
7 May	NATO planes accidentally bomb the Chinese embassy in Belgrade.
31 Dec.	As many countries in the world prepare to celebrate the new millennium, they also wait to see if Y2K computer bugs will cause catastrophic upheaval in technology systems, including government systems.

OVERVIEW

Closing the Century. A retrospective analysis of the 1990s is a synopsis of the century. The twentieth century was dominated by wars that began and ended in the Balkans. It was a century during which people struggled to reform politics, yet never made much change; many doors of opportunity were opened to formerly disenfranchised groups, only to inspire more people (including women, gays, and the disabled) to demand civil rights. It was a century driven by a technological revolution that began on the assembly line, threatened a nuclear holocaust, and ended in cyberspace. Conservation was championed at the beginning of the century and environmentalism at its end.

A Decade of Change. The issues of war, political reform, scandal, civil rights, technology, and environmentalism that structured the century also framed debate during the 1990s. The decade began with the breakup of the Soviet Union, the demise of communism, and the end of the Cold War. These events, which seemed to some to foreshadow international peace by eliminating political ideology as a basis for enmity, simply removed the lid from old ethnic and religious quarrels. Without the heavy hands of the two superpowers, the United States and the Union of Soviet Socialist Republics (U.S.S.R.), to confine them, many ethnic groups struggled for independence, often fighting against their neighbors, or tried to regain old-but-not-forgotten land claims. The states of the former Soviet Union were most susceptible to these disputes, yet no place was more divided than Yugoslavia, with its multicultural, ethnic, and religious problems. As events around the world seethed, internationalism, a prerequisite of the Cold War, was again questioned by Americans as the threat of nuclear holocaust became seemingly remote. The tendency to move toward isolationism, which had never really disappeared from the American political landscape, reappeared both as a reluctance to become entwined again in world affairs and through an emphasis on domestic affairs rather than foreign issues. At home, the country was consumed by the politics of scandal at the White House, culminating in a presidential impeachment, while the economy roared through unprecedented growth. The civil rights movement evolved as women and racial minorities continued to gain ground to the point that many, including the U.S. Supreme Court, questioned the need for affirmative action policies.

Gay and lesbian rights also became a leading issue as a result of the decision by the Clinton administration to open the military to homosexuals through a "Don't Ask, Don't Tell" policy. Finally, the country was galvanized by a series of natural disasters that spared no region and led to new initiatives for environmental control and emergency preparedness.

New World Order. Since before the American Revolution (1775–1783), Americans defined themselves in part by their enemies. Native Americans on the frontier, the French, British, Mexicans, Spanish, Germans, and Soviets have all played the role of the adversary against whom Americans could test themselves and prove their patriotism. Whatever else they argued about, Jacksonians and Whigs, Democrats and Republicans could usually agree on who the bad guys were. In 1990, however, for the first time in its history, the United States stood without a clear adversary. Communism had been overthrown in virtually all of Eastern Europe and was on the wane in the Soviet Union. By the end of 1991 the Soviet Union no longer existed. It had been replaced by a Commonwealth of Independent States in which the Communist Party was but one among many competing voices, and nationalism, not communism, was the dominant ideology. Though still heavily armed and retaining their nuclear arsenal, the Russians, Ukrainians, and other heirs to the Soviet empire needed U.S. and Western help just to stay afloat. The Cold War was over. If the United States had not precisely won the conflict, the ideals for which it stood—individual freedom, democracy, and the rule of law—had evidently prevailed. Of the remaining communist powers, only the People's Republic of China, Vietnam, Cuba, and North Korea remained under the sway of ruling communist parties. China, though rejecting democracy, was hurrying to open her economic system to market forces.

Simmering Conflicts. When President George Bush called for a "new world order" to replace the ideological conflicts of the Cold War era, he envisioned a future in which global security would no longer be based on "mutually assured destruction" but on diplomacy and international commerce in a world no longer plagued by the threat of nuclear war. Francis Fukuyama, in the *End of History and the Last Man* (1992), even argued that the end of the

Cold War represented an "end of history." Using Georg Wilhelm Friedrich Hegel's theory that history is moved forward by conflict, the seeming triumph of capitalism and democracy removed the basis for future conflict. Human history, in its broadest sweep, at any rate, had reached its pinnacle. His assessment proved premature, however, and the new world order proved to be anything but free of conflict. Long-simmering ethnic and religious tensions in the Balkans, southeast Asia, and Africa exploded into open violence and genocide. The Balkan peninsula—especially the former Yugoslavia—became, as it had a century earlier, an ethnic powder keg. National and religious identity, not political ideology, provided the basis for violent confrontations in Croatia, Bosnia, and Kosovo in southern Europe, as well as in Rwanda and Congo in Africa and East Timor in Indonesia. The United Nations (U.N.) and the North Atlantic Treaty Organization (NATO) expanded their peacekeeping roles and U.S. soldiers, sailors, airmen, and marines joined multinational peacekeeping forces to restore and maintain peace around the world. Nuclear technology from the former Soviet Union, as well as conventional arms, proliferated. As the danger of global thermonuclear war receded, the likelihood of limited nuclear, biological, or chemical exchanges between small, poor, but well-armed adversaries increased. The world after the Cold War was dangerous and unpredictable. Cold War U.S. military and political institutions had to scramble to deal with new and unexpected threats to American and global security.

Gulf War. President Bush's first challenge of the post–Cold War era came quickly. Saddam Hussein, the unsavory but politically skillful president of Iraq, invaded his oil-rich neighbor, Kuwait, in August 1990 and threatened to seize oilfields in Saudi Arabia. Saddam's actions, from his perspective, had little to do with global politics. He had been tacitly supported by the United States in the long Iran-Iraq war and had been assured that his border dispute with Kuwait was not an issue in which the Bush administration wanted to get involved. Saddam saw an opportunity and assumed, with good reason, that the time was right. His attack across the long-disputed and poorly-defended Kuwaiti border had far-reaching implications, however, which he had not taken into account. He had upset the balance of power in the Middle East and threatened global oil supplies. His behavior seemed frighteningly similar to that of Adolf Hitler's fifty years earlier. Significantly, President Bush, who had been a teenager at the outset of World War II and a fighter pilot during the conflict, equated Saddam's attack on Kuwait with Hitler's seizure of Czechoslovakia, an act that had been allowed by great powers who were unwilling to go to war for such seemingly small stakes. Bush believed that allowing such behavior to go unchecked only invited further aggression. He mobilized U.S. forces and drew a "line in the sand," demanding Iraqi withdrawal from Kuwait; won approval for military actions from the U.N. Security Council and the U.S. Congress; and contacted virtually every world head of state, garnering cooperation and assistance from traditional allies and former

adversaries alike. More importantly, he persuaded Israel to remain neutral. Bush recognized that Israeli participation would have permitted Saddam to transform the conflict over Kuwait into a holy war against Israel, driving a wedge into the fragile coalition of Middle Eastern, American, and European allies. When the U.S.-led coalition invaded Iraq in January 1991 in Operation Desert Storm, Iraqi resistance collapsed before the overwhelming military might of the allies. Kuwait was freed, but Saddam remained in power, alternatively cooperating with and thumbing his nose at U.N. demands that he destroy Iraqi weapons of mass destruction and permit inspections of facilities for making nuclear, biological, and chemical weapons. What had seemed a splendid little war—short, victorious, and nonnuclear—continued to absorb American resources throughout the decade as American pilots tried to enforce U.N. resolutions that had formally ended the war but had not resolved the conflict.

Clinton Presidency. In 1992 Arkansas governor Bill Clinton, young and articulate but with little national political experience and a penchant for making lengthy speeches, seemed the longest of long shots to win the U.S. presidency. He won the Democratic nomination, however, in part because other viable candidates did not want to run against the incumbent, President Bush, who was fresh from a victory in the Gulf War and riding high in public-opinion polls. Although in foreign policy Bush was strong, the U.S. economy had soured during his administration, and Clinton—a consummate campaigner—exploited this weakness. Reading the mood of the electorate, he challenged Bush's domestic and economic record. Clinton was elected with a plurality of votes, aided in part by the third-party candidacy of H. Ross Perot, whose populism and bluff talk took many more voters from Bush than Clinton. Though he was full of energy and capitalized on his status as the first baby boomer in the White House, his first term did not begin well. He fulfilled his campaign promise to address healthcare reform by appointing his wife, Hillary Rodham Clinton, to chair a commission to study the issue and propose sweeping reforms. Its proposals pleased no one, Congress refused to act, and millions of working but uninsured Americans continued to live in fear of a sickness or injury that could leave them bankrupt. Clinton also tried to address the problems faced by homosexuals who served, or wanted to serve, in the military by instituting a "Don't Ask, Don't Tell" policy that virtually institutionalized hypocrisy and did little to protect gays. Nor did charges that he had dodged the draft during the Vietnam War help his standing as commander in chief. To many, President Clinton did not seem to act presidential during his first year in office. As a result, Republicans dominated the midterm elections in 1994 and took control of both houses of Congress. Republican Newton Leroy "Newt" Gingrich (R-Georgia), an aggressive and outspoken critic of the president, became Speaker of the House of Representatives and, for a time, took the policy initiative away from the White House, but he proved to be a better underdog than policy maker. When Congress and the President deadlocked on a budget and left the government temporarily broke, voters blamed the Republicans. Clinton, ever the master politician, portrayed himself as a moderate as the Republicans found themselves being pushed by their leadership further and further to the Right, which alienated moderate voters. It did not help that in the 1996 presidential election, Senator Robert Joseph Dole (R-Kansas) ran a lackluster campaign against Clinton's masterful one. In November 1996 Clinton won a second term in the White House. The economy was soaring and America was the only remaining superpower.

Scandals and Impeachment. The Clinton administration coincided with one of the longest periods of U.S. economic expansion in history. In an economy powered by a growing technology sector and low gasoline prices, unemployment fell and inflation remained negligible. Deficit spending, which had grown enormously in the 1980s, was replaced with a budget surplus. President Clinton arguably should have been the most popular executive since Dwight D. Eisenhower and might have been had his personal life not tarnished his reputation. Even as a Rhodes Scholar at Oxford University, Clinton had been plagued with rumors of sexual misbehavior. As governor of Arkansas he allegedly sexually harassed a young woman named Paula Corbin Jones. Such allegations might have gone nowhere had he and his wife, Hillary Rodham Clinton, not become caught up while he was governor in a failed land deal called Whitewater. Kenneth W. Starr, appointed under the independent prosecutor law to investigate the Whitewater affair, found instead a young White House intern, Monica S. Lewinsky, who had become involved sexually with the president. When Clinton apparently lied to a grand jury about his relationship with Lewinsky, Starr pressed the House of Representatives to impeach the president. After extensive and heavily televised hearings, the House voted to impeach, mostly along party lines. While most Americans condemned the president's behavior, they saw the impeachment proceedings as a politically motivated attempt at a coup d'état. In the midterm elections of 1998, in the midst of the impeachment crisis, the Republicans lost ground. Gingrich, taking responsibility for the defeat, resigned his speakership and House seat. The Senate, nevertheless, tried the case but failed to convict; Clinton's legacy, and perhaps the presidency, was besmirched by the process. Critics predicted that Clinton would be crippled by the impeachment and unable to govern effectively during his last two years in office. Yet, ever the "come back kid," he put the issue behind him and continued to lead effectively. The country prospered, and many Americans acknowledged that, while disapproving of his personal behavior, they could not argue with the results of his governance.

All Politics Are Local. Although Americans talked about the virtues of a limited government, they continued to expect a great deal for their tax dollars. With the end of the Cold War, Congress could no longer justify enormous defense budgets, and the Reagan Revolution made regular tax cuts a political necessity. Government spending, and thus services, had to contract. Communities that had depended on military bases and defense contracting faced economic hardship as bases were closed and spending programs curtailed. National parks were forced to cut back on services and started charging higher fees to visitors. Programs from the National Endowment for the Arts (NEA) to the National Aeronautics and Space Administration (NASA) scrambled to defend not only their spending but also their existence. Hardest hit were the poor, who bore the brunt of welfare and other spending reforms. Despite budgetary cutbacks, the government continued to respond to natural disasters. Victims of hurricanes along the Gulf Coast and the Carolinas, floods and droughts in the Midwest, and forest fires in the West found that agencies such as the Federal Emergency Management Administration (FEMA), National Guard, and the Coast Guard were ready to help in the difficult and often dangerous tasks of rescue, recovery, and relief. Americans continued to criticize the government in general but appreciated the efforts of such agencies in times of need.

TOPICS IN THE NEWS

AFTER THE COLD WAR

End of the Cold War. Political revolutions never just happen. Rather, they are part of processes that begin long before they are discernable by political scientists or historians. Cold War ideological and military competition began in 1945 in the aftermath of World War II. The Soviet Union had driven the Nazis out of Soviet territory, across Eastern Europe, and back into Germany. After the war the Soviets insisted on establishing friendly governments in all Eastern European nations occupied by its forces; they also subverted other governments and formed a Soviet empire stretching from the western sectors of Germany across Europe and Asia to the Pacific Ocean. Communist revolutions in China (1949) and Cuba (1959) seemingly added to their empire, at least as it was perceived in the West. From 1945 to 1989 there was constant ideological competition between the United States and the U.S.S.R. for allies. That struggle was especially intense in Africa and Asia as many

Former president George Bush (l) and former Soviet premier Mikhail Gorbachev discuss the end of the Cold War at a 9 October 1995 conference in Colorado Springs, Colorado (AP/Wide World Photos)

The United States and the members of the North Atlantic Treaty Organization (NATO) struggled to redefine its role after the collapse of the Soviet Union. One hot spot was the genocide occurring in Bosnia and Herzegovina. The following is a portion of an article by Paul C. Warnke, "Who Needs NATO? Bosnia Does—But is the Alliance Still Relevant?"

As French Foreign Minister Alain Juppe observed at yesterday's meeting, it is clear that everything still depends on the international community's ability to gather the means necessary to meet the responsibilities outlined in the communique. NATO is the one international institution with an integrated military command that can bring to bear force or the threat of force to end military conflict. As recently as last December, the NATO foreign ministers met—with France in attendance—and declared their willingness to support peacekeeping operations under the auspices of the United Nations or the Conference on Security and Cooperation in Europe (CSCE). They also agreed that NATO military authorities should be instructed to plan and prepare forces for such missions. Again, the rhetoric has not been matched by the response.

The traditional NATO reluctance to intervene "out-of-area," if it remains relevant anywhere, certainly should exercise no inhibiting effect in Bosnia. The former Yugoslavia is bounded by NATO countries to the west, the south and to the east. An expansion of the conflict into other remnants of that shattered land could even find two NATO countries, Greece and Turkey, taking opposing positions.

The disappointing reaction of our European allies to the recent attempts of Secretary of State Warren Christopher to forge a NATO consensus should not be taken as final, nor should a continued effort to bring NATO into serious engagement be feared as causing an alliance rift. It is, I believe, understandable that some of our European friends questioned whether the prescription then advanced by the United States—arming the Bosnian Muslims and attacking Serbian targets—is the best way to bring about peace. But NATO, as the primary European security instrument, can justly be called upon by the United States to come up with a military plan that its members deem more appropriate to meet the crying need for a peaceful solution.

At the foreign ministers meeting yesterday, additional steps were outlined to improve and enlarge the safe havens in Bosnia, to patrol the borders and to prevent the conflict from extending outside the borders of Bosnia-Herzegovina. The United States offered to assist in this effort, but not with ground troops. But none of this in itself is apt to scare the war lords or spare the Bosnian people. There will be no safe havens and no end to the slaughter unless and until significant military forces are introduced into the area. Only NATO can do it. A unilateral American venture is, and should be, out of the question. But the United States should press NATO to design and implement such a plan without delay. The forces would be deployed in a peace-enforcing mission, but with authority to take aggressive military action against any activity that seeks to interfere with that mission. The United States, of course, must do its part as a member of NATO. Russian participation should be encouraged.

The NATO deployment would remain while the contending factions work out whatever compromise arrangements they can all live with. Whatever the starting point, the eventual result would in all likelihood have to be a Bosnian government and military arm that reflect a Muslim majority. . . .

There can, of course, be no certainty that strong NATO intervention will do the job. But there is good reason to think that it very well might. Most bullies are cowards and the present aggressors have thus far been in a "no lose" situation. If they are faced with the fact that their continued violations of human rights and international law will cost them heavily, they could well reconsider their present policy.

Bosnia is not Vietnam; NATO intervention there would not involve misguided ideologically-driven war. Nor would it replicate the courageous Serbian guerrilla resistance to the Nazi invaders. Serbian and Croatian soldiers are now fighting for national survival. The security and independence of their own countries is not challenged. The fighting now is about carving up another country.

Source: *Congressional Record*, 139, part 8, 103rd Congress, 1st session (20 May 1993–27 May 1993), pp. 10929–10930.

Third World states became independent from European colonial rule. The superpowers also delighted in activities designed to destabilize regimes friendly to the other side. In addition, they maintained a military rivalry that included arming these new countries and interfering in their domestic politics, as well as maintaining a complex system of nuclear weapons and nuclear deterrence. This competition planted the seeds for the destruction of one superpower, however, as it was unable to keep up with its technologically dominant opponent.

Demise of the Soviet Union. In 1985 Mikhail Gorbachev became General Secretary of the Communist Party of the Soviet Union. He immediately recognized that there were two undeniable realities that made it impossible for the Soviet Union to continue the superpower competition. Not only was the gap between Soviet and U.S. technological abilities huge, but it was also widening, which suggested that the Soviet Union could not continue to compete with the Americans. This understanding led to the second undeniable truth—that the Soviet economic system was in such poor shape that it was not capable of the innovations and economic output necessary to continue to compete. Reform of the command economy was necessary, but it was only possible if the Soviets could first settle their major international disputes, which took huge portions of the industrial and economic resources of their country. In the late 1980s Gorbachev moved to reduce military and nuclear tensions with the United States and by 1989 had also signaled to the Eastern European states that they were on their own. People in those nations quickly overthrew leaders who clearly could not remain in power without Soviet arms to back them up. The Berlin Wall was opened on 9 November 1989 and by 1 January 1990 all Eastern European regimes were in transition away from Soviet-style dictatorships. The internal structure of the Soviet Union also began to unravel. The basis of its system, constructed by the Bolsheviks in the 1920s, was rule by the Communist Party, a centralized and command economy, and a multinational state—maintained by force if necessary. When Gorbachev challenged the system by instituting economic change, while loosening the Communist Party's hold on the political system, he knocked the props out from under the entire rickety structure. The new ideas were democracy, free-market capitalism, and ethnic nationalism. The Soviet system crumbled as former republics began to secede and the U.S.S.R. ceased to exist at the end of 1991. In its place stood Russia, Kazakhstan, Ukraine, Belarus, Turkmenistan, and ten additional states.

World Without Superpower Competition. The decade was one of transition, from a military struggle between two superpowers based on ideology and national identity to economic and technological competition between businesses and financial enterprises that were unconcerned about national boundaries. Leaders had to change their thinking in response to this new development but were often reluctant to do so. While the United States was the only remaining superpower, the real basis of its power was that it effectively plugged into the economic and technical "revolution without borders." The sudden end of the Cold War called into question most of the assumptions that had governed world politics in the previous forty-five years. At first there was a reluctance to recognize that everything had changed; then there was a brief period of euphoria, when many believed that a new era of multilateral cooperation to resolve international problems had emerged; but by mid decade a new understanding dawned that there would be even greater change. The Persian Gulf War (1991) strengthened the belief in multilateral approaches through the United Nations, but the debacle in Somalia (1992–1993) dashed those hopes. The end of apartheid and the move to majority rule in South Africa indicated that local issues could be peaceably resolved in part because they were removed from Cold War influence. Yet, ethnic violence in Rwanda, Indonesia, the former Yugoslavia, and republics of the former Soviet Union reminded the world that the rise of ethnically-based nationalism would inevitably create a host of new conflicts, many of which would require international intervention. This rise of nationalism and the reality of globalizing processes were two dominating and clashing forces in the post–Cold War era.

Clash of Traditional and Global Forces. There were two simultaneous and conflicting trends that defined the world in its transition from the Cold War. In *The Lexus and the Olive Tree* (1999), Thomas Friedman argues that the car known as the Lexus symbolizes those parts of the world that are trying to globalize to compete not just in local markets, but around the world. The olive tree symbolizes that there are still many unresolved conflicts over who owns the ancient olive tree: conflicts concerning territory, nationality, past ethnic grievances, and the like. What made globalization so complicated as the world entered the twenty-first century was that some elements in a country will be concerned with "Lexus" and others with "olive tree" issues—sometimes both at the same time, even though they seem to be mutually exclusive. Many international concerns in the 1990s were from the "olive tree" branch of the equation. The difficulties in the ongoing peace process between Israel and its neighbors, including the Palestinians, were about who gets what land and at what cost. Similarly, ethnic conflicts in central Africa and the former Yugoslavia were traditional ones based on old animosities, competing claims, and a repetitive cycle of killing and oppression. In many ways the irony of the end of the Cold War was that it made the world safe for a resurrection of ethnic conflicts. Although there were some efforts to moderate these clashes (Kosovo, Bosnia), in many cases multilateral efforts were too little, too late, or not made at all (Rwanda, East Timor, and Chechnya). Issues of human rights were discussed at length at international conferences and in the media, but it became clear that people could not agree on the definition of human rights, what constituted abuses, or what solutions might be workable, should agreement be reached.

Globalization. Countries, markets, and technologies around the world were being integrated. Old ideas and animosities only got in the way of globalization, and countries that insisted on hanging on to old ways were being bypassed by the global system. Those that accepted the fact that the driving idea behind globalization was free market capitalism, and that organized their society and economy to allow the transparency required by free market systems, were more successful economically. Others that failed to do so fell deeper into an abyss of continued violence and poverty and were left behind by nations willing to become part of the global system. The last years of the decade were a struggle for those elites who were unsure of where they stood; they faced a dilemma. Often they were in power because of the support of traditional elites, and this base was threatened by the globalizing process. To not join the global system, however, would confine their country to a backward status—a difficult choice for many leaders.

Sources:

George Bush and Brent Scowcroft, *A World Transformed* (New York: Knopf, 1998).

Thomas L. Friedman, *The Lexus and the Olive Tree* (New York: Farrar, Straus and Giroux, 1999).

William R. Keylor, *The Twentieth-Century World: An International History,* fourth edition (New York: Oxford University Press, forthcoming).

BUSH'S GULF WAR

Kuwait. On 2 August 1990 the Iraqi army moved into neighboring Kuwait and seized control of the oil-rich sheikdom. The United States and Western Europe were caught off guard by the unprovoked action, which threatened not only the world supply of oil but also the stability of the Middle East. These Western nations immediately sought a United Nations (U.N.) resolution condemning the action of Iraq. Saddam Hussein, the Iraqi leader, was surprised by the Western reaction, because scarcely a week earlier (25 July 1990) U.S. ambassador April C. Glaspie had told him that the Iraq/Kuwait border dispute was an Arab, not American, issue. This interchange, a classic case of cultural miscommunication, ultimately resulted in war. Hussein thought he had been clear about his intentions; the ambassador thought Hussein was merely restating an old internal dispute. Once Iraq acted, however, the West could not ignore the situation.

Desert Shield. The U.N. coalition against Iraqi militarism was formed and led by President George Bush, who demonstrated his ability to deal with international relations. Bush contended that U.S. political and economic positions in the Middle East were threatened by the Iraqi action. First, Iraqi militarism threatened the balance of power in the Middle East. The United States had for two decades walked a delicate path in trying to balance Arab and Israeli interests. The Iraqi action had the potential of coalescing the Arab states in opposition to the West and Israel. Bush recognized the need for a swift response and dubbed his plan Operation Desert Shield. He worked in conjunction with British prime minister John Majors to get the support of the United Nations for economic and military sanctions. On 19 August 1990 the U.N. declared the Iraqi annexation of Kuwait invalid, and on 25 August it authorized military interdiction. Bush also worked quickly to support Saudi Arabia, which was threatened by Hussein's action and which Bush needed as a staging area for military actions against Iraq. Ultimately Bush was able to get not only Saudi Arabian cooperation, but also that of most Arab states in the region. Bahrain, Egypt, Kuwait, Oman, Qatar, Saudi Arabia, and Syria all contributed men and munitions in the fight against Iraq. The lone exception was Jordan, which felt particularly vulnerable in its geographic location between Israel and Iraq. In the meantime, Bush pressured Israel not to act hastily. It had long been rumored that Israel had developed nuclear bomb technology, and the United States did not want the situation to escalate to the point where they would be impelled to use it. Furthermore, the world supply of oil was threatened by Iraq. Kuwait had been a leading supplier of oil to Europe and Asia; Iraqi control of Kuwaiti oil fields, along with its own immense oil resources, would put much of the world at the mercy of the highly unpredictable Hussein. Because of the threat to world peace and the oil supply, Bush "drew a line in the sand." The United States told Iraq that if it did not withdraw its armies from Kuwait by 15 January 1991 that the United States and United

AIR WAR IN THE PERSIAN GULF

On 29 January 1991 U.S. pilot Michael Donnelly recorded a sortie:

Today I flew a 3.6-hour sortie into southern Iraq against the Republican Guard. We dropped four CBU-87s each. The most impressive thing was that there was a steady flow of A/C into the area. Bombs are falling there 24 hours a day.

There was very little in the way of air defense there. We dropped our bombs on a concentration of vehicles. There were a lot of things burning on the ground. The A-10s were in there killing tanks. The Iraqi Army cannot hide. They are being obliterated. Hussein must not know what is really happening there.

This is so easy, there must be something going on behind the scenes. We are all wondering what the trick will be that Hussein will pull out next. I'm betting it is chemicals. I hope not.

I wonder if I killed anyone today. I don't worry about it much, though. I think of it more as dropping bombs on things instead of people. I'm trying to destroy their ability to fight. I'm saving the life of our boys down on the ground every time I take out some of them. Besides, they sure as hell are trying to kill me, too! I don't intend on letting them. That is all cold hard fact.

Every day I fly, my heart rate jumps up, my nerves are on edge and I take everything and everyone seriously. When I cross the border into Iraq/Kuwait, it's the most alert, cautious and intense time of my life. Everything depends on it. I'm fighting for everything I believe in. I love you, Sue and Erin. My family must be going crazy at home. I wonder where Tim is now.

Source: Michael Donnelly, with Denise Donnelly, *Falcon's Cry: A Desert Storm Memoir* (Westport, Conn.: Praeger, 1998), pp. 108–109.

Nations would take retaliatory action. At this point the United States moved five hundred thousand land, air, and naval forces into the Middle East and prepared for war.

Desert Storm. Despite the "rattling of sabers," Iraq had reason to believe that it might be able to hold on to Kuwait. Its leaders, however, overestimated their own military strength and underestimated U.S. resolve. The military might of Iraq was considered by many observers to be the strongest in the Arab world—its army had spent ten years fighting Iran over the oil fields on their common border. Iraq was well prepared for war. Hussein's elite Republican Guard had a fearsome reputation as a first-rate fighting force. The Central Intelligence Agency (CIA) also had evidence that Iraqi agents were developing biological, chemical, and nuclear weapons. It was assumed that Hussein would not hesitate to use them. The Iraqis also questioned the resolve of the United States to enter into a bloody and protracted war. The legacy of Vietnam still affected American attitudes toward war. From August, when President Bush announced Desert Shield, until January 1991 there was continuous

A U.S. soldier guarding destroyed vehicles that were driven by Iraqis escaping from Kuwait City during the Persian Gulf War (AP/Wide World Photos)

debate in Congress and among the American people about the wisdom of waging a war with Iraq. Those opposed to the use of force argued that vital U.S. interests were not being threatened and that the administration was using the military to protect oil that was destined for Japan and Europe, not the United States. Those supporting armed intervention argued that vital interests were involved with Israel and Saudi Arabia and that if the United States did not intervene at this time, Iraq could control the Middle East and threaten the existence of the Jewish state. The debate continued until 12 January when a vote on the resolution supporting armed intervention in Kuwait and Iraq was passed by Congress. In the end, most of the lawmakers supported the president for fear that any other action would demonstrate weakness and possibly weaken U.S. credibility in foreign diplomacy. On 16 January 1991, U.S. missiles and warplanes began attacking the capital city, Baghdad, and other military targets in Iraq. The army had projected that the war would last many months and cost thousands of lives. Luckily the estimates were greatly overstated. The missile attacks, which preceded ground deployment, were effective, and by the time troops invaded Iraq and Kuwait on 23 February 1991, they met little resistance. On 27 February President Bush ordered a cease-fire at midnight Kuwaiti time, and on 3 March Iraq formally accepted these terms.

Aftermath. President Bush successfully restored American prominence in the world. He had managed to keep the Israelis out of the conflict by convincing them they could rely on U.S. protection. He guided the U.N. through this action. In May 1991 he had one of the highest ratings in popularity polls ever registered by a U.S. president. He looked like a

certainty for reelection in 1992; yet, that did not happen. The terms of the peace agreement imposed a no-fly zone over Iraq, installed economic sanctions, and required inspections of military installations by U.N. teams. It also allowed Hussein to remain in power in Iraq. Unbowed, Hussein continued to test the resolve of the United States and U.N. by attacking Kurdish settlements in Iraq; failing to cooperate with U.N. inspection teams as they looked for evidence of nuclear, biological, or chemical weapons of mass destruction; and generally resisting all efforts to undermine his power. What seemed Bush's greatest triumph became his biggest headache. Hussein was one of the issues that Arkansas governor Bill Clinton used to attack and ultimately defeat Bush in the 1992 presidential election. Yet, in his eight years in the White House, Clinton was no more successful than Bush was with Hussein. The decade ended as it had begun, with Hussein still in power in Iraq.

Sources:

W. Lance Bennett and David L. Paletz, eds., *Taken by Storm: The Media, Public Opinion, and the U.S. Foreign Policy in the Gulf War* (Chicago: University of Chicago Press, 1994).

Otto Friedrich, ed., *Desert Storm: The War in the Persian Gulf* (Boston: Little, Brown, 1991).

Mark Grossman, *Encyclopedia of the Persian Gulf War* (Santa Barbara, Cal.: ABC-CLIO, 1995).

THE ELECTION OF 1992

Clinton Elected. Governor Bill Clinton (D-Arkansas) was sworn in as the forty-second president of the United States on 20 January 1993, after a close race against the Republican incumbent George Bush. The victory was most surprising because of President Bush's

1992 PRESIDENTIAL ELECTION

State	Clinton Votes	Pct.	Bush Votes	Pct.	Perot Votes	Pct.	Electoral Vote* Clinton	Bush
Alabama	686,571	41	798,439	48	180,514	11	0	9
Alaska	63,498	32	81,875	41	55,085	27	0	3
Arizona	525,031	37	548,148	39	341,148	24	0	8
Arkansas	498,548	54	333,909	36	98,215	11	6	0
California	4,815,039	47	3,341,726	32	2,147,409	21	54	0
Colorado	626,207	40	557,706	36	362,813	23	8	0
Connecticut	680,276	42	575,778	36	347,638	22	8	0
Delaware	125,997	44	102,436	36	59,061	21	3	0
District of Columbia	186,301	86	19,813	9	9,284	4	3	0
Florida	2,051,845	39	2,137,752	41	1,041,607	20	0	25
Georgia	1,005,889	44	989,804	43	307,857	13	13	0
Hawaii	178,893	49	136,430	37	52,863	14	4	0
Idaho	136,249	29	201,787	43	129,897	28	0	4
Illinois	2,379,510	48	1,718,190	35	832,484	17	22	0
Indiana	829,176	37	970,457	43	448,431	20	0	12
Iowa	583,669	44	503,077	38	251,795	19	7	0
Kansas	386,832	34	444,599	39	310,458	27	0	6
Kentucky	664,246	45	616,517	42	203,682	14	8	0
Louisiana	815,305	46	729,880	42	210,604	12	9	0
Maine	261,859	39	207,122	31	205,076	30	4	0
Maryland	941,979	50	671,609	36	271,198	14	10	0
Massachusetts	1,315,016	48	804,534	29	630,440	23	12	0
Michigan	1,858,275	44	1,587,105	37	820,855	19	19	0
Minnesota	998,552	44	737,649	32	552,705	24	10	0
Mississippi	392,929	41	481,583	50	84,496	9	0	7
Missouri	1,053,040	44	811,057	34	518,250	22	11	0
Montana	153,899	38	143,702	36	106,869	26	3	0
Nebraska	214,064	30	339,108	47	172,043	24	0	5
Nevada	185,401	38	171,378	35	129,532	26	4	0
New Hampshire	207,264	39	199,623	38	120,029	23	4	0
New Jersey	1,366,609	43	1,366,609	41	505,698	16	15	0
New Mexico	259,500	46	212,393	38	91,539	16	5	0
New York	3,246,787	50	2,241,283	34	1,029,038	16	33	0
North Carolina	1,103,716	43	1,122,608	44	353,845	14	0	14
North Dakota	98,927	32	135,498	44	70,806	23	0	3
Ohio	1,965,204	40	1,876,445	39	1,024,598	21	21	0
Oklahoma	473,066	34	592,929	43	319,978	23	0	8
Oregon	525,123	43	394,356	32	307,860	25	7	0
Pennsylvania	2,224,897	45	1,778,221	36	896,177	18	23	0
Rhode Island	198,924	48	121,916	29	94,757	23	0	4
South Carolina	476,626	40	573,231	48	138,140	12	0	8
South Dakota	124,861	37	136,671	41	73,297	22	0	3
Tennessee	933,620	47	840,899	43	199,787	10	11	0
Texas	2,279,269	37	2,460,334	40	1,349,947	22	0	32
Utah	182,850	45	320,559	45	202,605	29	0	5
Vermont	125,803	46	85,512	31	61,510	23	3	0
Virginia	1,034,781	41	1,147,226	45	344,852	14	0	13
Washington	855,710	44	609,912	32	470,239	24	11	0
West Virginia	326,936	49	239,103	36	106,367	16	5	0
Wisconsin	1,035,943	41	926,245	37	542,660	22	11	0
Wyoming	67,836	34	79,558	40	51,209	26	0	3
Total	**43,728,275**	**43**	**38,167,416**	**38**	**19,237,247**	**19**	**370**	**168**

Source: *Facts on File* (5 November 1992), p. 827.

Hillary Rodham Clinton, President-elect Bill Clinton, Vice President-elect Al Gore, and Tipper Gore (l. to r.)
in front of the Old State House in Little Rock, Arkansas, celebrate their victory in the 1992
presidential election (AP/Wide World Photos)

popularity. Nevertheless, a slowing economy during the intervening months and a cutthroat three-way race among Clinton, Bush, and H. Ross Perot (I) allowed the victor to take office with 43.3 percent of the vote, while Bush garnered 37.7 percent and Perot took 19 percent. Clinton was a masterful campaigner and Bush failed to adequately defend his presidency. There was also a large measure of luck. Niccolò Machiavelli wrote in *The Prince* (1513) that one-half of success is based on ability and one-half on fortune (luck). Clinton's election in 1992 was a dramatic illustration of Machiavelli's observations—both ability and luck played critical roles.

The Campaign Staff. The foremost factor in Clinton's election was an especially talented and aggressive campaign staff led by James Carville, who recognized that the most critical issue for American voters was the economy. He hung a sign at campaign headquarters in Little Rock, Arkansas, which read: "It's the economy, stupid!" That slogan came to epitomize the central theme of the campaign and of the Clinton administration over the next eight years. The economy was in a slowdown after flying high in the 1980s; unemployment was higher than it had been since 1984; the Soviet menace was removed with the crumbling of the Berlin Wall

in 1989; and the Persian Gulf War had stabilized relations in the Middle East. Safe from an international threat, Americans were concerned with their pocketbooks. The Clinton campaign, more than its opponents, recognized the longing of many Americans for domestic tranquility and prosperity. The campaign staff also masterfully used the latest in communication technology to disseminate their message. They made use of fax machines and e-mail to rapidly communicate with the news media and campaign staffers around the country. Proficiency in the new technology gave Clinton and his staff a great advantage over their opponents' slower response mechanisms. Rumors could be, and were, squelched by rapid-fire, mass-fax responses, which prevented the media from being gatekeepers. Clinton's campaign staff was later rewarded: he made George R. Stephanopoulos, his Deputy Campaign Manager and Director of Communications, the Senior Adviser for Policy and Strategy; Dee Dee Myers became the first female White House press secretary; and longtime friend and adviser, Thomas "Mack" McLarty, became Chief of Staff. Carville, however, declined to take a position in the administration. Clinton's brilliant campaign staff did not fare well as part of his administration and before his first term was up, he found it necessary to replace almost all of the 1992 staffers and Arkansas cronies with more seasoned Washington politicians.

Bush. The second factor in Clinton's win was President Bush's style. Bush had a stellar resume: war hero, businessman, congressman, diplomat, vice president, and president. What he lacked was charisma—something both of his 1992 opponents had in abundance. His self-professed understated style was further reinforced by the lackluster campaign his staff ran. Not expecting to have any real competition, it was unprepared for the hard-hitting, aggressive style of campaigning waged by Clinton, whose staff painted Bush as an internationalist who knew more about foreign affairs than about the domestic struggles of common Americans. His aristocratic background and preppy demeanor did little to negate the images of Bush's aloofness in the average voter's mind. Clinton's down-home image—he grew up in the little town of Hope, Arkansas—was played up. Even his ivy-league education (B.A., Georgetown University, 1968; Rhodes Scholar, Oxford University, 1968–1970; and LL.B., Yale Law School, 1973) was portrayed as "the poor boy makes good"—a modern-day version of the Horatio Alger myth. Americans were cajoled into believing Clinton was just a "good ole boy." When he selected another baby boomer from the South, Senator Al Gore (D–Tennessee), as his running mate, observers hailed the tandem as the "Bubba" ticket, even though Gore had spent most of his life in Washington, D.C., as son of former senator Albert Gore Sr. The election was largely a campaign of image, not substance. Clinton created it; Carville sold it. Bush tried to recover by firing his campaign manager, but it was too late. Without the assistance of Harvey Leroy "Lee" Atwater, the mastermind of negative campaign tactics, who had died in 1991, Bush struggled while Perot hammered him about breaking his promise not to raise taxes, and Clinton painted him as a "wimp." Unable to deflect these attacks with a humorous quip like President Ronald Reagan used to do, Bush was left with the undeserved image of being untrustworthy, and Clinton won the election as another "teflon" president.

Perot. H. Ross Perot was a self-made billionaire iconoclast whose forays in politics included working for the freedom of American POWs in Vietnam, organizing a prison rescue mission in Iran, and spearheading a war on drugs in Texas. Sensing the alienation among many voters with the two major political parties, Perot organized United We Stand America as a platform for pressing his agenda and for a run for the presidency. His unorthodox views and methods made him attractive to the independent voter. Though Perot's 19 percent share of the total vote was not sufficiently strong in any single state to garner him any electoral votes, it was strong enough to influence the outcome of the election by seizing votes from Bush. Many observers believed that Bush would have won had Perot not been the "spoiler." With-

out Bush to attack, Perot turned his criticism on Clinton, remaining a thorn in his side through to the 1996 election, when he again challenged for the presidency under the banner of a newly formed Reform Party. Bush retired to his home in Kennebunkport, Maine, leaving a power vacuum in the Republican Party leadership that was quickly seized by Representative Newton Leroy "Newt" Gingrich (R–Georgia), who became a powerful foe of Clinton. In the end Clinton discovered, like many before him, that getting elected and governing are two different games.

Sources:

John William Cavanaugh, *Media Effects on Voters: A Panel Study of the 1992 Presidential Election* (Lanham, Md.: University Press of America, 1995).

Michael Nelson, ed., *The Election of 1992* (Washington, D.C.: Congressional Quarterly Press, 1993).

HEALTH CARE DEBATE

Major Debate. Health-care reform was one of the first and most divisive major-policy initiatives of the Clinton administration. Health care first became a public policy issue for Americans after World War II, when President Harry S Truman advocated national health insurance. The American Medical Association (AMA), however, vigorously opposed it, and it was not until 1965 that Medicare and Medicaid were finally established, covering retired persons and those on welfare, respectively. The remainder of the population was still responsible for paying for its own health care either through employers or out-of-pocket. The working poor were most at risk under these conditions because they did not qualify for Medicaid and generally did not work for employers that offered medical insurance. From the 1960s to the 1980s, health-care costs continued to rise because of inflationary trends and technological advances. By the 1990s even employers who furnished health-care plans found it difficult to continue to provide the level of protection to which workers had become accustomed without raising copayments and/or lowering benefits. Health maintenance organizations (HMOs) entered into this environment with the promise of lowering insurance costs by focusing on preventive care rather than corrective medicine. Though the premise was sound—save money by preventing expensive health problems—it assumed long-term cost savings that did not necessarily materialize in the short run. Other forms of cost savings had to be found. HMOs pursued efficiency by requiring that nonroutine procedures be authorized by insurance companies before being completed. Family doctors were replaced by medical groups, which lowered overhead but tended to make care impersonal. Despite the reduction in personal attention, costs continued to rise, as did insurance premiums.

Clinton's Task Force. President Clinton perceived that the political environment was ripe for a bold new plan of universal health care for all Americans. He chose the First Lady, Hillary

In April 1994, Representative Henry A. Waxman (D-California) chaired a congressional subcommittee that looked into the tobacco industry. The following is a portion of a report by Michael Wines on one of the hearings:

It was extraordinary, not so much for its telling blows—there were few—as for the spectacle of so many Grants and Lees matching hyperbole with obfuscation, graph with statistic, carefully calculated outrage with carefully calculated hurt.

It was also a battle that the tobacco industry—hauled onto Mr. Waxman's turf to defend a business that the Government blames for 400,000 deaths every year—could not, despite its best efforts, hope to win.

"It's theater," one contemptuous public-relations adviser to a cigarette maker, who demanded anonymity, said of Mr. Waxman's hearing. "What are they going to do next, bring out the goat boy?"

It was indeed theater, staged expertly by Mr. Waxman, a California Democrat who is an implacable foe of cigarette makers.

His staff placed television cameras so that the only shot of the nation's seven tobacco scions—leaders of Philip Morris U.S.A., the R. J. Reynolds Tobacco Company, the United States Tobacco Company, the Lorillard Tobacco Company, the Liggett Group Inc., the American Tobacco Company, the Brown & Williamson Tobacco Corporation—captured a huge placard directly on their left.

It read, "One American dies every 80 seconds from tobacco use," and was periodically replaced by charts depicting rising nicotine levels in cigarettes and grisly photographs of oral cancer.

Mr. Waxman's Democratic allies on the panel, like Representatives John Bryant of Texas and Mike Kreidler of Washington, bore their own arms. Mr. Bryant read a wrenching letter from a Florida woman Pat McLaughlin, whose father had died of emphysema "with a cigarette in his hand."

". . . You know, it would be hard for me to imagine that there's one of you gentlemen sitting here that has ever witnessed something like that," he said. "It's progressive. It just goes until you die. You can't get any breath."

By and large, the tobacco company executives did not explicitly deny that cigarettes were potential killers. Their defense was instead to deny that cigarettes caused any specific deaths, and to couch the entire topic of cancer, and emphysema and dying in the subdued locutions of scientists or sales marketers.

"I really don't accept that smoking is addictive," William I. Campbell, president of Philip Morris, told Mr. Kreidler, then added, "In terms of your own family situations, I can only feel the same kind of remorse that you reflect."

The chairman of R. J. Reynolds, James W. Johnston, told Mr. Kreidler: "I am sorry to hear about the McLaughlin family situation. I do not believe that Mr. McLaughlin was addicted to cigarettes." He later said that cigarettes were a "risk factor," but left unsaid what the risks were.

"Oral tobacco has not been established as a cause of mouth cancer," U.S. Tobacco's president, Joseph Taddeo, said seconds after being told that users of snuff were 50 times more likely to develop oral cancer than those who abstained.

When accused by Mr. Waxman of deliberately making cigarettes with high nicotine levels, so as to addict smokers, Mr. Johnson said nicotine was not addictive, but had a "mild pharmacological intent." An industry scientist testified that manufacturers monitored the nicotine level in cigarettes not to gauge their addictive potential, but to achieve "the target taste profile in the end product."

Mr. Waxman and others largely refused to accept the explanations. They cut off the executives in mid-sentence, mocked their answers and accused them of lacking corporate responsibility and distorting the truth.

Source: *The New York Times* (15 April 1994).

Rodham Clinton, to take the lead in overhauling the $915 billion health-care system and extending care to thirty-seven million uninsured Americans. Clinton trusted her abilities and she was anxious to make a new role for the First Lady as policy maker. While she had a sharp, analytical mind, it was the mind of a lawyer, not a politician—she made some early and critical mistakes. A blue-ribbon task force was organized to come up with a health plan, but she chose not to include any representatives from the AMA or the hospital administration field among its 511 members. She also chose to hold meetings in secret. These two decisions left the committee and her open to charges of attempting to undermine the democratic process and covertly promote a socialist agenda. The committee also had problems meeting its deadlines. President Clinton initially imposed a one-hundred-day deadline for the report; however, it was changed when the First Lady's father died. The report finally came out in September 1993 and was introduced into Congress in late October, but it was dead on arrival. The insurance industry and Republican Party had organized a media blitz against the plan, calling it "socialized medicine" and claiming that it would do away with a patient's freedom to choose his or her own doctor.

Health Security Act. The plan was not as bad as its critics charged. It had six major goals: security, comprehensive benefits, cost savings, quality care, individual choice, and paperwork reduction. Security would have been obtained by providing for "portability" of plans. Whenever a person lost or changed jobs, they would be allowed to take their plan to the next job. Comprehensive benefits focused on preventive health and included

With Senator Robert Joseph Dole (R-Kansas) listening, Hillary Rodham Clinton addresses reporters on Capitol Hill during the health-care debate, 30 April 1993 (AP/Wide World Photos)

screenings, physicals, and immunizations, as well as doctor visits, hospital care, emergency services, laboratory and diagnostic services, prescription drugs, mental-health care, hospice and home-health care, vision and hearing care, and children's dental care. It was projected that the plan would have been funded through employer and employee contributions, Medicare and Medicaid savings, federal taxes, savings through paperwork reduction, and fraud prevention. The plan was ambitious in its coverage and much too optimistic in its cost savings, particularly those it projected through Medicare and Medicaid. Ultimately, the possible benefits of the plan did not matter. After being introduced into Congress, it was assigned concurrently to several committees that held hearings over the next year. Parts of the plan eventually found their way into law, albeit in a different form, but most simply died in committee. Even President Clinton gave up supporting it, realizing it was a lost cause.

Reform Derailed. The failure of health-care reform was a classic example of what happens to public policies that have diffuse benefits and concentrated costs. The benefits of health-care reform would have been spread marginally over the whole population and would only be felt if someone were seriously ill. Since the probability of serious illness for any individual is unknown, the average person was not motivated to become politically active in the debate. Groups bearing the costs, for example, the doctors, hospitals, and insurance companies, had well-organized, well-heeled, experienced lobbyists who played on the fears of the weak and old. Even the American Association of Retired Persons (AARP), which had

initially supported Clinton's program, switched sides when its members began to fear that they would lose the option to choose their own doctors and other health-care providers. Without a strong support system among the public, lawmakers were unwilling to risk their political careers on the controversial proposal. Though a failure as legislation, the debate over health care continued throughout the decade.

Sources:
"The Health Security Act of 1993," *White House Electronic Publications,* 20 September 1993, Internet website.

Frank Marafiote, "In Sickness or in Health: Hillary Takes Charge," *Hillary Clinton Quarterly,* Internet website.

Bernard D. Reams Jr., ed., *Health Care Reform, 1993–1994: The American Experience: Clinton and Congress—Law, Policy, and Economics: A Legislative History of the Health Security Act* (Buffalo, N.Y.: Hein, 1996).

NATURAL DISASTERS

FEMA. Natural disasters are a relatively common occurrence in a country as large as the United States, yet the severity of the events in the 1990s was unusual. Floods, hurricanes, earthquakes, and tornadoes hit the United States repeatedly, causing billions of dollars in damage and taking many lives. These storms and resulting catastrophes tested the wherewithal of a new federal agency, the Federal Emergency Management Agency (FEMA), which had been established in 1979 to respond quickly to the needs of citizens suffering from a natural disaster. It was not until 1989 that FEMA was tested fully. Hurricane Hugo hit Charleston, South Carolina, in September 1989, causing $7 billion in damage. Because of the massive destruction caused by the hurricane, and the newness of FEMA, the

Federal Emergency Management Administration (FEMA) employees organizing boxes of toys donated to children in Raleigh, North Carolina, on 15 December 1999 following Hurricane Floyd (AP/Wide World Photos)

agency was unprepared to respond in a timely manner with sufficient resources. A second disaster hit scarcely a month later, on 17 October, when an earthquake measuring 6.9 on the Richter Scale rocked the Bay Area of California, damaging the Oakland Bay Bridge, causing fires in San Francisco, and collapsing a double-decker freeway. Known as the Loma Prieta earthquake, it killed more than 60 people, injured more than 3,700 others, displaced approximately 12,000 more, and caused direct damage estimated to be around $6.8 billion. Hoping not to repeat the errors of the South Carolina experience, FEMA rushed in supplies, yet again they were insufficient. Over the next ten years, FEMA had plenty of opportunities to perfect its operations as one disaster after another struck the nation.

South Struck Again. Hurricane Andrew was the first catastrophic storm of the 1990s. A category-five hurricane on the Saffir-Simpson Scale, it slammed into south Florida on 24 August 1992 with sustained winds in excess of 150 miles per hour. Homestead Air Force Base and the nearby town of Homestead were flattened. More than two million people were evacuated. After wrecking South Florida, Andrew headed out across the Gulf of Mexico and bore down on the Louisiana coast. It was only through luck that both Miami and New Orleans escaped the brunt of the storm. Had those cities been hit directly, the $26 billion in damage would have been even higher and more lives may have been lost. Nevertheless, twenty-six people died as a result of the storm, hundreds more were injured, and thousands lost all of their possessions.

Other Storms. A few weeks later a rare Pacific typhoon, Iniki, crashed ashore in Hawaii on the island of Kauai on 11 September 1992, resulting in nearly $2 billion in damage to the island. In March 1993 "the storm of the century" ravaged the East Coast with a late-winter storm that carried hurricane-force winds and left more than one hundred people dead. The following summer, June–August 1993, the worst flood to hit the Mississippi River valley in nearly two centuries inundated farmlands and communities from North Dakota to Missouri, causing more than $10 billion in damages and taking around fifty lives. An earthquake in Northridge, California, occurred in 1994, killing sixty-one people and injuring thousands. Over the next five years, hurricanes, tornadoes, floods, and wildfires continued to ravage the country and by the end of the decade, FEMA had spent more than $25 billion to help alleviate suffering. In addition to natural disasters, FEMA agents assisted at the site of the bombing on 19 April 1995 of the Alfred P. Murrah Federal Building in Oklahoma City.

Natural or Man-Made? The disasters of the 1990s were only partially attributable to climatic changes. They were mainly the direct result of poor planning on the part of individuals and governments to address the desire of a larger, wealthier population to live in areas subject to natural disasters. The hurricanes that struck during the decade were not only large and strong, but they also hit coastlines full of homes and vacation resorts rather than empty sea islands and marshes. The earthquakes were more costly because so many homes crowded along fault lines. The Mississippi floods were so damaging because there were no wetlands left to absorb the waters. It was evident that good emergency management was as much a function of prevention as relief. In 1997 FEMA and the Office of Energy Efficiency and Renewable Energy (EERE) of the Department of Energy (DOE) launched "Project Impact: Building Disaster Resistant Communities." Its purpose was to spread the idea of sustainable redevelopment, to help disaster-prone areas not only become safer and disaster resistant but also stronger and healthier from an environmental and economic standpoint. In the first two years of its operation, Project Impact began working with businesses and communities to improve their readiness for disasters. They developed a four-phase model, which leaders could use to make their communities less vulnerable, that involved building partnerships, assessing risks, prioritizing needs, and finally, keeping authorities informed of the actions taken. Special teams also inspected and assessed building materials and procedures to determine better construction methods. By becoming proactive, the federal government hoped to reduce property loss, just as improved weather forecasting had saved lives.

Sources:

FEMA.GOV, Internet website.

U.S. Senate, Committee on Governmental Affairs, *Rebuilding FEMA: Preparing for the Next Disaster: Hearing before the Committee on Governmental Affairs, United States Senate, 103rd Congress, first session, May 18, 1993* (Washington : U.S. GPO, 1994).

REPUBLICAN RENAISSANCE?

Gingrich. The congressional elections of 1994 resulted in a Republican landslide as voters across the country, angered by President Bill Clinton's liberal agenda and afraid of socialized medicine, turned en masse to the Republican candidates. Much of the credit for their success, however, must be attributed to Representative Newton Leroy "Newt" Gingrich (R-Georgia), who came to

---

FEMA FALLS SHORT

FEMA (Federal Emergency Management Agency), entrusted with coordinating emergency federal relief after a national disaster, faced a difficult task following the wake of Hurricane Andrew, which hit Florida on 24 August 1992. In May of 1993 the performance of the agency was investigated by a congressional committee.

In South Florida, State, local, and volunteer agencies fell far short of providing the amount of life-sustaining services needed in the immediate aftermath of Hurricane Andrew. For example, during the first 3 days after Hurricane Andrew, FEMA reports indicate that the combined efforts of Federal, State, local, and volunteer agencies provided enough meals to feed about 30,000 to 50,000 disaster victims a day, although Andrew left about 160,000 to 250,000 people homeless and potentially in need of mass care.

A number of disaster victims in South Florida told us that the relief effort was inadequate. They said that they survived by resorting to such actions as looting grocery stores to feed their families, drinking potentially contaminated water from leaking faucets, and staving off looters by living in makeshift dwellings set up in front of their homes.

In addition, local officials, who in many cases were victims of the storm, knew that they were unable to meet their citizens' needs for life-sustaining services. However, they were having trouble communicating with one another and with the State, and were unable to request specific quantities of assistance.

FEMA regional officials told us that they knew by the second day after the disaster that more resources beyond those of the American Red Cross would be needed to meet the mass care needs of the disaster victims. These officials then offered to provide the State with whatever assistance it requested. However, Florida did not immediately request significant amounts of additional mass care because it had the impression that the State/local/volunteer network was doing an adequate job. For example, according to the State official who co-managed Florida's emergency operating center, the American Red Cross officials informed him that it had established feeding centers in Homestead and Florida City. The Red Cross later learned that some of the mobile feeding units it sent to the areas were not able to reach these cities because debris was still blocking the roadways. In fact, Homestead and Florida City—perhaps the two hardest-hit areas—did not get large scale feeding operations until the military supplemented voluntary efforts with field kitchens there 5 days after the disaster.

By the second day after the disaster, FEMA headquarters officials said that they had realized that a massive amount of relief would be needed from the Federal Government—and that Florida was not requesting it. To deal with this problem, concurrent with the designation of the Secretary of Transportation to oversee relief operations, the President also directed increased Federal assistance, particularly from the military, to South Florida. At that point, significant amounts of relief supplies began flowing into the region.

Source: U.S. Senate, Committee on Government Affairs, 103rd Congress, first session, *Rebuilding FEMA: Preparing for the Next Disaster* (Washington, D.C.: Government Printing Office, 1994), p. 85.

Congress in 1978 with the goal of becoming Speaker of the House. As far-fetched as the goal may have seemed, Gingrich continued in this pursuit until 1990, when he was elected Minority Whip by the Republican Caucus. That position put him second in line to Minority Leader Robert Henry Michel (R-Illinois), a moderate, whose gentlemanly demeanor was at odds with the scrappy and antagonistic style of Gingrich. When Michel announced his retirement in 1994, Gingrich seized the opportunity for leadership by promoting a "Contract with America."

Republican Promises. The Contract with America promised eight legislative reforms in the first one hundred days of the 104th Congress and ten major pieces of legislation in the following one hundred days. The Republicans promised to clean up Congress by requiring that all federal legislation be applicable to Congress, reducing the number of committees, opening committee meetings to the public, requiring a three-fifths vote on tax bills, banning proxy votes, limiting the terms of committee chairs, and cleaning up budgeting and auditing processes. While these congressional reforms were rather sweeping, the proposed legislative agenda was even broader, as it included bills advocating a federal balanced-budget amendment, an anticrime package, programs to discourage teen pregnancy, stronger child-support enforcement, income-tax reform, litigation reform, and congressional term limits. Each of these areas struck a chord with the American people. There was general agreement that the federal government had become too big and pervasive, although there was not accord on which areas should be cut. The Contract seemed to be a rational solution to the perceived moral decay of the late twentieth century, and also had the advantage of putting many pet projects of the Republican leadership into a framework that was easy to understand. For many congressmen, it may have been too easy. Even congressmen who had strong apprehensions about the wisdom of a balanced-budget amendment, or who were personally opposed to congressional term limits, found it difficult not to sign the document. Democrats were forced into the uncomfortable position of seeming to favor crime or teenage pregnancy if they opposed the Contract or the Republicans.

Tug of War. The Republicans hammered on conservative moral themes during the 1994 election and had a heyday with President Clinton's actions and political positions. His amorous affairs and support of homosexuals in the military, as well as questions about his personal ethics relating to the Whitewater land deal and draft dodging, all created an aura of untrustworthiness. Not surprisingly, the Republicans won fifty-four seats in the House of Representatives and four seats in the Senate, gaining control of both chambers, and picked up several governorships. Gingrich wasted no time in pushing the Contract with America. During the first one hundred days of the 104th Congress, nine out of ten proposed articles were adopted into law. Only the issue of term limits was defeated, an unsurprising outcome in an institution based on seniority. Even President Clinton admitted defeat. Shortly after the election, he announced

to the American people that "he had gotten the message." The "Comeback Kid," as Clinton was nicknamed, did come back. He spent the next two years pursuing moderate economic policies—which led to a booming economy—and backtracking on his earlier liberal agenda. While Clinton pursued the moderate road, Gingrich and the Republican Congress seemed to be ideological zealots on a conservative crusade. By staking out the conservative electorate as their base of support, the Republicans left the large middle area for the Democrats; this area came back to haunt them two years later.

Startling Setback. Most political observers expected that the Republicans would fare well in the 1996 elections. Since President Richard M. Nixon had formulated the Southern Strategy in 1968, which combined the Sunbelt (California to the Carolinas) with the heartland (Midwest farming states) to form the nucleus of the party, Republicans had held an advantage in all presidential elections. That base should have held firm in 1996. However, a grueling Republican primary campaign, Clinton's moderate legislative agenda, an exceedingly strong economy, and the return of H. Ross Perot to the campaign trail all helped in the end to propel Clinton back into office. The early Republican primaries featured several important candidates: Senate Majority Leader Robert Joseph "Bob" Dole (R-Kansas), former congressman and Secretary of Housing and Urban Development (HUD) Jack French Kemp, multimillionaire businessman Malcolm S. "Steve" Forbes Jr., veteran candidate and television commentator Patrick J. Bucha-

---

NEWT RESIGNS

On 6 November 1998, Speaker of the House Newt Gingrich (R-Georgia) announced that he would not run for the post that year:

Today I have reached a difficult personal decision. I will not be candidate for Speaker of the 106th Congress. The Republican conference needs to be unified, and it is time for me to move forward where I believe I still have a significant role to play for our country and our party. My party will have my full support, and I will do all I can to help us win in 2000.

I urge my colleagues to pick leaders who can both reconcile and discipline, who can work together and communicate effectively. They have my prayers and my thoughts as they undertake this task.

I want to thank everyone whose friendship and support has made these years enjoyable. Marianne and I are grateful to the citizens of Georgia who gave us the wonderful opportunity to represent them and to my Republican colleagues who became our extended family. Thank you and God bless you.

Source: *Washington Post* (7 November 1998).

Representative Newton Leroy "Newt" Gingrich (R-Georgia) and Senate Majority Leader
Robert Joseph Dole (R-Kansas) meeting reporters on 2 December
1994 (AP/Wide World Photos)

nan, and former Tennessee governor Lamar Alexander. Dole, an able politician, locked up the most political support and handily won the nomination for president. He selected Kemp to be his running mate. Kemp, a former professional football player, had an easygoing style and was considerably younger than the seventy-year-old Dole. While Dole was favorably regarded by the American public for his heroic World War II record and his years in the Senate, he was unable to build a majority. He was handicapped by Perot's reentry into the race. While Perot represented the Reform Party he was unable to muster the same amount of interest or support he had generated four years earlier. Nevertheless, he continued to be a spoiler in favor of the Democrats by distracting independents and populist Republicans. Dole was also running against an incumbent president in peacetime, and the country was experiencing a strong economy. Clinton had used the two intervening years between the 1994 debacle and 1996 election to re-create himself as a moderate. Because Dole had been forced to fight for the conservative vote in the primaries, he entered the general election positioned further to the Right than where he felt comfortable and was unable to make up the difference by election day. Clinton won reelection relatively easily with 49.24 percent of the popular vote, defeating Dole (40.71 percent) and Perot (8.40 percent).

Moderate Retreat. After President Clinton's reelection, the Republican leadership was forced to moderate their legislative agenda. Despite their loss, they were not about to let Clinton have an easy second term. They simply changed the arena of combat from the legislature to the courts. They chose Kenneth W. Starr to be the independent counsel in charge of the Whitewater investigation. Starr was dogged in his pursuit of Clinton. The investigation was so unrelenting and seemed to many so mean-spirited, resulting in calls for impeachment of the president, that Americans turned their anger toward Starr and Gingrich and away from Clinton. Had the economy been weaker the Republicans might have achieved some midterm election victories, but despite Clinton's troubles, the Democrats gained seats in the 1998 election. This Democratic success was such a blow to the Republicans and Gingrich's leadership that a few days later he resigned both from his position as Speaker and his seat in the House of Representatives. While the Republicans continued to control both houses of congress, they no longer had a strong and aggressive leader. Robert Linlightgow "Bob" Livingston Jr. (R-Louisiana) was chosen to succeed Gingrich, but before he could be formally voted in, he resigned because of allegations of marital infidelity. On 6 January 1999 House Republicans chose John Dennis Hastert (R-Illinois) to serve as Speaker of the House. After Clinton's acquittal in the Senate trial, Hastert spent the rest of the year attempting to rebuild bridges in the House. The decade ended with a divided government and with the Republican Party gearing up for another shot at the presidency in 2000.

Sources:

Dan T. Carter, *From George Wallace to Newt Gingrich: Race in the Conservative Counterrevolution 1963–1994* (Baton Rouge: Louisiana State University Press, 1996).

Newt Gingrich, *To Renew America* (New York: HarperCollins, 1995).

Judith Warner and Max Berley, *Newt Gingrich: Speaker to America* (New York: Signet, 1995).

SCANDALOUS ADMINISTRATION

Campaign Rumors. The Clinton administration was plagued by scandals and allegations of corruption. Women, money, and power led to the impeachment trial of President Bill Clinton in 1998 by the House of Representatives and trial by the Senate in 1999. From the beginning of his 1992 campaign, rumors swirled about Clinton's penchant for women. The first scandal concerned a woman named Gennifer Flowers, who alleged that she had a twelve-year affair with Clinton while he was the governor of Arkansas. She also claimed that he got her a job in the state government because of their relationship. Clinton refused to admit the affair and went on national television with his wife, Hillary Rodham Clinton, claiming that even though they had had problems in their then seventeen-year marriage, they loved and supported each other. The appearance defused the rumors and seemed to end Clinton's personal problems, at least until after the inauguration.

Jones v. *Clinton.* The second womanizing scandal broke shortly after President Clinton's inauguration, when his opponents convinced a young woman in Arkansas, Paula Corbin Jones, to go public with an allegation of sexual harassment that had occurred in 1991. Jones claimed that at a political function Clinton had invited her up to his hotel room, where he exposed himself. Clinton denied the allegation and used his staff to attack Jones's veracity. Rather than disappearing, however, Jones filed suit in federal court on 6 May 1994, seeking $700,000 in damages for "willful, outrageous and malicious conduct." Clinton sought dismissal of the suit on the grounds of presidential immunity, a precedent established by President Thomas Jefferson whereby presidents have refused to acknowledge the right of the judicial branch to subpoena a sitting president because of the doctrine of separation of powers. U.S. District Court Judge Susan Webber Wright agreed with the precedent that a sitting president could not be tried, but did allow that fact-finding could continue. In 1996 a three-judge appeals panel of the Eighth U.S. Circuit Court reversed the lower court, ruling that the trial could proceed. The case was then appealed to the Supreme Court, which in May 1997 upheld the appeals-court holding. The trial date was set for 27 May 1998. During the next year lawyers for Clinton and Jones wrangled over the charges and evidence. Wright dismissed the lawsuit in April 1998. Jones promptly appealed to the circuit court. On 13 November 1998 an out-of-court settlement was reached when Clinton agreed to pay Jones $850,000, but he admitted to no wrongdoing.

Lewinsky. After the publicity surrounding the initial charges, the Jones case nearly disappeared until Kenneth W. Starr, special prosecutor for the Whitewater affair, started investigating charges of perjury by President Clinton in his testimony in federal court during the Jones hearing. Starr's investigation led him to other cases of womanizing by Clinton. One in particular led to the impeachment of Clinton: the case of a White House intern, Monica S. Lewinsky, who claimed to have had a sexual relationship with the president. Starr wanted Lewinsky to testify in the Jones case in order to discredit Clinton's testimony and prove perjury charges. Lewinsky had been surreptitiously taped by her friend and coworker, Linda R. Tripp, as she confessed her relationship in telephone conversations. Those tapes and the information contained on them became the center of the third major scandal, which eventually led to the impeachment of Clinton in late 1998.

Whitewater. Flowers, Jones, and Lewinsky were not enough by themselves to lead to impeachment. Other scandals, involving money and power, also stained the reputation of the Clinton administration. Four months into his first term, Clinton was accused of illegally firing employees of the White House travel office in order to give work to an Arkansas firm. A Federal Bureau of Investigation (FBI) inquiry ensued in what became known as Travelgate. This scandal was overshadowed when a more far-reaching controversy, known as Whitewater, surfaced. Whitewater was a land-development project in 1978 in which Bill and Hillary Rodham Clinton had invested with partners James B. and Susan McDougal. At the time of the investment Clinton was attorney general of Arkansas, and James McDougal was a fast-talking financier who bought the Madison Guaranty Savings and Loan in 1981 to help underwrite his deals. Within two years of purchasing Madison Guaranty, it was in trouble and McDougal had to contract with the Rose Law Firm, where Hillary Rodham Clinton was a partner, for help. Both Madison Guaranty and the Whitewater Development Corporation failed in the late 1980s because of financial mismanagement. The federal government spent $60 million to rescue investors, and McDougal became the center of a federal investigation. Over the next decade, government investigators tried to determine to what extent the Clintons were involved in the failure of Madison Guaranty. A pall was further cast over the Clinton administration when Deputy White House Counsel Vincent W. Foster Jr., who had been handling the Whitewater case for the Clintons, was found dead in a Washington park on 20 July 1993, causing the lunatic fringe to speculate about the alleged involvement of the Clintons in his death. In 1994 special counsel Starr, a Republican, began investigating the Whitewater-Madison Guaranty case. Between 1993 and 1999 a team of thirty lawyers and ten

On 20 July 1993 Vincent W. Foster Jr., the deputy legal counsel and life-long friend of President Bill Clinton, shot himself to death in Fort Marcy Park, Virginia. Rumors swirled and investigations were launched.

The tabloid *New York Post* claimed that after Foster's death, administration officials "frantically scrambled" to remove from his office safe a previously unreported set of files, some of them related to the Whitewater affair. A financial newsletter published an even more sensational—and equally unsubstantiated—report that Foster's body had been moved from an apartment in Virginia to the suburban park where it was found. On his radio show, conservative blunderbuss Rush Limbaugh embellished that report just a bit: he said the newsletter "claims that Vince Foster was murdered in an apartment owned by Hillary Clinton."

. . . .No, Hillary Clinton was not involved in a murder. In fact, there's still no credible evidence that Foster's death was anything but the depression-induced suicide that his family believes it to have been. Then why all the garish speculation? Partly because of the clumsy behavior of Foster's boss, former presidential counsel Bernard Nussbaum, and other White House staffers immediately after the suicide: leaving his office unsealed and spiriting documents away. Partly because of the enigmatic note that Foster left behind—unsigned, addressed to no one, torn into pieces—lamenting his own "mistakes" and the poisonous atmosphere of Washington, where "ruining people is considered sport." Partly because the Whitewater affair, one of the items on his desk, has resurged so dramatically. And partly because many people in the news media simply won't let Foster rest.

Some of the stories are nothing more that the cut and thrust of responsible news coverage. But all along, others have seemed determinedly partisan. There is continued grumbling from *The Wall Street Journal* editorial page, whose stinging criticism apparently contributed to Foster's depression ("WSJ editors lie without consequence," he complained in his note). There's a steady stream of innuendo from conservative *New York Times* columnist William Safire, who implied at one point that "intelligence matters" might have had something to do with the suicide. And on another level entirely, there is the florid hype and fantasy of the tabloids, designed more to entertain than inform. Some of the most raucous of those excesses have come from overseas. In Britain, Rupert Murdoch's *Sun* claimed, three days after the suicide, that Foster had a "deep personal friendship" with Hillary Clinton.

Last week one of the more overwrought American tabloids, the *New York Post,* charged that investigators "never took a crucial crime-scene photo of Vincent Foster's body before it was moved" out of the park where it had been discovered. The tabloid, which has begun to put quotation marks around the word "suicide" in stories about Foster, also asserted that "little blood loss" was evident at the scene—which could be taken as a sign that the fatal shot was fired into Foster's head somewhere else.

Partisan, if not downright malicious, speculation that the death might not have been suicide spread like a bad odor. Roger Ailes, the former Republican campaign consultant who is now president of the CNBC cable TV network, suggested in a radio interview with Don Imus that Foster's death could have been murder. Right-wing televangelist Pat Robertson devoted a segment of his "700 Club" show to the subject. "Suicide or murder? That's the ominous question surfacing in the Whitewater swell of controversy concerning Vincent Foster's mysterious death," he intoned.

Another major source of the rumors was conservative activist Floyd Brown and his Citizens United group, which feeds information to the news media and some Republicans. Brown employs a full-time investigator named David Bossie to dig up dirt on Clinton. Last week Brown claimed to have "new clues that suggest Foster did not commit suicide."

But the foul-play stories didn't stand up. Last Friday, ABC News, which apparently had been fed by the administration, said it had inspected a gruesome set of crime-scene photographs taken by investigators. It said the "grim and graphic" pictures—most of which were not shown on the air—dispelled speculation that there was little blood around the body. A close-up of Foster's hand showed his thumb still resting on the trigger of the revolver that had fired into his mouth, with what ABC said were powder burns visible on the hand. The network said it had seen a medical examiner's report in which "the burns and other gunpowder residue are listed as primary evidence that Foster shot himself."

Source: Russell Watson and Mark Hosenball, "Vince Foster's Suicide: The Rumor Mill Churns," *Newsweek* (21 March 1994): 32–33.

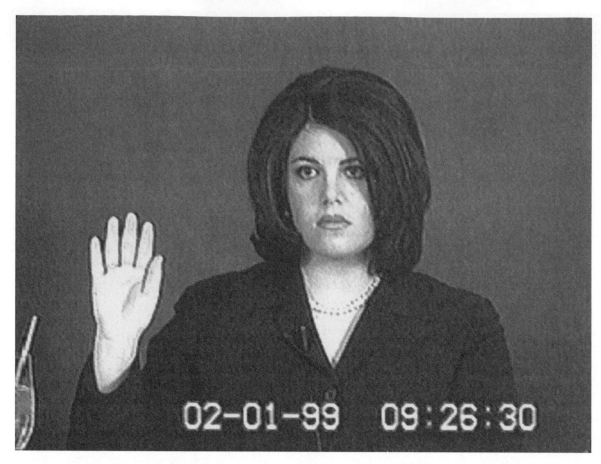

Monica S. Lewinsky being sworn in for her videotaped deposition (AP/Wide World Photos)

investigators worked on the case. During that time they spent millions of dollars and sent several defendants to jail, including the McDougals; Jim Guy Tucker, sitting governor of Arkansas; and Deputy Attorney General Webster Hubble, who had been Hillary Rodham Clinton's law partner. Starr, however, was not able to gather enough evidence to indict the president or Mrs. Clinton on criminal charges, so he used evidence of perjury in the Jones case to incriminate Clinton. (The Whitewater charges were eventually determined to be unfounded.) By the time Starr's report was sent to Congress in September 1998, it was 2,800 pages long, including graphic detail with thousands of footnotes, and contained accusations and recommendations relating to perjury and misconduct in office that formed the basis of the impeachment and trial of President Clinton.

Sources:

"Jones v. Clinton Special Report," *Washingtonpost.com*, Internet website.

Jeffrey Toobin, *A Vast Conspiracy: The Real Story Of The Sex Scandal That Nearly Brought Down A President* (New York : Random House, 2000).

"Whitewater Timeline," *Washingtonpost.com*, Internet website.

TRIALS OF A PRESIDENT

Impeachment. Since the founding of the Republic, only two presidents have been impeached by the House of Representatives: President Andrew Johnson in 1868 and President Bill Clinton in 1999. Neither man was convicted. Johnson was impeached because he refused to succumb to the dictates of the Radical Republicans in Congress when he fired Secretary of War Edwin M. Stanton in opposition to the Tenure in Office Act (1867). The issue for Johnson revolved around how to govern and what treatment was to be given the former confederates after the Civil War. Though Johnson was not a strong president, he has been viewed sympathetically by historians, much more so than by the Congress that impeached him. The impeachment of Clinton was simply a tawdry affair. The issue was whether the president had lied to a grand jury in the sexual harassment trial instigated by Paula Corbin Jones, used his influence to cover up the perjury, lied about his actions, and if his sexual relations with White House intern Monica S. Lewinsky entailed abuse of power. Unlike the Johnson case, it was personal action, not political activity, that led to impeachment.

High Crimes and Misdemeanors? The emphasis on personal morals and behavior was a legacy of the Vietnam War (ended 1975) and the Nixon administration (1969–1974). Both President Lyndon B. Johnson and President Richard M. Nixon lied to the American people about U.S. involvement in the Vietnam War. Nixon also lied about his involvement in the Watergate break-in (17 June 1972) and subsequent cover-up. If Nixon had not resigned the presidency in August 1974, he would have been impeached by the U.S. House of

As required by Section 595(c) of Title 28 of the United States Code, the Office of the Independent Counsel ("OIC" or "Office") hereby submits substantial and credible information that President William Jefferson Clinton committed acts that may constitute grounds for an impeachment. The information reveals that President Clinton:

lied under oath at a civil deposition while he was a defendant in a sexual harassment lawsuit;

lied under oath to a grand jury;

attempted to influence the testimony of a potential witness who had direct knowledge of facts that would reveal the falsity of his deposition testimony;

attempted to obstruct justice by facilitating a witness's plan to refuse to comply with a subpoena;

attempted to obstruct justice by encouraging a witness to file an affidavit that the President knew would be false, and then by making use of that false affidavit at his own deposition;

lied to potential grand jury witnesses, knowing that they would repeat those lies before the grand jury; and

engaged in a pattern of conduct that was inconsistent with his constitutional duty to faithfully execute the laws.

The evidence shows that these acts, and others, were part of a pattern that began as an effort to prevent the disclosure of information about the President's relationship with a former White House intern and employee, Monica S. Lewinsky, and continued as an effort to prevent the information from being disclosed in an ongoing criminal investigation.

Factual Background

In May 1994, Paula Corbin Jones filed a lawsuit against William Jefferson Clinton in the United States District Court for the Eastern District of Arkansas. Ms. Jones alleged that while he was the Governor of Arkansas, President Clinton sexually harassed her during an incident in a Little Rock hotel room. President Clinton denied the allegations. He also challenged the ability of a private litigant to pursue a lawsuit against a sitting President. In May 1997, the Supreme Court unanimously rejected the President's legal argument. The Court concluded that Ms. Jones, "[l]ike every other citizen who properly invokes [the District Court's] jurisdiction . . . has a right to an orderly disposition of her claims," and that therefore Ms. Jones was entitled to pursue her claims while the President was in office. A few months later, the pretrial discovery process began.

One sharply disputed issue in the *Jones* litigation was the extent to which the President would be required to dis-

close information about sexual relationships he may have had with "other women." Ms. Jones's attorneys sought disclosure of this information, arguing that it was relevant to proving that the President had propositioned Ms. Jones. The President resisted the discovery requests, arguing that evidence of relationships with other women (if any) was irrelevant.

In late 1997, the issue was presented to United States District Judge Susan Webber Wright for resolution. Judge Wright's decision was unambiguous. For purposes of pretrial discovery, President Clinton was required to provide certain information about his alleged relationships with other women. In an order dated December 11, 1997, for example, Judge Wright said: "The Court finds, therefore, that the plaintiff is entitled to information regarding any individuals with whom the President had sexual relations or proposed or sought to have sexual relations and who were during the relevant time frame state or federal employees." Judge Wright left for another day the issue whether any information of this type would be admissible were the case to go to trial. But for purposes of answering the written questions served on the President, and for purposes of answering questions at a deposition, the District Court ruled that the President must respond.

In mid-December 1997, the President answered one of the written discovery questions posed by Ms. Jones on this issue. When asked to identify all women who were state or federal employees and with whom he had had "sexual relations" since 1986, the President answered under oath: "None." For purposes of this interrogatory, the term "sexual relations" was not defined.

In January 17, 1998, President Clinton was questioned under oath about his relationships with other women in the workplace, this time at a deposition. Judge Wright presided over the deposition. The President was asked numerous questions about his relationship with Monica Lewinsky, by then a 24-year-old former White House intern, White House employee, and Pentagon employee. Under oath and in the presence of Judge Wright, the President denied that he had engaged in a "sexual affair," a "sexual relationship," or "sexual relations" with Ms. Lewinsky. The President also stated that he had no specific memory of having been alone with Ms. Lewinsky, that he remembered few details of any gifts they might have exchanged, and indicated that no one except his attorneys had kept him informed of Ms. Lewinsky's status as a potential witness in the *Jones* case.

Representative Ira William McCollum Jr. (R-Florida), one of the House managers in the impeachment trial of President Bill Clinton, making a point during closing arguments on the Senate floor on 8 February 1999 (AP/Wide World Photos)

Representatives. After the Nixon resignation, there was profound distrust of politicians and particularly of presidents. Politicians and would-be presidents had to demonstrate honesty in their personal and professional lives according to a much higher standard than earlier officeholders. Infidelity became a political test. Senator Gary Warren Hart (D-Colorado), the favored candidate for the 1988 Democratic nomination, was forced to drop out of the race when the media published evidence of his extramarital affairs. When President George Bush nominated Clarence Thomas to become an associate justice of the Supreme Court to replace the venerable Thurgood Marshall, Thomas's Senate hearing became the center of sexual harassment charges by his former coworker Anita F. Hill. Women's groups across the nation rushed to support Hill. Vietnam, Watergate, and the Thomas hearing coalesced to haunt Clinton. Patterning himself after President John F. Kennedy, Clinton saw himself as the torchbearer for the new generation of Baby Boomers, just as Kennedy had been for those who came of age during World War II (1939–1945). Like Kennedy, Clinton played on his sex appeal and charisma to get support. Kennedy was president at the beginning of the sexual revolution, however, when men still held power and sex was "cool." Clinton served at a time when extramarital affairs were no longer tolerated and when sex, because of the AIDS crisis, could kill. Whatever the logic or lack thereof, Clinton found himself in 1998 in a maelstrom largely created by his sexual misbehavior. Between November 1995 and April 1996 President Clinton had a consensual sexual relationship, characterized by oral sex, with Lewinsky. When first accused of the affair, Clinton denied having sex "with that woman." Only when confronted with physical evidence in the form of semen stains on one of her dresses did he recant. This action alone, however reprehensible, probably would not have led to impeachment hearings if it had not happened at a time when the conservative Republican leadership in Congress was already angered by a series of other scandals surrounding the president.

The Process. The impeachment process, like that of 1868, was driven by a congressional Republican Party anxious to control national politics; independent counsel Starr approached the investigation with missionary zeal. The Republican Party was rejuvenated in the last quarter of the twentieth century. The election of Ronald Reagan, a conservative Republican, represented a rejection by Americans of the liberalism of the Democratic Party. He was a master of the television camera and had a charming, folksy style that won the hearts of many. His leadership led to Republicans winning a majority of seats in the Senate and thus controlling it for the first time in almost thirty years. Over the next decade Republican voters increased steadily in both national and state elections. The only major setback in this trend was the Clinton election in 1992. By 1994 the Party was back on track, fueled by a reaction against Clinton's failed health-care plan, tax program, and policy about gays in the military. The House also had a new minority leader, Representative Newton Leroy "Newt" Gingrich (R-Georgia). He had none of the charm of President Reagan or the charisma of President Clinton, but he was a great tactician and relentless opponent. The difference in ideology of the two men led to a stalemate in domestic politics. The power struggle between Clinton and Gingrich fueled the Starr investigation. Gingrich and the Republican Congress were eager to discredit Clinton. The Democrats in Congress, now a minority party after sixty years of control, were unwilling to concede power to the Republicans. By the time the Judiciary Committee held hearings on the findings of the independent counsel, Congress was split according to party politics. It was at this strategic point that elections were held, which Gingrich expected would be a rejection of Clinton and the Democrats and another sweep for the Republicans. Instead, the Democrats picked up five seats and Gingrich resigned his position as Speaker.

Senate Trial. On 19 December 1998 the House of Representatives voted on the four articles of impeachment. Article I, alleging perjury before a grand jury, passed 228 to 206. Article II, accusing the president of perjury in a civil lawsuit, failed 229 to 205. Article III, alleging obstruction of justice, was approved 221 to 212. Article IV, charging abuse of power, failed 285 to 148. Except on Article IV, the votes, with few exceptions, lined up by party, with the Republicans voting for and Democrats voting against impeachment. Thirteen members of the House of Representatives, all white male Republicans, were tapped to be "managers" (prosecutors) of the case against the president in the Senate trial. President Clinton chose a more diverse defense team of lawyers, which included Cheryl D. Mills, a young, black, female attorney, who proved to be the most successful spokesman for the president. The trial began in the Senate chambers on 13 January 1999, with Chief Justice William Hubbs Rehnquist presiding. After opening motions, each side was given twenty-four hours to present its case, and the senators then had sixteen hours to question the parties. President Clinton did not appear during the trial, but Lewinsky testified using videotape and several of Clinton's confidants submitted depositions. After closed deliberations the Senate voted on 12 February 1999 to acquit. Neither of the two articles of impeachment brought by the House achieved a simple majority, much less the two-thirds necessary to convict Clinton of high crimes and misdemeanors. Article I, alleging perjury, was defeated on a forty-five to fifty-five vote. Article II, charging obstruction, failed on a fifty-fifty tie. All forty-five Democrats and five Republicans voted for full acquittal. The impeachment and trial of President Clinton thus ended as it had begun, full of salacious rumors, petty infighting, and a feeling of apathy and ennui among the American public.

Sources:

Eric Pooley and Michael Weisskopf, "How Starr Sees It," *Time*, 152 (28 December 1998): 82.

Richard A. Posner, *An Affair of State: The Investigation, Impeachment and Trial of President Clinton* (Cambridge, Mass.: Harvard University Press, 1999).

"The President on Trial: Timeline," *Time.com.*, Internet website.

Jeffrey Toobin, *A Vast Conspiracy: The Real Story of the Sex Scandal That Nearly Brought Down a President* (New York: Random House, 2000).

HEADLINE MAKERS

MADELEINE ALBRIGHT

1937-

U.S. REPRESENTATIVE TO THE UNITED NATIONS (1993-1997); SECRETARY OF STATE (1997-)

European Roots. Madeleine Korbel was born in Prague, Czechoslovakia, on 15 May 1937, only a little more than a year before the outbreak of World War II in Europe. Her Father was a Czech diplomat and was forced to move his family to England after the German invasion of their country. They went back after the war and her father was accredited as a Czech diplomat to the United Nations in New York. She came to the United States in 1948, and in the wake of the communist takeover of Czechoslovakia that year, her father asked for political asylum for himself and his family. It was granted and Madeleine ultimately became a naturalized citizen. She graduated from Wellesley College in 1959 with a Bachelor of Arts in political science; earned her Master of Arts in international affairs, with an emphasis on Soviet studies, from Columbia University in 1968; and was awarded a Ph.D. from Columbia in 1976. She married, was divorced, and raised three daughters.

Early Public Career. Achieving high office in the United States, whether elected or appointed, is never merely a matter of having merit. It requires that one meet the right people, impress them, and be in a position to take advantage of an opportunity should it arise. Albright began working for a series of Democrats who had the potential of reaching the White House: she coordinated the failed 1980 presidential campaign of Senator Edmund Sixtus Muskie (D-Maine); and was a foreign policy advisor to both 1984 Democratic presidential nominee Senator Walter Frederick Mondale (D-Minnesota) and vice-presidential nominee Representative Geraldine Anne Ferraro (D-New York). She also advised Democratic nominee Massachu-

setts governor Michael Stanley Dukakis in 1988, as well as Arkansas governor Bill Clinton in 1992. In addition to these political responsibilities, she pursued a career in government and academia. President Jimmy Carter's National Security Advisor Zbigniew Brzezinski prevailed on her to join the National Security Council (NSC) staff as a legislative liaison in 1978, and she stayed in that position until the end of the Carter administration in 1981. She then turned her considerable energies to scholarship and spent 1981–1982 writing a book, *Poland: The Role of the Press in Political Change* (1983). She accomplished this task while on fellowship at the Woodrow Wilson International Center for Scholars at the Smithsonian Institution. In 1982 she joined the faculty at Georgetown University in Washington, D.C., teaching courses in international affairs, U.S. foreign policy, and Soviet foreign policy. In 1989 she combined her role as a policy analyst with her political interests, taking over as president of the Center for National Policy, a Democratic policy-oriented think tank. All of these activities kept her in touch with the U.S. foreign policy establishment and with Democratic presidential hopefuls waiting out the Reagan and Bush years in academic institutions and think tanks in the Washington, D.C., area.

United Nations. In 1993 she was made U.S. Permanent Representative to the United Nations (U.N.). The United States was, of course, a major presence at the U.N., as one of only five permanent members of the Security Council, along with France, United Kingdom, Russia, and China. The United States is also, as Albright liked to say, "the indispensable nation." Its great power, democratic traditions, and wealth all gave it an edge in resolving international disputes. Her fluency in French and Czech in addition to English, and her reading and speaking skills in Russian and Polish, served her well in the U.N. councils. She aggressively pursued reform in the U.N. administration and budget, arguing that it was trying to do too much, that its many administrative offices were too independent, and that there was little accountability. It was a heady time at the U.N., as it seemed to be moving toward a more-active role denied it for forty-five years while it was caught in the crossfire between the two Cold War superpowers. Albright recognized that the U.N. was not really ready to take on all the new tasks effectively and urged attention to careful determination of its future role. Albright understood that while the U.N. was essential for American national interests, U.S. influence there was limited by the refusal of Congress to pay its dues to the organization, partly because of objections to U.N. family-planning initiatives. Albright was active in educating Americans that an effective and strong U.N. is in U.S. national interests.

Toughness and Charm. President Clinton's announcement in 1996 that he was nominating Albright to be his Secretary of State met with wide approval, partly because of her reputation as a plain-spoken and aggressive defender of U.S. interests in the U.N. Americans who paid attention to such things, the press, and, most important, influential members of Congress liked her tough style and her unwillingness to quietly allow the "America bashing" that was sometimes a staple of U.N. discourse to go unchallenged. Yet, she was also well known for her ability to talk to many different people with varying political agendas and to get them to agree on issues. Most dramatically, her willingness to find common ground with Sen. Jesse Helms (R-North Carolina), the powerful and querulous chairman of the Senate Foreign Relations Committee and a relentless critic of both the U.N. and the foreign policy of the Clinton administration, attests to her political and diplomatic skills.

Cabinet Officer. The office of Secretary of State is considered the highest-ranking cabinet position. Albright was confirmed by the Senate in 1997, making her the sixty-fourth Secretary of State, the first woman to hold the post, and the highest-ranking woman ever in the executive branch. From the beginning of her tenure, she showed her political acumen by courting Senator Helms, who had the ability to smooth the way in Congress for Clinton administration foreign-affairs appointments and initiatives, or to make it rough sledding indeed. While the administration and Helms continued to disagree on many issues, Albright's overtures lessened the public conflicts and helped resolve such issues as U.N. reform and payment of arrears. As Secretary of State, Albright is a member of the NSC and is responsible for advising the president on foreign affairs. In addition, in the last twenty to thirty years secretaries of state have increasingly taken personal charge of high-profile negotiations that were once left to local ambassadors, special emissaries, or even lower-ranking diplomats. Accordingly, she is heavily involved in attempting to solve a variety of intractable international issues. At the end of the decade the issues of peace in the Middle East and of national self-determination in the Balkans have been especially troublesome.

Challenges. There has always been a significant strain of isolationism in the United States. Many Americans have maintained that the country should stay out of international conflicts and problems in order to concentrate on domestic issues. After the end of World War II, however, Americans were convinced of the necessity to forego isolationist impulses to combat communism. With the fall of communist regimes in Europe, many Americans again felt comfortable resorting to isolationism, a trend reflected in Congress. Albright is an internationalist, putting her in conflict with many legislators from both major parties who want to cut back on foreign-aid commitments and end U.S. participation in peacekeeping operations in favor of greater emphasis on domestic interests. This sentiment has been her greatest challenge as secretary of state. Whether it be in reference to development efforts in Africa, support for economic reform in Latin America, ending human-rights abuses in the Balkans and peacekeeping operations there, or commitments to extending free trade, she faces stiff opposition from Congress and domestic constituencies that are suspicious of international involvement. Her efforts in public education may be as important in this regard as her negotiating skills.

Sources:

Madeleine Albright, "Remarks to the Business Council of the United Nations," 28 September 1998, *US State Department*, Internet website.

Ann Blackman, *Seasons of Her Life: A Biography of Madeleine Korbel Albright* (New York: Scribner, 1998).

Michael Dobbs, *Madeleine Albright: A Twentieth Century Odyssey* (New York: Holt, 1999).

GEORGE BUSH

1924-
PRESIDENT OF THE UNITED STATES (1989–1993)

Early Years. George Herbert Walker Bush was born in Milton, Massachusetts, on 12 June 1924, and was raised in Greenwich, Connecticut. His father, Prescott Sheldon Bush, was an investment banker and later a U.S. Senator from Connecticut (1952–1963). The younger Bush was in his last year of high school when the Japanese attacked Pearl Harbor on 7 December 1941. Like many young men of his generation, he joined the military at his first opportunity, enlisting in the U.S. Navy on his eighteenth birthday in 1942. He went to flight school and won his wings to become the youngest pilot in the Navy. He served in the Pacific and flew in fifty-eight combat missions against the Japanese. He was awarded the Distinguished Flying Cross for actions taken after his plane was shot down over the water where he was eventually rescued by a submarine. After he came back to the United States early in 1945, he married Barbara Pierce and entered Yale University. He graduated with a Bachelor of Arts in economics. Instead of entering his father's firm, Bush moved his family to west Texas to go into the oil business. He was quite successful and by 1954 was president of the Zapata Offshore Company.

Lure of Politics. Bush first entered into politics in the early 1960s as chairman of the Harris County Republican Party. He ran for Senate in 1964 but lost. Two years later he was elected to the House of Representatives and served two terms. He ran for the Senate in 1970, but again he was defeated. These defeats in many ways defined his political career. He was moderate in a state were the electorate was considerably more conservative than he was. While he had a largely conservative voting record, his more moderate votes were singled out for criticism by conservatives. This reputation for moderation later doomed his presidential bid in 1980, and seriously undercut his effectiveness with the conservative wing of his own party during his years as president.

A Public Career. After his defeat by Lloyd Millard Bentsen Jr. (D) for a Senate seat in 1970, Bush was appointed to a series of high-level positions by presidents Richard M. Nixon and Gerald R. Ford. Shortly after his 1970 electoral defeat, President Nixon appointed him U.S. Ambassador to the United Nations. In 1973 he became chairman of the Republican National Committee (RNC), and in 1974, President Ford appointed him the head of the U.S. Liaison Office in the People's Republic of China. His service in this latter position took place in the still-poisoned atmosphere of American-Chinese enmity stemming from the Cold War and their military clash during the Korean War. This service further fueled suspicions many conservatives harbored about Bush. At the end of 1975, President Ford appointed Bush to head the Central Intelligence Agency (CIA), which was under political pressure from investigations by the Church Committee in the Senate and the Pike Committee in the House of Representatives into alleged illegal covert actions. As CIA director he was widely credited with reforms that reined in unapproved covert activities. He negotiated a new relationship between the president and Congress for information sharing about, and approval of, covert missions. He left the CIA when Jimmy Carter, a Democrat, was elected president in 1976.

Unsuccessful Run. Carter's presidency was widely viewed by Republicans as a failure. In the months leading up to the 1980 election, many well-known Republicans decided to seek the nomination in November. Bush, for a while, looked like a front-runner. Soon, however, he fell behind the Ronald Reagan juggernaut and Reagan was nominated at the national convention, at which the Republicans adopted the most conservative Party platform in memory. It was in this celebration of conservative successes that Reagan offered the vice presidency to the moderate Bush. Reagan was initially cool to the idea of adding Bush to the ticket, but was reassured when Bush agreed that he would support the platform wholeheartedly. The Reagan-Bush ticket won the general election and was reelected in 1984. Bush served loyally and quietly in the shadow of Reagan, and remained in the background partly because of his own belief about his role and partly because Reagan's political handlers made sure that the vice president never became an independent political force within the administration.

The Presidential Years. After surviving a primary challenge by Sen. Robert Joseph "Bob" Dole (R-Kansas), Bush won the Republican nomination and defeated Democrat Michael Dukakis, former governor of Massachusetts, in the 1988 election. Within a few months it was clear that the Bush administration was not just an extension of the Reagan years. For instance, he put his own people in the cabinet and on the White House staff. In doing so, he alienated Reagan loyalists in the Republican Party both in and out of Congress. As Bush emerged from Reagan's shadow, many Republicans (especially conservatives who were suspicious of him anyway) found it difficult to support him. As president, Bush quickly established the reputation of specializing in foreign affairs with little real interest in domestic issues. Like any generalization, this one had a basis in fact while it also ignored other realities. Bush initiated a war on drugs, a historic agreement with Democrats in Congress to reduce the deficit, and moved to end the savings and loan crisis. Yet, his real interests remained foreign affairs.

Foreign Policy. The dramatic end of communism, invasion of Panama, and Persian Gulf War all occurred during the Bush presidency. As Bush took office in 1989, events that would lead to the downfall of communism, at least in Europe, were already in place and ready to burst forth in the fall of that year. Bush seemed initially unsure of how to deal with these dramatic events and remained aloof. Perhaps, as some supporters have argued, he did not want to embarrass Soviet leader Mikhail Gorbachev, through whom he believed the United States had to obtain a positive post–Cold War relationship. Detractors contend that he failed to understand the significance of what was happening and was slow to react and design an appropriate response. In the midst of the collapse of the Soviet Union, President Bush made the decision to invade Panama (December 1989) in an attempt to overthrow the regime of Manuel Antonio Noriega Moreno, who had interfered in the election there, threatened U.S. citizens, and was reputedly heavily involved in drug trafficking. The invasion was successful, Noriega was captured by U.S. forces and transported to Miami to face drug charges, and the rightful winners of the Panamanian elections were installed in office. The end of the Cold War was readily apparent to all international observers during the invasion, as the Soviet Union limited itself to only tepid criticism while President Bush carefully kept the Soviets informed of U.S. intentions. This kind of relationship between the Cold War superpowers would have been unimaginable just a few months earlier. In August 1990 Iraq invaded oil-rich Kuwait. This action violated international law and threatened Saudi Arabia, stability in the Gulf, and the world's oil supply. In what was perhaps his finest hour, President Bush organized a worldwide, U.N.-sanctioned coalition against Iraq. He mobilized the American people as well, sending more than four hundred thousand U.S. troops to the Gulf, and obtaining congressional approval for military action against Iraq. After several weeks of intensive bombardment, on 24 February 1991 an invasion was launched into Iraq and Kuwait. In fewer than one hundred hours the Iraqi military was either destroyed or in retreat, and the door was opened to Baghdad. Bush and the Gulf Coalition decided not to directly overthrow the regime of Saddam Hussein, opting instead for an agreement requiring Iraq to leave Kuwait, international inspections of Iraqi missile and nuclear facilities, and limits on Iraqi sovereignty over certain areas of the country. A great deal of ink was spilt throughout the 1990s arguing whether or not it might have been better to march into Baghdad, end Hussein's rule, and install an alternative government. The debate heated up after Hussein successfully ended inspections and sporadic military actions from the air had to be taken to enforce the no-fly zones in Iraq. An assault on Baghdad in 1991, however, would have meant many more casualties, would likely have threatened the Coalition itself, and would have removed Iraq as a counterweight to Iran in the Gulf region. At the end of the war, President Bush enjoyed a virtually unprecedented public approval rating of 91 percent of those polled.

Domestic Political Issues. President Bush's foreign-policy successes and his high approval rating may have led him to underestimate the centrality domestic, and especially economic, issues have with the American electorate. His willingness to compromise with Democratic congressional leaders to cut spending, and his decision to raise taxes to cut the budget deficit, violated his "no new taxes" pledge and alienated conservative Republicans. In the spring of 1991 there was a mild recession. Some of his advisers counseled him to aggressively attack the recession, but he refused to do so on the grounds that calling public attention to it might further undermine confidence in the basic stability of the economy and actually prolong the recession. As the Gulf War steadily receded into the background of the public consciousness and the recession continued, his popularity dropped. As the 1992 election approached, he was roundly criticized for being too concerned about foreign policy. In a way, his foreign-policy successes contained the seeds of his eventual electoral defeat. Gov. Bill Clinton of Arkansas painted Bush as too concerned about people overseas and insufficiently worried about those at home, and maintained a rigorous focus on the economy throughout the campaign. Combined with the third-party challenge of H. Ross Perot, Bush's foreign-policy successes seemed irrelevant. Bush received only 37 percent of the popular vote in the election to Clinton's 43 percent and Perot's 19 percent. After Clinton's inauguration in January 1993, Bush retired to private life in Texas.

Sources:

George Bush and Brent Scowcroft, *A World Transformed* (New York: Knopf, 1998).

David Mervin, *George Bush and the Guardianship Presidency* (New York: St. Martin's Press, 1996).

Charles Tiefer, *The Semi-Sovereign Presidency: The Bush Administration's Strategy for Governing Without Congress* (Boulder, Colo.: Westview Press, 1994).

BILL CLINTON

1946-
PRESIDENT OF THE UNITED STATES (1993-2000)

Lost Opportunities. Historians, political scientists, and psychologists will write at length about Bill Clinton and his presidency. First elected in 1992 with only 43 percent of the popular vote, and reelected in 1996, Clinton dominated the U.S. political landscape for most of the 1990s. He was the first president to be born after the end of World War II (1945) and he symbolized the rise to political maturity of the baby boomers. He began his presidency with the intention of resolving several high-profile, but seemingly intractable, political issues including national health insurance, balancing the budget, civil rights, and education. Like all presidents, Clinton soon learned that progress on any of these issues required spending political capital, and that significant progress on all of them was impossible. As the first president elected after the end of the Cold War, he enjoyed the benefits of an end to the hair-trigger military standoff with the U.S.S.R., but along with that came a host of new and unanticipated foreign-policy problems unleashed by the untidy demise of the Soviet Empire. Finally, his presidency has been forever tainted by his own personal behavior, including dishonesty about his draft status during the Vietnam War (ended 1975), whether he smoked marijuana as a young man, extramarital affairs, and the lies and half-truths that led to his impeachment. Although he was not convicted by the Senate, the sordid affair cast a moral and political pall over nearly all of his second term. His presidency was not without successes—for example, the balanced budget, peace negotiations and agreements in the Middle East, and the improved situation in Northern Ireland—yet, so much more could have been accomplished.

Southern Roots. William Jefferson Blythe IV was born in Hope, Arkansas, on 19 August 1946. Three months before his birth his father, Bill Blythe, was killed in an automobile accident. In 1947 his mother left the boy in the care of his maternal grandparents while she went to New Orleans and nursing school. For most of the next two years he was raised by his grandparents with only occasional visits with his mother. His mother married Roger Clinton when he was four years old. He took the Clinton name when he was in high school. When he was seven the family moved to Hot Springs, Arkansas, though he frequently stayed in Hope with his grandparents. A younger brother, Roger, was born when Bill was ten. Clinton was a fine student and a musician with enough skill and talent with the saxophone to earn music, as well as academic, scholarships. When he was a senior in high school he was an Arkansas delegate to Boys Nation held in Washington, D.C., where he met President John F. Kennedy. By all accounts this was a defining moment for young Clinton and may have been instrumental in his eventual decision to pursue a career in politics. He attended Georgetown University with the help of scholarships and student loans and graduated with a Bachelor of Science in International Affairs in 1968. Georgetown was an ideal place for a young man interested in politics. Its Washington, D.C., location allows students to be close to national politics. While a student there Clinton interned in the Senate office of one of his home-state senators, James William Fulbright (D). After graduation, Clinton was awarded a Rhodes Scholarship to study at Oxford University in England. After two years abroad, Clinton returned to the United States and began legal studies at Yale University. While there, he met Hillary Rodham, also a promising law student. He graduated with his law degree in 1973. He briefly taught law, as did Rodham, at the University of Arkansas. They were married in 1975 and became parents of a daughter, Chelsea, in 1980. His first run for public office was an unsuccessful try at the Arkansas Third District congressional seat in 1974. Two years later he was elected Attorney General and in 1978 he was elected governor when he was only thirty-two years old. He was defeated in his 1980 reelection bid but came back and won the governorship again in 1982, and he held it from that point until his 1992 run for the presidency.

Running for President. Clinton was a long shot to get the Democratic nomination in 1992 to run against President Bush. He did not have a high public profile nationally, and Arkansas is not usually thought of as a strong base for a presidential run. Clinton benefitted as several nationally prominent Democrats decided not to seek the nomination in part because they were intimidated by Bush's incredibly high approval ratings in public opinion polls. Unlike other potential Democratic candidates, Clinton was willing to take the chance. He believed that Bush was unlikely to be able to sustain the unprecedented poll numbers and that he was vulnerable on other issues—most notably, the economy. In the 1980s Clinton had positioned himself to be a new Democrat who could put together an electoral coalition to win the presidency. He believed that though the old Democratic coalition of labor, liberals, and blacks had been successful from the 1930 through the 1960s, now it had become increasingly prone to fracturing on important issues. Clinton believed that new issues, raised and discussed by the Democratic Leadership Council that included Clinton, and the associated think tank, the Progressive Policy Institute, were the framework for forming a new coalition. The broad outlines of this line of thinking included a continuing reliance on activist government and social issues such as civil rights, but with a simultaneous embrace of free enterprise on the domestic front and a commitment to a global free market trading system. There would be less welfare, to be replaced with a greater reliance on "workfare" and job-training programs. Unlike the old Democratic coalition, the new coalition would place an emphasis on reducing crime, and additional money would be committed to building prisons and putting more police on the streets. In addition, Clinton supported the use of the death penalty. All of these positions were a stark deviation from traditional Democratic paternalism, and his ability to position himself in the middle of the political spectrum was instrumental in securing the nomination and winning the general election campaign against Bush and H. Ross Perot. Perot's strong run as a third-party candidate in 1992 probably helped Clinton as well. Throughout the campaign, Bush and Perot engaged in a partly private, partly public feud that increased whatever negative impressions the public may have already had about them. Clinton focused on the economy, blaming President Bush for every negative economic reality. His campaign office posted a sign reminding the candidate and campaign workers that "It's the economy, stupid!" In November, Clinton barely won a plurality of the popular vote although he won a substantial victory in the Electoral College.

First Term. President Clinton got off to a difficult start. He had made promises to end discrimination against gays and lesbians in the U.S. military, and the homosexual community presumed that he would remove all restrictions on their military service. Clinton ran into a buzz saw of opposition to removing those restrictions, however, so he settled on a compromise position, ordering that the military not ask about sexual orientation. Gays and lesbians would be permitted to serve in uniform only if they did not tell others of their orientation. This satisfied neither the homosexual community nor those intent on maintaining traditional bans on their military service and earned Clinton the enmity of both sides. By the end of the decade, it had become clear that the "Don't Ask, Don't Tell" policy was a failure. President Clinton also appointed First Lady Hillary Rodham Clinton to head a task force charged with designing a new health-care insurance system for the United States. Providing adequate and affordable health care was one of the core promises Clinton had made in the 1992 campaign. It was a promise he could not keep as the insurance industry turned up the pressure on Congress and engaged in a public-relations blitz that crippled the effort before the proposals ever emerged from the commission. Clinton spent an enormous amount of political capital in this doomed effort. The suicide of Vincent W. Foster Jr., his deputy counsel at the White House and former law partner of Hillary Rodham Clinton, just six months after the new administration took office was to have long-term consequences. Not only was this tragic death of a friend a personal blow, but Foster's suicide became the focus of conspiracy theorists hoping to smear the president. Foster was Clinton's counsel handling charges that the Clintons had been involved in suspect land deals in Arkansas. This next round of investigations led to a web of further inquiries that turned up some shady dealings by a variety of people in and out of the administration, damaged the reputations of others not involved, and ultimately led to the president's impeachment in 1998 and trial in 1999. The biggest blow of all was the resounding Republican success in the 1994 midterm elections. Many political observers believed the congressional elections that year would be a referendum on Clinton and his policies, and the Democratic defeat was widely viewed as Clinton's defeat. There were successes as well, of course. Certainly the agreement in 1993 between Israel and Palestine to begin to carve out a Palestinian presence in occupied territories was a major victory, as was his success in getting Congress to approve the North American Free Trade Agreement (NAFTA) that same year. The economy was getting stronger, some categories of crime were in decline, welfare reform had been tackled in tandem with the Republican Congress, the Brady Handgun Violence Prevention Act imposing a waiting period on handgun purchases was passed, his national-service program (AmeriCorps) was created, and it was increasingly clear that the budget could be balanced after three decades of deficits.

The 1996 Election. In the months after the disastrous 1994 elections, it seemed unlikely that Clinton could sufficiently recover the political momentum necessary to secure a second term. Yet, he was once again the "Comeback Kid." He learned from his 1980 gubernatorial reelection defeat and his comeback victory two years later; from the Gennifer Flowers extramarital affairs charges that almost destroyed his candidacy before he got the nomination in 1992; and from the Republican success in capturing control of Congress in 1994. His opponents in 1996 were Robert Joseph "Bob" Dole (R-Kansas) and H. Ross Perot (Reform Party). Clinton successfully mobilized his constituencies around the New Democratic agenda; he was able to take credit for a strong economy, welfare reform, and reduced crime. He won the election by a wider margin than in 1992, but it was still only a plurality of the votes cast. He received 49 percent of the popular vote, while Dole garnered 41 percent and Perot trailed with 8 percent.

Second Term. The soaring economy provided the opportunity for Clinton and the congressional Republicans to reach an agreement on the historic balanced budget in 1997. This was so successful that by 1999 the major domestic political issue was how to use the ever-increasing budget surplus. In 1998 former Maine Senator George John Mitchell successfully led negotiations to end the violence between Catholics and Protestants in Northern Ireland and, while further negotiations continued at the end of the decade, this agreement and its successors constituted a major foreign-policy success for the administration. Yet, from the beginning of the second term ethical questions took center stage. First, there were allegations of illegal fundraising by the president's campaign, and by Vice President Al Gore personally. Then the investigations led by Special Prosecutor Kenneth W. Starr branched out from the original Whitewater investigation to look into Vincent W. Foster Jr.'s suicide, Paula

Corbin Jones's allegations of sexual misconduct on the part of Clinton when he was Arkansas governor, and new charges of improper conduct with a young intern, Monica S. Lewinsky. As 1998 wore on these matters increasingly consumed the press coverage of the president to the near exclusion of most matters of public policy. In August, Starr presented a report to Congress alleging that Clinton had perjured himself in the Jones and Lewinsky matters. On 19 December 1998 the House of Representatives voted, largely along party lines, to approve two of the possible four articles of impeachment, making Clinton only the second president in American history to be impeached (Andrew Johnson, in 1868, was the other). The dramatic Senate trial was held in January and February of 1999. Two-thirds of the senators had to vote "guilty" in order to remove the president from office. Like his sole impeached predecessor, Clinton survived that critical vote. On the first article, alleging grand jury perjury, the Senate failed to remove him from office by a vote of fifty-five to forty-five margin, with ten Republicans joining the Democrats; on the second article, alleging obstruction of justice, the Senate split fifty-fifty, as five Republicans broke ranks with their colleagues. Throughout the entire process opinion polls repeatedly indicated that while the public had some serious reservations about Clinton's character, they viewed the impeachment as a partisan political ploy and emphatically did not want Clinton removed from office.

Foreign Affairs. Of course, events around the world did not stop just for the impeachment battle. In the spring of 1999 issues of national self-determination in the Balkans again surfaced, this time in the Yugoslav province of Kosovo whose large Albanian population lived uneasily with a powerful Serb minority. In February and March increasing violence against the Albanians by Serbs supported by the Yugoslav army put the Balkans once again at the front of the foreign-affairs agenda. The North Atlantic Treaty Organization (NATO), comprising the United States and its European allies, decided in March to initiate a bombing campaign to drive the Serbs out of Kosovo. In the process, most of the Albanian Kosovar population became refugees and NATO relentlessly bombed Serbian assets, particularly the military, governmental, and economic infrastructure in the Serbian portions of Yugoslavia. In June an agreement was reached with the Serb political leadership that ended the bombing in exchange for Serb withdrawal from Kosovo, return of the Albanian refugees, and a multinational peacekeeping force in Kosovo led by NATO. While some peace was restored to the region, at the end of the decade it remained uncertain as to what the future would hold for Kosovo and its people.

Impact on American Politics. Clinton will be remembered as the president who was impeached and who, through the entire unsavory episode, was forced to publicly admit to embarrassing indiscretions, lies, and partial truths. Yet, in many ways his two terms in office were successful. The economy boomed, the budget was balanced, welfare reform was initiated, crime was reduced, several historic agreements were reached in foreign affairs, including movement toward peace both in the Middle East and Northern Ireland, major free-trade pacts were negotiated and implemented, and a national service program was instituted. Furthermore, he was instrumental in creating a new Democratic Party coalition that could effectively compete with Republicans on the national stage. Journalist Elizabeth Drew, quoting a friend of Clinton, said, "Bill has always been someone who has lived on the edge, politically and personally."

Sources:

Elizabeth Drew, *On the Edge: The Clinton Presidency* (New York: Simon & Schuster, 1994).

David Maraniss, *First in His Class: A Biography of Bill Clinton* (New York: Simon & Schuster, 1995).

Stanley A. Renshon, *High Hopes: The Clinton Presidency and the Politics of Ambition* (New York: New York University Press, 1996).

Martin Walker, *The President We Deserve: Bill Clinton, His Rise, Falls, and Comebacks* (New York: Crown, 1996).

NEWT GINGRICH

1943-
U.S. REPRESENTATIVE (1979-1998); SPEAKER (1995-1998)

Background. Newton Leroy "Newt" Gingrich was born in Harrisburg, Pennsylvania, on 17 June 1943 and spent most of his childhood years with extended family, or in following his stepfather to military postings in Europe. He learned the pleasures of reading early, and his years overseas influenced his interest in European history and led to his determination to be involved in politics. He graduated from Emory University (1965) and earned his Masters (1968) and Ph.D. (1971) degrees from Tulane University. Beginning in 1970 he served as an assistant professor of history at West Georgia College. While he was a popular teacher, he did not envisage a long career as an obscure academic and, instead, got involved in politics. After unsuccessful runs for a seat in Congress in 1974 and 1976, he was finally elected in 1978 after dropping his previous commitment to environmentalism and adding a strong conservative message.

Changing the Nature of Congressional Politics. Gingrich burst onto the political scene in 1979 as a brash young Republican congressman who was unwilling to quietly take his seat on the back benches of the minority party while waiting for sufficient seniority to accrue to allow him to be influential. He wanted influence immediately and his ambitions for himself and the Republican Party were unconcealed. He wanted to help develop a Republican majority in the House and his personal ambition was to be Speaker of the House. From the outset he clashed with congressional stalwarts from both parties. He was a new order politician—impatient, willing to step on colleagues' toes, and innovative. He entered the House at a time when there was a profound sense that the United States was directionless and that its people were hungry for new leadership. This view was reinforced by the election of Ronald Reagan to the presidency and a Republican majority in the Senate in 1980. Reagan's victory failed to translate into Republican success in the House, however, which remained in Democratic hands throughout the 1980s and early 1990s. In fact, Republicans suffered further losses in the House in the 1982 election. Over the next dozen years, Gingrich organized a movement and developed a political organization that led to a Republican majority in the House after the 1994 elections, propelled him to the speakership, and profoundly changed the fundamental assumptions and content of American politics for the remainder of the decade.

Fundamental Change. Although he was a member of the minority party and a newcomer in the House, a legislative body with 435 members that was notoriously slow in giving recognition to newly elected members, Gingrich moved quickly to make senior members take notice of him. He brought a new style that was neither genteel, nor quiet, nor deferential. His brashness quickly angered both the majority Democrats and many senior members of his own party. Nevertheless, he was appointed to lead a task force to develop a plan to obtain a Republican majority. Acting on the belief that the way to do so was not to get along with the Democrats, but to confront them whenever possible on both substantive and personal ethical issues, he developed a plan that included active and constant confrontation with the Democratic leadership. He used every opportunity and available medium to paint the Democrats as entrenched in power, unresponsive to the needs and desires of the electorate, and unethical. The first high-profile victim was Representative Charles Coles Diggs Jr. (D-Michigan), who became a target of Gingrich's ethics investigations and who was ultimately convicted of mail fraud. Gingrich's success ultimately led him to take on Speaker James Claude Wright Jr. (D-Texas), who resigned in 1989 in response to ethics charges initiated by Gingrich. In 1983 he created the Conservative Opportunity Society, which was made up of rebellious Republican conservative Representatives, and along with this core of true believers began laying the groundwork for a Republican majority. They used the new C-SPAN television channel to gain visibility and to get their message to the public (concealing the fact that they were often speaking to a nearly empty House chamber, which viewers did not see on the screen). A mixture of conservative themes such as supply-side economics, the war on drugs, concern about crime, and attacks on the welfare system were combined with a belief in the unlimited future of high technology, appeals for a balanced budget, and calls for a line-item veto and term limits in what became known as the Contract with America. In 1994 the Republicans used this new message to capture a majority of seats in the House.

New Republican Majority. The Contract with America was a stroke of political genius. Republicans could run for Congress behind a unified message. Republican candidates pledged to support: a balanced budget amendment and a line-item veto; an end to cuts from the defense budget and a ban on U.S. troops serving under international command; tax cuts; a rise in social security earnings limits; major modifications in welfare to encourage people to take benefits for only a short time; a cut in capital-gains taxes; measures to strengthen the family, including new enforcement provisions for child-support payments and strengthening the rights of parents; legal reforms that would put limits on punitive damages that juries could award in product liability cases; an anti-crime package; and term limits for members of Congress. These proposals were an ingenuous mixture of symbolism (term limits, no defense cuts, and an attack on crime) and substance (balanced budget amendment, line-item veto, welfare reform, and legal reform). Gingrich and the Contract with America must be credited for the resounding Republican electoral success in 1994, as they gained fifty-four seats in the House, becoming the majority for the first time since 1952. The Contract remained a motivating factor for many Republicans for the next four years, but the actual legislative record was mixed. The balanced budget amendment never went to the states for approval because, although it passed in the House, it failed in the Senate. The line-item veto was approved with President Bill Clinton's support, but was declared unconstitutional by the Supreme Court in 1998. The defense budget was reduced and a bill to ban U.S. troops from serving under U.N. command failed in the Senate. Some tax cuts (for example, tax credits for children) were implemented, but the social security earnings limit was not raised; welfare reform was initiated by giving money and discretion to the states; some adjustments in capital-gains taxes were instituted; a child-support enforcement bill was passed; legal reform was stymied in the Senate; more money was appropriated, with President Clinton's support, for the war on crime; and term-limits legislation failed in the House. While the record in implementing the Contract was mixed, Gingrich increasingly influenced American politics and dominated the political agenda between 1994 and 1996.

Leaving Politics. Not everything Gingrich touched turned into political or personal gold. Ethical questions about the use of GOPAC (a Republican political action committee) funds in his 1990 election campaign and a $4.5 million dollar book deal led to a House Ethics Committee investigation. In January 1997 he was fined $300,000 for violating House rules barring the use of tax-exempt foundations for political purposes. Furthermore, some House Republicans, restless under his leadership and believing that President Clinton regularly outsmarted him, attempted to replace Gingrich as leader in 1997. He survived that attempt but was politically weakened. In the 1998 congressional elections Republicans expected to make gains in the number of House seats because of the Lewinsky scandal and impeachment facing Clinton. Instead, the Democrats gained five seats. The media and many House colleagues pinned responsibility for the losses on Gingrich. At a minimum the losses revealed that the Republican Party that was so unified under his leadership in 1994 was now deeply divided over social and economic issues, as well as over Gingrich's leadership. On 6 November 1998 Gingrich announced that he would not seek the speakership and would resign his seat.

The Legacy. Gingrich brought a new style to American politics—media-savvy, in-your-face, partisan, and ideological. It has become the mainstay of much of the business of Congress, especially in the House; it sparked a national debate about the decline of civility in American political discourse. Furthermore, he was responsible for setting the political agenda that made the Republican Party the majority party in the House after four frustrating decades of wandering in the political wilderness of seemingly perpetual minority status. His Contract with America enjoyed some very real successes, notably in welfare reform, and the issues it raised remain a fundamental part of the American political landscape at the end of the decade.

Sources:
Ed Gillespie and Bob Schellhas, eds., *Contract with America: The Bold Plan by Rep. Newt Gingrich, Rep. Dick Armey and the House Republicans to Change the Nation* (New York: Times Books, 1994).

Mel Steely, *The Gentleman from Georgia: The Biography of Newt Gingrich* (Macon, Ga.: Mercer University Press, 2000).

H. ROSS PEROT

1930-

BUSINESSMAN, POLITICIAN

New Political Force. Third parties and third-party candidates typically share several characteristics on the American political stage: they do not get elected; they may attract significant voter interest in one election, but both the candidate and party soon thereafter disappear from the public's radar; they do not have an effective state-by-state grassroots organization; and any success they might enjoy contains the seeds for their eventual demise as the major issues they champion are absorbed by one or both of the major parties. H. Ross Perot, however, was not typical, nor was the third party he inspired and initially bankrolled. He ran for president as the Reform Party candidate in 1992 and 1996, and though he lost, he made a credible showing. The Reform Party continued to exist at the end of the decade, with several well-known political figures vying to run under its banner in the 2000 presidential election. In addition, it had success organizing on a grassroots and state-by-state level, and succeeded in electing a governor (Jesse Ventura, Reform-Minnesota). Finally, neither of the major parties successfully captured the major issues fueling support for the Reform Party. At the end of the decade, Ross Perot's political vision continued to draw support across the United States.

Texas Background. Henry Ross Perot was born on 27 June 1930 in Texarkana, Texas; it was here that he grew up and went to public school and junior college. His family was of modest means, and he and his sister enjoyed a close relationship with their parents. Perot won an appointment to the United States Naval Academy and graduated in 1953. He served several years on a destroyer and aircraft carrier before leaving the Navy in 1957. In 1956 he married Margot Birmingham and they raised five children. They settled in Dallas after his discharge from the Navy and he went to work for IBM as a salesman in the data processing division. Yet, Perot was neither content with, nor temperamentally suited for, the life of an IBM salesman. With the help of a $1,000 loan his wife provided from her job teaching school, he went into business for himself, starting a small data-processing company named Electronic Data Systems (EDS). The new business was wildly successful, becoming a multimillion-dollar corporation with thousands of employees. It also made Perot a well-known figure in both Texas and national political circles. He later sold this company to General Motors and earned a seat on the GM Board of Directors—a position he later resigned. Subsequently, he started a new business, Perot Systems.

Taking Control. Patiently waiting for events to play themselves out was never part of Perot's style. Instead, he was more comfortable taking matters into his own hands. In the 1960s and early 1970s American prisoners of war (POWs) held in North Vietnam became an increasingly serious domestic political issue. U.S. negotiators were well aware that the POWs served as a bargaining card for North Vietnamese authorities, an increasingly valuable chip as Americans focused on the POWs' plight and put pressure on the U.S. government to secure their release. It was in this context that Perot became involved in shadowy, ultimately unsuccessful schemes to rescue the POWs. In 1979 Perot directed a successful rescue effort of EDS employees who were being held hostage in Iran. His reputation as someone who could design solutions for seemingly intractable problems and make things happen led him to become

involved in attempts to solve serious public policy problems in Texas. He was chosen to lead the committee charged with stemming the flow of illegal drugs; five new laws were ultimately enacted into Texas law. He also worked to improve public education in Texas, and set a national trend by linking the issue with local economic development. When he was motivated, he was willing to pledge immense personal effort, and often a financial commitment, into its resolution.

Running for President. The decision to run for President of the United States can never be taken lightly, as an individual has to have enormous energy, an ability to inspire others to work hard with little obvious payoff, and the capability to raise vast sums of money or a willingness to spend one's own fortune. In addition, a prospective candidate must be able to tap into some strongly felt issue that concerns millions of Americans, but that is not being addressed suitably by other candidates. For Perot the task was even more difficult because the issues motivating his run forced him outside of the normal two-party structure of U.S. politics. He had to create a grassroots political movement and, ultimately, a political party that captured the imagination of Americans who somehow felt that they were not being adequately served by the political establishment and, in order to have a voice, to overcome the welter of disparate state laws and regulations that discouraged such candidacies. Against all odds, Perot overcame these hurdles, fueled in part by the political tract *United We Stand*, armies of paid and unpaid signature gatherers, and lawyers willing to go to court to get Perot on the ballot. In the process the movement became a third political party—the Reform Party. Many issues championed by Perot and his party were either ignored or only peripherally discussed by Republicans and Democrats in 1992. Yet, he struck a chord with many Americans who felt that politics and government had become a closed game for a self-serving elite that ignored the problems faced by the average people.

Policy Proposals. Perot's presidential campaign emphasized issues designed to appeal to those who normally feel left out of the political process. He argued that elected officials were living too well and doing so on the tab of the American taxpayers. Perot proposed that retirement systems and health coverage for members of Congress and the president should be more like those of average Americans, and that gifts and free meals be eliminated for these officials. He also argued for balancing the budget, a balanced-budget amendment to the Constitution, and a line-item veto. His campaign reform proposals included a shorter election cycle to lessen the financial burden of running for office and restrictions on raising money, including a ban on raising money from outside the district (for campaigns for House of Representatives) or state (for Senate campaigns). Perot also argued that House members should be limited to three terms and Senators to two terms. The North American

Free Trade Agreement (NAFTA), which had been negotiated by the Bush administration and signed in 1992, was designed to gradually eliminate trade barriers between Canada, Mexico, and the United States. Many Americans, however, felt it would accelerate the trend of manufacturing jobs leaving the United States; Perot picked up on this theme, saying that the "giant sucking sound" people could hear was that of jobs going to low-wage countries. This issue figured prominently in Perot's political appeal after NAFTA went into effect on 1 January 1994 and had a central place in his 1996 run for president. Other issues Perot proposed included designing a new and simpler tax system; reforming Medicare, Medicaid, and Social Security; and changing lobbying rules.

Election Results. Perot and the Reform Party ran a distant third in both the 1992 and 1996 presidential elections, but that should not obscure the importance of the man and party. In 1992 Perot received about twenty million votes, which was 19 percent of those cast for president. Subsequent analyses suggested that his appeal was most strongly felt by those who either did not normally vote or who usually voted Republican. Although he did not win a single Electoral College vote, his totals in several key states may have allowed Bill Clinton to capture those states from President George Bush. In other words, it is likely that Clinton owes his 1992 victory to Perot voters who might otherwise have voted for Bush. In addition, Perot's showing indicated that many voters felt that they were not being represented by the two major parties. In the 1994 congressional elections the Republican Party, under the leadership of Newton Leroy "Newt" Gingrich (R-Georgia), incorporated many of Perot's proposals into its Contract with America, which is credited with propelling the Republicans into control of the Congress that year. In 1996 Perot's second run under the Reform Party banner resulted in a much smaller vote total of just 8 percent, yet it was significant that this third party had survived the years between elections and remained a viable force. While many observers felt that the 1996 election showed that Perot was beginning to wear a little thin on the American electorate, his ideas continued to be salient.

Sources:

Albert J. Menendez, *The Perot Voters & the Future of American Politics* (Amherst, N.Y.: Prometheus Books, 1996).

H. Ross Perot and Paul Simon, *The Dollar Crisis: A Blueprint to Help Rebuild the American Dream* (Arlington, Tex: Summit Publishing Group, 1996).

Perot, *United We Stand: How We Can Take Back Our Country* (New York: Hyperion, 1992).

Gerald Posner, *Citizen Perot: His Life and Times* (New York: Random House, 1996).

Sean Wilentz, "Third Out: Why the Reform Party's Best Days Are Behind It," *New Republic,* 221 (22 November 1999): 23–25.

PEOPLE IN THE NEWS

Richard Keith Armey (R-Texas) came to Congress in 1985 as a supporter of President Ronald Reagan's economic policy. An economist, he quickly gained recognition in Congress as a leader of the conservative forces when he opposed President George Bush's tax compromise with the Democrats in 1990. In 1995, as the Republicans took control of the House for the first time in forty years, Armey sought and won the post of House Majority Leader. Upon taking office he delivered the line repeated often since, "The American people didn't give us power, they gave us responsibility." Armey continued as majority leader, even after the resignation of Newton Leroy "Newt" Gingrich (R-Georgia) as Speaker in 1998 and the election of John Dennis Hastert (R-Illinois) to succeed him.

Bill Bradley (D–New Jersey) retired from the U.S. Senate in 1996 after eighteen years of service. The ex–New York Knicks basketball star returned to politics in 1999 when he announced his candidacy for the Democratic Party presidential nomination in 2000.

In 1992 **Carol Moseley Braun** (D–Illinois) was elected as the first African American woman to serve in the Senate. She lost her bid for reelection in 1998 to state senator Peter G. Fitzgerald, largely because of charges that her campaign finances had been misused. On 10 November 1999 Braun was confirmed by the Senate as U.S. ambassador to New Zealand.

Ronald Brown (1941–1996) became the first African American to head a major U.S. political party as chairman of the Democratic National Committee (DNC) and the highest-ranking African American in the Clinton administration (Commerce Secretary). On 3 April 1996 an Air Force Boeing 737 carrying Secretary Brown and thirty others on a trade mission crashed into a mountainside near Dubrovnik airport in Croatia. At the time of his death, Brown was the major target of an independent counsel probe, headed by Daniel Pearson, which was looking into financial irregularities when he was chairman of the DNC.

Willie Lewis Brown Jr., longtime Democratic Speaker of the California Assembly (1980–1995), who lost his seat to term limits, was elected in 1995 as the first African American mayor of San Francisco.

George W. Bush, son of former President **George Bush,** was elected governor of Texas in 1994. A popular politician, he was reelected in 1998 to become the first Texas governor to serve two consecutive four-year terms. In 1999 he announced his candidacy for the Republican Party presidential nomination in 2000.

John Ellis "Jeb" Bush, son of former President **George Bush** and brother of Texas governor **George W. Bush,** was elected governor of Florida in 1998.

Ben Nighthorse Campbell (R–Colorado) became the first Native American (Northern Cheyenne) elected to the U.S. Senate in more than sixty years. Campbell was originally elected in 1992 as a Democrat but switched parties in 1995 after the Republicans took control of Congress that year. He was reelected in 1998 as a Republican. Campbell is the first Native American to chair the Indian Affairs Committee, and was also instrumental in getting the name of the Custer Battlefield Monument in Montana changed to the Little Bighorn Battlefield National Monument.

James Carville (the Ragin' Cajun) became the best-known Democratic political campaign strategist of the 1990s when he headed both of Bill Clinton's winning presidential campaigns in 1992 and 1996. Immediately after the election in 1992, he married **Mary Matalin,** a key Republican adviser to President George Bush.

Richard Bruce Cheney (R–Wyoming) left the U.S. House of Representatives on 17 March 1989 to become Secretary of Defense (1989–1993) for the Bush administration. As Secretary, Cheney was a key decision maker during the Persian Gulf War (1991).

Henry G. Cisneros, former mayor of San Antonio, Texas, was named Secretary of Housing and Urban Development (HUD) by President Bill Clinton during his first term in office. Cisneros was the rising star of the Hispanic community until rumors of his extramarital affairs began circulating, and he resigned in 1997 as a result of a Federal Bureau of Investigation (FBI) probe into payoffs he allegedly had made to a former mistress.

Richard M. Daley, Democratic mayor of Chicago (1989–), followed in the footsteps of his legendary father, Mayor **Richard Joseph Daley** (1955–1976). In 1996 he hosted the National Democratic Convention. Its success in showing off the city of Chicago did much to erase the memories of the debacle of the 1968 Democratic convention that turned into a riot and tarnished the reputation of his father.

Elizabeth Dole, Secretary of Labor in the Bush administration (1989–1990), which she left to become president of the American Red Cross. She left the organization to help her husband, **Robert Joseph Dole** (R-Kansas), campaign for the presidency in 1996. In 1999 she made a run for the presidency, but dropped out in November because of an inability to raise sufficient campaign funds to challenge front-runner **George W. Bush.**

Robert Joseph Dole (R-Kansas, 1969–1996) was Senate Majority Leader in the 103rd Congress. In 1996 he was nominated as the Republican canidate for president, but lost to **Bill Clinton,** 41 percent to 49 percent. After retiring from politics he became a spokesman for a variety of products including American Express and Viagra.

David Duke, former National Director of the Knights of the Ku Klux Klan, served one term in the Louisiana House of Representatives before losing a 1990 United States Senate race to **J. Bennett Johnston.** He then ran in 1991 for Louisiana Governor but lost to **Edwin W. Edwards.** A perennial candidate in Louisiana, he ran a losing Senate race in 1996 and again in 1999.

Louis Farrakhan (Louis Eugene Walcott), successor to **Elijah Muhammad** as head of the Nation of Islam, outraged many people when he made several disparaging comments about Jews. In 1995 he organized the Million Man March in Washington, D.C., which brought African American men together in a reaffirming spirit of the responsibilities of brotherhood and fatherhood.

In 1992 (Year of the Woman), **Dianne Feinstein** (D–California) and **Barbara Boxer** (D-California) were elected as the first female Senators from the state. Feinstein had served as mayor of San Francisco (1978–1988).

In 1994 Speaker of the House **Thomas S. Foley** (D–Washington) lost his bid for reelection in his home district as a result of the Republican landslide. His opponent, **George R. Nethercutt Jr.,** charged that he had lost touch with the values and views of people in his district. In 1997 President Bill Clinton appointed Foley as ambassador to Japan.

Malcolm S. "Steve" Forbes Jr., editor of *Forbes* and son of billionaire Malcolm Forbes, became one of a series of wealthy candidates without any previous political experience running for the presidency as a Republican in 1996. Because he did not take any federal matching funds he was able to outspend his opponents in the early primaries however, the money was not enough to overcome the handicaps of a stiff presence and a lack of political expertise.

Richard Andrew Gephardt (D–Missouri) became the Democratic Minority Leader of the U.S. House of Representatives after the Republicans gained control of the House, and Speaker **Thomas Stephen Foley** (D–Washington) lost his bid for reelection.

Rudolph W. Giuliani, popular Republican mayor of New York City (1994–), turned the $2 billion budget deficit he inherited into a $2 billion surplus. His targeted tax cuts and pro-business philosophy led to the highest five-year period of private sector job growth in the history of the city, while decreasing the crime rate to make it the safest large city in the United States.

Albert Gore Jr., former Democratic Senator from Tennessee, served as Vice President of the United States (1993–2000). He announced in 1999 that he would seek the Democratic nomination for president in 2000. An ardent environmentalist, he published a treatise, *Earth in the Balance: Ecology and the Human Spirit* (1992).

Vernon E. Jordan Jr., lawyer and civil-rights leader, was picked by President Bill Clinton to be co-chair of his presidential transition team in 1992–1993. Jordan again was thrust into the spotlight when he arranged to find **Monica S. Lewinsky** a job in New York City. Washington scuttlebutt voiced the opinion that it was in return for her silence in the **Paula Corbin Jones** civil case. Jordan denied those charges in his testimony under oath before the grand jury.

During the summer of 1995, **Monica S. Lewinsky** served as an intern in the White House. Her affair with President Bill Clinton became the central focus of his 1998 impeachment and 1999 Senate trial.

In July 1996 **Chester Trent Lott** (R–Mississippi) became the Senate Majority Leader upon the retirement of the former leader, **Robert Joseph Dole** (R–Kansas), after his failed presidential campaign. A southern gentleman, Lott, who was well liked and respected, was able to forge bipartisan ties with the Clinton administration.

Mary Matalin was Deputy Campaign Manager for President George Bush's reelection campaign in 1992. As the onboard planner who traveled with Bush throughout the campaign, she emerged as a vocal and occasionally controversial defender of the president and his policies. After his defeat, she became host of *Equal Time,* a political talk show on CNBC, and a frequent political commentator on the television networks. She coauthored with her husband **James Car-**

ville *All's Fair: Love, War and Running for President* (1994).

John Sidney McCain III (R–Arizona), a former U.S. Navy pilot who was a prisoner of war of the North Vietnamese (1967–1973), became a maverick congressman and senator. In 1991 he was implicated as one of the "Keating Five" in the Lincoln Savings and Loan scandal along with Senators **Alan Cranston** (D–California), **Dennis Webster DeConcini** (D–Arizona), **John Herschel Glenn Jr.** (D–Ohio) and **Donald Wayne Riegle Jr.** (D–Michigan). Although not found guilty of anything other than poor judgment, the event was the low point in his career. He was able to come back and in 1996 nominated **Robert Joseph Dole** (R–Kansas) for president at the Republican National Convention in San Diego. A strong national prominence led to his announcement in 1999 that he would be a presidential candidate in 2000.

Kweisi Mfume (Frizzell Gray), (D-Maryland, 1987–1997), served as head of the congressional black caucus. An outspoken civil-rights leader, he left Congress in 1997 to head the flagging National Association for the Advancement of Colored People (NAACP), which was losing membership because of corrupt and inept leadership. Mfume's energetic and forceful guidance quickly turned around the organization, making it again a leading voice for the African American community.

In 1993 **Dee Dee Myers** was named by President Bill Clinton as the first female White House Press Secretary. The youngest person ever to serve in the office, she left to become a political talk-show host and, later, the Washington editor of *Vanity Fair.*

General **Colin L. Powell** (U.S. Army, retired) was the first African American head of the Joint Chiefs of Staff (1989–1993), served in that office during the Persian Gulf War (1991), and became a leading figure in Republican politics after his retirement in 1994.

J. Danforth "Dan" Quayle, Vice President under President George Bush (1989–1993), tried a comeback in politics by running for President in 1996 and again in 1999. He could not garner much support or money, however, so he dropped out of both races.

General **H. Norman Schwarzkopf** (U.S. Army, retired) led North Atlantic Treaty Organization (NATO) forces during the Persian Gulf War (1991). A robust, genial, and forceful leader, he quickly became more popular with the American people than any other general since Dwight D. Eisenhower. Though there was wide speculation that he might run for president after he retired, Schwarzkopf showed no inclination to make politics a second career. In 1992 he retired from service and wrote his autobiography, *It Doesn't Take a Hero: General H. Norman Schwarzkopf, the*

Autobiography (1992), in collaboration with Peter Petre.

Kenneth W. Starr, a conservative Republican, was chosen by Congress as the independent counsel for investigation of President Bill Clinton's involvement in the Whitewater affair, a scandal concerning illegal loans made by a failed savings and loan. This investigation was later expanded to include Travelgate and allegations that the White House used the Federal Bureau of Investigation (FBI) to improperly collect background files. Starr was viewed by some as too partisan and out to destroy the Clintons. In 1997 he announced his decision to accept a position as dean of Pepperdine University law school. In the face of intense criticism, Starr reversed himself, but the action undermined his credibility. Starr's report to Congress was finally issued in September 1998 and he resigned his office on 18 October 1999.

George R. Stephanopoulos burst onto the national stage during the 1992 presidential campaign as director of communications for the Clinton/Gore campaign. After his election, Clinton named Stephanopoulos as senior adviser to the president, a position he held for four years. After leaving the administration, he became a journalist, television commentator, adjunct professor, and author. During the scandal surrounding the Lewinsky affair, Stephanopoulos broke with Clinton and publicly denounced his behavior. He wrote *All Too Human: A Political Education* (1999), an autobiographical account of his time with the Clinton team.

In 1991 **Clarence Thomas,** an African American federal appeals court judge, was nominated by President Bush to succeed Justice **Thurgood Marshall** on the U.S. Supreme Court when the latter retired because of advanced age and poor health. Thomas, a conservative Republican, had served as chairman of the Equal Employment Opportunity Commission (EEOC) between 1982 and 1990. During his confirmation hearings by the Senate Judiciary Committee, charges were made by a former co-worker, **Anita F. Hill,** that Thomas had used his position to make unwelcome sexual advances. Graphic testimony in the Senate chamber and demonstrations by women's groups around the country created a messy confirmation. Despite the uproar, the Republican majority in the Senate confirmed his nomination. Thomas has been relatively quiet on the Court, taking his lead from Justice **Antonin Scalia.**

James Strom Thurmond (R–South Carolina) in 1997 became the longest-serving U.S. senator in history [**John Cornelius Stennis** (D–Mississippi) and **Carl Trumbull Hayden** (D–Arizona) each served over forty-one years]. He entered the Senate as a Democrat in 1954, then switched to the Republican Party in 1964 over the issue of civil rights. As senator with the most seniority, he was named President Pro Tempore in 1987–1989 and again in 1995, when the Republicans regained control of the Senate. Reelected in 1996 at the age of ninety-four, he became the oldest senator in history and still served in his post at the end of the decade.

Jesse Ventura, former professional wrestler and mayor of Brooklyn Park, the sixth largest city in Minnesota, won the race for governor of Minnesota in 1998 on the Reform Party ticket. Ventura quickly became notorious for his unorthodox cultural and political views.

Christine Todd Whitman, Republican governor of New Jersey (1994–), became a leader as one of a handful of women in the Republican Party with national prominence. She was chosen by the party to deliver the response to President Bill Clinton's 1995 State of the Union Address and in 1996 was honorary cochair of the Republican National Convention.

DEATHS

Ralph David Abernathy, 64, minister, leader in the civil-rights movement of the 1950s and 1960s, cofounder of the Southern Christian Leadership Conference (SCLC), 12 March 1992.

Bella Savitsky Abzug, 77, outspoken feminist and Democratic representative from New York (1971–1977); first Jewish woman in Congress; known also for her outstanding collection of sometimes-outlandish hats, 31 March 1998.

Spiro Theodore Agnew, 77, Republican governor of Maryland (1967–1969) and vice president of the United States (1969–1973); resigned because he was facing bribery and tax evasion charges and eventually pleaded "no contest" to tax evasion, 17 September 1996.

Leslie "Les" Aspin Jr., 56, Democratic representative from Wisconsin (1971–1993) and Secretary of Defense (1993–1994), 21 May 1995.

Harvey Leroy "Lee" Atwater, 40, chairman of the Republican National Committee (1988–1990); infamous for designing negative political campaigns, especially the 1988 "Willie Horton" campaign against Democratic presidential nominee Massachusetts governor Michael Stanley Dukakis, 29 March 1991.

Daisy Lee (Gatson) Bates, 85, African American civil rights activist, who in 1957, at considerable risk to her own safety, supported and nurtured the nine African American students who integrated Little Rock (Arkansas) Central High School, 4 November 1999.

Terrel Howard "Ted" Bell, 74, Secretary of Education (1981–1985), appointed by President Ronald Reagan to phase out the Department of Education, but Bell changed his mind and, despite Reagan's objections, oversaw the writing and issuing of a report on schools (*A Nation at Risk,* 1987) calling for more help for education, 22 June 1996.

Ezra Taft Benson, 94, Secretary of Agriculture (1953–1961), known for his outspoken and extremely conservative views; president of the Church of Jesus Christ of Latter-Day Saints (1985–1994), 30 May 1994.

Rose Elizabeth Bird, 63, first female justice and chief justice of the California Supreme Court (1977–1986), controversial because of her views and decisions in opposition to the death penalty, 4 December 1999.

Harry Andrew Blackmun, 90, associate justice of the U.S. Supreme Court (1970–1994) who wrote the majority opinion in *Roe* v. *Wade* (1973), 4 March 1999.

Salvatore "Sonny" Bono, 62, Republican representative from California (1995–1998), best known for his singing and acting partnership *Sonny and Cher,* 5 January 1998.

Thomas Bradley, 80, Democratic mayor of Los Angeles (1973–1993), first African American to be elected to the Los Angeles city council and mayorship, 29 September 1998.

William Joseph Brennan Jr., 91, associate justice of the U.S. Supreme Court (1956–1990), wrote *Baker* v. *Carr* (1962) decision paving the way for reapportionment of state legislatures; *New York Times Co.* v. *Sullivan* (1964) reinforcing freedom of the press; and *Texas* v. *Johnson* (1989) affirming that burning the U.S. flag is political expression protected by the First Amendment. He was a critical part of the 1950s and 1960s liberal majority on the Court that ushered in a new era for civil rights and civil liberties, 24 July 1997.

Alfred Bryant Renton "Harry" Bridges, 88, Australian-born radical labor leader. He came to the United States in 1920 and later became a naturalized citizen; organized labor strikes on the West coast among longshoremen and maritime workers; was ordered deported several times, but he won court battles to stay in the United States; in 1950 he was convicted of perjury for denying Communist Party membership in his oath of naturalization and was sentenced to seven years in prison, but that too was overturned on appeal, 30 March 1990.

Edmund G. "Pat" Brown, 90, Democratic Governor of California (1959–1966); lost bid for a third term to Ronald Reagan (1966); father of Edmund. B "Jerry" (Governor Moonbeam) Brown Jr., 16 February 1996.

Ronald H. Brown, first African American chairman of the Democratic National Committee (DNC, 1989–1992); Secretary of Commerce (1993–1996), 3 April 1996.

McGeorge Bundy, 77, National Security Adviser to Presidents John F. Kennedy and Lyndon B. Johnson (1961–1966), one of the architects of increasing U.S. involvement in the war in Vietnam; president of the Ford Foundation (1966–1979), 16 September 1996.

Warren Earl Burger, 88, chief justice of the U.S. Supreme Court (1969–1986), wrote the decision in *United States* v. *Nixon* (1974) establishing that claims of executive privilege do not shield presidents from judicial subpoenas, leading to the release of Nixon's tapes and ultimately to his resignation from the presidency, 25 June 1995.

Anthony Joseph Celebrezze, 88, mayor of Cleveland, Ohio (1953–1962); first ethnically Italian cabinet member as Secretary of Health, Education and Welfare (1962–1965), 29 October 1998.

John Hubbard Chafee, 76, Republican governor (1963–1969) of, and senator (1976–1999) from, Rhode Island; Secretary of the Navy (1969–1972), 24 October 1999.

Lawton Mainor Chiles Jr., 68, Democratic senator (1971–1989) from, and governor (1991–1998) of, Florida, 12 December 1998.

Clark McAdams Clifford, 91, lawyer and adviser to Democratic presidents, including Harry S Truman, John F. Kennedy, Lyndon B. Johnson, and Jimmy Carter; helped draft the National Security Act of 1947, which set up U.S. institutional structure in foreign affairs; and, while Secretary of Defense (1968–1969), he convinced Johnson that the war in Vietnam was unwinnable, leading to Johnson's decision not to run for another term, 10 October 1998.

William Egar Colby, Central Intelligence Agency (CIA) agent and CIA director (1973–1976) cooperated with congressional investigations leading to the publicizing of intelligence operations and instituted reforms, 27 April 1996.

John Bowden Connally Jr., 76, Democratic governor of Texas (1963–1969); wounded while riding in the same car in which President John F. Kennedy was assassinated; switched to the Republican Party and served as President Richard M. Nixon's Secretary of Treasury (1971–1972); unsuccessfully ran for the Republican nomination for president (1980), 15 June 1993.

John Sherman Cooper, 89, Republican senator from Kentucky (1946–1949, 1952–1955, 1956–1973); ambassador to India (1955–1956) and East Germany (1974–1976); member of the Warren Commission that investigated the assassination of President John F. Kennedy; and was also one of the few Republican senators identified as opposing the war in Vietnam, 21 February 1991.

Charles Coles Diggs Jr., 75, Democratic representative from Michigan (1955–1980); founder and first chairman of the Congressional Black Caucus (1969–1971); first victim of Newton Leroy "Newt" Gingrich's (R-Georgia) strategy to target congressional Democrats on ethics issues in order to discredit them and help elect Republicans. Diggs was convicted (1978) of taking kickbacks from employees on his congressional office payroll, was censured (1979), resigned (1980), and was imprisoned for seven months (1980–1981), 24 August 1998.

John Daniel Ehrlichman, 73, chief domestic adviser to President Richard M. Nixon (1969–1973); authorized covert operations designed to discredit Dr. Daniel J. Ellsberg, who had delivered the *Pentagon Papers* (1971) to the press; was part of the Watergate cover-up; resigned at Nixon's request in 1973, and was convicted of conspiracy, obstruction of justice, and perjury. After his release from prison he wrote mildly interesting and fairly successful political novels, 14 February 1999.

Orval Eugene Faubus, 84, Democratic segregationist governor of Arkansas (1955–1967); mobilized the Arkansas National Guard to prevent nine African American students from attending Little Rock Central High School in 1957, and in doing so set off a national furor that increased nationwide support for integration, 14 December 1994.

Millicent Hammond Fenwick, 81, Republican representative from New Jersey (1975–1983); ambassador to the United Nations Agencies for Food and Agriculture (1983–1987); reputed to have inspired the character Lacey Davenport in the comic strip "Doonesbury," 16 December 1992.

Robert H. Finch, 70, campaign manager for Richard M. Nixon's unsuccessful 1960 presidential campaign, lieutenant governor of California (1966–1969); and Secretary of Health, Education, and Welfare (1969–1970), 10 October 1995.

Vincent Walker Foster Jr., 48, White House deputy counsel for President Bill Clinton and former Arkansas law partner of Hillary Rodham Clinton; oversaw the handling of the Whitewater investigation; his suicide prompted intensified investigations both into his death and the Whitewater scandal, 20 July 1993.

James William Fulbright, 89, Democratic representative (1943–1945) and senator (1945–1962, 1968–1974) from Arkansas; chairman of the powerful Senate Foreign Relations Committee (1959–1974); used committee hearings to question U.S. policy in Vietnam, 9 February 1995.

Arthur J. Goldberg, 81, Secretary of Labor (1961–1962); associate justice of the U.S. Supreme Court (1962–1965); wrote the *Escobedo* v. *Illinois* (1964) decision affirming that confessions by defendants who were deprived of counsel cannot be used in court; and ambassador to the United Nations (1965–1968), 19 January 1990.

Barry Morris Goldwater, 89, Republican senator from Arizona (1953–1965, 1969–1987); candidate for president in 1964; credited with being the godfather to the conservative political movement of the late twentieth century, although in his later years he disavowed some conservative positions and tactics. His acceptance speech at the Republican National Convention in 1964 contained the famous phrase: "extremism in the defense of liberty is no vice . . . moderation in the pursuit of justice is no virtue," 29 May 1998.

Albert Arnold Gore Sr., 90, Democratic representative (1945–1953) and senator (1953–1971) from Tennessee; early opponent of U.S. participation in the Vietnam War; father of Vice President Albert Arnold Gore Jr., 5 December 1998.

Harry Robbins "Bob" Haldeman, 66, chief of staff to President Richard M. Nixon until he was forced to resign, partly to protect the president, in the wake of the Watergate scandals, 12 November 1993.

Samuel Ichiye Hayakawa, 85, educator, linguist, and semanticist; senator from California (1977–1983); first came to the public's notice when he stood up in opposition to student demonstrators while president of San Francisco State College (1968–1973), 27 February 1992.

Alger Hiss, 92, State Department official and adviser to President Franklin D. Roosevelt; accused in 1948 by Whittaker Chambers, in testimony before the House Un-American Activities Committee, of being a communist spy, which he denied; was convicted and served five years in prison for perjury; spent the rest of his life asserting his innocence, 15 November 1996.

Roman Lee Hruska Sr., 94, Republican representative (1953–1954) and senator (1954–1976) from Nebraska; well known for trying to defend a Richard M. Nixon nominee to the Supreme Court who some said was mediocre, arguing the Court could use a little mediocrity, 25 April 1999.

Harold Everett Hughes, 74, Democratic governor (1963–1969) of, and senator (1969–1975) from, Iowa; unsuccessful candidate for presidential nomination (1972), 23 October 1996.

Richard Howard "Dick" Ichord II, 66, representative from Missouri (1961–1981); last chairman of the House Un-American Activities Committee (House Internal Security Committee after 1969), 25 December 1992.

Randolph Jennings, 96, Democratic representative (1933–1947) and senator (1958–1984) from West Virginia; drafted and secured passage of the 26th amendment to the U.S. Constitution, securing the right to vote for eighteen- to twenty-year-old citizens, 8 May 1998.

William Pat Jennings, 74, Democratic representative from Virginia (1955–1967), 2 August 1994.

Barbara Charline Jordan, 59, Democratic representative from Texas (1973–1979); first African American woman elected to Congress from the South, as well as to give the keynote at the Democratic National Convention (1976); was first noticed nationally because of her service on the Judiciary Committee considering the impeachment of Richard M. Nixon (1974), 17 January 1996.

Meir (Martin David) Kahane, 58, rabbi and founder of a radical Zionist movement, 5 November 1990.

Thomas Henry Kuchel, 84, Republican senator from California (1953–1969); refused to buckle to the demands of the fringe Right in California Republican politics, 21 November 1994.

Thurgood Marshall, 82, associate justice of the U.S. Supreme Court (1967–1991), the first African American to hold a seat there, who in 1954, as chief counsel for the National Association for the Advancement of Colored People (NAACP), argued *Brown* v. *Board of Education* before the Supreme Court, 24 January 1993.

John A. McCone, 89, chairman of the Atomic Energy Commission (1958–1961); director of the Central Intelligence Agency (1961–1965), 14 February 1991.

Wilmer David "Vinegar Bend" Mizell, 68, Republican representative from North Carolina (1969–1975); assistant Secretary of Commerce (1975–1976).

Before becoming a politician he was a pitcher in the major leagues (1950–1962), 21 February 1999.

George Lloyd Murphy, 89, actor, Republican senator from California (1965–1971), 3 May 1992.

Edmund Sixtus Muskie, 81, Democratic governor (1955–1959) of, and senator (1959–1980) from, Maine; U.S. Secretary of State (1980–1981); vice-presidential nominee (1968); and candidate for the Democratic nomination for president (1972), but his chances were dashed when he cried while defending his wife from scurrilous press attacks on her character, 26 March 1996.

Richard Milhous Nixon, 81, Republican representative (1947–1950) and senator (1950–1953) from California; vice president of the U.S. (1953–1961); unsuccessful candidate for president (1960); unsuccessful candidate for governor of California (1962); President of the United States (1969–1974). The Watergate scandal led to allegations that he had engaged in a cover-up, and as his impeachment by the House of Representatives looked increasingly likely, he resigned the presidency. He was later pardoned by President Gerald R. Ford and wrote several books on foreign affairs, 22 April 1994.

Thelma Catherine "Pat" Nixon (née Ryan), 79, wife of President Richard M. Nixon; first lady (1969–1973), 22 June 1993.

Thomas Phillip "Tip" O'Neill Jr., 81, Democratic representative from Massachusetts (1953–1987); Speaker of the House (1977–1987); author of *Man of the House: The Life and Political Memoirs of Speaker Tip O'Neill* (1987); famous for the piece of political wisdom that "all politics is local," 5 January 1994.

Lewis Franklin Powell Jr., 90, associate justice of the U.S. Supreme Court (1972–1987); wrote the decision in the *University of California Regents* v. *Bakke* (1978) that outlawed racial quotas, but allowed race to be a factor in university admissions policy, in effect confirming affirmative-action policies, 25 August 1998.

Dixie Lee Ray, 79, governor of Washington (1977–1981); supporter of nuclear power and last chairman of the Atomic Energy Commission (AEC), 2 January 1994.

Abraham Alexander Ribicoff, 87, Democratic representative (1949–1953) and senator (1963–1981) from Connecticut; governor of Connecticut (1955–1961); Secretary of Health, Education and Welfare (1961–1962). He is famous for denouncing the "Gestapo tactics" of the Chicago police at the 1968 Democratic National Convention, 22 February 1998.

Elliot Lee Richardson, 79, Republican politician; Under Secretary of State (1969–1970); Secretary of Health, Education, and Welfare (1970–1973); Secretary of Defense (1973); Attorney General (1973); U.S. Ambassador to the United Kingdom (1975–1976); and Secretary of Commerce (1976–1977). He is the only person to have headed four different cabinet departments;

resigned as Attorney General (1973) rather than carry out President Richard Nixon's orders to fire Watergate special prosecutor Archibald Cox, setting off a chain of appointments and firings known as the "Saturday Night Massacre"; author of *Reflections of a Radical Moderate* (1996), 31 December 1999.

George Wilcken Romney, 88, Republican governor of Michigan (1963–1969); unsuccessful candidate for the Republican nomination for president in 1968; served as Secretary of Housing and Urban Development in Richard M. Nixon's cabinet (1969–1973), 26 July 1995.

David Dean Rusk, 85, Secretary of State during the Kennedy and Johnson administrations (1961–1969); was an active participant in the deliberations in the executive branch during the Cuban Missile Crisis (1962); one of the architects of U.S. involvement in Vietnam, 20 December 1994.

Terrance "Terry" Sanford, 80, Democratic governor (1961–1965) of, and senator (1986–1993) from, North Carolina; candidate for the Democratic nomination for president (1972, 1976); president of Duke University (1969–1985), 18 April 1998.

Hugh Doggett Scott Jr., 93, Republican representative (1941–1945, 1947–1959) and senator (1959–1977) from Pennsylvania; Senate Minority Leader (1969–1977), 21 July 1994.

John Joseph Sirica, 87, federal judge; presided in the Watergate trial; subpoenaed the tapes that suggested that President Richard M. Nixon was involved in a cover-up, leading to his resignation, 14 August 1992.

Margaret Chase Smith, 97, Republican representative (1940–1949) and senator (1949–1973) from Maine; first woman elected to both houses of Congress, 29 May 1995.

Maurice Hubert Stans, 90, Republican administrator and fund-raiser; director of the Office of Management and Budget (OMB, 1958–1961) and Secretary of Commerce (1969–1972). Charged with violating fund-raising laws in Richard M. Nixon's 1972 reelection campaign; acquitted, but pleaded guilty to misdemeanor charges in 1975 and paid a fine, 14 April 1998.

John Cornelius Stennis, 93, Democratic senator from Mississippi (1947–1989); President Pro Tempore of the Senate (1987–1989). He was one of the Southern senators known for their opposition to civil rights legislation, 23 April 1995.

John Goodwin Tower, 65, Republican senator from Texas (1961–1985); chairman of the Tower Commission established to investigate the Iran-Contra scandal in the Reagan administration (1987); appointed by President George Bush to be Secretary of Defense (1989), but failed to gain confirmation in the Senate, 5 April 1991.

Paul Efthemios Tsongas, 55, Democratic representative (1975–1979) and senator (1979–1985) from Massachusetts; candidate for the Democratic Party nomination for president (1992), 18 January 1997.

Morris King Udall, 75, Democratic representative from Arizona (1961–1991); an early opponent of the Vietnam War and an environmentalist; unsuccessful candidate for the Democratic nomination for president (1976), 12 December 1998.

John Anthony Volpe, Republican governor of Massachusetts (1961–1963, 1965–1969); Secretary of Transportation (1969–1973); ambassador to Italy (1973–1977), 1998.

George Corley Wallace Jr., 79, segregationist governor of Alabama (1963–1967, 1971–1979, and 1983–1987), although he did change his stance by the 1980s; famous for refusing to allow African American students to enroll at the University of Alabama by standing in the door of the University to block their court-ordered admission (1963); ran for president as the American Independent Party candidate (1968); unsuccessful candidate for the Democratic Party nomination for president (1972 and 1976); paralyzed in the lower half of his body by a would-be assassin's bullet (1972), 13 September 1998.

Robert Clifton Weaver, 89, first African American cabinet member as Secretary of the Department of Housing and Urban Development (1966–1969), 17 July 1997.

Jamie Lloyd Whitten, 85, Democratic representative from Mississippi (1939–1993); chair of the House Appropriations Committee (1978–1992); served in the House longer than anyone in history, fifty-three years; opposed civil-rights legislation and channeled enormous amounts of federal spending into his state, 9 September 1995.

Ralph Webster Yarborough, 92, Democratic senator from Texas (1957–1971); only member of Congress from a southern state to vote for the 1964 Civil Rights Act; was riding in the automobile carrying Lyndon B. Johnson in the Dallas motorcade when President John F. Kennedy was shot (1963), 27 January 1996.

Coleman Alexander Young, 79, first African American mayor of Detroit (1974–1994) and first African American member of the Democratic National Committee (1968), 29 November 1997.

PUBLICATIONS

Ryan J. Barrilleaux and Mary E. Stuckey, eds., *Leadership and the Bush Presidency: Prudence or Drift in an Era of Change?* (Westport, Conn.: Praeger, 1992).

W. Lance Bennett and David L. Paletz, eds., *Taken by Storm: The Media, Public Opinion, and the U.S. Foreign Policy in the Gulf War* (Chicago: University of Chicago Press, 1994).

George Bush and Brent Scowcroft, *A World Transformed* (New York: Knopf, 1998).

Dan T. Carter, *From George Wallace to Newt Gingrich: Race in the Conservative Counterrevolution 1963–1994* (Baton Rouge: Louisiana State University Press, 1996).

Elizabeth Drew, *On the Edge: The Clinton Presidency* (New York: Simon & Schuster, 1994).

Thomas L. Friedman, *The Lexus and the Olive Tree* (New York: Farrar, Straus and Giroux, 1999).

Ed Gillespie and Bob Schellhas, eds., *Contract with America: The Bold Plan by Rep. Newt Gingrich, Rep. Dick Armey and the House Republicans to Change the Nation* (New York: Times Books, 1994).

Martin L. Gross, *The Great Whitewater Fiasco: An American Tale of Money, Power, and Politics* (New York: Ballentine, 1994).

Mark Grossman, *Encyclopedia of the Persian Gulf War* (Santa Barbara, Cal.: ABC-CLIO, 1995).

Michael Nelson, ed., *The Election of 1992* (Washington, D.C.: Congressional Quarterly Press, 1993).

Richard A. Posner, *An Affair of State: The Investigation, Impeachment and Trial of President Clinton* (Cambridge, Mass.: Harvard University Press, 1999).

Bernard D. Reams Jr., ed., *Health Care Reform, 1993–1994: The American Experience: Clinton and Congress—Law, Policy, and Economics: A Legislative History of the Health Security Act* (Buffalo, N.Y.: Hein, 1996).

Stanley A. Renshon, *High Hopes: The Clinton Presidency and the Politics of Ambition* (New York: New York University Press, 1996).

Charles Tiefer, *The Semi-Sovereign Presidency: The Bush Administration's Strategy for Governing Without Congress* (Boulder, Colo.: Westview Press, 1994).

Jeffrey Toobin, *A Vast Conspiracy: The Real Story of the Sex Scandal That Nearly Brought Down a President* (New York: Random House, 2000).

Martin Walker, *The President We Deserve: Bill Clinton, His Rise, Falls, and Comebacks* (New York: Crown, 1996).

George F. Will, *The Leveling Wind: Politics, the Culture, and the Other News, 1990–1994* (New York: Viking, 1994).

Bob Woodward, *The Agenda: Inside the Clinton White House* (New York: Simon & Schuster, 1994).

Reform Party conventioneers in Long Beach, California, on 11 August 1996 (AP/Wide World Photos)

LAW AND JUSTICE

by LISA S. MCLEOD

CONTENTS

1990

3 Jan.   Manuel Antonio Noriega Moreno, dictator of Panama (1983–1989), is arrested on drug smuggling, racketeering, and money-laundering charges.

12 Mar.   Clarence Thomas, who was nominated by President George Bush, takes the oath of office as a judge on the U.S. Court of Appeals for the District of Columbia Circuit.

26 July   President Bush signs the Americans with Disabilities Act, a wide-ranging bill intended to make public facilities, workplaces, and telecommunications more accessible to people with disabilities.

10 Aug.   Marion S. Barry Jr., mayor of Washington, D.C., is found guilty on one misdemeanor charge of cocaine possession.

9 Oct.   David Hackett Souter is sworn in as an Associate Justice of the U.S. Supreme Court.

1991

3 Mar.   Rodney King is beaten by Los Angeles police officers following a high-speed automobile chase.

22 July   Serial killer Jeffrey L. Dahmer is arrested in Milwaukee, Wisconsin. Convicted in 1992, he is killed by a fellow prisoner on 28 November 1994.

11 Oct.   The Anita Hill-Clarence Thomas hearings begin before the U.S. Senate Judiciary Committee. Hill accused the Supreme Court nominee of sexual harassment.

23 Oct.   Thomas takes the judicial oath as an Associate Justice of the U.S. Supreme Court.

1992

29 Apr.   Rioting erupts in South Central Los Angeles after four police officers accused of beating Rodney King are either acquitted or given light sentences. The rioting lasts until 2 May.

8 May   The Twenty-seventh Amendment to the U.S. Constitution is ratified; it restricts compensation, voted upon by senators and representatives for themselves, from going into effect until after an intervening election year.

21 Aug.   Samuel Weaver, the fourteen-year-old son of Randy Weaver, is shot and killed by a U.S. Marshal during a standoff between Weaver and federal agents at Ruby Ridge, Idaho. The following day, Weaver's wife, Vicki, is shot and killed by federal agents.

25 Sept.   Gregory Kingsley, a minor at the time, is legally emancipated from his biological mother by a Florida judge on the grounds she neglected and abused him.

1993

12 Jan.   President Bill Clinton asks Attorney General Janet Reno to appoint a special counsel to investigate the Whitewater real estate dealings.

5 Feb.	The Family and Medical Leave Act is enacted. The statute expands the rights of millions of American workers by mandating that employers provide covered employees up to twelve weeks of unpaid leave for certain family and medical problems.
26 Feb.	The World Trade Center in New York City is bombed, killing six and injuring more than a thousand people. Several Islamic extremists are later arrested and convicted for the attack.
28 Feb.	The standoff between federal agents and the Branch Davidians begins when ninety heavily armed Bureau of Alcohol, Tobacco, and Firearms (ATF) agents attempt to serve a search-and-arrest warrant at the Mt. Carmel compound near Waco, Texas. Four agents and several Davidians are killed.
19 Apr.	The fifty-day standoff at Mt. Carmel ends in a massive conflagration of the Branch Davidian compound.
8 July	Randy Weaver and Kevin Harris are found innocent of the death of a federal agent during the 1992 standoff at Ruby Ridge. Weaver is also acquitted on weapons-trafficking charges.
20 July	White House Deputy Counsel Vincent W. Foster Jr. is found dead in Fort Marcy Park, Virginia. The death was determined to be a suicide.
10 Aug.	Ruth Bader Ginsburg takes the oath as Associate Justice of the U.S. Supreme Court. She was nominated by President Clinton.

1994

21 Jan.	Lorena (Gallo) Bobbitt, charged with malicious wounding for cutting off the penis of her husband, John Wayne Bobbitt, is found not guilty by reason of insanity and is committed to a mental health facility for observation.
28 Feb.	The Brady Handgun Violence Prevention Act, or Brady Law, inspired by President Ronald Reagan's White House press secretary James Brady, who was shot during a 1981 assassination attempt on the president, goes into effect.
10 May	Convicted serial killer John Wayne Gacy Jr. is executed by lethal injection in Illinois. During the 1970s he killed thirty-three young men and boys.
3 Aug.	Stephen Gerald Breyer is sworn in as an Associate Justice of the U.S. Supreme Court of the United States. He was nominated by President Clinton.
13 Sept.	President Clinton signs the Violent Crime Control and Law Enforcement Act of 1994.
6 Dec.	Webster L. Hubbell, Associate Attorney General of the United States, pleads guilty to tax evasion and mail fraud. He spends eighteen months in prison.

1995

19 Apr.	A bomb explodes at the Alfred P. Murrah Federal Building in Oklahoma City, Oklahoma, killing 168 people and injuring more than 500. It is the most deadly domestic terrorist attack in U.S. history.

1996

12 Aug.	Shannon Faulkner becomes the first woman to attend The Citadel, a state-supported all-male military college in Charleston, South Carolina, as a member of its Corps of Cadets. She drops out of the school on 18 August.
19 Sept.	With the approval of the Federal Bureau of Investigation (FBI), *The New York Times* and *The Washington Post* publish the Unabomber Manifesto, which rails against modern technology and environmental destruction, two areas in which the bombing attacks had been targeted.
3 Oct.	O. J. Simpson is acquitted of the murders of his former wife, Nicole Brown Simpson, and Ronald Goldman.

26 Jan.	First Lady Hillary Rodham Clinton testifies before a grand jury in connection with the Whitewater investigation.
20 Mar.	Lyle and Erik Menendez are sentenced to life in prison without parole in the shotgun murders of their parents, Kitty and Jose Menendez.
3 Apr.	Theodore John "Ted" Kaczynski is arrested by FBI agents at his Montana cabin in connection with the Unabomber case. The FBI had been tipped off to the identity and whereabouts of the alleged bomber by his brother David.
17 May	President Clinton signs into law an amendment to the 1994 Violent Crime Control and Law Enforcement Act. Known as "Megan's Law," it requires the release of relevant information to protect the public from individuals convicted of sex offenses. The legislation was named after Megan Kanka, a murder victim of a convicted sex offender.
20 Aug.	Susan McDougal is sentenced to two years in prison for her role in obtaining an illegal loan for the Whitewater land deal. Less than a month later, before beginning this sentence, she is jailed for contempt of court for refusing to testify before a grand jury about President Clinton's possible involvement in Whitewater.
26 Dec.	Six-year-old JonBenet Ramsey is found dead in her Boulder, Colorado, home. While her parents, Patsy and John Ramsey are suspects, no arrest is made.

1997

14 Apr.	James B. McDougal is sentenced to three years in prison for his conviction on eighteen fraud and conspiracy charges in the Whitewater land deal.
27 May	The U.S. Supreme Court rules unanimously that President Clinton could not delay the civil suit brought against him by Paula Corbin Jones. He had wanted the proceeding to start after he left office.
2 June	Timothy James McVeigh is convicted on murder, conspiracy to commit murder, use of weapons of mass destruction, and conspiracy to use weapons of mass destruction charges in connection with the Murrah Federal Building bombing in Oklahoma City. On 14 August 1997 he is sentenced to death by lethal injection.
24 June	The U.S. Supreme Court refuses to hear President Clinton's appeal regarding his claim to lawyer-client privilege regarding subpoenaed notes dealing with Whitewater.

23 Dec.   Terry Lynn Nichols is convicted of conspiracy to use weapons of mass destruction and manslaughter in connection with the bombing of the Murrah Federal Building in Oklahoma City. He is sentenced to life in prison without the possibility of parole.

1998

3 Feb.   Karla Faye Tucker-Brown, convicted of two brutal murders in 1983, is executed in Texas. She is the first woman to be executed in the United States in the decade and the first in Texas since 1863. On 30 March, Judias V. Buenoano, who poisoned her husband, is electrocuted in Florida; she is the first female put to death in the state in 150 years.

4 May   Kaczynski pleads guilty in the Unabomber case and is sentenced to life in prison without parole.

9 Sept.   Independent Counsel Kenneth W. Starr submits his report to Congress on the possible offenses by President Clinton that could lead to impeachment.

21 Sept.   The video recording of President Clinton's grand jury testimony regarding his relationship with former White House intern Monica S. Lewinsky is televised.

18 Oct.   The U.S. House of Representatives begins impeachment hearings against President Clinton.

2 Dec.   A federal jury acquits former Clinton administration Agriculture Department secretary Albert Michael "Mike" Espy of corruption.

19 Dec.   The U.S. House of Representatives passes two Articles of Impeachment against President Clinton.

1999

7 Jan.   Members of the U.S. Senate are sworn in as jurors by U.S. Supreme Court Chief Justice William Hubbs Rehnquist in the impeachment trial of President Clinton.

14 Jan.   The impeachment trial begins.

12 Feb.   President Clinton is acquitted on both Articles of Impeachment.

12 Apr.   For the first time in U.S. history, a sitting president is held in contempt of civil court. U.S. District Court Judge Susan Webber Wright holds Clinton in contempt for "giving false, misleading and evasive answers that were designed to obstruct the judicial process" when he was asked about his relationship with Lewinsky. Clinton is required to pay the Court $1,200.

5 Nov.   A U.S. District Judge rules that computer software giant Microsoft Corporation is a monopoly.

OVERVIEW

Law and Society. In the 1990s public concern over various social and political issues was manifested in new legislation, litigation, and court decisions. Attention was focused on crime rates, the accessibility of guns, juvenile violence, the rights of minorities and women, and corporate liability for unsafe consumer products. Several highly publicized criminal trials played out before the American public and the world through the medium of television. Conflicts over the civil rights of minorities, women, and the terminally ill were debated in state legislatures, Congress, and courtrooms. The impact of scientific and technological developments also faced legal and political scrutiny. Reflecting the more conservative mood of the country, environmental conservation legislation met opposition from the growing property-rights protection movement. Various legal issues, as well, arose out of the impeachment trial of President Bill Clinton.

Crimes Rates. Concern over crime remained one of the most important public policy issues. In the early part of the 1990s, national crime rates rose slightly, but by mid decade they went down. This decrease was most dramatic in the number of violent crimes. Crime statistics in major urban areas and rural localities mirrored this general decline. Drug-related crimes, however, increased nationwide. Violent crimes committed by juveniles jumped in the first half of 1990s, but showed a slight decline in the latter part of the decade. At the same time, federal and state prison populations grew substantially. After the U.S. Supreme Court reinstated the death penalty in 1976, the number of prisoners on death row and executions experienced an upward climb. As spending by federal, state, and local governments increased for law enforcement personnel and prisons, the public's fear of becoming a victim of crime slowly diminished.

Juvenile Justice. Increases in violence committed by and against juveniles led state and federal agencies to search for innovative ways to curb youth crime and rehabilitate youthful offenders. With the support of courts and juvenile-justice agencies, pilot programs such as correctional boot camps, the use of mentors, and various intervention programs were instituted. The trend toward waiving youths from juvenile court to adult criminal court increased, however, indicating a nationwide effort to impose more-severe punishments on violent offenders. A spree of school shootings in suburban areas raised public awareness of the widespread problems of children and violence, and of the easy access that teenagers had to guns and drugs. These incidents also encouraged school officials and juvenile-justice agencies to explore the social, economic, and psychological causes of crime and violence.

Law and Order. With the support of the administrations of presidents George Bush and Bill Clinton, Congress addressed the ongoing public concern over crimes involving drugs and guns by legislating mandatory sentencing and background checks for handgun purchases, as well as criminalizing certain types of assault weapons. These restrictions led to debates over the Second and Fourteenth Amendments, and also were challenged in the courts. Several major terrorist attacks on American soil occurred during the decade, including the bombing of a federal building in Oklahoma City, Oklahoma (1995), the most deadly terrorist act in U.S. history; there were also attacks at the World Trade Center in New York (1993), the Olympics in Atlanta (1996), and Central Intelligence Agency (CIA) headquarters in Langley, Virginia (1993). These assaults shocked the public and caused law enforcement agencies and governments nationwide to increase and update security measures. The seventeen-year killing spree of the Unabomber ended with the capture and imprisonment of Theodore John Kaczynski. In response to public worries about terrorism and hate groups, federal and state governments began to search for new ways to track and prosecute these activities. In one such case a fringe religious group in Waco, Texas, engaged federal law enforcement officers in a fifty-one-day standoff that resulted in a conflagration at their compound and eighty deaths. The incident sparked public debate and a federal investigation into the handling of the case by government officials.

Ethics and Government. The public's concern over ethics in government focused on President Bill Clinton even before the 1992 presidential election. Clinton's alleged involvement in the Whitewater land-development scheme, his public denials and subsequent admission of an affair with a young White House intern, and the highly political nature of the 1998 impeachment trial led Americans to question the personal and political ethics of both the executive and Congressional members. The personal and financial scandals of several top presidential advisers, Cabinet members, and legislators, as well as growing questions about the impartiality of the independent counsel appointed to investigate the Whitewater affair, led to similar criticisms about the contempt for the law by government officials.

Equal Rights for Women. The struggle of women to achieve equal rights continued into the final decade of the twentieth century. In a gender discrimination case, *UAW* v. *Johnson Controls* (1991), the Supreme Court ruled that employers cannot bar women of child-bearing age from workplaces where they might be exposed to toxic substances. Rather, employers must make the workplace safe for all workers. In 1995 and 1996 two state-supported all-male military schools, The Citadel in South Carolina and the Virginia Military Institute, were required by state and federal courts to admit women. At the same time, pro-choice advocates received a setback with the banning of "partial-birth" abortions.

Affirmative Action. While women and minorities made some advances, the emergence of a rejuvenated Republican Party in the mid 1990s resulted in the constriction of employment and educational opportunities. State and federal governments began scaling back affirmative-action programs that had been aimed at increasing the prospects for racial minorities and women in the workplace and university admissions. Public, political, and judicial debates over the social and economic impact of the possible demise of affirmative action continued through the end of the decade.

Homosexual Rights. In the early part of the decade President Clinton, some state governments, and various large corporations publicly recognized the rights of homosexuals. The president instituted a "Don't ask, Don't tell" policy for gays in the U.S. military. The Hawaii Supreme Court laid the judicial groundwork to legalize same-sex marriages. Many states, however, enacted countermeasures; the federal legislature reacted by passing the Defense of Marriage Act (1996), which defined marriage exclusively as a union of a man and woman. The courts generally upheld this definition of marriage. Efforts to recognize the equal rights of same-sex couples were also made by some major businesses and universities, which offered their employees benefits for same-sex partners that were similar to those provided to traditional spouses. Increasing attempts by same-sex couples to adopt children also led to public debate and court battles.

Anti-Environment Decade. Important advances that had been achieved in environmental protection over the past two decades were challenged in the 1990s by the growing property-rights movement. Individual, interest group, and corporate proponents of strong property rights contested many major environmental laws, including the landmark Endangered Species Act (1973), in both the courts and legislatures. They argued that restrictions placed on property owners by these conservation efforts imposed undue economic burdens, jeopardized productivity, and endangered jobs. Following a trend that began at the end of the previous decade, court rulings increasingly interpreted the Fifth Amendment "takings" clause, which traditionally meant a complete and actual taking of property, to include "partial" regulatory takings, thereby requiring governments to reimburse property owners for economic losses sustained as a result of land-use restrictions.

Science and Technology. Developments in science and technology created new issues, opportunities, and problems for American justice. Testimony based on genetic testing grew rapidly as the use of DNA evidence in courtroom proceedings became routine; arguments and testimony that once could only be supported circumstantially were now more accurate with scientific procedures. The courts and Congress, however, often had difficulty keeping up with biotechnological advances. Legal implications of human cloning and genetic engineering came to prominence after British scientists successfully cloned a sheep. Concerns over this rapidly progressing field of science involved reproductive and privacy rights, as well as the property and patent rights of individuals who clone or genetically alter new organisms. As a result, several states banned human cloning and Congress considered similar legislation. Advances in computer technology also raised anxiety for the public, businesses, government, and the courts. The number of Americans with access to computers dramatically increased from 15 percent at the beginning of the decade to more than 50 percent by the end of the 1990s. Growing access to the Internet is one reason for the upward trend in computer use as one in five, or fifty-seven million, people three years old and older "surfed" the "Net" in 1997. While Internet use gave Americans easier access to information, it compelled the public, Congress, and the courts to address problems of privacy, censorship, intellectual property rights, and national security.

TOPICS IN THE NEWS

CIVIL RIGHTS AND CIVIL LIBERTIES

Affirmative Action. Since the 1970s many governments, businesses, and universities routinely used affirmative action policies in hiring and admissions to correct the lingering burdens of racism and gender discrimination. Beginning in the 1980s the Supreme Court, led by Chief Justice William Hubbs Rehnquist, an opponent of affirmative action, began limiting such programs and making it harder to prove employment discrimination. In an effort to overrule the position of the Justices, Congress passed the Civil Rights Act of 1991, which voided some attempts by the Court to scale back laws and policies designed to redress prior discrimination. The statute, however, prohibited the use of quotas in hiring, promotions, and college admissions. In 1996 the Supreme Court refused to review a 5th Circuit Court of Appeals ruling in *Hopwood* v. *Texas* that declared unconstitutional the race-based preference admissions system used by the University of Texas Law School. This ruling set a precedent by prohibiting separate standards for minority admissions. Affirmative action programs were also assaulted through the ballot. In California and Washington, initiatives limiting preferential hiring and race-based college admissions were adopted. In spite of strong opposition from civil-rights and women's groups, California voters in 1997 passed Proposition 209, which proscribed state and local governments, public universities, and schools from giving preferential treatment to any individual on the basis of race, sex, color, ethnicity, or national origin. In 1998 Washington voters approved a similar measure, known as Initiative 200, which ended racial preferences, quotas, and "reverse discrimination" by any governmental agency in hiring or admissions. Opponents, including the American Civil Liberties Union (ACLU), National Association for the Advancement of Colored People (NAACP), and Boeing Corporation, contended that the anti-affirmative action initiative would reduce student diversity and limit opportunities for minorities. In 1998 a public opinion poll showed that 41 percent of Americans favored affirmative action programs. There was a sharp difference, however, in the opinions held by blacks and whites. Only 35 percent of whites supported the programs, as compared to 79 percent of blacks.

Religion in Public Schools. The "Establishment Clause" in the First Amendment of the U.S. Constitution prohibits Congress from establishing a national religion. For decades the courts have fluctuated on the issue of prayer in schools. In 1984 Congress passed the Equal Access Act, which barred public schools from discriminating against student groups that wanted to meet at school on the basis of their religion, politics, or philosophy. The law was challenged and reviewed by the Supreme Court in 1990. The Court upheld the law in *Board of Education* v. *Mergens,* declaring that the denial of a request by a Christian Bible club to meet in a public high school classroom violated the Act. In *Lamb's Chapel* v. *Center Moriches Union Free School District* (1993) the Court also held that any religious groups must be allowed the use of public school facilities after hours if that access was granted to any other groups. Further lowering the wall between Church and State, the Court ruled in *Rosenberger* v. *University of Virginia* (1995) that the failure of school administrators to fund a student magazine written by a fundamentalist Christian group while it provided money for nonreligious publications violated the First Amendment. Justice David Hackett Souter dissented, arguing that "The Court today, for the first time, approves direct funding of core religious activities by an arm of the state."

The Right to Die. Most states, by statute or court rulings, have forbidden assisted suicide. Dr. Jack Kevorkian, referred to by the media as "Dr. Death," brought the right-to-die issue to the political and judicial forefront by repeatedly assisting terminally ill patients in ending their lives. In 1990 the Supreme Court, in *Cruzan* v. *Director, Missouri Department of Health,* ruled against the parents of a young, brain-injured, comatose woman who wished to remove their daughter's feeding tubes. Writing for the majority, Chief Justice Rehnquist refused to expand the rights of privacy and personal autonomy. The Court, however, did allow persons to withhold or terminate life-support measures if provisions were made in a "living will." Upholding several state laws, the Court declared in *Vacco* v. *Quill* (1997) that terminally ill persons did not

On 4 March 1996, Pontotoc County, Mississippi, school superintendent Jerry Horton walks past demonstrators who support and oppose his decision to end a half decade of in-school prayer and Bible study (AP/Wide World Photos).

have a constitutional right to physician-assisted suicide. Many Americans were less willing to accept these decisions, and juries have repeatedly refused to convict Kevorkian or family members who have assisted individuals in taking their own lives.

Homosexual Rights. Most Americans remained uncomfortable with extending rights to homosexuals, as evidenced when President Bill Clinton attempted to lift the ban on homosexuals serving in the armed forces. After much debate, an agreement was reached among Clinton, military leaders, and Congress. The compromise was the "Don't ask, Don't tell" policy, which ended the questioning of military personnel about their sexual orientation, but barred service members from revealing their preference under threat of being discharged. The gay community, which strongly supported Clinton in his bid for the presidency, opposed what they viewed as the "hide and lie" policy. Nonetheless, Clinton refused to pursue the issue further. At the state level, homosexual-rights groups lobbied for antidiscrimination legislation with mixed success. Colorado voters in 1992 passed a state constitutional amendment that nullified several homosexual-rights ordi-

nances. In 1996 the Supreme Court, in *Romer* v. *Evans,* struck down the Colorado amendment, the first time the Court had applied the Fourteenth Amendment to protect homosexuals from discrimination.

Same-sex Marriage. Controversy over same-sex marriages also erupted in the 1990s. The Hawaiian Supreme Court ruled in *Baehr* v. *Lewin* (1993) that a ban on homosexual marriage violated equal protection rights under the constitution of that state. The threat that Hawaii might possibly legalize same-sex marriage led more than half of the state legislatures in the country to pass measures barring recognition of such unions. In 1996 Congress passed the Defense of Marriage Act, which President Clinton signed. The "full faith and credit" clause of Article IV of the U.S. Constitution, however, leaves open the possibility of future challenges if states refuse to respect such marriages recognized in other states.

Medical Privacy. With the ever-expanding technological capabilities to disseminate information, such as through the Internet and various on-line computer networks, the privacy rights of Americans became difficult to protect. Confidential materials, such as medical records and personal information collected by state agencies, were increasingly violated. While most states protected the confidentiality of patient information, they seldom had up-to-date comprehensive health privacy laws. Although there were benefits to information technology, such as allowing physicians and researchers to diagnose and track diseases and the side effects of drugs more easily, as well as helping state and federal agencies uncover health insurance and Medicare fraud, the availability of patient information also led to abuses, such as the use of a patient's medical records to identify pre-existing conditions or other high-risk factors in order to exclude individuals from insurance coverages. Some feared that DNA profiling might reveal a person's genetic predisposition for developing certain diseases, which might be used to exclude them from medical coverage or hinder their ability to find employment. In order to provide more comprehensive protection of personal information, U.S. Department of Health and Human Services (DHHS) secretary Donna E. Shalala proposed in October 1999 the first-ever national standards to protect the privacy of medical records created by health care providers, hospitals, health plans, and health care clearinghouses that were transmitted or maintained electronically, as well as paper printouts.

Freedom of Expression. Advances in technology also created a new First Amendment problem. While the Supreme Court had ruled on obscenity laws in past decisions, the Internet made it easier to distribute allegedly obscene materials and images rapidly to millions of people, including minors. Concerned with the easy access that children had to computers and their possible exposure to obscene materials on-line, Congress passed the Communications Decency Act as part of the Telecommunications Reform Act (1996). The legislation assumed that the Internet was not the electronic equivalent to the printing press, and therefore does not merit the free speech protection of the First Amendment. Obscene materials were banned from the Internet, and the transmission of indecent speech and images to anyone under the age of eighteen was criminalized. In 1997 the Supreme Court overturned the law, in *Reno* v. *ACLU*, arguing that the statute was too broad and vaguely worded, thus violating free speech protections. Implicit in the decision was the view that the Internet was equivalent to the printing press and therefore protected from government regulation.

Miranda Challenged. On 6 December 1999 the Supreme Court announced that it would review the legal and constitutional basis for the *Miranda* v. *Arizona* (1966) ruling, focusing on whether Miranda warnings are rights based on the Fifth and Sixth Amendments or simply rules of evidence to prevent unfair treatment of prisoners. Miranda warnings grew out of the concern held by civil-rights organizations and some courts that police officers were using mental and physical abuse to coerce confessions. *Dickerson* v. *United States* challenged Miranda as

Section 3501, which was designed to tighten loopholes in Miranda by giving the courts the authority to decide on a case-by-case basis whether statements given by suspects in custody were voluntary and therefore admissible. The U.S. Justice Department and police departments nationwide routinely ignore the statute and, as a matter of course, give the Miranda warning to all suspects.

Sources:

Arthur Allen, "Exposed," *The Washington Post*, 8 February 1998.

Baehr v. *Lewin*, 74 Haw. 645, 852 P.2d 44 (1993).

George C. Edwards III, Martin P. Wattenberg, and Robert L. Lineberry, *Government in America: People, Politics, and Policy* (New York: Harper-Collins, 1996).

CRIME AND PUNISHMENT

Feeling Safer. Reflecting the downturn in crimes committed by and against adults, public opinion polls in the 1990s indicated that citizens felt safer in their homes and neighborhoods than they had in the 1980s. Polls also showed that in 1998, 48 percent of Americans thought that there was less crime in their local areas than in the previous year, while in 1989 only 18 percent responded that there was less crime. In 1998, in contrast to a poll taken ten years earlier, the number of people who thought there was less crime nationwide than in the previous year increased by 30 percent.

Crime Rates. While violent crimes increased early in the decade, a consistent and sharp downward trend began in 1993. As assaults and property offenses declined nationwide, however, crime increased in suburban areas. Crime rates were highest in large metropolitan areas; however, by the end of the decade, smaller cities outpaced larger ones. Rural areas were consistently less crime-ridden, and crime rates were highest in the South. In 1995 there were an estimated 5,278 crimes per one-hundred thousand persons, a drop of 11 percent from the 1991 level of 5,859. The 1998 national crime rate was 4,616 for every one-hundred thousand inhabitants, the lowest rate since 1973. More than 85 percent of crimes were property-related, primarily theft, while fewer than 15 percent were violent. Murder and rape accounted for the fewest offenses. Despite an overall

TREND IN ATTITUDES TOWARD LEVEL OF CRIME

Question: Is there more crime in your area than there was a year ago, or less?

	More	Less	Same	No Opinion
1998	30%	48%	16%	6%
1997	46	32	20	2
1996	46	24	25	5
1992	54	19	23	4
1990	50	18	24	8

Source: "Crime Issues," *The Gallup Organization*, Internet website.

decline in criminal activity, drug-related offenses increased, following an upward trend started in the 1980s. Experts suggested that the general decrease in crime was the result of improving economic conditions and lower levels of poverty. Another possible contributing factor was the effort by governments to impose stricter and longer sentences on offenders.

Mandatory Sentencing. In a nationwide effort to curb crime, particularly drug and gun-related offenses, the federal government and all fifty states enacted some form of mandatory sentencing laws by 1994. Most of these laws entailed two primary provisions: "truth in sentencing" and the "three strikes" mandate. Truth in sentencing required that convicts serve a certain percentage of their sentences. In order for states to qualify for federal aid, the Violent Crime Control and Law Enforcement Act of 1994 mandated that states require convicted offenders to serve at least 85 percent of their sentences. Three-strikes laws imposed mandatory prison sentences, often life sentences, for offenders convicted of their third felony. Some mandatory sentencing laws required incarceration for first-time drug offenders. While supported by some as a deterrent to crime, particularly those that were drug and gun-related, and as a way to incapacitate the most-serious habitual offenders, critics opposed mandatory sentences on the grounds that they unjustly imposed long prison sentences

for first-time drug offenders and eliminated the discretion of judges. Among those opposing some of these innovations was U.S. Supreme Court Chief Justice William Hubbs Rehnquist, who called mandatory drug sentencing an example of "the law of unintended consequences." He argued that justice requires consideration of individual

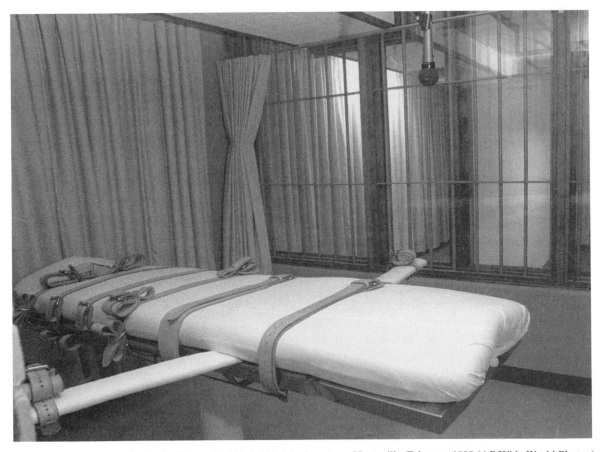

The Texas execution chamber in the Huntsville "Walls" Unit in downtown Huntsville, February 1998 (AP/Wide World Photos).

circumstances and that long prison sentences for first-time offenses were excessively harsh. Mandatory sentencing was also seen as having a disproportionate impact on racial and ethnic minority groups, which constituted a high percentage of drug-related arrests and convictions.

Prison Populations. State and federal prison populations increased over the decade. The number of inmates incarcerated for violent and drug-related crimes accounted for this upward trend, especially in state prisons. In 1985 there were 744,208 persons, 313 per one-hundred thousand, housed in prisons and jails. But during the 1990s, federal and state prison populations, as well as local jail populations, grew at the average annual rates of 8.3 percent, 6.6 percent, and 5.2 percent, respectively. In 1990 the number of inmates totaled 1,148,702, or 458 persons per one-hundred thousand. In 1998 U.S. prisons and jails incarcerated an estimated 1,802,496 persons, or 668 persons per one-hundred thousand. This dramatic increase caused overcrowding in many correctional facilities. By 1999, thirty-seven states, the District of Columbia, and the federal prison system reported operating at or higher above the intended capacity of their facilities. Utah, 84 percent of its prison beds filled, had the least crowded prison system. California, at slightly more than 200 percent capacity, had the most severe overcrowding problems.

Death Row. The number of prisoners on death row continued a sharp upward trend from the 1980s. In 1997 there were 3,335 persons with death sentences, compared to 2,356 in 1990 and 691 in 1980. As of mid 1999 California prisons housed the most death-row inmates (536), followed by Texas (437) and Florida (390). In 1980, three years after the U.S. Supreme Court lifted the moratorium on executions, no death penalties had been carried out; in 1990 there were twenty-three executions. In 1997 there were seventy-four executions; one year later there were sixty-eight. Throughout the decade the number of condemned whites was slightly higher than blacks in every state except Arkansas. In 1999 Texas led the country in executions, with twenty-eight. Women with death sentences remained under 4 percent of the total number of the death row population. Of the females on death row in mid 1999, 53 percent were white, 36 percent black, and 11 percent Latino. During the 1980s only one woman was put to death. Two women were executed in the 1990s: Karla Faye Tucker-Brown in Texas (3 February 1998) and Judias V. Buenoano in Florida (30 March 1998). The execution of Tucker-Brown, who was convicted of two pick-ax murders, received international attention and many clemency pleas, including requests from Pope John Paul II, Pat Robertson of the conservative Christian Coalition, one of the jurors who had convicted her, and the brother of one of her victims.

Decriminalization of Marijuana. In a 1996 referendum, California voters passed Proposition 215, which decriminalized marijuana use for medical purposes. This measure allowed physicians to prescribe marijuana to patients with cancer, AIDS, and other serious diseases. Some studies showed that the drug alleviates pain, relieves nausea, and increases appetites for those undergoing chemotherapy. State referenda in Alaska, Arizona, Colorado, Nevada, Oregon, and Washington also permitted the medicinal use of marijuana, although two of the votes were later invalidated. Most states that approved these measures faced court injunctions and litigation. U.S. Attorney General Janet Reno stated after the California referendum that federal law enforcement officials would continue to enforce the federal ban on the use of marijuana. A bipartisan majority of the U.S. House of Representatives and Barry R. McCaffrey, Director of the Office of National Drug Control Policy (ONDCP), contended that marijuana was a dangerous and addictive substance that acted as a gateway to even more dangerous drugs. McCaffrey opposed the use of marijuana under any circumstances. The American Medical Association (AMA) and the *New England Journal of Medicine,* however, spoke out in favor of more research on the medical benefits of marijuana. In addition, eleven states reduced the possession of small amounts of marijuana to a minor civil offense comparable to a traffic violation.

Sources:

Allen J. Beck and Christopher J. Mumola, *Prisoners in 1998* (U.S. Department of Justice, Office of Justice Programs, August 1999).

"Crime Issues," *The Gallup Poll Organization,* (8 November 1999), Internet website.

Darrell K. Gilliard, *Prison and Jail Inmates at Midyear 1998* (U.S. Department of Justice, Office of Justice Programs, March 1999).

Kathleen A. O'Shea, *Women and the Death Penalty in the United States, 1900–1998* (Westport, Conn.: Praeger, 1999).

Dale Parent, Terence Dunworth, Douglas McDonald, and William Rhodes, *Key Legislative Issues in Criminal Justice: Mandatory Sentencing* (U.S. Department of Justice, Office of Justice Programs National Institute of Justice Research in Action, January 1997).

U.S. Census Bureau, *Current Population Survey* (Washington, D.C.: U.S. Department of Commerce, Bureau of the Census, 1990, 1998, 1999).

DOMESTIC TERRORISM

Growing Hate Movement. During the 1990s a proliferation of extremist and militant activities emerged, ranging from Ku Klux Klan marches to murders and bombings. Tens of thousands of Americans joined various antigovernment and hate groups. Early in the decade right-wing domestic terrorism rose to a level not seen since the activities of left-wing student radicals and militants of the late 1960s and early 1970s. There were about five hundred active militia groups across the country, some with only a few members and others with thousands. Many of these groups were antigovernment, racist, and anti-Semitic; they were often well-organized, heavily armed, and held national meetings and local training sessions on a regular basis. While most groups did not use violence, there were some tragic examples of how far extremist individuals and organizations were willing to go in waging war against the government and other traditional targets of hate, namely racial and ethnic minorities. There were scores of arson attacks against black churches in the South. Homosexuals and Jews were also targeted. With the growth of the radical right, state and federal law enforcement agencies were assigned to monitor and control these groups. In some cases they failed in this task.

The Unabomber. One of the longest violent-crime cases of the Federal Bureau of Investigation (FBI), active for seventeen years, involved a series of fatal bombings. It was called the Unabomb case, a code name selected because some of the bombs were set off on university campuses and another was placed aboard an airliner. Beginning in 1978 the serial bomber, later identified as Theodore John Kaczynski, mailed or placed sixteen homemade explosive devices, killing three persons and injuring twenty-three others. A crucial development in the case occurred in early 1996 when the bomber sent a manuscript to *The New York Times* and *Washington Post*. With FBI approval, both papers published the 35,000-word treatise. The Unabomber argued that the purpose of the bombings was to call attention to the destabilizing effects of technology and "leftism" on modern society and traditional values. Publication of the manifesto led David Kaczynski to link it with earlier writings of his estranged brother Ted, who was living as a recluse near a small town in Montana.

Arrest. On 3 April 1996 Kaczynski, a former mathematics professor at the University of California, Berkeley, was arrested by FBI agents at his cabin. On 18 June he was formally indicted on ten counts relating to the transportation and mailing of explosive devices that killed or injured victims in California, New Jersey, and Connecticut. Supporting the government case was evidence found in the Montana cabin and DNA evidence from saliva taken from letters linked to the Unabomber.

Guilty Plea. A variety of difficulties faced both the defense and prosecution in pretrial proceedings in *United States* v. *Kaczynski*. For instance, the defendant refused to cooperate with mental-health professionals during psychiatric exams; Kaczynski also objected to undergoing neurological tests requested by his own lawyers. This refusal made it difficult for his defense team to pursue a diminished-capacity strategy. During these hearings Kaczynski was frequently observed muttering to himself and on one occasion he threw a pen across the courtroom. In a surprising move, the judge ruled that Kaczynski could represent himself if he was proven competent by a court-appointed mental-health expert. Kaczynski then agreed to the mental health exam. In January 1998, prior to opening statements, Kaczynski attempted suicide in jail and was placed under a twenty-four-hour watch. In spite of the serious nature of his crimes, the prosecution was reluctant to seek the death penalty. Had Attorney General Janet Reno decided to seek the death penalty, the defense would have had solid ground for a constitutional challenge. On 22 January 1998 Kaczynski accepted a plea bargain, entered an unconditional plea of guilty to all counts, and confessed to bombings for which he was not yet formally charged. He was sentenced on 4 May 1998 to life in prison without the possibility of parole.

Ruby Ridge. While antigovernment militia groups were active prior to the events at Ruby Ridge, Randy Weaver's

DAVID KORESH

Born Vernon Wayne Howell in Houston, Texas, in 1959 to a fifteen-year-old single mother, David Koresh never knew his father and was raised by his grandparents. From a young age, the high school dropout was interested in the Bible and music. In 1981 Koresh joined the Branch Davidians, a religious sect which in 1935 had settled ten miles outside of Waco. The Branch Davidians were a renegade sect of the Seventh Day Adventist Church, which had formally denounced the separatist group. In 1987 Koresh and the group's leader, George Roden, engaged in an armed power struggle in which Roden was shot. Koresh was tried for attempted murder. However, the trial judge declared a mistrial when the jury was unable to reach a verdict. Later the same year, Koresh assumed control over Mt. Carmel, and in 1990 he legally changed his name to Koresh. Reflecting his messianic mission, Koresh is a Hebrew word that refers to Cyrus, the name of the Persian king who allowed the Jews held captive in Babylon to return to Israel. The Davidians saw themselves as prophets, and Koresh claimed that he had been chosen by God to interpret the apocalyptic message in Revelation's seventh seal, which prophesied the last days of human history. Koresh regarded the siege by federal authorities, which began on 28 February 1993, as part of the prophecy of the seven seals. Koresh died on 19 April 1993 of a presumably self-inflicted gunshot wound.

standoff with federal authorities sparked increased interest in neo-Nazi, white supremacist groups such as the Ku Klux Klan, Aryan Nations, and Christian Identity. Hatred of the federal government, as well as racist and anti-Semitic sentiments, ran deep within these well-armed fringe organizations. Their objective was to reclaim the United States from an intrusive government, ethnic minorities, and Jews. In February 1991 Weaver, a U.S. Army veteran and survivalist, failed to appear for a trial on felony charges of selling sawed-off shotguns to an informant for the Bureau of Alcohol, Tobacco, and Firearms (ATF). Instead, Weaver, his wife, their son Samuel and two daughters, and Kevin Harris withdrew to the family home on Ruby Ridge, near Naples, Idaho. They remained there for eighteen months. Recognizing the potential for an armed confrontation, federal agents attempted to negotiate Weaver's surrender. On 21 August 1992 six U.S. Marshals were inspecting the woods around Weaver's cabin when they heard a dog barking. An agent shot the dog. They then heard shouting and gunfire. A marshal returned fire, shooting Weaver's fourteen-year-old son in the back and killing him. Harris then shot one of the agents, who also died. The following day, Weaver's wife, Vicki, was shot and killed as she held her infant in a doorway. The siege at Ruby Ridge contin-

The Alfred P. Murrah Federal Building in Oklahoma City, Oklahoma, shortly after it was bombed on 19 April 1995 (AP/Wide World Photos).

ued for eleven days with hundreds of FBI agents involved. On 30 August 1992 Harris, who was wounded, surrendered to federal agents. Weaver, with his remaining children, gave up the next day.

United States v. *Randy Weaver.* Along with Harris, Weaver was charged with capital murder. On 8 July 1993, however, a jury found both men innocent, believing that the government had provoked the entire incident by killing Weaver's dog, his son, and then his wife. The jury also found Weaver innocent of the original charge of trafficking in illegal weapons. His attorney, Gerry Spence, argued that his client had been entrapped. This defense required convincing jurors that Weaver was not predisposed to commit the crime. Despite Weaver's acquittal on the weapons charge, he was convicted of failing to appear for his original court date and sentenced to eighteen months in prison. With credit for time served while awaiting the trial, he was incarcerated for a few additional months.

Federal Responsibility. The federal government did not emerge from the incident unscathed, as the deaths of a young boy and of a woman holding an infant in her arms appeared to the public as abhorrent and criminal. The U.S. Attorney's Office, which was responsible for prosecuting the case, was widely criticized for pursuing the death penalty against Weaver. Assessment of the involvement of the FBI in the case was made more difficult because a senior agent destroyed documents relating to the case. The officer later pleaded guilty to obstruction of justice and, like Weaver, was sentenced to eighteen months in prison. After an extensive investigation the U.S. Department of Justice found that federal agents, particularly from the FBI, had overreacted to the threat presented by Weaver and questioned the "shoot-on-sight" policy. The investigation also criticized the federal agencies involved for failing to utilize proper investigative and enforcement procedures. These findings, in part, led to the Justice Department agreeing to pay Weaver and his surviving children $3.1 million.

Waco. Federal law-enforcement agencies apparently failed to learn from their mistakes at Ruby Ridge. On 19 April 1993, in full view of millions of television viewers, a fifty-one-day standoff between federal agents and a well-armed religious fringe group known as the Branch Davidians ended in a massive conflagration. Events leading up to this fiery conclusion began on 28 February 1993 when ninety heavily armed ATF agents attempted to serve a search-and-arrest warrant at the compound known as Mt. Carmel outside of Waco, Texas. Gunfire erupted and four federal agents were killed. The warrant, which was the result of almost a year of investigation and surveillance, was based on allegations that the residents possessed illegal firearms and were possibly converting semiautomatic rifles into machine guns. Later investigations found that the Davidians had stockpiled almost four hundred firearms, including forty-eight machine guns. During the standoff the activities at Waco dominated national news, and Davidian leader David Koresh became a household name.

Death at Mt. Carmel. After months of negotiations the standoff was finally brought to a close when federal tanks and armored vehicles punched holes in the walls of the compound and dozens of gas canisters were fired into the building in an attempt to force the Davidians out. Following the assault, smoke poured out of the structure and within minutes the entire compound was engulfed in flames. Seventy-six group members died, including twenty-five children under the age of fifteen. At least two dozen victims were later discovered to have died from gunshot wounds, either self-inflicted or caused by someone else in the compound. Nine Davidians escaped by fleeing the building.

Trial. Surviving Davidians were tried in federal court in 1994, charged with the murder of federal agents and various other crimes, including illegal weapons possession, manslaughter, and immigration violations. The Davidians argued that they had acted in self-defense against an unlawful assault conducted by the federal government. Koresh became a scapegoat for the defendants, who blamed their leader, along with the government, for the incident. Defense attorneys portrayed Koresh as delusional and paranoid. On 26 February 1994, almost one year to the day after the standoff began, the seven-week trial ended and all the Davidians were acquitted of the murder and conspiracy charges. Two were acquitted of all charges and freed. Seven others were convicted of lesser charges and fined or sentenced to prison terms.

Investigation. Over the next six years federal investigations attempted to resolve the questions of who fired first on 28 February and how the fire started. Did the Davidians commit mass suicide or were they killed by the fire? Did federal agents, as well as Attorney General Janet Reno, act within legal bounds? As late as 1999, Congress investigated the conduct of government agencies involved in the standoff. Allegations that the Justice Department had suppressed evidence that might have incriminated federal law-enforcement agencies surfaced in the late 1990s. In the midst of court orders for government attorneys to turn over all evidence from the siege or face contempt-of-court charges, as well as constant refusals and delays in submitting documents, Congress appointed a special investigative team, led by former senator John Claggett Danforth (R-Missouri), to continue the probe into the standoff at Waco. While some agencies submitted subpoenaed documents, the White House refused to turn over classified documents, citing executive privilege.

Wrongful Death Suits. In addition to the ongoing federal investigation into the conduct of law enforcement agencies, some survivors and family members of the Davidians filed a wrongful death suit against the government in civil court. The case claimed that federal agents fired on sect members first and that the government was responsible for setting the fire that engulfed the compound and resulted in scores of deaths. On 14 July 2000 a jury exonerated the government in the wrongful death suit; a week later Danforth's report declared that the agents were not responsible for the deaths at Waco.

Bombing in Oklahoma. Exactly two years after the final assault on the Mt. Carmel compound, a homemade bomb, hidden in a rented truck, exploded at the Alfred P. Murrah Federal Building in Oklahoma City, Oklahoma. The explosion killed 168 people and injured more than 500. It was the most deadly domestic terrorist attack in U.S. history. The Murrah Building housed a variety of federal agencies, as well as a daycare center for the children of federal employees. Nineteen children under the age of five were killed in the blast. According to federal prosecutors, the alleged motive for the bombing was antigovernment sentiments that had been inflamed by the raid on the Branch Davidians. An hour and a half after the blast Timothy James McVeigh was arrested on an unrelated weapons violation during a routine traffic stop. On 21 April, McVeigh, a U.S. Army veteran of the Persian Gulf War and a Bronze Star recipient, was charged by federal authorities in connection with the bombing. Terry Lynn Nichols, also a former soldier, was charged as an accomplice on 10 May 1995. On 11 August 1995 both McVeigh and Nichols were indicted by a grand jury for murder, conspiracy to commit murder, conspiracy to use a weapon of mass destruction, and use of a weapon of mass destruction. The murder charges pertained to eight federal agents who were killed in the explosion. In October, Attorney General Reno authorized federal prosecutors to seek the death penalty in both cases.

Cameras in the Courtroom. Because of the intense media coverage and the large number of individuals killed or injured in the attack, U.S. District Judge Richard P. Matsch moved the trial to Denver. Two pretrial issues involved in the case centered around whether television cameras would be allowed in the courtroom and whether the trial could be broadcast live. Matsch ruled in July 1996 that a closed-circuit telecast was constitutional and would be allowed. He refused, however, to permit bombing survivors and family members to watch the trial in person if they planned to testify. In March 1997 President Bill Clinton signed a bill allowing victims who were possible witnesses to attend the proceedings.

McVeigh's Trial. On 31 March 1997 jury selection began in the McVeigh trial and jurors were seated on 22 April. Opening statements began on 24 April. The federal prosecution team, led by assistant U.S. Attorney Joseph H. Hartzler, centered the case against McVeigh on evidence that the defendant rented the Ryder truck that carried the ammonium-nitrate bomb. Prosecutors also proved that McVeigh's fingerprints were found on a receipt for the purchase of forty fifty-pound bags of ammonium-nitrate fertilizer. Government prosecutors showed that clothing McVeigh wore when he was arrested was covered with bomb residue. Michael J. Fortier, a friend of the defendant, testified that he told law enforcement officials that McVeigh was angry about the federal assault on the Branch Davidians. McVeigh's defense, led by Oklahoma attorney Stephen Jones, attempted to sow reasonable doubt in the jurors's minds by emphasizing the circumstantial nature of the evidence. In particular, Jones criticized the competency of FBI crime lab procedures and analysis regarding the explosive residue on McVeigh's clothes. Jones contended that McVeigh was not the actual bomber. Rather, there was another person at the Murrah Building, "John Doe 2," who had accompanied McVeigh to rent the Ryder truck and who subsequently carried out the bombing. McVeigh did not testify. On 2 June 1997 he was convicted on all charges and on 14 August 1997 was sentenced to death by lethal injection. He is one of fewer than two dozen federal prisoners facing death sentences.

Nichols's Trial. Judge Matsch ordered that Nichols be tried separately from McVeigh, ruling that their rights could be compromised by a joint trial since Nichols had reportedly implicated McVeigh in the bombing. The judge concluded that to avoid self-incrimination Nichols could not be compelled to testify against McVeigh. On 23 December 1997 Nichols, who was never placed at the bomb scene, was convicted of conspiracy to use weapons of mass destruction and of eight counts of involuntary manslaughter for the deaths of the federal agents. He was sentenced to life in prison without the possibility of parole. Both Nichols and McVeigh had appeals pending in federal courts at the end of the decade.

Foreign Terrorists. Not all terrorist attacks in the United States originated domestically. On 26 February 1993 the World Trade Center in New York City was the target of a bomb that killed six and injured more than a thousand people. Evidence gathered by federal investigators indicated that the terrorist act was carried out by members of several different Muslim fundamentalist groups pursuing a jihad, or holy war, against America. The investigation also revealed the wide extent to which foreign terrorists lived and operated in the United States. At the time of the explosion about fifty thousand people were in the 110-story complex. The bomb, which was placed in a parking garage beneath the structure, was comprised of approximately twelve hundred pounds of explosives, including sodium cyanide. The attack caused $500 million in damage. It was the largest act of foreign terrorism on American soil; state and federal government buildings, as well as U.S. military installations around the world, were placed on alert.

Bombing Trials. Within a week and a half after the explosion, FBI agents tracked the vehicle suspected of carrying the bomb to Mohammed Salameh, a twenty-six-year-old Jordanian national. Salameh, along with Nidal Ayyad, a thirty-two-year-old chemist, Mahud Abouhalima, thirty-nine, and Ahmad Ajaj, thirty-four, were arrested. The four men were found guilty in March 1994 and sentenced to 240 years in prison. Another suspect, Ramzi Ahmed Yousef, the twenty-seven-year-old who was thought to have masterminded the attack, was arrested in February 1995 in Pakistan. Along with Eyad Ismoil, Yousef was tried on charges of murder and conspiracy. Federal prosecutors argued that Yousef and Ismoil had parked the bomb-laden vehicle in the garage. They were convicted in November 1997 and sentenced to 240-year prison terms. Other suspects are thought by federal agents to be at large. In February 1999 the first four militants convicted in the terrorist attack appealed their sentences, challenging the forensic evidence presented by federal prosecutors. In October 1999 a federal appeals court reduced their sentences by more than half. In another case involving foreign terrorists, cleric Sheik Omar Abdel-Rahman and nine other Muslims were convicted of seditious conspiracy for their role in a plot to bomb the United Nations (UN), FBI headquarters in Manhattan, two tunnels in New York, and a bridge connecting New Jersey with Manhattan—all in one day. Federal investigators also contend that they were co-conspirators in the World Trade Center bombing.

Sources:

FC, *The Unabomber Manifesto: Industrial Society and its Future* (Berkeley, Cal.: Jolly Roger Press, 1995).

Louis J. Freeh, *Ensuring Public Safety and National Security under the Rule of Law: A Report to the American People on The Work of the FBI, 1993–1998* (Washington, D.C.: U.S. Department of Justice, Federal Bureau of Investigation, 1999).

David Hoffman, *The Oklahoma City Bombing and the Politics of Terror* (Venice, Cal.: Feral House, 1998).

Harvey W. Kushner, *Terrorism in America: A Structured Approach to Understanding the Terrorist Threat* (Springfield, Ill.: Charles C. Thomas, 1998).

Michael Mello, *The United States of America versus Theodore John Kaczynski: Ethics, Power and the Invention of the Unabomber* (New York: Context Books, 1999).

Robert L. Snow, *The Militia Threat: Terrorists Among Us* (New York: Plenum Trade, 1999).

James D. Tabor and Eugene V. Gallagher, *Why Waco? Cults and the Battle for Religious Freedom in America* (Berkeley: University of California Press, 1995).

Gordon Witkin, "Making the Case," *U.S. News and World Report*, 122 (31 March 1997): 22–24.

ENVIRONMENTAL PROTECTION

Conservative Conservation. During the 1990s several judicial and legislative challenges were made to environmental protection laws passed in previous decades. Reflecting a growing property-rights movement that sought to strengthen the economic rights of landowners against government attempts to protect the environment, the federal courts, packed with conservative, probusiness Reagan and Bush administration appointees, tended to favor private-property owners and developers over environmental litigants. By mid decade the Republican-controlled Congress also worked to reduce or eliminate environmental programs and policies, as well as limit the scope of environmental protection regulations.

Court Trends. Targeting core environmental protection efforts, such as the National Environmental Policy Act (1969), Clean Air Act (1970), Clean Water Act (Federal Water Pollution Control Act, 1972), and Endangered Species Act (1973), advocates of strong property rights attempted to broaden the meaning of the "takings clause" of the Fifth Amendment to include partial takings. They also challenged state police powers to protect against public nuisances and to impose zoning restrictions. In a two-prong attack, developers and private landowners sought judicial remedies to prevent takings and for greater compensation. The due process clause of the Fourteenth Amendment guarantees that governments cannot take private property for public purposes without just compensation. Traditionally, this clause has been interpreted to mean total takings, that is, a government assuming ownership of a parcel of land. While the constitution does not prohibit the government from taking or regulating private property, it does require that when it does so, the government compensate the owner with the fair market value of the property. Beginning in the 1980s, however, courts began broadening the meaning of takings to include partial takings, something less than a total deprivation of the economically beneficial use of the property. The conservative Rehnquist Court favored business litigants who argued that overregulation amounted to taking property without due process.

Lucas v. *South Carolina Coastal Council.* In 1992 the U.S. Supreme Court reviewed a case from the South, *Lucas* v. *South Carolina Coastal Council*, which dealt with land-use restrictions and, more specifically, environmental protection legislation. The case involved a 1988 South Carolina law, the Beachfront Management Act, which prohibited the construction of new buildings in coastal areas subject to beach erosion. Structures were required to be set back a certain distance from the oceanfront. David Lucas, the petitioner, owned two vacant lots on the Isle of Palms, a barrier island off the coast of South Carolina. Because of the proximity of the lots to the coastline, the state prevented him from developing the land. He filed suit in state court for takings compensation, arguing that the environmental restrictions rendered the land valueless. The South Carolina trial court ruled that the state had, in fact, taken his property and required that $1.2 million be paid in compensation. The state appealed to the South Carolina Supreme Court, which reversed the decision. On 29 June

SCALIA ON TAKINGS

Justice Antonin Scalia, delivering the majority opinion in *Lucas* v. *South Carolina Coastal Council* (1992), noted:

We think, in short, that there are good reasons for our frequently expressed belief that, when the owner of real property has been called upon to sacrifice *all* economically beneficial uses in the name of the common good, that is, to leave his property economically idle, he has suffered a taking . . .

Whether Lucas's construction of single family residences on his parcels should be described as bringing "harm" to South Carolina's adjacent ecological resources thus depends principally upon whether the describer believes that the State's use interest in nurturing those resources is so important that *any* competing adjacent use must yield.

When it is understood that "prevention of harmful use" was merely our early formulation of the police power justification necessary to sustain (without compensation) *any* regulatory diminution in value; and that the distinction between regulation that "prevents harmful use" and that which "confers benefits" is difficult, if not impossible, to discern on an objective, value-free basis; it becomes self-evident that noxious-use logic cannot serve as a touchstone to distinguish regulatory "takings"—which require compensation—from regulatory deprivations that do not require compensation. *A fortiori*, the legislature's recitation of a noxious use justification cannot be the basis for departing from our categorical rule that total regulatory takings must be compensated.

Source: *Lucas* v. *South Carolina Coastal Council*, 112 Sup. Ct. 2886 (1992), majority opinion, 29 June 1992.

1992 the U.S. Supreme Court ruled, in a decision written by conservative Associate Justice Antonin Scalia, in favor of Lucas. Scalia argued that the state did not provide hard evidence that the proposed property use posed a public danger. In addition, and equally important, the Court defined "taking" as the loss of the economically beneficial or productive use of property rather than outright confiscation. In a move that could have long-range judicial implications, the Court left open the possibility that landowners who suffer a partial taking may have constitutional grounds to pursue an environmental regulatory taking claim. The decision established a "categorical rule" that when a regulatory action deprives a landowner of "all economically viable use of his property" and thus renders it "valueless," the owner is owed compensation. Scalia maintained that the only exception is when the use of land is already prohibited by law. In

Man-made dunes being bulldozed at Topsail Beach, North Carolina, on 21 September 1996, to protect homes built along the coastline (AP/Wide World Photos).

these cases, the state must "prove" that a real and imminent threat to the public exists. Thus, the opinion created a weighty burden of proof for governments seeking to regulate property usages. The decision also raised fundamental questions about the extent to which a landowner may be compelled to maintain the natural character of the land in order to protect ecological functions and biodiversity.

SLAPP Suits. In an effort to prevent environmental and consumer protection interest groups from participating in public hearings concerning land-use restrictions, lobbying zoning boards, and advertising against development projects, developers and other business interests initiated "Strategy Lawsuit Against Public Participation" (SLAPP) suits. This legal strategy was based on the contention made by property owners that interest groups defamed or libeled them by opposing development projects. While most SLAPP suits do not stand up in court, since they restrict First Amendment rights of free speech and the right to petition government for redress, they slowed the efforts of environmentalists and are often costly for activists.

Legislative Tactics. The 1994 elections gave Republicans a majority in both chambers of the U.S. Congress; environmental protection became a low legislative priority while property-rights protection became a prime objective. With the antiregulation agenda contained in the conservative "Contract with America," congressional Republicans fought to rein in what they regarded as the "regulatory beast." Democrats and the Clinton administration tried with equal vigor to protect public health and environmental protection accomplishments achieved over the past twenty-five years. The politics of

divided government, however, often led to partisan conflicts and gridlock. One of the successful tactics used by House and Senate Republicans to limit the scope of environmental regulations were riders, legislative policy stipulations often used to remake or eliminate federal programs, that were attached to appropriations bills. Most of these riders attempted to hinder the ability of federal agencies such as the Environmental Protection Agency (EPA) and the Department of Interior to enforce environmental laws. In July 1995 President Clinton signed one such appropriations bill that permitted extensive logging by private industries in old-growth forests on federal lands. Another legislative strategy to weaken environmental protection laws targeted the budgets of agencies charged with regulation and protection enforcement. Under the auspices of reducing the federal budget, Congress cut the funding of the EPA and similar agencies, including monies for the Superfund (used for environmental clean-up projects) and revolving loans to states for wastewater treatment and safe drinking water projects. In 1995 and 1996 a stalemate ensued between the White House and Congress, resulting in a temporary shutdown of many federal agencies. While the compromise budget reduced cuts initially proposed by Congress, the reductions were still significant.

Sources:

Michael E. Kraft, "Environmental Policy in Congress: Revolution, Reform, or Gridlock?" *Environmental Policy in the 1990s,* edited by Norman J. Vig and Kraft, third edition (Washington, D.C.: Congressional Quarterly Press, 1997), pp. 119–142.

Lucas v. *South Carolina Coastal Council,* 112 Sup. Ct. 2886 (1992).

Lettie McSpadden, "Environmental Policy in the Courts," *Environmental Policy in the 1990s,* edited by Vig and Kraft (Washington, D.C.: Congressional Quarterly Press, 1997), pp. 168–186.

FEDERAL JUDICIARY

Problems Plague the Courts. The 1990s was plagued by partisan fighting over the federal judiciary. In 1991 controversy arose over the confirmation of a U.S. Supreme Court justice who was accused of sexual harassment. By mid decade, as the political composition of the Congress moved increasingly to the right and tension between it and the White House heightened, scores of federal inferior court seats were left unfilled as the president and Republican senators fought over nominations.

The Supreme Court. During the 1990s there were four appointments to the U.S. Supreme Court. President George Bush appointed two associate justices. David Hackett Souter took office on 9 October 1990, filling the vacancy created by the retirement of the politically moderate Justice William Joseph Brennan Jr. On 23 October 1991 Clarence Thomas replaced renowned liberal justice Thurgood Marshall. President Bill Clinton also made two appointments. Ruth Bader Ginsburg took office on 10 August 1993, following the retirement of President John F. Kennedy appointee Justice Byron R. White, the only Democrat left on the Court at the time. On 3 August 1994 Stephen Gerald Breyer filled the vacancy created by the retirement of Justice Harry Andrew Blackmun, who had been appointed by President Richard M. Nixon.

The Rehnquist Court. While Clinton filled two seats with Democrats, the conservative appointees of Republican presidents from Nixon to Bush composed a clear majority on the Supreme Court. This was publicly noted by Justice Blackmun, who, several years before his retire-ment, declared that the Court was "moving to the right . . . where it wants to go, by hook or crook." With its conservative majority, led by Nixon appointee Chief Justice William Hubbs Rehnquist, Supreme Court decisions have shown a trend toward eliminating the liberal decisions of the Earl Warren Court (1953–1969) and the moderate decisions of the Warren Earl Burger (1969–1986) Court. The Rehnquist Court chipped away at affirmative action and abortion rights. Moreover, it no longer saw itself as the chief protector of individual and minority rights and liberties. Rather, decisions tended to defer to the federal and state governments.

Clarence Thomas and Anita Hill. With the retirement of Marshall in 1991, President Bush nominated a black, conservative federal appeals court judge to fill the position. Bush claimed that he was not employing quotas in his nomination of Clarence Thomas. While not everyone believed him, Senate liberals were placed in a difficult position. They favored another minority serving on the High Court, but realized that Thomas was not the liberal jurist that Marshall had been. The Senate Judiciary Committee sent Thomas's nomination to the Senate floor with a split vote. Just as the full Senate was about to vote on the nomination, charges of sexual harassment were leveled against Thomas. The committee hearings were reopened. University of Oklahoma law professor Anita Hill testified before the all-male committee. Before the television cameras, she described in graphic detail Thomas's alleged behavior. Thomas denied all the charges and then accused the Senate of racism for reviewing the

The 1994 U.S. Supreme Court: (l to r) justices Clarence Thomas, Antonin Scalia, Sandra Day O'Connor, Anthony M. Kennedy, David Hackett Souter, Stephen Gerald Breyer, John Paul Stevens, William Hubbs Rehnquist, and Ruth Bader Ginsburg. (AP/Wide World Photos).

issue. In a fifty-two to forty-eight decision, the smallest margin in more than a century, the Senate confirmed Thomas. Women's groups severely criticized the Senate for failing to take Hill's testimony seriously.

Gridlock in Lower Court Confirmations. While President Clinton was able to achieve a large percentage of judicial nominee confirmation in the first years of his administration—129 by 1994—partisan politics marred the selection process in the latter half of the decade. The Republican-controlled Senate slowed the process to a near standstill, leaving the courts severely backlogged and delaying justice. By the end of 1997 the tension between the White House and Senate Judiciary Committee was so severe that Chief Justice Rehnquist warned that if the high number of vacancies persisted, it would erode "the quality of justice that traditionally has been associated with the federal judiciary." Between 1996 and 1997 the Senate confirmed only fifty-six judges, barely more than the fifty-four judges confirmed on the average annually since 1979. In 1997 Senate Judiciary Committee chairman Orrin Grant Hatch (R-Utah) allowed only nine confirmation hearings. The tone of many of the hearings was highly partisan. Rather than focusing on the integrity, professional competence, and temperament of nominees, the hearings centered on whether they were judicial activists and liberals. During the first session of the 105th Congress, there were several proposals, including a constitutional amendment, to limit the terms of federal judges, thereby eliminating life tenure and the constitutional protection for judicial independence. Other measures proposed holding elections for federal judges. House Majority Whip Thomas Dale DeLay (R-Texas) even advocated impeaching federal judges based on their opinions. At one point during 1997 there were more than one hundred judicial vacancies, more than one-third of which were official "judicial emergencies," meaning that the seats had been vacant for more than eighteen months. The Clinton administration, however, did little to stop the attempt by the Senate majority to undermine presidential appointment power. Clinton provided minimal support for his nominees under fire. The stalemate continued throughout the remainder of the decade. By the end of 1999 twenty-four Appellate Court and thirty-two District Court seats were unfilled; fifteen were in a state of judicial emergency, while some had been vacant since 1994.

Composition. At the close of the decade there were 787 active District and Circuit Court judges. Eighty-three and a half percent (657) were white; 10.2 percent (80) were black; 5.1 percent (40) were Hispanic. Seven jurists were Asian Americans, two were Native American, and one was Arab American. Eighty percent (628) of federal judges were male and 20 percent (159) were women. Only nineteen black women served in federal judgeships. On the U.S. Supreme Court, there were six white men, one black man, and two white women. More than 60 percent of the women and 70 percent of the

blacks sitting on the federal judiciary at the end of 1999 were Clinton appointees.

Earnings. All federal judges receive salaries that are set by Congress. In 1998 the Chief Justice of the United States was paid $175,400. Associate Supreme Court Justices earned $167,900. Court of Appeals judges earned $145,000, while U.S. District Court judges received $136,700. Full-time Magistrate and Bankruptcy judges made $125,764, while the salaries of part-time Magistrate judges ranged from $3,167 to $58,065.

Technology and the Courts. An increasing amount of information about the federal and state courts, cases, and decisions became available to the public through technological means, such as the Internet. The television network *Court TV* gave Americans an inside look at courtroom proceedings. In addition, almost all federal and many state courts installed automated systems that allow for the search and retrieval of case-related information through personal computers and through a dial-in service called PACER (Public Access to Court Electronic Records). These technological advances allowed the public to gain direct, rapid, and easy access to official court information and records.

Sources:
1997 Report on the Judiciary (Washington, D.C.: Alliance for Justice, 1998).

George C. Edwards III, Martin P. Wattenberg, and Robert L. Lineberry, *Government in America: People, Politics, and Policy* (New York: Harper-Collins, 1996).

Judicial Selection Project (Washington, D.C.: Alliance for Justice, 1999).

GUN CONTROL

Public Opinion. Throughout the 1990s political parties established policy positions on gun control in their platforms, politicians vigorously campaigned on one side or the other of the gun-control issue, and interest groups lobbied Congress and the courts to increase or reduce restrictions on firearms ownership. The controversy centered around the need to curb crime, on one hand, and the Second Amendment right to bear arms, on the other. Pro-gun-control advocates claimed that the scales must be slightly tipped in favor of maintaining public order. Antigun-control proponents argued that law-abiding citizens have the constitutional right to protect themselves and their property with firearms. The issue, however, involved more than public and private security. At times, gun control became a Tenth Amendment issue. Some states contended that the federal government overstepped its bounds when it attempted to mandate that states perform background checks before allowing citizens to purchase handguns. These fundamental constitutional issues were often decided by the courts.

Brady Bill. Reflecting the public concern over violent and drug-related crime, Democratic President Bill Clinton worked with the Republican majority in Congress to pass groundbreaking crime-control legislation. Efforts to require background checks for handgun purchases had been debated in Congress since the attempted assassination of President Ronald Reagan on 30 March 1981, but there was not enough support for passage of stricter gun controls. In 1994, however, amid a flurry of public controversy and media coverage, the Brady bill became law. Named after Sarah Brady, antigun lobbyist and wife of James Brady, who was severely injured by a bullet from a handgun during the Reagan assassination attempt, the Brady Handgun Violence Prevention Act, or Brady Law, was signed into law on 30 November 1993 and went into effect on 28 February 1994.

Provisions. The Brady Law established a national five-business-day waiting period—a "cooling off" interlude—and required local law enforcement to conduct background checks on handgun purchasers. The waiting period applied only to handgun sales through licensed dealers. Transfers between private individuals, as well as sales at gun shows and through the Internet, were not included. Within one day of the proposed transfer, a dealer is required to provide information from the purchaser's statement to the chief law enforcement officer where the purchaser resides. This

CONCEALED WEAPONS PERMITTED

As the federal government imposed restrictions on firearms in the 1990s, states increasingly passed legislation that allowed private citizens to carry concealed weapons. In 1985 only eight states issued "carry permits." By 1998 thirty-one states had enacted "right to carry" laws.

Supporters of concealed weapons contended that citizens had the right to protect themselves against criminals, whether at home or on the streets. Moreover, they suggested that allowing private individuals to carry concealed weapons served as a deterrent to crime.

Opponents countered that carry permits posed a danger to both the carriers and law-abiding citizens, since most permits were issued with only minimal firearm-training requirements. They also argued that allowing private citizens to carry concealed guns would increase crime rates.

There are two general types of concealed-weapons laws. Some states have a "Shall Issue" provision in their state law, while others issue licenses on a "Discretionary" basis, which leaves more room to deny the permit. In both cases, background checks on applicants are conducted by local, state, or federal law enforcement agencies. In "Shall Issue" states, carry permits are easier to obtain than in "Discretionary" states. However, even if an individual has no criminal record, law enforcement officers in "Shall Issue" states have the authority to block the issuance of a permit, but must substantiate the reason—and the decision is open to appeal.

CHARLTON HESTON SPEAKS

In a 1997 interview on *Meet the Press* (NBC) Charlton Heston, president of the National Rifle Association (NRA), stated:

There are no good guns. There are no bad guns. Any gun in the hands of a bad man is a bad thing. Any gun in the hands of a decent person is no threat to anybody—except bad people. . . . You know, the Bill of Rights guarantees every citizen the right to own and bear firearms. It doesn't say anything about how many, how much you can pay for them. That's in the Bill of Rights. That's a sacred document in our country. There's no other country in the world that has such a document. And you know what its purpose is? To prevent the federal government from interfering with private citizens' rights.

Source: *Meet the Press*, 18 May 1997.

statement, verified by some form of photo identification, must include the purchaser's name, address, date of birth, and the date it was made. Local officials are then required to conduct a background check. The law made the theft of a gun from a federal firearms licensee a federal crime punishable by a fine of up to $10,000 and imprisonment up to ten years. It also increased the fee for a gun-dealer license to $200 for three years.

Challenges. The mandatory background check imposed on states by the Brady Act, a provision scheduled to expire in 1998, was struck down by the U.S. Supreme Court on 27 June 1997 in a five-to-four decision. In *Printz, Sheriff/ Coroner, Ravalli County, Montana* v. *United States* (1997) the Court ruled that requiring states to conduct background checks prior to the sale of handguns violated the principles of federalism protected in the Tenth Amendment. The five-day waiting period for handgun purchases, however, was unanimously upheld since it was directed at gun-store owners and was not a federal mandate to state officials. The Court rested its decision solely on the Tenth Amendment and its view of the federal-state relationship. In the majority opinion, Justice Antonin Scalia wrote, "The Federal Government may neither issue directives requiring the States to address particular problems, nor command the States' officers, or those of their political subdivisions, to administer or enforce a federal regulatory program." The Court made no mention of the "right to bear arms" provision of the Second Amendment. The ruling had no effect in twenty-seven states that enacted background-check laws. According to the Bureau of Alcohol, Tobacco, and Firearms (ATF), the Brady law was an effective deterrent to crime.

Instant Background Checks. In December 1998 Congress replaced the five-business-day "cooling off" period with a national "instant" felon-identification system to be used by dealers in screening all gun purchasers. Two mil-

The "Silent Shoes Speak" protest in Washington, D.C., on 30 September 1996, sponsored by Americans Against Gun Violence. Each pair of shoes represents a victim of gun violence (AP/Wide World Photos).

lion dollars in federal funds was made available to law enforcement agencies to assist in computerizing state criminal records and linking them to a national system. Responding to public concerns over the ease with which handguns could be purchased, Congress also introduced the Brady Waiting Period Extension Act in 1999. This bill, which was still pending in Congress at the end of the decade, calls for a mandatory seventy-two-hour waiting period for handgun purchases. It further requires that registration forms be sent to the chief law enforcement officers of the buyer's home locality, giving local police the opportunity to screen handgun purchasers to determine whether records indicate that the buyer is a prohibited purchaser.

Assault Weapons. In 1994 Congress passed the Violent Crime Control and Law Enforcement Act or "Assault Weapons Ban," which made illegal the sale of nineteen different types of semiautomatic weapons. Though many other rifles, shotguns, and handguns are semiautomatics, they were not included in the ban. At the time the law was passed, there were between one and two million semiautomatic assault weapons in circulation in the United States. The bill also banned "copies" or "duplicates" of the illegal weapons; failure to do so would have opened the door for widespread evasion of the legislation. Manufacturers were also prohibited from producing firearms with certain assault-weapon features, such as bayonet mounts and grenade launchers, as well as semiautomatic versions of fully automatic weapons. While the manufacture and importation of assault weapons was made illegal, existing weapons were grandfathered—guns lawfully possessed prior to the effective date could be legally retained, sold, or transferred to anyone entitled to own a firearm. The act also prohibited the production of magazines or ammunition-feeding devices capable of holding more than ten rounds. Like the exemption of prohibited semiautomatics owned prior to the ban, high-capacity magazines made before the date of enactment could be lawfully possessed, sold, or transferred. As a result, tens of thousands of such clips remained in circulation in the United States.

Protecting Children. On 17 June 1998, with bipartisan support, the 106th Congress passed a comprehensive bill crafted to address the problem of children gaining easy access to firearms. The Children's Gun Violence Prevention Act mandates that by the year 2001 new child-resistant safety devices be placed on guns manufactured and imported into the United States, including child-resistant safety locks, magazine disconnect safeties for pistols, and manual safeties. Furthermore, the act prohibited the sale of an assault weapon to anyone under the age of eighteen and increased criminal penalties for selling a gun to a juvenile.

Gun Control and the Courts. Scores of lawsuits were filed against gun manufacturers and dealers in a nationwide effort to regulate firearms. On 17 July 1997 the Florida Supreme Court handed down a landmark decision in *Kitchen* v. *KMart*, ruling that a retail gun dealer had a legal duty to refrain from selling a firearm to an intoxicated buyer and was liable for the harm that results when the purchaser then uses the gun to shoot an innocent third party. The victim in this case, Deborah Kitchen, filed suit against the discount store for injuries she suffered ten years earlier when her intoxicated former boyfriend purchased a rifle from KMart and shot her through the neck, rendering her a quadriplegic. In *San Diego County Gun Rights Committee* v. *Janet Reno* (1996), the U.S. Court of Appeals for the Ninth Circuit dismissed a legal challenge brought by two pro-gun groups against the federal law banning the manufacture and sale of assault weapons and large-capacity ammunition magazines. The Fourth Circuit Court of Appeals affirmed the dismissal of a similar case brought by a gun collector in *Kropelnicki* v. *United States* (1996). On 30 October 1998, New Orleans became the first city to file suit against the gun industry. In *Morial* v. *Smith & Wesson, et al.,* the city claimed that the industry, including well-known gun manufacturers Smith & Wesson, Beretta U.S.A., Colt, and Glock, was negligent for not incorporating safety systems into guns that would prevent widespread firearm misuse by unauthorized users, namely children, and was therefore liable for gun-related violence. Chicago followed with a lawsuit against the industry in November 1998. *Chicago* v. *Beretta U.S.A. Corp., et al.* attacked gun makers for their role in the problem of gun trafficking in the city.

Effects. While it is difficult to link directly the federal and state restriction on firearms with declines in the number of gun dealers, weapons purchases, and firearm-related crimes, the statistics are interesting to note. In 1993 Berkeley, California, had thirty-four licensed dealers; in 1996 it had two. During the same period gun dealerships in San Francisco dropped from 155 to 10. By the end of the decade three quarters of the gun dealers in New York City gave up their licenses. Overall U.S. pistol production fell nearly 60 percent, from 2.3 million to just under 1 million. While manufacturers of more expensive firearms reported only moderate decreases in production, companies that made less expensive guns claimed sharp declines. In 1993 Lorcin manufactured 341,243 inexpensive pistols and became for that year the leading pistol producer in the United States. In 1996 it manufactured only 87,497, a 74 percent reduction. During the same three-year period, the number of violent crimes committed with guns declined 20 percent. The number of homicides dropped by 23 percent and continued to fall throughout the rest of the decade.

Opposition. While gun control measures received support from many law enforcement agencies, Democrats in Congress, and large segments of the public, these efforts were strongly opposed by many firearms enthusiasts, interest groups, and Second Amendment supporters. One of the most vocal opponents of the restrictions was the National Rifle Association (NRA), which opposed the Brady Law, the Assault Weapons Ban, mandatory waiting periods, and restrictions on the manufacture, importation, and sale of any type of firearm, including semiautomatic "assault" weapons. The NRA claimed that such laws infringe on the Second Amendment, the right of citizens to "bear arms." Moreover, the organization contended that gun-control measures fail to keep career criminals from purchasing guns because they do not acquire them through licensed dealers, but from private individuals or through theft.

Sources:
Kitchen v. *Kmart*, 86 FL 812 (1997).

Kropelnicki v. *United States*, 92 F.3d 1179 (4th Cir. 1996).

Erik Larson, "Squeezing Out The Bad Guys: How ATF and Local Police Have Dramatically Turned the Tide in the Battle Against Crime Guns," *Time*, 154 (9 August 1999): 32.

Printz, Sheriff/Coroner, Ravalli County, Montana v. *United States*, 117 Sup. Ct. 2365 (1997).

San Diego County Gun Rights Comm. v. *Reno*, 98 F.3d 1121 (9th Cir. 1996).

Brian J. Siebel, *City Lawsuits Against the Gun Industry: A Roadmap For Reforming Another Deadly Industry* (Washington, D.C.: The Center to Prevent Handgun Violence, Legal Action Project, 1999).

IMPEACHMENT

Background. While the catalyst for the impeachment of President Bill Clinton was a 1998 report submitted to the U.S. House of Representatives by independent counsel Kenneth W. Starr, investigations into Clinton's background began shortly after he took office. In 1993 Attorney General Janet Reno appointed a special counsel to investigate his involvement in a failed real estate venture, known as Whitewater, and in a defunct Arkansas financial institution, Madison Guaranty Savings and Loan. Originally headed by former federal prosecutor Robert B. Fiske Jr., Starr took over as independent counsel in August 1995. The investigation was gradually broadened to include the suicide of Deputy White House counsel Vincent W. Foster Jr., whose files were discovered missing after his death; the truthfulness of Clinton's depositions in the sexual harassment case filed by Paula Corbin Jones, a former Arkansas state employee; and his alleged relationship with former White House intern Monica S. Lewinsky. On 17 January 1998 Clinton testified under oath to Jones's lawyers that he had not had a sexual relationship with Lewinsky. On 6 August 1998 Lewinsky testified before a grand jury convened by Starr that she had had a relationship with the President. On 17 August, Clinton gave his grand jury testimony via closed circuit television and admitted having had an inappropriate relationship with Lewinsky. On 9 September 1998 Starr submitted his report to Congress, which included possible offenses that might be grounds for impeachment, particularly perjury and obstruction of justice.

House Debates. On 18 October 1998 the House of Representatives voted 258 to 176 to hold an open-ended inquiry into President Clinton's conduct involving Lewinsky and Jones. After the November elections, in which the Democrats gained five House seats, Republicans on the House Judiciary Committee held a series of hearings but did not call any witnesses. On 19 December 1998, in a special Saturday session, the House passed two Articles of Impeachment against Clinton. One article, alleging that the President committed perjury before Starr's grand jury, was approved by a 228 to 206 vote. The charge of perjury in the Jones deposition was defeated 229 to 205. The third charge, obstruction of justice, passed narrowly by nine votes. The abuse of power article, stemming from written answers Clinton had given to the House Judiciary Committee, failed by a wide margin, 285 to 148, with nearly a third of House Republicans voting against it. The two adopted articles, for perjury and obstruction of justice, were approved by a strict party-line vote. Clinton was only the second president in U.S. history, the first being Andrew Johnson in 1868, to stand trial in the Senate and face possible removal from office.

Former Presidents. After the House passed the Articles of Impeachment, former presidents Gerald R. Ford and Jimmy Carter sent a joint statement to *The New York Times* on 21 December 1998 opposing Clinton's possible removal. Because impeachment carried many consequences for the executive office and the nation, Ford and Carter reasoned that a public statement was warranted. Their op-ed piece, titled "A Time to Heal Our Nation," called for reconciliation. Citing the pardon by Ford of President Richard M. Nixon and Carter's grant of amnesty for those who had avoided the Vietnam War draft, they proposed the Senate censure Clinton without a trial. A bipartisan resolution, censure would require that Clinton acknowledge that he had lied under

The House Managers

BOB BARR (R-Georgia), 50, elected 1994.
DUTIES: Outline how President Bill Clinton's conduct relates to obstruction of justice and perjury laws.

ED BRYANT (R-Tennessee), 50, elected 1994.
DUTIES: Outline factual case against President Clinton.

STEPHEN EARLE BUYER (R-Indiana), 40, elected 1992.
DUTIES: Address how Clinton's conduct meets constitutional test for removal from office.

CHARLES TERRANCE CANADY (R-Florida), 44, elected 1992, chairman House Judiciary Subcommittee on the Constitution.
DUTIES: Address how Clinton's conduct meets constitutional test for removal from office.

CHRISTOPHER B. CANNON (R-Utah), 48, elected 1996.
DUTIES: Outline how Clinton's conduct relates to obstruction of justice and perjury laws.

STEVE CHABOT (R-Ohio), 45, elected 1994.
DUTIES: Outline how Clinton's conduct relates to obstruction of justice and perjury laws.

GEORGE WILLIAM GEKAS (R-Pennsylvania), 68, elected 1982, chairman House Judiciary Subcommittee on Commercial and Administrative Law.
DUTIES: Outline how Clinton's conduct relates to obstruction of justice and perjury laws.

LINDSEY O. GRAHAM (R-South Carolina), 43, elected 1994.
DUTIES: Address how Clinton's conduct meets constitutional test for removal from office.

ASA HUTCHINSON (R-Arkansas), 48, elected 1996.
DUTIES: Outline factual case against Clinton on the obstruction of justice charge.

HENRY JOHN HYDE (R-Illinois), 74, elected 1974, chairman House Judiciary Committee.
DUTIES: Deliver opening and closing statements.

IRA WILLIAM "BILL" MCCOLLUM JR. (R-Florida), 54, elected 1980, chairman House Judiciary Subcommittee on Crime.
DUTIES: Summarize factual case against Clinton.

JAMES E. ROGAN (R-California), 41, elected 1996.
DUTIES: Outline case against Clinton on grand jury perjury and deliver closing remarks.

FRANK JAMES SENSENBRENNER JR. (R-Wisconsin), 55, elected 1978.
DUTIES: Deliver one hour introduction.

The President's Defense Team

CHARLES F. C. RUFF - Former chief Watergate prosecutor.

GREGORY B. CRAIG - Former State Department director of policy planning.

DAVID E. KENDALL - Clinton's Whitewater counsel and longtime friend.

CHERYL D. MILLS - Deputy White House counsel.

DALE BUMPERS - Retired Senator (D-Arkansas) and longtime Clinton friend.

BRUCE R. LINDSEY - Adviser to Clinton on Whitewater and Paula Corbin Jones cases.

LANNY A. BREUER - White House special counsel.

NICOLE K. SELIGMAN - Clinton's private defense lawyer and law partner with David E. Kendall.

Sources: "Defense Who's Who," *Washington Post,* 19 January 1999.

"Prosecution Who's Who," *Washington Post,* 14 January 1999.

oath, but would also entail immunity from further prosecution. Clinton privately and publically refused to admit to perjury, however, and the Senate trial proceeded.

Preparation. On 7 January 1999 Representative Henry John Hyde (R-Illinois), who led the House in the impeachment proceedings, along with the twelve other prosecutors or managers, formally submitted two Articles of Impeachment to the Senate. Later that day, with U.S. Supreme Court

Chief Justice William Hubbs Rehnquist presiding, the trial of President Clinton began with the senators being sworn in as impartial jurors. For the next week the Senate debated procedural rules that would govern the trial. During the Watergate scandal (1974), the Senate had established trial rules in anticipation of Richard M. Nixon's impeachment. While some rules of the Johnson and Watergate eras were adopted, new procedures were also formulated. Many senators, including

Secretary of the Senate Gary Sisco (left) receives the articles of impeachment against President Bill Clinton from House Judiciary chairman Henry John Hyde (R-Ill.) on 19 December 1998. Looking on (l to r) are representatives Bob Barr (R-Ga.),George William Gekas (R-Pa.), Ira William "Bill" McCollum Jr. (R-Fla.), and Frank James Sensenbrenner Jr. (R-Wis.) (AP/Wide World Photos).

Majority Leader Chester Trent Lott (R-Mississippi), wanted to avoid a long, chaotic trial. Some conservative senators, however, agreed with the House prosecutors and sought a full-fledged, open-ended trial with as many witnesses testifying as both sides wanted. The eventual compromise allowed House prosecutors to examine witnesses live, but only if a majority of senators consented, with each individual being considered on a one-by-one basis. This was an early defeat for the prosecution. The Senate also decided that most of the proceedings would be televised.

The Prosecution. On 14 January 1999 the House prosecutors began presenting their case. Their evidence and arguments focused on President Clinton's inconsistent sworn statements, gifts given to Lewinsky, his alleged coaching of secretary Betty Currie in preparation of her grand jury appearance, and Vernon E. Jordan Jr.'s assistance in finding Lewinsky a job. House manager Asa Hutchinson (R-Arkansas) identified the ways Clinton perjured himself and obstructed justice. He pointed out the conflicting and perjured statements made by Clinton concerning his relationship with Lewinsky. He argued that Clinton had repeatedly suggested to Jones's lawyers that they talk to Currie, because Clinton believed she would be called as a grand jury witness and because he allegedly had coached her in what to say. Hutchinson also cast doubt on the White House contention that the help Jordan, a friend of Clinton, and others gave Lewinsky in finding a new job had nothing to do with her testimony in the Jones case. The congressman pointed out that the assistance came in earnest only after Clinton learned

that Lewinsky's name was on the witness list. "The question here," Hutchinson said, "is not why did the President do a favor for an ex-intern? But why did he use the influence of his office to make sure it happened?" His answer: "To obstruct, impede justice." At this point, public-opinion polls indicated that most Americans believed Clinton had lied and obstructed justice, but they were mixed on whether to remove him from office.

The Defense. The lead defense attorney for Clinton, and by many accounts the most effective of his lawyers, was Charles F. C. Ruff, who argued that the wrongs committed were private indiscretions, not public crimes and not offenses that merited removal from office. Regarding the perjury charges, Ruff contended that Clinton's statements about his relationship with Lewinsky reflected his recollection of the events at the time of the sworn testimony. Ruff also argued that Clinton's impressions simply differed from other individuals' memories, including Lewinsky's. He quoted from a Supreme Court statement on perjury, that "Equally honest witnesses may well have differing recollections of the same event," and thus, "a conviction for perjury ought not to rest entirely upon an oath against an oath." In other words, it was a matter of differing interpretations. Ruff emphasized that House prosecutors had no eyewitnesses, tapes, or confessions indicating that the president obstructed justice in his testimony.

Witnesses. In early February the Senators voted to reject Lewinsky as a witness. This decision represented a bipartisan defeat for the Republican managers. The only concession the

Senate made was to allow them to use videotaped depositions of key witnesses, including Clinton, Lewinsky, Jordan, and White House aide Sidney Blumenthal. The best Hutchinson could do was to take strands of videotape testimony and contrast them with excerpts from the Paula Jones deposition, splicing together an argument that Clinton both lied and obstructed justice.

Motions to Dismiss or Censure. Prior to, and periodically during, the trial there were efforts to stop the proceedings by dismissing the charges, censuring the President, or issuing a finding-of-facts statement that catalogued the offenses that the senators believed had been proved against Clinton. None of these options received sufficient bipartisan support to be adopted. Many Republican and Democratic senators felt that such measures were unconstitutional since the House had already passed the Articles of Impeachment and the Senate was therefore required to try the president.

Acquittal. On 12 February the Senate voted on the two Articles of Impeachment. The outcome went as most expected. Public opinion polls showed that most Americans believed the president had lied and obstructed justice, but did not think he should be removed from office. The only surprise was the weakness of support for conviction. On the charge of perjury, the Senate acquitted Clinton fifty-five to forty-five, twenty-two votes short of the necessary two-thirds (sixty-seven) needed for conviction. All forty-five Democrats and ten Republicans voted not guilty, while forty-five Republicans voted guilty. On the allegation of obstruction of justice, all the Democrats and five Republicans voted not guilty; fifty Republicans voted to convict. The latter were seventeen votes short of the number needed for removal. At 12:39 P.M. Chief Justice Rehnquist declared President Clinton "Acquitted of the charges."

Legal Legacy. The various investigations into President Clinton's conduct and the consequent grand jury proceedings raised several important issues not only for Clinton, but for the presidency as well. Issues of presidential immunity, privacy and security, executive privilege, and lawyer-client confidentiality arose during the Jones case, Whitewater investigation, and Lewinsky affair. Clinton and his attorneys tried to block, or at least postpone, the civil action brought by Jones until his tenure as president was completed. They claimed that he should be immune from civil liability for unofficial acts. In January 1997 the U.S. Supreme Court heard arguments, with Robert S. Bennett, Clinton's lawyer in the Jones matter, arguing that a civil suit would interfere with the President's duties and set a dangerous precedent. On 27 May 1997 the High Court ruled unanimously that the private civil suit against Clinton could go forward. The Court upheld the individual rights of citizens to sue for redress against an abuse of power by an elected official, as well as against presidential prerogative. The justices required, however, that the federal court schedule the case with sensitivity "to the burdens of the presidency and the demands of the President's schedule." This order gave Clinton considerable leeway in delaying the case. Thus, the Court struck a balance between the constitutional principle of equal rights for all under the law and deference to a sitting president.

Insider Silence? In another case involving presidential prerogative, a panel of federal judges in July 1998 overturned a U.S. District Court ruling and required that Secret Service agents, who provide personal protection for the president, testify before a grand jury in the Lewinsky case. On 17 July 1998 Chief Justice Rehnquist refused to block the order on Secret Service testimony. The precedent meant that agents who in the line of duty overhear presidential conversations not already covered by other protections can be compelled to disclose the content of the communications. Some scholars argued that this practice could endanger presidents who may attempt to elude Secret Service protection to ensure their privacy. During the Starr investigations, the independent counsel also sought to compel President Clinton's lawyers, including Bruce Lindsey, to testify before a grand jury. A federal appellate court, and later Rehnquist, rejected Clinton's lawyer-client privilege appeal and ordered them to testify. The fallout carried over to the First Lady, Hillary Rodham Clinton. As part of Starr's investigation into missing Whitewater documents, he subpoenaed Mrs. Clinton to testify before a grand jury. She testified on 22 January 1995, the first time in U.S. history that a wife of a sitting president had been subpoenaed.

Sources:

Alan M. Dershowitz, *Sexual McCarthyism: Clinton, Starr, and the Emerging Constitutional Crisis* (New York: Basic Books, 1998).

Bob Woodward, *Shadow: Five Presidents and the Legacy of Watergate* (New York: Simon & Schuster, 1999).

JUVENILE CRIMINALS AND VICTIMS

Trends. The 1990s was a period of violence for the youth in the United States. The number of serious crimes committed by and against juveniles rose dramatically in the first half of the decade, reaching historically high rates. Although violent crime began to decline by mid decade, drug offenses continued to increase. National statistics also indicated that not only were youth committing more crimes, but they were increasingly the victims as well. There were also several highly publicized and deadly school shootings involving young assailants. The public, government, and courts struggled to find explanations for and solutions to teen violence.

Columbine. On 20 April 1999 gunfire erupted in a suburban high school in Littleton, Colorado, near Denver. Seniors Eric Harris, eighteen, and Dylan Klebold, seventeen, killed fifteen people total, and sent more than twenty others to hospitals with gunshot and shrapnel wounds, before turning their weapons on themselves. This attack was the deadliest school shooting in American history. Television images were broadcast nationwide of students fleeing from the building with their hands above their heads. Not shown were wounded victims still inside the school and beyond police help. Hundreds of officers from throughout the Denver area surrounded the school. Reflecting the ease with which children use technology, some students called their parents, the police, and television stations on cellular phones from inside the building. Nearby schools were locked and

PREVENTING SCHOOL VIOLENCE

"In your opinion, what is the single most important thing that could be done to prevent other incidences of school shootings by students, like the one in Littleton?"

More parental involvement and responsibility	32%
More security at school	16
Better gun control and gun laws	12
More counselors, counseling, and teachers at school	6
Left laws on disciplining children at school	6
Control media violence, video games, Internet	4
Better communication between students and parents and teachers	4
Raise morals, people's standards	3
Better education for students, parents, teachers	3
Put prayer back in schools and homes	3
Stricter punishment for children and stricter laws	2
Dress codes or uniforms at school	1
Others	4
None	1
No opinion	3
TOTAL	100%

The margin of error is +/- 3 percentage points

Source: Frank Newport, "Public Continues to Believe a Variety of Factors Caused Littleton," *The Gallup Organization*, Internet website, 13 May 1999.

students were prohibited from entering or leaving for hours. Law enforcement officers found dozens of explosives in the school and parking lot, including a twenty-pound propane bomb. For several days Federal Bureau of Investigation (FBI) agents and police SWAT teams searched for and removed devices that Harris and Klebold had hidden throughout the building.

Other School Shootings. The Columbine rampage was only one in a string of dozens of school shootings. On 2 February 1996 a fourteen-year-old student armed with a high-powered hunting rifle walked into his junior high school algebra class in Moses Lake, Washington, and killed two students and his teacher. On 19 February 1997 in Bethel, Alaska, a sixteen-year-old boy hid a shotgun in his pant leg until he reached school where he killed a classmate and the principal. After beating and stabbing to death his mother, a high school student in Pearl, Mississippi, shot and killed two students on 1 October 1997. Three students were killed and five others wounded on 1 December 1997 in West Paducah, Kentucky. The following year several individuals were killed in shooting incidents: a teacher was slain in Edinboro, Pennsylvania; four students and a teacher died in Jonesboro,

Arkansas; and two students, as well as the assailant's parents, were killed in Springfield, Oregon. Scores of youngsters were arrested for carrying weapons to, and for threatening violence at, their schools. While high-profile cases involved suburban, white, middle-class students, the majority of children killed at school were from lower income areas and were black.

Precautions. In the wake of suburban school shootings, administrators began increasing security measures, installing metal detectors, requiring see-though book bags, initiating routine checks of student lockers, employing security guards, instituting "zero-tolerance" policies for violence, and implementing early intervention programs for students with potential behavioral problems. Congress considered legislation that would make funds available to schools for security, impose stricter gun-control measures, restrict juvenile gun ownership, and hold parents criminally responsible when their children used their guns to commit crimes. Legislators also began searching for ways to limit children's access to Internet sites with violent content.

Why Kids Kill. The rash of school violence left parents, school administrators, and the nation wondering what causes middle-class, suburban children from two-parent homes to commit such crimes. Some blamed violent television programs, movies, video games, music, and the Internet. Others attributed responsibility to the ease with which youth have access to guns and a lack of parental guidance.

Rising Crime Rates. Violence by and against youth was not confined to schools. According to the FBI and the U.S. Department of Justice, juveniles between the ages of twelve and seventeen who were arrested for serious crimes such as murder, rape, assault, drug offenses, and robbery increased substantially, peaking in 1994. Juveniles accounted for 17 percent of all murder arrests and one of every ten convictions. In terms of race and gender, the juvenile homicide rate was highest among black males, followed by white males, and then black females. Young black males committed 175 murders per 100,000 in 1990; this figure peaked at 244 in 1993. Arrests of juveniles for robbery, aggravated assault, weapons violations, drug offenses, and motor vehicle theft also increased steadily early in the decade, almost doubling since the mid 1980s. This rapid increase, however, was followed by a steady decline. By the end of the decade, the juvenile violent-crime rate was at its lowest level, but still well above 1980s rates.

Teen Drug Use. While most youth crime began to decline, a notable exception was drug use. The number of teens illegally using alcohol also increased. In a 1998 survey, four out of five high-school seniors reported that they had tried alcohol at least once; half admitted to using it within the last month. Even among eighth graders the use of alcohol was high: one-half had tried alcohol and almost one-quarter said they had used it within one month prior to the survey. Of greater concern were juveniles who admitted to heavy drinking (five or more drinks consecutively). Thirty-one percent of seniors, 24 percent of tenth graders, and 14 percent of eighth graders reported this behavior. Tobacco use was less prevalent than alcohol abuse. Federal law prohibits the sale of tobacco prod-

Boot camp participants at the Youth Leadership Training Center, Camp Wilson, Wisconsin, on 16 May 1996 (AP/Wide World Photos).

ucts to individuals under the age of eighteen. In 1998, however, 65 percent of twelfth graders and 46 percent of eighth graders had tried cigarettes. Twenty-two percent of high school seniors, 16 percent of tenth graders, and 9 percent of eighth graders admitted to smoking cigarettes on a regular basis. More than half of high school seniors confessed to using illicit drugs (marijuana, stimulants, inhalants, LSD, cocaine, crack cocaine, steroids, and heroin). Marijuana was by far the most commonly used illicit drug. In 1998, 49 percent of twelfth graders said they had used marijuana. Just under 30 percent of seniors had used other illicit drugs. About one in ten twelfth graders reported having used cocaine and one in twenty admitted using crack cocaine. Studies also indicated that 15 percent of high school seniors had used inhalants, 13 percent had tried LSD, and 2 percent had abused heroin. Drug, alcohol, and tobacco use was more common among males than females, and more prevalent among whites and Hispanics than blacks. Statistics also showed that youth who used drugs were more likely to engage in other illegal activities, including robbery, assaults, and weapons violations.

Juvenile Victimization. As the juvenile crime rate rose, so too did the number of juvenile victims, most dramatically between 1990 and 1993. By 1996, however, the rate declined to its lowest point in the decade. Juveniles between the ages of fifteen and seventeen were more likely to be victims of rape, aggravated assault, and simple assault than persons in any other age group. They were also more likely to be victims of robbery than persons more than twenty-five years of age. One-third of all sexual assaults reported to law enforcement involved victims younger than twelve. Forty-three percent of these victims were assaulted by juveniles. Of sexual assault victims between the ages of seven and eleven, 34 percent of the

offenders were juveniles. Victims under the age of six were assaulted by juveniles 43 percent of the time. In most cases, the offender was either a family member or acquaintance. The murder rate for juveniles peaked in 1993 at 2,900, about four murders for every 100,000 persons under the age of eighteen. By 1997 this figure had dropped to 2,100, or about three murders per 100,000. Unlike the pattern for adult murders, however, youth homicides by the end of the decade were still substantially higher than levels in the mid 1980s, when about sixteen hundred juveniles were murdered annually. In 1997, 11 percent of all persons murdered were under the age of eighteen. Thirty-three percent were under the age of six and 50 percent were between the ages of 15 and 17; 70 percent were male, 47 percent were black, 56 percent were killed with a firearm, and 40 percent were slain by a family member.

Firearms. The rise in the juvenile murder rate was attributed to increased use of firearms. Homicides in which no firearms were involved remained relatively constant. Gun-related death rates rose substantially beginning in the late 1980s. Studies showed that when juveniles killed other children, the victims were usually acquaintances of the offender and firearms were commonly used.

Tougher Penalties. Unprecedented change was needed as states tried to reduce teen crime. By the end of the decade forty-seven states and the District of Columbia had enacted legislation that made juvenile justice more punitive. These laws generally included allowing, if not encouraging, juveniles charged with serious crimes to be transferred to adult criminal courts and then, if convicted, sentenced to adult correctional facilities. In 1987 just under seven thousand cases involving youth were transferred to adult criminal courts. This number increased to ten thousand by 1996. Most cases involved assaults, murders, and drug offenses. Ninety-five percent of juveniles transferred to adult courts were males, the majority of whom were older than sixteen. By the end of the decade thirty-five states automatically excluded serious drug offenses and crimes against persons from juvenile courts. Moreover, states increasingly eased confidentiality protection for youthful offenders and opened records to the public.

Behind Bars. The number of persons under age eighteen that were incarcerated in state and federal prisons decreased slightly from 6 percent of the population to 4 percent. Juveniles held in local jails, however, increased dramatically. In 1990, 2,301 young offenders were held in local jails. By 1997 this figure increased to 9,105. By mid decade youthful offenders held as adults significantly outpaced those detained as juveniles. A slight decrease in the juvenile population held in local correction facilities was evident at the end of the decade.

Boot Camp. In response to the increase in juvenile arrests and growing costs of incarceration, several states and many localities established juvenile boot camps. The first such programs, modeled after boot camps for adult offenders, emphasized military-style discipline and physical conditioning. In 1992 the Office of Juvenile Justice and Delinquency Prevention of the U.S. Justice Department funded three juvenile boot camps designed to address the special needs and circumstances of adolescent offenders. The programs were conducted in Cleveland, Ohio; Denver, Colorado; and Mobile, Alabama. Focusing on a target population of adjudicated, nonviolent offenders between the ages of thirteen and eighteen, boot-camp programs were designed as highly structured, three-month residential programs followed by six to nine months of community-based follow-up programs for continued rehabilitation and counseling. Most youths selected for the programs were nonviolent, repeat offenders. With a strong commitment to continued academic education, personal discipline, counseling, and a strong work ethic, the camps, usually located on the grounds of an existing correctional facility, imposed highly regimented programs with platoon-like organization. "Recruits" were provided with Spartan living facilities and required to wear uniforms and use military language, customs, and courtesies. There were onsite drill instructors with military backgrounds, teachers, and case managers. For 80 to 95 percent of recruits who completed the residential phase, there was a public graduation. By 1998 twenty-seven states had initiated boot camps for nonviolent youthful offenders.

Sources:

Kathryn A. Chandler, and others, *Students' Reports of School Crime: 1989 and 1995* (U.S. Department of Education, Office of Educational Research and Improvement, National Center for Education Statistics, and U.S. Department of Justice, Office of Justice Programs, Bureau of Justice Statistics, March 1998).

Tammerlin Drummond, "Battling the Columbine Copycats," *Time,* 153 (10 May 1999): 29.

Nancy Gibbs, "Death and Deceit," *Time,* 144 (14 November 1994): 43–48.

Eric Pooley, "Portrait of a Deadly Bond," *Time,* 153 (10 May 1999): 26.

JUVENILES IN PUBLIC/PRIVATE DETENTION, CORRECTIONAL, AND SHELTERED FACILITIES (OCTOBER 1997)

Offenses	Total Number (105,790)	Percentage
Violent Offenses	35,357	33.4%
Murder/manslaughter	1,927	1.8
Violent sex offense	5,590	5.3
Robbery	9,451	8.9
Aggravated assault	9,530	9.0
Simple assault	6,630	6.3
Others	2,229	2.1
Property Offenses	31,991	30.2
Household burglary	12,560	11.9
Motor vehicle theft	6,525	6.2
Theft	7,294	6.9
Others	5,612	5.2
Drug Offenses	9,286	8.8
Public order offenses (a)	9,718	9.2
Probation or parole violation	12,549	11.9
Other Offenses (b)	6,889	6.5

(a) Includes driving under the influence, obstruction of justice, weapons offenses, and others.

(b) Includes curfew violations, running away, truancy, underage alcohol offenses, and others.

Source: Catherine A. Gallagher, *Juvenile Offenders in Residential Placement, 1997* (Washington, D.C.: U.S. Justice Department, Office of Juvenile Justice and Delinquency Prevention, March 1999).

Prison and Jail Inmates at Midyear 1998 (Washington, D.C.: U.S. Department of Justice, Office of Justice Programs, Bureau of Justice Statistics, March 1999).

Howard N. Snyder and Melissa Sickmund, *Juvenile Offenders and Victims: 1999 National Report* (Washington, D.C.: U.S. Department of Justice, Office of Justice Programs, Office of Juvenile Justice and Delinquency Prevention, September 1999).

Anne L. Stahl, *Delinquency Cares Waived to Criminal Court, 1987–1996* (U.S. Department of Justice, Office of Justice Programs, Office of Juvenile Justice and Delinquency Prevention, April 1999).

THE LEGAL PROFESSION

Law School Enrollment. In 1990 there were 127,261 students enrolled in American Bar Association-approved law schools. This number increased to 129,397 in 1995, but dropped to 125,627 by 1998–1999. Despite the decline in total law school enrollment, the number of women in law programs rose consistently throughout the decade. In

In Topeka, on 25 April 1997, federal justices swear in 243 new lawyers to practice in federal and state courts in Kansas (AP/Wide World Photos).

1990 there were 54,097 women (43 percent) enrolled in 175 law schools; by 1998 the figure increased to 57,952 (46 percent) in 181 programs. The number of minority students also rose. In 1990 blacks, Hispanics, Asian/Pacific Islanders, Native Americans, and Puerto Ricans constituted 14 percent (17,330) of law students. By 1998 minority enrollment increased to an historic high of 25,266 or just over 20 percent. The attrition rate among law students increased slightly during the decade, the vast majority of whom quit in their first year. A slightly higher percentage of men dropped out than women—in 1990, 3,187 male and 2,245 female students quit; in 1997, 3,418 men and 2,469 women dropped out.

Degrees and Bar Admissions. The number of Juris Doctorate degrees awarded increased from 36,385 in 1990 to 39,455 in 1998. Women received 42 percent (15,345) of these degrees in 1990 and 45 percent (17,662) in 1998. Minorities awarded law degrees also increased from 4,128 in 1990 to 7,754 in 1998. Bar admissions rose from 47,174 in 1989–1990 to 57,875 in 1994, but they declined slightly to 56,629 in 1996.

Earnings. In the early 1990s law firms showed a decline in profits earned. During the second half of the decade, however, gross revenues and profits per partner increased. In 1999 the median salary for first-year associates ranged from $51,000 in firms of 225 attorneys or fewer to $85,000

LAW SCHOOL ENROLLMENT, NUMBER OF LAW SCHOOLS, AND BAR ADMISSIONS (1990-1999)

Year	Enrollment	Women Enrollment (%)	Law Schools	Bar Admissions
1998–1999	125,627	57,952 (46%)	181	na
1997–1998	126,886	56,915 (45%)	178	na
1996–1997	128,623	57,123 (44%)	179	56,629
1995–1996	129,397	56,961 (44%)	178	56,613
1994–1995	128,989	55,808 (43%)	177	57,875
1993–1994	127,802	55,134 (43%)	176	51,152
1992–1993	128,212	54,644 (43%)	176	57,117
1991–1992	129,580	55,110 (43%)	176	54,577
1990–1991	127,261	54,097 (43%)	175	43,286

Source: American Bar Association

MEDIAN COMPENSATION FOR LAWYERS IN PRIVATE FIRMS

Year	Entry-Level Salaries
1989	$50,000
1993	$50,000
1996	$52,000
1998	$55,000

Source: American Bar Association

in firms of 251 attorneys or more, with a first-year median of $70,000. Salaries for entry-level attorneys in larger firms and lawyers with expertise in specialized fields showed a noticeable increase during the decade. The average entry-level income for attorneys in larger New York firms ranged between $85,000 and $90,000. In some firms, first-year associates earned more than $100,000. The earnings of lawyers employed by state and federal agencies increased, but at a slower rate than in the private sector. By the end of the decade the salaries of entry-level county prosecutors averaged between $30,000 and $50,000. In 1999 the average income for State Attorneys General was between $55,000 and $150,000; U.S. attorneys made $118,400; federal public defenders ranged between $50,000 and $118,400; and public defenders at the county level could expect between $30,000 and $150,000.

Still Behind. The salaries and advancement of minorities and women remained lower than the national average. Only half of female associates and fewer than one third (30.8 percent) of minorities in large law firms perceived opportunities to advance to partnership as equitable. In smaller firms about 31 percent of female associates and 43 percent of minority associates perceived the criteria for advancement as being applied fairly. Minority partners in major law firms accounted for 2.95 percent; women accounted for 14.21 percent. Although minorities and women were underrepresented among partnerships, the figures documented a continuing, albeit small, increase from the early 1990s.

Sources:
ABA Network, American Bar Association, Internet website.

Amar Bhatia, "Lawyers Earnings Increase," *The Federal Lawyer,* 45 (August 1998): 19–20.

Margaret Cronin Fisk, "Most Lawyers Benefit From Boom," *National Law Journal,* 21 (14 June 1999): B7–B15.

National Association of Law Placement, *Perceptions of Partnership: The Allure and Accessibility of the Brass Ring* (NALP Foundation for Research & Education, 1999).

MICROSOFT MONOPOLY

United States of America v. *Microsoft Corporation.* Since the early 1990s computer software giant Microsoft had been the target of federal investigations. In November 1999

a federal judge issued a "finding of facts" that stated the company had used its monopolistic market position to aggressively stifle competition and harm consumers. Judge Thomas Penfield Jackson of the U.S. District Court for the District of Columbia heard testimony between October 1998 and June 1999 on the civil antitrust allegations that Microsoft had violated the Sherman Antitrust Act (1890) and various state statutes. In what was only an initial, albeit important, stage in the judicial process, the ruling in *United States of America* v. *Microsoft Corporation,* laid out the factual basis for determining that Microsoft had violated antitrust laws.

Antitrust Laws. The Sherman Act was passed to dismantle monopolies of the giant steel companies and other huge corporations that emerged in the U.S. industrial revolution after the Civil War (1861–1865). Antitrust laws are designed to protect competition and benefit consumers with more and better products at lower prices. The Federal Trade Commission (FTC) and the Justice Department enforce antitrust laws.

Findings. In a 207-page ruling, Judge Jackson stated that under the control of CEO William Henry "Bill" Gates III, Microsoft was a monopoly, which is not in itself illegal, but it had improperly abused its power to the detriment of competitors and consumers. The charges against the company, which controlled more than 90 percent of the computer software market and had a market value of $470 billion by 1999, represented serious violations of law. The judge's finding of facts alleged that Microsoft constricted its web browser competitor Netscape's access to the market by bundling its own browser, Microsoft Internet Explorer, with the popular computer operating system Microsoft

MONOPOLY STRUGGLE

"Microsoft had demonstrated that it will use its prodigious market power and immense profits to harm any firm that insists on pursuing initiatives that could intensify competition against one of Microsoft's core products."

Judge Thomas Penfield Jackson,
U.S. District Court for the District of Columbia.

"We respectfully disagree with a number of the Court's findings, and believe the American legal system ultimately will affirm that Microsoft's innovations were fair and legal, and have brought tremendous benefits to millions of consumers."

William Henry "Bill" Gates III,
Microsoft CEO.

Sources: Microsoft News Conference, 5 November 1999.

United States v. *Microsoft Corporation,* U.S. District Court for the District of Columbia (5 November 1999).

Courtroom sketch of Judge Thomas Penfield Jackson listening to Stephen Houck, lead lawyer for nineteen states in the Microsoft antitrust suit, on 21 September 1999 (AP/Wide World Photos).

Windows. This meant that all computer systems that used Windows contained Microsoft's own browser, thereby making the Netscape browser technically unnecessary. Agreeing with the Justice Department's lead attorney Joel I. Klein, the Court also found that Microsoft used strong-arm tactics to include its browser on Apple Computers and bullied computer chip-maker Intel into staying out of the software market. In addition to its aggressive approach to competitors, Judge Jackson further noted that by bundling the Explorer browser with the Windows operating system, Microsoft harmed consumers. Jackson found that this practice slowed down the operating system, increased the likelihood of system failures, and made the software more susceptible to viruses. In its defense, Microsoft attorneys argued that the company's practices were competitive but not illegal.

Remedies. The next step in the judicial process will likely take place sometime during early 2000. In this stage, Judge Jackson will issue orders to Microsoft detailing how it must remedy the antitrust violations. Unless Gates negotiates a deal with the Justice Department, these remedies could range from breaking up Microsoft, as was done in the early 1980s with the Bell telephone company, to forcing it to expose the secret code behind the Windows operating system. In any case, Microsoft is likely to appeal. It is possible, if not likely, that the case may stay in the courts for the next several years and the fate of the company eventually will be decided by the Supreme Court.

Sources:
Adam Cohen, "'Microsoft Enjoys Monopoly Power': In Uncommonly Harsh Language the Court Hands Gates a Devastating Defeat," *Time,* 154 (15 November 1999): 60.

Dori JonesYang, "The Empire Strikes Out," *U.S. News and World Report,* 127 (15 November 1999): 46–54.

RACE, JUSTICE, AND THE MEDIA

Conflicts over Rights. The Bill of Rights guarantees citizens freedom of expression, a free press, and the right to a fair trial. Journalists argued that they had the right to cover every trial based on the public's right to know. Lawyers and judges maintained that publicity should not affect judicial trials. During the 1990s, however, these rights appeared to be in conflict in two highly publicized cases, which were further complicated when some segments of the public perceived the incidents and verdicts to be racially tainted.

King Beating. On 3 March 1991 Rodney Glen King, a high school dropout who had served a year in prison for theft and aggravated assault, was driving on a California freeway with two friends. When Los Angeles Police Department (LAPD) officers attempted to stop him for speeding, King, who had been drinking and was still on parole, led the police on a high-speed chase and was finally forced off the road. During his arrest, several officers used force against King. They claimed that the six-foot, three-inch King charged them and resisted arrest; King contended that he was afraid of the white officers and had attempted to defend himself. While the incident was in progress, unknown to anyone at the scene, residents of a nearby apartment complex were awakened by the noise. One man videotaped part of the incident. Excerpts from the tape, showing a group of white police officers beating a black man lying on the ground, played repeatedly on television news around the world. King became an international symbol of police brutality and of the chasm between white and black justice.

Officers Indicted. Less than two weeks after the incident, on 15 March, four officers, Sergeant Stacey C. Koon and his subordinates Laurence M. Powell, Theodore J.

Briseno, and Timothy E. Wind, were indicted for unlawful assault and use of excessive force in beating King. The trial was moved out of Los Angeles to Simi Valley, a neighboring suburban city. Superior Court Judge Stanley Weisberg presided; a jury of six men and six women (ten whites, two Hispanics) was chosen. The trial began the first week in February 1992.

Prosecution's Case. The prosecution's case was straightforward. Using the eighty-one-second videotape of the incident, the state argued that the officers had wantonly abused their power and had betrayed the public trust. While many people believed that the beating was racially motivated, or at least partially so, prosecution attorneys also decided not to make race a primary issue given the majority white composition of the jury. These decisions proved to be strategic miscalculations.

The Defense. The defense argued that King was intoxicated, under the influence of an illegal drug, and aggressive. Addressing their state of mind during the incident, the officers testified that they believed, based on King's actions and the fact he was able to withstand two stun-gun darts, that he was under the influence of the drug Phencyclidine (PCP) or "angel dust," which produces erratic and aggressive behavior. Consequently, the officers judged that they were justified in using force to restrain King. The defense also used the videotape, playing it in slow motion and analyzing it frame by frame. They suggested that each blow delivered by the policemen was in response to specific actions by King in resisting arrest or in threatening the officers. The audio portion of the tape, which included racial epithets, was not played.

Rioting. After six weeks of testimony and six hours of deliberation, the jury found the officers not guilty. The end of the trial, however, only sparked violence. Between 29 April 1992, when the verdict was rendered, and 3 May, South Central Los Angeles, a low-income area populated largely by racial and ethnic minorities, was engulfed in chaos. Violence, looting, and mayhem ensued, leaving fifty-four dead, more than 2,500 injured, nearly 1,100 businesses destroyed, and an estimated $1 billion in property damage. The bedlam revealed the simmering tensions between race and justice. The public outrage over the state verdicts prompted a federal civil-rights trial in which all four officers were found guilty.

Denny Beating. One of the most heinous and publicized events during the riots was the beating of a white truck driver who was driving through the area. As news cameras fed live images to the nation, Reginald Denny was dragged from his truck and severely beaten. Crowds attacked whites, Latinos, Asians, and other blacks, many of whom lived and worked in the area. The National Guard was called in to restore order.

Federal Civil Rights Case. In response to the King verdicts and the outrage of the South Central Los Angeles community, the U.S. Justice Department filed federal charges against the four officers for violating King's civil

TELEVISIONS IN THE COURTROOM

In the late 1990s almost every state permitted still cameras in state courtrooms, while more than half allowed trials to be televised. The major argument in favor of cameras in courtrooms was that it gives ordinary citizens a glimpse into the workings of the judicial system. In addition, it enhances the Sixth Amendment right to a public trial. On the other hand, televised trials often encourage attorneys and judges to excessively posture for the cameras, thereby giving the audience a distorted view of courtroom proceedings. It can also make the judicial process more a matter of entertainment than justice. During the O. J. Simpson trial many television networks carried the entire proceedings live. This coverage came to mean that the attorneys on both sides, but particularly the defense, focused not only on directing its case toward the jury, but also toward millions of television viewers. Daily interviews were given by the attorneys. The judge, Lance A. Ito, even consented to an interview.

rights. In an unusual coalition, civil libertarians and right-wing conservatives objected to a federal trial as violating the Fifth Amendment prohibition against double jeopardy. Nevertheless, a jury of nine whites, two blacks, and one Hispanic was seated. On 17 April 1993, after six weeks of trial and thirty hours of deliberation, the jury found Powell and Koon guilty of violating King's civil rights. Powell was also found guilty of causing injury to King. Briseno and Wind were acquitted. With the LAPD on "tactical alert," the federal judge sentenced the two convicted defendants to thirty months in prison. The prosecution had recommended ten-year sentences. Explaining the sentence, Judge John G. Davies stated that King's actions had provoked the assault, that the defendants were unlikely to commit similar crimes in the future, and given that Powell and Koon had been prosecuted at both the state and federal levels, longer sentences would be unfair.

Assailants on Trial. Two months after the federal trial of the officers, three black men were tried for the beating of Denny, five other motorists, and two firefighters who had attempted to halt the assault. Damian Monroe Williams, nineteen; Antoine Miller, twenty; Henry Keith Watson, twenty-seven; and Gary Williams, thirty-three; had been identified on videotapes as the assailants and were arrested in late 1992. In the spring of 1993, Gary Williams pleaded guilty to charges of robbery and assault and was sentenced to three years in prison. Damian Williams and Watson were charged with multiple felony counts. Williams, who was allegedly seen on the video striking Denny in the head with a brick, was additionally charged with aggravated mayhem. The prosecution relied heavily on video footage. Defense attorneys challenged the videotape evidence, portrayed the defendants as victims of poverty and racial dis-

On 15 June 1995 O. J. Simpson, on trial for the murders of his wife, Nicole Brown Simpson, and her friend Ronald Goldman, tries on a leather glove he allegedly wore during the crime. He was acquitted of the charge (AP/Wide World Photos).

crimination, and relied on a group-contagion-theory defense, which suggests that individuals can become caught up in riotous behavior and lose sight of right and wrong. Reflecting the deep schisms between white and black views of the American criminal justice system, much of the local black community expressed support for Williams and Watson. On 18 October 1993, again with the LAPD on alert, the verdicts were announced. As controversial as the King verdict, the jury found Williams guilty of only one felony count of simple mayhem and one misdemeanor assault charge. He was sentenced to ten years in prison. Watson was found guilty of one misdemeanor assault charge, was credited with time served, and was released. Miller, who was tried separately from Watson and Williams, pleaded guilty to assault with a deadly weapon on 3 December; he was sentenced to time served and placed on probation.

Payback. Public reaction to the verdicts was strong, but mixed. Many in the press characterized the outcome as "payback" for the acquittals of the police officers in the initial King trial and the light sentences in the federal trial. A *Los Angeles Times* poll taken soon after the Williams and Watson verdicts in the Denny case found that 75 percent of Latinos, 66 percent of whites, and 53 percent of blacks believed the jurors were more motivated by fear for their own safety and of civil unrest than by fair and just consideration of the evidence. The poll also found that two-thirds of Latinos and whites disagreed with the verdicts and that

only a slight majority of blacks approved of the verdicts. Rodney King filed a $15 million civil suit against the city of Los Angeles for violating his civil rights, but two years after the South Central riots, a civil court refused to award him anything in punitive damages.

Simpson. Three years after the King beating, Los Angeles and the nation were once again polarized by racial divisions over a jury verdict. This time, however, the individual acquitted was Orenthal James "O. J." Simpson, a retired football star, sports announcer, television personality, and the prime suspect in the murders of his former wife, Nicole Brown Simpson, and her friend Ronald Goldman on 12 June 1994. Simpson, an African American, was arrested on 17 June 1994, after a lengthy, televised car chase on the Los Angeles freeway; both of the victims were white. In a July Gallup poll, 64 percent of black respondents believed Simpson would not receive a fair trial, while only 41 percent of whites held that opinion. By the time a grand jury was convened to review the evidence and determine if an indictment was warranted, Simpson had hired a cadre of celebrity lawyers, including Johnnie L. Cochran Jr., F. Lee Bailey, Robert Shapiro, and appeals expert Alan M. Dershowitz. The group was referred to by the media as the "Dream Team."

TV in the Courtroom. *The People of California* v. *Orenthal James Simpson* was called the "trial of the century" and made celebrities of many participants in the case, including the judge, Lance A. Ito. Several important juridical issues emerged, including the growing use of technology in judicial proceedings, the merits and problems of live television in the courtroom, and the reliability of DNA evidence, as well as more traditional problems, such as the use of race as a defense tactic. In a much debated move, Ito decided that the trial could be televised.

Prosecution's Case. The Simpson trial began on 23 January 1995 with hundreds of reporters from all over the world camped out in front of the courthouse. The jury consisted of eight blacks, two Hispanics, one white, and one person of mixed race; eight women, four men. The prosecution, led by attorneys Marcia Clark, Christopher Darden (the only black on the team), and William Hodgman, portrayed Simpson as abusive (several years earlier he had pleaded no contest to abusing his wife), jealous, and controlling. The evidence, however, was largely circumstantial; there was no weapon and there were no witnesses that directly linked the defendant to the crimes, but the prosecution presented a series of DNA experts who testified that blood found at the crime scene matched Simpson's DNA profile.

The Race Card. The defense argued that Simpson did not have the opportunity to commit the crimes, that his demeanor before and after the murders was not consistent with that of a murderer, and that the evidence presented was not only circumstantial, but may have been planted, particularly by Mark Fuhrman, a police detective whose history of racism was demonstrated in a series of audiotapes in which he used racial epithets. This evidence provided the Dream Team with the opportunity to introduce the so-called "race card." Over fellow defense attorney Shapiro's objections, Cochran suggested to the majority black jury that there was a widespread conspiracy against African Americans in the justice system. He even compared Simpson, a murder defendant, with Rodney King, a victim of police brutality.

The Verdict. On 2 October 1995 Judge Ito referred the case to the jury. At this time, even given the problems that plagued the prosecution, public-opinion polls indicated that more than half of Americans believed Simpson was guilty of the crimes. Whites were four times more likely than blacks, however, to hold this belief. Three hours and forty minutes after receiving the case, the jury informed Ito that they had reached a verdict. Fearing a replay of the civil disturbances after the 1992 King verdict, the judge delayed the reading until the next day to give the police department time to prepare. On 3 October, with millions of Americans watching television or listening to radio, the verdict was announced. Simpson was found not guilty.

Civil Case. Simpson's legal troubles did not end with the criminal trial. The following year the families of Nicole Brown Simpson and Ronald Goldman filed a civil suit against Simpson. Unlike in the criminal trial, the standard for a civil verdict is the lower criterion of "preponderance of evidence" rather than "beyond reasonable doubt." This trial lasted three months. A jury unanimously declared that Simpson was financially liable for the deaths. The families were awarded $8.2 million in compensatory damages and another $25 million in punitive damages.

Color of Justice. The issue of race and justice is a complicated one. The long history of discrimination against minorities in the United States and the racism that many minorities experience on a daily basis often lead them to regard traditional institutions, such as the legal system, with skepticism. After the King verdict, some analysts suggested that criminal justice reflected the values of the dominant white society. Upon viewing the beating of King, Americans of all races wondered whether the police would have behaved in a similar manner if he had been white. In the 1990s, as in previous decades, blacks were incarcerated at a much higher rate than whites. More young black men were in prisons and jails in the United States than were enrolled in colleges and universities. Another aspect of race and justice was money. While all criminal defendants are guaranteed the right to legal counsel by the Sixth Amendment, many minority defendants were unable to afford the quality of defense that many whites could. In 1998, 26 percent of blacks lived at or below the poverty level as compared to 8 percent of whites. The per capita income for blacks was $13,000 and $23,000 for whites. Some Americans and political analysts suggested that the Simpson verdict was not only bought, but was a deliberate "payback" for years of judicial injustices against minorities. Commenting on the verdict, George F. Will, a conservative columnist with the *Washington Post*, stated, "The jurors abused their position in order to send a message about racism or police corruption."

Sources:

Lou Cannon, *Official Negligence: How Rodney King and the Riots Changed Los Angeles and the LAPD* (New York: Times Books, 1997).

Gilbert Geis and Leigh B. Bienen, *Crimes of the Century: From Leopold and Loeb to O. J. Simpson* (Boston: Northeastern University Press, 1998).

Jewelle Taylor Gibbs, *Race and Justice: Rodney King and O. J. Simpson in a House Divided* (San Francisco: Jossey-Bass, 1996).

TOBACCO COMPANIES

Under Attack. For decades, tobacco companies rarely lost health-related lawsuits filed by consumers. This trend changed in the 1990s as the tobacco industry paid hundreds of billions of dollars in settlements. Law suits were filed by individuals, groups (class action suits), states, and cities. As a result, cigarette prices soared. Smoking was made even more expensive as sales taxes on cigarettes were increased in an effort to discourage smoking and to raise revenue. State and federal agencies, such as the U.S. Department of Health and Human Services, launched antismoking campaigns, primarily targeted at youth. According to the Centers for Disease Control (CDC), an estimated forty-seven million adults in the United States were cigarette smokers in 1999. While cigar smoking increased by almost 70 percent from the 1980s, mostly among males, overall adult smoking consistently declined during the decade. After a twenty-year downward trend, however, tobacco use among individuals under the age of eighteen increased by more than 30 percent. Tobacco use was responsible for more than 430,000 deaths each year, or one in every five deaths, and associated health costs were $100 billion.

States. On 14 November 1998 a settlement was reached between four of the largest cigarette manufacturers and forty-six states. In the largest civil settlement in U.S. history, Philip Morris, R. J. Reynolds, Lorillard, and Brown & Williamson agreed to pay $206 billion to cover the medical costs of smoking-related illnesses. The states were scheduled to receive $12 billion up front over the first five years. The rest would be paid in annual installments until 2025. In addition, the companies agreed to spend $1.7 billion on research programs aimed at discouraging smoking, especially among teenagers. The class action settlement also required that tobacco companies halt advertising on billboards and in transit stations, such as bus terminals and subways. Further, the companies were banned from selling clothing and merchandise that carried cigarette brand logos. The prohibitions meant that cartoon characters such as "Joe Camel" could not be used in advertising. While the settlement aimed at reducing smoking, it did not include any specific penalties if smok-

ing did not decline. There were also no penalties if underage smoking increased.

Jury Awards. There were also several jury verdicts against the tobacco industry. In *Widdick* v. *Brown & Williamson Tobacco Corporation,* Angela Widdick filed suit against the company for the death of her father, Roland Maddox. During the trial, thousands of pages of confidential Brown & Williamson documents surfaced and revealed that company officials had known about the dangers of smoking for decades. In one such document, a vice president stated that "nicotine is addictive. We are, then, in the business of selling nicotine, an addictive drug effective in the release of stress mechanisms." The jury found the company liable and noted that it was part of a larger industry-wide conspiracy to

Arkansas Attorney General Winston Bryant at a press conference, explains the November 1998 settlement between tobacco companies and the state of Arkansas (AP/Wide World Photos).

defraud the public. The company was ordered to pay the Maddox family $500,000 in compensatory damages. More importantly, the jury found that Brown & Williamson should pay the family $450,000 in punitive damages.

Class Action Suit. In July 1999 a Florida jury found the tobacco industry liable for illnesses of thousands of sick smokers. The suit was brought by pediatrician Howard A. Engle and eight other lead plaintiffs on behalf of approximately five hundred thousand sick smokers and heirs of deceased smokers. The defendants were the five largest U.S. tobacco companies: Philip Morris, R. J. Reynolds, Brown & Williamson, Lorillard, and Liggett. In addition, two industry organizations, the Council for Tobacco Research and the Tobacco Institute, were named in the suit. In the broadest ruling to date in the legal war against tobacco, the Miami jury concluded that cigarette makers "engaged in extreme and outrageous conduct," concealed the dangers of cigarettes, conspired to hide their addictiveness, and made a product that caused more than a dozen deadly diseases ranging from heart disease to lung cancer. If the verdict is not overturned on appeal, the plaintiffs could be awarded billions of dollars in damages.

Tobacco Victories. While states and individuals won major victories against the tobacco industry, cigarette companies were successful in some cases. They won a major victory in March 1999 when a federal court jury in Ohio ruled against 114 union health funds seeking to recover hundreds of millions of dollars spent to treat sick smokers. Following the lead of states that sued the industry to recover billions in Medicaid funds, the insurers charged that cigarette makers conspired to deceive the public about the dangers and addictiveness of smoking. In 1998 a Florida appeals court reversed a 1996 multi-million judgment against Brown & Williamson on a legal technicality. The appeals court ruled that Carter waited too long to file the suit. The statute of limitations in Florida for this type of civil case is four years. Carter filed suit four years and six days after being diagnosed with a lung disease.

Sources:

Saundra Torry, "Cigarette Firms Lose Fla. Class Action Suit," *Washington Post*, 8 July 1999.

Torry, "Tobacco Firms Win Suit Filed by Unions," *Washington Post*, 19 March 1999.

WOMEN'S ISSUES

Abortion. The right to abortion was affirmed by the Supreme Court in *Roe* v. *Wade* (1973). Since the 1980s, however, the Court has consistently allowed states to impose restrictions on this right. In *Planned Parenthood of Southeastern Pennsylvania* v. *Casey* (1992) the Court permitted Pennsylvania to limit abortions as long as state laws and regulations did not place an "undue burden" on pregnant women. The decision upheld a twenty-four-hour waiting period for abortions and parental consent requirements for minors seeking abor-

tions. While the ruling did not overturn *Roe* it limited the 1973 decision. During the 1990s Congress and the Clinton administration battled over abortion and reproductive rights. President Bill Clinton ended bans on fetal tissue research and abortions in military hospitals and lifted the "gag" rule enacted in 1987 that prevented public health clinics receiving federal funds from discussing abortion as a family planning option. He also lifted the ban on testing of RU-486, an "abortion pill." By mid decade, however, with the new Republican majority Congress, activities restricting abortions resumed.

Partial Birth Abortion. In 1996 and 1998 Congress passed bans on "partial birth" abortions, a procedure used late-term to terminate pregnancies. On each occasion, however, President Clinton vetoed the measures and Congress was unable to override them. Similar restrictions on "partial birth" abortions were passed in several state legislatures and many of these bans have been challenged in the courts. In October 1999 the 7th U.S. Circuit Court of Appeals upheld Illinois and Wisconsin laws that prohibited partial birth abortions. A month earlier, however, another federal appeals court threw out similar laws in Nebraska, Arkansas, and Iowa. The conflicting results made it more likely, though not certain, that the Supreme Court would step in to resolve the issue. In March 1998 the Court voted six to three not to review the invalidation by an appeals court of an Ohio law that banned the procedure. The Supreme Court has not heard an abortion case since the 1992 *Casey* case.

Fetal Protection and Workplace Rights. In 1990 the U.S. Supreme Court reviewed a class action suit involving gender-based workplace discrimination and fetal rights. Johnson Controls, a battery manufacturer, implemented a workplace safety policy aimed at protecting fetuses from exposure to lead, a primary ingredient in batteries. Occupational exposure to lead entails health risks, including potential harm to any fetus. After eight employees became pregnant while maintaining blood lead levels exceeding Occupational Safety and Health Administration (OSHA) standards for workers planning to have children, the company announced a policy barring all women, except those whose infertility was medically documented, from jobs involving actual or potential lead exposure. A group of employees filed a class action suit in district court, claiming that the policy constituted a sex discrimination violation of Title VII of the Civil Rights Act of 1964, as amended. The district court, and later a federal appeals court, ruled in favor of the company, arguing that the fetal-protection policy was reasonably necessary to ensure workplace safety. On appeal, the Supreme Court ruled in *International Union, United Automobile, Aerospace and Agricultural Implement Workers of America, UAW, et al.,* v. *Johnson Controls, Inc.* (1991) that while it is constitutional to protect fetuses, it is a violation of federal law to use a gender-based policy that discriminates against workers on the basis of their sex as a means for protecting fetuses. The Court threw out the fetal-protection policy that excluded all fertile women, regardless of their childbearing intentions, from certain higher paying jobs where they might be exposed to lead. Writing for the majority, Justice Harry Andrew Blackmun argued that in protecting women rather than improving working conditions for all employees, the company had practiced sex discrimination.

Faulkner. In early 1993 Shannon Faulkner was accepted to The Citadel, an all-male state-supported military college in South Carolina. On her application and transcripts all references to her gender had been removed. When The Citadel discovered that she was female, it withdrew her acceptance. Faulkner filed suit against the school. A U.S. district judge ruled that the school had to permit Faulkner to attend day classes, but allowed The Citadel to prohibit her from joining the Corps of Cadets or participating in military training until her lawsuit was settled. Before she could register, however, a 4th U.S. Circuit Appeals Court judge stayed the lower court order, thereby preventing Faulkner from attending The Citadel. Several months later the Appeals Court allowed her into day classes. In January 1994 Faulkner became the first woman to attend day classes at The Citadel. The school appealed the ruling, but in April 1994 the 4th U.S. Circuit Court of Appeals ruled that Faulkner could join the military Corps of Cadets, unless the state of South Carolina established a court-approved program with similar military leadership education and training for women. Because the state was unable to set up a separate, but equal, program for women before the court deadline, it appeared that The Citadel would be forced to admit Faulkner as a cadet. The Citadel appealed to the U.S. Supreme Court, hoping to block Faulkner's admission. Justices William Hubbs Rehnquist and Antonin Scalia refused to do so. On 11 August 1994, Faulkner became the first female cadet in the 152-year history of The Citadel. Accompanied by federal marshals, Faulkner reported to campus the following day. Less than a week after entering the school as a cadet, however, she dropped out, claiming that the stress of the two and a half year legal battle made her unable to continue.

VMI and Women. In 1996 the Supreme Court ruled that another all-male military school, the Virginia Military Institute (VMI), would have to admit women. The *United States* v. *Virginia et al.* ruling was perceived as also applying to The Citadel. VMI claimed that it did not have to admit women if the state provided a separate, but equal, military program for women. The Court rejected this argument in its seven to one decision (Justice Clarence Thomas did not participate in the case because his son was attending VMI). Writing for the majority, Associate Justice Ruth Bader Ginsburg argued that the exclusion of women from the education opportunities at VMI denied them equal protection. She further contended that providing women with a similar program at another facility "does not cure the constitutional violation."

DISSENTING OPINIONS

"Though the woman has a right to choose to terminate or continue her pregnancy before viability, it does not at all follow that the State is prohibited from taking steps to ensure that this choice is thoughtful and informed. Even in the earliest stages of pregnancy, the State may enact rules and regulations designed to encourage her to know that there are philosophic and social arguments of great weight that can be brought to bear in favor of continuing the pregnancy to full term and that there are procedures and institutions to allow adoption of unwanted children as well as a certain degree of state assistance if the mother chooses to raise the child herself. It follows that States are free to enact laws to provide a reasonable framework for a woman to make a decision that has such profound and lasting meaning. This, too, we find consistent with *Roe's* central premises, and indeed the inevitable consequence of our holding that the State has an interest in protecting the life of the unborn."

U.S. Supreme Court Justice Sandra Day O'Connor,
majority opinion

Source: *Planned Parenthood of Southeastern Pennsylvania* v. *Casey* (1992).

"There is no reason to believe that the admission of women capable of all the activities required of VMI cadets would destroy the institute rather than enhance its capacity to serve the more perfect union. . . . Neither the goal of producing citizen-soldiers nor VMI's implementing methodology is inherently unsuitable for women."

U.S. Supreme Court Justice Ruth Bader Ginsburg,
majority opinion

Source: *United States* v. *Virginia et al,* (941941), 518 U.S. 515 (1996).

"Today the court shuts down an institute that has served the people of the commonwealth of Virginia with pride and distinction for a century and a half. . . . I do not think any of us, women included, will be better off for its destruction."

U.S. Supreme Court Justice Antonin Scalia,
dissenting opinion

Source: *United States* v. *Virginia et al,* (941941), 518 U.S. 515 (1996).

Jeanie Mentavlos and Kim Messer, second and third from left, cheer along with other Citadel cadets at a 21 September 1996 football game (AP/Wide World Photos).

Sexual Harassment. After the Clarence Thomas nomination hearings, concerning whether or not he had sexually harassed Anita Hill, sexual harassment claims rose dramatically. Between 1990 and 1997, claims more than doubled. The Equal Employment Opportunity Commission (EEOC), a federal agency charged with enforcing civil rights in the workplace, reached record settlements with employers, increasing from $7.7 million in 1990 to $27 million in 1997. After the Supreme Court ordered admissions of women to The Citadel and VMI, several male cadets were suspended or expelled for sexually harassing female cadets, including the top cadet at VMI. Lawsuits followed these incidents. In November 1999 a female cadet who quit The Citadel settled a sexual harassment lawsuit against the school, a staff member, and two former cadets. Jeanie Mentavlos was awarded $135,000. Another former female cadet was awarded $34,000 in 1998 in her sexual harassment suit against The Citadel.

Sources:

"Chronology of Virginia Military Institute's Court Battle," *The* (Charleston, S.C.) *Post and Courier,* 16 June 1996.

International Union, United Automobile, Aerospace and Agricultural Implement Workers of America, UAW, et al., v. *Johnson Controls, Inc.,* (891215) 499 US 187 (1991).

Planned Parenthood of Southeastern Pennsylvania v. *Casey,* (91744), 505 U.S. 833 (1992).

Jessica Reaves, "Abortion Harking Back to the Supreme Court," *Time Daily,* 27 October 1999, Internet website.

United States v. *Virginia, et al.,* 518 U.S. 515 (1996).

HEADLINE MAKERS

JOHNNIE COCHRAN

1937–
ATTORNEY

Background. Johnnie L. Cochran Jr. was born in Shreveport, Louisiana, in the midst of the Great Depression. In 1943 he and his family moved to California. In 1955 Cochran enrolled in the University of California, Los Angeles and then graduated from Loyola Law School. During the early years of his private practice many cases he defended involved controversial and often racial issues. In 1966 he represented the family of a black man shot by Los Angeles police officers. He was the court-appointed attorney in 1969 for a case involving a member of the Black Panthers, an extremist civil-rights organization. In 1978 Cochran became an assistant district attorney in Los Angeles, the first black to serve in this capacity, and he initiated programs to assist victims of domestic violence and sexual assault. He left the District Attorney's office in 1982 to return to private practice and began to represent high-profile celebrity clients, including Elizabeth Taylor and Michael Jackson.

Representing Simpson. Cochran gained national notoriety in 1994 when he joined O. J. Simpson's defense team. Simpson, a former football player turned actor, was accused of murdering his former wife, Nicole Brown Simpson, and Ronald Goldman. Along with fellow defense attorney F. Lee Bailey, Cochran developed the "race card" strategy as a chief defense tactic. When it was discovered that a Los Angeles Police Department (LAPD) officer involved in the investigation, Mark Fuhrman, had recorded audiotaped notes in which he used racial epithets, Cochran persuaded the trial judge, Lance A. Ito, to consider their admissibility in the Simpson trial. Through a series of carefully orchestrated leaks, excerpts of the tapes appeared in several major newspapers in an attempt to increase public support for Simpson. Cochran was able to provoke one of the prose-cuting attorneys into having Simpson try on a pair of blood-stained gloves, one of which was found at the crime scene and the other at Simpson's residence. Cochran had earlier tried on the gloves and realized that they would not fit Simpson's hands. In open court, Simpson was directed to put on the gloves, which were clearly too small. This incident led to one of the most quoted statements of the trial, uttered by Cochran in his closing statement: "If the gloves don't fit, you must acquit." On 3 October 1995, Simpson was acquitted.

After O. J. Cochran continued in private practice after the Simpson case. In 1996 he co-authored an autobiographical book, *Journey to Justice.* He became the host in 1997 of a *Court TV* network program that offered commentary on various legal issues and cases.

Source:
Johnnie L. Cochran Jr. and Tim Rutten, *Journey to Justice* (New York: Ballantine, 1996).

MORRIS DEES

1936–
ATTORNEY, CIVIL-RIGHTS ACTIVIST

Beginnings. Born in Shorter, Alabama, the son of a farmer and cotton-gin operator, Morris Seligman Dees Jr. attended undergraduate school at the University of Alabama and then the University of Alabama School of Law. He founded a mail-order book publishing business, Fuller & Dees Marketing Group, which grew to be one of the largest publishing companies in the South. In 1969 Dees sold the company to Times Mirror, the parent company of the *Los Angeles Times.* In 1967 Dees began taking controversial cases that were unpopular within his white Southern community. For instance, he filed suit to stop construction of an all-white university in Alabama. He filed suit in 1968 to integrate the all-white

Montgomery YMCA. As he continued to pursue equal opportunities for minorities and the poor, Dees and his law partner Joseph J. Levin Jr. recognized the need for a nonprofit organization dedicated to seeking justice. In 1971 the two lawyers and civil-rights activist Julian Bond founded the Southern Poverty Law Center (SPLC).

Fighting Hate. Dees served as the chief trial counsel and chair of the executive committee for the SPLC during the 1990s. In this capacity he tracked and sued hate groups, as well as developed educational programs to teach tolerance to youth. In 1994, after uncovering links between white supremacist organizations and elements of the emerging antigovernment "Patriot" movement, the center established the "Militia Task Force." Six months before the 1995 Oklahoma City bombing, Dees warned the U.S. Attorney General that the growing hate movement in America could lead to large-scale violence. The Task Force currently monitors more than four hundred militias and other groups espousing extreme antigovernment views. Dees and the SPLC also file lawsuits against hate groups. After a rash of church-burnings in the South, Dees represented and won a conviction for the Macedonia Baptist Church in Manning, South Carolina, against the Christian Knights of the Ku Klux Klan, its state leader, and four other Klansmen. "That jury's decision was a day of reckoning for the Klan," said Dees. "The verdict shows that there are still some things sacred in the country, still some lines that no one can cross."

Teaching Tolerance. In 1991 Dees and the SPLC responded to an alarming increase in hate crimes among youth by establishing the Teaching Tolerance project. The program publishes an educational magazine, *Teaching Tolerance,* targeted at school-age children. Distributed free of cost twice a year to more than a half-million educators across the United States, the magazine includes articles and artwork that address themes of tolerance, respect, and community building. The Center also provides teaching kits for instructors at different school levels.

Recognition. Dees has received many awards in conjunction with his work at the Center. Trial Lawyers for Public Justice named him Trial Lawyer of the Year in 1987, and he was presented the Martin Luther King Jr. Memorial Award from the National Education Association (NEA) in 1990. The American Bar Association (ABA) gave Dees its Young Lawyers Distinguished Service Award and the American Civil Liberties Union (ACLU) honored him with its Roger Baldwin Award. Colleges and universities have recognized his accomplishments with honorary degrees, and the University of Alabama gave Dees its Humanitarian Award in 1993.

Publications. In 1991 the autobiography *A Season For Justice: The Life and Times of Civil Rights Lawyer Morris Dees* was published by Scribners. His second book, written with Steve Fiffer, was *Hate on Trial: The Case Against America's Most Dangerous Neo-Nazi* (1993). It chronicles the trial and $12.5 million judgment against white supremacist Tom Metzger, his son John, and the White Aryan Resistance (WAR) for their responsibility in the beating death of Mulugeta Seraw, a young Ethiopian immigrant and student

in Portland, Oregon. *Gathering Storm: America's Militia Threat* (1996), coauthored with Steven Corcoran, exposes the danger posed by domestic terrorist groups.

Sources:

Morris Dees, *A Season for Justice: The Life and Times of Civil Rights Lawyer Morris Dees* (New York: Scribners, 1991).

Southern Poverty Law Center, Internet website.

ANITA HILL

1956–
LAW PROFESSOR

Early Years. Anita F. Hill was born in 1956 in Okmulgee County, Oklahoma, the youngest daughter of farmers. A devoted Baptist, she attended Oklahoma State University and graduated in 1977. She earned her J.D. at Yale University in 1980 and took a position with Wald, Harkrader & Ross of Washington. In 1981 she met Clarence Thomas and began to work with him in his capacity as Assistant Secretary of Education for Civil Rights. In 1983 she accepted a teaching post at Oral Roberts University, and later taught law at the University of Oklahoma.

Reluctant Testimony. In September 1991 Hill was asked if she knew anything about allegations that U.S. Supreme Court nominee Thomas had sexually harassed women. After several inquiries, she acknowledged that she had been a victim. On 10 September the Senate Judiciary Committee opened hearings on Thomas's nomination. Initially, Hill resisted testifying. The committee voted thirteen to one to recommend Thomas as an Associate Justice on 8 October. Later that day, however, Senator Joseph Robinette Biden Jr. (D-Delaware), chair of the committee, informed Hill that hearings would be reopened and that she would be subpoenaed to testify. Hill was given less than three days to prepare. On 11 October the Thomas-Hill hearings began. Thomas testified first, categorically denying all of the allegations.

Harassment. With television cameras rolling, Hill's testimony began on 11 October. The questioning was highly partisan in nature, with all of the Republicans on the committee clearly supporting Thomas. Many Senators either indicated that they did not believe Hill and regarded her allegations as a partisan attempt to prevent Thomas's confirmation or considered Hill to have overreacted to Thomas's behavior. For nine hours Hill was required to discuss the most embarrassing incidents of the sexual harassment. She testified that in the early 1980s Thomas had sexually harassed her while they worked in the Office for Civil Rights, one of the chief federal enforcement agencies for combating race and gender discrimination. As Thomas's assistant, Hill investigated discrimination claims and researched the state of minority education and academic achievement. Hill testified that in 1981 Thomas began to pressure her to see him socially. Even though she declined, Hill stated that Thomas persisted in his pursuit of a personal relationship. Eventually, she claimed, Thomas became increasingly graphic and offensive. This behavior continued intermittently for several years. As a twenty-five-year-old just out of law school, according to Hill, she did not know how to effectively rebuff her supervisor's advances. In 1982 Thomas was offered a position at the Equal Employment Opportunity Commission (EEOC), which among other tasks investigates sexual harassment claims. Fearing that she might lose her job if she did not accompany Thomas to the new post, she agreed to follow him to the EEOC. Shortly thereafter, in July 1983, Hill resigned. After her testimony, Hill took a polygraph test, which indicated no deceptions in her responses.

Rebuttal and Confirmation. Thomas was given the opportunity to respond to Hill's allegations, all of which he denied. He portrayed himself as the victim and accused the Judiciary Committee of "high-tech lynching," denouncing committee Democrats as racists. Thomas further claimed that they had targeted him for ideological reasons, because he was a black conservative. After these allegations, the questioning became far less confrontational than Hill's had been. On 15 October the Senate voted fifty-two to forty-eight to confirm the nomination. This was the narrowest margin of confirmation for any Supreme Court nominee in history.

Postscript. Before the vote, Hill returned to the University of Oklahoma Law School to resume her teaching duties. Media interest, however, had not waned. For weeks she was pursued by reporters. While her Senate testimony did not block Thomas's confirmation, it highlighted the problems of sexual harassment in the workplace and exposed the fear that many women feel for their safety and jobs when they are targeted by this type of behavior. In 1997, Doubleday published Hill's *Speaking Truth to Power,* which recounts her life and experiences.

Source:
Anita Hill, *Speaking Truth to Power* (New York: Doubleday, 1997).

ASA HUTCHINSON

1950-

U.S. REPRESENTATIVE, IMPEACHMENT PROSECUTOR

Arkansas Roots. Asa Hutchinson was born in Gravette, Arkansas, on 3 December 1950. He attended Arkansas public schools and received a bachelor's degree in accounting from Bob Jones University in 1972. He earned his law degree from the University of Arkansas in 1975, where Bill Clinton taught, although Hutchinson did not take any of his classes. In 1986 the Arkansas Jaycees named him one of the ten outstanding young leaders in the state.

Political History. In 1977 Hutchinson assumed his first public office as city attorney for Bentonville, Arkansas. From 1982 to 1985 he served as U.S. Attorney for the Western District of Arkansas. Appointed by President Ronald Reagan, Hutchinson was, at age thirty-one, the youngest federal prosecutor in the country. During his tenure as U.S. Attorney, the Federal Bureau of Investigation (FBI) awarded Hutchinson a citation for his successful prosecution of a terrorist group in northern Arkansas known as the Covenant, Sword and Arm of the Lord. In 1984 he brought a cocaine-distributing charge against Roger Clinton, the half brother of Governor Bill Clinton. Roger Clinton pleaded guilty. Hutchinson then practiced law for the Fort Smith firm of Karr & Hutchinson. In 1986 he ran an unsuccessful campaign for the U.S. Senate seat from Arkansas. From 1990 to 1995 Hutchinson served as chairman of the Republican Party of Arkansas.

Congressman. In 1996 Hutchinson was elected to the U.S. House of Representatives from the Third Congressional District in Arkansas. He filled the seat vacated by his brother Timothy "Tim" Hutchinson, who left the House to run for the U.S. Senate. While in Congress, Hutchinson served on the Judiciary Committee (Constitution and Crime Subcommittees), Transportation and Infrastructure Committee (Aviation and Water Resources and Environment Subcommittees), and Government Reform Committee (Criminal Justice Subcommittee). As a House member, Hutchinson focused his attention on several national issues, including campaign finance reform and youth drug use. Hutchinson also served on the U.S. House Speaker's Task Force for a Drug-Free America. In 1995 he was appointed to represent the interests of the elderly as a delegate to the White House Conference on Aging.

Impeachment. As one of thirteen House prosecutors during the Senate impeachment trial of President Clinton, Hutchinson was assigned the critical job of proving the president had devised a scheme to obstruct justice in an effort to hide his relationship with former White House intern Monica S. Lewinsky. In his opening statement, Hutchinson argued that Clinton's sworn testimony established a pattern of "false statements, deceit, and obstruction." With these actions, he continued, the President moved beyond questionable and embarrassing private conduct into the public arena. The Arkansas congressman accused Clinton of not only lying under oath, but of obstructing justice by soliciting and encouraging false statements by others. Not to prosecute the president for these offenses would be tantamount to accepting that wealthy and powerful individuals are above the law, Hutchinson contended. After a failed attempt to call witnesses, Hutchinson, along with several other House managers, introduced to the Senate jurors both the written and videotaped testimonies of Clinton, Lewinsky, Vernon E. Jordan Jr., and Betty Currie. While many legal and political observers regarded Hutchinson as the strongest and most persuasive of the House lawyers, he, along with the other impeachment managers, was ultimately unsuccessful in his role as prosecutor. On 12 February 1999 the Senate acquitted Clinton on both Articles of Impeachment.

Sources:
Bob Woodward, *Shadow: Five Presidents and the Legacy of Watergate* (New York: Simon & Schuster, 1999).

PAULA CORBIN JONES

1966-

ARKANSAS STATE EMPLOYEE

Beginnings. Paula Corbin was born in Lonoke, Arkansas, in 1966. She graduated from high school in 1984, and worked as saleswoman, rental car clerk, and secretary. In 1991 she accepted a position as a clerk with the Arkansas Industrial Development Commission (AIDC); she also married Steven Jones. She moved to California in 1993.

Accusation. In February 1994 Jones publicly accused President Bill Clinton of sexual harassment. Jones claimed that the alleged incident occurred in 1991, when she was a state employee, during Clinton's tenure as the governor of Arkansas. Although she received little initial attention from the mainstream press, Jones, who said that she waited two years to make the charge because she feared not being believed, was soon supported by Clinton's political opponents. Jones alleged that on 8 May 1991, when she was working at a conference for the AIDC in Little Rock, Arkansas, a state trooper approached her, handed her a piece of paper with a hotel room number on it, and told her that Clinton wanted to meet with her. Jones went to the room, where she alleged Clinton made unwanted sexual advances toward her.

Paula Jones v. *Bill Clinton.* On 6 May 1994 Jones sued Clinton for sexual harassment. She contended that the purpose of the civil litigation was to redeem her reputation, not to acquire a financial settlement or politically harm Clinton. The suit was based on a federal law that prohibits gender discrimination, including sexual harassment, by government officials. Jones's attorneys, however, had a heavier burden than just proving harm. Because she did not file her complaint within six months of the alleged incident, Jones missed the deadline for filing a typical sexual harassment case, under which it would have been enough to prove that her career was harmed or that she was forced to tolerate a hostile work environment. Instead, she had to argue that she was deprived of her constitutional right to equal protection under federal employment law—a more difficult standard of proof. She had to show that Clinton was using his official position as governor of Arkansas to coerce her when he allegedly asked his state police guard to summon her to his hotel room and that Clinton intended to deprive her of her constitutional rights. Another legal problem for Jones was that she was forced to scale back her suit and remove any claims that she was "defamed." Some legal experts considered this a loss because even if she could not prove that Clinton made the unwanted advances, Jones conceivably could have proved that her reputation was damaged. Jones chose to abandon that claim because it would have opened the door for the President's lawyers to raise questions about her sexual past.

Delay Tactics. Facing reelection, President Clinton and his attorneys attempted to delay the proceedings, claiming presidential immunity. U.S. District Court Judge Susan Webber Wright ruled that Jones's lawyers were entitled to take depositions from witnesses who might have information concerning Clinton's behavior. In an effort to stall, Clinton's lawyers appealed to the U.S. Supreme Court. In May 1997 the Court ruled that Clinton could not postpone the civil suit until he was out of office. Several settlement offers were made, but no agreement could be established. During "discovery," Jones's attorneys sought evidence to show that Clinton had a history of this type of personal behavior, including affairs while he was governor and with White House employees.

Lewinsky. In January 1997 an anonymous phone call led Jones's attorneys to a former White House volunteer, Kathleen Elizabeth Willey, who claimed Clinton had sexually harassed her. In October 1997 they learned of Monica S. Lewinsky, who eventually alleged that she had a sexual relationship with the president while she was a White House intern. This charge led Jones's attorneys and independent counsel Kenneth W. Starr to Linda R. Tripp, who had taped several conversations with Lewinsky regarding her relationship with Clinton. Both Lewinsky and Tripp were subpoenaed to give depositions in the case. By January 1998 Starr's investigation into the failed Whitewater land venture had expanded to include Lewinsky. With the apparent revelations that Clinton had a relationship with Lewinsky, Jones's case appeared to be strengthened, at least in terms of public opinion.

Resolution. On 1 April 1998 Jones's case was dismissed by Judge Wright, who ruled that even if her claims were true, they did not constitute sexual assault or harassment according to the law. On 16 April Jones announced that she would appeal. In November 1998 Jones settled with Clinton for $850,000. Her legal fees were estimated to be more than $2 million. Ramifications of the Jones case were far-reaching, as the investigation into sexual harassment opened the door to Lewinsky, which would eventually lead to Clinton's impeachment trial.

Sources:
Ann H. Coulter, *High Crimes and Misdemeanors: The Case Against Bill Clinton* (Washington, D.C.: Regency, 1998).

Alan M. Dershowitz, *Sexual McCarthyism: Clinton, Starr, and the Emerging Constitutional Crisis* (New York: Basic Books, 1998).

WILLIAM REHNQUIST

1924-

CHIEF JUSTICE, U.S. SUPREME COURT

Background. William Hubbs Rehnquist was born on 1 October 1924 in Milwaukee, Wisconsin. He served in the Army Air Corps during World War II. After leaving the military he attended Stanford University where he received a B.A. in political science, and earned master's degrees in political science from both Stanford (1948) and Harvard (1950), before attending Stanford Law School. He graduated first in his class in 1952 with an LL.B. and was awarded the Order of the Coif. Rehnquist then served as a clerk to Supreme Court Justice Robert H. Jackson. During his tenure as a clerk, he drafted a memo for Justice Jackson that stated racial segregation in education was "right and should be affirmed." Following the clerkship, Rehnquist practiced law in Phoenix, Arizona. He then served as Assistant Attorney General for the Office of Legal Affairs in the Department of Justice. In 1971 President Richard M. Nixon nominated Rehnquist to be an associate justice on the Supreme Court, filling the seat vacated by Justice John Marshall Harlan. He served as an associate justice on the bench until 1986 when President Ronald Reagan nominated him to replace retiring Chief Justice Warren Earl Burger. Rehnquist is the sixteenth Chief Justice.

Conservative Court. During the 1990s the Supreme Court made noticeable moves to limit civil rights. Under the guidance of Rehnquist the Court restricted habeas corpus review, allowed greater scope for law enforcement agencies to conduct searches and administer drug tests without an individual's consent, and allowed states to admit evidence that under previous Courts was excluded. The Rehnquist Court has also narrowed personal privacy rights, such as abortion and homosexual rights. While not overturning the landmark 1973 ruling in *Roe* v. *Wade,* the Court increasingly allowed states to impose stricter regulations on abortion. The Court also refused to extend specific protections for homosexuals. Finally, it struck down affirmative action programs that used quotas. In general, the Court followed Rehnquist's position of mitigated judicial restraint. Ideologically, the Chief Justice consistently held that courts have the responsibility of extending the Constitution to cases that the framers might not have foreseen. Thus, the First Amendment protection of speech can be applied to modern communication technology, such as the Internet. On the other hand, Rehnquist rejected the more permissive reading of the constitution that permits courts to impose their own views in order to expand rights and liberties, such as with affirmative action.

Impeachment Trial. Following the constitutional requirements, on 7 January 1999 Chief Justice Rehnquist took an oath to do "impartial justice" during the impeachment trial of President Bill Clinton and then administered the oath to the senators who acted as jurors in the case. Rehnquist has the distinction of serving as the second Chief Justice in U.S. history to preside over an impeachment trial of a president and the first to conduct such proceedings before television cameras. Unlike at the Supreme Court where justices question attorneys and cast a vote, as presiding officer over the impeachment trial, Rehnquist's duties were more limited, primarily to rule on questions involving evidence. A simple majority of senators, however, could overrule Rehnquist's decisions. While the Senators were required to remain silent during the proceedings, they were allowed to submit questions to Rehnquist, who would relay them to the House prosecutors. Rehnquist did not have the authority to question the House managers. By almost all accounts, Rehnquist conducted the trial in a courteous and impartial manner. He was well acquainted with the impeachment process; his *Grand Inquests: The Impeachments of Justice Samuel Chase and President Andrew Johnson* (1992) detailed two impeachment trials that took place in the Senate, one of Associate Supreme Court Justice Samuel Chase in 1804, and the other of President Andrew Johnson, during the post-Civil War Reconstruction era (1868). *Grand Inquest* became so popular during the Clinton proceedings that the publisher reissued the book.

Source:
D. F. B. Tucker, *The Rehnquist Court and Civil Rights* (Aldershot, U.K. & Brookfield, N.H.: Dartmouth, 1995).

JANET RENO

1938-

ATTORNEY GENERAL OF THE UNITED STATES

Beginnings. Janet Reno was born 21 July 1938 in Miami, Florida, the daughter of Danish immigrants, both of whom were reporters. She graduated from Cornell University in 1960 and from Harvard Law School in 1963, one of only sixteen women in a class of more than five hundred. After graduation, Reno was denied a position with a major Miami law firm because she was a woman. After being in private practice for several years, she was named staff director of the Judiciary Committee of the Florida House of Representatives in 1971. In this position she helped to rewrite the state constitution and reform the court system. The following year she lost a bid for a seat in the state legislature. Reno then took a position in the state attorney's office, where she was assigned to the juvenile division. In 1978 she became the first woman to head a prosecutor's office in Florida.

Political Controversy. In 1993 Reno was nominated to the position of U.S. Attorney General by President Bill Clinton. When sworn in on 12 March 1993 she became the first woman ever to hold the position. Noted for her strong-willed, straightforward manner, Reno had a reputation for being willing to make difficult decisions. This characteristic was tested shortly after she took office. One of her first major decisions as Attorney General was to order the Federal Bureau of Investigation (FBI) to confront the Branch Davidians at their compound in Waco, Texas, by using tear gas in an attempt to draw out their leader David Koresh and his followers. When the compound erupted in flames, killing most of the Davidians, including many children, Reno publicly took full responsibility for the deaths. In 1999 an investigation into the Waco tragedy revealed that the FBI disregarded Reno's orders not to use pyrotechnic substances in the standoff, a possible cause of the deadly fire. After the beating of Rodney Glen King in Los Angeles in 1991, Reno ordered the federal civil-rights prosecution of the four Los Angeles Police Department (LAPD) officers responsible for the attack.

Battling Critics. Repeatedly Reno was called upon by members of Congress to step down from her post; she offered to resign after Waco, a gesture turned down by President Clinton. She often appointed independent counsels to investigate allegations of misconduct among members of the administration, angering some who thought she was not supporting Clinton strongly enough, although in several cases, such as when improper telephone solicitation of donors was alleged, she refused to do so. Despite being embattled on all sides, at the end of the decade Reno had served longer in her position than any former attorney general since the Eisenhower administration. During her tenure as attorney general she pushed for greater access to the justice system for ordinary citizens, prevention programs, stricter immigration laws, protection of the environment, and inclusion of minorities. Reno was active in developing new strategies to combat computer crime. In addition to the stressful nature of her job, Reno bravely battled Parkinson's disease, standing up to congressional and media critics even when trembling visibly, and refusing any suggestions that she step down because of her illness.

Source:

Paul Anderson, *Janet Reno: Doing the Right Thing* (New York: Wiley, 1994).

ORENTHAL JAMES "O. J." SIMPSON

1947-
FOOTBALL PLAYER, ACTOR, MURDER SUSPECT

Almost the American Dream. O. J. Simpson ran away with rushing and scoring records during his spectacular professional football career, but in 1994 he found himself publicly running from the law in what became the most bizarre murder investigation and trial of the decade. The June 1994 murder of Simpson's former wife, Nicole Brown Simpson, and her friend Ronald Goldman dominated media attention for nearly two years and turned the football hero and actor into a public pariah. Simpson's trial revealed deep divisions in the way Americans perceived the confluence of race, wealth, and justice, as lawyers, judges, detectives, friends, and family members became household names in a surreal, but very public, murder mystery.

Early Years. Orenthal James Simpson was born 9 July 1947 in San Francisco, California. He and his mother, Eunice, lived in the Petrero Hills public housing projects where there were few opportunities for African American children to succeed and many opportunities to get in trouble. Though Simpson spent his formative years at the neighborhood recreation center, his athletic potential was far from evident. Simpson wore braces for his bowed legs until he was two years old; although athletically talented, he was cut from the local Pop Warner Football team in 1961. Former baseball great Willie Howard Mays Jr. became Simpson's mentor after the teen spent a weekend in juvenile hall. Simpson's athletic star began to shine at Galileo High School. He married his eighteen-year-old high-school sweetheart, Marguerite, in June 1967. After playing football for City College of San Francisco, Simpson became the running back for the University of Southern California (USC). His breakthrough game came on 18 November 1967 against the number one ranked University of California at Los Angeles (UCLA), where a national championship, Rose Bowl bid, Pacific-8 title, and Heisman Trophy were all on the line. Although Simpson did not win the Heisman that year, he did in 1968. His 1,750-point victory over runner-up Leroy Keyes of Purdue University is still the largest margin ever in Heisman balloting. His first child, Aaren (who died in a boating accident in 1979), was born on the eve of Simpson winning the coveted trophy.

NFL Superstar. The Buffalo Bills of the American Football League (which would later merge with the National Football League and become the American Football Conference) made Simpson their first round draft pick in 1969. During his eleven-year pro football career, Simpson rushed for more than one thousand yards annually between 1972 and 1976, won four NFL rushing titles, and played in the 1969 AFL All-Star Football game and five NFL Pro Bowl games between 1972 and 1976. In 1973 Simpson became the first running back to rush for more than two thousand yards in a single season, reaching 2,003 yards thanks to a fourteen-game schedule. The Associated Press voted him the NFL's Most Valuable Player that year. Simpson recalled, "I was in the locker room all by myself before the game ended. I started walking around thinking how I could not wish to do anything more or be anyone else. I was part of the history of the game. If I did nothing else in my life, I had made my mark." The Bills traded Simpson to the San Francisco 49ers in 1978, where he retired the following year. During this time, he divorced Marguerite to be with Nicole Brown, an eighteen-year-old blond-haired, blue-eyed recent high school graduate who was working as a waitress in 1977.

Trial of the Century. After football, Simpson pursued a career in acting (most notably in *The Naked Gun* series of comedic farces), sports broadcasting with the National Broadcasting Company (NBC), and as spokesman for Hertz Rental Car. Simpson was inducted into the NFL Hall of Fame in 1985 and married Brown that same year. For a while, it appeared that he was living the American Dream. However, in 1989, Simpson pleaded no contest to beating his wife after police responded to a "911" call from Nicole. The couple divorced in 1992. Simpson later suggested jokingly that the relationship was not over, saying "This is to show you how smart I am. I am dating my ex-wife." On 13 June 1994 the bodies of Nicole Brown Simpson and Ronald Goldman, a waiter and aspiring model and actor, were discovered outside her home. Both had been repeatedly stabbed and slashed, but there were no witnesses to the assault. Simpson claimed he was en route to Chicago when the crimes were committed. Nonetheless, police charged Simpson with the deaths four days later, citing a trail of evidence linking him to the scene of the crime, including a bloody glove found outside the murder scene that allegedly matched one found at his estate.

The Chase. Simpson did not immediately surrender. Instead, he and lifelong friend Al Cowlings were spotted by police in a white Ford Bronco on a Los Angeles expressway. Simpson was thought to be carrying a gun and threatening to kill himself. The two men led police on a sixty-mile, low-speed pursuit through southern Los Angeles that ended at Simpson's Brentwood mansion. Simpson, clutching a family photo, then surrendered to police.

The Trials. He pleaded not guilty to the murders and the criminal trial began 23 January 1995, with Judge Lance A. Ito presiding. The jury acquitted Simpson in October 1995. The verdict shocked many white Americans who had become persuaded of Simpson's guilt, and elated many African Americans who were equally convinced he had been framed by a racially biased justice system. The Brown and Goldman families, not satisfied with the verdict and seeking some vindication, filed a wrongful death lawsuit against Simpson. The civil trial began 23 October 1996. Superior Court Judge Hiroshi Fujisaki banned still photographers and ordered lawyers and witnesses not to discuss the case with the media. Attorney Daniel M. Petrocelli portrayed Simpson as an egomaniac obsessed with his former wife and who routinely beat her, while defense attorney Robert Baker accused the plaintiffs of character assassination. Simpson again denied killing his wife and Goldman, but could not explain the physical evidence against him. As the civil trial unfolded, an Orange County, California, family court judge awarded Simpson custody of his two children over the objections of the Brown family. More troubles followed the beleaguered former star; the Internal Revenue Service (IRS) seized Simpson's Brentwood mansion and other property to collect the nearly $700,000 he owed in back taxes. On 4 February 1997 the jury found Simpson liable in the slayings and awarded $8.5 million in compensatory damages to the families of the deceased.

After the Trials. Simpson, who had remained quiet during most of the murder trials, attempted to rebuild his public image. Through carefully chosen interviews, a highly publicized but poorly selling video, and a book, *I Want to Tell You: My Response to Your Letters, Your Messages, Your Questions* (1995), written with the help of Lawrence Schiller, Simpson continued to insist on his innocence and his commitment to finding the "real" killers. He took part in a college debate at the Oxford Union and even made a spontaneous phone call to CNN's "Burden of Proof" television show, where he charged that his former wife's allegations of spousal abuse were written to get out of a prenuptial agreement. Only once, he argued, in 1989, did he ever fight with Nicole and leave her injured. He did not vary from the claim he made in his book, "I want to state unequivocally that I did not commit those horrible crimes." More tellingly, Simpson's attorney Alan M. Dershowitz described Simpson as "One of those rare defendants who could challenge the prosecution on a level playing field. Had he been just a regular indicted defendant denied the resources needed to challenge the prosecutors' forensic case, he might have well have gone to prison."

Sources:

Alan M. Dershowitz, *Reasonable Doubts: The Criminal Justice System and the O. J. Simpson Case* (New York: Simon & Schuster, 1996).

Elizabeth Hardwick, "Family Values," *New York Review of Books* (6 June 1996): 7–10.

O. J. Simpson, *I Want to Tell You: My Response to Your Letters, Your Messages, Your Questions* (Boston: Little, Brown, 1995).

Jeffrey Toobin, *The Run of His Life: The People Versus O. J. Simpson* (New York: Random House, 1996).

PEOPLE IN THE NEWS

In 1999 **Nathaniel Abraham,** thirteen, was tried and convicted as an adult for the 29 October 1997 murder of eighteen-year-old **Ronnie Greene Jr.** The case attracted national attention and sparked contentious debate over juvenile justice because he was only eleven years old when he was charged with first-degree murder under a controversial Michigan law that allows children under age seventeen to be tried as adults.

On 6 May 1994 **Deborah A. Batts** became the first openly homosexual woman to be appointed to the federal courts. A graduate of Radcliffe College and Harvard Law School, she served as an Assistant Attorney General in the U.S. Justice Department and an associate professor at Fordham University School of Law before her appointment to the U.S. District Court for the Southern District of New York.

In 1994 **Stephen Gerald Breyer** was appointed to the U.S. Supreme Court as an Associate Justice by President Bill Clinton. He was sworn in on 3 August 1994. His field of expertise is regulatory law.

In a racially motivated murder that drew national attention, **James Byrd Jr.** was beaten and decapitated in June 1998 as he was dragged behind a pickup truck in Jasper, Texas. Three men, **Shawn Allen Berry, John William King,** and **Lawrence Russell Brewer,** members of a hate group, the Texas Rebel Soldiers, a branch of the Confederate Knights of America, were convicted and sentenced to prison in 1999.

Marcia Clark, deputy district attorney in Los Angeles County, served as the lead prosecutor for the state of California in the 1995 O. J. Simpson trial.

On 22 July 1991 **Jeffrey L. Dahmer** was arrested for several murders in Milwaukee. The serial killer was found guilty, in 1992, of fifteen of the seventeen killings to which he had confessed. His insanity plea was rejected by the jury and he was sentenced to life in prison. On 28 November 1994 he was killed by a fellow prisoner.

Louis J. Freeh was sworn in as the director of the Federal Bureau of Investigation (FBI) on 1 September 1993. A native of New Jersey, Freeh served as an FBI special agent and was a federal judge in New York. During his tenure as director, Freeh has led investigations and prosecutions of crimes related to racketeering, drugs, organized crime, fraud, and terrorism.

Gil Garcetti, Los Angeles County district attorney who directed the prosecution of several high-profile cases that captured national attention, including the Rodney Glen King beating case (1991); O. J. Simpson murder trial (1995); and the trial of Lyle and Eric Menendez, two brothers convicted for killing their parents (1996).

On 3 August 1993 **Ruth Bader Ginsburg** was confirmed as an associate justice of the U.S. Supreme Court. Appointed by President **Bill Clinton,** she is the second woman, after **Sandra Day O'Connor,** to sit on the highest bench. Ginsburg was born in New York City and earned her J.D. at Columbia Law School (1959). She taught at Rutgers University Law School (1963–1972) and Columbia University Law School (1972–1980). She was a circuit judge on the U.S. Court of Appeals for Washington, D.C. (1980–1993). She led the Women's Rights Project while at Columbia. In 1996 she wrote the majority opinion allowing the admission of women to the Virginia Military Institute (VMI), a formerly all-male military school.

In December 1994 **Webster L. Hubbell,** former U.S. Associate Attorney General and former law partner of **Hillary Rodham Clinton,** was convicted on two counts of defrauding the federal government through tax evasion and mail fraud. He was sentenced to eighteen months in prison. His license to practice law was revoked in April 1995.

On 29 July 1994 seven-year-old **Megan Kanka** of Hamilton Township, N.J., was murdered by a convicted sex offender, **Jesse Timmendequas.** Through the lobbying of her parents, **Richard** and **Maureen Kanka,** more than forty states and the federal government passed "Megan's Laws," which require that communities be notified when convicted sex offenders are released from prison.

Gregory Kingsley (Shawn Russ), an eleven-year-old Florida boy, drew national attention when he sued his biological parents for "divorce" on the grounds that they were abusive and neglectful. Kingsley had been in and out of foster care for years. When his mother sought to regain custody from the court-appointed foster parents, **George** and **Lizebeth Russ**, Kingsley took his biological parents to court. The boy's natural father voluntarily relinquished his parental rights before trial. In September 1992 a Florida judge terminated the parental rights of the natural mother and approved his adoption by his foster parents. The ruling was hailed by many children's-rights advocates.

Marc Klass became an advocate for kidnapped children and their parents after the abduction and murder of his daughter **Polly Hannah Klass** in October 1993. Klass organized the KlassKids Foundation, which works with individuals, communities, and governments to protect children and locate missing children.

Joel I. Klein, head of the Antitrust Division of the U.S. Department of Justice, was the lead attorney for the Justice Department in *United States of America* v. *Microsoft Corporation*. In November 1999 the government won an important initial phase in its case against the software giant when a federal judge found that Microsoft was a monopoly that had engaged in illegal practices.

In May 1999 **Nancy Mace** became the first female graduate of the formerly all-male military school, The Citadel. Mace graduated with a 3.8 GPA and a degree in business administration. Her father, retired Brigadier General **J. Emory Mace,** was a 1963 Citadel graduate.

In 1991 **Nancie G. Marzulla** founded the Defenders of Property Rights, an interest group that lobbies and litigates on behalf of the property rights of individuals and businesses. A lawyer, she testified at congressional property-rights protection and regulatory takings compensation hearings during the 1990s.

In 1994 **Thomas E. Pope,** a state prosecutor in South Carolina, gained national attention when he prosecuted **Susan V. Smith**, the Union County woman who admitted to drowning her two children, **Alex** and **Michael,** after she alleged, at first, that her children had been kidnapped.

Millionaire businessman **John Ramsey** and his wife **Patricia** of Boulder, Colorado, were the chief suspects in the 26 December 1996 death of their six-year-old daughter, **JonBenet Ramsey**. Although the Ramseys maintained their innocence, Boulder investigators continued to question the parents in connection with the murder, but at the end of the decade the case had still not been solved.

In 1994 **Barry Scheck**, a DNA expert, served as one of **O. J. Simpson's** lawyers. He also defended **Louise Woodward,** the au pair accused of shaking eight-month-old **Matthew Eappen** to death on 4 February 1997. Scheck

is a law professor at Benjamin N. Cardozo School of Law, Yeshiva University in New York City.

Robert Shapiro, a defense attorney who specializes in representing high-profile clients, defended **O. J. Simpson** (1995) and **Christian Brando** (son of actor **Marlon Brando**) on a murder charge (1991). Other celebrity clients included **Johnny Carson, John DeLorean,** and baseball player **Darryl Strawberry.**

Gerry Spence, a Wyoming defense attorney, represented white-separatist **Randy Weaver** (1993). He also defended several men accused of beating **Reginald Denny** during the 1991 riots that occurred in Los Angeles after the verdict against the police officers who beat **Rodney Glen King** was announced. During the 1990s Spence frequently served as a legal commentator on various television news shows.

A lawyer and former U.S. Appeals Court judge, **Kenneth W. Starr** replaced New York attorney **Robert B. Fiske Jr.** as independent counsel investigating the Whitewater land deal in August 1994. His investigation led to the uncovering of a White House sex scandal involving intern **Monica S. Lewinsky** and **Bill Clinton**. In September 1998 Starr released a report to Congress detailing a case for impeachment against Clinton. He was born in Texas and served as a law clerk to Chief Justice **Warren E. Burger** (1975–1977) and as Solicitor General of the United States (1989–1993).

In June 1999 **Jean H. Toal** was appointed the first woman Chief Justice of the South Carolina Supreme Court. The South Carolina legislature also unanimously elected **Kaye Hearn** as the first woman to be Chief Judge of the state Appeals Court.

On 3 February 1998 **Karla Faye Tucker-Brown** became the first woman executed during the 1990s. She was convicted of two murders and was executed in Texas. In Florida, on 30 March 1998, **Judias V. Buenoano** became the second female executed in the decade.

Florida attorney **Norwood Wilmer** represented individuals filing suits against tobacco companies. His 1996 victory over Brown & Williamson Tobacco Corporation, the first time a major tobacco company had been found liable for smoking related illnesses, attracted national attention.

In 1997 **Louise Woodward**, a teenage British au pair living in the United States, was charged with shaking to death **Matthew Eappen**, a baby in her charge, on 4 February. Woodward had been hired by Massachusetts couple **Deborah** and **Sunil Eappen** in 1996 to care for their children. Woodward was initially convicted of first degree murder, but in a controversial decision, the judge reduced the sentence to involuntary manslaughter. She was allowed to returned to England.

DEATHS

Harry Andrew Blackmun, 90, associate justice of the U.S. Supreme Court (1970–1994) who wrote the majority opinion in *Roe* v. *Wade* (1973), 4 March 1999.

Nils Andreas Boe, 78, judge, U.S Court of International Trade and former governor of South Dakota, 30 July 1992.

William Joseph Brennan Jr., 91, associate justice of the U.S. Supreme Court (1956–1990), 24 July 1997.

Vincent L. Broderick, 74, judge, U.S. District Court of the Southern District of New York, 3 March 1995.

Vincent J. Browne, 80, civil-rights scholar at Howard University, 27 August 1997.

Warren Earl Burger, 88, chief justice of the U.S. Supreme Court (1969–1986) who wrote the decision in *United States* v. *Richard Nixon* (1974) establishing that claims of executive privilege do not shield presidents from judicial subpoenas, leading to the release of Nixon's tapes and ultimately to his resignation from the presidency, 25 June 1995.

Thomas Emmet Claire, judge, U.S. Court of Appeals for the Second Circuit, 24 September 1997.

Franklin T. Dupree, judge, U.S. District Court of the Eastern District of North Carolina, 17 December 1995.

Erika S. Fairchild, criminal-justice scholar at North Carolina State University, 25 November 1992.

Vincent W. Foster Jr., 48, lawyer, Deputy White House counsel to President Bill Clinton and former law partner of Hillary Rodham Clinton, 20 July 1993.

Ralph M. Freeman, 87, judge, U.S. District Court of the Eastern District of Michigan, 29 March 1990.

Arthur Joseph Goldberg, 81, associate justice of the U.S. Supreme Court (1962–1965), 19 January 1990.

Charles M. Hardin, 88, constitutional scholar at the University of California, Davis, 28 June 1997.

John R. Hargrove, judge, U.S. District Court of the State of Maryland, 1 April 1997.

Walter Edward Hoffman, 89, judge, U.S. District Court of the Eastern District of Virginia, 21 November 1996.

Frederick Landis, senior judge, U.S. Court of International Trade, 1 March 1990.

Lawrence T. Lydick, 79, judge, U.S. District Court of the Central District of California, 17 December 1995.

J. Daniel Mahoney, 65, judge, U.S. Court of Appeals for the Second Circuit, 23 October 1996.

Thurgood Marshall, 82, associate justice of the U.S. Supreme Court (1967–1991) who in 1954, as chief counsel for the National Association for the Advancement of Colored People (NAACP), argued *Brown* v. *Board of Education* before the Supreme Court, 24 January 1993.

William Hughes Mulligan, 78, judge, U.S. Court of Appeals for the Second Circuit, 13 May 1996.

Helen Wilson Nies, 71, judge, U.S. Court of Appeals for the Federal Circuit, 7 August 1996.

James E. Noland, 72, judge, U.S. District Court of the Southern District of Indiana, Indianapolis Division, 12 August 1992.

James Earl Ray, 70, assassin of Martin Luther King Jr. (4 April 1968), 23 April 1998.

Donald Russell, judge, U.S. Court of Appeals for the Fourth Circuit, 22 February 1998.

John Lewis Smith, judge, U.S. District Court of the District of Columbia, 4 September 1992.

Roszel C. Thomsen, judge, U.S. District Court of the State of Maryland, 11 March 1992.

William H. Timbers, judge, U.S. Court of Appeals for the Second Circuit, 26 November 1994.

PUBLICATIONS

Robert H. Bork, *Slouching Towards Gomorrah: Modern Liberalism and American Decline* (New York: Regan Books, 1996).

Ann H. Coulter, *High Crimes and Misdemeanors: The Case Against Bill Clinton* (Washington, D.C.: Regnery, 1998).

Alan M. Dershowitz, *Sexual McCarthyism: Clinton, Starr, and the Emerging Constitutional Crisis* (New York: Basic Books, 1998).

Steven J. Eagle, *Regulatory Takings* (Charlottesville, Va.: Michie, 1996).

Barry C. Feld, *Bad Kids: Race and the Transformation of the Juvenile Court* (New York: Oxford University Press, 1999).

Stanley H. Friedelbaum, *The Rehnquist Court: In Pursuit of Judicial Conservatism* (Westport, Conn.: Greenwood Press, 1994).

Leslie Friedman Goldstein, ed., *Feminist Jurisprudence: The Difference Debate* (Lanham, Md.: Rowman & Littlefield, 1992).

Anita Hill, *Speaking Truth to Power* (New York: Doubleday, 1997).

Peter Irons, *Brennan vs. Rehnquist: The Battle for the Constitution* (New York: Knopf, 1994).

Barbara Klier, Nancy R. Jacobs, and Jacquelyn Quiram, *Gun Control: Restricting Rights or Protecting People?* (Wylie, Tex.: Information Plus, 1999).

John R. Lott Jr., *More Guns, Less Crime: Understanding Crime and Gun Control Laws* (Chicago: University of Chicago Press, 1998).

G. Steven Neeley, *The Constitutional Right to Suicide: A Legal and Philosophical Examination* (New York: Peter Lang, 1994).

Kathleen A. O'Shea, *Women and the Death Penalty in the United States, 1900–1998* (Westport, Conn.: Praeger, 1999).

Richard A. Posner, *An Affair of State: The Investigation, Impeachment, and Trial of President Clinton* (Cambridge, Mass.: Harvard University Press, 1999).

William H. Rehnquist, *Grand Inquests: The Historic Impeachments of Justice Samuel Chase and President Andrew Johnson* (New York: Morrow, 1992).

David A. J. Richards, *Women, Gays, and the Constitution: The Grounds for Feminism and Gay Rights in Culture and Law* (Chicago: University of Chicago Press, 1998).

David G. Savage, *Turning Right: The Making of the Rehnquist Supreme Court* (New York: Wiley, 1992).

James F. Simon, *The Center Holds: The Power Struggle Inside the Rehnquist Court* (New York: Simon & Schuster, 1995).

Christopher E. Smith, *The Rehnquist Court and Criminal Punishment* (New York: Garland, 1997).

Patricia Smith, *Feminist Jurisprudence* (New York: Oxford University Press, 1993).

Rickie Solinger, ed., *Abortion Wars: A Half Century of Struggle, 1950–2000* (Berkeley: University of California Press, 1998).

Gerry Spence, *Give Me Liberty!: Freeing Ourselves in the Twenty-first Century* (New York: St. Martin's Press, 1998).

Kenneth Starr, *The Starr Report: The Findings of Independent Counsel Kenneth W. Starr on President Clinton and the White House Scandals* (New York: Public Affairs, 1998).

D. F. B. Tucker, *The Rehnquist Court and Civil Rights* (Aldershot, U.K. & Brookfield, N.H.: Dartmouth, 1995).

Franklin E. Zimring, *American Youth Violence* (New York: Oxford University Press, 1998).

ABA Journal, periodical

American Lawyer, periodical

National Law Journal, periodical

The Federal Lawyer, periodical

CHAPTER EIGHT

LIFESTYLES AND SOCIAL TRENDS

by MARK G. MALVASI and MEG GREENE

CONTENTS

Sidebars and tables are listed in italics.

1990

1 Jan.	Maryland becomes the first state to ban the sale of cheap handguns known as Saturday Night Specials.
22 Mar.	The first edition of Microsoft Windows 3.0 is shipped to consumers.
25 Mar.	An arson fire sweeps through an overcrowded Bronx social club killing eighty-seven persons, making it the deadliest blaze in New York City since the Triangle Shirtwaist Fire of 1911.
28 Mar.	President George Bush posthumously presents the Congressional Gold Medal to Jesse Owens, famous for having angered Adolf Hitler at the 1936 Berlin Olympics by winning four gold medals for his humanitarian contributions.
April	The minimum wage is raised to $3.80 an hour.
6 June	Greyhound Bus Lines files for bankruptcy.
1 Nov.	Under pressure from environmental groups, McDonald's agrees to replace styrofoam containers with paper wrappers.

1991

2 Feb.	The price of a first-class postage stamp is raised from 25¢ to 29¢ cents.
14 Feb.	Homosexual and unmarried heterosexual couples begin registering under a new law in San Francisco to be recognized as "domestic partners."
3 Mar.	Rodney Glen King is severely beaten by four Los Angeles police officers in a scene captured on home video.
16 Mar.	Members of the Irish Gay and Lesbian Organization march in the annual New York City St. Patrick's Day Parade.
April	The minimum wage is raised to $4.25 an hour.
22 April	Intel releases the 486SX computer chip.
20 May	The Red Cross announces stricter procedures for screening blood for the AIDS virus.
22 June	The remains of President Zachary Taylor are exhumed in Louisville, Kentucky, to determine whether Taylor died of arsenic poisoning; tests prove that arsenic was not present.
22 July	Milwaukee police arrest Jeffrey L. Dahmer, a suspect in the deaths of at least seventeen young men.
5–7 Sept.	Naval and Marine aviators attending the thirty-fifth annual Tailhook convention (named after an aircraft-carrier landing device) assault dozens of women, including fourteen fellow officers, in a drunken ritual called "the gauntlet."
Oct.	The first Planet Hollywood restaurant opens.
6 Nov.	The Food and Drug Administration (FDA) announces sweeping changes in food labeling practices, which will require a more detailed listing of contents.
26 Nov.	Condoms are handed out to thousands of New York City high-school students.

1992

7 Jan. AT&T releases a videotelephone.

16 Feb. Former Goodyear blimps are now painted yellow and blue.

24 Feb. General Motors Corporation announces a record $4.5 billion loss in 1991 and that it will close twenty-one plants; 74,000 workers will lose their jobs over the next four years.

6 Mar. Computer users braced themselves for the computer virus "Michelangelo"; only scattered cases of missing files are reported.

13 Mar. The U.S. House of Representatives votes unanimously to identify publicly the 355 former and current members who had overdrawn their accounts at the House bank.

15 Mar. Investigators report that pieces of an old airplane discovered on a remote Pacific island may be linked to the disappearance of Amelia Earhart, who vanished while on a round-the-world flight in 1937.

6 Apr. Microsoft releases Windows 3.1.

13 Apr. Crystal Pepsi, a clear cola soft drink, begins test marketing.

- The century-old tunnel system in Chicago, and adjacent basements, fill with more than 250 million gallons of water from the Chicago River, causing the downtown electrical system to fail.

5 June The unemployment rate jumps to 7.5 percent—the highest level in eight years.

9 June William Pinkney becomes the first African American to sail solo around the world.

23 June Pilot Jessica Hearns is reinstated by Continental Airlines after having a sex-change operation.

30 June The first pay bathroom opens in New York City at a cost of 25¢.

11 Aug. The Mall of America, the biggest shopping complex built in the United States, opens in Bloomington, Minnesota.

22 Sept. A structure thought to have been built by prehistoric Native Americans more than twelve thousand years in the past is discovered in Sharon County, Ohio.

1 Oct. The United States goes "metric" with the official adoption of the International Unit of Measure.

3 Oct. Microsoft founder William Henry "Bill" Gates III heads the list in *Forbes* of "400 Richest Americans" with an estimated net worth of $6.3 billion.

17 Oct. A Japanese exchange student, Yoshihiro Hattori, sixteen, is shot and killed by a Center, Louisiana, man after Hattori mistakenly knocked on the shooter's door while looking for a Halloween party.

8 Nov. To commemorate the tenth anniversary of the Vietnam Memorial, volunteers begin reading aloud the 58,183 names that are inscribed on the monument.

23 Nov. Ten thousand cellular phones have been sold in the United States.

29 Dec. David and Sharon Schoo of St. Charles, Illinois, are arrested at O'Hare Airport in Chicago upon their return from a trip during which they had left their young daughters at home alone.

1993

18 Jan.	The Martin Luther King Jr. national holiday is observed for the first time in all fifty states.
25 Jan.	Sears and Roebuck announces it will close its pioneering catalogue-sales department after ninety-seven years of operation.
30 Jan.	The city of Los Angeles officially opens the "Red Line," its first modern subway.
2 Feb.	Smoking is officially prohibited at the White House.
19 Feb.	A Massachusetts superior court rules that a gay group can march in the annual St. Patrick's Day Parade in South Boston.
March	Intel Pentium computer chip makes its debut.
12–14 Mar.	The "storm of the century," with record snowfalls and high winds, paralyzes the eastern seaboard, killing approximately 270 people.
19 Apr.	After a fifty-one-day stalemate, eighty members of the Branch Davidian cult, including at least seventeen children, die in a fire as the result of a botched assault by federal agents on their compound in Waco, Texas.
22 Apr.	The United States Holocaust Memorial Museum in Washington, D.C., is dedicated.
25 Apr.	Gay-rights activists and supporters march on Washington demanding equal rights and freedom from discrimination.
28 Apr.	The first "Take Our Daughters to Work Day," organized by the Ms. Foundation to boost young girls' self-esteem by visiting their parents' workplaces, takes place.
24 May	Microsoft launches Windows NT operating system.
14 July	In a move toward a more healthy product, Kentucky Fried Chicken (KFC) removes the word *fried* from its logo and unveils "Rotisserie Gold Roasted Chicken."
29 July	Ground is broken for the Vietnam Women's Memorial in Washington, D.C.
19 Aug.	Mattel Toys and Fisher-Price Toys merge.
11 Nov.	The Walt Disney Company announces plans to build a U.S. history theme park in northern Virginia; however, in the face of local opposition, the company later backs down.

1994

5 Feb.	White separatist Byron De La Beckwith is convicted of the 1963 murder of civil-rights leader Medgar Evers in Jackson, Mississippi, and is sentenced to life in prison.
8 Apr.	Smoking is banned at the Pentagon and all U.S. military bases.
26 June	Thousands of homosexuals gather in New York City for the twenty-fifth anniversary of the Stonewall Inn Riot, the birthplace of the gay-rights movement.
22 July	A federal judge orders the all-male military school The Citadel, a state-financed college in South Carolina, to admit women.
6 Aug.	In Wedowee, Alabama, an arson fire destroys the Randolph County High School, which had been the focus in recent weeks of tensions over the principal's stand against interracial dating.

3 Sept. In Alaska, a local Native American tribal council exiled two teenage Tlingit boys, who beat and robbed a pizza-delivery man, to an uninhabited offshore island for the period of one year.

12 Sept. The Netscape Navigator web browser is introduced.

11 Oct. The Colorado Supreme Court strikes down an anti-gay-rights measure as unconstitutional.

16 Nov. In a letter published in the press, former president Ronald Reagan discloses he has Alzheimer's disease.

6 Dec. Orange County, California, one of the wealthiest municipalities in the country, becomes the largest municipality to file for bankruptcy protection; because of risky and poor investments the county was $2 billion in the red.

1995

15 Feb. In a study done at Yale University, researchers conclude that men primarily use the left side of their brains and women use both the left and right sides equally.

18 Feb. The National Association for the Advancement of Colored People (NAACP) ousts Dr. William F. Gibson as president; Myrlie Evers-Williams, widow of Medgar Evers, is elected to the office.

21 Feb. A fifty-year-old Chicago stockbroker breaks the distance record for balloon travel with his 5,885-mile flight from South Korea to Canada, despite the heaters in the balloon breaking down.

13 Apr. Coretta Scott King, widow of slain civil-rights leader Martin Luther King Jr., loses a court battle in which she tried to regain possession of her husband's papers from Boston University.

19 Apr. A bomb explodes in front of the Alfred P. Murrah Federal Building in Oklahoma City, killing 168 people.

17 July The remains of Jesse James are exhumed in Kearney, Missouri, to determine the exact cause of the famed outlaw's death.

10 Aug. In Los Angeles, Hollywood madam Heidi Fleiss is found guilty of tax evasion and money laundering.

15 Aug. In an out-of-court settlement, the U.S. government pays $3.1 million to the family of white separatist Randall C. Weaver, whose wife and son were killed by government agents in 1992.

2 Nov. Paula Barbieri, model and fiancée of O. J. Simpson, announces that their relationship has ended.

7 Dec. *The New York Times* refuses to run an ad placed by a right-wing Japanese group wanting to rewrite Japan's war record.

12 Dec. Two black civilians are murdered by two white soldiers in North Carolina.

18 Dec. The stock market tumbles 101.52 points, making it the largest percentage decline in more than two years.

1996

1 Feb.	Congress votes to rewrite the sixty-one-year-old Communications Act, opening the way for television, phone, and computer companies to offer products in each other's fields.
16 Feb.	A U.S. District Judge bans government from enforcing a new law that would punish anyone making "indecent" material available to minors through computers.
1 Mar.	Pacific Bell introduces the toll-free 888 area code.
14 Mar.	AT&T introduces Internet access service.
25 Mar.	A new $100 bill, redesigned to inhibit counterfeiting, goes into circulation.
19 Apr.	On the first anniversary of the Oklahoma City bombing, hundreds of mourners observe 168 seconds of silence at the site where the federal building once stood.
23 Apr.	Sotheby's begins a four-day auction of possessions belonging to Jacqueline Kennedy Onassis; the auction will bring in $34.5 million.
2 May	The U.S. Senate passes an immigration bill making it more difficult for aliens to get jobs and access to social services.
5 May	The Federal Bureau of Investigation (FBI) releases figures showing that the number of serious crimes reported in the United States has dropped for the fourth straight year.
11 May	ValuJet Flight 592 crashes into the Florida Everglades; all 104 passengers and 5 crew members perish.
20 May	The U.S. Supreme Court strikes down a Colorado law that bans legislation protecting homosexuals from discrimination.
4 July	HotMail, a new free Internet e-mail service, begins operation.
12 July	The U.S. House of Representatives votes overwhelmingly to define marriage in federal laws as the legal union of men and women only, regardless of what individual states recognize.
17 July	TWA Flight 800 crashes into the Atlantic shortly after takeoff; all 230 persons on board are killed.
13 Aug.	Microsoft releases Internet Explorer 3.0 to compete with Netscape Navigator.
19 Sept.	IBM announces it will extend health benefits to partners of homosexual and lesbian employees.
21 Sept.	John F. Kennedy Jr. marries Carolyn Bessette in a private ceremony on Cumberland Island, Georgia.
29 Sept.	The Nintendo 64 video game debuts in the United States.
1 Oct.	The minimum wage is raised to $4.75 an hour.
12 Oct.	Thousands of Hispanic Americans march in Washington, D.C., to show support for a simplified citizenship process and a higher minimum wage.
27 Nov.	A federal judge blocks enforcement of California initiative that would dismantle state affirmative-action programs.
3 Dec.	A judge in Hawaii rules that the state must issue marriage licenses to same-sex couples.

1997

- The Mattel Company, manufacturer of the Barbie doll, announces that there are more Barbie dolls in existence (250 million) than the entire population of the United States.

- In a *Time*/CNN poll, 22 percent of Americans believe that aliens from outer space have been in contact with humans; another 13 percent believe that aliens have abducted human beings in order to observe them or perform experiments on them.

9 Aug. The city of Memphis declares 9–17 August "Elvis Presley Week" in honor of the twentieth anniversary of the singer-entertainer's death.

4 Nov. Voters in Houston, Texas, approve the retention of affirmative-action programs in the city.

7 Nov. The Department of Labor reports the jobless rate at 4.7 percent, the lowest since 1973.

10 Nov. MCI Communications, the second-largest long-distance phone company, agrees to merge with Worldcom for $43 billion, making the deal the largest merger in U.S. business history.

3 Dec. President Bill Clinton holds a "town meeting" in Akron, Ohio, to open a "national conversation" about race.

5 Dec. The U.S. government reports that 404,000 new jobs were created, that unemployment is now at 4.6 percent, and that hourly earnings have climbed 7 cents in the last year.

15 Dec. A special investigative panel urges the Pentagon to "roll back" the integration of men and women in basic- and advanced-training programs.

1998

- Betty Crocker, the homemaker icon created by General Mills, starts a website.

1 Jan. The Census Bureau estimates that the current population of the United States is 268,921,733 persons.

14 Jan. The first woman to enroll at the Virginia Military Institute (VMI) withdraws.

22 Jan. The states of New York and New Jersey argue before the Supreme Court to determine which state owns Ellis Island, the national historic gateway for more than sixteen million immigrants. The court will split ownership, with New Jersey being given approximately twenty-two acres, while New York retains five acres.

23 Jan. Netscape begins giving its browsers away free on the Internet.

6 Feb. Washington National Airport is renamed the Ronald Reagan National Airport.

10 Feb. A college dropout who had e-mailed threats to Asian students is convicted of committing the first "hate crimes in cyberspace."

6 Apr. The Dow Jones Industrial average hits a record 9,000 in single day's trading.

21 Aug. A former Ku Klux Klan wizard, Sam H. Bower, is convicted for the 1966 firebombing death of Vernon Dahmer Sr., who had registered blacks to vote at his store outside Hattiesburg, Mississippi.

1999

- Summer along the eastern United States brings serious rainfall shortages, with many states experiencing the worst drought on record.

10 Jan. The cost of a postage stamp is raised from 32 to 33 cents.

9 Feb. In an article published in his *National Liberty Journal,* the Reverend Jerry Falwell warns parents that the purple, purse-toting "Tinky-Winky" of the popular Public Broadcasting Service (PBS) children's program "Teletubbies" is a role model for homosexuality.

11 Feb. A federal jury in Brooklyn finds that gun manufacturers, in the first case of its kind, are liable for shootings done by illegally obtained handguns.

15 Mar. The Dow Jones index hits the 10,000 mark at 9:50 A.M.

11 Apr. A report from *The New York Times* states that tax returns from Americans earning more than $100,000 a year and from the larger corporations are escaping the scrutiny of the Internal Revenue Service (IRS).

3 May The Dow Jones index sets a record closing at 11,014.69 points.

8 July President Clinton ends a four-day tour of "poverty in America," which receives minimal coverage from the press.

13 July For the first time in history, a federal grand jury in Florida brings criminal charges for an airline accident against an airline-maintenance company in the 1996 ValueJet crash.

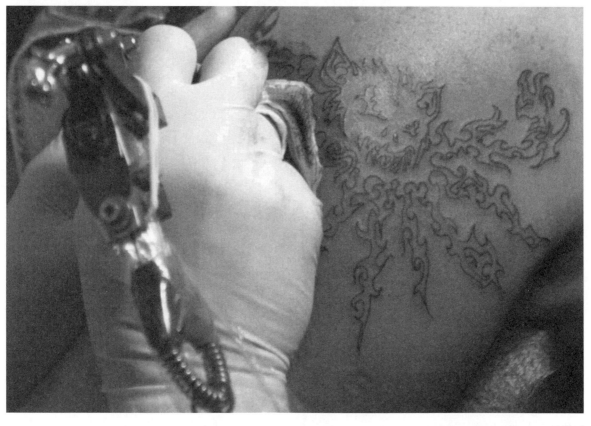

Tattoo artist working on a design at the Heart of America Tattoo Festival in Burlington, Iowa, 5 September 1999 (AP/Wide World Photos)

OVERVIEW

Extremes and Contradictions. The 1990s was a decade of extremes and contradictions. Americans built bigger and more-elaborate homes and drove more-expensive automobiles, but then worked longer hours than before to pay for them. The stock market and executive salaries soared, while the wages of many workers stagnated; many employees lost their jobs as the result of layoffs, mergers, and corporate downsizing. Politicians and policymakers, advertisers and marketers, all focused on children. Children, however, struggled to deal with the pressures of the adult world to which they were increasingly exposed; many were forced to adjust to new stepfamilies. Meanwhile, a disturbing number of adolescent and teenage boys went on deadly shooting rampages that left dozens dead or wounded, and a troubled nation asking "why?" Guns nevertheless found their way into more households during the 1990s even as Americans decried the rise in gun violence. Americans also lamented the widespread decline of civility and respect at the precise moment that the Internet enabled them to connect and communicate with one another more quickly and easily than ever before. Feminists quarreled among themselves. Men endured a crisis of masculinity. Gays and lesbians came closer to entering the American mainstream, yet faced violent assaults and an antigay backlash. Patterns of intermarriage revealed a marked demographic trend toward a multiethnic and multiracial future for the United States, a prospect that brought varied responses, including a challenge to preferential affirmative-action programs that benefited one group at the expense of others. Americans spent more, borrowed more, and went more deeply into debt. They drank more coffee and smoked more cigars. They pampered their pets and turned gambling into a national pastime. In general, they engaged in a round of consumption and material indulgence that had experts, such as those at The Trends Research Institute in Rhinebeck, New York, characterizing the decade as "The Narcissistic '90s." At the same time, many Americans devoted themselves to eradicating a variety of social problems and to seeking spiritual fulfillment. These activities, though, often led them back to considerations of work, money, and material success.

Home. The 1990s established new trends in home design and in the character of residential communities. Homes, at least for affluent Americans, became larger and contained a greater variety of expensive amenities such as media rooms, home theaters, home offices, and music rooms. There was a renewed emphasis on interior design, with experts such as Martha Stewart helping to establish the canons of good taste. Home security was an increasingly important concern. As a consequence, contractors began offering home-security systems as standard features on all the homes they built. To further enhance their sense of security, Americans also "forted up." That is, they bought homes in gated communities to escape the crime and violence that plagued many urban and suburban neighborhoods.

Family. The trend toward the formation of stepfamilies continued in the 1990s. As more divorced parents remarried, the number of stepfamilies increased; by 1999 there were 5.5 million such families in the United States. Estimates suggest that if the current trend continues, stepfamilies will outnumber nuclear families by the year 2007. These changes in the composition of the American family brought about several debates in family law about the rights and responsibilities of stepparents. In this regard, the efforts of the Step Family Association of America were instrumental in getting public-school officials and others to acknowledge the increasingly important role of stepparents. Cultural attitudes toward, and definitions of, the family also began to change. More marriage ceremonies included the children of previous unions as a way of acknowledging the past and, at the same time, of celebrating the new family. In addition, greeting-card companies such as Hallmark began issuing a series of cards designed specifically for stepparents and stepchildren.

Children. Children became the focus of considerable attention during the 1990s. Politicians and public-policy experts debated the rights of children and the proper role of the federal government in protecting them from poverty and abuse. Most Americans favored allocating additional tax dollars to programs designed to benefit children. During the decade, however, the number of children mired in poverty continued to grow. Schools began taking a more active role in helping children overcome many problems and disadvantages. Throughout the country educators came to advocate "full-service schools" that assumed the role of surrogate parents, taking responsibility for the physical and emotional welfare of children from birth, and in some cases before birth, to the age of twelve. Not surprisingly, children also came to the attention of advertisers and marketers, since youngsters spent approximately $14 billion a year on a variety of products. Experts in child psychology and child development, however, worried whether this affluence and buying power, coupled with the hectic pace at which many children lived, did not give them a false sense of sophistication, security, and power that ill fitted them for adulthood. By contrast, these experts were also concerned that children were being forced to assume adult responsibilities before they were emotionally prepared to do so.

Pets. Although the number of Americans owning pets declined during the 1990s, pet ownership was on the rise because of a growing number of multipet households. For those Americans who owned pets, the animals often came to be regarded as members of the family for whom their owners spared no expense. Americans spent more money on their pets than ever before, and retailers such as Wal-Mart were not slow to take advantage of this trend. With the rising costs of animal health care, pet Health Maintenance Organizations (HMOs) also became an increasingly popular and necessary expenditure. During the decade, legislation regulating the sale of pets and addressing the problem of animal overpopulation passed in more than twenty states and the District of Columbia, as similar legislation was pending at the federal level.

Work. During the 1990s Americans became the workaholics of the world, putting in far more hours on the job than Western Europeans or even the Japanese. Although Americans worked longer hours, as corporate profits and the stock market soared throughout the second half of the decade, the average American worker, including the white-collar middle manager and his or her family, did not consistently benefit from the boom. The gap between rich and poor grew steadily while the middle- and working-classes often endured economic stagnation. Those Americans who could, abandoned their low-paying jobs in search of better salaries and benefits packages. Overcoming company loyalty was the one sure way to get ahead in the competitive job market, at least in the short term. The decline in industrial jobs played a central role in the painful economic upheavals of the 1990s for many American workers. Unlike the previous transformation of the economy from agricultural to industrial, the new labor positions required education, sophisticated skills, and command of cutting-edge technology that average American workers lacked. Those unable to acquire the requisite training were condemned to declining fortunes. As a consequence, legions of American workers, left behind by the so-called knowledge revolution, never recovered what they lost in jobs and income during the recession of 1990–1991.

The Internet Revolution. The future is now. Once a fantasy, then a novelty, the Internet revolutionized how Americans work, shop, invest, transact business, gather information on an untold variety of subjects, search for a new home, go to school, listen to music, consult a physician, think, communicate, play, love, and live. Between 1990 and 1997 the number of households that owned computers increased from 15 percent to 35 percent, and the amount spent by the average household on computers and associated hardware more than tripled. Households with the highest levels of education had the highest levels of computer ownership. In 1997, 66 percent of households whose reference person had attended graduate school owned a computer as compared to only 12 percent of households headed by a person who did not finish high school. Among ethnic groups, Asians had the highest levels of computer ownership at 49 percent, followed by whites at 36 percent, and blacks at 18 percent. At the end of 1999, 196 million persons around the world regularly "surfed the Net," eighty million of them in the United States. Estimates suggest that by the year 2003 that number will increase to more than five hundred million. Advocates contended that the Internet enhanced both a sense of independence and of community by fostering free, open, and democratic communication. Many also saw the Internet as empowering. "Power is taken from the editors and distributors in huge over-cautious corporations," wrote Stewart Brand, "and handed to a no-longer-passive, radical everyone. Individuals on the Net initiate and control content to suit themselves and those they can interest." The Internet has permanently altered how the world communicates. Yet, persistent concerns remained about privacy, free speech, security, taxation, and regulation.

New Age Spirituality. Americans were not only concerned with cyberspace in the 1990s, but with "inner space." In their quest to discover richer spiritual lives they not only returned to mainstream churches but also explored an array of spiritual alternatives. New Age spiritualism both waned and prospered during the 1990s. Although the numbers of those willing to identify themselves as Spiritualists declined, the popularity of such New Age gurus as Deepak Chopra suggested that spiritualism continued to assert an influence in American life. Indeed, spiritualism surfaced in some unlikely settings. The phenomenon of "corporate spiritualism" transformed the workplace in many companies, large and small, and became popular as a means of motivating employees by emphasizing their individual autonomy, their obligations to the employer and to God, and their responsibility for their own happiness and fulfillment. Evangelical Christian entrepreneurs also worked to Christianize American society through business and commerce. These so-called Christian capitalists believed that religion not only belonged in the workplace but that it was essential to economic success. They regarded themselves as spiritual as well as economic leaders engaged in a covenant with God and a custodial relationship with their families, employees, and customers. Moreover, they asserted an intimate connection between American society, capitalism, and Christianity.

Incivility and Violence. Americans also worried about the decline of manners and the rise of incivility during the decade. A majority, in fact, regarded these dual problems as portents of a serious social crisis. Many experts were concerned that incivility was such an ingrained part of the American character that it would be impossible to eradicate, and that it was rooted in a fundamental lack of respect for the rights, property, and person of other human beings. Although statistics suggested that crime decreased during the decade, the increase in acts of violence seemed to bear out their fears. During the 1990s Americans witnessed a rash of mass shootings, many of them involving children or teenagers. While juvenile crime declined throughout the decade, the number of youths killed by gunfire increased by an alarming 153 percent. There was a growing sense among many Americans that no one was safe from unpredictable gun violence. Yet, the attitudes of Americans toward guns remained ambivalent. The percentage of U.S. households owning guns increased while membership in the National Rifle Association (NRA) declined. Legislation such as the Brady Handgun Violence Prevention Act (1993) was offset by the passage of right-to-carry laws in more than thirty states. Overwhelming opposition to assault weapons on the part of the American people was countered by the insistence of lobbyists and scholars that an armed citizenry deterred crime and saved lives.

Gender Issues. The women's movement, the male crisis, and the crusade for gay rights all made headlines during the 1990s. Although the feminist movement continued to enjoy success in promoting women's issues and women's rights, increasing numbers of women criticized feminism as a bastion of the elite and as being irrelevant to the lives of women who were not educated, white, or middle class. The decade also found the American male under siege, pressured to be masculine in a culture that no longer valued traditional codes of manhood. Experts did not agree on the origins of this crisis. Some blamed the feminists, while feminists argued that men were in crisis because women were at last effectively challenging male dominance. Even testosterone came under attack. A more complete consensus emerged about the implications of the crisis. Experts worried that masculinity had became a matter of display and ornament. The essence of masculinity, critics complained, had come increasingly to derive from appearances rather than from inner resources, since most men no longer had opportunities to participate meaningfully in public life.

Homosexuality. Just the opposite may have been the case for homosexuals, who made their presence felt in all aspects of public life during the 1990s and who inserted themselves into the mainstream of U.S. politics. Nevertheless, although the majority of Americans surveyed in 1998 believed that homosexual relations were acceptable, violence and a legal backlash against gay rights were familiar occurrences. Several surveys revealed ambivalence among Americans on the issue of homosexuality. An overwhelming majority believed that homosexual men and women ought not to face discrimination in housing or employment because of their sexual orientation. Most Americans also favored harsher punishments for those who committed violent assaults against gays and lesbians. By the same token, more than 50 percent of Americans opposed same-sex marriages, one of the hot-button political and social issues of the 1990s.

Race and Ethnicity. More than 90 percent of Americans surveyed in 1996 believed that the race problem was not serious enough to warrant attention from the federal government, even as relations among blacks, whites, Asians, and Hispanics continued to deteriorate. Race may have remained an obsession among intellectuals, journalists, academics, and politicians, but it was little more than an afterthought to most ordinary citizens. Perhaps the rate of intermarriage that took place during the 1990s, and the clear prospect of a population that in the near future would be predominantly multiracial and multiethnic, help to explain the increasingly relaxed attitudes toward race relations. Yet, one area in which the majority of Americans were not so casual was in the growing opposition to preferential forms of affirmative action, the very sorts of programs that President Bill Clinton wished to salvage when he announced his "conversation" on race in 1996. The debate over affirmative action pitted the belief in equal opportunities against the idea that hard work and merit, not race (or gender), ought to determine who prospers. Beneath the surface of this controversy lingered the growing sense that affirmative action represented another instance of government intrusion and social engineering, however much sympathy Americans might express for the victims of bias and discrimination.

TOPICS IN THE NEWS

CHILDREN

Politics. Among the most important and divisive issues in the cultural politics of the United States during the 1990s was the debate about the rights of children. From the outset, the Clinton administration, largely at the initiative of First Lady Hillary Rodham Clinton, gave the issue top priority. The emphasis on children, however, enabled activists and politicians alike to use the issue as political leverage. "I can win any argument by saying we need welfare reform, but not at the cost of the children," remarked Senator Edward M. Kennedy (D-Massachusetts) in 1995. For Marian Wright Edelman, founder and president of the Children's Defense Fund (CDF), poverty remained the single most devastating problem facing children in the United States. Her proposed solution was straightforward: the federal government must give poor families more money. Many of Edelman's opponents, however, charged that her focus on children masked her real objective—to end poverty for people of all ages through the expenditure of federal revenue. In a general sense, Edelman's basic position remained extremely popular with Americans throughout the decade. A *Time*/CNN poll conducted in 1996, for example, found that 73 percent of Americans surveyed favored allocating additional tax dollars to programs designed to benefit children. Yet, despite this apparent national consensus, as the 1990s drew to a close, statistics compiled by the federal government suggested that the number of children mired in poverty was growing at an alarming rate. According to a Department of Health and Human Services report the percentage of children living in "extreme poverty" doubled since 1975—at the end of the decade the number stood at 10 percent, or 6.3 million children. To experts in child development, such as Douglas Nelson, executive director of the Annie E. Casey Foundation, such statistics predicted a grim future for the United States. As Nelson explained in 1996: "It may well be that the nation cannot survive—as a decent place to live, as a world-class power or even as a democracy—with such high rates of children growing into adulthood unprepared to parent, unprepared to be productively employed and unprepared to share in mainstream aspirations."

Children and Education. The chief innovation in elementary education during the 1990s did not concern curricular reform. Rather, it involved the assumption on the part of schools, particularly those located in impoverished and crime-ridden neighborhoods, of responsibility for the emotional and social welfare of children from birth to age twelve. Theoretically, anything that affected a child became the business of the school, from nutrition to the prevention of drug abuse to health care to psychological counseling. Joy G. Dryfoos maintained in *Full-Service Schools: A Revolution in Health and Social Services For Children, Youth and Families* (1994) that "schools are being called on to be those 'surrogate parents' that can increase the 'teachability' of children who arrive on their doorsteps in poor shape." During the decade, therefore, schools expanded beyond traditional academics, but to many educators it was a logical evolution. One of the more far-reaching educational programs of the 1990s began in Missouri and had spread to forty-seven other states by 1996. This program employed so-called parent educators to offer advice on parenting skills to young families. Perhaps the most interesting aspect of this program was that it began by focusing on future parents in the third trimester of pregnancy. Bowling Park Elementary School in Norfolk, Virginia, which advertised itself as "A Caring Community," provided another notable example of the new directions in elementary education. Principal Herman Clark not only looked after the needs of his students, but provided object lessons for their parents in the form of field trips. One year Clark took them to the Greensville Correctional Center. On another occasion parents visited the woman's prison in Goochland County, Virginia. Perhaps the most memorable trip, however, was to death row at the Mecklenberg Correctional Center. "The parents are subjected to a shakedown body search," Clark said. "They hear the door slam. They look at the inmates and see the way the inmates look back at them. We ask the prisoners 'Was there something that led you to this life?' They say, 'Yes, my parents were not there when I was a kid. There was nothing to do, so I did this or that [crime].' It is frightening. It makes our parents realize: this is where their kid is heading." The shock-treatment field trips were just one of the methods that educators began to use to rescue not only children, but entire families. "School has to be about more than reading and writing," Clark declared. In 1992 Bowling Park was selected as the site of the first CoZi school, developed by

HARRY POTTER

Throughout the latter part of 1999, thousands of young children walked around with paste-on tattoos in the shape of a purple lightening bolt. Many adults were puzzled; for those in the know, however, the tattoos indicated that these kids were fans of the young, would-be wizard Harry Potter. The fictional character and his adventures, the creation of English author J. K. Rowling, captivated readers young and old. Three books, *Harry Potter and the Sorceror's Stone* (1998), *Harry Potter and the Chamber of Secrets* (1999), and *Harry Potter and the Prisoner of Azkaban* (1999), racked up record-breaking sales in the United Kingdom and the United States. The books also earned the distinction as one of the few children's books ever to crack the adult best-sellers list, remaining on *The New York Times* Best Sellers' List for more than thirty-eight weeks. By the fall of 1999, more than 7.5 million volumes were in print, translated into twenty-eight languages, with more than 650,000 lightning-bolt tattoos also being sold at local bookstores across the country. Why Harry Potter? For many readers, the visit to Harry's world of enchantment promises a brief respite from the uncertainties of the 1990s. Rowling, a single mother of a young daughter, plans to write four more books for the series.

Sources: "The Year of Harry Potter," *USA Today*, 18 (20 December 1999): 50.

"Hurry Harry," *Newsweek*, 134 (1 November 1999): 6.

Paul Gray, Elizabeth Gleick, and Andrea Sachs, "Hooked on Harry," *Time*, 154 (20 September 1999): 66–72.

James P. Comer and Edward Zigler of Yale University. The CoZi school model has since been adopted in more-affluent school districts throughout the United States. Operating year-round, CoZi schools became an exercise in cooperative management in which parents, teachers, administrators, and mental-health professionals jointly decided policy in an effort, as Zigler put it, to "make the success of the child in every aspect of development our constant focus."

The Market Place. Preteenage children, "tweeners" as they were known to advertisers and marketers, were active consumers. According to statistics compiled for the last quarter of 1999, preteens (ages eight to thirteen) spent approximately $14 billion a year throughout the 1990s, much of it on expensive, brand-name clothing and accessories. They also accounted for 9 percent of compact disc (CD) sales. James McNeal, professor of marketing at Texas A & M University, estimated that tweeners directly influenced more than $128 billion in family spending in 1997, the last year for which complete figures are available. "Kids invented the minivan," McNeil asserted, "and just recently, they've been encouraging their parents to sell them and get an SUV (sports utility vehicle) instead." Experts sug-

gested that children came to exert so much influence on family spending habits because of a dramatic change in family relations. "People treat each other more like members of a group," McNeil points out, "rather than as sons and daughters and moms and dads." This more democratic ideal of parenting not only gave children of the 1990s more individual freedom but more power within the family as well. Child psychologist Paula Rauch of Harvard Medical School expressed concern that during the decade it became harder for parents to set limits on their children's behavior, a failure that, in turn, gave children a false sense of power. "They may end up self-centered, self-absorbed, incapable of managing a successful social life, spoiled and unhappy because they're never going to get their own way all the time," concluded William Damon, director of the Stanford Center on Adolescence.

Sports. Paying for children to play sports was another major family expenditure of the 1990s. Some estimates placed the number of American children participating in organized sports during the decade at more than forty million. Parents on average paid close to $4,000 a year to enable their children to participate. These costs included not only equipment and uniforms, but club dues to help pay coaches' salaries, fees for private clinics and camps, and travel and hotel expenses. By the end of the 1990s, however, sports for children had succumbed to a cycle of rising expectations. "Nobody seems to want to play on the little neighborhood team for more than one season," said Judith C. Young, executive director of the National Association of Sport and Physical Education (NASPE) located in Reston, Virginia. The athletic lives of many children were consumed by practices, clinics, and competitive tournaments. There was no longer room for dilettantes or for what parenting manuals used to call "unstructured play." The objective of participating became more than experiencing the thrill of victory, winning a trophy, or molding a good character. Instead the prize was often a college scholarship, a place on an Olympic team, or a lucrative professional career. Experts and parents alike, however, pointed to the benefits of participation. A child busy with sports was less susceptible to the lure of drugs, gangs, and violence. Sports provided exercise, discipline, and camaraderie. Mark Goldstein, a child psychologist at Roosevelt University in Chicago, maintained that "we know from a lot of research that kids who participate in sports tend to do better academically. It forces them to be more organized with their time and to prioritize better." By contrast, critics increasingly cited the pressure that parents and coaches placed on children as the principal reason why 73 percent of them quit playing sports by age thirteen. Fred Engh, a coach and author of *Why Johnny Hates Sports* (1999) wrote that "they drop out because it ceases to be fun, and the pressures put on them by coaches and parents don't make it worthwhile. . . . There's nothing wrong with competition. . . . But children under the age of 10 don't necessarily want competition. What they want is to have fun."

Members of the under-nine Longview Soccer Club practice in Longview, Washington on 20 September 1999 (AP/Wide World Photos).

The 1990s Lifestyle. "They are a generation stuck on fast forward, children in a fearsome hurry to grow up," concluded writers Barbara Kantrowitz and Pat Wingert. "The girls wear sexy lingerie and provocative makeup . . . in order to complete what some parents call the Lolita look. The boys affect a tough-guy swagger—while fretting about when their voices will change." These were the children of the 1990s: educated, affluent, computer savvy, apparently obsessed with athletic competition, and often motivated by the dictates of consumption, fashion, and celebrity. Experts worried, though, that they might never grow up, mistaking the appearance for the substance of maturity. "What we're seeing is a superficial sophistication," lamented Damon. "There's been no increase in the values that help a kid get through the confusion of life in a steady, productive way." The lives of these well-to-do children moved at an increasingly frenetic pace. Ten-year-old Allie Terese Baron-Phillips of Tarzana, California, described her hectic daily routine to Kantrowitz and Wingert. "My life is really hectic right now. I'm doing what some people in the 1800s weren't doing until they were full-grown adults. I get up at 6:30 every morning, go to school and have to rush through all my classes, come home and work on my homework, go to ice skating lessons, watch a little TV, talk on the phone, do more homework and practice my violin. If I'm lucky, I get to sleep by 11. And then the entire ordeal starts again." The consequences of this constant pressure are difficult to quantify, but perhaps one indication of its effect was that physicians wrote an estimated five hundred thousand to one million prescriptions a year for antidepressants to treat children and teenagers. The pressure on children to behave like adults became almost irresistible during the decade. Children were "being exposed to adult things from birth," said Markus Kruesi, a child and adolescent psychologist at the University of Illinois Institute for Juvenile Research. Half were children of divorce. As young children they worried about being abducted by strangers and having their photograph appear on milk cartons. Before they had been on a date, they had heard about the perils of AIDS. Many were exposed to drugs, gangs, and violence before they entered junior high. Recent research has suggested that sexual activity and drug use among preteens have both increased dramatically. According to a study conducted in 1997 by the Centers for Disease Control (CDC) in Atlanta, Gerogia, 6.5 percent of ninth-grade girls and 14.7 percent of ninth-grade boys admitted to having had sex before the age of thirteen. A University of Maryland study completed in 1998 found that 29 percent of eighth graders had sampled illegal drugs. More than half (52.5 percent) said they had used alcohol, with 24.7 percent saying they have been drunk at least once. Researchers placed the responsibility for the attitudes and behavior of children primarily on parents. "This is a time when they're real curious about the world and they're soaking up other points of view," argued Mary Pipher, the author of *Reviving Ophelia: Saving the Selves of Adolescent Girls* (1994). "They're not getting enough of that from the people who love them. They're getting it from machines and people who want to sell them stuff." Still, despite the problems and pressures they faced, the children of the 1990s remained optimistic. According the "1998 Roper Youth Report: The Mood of Young America," 80 percent expected to have better lives than their parents.

Sources:

Joy G. Dryfoos, *Full-Service Schools: A Revolution in Health and Social Services For Children, Youth and Families* (San Francisco: Jossey-Bass, 1994).

Fred Engh, *Why Johnny Hates Sports* (Garden City, N.Y.: Avery, 1999).

Andrew Ferguson, "Inside the Crazy Culture of Kids Sports," *Time,* 154 (12 July 1999): 52–60.

Elizabeth Gleick, "The Children's Crusade," *Time,* 147 (3 June 1996): 30–35.

Sylvia Ann Hewlett, *When the Bough Breaks: The Costs of Neglecting Our Children* (New York: Basic Books, 1991).

Margot Hornblower, "It Takes a School," *Time,* 147 (3 June 1996): 36–38.

Barbara Kantrowitz and Pat Wingert, "The Truth About Tweens," *Newsweek,* 134 (18 October 1999): 62–72.

J. F. O. McAllister, "The Children's Crusade," *Time,* 150 (25 August 1997): 36.

"1998 Roper Youth Report: The Mood of Young America" (New York: Roper Starch Worldwide, 1998).

Mary Pipher, *Reviving Ophelia: Saving the Selves of Adolescent Girls* (New York: Putnam, 1994).

"Special Report: Troubled Kids," *Time,* 154 (31 May 1999): 33–59.

CRAZES, FADS, AND TRENDS

Coffee. Americans went crazy for coffee during the 1990s. They enjoyed gourmet coffees at neighborhood coffeehouses and bought specialty coffees to drink at home. In the 1980s such companies as Peet's Coffee & Tea and Starbucks Coffee helped to make gourmet coffees more widely available and thus enhanced their popularity. By the 1990s coffee bars and coffeehouses appeared everywhere, including in bookstores such as Barnes & Noble and Borders. Coffee bars became convenient places for men and women to meet and socialize. The appeal of coffee during the decade came about in part because the beverage gave consumers an opportunity to treat themselves to an affordable luxury.

Cigars. Among the most unexpected fads of the 1990s was the incredible popularity of premium cigars. Throughout much of the decade, the Cigar Manufacturers Association reported, the annual sale and price of premium cigars escalated at unprecedented rates. Between 1993 and 1998 sales of premium cigars more than tripled. Many industry experts trace the origins of the cigar boom to the introduction of *Cigar Aficionado,* a publication of Marvin Shanken Communications, that promoted not only cigar smoking, but the upscale lifestyle that apparently accompanied it. Cigar smoking had a special appeal among young men and women in their twenties and thirties, whose hobby prompted the appearance of smoke shops, cigar clubs and bars, and cigar-friendly restaurants and hotels. By the end of the decade, however, the demand for expensive, premium cigars had begun to decline. Prices fell dramatically, as did the value of stock shares, and companies that had begun to manufacture and sell cigars at the height of the boom declared bankruptcy, sold off their remaining

BEANIE BABIES

Launched by H. Ty Warner in 1993, Beanie Babies emerged as one of the hottest collectibles for kids and grown-ups alike. Seeing the need for a toy "in the $5 range that wasn't real garbage," Warner designed a whole series of small, understuffed, polyester plush toys filled with polyvinyl chloride pellets. Bypassing any kind of advertising campaign and refusing to court the big toy retailing giants such as Toys-R-Us, Warner instead shipped Beanie Babies to smaller retailers. What really pushed the toys, such as "Flitter the Butterfly" or "Cheeks the Baboon," was that no one store carried the entire collection. Add to that Warner's "retiring" of certain toys after a short period of time on the market and the quest for the complete line of Beanie Babies became something akin to a treasure hunt, with anxious collectors storming stores, advertising on the Internet, and stalking conventions in search of the ever-elusive Beanie to add to their collections. Prices for the rarer Beanies soared into the thousands of dollars, with one retailer offering to sell the entire collection he had put together for $175,000. Sales for Warner's company reached $1 billion by 1999, making Warner one of the richest men in the country. On 31 August 1999, Warner dropped the bombshell that as of 31 December his company would be retiring the line forever.

Sources: Tonya Davies, "Bidding Adieu to Beanie Babies," *Macleans,* 112 (13 September 1999): 10.

Margaret Mannix, "Beanie Babies Get Sandbagged," *U.S. News & World Report,* 127 (13 September 1999): 66.

inventory at a fraction of its former cost, and went out of business.

Museums. Americans visited history museums, art museums, science museums, children's museums, botanical gardens, zoos, and aquariums in record numbers in the 1990s. The American Association of Museums estimates that in 1997 there were 865 million visitors to museums in the United States. Attendance at the Metropolitan Museum of Art in New York City increased by one million persons between 1991 and 1996. New museums, such as the United States Holocaust Memorial Museum located in Washington, D.C., also drew many visitors. Fewer than five years after the museum opened, it welcomed its ten-millionth visitor. Many small museums did not report the number of visitors they received each year; therefore, museum attendance during the decade was probably higher than official estimates. In addition, many museums also had "virtual" visitors through their websites.

Patrons in the Torpedo Lounge in San Francisco, one of the first clubs to cater to smokers after the 1998 ban on tobacco use in public establishments in California (AP/Wide World Photos)

Community Service. The 1990s was a decade of volunteerism and community service. Americans of all ages worked to solve the problems of homelessness, illiteracy, drug addiction, crime, and violence by participating in a variety of community service projects. Even the federal government encouraged volunteerism. The National and Community Service Trust Act of 1993 created AmeriCorps and Learn and Serve America. AmeriCorps enabled young Americans to earn money to pay for college by performing community service. Learn and Serve America helped students to become involved in local volunteer programs. Many high schools across the United States began to require that students perform community service in order to graduate. Individuals convicted of breaking the law were also increasingly sentenced to terms of community service rather than time in jail.

Gambling. Gambling and spending became two of Americans' favorite pastimes during the 1990s. Wagering enjoyed both phenomenal growth and spawned feverish protests. Early nineteenth-century French aristocrat Alexis de Tocqueville believed that gambling was an indelible part of the American character. The tendency remained strong during the 1990s. A survey conducted by the gambling industry found that 89 percent of Americans had no objection to casino gambling, even though 33 percent said they would not go to a casino themselves. Proponents of gambling estimated that it brought $1.4 billion in tax revenue for state and local governments. Critics, such as John W. Kindt, University of Illinois Professor of Commerce, maintained that for every dollar gaming contributed in taxes, taxpayers spent at least three on everything from repairing streets around casinos to increasing police patrols to treating compulsive gamblers.

Spending. Americans also became infected with what Cornell University economist Robert H. Frank called "luxury fever." Accompanying the prosperity of the late 1990s was a "national culture of upscale spending," declared economist Juliet Schor in *The Overspent American: Upscaling, Downshifting, and the New Consumer* (1998). Yet Schor, among others, questioned the consequences. Americans accumulated record levels of debt during the decade in order to acquire bigger and more-expensive television sets, automobiles, and houses. According to Thomas J. Stanley and William D. Danko, authors of *The Millionaire Next Door: The Surprising Secrets of America's Wealthy* (1996), the turn toward bigger cars and houses represented a new wave of "hyperconsumption," much of it carried on by "under- accumulators" who based their financial decisions on "the best year they've ever had." To pay for their upscale purchases, Americans borrowed more money during the 1990s than at any time in history and also made use of a proliferation of low-interest credit cards and innovative lending instruments such as the 125-percent second mortgage. By mid decade there were signs of a modest rebellion against the escalating

SUVs

The preferred vehicle of the 1990s for many Americans was the Sports Utility Vehicle (SUV). Sales of SUVs doubled from 1990 to 1998, with more than three million being sold in 1998 alone, making it one of the most popular vehicle types ever manufactured. SUVs are classified as a light truck. Although they have been around for more than two decades, the SUV, first introduced by Jeep, was designed for off-road driving and the towing of trailers and boats. It was not until the early 1990s that the vehicle became trendy as a "family car" for adults with kids and pets. The vehicle offered plenty of room for passengers and cargo. Like trucks and vans, SUVS also made it easier for drivers to see traffic as they were built higher than a regular passenger car. To increase their popularity, designers made SUVs more comfortable to drive and ride in, while adding many of the amenities that people wanted in their vehicles such as CD stereo systems, cup holders, and leather interiors. By 1998, more than forty different models were available for consumers to choose from including offerings from Ford (which produced the most popular model in the Ford Explorer), Jeep, Chevrolet, GMC, Nissan, and Toyota. Even luxury-car manufacturers such as Mercedes Benz and Lexus offered a luxury SUV for the discriminating driver.

Sources: Jay Koblenz, "Booming SUVs," *Consumer Digest*, 38 (May/June, 1999): 58–62.

"Trend Watch," *Consumer Reports*, 64 (August 1999): 10.

cycle of spending. Many affluent Americans began to recognize, in the words of Richard M. Ryan, a psychologist at the University of Rochester, that "there's a very short half-life to the pleasure that comes from spending." Between 1990 and 1996, according to a survey conducted by EDK Associates, nearly 20 percent of the population made a voluntary effort to simplify their lives. Approximately 85 percent of these "downshifters" reported that they were happier as a result.

Sources:
Elise Ackerman, "The Cigar Boom Goes Up in Smoke," *U.S. News & World Report*, 127 (29 November 1999): 55.

Robert Goodman, *The Luck Business: The Devastating Consequences and Broken Promises of America's Gambling Explosion* (New York: Free Press, 1995).

James Lardner, "The Urge to Splurge," *U.S. News & World Report*, 126 (24 May 1999): 48–52.

Juliet Schor, *The Overspent American: Upscaling, Downshifting, and the New Consumer* (New York: Basic Books, 1998).

Joseph P. Shapiro, "America's Gambling Fever," *U.S. News & World Report*, 120 (15 January 1996): 52–61.

Thomas J. Stanley and William D. Danko, *The Millionaire Next Door: The Surprising Secrets of America's Wealthy* (Atlanta, Ga.: Longstreet Press, 1996).

FAMILY LIFE

The New Extended Family. The "new extended family," the stepfamily, the "recombinant family," the "blended family": by whatever name, such familial configurations became the standard in American society during the 1990s. The government estimated that by the year 2007, stepfamilies would outnumber traditional nuclear families. In 1999 there were already more than 5.5 million stepfamilies in the United States. Although the members of many stepfamilies made the necessary adjustments and compromises, there remained a sizable number of such families that struggled or failed. A variety of studies collectively demonstrated that stepchildren were more likely to become disciplinary problems, perform poorly in school, have to repeat a grade, or drop out of school altogether than children who lived in traditional, two-parent homes. American children living in stepfamilies were less likely to go to college or to receive financial support from their family if they did. Worse, according to the extensive research of Martin Daly and Margo Wilson of McMaster University in Ontario, stepchildren were more commonly the victims of physical and sexual abuse, and were one hundred times more likely to be killed by a stepparent than by their biological parents. Such studies fueled the conservative indictment of stepfamilies as unnatural arrangements and the consequent push for stronger "pro-family" social policies designed to discourage

A Washington State family at adoption proceedings at the Lewis County Courthouse on 30 December 1997 (AP/Wide World Photos)

divorce and preserve the traditional nuclear family. These measures included many ideas proffered by the nascent "marriage movement," such as marriage-friendly tax policies and "covenant marriages" that were intended to make divorce and remarriage more difficult. Meanwhile, critics argued that creating social policies to force unhappy and dysfunctional families to stay together was far riskier than life in a stepfamily.

Family Law. One possibility that emerged during the decade to strengthen stepfamilies was the effort to alter the legal status of stepparents. Like domestic partners, stepparents had almost no legal standing in most states, which meant that even when they assumed financial and emotional responsibility for their stepchildren, they had no corresponding rights. If the marriage ended, the stepparent had no legal right to request custody or visitation. During the 1990s family law was challenged in various ways in different jurisdictions with inconsistent results. Experts on the family will no doubt be arguing for legislation that will explicitly spell out both the rights and responsibilities of stepparents.

Changing Attitudes. Cultural and social change regarding stepfamilies came even more slowly than legal change. Yet, by the end of the 1990s, there were unmistakable indications that longstanding attitudes were beginning to erode. In Kansas City, Missouri, for example, the Reverend Roger Coleman began to perform marriage ceremonies specifically designed to include children from previous unions, and thereby to help them overcome their confusion and insecurity. Coleman's ceremonies aimed to legitimize and celebrate the "new family." Changes also began to occur in public schools across the country. Through the efforts of the Step Family Association of America, school officials began to acknowledge the increasingly important role of stepparents, for example, by accepting their signa-

GENEALOGY

The 1990s saw a veritable explosion of interest by people seeking to learn more about their roots. Thanks to a host of computer programs and websites devoted to the subject, finding out about your family became easier than ever. According to one study, genealogy ranked with sex, finance, and sports as one of the biggest areas of interest on the Internet. For instance, one site, RootsWeb, received more than 160 million messages through its site in a single month. In April 1999 the largest repository of genealogy in the United States, the Church of Latter Day Saints (Mormon Church) announced that it would host a website that eventually will catalogue more than six hundred million names in an effort to help those looking for pieces of their family history.

Sources: Margot Hornblower and Melissa August, "Roots Mania," *Time,* 153 (19 April 1999): 54–67.

David Jackson, "How to Program Your Family History," *Time,* 153 (19 April 1999): 58–60.

GENERATION X

Although overshadowed by the seventy-eight million members of the Baby Boom generation, the forty-five million children born between 1965 and 1977 made themselves heard during the decade of the 1990s. Known as "Generation X," these youths were at first depicted as cynical, drifting, and lazy. But this portrayal was far from accurate. Unlike the Baby Boomers, who tended to grow up in affluent circumstances and who have come to accept prosperity as their due, Generation X could never presume on that kind of success. They grew up in the 1980s during a recession, witnessed increased divorce rates and the hard reality of homelessness, lived and loved in the shadow of AIDS, and entered a job market that was tight and less rewarding. Despite these obstacles, the "Gen Xers" have shown themselves to be hardworking, ambitious, and confident. Committed to a variety of social causes and yet dedicated to making money, this group of young people took hold of their futures. Representing an impressive $125 billion in purchasing power a year, Generation X is also the first group to have grown up with computers, and they have shown themselves to be savvy in the business world as well. Many believe that working hard will provide the key to obtaining the high quality of life that they desire.

Sources: Margot Hornblower, "Great Xpectations," *Time,* 149 (9 June 1997): 58–65.

Karen Shoemer, "Talking 'Bout Our Generation," *Newsweek,* 124 (26 December 1994): 32–34.

tures on school registration forms and field-trip permission slips. Change was also evident in a marketplace eager to exploit a widening social trend. In a sign of the times, the Hallmark greeting-card company launched a line of cards devoted entirely to nontraditional families. The cards in the "Ties That Bind" series were aimed at persons who had come together as the result of remarriage. The message of some cards was straightforward: "There are so many different types and ways to be a family today." Others were more elliptical: "It's like looking at a puzzle where the pieces aren't where they used to be." Yet, all the cards were aimed at the vast and growing market of men, women, and children who no longer identified with the traditional definitions of family and were trying to find new ways to make their families work.

Sources:
Brad Edmondson and Judith Waldrop, "Married With Children," *American Demographics,* 15 (December 1993): 31–33.

Wray Herbert, Suzi Parker, and Stephen Sawicki, "When Strangers Become Family," *U.S. News & World Report,* 127 (29 November 1999): 58–67.

John K. Rosemond, "Blended Families . . . One Step At A Time," *Better Homes & Gardens,* 72 (February 1994): 56.

Elaine Fantle Shimberg, *Blending Families* (New York: Berkeley Books, 1999).

The Critique of Feminism. The rallying cry "women's liberation" entered the English language during the 1960s. More than thirty years later, few countries around the world were without a women's movement, and few governments were immune to its demands. During the 1990s traditional notions of female roles continued to erode, and the "gender gap" narrowed. The women's movement in the United States made enormous progress in ending discrimination in education, government, employment, and the law. Throughout the decade, however, more and more American women began to criticize the feminist agenda as irrelevant to their lives. "If you become a doctor, the feminists are right behind you," declared nurse midwife LaVonne Wilenken of Antelope Valley, California, in 1994, but "they've done very little for the average woman." This sentiment became more widespread. Women who were minorities, poor, fulfilling traditional roles of wife and mother, and doing traditional jobs all acknowledged their debt to feminism. At the same time, however, many of them charged that the movement had failed to broaden its base and that it remained composed primarily of white, educated, and affluent women who had not adequately addressed issues important to nonwhite, less-well-educated, and less-affluent women. The feminist movement of the 1990s, these women maintained, focused on abortion and lesbian rights rather than child care, on political equality rather than economic survival. The revolt against feminism, or at least the direction the movement had taken since the late 1980s, also surfaced in intellectual circles. In *Feminism Is Not the Story of My Life: How Today's Feminist Elite Has Lost Touch With the Real Concerns of Women* (1996), the most important critique of feminism produced during the 1990s, Elizabeth Fox-Genovese set out to measure the disparity between radical feminist characterizations of women's lives and how ordinary women actually lived, thereby exposing the "corruption" that "perverted" the feminist movement.

Accomplishments and Limitations. The progress that American women made during the 1990s was uneven. At the end of the decade, 40 percent of medical students and 50 percent of law students were women. But like men, women without education or marketable skills were being left behind. Women also continued to be paid less than their male counterparts. Labor Department statistics indicated that the wage gap closed, but only a little. In the 1990s women earned 71 percent of what men earned, compared with 64 percent in 1952. Poverty also continued to plague women to a greater extent than it did men. Sixty percent of single mothers lived in poverty according to a study released in 1994 by Women Work!, a training and advocacy group for displaced homemakers and single mothers. The study found that the annual median income for such women was $9,353. "The perception is that there's been dramatic change for women," concluded Jill Miller, executive director of Women Work! "The troubling thing about the survey is that it shows it's not really that way." Many women's organizations arose to address the issues that mainstream feminism ignored. Groups such as La Mujer Obrera, which organized Hispanic working women, and the Older Women's League, which lobbied for women older than forty-five, claimed that they were the real women's movement. These grassroots

Women praying in support of participants in the Million Man March (AP/Wide World Photos)

groups labored to produce a "fourth wave" of the movement for the coming millennium.

Crisis of Masculinity. The 1990s produced the phenomenon of "angry white man," the American male under siege, pressured to be masculine in a culture that no longer valued traditional codes of manhood. The so-called crisis of masculinity took many and diverse forms, including the navy's Tailhook scandal (5–7 September 1991); the debate over the admission of women into the formerly all-male, state-supported military colleges, The Citadel and Virginia Military Institute; the sexual athleticism of the Spur Posse, a gang of high-school students from the affluent suburb of Lakewood who achieved national notoriety in 1993 when a competition among members to see who could sleep with the most girls led nine boys to be charged with rape; inner-city "gangstas"; and schoolyard shootings across the country. More sedate, but equally revealing, was the masculine retreat to cigar clubs, strip joints, and lap-dancing emporiums, the increase in male cosmetic surgery, the abuse of steroids, and the brisk sale of Viagra (a drug that enhances sexual performance). By the hundreds of thousands, ordinary men confirmed the diagnosis of a male-identity crisis, convening both the Million-Man March (16 October 1995), under the leadership of the Nation of Islam, and the Promise Keepers rally (July 1991), inspired by evangelical Christians. There has been little agreement on the origins of the crisis. Feminist mothers and wives, indulgent liberals, and even testosterone came under attack. Feminists and antifeminists alike maintained that men were in crisis because women, properly or improperly, challenged male dominance. In *Stiffed: The Betrayal of the American Man* (1999), feminist journalist Susan Faludi admitted she mistakenly assumed "that the male crisis in America was caused by something men were doing unrelated to something being done to them." In the culture of the 1990s, experts worried that masculinity became a matter of display and ornament. The essence of masculinity, these critics complained, came increasingly to derive from appearances rather than from inner resources since most men no longer had opportunities to participate meaningfully in public life. Amid the crisis, many such as Faludi saw new opportunities for men to break free of old stereotypes and new paradigms of masculinity. "Their task is not, in the end, to figure out how to be masculine," Faludi concluded, "rather their masculinity lies in figuring out how to be human."

Sources:

Susan Faludi, *Backlash: The Undeclared War Against American Women* (New York: Crown, 1991).

Faludi, *Stiffed: The Betrayal of the American Man* (New York: Morrow, 1999).

Elizabeth Fox-Genovese, *Feminism Is Not the Story of My Life: How Today's Feminist Elite Has Lost Touch With the Real Concerns of Women* (New York: Nan A. Talese, 1996).

Fox-Genovese, *Feminism Without Illusions: A Critique of Individualism* (Chapel Hill: University of North Carolina Press, 1991).

Emily MacFarquhar, "The War Against Women," *U.S. News & World Report*, 116 (28 March 1994): 42–48.

Elizabeth Powers, "Feminism and Its Illusions," *National Review*, 48 (3 June 1996): 52–53.

GUNS IN AMERICA

Legislation. In the wake of the assassinations of the Reverend Martin Luther King Jr. (4 April 1968) and Senator Robert F. Kennedy (5 June 1968), the United States Congress passed the Gun Control Act of 1968. For more than thirty years this legislation defined federal gun policy. It banned most interstate sales of firearms, licensed most gun dealers, and barred felons, minors, and the mentally ill from purchasing and owning guns. Culturally, the law represented a brief national revulsion against gun violence. Recent gun-control legislation has been more contentious and less extensive. During the first years of the Clinton administration the Democratic Congress enacted the Brady Handgun Violence Prevention Act (1993), which required a five-day waiting period for the purchase of handguns and banned certain assault weapons. Since 1994, however, efforts to pass major antigun legislation have slowed. More modest pieces of legislation, such as a proposal for safety locks on guns, stand the best chance of success. Meanwhile, many state laws have begun to favor the rights of gun owners, including the right of any citizen without a criminal record to carry concealed weapons, which is now legal in thirty-one states.

Attitudes. According to a survey conducted by the Princeton Survey Research Associates during August 1999, 74 percent of Americans supported the registration of all handgun owners and 93 percent favored a mandatory waiting period for persons wishing to buy handguns. An additional 68 percent of those interviewed believed that military assault weapons ought to be outlawed, while 51 percent wanted to abolish gun shows at which weapons of all types can be bought and sold with little regulation. Wayne LaPierre, executive vice president of the National Rifle Association (NRA), countered that "the real target is the Second Amendment. . . . What is being offered is some utopian society where guns do not exist. I hate to tell people, you're never going to get there." Other advocates of the right to bear arms echoed LaPierre's sentiments. "Guns are for defense, [for] saving your own life," insisted Elizabeth Saunders, president and CEO of American Derringer.

Ownership. By 1998 the percentage of American households in which guns were present had declined slightly from approximately 45 percent to nearly 40 percent. Membership in the NRA had also dropped from 3.5 million in 1995 to 2.8 million, a decrease of 20 percent. At the same time, estimates suggested that Americans still owned more than 235 million guns. University of Chicago economist John R. Lott Jr. concluded in the controversial *More Guns, Less Crime: Understanding Crime and Gun-Control Laws* (1998) that in states enacting more-relaxed right-to-carry laws,

Confiscated guns being destroyed in Los Angeles in July 1992 (Flora Gruff)

murders fell an average of 8 percent, rapes an average of 5 percent, and aggravated assaults an average of 7 percent between 1977 and 1992. The longer such laws remained on the books, the more precipitous the decline in violent crime. After five years the number of murders fell by 15 percent and rapes by 9 percent. In addition, the average death rate from mass shootings in states with right-to-carry laws dropped by 69 percent. By comparison, Lott showed that in the United States as a whole during this same period the number of murders increased by 24 percent, rapes by 71 percent, and aggravated assaults by more than 50 percent. Gun-control lobbyists, criminologists, and other critics charged that Lott's research is spurious, his statistics unreliable, and his conclusion—that permitting citizens to own and carry guns will create a safer society—dangerous.

Guns and Violence. Americans witnessed during the 1990s a rash of mass shootings, many involving teenagers or children. Although juvenile crime declined throughout the decade, the number of youths killed by gunfire increased an alarming 153 percent. Recent statistics suggest that one in twelve high-school students was threatened or injured by a classmate with a gun every year. The growing sense among many Americans that no one was safe from unpredictable gun violence fueled the debate over gun control, a debate likely to continue among congressmen, state legislators, lobbyists, and the general public, and which almost certainly will be a major issue in the presidential election of 2000.

Sources:
"America Under the Gun," *Newsweek,* 134 (23 August 1999), special issue.

"The Atlanta Massacre," *Time,* 154 (9 August 1999): 22–39.

Constance Johnson, "Law and Disorder," *U.S. News & World Report,* 116 (28 March 1994): 35–37.

John R. Lott Jr., *More Guns, Less Crime: Understanding Crime and Gun-Control Laws* (Chicago: University of Chicago Press, 1998).

Bruce W. Nelan, "Guns and Poses," *Time,* 147 (3 June 1996): 42–44.

The following list provides a chronology of the major incidents of gun violence involving children and other mass shootings during the decade.

2 February 1996: Barry Loukaitis, 14, killed a teacher and two students and wounded another at Frontier Junior High School in Moses Lake, Washington. He is now serving two life sentences.

1 October 1997: Luke Woodham, 16, stabbed his mother to death and then drove to Pearl High School in Pearl, Mississippi, where he proceeded to kill two students, including his former girlfriend, and to wound seven others. Woodham was sentenced to life in prison.

1 December 1997: Michael Carneal, 14, killed three students and wounded five others who were attending a prayer meeting at Heath High School in Paducah, Kentucky.

24 March 1998: Mitchell Johnson, 13, and Andrew Golden, 11, killed a teacher and four classmates and wounded ten other persons at Westside Middle School in Jonesboro, Arkansas.

24 April 1998: Andrew Wurst, 14, killed a teacher at an eighth-grade graduation dance at James W. Parker Middle School in Edinboro, Pennsylvania.

19 May 1998: Jacob Davis killed another student in the parking lot of Lincoln County High School in Fayetteville, Tennessee. Davis claimed the other boy had been dating his former girlfriend.

21 May 1998: Kip Kinkel, 15, killed two students and wounded twenty-two others at Thurston High School in Springfield, Oregon. Kinkel, also charged with murdering his parents the previous day, was sentenced to 112 years in prison.

24 July 1998: Russell "Rusty" Watson, 41, killed a police officer and a federal guard and wounded a female tourist at the Capitol building in Washington, D.C. Watson was severely wounded by police.

15 April 1999: Sergei Babarin, 74, killed a woman and a security guard and wounded four others at the Mormon Family History Library in Salt Lake City, Utah. Police then shot and killed Babarin as they attempted to apprehend him.

20 April 1999: Eric Harris, 18, and Dylan Klebold, 17, killed twelve students and one teacher and wounded twenty-three others before taking their own lives at Columbine High School in Littleton, Colorado.

20 May 1999: Anthony "T. J." Solomon, 15, wounded six students at Heritage High School in Conyers, Georgia.

2–4 July 1999: Benjamin Nathaniel Smith, 21, killed two persons and wounded nine others during a rampage through Illinois and Indiana, after which he took his own life. Smith's killing spree was apparently motivated by racial animosity.

29 July 1999: Mark Barton, 44, a disgruntled day-trader, shot and killed nine persons and wounded thirteen others in Atlanta, Georgia, after bludgeoning to death his wife and two children. Barton then took his own life.

5 August 1999: Alan Eugene Miller, 34, killed at least two, and possibly three, persons in Pelham, Alabama.

10 August 1999: Buford O. Furrow, 37, wounded three children, a teenager, and a sixty-eight-year-old receptionist when he opened fire at a Jewish community center in Los Angeles, California. Furrow later shot and killed a postal worker.

HOME AND COMMUNITY

Safe and Sound. As diverse as their generation is, "security issues tie all baby-boomers together," observed Elizabeth Falconer, owner of Position By Design, located in Grand Prairie, Texas. Denver architect Michael Knorr agreed. "I don't know if it's growing up with the Cold War and surviving or what," Knorr declared, "but we seem to have an incredible need for security." The increased need for personal security among baby boomers prompted many builders during the 1990s to include home-security systems as standard features in all their units. Designers of luxury homes also offered "safe rooms" concealed underneath stairs, behind built-in bookshelves, or inside closets.

Home Design. Other trends in home design that became popular during the 1990s included the addition of media rooms, home theaters, home offices, megabaths, and special-interest rooms, such as reading and music rooms, to support a variety of interests and hobbies. Joan McCloskey,

building editor of *Better Homes and Gardens,* pointed out that boomers also wanted yards and neighborhoods with parks, wilderness areas, and gardens. As more elderly parents or adult children unable to find work, or if employed, unable to afford homes of their own, move in, baby boomers want flexible floor plans with rooms that can be used either as offices or bedrooms. With the ownership of pets becoming more common, many homes constructed during the 1990s contained a pet grooming area. Contractors also began preparing homes adapted to the needs of aging boomers, by incorporating into home designs such small but thoughtful touches as levers instead of knobs on doors and faucets, raised dishwashers, lowered light switches, wider platforms for bathtubs, and door frames designed to accommodate wheelchairs. Kitchens again became important, and home designers responded by building larger kitchens often with two stoves, several food-preparation areas, and more storage space. Homes

Entrance to the gated community of Jacaranda Point in Plantation, Florida

themselves, at least those of more affluent Americans, also became larger during the decade. If California is the harbinger, ten-thousand- and twenty thousand-square-foot residences will soon proliferate across the nation.

Community Life. Throughout the United States, affluent homeowners began "forting up" during the 1990s. That is, they retreated from their neighbors and shielded themselves from the outside world by barricading their families behind locked gates, walls, and barriers. By the end of the decade more than eight million Americans lived in an estimated twenty thousand gated communities, taking refuge from urban problems that had apparently become unsolvable. Eighty percent of planned urban communities were gated, and suburbanites "gated" as rapidly as those who lived in cities. The popularity of gated communities, however, had experts wondering about the future of civic and community life in the United States. In *Fortress America: Gated Communities in the United States* (1997), Edward J. Blakely and Mary Gail Snyder raised just such concerns. "In the new lexicon," wrote Blakely and Snyder, "we appear to be not citizens, but taxpayers who merely exchange money for services." "The thing that is most worrisome for me," Blakely added in an interview, "is this kind of 'forting up,' turning our backs on what I think is the nation's civic destiny—a more heterogenous, open society. We are a society that is seeking to bring people of all income levels and races together, but this is the direct opposition of that. How can the nation have a social con-

tract without having social contact?" Gated communities have brought a dramatic reduction in certain kinds of property crime, such as automobile theft, but seemed to reduce overall crime rates only marginally. Nevertheless, the overwhelming perception among residents remained that gated communities offered greater security for persons and property. Blakely and Snyder, though, noted other consequences. They observed, for instance, that as more private communities provide security, parks, maintenance, recreation, and garbage collection for their residents, those who cannot afford to live in such neighborhoods will have become more dependent on the reduced, and often inadequate, services of city and county governments. Then, too, Blakely concluded, "the more you lock places up . . . the places left unlocked become even more susceptible to problems, so are you going to lock everybody up? Where is that going to lead?"

Sources:
Edward J. Blakely, "Places to Hide," *American Demographics*, 19 (May 1997): 22–25.

Blakely and Mary Gail Snyder, *Fortress America: Gated Communities in the United States* (Washington, D.C.: Brookings Institution Press, 1997).

Martha Binig Drake, "Upscale Home Owners Cluster in New 'Gated Communities,'" *Houston Business Journal* (5 September 1995): 1–2.

James Lardner, "The Urge to Splurge," *U.S. News & World Report*, 126 (24 May 1999): 48–52.

Carol Tucker, "Gated Communities: The Barriers Go Up," *Public Management*, 80 (May 1998): 22–25.

Lisa M. Whiteney, "Homebuilders Prepare for Baby Boomers," *Phoenix Business Journal* (27 March 1998): 21–22.

CELLULAR PHONES

The hottest new personal communications device for many Americans during the decade was the cellular phone. Though cellular service had been available since the early 1980s, the sales of cell phones rose as service and equipment became more affordable. For most users, cellular service fell into three categories: 1) portable phones small enough to be carried in a purse or shirt pocket, 2) personal beepers that signaled the holder with a message, and 3) mobile phones that were often permanently installed in vehicles. By 1998 more than sixty-three million Americans were using some type of cellular phone service. With the rise of cellular use, however, society was confronted with a host of new problems resulting from noisy phones and beepers going off everywhere from churches to classrooms, movie theaters to restaurants. Perhaps the biggest problem debated was the use of cell phones while driving. According to a study published in the *New England Journal of Medicine*, people talking on a cell phone while driving were four times more likely to be in an accident than the average driver. Those odds placed the cell-phone driver on the same level as someone driving drunk. Several state legislatures and city halls proposed bills that would ban the use of cellular phones while driving.

Sources: Csaba Csere, "Driven to Distraction Digitally," *Car and Driver*, 45 (December 1999): 11.

Jacqueline Simmons, "Safe, Annoying," *Wall Street Journal*, 16 August 1996.

HOMOSEXUALITY

Gay Politics. The dynamic of homosexual politics in the 1990s consisted of gays and lesbians trying to establish themselves in mainstream American life and the efforts of conservatives to resist such a fundamental cultural change. Many Americans, meanwhile, seem to have drifted toward a somewhat uneasy accommodation with homosexuality. According to a *Time*/CNN poll conducted in 1998, 64 percent of those questioned believed that homosexual relations were acceptable, while 48 percent thought them morally wrong. Twenty years earlier, in 1978, 53 percent of Americans thought homosexual relations were morally unacceptable and only 41 percent found them permissible. Indisputably, there were more gay men and women visible in American society during the 1990s than at any other time in U.S. history. "I think we've done a great deal of persuading people that we are not a countercultural force," explained Andrew Sullivan, the author of *Love Undetectable: Notes on Friendship, Sex, and Survival* (1998) and former editor of the *New Republic*. "We are a mainstream force." As a consequence of the homosexual embrace of mainstream society, antigay activists had to alter their basic strategy. No longer able to demonize homosexuals, critics, such as Senate majority leader Chester Trent Lott

(R-Mississippi), compared them to individuals who were afflicted with alcoholism or kleptomania, regarding homosexuality as an illness that can be cured. A major effort in this respect came from Transformation Ministries, a branch of Exodus International, a nondenominational Christian fellowship dedicated to helping homosexuals change their orientation. According to a 1998 *Newsweek* poll, 56 percent of respondents believed that gay men and lesbians could alter their sexual orientation through therapy, will power, or religious conviction. Even as the debate raged over whether homosexuality was genetically inherited or the result of experience and environment, gay and lesbian organizations went from being outcasts to being an expected, and even welcomed, presence in politics, at least among Democratic coalitions. "The whole public attitude on gay issues has become much more mainstream," observed Al From, cofounder and president of the Democratic Leadership Council. "A lot more people are dealing with gays in their families."

The Clinton Administration. Many activists on both sides of the question regard the election of Bill Clinton as a turning point in the debate over gay rights, even though Clinton's support for gays was unsteady and equivocal. His policy of "Don't ask, Don't tell" for gays in the military satisfied no one. In addition, he signed the Defense of Marriage Act (21 September 1996), which denied federal recognition to same-sex marriages. Yet, Clinton also ended the federal policy of treating homosexuals as security risks and was the first president to invite gay activists to the White House. The message Clinton sent was that gays were not only a part of America but that they were becoming an important political constituency as well. Meanwhile, a new kind of gay-lobbying group emerged during the 1990s. Gone was the militant tribalism of ACT UP and Queer Nation. In their place was the Human Rights Campaign (HRC). Founded in 1980, the HRC corresponded to the impulses within the gay community to join the mainstream. As of 1998, membership in the HRC stood at 250,000. "The Clinton elections took the wind out of the sails of the street activists," declared John Gallagher, national correspondent for the *Advocate*, a gay monthly news magazine. "They used to be outside shouting. Now people have to be inside talking, which is a new experience." Even the Republican Party had to respond. In 1998, Jim Nicholson, chairman of the Republican National Committee (RNC), made a point of welcoming gays into the party. In the Senate, a small number of conservatives, including presidential candidates Orrin G. Hatch (R-Utah) and John S. McCain III (R-Arizona), quietly moved closer to gay advocacy groups on such issues as hate-crime legislation, although they remained aloof on the issue of gay marriage. Opponents on the Christian Right, however, became more adamant in their condemnation. One-time presidential candidate Gary Bauer, head of the Family Research Council, made opposition to gay rights a defining issue of his campaign. Pat Robertson, president of the Christian Broadcasting Network (CBN), insisted that "the

Two same-sex marriages performed outside the Raleigh, North Carolina, General Assembly on 17 July 1996 to protest state legislators who were debating a bill to ban recognition of such unions (AP/Wide World Photos)

acceptance of homosexuality is the last step in the decline of Gentile civilization."

Hate Crimes. Violent assaults against homosexuals were nothing new in the 1990s, but the savage attack on University of Wyoming student Matthew Shepard that took place in Laramie, Wyoming, on 7 October 1998 (Shepard died from his injuries on 12 October) focused renewed national attention on the issue. A *Time*/CNN survey conducted at the time, the results of which were no doubt influenced by Shepard's murder, revealed that 76 percent of those questioned favored increased penalties for those who commit "hate crimes" against homosexuals. By the end of the decade, forty-two states had passed hate-crime statutes, and twenty-two specifically listed homosexuals as a possible class of victims. Nevertheless, Kris Pratt, a policy advocate at HCR, argued that "America is still largely ignoring hate crimes against gays and lesbians." In part, Pratt and others have suggested, the rising violence against homosexuals was simply a response to the more visible public presence of gays in American life. "When the larger society is faced with the gay and lesbian experience," said Pratt, "the more violent segments of that society often react in very heinous ways by bashing back."

The Antigay Backlash. Less dramatic but equally revealing about American attitudes toward homosexuality was the growing backlash against gay rights. In West Hartford, Connecticut, in 1998, for example, the city council denied a gay couple the right to purchase a reduced-rate family pass to a municipal swimming pool. This incident,

hardly a major setback in the struggle for gay rights, nevertheless represented to many a new set of barriers that gays faced. Although partner benefits were not placed in jeopardy, the accumulation of similar setbacks raised questions about whether Americans had reached the limit of their tolerance for gay rights as the decade drew to a close. On the national level the backlash took familiar forms. Most glaring, the number of hate crimes rose while the overall crime rate declined. Despite the Clinton administration policy of "Don't ask, Don't tell" the dismissal of gay servicemen and servicewomen increased 67 percent between 1994 and 1997. At the same time, twenty-eight states enacted legislation outlawing gay marriages. In February 1998 Maine became the first state to reverse a gay-rights ordinance prohibiting discrimination in housing and employment. Although polls suggested that the majority of Americans accepted civil rights for gays, those same persons became uneasy with the morality of homosexuality. In a *Newsweek* survey conducted in 1998, 83 percent of those queried agreed that gays deserved equal rights to employment and 75 percent agreed that housing discrimination against gays ought to be against the law. Fifty-two percent believed that homosexuals ought to be able to inherit their partner's property and Social Security benefits. Yet, 54 percent declared that homosexual relations were sinful.

Same-Sex Marriage. Moral reservations also explained why most Americans during the decade did not support same-sex marriages. Despite this widespread opposition, however, scholars as well as advocates and critics of gay rights regarded the ruling of the Supreme Court of Vermont in the case of *Baker* v. *State* (December 1999) as a legal landmark in the controversy about equal marriage rights for homosexuals. The justices declared that "the extension of the Common Benefits Clause [of the Vermont Constitution] to acknowledge plaintiffs as Vermonters who seek nothing more, nor less, than legal protection and security for their avowed commitment to an intimate and lasting human relationship is simply, when all is said and done, a recognition of our common humanity." In response to the decision, the editors of the *New Republic* wrote: "legalizing gay marriage . . . is not a radical reformation of an unchanging institution. It is the long-overdue correction of a moral anomaly that dehumanizes and excludes a significant portion of the human race." Most Americans disagreed: a *Newsweek* survey showed that only 33 percent supported the legalization of gay marriage. In Vermont, 52 percent opposed the Supreme Court ruling.

Sources:

Scott Baldauf, "Do Homosexuals Need More Legal Protections?" *Christian Science Monitor* (14 October 1998): 3.

John Leland and Mark Miller, "Can Gays 'Convert'?" *Newsweek,* 132 (17 August 1998): 46–50.

Marc Peyser, "Battling Backlash," *Newsweek,* 132 (17 August 1998): 50–52.

"Separate but Equal?" *New Republic,* 222 (10 January 2000): 9.

Andrew Sullivan, *Love Undetectable: Notes on Friendship, Sex, and Survival* (New York: Knopf, 1998).

THE INTERNET REVOLUTION

E-Commerce. Wearing smart, tailored business suits or sneakers and khakis may not fit the stereotype, but Jeffrey P. Bezos, Meg Whitman, and Jay Walker were 1990s-style revolutionaries. Each heads a company that radically transformed the way Americans and people around the world shop. Although on-line shopping represented only a small fraction of total consumer sales, that fraction did not exist as recently as 1995. As of 1999 the estimated revenue generated from e-commerce exceeded $184 billion. Yet, this figure constituted only 1 percent of the American economy, and on-line sales accounted for approximately .2 percent of total retail sales. These statistics produced a few skeptics. Stephen Roach, chief global economist at Morgan Stanley Dean Witter, for instance, suspects that e-commerce is being "oversold." "I question if it'll ever be big," Roach admitted. Such doubts notwithstanding, a few years ago no one had heard of Bezos, Whitman, and Walker; now their companies are household names. Bezos built Amazon.com into the largest bookseller in the world and has recently expanded it to sell videos, compact discs, toys, tools, electronics, and a host of other items. Whitman, the CEO of the on-line auction site eBay.com, insists that "we are enabling a kind of commerce that didn't exist to any extent before and that's person-to-person contact." Corporate marketing expert Walker created Priceline.com, a service that initially enabled customers to name their own price for

---

Y2K

One of the biggest concerns during the last year of the decade was the "Y2K" bug. As early as 1997 it had been officially determined that many computers, from those operated in agencies of the federal government to those found in individual homes, might not "recognize" the year 2000. The result would be the crashing of systems everywhere from Automatic Teller Machines (ATMs) to electrical grids and hospital equipment to the possible detonation of atomic weapons. For many persons hearing the phrase "Y2K ready" on everything from their banks to national government agencies meant that all systems were in compliance. For others, though, the Y2K problem signaled nothing less than the possible end of the world. All over the country, people stocked up on power generators, dried and canned food, bottled water, guns, and ammunition in preparation for a New Year's Day that would begin in chaos. Y2K fears spawned a host of associated products and businesses from survival videos to websites to agencies that for a fee reserved places in Y2K-safe communities. Most Americans, however, took the whole thing in stride; as early as January of 1999 almost 40 percent of persons surveyed believed that the Y2K problem was not something about which to be terribly concerned.

Sources: "Auld Lang Sigh," *Time,* 154 (29 November 1999): 56–67.

"Y2K: Still Waiting," *Time,* 153 (15 March 1999): 26.

---

airline tickets. Subsequently, Walker extended the service to include hotel rooms, mortgages, and automobiles, and plans to apply the "name-your-own-price" scheme to groceries. Like other on-line moguls, Bezos, Whitman, and Walker are convinced that the Internet will drastically alter the way business is conducted and affect every industry on the planet, primarily by empowering consumers in ways unimaginable before the advent of the new computer technology.

Politics. "E-Campaigning has been upgraded from novelty to necessity," wrote Howard Fineman, the political correspondent for *Newsweek.* "Candidates must now compete in the wilds of the Web," Fineman continued, "a world with its own rules. Politics and governing may never be the same." With growing sophistication and urgency, political candidates in the 1990s turned to the Internet to advertise, organize, and influence, to say nothing of solicit donations. The Internet enjoyed its political coming of age in 1998 during the Minnesota gubernatorial campaign of Jesse Ventura. An independent candidate with no party structure and no political endorsements to support him, Ventura conducted much of his campaign through the Internet, from which he received 67 percent of his fund-raising pledges. "The Internet didn't win it for

---

An advertising manager for Coldwater Creek in Sandpoint, Idaho, preparing a company website for e-commerce (AP/Wide World Photos)

us," asserted Philip Madsen, Ventura's Webmaster, "but we couldn't have won without it." Presidential candidates were quick to adopt Ventura's methods. Al Gore, Bill Bradley, Steve Forbes, John S. McCain, and George W. Bush each established elaborate web sites. Forbes's campaign manager, Bill DalCol, even vowed to run "the first Internet-based campaign." A survey conducted by the University of California, Santa Barbara, suggested that these efforts were not misplaced because 50 percent of all adults living in the United States have access to the Internet either at home or at work. More than half that number use the Internet to explore political topics. In addition, the survey found that for 36 million Americans the Internet is the main source of news and information. These developments prompted Fineman to conclude that "the Internet is fast becoming a Virtual New Hampshire: a quirky but pivotal place where campaigns are launched or scuttled, where savvy organizers and voters roam in search of action, answers and influence."

Education. According to a Department of Education survey, 51 percent of American classrooms were connected to the Internet in 1998. In addition to providing students at virtually all levels access to a staggering quantity and variety of information, the Internet revolutionized education by allowing "distance learning," enabling students and teachers to interact despite the separation of distance. This nontraditional education appeals principally to adults completing bachelor's or master's degrees, or to those trying to enhance the knowledge and skills needed for their jobs. By the end of 1999 American colleges and universities offered more than six thousand accredited courses through the Internet. That number will likely grow as for-profit companies enter the market, many affiliating with accredited colleges and universities.

Privacy. Among the most alarming prospects to accompany the widespread use of the Internet is the invasion of privacy, which might include the theft of identity. All that is required is someone's name and Social Security number. Financial institutions such as banks and mortgage companies, HMOs and other health-care providers, and departments of motor vehicles are the most common businesses and agencies to use Social Security numbers to identify customers and clients. Eventually, that information ends up in an on-line data bank, even if the patron did not originally submit it through the Internet. Peter G. Neumann of SRI International called identity theft the "hidden downside of computing." Beth Grossman of the Federal Trade Commission (FTC) added, "Before, you had to go to the county courthouse to find that information. Not anymore." The Internet made it possible for criminals to access marriage licenses, property records, and motor-vehicle information with the click of a mouse. Even on-line commerce has inadvertently threatened privacy. According to Richard M. Smith of Phar Lap Software, a firm specializing in Internet security, the operator of any website can track and reconstruct the activities of any visitor. Smith likens the Internet to a VCR "constantly recording when you come in, who you talked to and maybe what you talked about." Some critics maintain that even e-mail can become an intrusive invasion of privacy by rendering an individual accessible to his or her employer day and night, across time zones, oceans, and continents, and thereby erasing the distinction between private life and work. Sociologist Sherry Turkle of the Massachusetts Institute of Technology has argued that American culture in the 1990s experienced a mass identity crisis, with men and women clinging to a former sense of privacy in a world in which technology has made it possible to probe the most intimate aspects of people's lives. "It's a very schizophrenic time," Turkle declared. "We have very unstable notions about the boundaries of the individual."

Security. Some breaches of Internet security can have even more far-reaching consequences than interfering with users' credit, tarnishing their good name, or placing them always on call. Hackers can compromise the integrity of corporations or threaten national security. Such was the case when hackers from the Russian Academy of Science targeted the computer systems at the Departments of Defense and Energy, as well as those at various defense contractors and civilian universities. They acquired a vast amount of sensitive data that included classified naval codes and information on missile-guidance systems. Pentagon officials declared that this attempt was nothing less than "a state-sponsored Russian intelligence effort to get U.S. technology." Deputy Secretary of Defense John Harme regarded this violation of security as so serious that he told colleagues that "We're in the middle of a cyberwar."

Regulation. The real problem, according to Kevin Kelly, executive editor of *Wired* magazine, is that although Americans claimed to value their privacy, they "think that privacy is about information, but it's not—it's about relationships." In Kelly's view, there was no privacy in the traditional village or small town. Everyone knew about their neighbor's affairs. Yet, that arrangement seemed comfortable and could even be reassuring. "There was a symmetry to the knowledge," Kelly has pointed out. "What's gone out of whack is we don't know who knows about us anymore. Privacy has become asymmetrical." In the 1990s computer and surveillance technology outpaced ethics and law. Nevertheless, Kelly opposed a federal privacy law as even more restrictive and intrusive. The key, experts such as Kelly agree, is to restore the balance between the need and desire to know and the respect for the privacy of the individual. As with other technological innovations, especially those such as the Internet that have the potential to alter fundamental social arrangements and relations, a vast array of social, political, and ethical questions will have to be addressed and answered to ensure that the instrument will be put to the most wholesome and beneficent uses possible.

Sources:

Bruce Bimber, "Research on Information Technology and Democracy," *Bruce Bimber Research Page, University of California, Santa Barbara, Department of Political Science,* Internet website.

Gary S. Becker, "How the Web is Revolutionizing Learning," *Business Week* (27 December 1999): 40.

Chandra Devi, "Potential of Internet-based Education," *New Straits Times-Management* (13 December 1999).

Joshua Quittner, "Invasion of Privacy," *Time,* 150 (25 August 1997): 28–35.

MANNERS

The Rise of Incivility. Incivility seemed to penetrate every aspect of American life during the 1990s. A survey conducted in February 1996 by *U.S. News & World Report* and Bozell Worldwide revealed that 90 percent of Americans believed incivility in speech and conduct was a serious social problem. Seventy-eight percent of respondents thought that the problem had worsened during the 1990s, and more than 84 percent saw in incivility evidence of social disorder portending crisis and collapse. The poll concluded that a vast majority of Americans felt themselves embattled, and perhaps imperiled, in their personal and professional lives by the rising tide of vulgarity, discourtesy, and inconsideration. Many Americans came to believe that the real issue underlying bad manners was the loss of a basic sense of respect for others. "You cannot have a complex society in which you do not hear the other party, the antagonist," explained Martin Marty, a noted scholar of religion, in 1996. "The alternative to civility is first incivility," Marty concluded, "and then it is war."

A Culture of Incivility? Americans in the 1990s were ambivalent about their own bad behavior. On the one

"ROAD RAGE"

American drivers became ruder, meaner, and more dangerous than ever in the 1990s. By 1998 "aggressive driving" incidents, in which an angry or impatient driver tries to hurt or in some cases even kill another driver, had risen by 51 percent since the beginning of the decade. In several cases studied, 37 percent of those drivers used firearms against other drivers; 28 percent used other weapons; and 35 percent used their cars. Fear of drivers and "road rage" has become so pervasive that in a 1996 poll, residents of Maryland, Washington, D.C., and Virginia listed it as a more pressing concern than drunk drivers. The phenomenon has since given rise to many books, articles, and special therapies that deal specifically with the problem. "Road Rage" has become so prevalent that legislation to punish offenders is currently under discussion in Congress. Experts agree that aggressive driving has become the "norm" for many drivers now, generating a new American subculture. Studies have shown that increased traffic and longer commutes pave the way for shorter tempers and in some cases aggressive and dangerous behavior. Other factors that have contributed to the problem are the increasing popularity of trucks and SUVs, which, because of their height and weight, give the driver a greater feeling of power and invincibility than those in regular-sized automobiles.

Sources: Sidney Callahan, "Oh Behave," *Commonweal,* 126 (17 December 1999): 8–10.

Michael A. Lipton and Jennifer Mendelsohn, *People,* 15 (10 May): 256–260.

A California state trooper investigates an apparent "road rage" accident on Interstate 5, near Sylmar, on 14 January 1998 (AP/Wide World Photos).

hand, Americans did not want children to talk rudely to parents, students to disrespect teachers, or politicians to insult one another. On the other hand, they continued to applaud rebels in government and popular culture who did not always play by the rules or rely on genteel courtesies to get what they wanted. Americans especially enjoyed the spectacle of a good fight, as the competitiveness of sports and politics, the violence and coarseness of television and the movies, and the aggressiveness and vulgarity of pop music made clear. Another symptom of the decline of civility during the 1990s was the spectacle of the public confession combined with the incessant invasion of privacy. "Popular culture shines its klieg lights on the most intimate corners of our lives," wrote Joshua Quittner of *Time*, "and most of us play right along. If all we really wanted was to be left alone, explain the lasting popularity of Oprah and Sally and Ricki tell-all TV. Memoirs top the best-seller lists, with books about incest and insanity and illness leading the way." The ambiguous attitudes about incivility had experts asking whether a certain level of incivility was not key to being an American.

The Return of Etiquette. Surprisingly, the popularity of etiquette returned in the 1990s. Such books as Marjabelle Young Stewart and Marian Faux's *Executive Etiquette in the New Workplace* (1994), Norine Dresser's *Multicultural Manners: New Rules of Etiquette for a Changing Society* (1996), Wendy Reid Crisp's *Do As I Say, Not As I Did: Perfect Advice from an Imperfect Mother* (1997), and Judith Martin's *Miss Manners' Guide to Excruciatingly Correct Behavior* (1982) proliferated. "Manners are the

new status accessory," suggested etiquette expert Stewart. "Pricier than a Rolex, more portable than a Day-Timer, and shinier than handmade shoes . . . polished graces can get you where you're going faster than a speeding BMW."

Sources:

Wendy Reid Crisp, *Do As I Say, Not As I Did: Perfect Advice from an Imperfect Mother* (New York: Berkley, 1997).

Norine Dresser, *Multicultural Manners: New Rules of Etiquette for a Changing Society* (New York: Wiley, 1996).

Owen Edwards, "End of the Rude," *Town & Country*, 146 (June 1992): 47–48.

John Marks, "The American Uncivil Wars," *U.S. News & World Report*, 120 (22 April 1996): 66–72.

Judith Martin, *Miss Manners' Guide for the Turn of the Millennium* (New York: Fireside, 1990).

Joshua Quittner, "Invasion of Privacy," *Time*, 150 (25 August 1997): 28–35.

Marjabelle Young Stewart and Marian Faux, *Executive Etiquette in the New Workplace* (New York: St. Martin's Press, 1994).

"No Norms," *Wall Street Journal*, 233 (22 April 1999): A22.

THE NEW SPIRITUALISM

New Age. In 1981 pollster Daniel Yankelovich estimated that 80 percent of Americans were affected, either strongly or marginally, by some form of spiritualism and the ethos of self-help and fulfillment. Ten years later a survey commissioned by the City University of New York to gather data on American religious beliefs and attitudes found only 28,000 Americans willing to identify themselves with significant aspects of New Age spiritualism. These statistics, which forecast the apparent demise of the New Age spiritualist movement in the United States, did not tell the full story. One indication that spiritualism con-

FENG SHUI

From the boardroom to the bedroom and in about every other living space possible, the principles of Feng Shui, or "wind and water," became one of the interior-design industry's hottest trends during the 1990s. Based on the ancient Chinese theory of organizing positive energy or "ch'i" in living and working spaces, Feng Shui seeks to create the most harmonious balance possible between the exterior and interior elements of one's environment, as well as the personal energy of the individual. Translating it into everyday applications, the serious practitioner of Feng Shui studies a space to make sure that everything from the placement of furniture to the room color to the pictures or mirrors hanging on the walls is in "balance" with the forces of nature. Architects also studied the theory in determining the best placement for a building so that positive energy forces would be utilized. Homeowners solicited the help of Feng Shui practitioners and priests to coordinate their homes and offices in order to avoid the pitfalls of financial ruin, bad luck, and tense family relations.

Sources: Skye Alexander, "Feng Shui," *Better Homes & Gardens*, 77 (April 1999): 90–93.

Winifred Gallagher, "How Places Affect People," *Architectural Digest*, 187 (February 1999): 74–80.

tinued to thrive in the United States during the 1990s was the market, numbering in the millions, for New Age books, audiotapes, and videos. The number of New Age bookstores in the United States during the 1990s exceeded five thousand. According to David S. Toolan, S. J., the "crystal gazers and psychic channelers are the lunatic fringe" of the spiritualist movement. Most 1990s New Agers, Toolan argued, although more liminal than most Americans, share with many of their middle-class brethren a sense that the "American Dream" had broken down and that economic, social, political, educational, and ecclesiastical institutions no longer functioned well. For New Agers, modern life is superficial, hollow, and meaningless. Yet, they have not responded to the crisis of American civilization by embracing conservatism, nostalgia, or despair. On the contrary, the spiritualist movement became aggressively millennialist and messianic. Spiritualists welcomed the death of the old America as the necessary, if painful, prelude to a major cultural realignment that would produce a paradigm shift in medicine, psychology, science, politics, business, education, and religion. These changes, asserted spiritualists, would not lead to the mending but the remaking of American society. New Age spiritualism is "certainly the culmination of the 1960s generation coming to power in America," explained Gene Taback, president of Bookpeople, one of the largest distributors of New Age literature. There is also a strong link between the New Age spiritualism of the 1990s and the drug culture of the 1960s. "A lot of people

got their starts in the 1960s running head shops selling the tremendous number of products for consumption of recreational drugs," Tabak explained. "The 1960s set transcendence as an individual quest rather than as a traditional religious quest. But the idea of pharmacological transcendence has turned into a transcendence with more spiritual overtones and become New Age in the 1990s." Curiously, given their origins, New Agers may be reactionaries of a sort, the only Americans still left who wholeheartedly subscribe to the historic mission of the nation to create a *novus ordo saeculorum* (new sacred order)—a city upon a hill.

Spirituality in the Workplace. Increasingly during the 1990s the phenomenon of "corporate spiritualism" came to be introduced as a means of motivating employees by emphasizing their individual autonomy and responsibility. Indebted to the New Age movement, the advocates of corporate spiritualism have posited that human beings are not victims or pawns, and are thus not limited by conditions or conditioning. They are independent agents, and their success or failure depends solely on individual imagination and initiative. Neither organizational nor institutional factors ought to hinder personal achievement, productivity, or fulfillment. Corporate spirituality, experts contended, can enhance workers' "intuition," "energy," and "commitment." In *Awakening Corporate Soul: Four Paths to Unleash the Power of People at Work* (1998), Eric Klein and John B. Izzo argued that such "life forces" bring "the deepest and most dynamic energies into work. . . . Corporate Soul is the expression of this primary life-giving energy in work and the workplace. When Corporate Soul is awake, work flourishes, overflows, and manifests as productivity, creativity, innovation, and inspiration." Thus, it followed, that the corporation provided individuals with a medium through which to satisfy their needs and realize their goals, ideally forming an alternate community and family. With enthusiasm and even love directed toward work, employees theoretically were supposed to transform what was once a chore into a tool to develop, nourish, and enrich their lives. Workers, maintained Klein and Izzo, must "accept primary responsibility for [their] sense of fulfillment," even if the conditions under which they labor prove less than satisfactory. Therefore, an employee ought to be willing to adjust to the needs of the corporation, to make personal sacrifices, and to work harder not because "I have to but because this job is the place were [sic] I become more myself." In an effort to cement the link between employee self-fulfillment, job performance, and corporate profits, spiritual "inner-renewal" training programs gained momentum throughout the 1990s. A clear indication of the growing popularity of corporate spiritualism was the combined $30 billion that American companies spent during the decade to promote it among their employees. The advocates of New Age corporate spiritualism thereby sought to foster employees' identification with a "spiritualized corporate image," making work the means of "self-actualization" and "self-fulfillment."

Buddhists meditating in Central Park, New York City,
in June 1999 (AP/Wide World Photos)

Evangelical Capitalism. Although a heterogenous group, evangelical Christians have shared a commitment to fashioning a social order grounded in the free enterprise system and the nuclear family and the elimination of government-sponsored welfare programs perceived to foster dependency on the state, undermine the family, alter traditional gender roles, and promote moral decay. Ultimately, this Christian society is anchored in the reconstruction of an idealized America that would promote devotion to family, patriotism, hard work, individual freedom, responsibility, and morality. In a sense, it can be argued that evangelicals have Christianized the self-help movement. During the 1990s evangelical Christians worked toward achieving their social vision not only through political action and religious conversion, but through business and commerce as well. They asserted an intimate connection between America, capitalism, and Christianity. Christian capitalists believed that religion not only belonged in the workplace but that it was essential to economic success. As a class, the Christian capitalists of the 1990s were primarily managers, professionals, and the owners of small businesses. They were mostly male, predominantly southern, and overwhelmingly members of nondenominational Protestant churches. Evangelical executives tended to regard themselves as spiritual and economic leaders, engaged in a covenant with God and a custodial relationship with their

families, their employees, and their customers. Jesus, for many of them, was the ultimate CEO. According to Laurie Beth Jones's popular manual *Jesus, CEO: Using Ancient Wisdom for Visionary Leadership* (1995), Christ adhered to all the basic precepts of effective organizational management: "Jesus regularly visualized the success of his efforts." "Jesus kept in constant contact with his boss." "Jesus knew his mission statement, and he did not deviate from it." Increasingly influential, Christian capitalists during the 1990s were determined to make their mark on American society. "Support of Christian businesses is one area where we can [regain control of] our culture and politics is another," asserted Bob Reese, vice president of Flowdata, a Dallas company that manufactures industrial meters. Many Christian capitalists, such as Norm Miller, chairman of Interstate Batteries, thus used a portion of their profits to finance conservative political causes. Miller, for example, donated large sums to the Free Market Foundation, which helps voters in Texas identify socially conservative political candidates. Some Christian capitalists have given money directly to the Republican Party, while others, such as S. Truett Cathy, CEO of Chick-Fil-A fast-food restaurants, have funded local or regional social-welfare programs. Such stewardship was among the most important responsibilities of successful Christian capitalists. "When one of your restaurant operators is sitting on a $500,000 investment and not doing anything with it," Cathy insists, "he is not being a steward of the Lord." Throughout the 1990s the economic and political power of conservative Christian capitalists and Christian groups continued to grow. These entrepreneurs and organizations clearly wanted to exercise greater influence on how the nation conducted business, promoting both individually responsible spiritual lives and a socially responsible economic system. "For too long," declared Republican strategist William Bennett, "religious conservatives have been ignored, and now they are trying to take back their institutions one by one."

Sources:

Laurie Beth Jones, *Jesus, CEO: Using Ancient Wisdom for Visionary Leadership* (New York: Hyperion, 1995).

Eric Klein and John B. Izzo, *Awakening Corporate Soul: Four Paths to Unleash the Power of People at Work* (Leucadia, California: Fair Winds Press, 1998).

Dan McGraw, "The Christian Capitalists," *U.S. News & World Report*, 118 (13 March 1995): 52–62.

David S. Toolan, S. J., "Harmonic Convergence and All That: New Age Spirituality," *Cross Currents*, 46 (Fall 1996): 369–379.

PETS IN THE 1990S

Ownership. Pets of all kinds became increasingly prominent in U.S. households during the 1990s. According to a 1996 survey undertaken by the American Veterinary Medical Association (AVMA), 59 percent of American households owned at least one pet. Yet, the same survey also indicated that as the population aged, the percentage of pet-owning households declined. In 1996, 27 percent of American households owned a cat, down from 31 percent in 1987. Those who did own pets, however, were likely to own more of them in the 1990s than a decade earlier. The average number of dogs in households was

A funeral for a greyhound in Brooklyn, New York, on 26 December 1997 (AP/Wide World Photos)

1.69 in 1996, up from 1.51 in 1987. The average number of cats was 2.19 in 1996, up from 1.95 in 1987. The total number of dogs owned increased from 52.4 million in 1987 to 52.9 million in 1996; cats increased from 54.6 million to 59.1 million during that same period. In addition to these animals, Americans during the 1990s owned 13 million birds, 4 million horses, 6 million rabbits, 6 million ferrets, 5 million rodents, 3.5 million reptiles, and 56 million fish. Sixty-eight percent of owners consider their pets members of the family. Thirty-seven percent carried pictures of their pets in their wallets; 31 percent took days off from work when their pets were ill; 28 percent talked to their pets on the telephone; 27 percent celebrated their pets' birthdays with a party; 79 percent allowed their pets to sleep with them.

Economic Impact. Pets may make life more pleasant, but owning them also makes it more expensive. In the 1990s only 48 percent of American households with incomes of less than $12,000 owned a pet compared with 61 percent with an income of between $25,000 and $39,999 and 65 percent with an income of $40,000 or more. During the decade the retail market in pet products increased at the rate of between 10 percent and 15 percent a year, according to Ken Banks, senior vice president of marketing, branding, and advertising for PetsMart. Other retailers were not slow to respond to the trend. Wal-Mart, Ames, and grocery-store chains such as Wegmans and Shop Rite all developed special pet shops to sell food, acces-

sories, and high-margin items. There was a simple explanation for all the effort in the opinion of pet expert Warren Eckstein, author, with Denise Madden, of *Memoirs of a Pet Therapist* (1998). Americans so cherish their pets that they become more and more willing to change their lives for them. "People will give up their own needs for their pets," Eckstein said, "so where they shop for pets can determine where they'll buy other items." Indeed, a fundamental change took place in the economic relations between Americans and their pets during the 1990s. Retail was only one part of the overall picture. By 1999 the pet business was a $23 billion industry comprised of pet superstores, Internet companies, medical organizations, and media ventures. Veterinarians also witnessed the transformation of their profession, as a growing number of Americans spent sums on pet health care that would have been unthinkable even a decade before. Pet care alone generated $11 billion in annual revenue during the second half of the decade. Inevitably, the rising costs of this medical care led to the creation of pet HMOs. In 1999, for example, Jack Stephens's company, Veterinary Pet Insurance, issued 850,000 policies in forty-six states.

Pets and the Law. The two chief animal-related problems requiring legislative attention during the 1990s were overpopulation and the prevention of pet shops from stocking dogs acquired from puppy mills. According to statistics compiled by the Humane Society of the United States, more than fifty thousand puppies and kittens were born each day throughout the decade, largely because of the uncontrolled breeding of pets. Between four and six million dogs and cats were destroyed each year because they were unwanted. Abandoned and stray animals also posed a health risk to humans and other animals. During the decade thirty-two states and the District of Columbia enacted legislation addressing the issue of animal overpopulation. Fifteen others, Arizona, Arkansas, California, Connecticut, Florida, Illinois, Maine, Minnesota, Nevada, New Hampshire, New York, Pennsylvania, South Carolina, Vermont, and Virginia, passed "lemon laws" for pets, compelling retailers to provide complete health information about the animals they sell and enabling consumers to return pets for a certain number of days after purchasing them. On the federal level, the Pet Safety and Protection Act of 1999 eliminated the purchase of dogs and cats from random sources, the alleged route whereby stolen pets end up in research facilities.

Sources:

Faye Brookman, "The Things People Do For Pets!" *Discount Store News*, 38 (25 October 1999): 17–21.

Warren Eckstein and Denise Madden, *Memoirs of a Pet Therapist* (New York: Fawcett Columbine, 1998).

Brad Edmondson and Josh Galper, "Pet Places," *American Demographics*, 20 (September 1998): 38–40.

Janice Sparhawk Gardner, "The Canine Legislative Beat," *Dog World*, 84 (August 1999): 82–86.

Chester Hicks, "Dog Day Legislation: Cats and Canines are of Concern at the Capitol," *State Government News*, 42 (April 1999): 31–32.

John Marks, "Tail of the Pampered Pooch," *U.S. News & World Report*, 126 (17 May 1999): 46–48.

RACE AND ETHNICITY

The Politics of Race Relations. In proposing a national "conversation" on race in 1996, President Clinton asked "can we fulfill the promise of America by embracing all our citizens of all races. . . . Can we become one America in the 21st century?" If the United States could become "the world's first truly great multiracial, multiethnic democracy," Clinton declared, then it would "rewrite the rules of human evolution." Clinton's avowed political purpose in announcing this dialogue was to defend preferential forms of affirmative action. Yet, despite the president's aspirations, only 4 percent of the respondents to a 1996 Pew Research Center survey thought race relations a serious enough problem to be a top priority of the federal government. Data complied from several sources suggested that the continued government policy of defining people according to racial criteria was in part responsible for the mounting tensions that surfaced during the 1990s among African Americans, whites, Asians, and Hispanics. These tensions were perhaps most dramatically exemplified by the trials of Rodney King and O. J. Simpson, in which many perceived blacks as feeling a stronger allegiance to the members of their racial group than to fellow citizens and to be more concerned with their own advancement than with the achievement of justice.

Racial and Ethnic Convergence. With an intermarriage rate of 40 percent among persons of Hispanic descent and

On 3 October 1995 students at Augustana College in Rock Island, Illinois, react to the acquittal of O. J. Simpson (AP/Wide World Photos).

This initiative measure is submitted to the people in accordance with the provisions of Article II, Section 8 of the Constitution.

This initiative measure expressly amends the Constitution by adding a section thereto; therefore, new provisions proposed to be added are printed in *italic type* to indicate that they are new.

PROPOSED AMENDMENT TO ARTICLE I

Section 31 is added to Article I of the California Constitution as follows:

SEC. 31. (a) The state shall not discriminate against, or grant preferential treatment to, any individual or group on the basis of race, sex, color, ethnicity, or national origin in the operation of public employment, public education, or public contracting.

(b) This section shall apply only to action taken after the section's effective date.

(c) Nothing in this section shall be interpreted as prohibiting bona fide qualifications based on sex which are reasonably necessary to the normal operation of public employment, public education, or public contracting.

(d) Nothing in this section shall be interpreted as invalidating any court order or consent decree which is in force as of the effective date of this section.

(e) Nothing in this section shall be interpreted as prohibiting action which must be taken to establish or maintain eligibility for any federal program, where ineligibility would result in a loss of federal funds to the state.

(f) For the purposes of this section, "state" shall include, but not necessarily be limited to, the state itself, any city, county, city and county, public university system, including the University of California, community college district, school district, special district, or any other political subdivision or governmental instrumentality of or within the state.

(g) The remedies available for violations of this section shall be the same, regardless of the injured party's race, sex, color, ethnicity, or national origin, as are otherwise available for violations of then-existing California antidiscrimination law.

(h) This section shall be self-executing. If any part or parts of this section are found to be in conflict with federal law or the United States Constitution, the section shall be implemented to the maximum extent that federal law and the United States Constitution permit. Any provision held invalid shall be severable from the remaining portions of this section.

Source: California Secretary of State, *Vote96,* Internet website.

---

50 percent among those of Asian descent, most students of racial and ethnic demographics agree that the United States faces a future in which the majority, or near majority, of its citizens will be of mixed race and ethnicity. Even the intermarriage of blacks and whites, despite the enduring cultural impediments to such unions, became more prevalent during the 1990s, especially among young, middle-class, college-educated blacks. Still, black-white intermarriage remained strikingly less common than intermarriage between the members of other groups. The prospect of a mixed racial and ethnic citizenry in the future has elicited varied responses. To some, this demographic projection has suggested that American society and government had better attend to the needs of its minority citizens and residents who will soon be in the majority. To others, it has meant that the federal government should restrict immigration in order to avoid the advent of a "non-white majority" in fifty or one hundred years. To civil-rights activists and those concerned to maintain the power of specific minorities, it has prompted objections to the official recognition of multiracial and multiethnic identities. Such unwieldy complexities, after all, would make it even more difficult to advance programs and legislation designed to end discrimination against a single, homogeneous group.

Changing Attitudes. An additional response to the changing racial and ethnic composition of the United States was the growing opposition to preferential forms of affirmative action. The majority of Americans during the 1990s, fully 67 percent according to a *Wall Street Journal/NBC News* survey conducted in 1995, opposed affirmative action. The increasingly angry and divisive debate posed a conflict between two cherished American ideals: the belief that all Americans deserve equal opportunities and the idea that hard work and merit, not race or gender, ought to determine who prospers and who does not. The debate intensified during the early-to-mid 1990s, which were years of slow economic growth, stagnation of middle- and working-class incomes, and corporate downsizing. In 1995, Clint Bolick, cofounder of the Institute for Justice, summed up the changing sentiments about affirmative action saying "there's a great deal of pent-up anger beneath the surface of American politics that's looking for an outlet." These anxieties combined in the 1990s with a growing sense that affirmative action represented another instance of government intrusion and social engineering. The logic of affirmative action, that those hobbled by generations of bias could not hope to enjoy equal opportunities, made sense to many Americans during the 1960s. By the 1990s, however, many had come to believe that the government was not only working to ensure equality of opportunity but equality of condition, not only to give the disadvantaged a fair chance but to guarantee their success. The opposition to affirmative action culminated in California's Proposition 209, which outlawed racial and gender preferences in admission to colleges and universities. At the end of a decade of controversy, however, the questions at the heart of the affirmative action debate remained unanswered.

Sources:

Christopher Clausen, "Once More Around the Race Track," *New Leader,* 80 (6 October 1997): 10–12.

Jerelyn Eddings, "Counting a 'New' Type of American," *U.S. News & World Report,* 123 (14 July 1997): 22–23.

Joel Perlman, "Multiracials, Intermarriage, Ethnicity," *Society,* 34 (September/October 1997): 21–24.

Steven V. Roberts, "Affirmative Action on the Edge," *U.S. News & World Report,* 118 (13 February 1995): 32–38.

"Truth-Telling on Race," *Nation,* 265 (15 December 1997): 3–4.

WORK, WORKERS, AND THE WORKPLACE

Hours. During the 1990s, Americans became the workaholics of the world. Between 1977 and 1997 the average workweek among salaried employees working at least twenty hours lengthened from forty-three to forty-seven hours. During that same twenty-year period, according to James T. Bond, vice president of the Families and Work Institute, the number of workers putting in fifty or more hours per week increased from 24 percent to 37 percent. Americans who once viewed the work habits of the Japanese with horrified awe became the people working the longest hours in the industrial world. The average American worked the equivalent of eight weeks a year longer than the average Western European. In Norway and Sweden, for example, workers commonly receive between four and six weeks of vacation and up to a year of paid parental leave. In France, a maximum workweek of no more than thirty-five hours, promoted by the socialist government of Prime Minister Lionel Jospin as a means of reducing unemployment, is becoming the law of the land. The longer hours Americans spend on the job, however, have thus far translated into lower unemployment rates and greater prosperity in the United States. Approximately 10 percent unemployment was the norm across Western Europe. In the United States, by contrast, unemployment hovered at around 4.2 percent and, as of January 2000, economic expansion had continued for an unprecedented 106 consecutive months. Work and money came to occupy a greater portion of American life. The gains in income and prosperity seemed clear, but the costs to family, children, and health were only beginning to be sorted out by the end of the decade. According to Ellen Galinsky, president of the Families and Work Institute, in *Ask the Children: What America's Children Really Think About Working Parents*

DILBERT

Launched in 1989, the cartoon creation of former engineer Scott Adams emerged as the "everyman" of the corporate office in the 1990s. Adams, who did not know a thing about cartooning, bought a book on how to draw and then started sending his ideas out. His hapless Dilbert, the bespectacled nebbish "cubicle slave," symbolized much of what was wrong with business in America and soon struck a chord with readers everywhere. Unable to control his tie—much less his boss—Dilbert, along with Adams's other characters, dutifully endures meaningless initiatives, silly mission statements, and out-of-touch managers. Although it got off to a slow start, *Dilbert* eventually found its audience, mostly among young males aged twelve to thirty, and by the end of the decade appeared in more than seventeen hundred newspapers in fifty-one countries. The success of the comic strip was also translated into toys, book compilations, and an animated television show. Adams credits the strip's success to the notion that "there is a very large cubicle class out there and they don't really have any way of expressing their views. They could tell their bosses but it would get them fired." A measure of the accuracy of Adams's take on the workplace was gauged in a study that found the more-cynical workers believed the comic strip reflected real-life workplace situations. The strip even coined a new word, *dilberted,* which described the state a worker might be in after being abused by the boss.

Sources: Steve Labadessa, "Dilbert," *People,* 46 (30 December 1996): 74–76.

Larry Reisman, "Dilbert Editor Skewers Work While in Pajamas," *American Editor* (June 1997): 28.

(1999), most children cared less about the hours their parents worked than about the work-related stress that made parents tired, impatient, and irritable. Experts agree that the challenge American workers will face in the future will be to learn how to achieve a healthy balance in their lives by managing their time more efficiently at work, at home, and in between.

Wages. Although corporate profits and the stock market soared throughout the second half of the 1990s, the average American worker, including the white-collar middle manager and his or her family, did not consistently benefit from the boom. The gap between rich and poor grew steadily while the middle and working classes often endured economic stagnation. On average, median family income remained at approximately the same levels for twenty-five years, although there were many more two-income households in the 1990s than during the mid 1970s. At the same time, real weekly wages have declined $23, or nearly 5 percent, since 1979. According to statistics compiled in 1994, fully 60 percent of American households were not keeping

An employee of Ernst and Young in San Jose, California, poses in his casual work clothes, 2 January 1998 (AP/Wide World Photos).

up with inflation. While the wealthy accumulated huge gains in the stock market, working- and middle-class Americans depleted their savings and ran up massive credit-card debt to compensate for stagnating wages. Of the income gains made between 1977 and 1990, 79 percent went to those already earning incomes in the top 1 percent. In the midst of unprecedented economic growth, a survey conducted by *U.S. News & World Report* in early 1996 found that only 22 percent of Americans believed the economy was expanding; 67 percent believed that it was either stagnating or declining.

Wealth. Throughout the 1990s executive pay and stock prices soared while wages slumped and jobs disappeared. As a result, average Americans worked longer hours, often at more than one job, just to keep their economic and financial heads above water. Government statistics compiled for the years 1995–1998, released in January 2000, require some revision of this assessment. In the economic boom of the mid 1990s, American families experienced a 17.6 percent increase in wealth. The net worth of American families rose to $71,600 in 1998, up from a net worth of $60,900 in 1995 after adjusting for inflation. At the same time, however, the statistics mark a decline of 20 percent in the median net worth of families earning $25,000 a year or less. The poorest families, those earning $10,000 or less annually, suffered a drop of 25 percent in net worth. By contrast, families earning between $50,000 and $99,999 enjoyed the largest increase in median net worth, a 20 percent jump to $152,000.

Casual Workplace. Casual dress, supposedly to improve workers' moods and hence increase their productivity, may have been a mistake. Companies are finding out that more-formal dress was a good idea after all. Yet, employees love casual-dress policies so much that 90 percent of American companies have adopted them, even if it is only on Fridays or for the summer. For employers, however, says Anne Pasley-Stuart, president of a human-resources consulting firm in Boise, Idaho, casual dress codes are "starting to cost a lot in terms of productivity and customer satisfaction." Managers are discovering that when employees dress casually, they also perform more casually in terms of the quality of their work, manners, and punctuality. Short of returning to formal business attire, many companies have now begun spelling out exactly what is acceptable and instructing managers to send home inappropriately dressed workers.

Disappearing Company Man. The old adage that quitters never prosper no longer applied in the 1990s. Based on a survey of resignation rates conducted by the Saratoga Institute, a workforce research company, approximately seventeen million Americans will quit their jobs in 2000 to take other positions for as much as a 10 to 20 percent increase over current salaries. On average, American companies will have to replace 14 percent of their current workforce in 2000. In the opinion of Stephen M. Pollan, coauthor with Mark Levine of *Live Rich: Everything You Need to Know To Be Your Own Boss, Whomever You Work For* (1998), the promise of more money is the principal motive for changing jobs. The "quit-to-win strategy," however, has a downside. "Jobhoppers," as they are called, have little chance of retiring with a company pension, and, in the event of an economic downturn, face the danger that the most recently hired and higher-paid employees will be the first fired. Companies, though, have also come to believe that a high turnover in their workforce is more cost-effective and profitable than giving large general raises, notwithstanding recruiting costs and hiring bonuses. Since 1991 corporate profits have risen on average 9.4 percent a year. During that same period companies have budgeted only 4 percent for annual merit and cost-of-living raises for salaried employees and slightly less for hourly workers. Large raises have gone only to a few indispensable employees who threaten to move to other companies. As a result, the take-home pay for the CEOs of large corporations rose by 13 percent a year during the 1990s. Since 1975, the ratio between the pay of CEOs and average American workers has risen from 41 to 1 to 225 to 1, according to compensation expert Graef S. Crystal, author of *In Search of Excess: The Overcompensation of American Executives* (1991). Economist Robert H. Frank of Cornell University concludes that "if you need to pay your top talent premium rates to keep them from going to the competition, it means you've got to keep the margins tight everywhere else." "To get a significant raise," says career counselor Leslie B. Prager, founder of the Prager-Bernstein Group, "you have to change jobs." As they abandoned their low-paying jobs and overcame their longstanding company loyalties, growing numbers of American workers in the 1990s were apparently coming to agree with this view.

American Economy. The decline in industrial jobs played a central role in the painful economic upheavals of the 1990s. In the place of industrial workers arose what management expert Peter Drucker called "knowledge workers." By 2000, approximately 33 percent of the American workforce fit this category. Unlike the previous transformation of the economy from agriculture to industry, new positions required education, sophisticated skills, and command of cutting-edge technology that average American workers lacked. Those unable to acquire the requisite training have been condemned to declining fortunes while the "knowledge workers" take home a growing share of income. As a consequence legions of American workers, left behind by the so-called knowledge revolution, have never recovered what they lost in jobs and income during the recession of 1990–1991. The victims of layoffs, mergers, buy-outs, and downsizing, these workers have either been forced to take jobs that pay anywhere from

between a third to a half less than their previous income, or else to remain permanently unemployed. Those who have managed to keep their jobs or find new ones must still deal with an unremitting job insecurity that has persisted despite sustained economic growth. In such industries as banking, retail, and telecommunications—where job insecurity has become the norm—wages rise slowly, in part because workers are too fearful of losing their jobs to demand more money. "Economic theory tells us that ultimately workers are paid their just reward," contends Stephen Roach, chief economist of Morgan Stanley Dean Witter, adding that "in the '90s, that has not been the case." Instead, productivity gains of approximately 2 percent a year until 1995 were accompanied by a meager compensation growth of 0.6 percent. Corporations have not turned their massive profits into increased wages, but rather have built up large reserves of cash and spent more on equipment such as computers and software. "There has been an extraordinary decoupling between productivity growth and compensation growth," declared Lawrence Perlman, chairman and CEO of Ceridian Corporation, an information-services company based in Minneapolis. Whether the disparity between productivity and pay is a temporary or structural problem remains to be seen. Nevertheless, for now experts agree that in a nation where work and job title are highly valued commodities, unemployment or diminished earning power imposes heavy psychological as well as economic burdens. A diminished sense of self-worth and self-esteem frequently accompany unemployment. "What it takes today to regard yourself as successful," explained Stanford University economist Paul Krugman in 1996, "is increasingly out of reach." As Steven V. Roberts wrote in *U.S. News & World Report:* "working hard and going nowhere is threatening the American dream."

Sources:

Don L. Boroughs, "Winter of Discontent," *U.S. News & World Report*, 120 (22 January 1996): 47–54.

Kim Clark and others, "Why it Pays to Quit," *U.S. News & World Report*, 127 (1 November 1999): 74–86.

Graef S. Crystal, *In Search of Excess: The Overcompensation of American Executives* (New York: Norton, 1991).

Melynda Wilcox Dovel, "New Wrinkles in Casual-Dress Codes, *Kiplinger's Personal Finance Magazine*, 53 (November 1999): 28.

"Family Wealth up 17.6%," *Richmond Times-Dispatch*, 19 January 2000, pp. A1, A7.

Robert H. Frank and Philip J. Cook, *The Winner-Take-All Society: How More and More Americans Compete for Ever Fewer and Bigger Prizes, Encouraging Economic Waste, Income Inequality, and an Impoverished Cultural Life* (New York: Free Press, 1995).

Ellen Galinsky, *Ask the Children: What America's Children Really Think About Working Parents* (New York: Morrow, 1999).

James Lardner and Trena Johnson, "World-Class Workaholics," *U.S. News & World Report*, 127 (20 December 1999): 42–53.

Robert McNatt, "Small Pleasures at Work," *Business Week* (6 December 1999): 6.

Stephen M. Pollan and Mark Levine, *Live Rich: Everything You Need to Know To Be Your Own Boss, Whomever You Work For* (New York: HarperBusiness, 1998).

Steven V. Roberts, "Workers Take It On the Chin," *U.S. News & World Report*, 120 (22 January 1996): 44–46.

"Was Casual Day a Mistake," *Des Moines Business Record*, 93 (3 November 1997): 48.

HEADLINE MAKERS

DEEPAK CHOPRA

1947-

NEW AGE GURU, DOCTOR, AUTHOR, ENTREPRENEUR

"The Bearer of True Enlightenment." One of the more influential New Age writers, educators, lecturers, and gurus to the rich and famous was Indian-born Deepak Chopra. A medical doctor by profession, Chopra, through a series of best-selling books, tapes, and lectures, made believers out of thousands of Americans with a message that combines medical and spiritual advice. His words have helped to soothe the sense of emptiness that many Americans confess is now a part of their lives.

Setting the Stage. Chopra arrived in the United States in 1970 as a Western-trained medical doctor. Gradually, he became known as "The Lord of Immortality," a prominent spokesman for the Maharishi Mahesh Yogi's Transcendental Meditation movement. Since that time he has emerged as a personality in his own right, having written nineteen books that have sold more than ten million copies and been translated into thirty languages. He has given on average fifty lectures a year, and has been the personal spiritual advisor to many celebrities, including Demi Moore, George Harrison, Madonna, and the late Princess Diana. He has even been called in to advise the troubled National Broadcasting Company (NBC) about how to recapture the top rating among television networks.

The Deepak Empire. By the end of the decade Chopra had built a large and growing personal empire. His various enterprises include a proposed worldwide chain of Centers for Well Being, a monthly newsletter, CDs, study groups, herbal supplements, massage oils, lectures, seminars, and movie scripts. His pronouncements, such as the one made on the Oprah Winfrey Show in 1993, that people did not have to grow old, spurred record sales of his then-current title *Ageless Body, Timeless Mind: The Quantum Alternative to Growing Old* (1993). Chopra is not without his critics, however. They charge him with being nothing more than a modern snake-oil salesman with an M.D. Still, his influence cannot be underestimated as he answers the spiritual and medical longings of many who are searching for inner peace.

Sources:

John Leland and Carla Power, "Deepak's Instant Karma," *Newsweek*, 132 (20 October 1997): 52–58.

Kevin Sean O'Donghue, "NBC Mum About Deepak," *Incentive*, 172 (December 1998): 9.

Degan Pener and Jacqueline Savaiano, "Hollywood Soul Man," *Entertainment Weekly* (24 May 1996): 12–14.

BILL McCARTNEY

1940-

FORMER FOOTBALL COACH, FOUNDER OF PROMISE KEEPERS

"The Game of His Life." All his life, Bill McCartney knew he was going to be a coach. "I never saw myself doing anything else," he once told an interviewer. After graduating from the University of Missouri in 1962, McCartney coached high-school football for twelve years before landing his first collegiate position as a defensive coordinator for the University of Michigan Wolverines in 1974. By 1982, McCartney and his family were on their way to the University of Colorado, located in Boulder, where McCartney had agreed to take on the floundering Buffaloes. In his determination to rebuild the ailing football program, however, McCartney neglected to check on the status of his own family.

Life With Father. In the next few years, McCartney saw his struggling program grow stronger. In 1989 he was named Coach of the Year. In 1991, almost a decade after arriving in Boulder, he led his seemingly invincible Buffaloes to victory over the Notre Dame Fighting Irish in the Orange Bowl. All the accolades, however, could not disguise trouble at home. One of his daughters became pregnant twice by different players on his football squad. His remaining children moved out, leaving him alone with a wife who suffered from depression. McCartney realized he had lost his way.

Promise Keepers. In 1990, struck by a vision of stadiums filled with men committed to leading Christian lives, McCartney, himself a devout Christian, founded Promise Keepers. The first conference was held in July 1991. This Christian male-only organization focuses on reestablishing the male voice and presence in American religious, family, and public life, while charging men to become better fathers, husbands, leaders, and human beings through commitment to the Seven Promises outlined in Scripture. To date, Promise Keepers boasts more than 1.5 million members nationwide. It is a movement that cuts across racial, economic, and religious boundaries. Although closely aligned with the Religious Right, Promise Keepers declares it has no political agenda. Yet, women's groups and civil liberties organizations are not so sure, claiming that the group could present a significant danger to the achievement of women's rights and civil liberties.

Sources:

Phyllis E. Alsdurf, "McCartney On the Rebound," *Christianity Today,* 42 (18 May 1998): 26–32.

Edd Doerr, "Promise Keepers: who, what and why?" *USA Today Magazine,* 126 (March 1998): 30–33.

Richard N. Ostling, "God, Football, And The Game of His Life," *Time,* 150 (6 October 1997): 38–39.

Ron Stodghill II, "God Of Our Fathers," *Time,* 150 (6 October 1997): 34–40.

FAITH POPCORN

1947-

FUTURIST

Popcorn, Please. Decried by some as nothing more than an old-fashioned scam artist, revered by others as nothing short of a miracle worker, professional futurist Faith Popcorn has been credited with coining and pinpointing several trends that marked the decade of the 1990s. Companies such as Reebok, BMW, IBM, Philip Morris, and American Express pay Popcorn and her New York firm, BrainReserve, millions of dollars to help them create marketing strategies and products, and, when necessary, to revamp old products with a new packaging. Her views on everything from throwaway products ("People just don't get attached to things the way they used to") to boxer shorts ("People think, 'Maybe if I wear them, everything will be alright'") have been quoted throughout the media.

The Way the World Is Going. Popcorn, born Faith Plotkin, started out working in advertizing. By the mid 1980s she had moved to BrainReserve where she hoped to show her clients "which way the world was going." Her early predictions included "Cocooning," that is, settling at home with fancy and expensive take-out food and a video instead of braving the increasingly mean streets of urban and suburban America. The demand for take-out food boomed in the 1990s, creating an industry worth more than $28 billion dollars by 1994. Other trends that Popcorn has been credited with predicting are "Clanning," the inclination to join up or belong to groups of all kinds, "Small Indulgences," rewarding yourself with small luxuries, and "Being Alive," embracing healthier lifestyles.

Safe-Clicking the Future. The key to Popcorn's success is what she has called "clicking," or searching for the right combination of elements to "future fit" one's life. Once one "clicks," life is filled with all kinds of exciting possibilities and opportunities. It is information about these possibilities and opportunities that Popcorn's clients are willing to pay for. Whether Popcorn will continue to dominate the business and cultural scene remains to be seen. Recently, she has missed on some of her predictions. Critics complain that she merely recycles old trends under new guises and that her predictions are based more on common sense than any real insight into what consumers think they want. But that common sense of what consumers desire, and what they are willing to pay for, is what "clicking" is all about. For the moment, Popcorn is looking beyond the marketplace. By the end of 1994, she and her company were exploring the possibility of offering their services to politicians unsure of how to present themselves to the voters. For Popcorn, the whole of society is one huge marketplace in which everything and everybody is a potential commodity waiting to be bought and sold. The question for her is what makes the product, whether a politician or take-out sushi, "click."

Sources:

Janet Cawley, "Interview," *Biography,* 2 (June 1998): 76–78.

Faith Popcorn and Lys Marigold, *Clicking: 16 Trends To Future Fit Your Life, Your Work, And Your Business* (New York: HarperCollins, 1996).

Ruth Shalit, "The Business of Faith," *New Republic,* 210 (April 18, 1994): 23–28.

DR. LAURA C. SCHLESSINGER

1947-
RADIO PERSONALITY/THERAPIST

"Dr. Laura." For three hours every day, Dr. Laura C. Schlessinger dispenses advice while pointing out the shortcomings of people who call in to her radio show, which reaches millions of listeners. On any given day, more than fifty thousand persons will jam the phone lines for a chance to converse with her about a myriad of problems—the state of marriage, abortion, relationships, and a host of other topics. For Dr. Laura, it is business as usual. For her listeners, it means an opportunity to solve puzzling difficulties or to hear that they are not alone. In addition, for those who do not listen to the radio, Dr. Laura's advice is also available in her syndicated columns running in at least fifty-five newspapers nationwide, or in her three popular books: *Ten Stupid Things Women Do To Mess Up Their Lives* (1995), *Ten Stupid Things Men Do To Mess Up Their Lives* (1997), and *How Could You Do That?: The Abdication of Character, Courage and Conscience* (1996). For many, Dr. Laura's success has come out of her ability to take aim and fire at the attitudes of the "Me Generation," which often amounted to an abdication of personal and moral responsibility.

"The Soul of a Hall Monitor." Born and raised in Brooklyn, Schlessinger is the first to admit that her childhood was anything but happy. Raised in a household often filled with the sounds of arguing between her Jewish father and Roman Catholic mother, she often felt lost, alone, and confused. Those feelings led the young Schlessinger to be overly sensitive to other people doing things they should not have been doing, such as ripping pages out of library books. Schlessinger early felt an urgent need to tell people when they were doing something wrong, even if it meant being unpopular and alone. After earning a Ph.D. in physiology from Columbia University, she went on to teach and eventually earned her license in marriage and family therapy. A chance call-in to a radio talk show in 1975 opened the way for a career in radio.

"Grow Up!" Dr. Laura's no-holds-barred approach to dispensing advice on everything from divorce to homosexuality has earned her a legion of devoted listeners, as well as many who call her an insensitive charlatan. Her ability to zero in on a caller's problem has made her the envy of ministers and therapists alike. Her tone, which at times can be moralistic, judgmental, and yet beneficent, has also sent a message that millions of Americans are apparently ready to hear: Grow up, take responsibility for your actions, and be good and helpful to others.

Sources:
Tom Allen and Laura C. Schlessinger, *A Closer Look at Dr. Laura: On Target or Off The Wall?* (New York: Horizon, 1999).

Schlessinger, *How Could You Do That?: The Abdication of Character, Courage and Conscience* (New York: HarperCollins, 1996).

Joannie M. Schrof, "No Whining!" *U.S. News & World Report*, 123 (14 July 1997): 48–55.

MARTHA STEWART

1941-
ENTREPRENEUR, PROFESSIONAL HOMEMAKER

"K-Martha." Teaching people how to set the right kind of table, or create an elegant dessert, or make the perfect Christmas wreath may have been enough for Martha Stewart in the 1980s. In the 1990s, however, Stewart set out to conquer the world. In 1997, aligning herself in a newly revised business partnership with the discount retailer K-Mart, Stewart unveiled a series of products from sheets to paint designed to increase the sales and profits of both K-Mart and herself. She also weighed in on issues from dyeing Easter eggs to collecting glass in her "askMartha" newspaper column that reached an estimated eighty-eight million readers a month, launched a new web business that combined how-to advice with the sales of related domestic merchandise, and appeared on her own television program. Probably the biggest event though of the Stewart story was the unveiling of Martha as stock entity when shares of Martha Stewart Living Omnimedia went public in October 1999.

The Everyday Martha. People across the United States have listened to Stewart's advice for years. The daughter of Polish American teachers, Stewart, a graduate of Barnard College and a former stockbroker, has amassed a small fortune showing people how to make simple things better and thereby to make their lives "nicer and prettier." She has offered her expertise on everything from baking the perfect sugar cookie to achieving just the right color for Easter eggs. She has influenced contemporary American taste and design to such an extent that many upscale furniture and interior-design companies, such as The Pottery Barn, rely on her vision to determine the products they sell. Like Ralph Lauren, Stewart has been credited not only with designing products to complement a particular lifestyle, but with helping to create and maintain that lifestyle itself.

"And That's A Good Thing." When K-Mart officials learned that more people trusted Stewart than their own doctors, they wasted no time in proposing a new partnership (she was already serving as a design consultant to the company) that not only netted Stewart a sizable profit up front, but guaranteed her a percentage of every "Martha Item" sold. The Stewart empire did not end there. Stewart also launched her own website, a mail-order catalogue, and a syndicated television show. Along with her magazine, *Martha Stewart Living,* launched in 1991, the new ventures made Stewart one of the most visible, recognized, and influential figures of the 1990s. During the decade, Stewart became for many Americans the last word in home decor, as well as cooking, baking, and entertaining.

Sources:

Diane Brady, "Martha, Inc.," *Business Week* (17 January 2000): 62–70.

Stacy Perman, "Attention K-Martha Shoppers," *Time,* 150 (6 October 1997): 54–60.

Martha Stewart, "My Big Bet On The Net," *Newsweek,* 132 (7 December 1998): 53.

PEOPLE IN THE NEWS

On 12 March 1992, **Jim and Tammy Faye Bakker**, partners in the multimillion-dollar television Praise the Lord (PTL) evangelism empire before he went to prison for fleecing his flock, notified the public they were divorcing. Tammy Faye had decided to divorce her husband after thirty-one years of marriage. He got the news at the Federal Medical Center in Rochester, Minnesota, where he was serving an eighteen-year sentence.

On 23 June 1993, in Manassas, Virginia, **John Wayne Bobbitt** reported to police that his wife, **Lorena,** had amputated his penis while he slept and threw it away while driving from the couple's home. It was later recovered, put on ice, and taken to the hospital where the appendage was reattached. Bobbitt was later acquitted of marital sexual assault; Lorena was acquitted of malicious wounding by reason of insanity.

In 1998, **Chuck Burris** was sworn in as the first African American mayor of Stone Mountain, Georgia, the longtime headquarters of the Ku Klux Klan.

In 1996 First Lady **Hillary Rodham Clinton** published *It Takes A Village and Other Lessons Children Teach Us,* a combined autobiographical account of her relationship with daughter **Chelsea** and her thoughts on childrearing. The book stayed on the best-seller chart for twenty weeks. Although criticized for her timing—publishing the work just prior to the reelection campaign of her husband President Bill Clinton—she had long been an advocate of child welfare. In 1997 she won a Grammy Award for her audio version of the book.

On 11 April 1996 seven-year-old **Jessica Dubroff**, who had hoped to become the youngest person to fly crosscountry, was killed with her father and a flight instructor when her plane crashed after takeoff from Cheyenne, Wyoming. The incident raised questions over the wisdom of a young child piloting a plane for long-distance trips.

On 16 October 1995, **Louis Farrakhan**, head of the controversial Nation of Islam, led four hundred thousand African American men on the "Million Man March" in Washington, D.C., the largest march by African Americans in U.S. history. Farrakhan's message to the marchers stressed respect for black women, the evils of drugs and rape, and the necessity of achieving economic self-sufficiency, self-respect, and self-discipline.

On 18 August 1995, **Shannon Faulkner**, who had won a long legal fight to become the first female cadet to attend The Citadel, an all-male military college in South Carolina, resigned after only four days at the school. Faulkner had attended orientation activities and the first day of training.

In 1997 San Antonio businesswoman **Linda Finch** completed her journey to retrace the final flight path of Amelia Earhart, who had disappeared in the South Pacific sixty years earlier. She flew the same make and model plane as Earhart, a restored 1935 Lockheed Electra 10E.

In 1997, **Lt. Kelly Flinn**, the first female bomber pilot, was allowed to resign from the U.S. Air Force rather than face a court martial on charges of disobeying orders, fraternizing with an enlisted officer, and adultery. The charges were criticized by many civilians as unfairly targeting women, while military personnel criticized the leniency of the Air Force in allowing her an "uncharacterized" (neither honorable nor dishonorable) discharge.

In 1998, **Martin Luther King III**, the son of the slain civil-rights leader, was elected as president of the Southern Christian Leadership Conference (SCLC), the group his father helped to found in 1957. The younger King vowed to reinvigorate the once-powerful civil-rights organization.

In April 1992 eleven-year-old **Gregory Kingsley** sued his biological parents for "divorce" in order to remain with his foster parents. A Florida judge awarded the divorce, and in September allowed Gregory to return home with his foster parents. Gregory has since changed his name to Shawn Russ.

In February 1998 decorated sailor **Timothy McVeigh** (no relation to the Oklahoma City bomber) was exonerated by a federal court; McVeigh, who had identified himself as a homosexual in an America Online e-mail exchange, was in danger of being dismissed by U.S. Navy authorities.

On 30 August 1994, **Rosa Parks**, whose refusal to give up her seat on a Montgomery, Alabama, bus in 1955, sparked the beginnings of the Civil Rights movement, was robbed and beaten in her Detroit apartment.

In 1996, **Jonathan Prevette**, a Lexington, North Carolina, first-grader, was removed from class and kept from a class party for kissing a girl on the cheek. School authorities defended the removal, calling Prevette's act "unwelcome touching." Prevette became an overnight celebrity as his case was debated around water coolers and on talk-show programs across the country.

In December 1999 cartoonist **Charles Schulz** announced that because of ill health he would no longer draw *"Peanuts,"* one of the most popular comic strips for more than fifty years.

In 1997, **Malcolm Shabazz**, twelve, pleaded guilty to arson and the juvenile equivalent of manslaughter for setting a fire that killed his grandmother, Betty Shabazz, widow of Malcolm X.

On 7 March 1995, **Carol Shaya-Castro** was dismissed from her job as a New York City policewoman for posing both nude and in her uniform for *Playboy* magazine.

On 6 October 1998, **Matthew Shepard**, 21, a gay student at the University of Wyoming, was beaten, tied to a fence, and left for dead. Shepard, who died a few days later, was a haunting reminder to Americans that "hate crimes" against homosexuals were still prevalent in American society.

In January 1993 authorities rescued **Jennifer Stolpa** and her infant son, after Stolpa's husband, **James**, succeeded in reaching help after the family's nine-day ordeal in the snow-covered Nevada desert.

On 24 April 1991, **Freddie Stowers**, an African American corporal who served in World War I (1914–1918) was posthumously awarded the highest U.S. military decoration, the Medal of Honor, for valor in combat.

On 3 February 1998, **Karla Faye Tucker**, a prisoner at the Texas State Prison in Huntsville, was executed by lethal injection. Convicted of a brutal pickax murder committed in 1983, Tucker made headlines with her claim to be a "born-again" Christian. Opponents of capital punishment campaigned for her sentence to be commuted to life in prison. She was the first woman to be executed since 1984.

On 5 February 1994 twelve-year-old **Vicki Van Meter** of Meadville, Pennsylvania, completed her transatlantic flight, landing in Glasgow, Scotland, making her the youngest girl ever to pilot a plane to Europe.

DEATHS

Ralph David Abernathy, 64, reverend, civil-rights activist, and chief aide to Martin Luther King Jr., 17 April 1990.

Cleveland Amory, 81, author of *Who Killed Society* (1960) and *The Cat Who Came For Christmas* (1988) and animal-rights activist who founded the Fund for Animals, 14 October 1998.

Erma Bombeck, 69, humorist and author whose experiences as wife and mother provided subjects for a syndicated column and six books, 22 April 1996.

Leo F. Buscaglia, 74, writer and lecturer who promoted the power of love as a healing force, known as the "Hug Doctor," 12 June 1998.

Stokely Carmichael (Kwame Ture), 57, civil-rights activist and revolutionary, 15 November 1998.

Carlos Castaneda, 72, author of ten books detailing his experiences with mysticism and psychedelic drugs during the 1960s, 27 April 1998.

Eldridge Cleaver, 62, Black Power advocate, author of *Soul on Ice* (1968), and leading member of the Black Panthers, 2 May 1998.

Henry Steele Commager, 95, U.S. historian, 2 March 1998.

Walter E. Diemer, 93, inventor of bubble gum, 8 January 1998.

Judith Campbell Exner, 65, alleged mistress of John F. Kennedy, 24 September 1999.

James Farmer, 79, civil-rights activist and cofounder of the Congress of Racial Equality (CORE), 9 July 1999.

M. F. K. Fisher, 83, writer whose work often used food as a cultural metaphor, 22 June 1992.

Eugene Fodor, 85, producer of travel guides used for more than half a century by American tourists, 18 February 1991.

Malcolm S. Forbes Sr., 70, publisher, flamboyant millionaire, father of presidential hopeful Malcolm S. "Steve" Forbes Jr., 24 February 1990.

Barry M. Goldwater, 89, longtime Arizona senator, presidential candidate in 1964, leading figure in American conservative movement that emerged following World War II, 29 May 1998.

John L. Goldwater, 83, creator of the *Archie* comics, 26 February 1999.

Charles Goren, 90, world expert on contract bridge, 3 April 1991.

Mary Elizabeth "Meg" Greenfield, 68, journalist, editor of the editorial page of the *Washington Post*, 13 May 1999.

Armand Hammer, 92, noted philanthropist and art collector, who actively promoted peace between the United States and the Soviet Union, 10 December 1990.

Bob Kane, 83, creator of the *Batman* comic strip, 3 November 1998.

Alfred Kazin, 83, literary critic, memorist, and teacher, 5 June 1998.

Michael Kennedy, 39, son of Robert F. Kennedy, 31 December 1997.

Rose Fitzgerald Kennedy, 104, matriarch of the Kennedy family, 22 January 1995.

Lane Kirkland, 77, labor leader and former president of the AFL-CIO, 14 August 1999.

Edwin Herbert Land, 81, inventor of the Polaroid Land Instant Camera, 3 March 1991.

Timothy Leary, 75, clinical psychologist at Harvard who in the 1960s introduced Americans to LSD, 31 May 1996.

William J. Levitt, 86, Long Island, N.Y., developer who built "Levittown," a prototype of the American suburb, after World War II, 22 January 1994.

J. Gordon Lippincott, 89, designer and engineer who created some of the most recognized corporate logos, such as those for Coca-Cola, Campbell Soups, and Betty Crocker, 29 April 1998.

Paul Mellon, 91, philanthropist and banker, 1 February 1999.

Willie Morris, 64, journalist, 2 August 1999.

Jeffrey A. Moss, 56, writer and creator of the Sesame Street characters Cookie Monster and Oscar the Grouch, and composer of the well-known song "Rubber Duckie," 24 September 1998.

Lewis Mumford, 94, city planner, author, cultural and political commentator, 26 June 1990.

Arthur Murray, 95, world-renowned teacher of ballroom dancing, 3 March 1991.

Jacqueline Bouvier Kennedy Onassis, 64, widow of President John F. Kennedy and Greek shipping magnate Aristotle Onassis, book editor, 19 May 1994.

Vance Packard, 82, journalist and social critic who warned against advertizing excesses and social climbing, 12 December 1996.

Laurence J. Peter, 70, author who satirized corporate climbers and coined the phrase the "Peter Principle," 12 February 1990.

Roger Tory Peterson, 87, ornithologist, author of *A Field Guide To the Birds* (1934), the bible for bird watchers, 20 July 1996.

Sylvia F. Porter, 72, author and columnist who interpreted the world of business and finance for many American readers, 5 June 1991.

Charles "Bebe" Rebozo, 85, wealthy businessman whose claim to fame lay in his close friendship with former president Richard M. Nixon, 8 May 1998.

James W. Rouse, 81, developer who created new towns in countrysides, shopping malls, and "festival" places such as Faneuil Hall in Boston, 9 April 1996.

Johnny Roventini, 86, icon for the popular ad "Call for Philip Morris," heard on radio and television, 30 November 1998.

Waldo L. Semon, 100, inventor of vinyl in 1928, 26 May 1999.

Betty Shabazz, 61, educator, civil-rights activist, widow of black nationalist Malcolm X, 23 June 1997.

B. F. (Burrhus Frederic) Skinner, 85, leading American psychologist who advocated behavior modification according to scientific principles, 8 August 1990.

Benjamin Spock, 94, pediatrician whose book *The Common Sense Book of Baby and Child Care* (1946) sold fifty million copies through seven editions, 15 March 1998.

Sam Moore Walton, 74, founder of Wal-Mart Department Stores, 4 April 1992.

Thomas J. Watson Jr., 79, chairman of IBM, brought the company and nation into the computer age, 31 December 1993.

William H. Whyte, 81, wrote about the American urban scene, author of *The Organization Man* (1956), 12 January 1999.

Evelyn Wood, 86, founder of the Evelyn Wood Reading Dynamics Institute, which promoted her method of speed-reading, 26 August 1995.

PUBLICATIONS

Edward J. Blakely and Mary Gail Snyder, *Fortress America: Gated Communities in the United States* (Washington, D.C.: Brookings Institution Press, 1997).

Robert Bly, *Iron John: A Book About Men* (Reading, Mass.: Addison-Wesley, 1990).

Faria Chideya, *The Color of Our Future* (New York: Morrow, 1999).

Deepak Chopra, *Ageless Body, Timeless Mind: The Quantum Alternative to Growing Old* (New York: Harmony Books, 1993).

Chopra, *Creating Affluence: Wealth Consciousness in the Field of All Possibilities* (San Raphael, Cal.: New World Publishing, 1993).

Hillary Rodham Clinton, *It Takes A Village and Other Lessons Children Teach Us* (New York: Simon & Schuster, 1996).

Stephen R. Covey, *The 7 Habits of Highly Effective Families: Building a Beautiful Family Culture in a Turbulent World* (New York: Golden Books, 1997).

Tom Diaz, *Making A Killing: The Business of Guns in America* (New York: New Press, 1999).

Esther Dyson, *Release 2.1: A Design For Living in the Digital Age* (New York: Broadway Books, 1998).

Susan Faludi, *Backlash: The Undeclared War Against American Women* (New York: Crown, 1991).

Faludi, *Stiffed: The Betrayal of the American Man* (New York: Morrow, 1999).

Elizabeth Fox-Genovese, *Feminism Is Not the Story of My Life: How Today's Feminist Elite Has Lost Touch With the Real Concerns of Women* (New York: Nan A. Talese, 1996).

Evan Gerstmann, *The Constitutional Underclass: Gays, Lesbians and the Failure of Class-Based Equal Protection* (Chicago: University of Chicago Press, 1999).

James Gleick, *Faster: The Acceleration of Just About Everything* (New York: Pantheon, 1999).

Richard J. Herrnstein and Charles Murray, *The Bell Curve: Intelligence and Class Structure in American Life* (New York: Free Press, 1994).

Patricia Hersch, *A Tribe Apart: A Journey into the Heart of American Adolescence* (New York: Fawcett Columbine, 1998).

Michael S. Hyatt, *The Millennium Bug: How To Survive The Coming Chaos* (Washington, D.C.: Regnery, 1998).

Jonathan Kozol, *Amazing Grace: The Lives of Children and The Conscience of a Nation* (New York: Crown, 1995).

Wayne R. LaPierre, *Guns, Crime, and Freedom* (Washington, D.C.: Regnery, 1994).

Michael Lerner, *The Politics of Meaning: Restoring Hope and Possibility In An Age of Cynicism* (New York: Addison-Wesley, 1996).

Judith Martin, *Miss Manners' Guide for the Turn of the Millennium* (New York: Fireside, 1990).

Michael Nava and Robert Dawidoff, *Created Equal: Why Gay Rights Matter to America* (New York: St. Martin's Press, 1994).

Camille Paglia, *Sex, Art, and American Culture: Essays* (New York: Vintage, 1992).

Faith Popcorn, *The Popcorn Report: Faith Popcorn on the Future of Your Company, Your World, Your Life* (New York: Doubleday, 1991).

Dan Rather, *Deadlines and Datelines* (New York: Morrow, 1999).

Shelby Steele, *A Dream Deferred: The Second Betrayal of Black Freedom in America* (New York: HarperCollins, 1998).

Andrew Sullivan, *Virtually Normal: An Argument About Homosexuality* (New York: Knopf, 1995).

Steven A. Tuch and Jack K. Martin, eds., *Racial Attitudes in the 1990s: Continuity and Change* (New York: Praeger, 1997).

Naomi Wolf, *The Beauty Myth: How Images of Beauty Are Used Against Women* (New York: Morrow, 1991).

Cigar Afficionado (periodical).

George (periodical).

Martha Stewart's Living (periodical).

Newsweek (periodical).

People Magazine (periodical).

Time (periodical).

Vanity Fair (periodical).

Customers line up to purchase Powerball Lotto tickets at the Kwik Stop Gas & Groceries in Malad, Idaho, on 19 May 1998 (AP/Wide World Photos)

The Millennium Clock in Times Square, New York City, counting down to 2000 (AP/Wide World Photos)

MEDIA

by SUSAN M. SHAW

CONTENTS

Sidebars and tables are listed in italics.

1990

22 Feb.	Hughes Communications, News Corp, National Broadcasting Company (NBC), and Cablevision Systems Corporation create Sky Cable, a joint effort to launch direct-broadcast satellite TV program service with as many as 108 channels.
6 Mar.	Whittle Communications LP airs its first installment of *Channel One*, a daily news program for high school students.
4 Apr.	Columbia Broadcasting System (CBS), NBC, and American Broadcasting Company (ABC) announce the formation of Network Television Association, designed to promote network television to advertisers and agencies.
8 Apr. to 10 June 1991	ABC TV series *Twin Peaks* runs, causing viewers to ask, "Who killed Laura Palmer?"
18 May	*The Forward*, a new national English-language Jewish newspaper, based on the Yiddish *Forverts* (starting 1897), begins publication.
30 May	The sitcom *Seinfeld*, a show about "nothing," begins its highly successful eight-year run.
13 Sept.	The police/courtroom drama *Law and Order* debuts.
25 Sept.	Three hundredth anniversary of *Publick Occurrences*, the first newspaper published in what is now the United States (Boston).
9 Nov.	The Cable News Network (CNN) defies a federal judge's orders and airs taped phone conversations between former Panama dictator Manuel Antonio Noriega Moreno and members of his legal defense team. The network argues no court has the right to decide what the news media may broadcast.

1991

21 Jan.	CNN dominates Persian Gulf War coverage.
16 Apr.	NBC News names the alleged victim of the William Kennedy Smith rape. The next day the *New York Times* also publishes her name.
Oct.	Liberal magazine the *New Republic* appoints conservative and gay Andrew Sullivan as editor.
6 Oct.	National Public Radio (NPR) and *Newsday* announce Anita F. Hill's allegations of sexual harassment against Supreme Court nominee Clarence Thomas.
4 Dec.	Associated Press correspondent Terry Anderson is freed after seven years as a hostage in Beirut.
21 Dec.	Media mogul Robert Edward "Ted" Turner III marries actress Jane Fonda.

1992

29 Apr.	Rioting erupts in Los Angeles hours after four Los Angeles police officers are found not guilty of beating black motorist Rodney Glen King. The videotape of the beating had been widely broadcast before the trial.
19 May	Vice President Dan Quayle attacks sitcom character Murphy Brown during a campaign speech, saying that the character is fostering lax family values.
23 Sept.	Sitcom *Mad About You* with Helen Hunt and Paul Reiser premieres.

1993

19 Apr.   The Branch Davidian compound in Waco, Texas, burns following a standoff with the Federal Bureau of Investigation (FBI).

1 June   Dan Rather and Connie Chung co-anchor the *CBS Evening News* for the first time.

10 Sept.   *The X-Files*, a drama about two FBI special agents who investigate unexplained cases, premieres on the FOX network.

16 Sept.   *Frasier*, a sitcom spinoff from the highly acclaimed *Cheers*, debuts.

24 Sept.   *60 Minutes* celebrates its twenty-fifth anniversary.

1994

Jan.   *Women's Wire*, a San Francisco-based on-line service for women, is launched. Beset by financial woes, the formerly feminist service was taken over in 1995 and relaunched as a cyberspace version of a traditional women's magazine.

3 Apr.   Charles Kuralt, TV journalist and *CBS News Sunday Morning* commentator, retires at age 59.

27 May   TV talk show host Arsenio Hall calls it quits after five years on the air in the late-night wars.

17 June   O. J. Simpson is charged with the murder of his ex-wife Nicole Brown Simpson and her friend Ronald Goldman. Media helicopters televise Simpson's flight from the police in a white Ford Bronco along a Los Angeles freeway.

Sept.   *She TV*, a breakthrough sketch comedy show focusing on and creatively developed by women, premieres.

19 Sept.   *ER*, a hospital emergency room drama, premieres.

22 Sept.   The sitcom *Friends* debuts.

Sept.   Ken Burns's eighteen-hour documentary on baseball airs on Public Broadcasting Service (PBS).

31 Dec.   *Far Side* creator Gary Larson retires from his daily cartoons, which ran in nearly 1,900 newspapers.

1995

19 Apr.   A bomb blast at the Alfred P. Murrah Federal Building in Oklahoma City kills 168 people.

21 Aug.   ABC News apologizes to tobacco giant Philip Morris for a story it ran on *Day One* claiming the industry spiked cigarettes with nicotine.

9 Nov.   CBS pulls a *60 Minutes* segment on the tobacco industry.

1996

- Pressured by the Federal Communications Commission (FCC), television broadcasters agree to include three hours of educational children's programming in their schedules.

7 Feb.   President Bill Clinton signs the Communications Decency Act, part of the Telecommunications Reform Act of 1996.

27 July   A bomb explodes in Centennial Olympic Park in Atlanta. Later the *Atlanta Journal Constitution* identifies Richard Jewell as a suspect in the bombing, but he is cleared on 26 October.

17 Sept.   The O. J. Simpson civil trial begins, and cameras are banned from the courtroom.

26 Dec.   The body of young beauty pageant queen JonBenet Ramsey is found in the basement of her parents' Boulder, Colorado, home.

1997

23 Jan.   A North Carolina jury ordered ABC to pay Food Lion supermarkets $5.5 million for a story on unsanitary conditions in food preparation areas. The case did not attack the truthfulness of the report, but charged fraud in the manner in which the reporters obtained their information. The judgment was later reduced to $315,000.

4 Mar.   *The Practice,* a one-hour drama about lawyers, premieres.

20 May   After a nine-year run on ABC, the successful sitcom *Roseanne,* starring "domestic goddess" Roseanne Barr, ends.

11 Aug.   *The View,* a critically acclaimed talk show on ABC featuring Barbara Walters and four other high-powered women discussing the most important topics of the day, premieres.

8 Sept.   *Ally McBeal,* a one-hour comedy-drama about a quirky law firm in Boston, premieres on FOX.

1 Dec.   A U.S. District Judge rules that New York City Mayor Rudolph Giuliani must put ads mocking the mayor back on city buses. The ads had been yanked in November.

16 Dec.   President Clinton signs the No Electronic Theft Act, which imposes criminal penalties on copyright violators who do not profit from their actions, into law.

1998

5 Jan.   Pope John Paul II honors media mogul Rupert Murdoch with a papal knighthood.

9 Jan.   *People* owner Time Inc. launches *Teen People,* a new monthly aimed at teenagers.

17 Jan.   Internet reporter Matt Drudge publishes the story of Clinton's alleged affair with White House intern Monica S. Lewinsky on-line in his infamous *Drudge Report,* scooping the traditional media.

21 Jan.   Broadcast and cable networks televise the Pope's visit to Cuba.

26 Jan.	A black-owned weekly newspaper, the *Jackson* (Miss.) *Advocate*, is firebombed. The *Advocate* is known for its investigations and battles with local officials.
2 Feb.	Two paparazzi, Giles Harrison and Andrew O'Brien, are found guilty of misdemeanor false imprisonment stemming from a May run-in with Arnold Schwarzenegger and Maria Shriver.
20 Feb.	The *Nashville Banner* ceases publication after 122 years.
27 Feb.	The Virginia Supreme Court upholds the dismissal of a Virginia Tech administrator's defamation lawsuit against the school newspaper, the *Collegiate Times*.
3 Mar.	*Time* magazine celebrates its 75th anniversary.
20 Apr.	Associated Press celebrates its 150th anniversary.
2 Nov.	Twenty-four hundred unionized ABC employees walk off the job in New York, San Francisco, Los Angeles, Chicago, and Washington, D.C., in a dispute over health benefits.
19 Dec.	The House of Representatives votes to impeach President Clinton.

1999

12 Feb.	President Clinton is acquitted by the U.S. Senate on charges of perjury and obstruction of justice.
9 Nov.	Members of the Feminist Coalition on Public Broadcasting meet with PBS representatives to discuss the network's airing of an antifeminist series, particularly in the context of a PBS lineup that underrepresents women and people of color.
12 Nov.	CBS resolves the contempt case of producer Mary Mapes, who was cited for contempt for failing to turn over unaired video of a Dan Rather interview with murder defendant Shawn Allen Berry. The interview aired on *60 Minutes II* on 28 September.
20 Dec.	*Time* magazine runs an exclusive story based on the content of homemade videotapes recorded by Eric Harris and Dylan Klebold in the weeks before they killed twelve Columbine High students, a teacher, and themselves.

OVERVIEW

Transition. The decade of the 1990s was a period of rapid change in media fueled by advances in technology, the continued merging of companies, and the explosion of "trash" media. Developments in technology led to debates about censorship and protecting children from violent or pornographic images. It also provided quick and easy access to information through the increased availability of the World Wide Web in most homes and offices in the country. Yet, while technological options expanded, authentic diversity in media voices contracted as more and more media sources were merged into large corporations. From reality-based television programming to television and radio talk shows to network news, high-decibel confrontations, innuendo, and intimate sexual details dominated the media. Even, however, as the public cried out against lowering standards in the media, people tuned in to listen and bought sensational editions in record numbers.

Technology. Advances in computer technology in the 1990s led to unprecedented growth in media access. Either at home, work, school, or the public library, almost every American could get to the information superhighway on the Internet. Such access made electronic publishing a lucrative industry, with advertisers lining up to have a link on an electronic newspaper or magazine page. Many long-time print newspapers and magazines added on-line versions, while new Internet-only publications cropped up at every turn. Of course, unlimited access to web-surfers was not without its problems. Of particular concern was the easy availability to children of pornography on the web. While software was being developed to block children's access to adult sites, the debate about porn on the web was still raging at the end of the decade. Technology also made possible growth in television opportunities. Digital cable provided room for an enormous expansion in the number of channels available to consumers, while digital satellite TV increased offerings even more. WebTV allowed couch potatoes to surf the web from their sofas, and interactive television was becoming a reality as shows provided links on WebTV. Again, such open access raised questions about inappropriate content for children, and by 1999 half of all televisions manufactured were required to carry a v-chip that would allow parents to block children from opening sites with violent, sexually explicit, or graphic television

content. After 1 January 2000 all new televisions had to meet this requirement.

Trash. The 1990s was a decade of trash television, radio, and even news. The television ratings winners were "shockumentaries," a genre of reality-based TV that featured shocking footage of everything from police chases to animal attacks. Especially popular in the important eighteen to forty-nine demographic, these shows proliferated on the FOX network but appeared even from such respected producers as *National Geographic*. While violence on television declined on the whole throughout the decade, the shockumentary was the exception. Shockumentaries, however, were not the only place trash flourished, as TV talk shows reached a new low when they moved from exploring controversial subjects to initiating confrontation. Day by day guests appeared to air their grievances with friends and lovers, while hosts and producers encouraged louder and more-vicious arguments to keep the shows lively. In particular, Ricki Lake and Jerry Springer paraded out people to exploit their private pain on national television. A murder followed the taping of one Jenny Jones Show, in which a young man revealed his crush on his male neighbor. Cultural critics began to refer to these shows as "exploitalk." Americans' romance with real TV also grew to include courtroom television. From Courtroom Television Network (Court TV), which aired such infamous cases as the Lyle and Erik Menendez murder trial (1995–1996), to the live broadcast of the O. J. Simpson murder trial (1995) on CNN and other networks, to television courtroom shows such as *Judge Judy* and *The People's Court*, Americans tuned in to watch the justice system at work, particularly if the cases were sensational. Talk radio also added its share of trash to the air, often generating extreme emotion and misinformation. Rush Limbaugh's variety of political conservatism found an audience in antifeminist, anti-environmentalist, white, Republican listeners, while Laura C. Schelssinger pandered to troubled people needing definitive answers and a quick fix. Probably the greatest trash-monger of them all, however, was Howard Stern, a radio shock jock and self-proclaimed "King of All Media." Specializing in the offensive and scatological, Stern netted more than $2 million in Federal Communications Commission (FCC) fines for his on-air vulgarity. Neither was print immune from this tendency toward the salacious. Supermarket tabloids began to scoop mainstream press, and the mainstream press began to run stories one would have expected to have found only in the pages of the *National Enquirer* or *Star*. In particular, the death of Diana, Princess of Wales (31 August 1997), and the sex scandal surrounding President Bill Clinton brought tabloid journalism and mainstream media closer together.

Covering Terror. While for most of its history the United States had been immune from terrorism carried out on its shores, the 1990s brought about an escalation of wide-scale violence. The Unabomber's deadly attacks continued until Theodore John "Ted" Kaczynski was captured (3 April 1996) and found guilty of a seventeen-year (1978–1995) bombing spree that killed three and wounded twenty-three. The World Trade Center in New York was bombed on 26 February 1993, and the Alfred P. Murrah Federal Building in Oklahoma City was blown up on 19 April 1995. A homemade pipe bomb exploded in the Centennial Olympic Park in Atlanta (27 July 1996). School shootings began to occur at an unthinkable rate. The most widely covered incidents were at Pearl, Mississippi (1 October 1997); West Paducah, Kentucky (1 December 1997); Jonesboro, Arkansas (24 March 1998); Springfield, Oregon (21 May 1998); Littleton, Colorado (20 April 1999); and Conyers, Georgia (20 May 1999). Responses to these events posed many dilemmas for the media, who immediately immersed readers and viewers in the crisis, especially with the availability of twenty-four-hour news channels that carried almost nonstop coverage of each tragedy. Journalists found it particularly difficult to walk the line between reporting the news and sensationalizing or oversentimentalizing it.

Mergers. Like the 1980s, the 1990s witnessed continued centralization of the media in the hands of fewer and fewer corporations. Hometown newspapers were gobbled up as business investments by groups such as Community Newspaper Holdings (CNHI) and Liberty Group Publishing. Buying newspapers in geographic clusters was a trend that led major publishers such as Knight Ridder, Cox, Gannett, and others to swap holdings like cards in a game. The idea was that newspapers in close geographic proximity could share resources and thereby lead to greater profits. For many communities, however, this change meant the end of any sort of competition between papers and the decreasing of journalistic voices available to readers. Likewise, television companies merged, with AT&T becoming the largest cable operator in the country after buying TCI. The Walt Disney Company bought Capital Cities/ABC, Time Warner bought Turner Broadcasting System (TBS), Viacom bought Paramount and then Columbia Broadcasting System (CBS). Even in publishing the number of publishing houses grew smaller, and Pearson Education became the largest educational publisher in the world when Addison Wesley Longman and Simon & Schuster education, business, professional, and references businesses merged.

Dealing with Diversity. Some headway was made in the 1990s in terms of diversity in media, although disparities and stereotypes certainly remained at the end of the decade. Women moved into greater visibility as news anchors and sportscasters, although television jobs were still dominated by men and whites. Television, newspapers, and magazines provided more coverage of women's sports, and magazines focusing specifically on this area, such as *Sports Illustrated for Women* and *Women's Sports and Fitness*, started up. African Americans also began to have greater representation in sitcoms, especially on the United Paramount Network (UPN), FOX, and Warner Brothers (WB), but still the number of ethnic minorities on television shows remained abysmally low. Gay characters began to populate television shows with regularity, and in 1997 Ellen DeGeneres's character on *Ellen* became the first openly gay lead on a sitcom.

Media Responsibility. In the wake of the news media coverage of major events, especially the presidential sex scandal, many Americans seemed fed up with the press. The broadcast and publication of sordid details left consumers disgusted and questioning the credibility of the news media. Decisions such as the $5.5 million Food Lion lawsuit against ABC News for manipulative reporting indicated the degree to which the public was outraged with sensational and untrustworthy journalistic tactics. The burgeoning news sources on the Internet also provided forums for gossip and innuendo at a rapid pace that defied checking facts and sources. Yet, despite their concerns, at the end of the decade most Americans still relied on the mainstream media for most of their news and information. Broadcast news was trusted more than print news. Prime-time TV news magazines, CNN, public television news, and local TV newscasts were more trusted than network nightly news. TV news magazines were also more trusted and more utilized than print magazines such as *Time*, *Newsweek*, and *U.S. News & World Report*. Yet, few Americans relied on the Internet for news. Apparently, they did not so much believe that the press was inaccurate in presenting titillating information about scandals and tragedies, but rather, it seems, they thought the media should not be presenting such information at all.

Source:

Frank Newport and Lydia Saad, "A Matter of Trust," *American Journalism Review*, 20 (July/August 1998): 30–33.

TOPICS IN THE NEWS

THE BUSINESS OF BOOKS

Selling Books. Novelists, poets, and writers of nonfiction plied their craft in the 1990s pretty much as they had since the invention of movable type, but the business of publishing and marketing books evolved at a pace that left industry analysts wondering if these were the best of times, worst of times or, more likely, both at once. While there was no shortage of writers clamoring to see their work in print, and readers continued to buy books, the industry found itself in a crisis. Commending a book to the printing press had always been an act of faith for the publisher. Unless the writer could be persuaded to pay the costs of printing out of pocket, publishers risked a substantial sum of money producing books that might never sell. Of course, publishers advertised and tried to persuade bookstore owners to stock and prominently display new titles, but if copies remained unsold, booksellers could return them to the publisher, who either pulped them or sold them at a loss. Since end-of-the-year inventories were taxed, neither publishers, distributors, nor retailers wanted a large backlog of unsold books.

Profit-driven Publishers. According to Jason Epstein, former editorial director of Random House, "book publishing has deviated from its true nature by assuming, under duress from unfavorable market conditions and the misconceptions of remote managers, the posture of a conventional business. Book publishing is not a conventional business. It more closely resembles a vocation or an amateur sport in which the primary goal is the activity itself, not its financial outcome. For owners and editors willing to work for the joy of the task, book publishing . . . has been immensely rewarding. For investors looking for conventional returns, it has been disappointing." Although there were thousands of publishers in the United States, some organized on a not-for-profit basis while others were simply unprofitable, most books were produced and distributed by a small number of major firms. Many of the venerable publishing houses had merged with large conglomerates. For example, Simon & Schuster, which had been established in 1924, became in the 1990s a subsidiary of Viacom, whose media holdings included Blockbuster (a chain of video rental stores), a cable-television business, and a movie studio. Prentice-Hall, a publisher of text-

books, became a subsidiary of Pearson Education, a British-based corporation (that included Simon & Schuster's education division), whose goal was to become "an educational company, not a book company." Although such mergers brought with them economies of scale, they also put increased pressure on publishers to maintain their share of the corporate bottom line. Promising, but unknown, authors whose works might—given adequate attention and marketing—find an audience, were often rejected by the big publishing houses. Economies of scale, however, could also work in reverse. Books published by small, niche publishers and university presses continued to find readers, though their press runs tended to be in the hundreds or thousands rather than hundreds of thousands. Occasionally such books were discovered by a wider audience, as was the case with Norman Maclain's *A River Runs Through It, and Other Stories* (1976), which was reissued in 1983 and made into a movie in 1992. Oprah Winfrey's book-club selections could propel little-known titles onto the best-seller lists virtually overnight, as could a movie based on a new work. Books that were connected with a specific event, such as the trial of O. J. Simpson (1994) or the Clinton-Lewinsky scandal (1998) could sell well, but they required massive and costly press runs and often had to make their mark within a matter of days before the buying public lost interest. At the back of every publisher's mind was the fear that Americans were not reading as many books as they had in decades past.

Superstores. The traditional bookstore was often a small, quaint place, with a particular odor and ambiance, run by an owner/manager who got into the business out of a love for books. Customers wandered in, looked around, and bought something more-or-less on impulse because it looked interesting or the owner recommended it. Though the percentage of the total market cornered by a single bookstore was minute, as a group independent dealers had enormous influence. They ordered books they thought would sell and promoted ones they liked. *The New York Times* best-seller list—the benchmark of literary success—was based on sales reports from such independent establishments, and inclusion on the list, if nothing else, promoted further sales. In the early 1990s, however, a new kind of bookstore entered the marketplace. Barnes and

Noble, Borders Books and Tapes, and Books-A-Million built warehouse-size stores—usually in or near shopping malls—stocked with inventories far larger than independent booksellers could afford. Because the larger stores bought books in mass quantity, they could demand deep discounts from the publishers and undercut independent retailers. They also sold coffee and cappuccino in the store, so shoppers could browse, buy something to read, and enjoy a drink while reading the first chapter. Though some independent bookstores were unable to survive in competition with the superstores, others held their own by offering customers better service, an intimate atmosphere, and, copying an idea from their competition, a shot of espresso. Whether or not the superstores increased total readership, or simply homogenized the market, remained to be seen at the close of the decade.

Digital Publishing. The digital revolution represented a fundamental change in the way information was stored, edited, and distributed. Since these functions were how publishers had traditionally made money, it seemed inevitable that this new technology would cause major upheavals in the publishing business. Books, for example, no longer had to be typeset. Rather, a writer could deliver a text on a disk, or through the Internet; an editor could convert it to a camera-ready format and send it to the press or, bypassing paper and ink altogether, distribute it directly to consumers on the World Wide Web. While only a few on-line magazines won a foothold on the web, most notably *Salon,* by 1999 virtually every major newspaper and news magazine offered readers an on-line version, usually for free. The Gutenberg Project posted thousands of copyright-free books on the web, and in 2000 suspense novelist Stephen King published *Riding the Bullet* entirely online. As early as 1993, well before the World Wide Web became popular, Charles Ellis of Houghton Mifflin observed that electronic publishing would become, "a very significant part of our future. There seems to be a greater sense that it's now more a question of how and when the explosion will happen, not if." By the end of the decade, however, the impact of electronic publishing was just beginning to be felt. It was hindered largely by a reluctance on the part of consumers to pay for anything on the web. Readers complained that looking at pages of text on a computer screen was not nearly as appealing as sitting down with an old-fashioned book. Nonetheless, if electronic publishing was still in its early stages of evolution, the Internet proved to be a powerful sales tool. Amazon.com, billing itself as the "world's largest bookstore," started selling books directly to consumers from its website. Without having to rent store space, Amazon.com could maintain an enormous inventory through which customers could browse from home. By placing an order electronically, a consumer could have his book delivered in a few days. By the end of the decade Amazon.com branched out, offering toys, music, and gourmet food as well as reading material. Books, in the new world of the digital era, became commodities to be bought and sold like pork bellies and soybeans. To readers and

writers, however, the magic of the written word transcended even the unbending realities of the marketplace.

Sources:
John F. Baker, "The Year of Living Dangerously," *Publishers Weekly* (6 January 1997): 35.

Baker and Richard Curtis, "Hard Times, Hard Choices," *Publishers Weekly* (4 January 1993): 45.

Baker and Jim Milliot, "Whatever Happened to the Book Market," *Publishers Weekly* (6 January 1997): 36.

Paul Hilts, "Looking at a New Era," *Publishers Weekly* (8 May 2000): 26.

CARTOONS IN PRIME TIME

Not Just for Kids. At the end of the decade, what was the longest-running situation comedy in prime time? *The Simpsons.* With the success of this show, television executives learned that cartoons were not just for kids on Saturday morning. By the end of the 1990s, FOX, MTV, and WB were all running prime-time cartoons. While *The Simpsons* was by far the most consistently excellent animated series, several other shows provided prime-time laughs and acquired devoted followings.

The Simpsons. Cartoonist Matt Groening introduced *The Simpsons* in 1987 on *The Tracey Ullman Show* (1987–1990). Before creating *The Simpsons,* Groening was best known for his *Life in Hell* comic strip that first appeared in 1977 and became syndicated in more than 250 newspapers worldwide. Following their stint on *The Tracey Ullman Show, The Simpsons* got their own Christmas special in 1989, and a prime-time series was launched 14 January 1990 with "Bart the Genius." In this episode Bart learned his lesson when he cheated on an aptitude test and then ended up in a school for exceptional children. The Simpson family—Homer, Marge, Bart, Lisa, and Maggie—fast became cultural icons and the instruments of hilarious and surprising social satire. Perhaps one testimony to the success of *The Simpsons* is the long list of stars who have lent their voices, and sometimes their images, to the show, including Elizabeth Taylor, Winona Ryder, Michael Jackson, Gillian Anderson, and David Duchovny. In 1994, *The Simpsons* became the first regular prime-time series to be simulcast in Spanish, and in February 1997 it became the longest-running cartoon on prime time, surpassing the record set by *The Flintstones* (1960–1966).

Beavis & Butt-head. Mike Judge made his first cartoon in 1991 and, not knowing what to do with it, mailed it to addresses he found in the phone book. Comedy Central called, and then the Sick and Twisted Festival of Animation, and within a year Judge had produced four animated shorts. In 1992 his "Frog Baseball," which featured two dumb, ugly teens playing the game of the title, aired on MTV, and the channel commissioned the *Beavis & Butt-head* series, which debuted in 1993. The first season featured the two unbelievably stupid male adolescents who sat on their couch reviewing music videos (which were either "cool" or "sucked") while making crass and idiotic remarks, which on occasion hit home with their piercing insight into 1990s American culture. The show was an immediate success, although some media commentators took it too seri-

Cover commemorating the debut of the first prime-time TV cartoon series

ously as an example of the "dumbing down" of America. "Just because you do a show about dumb guys doesn't make it a dumb show," Judge responded. "I think that's a dumb way to look at it. Like if you did a show about straight-A students, that would be a smart show." Judge animated the series and did most of the male voices for seven seasons, ending his work on the series to devote more time to his new animated show, *King of the Hill*.

King of the Hill. Following his success with *Beavis & Butt-head*, Judge teamed up with Greg Daniels, who had written for *The Simpsons*, to create *King of the Hill* for FOX. The series debuted 12 January 1997, following the televised broadcast of Super Bowl XXXI. *King of the Hill* centered on the Hill family of Arlen, Texas—Hank, who sold propane and propane accessories; Peggy, a substitute school-teacher and champion Boggle player; Bobby, their middle-school-aged son; Luanne, the ditzy niece who lived with them; and their neighbors—Dale, Boomhauer, and Bill. Unlike *The Simpsons*, *King of the Hill* presented a family based in the reality of working-class suburbs, the world of Wal-Mart and pickup trucks with gun racks. While the show often explored some of the misfits of Texas storytelling tradition, on the whole it relied on Hank's sense of values and populist notions to create its understated humor.

South Park. It was called "Peanuts on acid," and it won a place on the *New York Times* and *Newsday* ten-best lists for 1997 television. Created by Randolph Trey Parker III and

Matt Stone, *South Park* focused on the adventures and misadventures of four third-graders living in the fictional Rocky Mountain town of South Park. Parker caught the attention of FoxLab executive Brian Graden who commissioned Parker and Stone to create a video Christmas card to send his friends. The duo came up with a five-minute short, *Spirit of Christmas*, which featured Jesus and Santa Claus battling over who would own the holiday, while the *South Park* gang looked on. The short was a success, and the series was born. *South Park* debuted on Comedy Central on 13 August 1997 and became the highest rated original series in Comedy Central history. It won a Cable ACE award for Best Animated Series.

Futurama. Groening followed his success with *The Simpsons* by launching another prime-time cartoon on FOX—*Futurama*, which debuted 3 March 1999. This show was set in New York City a thousand years in the future. Fry, the show's protagonist, was a twenty-five-year-old pizza-delivery boy who made a delivery to a cryogenics lab and accidentally froze himself on 31 December 1999. When he woke up, it was the year 3000 and he had a chance to make a new start. So he went to work for the Planet Express Corporation, a delivery service that transported packages to all five quadrants of the universe. His spaceship companions included the captain, Leela, a beautiful one-eyed alien, and Bender, a robot with very human flaws and emotions.

Family Guy. Twenty-five-year-old Seth MacFarlane created a short animation entitled "The Life of Larry" while he was a student at the Rhode Island School of Design. That effort brought his talent to the attention of FOX executives, who gave him the opportunity to create an animated prime-time series. MacFarlane came up with *Family Guy*, which presented the everyday trials and tribulations of family life with its own special spin. The show premiered 6 April 1999, with Peter Griffin, the protagonist, accidentally destroying the satellite dish that provided television service to his town and then pinning the catastrophe on his teenage daughter. The show then focused on his attempts to live without his beloved tube. A subplot featured Stewie, Peter's evil genius toddler son, who had been forced to eat broccoli, creating a weather machine to destroy broccoli while it was still on the farm.

Daria. A spinoff of *Beavis & Butt-head*, *Daria* was MTV's clever and consistently sarcastic portrayal of teenage life. Daria Morgendorffer was an above-average-intelligence adolescent who struggled to hold on to her individuality in the world of high school. Judge, who created *Beavis & Butt-head*, did not create *Daria*, however. Rather, she was developed by Glenn Eichler and Susie Lewis, who worked on *Beavis & Butt-head*. After that show ended, Eichler and Lewis pitched the idea for *Daria* to MTV Animation, and *Daria* got her own show, which premiered 3 March 1997.

The PJ's. Diversity in prime-time cartoons was represented by *The PJs*, a show about a grumpy African American building supervisor, Thurgood Stubbs, his family, and neighbors in the Hilton-Jacobs Projects. The brainchild of comedian Eddie Murphy, who envisioned a show loosely based on puppetry set in an urban environment, the concept was pitched to FOX executives in 1998. *The PJs*, produced by Will Vinton Studios using a "foamation" technique and with Murphy providing the voice of Stubbs, debuted in January 1999.

Sources:
Comedy Central, Internet website.

FOX Network, Internet website.

MTV, Internet website.

COURT TELEVISION

Real-life Drama. In the 1990s the American appetite for "real" TV grew. In addition to the many "shockumentaries" that showed footage of everything from police chases to animal attacks, Americans began to tune in to courtroom television. Two subgenres experienced increasing popularity throughout the decade—televised coverage of criminal trials and shows starring theatrical judges who generally heard civil cases brought by friends, relatives, neighbors, and business associates against each other.

Cameras in the Courtroom. On the whole, the decision whether or not to allow cameras in the courtroom has tended to be left to state supreme courts. In 1965, however, the U.S. Supreme Court held in *Estes* v. *Texas* that television coverage of a trial could not be conducted in a circus-like atmosphere, but it did not say that this coverage was inherently unconstitutional. In its *Chandler* v. *Florida* (1981) decision, the Court ruled that TV coverage of criminal trials could be allowed providing they did not violate the defendants' rights. Following that ruling, courtrooms across the nation began to welcome television cameras, and by the 1990s almost every state allowed them into some judicial proceedings and about two-thirds freely allowed them into trial courts at the judge's discretion. The 1995 O. J. Simpson case, however, led to a rethinking of the impact of courtroom cameras. Simpson, the former football star, was charged with murdering his former wife Nicole Brown Simpson and her friend Ronald Lyle Goldman. The murder trial was broadcast live by several news networks, including CNN. Judge Lance Ito did not handle the trial well, and the cameras allowed the world to view the spectacle. Following the not-guilty verdict, many people blamed television coverage for influencing the trial, and many judges began to reconsider allowing cameras in their courtrooms. Particularly, in several high-profile cases, cameras were banned following the Simpson debacle—Susan Smith's child-drowning trial in South Carolina (July 1995); the Texas murder trial of Yolanda Saldivar (October 1995), accused of killing singing star Selena Quintanilla-Perez on 31 March 1995; the New Jersey child-murder trial of Jesse K. Timmendequas (May 1997), whose crime, the murder of seven-year-old Megan Kanka, inspired "Megan's law," requiring the notification of neighbors that a convicted sex offender would be living in their community; and the trial of Richard Allen Davis in California (February–June 1996), whose rape and murder of Polly

LEGAL BATTLE OVER LEGAL SELF-HELP

A California publisher of books and software giving detailed instructions on how to complete legal tasks had to go to court in Texas to fight an accusation that the company was engaging in the unauthorized practice of law (UPL). As early as 1992, Texas banned a manual that contained forms and instructions for creating a will. Next the UPL was applied to Parsons Technology's *Quicken Family Lawyer,* a computer program that helps consumers prepare several different legal forms, which a federal judge banned in January 1999 from being sold in Texas. Nolo Press, the most prominent publisher of self-help legal aids in the United States, was accused in 1998 of violating the Texas law and was under investigation by the Unauthorized Practice of Law Committee when the publisher filed a lawsuit in district court in March 1999 against the Committee. The lawsuit asked that the court declare that Nolo's books and software did not practice law and that, consistent with the free-speech provision of the Texas Constitution, they could not be banned from Texas.

Before the lawsuit was heard, the Texas legislature got into the act and amended the government code to address the issue. HB 1507, which was passed by the House on 21 April 1999 and the Senate on 21 May 1999, clarified "practice of law" to exclude legal self-help publications and software as long as the products conspicuously stated that they were not substitutes for the advice of an attorney. Based on that legislative change, the UPL Committee ended their investigation of Nolo Press, and in July 1999 the U.S. Fifth Circuit Court of Appeals ruled that Parsons could sell *Quicken Family Lawyer* in Texas.

Sources: Associated Press, "Federal Judge Bars Distribution of Self-Help Legal Software in Texas."

John Greenwald, "A Legal Press in Texas," *Time,* 3 August 1998.

"Nolo v. Texas—Nolo Declares Victory," *Nolo.com,* Internet website.

James E. Powell, "Quicken Family Lawyer Once Again Legal in Texas," *Winmag.com,* Internet website.

Hannah Klaas led to the "three strikes and you're out" laws against repeat offenders. Critics argued that courtroom television did not present trials in an appropriate way, relying too heavily on sound bites and omitting in-depth explanation and analysis. Particularly in high-profile cases such as the Simpson trial, television, they contended, focused on the sensational and influenced the proceedings. Journalists, on the other hand, argued that the problem was not that cameras were in the Simpson courtroom but that Ito's inability to control the courtroom and lawyers' attempts to manipulate public opinion with statements outside the courtroom created most of the problems in the

INDUSTRIAL SOCIETY AND ITS FUTURE (THE UNABOMBER MANIFESTO)

INTRODUCTION

1. The Industrial Revolution and its consequences have been a disaster for the human race. They have greatly increased the life-expectancy of those of us who live in "advanced" countries, but they have destabilized society, have made life unfulfilling, have subjected human beings to indignities, have led to widespread psychological suffering (in the Third World to physical suffering as well) and have inflicted severe damage on the natural world. The continued development of technology will worsen the situation. It will certainly subject human beings to greater indignities and inflict greater damage on the natural world, it will probably lead to greater social disruption and psychological suffering, and it may lead to increased physical suffering even in "advanced" countries.

2. The industrial-technological system may survive or it may break down. If it survives, it MAY eventually achieve a low level of physical and psychological suffering, but only after passing through a long and very painful period of adjustment and only at the cost of permanently reducing human beings and many other living organisms to engineered products and mere cogs in the social machine. Furthermore, if the system survives, the consequences will be inevitable: There is no way of reforming or modifying the system so as to prevent it from depriving people of dignity and autonomy.

3. If the system breaks down the consequences will still be very painful. But the bigger the system grows the more disastrous the results of its breakdown will be, so if it is to break down it had best break down sooner rather than later.

4. We therefore advocate a revolution against the industrial system. This revolution may or may not make use of violence: it may be sudden or it may be a relatively gradual process spanning a few decades. We can't predict any of that. But we do outline in a very general way the measures that those who hate the industrial system should take in order to prepare the way for a revolution against that form of society. This is not to be a POLITICAL revolution. Its object will be to overthrow not governments but the economic and technological basis of the present society.

5. In this article we give attention to only some of the negative developments that have grown out of the industrial-technological system. Other such developments we mention only briefly or ignore altogether. This does not mean that we regard these other developments as unimportant. For practical reasons we have to confine our discussion to areas that have received insufficient public attention or in which we have something new to say. For example, since there are well-developed environmental and wilderness movements, we have written very little about environmental degradation or the destruction of wild nature, even though we consider these to be highly important.

Source: "The Unabomber Case," *CNNiN interactive Time,* Internet website.

---

trial. The issue for journalists was instead the public's right to know and to witness the execution of justice. Even Associate Justice of the Massachusetts Superior Court Robert Barton said, "The courts belong to the public. They don't belong to the judge, the lawyers or the litigants." In 1990 the Federal Judicial Conference approved a three-year experiment allowing cameras in some federal courts. The report on the experiment recommended that coverage continue, but the conference voted against coverage. At the end of 1999 the "Sunshine in the Courtroom Act," which would allow cameras in federal courtrooms, was pending congressional approval. Interestingly enough, the U.S. Supreme Court itself still refused to permit coverage of its proceedings at the end of the decade.

Court TV. Because of access to many courtrooms and public interest in the American judicial system, the Courtroom Television Network (Court TV) was launched in July 1991 by Steven Brill. While it was initially a small cable network, it had surprisingly good ratings, even reaching number four during the day among cable viewers who received it, according to the first Nielsen survey of its viewers done in 1993. The network aired several high-profile cases, including the William Kennedy Smith rape trial (1991), the insanity defense of serial killer Jeffrey L. Dahmer (1992), the parole hearing of Charles Manson, the Oklahoma City bombing trial of Timothy McVeigh (April–June 1997), and the "nanny murder trial" of Louise Woodward (October 1997). The case that really engaged the American public, however, was the trial of Lyle and Erik Menendez (1994), two Beverly Hills brothers accused of murdering their parents. The jurors could not reach a verdict, and cameras were banned from the courtroom during their retrial in 1995–1996. This time the brothers were convicted of first-degree murder. Following its beginnings in live trial coverage, the network added other forms of programming—judicial news updates, segments on consumer law, small claims courts, and parole and death penalty issues, for example. Critics of Court TV, however, argued that the net-

Media surrounding Stephen Jones, lawyer for Timothy James McVeigh, accused bomber of the
Alfred P. Murrah Building in Oklahoma City (AP/Wide World Photos)

work aired mostly sensational cases in order to garner ratings. Court TV responded by noting that most of its airtime was devoted to unspectacular cases such as medical malpractice and business lawsuits.

Here Comes the Judge. Real-life TV courtroom trials began with *Divorce Court,* which ran from 1957 to 1969 and again from 1986 to 1991, but its popularity was eclipsed by Judge Joseph A. Wapner's *The People's Court,* which aired from 1981 to 1993. After Wapner's tenure, the genre waned and was only revived when Judge Judith "Judy" Sheindlin took to the air in 1996, spawning several other court shows featuring tough judges doling out justice for the TV-viewing public. Sheindlin's career began in family court in 1972 when she was a juvenile prosecutor for the state of New York. In 1982 then-Mayor Ed Koch appointed Sheindlin to the bench as a judge in family court, and in 1986 she was appointed supervising judge in Manhattan. Sheindlin quickly earned a reputation as a no-nonsense judge who delivered tough, direct admonitions to defendants. An article about Sheindlin in the *Los Angeles Times* in 1993 caught the attention of *60 Minutes,* which did a segment on her. After that exposure she was approached by Big Ticket Television about presiding over a television courtroom. Sheindlin was attracted to the notion of a national audience for her message of justice, and *Judge Judy* premiered in national syndication on 16 September 1996. Sheindlin was to-the-point but also injected her show with wit and humor. By 1999 her show had seven million viewers in an average week and she had garnered an Emmy Award nomination. Following *Judge Judy's* success, other court shows took to the air. Wapner moved to *Animal Court,* and Koch brought *The People's Court* back to daytime television. Judge Joe Brown, Judge Greg Mathis,

and Judge Mills Lane all handed out justice on their own programs, though none was as successful as Sheindlin's show. Even *Divorce Court* made a comeback, returning to television in late 1999. According to Bill Carroll, executive vice president at Katz Television Group, "If it is done correctly, the court format is a little bit game show, a little bit talk show." It presents real-life drama with a resolution to the problems presented, and "that is a pretty strong draw for audiences," Carroll said.

Sources:
Fred Graham, "Doing Justice with Cameras in the Courts," *Media Studies Journal,* 12 (Winter 1998): 326–332.

Manuel Mendoza, "Starting this Fall, the Defense Never Will Rest," *Dallas Morning News,* 26 August 1998.

"No Cameras in the Courtroom for Menendez Retrial," 7 October 1995.

Donna Petrozzello, "Court Shows Pack Big Appeal," *New York Daily News Online,* 12 July 1999.

"Television on Trial," *The Economist,* 349 (19 December 1998): 23.

CYBERPORN

A Pitfall on the Information Superhighway. The Internet brought quick, easy access to information into homes and offices worldwide in the 1990s. Bright entrepreneurs developed various e-commerce sites, and the web became a viable place of business for many, including those who offer sexually explicit images. Unlike seedy adult bookstores, many pornographic sites in cyberspace are easily accessible to anyone at a computer keyboard, including children. That recognition set off a raging debate about the legality of pornography on the web. At the core of this debate was the question raised by the new technology—was the web more like print media and therefore protected by the First Amendment from much regulation at all, or

Osborne v. *Ohio*, 18 April 1990

The Supreme Court held that a state could consti-tutionally proscribe the possession of child pornog-raphy because protection of the victims of child pornography outweighed other concerns. The case arose when Ohio police found explicit pictures of adolescent males during the execution of a search warrant. The resident was found guilty of violating an Ohio law that prohibits possession of child por-nography.

Leathers v. *Medlock*, 16 April 1991

By a seven-to-two vote, the Supreme Court found that a differential tax structure for various media did not interfere with First Amendment rights and did not present the potential for censorship of ideas. The case brought by Arkansas's cable industry argued that the state's policy of taxing cable but not print media was unconstitutional because the law might suppress the expression of a particular point of view.

Masson v. *New Yorker Magazine, Inc.*, 20 June 1991

By a nine-to-zero vote, the Supreme Court found that a public figure can recover libel damages from the publisher of an article that attributes altered quotations to the public figure if the alteration results in a material change in the meaning of the statement.

Cohen v. *Cowles Media Co.*, 24 June 1991

By a five-to-four vote, the Supreme Court held that a newspaper could be sued under a state's promis-sory estoppel law (right to sue as a result of a broken promise) because the law does not discriminate against the press. The case arose when a Minnesota gubernatorial campaign worker offered documents about another candidate to newspapers on the basis of a promise of confidentiality. The newspapers then published the worker's name.

Simon & Schuster v. *NY Crime Victims Board*, 10 December 1991

The Court ruled that New York's 1977 "Son of Sam" law, which ordered that proceeds from crimi-nals' selling of their stories be turned over to the New York State Crime Victims Board, violated the free speech clause of the First Amendment.

Turner Broadcasting v. *FCC*, 27 June 1994

The Supreme Court held that the must-carry provi-sion of the Cable Television Consumer Protection and Competition Act of 1992 was not a violation of the First Amendment. Part of the Act required cable companies to allocate a percentage of their channels to local public broadcast stations. The Court found that this Act promoted fair competi-tion and did not determine programming content.

Denver Area Consortium v. *FCC*, 28 June 1996

In a six-to-three decision, the Supreme Court held that the 1992 Cable Television Consumer Protec-tion and Competition Act allowed leased channel cable operators to restrict the transmission of patently offensive or indecent programming, but it did not allow them to ban offensive or indecent pro-gramming on public-access channels.

Arkansas Educational Television Commission v. *Forbes*, 18 May 1998

In a six-to-three decision, the Supreme Court found that the exclusion of a ballot-qualified candidate from a debate sponsored by a state-owned public television broadcaster did not violate the candidate's First Amendment right to freedom of speech. Dur-ing a congressional race the Arkansas Educational Television Commission had excluded an indepen-dent candidate with little popular support from its debate between major party candidates. The Court held that as long as the debates were not designed as public forums, public broadcasters could selectively exclude candidates.

Hanlon v. *Berger* and *Wilson* v. *Layne*, 24 May 1999

By nine-to-zero and eight-to-one votes, the Supreme Court ruled that law enforcement officials violate the Fourth Amendment by allowing the media to enter private homes on execution of a search warrant and that officers were entitled to qualified immunity because it was not yet a clearly established violation of the Fourth Amendment. A reporter and photographer from *The Washington Post* accompanied law enforcement officials during the execution of a search warrant, and the residents sued, alleging the officers had violated their rights to privacy.

Source: The Oyez Project, Northwestern University, First Amendment Cen-ter, Supreme Court Files.

was it more like broadcast media, which are much more open to federal regulation?

Porn on the Web. New technologies made pornography on the web accessible and profitable. "Adult" sites on the web were a billion-dollar business by 1998, and more than half the requests on search engines were adult-oriented. While many pornographic sites required identification and a credit card, many others could be accessed by anyone with web service. One survey found that 25 percent of teens said they had visited X-rated websites. Almost all on-line consumers of porn were men, and a great deal of the adult material available consisted of images not readily available in the average porn-magazine market—including bondage, sadomasochism, bestiality, and pedophilia.

Case of the Thomases. Robert Alan and Carleen Thomas operated the Amateur Action BBS (bulletin board service) out of Milpitas, California. The two entrepreneurs were indicted in 1994 for transmitting pornographic material to a government agent in Tennessee. A Memphis jury decided the images were obscene, and the Thomases were found guilty of violating federal obscenity laws by allowing residents in Tennessee to download explicit images and by sending explicit videotapes into Tennessee by United Parcel Service (UPS). Their conviction was affirmed by the U.S. Court of Appeals in February 1996, and the Supreme Court declined to review the case in October 1996. Federal obscenity law requires the court to consider the standards of the local community into which pornography is sent in determining whether or not the material is obscene. The American Civil Liberties Union (ACLU) and other free-speech advocates argued that the images on the web were not sent specifically to Tennessee and that to find the Thomases guilty in that state would mean that anyone posting explicit material on the web could be liable for prosecution in any community that had access to the information. The Supreme Court did not address the larger issue because the Court found that Thomas required the name, age, address, and phone number of each subscriber before he gave them a password to download images from his BBS. Thus, the Thomases knew their customer was in Tennessee and knew they were providing access to someone in a community with strict obscenity standards. Had they not wished to subject themselves to liability, they could have refused to provide a password to consumers in those communities. In other words, the Court ruled that because the Thomases knew the addresses of customers, their business was essentially no different than *Playboy* or *Hustler* or any "adult" business that ships videotapes or printed material.

Communications Decency Act. As cyberporn began to come to wider public attention in the mid 1990s, lawmakers began to wonder how to regulate it on the web. Despite protests from various constituencies concerned with civil liberties and free speech, the U.S. House voted 416 to 9 and the U.S. Senate 91 to 5 in favor of the 1996 Telecommunications Reform Act, which included the Communications Decency Act. The CDA called for up to two years in prison and fines up to $250,000 for Internet content pro-

As part of the effort to control child pornography, Vice President Al Gore displays the "Parents Guide to the Internet" at a 2 December 1997 conference in Washington, D.C. (AP/Wide World Photos).

viders who displayed "patently offensive material" that could be viewed by a minor or for Internet users who knowingly transmitted indecent material to a minor. Clinton signed the bill into law. In response, ACLU associate director Barry Steinhardt said, "It's a sad day for free speech in America," and the ACLU immediately filed a lawsuit to prevent implementation of the CDA while it was reviewed in the courts. Even among those who voted for the bill, doubts arose about the constitutionality of the measure. A year and a half later the Supreme Court rejected the CDA, declaring it unconstitutional in its abridgement of free-speech rights. The Court voted unanimously against the provision aimed at "patently offensive display," which could have included speech both on websites and in chat rooms, and split seven to two on the transmission provision.

Free Speech on the Internet. In its decision against the Communications Decency Act, the Supreme Court ruled that the provisions of the law unconstitutionally undermined free speech. While affirming the importance of protecting children from inappropriate material, the Court concurred with a lower court ruling that the Act abridged First Amendment rights. In making its ruling, the Court concluded the broadcast standards used to censor obscenity do not necessarily apply to the Internet and that the need to protect children from explicit sexual materials on-line does not supersede the rights of adults to have access to such content. Chris Hansen, lead counsel for the ACLU, which brought suit over the Act, commented that the decision "is recognition that speech over the Internet is entitled to the same First Amendment protection that books and magazines have always enjoyed." Representative Anna Georges Eshoo (D-California) added, "The Supreme Court has demonstrated a far better understanding of free-speech issues on the Internet than Congress did in its rush to address questionable online materials. Today's ruling erects a high legal barrier around online free speech that Congress would be wise not to attempt to breach." Ultimately, then, in the eyes of the Supreme Court justices, preventing children from accessing graphic materials on the Internet is the parent's responsibility.

Blocking Porn. At the end of the decade two technologies existed to help block porn on the Internet, although neither was foolproof. The first is a filtering software that blocks access to sites that contain certain words or phrases associated with sexually explicit material. One of the problems, however, is that such software often also blocks legitimate sites such the National Organization for Women (NOW) or sites that deal with social issues such as violence, sexuality, rape, or homosexuality. Additionally, the software does not always block pornographic pages. The second technology for blocking pornography is a ratings system. Web developers can label sites with invisible tags that indicate the type of content on the site. Users then utilize a ratings system developed by an organization they trust, such as the Parent-Teacher Association (PTA), and program their browsers to access only sites whose content meets the standards of the organization. While both technologies have their problems, opponents to the CDA argue that filtering software and ratings systems are still better options than censorship. Following the Supreme Court decision, Clinton stated, "We will study the opinion closely. We can and must develop a solution for the Internet that is as powerful for the computer as the V-chip will be for television and that protects children in ways that are consistent with America's free-speech values."

MERGERS

Bigger? Yes. Better? Remains to Be Seen. The trend toward consolidation begun in the 1980s continued with renewed vigor in the 1990s. Publishing houses, newspapers, radio and television stations all were swallowed up in the ongoing series of mergers that created larger and larger companies while reducing genuine diversity in ownership and perspective, as well as occasionally creating strange bedfellows.

Newspapers for Sale. The hometown newspaper, a staple of American life, was undergoing a major change in the 1990s that may completely alter the nature of local news. Half of the 1,489 daily U.S. newspapers had circulations under thirteen thousand, but these small papers were being bought up as business investments at an amazing rate—

more than 380 were sold in a five-year period. The hometown daily constituted 70 percent of daily newspaper sales, making the small paper a profitable business for their owners, usually large businesses that bought up and trimmed down these local papers. Community Newspaper Holdings (CNHI), for example, owned ninety-five papers; Liberty Group Publishing owned sixty-three. Hometown dailies were especially appealing because, unlike large metro papers, they usually faced little or no competition, had fewer pages and therefore required less newsprint per copy, rarely had unionized workers, employed cheap labor, and tended to have stable bases.

Fast-Growing Empires. Two of the fastest-growing newspaper empires were CNHI and Liberty, which only came into existence in 1997 and 1998, respectively. Based in Birmingham, Alabama, CNHI owned ninety-five dailies by 1999 with a total circulation of eight hundred thousand and another 102 nondaily publications. Ralph Martin, founder and president of CNHI, worked for Park Communications as vice president of newspaper operations. When Park was sold to Media General, Martin discovered the new owner did not intend to keep all of Park's 106 newspapers. Preferring to avoid a public offering of the small papers he wanted to buy, Martin went to the Alabama pension fund, which put up the money for the venture, enabling CNHI to buy such small dailies as the *Lumberton* (N.C.) *Robesonian,* the *Jacksonville* (Texas) *Daily Progress,* and the *Jeffersonville* (Ind.) *Evening News.* Likewise, in 1998, Leonard Green made a $310 million deal with Hollinger International and created Liberty Group Publishing in Northbrook, Illinois. Liberty's sixty-five papers had a circulation of 275,000, and the company owned another 237 nondaily publications.

Geographic Clusters. A further trend that emerged in all the transfers of local newspapers was clustering, the buying up of newspapers in towns located in geographic proximity. All of the major newspaper publishers—Thomson, Knight-Ridder, Cox, Media General, Hollinger, Gannett, Donrey, and MediaNews—engaged in swapping properties to fit their geographic strategies and tightening the concentration of ownership. The reason for clustering was economic. Newspapers in close geographic proximity could share resources—accounting, for example, or state and regional coverage. Best of all, some papers could share the same printing plant. Geographic concentration also appealed to large retail advertisers who could create a single ad sheet for several newspapers and could make a single purchase on a cost-per-thousand basis rather than buying ad space in bits and pieces.

Reduced Diversity. While building clustered newspaper empires made economic sense for investors, the strategy had its drawbacks. Often newly purchased newspapers found themselves facing staff and budget cuts. When MediaNews bought the *Long Beach* (Cal.) *Press-Telegram,* it slashed newsroom salaries, and more than half the staff left. Twenty-five employees were cut

Costumed ABC employees on strike outside the main gates of the Walt Disney Company on 6 November 1998 (AP/Wide World Photos).

at the *Times Herald* in Norristown, Pennsylvania, by the Journal Register Company; fifty-five editorial positions were cut when Gannett bought the *Asbury Park Press* in New Jersey. Perhaps the greater worry for readers, however, was the reduction in authentic diversity of journalistic voices as newspaper ownership was concentrated into fewer and fewer hands. In twenty-two states a single company owned at least 20 percent of the daily newspapers. For example, CNHI owned more than half of the dailies in Oklahoma, and Media General owned one-third of the papers in Virginia. With newspapers being owned by widely diversified financial corporations, the possibility of conflicts of interest rose greatly. The trend toward corporate ownership also raised the issue of community involvement. With ownership of the paper removed from the local community, many newspapers became less involved in local issues because owners did not see such participation as contributing to the bottom line.

AT&T and TCI. In 1999 a phone company became the largest cable operator in the nation when AT&T bought TCI for $48 billion. For most of its history, the cable industry was a sort of family affair, with small cable companies being owned by local businessmen. As a result of deregulation, competition, and consolidation, however, cable companies quickly became part of larger corporations. At the end of the decade analysts were predicting that eventually four or five cable companies would dominate, with AT&T, Time Warner, and Comcast among the leaders. In June 1999 a federal judge ruled in favor of a lawsuit brought by Portland, Oregon, and surrounding Multnomah County, to require AT&T to open its cable networks to competition. Cable networks in the late 1990s began to deliver more than television, as technological advances allowed them to carry advanced digital services such as the Internet and telephone service. The Portland lawsuit was an attempt to force AT&T to sell access to its network to Internet providers such as America Online (AOL) and MindSpring. AT&T appealed the decision in the U.S. Court of Appeals, but in December it agreed to allow broadband customers a choice of Internet Service Provider (ISP). In a letter to Federal Communications chair William E. Kennard, AT&T's vice president and general counsel James W. Cicconi wrote that the company would allow high-speed Internet access over its cable, giving customers a choice of ISPs beginning in 2002 when its contract with Excite@Home expired.

Disney and ABC. In 1995 Walt Disney Company chair Michael D. Eisner led the Magic Kingdom to spend $19 billion to buy Capital Cities/ABC in a deal that united theme parks, movie and television studios, a major network, and a variety of cable channels, including ESPN and Lifetime TV. Disney's romance with American Broadcasting Company (ABC) began more than forty years earlier when ABC helped Walt Disney finance his dream of a theme park, and talks of merger had been surfacing from time to time throughout the previous decade. Wall Street reacted positively to the merger, and, by the end of the week after the merger announcement, the combined value of the two companies topped $48 billion.

Time Warner and Turner. In 1996 a $7.5 billion merger occurred between Time Warner and Turner Broadcasting System (TBS), creating the world's largest media and entertainment company at the time. Robert Edward "Ted" Turner III, founder and chair of TBS, became vice chair and the largest single shareholder of the newly merged company. The deal left the company owning film and TV studios, a cable system, cable networks, music groups, magazines, publishing houses, the Atlanta Braves, the Atlanta Hawks, and other interests.

Viacom and Paramount. In 1994, Viacom, best known for its ownership of MTV, acquired Paramount Communications for $9.8 billion in a battle with Barry Diller, chairman of QVC Network, who also was trying to buy the company. By building an alliance with Blockbuster Entertainment Corporation, the largest retail video store operator in the world, Viacom was able to close the deal, creating a media empire that included movie and TV studios, a cable system, cable networks, broadcasting stations, publishing houses, motion picture theaters, 3,500 Blockbuster Video stores in ten countries, the New York Knicks and the New York Rangers, and many other interests.

A SAMPLE OF WHAT THEY OWNED: THREE MAJOR MEDIA CORPORATIONS

Time Warner/Turner

Castle Rock

Hanna-Barbera Cartoons

New Line Cinema

Cartoon Network

CNN International

Comedy Central

Court TV

Home Box Office

Headline News

Elektra Entertainment

Atlantic Records

Warner Brothers Records

Time

Fortune

Sports Illustrated

People

Book of the Month Club

Little, Brown & Co.

Atlanta Braves

Atlanta Hawks

DC Comics

World Championship Wrestling

Disney/ABC

Buena Vista Pictures

Miramax Films

Touchstone Pictures

Touchstone Television

The Disney Channel

ESPN and ESPN2

Lifetime TV

Hollywood Records

Discover Magazine

Anaheim Mighty Ducks

Disneyland

California Angels (25 percent)

Viacom/Paramount

Republic Pictures (37 percent)

Spelling Entertainment (70.5 percent)

MTV

Nickelodeon

Showtime USA Network

Three NBC and two CBS affiliates

Four independent and three FOX affiliates

14 radio stations

Pocket Books

Prentice-Hall Imprints

Simon & Schuster Publishers

New York Knicks

New York Rangers

Regional theme parks

Motion picture theaters

Music Plus retail chain

Source: John Pungente, S.J., "Trans-National Media Corporations: What They Own and How Much They Earn," *Mediacy* (1996): 18.

Viacom and CBS. In September 1999, Viacom agreed to purchase Columbia Broadcasting System (CBS) for $34.8 billion. Viacom chair Sumner M. Redstone was slated to be chair and chief executive (CEO) of the new company that was planning to keep the Viacom name. To put Viacom in a strong financial position for the deal, Redstone sold a minority stake in Blockbuster in a public stock offering and planned to sell the remaining stakes within a few months. The merger put the future of Viacom's stake in United Paramount Network (UPN) in jeopardy because government rules prevent a company from owning more than one TV network.

Pearson Education. On 30 November 1998 Pearson Education was launched from the merger of Addison Wesley Longman with Simon & Schuster education, business, professional, and reference divisions to form the largest educational publisher in the world. The newly formed publishing house offered publications in elementary, secondary, professional, and higher education, as well as English Language Teaching and educational technology. Its imprints included Prentice-Hall, Scott Foresman, Allyn & Bacon, Macmillan Computer Publishing, and Modern Curriculum Press.

Sources:

"AT&T to Allow Broadband Cable Internet Access Customer Choice of ISP," *Tech Law Journal,* 7 December 1999, Internet website.

Jack Bass, "E Pluribus Unum," part 13 in "The State of the American Newspaper," *American Journalism Review,* Internet website.

"FTC Approves Turner-Time Warner Merger," *U.S. News Story Page,* CNN Interactive, 12 September 1996, Internet website.

Nancy Gibbs, "Easy as ABC," *Time,* 146 (14 August 1995): 24–30.

John Greenwald, "The Deal that Forced Diller to Fold," *Time,* 143 (28 February 1994): 50–53.

Corey Grice, "The Changing Face of Cable," *CNET News.com,* 10 May 1999, Internet website.

Grice and John Borland, "Cable Open Access Fight Far From Over," *CNET News.com,* 7 June 1999, Internet website.

Steve Lipin, Martin Peers, and Kyle Pope, "Viacom Agrees to Buy CBS," *Wall Street Journal,* 7 September 1999.

Jeff Peline, "AT&T to buy TCI for $48 billion," *CNET News.com,* 24 June 1998, Internet website.

"U.S. Regulator Clears Pearson's $4.6 Billion Simon & Schuster Acquisition," *Computer Curriculum Corporation,* 23 November 1997, Internet website.

Mary Walton, "Forged Chains: Hungry New Investors are Gobbling Up America's Hometown Newspapers," *AJR Newslink,* May 1999, Internet website.

SHOCKUMENTARY

Ratings Winners. In the 1990s the most successful documentaries and ratings winners on television were "shockumentaries," a form of reality-based television that uses a "greatest hits" format to showcase shocking, violent, and gory footage of everything from police shootouts to unbelievably large tumors to natural disasters. They are inexpensive to make and highly successful in garnering high ratings, especially in the all-important eighteen- to nine-nine-year-old demographic. The shockumentary trend began in 1995 when Columbia Broadcasting System (CBS) aired *World's Most Dangerous Animals,* but FOX perfected the genre with *When Animals Attack.* In fact, the second installation of the show was so successful that FOX ran it twice during the November 1996 rating sweeps period.

Shock Predecessor. One of the most successful reality-based programs began in 1989 and had aired more than four hundred episodes by the end of 1999. *COPS* broadcast everyday experiences of law enforcement officers, such as chasing fleeing suspects, intervening in domestic disputes, and apprehending murder suspects. The show was nominated for four Emmys and won its timeslot in the eighteen- to forty-nine-year-old adult demographic during the 1998 May sweeps. At the end of the decade, *COPS* was one of the longest-running programs on television, joining the ranks of *60 Minutes, 20/20,* and *48 Hours.* While *COPS* was an innovator in the reality genre, its images of police experiences were mild compared with the shock specials that came to the fore in the middle of the decade.

Behind the Shock. The brains behind shockumentary programs on FOX was Mike Darnell, executive vice president of specials. Darnell began his TV career as a tape librarian at the local FOX station in Los Angeles. He worked his way up the ranks and was eventually invited to work on *Alien Autopsy: Fact or Fiction* (1995), which became FOX's highest-rated special ever. Based on the success of *Alien Autopsy,* Darnell was placed in charge of specials for the network. Drawing on the success of animal specials produced by *National Geographic,* Darnell decided to put together a show from footage of animals attacking people, and *When Animals Attack* was born.

Animal Snuff Films. NBC executive Don Ohlmeyer likened *When Animals Attack* to a "snuff film," a form of pornography in which women are brutally killed. FOX responded by pointing out that *Dateline* on NBC had aired footage of a man being gored by a bull. Later FOX volunteered not to air the attack-genre specials anymore. During the 1997 sweeps, however, FOX broadcast *World's Deadliest Swarms, When Stunts Go Bad, Cheating Death: Catastrophes Caught on Tape,* and *World's Scariest Police Shootouts.* An advertisement for *When Good Pets Go Bad* encouraged viewers to send in their footage of "performing animals that strike back against trainers or rebel in performance, companion animals trained to fight, animals making mad dashes to freedom, frightening scenes of animals displaying their wild natures, humans under attack—bitten by snakes, pecked by birds, scratched by cats, ravaged by dogs." While *When Animals Attack* was canceled in 1998, its effects continued throughout the industry. The American Broadcasting Company (ABC) aired *World's Deadliest Volcanoes,* FOX developed *When Disaster Strikes,* CBS presented *Forces of Nature,* and even the venerable *National Geographic* created a documentary called *Deadly Encounters* that featured black widow spiders, rattlesnakes, and bears. FOX also developed *Guinness World Records: Primetime,* which debuted 27 July 1998, featuring a three-hundred-pound tumor. Other

Guinness episodes included the man with the longest fingernails, the boy who had his head reconstructed, the "living skeleton," and "werewolf" boys. Another FOX series was the *Busted* specials that showed surveillance video of people doing things they should not have been doing—urinating in a coffeepot, stealing donuts, or copying their breasts on the office copier.

Real TV. Paramount also offered its share of shock with a series called *Real TV.* Premiering 9 September 1996, *Real TV* showed viewers clips from Margot Byra "Margaux" Hemingway's private therapy sessions four years prior to her 28 June 1996 suicide. *Real TV* presented footage of celebrities before they were stars, high-drama rescues, amazing stunts, natural disasters, and bizarre people. Episodes included a man falling onto the concrete bottom of his empty swimming pool, people who survived a shootout at a North Hollywood bank, a Russian kidnapping, a high-rise fire in Chile, and the removal of an arrow from a horse that had been shot at point-blank range. By February 1997 viewership was up 62 percent from its premiere episode.

Shock Promos. Of course, the success of shockumentaries was based on the ability of networks to get people to watch their shows, hence, the shock promotion. While viewers certainly had the choice not to watch the actual shows, the promos were a different matter. These brief glimpses of car crashes, attacking bears, havoc-wreaking tornadoes, and human deformities appeared as commercials during other programs. In the middle of watching *The Simpsons* or *Ally McBeal,* unsuspecting viewers often found themselves confronted with station-break promotions of carnage shows, whether they wanted to see it or not. One commentator wrote, "I'm sure many people who see the promos will tune in so they can survey the rest of the disaster scene . . . I don't want shocking things flashed in front of my eyes without warning. They put warnings before shows like that air in their entirety. Why do they feel it's OK to shove it in my face when I'm unsuspecting?"

Real Violence—Real Problem. A 1998 report based on a three-year study by researchers at UCLA found that overall depictions of violence on television had decreased through the decade, with the exception of the shockumentary. While the genre was virtually nonexistent in the first year of the study, specials that elicited concern over violent content grew from five in the second year to sixteen in the third. Jeffrey Cole, director of the UCLA Center for Communications Policy explained, "Overall, the trend is toward less violence on network television. While the majority of programming deals responsibly with violence issues, reality-based specials do not." In particular, the study cited FOX's *World's Scariest Police Shootouts* and CBS's *The World's Most Dangerous Animals* for their violent and gory content. Cole said that such shows depicted "violence without any context." Darnell disagreed, explaining that the specials depicted the same violence shown on local news everyday. Despite the debate, shockumentaries were

highly successful in the late 1990s. *World's Wildest Police Videos* and *Shocking Moments Caught on Tape* helped FOX capture its best ratings in the eighteen- to forty-nine-year-old demographic in nearly six years.

TABLOID JOURNALISM

News Lite. In the 1990s the line between serious journalism and tabloid reporting blurred substantially. Supermarket tabloids such as the *National Enquirer, Star,* and *Weekly World News* broke and reported top news stories, and more and more the stories that appeared in print and television news began to look like reports from the *National Enquirer.* In fact, *Inside Edition* won a Polk Award for a piece on abuses in the insurance industry in Arkansas, and major networks provided almost nonstop coverage of the woes of Michael Jackson, O. J. Simpson, Patsy and John Ramsey, and Bill Clinton. News anchor Dan Rather called this trend toward the sensational "news lite." On the one hand, Americans assailed the journalistic world for reporting the sordid details, of Clinton's sex scandal, for example, and yet they could not seem to get enough of them. The decade ended with debates still raging about journalistic ethics and the intrusion of the press into the private lives of public figures.

Diana and the Paparazzi. Diana, Princess of Wales, had often complained of the paparazzi who seemed to follow her everywhere after she came to public attention when she was courted by Prince Charles and later married him. When she died in a car accident in Paris on 31 August 1997 while being chased by photographers, her plight raised public interest and anger over the ways news was gathered. While blood alcohol tests revealed that Diana's driver was drunk that night, many people, including Diana's brother, blamed paparazzi for their role in the accident. Not only did they chase Diana, but they immediately snapped pictures of the accident scene. In his statement the day of his sister's death, Earl Spencer said, "I always believed the press would kill her in the end. But not even I could imagine that they would take such a direct hand in her death as seems to be the case. It would appear that every proprietor and editor of every publication that has paid for intrusive and exploitative photographs of her, encouraging greedy and ruthless individuals to risk everything in pursuit of Diana's image, has blood on his hands today." Diana had long pled with the paparazzi for privacy and had even filed a restraining order against one photographer the year before her death. Other celebrities joined in recounting their frustrating experiences with paparazzi, and some U.S. legislators called for measures to limit access to public figures, but journalists argued that laws on the books already addressed the issue and further limitations would prove unconstitutional and unnecessary. Some supermarkets even refused to carry any tabloid newspapers that published accident-scene photographs. Still, coverage of Diana's death in the mainstream media was itself a feeding frenzy. *Time* and *Newsweek* redid their covers and devoted many pages to stories about Diana. In fact, *Time*'s first

Diana, Princess of Wales, passing paparazzi on 3 December 1993 (Michel Stephens/"PA Photos")

issue about Diana's death sold 850,000 newsstand copies—650,000 more than normal—and the commemorative issue sold 1.2 million copies, making these editions the two largest sellers in *Time*'s history. *USA Today*'s circulation for the week following the accident was well above normal, and *The Washington Post* sold more than 20,000 copies above the normal rate of its Sunday editions the day Diana died and the day after her funeral. CNN experienced a dramatic increase in its viewership, and more than fifteen million people watched the *60 Minutes* edition devoted to the princess. More than twenty-six million households tuned in to watch Diana's funeral. Some journalists decried the "tabloid-laundering" of many of the mainstream media—writing about the tabloids and running pictures of the photographs to show how terrible they were. Other journalists defended the practice, saying the photos illustrated serious issues and were not meant to titillate or entertain. In either case, the coverage of Diana's death certainly illustrated the blurring line between tabloid and mainstream journalism, in addition to the increasing pressure on the press to provide entertainment as well as news.

Monicagate. The story that led to the impeachment of President Clinton by the House of Representatives was broken not in the mainstream media but by Internet gossip Matt Drudge on 18 January 1998. Three days later the *Washington Post, Los Angeles Times,* and American Broadcasting Company (ABC) reported the allegations that the president had had an affair with a White House intern, which Clinton denied, and the media frenzy began, with innuendo often replacing fact. Interestingly enough, *Newsweek* lost the scoop because the magazine wanted to act responsibly. Michael Isikoff had been pursuing the story as a follow-up to Paula Corbin Jones's allegations of sexual misconduct against Clinton. In March 1997, Isikoff met with Linda Tripp, a Pentagon public-affairs officer and confidant of Monica Lewinsky, who had taped phone conversations in which Lewinsky discussed her affair with the president. *Newsweek* had held up the story, but when other media published the allegations, *Newsweek* decided to put the details online. The ensuing coverage eclipsed even the media attention that had been given to the O. J. Simpson trial or the death of Princess Diana. Suddenly Americans learned on the nightly news details that would have required a parental-warning label had they appeared in a prime-time show. Night after night television audiences heard about oral sex, adultery, and a semen-stained dress. Newspapers and television consistently used phrases such as "sources said" or "reportedly" to bring every lurid detail, allegation, and innuendo to the public's attention. Eventually, however, people tired of the coverage of the scandal, seeing the media's preoccupation as sordid and excessive. In fact, as the scrutiny intensified, Clinton's popularity increased. An outpouring of anger at the media occurred, and yet people continued to

BEST-SELLERS OF THE 1990S (1990-1998)

Rank	Title	Author	Number Sold	Years as bestseller
1.	*The Pelican Brief*	by John Grisham	11,200,000+	(1993–1994)
2.	*The Client*	by John Grisham	8,100,000	(1994)
3.	*Men are from Mars, Women are from Venus*	by John Gray	6,600,000+	(1993–1997)
4.	*Jurassic Park*	by Michael Crichton	6,400,000+	(1993)
5.	*The Firm*	by John Grisham	6, 175,000+	(1993)
6.	*In the Kitchen with Rose*	by Rosie Daley	5,900,000+	(1994–1995)
7.	*The Bridges of Madison County*	by Robert James Waller	5,800,000+	(1993–1995)
8.	*Rising Sun*	by Michael Crichton	5,600,000	(1993)
9.	*The Chamber*	by John Grisham	5,000,000	(1995)
10.	*The Runaway Jury*	by John Grisham	4,995,000+	(1997)

Source: *Publishers Weekly*

read and tune in. For many critics of the media, coverage of the White House scandal indicated the extent to which tabloid and mainstream journalism had become closely aligned. TV critic Tom Shales wrote in the *Washington Post*, "Once more, as seems to be happening with greater frequency, the lead story on 'Inside Edition' and 'Hard Copy' is the same as the lead story on 'The CBS Evening News.'" Media critic Jon Katz likewise worried that the ramifications of the salacious coverage of the scandal would transmit a dangerous message to the public: "that there is no difference between us and the tabloids."

Sources:

Reese Cleghorn, "The News: It May Never be the Same," *American Journalism Review*, 20 (March 1998): 4.

James McCartney, "News Lite," *American Journalism Review*, 19 (June 1997): 18–25.

Sherry Ricchiardi, "Double Vision," *American Journalism Review*, 20 (April 1998): 30–35.

Ricchiardi, "Standards are the First Casualty," *American Journalism Review*, 19 (March 1998): 30–35.

Jacqueline Sharkey, "The Diana Aftermath," *American Journalism Review*, 20 (November 1997): 18–25.

Alicia C. Shepard, "A Scandal Unfolds," *American Journalism Review*, 20 (March 1998): 21–28.

TALK RADIO

Conservative Media. Through the last few decades of the twentieth century, conservative politicians, religious leaders, and other public figures often decried the "liberal media," but in the 1990s conservatives themselves found their media niche—talk radio. By far, talk-radio shows across the nation were dominated by conservative ideologues who attacked everything from feminism and welfare to gun control and the president, although a few liberals remained on the air. By the middle of the decade talk radio was the second most pervasive radio format in the nation, following only country music, and the number of talk stations had increased to one thousand, up from two hundred only ten years before. One talk station manager suggested the reason that conservatives dominated was that they were simply more entertaining. Liberals, he said, "are genetically engineered not to offend anybody. People who go on the air afraid of offending are not inherently entertaining." Certainly most conservative radio talk-show hosts in the 1990s did not shy away from offending people. For example, Rush Limbaugh, probably the top conservative radio talk-show host of the decade frequently targeted women, the poor, and people of color with his on-air comments. Ken Hamblin, a black conservative whose show was syndicated to more than sixty stations nationwide, at one time railed against gun control and against James Brady, whom he called "the cripple guy," for promoting it. Apparently these shows had a lot of influence too. A 1993 Times Mirror Center for the People and the Press survey found that 44 percent of Americans named talk radio as their primary source for political information. One congressman even suggested that Limbaugh was partly responsible for the GOP's 1994 election victories.

Dittoheads and Feminazis. The number one radio talk-show host of the nineties was Rush Limbaugh, whose three-hour show was heard daily by twenty million listeners. Limbaugh was born in Cape Girardeau, Missouri, in 1954 and began working in radio for a Top-40 station when he was only sixteen. After attending Southeast Missouri State University, he started his radio career at American Broadcasting Company's (ABC) affiliate in Pittsburgh. From there he moved to Kansas City, where he eventually left broadcasting for a few years to work with the Kansas City Royals baseball franchise. In 1983 he returned to broadcasting as a political commentator for KMBZ in Kansas City, and in 1984 he began to host a daytime talk show on KFBF in Sacramento. In 1988 he began his nationally syndicated network talk show. He received the Marconi Award for Syndicated Radio Personality of the Year in 1992 and in 1993 was inducted into the Radio Hall of Fame. Limbaugh's willingness to lambaste the Left, sometimes with complete disregard of the facts, earned him a devoted following, usually white, male, and working class, who agreed with his views and quickly became known as "dittoheads." His comments were often inflammatory and raised the ire of organizations such as the National Organization for Women (NOW) and Fairness and Accuracy in Reporting (FAIR). NOW began a "flush Rush" campaign to encourage advertisers to pull their spots from his show, and FAIR released a report documenting the misinformation (called "disinformation" by some) in many of Limbaugh's comments. For example, Limbaugh contended that volcanoes did more to harm the ozone layer than human-produced chemicals. He claimed that the only people who worried about the ozone layer were "environmental whackos" and "dunderheaded alarmists and prophets of doom." He outraged feminists by referring to them as "feminazis," and in his "Thirty-Five Undeniable Truths" (February 1994) he argued that "Feminism was established to allow unattractive women easier access to the mainstream of society."

Radio Therapy. Close on the heels of Limbaugh's popularity was Dr. Laura C. Schlessinger, whose three-hour daily radio talk show drew twenty million listeners, with fifty thousand of them vying each day to consult her on the air. She was heard on 450 stations in the United States and 35 in Canada. The format of her show was simple. People called in with their problems, and Schlessinger offered them quick—often simplistic and untenable—solutions. Her answer to women who complained about the men in their lives? "Pick better!" A man confessed to a sex addiction problem, and she told him, "No, you have a character problem." Schlessinger's credo was "Grow up." For many Americans searching for a definitive answer in the instability of postmodernism, Schlessinger provided an avenue of certainty. Judgmental and moralistic, she berated callers' behaviors and ordered them around like a media mother. Schlessinger herself was raised without religion by a Jewish father and Catholic mother, and recalled her childhood as an unhappy one. She earned a Ph.D. in physiology from Columbia University Medical School and became a professor at the University of Southern California and Pepperdine University. Eventually she received a license in marriage and family therapy and went into private practice. One day in 1975 she called in to Bill Ballance's radio talk show, and her banter with him went so well that he began to feature her as a regular guest. Within a few years she had her own show. While Schlessinger immersed herself in Judaism, she was supportive of all religions but became a darling of the evangelical Right. Her antifeminist message played especially well amidst the backlash against activist women during the decade. Schlessinger claimed she had once been a feminist, but "all that feminist stuff fell off me like bad dandruff and I knew there was something more important than me and my success." "There is no oppression of women in this country," she said. Feminists "nauseate and sicken me. They've destroyed the sanctity of motherhood." Of course, Schlessinger herself managed a highly successful career and certainly seemed to benefit from advances brought about by the women's movement. Along the way, she managed to offend most people who knew her. Even Ballance, her mentor, referred to her as an "ogre." Still, at the end of the decade her show had already surpassed Howard Stern's and was rivaling Limbaugh's.

Shock Jock. The self-proclaimed "King of All Media," Howard Stern, was the third leading radio host in the decade, delivering a foul-mouthed, offensive, and highly successful show. The best known of the "shock jocks," Stern's show netted him more than $2 million in Federal Communications Commission (FCC) fines throughout the decade for graphic and indecent speech on air. A 1997 Gallup Poll found that 90 percent of Americans were familiar with Stern, but 75 percent of those in the sample held an unfavorable opinion of him, especially women, older people, and better-educated people. Still, when Stern spoke, people listened, and, in fact, his endorsement of George E. Pataki for governor of New York in 1994 was considered a significant factor in the Republican's defeat of incumbent Democrat Mario M. Cuomo. In 1993 Stern endorsed Republican Christine Todd Whitman for governor of New Jersey, and in return she named a rest stop along I-295 in Springfield after him, complete with a plaque featuring Stern peeking from an outhouse. Stern was born in New York in 1954 and graduated from Boston University in 1976. He began work with Infinity Broadcasting in 1985 after being fired from WNBC in New York. The next year his show moved to the morning drive slot in Los Angeles. In August 1986 the show was simulcast in Philadelphia and Washington, D.C. In 1990 Stern finally got the right to syndicate the show, and its expansion began. In 1998 he began a nightly television show on E! Entertainment Television, which earned an MA (mature audiences) rating for its raunchy content. Critics called the show "a low point in television history" and "the dregs of the dregs." Perhaps Stern's lowest point came in 1999 when he found a way to worsen the horror and tragedy of the Columbine High School shootings in Littleton,

Shock-jock Howard Stern (AP/Wide World Photos)

Colorado. While considering the motives for the murders, Stern said, "There were some really good-looking girls running out with their hands over their heads. Did those kids try to have sex with any of the good-looking girls? They didn't even do that. At least if you're going to kill yourself and kill all the kids, why wouldn't you have some sex? If I was going to kill some people, I'd take them out with sex."

Not Necessarily the Facts. The radio talk shows of the 1990s relied more on emotion than reality. While wildly popular, these conservative hosts seemed more concerned with rhetoric, especially that which drew in an audience, than substance or reality. Often the tone of their shows was mean, if not downright vicious. Mike Hoyt, in a 1992 edition of the *Columbia Journalism Review,* explained that the flavor of these talk shows was dictated by the hosts. "There are demagogues, semi-demagogues, and no shortage of hosts who dance around the edge, at least, of hostility toward women, gays, Jews, or blacks." Nonetheless, talk radio seemed to provide a forum for many Americans to have their say or at least to have someone say it for them.

Sources:
"Action Alert: Howard Stern Advocates Rape of Littleton Victims," *Fairness and Accuracy in Reporting (FAIR),* 28 April 1999, Internet website.

Richard Corliss, "Look Who's Talking," *Time,* 145 (23 January 1995): 22–25.

Mike Hoyt, "Turning Up the Volume," *Columbia Journalism Review* (November/December 1992), Internet website.

Frank Newport, "Howard Stern Well Known Across America but Unfavorably Viewed," *Gallup Poll Monthly,* 379 (April 1997): 22–23.

Jennifer L. Pozner, "'I'd Take Them Out with Sex': Journalists Trivialize Howard Stern's Advocacy of Rape as 'Insensitivity,'" *Fairness and Accuracy in Reporting (FAIR),* July/August 1999, Internet website.

Steve Rabey, "Howard Stern Radio Show," *Christianity Today,* 42 (26 October 1998): 15.

"Rush Limbaugh," *Talkwire.com,* Internet website.

Joannie M. Schrof, "No Whining," *U.S. News & World Report,* 123 (14 July 1997): 48–53.

"The Way Things Aren't: Rush Limbaugh Debates Reality," *Fairness and Accuracy in Reporting (FAIR),* July/August 1994, Internet website.

TV TALK SHOWS

Trash TV. The most popular television talk show, *The Oprah Winfrey Show,* took the high ground in the explosion of talk shows in the 1990s. While Winfrey focused on personal empowerment, social activism, and books, other talk shows relied on raucous confrontations and tell-all revelations, culminating with the murder of a *Jenny Jones Show* guest who had revealed on a program his crush on another male participant. Guests came on talk shows voluntarily to air their grievances; reveal deep, dark secrets; or be reunited with mysterious people from their pasts. According to

In March 1995, Jonathan Schmitz, 26, appeared on the *Jenny Jones Show* to meet a secret admirer. Although *Jones* producers insist that Schmitz knew his admirer could be a woman or a man, Schmitz was shocked and embarrassed when the admirer turned out to be his gay neighbor, Scott Amedure, 32. Three days after the taping, Schmitz took a twelve-gauge shotgun to Amedure's home and fired twice at close range into Amedure's chest. Minutes later, Schmitz called 911 and said, "I just walked in the room and killed him." Schmitz's lawyer claimed that Schmitz was deceived by *Jenny Jones* representatives and then snapped three days later when he found a sexually suggestive note on his doorstep and assumed it was from Amedure. Schmitz was found guilty of second-degree murder and illegal possession of a firearm in commission of a felony, but his conviction was overturned because of the mishandling of jury selection. A second guilty verdict was handed down in August 1999. The episode on which he and Amedure appeared never aired.

Meanwhile, Amedure's family filed a civil suit against the *Jenny Jones Show*, alleging that the show was negligent and responsible for the events that led to Amedure's death. The defendants in the case were Telepictures, which produces the show, and Warner Bros. Television, which syndicates it. Both entities are owned by Time Warner. In May 1999 a Michigan jury found in favor of the Amedure family and awarded them $25 million. If the decision is upheld, the case could have far-reaching effects in the talk-show industry.

Attorneys for Warner Bros. argued that the verdict could have a chilling effect on free speech on talk shows, but Geoffrey Fieger, attorney for the Amedure family (and for Dr. Jack Kevorkian), argued that the issue was not free speech but exploitation by TV talk shows. He claimed that the show was reckless in its use of an unstable man for entertainment and did not think about the consequences of the situation in which they placed Schmitz and Amedure. In fact, he went on to condemn not only the *Jenny Jones Show* but all of talk TV, contending that such shows are undermining U.S. culture.

Jenny Jones said she was shocked and outraged by the jury's judgment. She suggested that the reaction to the murder would not have been the same had the murder followed a "heterosexual show." Rather, she argued, the response was about homophobia. Nonetheless, the decision sent shockwaves through the industry, suggesting that the public was ready for talk TV to take some responsibility.

many guests, producers often tried to whip them into a frenzy before they went on the air. The resultant televised emotional outbursts proved entertaining for audiences and took hosts such as Ricki Lake and Jerry Springer to the top of daytime television.

Talk TV in the 1990s. Coming into the 1990s, longtime talk-show host Phil Donahue led the pack, closely followed by Geraldo Rivera, Sally Jesse Raphael, and Winfrey. Donahue and Winfrey, in particular, had fostered a genre of talk show that focused on exploring information and relationships, while encouraging listeners to be better people. All of that changed quickly in the early 1990s when talk shows proliferated with what one cultural critic called "exploitalk." The bar for talk shows had been set low when in 1988 a melee by white supremacists erupted on *Geraldo*, and one of the guests broke the host's nose with a chair. When Maury Povich, Montel Williams, and Jenny Jones took to the air in 1991, Jerry Springer in 1992, and Leeza Gibbons and Ricki Lake in 1993, trash TV emerged to dominate daytime television. While the earlier talk shows had not shied away from controversy, these newcomers added the element of confrontation, and suddenly screaming matches and fistfights became part of daytime talk show fare. With topics such as "Woman in love with a serial killer" and "Girlfriend, I slept with your man and I'll do it again," these shows played to whooping audiences who, along with the hosts and producers, encouraged the escalation of mud-slinging and temper-flaring. In fact, the confrontation format was so successful that in February 1998 the *Jerry Springer Show* nudged Winfrey out of the number one slot she had held since 1987. The debut of the *Rosie O'Donnell Show* in June 1996 signaled an attempt by several performers to clean up daytime TV. Barbara Walters launched *The View*, a daytime show hosted by a group of women, in 1997; Donny and Marie Osmond and Roseanne established shows in 1998; and hip-hop star Queen Latifah debuted her show in 1999. Their impact was widely felt in the industry. Geraldo cleaned up his act and became a serious journalist, leaving his talk show in 1998 to move on to *NBC News*. Even Springer agreed to eliminate the foul language and fistfights, and his ratings slipped 17 percent, allowing *The Oprah Winfrey Show* to regain the number one spot.

A New Television Low? While daytime talk shows brought to television issues that were often silenced in societal discourse, the exploitative aspects highly outweighed the educational benefits they claimed to provide. Quite often the recruiting practices of these shows bordered on the deceptive, and many guests left feeling they had been set up for humiliation. One talk show producer told *TV Guide*, "When you're booking guests, you're thinking, 'How much confrontation can this person provide me?' The more confrontation, the better. You want people just this side of a fistfight." Ambushing guests was a typical tactic. One guest invited to the *Jerry Springer Show* found out, in front of the studio and TV audience, that her husband was still involved with his former girlfriend and that he also

Headline for the 23 April 1998 cover story attacking the
most popular television talk show of the year

had a male lover. She had to encounter them both on camera, and the former girlfriend even assaulted her. The guest, however, saw the experience as a mixed bag. For her, finding out the whole truth was in some ways a relief, and the show offered to pay for counseling for her and her husband. Of course, the appeal of these shows was therapy as entertainment, and in the name of therapeutic disclosure hosts encouraged their guests to reveal intimate and titillating details of their personal lives. While disclosure may have proven helpful to some guests, the fact was that they were simply objects of entertainment for the audience—who were fulfilling their voyeuristic desires. The point of these shows was not really to help guests but to garner ratings by dragging out true confessions. Although the tenor of these shows was generally nonjudgmental, audience members often viewed guests with contempt or watched their misfortunes with a sadistic sort of glee. As one cultural critic explained, "This is one of the more shameless aspects of the talk show spectacle. As passive witnesses, we consume others' misfortunes without feeling any responsibility to do anything to intervene."

Sources:

Vicki Abt, *Coming After Oprah: Cultural Fallout in the Age of the TV Talk Show* (Bowling Green, Ohio: Bowling Green State University Popular Press, 1997).

Abt, "How TV Talkshows Deconstruct Society," *Research/Penn State*, March 1996.

Gina Bellafante, "Playing 'Get the Guest,'" *Time*, 145 (27 March 1995): 77.

James Collins, "Talking Trash," *Time*, 151 (30 March 1998): 63–66.

Joshua Gamson, "Freak Talk on TV," *The American Prospect Online*, 23 (Fall 1995), Internet website.

Richard Huff, "Tamer 'Springer' Losing Ratings Punch," *New York Daily News Online*, 24 June 1999.

Richard Zoglin, "Talking Trash," *Time*, 145 (30 January 1995): 77–78.

TV TECHNOLOGY

More Options. Television options expanded rapidly in the 1990s with new cable networks, digital satellite signals, and WebTV. By the end of the decade, more than two hundred broadcast networks and cable channels were available, and viewers were able to interact with many of their favorite television programs from the comfort of their couch.

Cable Expansion. Throughout the decade the number of cable channels grew sharply, although most new channels were not available to basic cable subscribers. In the early 1990s new channels tended to reflect the programming of existing networks, which targeted broad-based audiences. Instead of offering programs devoted to specific interests, viewers were given more of the same fare by these channels. For example, FX was launched in 1994, featuring a morning show, familiar reruns, a pet show, a collectibles program, and a *Nightline*-style interview show. Nonetheless, the channel, created by FOX, opened up with eighteen million subscribers, the largest start-up figure for any cable service in history. One problem in developing greater diversity was the limitation of the cable system itself, which only allowed about forty slots for programming. Additionally, the cable industry complained that the Cable Television Consumer Protection and Competition Act (1992) took away incentives to add new programming to basic service because the cost the industry was allowed to pass on to the consumer did not make carrying these channels lucrative. Instead, the cable companies focused on adding channels that were not hindered by federal rate caps—premium service, home-shopping networks, and pay-per-view movies. In fact, one of the largest growth areas was adult movie channels, which provided a substantial profit for cable operators. At the end of the decade, however, digital cable technology made possible the expansion of channels into highly specialized areas, and viewers were able to watch channels that were devoted to animals, health, cars, golf, gardening, comedy, science fiction, history, and the outdoors. News, movie, music, and sports channels were especially prolific; channels targeting specific ethnic minorities even went on the air. Many premium movie channels developed multiplexed versions so that, for example, subscribers to Encore also received Encore Love Stories, Encore Westerns, Encore Mystery, Encore Action, and Encore True Stories and Drama. By 1999 just about anyone could find a channel, from the Adam and Eve channel to Z Music, to suit his or her interest.

Crisp Images and Quality Sound. Digital satellite services were first offered in 1994, providing a system for delivering crisp images and quality sound by a digital signal

404

Students used to do their research at the library, searching through card catalogs and journal indices, checking out books, and copying articles. At the end of the 1990s, electronic publishing had changed all that. Everything from newspapers to magazines to books could be found with a point and a click on the web. And at the end of the decade, most of these sites could be surfed free of charge. While some print newspapers essentially reproduced their stories on the web with few changes other than a few hypertext words offering links to other stories, many web publications, such as HotWired, were creating a new genre of media. Editor David Weir explained, "I think what you're looking at is honestly the birth of a new mass media. It's happening right before our eyes." Not everyone was exuberant about the move toward electronic publishing. Many journalists and newspaper publishers found themselves wondering if they were fast becoming dinosaurs. As one journalist put it, "Round One is over and America Online has won." The *New York Times* discovered, for example, that half of its 3 million registered on-line users had never bought a copy of the paper, and a Pew Research Center survey found that the percentage of Americans getting news on-line at least once a week had tripled to over 36 million from 1996 to 1998. Forty-seven percent of under-30 college graduates were reading their news on-line. Unfortunately, often accuracy was sacrificed for speed in the world of the web where immediate posting of information was possible. *Newsweek* columnist and media critic Jonathan Alter summed it up: "The time when newspapers were the gatekeepers of information is over. What newspapers are now becoming is the authenticators of information, the quality control instruments on a huge river of rumor—and for that you have to have reporters. Newspapers will continue to be the primary instruments of newsgathering, but when you have so many sources of information, any one pundit has less influence. Even if there were a Walter Lippmann today, he'd just be another guy with a link to the Drudge Report."

Sources: Carol Pogash, "Cyberspace Journalism," *American Journalism Review News Link,* Internet website.

"Romancing the Abyss," *American Journalism Review News Link,* Internet website.

"Vanity and Panic," *American Journalism Review News Link,* Internet website.

broadcast. An orbiting satellite beamed down signals that provided better-quality pictures than air or cable broadcasts. Another advantage of digital satellite was its availability. While still offered only in limited markets at the end of the decade, digital satellite television was available anywhere a viewer could put a dish with an unobstructed view of the sky. The drawback was that digital satellite services did not provide access to local programming. Network stations were available, but they could be from anywhere in the United States—the American Broadcasting Company (ABC) affiliate in New York or the Columbia Broadcasting System (CBS) affiliate in Los Angeles. The problem was that for most people that meant no access to local news or weather. Digital satellite service was begun by DIRECTV, who actually owned the rights to the acronym DSS (digital satellite systems). Within the first six months of operation, more than half a million people had signed up for service, and by the end of the decade DIRECTV claimed more than half of the satellite-dish market share and offered more sports programming than any other network. The initial setup was expensive, however, and ordering services was complicated. The second of the three biggest satellite companies, Primestar, provided equipment and made its pricing highly competitive, but it required larger dishes, offered fewer channels and sports events, and charged more for pay-per-view movies. The third major player, the DISH Network, offered an aggressive pricing scheme if viewers were willing to commit to one year of premium service. DISH offered many channels not available with the other services, including BBC America, NASA TV, and an extensive collection of international and religious channels, and also was making an attempt to provide local network programming, offering local packages in thirteen major cities. To get all of the channels, however, consumers had to put two or even three dishes on the roof or in the backyard because the network broadcast various stations from different satellites. As an interesting side note, satellite dishes gave rise to another product, the Rock-On, a hollow faux-granite boulder used to camouflage the eighteen-inch dishes.

The Web for Couch Potatoes. Former Apple prodigy Steve Perlman designed the Web TV box in 1995 to adapt computer data so it could be browsed on a television set remote control. The WebTV-based Internet Terminal appeared in stores in October 1996. A year later, WebTV Networks introduced the WebTV-based Internet Receiver that integrated television programming with Internet content and services. Interactive Television Links allowed subscribers to supplement their television viewing with related information from the Internet. WebTV Networks was acquired by Microsoft in August 1997. In 1999 WebTV Networks joined with EchoStar Communications to make Internet TV service available through satellite. The Echo-Star satellite receiver came equipped with an ultrafast, multigigabyte hard drive that made possible such features as TV Pause (freezing a show for up to thirty minutes and then resuming when the viewer is ready to watch again), DVR (automatic recording of several hours of high-quality digital video), and downloadable video games. By the end of 1999, television viewers with WebTV could play along with *Jeopardy,* vote in a live poll while watching *Judge Judy,* access sports stats, and get up-to-the-minute news coverage with *NBC Nightly News.*

Sources:

"Microsoft to Acquire WebTV Networks," 6 April 1997, *WebTV*, Internet website.

Cindy Vanous, "Satellite TV: The Dish on the Dish," *CNET*, 21 December 1999, Internet website.

Richard Zoglin, "Cable's Big Squeeze," *Time*, 143 (27 June 1994): 66–68.

THE V-CHIP

Responsible Viewing. With the explosion of new networks and greater availability of ever-increasing violence on television, parents and politicians became concerned in the 1990s about children's access to violent programming. As early as 1992 the technical standards for a "violence chip," to provide parents with a way to block particular television programs, were discussed at meetings of the Electronic Industries Association. The v-chip reads information encoded in a rated program and blocks programs based on the parent's selections. In 1992 the v-chip was shot down by broadcasters who were afraid it might limit audiences and advertising revenue, but by 1994 the industry group agreed to begin including the device in more-expensive televisions.

Telecommunications Reform. In the midst of the ever-growing telecommunications industry, Congress, along with President Bill Clinton, recognized the need for reform in order to promote competition, stimulate private investment, improve access to information, and provide parents with technology to help them control programming in their homes. In 1996 Congress passed, and on 8 February Clinton signed, the Telecommunications Reform Act. This law provides the industry with guidance in several areas: (1) universal service, ensuring that schools, libraries, hospitals, and clinics have access to advanced telecommunications services; (2) media ownership, preventing undue concentration of television, newspaper, and radio ownership; (3) phone service, removing regulations that kept local Bell Telephone companies and long-distance companies from competing with one another; and (4) the v-chip. The Act calls for a v-chip to be installed in every new television set. In response to this legislation the TV industry in 1997 submitted a voluntary system of parental guidelines for rating television programming to the Federal Communications Commission (FCC) for review, and in March 1998 the FCC found the rating system was acceptable and adopted technical requirements for the v-chip.

President Bill Clinton shows off a v-chip at the Library of Congress on 8 February 1996, where he signed the Telecommunications Reform Act (AP/Wide World Photos).

The following are the ratings established to guide parents in their viewing selection for their children as described by the FCC:

TV-Y (All children—this program is designed to be appropriate for all children). Whether animated or live-action, the themes and elements in this program are specifically designed for a very young audience, including children from ages two through six. This program is not expected to frighten younger children.

TV-Y7 (Directed to Older Children—this program is designed for children age seven and above). It may be more appropriate for children who have acquired the developmental skills needed to distinguish between make-believe and reality. Themes and elements in this level may include mild fantasy or comedic violence, or may frighten children under the age of seven. Therefore, parents may wish to consider the suitability of this program for their younger children.

TV-G (General Audience—most parents would find this program suitable for all ages). Although this rating does not signify a program designed specifically for children, most parents may let younger children watch this program unattended. It contains little or no violence, no strong language, and little or no sexual dialogue or situations.

TV-PG (Parental Guidance Suggested—this program contains material that parents may find unsuitable for younger children). Many parents may want to watch with their younger children. The theme itself may call for parental guidance and/or the program contains one or more of the following: moderate violence (V), some sexual situations (S), infrequent coarse language (L), or some suggestive dialogue (D).

TV-14 (Parents Strongly Cautioned—this program contains some material that many parents would find unsuitable for children under fourteen years of age). Parents are strongly urged to exercise greater care in monitoring this program and are cautioned against letting children under the age of fourteen watch unattended. This program contains one or more of the following: intense violence (V), intense sexual situations (S), strong coarse language (L), or intensely suggestive dialogue (D).

TV-MA (Mature Audiences Only—this program is specifically designed to be viewed by adults and therefore may be unsuitable for children under seventeen). This program contains one or more of the following: graphic violence (V), explicit sexual activity (S), or crude, indecent language (L).

FCC V-Chip Rules. According to the FCC, all TV sets with picture screens thirteen inches or larger must be equipped with the v-chip. Half of all televisions manufactured after 1 July 1999 were required to carry the v-chip, and all thirteen-inch or larger sets made after 1 January 2000 had to meet this requirement. Set top boxes were made available to allow parents to use v-chip technology on their existing televisions. The rating system established by the National Association of Broadcasters, the National Cable Television Association, and the Motion Picture Association of America is known as "TV Parental Guidelines." Ratings are shown on the TV screen for the first fifteen seconds of a rated program.

The V-Chip and the First Amendment. V-chip legislation was carefully crafted to avoid infringing on First Amendment free-speech rights. While television manufacturers would be required to install the v-chip, the program ratings system would be devised and implemented by the television industry. The v-chip would allow parents to block programs they found inappropriate for their children, but it would not require programmers to alter their content to conform to decency standards. Additionally, no requirement was made that programs be labeled. That allowed the TV industry to administer and apply the rating system to specific programs.

V-Chip Task Force. In May 1999 FCC chairman William E. Kennard established the FCC V-Chip Task Force to ensure the success of the v-chip. The goals of the Task Force were: (1) ensure that blocking technology was available and that programmers were encoding ratings information in conformance with their voluntary commitment; (2) educate parents about the v-chip; (3) encourage distribution of information about the v-chip at the time consumers purchase televisions; (4) encourage labeling v chip equipped sets; and (5) gather information about the availability, usage, and effectiveness of the v-chip. According to Task Force chairperson Gloria Tristani, 90 percent of television manufacturers should be in compliance with v-chip technical requirements by the July 1999 and January 2000 deadlines, although a FCC survey found that many programmers were lagging behind in actually encoding ratings.

WOMEN IN THE NEWS

Girl Power. While the second wave of the women's movement began in the late 1960s and early 1970s, the 1990s witnessed several significant developments in women's progress. Research on girls' loss of self-esteem at puberty led to efforts to boost their self-esteem and to encourage girls to consider the entire range of possibilities available to them. Girls went to work with their parents, were encouraged to go into math and science, and scored goals, baskets, and runs in sports. While equality was not fully achieved, important steps were taken, although a backlash had begun by the last few years of the decade as detractors claimed that girls' progress had come at boys' expense. Women, as well, made important steps in the decade, particularly in the areas of politics and sports.

Prior to the mid 1990s few television shows, made-for-TV movies, or specials featured gay and lesbian characters. While *That Certain Summer* (1972) on ABC had featured Hal Holbrook and Martin Sheen as a gay couple, and Billy Crystal had played a bisexual man on *Soap* in the late 1970s, only the occasional gay character appeared on the small screen. As gay rights came to the front of American politics, however, gay characters came to television. A list of examples follows:

In 1992 Guy Savant played a gay character, Matt Fielding, on *Melrose Place.*

A 1994 Ikea ad featured two men shopping for a table together.

Roseanne was kissed by Mariel Hemingway in a gay bar on a *Roseanne* episode entitled "Don't Ask, Don't Tell," which aired on 1 March 1994.

In 1995 Chris Bruno played a gay schoolteacher on *All My Children.*

The 11 January 1997 episode of *Relativity* showed two women engaged in passionate kissing.

In May 1997 Maggie Doyle's character on *ER* came out as a lesbian.

In July 1997 *TV Guide* included two gay-focused shows on its list of *The 100 Greatest Episodes of All Time*—Ellen DeGeneres's coming-out episode and an episode of *My So-Called Life* in which Wilson Cruz's character Rickie, who is gay, had a crush on Corey, played by Adam Biesk.

Will and Grace, a sitcom centering on two gay men and their heterosexual women friends, debuted in the fall of 1998.

In 1999 Warner Bros.'s *Dawson Creek* featured a gay character whose experiences reflected those of series creator Kevin Williamson.

In early 1999 a gay clerical assistant in the detectives' squad room, who had appeared intermittently on *NYPD Blue*, became a permanent character on the show.

On 8 April 1999, the *Cathedral of Hope* aired a program by and for lesbians and gays.

The Simpsons character Waylan Smithers had an obvious crush on his boss, Montgomery Burns.

Oh, Grow Up debuted with newly divorced and newly outed lead.

Animated *Mission Hill* featured Wally and Gus, who had been a couple for forty years and are the only gay couple who enjoyed an on-screen kiss.

Other shows featuring gay characters included *Friends, Mad about You, Spin City, Wasteland, Popular,* and *Action. Drew Carey* featured Drew's cross-dressing heterosexual brother.

The Year of the Woman. Energized by the 1991 Clarence Thomas–Anita Hill hearings, women stormed into the political world in 1992. More female candidates than ever ran for House and Senate seats. Five Democratic women were elected to the Senate—Barbara Boxer and Dianne Feinstein from California, Blanche Lambert Lincoln from Arkansas, Carol Moseley-Braun from Illinois, and Patty Murray from Washington—bringing to eight the total number of women in the Senate. Forty-eight women were elected to the House, and women helped elect Democratic presidential candidate Bill Clinton. The press quickly labeled 1992 as "The Year of the Woman." Nonetheless, the media still tended to focus on trivial stories about Barbara Bush and Hillary Rodham Clinton rather than on serious stories about women candidates. Election coverage still tended to be male dominated and focused on male candidates. Still, when so many women swept into Congress and Clinton was elected, many feminists thought that significant women's issues would at last be addressed, but the hopes of liberal women in 1992 were short-lived. In 1994 the Republicans announced their "Contract with America" and took a majority in both the House and Senate, leading to a new era of cutbacks in abortion rights and welfare.

The 1996 Olympics. The 1996 Olympics in Atlanta marked a turning point in women's sports and in media coverage of female athletes. More women participated than ever before—3,626 women or 36 percent of all Olympic athletes that year—in part a result of the recognition of women's soccer, softball, and triple jump as Olympic events. In many ways the American women athletes were the beneficiaries of Title IX (Education Amendments of 1972), which required gender equity in education, including sports. While its goals had yet to be realized at the end of the decade, its effects were beginning to be seen in women athletes. Donna Lopiano, executive director of the Women's Sports Foundation, explained, "You're seeing the first generation of women who've had a lifetime of opportunity to play. What you see is the female athlete as a rule, not the exception." American women won team gold medals in basketball, soccer, softball, and gymnastics, opening the way for new

First Lady Hilllary Rodham Clinton (center) with senators (l to r) Carol Moseley-Braun (D-Ill.), Patty Murray (D- Wash.), Barbara Ann Mikulski (D-Md.), Barbara Boxer (D-Cal.), Dianne Feinstein (D-Cal.), and Nancy Landon Kassebaum (R-Kans.) (Official White House Photo)

professional leagues in basketball and softball. NBC covered the Olympics and was criticized for hiring only eleven women for its team of fifty-one reporters and commentators, as well as for not providing ample coverage of women's soccer. Recognizing the growing power of women athletes, General Mills placed a photo of the gymnastics team on a box of Wheaties, and Nike made basketball player Sheryl Swoopes the first female athlete to have a sneaker named after her.

Success and Inequality. The success of female athletes at the 1996 Olympics opened the way for the expansion of women's sports in the United States. The American Basketball League (ABL) tipped off its first season on 18 October 1996 with eight teams, featuring Olympic stars Teresa Edwards and Katy Steding. While the league inspired devoted fans, it was unable to stay afloat financially and folded in December 1998. Several commentators attributed its demise, at least in part, to a lack of television exposure. Meanwhile, the Women's National Basketball Association (WNBA) got off the ground 21 January 1997. Rebecca Lobo, Swoopes, and Lisa Leslie all signed to play in the inaugural season. The WNBA received more television coverage, especially from Life-

time TV, a cable channel devoted to women's issues and interests. Perhaps American women's greatest success in sports and sports coverage in the 1990s was women's World Cup soccer. The 1999 championship sold more than 650,000 tickets and grabbed headlines rarely seen for soccer or women's sports in the United States. A crowd of 90,185 at the Rose Bowl in Pasadena watched as the U.S. women defeated China in a sudden-death overtime after 120 scoreless minutes. The game was one of the most-watched sporting events in the decade for women or men. With the growth of televised women's sports, in particular, more women were also given the opportunity to work as sportscasters, with some even moving into the realm of men's sports, including football. Much of the credit for providing career opportunities in sportscasting to women was given to ESPN, which hired Gayle Gardner in 1983. Still, at the end of the 1990s women had a long way to go in achieving gender equality in sports and sports coverage. Few colleges were in full compliance with Title IX. The purse for women's sports was still smaller than men's in the same sport, and salaries for female athletes still ranked far below their male counterparts. Coverage of women's sports also lagged behind.

HEADLINE MAKERS

ELLEN DEGENERES

1958-

COMEDIENNE AND ACTRESS

Coming Out. Depending on whom one asks, it was either a triumph for social justice or a further indicator of the moral decline of Western civilization. In April 1997 actor and comedian Ellen DeGeneres revealed that she was a lesbian, and her character, Ellen Morgan, also came out, making *Ellen* the first sitcom ever with a gay lead character. News of this impending declaration leaked in September 1996, setting off a sensational debate about gays both on TV and in American life. In March of 1997, ABC finally announced that Ellen Morgan would indeed come out on a special one-hour episode the last day of April. For DeGeneres, her declaration was something she had put off for a long time, attempting to keep her personal life separate from her professional one. When DeGeneres approached ABC about having her character discover that she is a lesbian, however, she knew that the time had come for her to be more open and honest about her own life. Furthermore, when she made her decision to go public, she did so in a big way, making the cover of *Time* magazine and appearing with her partner, actor Anne Heche, on *The Oprah Winfrey Show.*

Taking the Heat. While Ellen at last breathed a sigh of relief at having made her decision, ABC and Touchstone Television, which coproduced *Ellen* and were part of The Walt Disney Company, began to feel the heat from anti-gay commentators. Reverend Jerry Falwell referred to the star as "Ellen DeGenerate," and Reverend Donald E. Wildmon and his American Family Association issued threats to boycott advertisers of the show. Two occasional advertisers, J. C. Penney and Chrysler, announced that they would no longer sponsor the show. Nonetheless, *Ellen* was aired on schedule.

Background. DeGeneres was born in 1958 in Metairie, Louisiana. After graduating from high school in 1976, she worked a series of dead-end jobs around New Orleans. Her friends began to tell her how funny she was, and in 1981 she took the stage at an amateur hour at a local coffee house. In 1982 she entered and won Showtime's *Funniest Person in America* competition, which became the springboard for her career as a standup comic. In 1986 she appeared on the *Tonight* show, and, following her routine, Johnny Carson invited her to take a seat, making her the first woman comic to receive the invitation on a debut appearance on the show. She was offered her own sitcom, which appeared in 1994 as *These Friends of Mine* and then, following some rethinking and recasting, became *Ellen* (1994–1998).

"The Puppy Episode." The first three years of *Ellen* were fairly lackluster, to the point that producers suggested the lead character get a puppy to liven up the show. Instead, as an inside joke, writers named the coming-out show "The Puppy Episode." In this show Ellen Morgan realizes that she is gay when she meets Susan, played by Laura Dern. The episode deals with Ellen's struggles and feelings about her realization. Oprah Winfrey appears as Ellen's therapist, and a dream sequence includes cameos by Demi Moore and Billy Bob Thornton. Ellen's lesbian friends Melissa Etheridge and k. d. lang also made guest appearances. *Ellen* scored its highest rating ever with "The Puppy Episode" and garnered five Emmy nominations. The show won an Emmy for best comedy writing and a Peabody Award. The fourth season concluded with episodes in which Ellen Morgan came out to her family and to her employer, with mixed results. In accepting the Emmy, DeGeneres said, "On behalf of the people— and the teenagers especially—out there who think there is something wrong with them because they're gay: There's nothing wrong with you, and don't let anyone make you ashamed of who you are."

Parental Warnings and Cancellation. In its fifth season the show began to explore Ellen Morgan's newly identified sexuality and was frequently rewarded with a parental advisory label that appeared before the show for such potentially "offensive" acts as kissing her girlfriend or discussing her lesbianism. Ratings for the series began to slip, and in April 1998 ABC announced that it would not continue the show.

Sources:

"ABC Axes *Ellen*," *Mr. Showbiz*, 24 April 1998, Internet website.

Elizabeth L. Bland, William Tynan, and Jeffrey Ressner, "Roll Over Ward Cleaver," *Time*, 149 (14 April 1997): 78–85.

Hilary de Vries, "Ellen DeGeneres: Out and About," *TV Guide*, 45 (11–17 October 1997): 20–27.

"Ellen DeGeneres," *Mr. Showbiz*, nd., Internet website.

Rich Marin and Jolie Solomon, and others, "Ellen Steps Out," *Newsweek*, 129 (14 April 1997): 64–67.

IRA GLASS

1959-
JOURNALIST

Revolutionary Journalism. At the end of the 1990s Ira Glass was changing the face of American journalism with his weekly radio program, *This American Life*. Run out of Chicago public radio station WBEZ, *This American Life* was a show of stories held together by a theme. After only three and a half years on the air the program aired on 350 public radio stations to an audience of more than 830,000. The show began when WBEZ received a MacArthur Foundation grant to create a weekly arts/news show and asked Glass to produce it. Instead, Glass pitched the station his idea for a human interest show he wanted to host featuring stories about everyday Americans. WBEZ bought the idea, and the show began broadcasting in November 1995 with an annual budget of $224,000. In its first year it won a Peabody Award and in its second year was awarded a $350,000 grant from the Corporation for Public Broadcasting. Later the Ford Foundation and the National Endowment for the Arts became underwriters, and the show developed a collaboration with Amazon.com that brought in about $125,000 per year. Even Hollywood had contacted Glass about a possible television version of the show.

Background. Glass grew up in Baltimore and then attended Northwestern University and Brown University. His first radio job was selling one-liners to a shock jock in Baltimore. After his first year in college, he volunteered to produce promotional announcements at National Public Radio (NPR) and eventually worked that position into a paying job. For the next sixteen years he worked as a producer and reporter for NPR before becoming host of *This American Life*.

Telling Stories. According to Glass, the aim of *This American Life* was to tell stories that go straight to the heart. He introduced the show as "documentaries, monologues, overheard conversations, found tapes, anything we can think of." He also kept in a lot of the voices and moments edited out of other shows, producing a more raw, realistic sound than most TV or radio programs. While realistic television tended to play toward the prurient, *This American Life* presented reality without tabloid hype, presenting stories about ordinary lives in old-fashioned ways. Glass credited the Readings section of *Harper's* magazine for some of the ideas of *This American Life*. Like the magazine section, *This American Life* was a collection of odds and ends—performance pieces, memoirs, reported pieces, some by big-name writers who normally commanded exorbitant fees but who worked for a few hundred dollars just to be on Glass's show. The program has included a piece about a secular Jew who journeyed to Colorado Springs to try to understand a group of evangelicals who spent their days praying for strangers and a story about a middle-class couple who moved to a poor Missouri town to try to improve things—with very bad results. One show, on the kindness of strangers, featured pieces on a locksmith rescuing a stranded motorist, a white teenager who ran away from home to move in with a black father figure in Harlem in the 1950s, a crazy woman who posted notices on the door of her neighbors accusing them of being drug dealers, and a man who entertained his block with Sinatra songs. Journalist Bill McKibben wrote in *The Nation* in November 1997, that *This American Life* is "simultaneously 'light,' in that it doesn't discuss Madeleine Albright/global warming/the Teamsters election/budget deficits/the Gephardt campaign, and 'deep,' in that it gets at what matters to us most of the time. It is, for instance, almost the only journalism I've ever come across that manages to cover religion as the experience it is in contemporary America. And at the same time there's room for a report from rock-and-roll fantasy camp."

Exerting Influence. The impact of Glass's use of stories told in authentic voices was felt across the world of journalism. *NBC Nightly News* created a segment called "In His Own Words," in which the subject told his or her own tale. *The New York Times, Washington Post, St. Petersburg Times, Baltimore Sun*, and *Philadelphia Inquirer* all began to use more narrative, including even the occasional fictional piece, and more and more they turned to stories of ordinary people. Paul Tough, editor of the Canadian monthly *Saturday Night*, modeled his magazine's front-of-the-book section on the program. Tough described *This American Life* as "applying the tools of journalism to everyday lives, personal lives." At the end of the decade that was still the kind of journalism Glass preferred: "I feel the stories in my heart. There's still a huge, undiscovered country."

Sources:

"About the Show," *This American Life,* Internet website.

Marc Fisher, "It's a Wonderful Life," *American Journalism Review,* 21 (July/August 1999): 40–45.

Steve Ramos, "Radio Head," *CityBeat,* 29 July 1999, Internet website.

THEODORE JOHN KACZYNSKI

1942-

TERRORIST

Antitechnology Serial Killer. Over a seventeen-year period, a mysterious terrorist mailed or planted sixteen package bombs that killed three people and wounded twenty-three others, and he managed to elude the Federal Bureau of Investigation (FBI), the U.S. Postal Service, and the Bureau of Alcohol, Tobacco, and Firearms until 3 April 1996. He was dubbed the "Unabomber" because his first targets were related to universities (un) and airlines (a). His identity became known only when his brother recognized his antitechnology rantings in a manifesto published in the *Washington Post* and contacted federal authorities.

Background. Theodore John Kaczynski was born in Chicago on 22 May 1942. He went to Harvard on scholarship at age sixteen and then earned a Ph.D. in math from the University of Michigan. Upon graduation in 1967, he was appointed assistant professor of mathematics at the University of California, Berkeley. He resigned suddenly from that post in 1969 and then lived and worked in Salt Lake City through the mid 1970s. In 1978 he moved back to Chicago. In 1988 and again in 1991, Kaczynski wrote letters to mental-health professionals requesting counseling by mail rather than face-to-face sessions. In one of the letters he detailed his lack of friends, absence of social contact, and lack of social skills and self-confidence that led to his isolation. Kaczynski eventually began to live in a cramped hand-built cabin on a small plot of land he and his brother owned in Montana. That is where federal agents eventually found and arrested him.

The Bomb is in the Mail. The Unabomber first struck in May 1978. A package was found in a parking lot at the University of Illinois in Chicago with a return address of a Northwestern University professor. The package was addressed to a professor at Rensselaer Polytechnic Institute in Troy, New York. On 26 May the package was returned to Professor Buckley Crist at Northwestern, who was suspicious and contacted the University's Department of Public Safety. Public Safety officer Terry Marker opened the package, which exploded, leaving Marker with minor injuries. Over

time the FBI came to realize that the Unabomber often addressed packages so that the return addressee was the intended recipient. Over the next nine years the Unabomber struck at Northwestern University, American Airlines, United Airlines, the University of Utah, Vanderbilt University, UC-Berkeley, Boeing, the University of Michigan, Rentech computer store in Sacramento, and CAAMS, Inc., in Salt Lake City. With the attack on American Airlines president Percy A. Wood in June 1980, the Unabomber began to use the initials "FC" to mark his work. During the 20 February 1987 attack at CAAMS, a secretary saw a man with a mustache in a sweatshirt placing a bomb next to a car. The employee's description became the basis for the widely used sketch of the Unabomber. After the CAAMS bombing, the Unabomber's attacks seemed to stop until 1993, when in June they resumed with mail bombs being sent to a geneticist at the University of California, San Francisco, and a computer science professor at Yale University. The same day a bomb exploded at Yale, *The New York Times* received a letter mailed from Sacramento connecting "FC" to the two attacks and providing a nine-digit social security format number that it claimed would be used to authenticate future communications from "FC." In July of that year the UNABOM Task Force formed in San Francisco, made up of agents from the FBI, Treasury Department, and U.S. Postal Service.

The Unabomber Speaks. In December 1994 and April 1995, the Unabomber struck again, killing an advertising executive in New Jersey and a Forestry Association president in California. The same day as the Forestry killing, a number of letters with the "FC" identifying mark were received. A victim of one of the 1993 bombs received a letter stating that "there are a lot of people out there who resent bitterly the way techno-nerds like you are changing the world." Two researchers received letters warning them to stop their genetic research. That same day *The New York Times* received a letter from "FC" with the identifying number given in 1993. The author of the letter claimed to be part of an anarchist group and suggested that if *Time, Newsweek,* or *The New York Times* would publish a lengthy article telling his story the group would cease its "terrorist activities," although the group retained the right to engage in "sabotage," which was defined as the destruction of property. On 27 June 1995 *The Washington Post* received a letter from "FC" that repeated the offer to cease its terrorist activities if the *Post* would publish an enclosed manuscript. The next day *The New York Times* received another letter from "FC," including the same 35,000-word manuscript that was sent to the *Post.* The following day *Penthouse* received a letter in response to an earlier offer to publish the manuscript in the magazine. The letter expressed a preference for publication in the more "respectable" *Post* or *Times* and stated conditions for publication, although the group reserved the right to one additional bombing after the *Penthouse* publication. These letters left the publications with an ethical dilemma. On the one hand, if they published the manifesto, they could possibly save potential bombing victims. On the other, they would be acceding to terrorist demands and may well open the door for other murderous social critics to demand publication of their manifestos. Not to publish the document, however, could lead to public perception of the publications as accomplices if the Unabomber struck again. On 19 September 1995 *The Washington Post* and *The New York Times* split the cost of publication of the Unabomber's manifesto in the *Post*. Their joint statement also explained that they had chosen to print the document based on recommendations from the FBI and because of "public safety reasons." The rambling document was essentially an indictment of a technocratic society that crushed human freedom.

Caught. In February 1996, David Kaczynski contacted the FBI, voicing his suspicions that his brother may be the Unabomber. Federal agents arrested Ted Kaczynski at his Montana cabin on 3 April 1996. Kaczynski's trial began with jury selection on 12 November 1997. On 22 January 1998, Kaczynski pled guilty to thirteen counts for attacks in California, New Jersey, and Connecticut that killed three and injured two. He was sentenced to four consecutive life sentences without the possibility of parole.

Sources:
John Elson, "Murderer's Manifesto," *Time,* 146 (10 July 1995): 32–33.

Michael D. Lemonick, "The Bomb is in the Mail," *Time,* 145 (8 May 1995): 70–72.

"The Unabomber: A Chronology," *CourtTV Online,* Internet website.

DAVID E. KELLEY

1956-

TELEVISION PRODUCER

Producer of the Decade. At the end of the 1990s, David E. Kelley had five shows on television and Emmys for Best Drama and Best Comedy. Without a doubt, Kelley was the most influential TV producer of the decade. Kelley started his TV career as a story editor for *L.A. Law* (1986–1994). The next year he became executive story editor and then supervising producer. When Steven Bochco left the show after its third season, Kelley became executive producer. Following *L.A. Law,* Kelley was creative consultant for *Doogie Howser, M.D.* (1989–1993), another Bochco production, and then executive producer of *Picket Fences* (1992–1996), *Chicago Hope* (1994–), *Ally McBeal* (1997–), *The Practice* (1997–), and *Snoops* (1999–). His shows have won seven Emmys for Outstanding Drama and Outstanding Comedy.

Background. Kelley was born in Maine in 1956. He attended Princeton University and Boston University Law School. An associate at a law firm in 1983, he used his legal experience as the basis for a movie script that was produced as *From the Hip* (1987), starring Judd Nelson, Elizabeth Perkins, and John Hurt. When Bochco was planning *L.A. Law,* he began to look for writers with some legal expertise. He saw Kelley's script and invited him to discuss the possibility of writing an episode of *L.A. Law.* The meeting was so successful that Bochco hired Kelley as a story editor for the show. Bochco was Kelley's mentor, and when he left the show to produce *NYPD Blue* (1993–), Kelley stepped into his shoes as executive producer and continued to write scripts for the show. In 1993, Kelley married actress Michelle Pfeiffer.

Quirky, Vulnerable Characters. The one thing Kelley's vast array of programs had in common was characters who were vulnerable, needy, quirky, ridiculous, and often embarrassed; they struggled with difficulties, as well as complex moral and ethical questions. Five-time Emmy Award–winning *Chicago Hope* followed the personal and professional dilemmas of medical personnel in a leading urban hospital. Against the backdrop of high-tech medicine and the ever-changing world of modern health care, the staff members attempted to maintain sanity in a place with a reputation for being "the last, best hope," a hospital that provided treatment no other institution could or dared to give. *Ally McBeal* and *The Practice* could be considered two sides of the same coin. One a comedy and the other a drama, both were set in the world of the courtroom. *Ally McBeal* focused on a young, single lawyer who joined a rather unconventional law firm in which her former longtime boyfriend worked. One of the most interesting elements of the show was its blending of fantasy with reality—Ally's interior life often appeared on the screen—dancing babies and unicorns, for example. Neither did the show shy away from controversial issues, often engaging and offending viewers at the same time. It was an immediate hit, pulling in an average of 11.4 million viewers a week in its first season. *The Practice,* a more serious courtroom drama focusing on the complexities and moral ambiguities of the legal system, premiered on 4 March 1997 to immediate high acclaim. In 1999 *The Practice* was nominated for thirteen Emmy Awards and won the Emmy for Outstanding Drama Series, as well as a Golden Globe for Best Dramatic Series and the George Foster Peabody Award for overall excellence. Kelley's last production of the decade was *Snoops,* a detective show in which three female private eyes teamed up with a surveillance expert to solve cases, which premiered 26 September 1999.

JOHN FITZGERALD KENNEDY JR.

1960-1999
LAWYER AND PUBLISHER

Another Kennedy Tragedy. John F. Kennedy Jr. was only thirty-eight when he died Friday, 16 July 1999, when the small plane he was piloting crashed off the coast of Martha's Vineyard in Massachusetts. Killed along with him were his wife, Carolyn Bessette Kennedy, and her sister, Lauren Bessette. They were on their way to cousin Rory Elizabeth Katherine Kennedy's wedding. When Kennedy did not arrive, a family member contacted the Coast Guard, which launched an intensive search Saturday morning. That afternoon debris from the plane began to wash up on shore. The nation waited in shock as television provided around-the-clock coverage of the search. By Sunday hope was all but gone, and finally the Coast Guard announced that it had changed its search-and-rescue mission to search-and-recover. The bodies, still in the fuselage, were recovered Wednesday; Kennedy was cremated and buried at sea within twenty-four hours.

America's Crown Prince. America's fascination with "John-John" Kennedy began when his father was elected president in 1960, seventeen days before John Jr.'s birth on 25 November. He is probably best remembered for the famous photograph of him, clad in coat and shorts, on his third birthday, standing and saluting the coffin bearing his father's body. Kennedy grew up in the media spotlight, and most people expected him to follow in his family's political footsteps. He graduated from Brown University and New York University Law School, and, though he initially failed the bar exam, he eventually became an assistant district attorney in Manhattan. In 1988 he gave the keynote speech at the Democratic National Convention. Throughout the 1980s and early 1990s, he was the most eligible bachelor in the country and was named "The Sexiest Man Alive!" by *People* magazine. In 1996 he married former fashion publicist Carolyn Bessette in a secret ceremony on Cumberland Island just off the Georgia coast. Despite his good looks and celebrity status, Kennedy was a kind and compassionate man who maintained his family's sense of obligation to disadvantaged Americans, and his sense of humor about himself and "regular guy" demeanor endeared him to the public.

Not Politics as Usual. In 1995, Kennedy surprised most people when, instead of going into politics, he entered the world of publishing, founding *George* magazine, a blend of pop culture and politics. He got Hachette Filipacchi Magazines, publisher of such magazines as *Car and Driver, Elle, Mirabella, Premiere,* and *Woman's Day,* to invest $20 million in the new magazine, and it quickly became the most successful political magazine ever, with a circulation of 419,000, four times that of a serious political magazine such as *New Republic.* The magazine never turned a profit, however, and just before Kennedy's death, Hachette Filipacchi was considering whether or not it would continue its support and Kennedy was reportedly seeking other investors. Kennedy was also editor in chief of the magazine and played a hands-on role in its production. He regularly interviewed hard-to-get celebrities, such as George C. Wallace, Louis Farrakhan, Bill Gates, Colin L. Powell, and the Dalai Lama. Kennedy made *George* a nonpartisan publication, which resulted in its never quite being embraced in Washington. This did not seem to faze Kennedy, who aimed for a more populist approach. Kennedy on occasion exploited his own celebrity status, once posing nude, although strategically shadowed, and he criticized some of his own family members, describing them as "poster boys for bad behavior." Kennedy admitted, "I can't pretend that my last name didn't help sell this magazine or that it didn't help bring it to people's attention."

The Future of *George*. Kennedy's last issue of *George* hit newsstands 31 August 1999 just as he left it. The issue included an interview with Attorney General Janet Reno, an article on Elizabeth Dole, and a listing of the "20 most fascinating women in politics." Much of the October issue was dedicated to commemorating Kennedy. At the end of 1999 the future of *George* was still in question despite a Hachette Filipacchi commitment to keep the publication alive, although with fewer issues, following Kennedy's death. The magazine had experienced a 20-percent drop in advertising in the first half of 1998, and newsstand sales were off by 28 percent. Nonetheless, advertisers were being promised that starting with the February 2000 issue, circulation would reach 450,000. In Kennedy's final issue the staff's letter, which was usually written by Kennedy, explained that the magazine was a reflection of his ideals about politics: "He edited *George* because the magazine manifested certain beliefs he wanted to promote. . . . That for all its imperfections, politics is a noble profession, and given his unique perspective on and place in the political world, he could make a difference by saying so."

Sources:

"*George* to Stay on the Stands," *ABCNews.com.*, nd., Internet website.

Michael Grunwald, "JFK, Jr. Feared Dead in Plane Crash," *Washington Post,* 18 July 1999.

Brian Hartman, "A Man in Full," *ABCNews.com.*, Internet web site.

Howard Kurtz, "From Media Magnet to Media Magnate," *Washington Post,* 18 July 1999.

David Phinney, "The Magazine Left Behind," *ABCNews.com.*, Internet website.

Michael Powell, "JFK Jr.: As Child and Man, America's Crown Prince," *Washington Post,* 18 July 1999.

BRIAN WILLIAMS

1959-

CORRESPONDENT AND NEWS ANCHORMAN

A Road Less Traveled. Brian Williams was a fast-rising star as the White House correspondent on *NBC News* when he took an unusual career turn for an aspiring nightly anchor. He accepted an offer to become anchor on an all-news cable channel launched in 1996 by NBC and Microsoft. Most journalists travel in the other direction, from cable to network news, but Williams had no trouble making the decision to front his own hour-long news program on MSNBC, *The News with Brian Williams.* He continued to anchor the Saturday edition of *NBC Nightly News,* however, and is rumored to be a possible future replacement for Tom Brokaw.

Background. Williams dreamed of being a news anchor as a child in Middletown, New Jersey. He worked his way through a Catholic high school and took classes at Catholic University and George Washington University. He never graduated and instead chose a low-level job in the White House during Jimmy Carter's presidency. From there, Williams spent a short while running the political action committee of the National Association of Broadcasters and then landed his first TV job as a reporter in Pittsburgh, Kansas. He moved to Washington, D.C., then to Philadelphia, and finally to WCBS-TV in New York, where he was a reporter and noon anchor for five years. While at WCBS he won two Emmys for his coverage of the 1987 stock market crash and the 1989 collapse of the Berlin Wall. In 1993 he was recruited to NBC and became Saturday night news anchor after only five months on the job. He won another Emmy for his coverage of the Iowa flood in 1993, and he and Brokaw were nominated for a 1994 Emmy for coverage of the California earthquakes. In 1994 he was assigned by NBC to the White House as its chief correspondent, while continuing to anchor the *Nightly News* on Saturdays. While working as White House correspondent, he accompanied President Bill Clinton on *Air Force One,* and he was the only TV news correspondent to accompany Clinton and former presidents George Bush and Jimmy Carter to the funeral of Yitzhak Rabin in Israel. In 1996 he took the position with MSNBC and got his own program. Although a serious journalist, Williams also exhibited a great deal of charm and wit. He appeared as a guest on *The Tonight Show with Jay Leno, Late Night with Conan O'Brien,* and *The Late Show* with David Letterman, and he was so entertaining on *The Tonight Show* that he was invited back several times.

MSNBC. Williams's willingness to shift to cable news was a significant indicator of how news was changing in the 1990s. MSNBC, a twenty-four-hour news channel, resulted from a $500 million deal between NBC and Microsoft. NBC president Robert Wright convinced Microsoft CEO Bill Gates to pay NBC for half-interest in America's Talking, a cable network owned by NBC that was shut down to make way for MSNBC, and then to put up another $250 million for Microsoft's share of building the new network over five years. By 1997 MSNBC reached 25 million homes (compared with 70 million for CNN), but the network anticipated reaching 55 million homes by 2000. The early success of MSNBC could perhaps be gauged by the talent it has attracted. John Hockenberry left ABC to host his own weekend program, *Edgewise,* and MSNBC's nightly talk show, *InterNight,* included Brokaw, Katie Couric, Byrant Gumbel, Bob Costas, and Bill Moyers in its rotation of hosts. Because cable news reached an audience more interested in news than entertainment, MSNBC was able to provide Williams with a place to develop his unique style of journalism without some of the constraints of network news.

The News with Brian Williams. Cable news gave Williams an opportunity to do serious, in-depth news on television. Without the ratings pressure of network TV, he was able to cover the kinds of stories that interested him—politics, government, business, and the like. Assuming an audience actually interested in news, Williams and executive producer Kathy Sciere were able to run longer stories than would generally be seen on network news, as well as more foreign news and lengthier live interviews. While the show developed hard news rather than lighter features, it also allowed Williams to develop a conversational tone and inject his wit on air. Vice president and general manager of MSNBC Cable Mark Harrington explained, "Brian brings a great sense of tone. He's serious when he needs to be, because the news does deal with tragedy and sadness, and at other times wry and filled with amusement. He can have fun with things." Williams's continuous coverage of the death of Diana, Princess of Wales, on MSNBC, which was simulcast on NBC worldwide, brought praise from TV critics, and after his coverage of the crash of TWA Flight 800 and the death of John F. Kennedy Jr., *New York Magazine* called him the "complete package," and *GQ* named him "the most interesting man in television today."

Sources:

Marc Gunther, "The Cable Guy," *American Journalism Review,* 19 (January/February 1997): 40–46.

"Brian Williams," *MSNBC.com,* Internet website.

OPRAH WINFREY

1954-
ACTRESS AND TALK SHOW HOST

At The Top. *Time* named Oprah Winfrey one of the most important people of the twentieth century, and in 1998 *Entertainment Weekly* ranked her first in its annual list of the most influential people in Hollywood. In 1997 *Newsweek* named her the most important person in books and media, and *TV Guide* called her the television performer of the year. She received the George Foster Peabody Individual Achievement Award and the International Radio and Television Society (IRTS) Gold Medal Award in 1996, as well as the National Academy of Television Arts and Science's Lifetime Achievement Award in 1998. She has won seven Emmy Awards for Outstanding Talk Show Host and nine Emmys for Outstanding Talk Show. The first African American woman to own her own production studio, Winfrey revolutionized television talk shows. Since her show began in syndication in 1986, it remained the number one talk show for twelve consecutive seasons and boasted an audience of thirty-three million viewers every weekday in the United States. The show was also broadcast in 135 countries worldwide. In 1999, Oprah, with an estimated $725 million fortune, showed up as number 348 on the *Forbes* list of the 400 wealthiest Americans. In 1998 she signed a contract to continue her show until 2002.

Background. Winfrey was born on 29 January 1954 in Kosciusko, Mississippi, where she was reared by her grandmother until she was six, when she moved to Milwaukee with her mother. At thirteen she ran away from the abuse in her home and ended up being sent to live with her strict father in Nashville. She began her broadcasting career in 1973 at WVOL radio in Nashville and two years later joined WTVF-TV in Nashville as a reporter and anchor. In 1976 she moved to WJZ-TV in Baltimore and in 1978 became cohost of the station's *People are Talking* talk show. In January 1984 Winfrey moved to Chicago to host WLS-TV's faltering local talk show, *AM Chicago,* and, in less than a year, she turned the program into one of the most popular shows in town. The format expanded to an hour and in 1985 was renamed *The Oprah Winfrey Show.* The show went national in 1986 and quickly became the number one talk show in the nation. In 1987 it received three Daytime Emmy Awards for outstanding host, outstanding talk/service program, and outstanding direction. Winfrey's talents were not limited to the small screen. In 1985 she was nominated for an Academy Award and a

Golden Globe as Best Supporting Actress for her performance in Steven Spielberg's *The Color Purple.* Additionally, in 1986 she became the first black woman to form her own production company, HARPO Productions, Inc., and, when in 1988, HARPO assumed ownership and production responsibilities for *The Oprah Winfrey Show,* Winfrey became the first woman ever to own and produce her own talk show. HARPO also produced a made-for-TV adaptation of Gloria Naylor's *The Women of Brewster Place* (1989) and a feature film in 1998 based on Toni Morrison's *Beloved: A Novel* (1987), both starring Winfrey. In 1996 she introduced *Oprah's Book Club,* an on-air reading club that featured such titles as Ursula Hegi's *Stones from the River* (1994), Kaye Gibbons's *Ellen Foster: A Novel* (1987), Wally Lamb's *She's Come Undone: A Novel* (1992), and Maya Angelou's *The Heart of a Woman* (1981). Each book selected for the show became an instant best-seller. In 1997, Winfrey launched Oprah's *Angel Network,* a humanitarian effort to encourage people to help others in need. One *Angel* program raised enough money to provide college scholarships for 150 students, and the *Angel* network teamed with Habitat for Humanity to provide funding and volunteers to build almost two hundred houses for disadvantaged families across the country. Winfrey also used her clout as a political activist. In 1991 she testified before the U.S. Senate judiciary committee to establish a national database of convicted child abusers. The "Oprah Bill" was signed into law 20 December 1993 by President Bill Clinton.

Oprah's Appeal. According to communications expert Deborah Tannen, Winfrey's appeal resulted from her ability to blend public and private in such a way that viewers, especially women, felt as if she were a friend. Contrasting Winfrey's "rapport-talk" with the "report-talk" typical of male talk show hosts, Tannen explains, rather than focusing on information, Winfrey focused on self-revealing intimacies that are the basis of female friendship. "She turned the focus from the experts to ordinary people talking about personal issues," and divulged her own secrets, making the show more immediate, confessional, and personal. Her show became a medium, then, not only to inform and entertain but also to empower.

Oprah vs. the Cattlemen. Winfrey probably received the most press in the 1990s when she became embroiled in a lawsuit with Texas cattlemen. In an April 1996 show about dangerous foods, vegetarian activist Howard Lyman explained that feeding ground-up animal parts to cattle could spread mad cow disease in the United States. Winfrey exclaimed that the information stopped her from eating another burger. Cattlemen in Texas, led by Amarillo rancher Paul Engler, alleged that the broadcast caused the cattle industry to lose millions of dollars in the beef futures market. Engler and six other plaintiffs brought suit under Texas's False Disparagement of Perishable Foods Products law. The suit claimed that

Winfrey knew the information presented on the show was false and misleading. The case was to be the most significant test of so-called "veggie libel" laws to date, but U.S. District Judge Mary Lou Robinson ruled that the case would not proceed under the "veggie libel" law, but would be tried as a business disparagement case. In this instance, then, cattlemen had to prove that Winfrey maliciously and intentionally sought to harm the beef industry. Attorneys for the cattlemen argued that Winfrey had knowingly produced a show that was unfairly biased against the beef industry. Winfrey's attorney countered that the case was actually about the First Amendment. On 26 February 1998 the jury decided the case in favor of Winfrey, determining that the state-ments did not constitute libel. After the verdict, Winfrey exclaimed, "Free speech not only lives, it rocks!"

Sources:

"About Oprah," *Online with Oprah*, Internet website.

Shanna Foust-Peeples, "Oprah Shunning Offer to Settle, Lawyer Says," *Amarillo Globe-News*, 11 July 1997.

"Oprah Winfrey: Entertainment Executive," *American Academy of Achievement*, Internet website.

"Oprah's Angel Network," *Online with Oprah*, Internet website.

"Spielberg, Oprah Make Forbes' Wealthiest List," *Mr. Showbiz*, 27 September 1999, Internet website.

Deborah Tannen, "Oprah Winfrey," *Time*, 151 (8 June 1998): 196–198.

"Texas Cattlemen Lose Suit Against Oprah," *CNN.com*, Internet website.

"Texas Cattlemen v. Oprah Winfrey," *Media Libel*, University of Houston, School of Communications, Internet website.

PEOPLE IN THE NEWS

On 4 June 1997 United Press International (UPI) names **James Adams,** Washington bureau chief for the *Sunday Times* of London, as its chief executive officer.

On 18 June 1997 **John J. Agoglia** resigns as president of NBC Enterprises. He was directly responsible for the network's dealings with the entertainment industry.

On 25 September 1997 TV sportscaster **Marv Albert** pleads guilty to misdemeanor assault and battery in a sex scandal that leads to his firing from NBC. He receives a twelve-month suspended sentence and is ordered to undergo counseling, and returns to sports broadcasting in July 1999.

Disgraced TV evangelist **James Orsen Bakker** is released after serving 4.5 years in a federal prison. He was convicted in October 1989 on charges of selling $158 million worth of essentially nonexistent timeshares at his Heritage USA Christian theme park.

In August 1998 *Boston Globe* columnist **Mike Barnicle** is suspended for two months after the newspaper discovered he had used jokes from George Carlin's *Brain Droppings* (1997) in his column, as well as fabricated facts and sources. He resigned shortly thereafter and went to work for the *Sunday Daily News.*

In July 1994 **Jeffrey P. Bezos** founds Amazon.com, an Internet retailer of books, music, and videos. By 1998 Amazon.com is the leading on-line shopping site with sales topping $500 million, and Bezos was named *Time* Person of the Year in 1999.

Charles Boesch, a former executive of the *Los Angeles Times,* is sentenced on 7 January 1998 to four years in prison for billing the newspaper more than $775,000 for freelance articles that were never written. He is also ordered to pay all of the money back to the company.

Benjamin C. Bradlee, retired executive editor of *The Washington Post,* is honored 9 December 1997 by the National Constitution Center for his decision to publish the *Pentagon Papers* in 1971 despite threats of punishment and for pursuing the Watergate story and improprieties in the Nixon administration.

Tina Brown, former editor in chief of *Vanity Fair* and *The New Yorker* magazine, joins forces with Miramax and Hearst Corporation to found *Talk,* a new general interest magazine. The magazine is launched 3 August 1999 with an initial press run of one million copies, which quickly sold out, necessitating a second press run of an additional three hundred thousand, making *Talk* the fastest selling title in Hearst history.

In 1990 **Connie Chung** becomes anchorwoman and senior correspondent for the Emmy-winning prime-time news series, *Face to Face with Connie Chung,* on CBS. From 1993 to 1995 she coanchors the *CBS Evening News with Dan Rather and Connie Chung.* She joined *ABC News* in November 1997.

On 8 September 1999, CBS announces that **Jane Clayson,** a Los Angeles-based correspondent for ABC, is named coanchor with **Bryant Gumbel** on *The Early Show.*

Steve Coll is named managing editor of *The Washington Post* on 9 March 1998. Prior to his appointment he was editor and publisher of the *Washington Post Magazine.*

Katie Couric joins the *Today* show in June 1990 as its first national correspondent, serves as substitute anchorwoman from February 1991 to 5 April 1991, when she becomes permanent anchorwoman.

James Fallows is fired as editor of *U.S. News & World Report* in June 1998 after twenty-two months on the job. Reportedly Fallows's departure was the result of disagreements with magazine owner Mortimer Zuckerman.

In May 1998 reporter and associate editor Stephen Glass is fired by *The New Republic* editor Charles Lane, when Glass's penchant for creating his stories comes to light. Glass fabricated quotations, people, corporations, organizations, and even cities. *The New Republic* had published forty of his articles since December 1995.

On 2 April 1997 Amy Gross resigns as editor in chief of *Mirabella* magazine, which she helped found in 1988. Hachette Filipacchi Magazines, which owns *Mirabella,* cites "creative differences" as the reason for the resignation.

Byrant Gumbel, who coanchored the *Today* show with Katie Couric until late 1996, leaves NBC for his own prime-time news magazine, *Public Eye with Bryant Gumbel,* on CBS. The program is canceled in 1998, and Gumbel returns to the morning routine of *The Early Show,* which airs opposite his former cohost.

On 1 January 1997 Ted Harbert resigns as chair of ABC Entertainment.

On 9 January 1998 Dow Jones & Company names executive editor Paul Ingrassia as president of its *Newswires* operation. He won a Pulitzer Prize in 1993 with colleague Joseph B. White for coverage of management turmoil at General Motors.

On 20 January 1997 Julia Kagan is promoted from deputy editor to editor of *Consumer Reports.*

Robert G. Kaiser resigns as managing editor of *The Washington Post* on 30 June 1998. Kaiser held the post for seven years, having joined the paper staff in 1967 after two summers as an intern.

Richard Kaplan becomes president of CNN/USA in August 1997 after seventeen years at ABC, where he was executive producer of *World News Tonight, Prime Time Live,* and *Nightline.*

In July 1990 television reporter Brian Karem from KMOL-TV serves two weeks of a six-month sentence in a San Antonio jail for refusing to give the names of the people who helped arrange a phone interview with accused cop-killer Henry David Hernandez. Karem is released when he informs the judge that the source agreed to be named.

On 9 April 1998 CBS names Mel Karmazin president and CEO. He had been chair and CEO of the CBS Station Group since May 1997.

In 1997 Michael Kelly, editor of *New Republic,* is fired by owner Martin Peretz after only two months on the job and is replaced by Charles Lane. Peretz was unhappy with Kelly's columns that were critical of his friend Vice President Al Gore.

On 11 November 1998 Kevin Klose was named president and CEO of National Public Radio (NPR). Prior to joining NPR, Klose was director of U.S. International Broadcasting and president of Radio Free Europe/Radio Liberty.

In June 1998 Kay Koplovitz, founder of USA Networks, resigned as chair and president. She took the cable network from an idea to a $3.5 billion company in her twenty years in the industry.

On 21 May 1999, after nineteen years of nominations, Susan Lucci finally wins an Emmy for best daytime actress on 21 May 1999, for her role as Erica Kane in the daytime soap *All My Children* (ABC).

On 27 January 1997 Christopher Ma, former *U.S. News & World Report* deputy editor, is named executive producer of the *Washington Post* on-line venture *Digital Ink,* which had been launched October 1993.

In October 1998 Mike McCurry resigns as White House Press Secretary, a job he held since 1995. Prior to that appointment he worked at the State Department and in the presidential campaigns of Jimmy Carter, Walter Mondale, and Michael Dukakis.

Politician-turned-morning-show-host Susan Molinari is released as anchor for *CBS News Saturday Morning* on 23 June 1998. Molinari took the job in September 1997 after a career as a Republican congresswoman from New York City's Staten Island. Audiences did not respond to Molinari, and ratings for her show were quite low.

On 14 April 1998 FOX News Channel hires former presidential adviser Dick Morris, who had resigned August 1996 because of a sex scandal, as a political commentator.

On 30 March 1998 *The New York Post* names James Murdoch, son of media mogul and *Post* owner Rupert Murdoch, as deputy publisher. He was previously president of News America Digital Publishing.

After four years as metropolitan editor for *The New York Times,* Michael Oreskes switches roles to become its Washington bureau chief in September 1997.

In 1998 *Dateline NBC* signs anchorwoman Jane Pauley for another five years with a $5.5 million contract. Pauley had been making around $4.5 million annually.

On 10 June 1990, because of his erratic and often irresponsible behavior, Hutchinson Pearson resigns as editor in chief of *Street News.* He had founded the paper to help homeless people help themselves by selling it on the street.

In January 1995 Norman Podhoretz steps down as editor in chief of *Commentary.* During his thirty-five-year tenure, Podhoretz transformed the previously liberal Jewish monthly into a promoter of neoconservatism.

On 13 February 1998 **William L. Pollak** is named president and chief executive officer for American Lawyer Media, Inc., a publisher of legal journals, newspapers, and other resources. Previously, Pollack was executive vice president for circulation for *The New York Times*.

On 14 July 1998 **David Remnick** is named editor of *The New Yorker*. He had been a staff writer at the magazine since 1992 and had won the Pulitzer Prize for nonfiction in 1994 for *Lenin's Tomb: The Last Days of the Soviet Empire* (1993).

In October 1997 **Lucie Salhany,** the top-ranking woman executive in broadcast television, leaves the United Paramount Network (UPN) to become a board member of BHC Communications and to operate JH Media. Before moving to UPN, she had worked for the FOX Network.

On 18 June 1998 **Patricia Smith,** a columnist for *The Boston Globe,* is forced to resign after the newspaper discovered that she had fabricated characters and quotations in some of her columns. Smith had won the American Society of Newspaper Editors Distinguished Writing Award and had been named a Pulitzer Prize finalist in the commentary category.

On 11 February 1997 home decorator par excellence **Martha Stewart** leaves the *Today* show on NBC to join *CBS This Morning*. Stewart had appeared on *Today* since 1992.

On 26 August 1999 **Jamie Tarses** resigns as president of ABC Entertainment. Her brief three-year tenure with the network had been marked by controversy.

On 4 March 1998 **Carolyn Wall** is named publisher of *Newsweek*. Previously, she had been publisher of *New York* magazine, as well as vice president and general manager of the FOX affiliate in New York City.

On 16 December 1997 **John Walston** is named editorial director of United Press International (UPI). Previously he worked for *USA Today*, the *San Jose Mercury News*, and the *Dallas Times Herald*.

On 13 December 1997 **Gary Webb,** the reporter whose series linked the Central Intelligence Agency (CIA) to crack cocaine sales, resigns from the *San Jose Mercury News*. Webb had been criticized by other newspapers and U.S. officials for the story.

On 21 July 1998 **Betsy West,** an ABC executive who helped launch *PrimeTime Live* and *Turning Point,* joins CBS to oversee its prime-time news broadcasts. West won eighteen Emmy Awards during her tenure at ABC.

Revered *Glamour* editor **Ruth Whitney** is ousted in August 1998 and replaced by her rival, *Cosmopolitan* editor **Bonnie Fuller.** Under Whitney, *Glamour* became one of the most-read women's magazines in the nation with 2.2 million readers (compared with *Cosmopolitan*'s 2.7 million) and won several National Magazine Awards. Fuller was succeeded by *Redbook* editor **Kate White.**

AWARDS

EMMY AWARDS

1990

Outstanding Drama Series: *L.A. Law* (NBC)

Outstanding Comedy Series: *Murphy Brown* (CBS)

Outstanding Variety Series: *In Living Color* (FOX)

1991

Outstanding Drama Series: *L.A. Law* (NBC)

Outstanding Comedy Series: *Cheers* (NBC)

1992

Outstanding Drama Series: *Northern Exposure* (CBS)

Outstanding Comedy Series: *Murphy Brown* (CBS)

Outstanding Variety Series: *The Tonight Show Starring Johnny Carson* (NBC)

1993

Outstanding Drama Series: *Picket Fences* (CBS)

Outstanding Comedy Series: *Seinfeld* (NBC)

Outstanding Variety Series: *Saturday Night Live* (NBC)

1994

Outstanding Drama Series: *Picket Fences* (CBS)

Outstanding Comedy Series: *Frasier* (NBC)

Outstanding Variety Series: *Late Show with David Letterman* (CBS)

1995

Outstanding Drama Series: *NYPD Blue* (ABC)

Outstanding Comedy Series: *Frasier* (NBC)

Outstanding Variety Series: *The Tonight Show with Jay Leno* (NBC)

1996

Outstanding Drama Series: *ER* (NBC)

Outstanding Comedy Series: *Frasier* (NBC)

Outstanding Variety Series: *Dennis Miller Live* (HBO)

1997

Outstanding Drama Series: *Law & Order* (NBC)

Outstanding Comedy Series: *Frasier* (NBC)

Outstanding Variety Series: *Tracey Takes On. . .* (HBO)

1998

Outstanding Drama Series: *The Practice* (ABC)

Outstanding Comedy Series: *Frasier* (NBC)

Outstanding Variety Series: *Late Show with David Letterman* (CBS)

1999

Outstanding Drama Series: *The Practice* (ABC)

Outstanding Comedy Series: *Ally McBeal* (FOX)

Outstanding Variety Series: *Late Show with David Letterman* (CBS)

PULITZER PRIZES FOR JOURNALISM

1990

Public Service: *The Washington* (N.C.) *Daily News.* For revealing that the city water supply was contaminated with carcinogens, a problem that local officials neither disclosed nor corrected over a period of eight years.

The Philadelphia Inquirer. For reporting by Gilbert M. Gaul that disclosed how the American blood industry operates with little government regulation or supervision.

General News Reporting: The Staff, *San Jose* (Cal.) *Mercury News.* For its detailed coverage of the 17 October 1989 Bay Area earthquake and its aftermath.

National Reporting: Ross Anderson, Bill Dietrich, Mary Ann Gwinn, and Eric Nalder, *The Seattle Times.* For coverage of the Exxon Valdez oil spill and its aftermath.

International Reporting: Nicholas D. Kristof and Sheryl Wu Dunn, *The New York Times.* For knowledgeable reporting from China on the mass movement for democracy and its subsequent suppression.

Editorial Writing: Thomas J. Hylton, *The Pottstown* (Pa.) *Mercury.* For his editorials about a local bond issue for the preservation of farmland and other open space in rural Pennsylvania.

Editorial Cartooning: Tom Toles, *The Buffalo News.* For his work during the year as exemplified by the cartoon "First Amendment."

1991

Public Service: *The Des Moines Register.* For reporting by Jane Schorer that, with the victim's consent, named a woman who had been raped—which prompted widespread reconsideration of the traditional media practice of concealing the identity of rape victims.

Spot News Reporting: The Staff, *The Miami Herald.* For stories profiling a local cult leader, his followers, and their links to several area murders.

National Reporting: Marjie Lundstrom and Rochelle Sharpe, Gannett News Service. For reporting that disclosed hundreds of child-abuse-related deaths undetected each year as a result of errors by medical examiners.

International Reporting: Serge Schmemann, *The New York Times.* For his coverage of the reunification of Germany.

Caryle Murphy, *The Washington Post.* For her dispatches from occupied Kuwait, some of which she filed while in hiding from Iraqi authorities.

Editorial Writing: Ron Casey, Harold Jackson, and Joey Kennedy, *The Birmingham* (Ala.) *News.* For their editorial campaign analyzing inequities in Alabama's tax system and proposing needed reforms.

Editorial Cartooning: Jim Borgman, *The Cincinnati Enquirer.*

1992

Public Service: *The Sacramento* (Cal.) *Bee.* For "The Sierra in Peril," reporting by Tom Knudson that examined environmental threats and damage to the Sierra Nevada mountain range in California.

Spot News Reporting: The Staff, *New York Newsday.* For coverage of a midnight subway derailment in Manhattan that left five passengers dead and more than two hundred people injured.

National Reporting: Jeff Taylor and Mike McGraw, *The Kansas City Star.* For their critical examination of the U.S. Department of Agriculture.

International Reporting: Patrick J. Sloyan, *Newsday,* Long Island, N.Y. For his reporting on the Persian Gulf War, conducted after the war was over, which revealed new details of American battlefield tactics and "friendly fire" incidents.

Editorial Writing: Maria Henson, *Lexington* (Ky.) *Herald-Leader*. For her editorials about battered women in Kentucky, which focused statewide attention on the problem and prompted significant reforms.

Editorial Cartooning: Signe Wilkinson, *Philadelphia Daily News*.

1993

Public Service: *The Miami Herald*. For coverage that not only helped readers cope with Hurricane Andrew's devastation but also showed how lax zoning, inspection, and building codes had contributed to the destruction.

Spot News Reporting: The Staff, *Los Angeles Times*. For balanced, comprehensive, penetrating coverage under deadline pressure of the second, most destructive day of the Los Angeles riots.

National Reporting: David Maraniss, *The Washington Post*. For his revealing articles on the life and political record of candidate Bill Clinton.

International Reporting: John F. Burns, *The New York Times*. For his courageous and thorough coverage of the destruction of Sarajevo and the barbarous killings in the war in Bosnia-Herzegovina.

Roy Gutman, *Newsday*, Long Island, N.Y. For his courageous and persistent reporting that disclosed atrocities and other human rights violations in Croatia and Bosnia-Herzegovina.

Editorial Writing: *No Award*

Editorial Cartooning: Stephen R. Benson, *The Arizona Republic*.

1994

Public Service: *Akron Beacon Journal*. For its broad examination of local racial attitudes and its subsequent effort to promote improved communication in the community.

Spot News Reporting: The Staff, *The New York Times*. For its comprehensive coverage of the bombing of Manhattan's World Trade Center.

National Reporting: Eileen Welsome, *The Albuquerque Tribune*. For stories that related the experiences of Americans who had been used unknowingly in government radiation experiments nearly fifty years ago.

International Reporting: *The Dallas Morning News* team, *The Dallas Morning News*. For its series examining the epidemic of violence against women in many nations.

Editorial Writing: R. Bruce Dold, *Chicago Tribune*. For his series of editorials deploring the murder of a three-year-old boy by his abusive mother and decrying the Illinois child welfare system.

Editorial Cartooning: Michael P. Ramirez, *The Commercial Appeal*, Memphis, Tenn. For his trenchant cartoons on contemporary issues.

1995

Public Service: *The Virgin Islands Daily News*, St. Thomas. For its disclosure of the links between the region's rampant crime rate and corruption in the local criminal justice system. The reporting, largely the work of Melvin Claxton, initiated political reforms.

Spot News Reporting: The Staff, *Los Angeles Times*. For its reporting, on 17 January 1994, of the chaos and devastation in the aftermath of the Northridge earthquake.

National Reporting: Tony Horwitz, *The Wall Street Journal*. For stories about working conditions in low-wage America.

International Reporting: Mark Fritz, Associated Press. For his reporting on the ethnic violence and slaughter in Rwanda.

Editorial Writing: Jeffrey Good, *St. Petersburg* (Fla.) *Times*. For his editorial campaign urging reform of Florida's probate system for settling estates.

Editorial Cartooning: Mike Luckovich, *The Atlanta Constitution*.

1996

Public Service: *The News & Observer*, Raleigh, N.C. For the work of Melanie Sill, Pat Stith, and Joby Warrick on the environmental and health risks of waste disposal systems used in North Carolina's growing hog industry.

Spot News Reporting: Robert D. McFadden, *The New York Times*. For his highly skilled writing and reporting on deadline during the year.

National Reporting: Alix M. Freedman, *The Wall Street Journal*. For her coverage of the tobacco industry, including a report that exposed how ammonia additives heighten nicotine potency.

International Reporting: David Rohde, *The Christian Science Monitor*. For his persistent on-site reporting of the massacre of thousands of Bosnian Muslims in Srebrenica.

Editorial Writing: Robert B. Semple Jr., *The New York Times*. For his editorials on environmental issues.

Editorial Cartooning: Jim Morin, *The Miami Herald*.

1997

Public Service: *The Times-Picayune*, New Orleans, La. For its comprehensive series analyzing the conditions that threaten the world's supply of fish.

Spot News: Staff of *Newsday*, Long Island, N.Y. For its enterprising coverage of the crash of TWA Flight 800 and its aftermath.

National Reporting: Staff of *The Wall Street Journal*. For its coverage of the struggle against AIDS in all of its aspects, the human, the scientific, and the business, in light of promising treatments for the disease.

International Reporting: John F. Burns of *The New York Times*. For his courageous and insightful coverage of the harrowing regime imposed on Afghanistan by the Taliban.

Editorial Writing: Michael Gartner of *The Daily Tribune*, Ames, Iowa. For his commonsense editorials about issues deeply affecting the lives of people in his community.

Editorial Cartooning: Walt Handelsman of *The Times-Picayune*, New Orleans, La.

1998

Public Service: *Grand Forks* (N.D.) *Herald*. For its sustained and informative coverage, vividly illustrated with photographs, that helped hold its community together in the wake of flooding, a blizzard, and fire that devastated much of the city, including the newspaper plant itself.

Breaking News Reporting: *Los Angeles Times* Staff. For its comprehensive coverage of a botched bank robbery and subsequent police shoot-out in North Hollywood.

National Reporting: Russell Carollo and Jeff Nesmith of the *Dayton Daily News*. For their reporting that disclosed dangerous flaws and mismanagement in the military health care system, and prompted reforms.

International Reporting: *The New York Times* Staff. For its revealing series that profiled the corrosive effects of drug corruption in Mexico.

Editorial Writing: Bernard L. Stein of *The Riverdale* (N.Y.) *Press*. For his gracefully written editorials on politics and other issues affecting New York City residents.

Editorial Cartooning: Stephen P. Breen of the *Asbury Park Press*, Neptune, N.J.

1999

Public Service: *The Washington Post*. For its series that identified and analyzed patterns of reckless gunplay by city police officers who had little training or supervision.

Breaking News Reporting: *The Hartford Courant* Staff. For its clear and detailed coverage of a shooting rampage in which a state lottery worker killed four supervisors then himself.

National Reporting: *The New York Times* Staff. For a series of articles that disclosed the corporate sale of American technology to China, with U.S. government approval despite national security risks, prompting investigations and significant changes in policy.

International Reporting: *The Wall Street Journal* Staff. For its in-depth, analytical coverage of the Russian financial crisis.

Editorial Writing: Editorial Board of the *Daily News*, New York, N.Y. For its effective campaign to rescue Harlem's Apollo Theatre from the financial mismanagement that threatened the landmark's survival.

Editorial Cartooning: David Horsey of the *Seattle Post-Intelligencer*.

DEATHS

Morey Amsterdam, 83, vaudeville performer, composer, and actor best known as Buddy Sorrell on *The Dick Van Dyke Show*, 28 October 1996.

Robert Angus, 74, producer of *The Adventures of Ozzie and Harriet* and *The Mary Tyler Moore Show*, 5 February 1996.

Harry S. Ashmore, 81, 1958 Pulitzer Prize–winner for his editorials during the school integration crisis at Central High School in Little Rock, Arkansas, 20 January 1998.

Gene Autry, 91, actor, the original singing cowboy, and composer of "Rudolph the Red-Nosed Reindeer," 2 October 1998.

Keyes Beech, 76, foreign correspondent who won a Pulitzer Prize in 1951 for his coverage of the Korean War, 15 February 1990.

Bob Bell, 75, TV's Bozo the Clown for twenty-five years, 8 December 1997.

Erma Bombeck, 69, humorist and housewife-turned-columnist, 22 April 1996.

Sonny Bono, 62, singer, costar of the 1970s hit variety show *The Sonny and Cher Show,* and U. S. congressman from California, 5 January 1998.

Jack Brickhouse, 82, sportscaster and the first voice heard on WGN-TV when it signed on the air in 1948, 6 August 1998.

Wally Bruner, 66, host of the TV game show *What's My Line* from 1968 to 1972, 3 November 1997.

George N. Burns (Nathan Birnbaum), 100, comedian, actor, screenwriter, straightman to his wife Gracie Allen, and star of the *Oh, God!* movies, 9 March 1996.

Raymond Burr, 86, actor and star of *Perry Mason* and *Ironsides,* 12 September 1993.

Herb Caen, 80, San Francisco columnist, Pulitzer Prize–winner, 1 February 1997.

John Joseph Carroll, 77, former city editor for the Associated Press in New York City, 6 June 1997.

Mary Margaret "Peggy" Cass, 74, former *To Tell The Truth* game show panelist, 8 March 1999.

Joseph Cates, 74, TV and Broadway producer, creator of *The $64,000 Question,* and the man who hired Art Carney to play Ed Norton in *The Honeymooners,* 10 October 1998.

John Chancellor, 68, journalist and TV news anchor for NBC, 12 July 1996.

Sey Chassler, 78, former *Redbook* editor who pushed women's magazines to promote equal rights, 11 December 1997.

Virginia Christine (Kraft), 76, actor best remembered for her portrayal of the kindly Swedish lady who offered everyone a cup of Folger's coffee, 24 July 1996.

Nancy Claster, 82, the original *Romper Room* host, "Miss Nancy," 25 April 1997.

Norma Connolly, 71, actor, Ruby Anderson on *General Hospital* for twenty years, 17 November 1998.

William Lawrence Cullen, 70, original host of *The Price is Right,* 7 July 1990.

Adelaide Hawley Cumming, 93, actor, Betty Crocker for General Mills on radio and television, 21 December 1998.

Gail Davis, 71, actor, star of *The Annie Oakley Show* (1953–1956), 15 March 1997.

Jeanne L. Dixon, 79, astrologer and psychic, 25 January 1997.

Stephen Donaldson, 49, Associated Press reporter who was best known as the first survivor of prison rape to speak out on the issue publicly. Donaldson was jailed in 1973 for trespassing at the White House during a peaceful Quaker protest against the bombing of Cambodia. The warden, suspecting Donaldson of writing an exposé, transferred him to a cellblock with violent offenders where he was repeatedly gang-raped over a two-day period, 18 July 1996.

Robert E. Dore, prize-winning editor and producer for NBC and National Public Radio, 7 January 1998.

Douglas Edwards, 73, pioneering broadcast journalist and CBS newsman, 13 October 1990.

Christopher Crosby Farley, 33, comedian and actor, cast member on *Saturday Night Live,* 18 December 1997.

Norman Fell, 74, actor, known best as Mr. Roper from TV's *Three's Company,* 14 December 1998.

Hugh Finn, 44, Louisville, Kentucky, news anchorman, 9 October 1998.

Art Fleming, 70, the original host of the TV game show *Jeopardy* (1964–1975), 25 April 1995.

Chet Forte, 60, producer and director of *Monday Night Football* for twenty-five years, 18 May 1996.

Redd Foxx (John Elroy Sandford), 68, comedian, star of *Sanford and Son,* 11 October 1991.

Mary Frann (Mary Frances Luecke), 55, actor who played Joanna Louden on *Newhart,* 23 September 1998.

Isadore "Friz" Freleng, 89, animator of Bugs Bunny, Porky Pig, Daffy Duck, and Yosemite Sam. He won five Oscars for his work, 26 May 1995.

Fred Friendly (Ferdinand Friendly Wachenheimer), 82, president of CBS News in the 1960s, helped create the Corporation for Public Broadcasting, 3 March 1998.

Eva Gabor, 74, actor, star of sitcom *Green Acres,* 4 July 1995.

William M. Gaines, 70, publisher, father of comic book horror, helped launch *Mad* magazine, 3 June 1992.

Martha Gellhorn, 89, pioneering American war correspondent and third wife of Ernest Hemingway, 15 February 1998.

Gale Gordon, 89, actor, Mr. Mooney on *The Lucy Show* (1962–1968) and Harrison Carter on *Here's Lucy* (1968–1974), 30 June 1995.

Virginia Graham, 86, substitute host on *The Jack Paar Show,* and host of *Girl Talk* (1963–1969) and *The Virginia Graham Show* (1970–1972), 22 December 1998.

Lewis M. Grizzard Jr., 47, humorist, author, and syndicated columnist, 20 March 1994.

Frederick Hubbard Gwynne, 66, actor, Herman Munster on *The Munsters,* 2 July 1993.

Alan Hale Jr., 71, actor, the Skipper on *Gilligan's Island,* 2 January 1990.

Mark Harrington, 51, producer of the *Evening News with Walter Cronkite,* joined NBC in 1996 to help launch MSNBC, a twenty-four-hour news channel, 25 June 1998.

Don Harrison, 61, CNN news anchorman, 2 May 1998.

Phil Hartman, 49, actor and comedian, *Saturday Night Live* star, and the voice of Troy McClure on *The Simpsons,* 28 May 1998.

George A. Heinemann, 78, creator of *Ding Dong School, Shari Lewis and Lamb Chop,* and other children's and educational programs, 21 August 1996.

Shirley Hemphill, 52, actor, the smart-talking waitress Shirley Wilson on the 1970s *What's Happening!,* 10 December 1999.

William A. Henry III, 44, senior writer and theater critic for *Time* from 1981 to 1994, won two Pulitzer Prizes while at the *Boston Globe,* and wrote the 1990 Emmy Award–winning PBS documentary on Bob Fosse, 28 June 1994.

Jim Henson, puppeteer, creator of the Muppets, 16 May 1990.

Ed Herlihy, 89, radio announcer and the voice of Kraft Foods for forty years, 30 January 1999.

John Holliman, 49, CNN news correspondent, 12 September 1998.

Jack Rohe Howard, 87, former president and general manager of E. W. Scripps, 22 March 1998.

Anne Schumacher Hummert, 91, creator of the radio soap opera, including *Stella Dallas* and *Mystery Theater,* 5 July 1996.

Robert M. Hunt, 69, former president and CEO of the *Chicago Tribune,* and former publisher and president of the *New York Daily News,* 27 December 1997.

Wolfman Jack (Robert Weston Smith), 57, disc jockey, 1 July 1995.

Dennis James, 79, television emcee and host of variety and game shows such as *The Price is Right* and *Name That Tune,* 3 June 1997.

Graham Jenkins, 80, reporter for Reuters sent to cover Communist China. After being detained by the ruling Nationalists in Shanghai, he was returned to Hong Kong, where he founded *The Star,* a daily tabloid, in 1965, 3 March 1997.

Bob Kane, 83, cartoonist and creator of *Batman,* 3 November 1998.

Leonard Katzman, 69, executive producer, writer, and director for the TV series *Dallas* and producer of the Chuck Norris series *Walker, Texas Ranger,* 2 September 1996.

Brian Keith (Robert Keith Richey Jr.), 75, actor, best known for his portrayal of Uncle Bill on CBS's *Family Affair* (1966–1971), 24 June 1997.

James L. Knight, 81, cofounder of the Knight newspaper chain, 5 February 1991.

James Komack, 70, actor, writer, TV producer of *My Favorite Martian, The Courtship of Eddie's Father, Chico and the Man,* and *Welcome Back, Kotter,* 24 December 1997.

Charles Kuralt, 62, CBS newsman, best known for his "On the Road" series on *CBS News,* and host of *Sunday Morning,* 4 July 1997.

William G. Lambert, 78, investigative journalist, Pulitzer Prize–winner whose 1969 article in *Life* magazine led to the resignation of U.S. Supreme Court justice Abe Fortas, 8 February 1998.

Michael Landon (Eugene Maurice Orowitz), 54, actor, star of *Bonanza, Little House on the Prairie,* and *Highway to Heaven,* 1 July 1991.

Walter Lantz (Walter Lanza), 93, cartoonist and creator of Woody Woodpecker, 22 March 1994.

Frances Lear, 73, former wife of producer Norman Lear, who took her divorce settlement and began a women's magazine called *Lear's.* After the magazine folded in 1974, she began *Lear Television,* which was also geared toward women, 30 September 1996.

Shari Lewis, 64, puppeteer and creator of puppets Lamb Chop, Charlie Horse, and Hush Puppy, host of *The Shari Lewis Show,* 2 August 1998.

Audra Lindley, 79, actor, Mrs. Roper on *Three's Company,* 16 October 1997.

Jack Lord (John Joseph Patrick Ryan), 77, actor, Detective Steve McGarrett on the longest-running police show on television, *Hawaii Five-O* (1968–1980), 21 January 1998.

Frederick Martin MacMurray, 83, actor, the father on *My Three Sons,* 5 November 1991.

Bill MacPhail, 76, founder of CNN Sports, 4 September 1996.

Robert Magness, 72, creator of cable television; merged Community Television Inc. and its microwave distribution partnership, Western Microwave Inc., to create Tele-Communications, Inc. (TCI), 15 November 1996.

Roy Ketner McDonald, 88, publisher of *Chattanooga News-Free Press* and chair of Chattanooga Publishing Company, 19 June 1990.

Audrey Meadows, 71, actor, Alice Kramden in the 1950s sitcom *The Honeymooners,* 3 February 1996.

Tom Mees, 46, ESPN sports anchorman (1979–1993) and play-by-play announcer for the National Hockey League (NHL) on ESPN2, 14 August 1996.

Burgess Meredith, 89, actor, The Penguin on *Batman,* 9 September 1997.

John Paul "Jay" Monahan III, 42, attorney and legal analyst for NBC News and husband of *Today* show anchorwoman Katie Couric, 24 January 1998.

Elizabeth Montgomery, 57, actor, starred as Samantha Stevens on 1960s sitcom *Bewitched,* 18 May 1995.

Clayton Moore (Jack Carlton Moore), 85, actor, *The Lone Ranger* on TV, 28 December 1999.

Jeffrey A. Moss, 56, helped create such Muppet characters as Cookie Monster and Oscar the Grouch, 25 September 1998.

Jim Murray, 78, sportswriter for the *Los Angeles Times*, 16 August 1998.

Gary Morton, 74, comic, TV producer, husband of Lucille Ball, 30 March 1999.

Harriet Hilliard Nelson, 85, radio and TV actor, best known as the wife and mother in *The Adventures of Ozzie and Harriet*, which ran on radio and TV from 1944 to 1966, 2 October 1994.

Jeanette Nolan, 86, actor, best known for appearances in TV westerns such as *Gunsmoke*, *The Virginian*, and *Wagon Train*, 5 June 1998.

William Samuel Paley, 89, founder of CBS, 15 November 1990.

Mary Phelan, 37, St. Louis KMOV-TV news anchorwoman, 20 December 1998.

Dana Michelle Plato, 34, actor, child star of *Diff'rent Strokes*, 8 May 1999.

Antonio Prohias, 77, cartoonist for *MAD* magazine and artist for *Spy vs. Spy* cartoon strip, 24 February 1998.

Eugene S. Pulliam, 84, publisher of *The Indianapolis Star* and *The Indianapolis News*, 20 January 1999.

Gene Rayburn, 81, game show host for *Concentration, Joker's Wild*, and *The Match Game*, 29 November 1999.

Harry Reasoner, 68, journalist, TV news anchorman, correspondent on *60 Minutes*, 6 August 1991.

Robert Reed, 59, actor, father on the sitcom *The Brady Bunch*, 12 May 1992.

Tommy Rettig, 54, actor, the first boy to star alongside Lassie in the TV series debut, 15 February 1996.

William Roberts, 83, creator of *The Donna Reed Show*, 5 March 1997.

Eugene Wesley "Gene" Roddenberry, 70, TV producer and creator of *Star Trek*, 24 October 1991.

Roswell B. Rogers, 87, Emmy-nominated head writer for *Father Knows Best*, 6 August 1998.

Roy Rogers, 86, actor, Hollywood cowboy, starred in NBC's *The Roy Rogers Show* from 1951 to 1957 and *The Roy Rogers and Dale Evans Show* on ABC in 1962. He also made more than one hundred feature films, 6 July 1998.

Esther Rolle, 78, actor, created the role of Florida Evans in *Maude* and then starred in that role in the spin-off *Good Times*, 17 November 1998.

Cesar Romero, 86, actor, the Joker on *Batman*, 1 January 1994.

Bob Ross, 52, host of the hit show *The Joy of Painting* on PBS, 4 July 1995.

Virgil Ross, 88, animator and creator of Bugs Bunny, Sylvester the Cat, Tweety Bird, and Yosemite Sam, 15 May 1996.

Roy Rowan, 78, warm-up man and announcer for *I Love Lucy*, 10 May 1998.

Mike Royko, 64, columnist for the *Chicago Tribune* and winner of a 1972 Pulitzer Prize, 29 April 1997.

Harrison Salisbury, 84, former *New York Times* editor, 5 July 1993.

Dick Sargent, 61, actor who replaced Dick York as Darrin on *Bewitched*, 8 July 1994.

Natalie Schafer, 90, actor, Mrs. Howell on *Gilligan's Island*, 10 April 1991.

Jeffrey Schmalz, 39, *New York Times* reporter who wrote of his own battle with AIDS, 6 November 1993.

Bess Whitehead Scott, 107, the first woman to hold a hard-news job at the *Houston Post*, where she began her reporting job in 1915.

Robert J. Shaw, 79, writer for the hit drama series *Dallas*, wrote the famous "Who Shot J. R." episode, 30 March 1996.

Joe Shuster, 77, cartoonist and co-creator of *Superman*, 30 July 1992.

Gene Siskel, 53, movie critic for the *Chicago Tribune*, 20 February 1999.

Richard B. "Red" Skelton, 84, comedian and clown, 17 September 1997.

"Buffalo" Bob Smith, 80, creator and cowboy host of *The Howdy Doody Show*, 30 July 1998.

Barbara Stanwyck (Ruby Stevens), 83, actor, star of *The Big Valley* and *Dynasty*, 20 January 1990.

McLean Stevenson, 66, actor, Lt. Col. Henry Blake on *M*A*S*H*, 15 February 1996.

Brandon Tartikoff, 48, the youngest executive to run an entertainment division, made NBC the highest rated network for six years in a row, 27 August 1997.

Danny Thomas, 79, star of *Make Room for Daddy* and *The Danny Thomas Show*, founder of St. Jude's Children's Hospital, 6 February 1991.

Jack D. Tippit, 71, cartoonist whose work appeared nationally in newspapers, as well as in the *New Yorker* and *Saturday Evening Post*, 14 October 1994.

Sylvia Field Truex, 97, actor, Mrs. Wilson on *Dennis the Menace*, 31 July 1998.

Mark Edward Warren III, 60, director for *The Cosby Show*, *Sanford & Son*, *Barney Miller*, *What's Happening!*, and *Fish*, won an Emmy for his work on *Rowan and Martin's Laugh-In* and an NAACP Image Award for best director for his work on *The Cosby Show*, 11 January 1999.

Lawrence Welk, 89, orchestra conductor, star of *The Lawrence Welk Show* (1955–1982), 17 May 1992.

Paul West (Paul Hersey), 86, radio and TV writer, one of the CBS writers of the first soap opera, *Sally of the Star* (1936), 15 June 1998.

David White, 74, actor, Mr. Tate on *Bewitched,* 27 November 1990.

Clerow "Flip" Wilson, 64, comedian and star of *The Flip Wilson Show,* the first successful television variety show hosted by an African American, 25 November 1998.

Nancy Jane Woodhull, 52, president of Gannett News Service and a founding editor of *USA Today,* 1 April 1997.

Alma Kitchell Yoder, 103, the first lady of radio, whose voice was transmitted by the Amateur Radio Corps of America from an experimental station off New York harbor in 1917, sang on the first televised soap opera, and presided over the first television cooking show, 13 November 1996.

Dick York, 63, actor, Darrin on *Bewitched,* 20 February 1992.

Robert Young, 91, actor, star of *Father Knows Best* and *Marcus Welby, M.D.,* 21 July 1998.

Michael Zaslow, 54, soap opera actor who appeared on *Search for Tomorrow, Love is a Many-Splendored Thing,* and *One Life to Live,* 6 December 1998.

PUBLICATIONS

Beulah Ainley, *Black Journalists, White Media* (Stoke on Trent, England: Trentham Books, 1998);

Robin Andersen, *Consumer Culture and TV Programming* (Boulder, Colo.: Westview Press, 1995);

Stephen Ansolabehere, Roy Behr, and Shanto Iyengar, *The Media Game: American Politics in the Television Age* (New York: Macmillan, 1993);

Joey Anuff and Ana Marie Cox, eds., *Suck: Worst-case Scenarios in Media, Culture, Advertising, and the Internet* (San Francisco, Cal.: Wired, 1997);

Ben H. Bagdikian, *The Media Monopoly* (Boston: Beacon, 1983);

James Baughman, *The Republic of Mass Culture: Journalism, Filmmaking, and Broadcasting in America Since 1941* (Baltimore: Johns Hopkins University Press, 1992);

Margaret A. Blanchard, ed., *History of the Mass Media in the United States: An Encyclopedia* (Chicago: Fitzroy Dearborn, 1998);

Leo Bogart, *The American Media System and its Commercial Culture* (New York: Gannett Foundation Media Center, Columbia University, 1991);

Charlotte Brunsdon, Julie D'Acci, and Lynn Spigel, *Film and Politics in America: A Social Tradition* (New York: Oxford University Press, 1997);

Lionel Chetwynd, *Life, Liberty and the Pursuit of Sleaze: Media and Politics,* video (Virginia: PBS Home Video, 1999);

Lloyd Chiasson Jr., ed., *The Press in Times of Crisis* (Westport, Conn.: Greenwood Press, 1995);

Cynthia Crossen, *Tainted Truth: The Manipulation of Fact in America* (New York: Simon & Schuster, 1994);

David Croteau and William Hoynes, *By Invitation Only: How the Media Limit Political Debate* (Monroe, Maine: Common Courage, 1994);

Peter Dahlgren, *Television and the Public Sphere: Citizenship, Democracy and the Media* (London & Thousand Oaks, Cal.: Sage Publications, 1995);

Dahlgren and Colin Sparks, eds., *Journalism and Popular Culture* (London & Newbury Park, Cal.: Sage Publications, 1992);

John Dart and Jimmy Allen, *Bridging the Gap: Religion and the News Media* (Nashville, Tenn.: Freedom Forum First Amendment Center at Vanderbilt University, 1993);

Richard Davis, *The Press and American Politics: The New Mediator* (New York: Longman, 1992);

Linda Degh, *American Folklore and the Mass Media* (Bloomington: Indiana University Press, 1994);

Gail Dines and Jean M. Humez, *Gender, Race, and Class in Media: A Text-Reader* (Thousand Oaks, Cal.: Sage Publications, 1995);

C. K. Doreski, *Writing America Black: Race Rhetoric in the Public Sphere* (Cambridge & New York: Cambridge University Press, 1998);

Susan J. Douglas, *Where the Girls Are: Growing Up Female with the Mass Media* (New York: Times Books, 1994);

Bonnie J. Dow, *Prime-time Feminism: Television, Media Culture, and the Women's Movement Since 1970* (Philadelphia: University of Pennsylvania Press, 1996);

Susan J. Drucker and Robert S. Cathcart, *American Heroes in a Media Age* (Cresskill, N.J.: Hampton Press, 1994);

Bosah Ebo, ed., *Cyberghetto or Cybertopia: Race, Class, and Gender on the Internet* (Westport, Conn.: Praeger, 1998);

James S. Ettema and D. Charles Whitney, *Audiencemaking: How the Media Create the Audience* (Thousand Oaks, Cal.: Sage Publications, 1994);

James Fallows, *Breaking the News: How the Media Undermine American Democracy* (New York: Pantheon, 1996);

Robert Ferguson, *Representing "Race": Ideology, Identity and the Media* (London & New York: Arnold, 1998);

Martha A. Fineman and Martha T. McCluskey, eds., *Feminism, Media, and the Law* (New York: Oxford University Press, 1997);

Alec Foege, *The Empire God Built: Inside Pat Robertson's Media Machine* (New York: John Wiley & Sons, 1996);

Herbert N. Foerstel, *Banned in the Media: A Reference Guide to Censorship in the Press, Motion Pictures, Broadcasting, and the Internet* (Westport, Conn.: Greenwood Press, 1998);

Jean Folkerts and Dwight L. Teeter Jr., *Voices of a Nation: A History of Mass Media in the United States* (New York: Macmillan, 1994);

John Gabriel, *Whitewash: Racialized Politics and the Media* (London & New York: Routledge, 1998);

Glasgow University Media Group, *Getting the Message: News, Truth and Power*, edited by John Eldridge (London & New York: Routledge, 1993);

Philip Goldstein, ed., *Styles of Cultural Activism: From Theory and Pedagogy to Women, Indians, and Communism* (Newark: University of Delaware Press, 1994; London & Cranbury, N.J.: Associated University Presses, 1994);

Tim Graham, *Pattern of Deception: The Media's Role in the Clinton Presidency* (Alexandria, Va.: Media Research Center, 1996);

Marilyn Greenwald and Joseph Bernt, eds., *The Big Chill: Investigative Reporting in the Current Media Environment* (Ames: Iowa State University Press, 2000);

Jostein Gripsrud, *The Dynasty Years: Hollywood Television and Critical Media Studies* (London & New York: Routledge, 1995);

Larry Gross and James D. Woods, eds., *The Columbia Reader on Lesbians and Gay Men in Media, Society, and Politics* (New York: Columbia University Press, 1999);

Lawrence Grossberg, Ellen Wartella, and D. Charles Whitney, *Mediamaking: Mass Media in a Popular Culture* (Thousand Oaks, Cal.: Sage Publications, 1998);

Janice D. Hamlet, ed., *Afrocentric Visions: Studies in Culture and Communication* (Thousand Oaks, Cal.: Sage Publications, 1998);

John Hartley, *Popular Reality: Journalism, Modernity, Popular Culture* (London & New York: Arnold, 1996);

Darnell M. Hunt, *O. J. Simpson Facts and Fictions: News Rituals in the Construction of Reality* (Cambridge & New York: Cambridge University Press, 1999);

Earl Ofari Hutchinson, *Beyond O. J.: Race, Sex, and Class Lessons for America* (Los Angeles: Middle Passage Press, 1996);

It's Elementary Talking About Gay Issues in School, video, Debra Chasnoff, director, Helen S. Cohen and Chasnoff, producers (San Francisco: Women's Education Media, New Day Films, 1996);

Haynes Johnson and James M. Perry, *Contemporary Views of American Journalism* (Chestertown, Md.: Literary House Press at Washington College, 1993);

Alexandra Juhasz, *AIDS TV: Identity, Community, and Alternative Video* (Durham, N.C.: Duke University Press, 1995);

Yahya R. Kamalipour and Theresa Carilli, eds., *Cultural Diversity and the U.S. Media* (Albany: State University of New York Press, 1998);

Sara Kiesler, ed., *Culture of the Internet* (Mahwah, N. J.: Lawrence Erlbaum Associates, 1997);

Markos Kounalakis, Drew Banks, and Kim Daus, *Beyond Spin: The Power of Strategic Corporate Journalism* (San Francisco: Jossey-Bass, 1999);

Elisabeth Kraus and Carolin Auer, *Simulacrum America: The USA and the Popular Media* (Rochester, N.Y.: Camden House, 2000);

Howard Kurtz, *Media Circus: The Trouble with America's Newspapers* (New York: Times Books, 1993);

Paul Leslie, ed., *The Gulf War as Popular Entertainment: An Analysis of the Military-Industrial Media Complex* (Lewiston, N.Y.: Mellen, 1997);

Lisa A. Lewis, ed., *The Adoring Audience: Fan Culture and Popular Media* (London & New York: Routledge, 1992);

Peter Lewis, ed., *Alternative Media: Linking Global and Local* (Paris: UNESCO Publishing, 1993);

Jeremy Harris Lipschultz, *Free Expression in the Age of the Internet: Social and Legal Boundaries* (Boulder, Colo.: Westview Press, 2000);

James Lull and Stephen Hinerman, eds., *Media Scandals: Morality and Desire in the Popular Culture Marketplace* (New York: Columbia University Press, 1997);

Catharine Lumby, *Bad Girls: The Media, Sex and Feminism in the '90s* (St. Leonards, NSW, Australia: Allen & Unwin, 1997);

Maxwell McCombs, Edna Einsiedel, and David Weaver, *Contemporary Public Opinion: Issues and the News* (Hilldale, N.J.: L. Erlbaum, 1991);

Jonathan Mermin, *Debating War and Peace: Media Coverage of U.S. Intervention in the Post-Vietnam Era* (Princeton: Princeton University Press, 1999);

Susan D. Moeller, *Compassion Fatigue: How the Media Sell Disease, Famine, War, and Death* (New York: Routledge, 1999);

Wayne Munson, *All Talk: The Talkshow in Media Culture* (Philadelphia: Temple University Press, 1993);

Brigitte L. Nacos, *Terrorism and the Media: From the Iran Hostage Crisis to the World Trade Center Bombing* (New York: Columbia University Press, 1994);

Brian Neve, *Film and Politics in America: A Social Tradition* (London & New York: Routledge, 1992);

Scott Robert Olson, *Hollywood Planet: Global Media and the Competitive Advantage of Narrative Transparency* (Mahwah, N.J.: L. Erlbaum, 1999);

Richard Osborne and David Hewitt-Kidd, eds., *Crime and the Media: The Postmodern Spectacle* (London & East Haven, Conn.: Pluto Press, 1995);

David L. Paletz, *The Media in American Politics: Contents and Consequences* (New York: Longman, 1998);

John Pilger, *Hidden Agendas* (London: Vintage, 1998);

Jorge Quiroga, *Hispanic Voices: Is the Press Listening?* (Cambridge, Mass.: Joan Shorenstein Center Press, 1995);

M. L. Rantala, *O. J. Unmasked: The Trial, the Truth, and the Media* (Chicago: Catfeet Press, 1996);

Casey Ripley Jr, ed., *The Media & the Public* (New York: Wilson, 1994);

Clara E. Rodriguez, *Latin Looks: Images of Latinas and Latinos in the U.S. Media* (Boulder, Colo.: Westview Press, 1997);

Karen Ross, *Black and White Media: Black Images in Popular Film and Television* (Cambridge, Mass.: Polity Press, 1996);

Douglas Rushkoff, *Media Virus!: Hidden Agendas in Popular Culture* (New York: Ballantine, 1994);

Paddy Scannell, Philip Schlesinger, and Colin Sparks, *Culture and Power: A Media, Culture & Society Reader* (London & Newbury Park, Cal.: Sage Publications, 1992);

Janice Schuetz and Lin S. Lilley, eds., *The O. J. Simpson Trials: Rhetoric, Media, and the Law* (Carbondale: Southern Illinois University Press, 1999);

Martin H. Seiden, *Access to the American Mind: The Impact of the New Mass Media* (New York: Shapolsky Publishers, 1991);

William Shawcross, *Murdoch: The Making of a Media Empire,* revised edition (New York: Simon & Schuster, 1997);

Pamela J. Shoemaker, *Gatekeeping* (Newbury Park: Sage Publications, 1991);

William David Sloan and Emily Erickson Hoff, eds., *Contemporary Media Issues* (Northport, Ala.: Vision Press, 1998);

Erna Smith, *Transmitting Race: The Los Angeles Riot in Television News* (Cambridge, Mass.: Harvard University Press, 1994);

Norman Solomon and Jeff Cohen, *Wizards of Media Oz: Behind the Curtain of Mainstream News* (Monroe, Maine: Common Courage Press, 1997);

C. John Sommerville, *How the News Makes Us Dumb: The Death of Wisdom in an Information Society* (Downers Grove, Ill.: InterVarsity Press, 1999);

A. M. Sperber, *Murrow, His Life and Times* (New York: Freundlich Press, 1986);

Sasha Torres, ed., *Living Color: Race and Television in the United States* (Durham, N.C.: Duke University Press, 1998);

Jeremy Tunstall and Michael Palmer, *Media Moguls* (London & New York: Routledge, 1991);

James B. Twitchell, *Carnival Culture: The Trashing of Taste in America* (New York: Columbia University Press, 1992);

Teun A. van Dijk, *Racism and the Press* (London & New York: Routledge, 1991);

Robert Venturi and Denise Scott Brown, *Two Responses to Some Immediate Issues* (Philadelphia: Institute of Contemporary Art, 1993);

Jim Willis, *The Age of Multimedia and Turbonews* (Westport, Conn.: Praeger, 1994);

James Winter, *Common Cents: Media Portrayal of the Gulf War and Other Events* (Montreal & New York: Black Rose Books, 1992);

Michelle A. Wolf and Alfred P. Kielwasser, eds., *Gay People, Sex, and the Media* (New York: Haworth Press, 1991);

Nancy J. Woodhull and Robert W. Snyder, *Media Mergers* (New Brunswick, N.J.: Transaction Publishers, 1998).

CHAPTER TEN

MEDICINE
AND
HEALTH

by ROBERT J. WILENSKY

CONTENTS

Sidebars and tables are listed in italics.

1990

- The National Practitioner Data Bank (NPDB), established by the Health Care Quality Improvement Act of 1986 to record malpractice data on physicians, dentists, and other health care providers, is put into operation.

3 Jan. First Lady Barbara Bush receives radiation to relieve double vision caused by Graves' disease (hyperthyroidism).

15 Jan. The Food and Drug Administration (FDA) rescinds its approval of the Jarvik-7 artificial heart.

22 Jan. Dr. Charles S. Lieber of the Mt. Sinai School of Medicine reports greater susceptibility of women than men to alcohol intoxication. A woman who drinks the same amount as a man will have a higher blood alcohol level.

5 Feb. The Shanghai flu reaches epidemic proportions, affecting fifty to sixty million Americans in forty states.

25 Feb. Smoking is banned on all U.S. domestic flights of less than six hours' duration.

4 Mar. Hank Gathers collapses and dies of heart failure while playing in a basketball game for Loyola Marymount University, raising questions of why his medication for heart arrhythmia had been reduced and why he was allowed to continue competing.

9 Mar. Dr. Antonia Novello becomes the first female and first Hispanic U.S. Surgeon General.

16 Mar. Dr. Jonathan Mann, director of the United Nations Global Program on AIDS, resigns over policy disputes with his boss, Dr. Hiroshi Nakajima of the World Health Organization (WHO).

29 Apr. Representative Morris King Udall (D–Arizona) resigns because of Parkinson's disease; he dies on 12 December 1998.

13 Aug. The FDA approves the production and sale of Exosurf Intratracheal Suspension, a synthetic surfactant for the treatment of premature babies with respiratory distress, manufactured by Burroughs Wellcome.

14 Sept. U.S. geneticist W. French Anderson performs the first gene therapy on a human, injecting engineered genes into a four-year-old child to repair her faulty immune system, at the National Institutes of Health (NIH) in Bethesda, Maryland.

10 Dec. Norplant, an implantable contraceptive device for women, is approved by the FDA.

14 Dec. A Jasper County, Missouri, judge rules that the feeding tube keeping alive Nancy Beth Cruzan, thirty-three, may be removed. She had been in a coma since an auto accident on 11 January 1983. She dies on 26 December.

1991

19 Apr. President George Bush is hospitalized overnight with atrial fibrillation (abnormal heartbeat).

15 July Football player Lyle Martin Alzado announces he has brain cancer, possibly related to use of banned substances (steroids) during his playing days. He dies on 14 May 1992.

23 Oct. Marjorie Lee Wantz and Sherry Ann Miller commit suicide in Michigan with the aid of Dr. Jack Kevorkian.

7 Nov.	Earvin "Magic" Johnson announces that he has contracted the Human Immuno-deficiency Virus (HIV) virus and retires from professional basketball.
20 Nov.	Kevorkian's medical license is suspended in Michigan.
30 Dec.	Robert "Bob" Dole (R-Kansas), Senate Minority Leader, undergoes surgery for cancer of the prostate.

1992

•	An American Academy of Pediatrics task force recommends that babies be placed on their backs to sleep, leading to a decrease in Sudden Infant Death Syndrome (SIDS).
15 June	Earvin Johnson III, son of Magic and Cookie Johnson, is born. Mother and child are HIV negative.
6 Oct.	President Bush signs the 1993 appropriations bill for the Department of Health and Human Services (HHS), including millions of dollars for the Agency for Health Care Policy and Research.

1993

20 Jan.	Donna E. Shalala, former chancellor of the University of Wisconsin, is named Secretary of HHS.
Mar.	HHS approves the request from Oregon for a federal waiver that will allow the state to implement programs to expand Medicaid enrollment to all residents who have annual income at or below 100 percent of the federal poverty level.
30 June	Dr. Antonia Novello completes her term as Surgeon General.
July	The HHS approves a waiver for Hawaii to allow the state to integrate Medicaid with two state programs for uninsured residents and to create a large public purchasing pool that will allow medically indigent individuals to purchase health-care coverage through a process in which managed-care plans will engage in competitive bidding.
19 July	President Bill Clinton nominates the controversial African American pediatrician Joycelyn Elders, who advocates the distribution of condoms in schools and is pro-choice, to be Surgeon General. While governor of Arkansas, he had appointed her Director of the Arkansas Department of Health.
8 Sept.	Elders is confirmed as Surgeon General.
27 Oct.	Embryologist Jerry Hall of George Washington University reports the first cloning of a human embryo.
27 Oct.	President Clinton's 1,342-page Health Plan is delivered to Congress.

1994

21 Feb.	Jacqueline Kennedy Onassis announces that she has been diagnosed as having non-Hodgkin's lymphoma; she succumbs to the disease on 19 May.
2 May	Kevorkian is acquitted of charges stemming from the assisted suicide of Thomas Hyde, in Detroit, Michigan.
29 Aug.	Vice President Albert Gore is hospitalized after rupturing his Achilles tendon during a basketball game with former Senate colleagues.
Nov.	In an open letter to the American public, former president Ronald Reagan announces that he has Alzheimer's disease.
15 Dec.	The FDA permits the first U.S. test of RU-486, an abortion-inducing pill, in Des Moines, Iowa.
19 Dec.	Paul Jennings Hill, a former minister and antiabortion activist, is sentenced for the 29 July murder of Dr. John Bayard Britton and his bodyguard, James H. Barnett, outside of a Pensacola, Florida, abortion clinic.
31 Dec.	Elders is forced to resign as Surgeon General, following controversial remarks about sex education, abortion, and drugs; she returns to the University of Arkansas Medical Center as professor of pediatrics.

1995

Mar.	The FDA approves the first U.S. vaccine to prevent chicken pox, a childhood disease afflicting 3.7 million people each year.
6 Mar.	Olympic gold-medal diver Greg Louganis announces he is HIV positive in his autobiography, *Breaking the Surface,* written with Eric Marcus.
12 June	Christopher Reeve, the actor known for his leading role in *Superman* (1978) and three sequels, is hospitalized with a neck fracture, spinal injury, and paralysis after a horseback-riding accident. He becomes an outspoken advocate of spinal-injury research.

1996

11–13 Apr.	Macaques monkeys shipped from the Philippines to labs in Texas are found to have Ebola Reston virus, resulting in the destruction of forty-nine animals. The Centers for Disease Control (CDC) states that this strain of Ebola is not the same as the one that causes the disease in humans. The first such discovery of infected monkeys occurred in 1989 in Reston, Virginia.
13 May	The FDA approves the first new antiobesity drug in twenty-three years, Redux (dexfenfluramine), manufactured by Wyeth-Ayerst. In August 1997 the FDA will rescind its approval after several diet patients die.
14 May	Kevorkian is acquitted of assisted suicide charges for the third time, in Pontiac, Michigan.
Nov.	Massachusetts legislators pass the first state law to permit consumers unlimited access to basic background information about physicians, including medical malpractice data.

1997

- Driver and passenger side airbags are required to be installed in all new cars.

1 Jan. Dr. David Da-i Ho is named "Man of the Year" by *Time* for his AIDS research.

18 Aug. The birth of Gene, the first bull calf cloned from fetal stem cells, is revealed by ABS Global Inc., in DeForest, Wisconsin.

19 Aug. The American Medical Association (AMA) endorses Sunbeam Corporation products in an effort to raise money. It is later forced by public and physician pressure to rescind its endorsement.

20 Oct. A $300-million settlement is reached between the tobacco industry and Norma Brown, the lead plaintiff in a $5-billion lawsuit filed on behalf of sixty thousand flight attendants seeking damages for illness attributed to secondhand smoke.

15 Dec. The FDA announces the approval of nuclear irradiation to rid beef of *E. coli* and other bacteria.

1998

19 Aug. Nushawn Williams, a twenty-year-old New York man, is indicted on charges of felony reckless endangerment and attempted assault for knowingly exposing a fifteen-year-old girl to HIV while having sex. He pleads guilty on 19 February 1999; he is suspected of having exposed dozens of other women to the disease as well.

2 Sept. The FDA approves the Preven Emergency Contraceptive Kit, which includes high-dosage birth control pills that prevent pregnancy if taken up to seventy-two hours after intercourse.

21 Oct. President Clinton signs the 1999 Omnibus Appropriations Bill that requires health plans to cover postmastectomy breast reconstruction.

1999

15 Feb. Former Chicago Bears running back Walter Payton announces that he has a rare liver ailment, *primary sclerosing cholangitis.* He dies on 1 November 1999.

26 Mar. Kevorkian is found guilty of second-degree murder and the delivery of a controlled substance by a Michigan jury and is sentenced on 13 April to serve ten to twenty-five years in prison.

25 July Lance Armstrong, who has recovered from metastatic testicular cancer, wins the most famous bicycle race in the world, the *Tour de France.*

22 Sept. The U.S. Department of Justice files suit against tobacco companies to recover the costs of medical care that is the result of the use of tobacco.

24 Sept. The U.S. Court of Appeals for the Eighth Circuit strikes down as unconstitutional "partial birth" abortion statutes in Nebraska, Arkansas, and Iowa.

7 Oct. The U.S. House of Representatives passes "Patient's Rights" that would give patients the right to sue their Health Maintenance Organization (HMO). The bill does not become law without Senate concurrence.

12 Oct. Schering-Plough Corporation is ordered by the FDA to cease gene therapy studies after the death of Jesse Gelsinger on 17 September.

15 Oct.	Doctors Without Borders, the rapid-reaction group of medical volunteers who have championed and led humanitarian interventions around the world, is awarded the 1999 Nobel Peace Prize.
18 Oct.	ABC News announces the closing of the Ryan White AIDS Charity Foundation. Donations had dropped because many people felt (incorrectly) that the AIDS crisis in the United States was over.
1 Dec.	Scientists from the United States, Japan, and England announce the first mapping of an entire human genome, part of the Human Genome Project. This event has significance for the determination of causes of genetic disorders and possible treatment.
12 Dec.	Ophthalmologists at Johns Hopkins University announce the use of a computerized miniature video camera and a chip imbedded in the eye to restore sight.
28 Dec.	Mary Elizabeth "Tipper" Gore, wife of the Vice President, has a benign lump removed from her thyroid.
28 Dec.	Rhode Island becomes the last state in the country to approve the use of prescription drugs, including mifepristone (RU-486), as an alternative to surgical abortion.

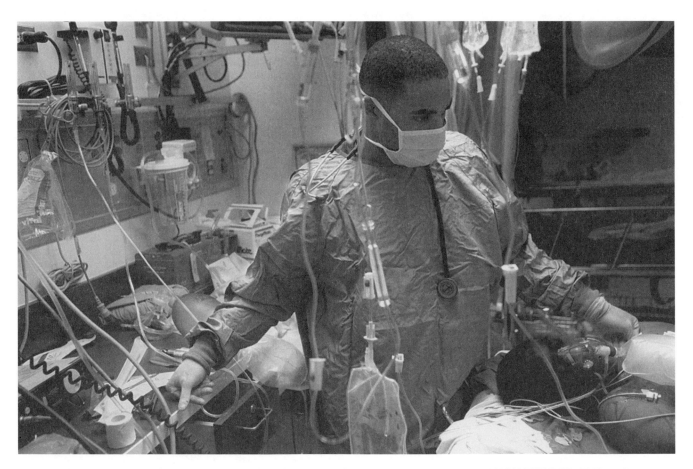

A trauma doctor at Cook County Hospital in Chicago cares for a gunshot victim, 6 January 1996 (AP/Wide World Photos)

OVERVIEW

Advances and Challenges. American medicine in the 1990s underwent great technological advances in areas ranging from plastic surgery to techniques that greatly improve a person's vision. General surgery, which had been a shrinking specialty, achieved new heights with advances led by the development of small incisional and endoscopic surgical procedures. Rapid improvements in medical technology, however, raised troubling ethical and legal questions. Attempts to define precisely the moment that a life begins and ends went from research labs into the courtrooms and, ultimately, became the subject of television talk shows and political debate. The AIDS epidemic, first identified in the 1980s, continued, along with a resurgence of infectious diseases such as tuberculosis, which had been thought to have been eradicated. As the population aged and health care became more expensive, the political and economic consequences of every health-care decision became subject to drawn-out national debate.

Testing Difficulties. Other debates received less media attention, although their outcomes were equally momentous for the future of medical research. The effectiveness of new drugs and treatment strategies can be determined only through carefully monitored studies. When new, promising treatments were offered, however, few patients were willing to be treated by older, possibly less effective methods. Thus, the inability to enroll subjects in controlled studies made it impossible to determine the statistical validity of some treatments. In a study of the use of bone marrow transplantation in the treatment of breast cancer, researchers were unable to enroll an adequate number of test patients. Almost no one was willing to be in the control group. A similar study, evaluating the use of bone marrow in ovarian cancer patients, was canceled for this same reason. At the 1999 meeting of the American Society of Clinical Oncology, researchers presented five studies of bone marrow treatment in breast cancer patients that reflected no differences in survival rates between those women who had the transplants and those who received conventional therapy. This procedure, however, became a popular and profitable treatment, and the lack of evidence for its effectiveness did little to dissuade those who profited from their continuation. Scientific conclusions also did not deter patients who felt they had no other alternative therapies available to them.

Reemergence of Old Diseases. Some diseases thought to be under control presented new challenges for medical providers. Bacterial infections unresponsive to antibiotic therapy were a major challenge. Not only were resistant strains of tuberculosis seen in immuno-suppressed patients (especially those with AIDS), but also infections that were previously easy to treat presented new problems. Strains of *Streptococcus-A* appeared that consumed the flesh of their victims (and was promptly labeled "flesh eating bacteria" in the popular press) and proved resistant to normal antibiotic therapy. Highly resistant forms of *Staphylococcus aureus,* normally seen only in hospitals and nursing homes, appeared among the general population. Many of these problems were traced to improper handling and overutilization of antibiotics. Failure to complete courses of treatment resulted in eradicating only the weak bacteria, allowing strong ones to remain and adapt to the medications.

Bacterial Problems. At the same time, diseases whose causes had been widely accepted as noninfectious were proved or suspected to be a result caused by bacterial infections. Dr. Barry J. Marshall argued that a bacterium (*Helicobacter pylori*) was the cause of peptic ulcer disease. This conclusion changed the entire approach to the problem: from a surgical one dating back to the time before the great German surgeon Theodore Billroth in the mid nineteenth century, to a medical problem utilizing antibiotics in treatment. The medical profession was slow to accept this change in orientation, but by the end of the decade antibiotics became the first line of defense against peptic ulcer disease. In an amazing series of studies it was shown that *h. pylori* caused peptic ulcer disease and that the eradication of the bacteria cured it and prevented its recurrence in the majority of patients. The same bacteria was also implicated as a cause of both gastric cancer and gastric lymphoma. Investigations underway in the late 1990s suggested that many cases of heart disease may be either caused or worsened by infection with *Chlamydia pneumoniae.* Trials with antibiotics in cardiac patients showed promising results.

TOPICS IN THE NEWS

AGING

Growing Older. With a declining birthrate, longer life spans, and the inevitable aging of the baby boom generation, the American population grew older throughout the 1990s. This demographic change created demands for new therapies to combat the challenges of aging. In March 1997, for instance, the Food and Drug Administration (FDA) approved Viagra, the first pill for treatment of male impotence. By the third week in April, doctors were writing 120,000 prescriptions a week for the drug, and Pfizer stock jumped to new highs. Michael Podgurski, director of pharmacy at the four thousand-outlet Rite Aid drugstore chain, said, "It's the fastest takeoff of a new drug that I've ever seen, and I've been in the business for 27 years." In spite of its popularity and promise, Viagra was not a wonder drug and problems began to appear. Some men found it ineffective and, more seriously, by October 1998, at least sixty-nine men had died after taking the drug. New prescriptions fell from a high of 280,000 to around 100,000 per month. Health insurers and Health Maintenance Organizations (HMOs) debated whether they should cover the cost of what some described as a recreational drug. Men also tried to counter other signs of middle age, with greater and lesser degrees of success. Hair loss, weight gain, decreased libido, and urinary problems—all once assumed to be a natural part of the aging process—were treated with a variety of drugs to forestall or reverse these changes. Melatonin, testosterone, dehydroepiandrosterone (DHEA, an over-the-counter supplement), and Human Growth Hormone all purported to restore vigor and youthfulness. Increasing numbers of men also opted for cosmetic surgery, especially face-lifts, hair transplants, and liposuction to remove abdominal love handles.

The Other Side. Women also had to deal with the problems of aging. Menopause (the cessation of the menstrual period) usually occurs between the ages of forty-five and fifty-five, with an average age of fifty-one. A drop in the production of estrogen affects around three hundred different bodily functions. The most effective treatment was hormone replacement therapy (HRT), usually given as a regimen of estrogen and progesterone. It reduced the incidence of hot flashes, osteoporosis, and heart disease; but estrogen given alone also increased the risk of uterine cancer, and progesterone appeared to detract from the protection estrogen provided against heart attacks. The therapy also occasionally caused bloating, irritability, and breakthrough bleeding.

Alzheimer's Disease. In November 1994 former President Ronald Reagan wrote an open letter to the American people announcing that he had been diagnosed with

Maureen Reagan, the daughter of former President Ronald Reagan, at a candlelight vigil at the Lincoln Memorial in Washington, D.C., for victims of Alzheimer's disease (AP/Wide World Photos)

ISOLATED IN ANTARCTICA

In June 1999 the only doctor at the U.S. Amundsen-Scott research base at the South Pole, Antartica, a forty-seven-year-old woman, discovered that she had a lump in her breast. As it was midwinter there, and the temperature averaged eighty degrees below zero, there was no way to evacuate her for diagnosis or treatment. In a dangerous and challenging mission, an Air Force C-141 Starlifter made a fifteen-hour round trip from New Zealand and air-dropped medical supplies for diagnosis and treatment. She directed her own breast biopsy. Digital microscopic images of the lump cells were transmitted back to pathologists in the United States, where the diagnosis of breast cancer was confirmed. Medical treatment was instituted. She was successfully evacuated in early December and subsequently underwent a mastectomy in the United States.

Source: Thomas Hayden and Adam Rogers, "Nowhere to Go for Help," *Newsweek,* 134 (26 July 1999): 68.

Alzheimer's disease and was withdrawing from public life. Because Alzheimer's takes away the memory from otherwise healthy people, older Americans feared it even more than cancer and heart disease. Striking unpredictably, the disease affected four million Americans—one in ten older than sixty-five and nearly half of those older than eighty-five. In 1995 the cost of caring for patients with the disease reached $100 billion. An eye-drop test using a diluted solution of tropicamide offered a clue to earlier diagnosis, but no hope of effective treatment of Alzheimer's emerged. Some studies suggested that the use of anti-inflammatory medicines, such as ibuprofen, might have some benefit against the disease, but a vaccine to prevent or treat it remained elusive.

Sources:
Jerry Adler, "Take a Pill and Call Me Tonight," *Newsweek,* 131 (4 May 1998): 48.

Melinda Beck, "Alzheimer's Terrible Toll," *Newsweek,* 126 (2 October 1995): 36.

Geoffrey Cowley, "Attention: Aging Men," *Newsweek,* 128 (16 September 1996): 68–75.

Cowley, "Cardiac Contagion," *Newsweek,* 129 (28 April 1997): 69–70.

Cowley, "Outsmarting Alzheimer's," *Newsweek,* (19 July 1999): 59.

Mary Hager and Marc Peyser, "Battling Alzheimer's," *Newsweek,* 129 (24 March 1997): 66.

Bruce Handy, "The Viagra Craze," *Time,* 151 (4 May 1998): 50–57.

John Leland, "Not Quite Viagra Nation," *Newsweek,* 132 (26 October 1998): 68.

Marc Peyser, Esther Pan, and Elizabeth Roberts, "Home of the Gray," *Newsweek,* 133 (1 March 1999): 50–53.

Jean Seligmann, "Every Woman for Herself," *Newsweek,* 119 (25 May 1992): 80–81.

Seligmann, "Not Past Their Prime," *Newsweek,* 116 (6 August 1990): 66–68.

Seligmann, "Progress on Alzheimer's," *Newsweek,* 124 (21 November 1994): 80.

AIDS

A Continuing Epidemic. Throughout the 1990s the worldwide Acquired Immunodeficiency Syndrome (AIDS) epidemic continued to take a devastating toll in human lives. In 1999 2.6 million people worldwide died from the disease, bringing the total number of deaths attributed to AIDS to 16.3 million. Although its effects were felt globally, by the end of the decade more than 70 percent of those infected with the Human Immunodeficiency Virus (HIV) lived in sub-Saharan Africa. In the United States forty thousand new cases of AIDS were reported each year. In spite of these numbers, mortality rates in the United States declined dramatically. With the advent of new, expensive multidrug "cocktails" of potent, antiviral drugs, often including reverse transcriptase and protease inhibitors, a positive blood test for HIV was no longer seen as an immediate death sentence. AIDS fell from being the eighth leading cause of death in 1996 to fourteenth a year later. Because the virus could be reduced to undetectable levels, and the onset of the symptoms of AIDS delayed for many years, HIV positive men and women continued to live productive lives for many years. AIDS remained incurable but was considered a chronic condition rather than immediately lethal. This treatment had significant implications for health insurance coverage and hospital costs. Many AIDS patients exhausted the coverage limits permitted by their insurers and were forced to deplete their life savings to pay for expensive, but vital and necessary, drug therapies.

Politics. Since the first appearance of AIDS in the 1970s, the fight against it has been political as well as scientific. Dr. Robert C. Gallo of the Tumor Cell Biology Laboratory (TCBL) of the National Cancer Institute in the United States and his French rival, Dr. Luc Montagnier of the Pasteur Institute in Paris, both claimed to have been the first to isolate and identify the HIV virus. More was at stake than pride, since the claim determined control over patent rights for increasingly important diagnostic tests. Other issues in the debate were hotly contested. Since AIDS was often perceived as being transmitted by homosexual activity and intravenous drug use, some members of the religious Right argued that the disease represented divine retribution for immoral behavior. Because research and treatment were costly—a lobby developed, especially among the homosexual community, which pressed pharmaceutical companies and the government for increased spending in the war on AIDS. Many of the activists, including ACT UP (AIDS Coalition To Unleash Power), founded by Larry Kramer in 1987, took a confrontational stance. Their passionate calls for immediate action often threatened to disrupt more reasoned scientific discussions. Although effective in prolonging life, anti-AIDS drugs were expensive, and companies that made them faced criticism for profiting from the suffering of desperately sick people. Pharmaceutical companies were also attacked for not supplying the drugs at reduced cost to poverty-stricken areas of the world, such as Africa, where the disease was rampant. The Food and Drug Administration (FDA) came under attack by activists both for being

THALIDOMIDE

In the late 1950s and early 1960s more than ten thousand deformed babies were born to mothers who had taken Thalidomide for morning sickness. The deformities were major: infants were born without limbs, had small hands extended out from the shoulders, and many children lacked eyes and ears. Most cases occurred in Europe, as the drug did not pass Food and Drug Administration (FDA) screening procedures in the United States. Subsequent research showed that thalidomide blocked the formation of new blood vessels and slowed the immune-system production of a chemical called Tumor Necrosis Factor-alpha (TNF-alpha). The first effect accounted for the disastrous consequences to the developing fetus, but the drug had potential benefits for people with cancer or other diseases where new vessel growth causes trouble. The ability to stop production of TNF-alpha has the potential to be of use in treating diseases such as type-1 diabetes, in which the immune system attacks tissues in its own body.

By the 1970s researchers had found that thalidomide could forestall the fever, skin nodules, and joint pain associated with leprosy. The chemical was also determined to be of benefit for sufferers of the symptoms of lupus erythematosus, multiple sclerosis, and rheumatoid arthritis, as well as to combat AIDS-related wasting. It may be useful in treating such diseases as diabetic retinopathy and macular degeneration, the two leading causes of blindness in the United States, which result from the overgrowth of blood vessels in the eye. On 16 July 1998 the FDA approved its use only against the lesions associated with leprosy. It will be dispensed with great limitations on supply (prescriptions to last only four weeks with no refills) and dramatic warning systems. Still, the likelihood exists that more fetuses will be exposed with resulting deformities.

Sources: Geoffrey Cowley, "Bitter Pill: Thalidomide Is Coming Back; Will It Be Safer This Time?" *Newsweek*, 130 (6 October 1997): 57.

Anne Underwood, "A 'Bad' Drug May Turn Out To Do Good," *Newsweek*, 124 (19 September 1994): 58–59.

too slow to approve new anti-AIDS drugs and for approving drugs too hastily to assure their safety and efficacy.

Many Problems and Allegations. Because AIDS was most often transmitted through unprotected sexual relations and had long been associated with homosexual activity, many people sought to hide their HIV status. A few infected individuals were even prosecuted for not telling their partners of their HIV status before having unprotected sex. On several occasions individuals were charged with having used the HIV virus as a murder weapon by intentionally infecting others with the disease. Though no evidence was found to support the allegation, some African American activists accused the white political establishment of using AIDS as a tool of genocide and demanded funding for treatment programs that sometimes lacked scientific justification. The fear of infections so spread that even patients undergoing routine medical procedures insisted on knowing the HIV status of their health-care providers.

Rebounding Disease. Immunosuppressed patients were more susceptible to opportunistic infections, and during the decade a resurgence in the incidence of tuberculosis, a disease that had all but disappeared from the United States before the AIDS epidemic, occurred. New strains of the disease emerged that seemed impervious to traditional treatments. Tuberculosis patients themselves contributed unwittingly to the problem when they stopped treatment too soon. As a result of this action and the weakened immune systems of HIV positive tuberculosis patients, the bacteria that caused the disease developed antitubercular drug resistance. A few strains of the disease became resistant to all known antibiotics. Other rarely seen diseases occurred with frightening regularity among HIV positive patients, including *Pneumocystis carinii pneumonia*, toxoplasmosis, Mycobacterium avium complex infection, fungal infections, and cytomegalovirus disease.

Culture. AIDS entered the arena of public culture as well. A major American play of the early 1990s, Tony Kushner's "Angels in America," winner of four Tony Awards and the Pulitzer Prize for drama (1993), focused on AIDS. Jonathan Larson's hit musical "Rent" (1996), which brought "La Bohème" (1896) up-to-date, substituting AIDS for tuberculosis, also won the Pulitzer Prize for drama and four Tonys. In the movies Tom Hanks gave an Academy Award-winning performance as an AIDS-infected lawyer fighting for his job in *Philadelphia* (1993). Other movies in which AIDS played a prominent role were *Longtime Companion* (1990), *The Cure* (1995), and *Love! Valor! Compassion!* (1997). The acclaimed made-for-television movie, *And The Band Played On* (1993), told the story of the discovery of AIDS. Perhaps because the disease struck hard against the arts community, Hollywood took up the fight against AIDS. Almost everyone who attended the Academy Awards ceremonies in the 1990s wore a small red ribbon in token of their commitment to preventing and curing AIDS and of caring for its victims.

No Solution. Though the search for either a cure or vaccine for AIDS continued throughout the decade, progress was painfully slow. Like the virus that causes the common cold, the HIV virus tended to mutate readily. A vaccine or cure for one strain would be worthless against any other. The only known ways to prevent the spread of the disease, abstinence from unprotected and promiscuous sex and from sharing intravenous drug needles, demanded changes in widespread patterns of behavior. However, as the late Dr. Jonathan Mann (former head of the Global Program on AIDS of the World Health Organization) said, people don't like that answer and want a different one. At the close

Panels of the AIDS quilt covering the mall from the Washington Monument to the Capitol building, 11 September 1996 (AP/Wide World Photos)

of the decade, unsafe sexual practices, including sex among teenagers, were again on the upswing in the United States.

Sources:

David Brown, "AIDS Toll Will be Record 2.6 Million," *Washington Post*, 24 November 1999.

Brown, "Life Expectancy at Record High: AIDS Leaves U.S. List of Top Killers," *Washington Post*, 7 October 1999.

Geoffrey Cowley, "The Angry Politics of Kemron: Pushed by Black Activists, an AIDS Drug Gets a Trial," *Newsweek*, 121 (4 January 1993): 43–44.

Cowley, "The French Connection II: An International AIDS Dispute is Reborn," *Newsweek*, 115 (2 April 1990): 65.

Cowley, "Living Longer with HIV," *Newsweek*, 127 (12 February 1996): 60–62.

Cowley, "A New Face for an Old Nemesis," *Newsweek*, 118 (2 December 1991): 70.

Cowley, "A Ruling on Doctors with AIDS: Is Full Disclosure Really Necessary?" *Newsweek*, 117 (6 May 1991): 64–65.

Cowley, "Tuberculosis: A Deadly Return," *Newsweek*, 119 (16 March 1992): 53–57.

Mary Curtis, "S. F. Reports Upsurge in Risky Sex by Gay Men," *Los Angeles Times*, 6 September 1999.

Kenneth A. Freedberg, and others, "The Cost-effectiveness of Preventing AIDS-Related Opportunistic Infections," *Journal of the American Medical Association*, 279 (14 January 1998): 130–136.

Richard Goldstein, "The Impact of AIDS on American Culture," in *AIDS and the Public Debate*, edited by Caroline Hannaway, Victoria A. Harden, and John Parascandola (Washington, D.C.: IOS Press, 1995), pp. 132–136.

"Increases in Unsafe Sex and Rectal Gonorrhea among Men Who Have Sex with Men—San Francisco, California, 1994–1997," *Mortality and Morbidity Weekly Review*, 48 (29 January 1999): 45–58.

Barbara Kantrowitz and Mark Miller, "A Deadly Attraction: Did a Doctor Inject His Former Lover with HIV?" *Newsweek*, 128 (19 August 1996): 64.

Kantrowitz, "Doctors and AIDS," *Newsweek*, 118 (1 July 1991): 48–57.

Daniel Pedersen and Eric Larson, "Too Poor to Treat: States are Balking at Paying for Pricey AIDS Drugs," *Newsweek*, 130 (28 July 1997): 60.

ALTERNATIVE MEDICINE

No Doctors. Various alternative medicines and remedies became popular during the 1990s, some of which faded from view as rapidly as they entered the popular consciousness. Because they were classified by the Food and Drug Administration (FDA) as food supplements rather than medications, they received no federal approval and could be

EAT AND GET THIN

In the late 1990s it seemed everyone in the United States was trying to lose weight, and the preferred diet of the era was a high-protein, low-carbohydrate regime. Popularized by "the diet doctor," Dr. Robert C. Atkins, and his best-selling books, the diet did not limit the amount a person could eat. He maintained that by changing what people ate they could change their metabolism so that fat stores were mobilized and consumed, and weight loss would occur in the absence of limited portions or hunger.

The fundamental concept is that carbohydrates disrupt the balance of sugars and the natural hormone, insulin, which regulates them, thus promoting fat storage and weight gain. By eliminating carbohydrates the body goes into ketosis with resulting weight loss. Nutritionists and physicians questioned the safety of the low-carbohydrate plans. The absence of fiber found in cereals or vegetables, for example, caused bowel disturbances in some dieters. Cardiologists voiced concern with a diet that is high in meat, cheese, eggs, and cream. Atkins maintained that those who followed his regime would experience a lowering of their serum lipids and an improvement in high-to-low density ratios. He also argued that much of the criticism came from economic interests, because many of the foods used in his diet meant minimal profits to the food industry.

The benefits of Atkins's diet were inconclusive. There was no research to indicate that the diet kept weight off. Even Atkins admitted that there were no long-term weight loss studies of his diet—and losing weight and keeping it off are really two different problems.

Source: Carole Sugarman, "Eat Fat, Get Thin?" *Washington Post Health Magazine* (23 November 1999): 11–14.

Workers harvesting echinacea flowers, used as an herbal remedy, in a Leyden, Massachusetts, field in the summer of 1998 (AP/Wide World Photos)

purchased without a prescription. Melatonin, a naturally occurring inexpensive sleep medicine, took the nation by storm in 1995 as a remedy for jet lag. Herbal medicines such as St. John's Wort (for depression), ginkgo biloba (for Alzheimer's disease), milk thistle (for liver disease), saw palmetto (for prostate problems), or *Garcinia cambogia* (for weight loss) flooded the market. The manufacturers of Metabolife, a weight-loss product, saw sales zoom to close to $1 billion in 1999 in spite of concerns by physicians that some of its components might be dangerous without proper monitoring. Though Americans spent as much as $27 billion a year on herbal remedies, the major drug companies showed little interest since the naturally occurring ingredients could not be patented. As a result, research lagged far behind the enthusiasm for natural, but often potent and sometimes dangerous, remedies.

Muscle Drugs. Herbal formulas such as creatine also gained popularity among some athletes. When Mark McGuire hit his record-breaking seventieth home run in 1998, he was taking a supplement, androstenedione, to build his muscles. He stopped taking the medication after the 1998 season, however, and had almost as good a year in 1999 without it. He ceased using the supplement in order not to encourage its use by young athletes. Phoenix Suns forward Tom Gugliotta's seizure and respiratory arrest was attributed to the use of an over-the-counter herbal supplement containing gamma butyrolactone, which supposedly hastens muscle recovery and serves as a sleep aid.

Yoga and Touch. Traditional forms of nonmedical treatment also gained in popularity. Massage, or touch therapy, was reputed to help not only muscle aches and pains, but also

to reduce blood pressure, improve the immune system, and raise levels of the mood-elevating brain chemical serotonin. Though less risky than some supplements, not all of the claims of its enthusiasts could be supported. Emily Rosa, a fourth-grade student in Colorado, did an experiment that was reported in *The Journal of the American Medical Association,* debunking the idea that an energy field is generated by therapeutic touch. Acupuncture, on the other hand, was found to be effective by a National Institute of Health (NIH) panel in treating painful disorders of the muscles and skeletal system.

Insurance. Dr. Dean Ornish of Sausalito, California, believed that even blocked arteries could be opened without surgery, using a regime of meditation, yoga, group support, and a low-fat vegetarian diet. His documented results are so good that forty major insurance companies decided to cover the program as an alternative to surgery. His program cost $5,500 rather than the $15,000 for an angioplasty or $40,000 for bypass surgery. Insurance companies that had been reluctant to pay for alternative therapies became more enthusiastic when they discovered that they usually cost far less than traditional medicine and surgery. The Health Care Financing Administration (HCFA) in the Department of Health and Human Services (HHS) began funding a demonstration study in late 1999 to determine if Medicare coverage of the program would save that program money. Chiropractic care, long despised by physicians and insurance companies, also came to be covered by many insurance companies, though often under state mandate. A few insurance companies also covered acupuncture.

Sources:
Geoffrey Cowley, "Healers," *Newsweek,* 131 (16 March 1998): 50–54.

Cowley, "Melatonin," *Newsweek*, 126 (7 August 1995): 46–49.

Cowley and Patricia King, "Going Mainstream," *Newsweek*, 125 (26 June 1995): 56–57.

Cowley and Jamie Reno, "Mad About Metabolife," *Newsweek*, 134 (4 October 1999): 52.

John Greenwald, "Herbal Healing," *Time*, 152 (23 November 1998): 60–67.

"Herbal Supplement Might be Factor in Gugliotta's Seizure," *USA Today*, 28 December 1999.

Michael D. Lemonick, "Emily's Little Experiment," *Time*, 151 (13 April 1998): 67.

Karen Springen and Marc Peyser, "The New Muscle Candy," *Newsweek*, 131 (12 January 1998): 68.

Ann Underwood, "The Magic of Touch," *Newsweek*, 131 (6 April 1998): 71–72.

CANCER

Research and Treatment. In 1993 1.1 million new cases of cancer were reported in the United States. Cancer of the lung ranked first in number of occurrences, followed by cancer of the colon. Researchers found that a faulty MSH2 gene, detectable by a blood test, predisposed one in two hundred people to the development of colon cancer. Another blood test, the PSA (prostate specific antigen), showed an elevation in the presence of prostate cancer and became an effective screening technique for the early stages of the disease. Basic research on multiple fronts sought new ways to treat or prevent cancer. Dr. Judah Folkman, director of the Surgical Research Laboratories, Children's Hospital of Boston, discovered two drugs, endostatin and angiostatin, which could cure cancer in mice by altering new blood vessel growth. Although there was no evidence that this treatment would work in humans, the price of stock in his biotech firm increased from $12 to $85 a share. Folkman once quipped, "As long as there is an unconquered disease, we have an obligation to pursue research. . . .[For now], if you have cancer and you are a mouse, we can take good care of you." On a less high-tech level, phytochemicals (plant-derived nutrients) and other naturally occurring compounds were promoted as cancer preventives and widely marketed as food supplements.

Breast Cancer. Women became more politically active and vocal in asserting their demands for research into breast cancer and other diseases that affected them. In 1990 there were 43,700 deaths from breast cancer, while annual government research funding was $77 million; the same year 23,739 people died from AIDS, whereas funding for research into this disease was $1.1 billion. By 1997 research funding for breast cancer increased to $340 million per year (compared to $220 million for AIDS and

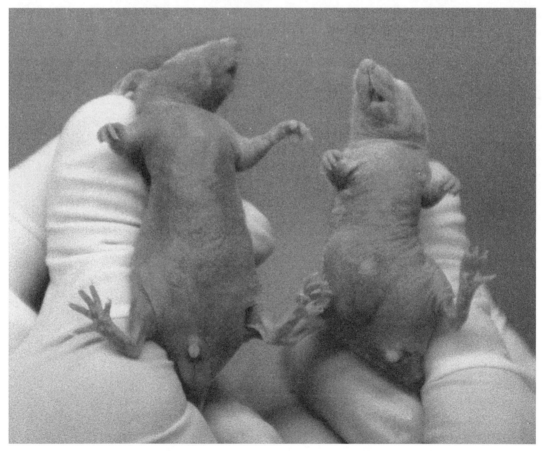

Two mice treated with the experimental IL 13 Toxin cancer drug at the National Institutes of Health in Bethesda, Maryland (AP/Wide World Photos)

$125 million for lung cancer). Despite the paucity of funding, new techniques for diagnosis were developed, such as the stereotactic biopsy, where the suspicious mass is marked with a wire and the nonsurgical, needle biopsy is carried out under digitalized X-ray control. Clinical trials with medications such as B-Oval (a birth control pill) and tamoxifen (an estrogen inhibitor) were undertaken; the latter seemed to decrease the incidence of breast cancer in high-risk women. A Mayo Clinic study showed that prophylactic mastectomy (the removal of a breast with no known disease) could reduce the risk of developing breast cancer by 90 percent. In the area of early detection, a debate raged over recommendations regarding mammography for younger women. The National Cancer Institute reversed its original recommendation and backed mammography for women beginning at age forty. This change was significant since insurance companies might have balked at paying for the screening study if the first recommendation had remained in effect. Politicians endorsed the new shift, but changing a medical policy because of public pressure rather than new data troubled some scientists.

Politics and Smoking. Public pressure, along with concern by state governments about medical-care costs, led to an attack on the cigarette industry. As Dr. Thomas D. MacKenzie argued in a *New England Journal of Medicine* (1994) article, "cigarettes remain the only consumer product sold legally in the U.S. that is unequivocally carcinogenic when used as directed." Dr. William L. Roper, director of the Centers for Disease Control and Prevention (CDC), noted in 1991 that it can take up to twenty years for cancer caused by smoking to develop. In 1993 the University of California and the CDC calculated that the cost of tobacco-related illness was at least $50 billion per year. Secretary of the Department of Health and Human Services (HHS), Dr. Louis W. Sullivan, denounced the tobacco industry for test-marketing cigarettes aimed at African Americans, and the R. J. Reynolds Company canceled the introduction of a new brand aimed specifically at blacks. Sullivan also criticized tobacco industry sponsorship of athletic events, as well as ads directed toward women, minorities, and the young. "Joe Camel" ads, featuring a suave cartoon camel, came under the strongest attacks since they seemed to effectively target children; the macho image of the "Marlboro Man" was also targeted. Americans were not the only people vulnerable to these illnesses and advertisements. In order to offset domestic declines in cigarette consumption the U.S. tobacco companies aggressively marketed their product abroad.

GULF WAR SYNDROME

About 697,000 men and women of the U.S. military served in the Persian Gulf War during 1990 and 1991. Some returned home with various illnesses such as rash, asthma, short-term memory loss, fatigue, muscle aches and pains, and weakness. This grouping of diverse symptoms affecting returning veterans became known as the Gulf War syndrome. In spite of receiving medical discharges, some veterans were denied full disability pay. The military and the Veterans Affairs Department initially dismissed the complaints as not being related to service in the Persian Gulf.

Spouses of some veterans came down with some of the symptoms as well, and some of the pregnancies following service in the Gulf resulted in premature births and an elevated incidence of birth defects and neonatal illnesses. The potential causes of the syndrome are as varied as its symptoms. Soldiers breathed smoke from burning waste dumps and oil wells and encountered a variety of paints, solvents, and pesticides. Some veterans believe they were exposed to chemical or germ warfare agents that were dispersed into the air after the allied bombing of Iraqi storage facilities. The Pentagon acknowledged that it had detected minute traces of sarin (a nerve agent) and mustard gas in the desert. Another potential source of the problem may have been medications administered to the soldiers, such as pyridostigmine bromide, a drug given to four hundred thousand soldiers to protect them against chemical weapons.

Researchers at Duke University and the University of Texas linked the veterans' problems to chemicals used to protect them from insects and nerve gas. The study showed that even in small amounts, cholinesterase inhibitors used in combinations can cause an illness resembling Gulf War syndrome. Animals treated with only one of the drugs in question did not develop illnesses, but those receiving both the anti-nerve-gas pill and the insect repellents did exhibit symptoms.

In 1999 a report prepared for the Defense Department "could not rule out" the drug pyridostigmine bromide (PB) as a possible cause of the syndrome. The Defense Department has spent $100 million on Gulf War Health Research since 1994, and had $17 million worth of studies on PB underway. While no definitive answer was determined as to the etiology of the Gulf War illness, the Department of Veterans Affairs and the Department of Defense now recognize that the syndrome is a real entity.

Sources: David Brown, "'Gulf War Syndrome' Study Looks at Nerve Gas Protection," *The Washington Post,* 19 October 1999.

Geoffrey Cowley, "Coming Home to Pain: Why Are So Many Gulf War Veterans So Sick?" *Newsweek,* 121 (28 June 1993): 58–59.

Cowley, "Tracking the Second Storm," *Newsweek,* 123 (16 May 1994): 56–57.

Cowley and Mary Hager, "Poisoned in the Gulf?: New Clues to the Veterans' Mysterious Illness," *Newsweek,* 127 (29 April 1996): 74.

Side Effects. Secondhand smoke was implicated in multiple health problems. The Environmental Protection Agency (EPA) reported that such smoke caused 3,000 lung cancer deaths, contributed to 105,000 to 300,000 respiratory infections in infants, triggered 8,000 to 26,000 new cases of asthma, and exacerbated symptoms in 400,000 to 1 million asthmatic children per year. Based on this evidence, multiple lawsuits were filed against cigarette manufacturers. They had faced suits before but were uniformly victorious in the courtrooms, utilizing the defense that they produced a legal product that people could use or not as they wished, and if they chose to use it, they were freely accepting any risks involved.

Tobacco Under Attack. During the new legal siege, executives of the cigarette-producing companies were forced to give testimony. Each new suit seemed to introduce new information about what the tobacco company executives knew concerning the health hazards of the product, such as whether it caused cancer and was addictive, as well as about alleged manipulation of cigarette ingredients to increase nicotine levels. Evidence mounted that the industry targeted teenagers in order to maintain a steady supply of customers. After contentious argument within Congress and between Congress and President Bill Clinton, a deal was finally reached. The industry agreed to a settlement of close to $400 billion, in part to stop the onslaught of suits in virtually every state. Data for 1999 showed a 7 to 9 percent decrease in cigarette consumption, which may be attributed to the price jump of 45 cents per pack. Many of the states chose to use the money as general revenue rather than designating it for antismoking or education programs or for health programs. According to the National Conference of State Legislatures, only 8 percent of the $206 billion that the tobacco companies were to pay the states under the settlement went to antismoking efforts.

Sources:
Carl E. Bartecchi, Thomas D. MacKenzie, and Robert W. Schrier, "The Global Tobacco Epidemic," *Scientific American*, 272 (May 1995): 44–51.

Melinda Beck and Lucille Beachy, "The Politics of Breast Cancer," *Newsweek*, 116 (10 December 1990): 62–64.

Sharon Begley, "Beyond Vitamins," *Newsweek*, 123 (25 April 1994): 45–48.

Begley, "The Mammogram War," *Newsweek*, 129 (24 February 1997): 54–57.

Begley, "New Hope for Women at Risk," *Newsweek*, 131 (20 April 1998): 68–70.

Begley and Claudia Kalb, "One Man's Quest to Cure Cancer," *Newsweek*, 131 (18 May 1998): 55.

Geoffrey Cowley, "Are Supplements Still Worth Taking," *Newsweek*, 123 (25 April 1994): 47.

Cowley, "I'd Toddle a Mile for a Camel," *Newsweek*, 118 (23 December 1991): 70.

Cowley, "A Needle Instead of a Knife," *Newsweek*, 119 (13 April 1992): 62.

Cowley, "Poison at Home and at Work," *Newsweek*, 119 (29 June 1992): 55.

"A Grim Legacy for Longtime Smokers," *Newsweek*, 118 (11 February 1991): 58.

Claudia Kalb, "Hype, Hope, Cancer," *Newsweek*, 132 (28 December 1998): 73.

Jeffrey Kluger, "Mammogram Two-Step," *Time*, 149 (7 April 1997): 67.

Richard Lacayo, "Smoke Gets in Your Aye," *Time*, 151 (26 January 1998): 50.

Charles Leerhsen, "Searching for a Better Pill: Can It Deter Breast Cancer?" *Newsweek*, 117 (8 April 1991): 56.

John Leland, "A Whiff of Smoking Guns," *Newsweek*, 126 (7 August 1995): 56–57.

Thomas D. MacKenzie, Carl E. Bartecchi, and Robert W. Schrier, "The Human Costs of Tobacco Use (Second of Two Parts)," *New England Journal of Medicine*, 330 (7 April 1994): 975–980.

Tom Morganthau, "Sullivan: Bush's Aide Makes Waves," *Newsweek*, 115 (5 March 1990): 19.

"A Radical Solution," *Newsweek*, 133 (25 January 1999): 68.

"Tobacco Wars, Still," *Washington Post*, 29 December 1999.

ETHICAL QUESTIONS

Right To Die. During the 1990s Dr. Jack Kevorkian forced a major ethical controversy into the public arena. Although some physicians had for years quietly provided painkillers in amounts they (and their terminally ill patients) knew would shorten life, Kevorkian, a retired Michigan pathologist, publicly and openly assisted in the suicide of his "patients." He even introduced a device called the "Suicide Machine." In June 1990 Kevorkian helped Janet Elaine Adkins of Portland, Oregon, end her own life. The fifty-four-year-old Adkins had been diagnosed with Alzheimer's disease and preferred to take her own life rather than slowly lose her mind. Kevorkian's actions put the debate about such controversial decisions into the open, and even though he was widely and harshly criticized, the public no longer wished to leave such matters in the hands of physicians. Many doctors, fearing the legal consequences of inaction, often ignored the patient's wish to be permitted to die.

Contested Issues. Kevorkian helped scores of terminally ill people to commit suicide and was charged repeatedly with murder, even though no jury could be found to convict him. The Michigan legislature specifically outlawed assisted suicide; Kevorkian ignored the laws and dared the state to do something about it. In November 1998, perhaps wanting to force the hand of the state, Kevorkian videotaped the death of one of his "patients." Rather than setting up the equipment and having the patient activate it (as he had in previous suicides), he injected the patient with the lethal drugs himself. The videotape was later shown on the CBS news program *60 Minutes*. With such unambiguous evidence the State of Michigan charged the former pathologist with first-degree murder. In April 1999 he was found guilty and sentenced to life imprisonment. While some people thought it healthy to bring the debate about euthanasia and end-of-life decisions into the public arena, many questioned Kevorkian's method of doing so. Kevorkian's critics felt that decisions about life and death should not rest solely with the patient and physician. They called for the establishment of committees that would include ethicists, physicians specializing in care of the elderly, members of the clergy, social workers, and

Dr. Jack Kevorkian and one of his suicide machines (AP/Wide World Photos)

family members, to provide safeguards against premature, precipitous, and irreversible actions.

Abortion Struggle. As it had during the 1980s, abortion continued to divide the nation. While street protests in front of clinics continued, a few antiabortion advocates adopted terrorist tactics, murdering doctors who provided abortion services in Florida and New York. On 10 March 1993 antiabortionist Michael Frederick Griffin gunned down Dr. David Gunn at the entrance of a Pensacola, Florida, clinic where abortions were performed. Griffin was convicted of murder and sentenced to serve a life term in prison. Less than a year and a half later, on 29 July 1994, Dr. John Bayard Britton, who performed abortions, and his escort, James H. Barnett, were murdered by Paul Jennings Hill, a former Presbyterian minister. Other clinics were bombed and staff assaulted. The availability of antiprogesterone mifepristone, a drug that terminates pregnancy, also changed the nature of the debate. The pills had been in use in Europe, marketed in France as RU-486, since 1988, but the threat of boycotts had scared potential manufacturers away from seeking approval to distribute the drug in the United States. Other drugs such as methotrexate, an anticancer medication, were successfully used to terminate pregnancies. Oral contraceptives taken in high doses were also found to be effective in terminating pregnancies more than 75 percent of the time. One of the most contested issues was partial birth abortions, with the added controversy over the use of cells removed from the aborted fetuses to be used for medical therapies and experiments. In 1996 and 1998 Congress passed bans on such late-term proce-

dures, though they were vetoed each time. At the end of the decade the conflict had moved to the Supreme Court for adjudication.

Pregnancy Prevention. The use of Norplant, a contraceptive implant made by Wyeth-Ayerst, also was criticized. By slowly releasing antifertility hormones, Norplant can prevent pregnancy for five years after its insertion beneath the skin. If inserted improperly, however, it can cause pain, scarring, and nerve damage. More reliable than birth-control pills, which require daily dosages to be effective, many poor women were encouraged to have the device implanted. Some women reported being pressured to use Norplant by government agencies more willing to bear the cost of the implant than the expense of a pregnancy and later childcare. Other women had trouble getting the device removed after experiencing mood swings, weight gain, and irregular or absent menstrual periods; some women simply wanted the device taken out after deciding to become pregnant.

Sources:

Katrine Ames, "Last Rights," *Newsweek,* 118 (26 August 1991): 40–41.

Melinda Beck, "The Doctor's Suicide Van," *Newsweek,* 115 (18 June 1990): 46–48.

Sharon Begley, "Abortion by Prescription," *Newsweek,* 126 (11 September 1995): 76.

Adam Cohen, "Showdown for Doctor Death," *Time,* 152 (7 December 1998): 46–47.

Geoffrey Cowley, "The Norplant Backlash: Is It Dangerous, Or Are Lawyers Exploiting It?" *Newsweek,* 126 (27 November 1995): 52.

Douglas Frantz, "The Rhetoric of Terror," *Time,* 145 (27 March 1995): 48–51.

A Harvard School of Public Health College Alcohol Study (1999) found that 44 percent of all college students "binge drink," defined as regularly consuming four or five drinks in a short space of time in order to get drunk. The survey also discovered that members of fraternities or sororities were four times more likely to be binge drinkers than were other students. White students were twice as likely to binge drink as were members of minority groups. Among those who identified themselves as binge drinkers, 30 percent reported engaging in unplanned sexual activity as a result of their drinking. One student in five reported that they abandoned safe-sex practices when drunk.

The increase in binge drinking coincided with the rise in the legal drinking age from eighteen to twenty-one. To the under-twenty-one college crowd, it was like a mini-Prohibition in full swing. Some people have argued that the change in the drinking age may have actually contributed to binging, because if a student had alcohol in his possession—that he is not supposed to have in the first place—there may have been a tendency for him to finish it off rather than try to hide it.

In 1999 7 percent of the sixteen thousand students enrolled at Ohio University were disciplined for alcohol abuse. Campus rioting occurred at Michigan State University when authorities attempted to close a field used by students for pregame partying near the football stadium. University of Colorado, University of Iowa, and Ohio State University have all experienced "beer riots." Student deaths as a result of alcohol abuse occurred all across the country. In August 1997 Benjamin Wynne, a twenty-year-old freshman pledge trying to join a fraternity, died at Louisiana State University after a night of celebration, though the university had a school-wide no-alcohol policy in effect. Three other students were hospitalized in the same incident. On 12 May 1996 (Mother's Day), five students died in a University of North Carolina-Chapel Hill fraternity house fire after a long night of commencement celebration partying—four of the victims may have been too intoxicated to escape the flames. On 29 September 1997 an eighteen-year-old freshman with a blood alcohol level of .41, more than five times the legal limit for driving an automobile in the state, died at the Massachusetts Institute of Technology. The fraternity he was trying to pledge was indicted a year later for contributing to his death. Of course, drinking on campuses was not a new phenomenon. Drunken depravity was a problem at the medieval University of Paris. Thomas Jefferson had to contend with a group of intoxicated rowdies who nearly caused a riot at the school he founded, the University of Virginia.

Despite the image of drunken rowdiness commonly attributed to college life, many students and institutions began to fight this trend. Some students rebelled against excessive partying, and alcohol-free dorms were formed on several campuses. Alcoholics Anonymous groups were not uncommon at many universities and colleges. After being labeled by *The Princeton Review* as the top "party school" for two years in a row, Rhode Island University banned alcohol at all campus social events.

Sources: Jerry Adler, "The Endless Binge," *Newsweek*, 124 (19 December 1994): 72–73.

Adam Cohen, "Battle of the Binge," *Time*, 150 (8 September 1997): 54–56.

Jack Hitt, "The Battle of the Binge," *New York Times Magazine*, 149 (24 October 1999): 31–32.

Claudia Kalb, "Drinking and Dying: A Death at MIT Puts Campuses on Edge," *Newsweek, 130* (13 October 1997): 69.

Julie Grace, "Curtains for Dr. Death," *Time*, 153 (5 April 1999): 48.

Barbara Kantrowitz and Pat Wingert, "The Norplant Debate," *Newsweek*, 121 (15 February 1993): 39–41.

Rick Mann and Charles Fleming, "Contraceptive Controversy," *Newsweek*.

LEADERS IN NATIONAL HEALTH CARE POLICY

Bush Appointees. Dr. Louis W. Sullivan, the first African American to be Secretary of the Department of Health and Human Services (HHS), was in office at the start of the decade, having been appointed by President George Bush and serving from 1989 to 1993. His term ended with the inauguration of President Bill Clinton, and he returned to the presidency of Morehouse School of Medicine in Atlanta. Dr. Antonia C. Novello, who was born and reared in Puerto Rico, was the first female and Hispanic to become Surgeon General of the United States. During her tenure in office, Novello focused attention on the health of women, children, and minorities, as well as on underage drinking, smoking, and AIDS. She worked to discourage illegal tobacco use by young people and criticized the tobacco industry for appealing to the youth market through the use of cartoon characters such as "Joe Camel." She left the post on 30 June 1993 to become the Special Representative for Health and Nutrition for the United Nations Children's Fund (UNICEF), a position she held until 1996.

Clinton Appointees. Novello was succeeded in the post of Surgeon General by the first African American

President Bill Clinton (l) and Vice President Al Gore flank the newly sworn-in Surgeon General,
Dr. David Satcher, after the ceremony at the White House on
13 February 1998 (AP/Wide World Photos)

to hold that position, Dr. Joycelyn Elders, a doctor and professor of pediatrics. Appointed by President Clinton in 1993, Elders had served as State Health Director in Arkansas for five years (1987–1992) during Clinton's second tenure as governor there (1982–1992). As Surgeon General she argued for universal health coverage and advocated a program of comprehensive health education for school children that would include age-appropriate information about human sexuality. She was an outspoken advocate for school-based health clinics, which would have made contraception pills and devices available to sexually active teenagers. This advocacy of condom distribution in the public schools, as well as her open discussion of masturbation, sparked widespread criticism and led to her forced resignation in December 1994. Clinton selected Donna E. Shalala, former president of Hunter College, to replace Sullivan as head of HHS. Shalala was sworn in on 22 January 1993 and became the longest-serving secretary in that post by the end of the decade. She concentrated on expanding immunization to more children, broadening accessibility to health insurance, continuing the fight against tobacco, and pushing women's health issues.

Less Controversial Surgeon General. After the controversial Elders resigned, the post remained vacant until 13 February 1998 when Dr. David Satcher was sworn in as the sixteenth Surgeon General and Assistant Secretary for Health. The first African American male appointed to the position, and only the second person to hold both posts simultaneously, Satcher had been president of Meharry Medical College in Tennessee prior to serving as Director of the Centers for Disease Control and Prevention (CDC) in Atlanta. He decided that the focus of his tenure would be improved prenatal and child care, better mental health services, promotion of healthy lifestyles, and the prevention and treatment of HIV/AIDS. He also wanted to maintain a focus on preventive medicine.

Sources:

Department of Health and Human Services, 13 February 1998.

Joel D. Howell, *Technology in the Hospital: Transforming Patient Care in the Early Twentieth Century* (Baltimore: Johns Hopkins University Press, 1995).

POLITICAL ISSUES

Health Care. Throughout much of the 1990s, health care was a political issue. Calls for reform came from across the political spectrum. Although most people agreed that something needed to be done to hold down spiraling costs

DATE-RAPE DRUG

Rohypnol, a treatment for insomnia, was legally available in more than sixty countries, and U.S.-bound travelers could bring a three-month supply into the country for their own personal use. On the street the drug acquired such monikers as roofies, rope, the forget pill, and roach. The drug is a sedative related to Valium but is ten times stronger than the latter. At $1 to $5 per pill, it was cheap and therefore popular with teenagers, who liked to combine it with alcohol. Demand for the pills inspired trafficking in the drug into the United States from Colombia and Mexico. Although it was confiscated by police in more than thirty states, its use appeared heaviest in Florida and Texas.

Local authorities soon had a new problem to face besides teenagers abusing the drug at rave parties. Like alcohol, roofies made some of its users fearless and aggressive. The drug also was capable of causing a blackout, with complete loss of memory. Easily spirited into the drink of an unsuspecting victim, rohypnol soon became known as the "date-rape drug." Reports of such attacks popped up throughout the country. Perpetrators were difficult to prosecute, however, as the women often had no recollection of the events that occurred after being administered the drug. One Florida man, who bragged to friends about drugging and raping dozens of women, was convicted and sentenced to eight years in prison. Bar and party patrons were advised to be aware of the drug, and federal authorities considered placing the sleeping pill on tighter restrictions.

Source: Jean Seligmann and Patricia King, "'Roofies': The Date-Rape Drug," *Newsweek*, 127 (26 February 1996): 54.

and to provide better health care coverage for the uninsured, there was no agreement on how reform might be implemented. In 1990 the bipartisan Pepper Commission proposed creating two new programs to address the crisis. One program would have provided basic health insurance to those currently uninsured. Employer mandates would have required employers to either provide health insurance for their employees or to pay into a government fund to provide the insurance. Another program would have underwritten the costs of long-term care. The annual cost of the two programs was estimated at $66.2 billion. Neither program, however, was passed into law. A revised reconciliation budget was passed and signed into law in 1990 (HR 5835), which reduced spending on Medicare by $44.2 billion over five years. Most of the reduction, $34 billion, was achieved by lowering payments to providers. The rest came from out-of-pocket increases for beneficiaries. Senate supporters of rural hospitals were concerned that such institutions were absorbing a disproportionate share of the reduction. In 1991 more than three dozen health care

reform bills were introduced in Congress. None of them were acted upon during the year. After extensive lobbying by the Bush administration Congress passed restrictions on the ways states could raise funds to pay for their share of Medicaid. Restrictions were placed on the amount of revenue that could be raised from taxing providers, "voluntary" donations from providers were banned as a source of future funding, and a permanent cap of 12 percent of expenditures was placed on the amount states could pay to hospitals that treated a "disproportionate share" of Medicaid patients.

New Reform Plans. In 1992 health care became a major election issue. In February President George Bush presented a health-care reform plan in the form of a ninety-four-page white paper. The plan sought to build on the existing Medicare system, including low-income vouchers, tax incentives, insurance streamlining, and a reduction in the amount of red tape. It promised to cover the more than thirty-five million Americans without health insurance and to stop the spiraling costs for the Medicare system by limiting malpractice awards, increasing preventive health care, encouraging coordinated care, and encouraging healthy life styles. The legislation died in Congress.

Health Security. On 27 October 1993, with much fanfare, President Bill Clinton introduced his health care reform bill, called the National Health Security Act, which would have reformed the entire U.S. health care system. A key objective was to provide health insurance for all Americans. The plan was to be financed through a combination of savings in existing programs, new revenues, and a series of cross subsidies. It would have required employers to pay for 80 percent of their employees' health insurance, with the government providing subsidies to low-income workers and some small businesses. There would have been a 75¢ per-pack cigarette tax. All insurance would be purchased through regional health alliances that would be under government control. The plan placed controls on the number and distribution of residency programs and required that half of U.S. medical school graduates be trained in primary care fields. After a storm of criticism and harsh attacks from a variety of interests, the plan failed to make its way through Congress.

Competing Legislation. More than twenty competing health care bills were introduced in 1993. Among the more important offerings in the Senate were a moderate Republican bill sponsored by John Hubbard Chafee (R–Rhode Island); a conservative Republican bill sponsored by Donald Lee Nickles (R–Oklahoma) and Connie Mack III (R–Florida); and a bipartisan bill sponsored by John Berlinger Breaux (D–Louisiana) and David Ferdinand Durenberger (R–Minnesota). On the House side, proposals included a single-payer plan sponsored by James A. McDermott (D–Washington), and bipartisan bills sponsored by James Hayes Shofner Cooper (D–Tennessee) and Frederick Lawrence Grandy (R–Iowa) as well as by Roy Roland (D–Georgia) and Michael Bilirakis (R–Florida). The House Republican bill garnered the most votes, but none of the legislation passed. The omnibus deficit-reduc-

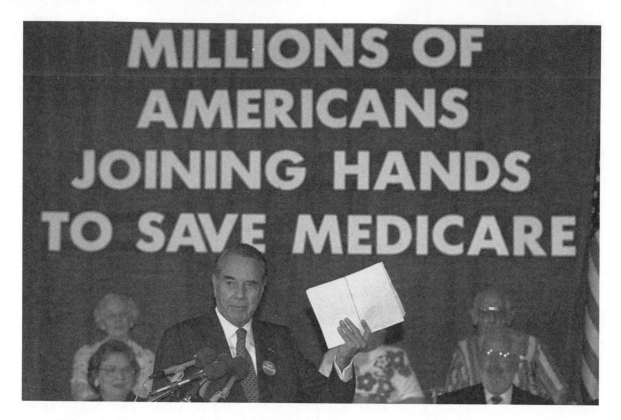

Senate Majority Leader Robert Joseph Dole (R-Kansas) at a meeting on Medicare
in Washington, D.C., in August 1995 (AP/Wide World Photos)

tion bill of 1993 enacted increased reimbursement for primary care physicians while cutting reimbursement for specialists, cuts to hospitals for overhead costs, attempts to reduce loopholes in the system, and increased spending for children's health care. The bill cut Medicare by $62.9 billion and Medicaid by $7.1 billion over five years.

Continuing Debate. In 1994 the debate over the various health plans continued, as Senators McDermott (D–Washington) and Paul David Wellstone (D–Minnesota) introduced a single-payer plan modeled after that utilized in Canada. Representative Fortney Hillman "Pete" Stark Jr. (D–California), offered a plan that differed from the one offered by the president by mandating tight budget controls over health care costs. Plans put forward by Nickles, Mack, Robert Joseph "Bob" Dole (R–Kansas), and William Philip "Phil" Gramm (R–Texas) called for substantially less government involvement. On 8 November the Republicans won control of both the House and Senate. Many attributed this change in control as a rejection of the Health Security Act. In 1995 political wrangling continued unabated. The Republicans refused to pass the Clintons' bill, and the President vetoed the Republican Medicare Preservation Act. Republicans blamed Democrats for being indifferent to the impending bankruptcy of Medicare and Democrats blamed Republicans for trying to make deep spending cuts at the expense of senior citizens. A minor managed-care pilot program within Medicaid was passed by Congress and signed into law by the president.

Stagnation. In 1996 most major reform efforts continued to stagnate. The Health Insurance Portability and Accountability Act (HIPAA) was passed into law. In mid 1997 the logjam was finally broken. Congress by a large margin passed a Balanced Budget Act (BBA), with Administration support. It included $112 billion in Medicare cuts over five years, mostly in payments to hospitals, home-health services, and other providers. Several managed-care options were introduced into Medicare with the objective of increasing choices to seniors. The measures were thought to be a short-term fix, delaying the expected depletion of the Medicare Part A trust fund by several years. The package expanded Medicare benefits to include coverage of preventive-health measures such as cancer screening and imposed tough anti-fraud measures. The BBA included the Children's Health Insurance Program (CHIP), which allocated $23 billion to allow states to provide coverage for children whose families earned up to 300 percent of the official poverty level. This coverage could be either through Medicaid or through another program subject to HCFA approval. The balanced budget bill established a seventeen-member national bipartisan commission on the future of Medicare. It was unable, however, to report back to Congress by its 1 March 1999 deadline. The members could not muster the required eleven votes needed even to bring a recommendation.

Medicare. In January 1998 President Clinton proposed expanding Medicare to displaced workers and retirees ages fifty-five to sixty-four on the basis that these groups often found it hard to obtain private health insurance. The proposal was not adopted. The following year he proposed a Medicare drug benefit, but this measure also was not adopted. Revised projections from the Congressional Budget Office showed that Medicare spending had slowed much more than Congress had intended, dropping at a rate of $206 billion rather than $115 billion. Congress passed a bill late in 1999, inserted into the fiscal year 2000 omnibus budget bill, which granted some relief to those institutions hardest hit by the BBA. It became law on 29 November 1999, and provided $16 billion in relief over five years and $27 billion over ten years. For all of the legislative activity, by the end of the decade the U.S. system of private insurance and market-driven health care remained unchanged. Tinkering with funding, however, served to prolong the solvency of the Medicare Trust Fund.

Sources:
Joel D. Howell, *Technology in the Hospital: Transforming Patient Care in the Early Twentieth Century* (Baltimore: Johns Hopkins University Press, 1995).

TECHNOLOGICAL ADVANCES AND CHALLENGES

Eyes That See Better. Oculoplastic and refractive surgery, procedures that use a laser or scalpel to change the eyes and improve them, began being used. Although I. G. Pallikaris reported the procedure in the *Archives of Ophthalmology* in 1991, the operations did not become commonplace until late in the decade. Oculoplastic surgery is reconstructive surgery of the eye and eyelid to change the function and structure of the lids, tear ducts, and eye socket. The most common conditions that this surgery treats are loose, droopy, or baggy eyelids, tear duct blockages, and eyelid damage from injuries. Refractive surgery changes the natural structure of the eye to alter its focusing power, which previously could only be changed by glasses or contacts; this surgery permanently eliminates the need for glasses or contacts. Although insurance companies declined to cover the cost of the operation ($1,500 to $2,000 per eye), many patients were eager to get rid of their eyeglasses and contact lenses. Radio and television advertising for the operation increased dramatically, with well-known athletes endorsing the procedure. A few surgeons opened offices in shopping malls and advertised the operation as quick and painless. Patients could walk in and, in less than an hour, leave without their glasses. The new procedure was a major financial boon to ophthalmology.

Computers and Medicine. Radiology was perhaps the greatest beneficiary of the marriage of computer-imaging techniques and medical practice. Traditionally, materials that would absorb X-rays had to be put into the heart and great vessels through catheters. When the X-ray was taken, these radio-opaque materials permitted physicians to trace the course of the blood vessels and other soft tissues. Procedures refined in the 1990s were far less invasive and generated detailed, often beautiful, images of internal structures and defects. Radioactive isotopes were simply injected into a vein, and with the use of computer-driven techniques such as the CT (computerized tomography), MR (magnetic resonance), or PET (positron emission tomography) scans, visualization of soft tissue

BREAST IMPLANTS

Silicone implants for cosmetic enlargement of the breast were developed in 1964. By the late 1990s between 1.5 and 1.8 million American women had implants in place. Because the use of these implants preceded 1976 legislation requiring Food and Drug Administration (FDA) approval, they were "grandfathered" and "assumed to be safe." In the early 1990s the FDA finally requested data to prove their safety and efficacy.

The FDA held hearings regarding the implants in May 1992. The panel found that the implants had not been proven to be safe, but neither was there conclusive evidence that they were harmful. In April 1993 the FDA instituted a moratorium on the use of silicone gel implants for cosmetic purposes while studies continued. In spite of the inconclusive nature of the evidence and ongoing research, the implant crisis provided a new and potentially lucrative arena for lawyers. Patients with complaints or problems that they felt were attributable to their breast implants appeared on television talk shows, and their faces were on the covers of magazines. They also found their way to lawyers' offices.

Mounting scientific evidence that the implants did not cause cancer or other systemic diseases did little to influence juries. Multimillion dollar verdicts were returned against the implant manufacturers. The largest manufacturer, Dow-Corning, decided to cut its losses and withdraw from the business. Conflicting scientific testimony caused judges to question and bar experts from the courtroom. Ultimately, Dow-Corning agreed to settle the class-action suit against it in order to end the legal ordeal and the financial uncertainty.

Sources: Sharon Begley, "The Trials of Silicone," *Newsweek,* 128 (16 December 1996): 56–58;

Tamala M. Edwards, "Slights of Silicone: The Legal Wrangling over Breast Implants May Test the Ability of Science to Stand up in Court," *Time,* 150 (1 September 1997): 64.

Daniel McGinn, Karen Springen, and Keara Ketchum, "Disorder in the Court," *Newsweek,* 132 (20 July 1998): 53.

John Schwartz, "They're Only Trying to Help: For Lawyers, Breast Implants Mean New Business," *Newsweek,* 119 (27 January 1992): 47.

Jean Seligmann, "The Hazards of Silicone: Questioning the Safety of Breast Implants," *Newsweek,* 117 (29 April 1991): 56.

Seligmann, "A Vote of No Confidence: An FDA Panel Advises Limiting Breast Implants," *Newsweek,* 119 (2 March 1992): 75.

structures and abnormalities reached new heights. These procedures were virtually painless to the patient and carried few risks. The images were often displayed on computer screens rather than X-ray film. This change made it possible to transmit the images anywhere in the world.

Physicians could consult with experts and specialists almost instantly. No longer was it necessary to send patients to different specialists for diagnosis or to undertake the cumbersome and time-consuming task of mailing films around the world. In addition to these new procedures Johns Hopkins University reported another potential use of computer technology. An implanted chip effectively restored vision to a seventy-two-year-old man who had been blind for decades. Using a computerized, miniature video camera mounted on a pair of eyeglasses and a computer chip implanted in the eye, this experimental system captured and transmitted images to the brain to create sight. Seventeen implants were successfully tested in the initial stages of research.

Privacy Issues and Technology. In spite of the promises of new technologies, the use of computers to electronically store and transmit medical records created unforeseen problems. New websites offered medical services on-line, allowing the public to consult directly with specialists and bypass their family physician. Other sites invited the public to obtain prescriptions electronically after answering a few questions on the computer. This new technological access to advice and treatments raised troubling questions about the legitimacy of physicians practicing medicine and prescribing drugs without physi-

cally examining, or even meeting, their patients. Another troubling revelation was that the storage of medical records on computers made it more difficult to guarantee their confidentiality. Although no one was supposed to be able to obtain confidential medical information without the patient's permission, the lack of security in many electronic systems had the potential to allow unauthorized individuals to access these records. Many privacy advocates feared that if insurers or employers obtained sensitive information regarding an individual's mental health or HIV status, the knowledge would unfairly affect the individual's ability to obtain health insurance or get a job.

Computer Assisted Diagnosis and Gene Therapy. Computers also helped doctors to make diagnostic and therapeutic decisions. Programs to detect abnormal PAP smears were accurate in 92 percent of cases that were previously misdiagnosed as normal. A more controversial program, named APACHE III (Acute Physiology, Age, and Chronic Health Evaluation), was used to predict survival rates of intensive-care patients. Some feared that such a program might be used to limit care for patients predicted not to survive. Medical progress also led to discussions of the appropriate use of new technologies. Gene therapy became a widely discussed topic. A gene is a linear sequence of DNA that codes for a particular protein.

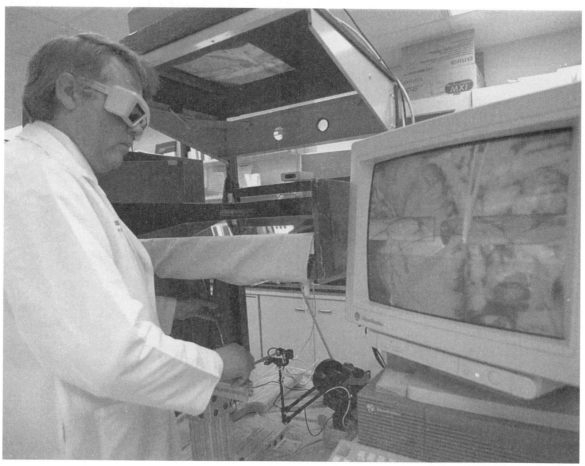

Electrical engineer demonstrating a Phantom machine at the Milton S. Hershey Medical Center, Hershey, Pennsylvania. The device is used to train medical students in new technical operations (AP/Wide World Photos).

Gene therapy is a technique whereby an absent or faulty gene is replaced by a working gene so that the body can make the correct enzyme or protein and eliminate the cause of a disease. There are two types of gene transfers used in gene therapy. One is a *in vivo* transfer, which is the introduction of genes into cells at the site where they are found in the body; *ex vivo* transfer is when cells are removed from the body and treated, then returned to the body. In May 1990 a four-year-old girl suffering from a rare immune deficiency became the first person to receive genetic therapy. There were setbacks, however. On 17 September 1999 Jesse Gelsinger, an eighteen-year-old with genetic liver disease, became the first patient to die as a result of gene therapy. Her death led to demands for increased oversight of genetic therapy and research and forced researchers to publicly defend their program.

Cloning. Even more startling than gene therapy was cloning, the creation of an entire animal from one cell of another animal. In July 1996 scientists in Scotland announced the birth of Dolly, a cloned sheep. She differed from previous cloning experiences in that she originated from an adult cell. The event brought humankind to another crossroads of scientific research and ethical concerns. The possibility of Dolly's not being a true clone was raised, but as other successful cloning experiments were published, this controversy faded. Physicist Richard Seed announced a scheme to open a commercial cloning clinic for humans in Chicago, creating more serious discussions, but backlash created by publicity doomed the project. President Bill Clinton responded by using executive powers to ban federal funding of human cloning research in the United States. He asked the National Bioethics Advisory Commission to review the ethical and legal implications of this new technology. It recommended that geneticists inform the public when future research would "affect important cultural practices, values and beliefs." Some scientists were concerned a cloning ban would restrict potentially beneficial research. Cloning could produce animals that possess a desirable genetic trait: for example, provide new clues to aging and cancer and assist in the development of new medications.

Fertility Treatments. While many families sought to prevent unwanted and unplanned pregnancies, others took advantage of new techniques in the treatment of infertility in an effort to have children. Most insurance plans, however, did not cover the costs of such infertility treatment. Among the most promising and expensive of the new procedures was invitro-fertilization (IVF), in which an ovum was harvested, fertilized outside the body, and reimplanted in the prospective mother's uterus. A single attempt could cost up to $11,000, and several implantations were often necessary to achieve a successful pregnancy. Some families, desperate to have children of their own, spent up to $100,000 in unsuccessful attempts for pregnancies. Not only was this quest for children expensive and often frustrating, but it also carried significant dangers for women. Some fertility drugs, such as

Clomiphene, were implicated in increasing the incidence of gynecological cancers. Since fertility drugs stimulated the production of ovum, use of the drugs also resulted in a high incidence of multiple births. In one sensational example, Mandy Allwood, who was seeking to overcome her infertility, took Metrodin. She conceived eight babies. Rather than opting for reduction in the number of fetuses, she elected to try and retain them all and sold her story to the London *News and World Tabloid*. The amount she would receive depended on the number of live births. In the end she miscarried all of the fetuses at about nineteen weeks. Fertility drugs could also reverse a woman's biological clock and substantially raise the upper age limit of prospective mothers. In California a sixty-three-year-old woman, who lied to the fertility clinic about her age, became a first-time mother, the oldest woman known to do so.

Smaller Cuts. In the 1960s and 1970s surgery almost always required large incisions and lengthy periods of recovery. By the late 1990s this situation was no longer true. Minimally invasive surgery, utilizing endoscopes and fiberoptics, enabled surgeons to see structures inside of cavities through small incisions, leaving smaller scars and causing less pain, as well as resulting in shorter recovery times. Much of endoscopic surgery began in the specialty of gynecology and then was picked up by other specialties such as orthopedics, plastic surgery, and general surgery. Knee surgery, appendectomies, and even the removal of the gall bladder could be carried out as outpatient procedures rather than requiring the previous three to five days of hospitalization. Even coronary artery bypass surgery could be performed through small incisions, with only two or three days of hospitalization required.

Sources:

Sharon Begley, "The Baby Myth," *Newsweek*, 126 (4 September 1995): 38–45.

Begley, "Little Lamb, Who Made Thee?" *Newsweek*, 129 (10 March 1997): 53–59.

"Computerizing the PAP Smear," *Newsweek*, 126 (21 August 1995): 61.

Frederic Golden, "Dolly, You're History," *Time*, 152 (3 August 1998): 64–65;

James G. Hodge Jr., Lawrence O. Gostin, and Peter D. Jacobson, "Legal Issues Concerning Electronic Health Information: Privacy, Quality, and Liability," *Journal of the American Medical Association*, 282 (20 October 1999): 1466–1471.

Claudia Kalb and Deborah Branscum, "Doctors Go Dot.Com," *Newsweek*, 134 (16 August 1999): 65.

Marc Kaufman, "A Ray of Hope for the Blind," *Washington Post*, 12 December 1999.

Bettyanne Holtzmann Kevles, *Naked to the Bone: Medical Imaging in the Twentieth Century* (New Brunswick, N.J.: Rutgers University Press, 1997).

Annetta Miller, "Baby Makers Inc.," *Newsweek*, 119 (29 June 1992): 38–39.

J. Madeline Nash, "Cloning's Kevorkian," *Time*, 151 (19 January 1998): 58.

Nash, "Was Dolly a Mistake?" *Time*, 151 (2 March 1998): 65.

Deborah Nelson and Rick Weiss, "Calls Grow for More Oversight of Gene Therapy," *Washington Post*, 24 November 1999.

Nelson and Weiss, "Gene Researcher Defends Test on Teen," *Washington Post*, 9 December 1999.

Nelson and Weiss, "Researchers Claim No Error in Gene Therapy Death," *Washington Post*, 2 December 1999.

I. G. Pallikaris and others, "A Corneal Flap Technique for Laser in Situ Keratomileusis Human Studies," *Archives of Ophthalmology*, 12 (1991): 1699–1702.

Adam Rogers, "The Mice that Roared," *Newsweek*, 132 (3 August 1998): 54–55.

Lawrence N. Rothenberg, and others, "A Perspective on the New Millennium," *Radiology*, 209 (December 1998): 600–603.

T. Seiler and P. J. McDonnell, "Major Review: Excimer Laser Photorefractive Keratectomy," *Survey of Ophthalmology*, 40 (September–October 1995): 89–112.

Jean Seligmann, "A Light for Poor Eyes: Correcting Nearsightedness With A 'Cool' Laser," *Newsweek*, 117 (17 June 1991): 61.

Seligmann, "Software for Hard Issues," *Newsweek*, 119 (27 April 1992): 55.

Ellyn E. Spragins and Mary Hager, "Naked Before the World: Will Your Medical Secrets be Safe in a New National Data Bank?" *Newsweek*, 129 (30 June 1997): 84.

James H. Thrall, "Directions in Radiology for the Next Millennium," *American Journal of Radiology*, 171 (Dec 1998): 1459–1462.

HEADLINE MAKERS

W. FRENCH ANDERSON

1936-
GENETICIST/GENETIC SURGEON

Weird Little Boy. W. French Anderson admits that he was "a rather weird little boy." Born on 31 December 1936 in Tulsa, Oklahoma, Anderson could read, write, and do arithmetic by the time he entered kindergarten, skills, he said, that "did not endear him to the other schoolchildren." When he was eight years old Anderson was working his way through college medical textbooks in order to satisfy the love of science and medicine that he had developed at age three—a passion he has carried with him for the rest of his life. While an undergraduate at Harvard University, from which he graduated at seventeen in 1958, Anderson discovered his life's work. Attending a lecture about sickle-cell anemia, an inherited and usually fatal disease characterized by crescent-shaped blood cells, Anderson exclaimed: "You could actually change the genes and correct sickle-cell anemia." "What a stupid thing to say," the lecturer retorted, "This is a serious scientific session." Anderson was humiliated. One of his chemistry professors, however, told him that his idea was "interesting." That was all the encouragement Anderson needed. From that day Anderson remained steadfast in his determination to cure hereditary disorders and diseases by repairing or replacing faulty genes. He earned an M.A. in Natural Sciences from Trinity College, Cambridge University (England) in 1960 and an M.D.

from Harvard Medical School in 1963. What was science fiction in the 1950s became science in the 1990s. Combining intuition and imagination with painstaking research and rigorous experimentation, Anderson is one of the thousands of scientists and physicians who are transforming the dream into reality.

Genetic Revolution. In September 1990 Anderson, then director of the Molecular Hematology Branch of the National Heart, Lung, and Blood Institute in Bethesda, Maryland, and his colleagues, Dr. R. Michael Blaese and Dr. Kenneth Culver of the National Cancer Institute (NCI), ushered in a new era in medicine. They conducted the first genetic procedure on a human being, aimed at curing a hereditary ailment. The patient was Ashanti DeSilva, a four-year-old girl born with Adenosine Deaminase Deficiency (ADA), a form of Severe Combined Immunodeficiency (SCID). ADA is caused by a genetic defect that blocks the production of the enzyme adenosine deaminase, the absence of which immobilizes the white blood cells and prevents the immune system from fighting off infection. Anderson's team extracted DeSilva's defective white blood cells, inserted normal ADA genes into the cells, and then reinjected them into the girl's body. The hope was that the white blood cells would begin producing enough ADA on their own to enable the immune system to function normally. The therapy worked. On 31 January 1991 Anderson's team began treating another patient, a nine-year-old girl, with equally encouraging results. Anderson and other experts now believed that gene therapy promised to have applications far beyond the treatment of hereditary diseases. He rather flamboyantly predicted that doctors will eventually employ "gene transfer techniques" to induce cells naturally to correct or reverse any disorder, including heart disease, diabetes, cancer, AIDS, and even the aging process. Anderson's obsession is to discover and release the natural "drugs" hidden in every cell so that physicians can simply diagnose an illness, replace or repair the defective cells, and send the patient home cured. In leading the campaign to put human gene therapy to use in the treatment and prevention of a wide range of disorders and diseases, Anderson plotted nothing less than a genetic revolution.

Problems, Prospects, and Concerns. As impressive as Anderson's experiment was, he and his collaborators knew they had treated, but not cured, their patients. After several months the altered white blood cells died and needed to be replaced. To achieve a cure they had to insert stem cells into the bone marrow so that the body could steadily produce its own supply of healthy white blood cells. In 1994 Blaese successfully carried out such a procedure when he inserted healthy ADA genes into stem cells extracted from the bone marrow of the two original patients. In 1994 Anderson predicted that "twenty years from now, gene therapy will have revolutionized the practice of medicine. Virtually every disease will have gene therapy as one of its treatments." Critics, however, raised troubling questions about the likelihood that an individual's genetic code may someday also be used to harm rather than to help them. Jeremy Rifkin, an outspoken opponent of genetic engineering, perceived a new threat to civil liberties accompanying the advent of the genetic age. "Genetic privacy," Rifkin declared, "will be the major constitutional issue of the next generation." Anderson readily acknowledges that critics such as Rifkin express legitimate concerns. "It's bad enough to have your mind manipulated through advertising, or into eating artificial substances in foods," he said in an interview conducted in 1991. "So the notion of manipulating genes—which make us who we are—is frightening. I feel strongly that gene therapy should be applied only for the treatment of disease. Very firm lines should be drawn to ensure that genetic engineering is used for no other purpose." Anderson, who since 1994 has been director of research at the University of Southern California Gene Therapy Laboratories, insists the work must go forward. There must be strict guidelines and regulations governing all research and experimentation involving human gene therapy, he concedes, but these rules must in no way impede progress. Anderson believes that if we continue to pile up toxins and carcinogens in the environment, "everybody may need gene therapy . . . to protect against harmful radiation from the sun [or]. . . to . . . detoxify dangerous compounds." In the future gene therapy may be essential to the survival of the species. Of more immediate concern to Anderson, however, were those who could be cured at the moment. "What's the rush?" he wondered, "Ask the cancer patient who has only a few months to live. Ask the AIDS patient whose body is shriveling. . . . The 'rush' arises from our human compassion for our fellow man who needs help now. . . . The sooner we begin, the sooner patients will be helped."

Sources:

Faith Hickman Brynie, "Gene Therapy: The Impossible Dream?" *Odyssey*, 7 (February 1998): 32–36.

Philip Elmer-DeWitt and David Bjerklie, "The Genetic Revolution," *Time*, 143 (17 January 1994): 46–53.

Leon Jaroff, "Battler for Gene Therapy," *Time*, 143 (17 January 1994): 56–57.

Kathleen McAuliffe, "An Interview with W. French Anderson," *Omni*, 13 (July 1991): 62–69;

Larry Thompson, *Correcting the Code: Inventing the Genetic Cure for the Human Body* (New York: Simon & Schuster, 1994).

ROBERT C. ATKINS

1930-
CARDIOLOGIST AND DIET DOCTOR

Eggs and Sausage. Dr. Robert C. Atkins graduated from Cornell University Medical School (1955) and is the founder and executive director of the Atkins Center for Complementary Medicine in New York City. Every morning for breakfast he enjoyed a plate full of scrambled eggs and sausage. Contrary to prevailing medical opinion, Atkins insisted that it was just what the doctor ordered. Controversial though Atkins's ideas were about diet and nutrition, they were also wildly popular. Atkins first came to prominence during the 1970s when he published *Dr. Atkins' Diet Revolution: The High Calorie Way to Stay Thin Forever* (1972), which, nearly twenty-five years later, remained one of the fifty best-selling books of all time. (It has sold in excess of 10 million copies.) In the 1990s, after a decade of low-fat, high-carbohydrate diet plans left 55 percent of Americans, and 25 percent of children, overweight, Atkins returned with a vengeance, advancing his theories in *Dr. Atkins' New Diet Revolution* (1996), which has stayed on the *New York Times* Best Seller list since 1997. Atkins promoted eating meats, cheeses, eggs, and other foods high in fat and protein instead of filling up on fruits, vegetables, and whole grains, which are low in fat but high in carbohydrates and soluble fiber. He advised dieters to consume only twenty grams of carbohydrate a day, the amount in just seven crackers, one large apple, or a slice and a half of bread. Dieters could, by contrast, eat as much meat as they wanted. "I've met hundreds of people who've been on every diet there is but never cut out carbohydrates," Atkins declared, "Now they are aware that there is an option for losing weight." His advice was to eat a cheeseburger a day, but first discard the bun.

Critics Weigh In. Although many celebrities, including actress Whoopi Goldberg and singer Stevie Nicks, endorsed Atkins's diet, the medical establishment roundly condemned it. The American Dietetic Association characterized Atkins's and other low-carbohydrate diets as dangerous to long-term health. "Atkins makes me want to tear out what's left of my hair," laments Dr. Dean Ornish, the author of *Eat More,*

Weigh Less: Dr. Dean Ornish's Life Choice Program for Losing Weight Safely While Eating Abundantly (1993), a low-fat, vegetarian diet plan. "What's the evidence?" Ornish asked, "None of these authors [advocating high-fat, high-protein, low-carbohydrate diets] have ever published any data validating their claims." Ornish found the popularity of Atkins's and similar diets particularly appalling "at a time when there's more information than ever about the importance of a low-fat, plant-based, whole-food diet." Atkins, who long viewed the medical establishment with disdain, dismissed his critics. "People in power have a tough time admitting they were wrong. . . . Low-carb eating," he insisted, "is the magic breakthrough for every overweight citizen."

Carb Fears. The paranoia about carbohydrates struck in the 1990s when Americans discovered that fat-free foods they had been consuming had made them fat. Such diet plans as Susan Powter's "Stop the Insanity!" sent people rushing to the supermarket to buy low-fat processed foods such as SnackWells and frozen yogurt. Those treats, it turned out, were high in both sugar and calories. People trying to lose weight ate them and gained weight. In reaction, people embraced high-fat, high-protein, low-carbohydrate diets as a way of eliminating sugar. Although Atkins's high-fat, high-protein regimen drew widespread criticism from the medical community, the diet also has its expert adherents. Dr. Dennis Gage, an endocrinologist at Lenox Hill Hospital in New York City, eliminated pasta and white bread from his patients' diets. Gage argued that the critics of Atkins's diet relied on outdated science. "Some of the registered dietitians trained the old-fashioned way, saying you have to have 50% carbohydrates. The government is always behind. The next update will probably correct that." The majority of nutritionists, dietitians, and doctors, however, remained skeptical of Atkins's low-carbohydrate diet, favoring a more traditional carbohydrate-laden food pyramid accompanied by a reduction in calories and an increase in exercise. "Most Americans don't eat enough fruits and vegetables," complained Franca Alphin, administrative director of the Duke University Diet and Fitness Center, "and now you have diets like Atkins that say don't eat sweet potatoes, don't eat carrots, don't eat corn. Those foods are so beneficial. It's really frustrating." There is nothing new about Atkins's diet, points out Marion Nestle, chairman of the Department of Nutrition and Food Studies at New York University. "They're just a rehash of an old thing that didn't work then. And won't work now."

Sources:

Robert C. Atkins, *Dr. Atkins' New Diet Revolution* (New York: M. Evans, 1996).

"Dr. Robert Atkins," *People*, 52 (31 December 1999): 62.

Timothy Gower and Anita Leclerc, "Protein Pushers," *Esquire*, 126 (August 1996): 40–41.

Wendy Marston, "The New Diet Food," *Health*, 10 (September 1996): 98–101.

Joel Stein, and others, "The Low-Carb Diet Craze," *Time*, 154 (1 November 1999): 72–79.

Lauren Swann, "Best Diets, Worst Diets," *Heart & Soul*, 22 (August-September 1997): 42–43.

JOYCELYN ELDERS

1933-
SURGEON GENERAL

Sharecropper's Daughter. Joycelyn Elders (Minnie Joycelyn Jones) was the first African American and woman to serve as U.S. Surgeon General. She was born 13 August 1933 in Schaal, Arkansas, into a sharecropping family. Her mother believed that the only way her children could succeed was through a good education. Even with the heavy chores that Elders and her siblings did, they were not permitted to neglect their schoolwork. Elders graduated as the valedictorian of her high-school class and received a full-tuition Methodist scholarship to Philander Smith College. She then served a stint in the U.S. Army Women's Medical Specialist Corps (1953–1956). In 1956 she entered the University of Arkansas Medical School with funding from the GI Bill. She graduated in 1960 with a specialty in pediatrics and then became a professor at the University of Arkansas Medical School.

Public Service in Arkansas. In 1987 Bill Clinton, governor of Arkansas, appointed Elders as director of the Arkansas Department of Health. During her service in that post Elders worked for increased medical care for school children and the elderly. She also began advocating the distribution of condoms to teenagers in an effort to reduce the risks of pregnancy and becoming infected with AIDS. In addition, her pro-choice views and open support of the medical uses of marijuana sparked considerable controversy in Arkansas. In 1993 President Bill Clinton nominated her for Surgeon General of the United States. After a lengthy confirmation debate in Congress, in which questions were raised about her open support of giving out condoms in school, sex education, as well as her positions on abortion and health issues in general, she was finally confirmed.

Outspoken Surgeon General. Eventually, her outspoken advocacy of such unpopular views began to erode support from those who had previously stood behind her. These issues included legalizing drugs as a possible solution to drug violence, and her continued support of broad sex education in schools. She issued various controversial statements about guns, homosexuality, and other "hot button" issues. In 1994, during the World AIDS Day at the United Nations, the controversy over Elders reached its apex when she suggested that masturbation should be encouraged as a way to prevent teenagers from engaging in other sexual activities. The next day Clinton requested and received Elders's resignation. She stated that she did not regret anything she had said. Elders returned to her post as professor of pediatrics at the University of Arkansas Medical School and continued to openly express her views on issues concerning the youth of the nation.

Sources:

Leon Dash, "Joycelyn Elders," *Washington Monthly*, 29 (January–February 1997): 58

Joycelyn Elders and David Chanoff, *Joycelyn Elders, M.D.: From Sharecropper's Daughter to Surgeon General of the United States of America* (New York: Morrow, 1996).

Paula Wilson, "Rise & Fall of the Surgeon General: The Nation Wasn't Ready for Joycelyn Elders' Blunt Messages About Sexuality," *USA Today*, 125 (May 1997): 58

DAVID DA-I HO

1952-

VIROLOGIST, AIDS RESEARCHER

An Immigrant Success Story. Born on 3 November 1952, Da-I Ho was the first child of Paul Ho, an engineer, and Sonia Ho. In 1955, when Ho was three, his father left Taichung, Taiwan, and immigrated to the United States. Da-I did not see his father for nine years. In 1965 Ho left Taiwan with his mother and brother to join his father in Los Angeles. Ho's father renamed him David and his brother Phillip. A third child, born in the United States after the reunion, was named Sydney. In 1996 Ho told Judy Woodruff of the Cable News Network (CNN) that his parents early impressed upon him the importance of getting a good education. Their sacrifices in the effort to make a better life for their family furthered his determination to excel academically. Surmounting his early difficulties with English, which he did not know at all when he arrived in the United States, Ho achieved academic success in high school. After graduation he attended the Massachusetts Institute of Technology (MIT) in Cambridge for a year before transferring to the California Institute of Technology (Cal Tech) in Pasadena. During his undergraduate career, Ho frequented the blackjack tables in Las Vegas, where he became so adept at memorizing and counting cards that several casinos banished him. Ho graduated summa cum laude from Cal Tech in 1974, having changed his emphasis from physics to medical research. He returned to Cambridge and enrolled at Harvard Medical School, earning an M.D. in 1978. After completing his residency in internal medicine at the Cedars Sinai Medical Center in Los Angeles in 1981, Ho served for a year as chief medical resident.

Discovery of HIV. During this period Ho began to encounter otherwise healthy homosexual men suffering from infections that ordinarily did not afflict those with functioning immune systems. Soon other patients with similar infections began arriving at the hospital in increasing numbers. They included not only gay men, but also intravenous drug users, hemophiliacs, those who had received blood transfusions, and babies. Each of the cases was distinct, but all had one element in common: whatever was making these people sick attacked the T-cells and destroyed the immune system, making it vulnerable to even the most harmless of infections. From the beginning Dr. Ho suspected a virus was responsible. He was not the first, however, to isolate the virus that causes AIDS. That honor went to Dr. Luc Montagnier of the Pasteur Institute in Paris, Dr. Robert C. Gallo of the National Cancer Institute in Bethesda, Maryland, and Dr. Jay Levy of the University of California, San Francisco. An immunologist at UCLA, Dr. Michael Gottlieb, reported the first documented cases of "gay pneumonia."

Big Breakthrough. Ho, working alone or in concert, altered the way in which scientists and physicians understood HIV and AIDS. His research during the 1980s and 1990s showed how HIV attacked the immune system and how the body combats the infection in its early stages. He thus prompted a major shift in the treatment of AIDS, emphasizing the early instead of the latter stages of the illness. Ho demonstrated that there was no initial dormant stage of infection, as AIDS researchers had once believed. From the beginning the body fights the disease, launching billions of immune cells to counter the threat. As long as doctors thought the virus was not very active in the early stages of infection, it made sense to delay radical treatment until it emerged from hibernation and began to ravage the immune system. Ho concluded, however, that the most effective treatment ought to be administered in the earliest stages of the disease, before it had utterly depleted the natural defense mechanisms.

Daring Experiment. In 1995 Ho, then scientific director and chief executive officer of the Aaron Diamond AIDS Research Center in New York City, began a daring experiment. To treat patients infected with HIV (Human Immunodeficiency Virus), the virus that causes AIDS, he began administering powerful new drugs called protease inhibitors in combination with standard antiviral medications. Other physicians, such as Dr. George Shaw of the University of Alabama at Birmingham, had done the same. Ho's bold innovation was to give the protease-inhibitor medication to patients in the earliest stages of infection. With this approach Ho came tantalizingly close to eliminating the virus from the blood. Within weeks of beginning the treatment the levels of HIV in his patients' blood dropped so low that it could no longer be measured. Ho suggested that if the disease is detected and treated within three months of infection, the patient stands a good chance of being entirely free of infection within two or three years. Ho was quick to caution, however, that his treatment is neither a preventive nor cure for AIDS and that it offers little hope to those suffering from the advanced stages of the disease. In those cases Ho's therapy may temporarily improve a patient's health but does not offer the prospect of long-term recovery. Ho was among the first to point out additional complications. The treatment was expensive, costing approximately $20,000 per year, and was thus unavailable to all but the wealthiest or best-insured patients. For twenty million victims of HIV in the developing world such remedy was out of the question. Moreover, Ho and other AIDS researchers were concerned lest the medication itself inadvertently produce a mutant strain of the virus immune to available drugs and thereby spawn a new and even more devastating epidemic. Yet, Ho's research brought a sense of hope, however tentative it might have been, to those who suffered from HIV. For the first time someone demonstrated that HIV was not invulnerable and that AIDS might not be a death sentence. Ho told Judy Woodruff in 1996, "We basically have, for the first time, staggered the virus, and the new optimism comes from the fact that we now realize maybe, just maybe, the virus is not as invincible as we had previously thought."

Sources:

Howard Chua-Eoan and Dan Cray, "The Tao of Ho," *Time Australia*, 1 (30 December 1996): 44–45.

Philip Elmer-Dewitt, "*Time's* Man of the Year for 1996: Dr. David Da-i Ho," *Time*, 148 (30 December 1996): 52–55.

Christine Gorman and Alice Park, "The Disease Detective," *Time Australia*, 1 (30 December 1996): 36–43.

Miriam Helbok and Sidney Ho, "In-Depth Biography: Dr. David Ho," *Click2Asia.com*, Internet website.

JACK KEVORKIAN

1928-

ADVOCATE FOR DOCTOR-ASSISTED SUICIDE

Dr. Death. Jack Kevorkian was born on 26 May 1928 in Pontiac, Michigan, the only son of immigrant Armenian refugees. Kevorkian graduated from the University of Michigan School of Medicine in 1952 and was licensed to practice medicine the following year, earning a residency in pathology at the University of Michigan Hospital. He completed his internship at Pontiac General Hospital and was associated with Pacific Hospital, Long Beach, California, until 1982. Kevorkian first earned the nickname "Doctor Death" when he performed research on the eyes of dying patients. He photographed the retinas at the moment of death and discovered that corneas become invisible at death. He published this discovery in the hopes that it would help doctors distinguish between death and comas. In 1958 Kevorkian presented a paper to a scientific society proposing that death-row inmates be anesthetized instead of executed and their living bodies be used by medical science. In that way, he reasoned, condemned prisoners could benefit from a painless death, and society could benefit by obtaining medical data and body parts for procedures like organ transplants. In 1960 Kevorkian testified before a judiciary committee, trying to get the death penalty revised to legal-ize medical experiments on condemned inmates. His campaign was undercut by a swing at that time in public opinion against capital punishment. He assisted his first suicide in 1989.

Assisting in Death. Kevorkian has attended at least forty-seven deaths since 1990. Some estimate that the number is actually closer to 120. His actions have lead to intense debates about the right to die. Kevorkian was acquitted of assisting a suicide three times, and a fourth trial ended in a mistrial. In 1999 he was convicted of second-degree murder and on delivery of a controlled substance charges. Instead of hooking a man up to his suicide machine, which enabled patients to kill themselves, he lethally injected a man. The videotape of this incident was shown on *60 Minutes*. He then challenged prosecutors to charge him, which they did. A jury decided that he had crossed the line between assisted suicide and murder.

Publications. Kevorkian's research has been printed in such publications as the *American Journal of Pathology*, *Journal of Criminal Law, Criminology and Police Science*, *Journal of the American Medical Association*, *Medicine and Law*, and *American Journal of Clinical Pathology*. His books include *Medical Research and the Death Penalty* (1960); *Prescription: Medicide: The Goodness of Planned Death* (1991); a medical history, *The Story of Dissection* (1959); a philosophic statement, *Beyond Any Kind of God* (1966); and nutritional advice written in rhyme, *Slimmeriks and the Demi-Diet* (1978). In June 1997 Kevorkian released a compact disc of twelve jazz tunes, "A Very Still Life," on which he plays flute and organ, accompanied by a quintet.

Sources:

Patricia Anstett, and others, "The Suicide Machine," (special report), *Detroit Free Press: FREEP*, Internet website.

Michael Betzold, *Appointment with Doctor Death* (Troy, Mich.: Momentum, 1993).

"Jack Kevorkian: A Short Biography," *wordarchive.com*, Internet website.

Rita L. Marker, "Prisoner Number 284797," *Human Life Review*, 25 (Summer 1999): 65.

ANTONIA NOVELLO

1944-

SURGEON GENERAL OF THE UNITED STATES

Difficult Childhood. Antonia Coello was born 23 August 1944 in Fajardo, Puerto Rico, to Antonio Coello and Ana Delia Coello. She suffered from congenital megacolon, and her difficult childhood experiences with this disease, resulting in her being hospitalized every year. She was supposed to have surgery to repair her colon when she was eight; however, she lived thirty-two miles from the hospital, and her mother, a school principal, could only take her on a Saturday. Her father died when she was eight and her mother remarried. She was finally able to have the surgery when she was eighteen, but she had to miss a semester of school and then wore diapers for the next six months. Through her health difficulties she developed a positive attitude that she could do anything, as well as an extraordinary sensitivity for patients. In 1970 she married a U.S. Navy surgeon, Dr. Joseph R. Novello.

Public Health Career. Antonia Novello graduated from the University of Puerto Rico with a Bachelor of Science degree in 1965 and M.D. degree in 1970. She served her pediatric internship and residency at the University of Michigan, Ann Arbor (1970–1973), where she was selected Intern of the Year in 1970. Dr. Novello completed her subspecialty training in pediatric nephrology at Georgetown University in Washington and in 1982 earned a Master's in Public Health from Johns Hopkins University. Novello spent several years in private practice in pediatrics and nephrology. She joined the U.S. Public Health Service in 1978 and spent most of her public-service career at the National Institutes of Health in Bethesda, Maryland, rising to deputy director of the National Institute of Child Health and Human Development. She also chaired the USPHS Work Group during the reorganization of the USPHS Commissioned Corps and the HHS Task Force on Pediatric HIV/AIDS; and she cochaired the NIH Advisory Committee on Women's Health Issues. While at NIH, Novello gained experience on Capitol Hill, where she was detailed to the Senate Committee on Labor and Human Resources.

Surgeon General. On 1 November 1989 President George Bush nominated Novello to become Surgeon General, and she was confirmed and sworn in on 9 March 1990 as the fourteenth leader of the U.S. Public Health Service, becoming the first woman and Hispanic-Puerto Rican to hold the position. Her initial health programs targeted youth and children. She frequently focused on problems of smoking, alcohol abuse, and domestic violence. In 1991 she started a spring-break program that attacked drinking in college and the problems that resulted from it, such as date rape, vandalism, injury, death, and dropping out of school. With younger children she focused on immunizations, pediatric AIDS, and injury prevention.

Teaching and Advocating for Health. After her tenure as Surgeon General, Novello served as the United Nations Children's Fund (UNICEF) Special Representative for Health and Nutrition. In particular, she provided leadership toward global efforts to eliminate iodine and Vitamin A deficiency disorders, immunizing children, and preventing smoking and substance abuse in youth. She served as a board-certified pediatrician and clinical professor of pediatrics at Georgetown University School of Medicine and the Uniformed Services University of Health Sciences. She was also adjunct professor of pediatrics and communicable diseases at the University of Michigan and adjunct professor of International Health at the Johns Hopkins School of Public Health. She was a member of Alpha Omega Alpha, the national honorary medical society. Novello published extensively and holds more than thirty honorary doctoral degrees. In addition, she received many awards and honors including the Surgeon General's Exemplary Service Medallion and Medal; the U.S. Army Legion of Merit; the U.S. Department of the Navy Distinguished Public Service Award; the Congressional Hispanic Caucus Medal; the Johns Hopkins Society of Scholars Award; and the University Alumni Association's Woodrow Wilson Award for Distinguished Government Service.

Sources:

"Antonio Novello," *National Women's Hall of Fame*, 1998, Internet website.

Joan C. Hawxhurst, *Antonia Novello: U.S. Surgeon General* (Brookfield, Conn.: Millbrook, 1993).

"The Week's Famous and Infamous Women," *Women's Stories*, Internet website.

PEOPLE IN THE NEWS

On 16 April 1990 **Marissa Eve Ayala** was born, having been conceived by her parents to serve as a bone marrow donor for their daughter, **Anissa**, eighteen, who was suffering from myelogenous leukemia.

On 16 December 1991 **David Baltimore**, Nobel Prize-winning biochemist (1975), resigned from the presidency of the Rockefeller University after being charged with falsifying research data. The charges were upheld by a National Institutes of Health (NIH) investigation. In 1996 a federal appeals panel overturned the charge and a year later he was appointed president of the California Institute of Technology.

On 13 July 1998 the remains of First Lieutenant **Michael Joseph Blassie**, shot down in Vietnam (11 May 1972), were positively identified through DNA testing. His remains had been interned at the Tomb of the Unknown Soldier in Washington, D.C., for fourteen years.

On 19 August 1996 **Grady Carter,** a former smoker and survivor of lung cancer, was awarded $750,000 in a liability suit against the Brown & Williamson Tobacco Company.

On 30 September 1991 **Dr. Frances Conley** rescinded her resignation as professor of neurosurgery at Stanford University School of Medicine. She had announced her resignation in May to protest alleged sexual harassment and the promotion of a male colleague but decided to stay after the university acted on her complaints.

On 8 October 1999 **Catherine D. De Angelis,** vice dean of Johns Hopkins University Medical School, was named editor of the *Journal of the American Medical Association (JAMA),* the first woman to hold that position.

On 17 September 1999 **Jesse Gelsinger,** an eighteen-year-old Arizona man who was suffering from ornithine transcarbamylase (OTC) deficiency, became the first person to die after receiving gene therapy at the University of Pennsylvania.

On 14 November 1991 basketball great **Earvin "Magic" Johnson** announced he is HIV (Human Immunodeficiency Virus) positive and retired.

On 2 March 1992 **Virginia Eshelman Johnson** and **William Howell Master,** sexologists who cowrote *Human Sexual Response* (1966), were divorced after twenty-one years of marriage.

On 13 June 1996 U.S. political asylum was granted to **Fauziya Kasinga,** a nineteen-year-old woman who fled Togo to avoid genital mutilation (female "circumcision").

In 1993 **Ira C. Magaziner** served as an adviser on health-care reform to the committee chaired by First Lady Hillary Rodham Clinton. His complicated and unwieldy solutions were incorporated in a lenghty report that was panned by conservatives and professional health-care providers.

In 1994 **Maclyn McCarty** received a Special Recognition Award in Medical Science for his seminal and historic investigation in the 1940s and 1950s that revealed that DNA is the chemical substance of heredity and for ushering in a new era of contemporary genetics.

On 19 November 1997 **Bobbi McCaughey** gave birth to seven children, the first live birth of living septuplets, in Carlisle, Iowa.

In April 1995 pioneering transplant surgeon **Dr. John Najarian,** of the Minnesota Anti-Lymphocyte Globulin (MALG) Program at the University of Minnesota, was indicted by a Federal Grand Jury for embezzlement, income tax evasion, and conspiring to deceive the Food and Drug Administration (FDA). He had been forced out as department chairman in 1993.

On 11 August 1997 **Amoret Powell** was charged with murder because her heroin-laced breast milk allegedly led to the death by oxygen deprivation of her seven-week-old daughter, **Eve,** in Tucson, Arizona.

On 10 November 1996 **Cheyenne Pyle,** a newborn, became the youngest heart-transplant recipient in the nation, undergoing the operation ninety minutes after her birth at the University of Miami-Jackson Children's Hospital. Despite the procedure, she died on 16 November.

On 13 February 1998 **David Satcher** became Surgeon General after being head of the Centers for Disease Control (CDC). The position had been empty for three years.

On 19 August 1991 **Arlette Schweitzer,** forty-two, of South Dakota, announced her surrogate pregnancy with her own grandchildren, in order to help her daughter, who had no uterus.

On 25 January 1999 **Matthew Scott** underwent the first hand transplant in the United States, in Louisville, Kentucky.

On 19 January 1993 **Dr. Louis W. Sullivan,** the first African American to serve as Secretary of Health and Human Services (HHS), completed four years in that position and returned to the Presidency of Morehouse College.

On 4 July 1990 Christian Scientists **David R.** and **Ginger Twitchell** were convicted of involuntary manslaughter in Boston, Massachusetts. They believed prayer would cure their infant son, **Robyn,** who died of a bowel obstruction on 8 April 1986. The ruling was later overturned on a technicality by the Massachusetts Supreme Court.

AWARDS

NOBEL PRIZE WINNERS IN MEDICINE OR PHYSIOLOGY

1990

Joseph E. Murray and **E. Donnall Thomas** for their studies concerning organ and cell transplantation in the treatment of human disease.

1991

No American Winner

1992

Edmond H. Fischer and **Edwin G. Krebs** for their discoveries concerning reversible protein phosphorylation as a biological regulatory mechanism.

1993

Richard J. Roberts and **Phillip A. Sharp** for their discoveries of split genes.

1994

Alfred G. Gilman and **Martin Rodbell** for their discovery of G-proteins and the role of these proteins in signal transduction in cells.

1995

Edward B. Lewis, Christiane Nüsslein-Volhard (Germany), and **Eric F. Wieschaus** for their discoveries concerning the genetic control of early embryonic development.

1996

No American Winner

1997

Stanley B. Prusiner for his discovery of prions—a new biological principle of infection.

1998

Robert F. Furchgott, Louis J. Ignarro, and **Ferid Murad** for their discoveries concerning nitric oxide as a signaling molecule in the cardiovascular system.

1999

Günter Blobel for discovering how proteins get shipped to their proper destinations within the body after being manufactured within cells.

ALBERT LASKER AWARDS

The Albert Lasker Awards are given in honor of medical research or public service of a pioneering nature.

1991

Edward B. Lewis for fundamental research on the Bithorax Complex, which established the role of homeotic genes in the development of cell patterns and provided a foundation for current studies of embryonic development. **Christiane Nüsslein-Volhard** (Germany) for charting new paths in developmental biology through investigations that led to the discovery of nearly all genes responsible for organizing basic body patters.

1992

No award

1993

Günter Blobel for landmark discoveries concerning the processes by which intercellular proteins are targeted across cell membranes.

1994

Stanley B. Prusiner for landmark revolutionary work that established the existence of an entirely new class of infectious agents, and which opened new understanding of the pathogenesis of several baffling neurodegenerative diseases.

1995

Peter C. Doherty (Australia) for the epochal discovery of MHC Restriction of T-cell Recognition and the Single T-cell receptor Altered-Self Hypothesis. Jack L. Strominger for pioneering the isolation of and solution to the structures of Class I and Class II MHC proteins and their peptide complexes. Emil R. Unanue for seminal discoveries in antigen processing and MHC-peptide binding which deciphered the biochemical basis of T-cell recognition. Don C. Wiley for visualizing the three-dimensional structures of Class I and Class II proteins and their complexes with antigens and superantigens. Rolf M. Zinkernagal for the landmark discovery of MHC Restriction of T-cell Recognition, and the Altered-Self Hypothesis.

1996

Robert F. Furchgott for the landmark discovery of endothelium-derived relaxing factor (EDRF), now known to be nitric oxide. Ferid Murad for ingenious elucidation of the cyclic GMP signaling pathway of nitric oxide and for essential discoveries that led to establishing the link between the endothelium-derived relaxing factor and nitric oxide.

1997

Mark S. Ptashne for elegant and incisive discoveries leading to the understanding of how regulatory proteins control the transcription of genes.

1998

Lee Hartwell, Paul Nurse (England), and Yoshio Masui (Canada) for pioneering genetic and molecular studies that revealed the universal machinery for regulating cell division in all eukaryotic organisms, from yeasts, to frogs, to human beings.

1999

Clay M. Armstrong, Bertile Hille, and Roderick MacMinnon for elucidating the functional and structural architecture of ion channel proteins, which govern the electrical potential of membranes throughout nature, thereby generating nerve impulses and controlling muscle contraction, cardiac rhythm, and hormone secretion.

CLINICAL MEDICAL RESEARCH AWARDS

1990

No award

1991

Yuet Wai Kan for his pivotal contributions to the development of human genetics, most importantly in the area of the hemoglobinopathies using recombinant DNA technology.

1993

Donald Metcalf for his outstanding discovery of the colony-stimulating factors, two of which are widely used to treat patients with cancer and disease of blood cell formation.

1994

John Allen Clements for his brilliant studies defining and describing the role of pulmonary surfactant and in developing a life-saving artificial surfactant now used in premature infants around the world.

1995

Barry J. Marshall for the visionary discovery that *Helicobacter pylori* causes peptic ulcer disease.

1996

Porter Warren Anderson Jr. for groundbreaking work in the development and commercialization of the Hemophilus influenza type b vaccine. David H. Smith for visionary leadership in bringing the life-saving Hemophilus influenza type b vaccine to the world market. John B. Robbins for bold and imaginative leadership in developing polysaccharide conjugate vaccine against Hemophilus influenza type b. Rachael Schneerson for pioneering discoveries in vaccines leading to the eradication of Hemophilus influenza type b, typhoid, and pneumococcus.

1997

Alfred Sommer for the understanding and demonstration that low-dose vitamin A supplementation in millions of third-world children can prevent death from infectious diseases, as well as blindness.

1998

Alfred G. Knudson Jr., Peter C. Nowell, and Janet D. Rowley for incisive studies in patient-oriented research that paved the way for identifying genetic alterations that cause cancer in humans and that allow for cancer diagnosis in patients at the molecular level.

1999

David W. Cushman and Miguel A. Ondetti for developing an innovative approach to drug design based on protein structure and using it to create the ACE inhibitors, powerful oral agents for the treatment of high blood pressure, heart failure, and diabetic kidney disease.

PUBLIC SERVICE AWARDS

1991

Robin Chandler Duke for her dedicated efforts to enhance the lives of the worldwide community through family planning and population control. **Thomas P. O'Neill Jr.** for his tireless dedication to increasing the nation's commitment to biomedical research, and a lifetime of public advocacy for the disadvantaged.

1993

Paul G. Rogers for tireless leadership in advancing the cause of American health care through his initiatives both as a legislator and as a private citizen. **Nancy S. Wexler** for her groundbreaking work in the scientific community toward finding a cure for Huntington's disease and for increasing awareness of all genetic disease.

1995

Mark O. Hatfield for energetic leadership and enduring advocacy in support of biomedical research.

SPECIAL ACHIEVEMENT IN MEDICAL SCIENCE

1994

Maclyn McCarty for his seminal and historic investigation which revealed that DNA is the chemical substance of heredity and for ushering in a new era of contemporary genetics.

1996

Paul C. Zamecnik for brilliant and original science that revolutionized biochemistry and spawned new avenues of scientific inquiry.

1997

Victor A. McKusick for a lifetime career as founder of the discipline of clinical genetics.

1998

Daniel E. Koshland Jr. for his accomplishments on diverse fronts as a visionary biochemist, tireless institution-builder, and eloquent public communicator.

1999

Seymour S. Kety for a lifetime of contributions to neuroscience, including discovery of methods for measuring cerebral blood flow that led to current brain imaging techniques, studies of adopted individuals with schizophrenia that established the importance of genetics in causing the disease, and visionary leadership in mental health that ushered psychiatry into the molecular era.

GENERAL MOTORS CANCER RESEARCH FOUNDATION AWARDS

The Charles F. Kettering Medal

Awarded for outstanding contributions to the diagnosis or treatment of cancer.

1990—Sir David Cox

1991—Victor Ling

1992—Lawrence H. Einhorn

1993—Gianni Bonadonna

    —Bernard Fisher

1994—Laurent Degos

    —Wang Zhen-Yi

1995—Norbert Brock

1996—Malcolm A. Bagshaw

    —Patrick C. Walsh

1997—Herman D. Suit

1998—H. Rodney Withers

1999—Ronald Levy

Charles S. Mott Prize

For the most outstanding recent contribution related to cause or ultimate prevention of cancer.

1990—Webster K. Cavennee

    —Raymond L. White

1991—Peter K. Vogt

1992—Brian MacMahon

1993—Carlo M. Croce

1994—Tony Hunter

1995—Frederick P. Li

    — Joseph F. Fraumeni

1996—Paul L. Modrich

    —Richard D. Kolodner

1997—M. Judith Folkman

1998—Suzanne Cory

    —Stanley J. Korsmeyer

1999—Arnold J. Levine

Alfred P. Sloan Prize

Awarded for the most outstanding contribution to basic science research related to cancer.

1990—Mark S. Ptashne

1991—Leland H. Hartwell

1992—Christiane Nüsslein-Volhard

1993—Hidesaburo Hanafusa

1994—Mario R. Capecchi

—Oliver Smithies

1995—Edward E. Harlow Jr.

1996—Mark M. Davis

—Tak W. Mak

1997—Paul M. Nurse

1998—H. Robert Horvitz

—Robert G. Roeder

—Robert Tjian

1999—Robert G. Roedner

AMERICAN MEDICAL ASSOCIATION DISTINGUISHED SERVICE AWARDS

Honors a member of the association for general meritorious service.

1990—Clarence S. Livingood

—John M. Smith Jr.

1991—W. Montague Cobb

—John Henry Burkhart

1992—John W. Eckstein

1993—John J. Connley

— Seymour F. Ochsner

1994—Henry P. Pendergrass

1995—Charles A. LeMaistre

—Theodore Englas Woodward

1996—William R. Felts

1997—David B. Carmichael

—Denton A. Cooley

1998—Jack Perry Strong

1999—Luther W. Brady

DEATHS

Janet Elaine Adkins, 54, Alzheimer's patient, suicide aided by Dr. Jack Kevorkian, 12 June 1990.

Lyle Martin Alzado, 43, professional football player for the Denver Broncos, Cleveland Browns, and Oakland Raiders, who developed brain cancer thought to be caused by steroids taken to build up his body and increase his strength, 14 May 1992.

Arthur Ashe, 49, African American tennis star who acquired AIDS through a blood transfusion in 1983 during a heart surgery, 6 February 1993.

Oscar Auerbach, 92, American pathologist who examined thousands of slides of human lung tissue to document the anatomical link between smoking and lung cancer, 15 January 1997.

Charles P. Bailey, 82, pioneering heart surgeon; first person to repair a hole between the two sides of the heart; preformed first closed mitral valve operation in the United States, 18 August 1992.

Theodore H. Benzinger, 94, inventor of the ear thermometer, 26 October 1999.

Kimberly Ann Bergalis, 23, first patient known to be infected with AIDS by a medical caregiver, in this case by bisexual dentist Dr. David Acer, in Florida, 8 December 1991.

Leroy Edgar Burney, 91, Surgeon General (1956–1961) and first in the office to implicate smoking as a cause for lung cancer; established the National Library of Medicine (1956) and National Center for Health Statistics (1960), 31 July 1998.

Michelle Siarra Carew, 18, from leukemia while awaiting bone marrow transplant; daughter of baseball great Rod Carew, who became an advocate for minority and biracial transplant candidates, 17 April 1996.

John J. Conley, 87, New York otolaryngologist, developed operations for improving the speech of patients who had lost their voice boxes to cancer and for reconstruction of the jawbone after loss of the bone to cancer, 21 September 1999.

Norman Cousins, 78, holistic health pioneer and editor of *The Saturday Review* (1942–1972), 30 November 1990.

Hugh J. Davis, 69, developer of the Dalkon Shield intrauterine birth-control device, which was recalled in 1984 after eighteen patients using the device died, 23 October 1996.

Charles Dederich Sr., 83, founder of the drug rehabilitation program Synanon, 2 March 1997.

Gertrude Belle Elion, 81, researcher and Nobel Prize winner (1988) who helped develop the first drug to combat leukemia and herpes effectively, and oversaw the development of the anti-AIDS drug AZT, 21 February 1999.

Robert H. Finch, 70, former Secretary of Health, Education and Welfare (1969–1970) under President Richard M. Nixon, 10 October 1995.

Josephine Smith Fox, 92, pioneer in developing swimming therapy for the disabled, 16 September 1999.

Ray Fuller, 60, codeveloper of the antidepressant drug Prozac, 11 August 1996.

Gerald E. Gaull, 66, pediatrician who identified taurine, the amino acid in milk important in brain development, 1 April 1997.

Elizabeth Glaser, 47, AIDS activist, wife of actor Paul Michael Glaser and speaker at the 1992 Democratic National Convention; became HIV positive in 1981 after a blood transfusion following the birth of her child; galvanized the Hollywood anti-AIDS community, 3 December 1994.

Janet Good, 73, aide to Jack Kevorkian, championed the right to die and began the Hemlock Society chapter in Michigan; suffered from pancreatic cancer and appears to have taken her own life, 26 August 1997.

Robert Klark Graham, 90, optical physicist who developed shatterproof plastic eyeglass lenses and established a controversial sperm bank that included donations collected from Nobel Prize winners, 13 February 1997.

Arthur B. Hardy, 78, psychiatrist who pioneered treatment of agoraphobia (fear of going outdoors), 26 October 1991.

Robert G. Heath, 84, found a protein antibody called taraxein in the blood of schizophrenics, providing early evidence that the disease was of biochemical origin, 21 September 1999.

Christy Henrich, 22, world-class gymnast, of multiple organ failure caused by anorexia nervosa; weighed only sixty pounds at the time of her death, 26 July 1994.

Oveta Culp Hobby, 90, first secretary of the Department of Health, Education and Welfare (1953–1955), 16 August 1995.

Hamilton Holmes, 54, orthopedic surgeon who in 1961 became one of first African Americans admitted to the University of Georgia, 26 October 1995.

Evelyn Hooker, 89, UCLA psychologist whose research in the 1950s led to the removal of homosexuality as a psychological disorder by the American Psychiatric Association from its *Diagnostic and Statistical Manual of Mental Disorders,* 18 November 1996.

Walter Hudson, 46, at 1,400 pounds he was the fattest man in the world in 1987; although he lost 800 pounds, he regained the weight to 1,125 pounds at the time of his death, 24 December 1991.

Charles Brenton Huggins, 95, Canadian-born medical researcher who won the Nobel Prize (1966) for hormone studies leading to the use of drug therapy in cancer, 12 January 1997.

Richard Joseph Hughes, 83, former Governor (1962–1970) and Chief Justice of New Jersey (1973–1981), who had ruled that the parents of Karen Ann Quinlan be allowed to remove her from life support in 1975, upholding the right to refuse medical treatment, 7 December 1992.

James J. Humes, 74, lead pathologist during the autopsy of President John F. Kennedy, 6 May 1999.

Nathaniel Kleitman, 104, physiology professor at the University of Chicago, pioneer sleep expert and codiscoverer of REM (Rapid Eye Movement) sleep in 1953; established sleep research as a separate medical field, 13 August 1999.

Sarah Knauss, 119, the oldest person in the world at the time of her death, in Pennsylvania, 30 December 1999.

Margaret E. "Maggie" Kuhn, 89, crusader against age discrimination and in 1970 one of the founders of the Gray Panthers, 22 April 1995.

Rose Kushner, 60, crusader for women with breast cancer, who worked for obtaining a less-radical surgery for treatment of that disease, 7 January 1990.

Mary Lasker, 93, philanthropist, in 1942 founded the Lasker Foundation with her husband, Albert. The Lasker Awards annually recognize advances in medicine, 21 February 1994.

Morton L. Levin, 91, epidemiologist and one of the first medical researchers to link tobacco and lung cancer (*Journal of the American Medical Association,* 1950), 7 July 1995.

C. Walton Lillehei, 80, surgical pioneer who performed the first successful open-heart surgery on a five-year-old girl (1952), 5 July 1999.

Jonathan Mann, 51, founder of the Global Program on AIDS (1986) of the World Health Organization (WHO), and his wife, Mary Lou Clements-Mann, a professor of international health, on the Swiss Air Flight 111 crash, 2 September 1998.

Shirley Ardell Mason, 75, the real-life model for "Sybil," the first well-publicized multiple personality disorder (MPD) patient, 26 February 1999.

Jean Mayer, 72, nutritionist who was a pioneer researcher in the relationship between food and poverty, aging, and obesity; established the first U.S. school of nutrition at Tufts University, 1 January 1993.

Barbara McClintock, 90, geneticist, revolutionized genetic science by showing that heredity can work in dynamic and irregular ways; received the Nobel Prize (1983), 2 September 1992.

Karl A. Menninger, 96, father of American psychiatry and in 1925 cofounder, with his father, C. J., and brother, Will, of the Menninger Clinic in Topeka, Kansas, 18 July 1990.

Anne Sheafe Miller, 90, believed to be the first patient in the United States saved by penicillin (1942), when it was still an experimental drug, 7 June 1999.

Victor Mills, 100, inventor of the disposable diaper, 1 November 1997.

Richard Overholt, 88, chest surgeon and pioneer in U.S. anti-smoking crusade, 16 July 1990.

Linus Carl Pauling, 93, a two-time winner of the Nobel Prize (1954, 1962), advocated vitamin C as a preventive and virtual cure-all, 19 August 1994.

John Peters, 67, supreme medicine man for the Wampanoag Nation who fought for legislation recognizing such Native American customs as the ritual use of peyote, 10 November 1997.

Joseph Quinlan, 71, pioneer of the right-to-die movement, who led a successful legal crusade to allow his daughter Karen Ann Quinlan to "die with dignity" after she slipped into a coma, 7 December 1996.

David Platt Rall, 73, toxicologist, Assistant Surgeon General (1971–1990), and pioneer in the environmental health field; former associate scientific director of the National Cancer Institute in Bethesda, Maryland; and founding director of the National Toxicology Program, 28 September 1999.

Richard "Ricky" Ray, 15, AIDS patient who, along with his two brothers, was barred from school in Arcadia, Florida, after becoming HIV positive during hemophilia treatments, 13 December 1992.

Albert Bruce Sabin, 86, microbiologist, developer of the oral polio vaccine, 3 March 1993.

Jonas Salk, 80, virologist, developed the first polio vaccine in 1955, 23 June 1995.

Harold Glendon Scheie, 80, noted ophthalmologist and founder of the Scheie Eye Institute adjacent to Presbyterian Hospital, Pennsylvania; treated and saved the eye of Lord Louis Mountbatten in the China-Burma-India theater in World War II; in 1964 he retired as a Brigadier General from the U.S. Army, 5 March 1990.

Jeffrey Schmalz, 39, *New York Times* reporter who wrote movingly of his fight against AIDS, 6 November 1993.

Florence Barbara Seibert, 93, biochemist who invented the process that made intravenous transfusions safe and refined an accurate skin test for tuberculosis, 23 August 1991.

Elizabeth Sherouse, 26, thought to be the first female prostitute in the United States charged with attempted manslaughter for risking transmission of AIDS to her clients, 22 January 1990.

John L. Simon, 86, psychiatrist who served as a medic during the Spanish Civil War (1936–1939) and as assistant to the surgeon of the Abraham Lincoln Brigade.

B. F. (Burrhus Frederic) Skinner, 86, pioneer of behavioral psychology and inventor of the "Skinner Box," 18 August 1990.

George Davis Snell, 92, Nobel Prize–winning biologist whose work on mouse genetics laid the basis for organ transplantation, 6 June 1996.

George Speri Sperti, 91, inventor of Preparation H hemorrhoid treatment and Aspercreme for arthritis relief, 29 April 1991.

Benjamin Spock, 94, revolutionized child care with *The Common Sense Book of Baby and Child Care* (1946), which sold almost fifty million copies. He later was a strong antiwar protestor, feeling that this continued his support of the lives of the children he helped rear, 15 March 1998.

Philip Strax, 90, championed early detection of breast cancer and helped lead the sixty-two thousand woman study in 1960 that found that mammography could reduce fatalities, 8 March 1999.

Michael Sveda, 87, researcher who discovered the sugar-substitute cyclamate (1937), 10 August 1999.

Michel M. Ter-Pogossian, 71, scientist who led the team that made the positron emission tomography (PET) scanner into a practical diagnostic tool, 19 June 1996.

Lewis Thomas, 80, scientist and writer of *The Lives of a Cell: Notes of a Biology Watcher* (1974) and *The Medusa and the Snail: More Notes of a Biology Watcher* (1979), which unlocked the mysteries of life for a broad audience, 3 December 1993.

William B. Walsh, 76, heart specialist, former physician to President Dwight D. Eisenhower, founder of Project HOPE (1958); he was the first American physician on the ground to treat victims after the atomic bomb was dropped on Hiroshima (6 August 1945) at the end of World War II, 27 December 1996.

Josef Warkany, 90, pediatrician, who in 1940 demonstrated that dietary deficiencies in mothers during pregnancy could cause birth defects, 22 June 1992.

Karen E. Wetterhahn, 48, chemistry professor at Dartmouth College, who studied how toxic metals inhibit DNA repair, from exposure in her lab to a rare mercury compound, 8 June 1997.

Carrie C. (Joyner) White, 116, in Palatka, Florida, the oldest living person in the world at the time of her death, 14 February 1991.

Allan C. Wilson, 56, leading researcher on human evolution and author of theory that all humans descended from one woman in Africa two hundred thousand years ago, 21 July 1991.

Ernst Wynder, 77, co-authored the 1950 landmark study linking cigarettes and lung cancer, 14 July 1999.

PUBLICATIONS

Robert C. Atkins, *Dr. Atkins' New Diet Revolution* (New York: M. Evans, 1996).

John Duffy, *From Humors to Medical Science: A History of American Medicine* (Urbana: University of Illinois Press, 1993).

Michael Fumento, *The Myth of Heterosexual AIDS* (New York: BasicBooks, 1990).

Edward S. Golub, *The Limits of Medicine: How Science Shapes our Hope for the Cure* (New York: Times Books, 1994).

Elizabeth Haiken, *Venus Envy: A History of Cosmetic Surgery* (Baltimore: Johns Hopkins University Press, 1997).

Caroline Hannaway, Victoria A. Harden, and John Parascandola, eds. *AIDS and the Public Debate: Historical and Contemporary Perspectives* (Amsterdam & Washington, D.C.: IOS Press, 1995).

Joel D. Howell, *Technology in the Hospital: Transforming Patient Care in the Early Twentieth Century* (Baltimore: Johns Hopkins University Press, 1995);

Alan M. Kraut, *Silent Travelers: Germs, Genes, and the "Immigrant Menace"* (New York: BasicBooks, 1994).

Katherine Ott, *Fevered Lives: Tuberculosis in American Culture since 1870* (Cambridge, Mass.: Harvard University Press, 1996).

George Rosen, *A History of Public Health* (Baltimore: Johns Hopkins University Press, 1993).

Charles E. Rosenberg, *Explaining Epidemics and Other Studies in the History of Medicine* (Cambridge & New York: Cambridge University Press, 1992).

Rosenberg and Janet Golden, eds., *Framing Disease: Studies in Cultural History* (New Brunswick, N.J.: Rutgers University Press, 1992).

David J. Rothman, *Strangers at the Bedside: A History of How Law and Bioethics Transformed Medical Decision Making* (New York: BasicBooks, 1991).

Sheila M. Rothman, *Living in the Shadow of Death: Tuberculosis and the Social Experience of Illness in American History* (New York: BasicBooks, 1994).

John W. Rowe and Robert L. Kahn, *Successful Aging* (New York: Pantheon, 1998).

Nancy Tomes, *The Gospel of Germs: Men, Women, and the Microbe in American Life* (Cambridge, Mass.: Harvard University Press, 1998).

United States Presidential Advisory Committee on Gulf War Veterans' Illnesses, *Presidential Advisory Committee on Gulf War Veterans' Illnesses: Final Report* (Washington, D.C.: U.S.G.P.O., 1996).

Jacqueline Van de Kamp and John H. Ferguson, *Persian Gulf Experience and Health* (Bethesda, Md.: U.S. Dept. of Health and Human Services, Public Health Service, National Institutes of Health, National Library of Medicine Reference Section, 1994).

An Alzheimer's disease patient at Senior Adult Services in Carbondale, Illinois, in 1995 (AP/Wide World Photos)

RELIGION

by CAROL GRIZZARD and TANDY MCCONNELL

CONTENTS

Sidebars and tables are listed in italics.

1990

- The *New Revised Standard Version of the Bible,* the first translation into English that is gender neutral, is published.

17 Apr. In *Employment Division, Department of Human Resources of Oregon* v. *Smith,* the Supreme Court rules that two members of the Native American Church are not entitled to unemployment benefits. They had been fired from their jobs as drug and alcohol counselors after using peyote in a religious service.

4 June In *Westside Community Board of Education* v. *Mergens,* the Supreme Court rules that public schools must give student-led religious groups the same access to school facilities allowed other student groups.

12–14 June After nearly two decades of coordinated effort, fundamentalists take undisputed control of the Southern Baptist Convention.

25 June The Central Conference of American Rabbis (Reform Judaism) votes to allow all rabbis to serve, regardless of sexual orientation.

4 July Christian Scientists David and Ginger Twitchell are convicted in Boston of manslaughter in the death of their two-year-old son, Robyn, in 1986. The Massachusetts Supreme Court overturns their conviction in 1993 on a technicality but states that parents have a legal duty to provide medical care for their children.

29 Sept. The Washington National Cathedral, whose construction began on 29 September 1907, is formally dedicated by President George Bush.

14 Dec. Former television evangelist James Orsen Bakker is found liable for $130 million in damages in a class action suit on behalf of 145,000 "lifetime partners" in his PTL Club. In 1989 he had been sentenced to forty-five years in prison for defrauding PTL members.

1991

1 May Pope John Paul II issues the encyclical *Centesimus Annus* (On the Hundredth Anniversary of Rerum Novarum), urging capitalist nations to right the injustices within their economic systems.

9–11 May Six thousand "moderate" Southern Baptists meet in Atlanta to organize the Cooperative Baptist Fellowship to provide a place for people who are no longer comfortable with, and whose ideas differ from, the increasingly conservative direction taken by the Southern Baptist Convention.

4–6 June The Southern Baptist Convention cuts all funding to the Baptist Joint Committee on Public Affairs, a religious liberty watchdog agency of several Baptist denominations, because its stand on several church-state and other issues are at odds with the leadership of the SBC.

16 Aug. After a month-long anti-abortion protest at a clinic in Wichita, Kansas, President George Bush calls the tactics of Operation Rescue "excessive."

22 Sept. The general public is allowed access to some of the Dead Sea Scrolls material for the first time when the Huntington Library in San Marino, California, puts its three hundred photograph negatives on display.

1992

12 June April Ulring Larson of the LaCrosse (Wisconsin) Area Synod of the Evangelical Lutheran Church in America becomes the first female Lutheran bishop in the United States.

24 June The Supreme Court rules in *Lee* v. *Weisman* that public schools may not include prayers as part of their graduation ceremonies. President Bush calls for a constitutional amendment to permit public prayer in school.

17–21 Aug. Pat Robertson and the Christian Coalition dominate the Republican National Convention and its platform; Patrick J. Buchanan uses the phrase "culture wars" to describe the conflict of values in American society.

Oct. Randall Terry, founder and leader of the activist, pro-life, anti-abortion organization Operation Rescue, says in a pamphlet that voting for Bill Clinton in the presidential election is a sin.

16 Nov. The Roman Catholic Church issues a new catechism that includes a statement that the Jews as a group were not responsible for Christ's death.

1993

28 Feb. Agents of the Bureau of Alcohol, Tobacco, and Firearms (ATF) storm the Branch Davidian compound near Waco, Texas, in order to arrest David Koresh and investigate charges that the religious group is stockpiling weapons. Four agents are killed in the botched raid.

10 Mar. Dr. David Gunn is killed by anti-abortionist Michael Frederick Griffin while entering a Pensacola, Florida, clinic where abortions were performed. Griffin claims that a vision from God led him to murder Gunn, but he is convicted and sentenced on 6 March 1994 to serve a life sentence.

26 Mar. R. Albert Mohler Jr. is elected president of the Southern Baptist Theological Seminary in Louisville, Kentucky.

13 Apr. The outspoken religious journal *Christianity and Crisis* publishes its last issue.

19 Apr. The Branch Davidian compound near Waco, Texas, is destroyed by fire as Federal Bureau of Investigation (FBI) agents try to end a fifty-one-day standoff. Nearly everyone inside is killed.

6–8 June Ten thousand people attend Global Vision 2000 in Washington, D.C., to honor the one hundredth anniversary of the arrival of Swami Vivekananda (Narendranath Datta) in the United States. He began the Hindu Vedanta movement in this country.

7 June In *Lamb's Chapel* v. *Center Moriches Union Free School District*, the Supreme Court rules that public schools allowing secular groups to use their facilities after school hours must grant equal access to religious groups.

11 June In *Church of Lukumi Bablu Aye, Inc.* v. *City of Hialeah*, the Supreme Court overturns a Hialeah, Florida, ban on animal sacrifices because it discriminated against practitioners of Santeria.

28 Aug. –5 Sept. The Second Parliament of the World's Religions convenes in Chicago a century after the first meeting. Six to eight thousand people attend, representing two hundred different religions, including Native American, Rastafarian, and other groups.

Oct.   The Evangelical Lutheran Church in America issues its controversial report on human sexuality.

27 Oct. The Religious Freedom Restoration Act is passed by the Senate by a vote of ninety-seven to three and is approved by the whole Congress on 16 November. The bill is a response to the Supreme Court decision in *Employment Division, Department of Human Resources of Oregon* v. *Smith* (1990).

4–7 Nov. The feminist "Re-Imagining Conference," sponsored by several mainstream denominations, outrages some when it includes a worship experience directed to Sophia, the feminine Wisdom of God.

7 Nov.   As the Roman Catholic Church prepared to discuss clerical sexual abuse, Cardinal Joseph Bernadin is accused of the crime by Steven Cook, a former seminarian who claimed to have recovered memories of the experience. Bernadin denied the accusations and Cook recanted completely in March 1994.

15 Dec. Steven Spielberg's movie, *Schindler's List*, opens, raising public awareness of the Holocaust.

1994

26 Feb. Five members of the Branch Davidian community are found guilty of aiding and abetting in the voluntary manslaughter of federal officials in connection with the ATF raid on 28 February 1993.

27 June In *Board of Education of Kiryas Joel Village School District* v. *Louis Grumet*, the Supreme Court declares the creation of a public school district solely for learning disabled and handicapped Hasidic Jewish children to be unconstitutional.

29 July Dr. John Bayard Britton, a physician at the Pensacola, Florida, Aware Woman Center for Choice, and James H. Barnett, his escort, are murdered by Paul Jennings Hill, a former Presbyterian minister seeking to stop abortions.

21 Sept. The television show *Touched by an Angel*, featuring angels helping people straighten out their lives, premieres on Columbia Broadcasting System (CBS).

Dec.   Bakker is released on probation. In 1991 his sentence was reduced to eighteen years, making him eligible for parole after serving five.

1995

•   The Church at Pierce Creek, New York, loses its tax-exempt status for publicly endorsing and opposing candidates in 1992. Randall Terry of Operation Rescue was a member. Pat Robertson's American Center for Law and Justice defended the church in court.

Jan.   The *Memphis Commercial Appeal* reports that a fire that had destroyed an area church the previous week might have been connected to fires at three black churches in western Tennessee a year earlier, beginning a nationwide media focus on the plight of black churches attacked by racially motivated arsonists.

30 Mar. Pope John Paul II issues the encyclical *Evangelium Vitae* (The Gospel of Life) in which he condemns abortion, in vitro fertilization, birth control, and euthanasia. He also says that the death penalty is rarely, if ever, necessary in modern society.

17 May	The Christian Coalition releases its "Contract with the American Family."
15–17 June	The National Conference of Catholic Bishops issues a statement critical of the United States for its participation in the international arms trade.
21 June	The Southern Baptist Convention formally apologizes for its history of racism.
29 June	In *Ronald W. Rosenberger* v. *Rector and Visitors of the University of Virginia,* the Supreme Court decides that the University must give the same funding to student-run religious publications as to student-run secular publications.
5 July	The Presbyterian Church, USA says that all clergy must be faithful in marriage or celibate in singleness; this allows nonactive homosexuals to be ordained.
16 Oct.	Louis Farrakhan (Louis Eugene Walcott) leads the Million Man March in Washington, D.C.

1996

28 Mar.	The Central Conference of American Rabbis passes a resolution endorsing civil marriages for homosexuals.
15 May	An Episcopal Church court dismisses heresy charges against Bishop Walter C. Righter for his 1990 ordination to the diaconate of Barry Stopfel, who was in a committed homosexual relationship. The court says that there was "no clear doctrine" involved.
12 June	The Southern Baptist Convention votes to boycott Disney movies, theme parks, and other entertainment outlets in part because the Disney Company recognizes homosexual relationships for insurance purposes. The Catholic League for Religious and Civil Rights began the boycott on 28 March 1995.
16 Oct.	The Public Broadcasting Service (PBS) airs the first of ten episodes of *Genesis: A Living Conversation with Bill Moyers.*
6 Nov.	Ruth Hoffman becomes the first ordained woman in the Christian Reformed Church.

1997

17–19 Jan.	The Landmark Conference on the Future of Buddhist Meditative Practice in the West meets in Boston.
14 Feb.	The First Baptist Church of Berryville, Arkansas, announces that it will close its daycare center in one month because its existence encourages women to work outside the home, contrary to the church's understanding of biblical teaching.
26 Mar.	Thirty-nine members of the Heaven's Gate religious cult commit suicide in their home near San Diego. They anticipated being taken to a higher level of being in a flying saucer supposedly trailing the Hale-Bopp comet.
24 May	The Dalai Lama dedicates the Great Buddhist Hall at the Chuang Yen Monastery in New York; it contains the largest statue of Buddha in the Western Hemisphere.

23 June   The Supreme Court overturns *Aguilar* v. *Felton* (1985), allowing public school teachers to provide remedial instruction for disadvantaged students attending religious schools.

25 June   The Supreme Court finds the Religious Freedom Restoration Act (1993) unconstitutional. The Court asserted that the act unduly burdened state and local governments by forcing them to recognize individual rights not specifically guaranteed in the Constitution.

17 Sept.   The television show *Nothing Sacred*, about an inner-city Roman Catholic church dealing with issues such as abortion and clerical celibacy, premieres on the American Broadcasting Company (ABC) network. Protests about the show begin before its premiere and lead to its cancellation six months later.

8 Oct.   The movie *Seven Years in Tibet* is released. It is based on the story of an Austrian mountaineer's introduction to Tibetan Buddhism and the Dalai Lama; it also introduces Buddhism to millions of Americans.

25 Dec.   *Kundun*, a movie that focuses on the life story of the Dalai Lama, is released.

1998

13 Mar.   United Methodist pastor Jimmy Creech is acquitted of violating denominational policy by officiating at a same-sex marriage.

16 Mar.   The Roman Catholic Commission for Religious Relations with the Jews issues *We Remember: A Reflection on the Shoah*.

28 Mar. –5 Apr.   At the World Conference of the Reorganized Church of Jesus Christ of Latter-Day Saints, Linda L. Booth and Gail E. Mengel become the first women appointed to the Council of Twelve Apostles.

6 June   The Southern Baptist Convention votes to add a clause to the *Baptist Faith and Message*, stating that a wife should submit graciously to the leadership of her husband.

10 Aug.   Kay Ward becomes the first female bishop in the Moravian Church of America.

11 Aug.   United Methodist Church Judicial Council says that same-sex marriages cannot be endorsed by the church and that pastors conducting such marriages can be punished.

Sept.   After a twelve-year-long audit, the Internal Revenue Service (IRS) revokes the tax-exempt status of Pat Robertson's Christian Broadcasting Network (CBN) because of "intervention in political campaign activities" in 1986–1987.

4 Oct.   The Evangelical Lutheran Church in America, the Presbyterian Church, the Reformed Church, and the United Church of Christ celebrate full communion for the first time.

16 Oct.   Anti-gay protestors, some of them Christians, demonstrate outside the funeral of twenty-one-year-old Matthew Wayne Shepard, a gay student at the University of Wyoming who died 12 October after having been beaten on 7 October.

23 Oct.   Dr. Barnett Slepian, an obstetrician who performed abortions, is killed at his home in Buffalo, New York.

1999

27 Oct.	President Bill Clinton signs the International Religious Freedom Act. The bill is intended to combat religious persecution overseas, calls on the president to assign an ambassador to monitor religious freedom outside the United States, and authorizes the imposition of diplomatic and economic sanctions against any country that violates the religious rights of its citizens.
18 Dec.	Disney releases the feature-length animated movie, *The Prince of Egypt,* a fictionalized account of the story of Moses.
Feb.	Jerry Falwell warns in his *National Liberty Journal* that Tinky Winky, a character on the children's television show *The Teletubbies,* promotes a homosexual lifestyle.
20 Apr.	Two students at Columbine High School in Colorado kill twelve students and a teacher, then commit suicide. Among the dead is seventeen-year-old Cassie Bernall, who reportedly was asked by the killers if she believed in God and was shot when she answered, "Yes, I believe in God."
11 Aug.	The Kansas Board of Education decides that the state will no longer test students on evolution, though it may still be taught.
Sept.	Feminist professor and scholar Mary Daly is fired by Boston College for refusing to allow men into her classes.
9 Sept.	Robert A. Seiple, Ambassador-at-Large for Religious Freedom, presents to Congress the first annual Report on International Religious Freedom, documenting harsh treatment of religious groups in 194 countries.
15 Sept.	Having already killed two people, Larry Gene Ashbrook opens fire on a group of young people meeting at the Wedgewood Baptist Church in Fort Worth, Texas, saying, according to one witness, "It's all bulls___, what you believe." He kills five worshipers and injures seven others before killing himself.
13 Dec.	The Supreme Court decides that the state of Vermont was acting constitutionally by subsidizing secular but not religious private education.

OVERVIEW

A Religious People. In the 1990s Americans continued to identify themselves by their religious belief. As in past decades, Protestants and Catholics dominated the religious landscape; Jews remained a small but influential minority; increasing, but still small, numbers of Americans identified themselves as Buddhists, Muslims, or Hindus. Though there was some evidence that people overreported their attendance at religious services, overall levels of participation were largely unchanged from previous decades. About 40 percent of Americans consistently reported attending religious services on a regular basis, a number virtually unchanged since the 1960s. More than 95 percent identified themselves as believing in God.

Religion in Public Life. The idea of a "moral majority" who shared a common commitment to traditionally conceived Judeo-Christian values and behavioral norms gave way in the decade to a sense among religious and cultural conservatives that American culture had lost its ethical moorings. The moral failings of President Bill Clinton, the increased public acceptance of homosexual and other alternative lifestyles, and the continued inability of the religious Right to outlaw abortion only confirmed this feeling of despair. Liberal religious groups did not fare any better. Indeed, the traditionally mainstream churches, represented by the National Council of Churches of Christ in the United States of America (NCC), found few issues around which to unite, and though several denominations made progress toward ecumenical unity, the Council itself struggled to remain financially solvent and culturally relevant. Increasing numbers of Americans identified themselves with nondenominational—or only vaguely denominational—"superchurches" that boasted tens of thousands of members, family-oriented programming, uplifting worship services, and relatively little concern for theology.

Religion and Politics. At the beginning of the decade, the Supreme Court rewrote the rules governing the way governments could regulate religious activity. In *Employment Divi-*

sion, Department of Human Resources of Oregon v. *Smith* (1990) the Court ruled that religious behavior is not exempt from governmental regulation as long as the intent of the regulation is general in scope and not intended to help or hinder religion. Thus, as long as the burden placed on a religious activity was incidental and not the purpose of the law, it was not constitutionally privileged. This set aside previous interpretations of the First Amendment that such regulations had to reflect an overriding state interest and should be minimally intrusive. Congress tried twice to restore the earlier interpretation, but the Court struck down the Religious Freedom Restoration Act (1993), and the subsequent Religious Liberty Protection Act (1999) failed to pass. Congress did approve an International Religious Liberty Protection Act (1998), which increased the attention paid to religious oppression around the world and required the president to respond to such actions with diplomatic and economic sanctions. Furthermore, although President Clinton and Vice President Al Gore were members of Southern Baptist churches, neither embraced the increasingly politicized conservatism of the denomination.

Religion and Violence. Some of the most violent events of the decade, including the bombing of the Alfred P. Murrah Federal Building in Oklahoma City (1995) and the shootings at Columbine High School (1999), had religious elements. One of the most visible and controversial incidents was the disastrous attempt by federal agents to take control of the Branch Davidian compound near Waco, Texas, and arrest its leader, David Koresh (1993). In other areas where violence intruded into the religious world, anti-Semitic and racist hate groups used the Bible to justify their attacks on civil society, while doctors who performed abortions were targeted and murdered by "right to life" advocates. Several of these assailants claimed that their actions had been in obedience to the laws of God. Similar attacks on homosexuals were defended by some as divine retribution for a sinful lifestyle.

TOPICS IN THE NEWS

CONTROVERSY OVER WOMEN'S ROLES

Theology and Language. As had been true for several decades, issues dealing with women—their rights and roles in reproduction, in the family, and in the workforce—were controversial in all areas of U.S. society. Jewish and Christian groups grappled with what kind of leadership, if any, women should exercise in their synagogues and churches. Women attended seminaries, were ordained, and found work on church and synagogue staffs in increasing numbers, but were still seldom senior rabbis, pastors, and denominational executives or bishops. Women's roles were particularly problematic in Judaism, Christianity, and Islam because the Bible and Koran were written in and about patriarchal societies, as were other works important in Jewish and Christian con-texts (for example, the Talmud, Church Fathers, and Hadith). All of this literature takes for granted that men have absolute authority over all members of their households (including male children and slaves) and that they head governments. A society that counts descent through the male line will find female sexuality dangerous, because the free exercise of it could lead to a confusion of male bloodlines; for this reason the Old Testament requires women to be virgins until marriage, but no such standard is held for men. As religious groups experienced internal conflict between conservative and liberal elements, the understanding of women often became a test case: is the patriarchal culture found in the Bible divinely inspired, which means that the passages limiting women's roles are God's will and therefore still in effect,

Episcopal church service led by female priests (AP/Wide World Photos)

Blessing over Milk and Honey

Our mother Sophia, we are women in your image:
With the hot blood of our wombs we give form to new life.
With the courage of our convictions we pour out our life
*   blood for justice.*

Sophia-God, Creator God,
let your milk and honey pour out,
showering us with your nourishment.

Our mother Sophia, we are women in your image:
With the milk of our breasts we suckle the children;
With the knowledge of our hearts we feed humanity.

Sophia-God, Creator God,
let your milk and honey pour out,
showering us with your nourishment.

Our sweet Sophia, we are women in your image:
With nectar between our thighs we invite a lover, we
*   birth a child;*
With our warm body fluids we remind the world of its
*   pleasures and sensations.*

Sophia-God, Creator God,
let your milk and honey pour out,
showering us with your nourishment.

Our guide, Sophia, we are women in your image:
With our moist mouths we kiss away a tear, we smile
*   encouragement.*
With the honey of wisdom in our mouths, we prophesy
*   a full humanity to all the peoples.*

Sophia-God, Creator God,
let your milk and honey pour out,
showering us with your nourishment.

Thanksgiving for the Shared Milk and Honey

Sophia, we celebrate your life-giving energy which
*   pulses through our veins,*
We celebrate women attempting to preserve life while
*   surrounded by war, famine and disease.*

We celebrate women's willingness to pour out their lifeblood for
*   others; to celebrate, to fight, and to protect both what they*
*   believe in and those whom they love.*
We celebrate your wisdom poured out upon women for eons.
We celebrate our unique perspectives, intelligence,
*   intuitions, and processes.*
We celebrate our mentors, our guides, our spiritual mothers,
*   our models.*

We celebrate the nourishment of your milk and honey.
Your abundance drips through your fingers onto us and
*   we in turn feed others.*
Through the sharing of this holy manna we enter into
*   community which strengthens and renews us for*
*   the struggle.*

We celebrate the sensual life you give us.
We celebrate the sweat that pours from us during our labors.
We celebrate the fingertips vibrating upon the skin of a love.
We celebrate the tongue which licks a wound, or wets our lips.
We celebrate our bodiliness, our physicality, the sensations
*   of pleasure, our oneness with earth and water.*

Source: Hilda A. Kuester, "Milk and Honey Ritual," in *Re-Membering and Re-Imagining,* edited by Nancy J. Berneking and Pamela Carter Joern (Cleveland, Ohio: Pilgrim, 1995).

---

or is the patriarchal culture and its understanding of women merely a human phenomenon and therefore not binding? The controversy was deeper and more significant because it involved the nature of Scripture and tradition as well as concern over the role of women. Language itself became not only a means of but also a subject of controversy as biblical translations, hymnals, and theologians using gender-neutral or feminine language in speaking of God were seen as departing unforgivably from centuries of tradition, while those who adhered to traditional ways were rejected by liberals as sexist and oppressive. The *New Revised Standard Version of the Bible* (1991) used inclusive language for people while retaining masculine wording for God; *The Presbyterian Hymnal: Hymns, Psalms, and Spiritual Songs* (1990) used inclusive language for both. Both works were consequently rejected by some congregations.

Family. Concern with women's roles in religion involved both the family and the broader worshiping community. The "traditional" American family has usually been understood as having a male breadwinner and a female homemaker, although this model was not as widely found in previous generations as many believe; in fact, it was always a largely upper- and middle-class phenomenon, since poorer families needed all adults to work. Wealthy individuals depended on poorer women to leave their own children in order to serve as nannies, cooks, and maids. In the latter decades of the twentieth century divorce rates and households consisting of a single parent and child or of cohabiting unmarried adults increased. A 1998 study by the University of Chicago found that 18.2 percent of children lived with single parents as opposed to 4.7 percent in 1972, while only 51 percent lived with both parents in 1998 as opposed to 73 percent in 1972. The study reported that families consisting of young children and two married parents, only one of whom worked outside the home, dropped from 45 percent to 26 percent between 1972 and 1998. In 1998 this type of household was less common than cohabiting childless couples or married childless couples. Many who saw these trends as alarming believed that the cause lay with feminism and its emphasis on self-fulfillment, requiring a career outside the home. In 1992 Pat Robertson referred to the feminist agenda as an "anti-family political movement." Because of concerns about the role of mothers in the family and the status of biblical texts defining that role, the issue of women in the workforce became a religious matter; as a result, religious groups paid particular attention to preserving the traditional family. In this spirit the First Baptist Church of Berryville, Arkansas, closed its daycare center (which served twenty-seven children) in March 1997. The church declared that by running a daycare center it was encouraging women to work; by closing the center the church urged families to live on one salary, giving up luxuries such as "big TVs, a microwave, new clothes, eating out and nice vacations." Biblical statements, such as Titus 2:5, which calls women "keepers at home," were used to justify the new policy.

Authority. In May 1994 Pope John Paul II issued *Ordinatio Sacerdotalis* (Priestly Ordination), saying that the Roman Catholic Church "has no authority whatsoever to confer priestly ordination on women" and that "this judgment is to be definitively held by all the church's faithful." In November 1995 the head of the Vatican's Congregation for the Doctrine of the Faith said, with papal approval, that the ban on women priests was "founded on the written Word of God" and was infallible. Bishop Anthony M. Pilla of Cleveland, president of the National Conference of Catholic Bishops (NCCB), said to those who favored women's ordination, "I ask you now prayerfully to allow the Holy Spirit to fill you with the wisdom and understanding [to] enable you to accept it." Still, approximately 60 percent of American Catholics consistently favored the ordination of women to the priesthood. The same week as the Vatican ruled against it, approximately one thousand women and men gathered in Washington, D.C., to celebrate the twentieth anniversary of the "Women's Ordination Conference." Speakers made it clear that they would continue to "keep the focus on ordination" while advocating broader changes in the hierarchical and male-dominated Roman Catholic Church.

The Re-Imagining Conference. The feminist and women-led ecumenical "Re-Imagining Conference" in November 1993 (sponsored by the Presbyterian Church of the United States of America, the United Methodists, the Evangelical Church in America, the American Baptist Convention, and the United Church of Christ, among others) was seen as embodying the anti-scripture, anti-family, and anti-authority attitudes that had concerned conservative Christians. These Christians were upset at the use of feminine pronouns and images to describe God at the conference, particularly in the context of a worship service directed to "Sophia," the personified-as-female Wisdom of God who often speaks in the biblical book of Proverbs ("Sophia" is the Greek word for "wisdom"). In another event that troubled conservatives, Delores S. Williams, a Union Theological Seminary professor, reportedly dismissed the relevance of the crucifixion: "I don't think we need folks hanging on crosses and blood dripping and weird stuff . . . we just need to listen to the God within." Conference sponsors were also accused of blasphemy and idolatry. Members of the United Methodist "Good News Movement" and the Presbyterian Lay Committee called "the worship of the Goddess Sophia" the "worst heresy in 1500 years of Christianity." Mary Ann Lundy lost her job as Director of Women's Ministries at denominational headquarters for the Presbyterian Church USA as a result of her support for "Re-Imagining." Advocates of the conference, however, said statements were taken out of context. Catherine Keller of Drew University argued that "the goddess Sophia" was an invention of conference critics and that Sophia is "simply a biblical female metaphor for the Holy." The conference, she said, was simply a chance for women to celebrate "the sacredness of women's lives as reflecting the image of God in which we were all created."

Ordination. Since women had been substantially represented in the secular workforce for several decades, some religious leaders felt that it was time for the religious world to catch up. Others perceived the interest in women's ordination to be an indication churches and synagogues were compromising with society rather than holding fast to the laws and traditions that guided them for centuries. Those on both sides of the issue were able to claim some victories in the decade. Several Christian groups ordained or otherwise placed women in specific leadership positions for the first time. In 1992 April Ulring Larson became the first female Lutheran bishop of the Evangelical Lutheran Church in America (less than three months after Maria Jepsen in Germany became the first female Lutheran bishop worldwide); in 1996 Ruth Hoffman was the first woman ordained in the Christian Reformed Church; in 1998 The Reorganized Church of Jesus Christ of Latter-Day Saints appointed Linda L. Booth and Gail E. Mengel as the first women on the Council of Twelve Apostles; also in that year Kay Ward became the first female bishop in the Moravian Church of America. Nevertheless, feminism in general was increasingly demonized: in a 1992 mailing Robertson said, "The feminist agenda is not about equal rights for women. It is about a socialist, anti-family political movement that encourages women to leave their husbands, kill their children, practice witchcraft, destroy capitalism, and become lesbians." In 1998 the Southern Baptist Convention amended its articles of faith (*The Baptist Faith and Message*) for the first time in thirty-five years to say that a woman should "submit graciously to the servant leadership" of her husband, who has the "God-given responsibility" to provide for and lead the family. On the other hand, on 11 November 1999, the Texas Baptist Convention voted to reject this amendment.

Sources:

Nancy J. Berneking and Pamela Carter Joern, eds., *Re-Membering and Re-Imagining* (Cleveland, Ohio: Pilgrim, 1995).

"Citing the Bible, Church Closes Day Care," *Christian Century*, 114 (23–30 April 1997): 405–406.

"A Converted Conference," *Christian Century*, 111 (16 February 1994): 160–162.

Stephanie Coontz, *The Way We Never Were: American Families and the Nostalgia Trap* (New York: BasicBooks, 1992).

James R. Edwards, "Earthquake in the Mainline," *Christianity Today*, 38 (14 November 1994): 38–43.

"An 'Infallible' No from Rome," *Christian Century*, 112 (13 December 1995): 1207–1208.

Martha Irvine, "Single Parents, Divorce More Accepted," *Louisville Courier-Journal*, 24 November 1999.

Catherine Keller, "Inventing the Goddess: A Study in Ecclesial Backlash," *Christian Century*, 111 (6 April 1994): 340–342.

Jane Redmont, "The Women's Ordination Movement, Phase Two," *America*, 173 (9 December 1995): 16–19.

William H. Shannon, "Tradition and the Ordination of Women," *America*, 174 (17 February 1996): 8–9.

ECUMENISM

National Council of Churches. When the churches of the American Protestant establishment—Lutherans, Methodists, Presbyterians, and Episcopalians—joined together in 1950 to establish the National Council of Churches of Christ in the United States of America (NCC), their postwar self-confidence and long-established respectability seemed to promise success in their ultimate goal, the restoration of Christianity as a single, unified body of believers. In midcentury America their rather modest theological differences and historical antagonisms seemed eminently less important than the goal of restoring the unity of the body of Christ. Just as importantly, the Protestant mainstream seemed to share common cultural expectations, language, and experiences. Sharing communion and creed did not seem too difficult to achieve with an adequate supply of goodwill. Such expectations were not misplaced. By the end of the century, enormous ecumenical strides had been made within the mainstream. On 31 October 1999, the anniversary of Martin Luther's posting of his Ninety-Five Theses, official representatives of the Roman Catholic Church and the Churches of the Lutheran Federation signed a Joint Declaration on the Doctrine of Justification—a key area of disagreement between Protestant and Catholic theologians—in the Sankt Anna Kirche in Augsburg, Germany. The agreement proclaimed "a consensus in basic truths" on how sinners are justified, or deemed righteous, in God's sight. Lutherans and Roman Catholics declared that the condemnations each side had leveled against the other for centuries no longer applied. The Joint Declaration allowed both traditions to retain their distinctive ways of talking about growth in holiness and the persistence of sin in the life of the believer—issues that remained controversial and theologically complex. It was a substantial move toward healing divisions that had divided Protestants and Catholics since the sixteenth century. Still, these and other ecumenical breakthroughs could not overcome the perception that the thirty-five denominations, with their combined fifty-two million members, that made up the NCC, were finding it impossible to speak with a single voice. The Christian Right, far more unified and clear in its agenda, was heard with much greater clarity than that of the NCC. Even more critical for the future of ecumenism, denominationalism itself seemed to be in decline in the United States.

Unity and Fragmentation. Though Catholics, Lutherans, Episcopalians, and Presbyterians reached unprecedented agreements, there was a wide perception that the NCC, though it had created an "ecumenical climate" that made intra-denominational conversations possible in the first place, had outlived its usefulness. Andrew Young, who became president of the NCC for 2000–2001, summarized the problem, saying that American Protestantism "is at a crisis moment" needing "a dramatic infusion of the Spirit . . . It's not just that people are losing interest in the ecumenical movement. They're losing interest in their own denominations and in the mainstream local churches." The continued success of nondenominational churches, such as the Willow Creek Community Church in South Barrington, Illinois, seemed to bear out Young's observations. Established in 1975 by Bill Hybels, Willow Creek sought to provide a "comfortable place" for people who felt uncomfortable with traditional liturgy and preaching, and were uninterested in denominational labels. Although the theology taught there was distinctly conservative and evangelical, it was doggedly nonsectarian. Its ministers, who were not usually seminary graduates, rarely emphasized theology. The services incorporated contemporary music, drama, and video, and Hybel's sermons focused on the role of faith in the everyday lives of middle-class suburbanites. The second largest church in America, Willow Creek became a defacto denomination when it established the "Willow Creek Association" of 1,400 other churches that shared its "seeker friendly" methods. With increasing numbers of churches and churchgoers rejecting denominational traditions, the NCC found itself struggling to carve out a new role for itself in a climate where the old mainline churches, that had been its core support, were increasingly marginalized.

Ecumenism at the End of the Century. Joan Brown Campbell, executive secretary of the NCC for most of the decade, acknowledged, "One of our big challenges is to deepen the unity between the churches that are National Council of Churches members. We are beyond the getting-to-know-one-another phase. It's time for churches to be more intentional about their unity regarding some of the topics about which they are uncomfortable." That would prove to be virtually impossible. While nondenominational churches could find unity fairly easily on key issues, and Evangelicals managed to define their positions clearly, the mainstream NCC had become too large and diverse to find many points of unity. Campbell said, "One of the things that the presence of the Christian Coalition reveals is that,

Various religions and denominations in late the twentieth-century United States experienced growth and revival, but increasing numbers of people identified themselves with particular affiliations without necessarily accepting all those traditions taught or becoming part of a local community of faith. A 1999 Gallup Poll indicated that 39 percent of Americans said that "there are a lot of things taught in my religion that I don't really believe," 45 percent said they paid more attention to "their own views" than to religious teaching in how they lived their lives, and 30 percent considered themselves "spiritual but not religious." This individualizing-of-religion phenomenon accompanied a trend toward "feel-good" religion, one that offered hope and comfort without a great deal of challenge. Examples of this trend were found in television shows such as *Touched by an Angel* and *Nothing Sacred*. The former dealt with compassionate angels who each week helped different individuals (seldom part of a religious community) deal with alienation, despair, sin, and death in a definitely religious and moral but nondenominational context. Theology was at a minimum. *Touched by an Angel* premiered in 1994 and was still popular at the end of the decade. On the other hand, *Nothing Sacred* was a serious and realistic look at an inner-city parish whose clergy and lay people were, from a specifically Catholic perspective, confronting controversial issues without simple answers—abortion, clerical celibacy, ordination of women, U.S. policies toward Central America, and homelessness, among others. It offered no miracles, coming closer to the actual experience of twentieth-century Christians in America than *Angel* did, and it did not last the entire 1997–1998 season.

The increasing popularity of angels was itself a part of this individualistic, comforting religious trend. According to a 1993 poll by *Time,* 69 percent of Americans believed in angels, 46 percent believed they had a guardian angel, and 32 percent said that they had felt the presence of an angel in their lives. In popular thought angels offered greater-than-human help without the awe-inspiring presence of God. They were, to use a common term, "user-friendly": supernatural help without supernatural demands. Interestingly, while 69 percent of Americans believed in helpful angels, only 49 percent believed in demons, their less comforting counterparts.

The movie *What Dreams May Come* (1999) was an excellent example of undemanding religious security. Angels abounded in this movie, although most were the souls of human dead (which no Jewish, Christian, or Islamic theology recognizes as angels). These characters inhabited a Heaven in which each individual is able to create his or her own perfect paradise; there is no ultimate reality except personal preference. While these angelic beings refer two or three times to God, there is in no sense such a character to be taken into account—the same is true of *Prophecy* (1995) and *End of Days* (1999), where Satan is an active and compelling character but God is not present; *Dogma* (1999) reversed this trend by presenting God but not Satan. Like *Ghost* (1990) and *Jack Frost* (1998), *What Dreams May Come* offered the dead hero a chance to make amends to a loved one for things never said or done in life. Many other movies, especially toward the end of the decade, dealt with survival after death without any kind of deity. In 1999 viewers learned about undying evil in *The Blair Witch Project*—or did they?—while *The Sixth Sense* and *Stir of Echoes* featured individuals who alone could see and offer help to the tormented dead.

As American culture became increasingly secularized, the religious issues of meaning in life, redemption in human relationships, and the nature of death and a future beyond it, were as important and widely discussed as ever. Movies offered traditional and moving views of religion—as in *Schindler's List* (1993), *Seven Years in Tibet* (1997), and *Kundun* (1997)—but the treatment of Christianity, the dominant faith in the United States, tended to be nontraditional and revisionist, as in *Stigmata* (1999) and *The Omega Code* (1999). *Dogma*, which took Catholicism far more seriously than any other major film of the decade, was widely protested by Catholics even before its release. More and more, religious issues were being presented without any sort of religious context. Many popular movies showed the universe as hostile, dangerous, and out of control: aliens nearly destroyed the human race in *Independence Day* (1996) and *Mars Attacks* (1996), while *Deep Impact* (1998) and *Armageddon* (1998) were about giant asteroids endangering Earth. *Godzilla* (1998) menaced New York. *Gattaca* (1997) presented a nightmarish, futuristic, scientifically based society in which there could be no privacy, and *The Truman Show* (1998) took reality-based TV to its paranoid limits by creating a hero who was unaware that his entire life had been manipulated for broadcast to the world with the participation of his "family" and friends. *Matrix* (1999) went one step farther, positing that all human reality is an illusion engineered to hide the fact that the human race is being used by aliens as carbon-based batteries. Such popular entertainment emphasized modern life as painful and meaningless. It is, therefore, not surprising that of the five movies nominated for Best Picture of 1998, three dealt with World War II (1939–1945)—*Saving Private Ryan, The Thin Red Line,* and *Life Is Beautiful*—while the other two were set in fifteenth and sixteenth century England, *Elizabeth* and *Shakespeare in Love.*

Sources: Nancy Gibbs, "Angels Among Us," *Time* (27 December 1993): 56–65.

Cathy Lynn Grossman, "In Search of Faith," and "An Unbound Spirit," *USA Today,* 23 December 1999.

Interfaith service led by John Cardinal O'Connor in New York on 20 April 1999 (AP/Wide World Photos)

by comparison to the NCC, the Coalition is a group of like-minded people." The coalition claims 1.5 million members. The NCC has in its member churches 49 million people, and their viewpoints are diverse. Even the historic role of the NCC as an advocate for social justice proved problematic. The NCC played a major role in publicizing the plight of African American churches burned in 1996 and 1997, as well as raising funds for rebuilding, in what was seen as an upsurge in hate-motivated arson attacks. Its uncritical advocacy, however, was assailed by critics who questioned whether the arsons were racially motivated and whether the Council was using the problem for its own purposes. Symptomatic of the malaise in the NCC was a funding crisis. In 1999 it reported a $4 million shortfall in its $70 million budget. The deficit was blamed on $2.5 million in consulting fees paid to find ways to streamline the organization, as well as a $500,000 error in the 1995 employee retirement fund and $330,000 paid into a fund to help restore burned churches. Concerned that the NCC was not adequately addressing underlying financial problems, the United Methodist Church suspended payment of more than $300,000 until things were cleared up. The Methodists were concerned about the failure of the NCC to maintain a budget based on its actual—rather than anticipated—income, and "lack of clarity on future liabilities." Other denominations raised questions as well. Robert W. Edgar, elected General Secretary in November 1999, said that the NCC got into financial trouble because it was "not very systematized or organized," was "coasting on a 1950s reputation," failed to maintain "a very good identity or clarity about our work," and did not keep adequate control of spending. The Methodist funds were restored early in 2000, but some critics and supporters of the NCC saw a troubled future for the fifty-year-old organization.

Sources:

"The Ecumenical Climb: An Interview with Joan Brown Campbell," *Christian Century*, 112 (8 November 1995): 1048–1052.

Joseph A. Fitzmyer, "The Augsburg Signing—An Overview of the Joint Declaration on Justification," *America*, 182 (19 February 2000): 17–21.

"NCC Chief: No More 'hemorrhaging'," *Christian Century*, 117 (8 March 2000): 266–267.

Jeffery L. Sheler, "Christians Unite!" *US News and World Report*, 127 (15 November 1999): 100.

HOMOSEXUALITY AND THE CHURCHES

Entering the Mainstream. Although gays and lesbians increasingly entered the mainstream of American society in the 1990s, their welcome was distinctly muted among broad sectors of the culture, particularly within religious institutions. Protestant, Catholic, and Jewish communities struggled to respond to the insistent demands from their homosexual members for recognition of their needs and contributions. When these demands included the recognition of same-sex marriages and the ordination of homosexual women and men, however, most mainstream churches retreated. New scientific theories further countered traditional definitions of homosexuality. Studies by the UCLA School of Medicine indicated that the brain structure of homosexual males differs from those of heterosexuals. The National Cancer Institute Laboratory of Biochemistry found evidence that male homosexuality may be inherited, and scientists at the National Institute of Health believed they found evidence that homosexuality is carried in DNA. This evidence, while not conclusive and dealing entirely with males, suggested that sexual orientation is inborn rather than chosen. These arguments were greeted by some Jews and Christians as yet more evidence of scientific hostility to religion; others reacted with relief, as the new information was seen as a means of offsetting the biblical statements on homosexuality.

Sacraments. In 1998 the Judicial Council of the United Methodist Church stated that same-sex marriages were not endorsed by the Church and that pastors who presided over such ceremonies could suffer the loss of their clerical status. American Episcopalians were forced to deal directly with the issue when Bishop John Shelby Spong of Newark, New Jersey, presented "A Statement in Koinonia" to the 1994 General Convention of the Episcopal Church. He argued that, whatever one's sexual orientation, sexuality is itself morally neutral, and nothing in Scripture prevents a homosexual relationship from being any less holy than a heterosexual one. Thus, homosexuals "who choose to live out their sexual orientation in a partnership that is marked by faithfulness and life-giving holiness" should not be excluded from the ordained ministry. Spong's statement revealed the depths of the division over homosexuality in American churches. Though Spong was widely criticized, others would be threatened with formal charges of heresy. When in 1994 Bishop Walter C. Righter ordained a homosexual man to the priesthood, he faced charges that in doing so he broke his ordination vows and was guilty of false teaching. In 1996 the church court formed to try the case dismissed the charges, finding that Righter's actions had violated "no clear doctrine."

The United Methodist Church. As the second largest, and perhaps most diverse, Protestant denomination in the United States, the United Methodists could scarcely avoid being caught up in what came to be seen as a fundamental question of morality. In 1996 the General Conference of the 8.5-million-member denomination, after a contentious debate, inserted a clause in the *United Methodist Social Principles* saying "ceremonies that celebrate homosexual unions shall not be conducted by our ministers and shall not be conducted in our churches." When Jimmy Creech, senior pastor at the First United Methodist Church of Omaha, Nebraska, challenged the new rule by performing a marriage ceremony for a lesbian couple on 14 September 1997, he was tried by a church court for a violation of church law. Creech argued, "There was no way I was going to say 'no' to the two women. I will not treat them with disrespect. I will not question their dignity and their right to love and commit themselves to the persons they love and are committed to." The jury found that, though his actions violated the Social Principles, they were not punishable in church court since it was not clear whether they were binding or simply advisory. In 1998 the United Methodist Judicial Council, the highest legislative body of the denomination, clarified the situation by stating that the prohibition against clergy's performing same-sex unions was not simply advisory but had the force of church law. When Creech performed a same-sex union ceremony for Larry Ellis and James Raymer on 24 April 1998 in Chapel Hill, North Carolina, he was charged, convicted, and unfrocked in November 1999. Creech was not alone in his opposition to the rejection of homosexuals by his church.

A Lutheran church service performed by and for homosexuals (AP/Wide World Photos)

After the Judicial Council ruling, the California-Nevada Annual Conference spent several days in "spiritual discernment" during which the 1600 delegates tried to understand God's will in the matter. They resolved to encourage local congregations within their jurisdiction to become "welcoming" of everyone without regard to sexual orientation. In response, the Kingburg United Methodist Church in California resolved that "in Christian conscience" it could no longer remain identified with the United Methodist Church. On 28 July 1998 the congregation voted to transfer its membership to the newly created Kingburg Community Church. In March 1999 the ban on clergy performing same-sex marriages was again put to the test when Gregory R. Dell, a United Methodist minister from Chicago, was found guilty of violating church law for performing several such ceremonies. He was suspended from the ministry for a year. By 1999 the issue threatened to create schism in the United Methodist Church. In January 1999, in Sacramento, California, ninety-two Methodist ministers, along with clergy from other denominations, took part in blessing the "holy union" of a lesbian couple in a service at St. Mark's United Methodist Church; complaints were filed against many of the participants. The United Methodist Board of Church and Society and Commission on Christian Unity and Inter-religious Concerns called on the Judicial Council to moderate its position against homosexuality. At the same time, leaders of Good News—a conservative caucus within the denomination—urged Methodists who favored church approval of same-sex unions "to formally withdraw from (Methodism's) covenant and seek another avenue in which they can faithfully express their heartfelt beliefs."

Presbyterians. In 1978 the Presbyterian Church USA stated that "homosexual persons are encompassed by the searching love of Christ. The church must turn away from its fear and hatred to move toward the homosexual community in love and to welcome homosexual inquirers to its congregations." The welcome was not without limits, however. In 1991 the General Assembly clarified its position regarding homosexual marriage, forbidding "the use of church facilities for a same sex union ceremony." Furthermore, it stated that "since a Christian marriage performed in accordance with the Directory for Worship can only involve a covenant between a woman and a man, it would not be proper for a minister of the Word and Sacrament to perform a same sex union ceremony that the minister determines to be the same as a marriage ceremony." This pronouncement did not prohibit ministers from blessing same-sex unions as long as the ceremony was not a wedding. In 1993 the General Assembly adopted a statement that "self-affirming, practicing homosexual persons may not be ordained as ministers of the Word and Sacrament, elders, or deacons." In 1997 the *Book of Order* was changed to read "Those who are called to office in the church are to lead a life in obedience to Scripture and in conformity to the historic confessional standards of the church. Among these standards is the requirement to live either in fidelity within the covenant of marriage between a man and a woman, or chastity in singleness. Persons refusing to repent of any self-acknowledged practice which the confessions call sin shall not be ordained and/or installed as deacons, elders, or ministers of the Word and Sacrament." Thus, homosexuals could be ordained, but had to commit themselves to lives of celibacy or, as critics pointed out, lie about their behavior. In an effort not to limit its ministry to homosexuals, the Hudson River Presbytery of the Presbyterian Church USA voted overwhelmingly to allow ministers to perform same-sex holy unions, provided that they were not called marriages, and a church tribunal upheld the right of the First Presbyterian Church of Stamford, Connecticut, to elect an openly gay elder to its governing board. On the matter of gay ordination, in 1999 the General Assembly opted for a measure calling for two years of study on the issue. That "decision not to decide" was called into question, however, when a church tribunal ruled in November that a group of Presbyterian congregations in New Jersey did not violate church laws by accepting a gay man as a candidate for ordination.

Lutherans. In 1993 the Evangelical Lutheran Church in America (ELCA) discussed an extensive and detailed statement on human sexuality that called for celibacy in singleness and fidelity in marriage. It also said that homo-sexuality was like any kind of sexuality; it was an integral part of one's identity. Without endorsing homosexual behavior, the statement avoided referring to it as either choice or sin, and concluded, "We trust in the power of the Holy Spirit to guide and unite us in Christ as we continue to deliberate on those questions and issues of homosexuality on which we are presently divided. In 1996 the ELCA Church Council adopted *A Message on Sexuality: Some Common Convictions.* In order to avoid the controversy that any such discussions inevitably raised, the statement did not address ethical questions related to homosexuality. In August 1999 the ELCA issued a guide for congregations, *Talking Together as Christians about Homosexuality.* The introduction acknowledged, "When the ELCA attempted to set forth its understanding of human sexuality in a social statement in 1993, it became clear that, on the topic of homosexuality, though the inherited tradition continues to guide the consciences of many people, it does not express for others an adequate understanding of the Christian life in light of the gospel and human experiences." The guide reflected the lack of consensus among Lutherans on the issue without attempting an authoritative statement. Gilbert Meilaender Jr., a Missouri Synod Lutheran pastor and Christian ethicist, contended that "By turning against the created meaning of our humanity as male and female, homosexual behavior claims the freedom to give our own meaning to life and thereby symbolically enacts a rejection of God's will for creation." Yet, Paul Thomas Jersild, a theologian and ethicist at Lutheran Theological Southern Seminary in Columbia, South Carolina, argued, "As a Christian community we need to move away from the kind of rational, universal thinking about human sexuality that coerces everyone into the same heterosexual mold, often with great human cost. We should be more concerned to address a people's humanity than their sexuality and to understand their sexuality as much more than genital activity."

Conservatives and Evangelicals. Conservative and evangelical churches had fewer qualms about dealing with homosexuality. Outraged first at President Bill Clinton's unpopular policy of "don't ask; don't tell" regarding gays serving in the military, and then by the increasing presence of homosexual characters and situations on television, many saw the increased visibility of homosexual lifestyles as a sign of moral decay and depravity. Dwayne Hastings, communications director for the Ethics & Religious Liberty Commission of the Southern Baptist Convention, described the problem homosexuality presented for conservative Southern Baptists. "We want to be compassionate people. While the Bible speaks very strongly against homosexuality, we're not saying we don't like people. It's a hate the sin, love the sinner sort of thing. We don't want it to come out in a homophobic way." In 1996 the Southern Baptist Convention (SBC), the largest Protestant body in the nation, voted to urge the Walt Disney Company to reverse its "gay friendly" policies, which included allowing the same-sex partners of gay employees to enjoy the same benefits as opposite-sex spouses. Disney, which owned, among other things, the American Broadcasting Company (ABC) television network, virtually ignored the SBC and broadcast a controversial episode of the television series *Ellen* in which the title character, played by Ellen DeGeneris, acknowledged and started to come to terms with her homosexuality. In 1997 the denomination voted to urge Christians to stay away from Disney World and Disneyland, and to boycott the vast array of entertainment enterprises owned by Disney, until it returned to its more "family friendly" beginnings. Though the boycott was widely ignored, even by Baptists, and appeared to have had a negligible impact on corporate profits, the SBC continued to urge Disney and other corporations to promote a more traditional, family-centered American culture. Less publicly, but with perhaps greater ramifications for the congregational polity, two Southern Baptist churches were expelled from the Georgia Baptist Convention in 1999 for violating the 1998 amendment to the constitution stating that "a cooperating church does not include (one) which knowingly takes, or has taken, any action to affirm, approve, or endorse homosexual behavior." This was the first time in the 177-year history of the Georgia convention that a church had been banned for theological nonconformity.

Sources:
"ELCA Prepares Sex Statement," *Christian Century*, 110 (3 November 1993): 1080–1081.

Jeff Flock and John Holliman, "Methodist Church Weighs Homosexual Marriage," *CNN Interactive*, 12 March 1998, Internet website.

William A. Henry, "Born Gay?" *Time*, 142 (26 July 1993): 36–39.

Brian Hicks, "Baptists Address Sexuality: Commission Pushes Abstinence, Compassion for Gays," *Charleston Post and Courier*, 3 March 1998.

"Homosexuality," *PresbyTel, The Reference Desk for the Presbyterian Church USA*, Internet website.

Bill Lancaster, "Assembly Opts for Unity/Diversity Dialogue, Not Another Amendment on Homosexual Issue," *General Assembly News* (Fort Worth, Texas), 25 June 1999, Internet website.

"Lutherans Issue Guide on Homosexuality," *ELCA News Service*, 13 September 1999.

"Methodist Jury Finds Minister Innocent in Case Challenging Homosexual Policy," *Athens* (Georgia) *Daily News*, 14 March 1998, *Online Athens*, Internet website.

John D. Pierce, "Georgia Church Could Face Ouster From State Over Homosexual Stance," *Baptist Press*, 20 September 1999.

"Prohibition against Performing Homosexual Unions Ruled Enforceable," *United Methodist News Service*, 11 August 1998, Internet website.

Paul Recer, "Brain Structure Different in Gay Men, Study Finds," *The Louisville Courier-Journal*, 1 August 1992.

James Solheim, "Court for Trial of a Bishop Responds to Pre-trial Motions," *Episcopal News Service Note*, 1345 (12 February 1996).

Larry Thompson, "A Search for a Gay Gene," *Time*, 145 (12 June 1995): 60–61.

LANGUAGE AND VIOLENCE

Increasing Concerns. The debate about "political correctness" begun in the 1980s continued in the 1990s. There were increasing protests about racism and sexism, particularly in humor and popular music. Some forms of visual and aural entertainment used violent images; some advocated violence against specific kinds of people. For decades there had been concern about a possible connection between violence shown on television and violent behavior, but the focus widened to include words and not just visual images. Violent lyrics became big news in 1992 when the rapper Ice-T (Tracy Morrow) recorded "Cop Killer" on his *Body Count* album. Although Ice-T said the song was about a character's avenging Rodney Glen King's beating by shooting Los Angeles policemen, but not an endorsement of the act itself, many felt that giving this character a voice could lead to the violent actions he described. Law enforcement officers and others protested until Time Warner released Ice-T from his contract and reissued *Body Count* without the controversial song. As far too many schools dealt with students

EVOLUTION AND THE PUBLIC SCHOOLS

The debate on evolution captured public attention when the Kansas Board of Education adopted on 11 August 1999 a new science curriculum that removed requirements on teaching evolution. Although local school boards can still permit the theory of evolution to be taught, questions on evolution—especially as they relate to human origins—will not be included in state assessment tests. Teachers with limited class time and boards with tight budgets will be less likely to teach a subject for which students will not be held accountable. Efforts to promote "scientific creationism" began in the 1960s. Creationists argue that much of the physical evidence that has been explained by Charles Darwin's theory of evolution can better be accounted for by a "scientific" but still literal interpretation of the Bible. Thus, when a 1968 Arkansas law forbidding the teaching of evolution was struck down by the Supreme Court, Louisiana tried to circumvent the consitutional problem by requiring that teachers who discussed evolution give "balanced treatment" to scientific creationism. This too was struck down in 1987 in *Aguillard* v. *Edwards*. Thus the Kansas Board of Education neither forbade the teaching of evolution nor required the teaching of creationism, but simply left the subject out of the curriculum altogether. This action sparked similar efforts in other states. In Kentucky, officials moved to replace the emotionally charged word "evolution" with "change over time." In New Mexico, however, the Board of Education made a countermove, effectively excluding creationism by limiting the state-wide science curriculum to the teaching of evolution as an explanation of human origins.

Source: Stephen Jay Gould, "Dorothy, It's Really Oz: A Pro-Creationist Decision in Kansas Is More than a Blow against Darwin," *Viewpoint*, 154 (23 Aug 1999).

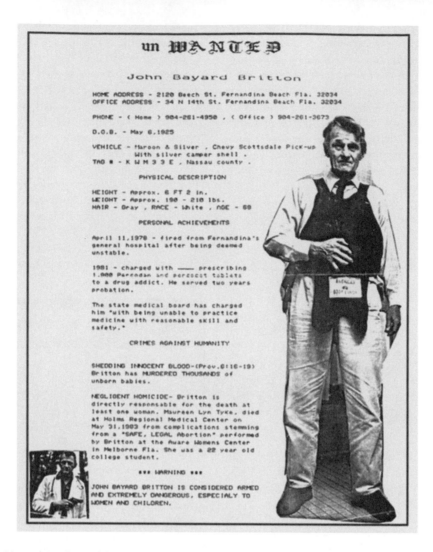

un WANTED

John Bayard Britton

HOME ADDRESS - 2120 Beech St. Fernandina Beach Fla. 32034
OFFICE ADDRESS - 34 N 14th St. Fernandina Beach Fla. 32034

PHONE - (Home) 904-261-4950 , (Office) 904-261-3673

D.O.B. - May 6,1925

VEHICLE - Maroon & Silver , Chevy Scottsdale Pick-up
          With silver camper shell .
TAG # - K W M 3 3 E , Nassau county .

PHYSICAL DESCRIPTION

HEIGHT - Approx. 6 FT 2 in.
WEIGHT - Approx. 190 - 210 lbs.
HAIR - Gray , RACE - White , AGE - 68

PERSONAL ACHIEVEMENTS

April 11,1978 - fired from Fernandina's
general hospital after being deemed
unstable.

1981 - charged with ——— prescribing
1,900 Percodan and percocet tablets
to a drug addict. He served two years
probation.

The state medical board has charged
him "with being unable to practice
medicine with reasonable skill and
safety."

CRIMES AGAINST HUMANITY

SHEDDING INNOCENT BLOOD-(Prov.6:16-19)
Britton has MURDERED THOUSANDS of
unborn babies.

NEGLIGENT HOMICIDE- Britton is
directly responsible for the death at
least one woman. Maureen Lyn Tyke, died
at Holms Regional Medical Center on
May 31,1983 from complications stemming
from a "SAFE, LEGAL Abortion" performed
by Britton at the Aware Womens Center
in Melborne Fla. She was a 22 year old
college student.

*** WARNING ***

JOHN BAYARD BRITTON IS CONSIDERED ARMED
AND EXTREMELY DANGEROUS, ESPECIALLY TO
WOMEN AND CHILDREN.

A poster, designed by antiabortion activists, that targeted Dr. John Bayard Britton of Pensacola, Florida. Bayard, and his escort, James H. Barnett, were murdered by Paul Jennings Hill on 29 July 1994.

who shot, and sometimes killed, their classmates and school personnel, the possibility of a cause-and-effect relationship between popular culture and violence was explored more deeply. This inquiry raised questions concerning First Amendment rights: when, if ever, is the right to say what one pleases superceded by fears that this speech could lead others, whom the speaker might not even know, to commit violence?

Abortion. Abortion had been a controversial issue since the *Roe* v. *Wade* (1973) decision by the Supreme Court. Several clinics that offered abortions were bombed in the 1980s as Catholic and evangelical Christians, among others, maintained an intensifying campaign for the sanctity of unborn human life. Abortion-rights activists, both secular and religious, argued that women had a fundamental right to control what happened within their bodies. With no room for compromise, both abortion-rights advocates and opponents tended to demonize their opponents. Beginning in 1993, however, a murderous dimension was added to the already-violent issue when on 10 March an antiabortionist killed Dr. David Gunn at a Pensacola, Florida, clinic that performed abortions. Several other abortion providers were

also murdered during the decade. In 1994 there were twelve attempted or actual murders, as well as twelve additional attacks on clinics by bombs or fire. Michael Frederick Griffin, who murdered Gunn, claimed at his trial that he had been brainwashed by John Burt, an antiabortion activist and member of the Christian prolife organization Rescue America. Griffin did not prove his claim and was sentenced to life imprisonment, but it did raise the question of the influence that Christian protesters had on those who used violence to stop abortions. There was even an Internet website known as "The Nuremberg Files" that compiled dossiers on medical personnel who performed or assisted with abortions and judges who protected them; information offered included family photos and home addresses. The site featured photographs of bloody fetuses and whenever an abortion provider was killed or injured, it would be reflected on the list. Spokespeople for both Planned Parenthood and the National Abortion Federation considered the sponsors of the site responsible for antiabortion violence; a federal court agreed and on 2 February 1999 shut it down. Many abortion foes, however, pointedly argued against using violence to end abortion. A "Pro-life

Proclamation Against Violence" was endorsed by more than thirty pro-life groups (not including Operation Rescue). Others did not consider their language to be too extreme in such an important cause. Michael Bray, convicted in seven clinic bombings in the 1980s, saw prolife evangelicals as at war against a foe "comparable to Nazi Germany"; this struggle therefore justified violence against the enemy. Randall Terry, founder of Operation Rescue, spoke of Supreme Court justices Harry Andrew Blackmun and John Paul Stevens as "enemies of Christ" and said that "they're going to be remembered with Adolf Hitler and Joseph Stalin." Paul Jennings Hill, a minister who murdered Dr. John Bayard Britton on 29 July 1994, wrote on Bray's *Capitol Area Christian News* Internet website that "the joy I felt after shooting the abortionist, and still feel today, is the joy of having freely obeyed Christ after long being enslaved to fearful obedience to men."

Intolerance of Homosexuality. The demonizing rhetoric found in the abortion controversy also surfaced in some Christian references to homosexuals. Pat Robertson described gays as indistinguishable from Nazis and Satanists on the 21 January 1993 edition of *The 700 Club.* When Matthew Wayne Shepard, a young gay man, was murdered in October 1998, in Wyoming, his funeral was picketed by members of Westboro Baptist Church of Topeka, Kansas, under the leadership of their pastor, Fred Phelps. They carried signs saying, "Matt's in Hell" and "God Hates Fags" and put up a "Westboro Baptist Church's Perpetual Gospel Memorial to Matthew Shepard" Internet website featuring a picture of Shepard burning in hell, along with the count of how many days they believed he had been there. Part of its Internet address was "godhatesfags." On 4 November 1999 Benjamin Matthew Williams, who was jailed for shooting a gay couple to death in California, said he was not guilty because homosexuality breaks God's law. In words similar to those used by Hill, the antiabortion activist who murdered Britton, Williams proclaimed: "I'm not guilty of murder. I'm guilty of obeying the laws of the Creator."

Sources:

Gary Delson and Sam Stanton, "Invoking God's Name to Justify Killing," *The Sacramento Bee,* 6 November 1999.

Douglas Frantz, "The Rhetoric of Terror," *Time,* 145 (27 March 1995): 48–51.

Paul Hill, "The Defensive Action Statement," Internet website.

Mark Juergensmeyer, "Christian Violence in America," *Annals of the American Academy of Political and Social Science,* 558 (July 1998): 88–100.

Melissa Manning, "Bathroom Rhetoric Hurts Debate," *The Daily Tar Heel,* 6 April 1999.

B. A. Robinson, "Violence & Harassment at U.S. Abortion Clinics," *Ontario Consultants on Religious Toleration,* Internet website.

MASCULINITY AND RELIGION

Crisis of Masculinity. The politicization of the American family as a religious and social ideal became institutionalized in the 1990s. In the traditional, idealized household, the husband and father earned most or all of the income. In return, his wife took care of the house and children. The husband led; the wife followed. God was honored, and everyone prospered. Since the 1960s the ideal had suffered continuous insult from broad social changes, a rising rate of divorce, and increased employment (and empowerment) of women. Most evangelical Christian leaders had merely fretted over such changes in the 1980s, but turned to social and political activism in the 1990s. The secular men's movement, represented by Robert Bly's figure, Iron John, was displaced by two distinctly religious responses. The Million Man March, organized in 1995 by Nation of Islam leader Louis Farrakhan (Louis Eugene

PROMISE KEEPERS: SEVEN PROMISES

1. A Promise Keeper is committed to honoring Jesus Christ through worship, prayer, and obedience to God's Word in the power of the Holy Spirit.

2. A Promise Keeper is committed to pursuing vital relationships with a few other men, understanding that he needs brothers to help him keep his promises.

3. A Promise Keeper is committed to practicing spiritual, moral, ethical, and sexual purity.

4. A Promise Keeper is committed to building strong marriages and families through love, protection, and biblical values.

5. A Promise Keeper is committed to supporting the mission of his church by honoring and praying for his pastor, and by actively giving his time and resources.

6. A Promise Keeper is committed to reaching beyond any racial and denominational barriers to demonstrate the power of biblical unity.

7. A Promise Keeper is committed to influencing his world, being obedient to the Great Commandment (see Mark 12:30-31) and the Great Commission (see Matthew 28:19-20).

Love the Lord your God with all your heart and with all your soul and with all your mind and with all your strength. The second is this: Love your neighbor as yourself. (NIV)

Mark 12:30-31

Therefore go and make disciples of all nations, baptizing them in the name of the Father and of the Son and of the Holy Spirit, and teaching them to obey everything I have commanded you. And surely I am with you always, to the very end of the age. (NIV)

Matthew 28:19-20

Source: *Promisekeepers,* Internet website.

Participants in the Million Man March in Washington, D.C., on 16 October 1995 (AP/Wide World Photos)

Walcott), brought nearly that number of black men to the Mall in Washington, D.C., to hear a call to greater involvement by black men in the lives of their families and communities. The Sacred Assembly of Men, organized by the Promise Keepers, also brought hundreds of thousands of mostly white, middle-class men to the same space in the capital to hear a similar message. Though addressing broad social problems, both events were self-consciously religious and intensely spiritual.

The Men's Movement. Bly's *Iron John: A Book About Men* (1990) addressed a growing uneasiness shared by a great many Baby Boomer males. They seemed to be missing something. Their fathers and grandfathers had fought in wars that were clear-cut contests of good and evil. They had been farmers and construction workers; they had worn their masculinity with an ease that suggested they were not even aware of its presence. The women's movement and the increasing complexity of family and social life, as well as the disappearance of male-only bastions in business, industry, and the military, demanded a redefinition of masculinity. Bly's novel provided a puzzling narrative based on ancient myths of the "wild man." Modern males, he suggested, had lost contact with their manhood. Young boys, raised by their mothers in the absence of father figures, were no longer learning about masculinity from other men. They grew up unable to understand themselves as men and unable to project the certainty of their forefathers. Thus, men behaved irresponsibly, found themselves paralyzed by fear, and were generally frustrated in their pursuit of fulfillment. The answer, Bly suggested, was to be found in reestablishing bonds with other men. The "wild man" within, stunted by years of neglect in a hostile culture, had to be rediscovered and given an opportunity to grow strong.

Recovering Masculinity. During the first years of the decade, a few men sought to recover their masculine ideal by joining men's groups where they beat on drums, chanted, and bonded with each other during weekend retreats in the woods. Though this secular movement addressed a real need, it became more popular as an object of derision than a serious social outlet. Lacking an organizational framework, ideological basis, and effective marketing, the early men's movement failed to establish itself within the fabric of American culture.

Million Man March. Farrakhan seemed a surprising, indeed a problematic, figure to be at the center of a gathering of black men focusing on unity and atonement. As leader of the Nation of Islam, Farrakhan had repeatedly spoken harshly about whites, Jews, and American culture in general. His commitment to Islam and black separatism put him at odds with the Christian and largely Protestant core of the traditional civil-rights movement and its most prominent leader, the Reverend Jessie Louis Jackson Sr. Yet, Farrakhan insisted that he called for the march because God wanted him to. And millions of black men, Christian and Muslim, agreed with Henry G. Cisneros, U.S. Secretary of Housing and Urban Development, that "things were profoundly wrong" and that the racial divide in American culture was profoundly damaging to them. Black men had a life expectancy of sixty-five years, eight years less than white males. Young black males were more likely to die of violence than disease, accident, or any other cause of death. Of every three black men between the ages of twenty and twenty-nine, one was in prison, on probation, or on parole. Though the media reported the march primarily as a political event, those men who attended it experienced a spiritual revival, a moment of repentance, change and renewal, and a call to replace division with unity. One speaker quoted 1 Cor. 1:10, "Now I beseech you, brethren, by the name of our Lord Jesus Christ, that ye all speak the same thing, and that there be no divisions among you; but that ye be perfectly joined together in the same mind and in the same judgment." Hugh B. Price, president of the National Urban League, called for black men to respect women and to take seriously their responsibilities as fathers at "the largest family-values rally in the history of America." Clarence Page, a black writer for the *Chicago Tribune*, noting the divisiveness of Farrakhan's own rhetoric, wrote, "I wish a black leader who was less incendiary than Farrakhan had issued the call for black men to come out to the Million Man March. But they didn't and he did. He stuck his neck out and it paid off."

Promise Keepers. A tightly organized religious movement that attracted millions of men to its rallies, Promise Keepers addressed many of the same feelings that something was terribly wrong in the lives of men. At its height in 1997, an estimated five hundred thousand men traveled from around the country to join in a "Stand in the Gap Sacred Assembly of Men" on the Mall in Washington, D.C. Founded in 1991 by former University of Colorado football coach Bill McCartney, the organization drew 4,200 men to its rallies during its first year of existence. At its height in 1997, more than one million men paid $60 each to attend six hour-long rallies—usually held in packed outdoors sports arenas—where they sang, prayed, cried, and promised to be better husbands and fathers. Almost from the outset, the Promise Keepers drew as much criticism as praise. Though many women, especially the wives of Promise Keepers, were enthusiastic about the changes the organization had wrought in their husbands, feminists were made distinctly uneasy by the message of separate roles for husbands and wives. Tony Evans, a popular speaker at Promise Keeper events, advised men to: "Sit down with your wife and say something like this: 'Honey, I've made a terrible mistake. I've given you my role. I gave up leading this family, and I forced you to take my place. Now I must reclaim that role.' I'm not suggesting you ask for your role back, I'm urging you to take it back . . . there can be no compromise here. You're going to lead, you must lead. . . . Treat the lady gently and lovingly. But lead!" Among the largely white, Protestant, and conservative group that attended these events, the message hit home. At these rallies men confessed their sins, sang, and wept with abandon—acts many would have found impossible to do in the presence of women. They promised to honor their wives, but insisted on asserting their responsibility to recover the leading role in their families, churches, and communities that they felt had been abdicated to women. They promised to support their church and its pastor and committed themselves to "practicing spiritual, moral, ethical, and sexual purity." Recognizing the importance of masculine community in keeping such promises, they committed themselves to "pursuing vital relationships with a few other men." Though claiming to be nondenominational and nonpartisan, Promise Keepers leaders made no secret of their hostility to abortion rights and insisted that gays and lesbians were "an abomination" who could, if they only would, convert from their lifestyles. They also rejected the leadership of female clergy. The great majority of men attending these events also attended fundamentalist or charismatic churches. With an exuberant and growing constituency, the Promise Keepers seemed destined to play a major role in religious culture—and perhaps in politics. The "Stand in the Gap" rally in Washington focused unprecedented attention on the organization. Much of the criticism leveled by feminists and others was dismissed. Columnist David Gergen complained shortly before the event that though "A growing chorus of critics . . . portrays them as cryptofascists with a thinly disguised agenda of religious extremism intent on putting white men back on top, women at their feet, and gays in a tightly locked closet," they were missing the point. Promise Keepers were not, he argued, about putting women down, but about building up strong families in which husbands and wives served each other. In 1997 the organization may have reached its zenith. At the Washington rally, McCartney announced that Promise Keepers would no longer charge the $60 registration fee to attend its rallies—most of which cost nearly $1 million to stage. Rather, it would depend on donations from members, friends, and churches. The decision plunged the organization into a financial crisis. The organization's 345-member force of full-time staffers was laid off in March 1998. Though most were rehired a few months later, the organization was in the midst of structural reorganization at the end of the decade, holding fewer rallies, and putting greater emphasis on extending the influence of its small "accountability groups" of men committed to transforming their families, churches, and communities.

Sources:

"Coors Foundation Buys a Round for Promise Keepers," *Church and State*, 51 (November 1998): 19.

Edd Doerr, "Promise Keepers: Who, What, and Why?" *USA Today Magazine*, 126 (March 1998): 30.

David Gergen, "Promises Worth Keeping: Critics Miss the Positive Force Behind a Christian Men's Movement," *U.S. News and World Report*, 123 (29 September 1997): 78.

John W. Kennedy, "Up From the Ashes?" *Christianity Today*, 42 (18 May 1998): 29.

RELIGIOUS LIBERTY

Religion, the Supreme Court, and the Constitution. The diversity in American religious practice led to increased tensions when the First Amendment limitations on the powers of the government to regulate religious practice came into conflict with governmental obligations to protect society at large. During the 1980s the Supreme Court had insisted that religious activity could not be regulated by the state unless the state had a compelling interest and the proposed regulation was the least restrictive means of doing so. A Supreme Court ruling in 1990, however,

Religious Equality

Passage of the Religious Equality Amendment to protect the religious liberties of Americans in public places.

The amendment would not restore compulsory, sectarian prayer or Bible-reading dictated by government officials. We seek a balanced approach that allows voluntary student- and citizen-initiated free speech in non-compulsory settings such as courthouse lawns, high school graduation ceremonies, and sports events.

Local Control of Education

Transfer funding of the federal Department of Education to families and local school boards.

Return greater power and control over education to parents and local communities. This reform begins by transferring funds for the U.S. Department of Education to families and local boards to administer as they see fit. Reform should include repealing Goals 2000.

School Choice

Enactment of legislation that will enhance parents' choice of schools for their children.

S. 618, the Coats-Lieberman Low-Income School Choice Demonstration Act, establishes 20 demonstration projects providing assistance to help low-income parents send their children to public or private schools of their choice. We urge swift passage of school choice legislation.

Family-Friendly Tax Policy

Reduce the tax burden on the American family, eliminate the marriage penalty, and pass the Mothers and Homemakers Rights Act.

1. Christian Coalition favors the $500 tax credit for children awaiting action in the Senate. We also support in concept a flat tax or flattened tax (with generous personal exemptions for children) as an ultimate goal.

2. H.R. 1215 makes married couples eligible for a tax rebate of up to $145 if their tax liability goes up as a result of being married. The Senate should pass this legislation to encourage marriage and ease the burden on families.

3. The Mothers and Homemakers Rights Act will allow homemakers to contribute up to $2000 annually toward an IRA [Individual Retirement Account], thereby providing equitable treatment to spouses who work at home. S. 287, sponsored by Sens [Kay] Hutchison [R, Texas] and [Barbara] Mikulski [D, Md.] would enact such policy.

Restoring Respect for Human Life

Protecting the rights of states that do not fund abortion, protecting innocent human life by placing real limits on late-term abortions, and ending funds to organizations that promote and perform abortions.

1. Legal protection to children in the latter months of pregnancy and an end to "partial-birth" abortions. Real restric-

tions on late-term abortions and an end [sic] the practice of D&X abortion.

2. Reverse Clinton administration policy requiring states to use Medicaid dollars for abortions. We urge passage of the Istook/Exxon [sic] Amendment.

3. Title X and international family planning assistance funding subsidizes organizations that promote and perform abortions. We urge Congress to end such funding.

Restricting Pornography

Protecting children from exposure to pornography on the Internet and cable television and from the sexual exploitation of child pornographers.

1. Enact legislation to protect children from pornography on the Internet.

2. Enact legislation requiring cable television companies to completely block video and audio on pornography channels to non-subscribers.

3. Amend federal child porn laws to make *any* possession of child pornography illegal.

Privatizing Federal Funding of Culture

The National Endowment for the Arts and Humanities, the Corporation for Public Broadcasting, and the Legal Services Corporation should become voluntary organizations funded through private contributions.

Support for Private Charities

Enact legislation to enhance contributions to private charities as a first step toward transforming the bureaucratic welfare state into a system of private and faith-based compassion.

Protecting Parental Rights

Enact a Parental Rights Act and defeat the U.N. [United Nations] Convention on the Rights of the Child.

Ensure that parents' rights over the care and nurturing of their children are not violated. Reps. Steve Largent (R, Ok) and Mike Parker (D, Miss.), and Sens. Charles Grassley (R, Iowa) and Howell Heflin (D, Ala.), are drafting parental rights legislation to address this critical problem.

The Coalition urges Congress to reject the U.N. Convention on the Rights of the Child because it interferes with the parent-child relationship, threatens the sovereignty of U.S. law, and elevates as "rights" such dubious provisions as access to television and mass media.

Punish Criminals, Not Victims

Funds given to states to build prisons should encourage work, study and drug testing requirements for prisoners in state correctional facilities and should require restitution to victims subsequent to release.

Source: *Facts on File*, 1995, p. 715.

Practitioner of Santeria saying prayer to the diety Chango (AP/Wide World Photos)

loosened those restrictions on local, state, and federal governments. The case, *Employment Division, Department of Human Resources of Oregon* v. *Smith* (1990) involved two members of the Native American Church who were fired from their jobs as addiction counselors after having consumed peyote in a traditional religious ceremony. When they applied for unemployment compensation, their application was denied because they had been fired for drug use. Claiming that their use of peyote was protected by the First Amendment, they filed suit. The Court found for the Employment Division, and in so doing altered the previous standard for adjudicating conflicts between governmental and religious interests. It ruled that a religious act was not protected if it violated a general law not aimed specifically at religious behavior. Only laws aimed at specific religious practices were unconstitutional. The Court made this clear in 1993 in *Church of Lukumi Babalu Aye* v. *Hialeah, Florida* when it found that a city ordinance banning animal sacrifice was aimed specifically at outlawing a practice of Santeria, a religion, since it did not forbid killing animals in meat-packing plants or hunting. Congress, with the support of most religious-rights organizations and many denominations, tried to restore the "compelling interest" and "least restrictive" standards that had been set aside in the *Employment Division* decision by passing the Religious Freedom Restoration Act (RFRA, 1993). The act said that the "government may substantially burden a person's exercise of religion only if it demonstrates that application of the burden to the person 1) is in furtherance of a compelling state interest, and 2) is the least restrictive means of furthering that compelling interest."

Counter Rulings. The RFRA proved to be short-lived. In 1997 the Supreme Court heard another case in which the legitimate interests of government competed with religious practice. In this case, a Catholic church in Boerne, Texas, wanted to build a new sanctuary for its growing congregation. Because the old building and property were in a designated historic district, the congregation was denied a building permit. When the Archbishop of San Antonio, Patrick F. Flores, sued the city on behalf of the church, claiming that its actions were protected by the RFRA, the Supreme Court used the occasion to strike down the act as an unwarranted intrusion by Congress on state and local governments. In 1998 and 1999, a new bill, the Religious Liberty Protection Act, was introduced in Congress but had not passed by the end of the decade. In another related case, *Lee* v. *Weisman* (1992), the Court ruled that prayer at public school graduations violated the "no establishment" clause, as did an attempt by New York to carve out a special school district strictly for a community of Orthodox Jews, *Board of Education of Kiryas Joel Village School District* v. *Louis Grumet* (1994). On the other hand, in *Agostini* v. *Felton* (1997) the Court overturned a 1985 decision (*Aguilar* v. *Felton*) and permitted public school districts to provide remedial instruction to disadvantaged students in religious schools. Given the complexity of negotiating the complex of laws, on 14 August 1997, President Bill Clinton issued *Guidelines on Religious Exercise and Religious Expression in the Federal Workplace.*

International Religious Liberty. Even as American lawmakers and judges struggled to balance the right of free exercise of religion with the constitutional prohibition against governmental support or interference, Congress enacted legislation directing the president to take action whenever evidence is presented of religious oppression anywhere in the world. The International Religious Liberty Protection Act, which President Clinton signed into law on 27 October 1998, committed the United States to "take diplomatic and other appropriate action with respect to any country that engages in or tolerates violations of religious freedom." Although the president was granted substantial latitude in the application of the law, it provided the State Department, as well as people around the world whose lives and liberty were threatened by virtue of their religion, a way of insisting that the oppression of religious minorities worldwide would, at the least, be reported to Congress. Although the law made no distinctions among religions or oppressing governments, critics complained that much of the onus of persecution fell onto Islamic nations and most of the beneficiaries were likely to be Christian minorities. Robert A. Seiple—whom Clinton named as the first Ambassador-at-Large for Religious Freedom and chair of a nine-member commission assigned by Congress with the responsibility of reporting on religious persecution— argued that "The bill was written to promote religious free-

dom everywhere in the world. If some people are nervous about that, perhaps they should be." On 9 September 1999 Seiple released the first report mandated by the act; although 194 countries were included, Afghanistan, Iran, Iraq, China, Saudi Arabia, and Sudan were reported to be among the worst offenders against religious freedom. It also pointed out that the protection of religious freedom included the right not to believe and was based not on "the American Way" but the Universal Declaration of Human Rights that had been adopted by virtually all nations. Article 18 states that everyone "has the right to freedom, conscience and religion; this right includes freedom to change his religion or belief and freedom, either alone or in community with others, and in public or in private, to manifest his religion or belief in teaching, practice, worship or observance." The report did not call for economic sanctions against violators and pointed out that it was, in many cases, impossible to separate persecution based on religious antagonisms from ethnic and political persecution.

Sources:

Robert F. Drinan, "Survey Documents Religious Freedom Abuses," *National Catholic Reporter*, 35 (8 October 1999): 20.

"Protecting Persecuted Christians," *Christian Century*, 115 (2 December 1998): 1136.

HEADLINE MAKERS

MARSHALL HERFF APPLEWHITE

1931-1997
CULT LEADER

Do and Ti. Marshall Herff Applewhite was the son of a Presbyterian minister in Texas and was interested in becoming a preacher when he was young. He excelled in music: he sang in local choirs in Colorado and Texas, and even captured stage and operatic roles. He married and had two children. In the early 1970s, after divorcing his wife and losing his job teaching music, he spent some time in a mental hospital in Texas. There he met a nurse, Bonnie Lu Trusdale Nettles; she took the name "Ti" and left her family to travel with him

after he left the hospital. Applewhite considered her his teacher, and he took the name "Do." By 1974 they had both cut ties with all their kin. For the next twenty years they created and led a series of groups around the country that combined gnosticism, Christian millenarianism, and belief in benign space aliens. In 1975 they began to claim that they themselves were aliens incarnated in human bodies. Their followers were urged to separate themselves from human desires, activities, and former ties; Applewhite and Nettles said that they, although inseparable, had a purely platonic relationship. They taught that extraterrestrials would bodily take them and their followers to a higher plane of existence, the literal "Kingdom of God," and that the simple lifestyle they lived would prepare them for that transition. They claimed to come from the "Evolutionary Level Above Human," explaining that periodically individuals from that level visited Earth because it is a training ground for souls, where they can prepare to move to the next plane. Applewhite said that he and Nettles had moved into middle-aged human bodies (which would have been in the 1970s) for this purpose. Jesus, who they argued was also a visitor from the Level Above Human, had similarly entered a thirty-year-old human body. These bodies (essentially "plants" with no souls of their own) were tagged from birth to be available to the extraterrestrials who would inhabit them. Like Jesus, Nettles and Applewhite believed they had brought with them souls that had already had some training preparatory to being incarnated in human form; this late-twentieth-century experience would be their final preparation before being taken to the next level. Applewhite said that this cycle of Earth civilization was winding down and that his stay would be the last visitation from the next level for some time.

Suicide. Nettles died in 1985. Applewhite continued to speak and recruit members. In October of 1996 Applewhite and his followers, now known as "Heaven's Gate," rented a large house in Rancho Santa Fe, near San Diego, California. The group owned and operated Higher Source, a computer programming company that also specialized in security services. The appearance of the comet Hale-Bopp was the sign Applewhite had been looking for, that it was time to return to the next level. Since the 1960s there had been groups that believed comets transported aliens to Earth. Applewhite said a "spaceship"—the last to come for a long time—was hidden by the tail of the comet. The Atlanta-based Farsight group, with no ties to Heaven's Gate, said they were also aware of a spaceship trailing Hale-Bopp, although astronomers said the bright object referred to was a star. Nettles and Applewhite had earlier believed that they and their followers would be physically transported to the Level Above Human, but now Applewhite said they would have to "shed their containers" to make the jump. He may have believed that he had cancer: he certainly told his followers that he did, as they mentioned in their farewell message that the approaching death of their "Elder Member" left them no reason to stay on this planet. Applewhite's autopsy, however, revealed no sign of the disease. Neighbors and business associates were shocked by the 26 March 1997 suicide of thirty-nine men and women who lived in the house with Applewhite (because of their unisex hairstyling and dressing, initial reports said that they were all male). Two more members attempted suicide several weeks later; one survived. Apparently the mass suicide had occurred in two groups of fifteen, assisted by others who followed later; a final group of nine then killed themselves. They ingested phenobarbital and alcohol; some had been smothered. Most of the identically-dressed bodies were cleaned, composed, and then covered with purple shrouds. The group left behind three major sources of information: their website, videotaped interviews with Applewhite, and a computer disc they sent to a Heaven's Gate member who had left in February, to tell him where to find their bodies.

Another David Koresh? While there were those who believed that the Branch Davidians were killed by the Federal Bureau of Investigation (FBI), there is no doubt that Heaven's Gate members killed themselves. In some ways their group was like the Davidians: they believed that a higher power was about to intervene on their behalf, they connected that power to Jesus Christ, and they thought they were misunderstood. The Heaven's Gate website referred to the Davidians and to the shoot-out at Ruby Ridge, Idaho, in August of 1992, as reasons to prepare themselves for persecution. Both David Koresh and Applewhite were charismatic and mesmerizing speakers who convinced their followers that they had absolute authority and understood the secrets of human existence because they were incarnations of a higher form of life. Koresh trained his followers to perceive the world as hostile and to expect persecution and death as a result; Applewhite taught that the world would write his group off as cultists. Both men prepared those who trusted them to see the failure of the world, to understand them as a sign that they were correct. The two men, however, were also different: Koresh derived his beliefs from the Bible, while Applewhite based his concepts largely on his interest in UFOs and was not particularly concerned with Judeo-Christian Scripture; Koresh taught that his status allowed him particular perks, especially sexual ones, while Applewhite insisted on absolute celibacy and even had himself castrated because of his commitment to it.

Sources:
Marshall Applewhite, "'95 Statement by an E.T. Presently Incarnate," *Trancenet.org News,* Internet website.

"Our Position Against Suicide," *Trancenet.org News,* Internet website.

JOSEPH CARDINAL BERNADIN

1928-1996
ROMAN CATHOLIC ARCHBISHOP OF CHICAGO

Southern Roots. Born in Columbia, South Carolina, in 1928, the son of Italian immigrants, Joseph Louis Bernadin attended public high school and started premedical studies at the University of South Carolina. He graduated, however, from St. Mary's Seminary in Baltimore and earned a Master's degree in Education at Catholic University in Washington, D.C., before being ordained to the priesthood in the diocese of Charleston, South Carolina. Bernadin served as a priest in South Carolina from 1952 to 1966, when he was consecrated a bishop and assigned to serve as auxiliary to Archbishop Paul J. Hallinan of Atlanta, a leader in the post-Vatican II effort to renew the church. At age thirty-eight, Bernadin was the youngest Catholic bishop in the nation. In 1968

Bernadin went to Washington, D.C., to serve as general secretary of the National Conference of Catholic Bishops and of its social-action agency, the United States Catholic Conference. Bernadin's skills as a mediator were recognized even by those who might have favored a less conciliatory approach. Russell Shaw, spokesman for the conference, recalled, "Over and over again I watched him at meetings where factions were wrangling and apparently irreconcilable. All of a sudden, Bernadin would just begin talking quietly and identify the issues in the debate and . . . weave together a kind of synthesis." Bernadin was appointed Archbishop of Cincinnati in 1972, in which capacity he spoke out against the U.S. bombing of North Vietnam and, in a White House homily, called on the president to help "keep alive in our society a profound sense of compassion for the poor, the suffering, and the oppressed." In August 1982 Bernadin was installed as Archbishop of Chicago, the second largest Catholic diocese in the United States. In 1983 Pope John Paul II elevated Bernadin to cardinal. The same year, as chair of the Bishops Committee for Pro-Life Activities, Cardinal Bernadin, in an address at Fordham University, restated the opposition of the Church to abortion as part of a consistent ethic of life that should include other issues, such as poverty, capital punishment, and the nuclear-arms race. Though he held firmly to Church doctrines, he continually sought to maintain dialogue among dissenting voices.

Ministry of Reconciliation. At a time when the Roman Catholic Church seemed to be positioning itself increasingly apart from the mainstream of American society—and from the lives of ordinary Catholics—Bernadin presented a powerful, consistent voice for reconciliation. As religious rhetoric became increasingly polarized over issues ranging from abortion, poverty, racism, euthanasia, and peacemaking, Bernadin identified a fundamental ethical question from which to begin discussion—the defense of life. One of the first leaders to articulate the "consistent ethic of life" as a thesis uniting Catholic teaching in opposition to capital punishment and abortion, and in defense of the poor and oppressed, Bernadin refused to be identified either with the Left or Right in political discourse. In the last years of his life, he launched the "Catholic Common Ground Project" to begin respectful and constructive dialogue on pastoral issues that divided the Church.

Troubling Charges. In 1991, amidst a storm of allegations of sexual abuse against priests in Chicago and elsewhere, Bernadin reversed the previous unspoken policy of quietly moving priests against whom accusations had been made to other locations. He established a committee, dominated by laypeople, to investigate charges, recommend disciplinary actions, and assist victims. In 1993, when Steven Cook, a thirty-four-year-old former seminarian, accused Bernadin of sexual abuse while Bernadin had been Archbishop of Cincinnati, Bernadin responded to the public charges: "I have never abused anyone, at any time and at any place. I can assure you that in all my life I've led a chaste, celibate life." Although he strenuously denied the accusation, he refused to attack the credibility or dignity of his accuser. Four months later, Cook withdrew the charges,

acknowledging that his memories of the episode had emerged first during a therapy session with an amateur hypnotist and were likely false. Though the Cardinal was praised for his handling of the episode, it was personally humiliating and painful. Yet, he met and prayed with Cook, then dying of AIDS, in late 1994. Less than a year later, Bernadin, who was being discussed as a potential successor to John Paul II, was diagnosed with pancreatic cancer.

Final Contributions. The last months of Bernadin's life brought him to a new phase of ministry. In September of 1995, after several months of treatment, the Cardinal resumed his episcopal duties, adding to them a pastoral ministry to hundreds of other terminally ill patients. He also visited and prayed with a death-row inmate, saying, "In a sense, he and I are in the same boat." More controversially, he helped launch the "Common Ground Project" of the Chicago Archdiocese to find room for Catholics with differing points of view to discuss, among other things, the changing roles of women, the liturgy, and the gap between Church teachings on sexuality and the convictions of many of the faithful. When criticized for encouraging confusion about and dissent from church teaching, Bernadin responded, "We anticipated criticism from some groups on the right or left who are convinced that anything not explicitly committed to their respective agenda will only strengthen their adversaries or legitimate the status quo. They simply do not see the situation as we do." Shortly after his diagnosis, Bernadin told reporters that he thought his greatest contribution would be in the way he died. Death, though he did not welcome it, came to him "as a friend, as the transition from earthly life to life eternal."

Sources:

"Called to be Catholic," Archdiocese of Chicago, Internet website.

Peter Steinfels, "Cardinal Bernadin Dies at 68; Reconciling Voice in Church," *New York Times*, 15 November 1996.

Jim Wallis, "The Passing of a Leader," *Sojourners*, 26 (January 1997): 9–10.

James Webb, "Bernadin's Call for Dialogue Has Split His Fellow Archbishops," *Philadelphia Inquirer*, 30 August 1996.

CASSIE BERNALL

1982-1999
STUDENT, VICTIM

Troubled Youth. Earlier in her life, Cassie Bernall, a seventeen-year-old student at Columbine High School in Littleton, Colorado, had experimented with drugs and alcohol and had once even discussed killing her parents. She had, however, converted to Christianity at an evangelical summer camp and had abandoned her flirtations with witchcraft for youth-oriented Bible studies and a "WWJD" (What Would Jesus Do) bracelet. When on 20 April 1999 Eric Harris and Dylan Klebold entered the Columbine High School library during a shooting rampage that would leave twelve students, a teacher, and the gunmen dead, Bernall hid under a table. Reportedly, one of the gunmen stood over her and asked if she believed in God. She answered, "Yes, I believe in God." The gunman asked, "Why?" but before she could respond, he shot her to death.

Unlikely Martyr. Bernall's parents, Misty and Brad, were evangelical Christians and were concerned that their son and daughter follow in their faith. When Cassie was an eighth and ninth grader she rebelled against her parents and their religious and social values, telling her mother that she had "given her soul to Satan." She started sniffing glue, smoking marijuana, and drinking. She experimented with occult practices and discussed having another boy kill her parents. When her parents became aware of their daughter's problems, they separated her from her friends, put her in a Christian academy, and limited her social outlets to church youth-group activities. Cassie responded to her parents' "tough love" approach, converted to Christianity, and as a high school student identified herself with other evangelical Christians. Klebold and Harris targeted Christians, as well as Jews, blacks, and athletes, during their shooting rampage.

"She Said Yes." Almost immediately after the story of Bernall's last words, she was marked as a hero and martyr to her faith, particularly among evangelical Christians. Reverend George Kirsten, her pastor, assured the two thousand mourners who attended her funeral, "she went to the martyrs' hall of fame." The phrase, "Yes, I believe," started to appear on lapel buttons and T-shirts. Christian youth rallies and concerts appealed to her memory. Michael W. Smith, a popular Christian musician and performer, recorded a song based on her story. Her mother wrote a biography of her daughter, *She Said Yes: The Unlikely Martyrdom of Cassie Bernall* (1999).

Who Said What? The story of Bernall's martyrdom became more muddled, however, in September 1999, when an article in the on-line magazine *Salon* challenged several of the widely reported—and believed—reports about the Columbine massacre, including her conversation with Harris and Klebold. According to the story by Dave Cullen, "an alternate scenario is far more likely: The killers asked another girl, Valeen Schnurr, a similar question, then shot her, and she lived to tell about it. Schnurr's story was then apparently misattributed to Cassie." While some witnesses, in the confusion and terror of the moment, were uncertain whether the words attributed to Bernall were spoken by her, by Schnurr, or both, others insist that they heard the killer's question and Bernall's response.

Sources:

Misty Bernall, *She Said Yes: The Unlikely Martyrdom of Cassie Bernall* (Nashville: Word Publishers, 1999).

Dave Cullen, "Inside the Columbine High Investigation: Everything You Know about the Littleton Killings Is Wrong, But the Truth May Be Scarier Than the Myth," *Salon.com*, 23 September 1999, Internet website.

Amy Goldstein, "Deaths Seen in Christian Context," *Washington Post*, 27 April 1999.

"A Surge Of Teen Spirit: A Christian Girl, Martyred at Columbine High, Sparks a Revival Among Many Evangelical Teens," *Time*, 153 (31 May 1999): 58.

Kenneth L. Woodward, "The Making of a Martyr," *Newsweek*, 133 (14 June 1999): 64.

LOUIS FARRAKHAN

1933-
NATION OF ISLAM LEADER

The Charmer. Born Louis Eugene Walcott in the Roxbury section of Boston in 1933, Gene was the younger of two sons of Mae Clark, an immigrant from Barbados. Walcott's father, a Jamaican immigrant, was largely absent in Gene's life, but his mother more than made up for the absence. Her children attended St. Cyprian's, an Episcopal church, and were close with the pastor, Nathan Wright. She also paid for her sons to take music lessons. Gene became an accomplished violinist, scholar, and athlete, winning an athletic scholarship to college in North Carolina. Frustrated with the racism he encountered in the South, he dropped out of school to take up a career as a calypso singer and became known as "the Charmer." He was losing patience with the religion of his youth and told Henry Louis Gates, "I couldn't understand why Jesus would preach so much love and why there was so much hate demonstrated by white Christians against black Christians." In 1955, after hearing Elijah Muhammad and Malcolm X speak, he converted to the Nation of Islam, a branch of Islam established in the 1930s by Wallace D. Fard in the black community of Detroit. Walcott took the name Louis X in keeping with Fard's teaching. Fard had taught that black people were the original people of the earth. Whites, the "blue-eyed devils," were interlopers. Their oppression of black people was destined to end when blacks woke up and discovered their real humanity, rejected their "slave names," and began to adopt the diet and pure lifestyles of their African ancestors. Fard disappeared in June 1934. His successor, Elijah Muhammad, proclaimed Fard a Prophet and Savior, and 26 February came to be celebrated as Savior's Day. Louis X led a temple in Boston from 1956 until the assassination of Malcolm X in 1965. He changed his name again, to Louis Farrakhan, and took over leadership of Temple No. 7 in New York City. When Muhammad died in 1975, leadership of the Nation of Islam passed to his son, Wallace Deen Muhammad, who steered the organization toward orthodox Sunni Islam. In 1977 Farrakhan broke with Wallace Deen Muhammad to reestablish the Nation of Islam according to the teachings of Fard.

Anti-Semitism. Under Farrakhan's leadership the new Nation of Islam enjoyed a period of financial and organizational growth; its membership—perhaps thirty thousand strong—and racially exclusive ideology left it at the fringe of American religious movements. In 1984, however, Jessie Louis Jackson's campaign for the U.S. presidency pushed Farrakhan into the national spotlight. Registering to vote for the first time, Farrakhan offered Jackson's campaign his clean-cut and bow-tied security force, the "Fruit of Islam," to protect the candidate. Farrakhan's rhetoric, always fiery and racially charged, discredited Jackson's campaign among white liberals and black moderates. When a black reporter quoted Jackson's reference to New York City as "Hymietown," Farrakhan further inflamed the situation by threatening the reporter with reprisal. Later that year Farrakhan criticized the state of Israel and complained that Jews used "God's name to shield your dirty religion." It would have been hard in any case for Farrakhan to distance himself from charges of anti-Semitism, and though he claimed repeatedly not to be anti-Semitic, he regularly referred to the existence of a powerful and secretive Jewish cabal.

Voice for Black Unity. The best known and most outspoken leader of the Nation of Islam, Farrakhan seemed to revel in controversy. His anti-white, anti-Semitic, anti-American culture rhetoric left few people unmoved. Even his supporters cringed when, in an interview on Reuters Television, he argued that "Many of the Jews that owned homes, the apartments in the black community, we considered them bloodsuckers because they . . . didn't offer anything back to our community." Farrakhan accused the U.S. government of introducing crack cocaine to the inner cities "as a method of exterminating blacks." Still, Farrakhan and his supporters insisted that his basic message was positive. He called for black unity in the face of white intolerance and oppression; he wanted blacks to face the threats to their culture and identity by building stronger character within stronger communities. Blacks, he argued, needed to exercise their power to rebuild "a more perfect union."

Million Man March. As the guiding voice behind the Million Man March, Farrakhan moved beyond his formal role as simply the outspoken leader of a fringe Islamic sect. Though he did not abandon his racial and religious extremism, his leadership of the march in Washington on 16 March 1995 marked the beginning of Farrakhan's move toward the mainstream of the civil-rights movement. Working with Christian and secular leaders of the African American community, Farrakhan called for black men from around the country to come to the National Mall for a day of speeches and community building. The march was held on a weekday so that the men who attended would have to sacrifice a day of work or school to attend. He encouraged women to stay at home in order to embody the ideal of family values as the men were being called to take more responsibility for their children and communities. Though its implications were clearly political, Farrakhan believed the March had "essentially a religious theme—atonement—disconnected from public policy."

Beyond the March. In January and February of 1996, responding to what Farrakhan claimed was divine inspiration, he made a "World Friendship Tour," meet-

ing with leaders of Third World countries, including Mu'ammar al-Qaddafi of Libya, Mobutu Sese Seko of Zaire, and Omar Hassan al-Bashir of Sudan, some of the most distasteful dictators in the world. Molefi Kete Asante, an Afrocentric scholar, complained that "What Farrakhan did, in my judgment, was to take the legitimacy of the march and put it in his back pocket, and march around to these terrible governments, as if somehow he was the leader of a million black people." In 1999 Farrakhan, though being treated for prostate cancer, remained among the most controversial religious leaders. Respected as a legitimate and powerful voice by many black Americans, feared or dismissed by most whites, his political and racial identity was inseparable from his religious worldview.

Sources:

Henry Louis Gates Jr., "The Charmer," *New Yorker,* 72 (29 April & 6 May 1996): 116–132.

Mortimer B. Zucker, "Louis Farrakhan's White Noise," *US News and World Report,* 119 (6 November 1995): 96.

DAVID KORESH

1959-1993
CULT LEADER

Davidian Foundations. Vernon Wayne Howell was born on 17 August 1959. In 1968 he and his mother joined the Seventh-Day Adventist Church (established in 1863). Adventists consider themselves to be the true people of God, awaiting Christ's imminent return and attempting to understand all parts of the Bible that foreshadowed that return. Dissatisfied with their teachings, Howell eventually moved on to the Branch Davidians. An energetic and charismatic man, he taught that the Seven Seals of Rev. 6 provide the only hope for salvation. By 1985 he came to believe that he was God's prophet chosen to deliver the Adventists from error, a doctrine they rejected. This increased Howell's sense of alienation. He saw himself as a modern Cyrus the Great, the Persian king who defeated Babylon and is called God's Messiah in Isaiah 45:1. Because he was able to explain the Seals, and Rev. 5 says that only the Lamb of God, who is Christ, can explain them, Howell eventually claimed to be the Christ-Lamb. He legally changed his name to David Koresh: "Koresh" is the Hebrew form of "Cyrus," and David, like Cyrus, is referred to as "Messiah" (2 Sam. 22:51, 23:1).

Religious Offshoot. In the 1930s Adventist teacher Victor T. Houteff created The Shepherd's Rod, a splinter group, and moved them to Waco, Texas. There he began calling the group the "Davidian Seven Day

Adventists." In 1962 a new prophetic figure, Ben Roden, changed the name to Branch Davidian Seventh Day Adventists as a result of a personal revelation. Several communities were established. After Roden's death his widow, Lois, assumed leadership. She was impressed by Koresh, a young man who joined the movement in 1981, and established him in the hierarchy so that when she died he would eventually take control of that group. Like Roden and Houteff before him, Koresh stressed personal purity for his followers (this included dietary as well as sexual matters). As the Lamb, however, Koresh was exempt from these strictures. He said his special status gave him the obligation to father a holy race and to that end he "married" many times; some of his "brides" were as young as twelve. By late 1992 government agencies began investigating the situation, partly at the instigation of noncustodial parents who were not part of the group. Koresh also taught that Christ's triumphant return was delayed because his true people—the Davidians—were impure and independent, unwilling to submit, and that (according to the Fifth Seal in Rev. 6:9–11) they must be willing to accept the martyrdom required before Christ's return in victory.

The Raid and the Siege. The Davidians began to stockpile guns in anticipation of the persecution they were sure was coming. When the Bureau of Alcohol, Tobacco, and Firearms (ATF) began investigating them, it seemed like the fulfillment of Koresh's prophecies. On 28 February 1993, ATF agents attempted to raid the compound. Koresh had been tipped off in advance, and the Davidians fired on the federal agents; four were killed and sixteen wounded, but they did not gain access to the compound. Koresh said five of his people were killed. The Federal Bureau of Investigation (FBI) was called in and a fifty-one-day siege began. During the standoff the FBI tried to force the Davidians out of the compound—shining bright lights, playing loud music, and cutting off their electricity and water. This treatment, of course, seemed to confirm to those inside that they were the persecuted Remnant of God. As this ordeal was happening, Koresh continued to speak with the FBI, give interviews, and communicate with biblical scholars. He agreed to write his interpretation of the Seven Seals of Revelation, after which he would surrender, but he completed only an introduction and an explanation of the First Seal. Whether his pledge to surrender was genuine continued to be a matter of some debate at the end of the decade.

Apocalypse. The FBI, holding Koresh responsible for the deaths of four ATF agents and feeling pressure to bring the standoff to an end, moved in on Sunday, 19 April 1993. After knocking holes in the main campground building with a specially equipped armored personnel carrier, FBI agents launched tear gas canisters inside. Whether the Davidians themselves set the fire that destroyed the campground or whether the canisters—some of which were incendiary—did, remains a fiercely debated issue at the end of the decade. There were approximately eighty casualties from the fire, all Davidians. Because of the incredible heat of the fire and the different claims made by Koresh to the FBI and by escaping Davidians as to how many people were in the compound that day, it may never be known exactly how many died. Nearly a quarter were children: thirteen of the dead, including Koresh, had been shot. Like Jesus at his death, Koresh was just thirty-three years old. At the end of the decade it still remained unclear whether the fire was set accidentally by flames from the tear gas canisters or whether they were intentionally set on orders from Koresh himself in a suicide pact similar to that of Jim Jones and the People's Temple in Guyana, in 1978. The nine Davidians who escaped the fire denied that there was any such pact. The FBI had considered the possibility that the group might commit suicide rather than surrender, but they counted on the Davidians' instinct to protect their children being stronger than their desire for martyrdom. Had they understood apocalyptic groups like the Davidians in general and the book of Revelation in particular, they should have known better: for people who believe that an attacking group are agents of Satan, surrendering children to them is not the most loving thing to do.

Aftereffects. Some groups with no affinity for Koresh's theology were disturbed by the actions of the government against people who were trying to live according to their own beliefs; the fact that the possession of weaponry helped lead to the original raid alarmed ardent supporters of the Second Amendment as well. A Justice Department probe in 1993 blamed Koresh for the deaths and found no evidence that the FBI had caused the fire. Nonetheless, in a phenomenon reminiscent of the reaction to the assassination of President John F. Kennedy in 1963, there were many suggestions in print and on the Internet that what happened at Waco was the result of a government conspiracy. Links were made between Waco and the 1992 incident at Ruby Ridge, Idaho, in which Christian white separatist Vicki Weaver and her son Sam were killed during a nine-day standoff with the FBI. On the second anniversary of the Waco fire the Alfred P. Murrah Federal Building in Oklahoma City was blown up, killing 168 people, partially in protest of the governmental action against the Branch Davidians. In August of 1999 U.S. Attorney General Janet Reno called for a review of the evidence from Waco after previously unseen FBI tapes indicated that the FBI fired two incendiary grenades at the compound the morning of the 19 April raid.

Sources:

Nancy Gibbs, "Fire Storm in Waco," *Time*, 141 (3 May 1993): 29–43.

David Koresh, *The Decoded Message of the Seven Seals of the Book of Revelation* (Green Forest, Ark.: Stewart Waterhouse, 1993).

James D. Tabor, "Apocalypse at Waco," *Bible Review*, 9 (October 1993): 24–33.

R. ALBERT MOHLER JR.

1959-
PRESIDENT, SOUTHERN BAPTIST THEOLOGICAL SEMINARY

Florida Roots. A native of Lakeland, Florida, R. Albert Mohler Jr. attended Florida Atlantic University before receiving his Bachelor of Arts degree from Samford University in Birmingham, Alabama, in 1980. He earned a Master of Divinity degree and a Ph.D (in systematic and historical theology) from Southern Seminary, during which time he served on then President Roy Lee Honneycutt's staff.

Holy War. When in 1993 the trustees of the Southern Baptist Theological Seminary (SBTS) in Louisville, Kentucky, elected thirty-three-year-old R. Albert Mohler Jr. to the presidency of the oldest seminary of the largest U.S. Protestant denomination, they signaled an end to the twenty-year struggle by conservatives to control the Southern Baptist Convention (SBC) and its institutions. Mohler's predecessor had called the struggle a "holy war" and had fought to maintain the independence of the school, even as the board of trustees that employed him was increasingly dominated by conservatives. Yet, that same board's choice of Mohler to succeed Honeycutt was surprising: although he had earned Master of Divinity and Ph.D. degrees from SBTS, he had neither been a pastor or teacher, nor had he accumulated much experience as an administrator. As a result of his selection, five administrators had resigned by the time he took office on 31 July, and enrollment had dropped. Moderates suggested that Mohler's tenure as president would be brief and that he would be merely a transitional figure with little impact beyond the school. They were wrong; he proved himself far more adroit in moving through the dangerous period of transition than his critics anticipated. As an articulate spokesperson for conservative evangelicalism, he wrote regularly for Religion News Service and various newspapers, as well as appeared frequently on television talk and news shows. In its 5 December 1994 issue, *Time* profiled him as one of the top fifty national leaders under fifty years of age in any field.

Social and Religious Conservative. Mohler saw modern Protestantism as too eager to compromise with secular society and urged churches not to substitute entertainment for worship. He publicly supported the Southern Baptist apology for slavery in 1995, its boycott of the Disney Corporation begun in 1996, its statement regarding the place of women in the family in 1998, and its targeting of Jews for evangelism during the High Holy Days in 1999. He urged President Bill Clinton's home church (Immanuel Baptist Church of Little Rock, Arkansas) to exercise church discipline against him because of his affair with Monica S. Lewinsky and Clinton's subsequent handling of that crisis. He said that the sinfulness of homosexuality could not be emphasized too much and that tolerance for gays was evidence of how morally degraded society had become. These public statements led many non-Baptists to see him as a spokesperson for traditional values. It was within his own denomination that Mohler was most controversial. Serious problems arose at SBTS involving his relationship with the tenured faculty who were already part of the seminary before his presidency began. SBTS had built a reputation for scholarship and social activism, and its faculty had often pushed the boundaries of Southern Baptist orthodoxy. To many conservatives within the denomination, the liberal (by Southern Baptist standards) faculty represented all that was wrong with the Southern Baptist Convention.

Controversy at the Seminary. One of Mohler's goals was to bring the faculty—many of whom had been his teachers—in line with the Abstract of Principles of the school, as the 1858 seminary charter requires all faculty to sign. The Abstract contains twenty articles covering such topics as the Scriptures, God, the Fall, perseverance of the saints, and liberty of conscience, all of which use masculine language for God and for people. In August of 1994 Mohler asked Molly Marshall, a professor of theology, to resign because he felt that her work was not in accordance with the Abstract in the areas of atonement and Scripture; Marshall was the first female theology professor at any Southern Baptist seminary. Students and faculty rallied to her defense, taking out a full-page ad in the *Louisville Courier-Journal,* urging people to sign a statement supporting her, but to no avail.

Another Crisis. Less than a year later a larger crisis began, again involving faculty fidelity to conservative beliefs. In March of 1995 Diana Garland, dean of the Carver School of Social Work, recommended the hiring of a new faculty member. Mohler refused to hire the candidate because the scholar believed women could serve as pastors; he also did not answer questions on abortion and homosexuality to Mohler's satisfaction. When Garland protested Mohler's decision, he fired her as dean (although she was still a tenured faculty member). Students and faculty rallied to defend Garland and the Carver School, but the effort was not successful. On 19 April the trustees said that no new faculty would be hired who believed that women could serve as pastors. At the same meeting they supported the firing of Garland and restricted the right of faculty members to criticize the seminary or its administration, an action that came to be called "a gag order." As a result, in February 1996 the Association of Theological Schools (the primary accreditation agency of SBTS) found deficiencies in academic freedom and in faculty involvement in hiring and discipline that injured its "capacity to provide significant theological education and ministerial training." The Council on Social Work Education had already said that accreditation of Carver School would not be renewed after May of 1997 because of the conflict between the social work profession's refusal to discriminate on the basis of race, sex, or sexual orientation and the theological imperatives of the new conservatism of SBTS. Mohler himself said that he felt there was a "dissonance" between the values of evangelical Christians and those of social workers. In 1998 the Carver School moved to Campbellsville University, a Baptist school in Campbellsville, Kentucky. By the end of the decade enrollment at the seminary was up and its accreditation problems were overcome. Virtually all of the faculty that had been in place when Mohler became president had retired or resigned. Mohler had created a faculty and student body that were, as he wished, more conservative than the ones he found when he took office.

Sources:

Michael Jennings, "Accrediting Agency Finds 'Deficiencies' at Baptist Seminary," *Louisville Courier-Journal*, 27 February 1996.

Mark McCormick, "Baptist Seminary Board Curbs Faculty Influence," *Louisville Courier-Journal*, 20 April 1995.

R. Albert Mohler Jr., "Don't Just Do Something; Stand There: Southern Seminary and the Abstract of Principles," convocation address at Southern Baptist Theological Seminary, 31 August 1993.

Leslie Scanlon, "Carver School's Move From Seminary Hits Snag," *Louisville Courier-Journal*, 10 October 1995.

RALPH REED

1961-

EXECUTIVE DIRECTOR, CHRISTIAN COALITION

Young Conservative. Born in Portsmouth, Virginia, the son of a Naval physician, Ralph Reed became fascinated by politics as a student at Cutler Ridge Junior High School near Miami when he ran for class president. As a student at the University of Georgia, he joined the College Republicans and served an extended internship as a Senate aide in 1980–1981. In 1983 he became president of the National College Republicans. He was also "born again, both politically and religiously. As a campus politician, he had earned a reputation for ruthlessness that he came to regret and later apologized to some of his earlier opponents. He earned a Ph.D. in American History at Emory University shortly before joining the Christian Coalition.

Political Strategist of the Religious Right. Ralph Reed served as executive director of the Christian Coalition from 1989 until 1997. He had previously been the executive director of the College Republican National Committee (1982–1984) and a political organizer for Senator Jesse Helms (R-North Carolina). During his eight years with the Christian Coalition he reached beyond the conservative Protestant base of the Christian Right to include socially conservative Catholics and Jews and addressed issues of tax and welfare reform, poverty, drug abuse, and racial reconciliation. He also wrote two books, *Politically Incorrect: The Emerging Faith Factor in American Politics* (1994) and *Active Faith: How Christians Are Changing the Soul of American Politics* (1996), and was a contributor to *The New York Times, The Wall Street Journal,* and *National Review,* as well as a frequent guest on television talk shows. In 1994 *Time* called him "the single most important strategist for the religious right."

New Directions. The Christian Coalition was established by Pat Robertson in 1989, the year following his failed bid for the presidency of the United States. Robertson had many other ventures as well, such as running the Christian Broadcasting Network (CBN) and the Family Channel, as well as hosting the 700 Club, which had seven million viewers in the 1990s, so he chose Reed to head the Coalition. Reed was given five basic goals: to represent Christians and their concerns at every political level, train them to be effective in the political arena, inform them of issues and legislation of particular concern, speak out publicly on religious issues, and protest discrimination against Christians and defend their legal rights. None of these concerns were new to politically active Christians; the "New Religious Right" had been old news for years by the time Reed, still in his twenties, became Executive Director. Nevertheless, he put a new face on conservative evangelical political activism. He attempted to make it mainstream, focusing on what he, and others, called "pro-family" stances rather than specifically Christian ones and making efforts to broaden the white Protestant image of the movement. He also muted the antagonistic rhetoric often used by other religious conservatives such as Patrick J. Buchanan. When he announced the release of the "Contract with the American Family" on 17 May 1995, Reed said, "This agenda is not a Christian agenda, a Republican agenda, or a special interest agenda. It is a pro-family agenda that is embraced by the American people, Republican and Democrat, Christian and Jew, Protestant and Catholic." At its height, the Coalition claimed an active membership of 1.9 million, with affiliates in every state, although others suggested that it was claiming as "active members" anyone who had ever made a donation.

Work at the Grassroots. Reed brought great organizing skills and a strong practical approach to the issues that interested conservative Christians. He understood the political process: targeting low-profile elections at first, building a grassroots base, and concentrating on urging conservative churches to get their members to the voting booths. He oversaw the running of hundreds of training seminars for Coalition volunteers on political organizing and communication. As the Coalition grew, he became a power broker on much grander levels. Reed and the Coalition took credit for the success of the Republican midterm sweep in 1994. This victory made Reed a powerful figure at the Republican National Convention in 1996, where he was instrumental in keeping a constitutional amendment outlawing abortion as part of the platform, even though many in the Party, including its nominee, Senator Robert Joseph "Bob" Dole (R-Kansas), disliked taking an extreme position on such a divisive issue.

Voting Guides. A key element of Coalition tactics was the voter guides that were sent out to churches. These guides rated candidates according to their statements and voting records on the issues that the Coalition considered to be most important, such as the establishment of prayer in schools; the denial of government funding to medical facilities performing abortions and to the National Endowment for the Arts; the outlawing of all abortions; and vouchers or tax relief for private school tuition. According to the Coalition, forty million of these guides were sent out for the national elections in 1992 and thirty-four million in 1994. These pamphlets caused much trouble for the Coalition. In 1996 the Federal Election Commission (FEC) filed suit against the Coalition on the grounds that the supposedly nonpartisan voter guides actually endorsed candidates (mostly Republican), creating $1.4 million in illegal campaign contributions; the FEC also claimed that the Coalition had worked with Republican campaigns. On 1 August 1999 District of Columbia Federal Court Judge Joyce Hens Green dismissed most of the charges because the federal campaign-spending laws were so vague. She upheld only two of the FEC contentions, saying that Coalition involvement in the 1994 campaign of Representative Newton Leroy "Newt" Gingrich (R-Georgia), as well as Oliver North's run for the U.S. Senate seat from Virginia, had been illegal. This victory was offset in the same year by the denial of tax-exempt status to the Coalition by the Internal Revenue Service (IRS), which was not only an economic problem for Reed's group but also raised the concern that churches using the voter guides could imperil their tax-exempt status.

Century Strategies. Reed resigned from the Christian Coalition on 23 April 1997, after the FEC suit was filed but before it was resolved. He said he wanted to be able to work more closely with the Republican Party and to that end formed his own political consulting agency, Century Strategies. The two men who replaced him at the Coalition, Donald P. Hodel as president and Randy J. Tate as executive director, each lasted less than a year in those positions. Reed was a popular consultant and ended the century working as an adviser to the George W. Bush presidential campaign.

Sources:

David van Biema, "A New Generation of Leaders," *Time*, 144 (5 December 1994): 48–67.

Stephen Glass, "After the Fall," *New Republic*, 216 (19 May 1997): 14–16.

Bill Miller and Susan B. Glasser, "A Victory for Christian Coalition," *Washington Post*, 3 August 1999.

Ralph Reed, "Statement on the Occasion of the Release of the Contract with the American Family," 17 May 1995.

JOHN SHELBY SPONG

1931–
EPISCOPAL BISHOP OF NEWARK

Stirring the Waters. Had John Shelby Spong not been an Episcopal bishop, his challenges to traditional Christian belief and practice would still have sparked controversy. Coming from the Bishop of the Episcopal Diocese of Newark, New Jersey, Spong's unapologetic rejection of some of Christianity's fundamental assumptions, and his willingness to use his Episcopal office as a bully pulpit for his message of postmodern Christian faith, made him a favorite target for conservative Christians. Born in Charlotte, North Carolina, Spong attended the University of North Carolina and Virginia Theological Seminary before being ordained to the Episcopal priesthood in 1955. He served as rector of churches in Durham and Tarboro, North Carolina, and in Lynchburg and Richmond, Virginia. A popular speaker and writer, he had already provoked controversy when he was elected Bishop of Newark, New Jersey, on 6 March 1976. Some years earlier, while pastor of St. Paul's Episcopal Parish in Richmond, Spong had responded to a rabbi's question about the Christian doctrine of the Incarnation with the words, "The Bible never says in a simplistic way that Jesus is God. Jesus prays to God in the Gospels. He is not talking to himself. Jesus dies on the cross. It makes no sense to say that the holy God died. The Bible only says that What God is, Jesus is; that God is met in Jesus; that to see Jesus is in some sense to see God." This rather careful statement was immediately interpreted by several local newspapers as a rejection of the Christian doctrine that God was fully incarnate in the person of Jesus of Nazareth.

Controversial Bishop. Spong emerged as a controversial figure again in 1987, when the Diocese of Newark called on the worldwide Anglican communion to permit the ordination of gays and lesbians to the priesthood and, similarly, to permit Anglican priests to "bless publicly the sacred commitments of gay and lesbian couples." On 16 December 1989 Spong ordained Robert Williams, an otherwise well-qualified man living openly in a homosexual relationship, to the Anglican priesthood. With the publication in 1991 of his *Rescuing the Bible from Fundamentalism: A Bishop Rethinks the Meaning of Scripture,* Spong effectively declared theological war on religious conservatives, most moderates, and quite a few liberals. Spong argued that the writers of the Bible reflected prescientific worldviews that could not be rationally sustained by modern people except by radically divorcing themselves from the findings of modern science and biblical scholarship. Thus, he proposed, the virgin birth, miracle stories, the Resurrection, and the Ascension of Jesus should be interpreted symbolically. Insisting on the literal accuracy of the biblical account, Spong believed, undermined their real, spiritual meaning. Most provocatively, he suggested that the Apostle Paul was "a deeply repressed, self-rejecting gay man." In *Born of a Woman: A Bishop Rethinks the Birth of Jesus* (1992), Spong suggested that the biblical birth narratives in Matthew and Luke were manufactured in response to charges that Jesus had been born illegitimately. He also suggested that the New Testament hints that Jesus had been married to Mary Magdalene. Spong's ideas were roundly condemned even by many of his fellow Episcopal and Anglican bishops. In June 1998 Robert W. Duncan, Bishop of Pittsburgh, wrote that Spong's teachings were nothing less than "an explicit denial of the Christian faith." Still, Spong's critique was not altogether negative. Calling himself a believer in exile, he addressed himself to others who wanted to embrace Christianity but could not accept what Spong saw as the anti-intellectual dogmatism of traditional "orthodox" Christianity. Spong's *Why Christianity Must Change or Die: A Bishop Speaks to Believers in Exile* (1998) summarized his decades-long struggle to liberate what he understood as the Gospel of Jesus Christ from the limitations of theological and biblical authority.

Sources:

Ellen Barrett, "Profile of a Bishop," *The Voice: The Newspaper of the Diocese of Newark,* September and October, 1997.

Richard N. Ostling, "More Spontaneous Eruptions," *Time,* 137 (18 February 1991): 62.

John Shelby Spong, *Rescuing the Bible from Fundamentalism: A Bishop Rethinks the Meaning of Scripture* (New York: HarperSanFrancisco, 1991).

Spong, *Why Christianity Must Change or Die: A Bishop Speaks to Believers in Exile* (New York: HarperSanFrancisco, 1998).

PEOPLE IN THE NEWS

In December 1994 former television evangelist **James Orsen "Jim" Bakker,** whose PTL Club and Heritage USA theme park cost his investors, the "lifetime partners," millions of dollars, was released from federal prison. His former wife and partner, **Tammy Faye Bakker,** had since married building contractor **Roe Messner.**

In August 1998 Father **James Callan,** who for twenty-two years had served the Corpus Christi parish in Rochester, New York, was suspended from the Roman Catholic Church. He was charged with having performed same-sex weddings, offering Communion to non-Catholics, and permitting a woman, **Mary Ramerman,** to wear a clerical stole and serve at the altar in a manner reserved for priests. In February 1999 he was excommunicated for starting a new church.

In 1991 **Joan Brown Campbell** was installed as general secretary of the National Council of Churches of Christ in the United States of America (NCC), the first ordained woman to hold that post.

James Earl "Jimmy" Carter, who used the prestige of his former office to undertake the role of peacemaker around the world, told the *Christian Century* part of the secret of his success: "I can get anyone to return my calls because I am a former President of the United States."

In September 1999 radical feminist theologian and scholar **Mary Daly** was dismissed from her tenured professorship at Boston College after she refused to admit men to her class.

In 1999 **Robert W. Edgar,** former U.S. congressman and president of Claremont School of Theology, replaced **Joan Brown Campbell** as executive secretary of the NCC. Edgar's first task was to restore the troubled finances of the organization that had deteriorated during Campbell's tenure.

William Franklin "Billy" Graham, though increasingly suffering from Parkinson's disease, continued to preach at evangelistic crusades and to lead the Billy Graham Evangelistic Association. His son, **William Franklin Graham III,** was increasingly recognized as Graham's successor—both as head of the association and as a forceful voice for evangelical Christianity. Billy, and his wife, **Ruth Bell Graham,** were awarded the Congressional Gold Medal in 1996.

In 1995 **Gordon B. Hinckley** was elected as the fifteenth president of The Church of Jesus Christ of Latter-Day Saints (Mormons) upon the death of his predecessor, **Howard W. Hunter.**

Rabbi **Harold S. Kushner,** whose book *When Bad Things Happen to Good People* (1981) comforted millions of Americans, in 1996 asked *How Good Do We Have to Be?* in a new work on morality and religion.

In 1999 **Henry J. Lyons,** former president of the National Baptist Convention USA, was sentenced to serve five and a half years in a Florida prison on charges of grand theft and racketeering.

In August 1994 **Molly Marshall,** the first and only theology professor at a Southern Baptist seminary, was fired from the Southern Baptist Theological Seminary for teaching not consistent with the new conservative direction of the institution.

Protestant church historian **Martin E. Marty** won the 1991 Campion Award from the Catholic Book Club.

In 1994 **Mary Adelia McLeod** became the first woman to head an Episcopal diocese, as Bishop of Vermont.

Benjamin F. Chavis Muhammad, a former United Church of Christ minister and head of the National Association for the Advancement of Colored People (NAACP), announced in February 1997 that he had converted to the Nation of Islam and added Muhammad to his name.

John Richard Neuhaus, a Lutheran theologian, announced in 1990 that he was converting to Roman Catholicism.

Irish rock singer **Sinead O'Connor,** an outspoken critic of the Pope, startled viewers of the late-night comedy show "Saturday Night Live" by concluding a 1992 performance by ripping up a photo of **Pope John Paul II** and telling the audience, "Fight the real enemy."

Sister **Helen Prejean** of Louisiana, who worked with condemned prisoners, was awarded the Pope Paul VI Teacher of Peace Award and the Notre Dame Laetare Medal, both in 1996.

Robert A. Seiple served as the first ambassador-at-large for international religious freedom for the State Department, a position mandated by passage of the International Religious Freedom Act of 1998.

Archbishop **Spyridon,** head of the Greek Orthodox Archdiocese of America, resigned in the wake of a three-year campaign against him by bishops and laity who saw him as autocratic and not in tune with American ways. He was replaced in 1999 by the Greek-born and Harvard-educated biblical scholar, Archbishop **Demetrias Trakatellis.**

In February 1999 **Paul Weyrich,** who, with **Jerry Falwell,** was one of the architects of the Moral Majority, announced, "I no longer believe that there is a moral majority. I do not believe that a majority of Americans actually shares our values." Weyrich was frustrated by the inability of Congress to remove President Bill Clinton from office in the impeachment process.

AWARDS

TEMPLETON PRIZE FOR PROGRESS IN RELIGION

Awarded since 1972 to a living person who has shown "extraordinary originality in advancing humankind's understanding of God and/or spirituality."

1990 L. Charles Birch, scholar at several U.S. universities, researcher of science and faith

1991 no American winner

1992 no American winner

1993 Charles W. Colson, founder of Prison Fellowship International

1994 Michael Novak, religious philosopher

1995 no American winner

1996 William R. "Bill" Bright, founder of Campus Crusade for Christ

1997 no American winner

1998 no American winner

1999 Ian Barbour, scholar of science and religion

GRAWEMEYER AWARD IN RELIGION

Awarded annually since 1990, the Award honors "ideas rather than lifelong or personal achievement." Thus winners are listed with the book for which they were recognized.

1990 E. P. Sanders, *Jesus and Judaism* (1985)

1991 John Harwood Hick, *An Interpretation of Religion: Human Responses to the Transcendent* (1989)

1992 Ralph Harper, *On Presence: Variations and Reflections* (1991)

1993 Elizabeth A. Johnson, *She Who Is: The Mystery of God in Feminist Theological Discourse* (1992)

1994 Stephen L. Carter, *The Culture of Disbelief: How American Law and Politics Trivialize Religious Devotion* (1993)

1995 Diana L. Eck, *Encountering God: A Spiritual Journey from Bozeman to Banaras* (1993)

1996 no award

1997 Larry Rasmussen, *Earth Community, Earth Ethics* (1996)

1998 Charles Marsh, *God's Long Summer: Stories of Faith and Civil Rights* (1997)

1999 no award

DEATHS

Paul Abels, former pastor of Washington Square United Methodist Church in New York (1973–1984); gay-rights activist, 12 March 1992.

Ralph David Abernathy, 64, civil-rights activist and cofounder of Southern Christian Leadership Conference (SCLC), 17 April 1990.

John Maury Allin, 76, presiding bishop of the Episcopal Church, who oversaw revisions to the *Book of Common Prayer* and the 1976 decision to ordain women to the priesthood, 6 March 1998.

James Barbour Ashbrook, 73, nominated for the Templeton Prize in Religion and Science for co-authorship of *The Humanizing Brain: Where Religion and Neuroscience Meet* (1997); researcher on the correlation between the brain and religion, 2 January 1999.

Joseph Cardinal Bernadin, 68, Archbishop of Cincinnati (1927–1982); Archbishop of Chicago (1982–1996), 14 November 1996.

Cassie Bernall, 17, student, killed during the Columbine High School shooting, allegedly for professing her faith in God, 20 April 1999.

Raymond E. Brown, 70, Roman Catholic priest and New Testament scholar, best known for his work on the Gospel of John, who taught at Union Theological Seminary in New York City, 8 August 1998.

Charles Earl Cobb, 82, first executive director of the Commission for Racial Justice of the United Church of Christ and cofounder of the National Conference of Black Christians, 27 December 1998.

Sholom D. Comay, president of the American Jewish Committee, 18 May 1991.

A. Roy Eckert, 79, United Methodist minister and special consultant to the President's Commission on the Holocaust; spoke out against anti-Semitism in Christian teaching, 5 May 1998.

Milton B. Engebretson, 75, sixth president of The Evangelical Covenant Church; former president of the International Federation of Free Evangelical Churches; and former convening chairman of the U.S. Church Leaders, 10 December 1996.

Joseph Fletcher, 86, Episcopal priest and scholar of biomedical ethics; as an advocate of "situation ethics," he argued that ethical decisions should be based on principles, not laws, 28 October 1991.

John Garcia Gensel (Juan Garcia Velez), 80, pastor to a jazz community out of St. Peter's Lutheran Church in New York City and subject of Duke Ellington's "The Shepherd (Who Watches Over the Night Flock)" (1968), 6 February 1998.

Rachel Henderlite, 86, theologian and professor, first woman ordained by the Presbyterian Church, USA (1965), 6 November 1991.

Howard W. Hunter, 87, fourteenth president of The Church of Jesus Christ of Latter-Day Saints (Mormons), 30 March 1995.

Blahoslav Hruby, 78, executive director of Research Center for Religion and Human Rights in Closed Societies, 22 October 1990.

Maude Keister Jensen, 94, the first woman to receive full clergy rights as a Methodist pastor (1956), 12 October 1998.

Bob Jones Jr., 86, chairman of Bob Jones University in Greenville, S.C., 12 November 1997.

Meir (Martin David) Kahane, 58, rabbi and founder of a radical Zionist movement, 5 November 1990.

Thomas Kilgore Jr., 84, first black president of the American Baptist Convention; leader of the Progressive National Baptist Convention (1976–1978); and advocate for racial justice, 4 February 1998.

Harold Lindsell, 84, former editor of *Christianity Today* (1968–1978), 15 January 1998.

Maurice F. McCracken, 92, pastor, peace advocate, and pacifist who went to jail for not paying taxes, was unfrocked and later reinstated by Cincinnati Presbytery.

Marshall T. Meyer, rabbi, founder of the progressive Jewish journal *Tikkun,* 29 December 1993.

Dwight L. "Dale" Moody, Southern Baptist theologian, and preacher; former member of the World Council of Churches' Faith and Order Commission, 22 January 1992.

Wayne E. Oates, 89, pioneer in pastoral care; one of the first scholars to advocate using principles of psychiatry and psychology in ministry; professor at Southern Baptist Theological Seminary and University of Louisville School of Medicine, 21 October 1999.

Madalyn Murray O'Hair, 76, atheist and outspoken opponent of public religion; disappeared in August 1995 with her two adult children, Jon Garth Murray and Robin Murray—all three were believed to have been murdered.

Norman Vincent Peale, 95, preacher and author of *The Power of Positive Thinking* (1952), 24 December 1993.

Marvin Pope, 80, scholar, writer, and professor of Near Eastern languages and civilization at Yale University, 15 June 1997.

Samuel DeWitt Proctor, 75, preacher, teacher, administrator in the National Council of Churches and Peace Corps; president of Virginia Union University, 22 May 1997.

Bruce Ritter, 72, Catholic priest; founder in 1969 of Covenant House, a Manhattan refuge for runaway children and teens, from which he resigned in February 1990 amidst charges of sexual misconduct, 7 October 1999.

Menachem Mendel Schneerson, 92, rebbe, seventh leader of the Chabad Lubavich movement within Orthodox Judaism; thought by some of his followers to be the messiah, 12 June 1994.

Betty Shabazz, 61, college administrator and professor, wife of Malcolm X, 23 June 1997.

Ira Silverman, first director of the Institute for Jewish Policy Planning and Research, former president of the Reconstructionalist Rabbinical College, 23 June 1991.

Glenn Smiley, associate of Martin Luther King Jr. during the Montgomery Bus Boycott (1956), 14 September 1993.

Joseph Dov Ber Soloveitchik, 90, rabbi, writer, and influential leader of mainstream American Orthodox Judaism, 8 April 1993.

Harry C. Spencer, 91, chair of the Broadcasting and Film Commission, National Council of Churches (1952–1973); recipient of the 1973 Award of Excellence in the Arts of Communication by the School of Theology at Claremont, California; and president of the First Assembly of the World Association of Christian Communication in Nairobi, Kenya (1968), 18 December 1996.

Timothy J. Tester, first American Buddhist monk to complete a Three-Steps-One-Bow Pilgrimage, 15 December 1998.

Nelson W. Trout, 75, pastor and professor; first African American Lutheran bishop (1983), 20 September 1996.

David Elton Trueblood, 94, Quaker theologian and author, 20 September 1996.

Deena Marie Umbarger, 35, American aid worker with the United Methodist Committee on Relief, who was shot and killed along the Kenya-Somalia border, possibly by Islamic fundamentalists, 20 March 1999.

Paul Matthews Van Buren, 74, theologian, associated with the "Death of God" school of theology (1960s)—though he rejected the term, 18 June 1998.

John Wimber, 63, founder of the Charismatic Association of Vineyard Churches, 17 November 1997.

PUBLICATIONS

Karen Armstrong, *A History of God: The 4000-Year Quest of Judaism, Christianity, and Islam* (New York: Knopf, 1993).

The Book of J, translated by David Rosenberg, interpreted by Harold Bloom (New York: Grove-Weidenfeld, 1990).

Raymond E. Brown, *The Death of the Messiah: From Gethsemane to the Grave: A Commentary on the Passion Narratives in the Four Gospels* (New York: Doubleday, 1994).

Donald J. Dietrich, *God and Humanity in Auschwitz: Jewish-Christian Relations and Sanctioned Murder* (New Brunswick, N.J.: Transaction Publishers, 1995).

Michael Drosnin, *The Bible Code* (New York: Simon & Schuster, 1997).

Richard Elliott Friedman, trans., *The Hidden Book in the Bible* (San Francisco: HarperSanFrancisco, 1998).

Robert W. Funk, Roy W. Hoover, and the Jesus Seminar, eds., *The Five Gospels: The Search for the Authentic Words of Jesus: New Translation and Commentary* (New York: Macmillan, 1993).

Dean R. Hoge and others, *Vanishing Boundaries: The Religion of Mainline Protestant Baby Boomers* (Louisville, Ky.: Westminster/John Knox, 1994).

Luke Timothy Johnson, *The Real Jesus: The Misguided Quest for the Historical Jesus and the Truth of the Traditional Gospels* (San Francisco: HarperSanFrancisco, 1996).

Mark Jurgensmeyer, *Terror in the Mind of God: The Global Rise of Religious Violence* (Berkeley: University of California Press, 2000).

Rodger Kamenetz, *Stalking Elijah: Adventures with Today's Jewish Mystical Masters* (San Francisco: HarperSanFrancisco, 1997).

Don Morreale, ed., *The Complete Guide to Buddhist America* (Boston: Shambhala Publishers, 1998).

Bill Moyers, *Genesis: A Living Conversation* (New York: Doubleday, 1996).

Sulayman S. Nayang, *Islam in the United States of America* (Chicago: Kazi Publishers, 1999).

Kathleen Norris, *Amazing Grace: A Vocabulary of Faith* (New York: Riverhead, 1998).

Bruce Perry, *Malcolm: The Life of a Man Who Changed Black America* (New York: Talman, 1991).

Ralph Reed, *Politically Incorrect: The Emerging Faith Factor in American Politics* (Dallas: Word Publishers, 1994).

Michael Warner, *American Sermons: The Pilgrims to Martin Luther King Jr.* (New York: Library of America, 1999).

Jack Wertheimer, *A People Divided: Judaism in Contemporary America* (New York: BasicBooks, 1993).

The Christian Century, periodical.

Christianity and the Arts, periodical.

Christianity Today, periodical

International Journal of Hindu Studies, periodical.

International Journal for the Psychology of Religion, periodical.

Medieval Philosophy and Theology, periodical.

Religion and American Culture: A Journal of Interpretation, periodical.

Sojourners, periodical.

Studies in World Christianity, periodical.

Tikkun, periodical.

Tricycle: The Buddhist Review, periodical.

The Matthews-Murkland Presbyterian church in Charlotte, North Carolina, aflame on 6 June 1996 (AP/Wide World Photos)

A worshipper kissing the hand of Pope John Paul II at Mile High Stadium in Denver, Colorado, on 12 August 1993 (AP/Wide World Photos)

CHAPTER TWELVE

SCIENCE AND TECHNOLOGY

by HOPE CARGILL

CONTENTS

Sidebars and tables are listed in italics.

1990

24 Apr.   The Hubble Space Telescope (HST) is placed into orbit by the space shuttle *Discovery.*

22 May   Microsoft releases Windows version 3.0, which sells close to thirty million copies in a year; Windows soon becomes the industry standard consumer operating system.

1 June   U.S. president George Bush and Soviet premier Mikhail Gorbachev sign a bilateral agreement to stop producing chemical weapons and to begin destroying stocks of agents by the end of 1992.

Sept.   American geneticist W. French Anderson performs the first gene therapy on a four-year-old girl with an immune-system disorder called Adenosine Deaminase (ADA) deficiency.

Oct.   The Human Genome Project (HGP) is formally launched.

1991

- Linus Torvalds, a student at the University of Helsinki, writes the code for the open-source Linux operating system and releases it over the Internet under a free public license.

3 Apr.   U.N. Security Council approves a Gulf cease-fire resolution that includes stripping Iraq of its weapons of mass destruction.

14 Aug.   Scientists report that a worldwide band of volcanic dust from the eruptions of Mount Pinatubo (June/July 1991) in the Philippines could be temporarily cooling the climate worldwide.

26 Sept.   Four men and four women begin a two-year stay inside a sealed-off structure in Oracle, Arizona, called "Biosphere Two."

1992

- American pharmaceutical house Merck agrees to pay the Costa Rican National Institute of Biodiversity (*El Instituto Nacional de Biodiversidad,* or INBio) $1 million over two years for the right to search for new drugs in the tropical forests of Costa Rica.

- The U.S. Army begins collecting blood and saliva samples from all new recruits as part of a "genetic dog tag" program aimed at better identifying soldiers killed in combat.

- American and British scientists unveil a technique for testing embryos *in vitro* for genetic abnormalities such as cystic fibrosis and hemophilia.

6 Mar.   A computer virus called "Michelangelo" strikes thousands of personal computers around the world.

7–16 May   During a space shuttle mission, three astronauts from the *Endeavor* simultaneously walk in space for the first time, retrieving and repairing the Intelsat-6 satellite; their walk lasts 8 hours, 29 minutes.

9 June	The largest ever environmental summit opens in Rio de Janeiro, Brazil, with representatives from 178 nations taking part. The United Nations Conference on Environment and Development (UNCED), otherwise known as the Earth Summit, ambitiously attacks environmental problems on fronts ranging from climate change to population control, but meets with mixed success.
28 June	Two earthquakes hit southern California, including the third strongest in the United States during the twentieth century, registering at 7.4 on the Richter scale.
12 Sept.	Space shuttle *Endeavor* takes off with a crew that includes Mark C. Lee and N. Jan Davis, the first married couple in space.

1993

- Biochemists at the U.S. National Cancer Institute announce that they have found at least one gene relating to homosexuality, residing on the X chromosome inherited from the mother.

- George Washington University researchers clone human embryos and nurture them in a petri dish for several days. The project provokes protests from ethicists, politicians, and people opposed to genetic engineering.

- An international research team, led by Daniel Cohen of the Center for the Study of Human Polymorphisms (*Centre d'Etude du Polymorphisme Humain* or CEPH) in Paris, produces a rough map of all twenty-three pairs of human chromosomes.

- The curbside recycling revolution takes off, with an 85 percent increase since 1988 in the number of U.S. communities that recycle.

3 Jan.	Russian president Boris Yeltsin and U.S. president George Bush sign the Start II Treaty, aimed at eliminating about two-thirds of the nuclear stockpiles of their nations.
Feb.	The National Center for Supercomputing Applications (NCSA) releases the first alpha version of Marc Andreessen's "Mosaic for X" web browser. There are fifty known Web servers.
Mar./Apr.	The first issue of *Wired,* a magazine covering computers, the Internet, and culture related to high technology, is published.
30 Apr.	A declaration by European Organization for Nuclear Research (CERN, *Conseil European pour la Recherché Nucleaire*) directors announces that World Wide Web technology will be freely usable by anyone, with no fees being paid to CERN.
6 May	The Strategic Defense Initiative (SDI, or "Star Wars"), the futuristic defense program initiated by former president Ronald Reagan, is downgraded by the Pentagon.
Aug.	Andreessen and coworkers release five versions of Mosaic for Macintosh and Windows. Windows NT is introduced.
Sept.	NCSA releases a working version of the Mosaic browser for all common platforms: X, PC/Windows, and Macintosh.
6 Sept.	The "Doomsday 2000" article, warning about possible Y2K (Year 2000) problems, is published in *Computerworld* by Canadian Peter de Jager.

9 Dec. U.S. astronauts finish a grueling five-day repair job on the $3 billion Hubble Space Telescope.

1994

- Scientists discover three planets orbiting the dim remnants of a star that exploded long ago, evidence of a solar system beyond our own.

- The revised open-source operating system Linux 1.0 is released over the Internet.

10 Jan. President Bill Clinton announces a deal under which Ukraine would give up its nuclear arsenal, the third largest in the world.

Feb. Bovine Growth Hormone (BGH), a genetically engineered hormone that boosts milk production in cows by as much as 15 percent, goes on sale after nearly ten years of legal battles.

11 Feb. Five astronauts and a cosmonaut return to Earth aboard *Discovery* after the first joint U.S.-Russian space shuttle mission.

15 Feb. North Korea ends a year-long standoff with the International Atomic Energy Agency (IAEA), allowing agency inspectors to check seven declared nuclear plants.

Mar. Andreessen and colleagues leave NCSA to form "Mosaic Communications Corporation," which soon becomes "Netscape Communications Corporation."

23 Apr. Physicists at the U.S. Department of Energy's Fermi National Accelerator Laboratory in Chicago find evidence for the existence of the subatomic particle known as the top quark, the last of six quarks (thought to be the building blocks of all matter) that are believed to exist.

May-June Andreessen and coworkers create the original Netscape Navigator Internet browser. There are fifteen hundred known Web servers.

July Nearly two dozen mountain-sized chunks of the fragmented comet Shoemaker-Levy 9 crash into Jupiter, creating two-thousand-mile-high fireballs that are visible from backyard telescopes on Earth. Scientists learn about Jupiter's atmosphere, comets, and how a similar impact on earth sixty-five million years ago might have killed off the dinosaurs.

15 Dec. Netscape Communications Corporation releases its graphical browser, Netscape Navigator 1.0, initiating a communications revolution. Within four months 75 percent of all Net users are accessing the web using the Netscape browser. The company goes public, gaining the largest IPO (Initial Public Offering) in Wall Street history.

1995

- Craig Venter and Hamilton Smith publish a paper in *Science* announcing that they have successfully mapped the entire genome of *Haemophilus influenzae.*

- The hottest year to date is recorded by scientists, a fact taken by some as the first concrete sign of global warming.

- Java, a miniaturized programming language from Sun Microsystems, is introduced.

2 Jan. The most distant galaxy yet discovered is found by scientists using the Keck telescope at the W. M. Keck Observatory in Mauna Kea, Hawaii. The galaxy is estimated to be fifteen billion light years away from Earth.

14 Mar. Norman E. Thagard becomes the first U.S. astronaut to fly in a Russian rocket on a mission to the Mir space station.

May Researchers at Duke University Medical Center transplant hearts from genetically altered pigs into baboons. All three transgenic hearts survived at least a few hours, proving that cross-species operations are possible.

14 June The Senate passes the Communications Decency Act (CDA), part of the Telecommunications Reform Act, intended to regulate "lewd and obscene" content on the World Wide Web.

Aug. A group of schoolchildren on a biology field trip in Minnesota discover deformed frogs, leading to a national fear that pesticides, toxins, and global warming are wreaking havoc on the environment.

24 Aug. Windows 95 is released.

3 Oct. Former football star O. J. Simpson is found not guilty in a high-profile double-murder trial in which Polymerase Chain Reaction (PCR) and DNA fingerprinting play a prominent but unpersuasive role.

7 Dec. A probe from the spacecraft Galileo successfully enters the atmosphere of the planet Jupiter.

10 Dec. National Aeronautics & Space Administration (NASA) scientists receive the first data from the space probe Galileo—a message beamed over 2.3 billion miles (3.7 billion km).

1996

- Genetically modified corn, known as Bt corn, is approved by the Environmental Protection Agency (EPA). The corn contains DNA spliced from the common soil bacterium *Bacillus thuringiensis*, which allows the corn to exude a toxin that is lethal to corn borers.

- The first commercially grown gene-spliced food crops are planted.

- The first genetically engineered insect, a predator mite that researchers hope will eat other mites that damage strawberries and other crops, is released in Florida.

- The first U.S. Congressional hearing on the Y2K problem is held, focusing on how federal agencies will prepare their computer systems for the year 2000.

1 Feb. Both houses of Congress vote overwhelmingly to approve the Telecommunications Reform Act, including the CDA.

8 Feb. President Clinton signs the Telecommunications Reform Act into law. On the same day, the American Civil Liberties Union (ACLU) and nineteen other groups file suit challenging its constitutionality.

Apr.	Genzyme Transgenics announces the birth of Grace, a transgenic goat carrying a gene that produces BR-96, a monoclonal antibody being tested and developed to deliver conjugated anticancer drugs.
13 Aug.	Data sent back by the Galileo space probe indicates that there may be water on one of Jupiter's moons, heightening the possibility that it could support a primitive life-form.
25 Sept.	NASA biochemist Shannon W. Lucid returns home after spending six months aboard the Russian space station Mir, earning her the title of America's most experienced astronaut.

1997

- Farmers in the U.S. plant genetically modified soy on more than 8 million acres and genetically modified corn on more than 3.5 million acres.

Feb.	Researchers at PPL Therapeutics, in Virginia, announce the birth of a transgenic calf named Rosie, whose milk contains alpha-lactalbumin, a human protein that provides essential amino acids, making it nutritious for premature infants who cannot nurse.
Mar.	The Hale-Bopp comet soars close to earth (122 million miles).
21 Apr.	The ashes of 1960s LSD guru Timothy Leary and *Star Trek* creator Gene Roddenberry are blasted into space in the first space funeral.
11 May	The IBM supercomputer Deep Blue makes chess history by defeating Gary Kasparov, the first time a reigning world champion is beaten in a match by a machine.
26 June	The U.S. Supreme Court rules the Communications Decency Act, meant to regulate "indecent" material on the Internet, unconstitutional.
4 July	The U.S. Pathfinder space probe, carrying the Sojourner rover, makes an historic landing on Mars.
2 Oct.	Several scientists deliberately freeze their ship, the Canadian icebreaker *Des Groseilliers*, into the Arctic ice for a yearlong study of changes in weather patterns in the far north.
Dec.	Representatives from 160 countries meet in Kyoto, Japan, to discuss climate change and agree to strictly control the release of greenhouse gases associated with global warming by the year 2012.

1998

- University of Hawaii scientists, using a variation of Ian Wilmut's "Dolly" technique, clone a mouse, creating not only dozens of copies but three generations of cloned clones.

- President Clinton names Eileen M. Collins as the first woman to lead a U.S. space mission.

- Craig Venter, with his private research company, Celeva, announces ambitious plans to decode the entire human genome by 2001, years ahead of the Human Genome Project deadline.

- DNA testing proves that U.S. president Thomas Jefferson had at least one child with Sally Hemings, one of his slaves.

16 Jan. NASA announces that former astronaut John Herschel Glenn Jr., age 76, has been approved for an October shuttle flight.

21 Jan. Theodore John Kaczynski pleads guilty to being the antitechnology Unabomber in exchange for a sentence of life in prison without parole.

24 Jan. The National Research Council, of the National Academy of Sciences, conducts a workshop on failed stars and superplanets.

Feb. 21.74 inches of rain fall on Santa Barbara, California, its highest monthly total on record. Scientists speculate that this deluge is the result of weather changes caused by global warming.

22–23 Feb. Severe El Niño-powered storms hit in and around Orlando, Florida, spawning tornadoes that kill at least thirty-six people and damage or destroy scores of buildings.

26 Feb. The last total solar eclipse visible from the Western Hemisphere of the millennium occurs.

5 Mar. NASA releases initial findings of the *Lunar Prospector.*

May India performs five underground nuclear tests, despite strong international disapproval. Pakistan answers with tests of its own.

19 May A failure of its onboard control system causes the Galaxy IV satellite to rotate out of position, disrupting pager and television service for millions of people in the U.S. and the Caribbean, as well as some ATM services for banks.

4 June Space shuttle *Discovery* docks with Russian space station Mir to collect astronaut Andrew Thomas after he spends four months aboard Mir.

6 June The National Research Council holds a forum in Los Angeles on the risk of an asteroid striking the Earth.

25 June Windows 98 is released.

30 July Monica S. Lewinsky hands over to Independent Counsel Kenneth W. Starr a dress she alleges may contain evidence of a sexual relationship with President Clinton. DNA analysis of semen stains on the dress match DNA from a blood sample given by Clinton.

23 Sept.–
1 Oct. NASA sponsors Challenge Mission, an eight-day deployment of the Carpenter Space Analog Station on the sea floor off Key Largo, Florida.

28 Oct. President Clinton signs into law the Digital Millennium Copyright Act.

29 Oct. Space shuttle *Discovery* launches with Senator and former astronaut Glenn, 77, aboard as a payload specialist.

Nov. Two research teams succeed in growing embryonic stem cells.

15 Nov. Young people aged ten to sixteen from fifty-four countries gathered in Cambridge for the Massachusetts Institute of Technology (MIT) Junior Summit '98.

17 Nov. The Leonid meteor shower, said to be the most intense meteor shower in thirty years, occurs, threatening five hundred satellites circling Earth.

9 Dec. Scientists announce that the nematode worm, *caenorhabditis elegans,* has become the first animal to have its genome completely mapped.

1999

- 5,800 pairs of bald eagles flourish in the Continental United States; the birds are removed from the endangered species list.

26 Mar. The "Melissa" computer virus makes its appearance, wreaking havoc on e-mail systems around the nation and affecting 19 percent of U.S. corporations, but causing little permanent damage.

2 Apr. David L. Smith is arrested for authoring the Melissa virus; he is tracked using the same technology that allows his virus to spread so freely.

25–27 Apr. International Data Group, one of the largest technology consultants in the world and publisher of high-tech periodicals, sponsors the first EnterTech conference in Carlsbad, California, bringing together the Silicon Valley and Hollywood executives to explore the union of technology and movies.

30 Apr. *Science* publishes two companion articles indicating that the deformities of the so-called "sentinel frogs" found in Minnesota and other states are primarily caused by a parasite, not by global warming or pesticides as was previously theorized.

May Researchers discover signs of premature aging in the cells of Dolly, the first sheep cloned from the cell of an adult ewe.

5 May Windows 98 Special Edition is released.

June The computer virus "Worm.Explore.Zip" infiltrates systems around the nation through e-mail, burrowing into software, erasing files, and shutting down networks. Microsoft's system is down for a few hours, and Boeing's for several days.

July New York City has its warmest and driest July on record, with temperatures climbing above 95 degrees F (35 degrees C) for eleven days. Scientists speculate that the extreme weather is the result of global warming.

Aug. The Working Group is established under the leadership of Attorney General Janet Reno to address the issue of cybercrime.

Nov. /Dec. In the world of e-commerce, on-line holiday sales tripled from the total of $73 million in 1998 to $3.17 billion.

20 Dec. In New Orleans, Jazz, an endangered African wildcat, becomes the first mammal to be born from a frozen embryo implanted in the womb of a common species, in this case, a house cat.

OVERVIEW

Optimism and Empowerment. As the century drew to a close, the potential for human invention and understanding appeared boundless. Scientific understanding expanded daily, from the fundamental building blocks of matter to the source code of all life to the origins, and perhaps the eventual demise, of the universe. The technological advances of the 1990s ushered in what appeared to be a social and economic revolution that would rival the Industrial Revolution two centuries earlier, creating a new society of technologically connected citizens with a world of digitized information, commerce, and communication at its fingertips. The new "Digital Age," represented by the "Information Superhighway" was not all-inclusive, threatened to leave many behind, including older citizens and those who could not afford the new technology. Still, by 1999 more than three-quarters of the U.S. population was "plugged in" to the new digital society, and most Americans felt that technological advances were improving their quality of life. Optimism was the reigning tone of the decade. New advances in science and technology seemed to promise eventual solutions to problems ranging from eliminating toxic waste to grocery shopping—genetic engineers developed microbes that would eat industrial sludge and researchers at the Massachusetts Institute of Technology's (MIT) Media Lab worked to devise a refrigerator that could sense when it was out of milk and use the Internet to order more. The 1990s allayed the fear that a technologically advanced society was necessarily heavily centralized, with Big Brother watching every move. Instead, with the creation of the Internet and the World Wide Web, and their emphasis on decentralization, equality, and the open sharing of resources, many individuals found that greater access to information increased their sense of personal freedom and power.

Ethics and the Natural. With the explosion of knowledge came public concern over where all of these new discoveries and technologies might be taking society. The cloning of an animal in 1997 suggested that human cloning had become viable as well, raising concerns—no longer quite theoretical—that humanity might be moving toward a "brave new world" of genetically engineered people. The Human Genome Project, launched in 1990 with a mission to decode the entire human genetic makeup, held promises for an end to genetic disorders, but threatened to open the way for "designer babies," who could be genetically altered to suit their parents' wishes. While many argued that plant and animal breeders had been fooling around with genetics for centuries in order to better the lot of humankind, others pointed out that new advances in genetics allowed researchers to cross boundaries set by nature, implanting human genes in animals in order to turn them into medicine factories, creating plants that produced plastics and glowed in the dark, even attempting to create "terminator" seeds that stifled their own reproductive capacity in order to maintain the seed manufacturer's cash flow. The question of what was "natural" came under serious consideration, as no aspect of the environment and the organisms in it seemed safe from genetic tinkering. Yet, while experiments with human cloning or customizing a child's genetic makeup seemed abhorrent to most Americans, there was general support for genetic research that could help to identify and cure genetic diseases or make food sources healthier and more plentiful for a growing global population.

Privacy. Privacy was an overarching concern with many of the technological and scientific advances of the 1990s. The Internet was an amazing new tool for sharing information, yet it was also a powerful means for finding information that was intended to be private, including government and military secrets, the source codes to proprietary software, and even a neighbor's social security number. Companies and individuals alike worried that their private information would be compromised when sophisticated computer technologists could "hack" into protected computer systems and erase or steal important data. Computer viruses, self-replicating codes written by malicious individuals, could steal into personal computer systems through e-mail or the Web and wreak havoc with the data stored there. Protecting privacy over the Internet was not easy, and many people worried that government attempts to intervene would only cripple the development of the Internet. Similar fears were sparked when concerned groups lobbied the government to outlaw pornography and other disturbing materials on the Web in the name of "protecting the children." While most Americans agreed that children should not be exposed to such material, attempts to regulate the content of individual Web pages and newsgroups conflicted with the idea of the Internet as an open, decentralized mass medium, where even the most absurd or repellant ideas could receive a hearing. Digital surveillance in the workplace also became an issue, as some companies spied on their workers' use of the Internet and e-mail.

Genetics and Privacy. Advances in genetics also threatened personal privacy. With the Human Genome Project scheduled to be finished early in the twenty-first century, and private companies competing to win patents on genetic discoveries, many individuals worried about what scientists might do with a complete understanding of the human genetic code. While genetic diseases could be discovered and perhaps cured, this information might also be used to discriminate against people predisposed to certain genetic malfunctions, or to group individuals based on their genetic data. The idea that scientists would own patents on the human genetic code was disturbing, as well, as it meant that human life could become a proprietary resource.

Big Science and Little Science. The National Aeronautics and Space Administration (NASA) continued to wow the world, sending the giant Hubble Telescope into orbit to gather and transmit never-before-seen images of deep space that offered increasingly tantalizing clues to the origins of the universe. The search for extraterrestrial life continued during the decade, as NASA scientists found possible evidence of bacterial life in a meteor from Mars, and distant planets were discovered that might contain water. NASA sent space probes to land on the surface of Mars, sent national hero John Herschel Glenn Jr. back into space to study aging, and made plans to build an International Space Station with research teams from other countries. Still, some critics wondered if all of the money spent on space research might not be better used to fund new discoveries here on Earth, almost as if the diversion of space was no longer as necessary when there were so many new and interesting projects going on right here. One of the most fascinating new realms of study was nanotechnology, a field of research that attempted to manipulate matter at the molecular level, building new devices atom by atom that could be used in miniaturized manufacturing, drug-delivery systems, and tiny nanocomputers. With the discovery of a new family of carbon molecules known as fullerenes, nanotechnology researchers had a new raw material to work with. The science was still very experimental at the turn of the century, but researchers and government officials saw great potential for this science of the tiny.

TOPICS IN THE NEWS

THE ENVIRONMENT

Global Warming. During the 1990s global warming became a major concern for scientists and the public. Many scientists warned that carbon dioxide and other gases from the burning of fossil fuels were collecting in the atmosphere and acting like the glass walls of a greenhouse, trapping heat on the surface of the Earth. They predicted that average temperatures could rise as much as 6.3 degrees F (3.5 degrees C) over the next century, threatening coastal areas with flooding as the polar ice caps melted and warmer sea waters expanded, and causing massive climate changes throughout the world. They cited evidence of heat waves, shrinking polar ice, and rising seas, all thought to be caused by global warming, and pointed to specific evidence that global warming was no longer a potential but a real threat to the environment. In Antarctica, Adelie penguin populations declined 33 percent in twenty-five years because the sea ice where they lived was shrinking. In Bermuda and Hawaii, rising seas killed coastal mangrove forests and caused beach erosion. Skeptics questioned the presumed connection between human activity and global warming, arguing that while the global temperature might be rising, it could be the result of normal changes in weather patterns. They pointed out that Earth had undergone several major climate shifts throughout its known history and suggested that these normal shifts, not the burning of fossil fuels, were responsible for the changes in global-weather patterns. Scientific experiments and research, as well as international conferences throughout the decade, addressed concerns about global warming, and though the majority of climatologists accepted the premise that the burning of fossil fuels and the subsequent rise in carbon dioxide levels in the atmosphere was causing the planet to grow warmer, there was no consensus on how global warming might be reversed. Civilization had, since the nineteenth century, become too dependent on coal, oil, and natural gas to easily change its ways.

Biosphere II, near Oracle, Arizona, in 1991 (AP/Wide World Photos)

Arctic Ice Cap. In October 1997 several scientists deliberately froze their ship, the Canadian icebreaker *Des Groseilliers,* into the Arctic ice for a year-long study of changes in weather patterns in the far north. They discovered that the polar ice was less than half as thick as ice measured in the same area in earlier years, down from between six and nine feet to less than four feet thick. They also found that the water below the ice had far less salt than normal, indicating that the ice was melting at an alarming rate, flooding the sea with fresh water. Scientists had known for some time that the Arctic ice cap was shrinking, especially since 1990, but did not expect the changes to be as great as they appeared. Scientists warned that the changing weather in the far north could in turn affect weather around the globe. A warmer Arctic could slow the transport of warmer waters north from the equatorial region, thus influencing weather over a huge area. Shifting circulation patterns in the Arctic contributed to weather changes in Northern Europe and across the Northern Hemisphere. No one knew if the changes in the Arctic weather resulted from burning fossil fuels, which supposedly created the "greenhouse-effect" by causing the atmosphere to hold more heat, or whether the changes were simply a temporary fluctuation in the weather. Many scientists suspected that the dramatic changes found in the Arctic ice in the 1990s suggested that the greenhouse effect was, in fact, to blame. They believed that the theorized global warming of the planet through the greenhouse effect would have the most dramatic impact in the far north and speculated that someday the polar ice caps might melt altogether in the summer, refreezing only during the winter months.

Biosphere II. A totally enclosed greenhouse, Biosphere II, was designed to mimic conditions on Earth (or Biosphere I) in a sealed, controlled environment. It was completed in 1991 and was bankrolled by Texas billionaire Edward P. Bass. Bass envisioned Biosphere II, located near Tucson, Arizona, as the first step toward the colonization of Mars. Inside the sealed environment, which contained five "wilderness areas," ranging from a rain forest to a desert and even an ocean, "biospherians" were to learn to live off the land, totally isolated—even from the Earth's atmosphere—except for communications. Eight biospherians lived inside the structure from 1991 to 1993; the experiment, however, disappointed its designers. Oxygen levels inside the complex dropped so low, and trapped nitrous oxide levels rose so high, that emergency steps were required to protect the lives of the eight researchers. Oxygen was pumped in, violating the ideal of total isolation, and some reports suggested that food production was so low that extra food was smuggled in as well. Nearly all of the birds, animals, and insects that were brought into the environment and expected to thrive there, died, though ants and cockroaches ran rampant. Later research showed that oxygen in Biosphere II had been absorbed by the massive concrete structure that supported the greenhouse. The biospherians eventually evacuated the structure, and Bass turned Biosphere II over to Columbia University to manage as a research project. The university took control over Biosphere II, using it as a teaching and research tool for environmental science education and research. Scientists experimented with using Biosphere II to simulate global warming, exposing some areas to increased levels of carbon

In 1997 Americans threw away more than 430 billion pounds of garbage. On top of that municipal solid waste, U.S. industries in the 1990s dumped more than 2.5 billion pounds of toxic waste per year. The alarming rate at which Americans produced waste was compounded by the fear that, as other countries developed, they would follow suit, dramatically increasing the global amount of trash.

Finding new ways to decrease and recycle garbage became a major concern. By the end of the decade, eco-industrial parks were being developed around the world, where several companies would share resources, with the waste products of one company serving as raw materials for the production process of another business. In addition, biotechnology was finding new tools to cope with waste. There were microbes that could take toxic substances in contaminated soil or sludge—including organic solvents and industrial oils—and convert them into harmless byproducts. Genetic engineers were working on making corn plants with a fiber content that paper companies could use, which could turn some agricultural waste into an industrial ingredient. In consumer markets, the emphasis on recycling spawned trends such as jackets made from discarded plastic bottles, briefcases from worn-out tires, and belts from beer-bottle caps. By 1999 some 25 percent of the 430 billion pounds of municipal garbage in the United States was being recycled. Experts predicted that this number would increase as industries developed materials that were easier to reuse. In addition, attempts to decrease the amount of garbage made in the first place was translated into new products, such as thinner aluminum soda cans and plastic bottles.

One of the greatest hopes for trash reduction lay in nanotechnology. Many scientists hoped that nanotechnology, with its atom-by-atom approach to creating goods, would eliminate much of the waste associated with traditional manufacturing. In addition, items could be made that were much smaller and more efficient.

Experts hoped that changes in lifestyle, associated with the new technology of the Information Age, might also decrease waste. For example, telecommuting (working at home via the personal computer and a modem hookup) meant less reliance on cars, and downloading music from the Web reduced demand for plastic compact disc (CD) cases. Moreover, many people hoped that as the economy became information-, rather than manufacturing-, based, resources could be more efficiently utilized, reused, and recycled.

Source: Ivan Amato, "Can We Make Garbage Disappear?" *Time*, 154 (8 November 1999): 116+.

---

dioxide to determine possible effect on the environment. With these studies, they hoped to find some indications of how Earth's environment would react to similar levels of the gas. In addition, students from all over the country came to study at Biosphere II. Despite the failure of its initial mission, as a research facility, it proved to be a useful tool for studying the mysteries of the environment.

Earth Summit. In 1992, more than one hundred heads of state met in Rio de Janeiro, Brazil, for the first United Nations Conference on Environment and Development (UNCED), or International Earth Summit. This meeting was convened to address problems of environmental protection and socio-economic development. The assembled leaders discussed global issues ranging from an increase in population, global warming, protecting biodiversity, and the distribution of resources and power among different countries. They created organizations to study global warming and the extinction of plant and animal species. They also endorsed the Rio Declaration and the Forest Principles, which called for sustainable development, equitable distribution of resources, and more-thoughtful exploitation of forest resources. Still, the Earth Summit met with mixed success, with critics charging that the most advanced countries, including the United States, were trying to regulate the development of poorer countries while they themselves were the worst environmental offenders. The Commission on Sustainable Development was created to monitor and report on the implementation of the Earth Summit agreements. In 1997 a five-year review of Earth Summit progress was made by the United Nations (U.N.) General Assembly meeting in special session. One of the findings of the U.N. Report indicated that global water supplies could be in danger. The supply of fresh, clean water, already threatened by growing levels of pollution, was found to be growing so scarce in some areas that two-thirds of humanity could suffer moderate to severe water stress by 2030, according to the report. It blamed poor water allocation, wasteful use of water, and lack of adequate water management for the potential problem.

Sentinel Frogs. In 1995 a group of schoolchildren on a biology field trip in Minnesota came across some unusual-looking frogs. One was missing a leg, some had withered arms, others had shrunken eyes. Of the twenty-two frogs caught that day, eleven were deformed in some way. After their teacher told officials, reports of more deformed frogs began pouring in, coming from other parts of Minnesota, as well as other states and parts of Canada. Herpetologists and environmentalists were puzzled as to what could be causing the deformities. Because frogs spend much of their lives in water, pesticides and toxic metals were prime suspects. Later suspected culprits included acid rain, global warming, and increased ultraviolet light. Some scientists feared that the deformed frogs could be a sign that something was wrong in the environment and that whatever was causing the abnormalities in the frog populations would eventually harm humans as well. Frogs were considered a "sentinel species": because their skin soaks up whatever is in the water or air, frogs could provide an early warning of environmental problems for other species, including humans. In April 1999, however, *Science* published two companion articles that indicated that the deformities were caused by a parasite. These findings were repeated among five species of frogs in twelve different locations in the United States. Many viewed these findings as conclusive proof that fears of environmental toxicity were unnecessary and reactionary. Still, others speculated that even though a parasite was found to be the cause of the abnormalities, toxins and global warming must have helped to create conditions for these parasites to thrive, maiming and killing frogs in unusually high numbers. Thus, the "sentinel frog" issue became fodder for both sides in the ongoing debate between environmental activists and those with a more conservative outlook.

Sources:

Anne T. Denogean, "It's Lessons Learned, Biosphere 2 Seeks Niche as Teaching Center," *Tucson Citizen,* 17 April 1998.

Lee Dye, "Arctic Scientists on Thin Ice," *ABCNEWS.com,* 25 March 1998, Internet website.

Dye, "Biosphere 2 A Joke No Longer," *ABCNEWS.com,* 10 June 1998, Internet website.

Michael Fumento, "With Frog Scare Debunked, It Isn't Easy Being Green," *Wall Street Journal,* 12 May 1999.

"Greenhouse Effects: Global Warming is Well Under Way," *Time,* 154 (13 December 1999): 54.

Christopher Hallowell, "Trouble in the Lily Pads," *Time,* 148 (28 October 1996): 87.

"Is a New DDT Killing the Frogs?" *ABCNEWS.com,* 30 September 1998, Internet website.

Kary Mullis, *Dancing Naked in the Mind Field* (New York: Vintage, 1998).

United Nations Department of Public Information, "General Information," *Earth Summit+5,* 23–27 June 1997, Internet website.

United Nations Department of Public Information, "Global Water Supplies in Peril, UN Report Finds," *Earth Summit+5,* 23–27 June 1997, Internet website.

GENETICS

The Human Genome Project. The International Human Genome Project (HGP) officially launched in 1990, was a multibillion dollar effort to map all of the estimated one hundred thousand genes on the twenty-three pairs of human chromosomes and read their entire sequence. In the center of any normal human cell there are forty-six X-shaped chromosomes, and within each chromosome is bundled a double-stranded helix of deoxyribonucleic acid (DNA). Made up of varying combinations of four different nucleotides within the DNA molecule, each gene carries instructions for everything from hair color and height to how the brain is organized. All of the genes together are collectively called the genome. Thus mapping or decoding all of the genes in the human genome would give scientists unprecedented understanding of the human body and could point to the eventual diagnosis, cure, or elimination of many genetic diseases. Francis S. Collins, director of the National Human Genome Research Institute (NHGRI) at the National Institutes of Health (NIH), asserted that this research was the most important organized scientific effort that humankind had ever attempted. By 1999 one-quarter of the human genome code had been spelled out by teams of scientists working on the HGP and by its corporate competitors. Computer technology played an important role in making genetic research possible, providing the communication and organizational medium to manage the genetic information that was discovered, and providing the tools to create machines that made it easier to sequence genes. By December 1999 scientists at the HGP had sequenced the first human chromosome. The second smallest, chromosome twenty-two, was chosen to be sequenced first because it was one of the most densely packed, with 33.5 million pieces, or chemical components. Researchers were able to find only 97 percent of the genetic material, but the results were considered complete for the time. More than thirty human disorders were already associated with changes to the genes of this chromosome, including a form of leukemia, disorders of fetal development and the nervous system, and schizophrenia. Scientists expected the decoding of the rest of the genome to come quickly.

Race to Finish. In addition to the government-funded HGP, private companies were working to map the human genome and, they hoped, to beat the HGP to the finish line in order to win lucrative patents on new genetic discoveries. Craig Venter, president of Celera Genomics Corporation, declared in 1998 that his company would have a map of the entire human genome

OTZI

In 1991 a hiker in the Otztal Alps, northwest of Merano, Italy, discovered a 5,300-year-old human body that had recently been uncovered by retreating glaciers. It was the oldest intact human body ever to be found. Nicknamed "Otzi," the prehistoric man died while he was between twenty-five to thirty-years old. He was dressed in a robe made from the furs of ibex, chamois, and deer, and he wore a fur cap. His leather shoes were insulated with grass and he carried a small arsenal: a dagger fashioned from flint, a bow made of yew, fourteen viburnum and dogwood arrows carried in a fur quiver, and a copper-bladed ax. Archaeologists conjectured that he was exhausted and suffering from exposure when he lay down in a shallow rock cavity at an elevation of 10,500 feet.

Source: Joseph Poindexter, "The Century in Science: The Iceman," *Discover,* 21 (January 2000): 52.

Demonstrators in Chicago protest at Food and Drug Administration (FDA) hearings on the safety of genetically altered food on 18 November 1999 (AP/Wide World Photos)

ready in 2001, years ahead of the original HGP estimated date of completion of 2005. His announcement forced the leaders of the HGP to move their deadline to 2003 for a finished product and 2001 for a "working draft." Critics of Venter and other private researchers argued that racing to decode the entire human genome would make for sloppy and incomplete results, but private companies retorted that the painstakingly precise research done at the HGP was unnecessarily slow and unnecessary. They argued that mapping all of the genes in encyclopedic detail delayed scientists from finding and concentrating on the really important genes that could be analyzed to help prevent or cure genetic diseases, and that details of a rough map could be filled in later. Scientists at the HGP predicted that Venter's genome map would be full of holes and worried that his financial backers would lock it up with patents, blocking the advancement of science. Many felt that allowing patents on human genes was unethical, anyway, since no one should "own" the human genetic code. In addition, patents on genetic information could deter scientists from doing important research since only the company or government institution that held a patent could profit from new discoveries that pertained to the patented information. Still, as long as patents on genetic discov-

eries were being awarded, the promise of these lucrative rights and scientific prestige drove researchers in the private and public sector to hasten their efforts toward a finished map of the human genome. In the summer of 2000, Celeva and HGP jointly announced the completion of the mapping project. All researchers agreed that once the gene sequence was completed, the next step would be to look into how genes varied from one person to the next, decoding, in effect, the genetic basis of human individuality.

The Nematode Worm. On 9 December 1998 scientists announced that they had finished the first complete genetic blueprint of a multicelled animal, the nematode worm. The worm, *Caenorhabditis elegans,* was less that one millimeter long, about as big as the head of a pin. It took researchers at Washington University and the Sanger Center in Cambridge, England, eight years to break the DNA code of the nearly twenty thousand genes of *C. elegans.* At least 40 percent matched genes found in other animals, researchers said. Genes involved in cancer and immune diseases were found in the worm, as well as genes necessary to make a nerve or muscle cell. This discovery meant that understanding the worm's genetic code could give researchers clues about human genes. Thanks to the worm, scientists were able to isolate a gene linked to Alzheimer's disease in humans. Many scientists hoped that the genetic map of the worm might act as a kind of Rosetta stone to help decode the information held in DNA.

Sources:

Ann Kellan and Reuters, "Scientists Crack Genetic Code of Lowly Worm," *CNN.com*, 11 December 1998, Internet website.

Jeffrey Kluger, "Who Owns Our Genes?" *Time*, 153 (11 January 1999): 51.

Michael D. Lemonick and Dick Thompson, "Racing to Map Our DNA," *Time*, 153 (11 January 1999): 44.

Rhonda Rowland and the Associated Press, "Scientists Sequence First Human Chromosome," *CNN.com*, 1 December 1999, Internet website.

Dick Thompson, "Gene Maverick," *Time*, 153 (11 January 1999): 54.

GENETIC ENGINEERING

Cloning. In 1997 Ian Wilmut at the Roslin Institute in Scotland successfully cloned a sheep named Dolly from the cell of an adult ewe. Wilmut replaced the DNA in a normal sheep egg with the DNA from the ewe's mammary gland, and then inserted the egg into the womb of another sheep, where it grew into an exact replica of the donor. This achievement was the first time that an animal had been cloned from an adult cell, not an embryo. It was a milestone in genetic engineering, indicating that it was possible to mass produce identical copies of a mammal. Many people worried about the ethical implications of this new technology, since the same techniques used to make Dolly might one day be used to clone humans. In 1993 researchers at George Washington University had cloned human embryos and nurtured them in a petri dish for several days. Their project had provoked protests from ethicists and politicians, and raised concerns about genetic engineering in general. When a group of scientists experimented with creating headless mice that could provide organs and tissues to others, people feared that headless human clones kept solely as organ donors for their "parent" might be a tempting next step. Fearing the moral implications of such a future, President Bill Clinton issued a moratorium banning research into human cloning in all federally sponsored laboratories and asked that private researchers also comply with the ban. In January 1998, however, physicist Richard Seed announced his intention to attempt human cloning. Research into animal cloning continued. In 1998 mice and calves were replicated, and a second sheep was cloned with a gene added so that she would produce a blood-clotting factor in her milk. China announced that it would use cloning to reproduce giant pandas in order to save the treasured species. In 1999 researchers found evidence that cloning may have its limits. They discovered that Dolly, then three years old, had DNA typical of a much older animal. This suggested that she was genetically older than her birth date, possibly because she was cloned from the cells of a six-year-old ewe. Despite the controversy and potential limitations, scientists argued that cloning could have beneficial uses for

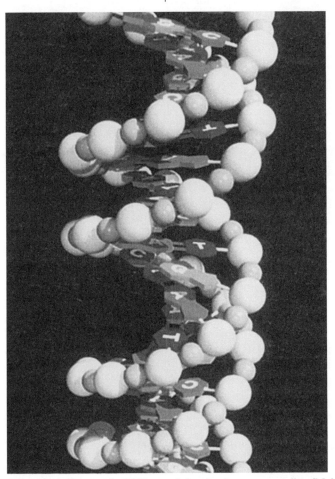

A computer-generated image of a DNA strand showing its genome coding (Mel Prueitt)

In the 1990s DNA fingerprinting, or the identification of an individual through a sample of his or her DNA, became an indispensable tool in investigations of murder, rape, and other crimes where the offender might leave at the scene a trail of physical evidence in the form of hair, skin, or bodily fluids. In 1998 the Federal Bureau of Investigation (FBI) opened a national DNA database of people convicted of certain serious offenses. DNA testing was also used in some cases to prove the innocence of convicted prisoners. A group called the Innocence Project sought DNA testing for convicted rapists and murderers, and by 1999, at least sixty-one inmates had been exonerated.

DNA fingerprinting had other uses as well. In 1992 the U.S. Army began collecting blood and tissue samples from all new recruits as part of a "genetic dog tag" system, aimed at better identifying the remains of soldiers killed in combat. Paternity testing using DNA became widespread during the decade, and billboards proclaiming, "Who's the Father? Call 1-800-DNA-TYPE" could be seen in major cities across the country. DNA testing was also used to identify the remains of historical figures. In 1993 British scientists used DNA fingerprinting to identify the bones of the Russian Tsar Nicholas II and members of his family.

The use of DNA fingerprinting played a major role in two of the most publicized legal cases of the decade: In the 1995 murder trial of former football star O. J. Simpson, and in the 1998 federal investigation of President Bill Clinton's affair with White House intern Monica Lewinsky. In the Simpson case, prosecutors claimed that DNA samples taken from the crime scene proved that Simpson was involved in the murder, but jurors sided with the defense, who claimed that the samples were contaminated or had been planted as part of a conspiracy against Simpson. The Simpson case was important in pointing out that DNA testing was not foolproof. The methods used to collect, store, and test the DNA samples had to be precise and scientifically controlled for the results to be accepted as conclusive. In the investigation that led to Clinton's impeachment, DNA tests proved that semen stains on Lewinsky's dress were the president's.

Sources: Wolf Blitzer, John King, and Bob Franken, "Sources: Lewinsky testifies she had a dozen sexual encounters with Clinton," *CNN.com*, 6 August 1998, Internet website.

"O.J. Simpson Main Page: The Evidence." *CNN.com*, Internet website.

"Innocent Man Freed After 16 Years in Prison," apbnews.com, 16 June 1999, Internet website.

James Shreeve, "Secrets of the Gene," *National Geographic*, 196 (October 1999): 42–75.

society, including preserving endangered species and advancing medical understanding of aging and diseases.

Pharming. When Wilmut began working on cloning sheep, his goal was to create genetically altered farm animals that would manufacture therapeutic proteins in their milk. In this field of genetic engineering, often referred to as "pharming," animals were created whose bodies manufactured drugs to treat human diseases. Scientists could alter the DNA of animal cells and embryos, often by adding human genes, in order to "engineer" animals that produced milk containing specific proteins for medicines or that had organs that would not be rejected after being transplanted. Cloning technology could then be used to breed genetically identical flocks of these animals. Polly, Dolly's playmate at the Roslin Institute, was both a transgenic and cloned animal. Her milk produced human Factor IX, a blood-clotting protein used to help treat hemophilia B. By the end of the decade, the Scottish firm had also created sheep whose milk contained a protein used to treat cystic fibrosis, and a transgenic calf whose milk contained a human protein that provided essential amino acids, making it nutritious for premature infants who could not nurse.

Other companies were also successful in creating animals that produced pharmaceutical products, medicines, or nutrients for humans. In 1996, for example, Genzyme Transgenics announced the birth of Grace, a transgenic goat carrying a gene that produced BR-96, a monoclonal antibody that was being tested and developed to deliver conjugated anticancer drugs.

Frankenfood. Genetic modification of food crops, which helped to make them impervious to insects and the elements, was a boom industry in the 1990s. Globally, sales of the technology rose from $75 million in 1995 to $1.5 billion in 1998. It also sparked heated debates, however, about the safety of modified crops and the effects that genetic modification might have on other plants and animals. In February 1994 Bovine Growth Hormone (BGH) was approved by the Food and Drug Administration (FDA) and entered the market. The hormone, a natural protein found in cows, was artificially manufactured in vats of genetically altered bacteria. When cows were given extra doses of the hormone, their milk production rose by as much as 15 percent. Monsanto, the company that marketed BGH, claimed that milk from BGH-treated cows was indistinguishable from ordinary milk. The FDA, National Institutes of Health (NIH), and American Medical Association (AMA) concurred. Critics of BGH nevertheless pointed out that cows treated with the hormone were more susceptible to udder infections, and they worried that antibiotics used to treat these infections would be present in the milk. Some milk retailers responded by asking that their suppliers not use BGH, but its use by the end of the decade was still widespread. By 1999 the debate over genetically modified foods had grown hotter. A Cornell University researcher reported in May that genetically altered corn crops, approved and planted since 1996, were killing off monarch butterflies. The corn (known as Bt corn) contained a gene spliced from the common soil bacterium *Bacillus thuringiensis*, which allowed the corn to give off a toxin that was lethal to corn borers, but supposedly harmless to humans and other insects. Yet, pollen from the corn was found to kill monarchs. The Bt gene was also regularly spliced into potatoes (as protection against the Colorado potato beetle) and cotton (against the boll weevil). Later, an article in the British medical journal, *Lancet,* outlined preliminary findings that genetically altered potatoes were linked to intestinal problems in lab rats. Genetically modified food was much more closely regulated in Europe, where the European Union (EU), unlike the United States, required labels on products containing genetically modified produce. For most of the decade, Europeans were much more concerned about genetically altered foods than Americans. By 1999, however, American protesters began loudly to question the safety of genetically modified crops. By then, half of all soybeans, about a third of the corn crop, and substantial quantities of the potatoes grown in the United States came from plants that had been genetically altered. Proponents of genetically modified foods argued that they could help to feed an ever-more crowded world, making foods richer in nutrients, less prone to spoilage, and easier to grow. Opponents worried that plants with an innate herbicide might breed a new species of resistant "super-insects," or that modified seeds might cross-pollinate with other plant species, resulting in potentially dangerous consequences. In addition, they argued that the health risks to humans had not been adequately studied. Monsanto heightened the controversy by announcing plans to create "terminator" seeds that would contain a set of genetic instructions to render themselves sterile after just one planting, thus enforcing the patent right on the seeds. The United Nations expressed concern that terminator seeds would force farmers into total dependence on seed companies. Others worried that cross-pollination might render other plants sterile. Finally, after huge public outcry, Monsanto abandoned its research into its terminator seeds. By the turn of the century, however, the debate over other genetically modified crops had not been resolved.

Sources:

"Animal Pharm," *Discover,* 21 (January 2000): 26.

"Cloning," *The 20th Century, CNN.com,* Internet website.

"Cloning Technology Progresses Despite Controversy," *CNN.com,* 13 January 2000, Internet website.

"Dolly Had a Little Lamb," *Time International,* 150 (4 May 1998): 40.

Philip Elmer-Dewitt, "Brave New World of Milk," *Time,* 143 (14 February 1994): 31.

Mike Eskenazi. "Frankenfood: Why Does Europe Find It Scarier?" *Time Daily,* 18 October 1999, Internet website.

"The Genetics Revolution: Plant and Animal Applications," *Time Daily,* 1999, Internet website.

Frederic Golden, "Who's Afraid of Frankenfood?" *Time,* 154 (29 November 1999): 49+.

J. Madeleine Nash, "Dr. Ian Wilmut . . . and Dolly," *Time,* 150 (29 December 1997/ 5 January 1998): 98–99.

"Of Corn and Butterflies," *Time,* 153 (31 May 1999): 80+.

INTERNET

Information Superhighway. The revolutionary technology of the Internet and the World Wide Web created a whole new digital culture in America during the 1990s. The idea of an "Information Superhighway" that could link anyone in the world through nearly instantaneous data transmission became a reality, and terms such as "cyberspace" and "the Net" became part of everyday speech. The introduction of the Internet into mainstream American society changed the ways that business and commerce was conducted, information exchanged, and social interaction carried out.

ARPANET. Joseph C. R. Licklider, a psychologist at M.I.T., first envisioned the idea of an Internet, or an interconnected computer network. In August of 1962 he wrote a series of memos discussing his "Galactic Network" concept. He envisioned a globally interconnected set of computers through which anyone with a computer terminal could quickly access data and programs from another computer. In 1962 Licklider became the first head of the computer research program at the Advanced Research Projects Agency (ARPA), a bureau of the Department of Defense. Created in 1958 by President Dwight D. Eisenhower, ARPA was the first U.S. response to the Soviet launching of *Sputnik* (4 October 1957). The mission of ARPA was to ensure that the United States maintained a lead in applying state-of-the-art technology for military capabilities and to prevent technological surprises from an enemy. In 1969 scientists at ARPA created the first-ever computer network, known as the ARPANET. It was originally intended to promote access to big, time-sharing supercomputers among U.S. researchers through a cooperative network. From these humble origins, it grew into the worldwide phenomenon known as the Internet.

Packet Switching. One of the key innovations that made the Internet possible was packet switching. A telephone used "circuit switching," by which a circuit was opened between two machines, forming a connection that allowed information to be passed back and forth. Each circuit was "dedicated," meaning only those machines it connected could exchange information. Circuit switching was problematic, however, because if for any reason the connection was broken, the entire communication was lost. In the 1960s, fearing a loss of communication in the event of Soviet attack, the U.S. military began to experiment with ways around circuit switching. To ensure national commu-

An image of William Henry Gates III, of Microsoft, projected behind Apple Computer cofounder Steven Jobs, who is announcing the alliance formed between their two companies, on 6 August 1997 (AP/Wide World Photos)

nication even without telephones, the United States needed an indestructible communications network. Moreover, this network needed to have no central control station that would be an obvious target for enemy bombs. Paul Baran of the RAND Corporation, the foremost Cold War think tank, proposed a system of decentralized packet switching. Using packet switching, a message could get to its final destination even if part of the network was destroyed. The message to be sent was divided into "packets" and launched into the network. Each packet was like a postcard carrying some part of the message, with a "to" and "from" address, or a header, indicating where it wanted to go. Unlike a telephone system, there was no dedicated circuit opened from point A to point B; rather, the packets found their way through the network along any paths that were open to them, moving from node to node along the network. A node was like a post office that sent the postcards along toward the recipient. Each node kept copies of the packets and continued to send them out until the packets successfully reached the next node. When all of the packets reached the final destination, they were reassembled and the complete message was delivered to the recipient. Packet switching worked better than circuit switching because as long as some part of the network was still functioning, the message could successfully get through.

IMPs. To build the first ARPANET, which would link four heterogeneous mainframe computers, ARPA scientists found that the easiest way to connect the mainframes was to build identical special purpose minicomputers to form a network and to tie each mainframe to one of them. This way, the mainframe computers did not have to change to be able to communicate with each other. These minicomputers were called Interface Message Processors (IMPs). The first ARPANET used four identical IMPs, utilizing packet switching technology, to link four different mainframe computers in four different locations: a Sigma 7 at the University of California at Los Angeles (UCLA), an SDS 940 at Stanford Research Institute, an IBM 360/75 at the University of California Santa Barbara (UCSB), and a PDP-10 at the University of Utah. Since the first networks had to use telephones, and thus circuit switching, to communicate, special hardware and software was built so that if the telephone circuits failed, the IMPs, using packet switching, could try to retransmit the message. On 1 September 1969 the first IMP was plugged into the UCLA mainframe. By December 1969 all four computers were interconnected and the first network was successful. By April 1971 the ARPANET had eighteen mainframe computers hooked into its network. In October 1972 ARPA demonstrated its computer network in Washington, D.C., at the International Computer Communications Conference. This event was the first international conference on computers and communication sponsored by ARPA. At the time, ARPA had fewer than twenty-five sites on-line. After the conference the development of computer networks took off, and networks began to multiply throughout the Western world. In 1974 Bolt, Baranek and Newman (BBN), the company that built the first IMPs, opened Telnet, the first commercial version of the ARPANET.

E-mail. At first, the ARPANET could only be used to transfer data files from computer to computer. In 1971 Raymond S. Tomlinson at BBN wrote the first "killer app": e-mail. He developed the code for e-mail on his own time, for fun. Tomlinson later said, "It seemed like a neat idea." He was the first person to use the now-ubiquitous @-sign. In 1972 he modified his electronic-mail program for use on the ARPANET, where it became a quick hit with other users. E-mail quickly became the most popular application on the ARPANET, with people using it to collaborate on research projects and discuss various topics.

TCP/IP. With the proliferation of networks, a new problem emerged. Each individual Local Area Network (LAN) or Wide Area Network (WAN) essentially spoke its own language. There was as yet no communal networking language that could allow separate networks to communicate with each other. In 1973 Vinton Gray "Vint" Cerf and Robert E. Kahn teamed up to develop TCP/IP (Transmission Control Protocol/Internet Protocol), which was a set of rules, or protocols, that would allow different networks to pass their messages back and forth. The computer used to connect the networks that would know this protocol was called the gateway or router. The gateway interconnected the networks to each other, and could encapsulate packets coming from host computers and send them out to other networks. No information was retained by the gateways about the individual flow of packets passing through them, thereby keeping them simple. Even though networks were connected, there was no central agency that controlled the flow of information. In 1983 TCP/IP was adopted as the universal standard for networks, a milestone in the development of the Internet. It made possible a common, interconnected network. For the first time, the loose collection of networks that made up the ARPANET was seen as an "internet," and the Internet that would transform business, entertainment, and education in the 1990s was born.

Open Architecture. The Internet was built with an open-architecture, meaning that there were no set rules as to what it could and could not be used for. The ideas of inclusion and generality of purpose were central to the growth of the Internet. Since it was not controlled by one central source, it could be adapted to a variety of ideas and applications. In an open-architecture network, the individual networks that connected to the Internet could be separately designed and developed. Each could have its own unique interface that it offered to users and/or other providers. Thus, each network could be designed in accordance with the specific environment and user requirements of that network. The rate of evolution of the Internet was high because so many people from different areas were contributing to it, adding applications and designs that were not even thought of when the Internet was first created. There was no board of directors that dictated how the Internet could be used, or what information could be passed along it. The Internet belonged to everyone and no one.

Growth of the Internet. The mid 1980s marked a boom in the personal computer and super-minicomputer industries. The combination of inexpensive desktop machines and powerful, network-ready servers allowed many companies to join the Internet for the first time. Corporations began to use the Internet to communicate with each other and with their customers. Throughout the 1980s, more and more small networks were linked to the Internet, including those of the National Science Foundation, NASA, the National Institutes of Health, and many foreign, educational, and commercial networks. The nodes in the growing Internet were divided up into Internet "domains," known as "mil," "org," "com," "gov," "edu," and "net." "Gov," "mil," and "edu" denoted government, military, and educational institutions, which were the pioneers of the Internet. "Com" stood for commercial institutions that were soon joining in, along with nonprofit "orgs," while "net" computers served as gateways between networks.

The ARPANET was originally developed as a tool for defense research and was restricted to certain universities and think tanks engaged in government projects. For this reason, private networks such as Prodigy, Compuserve, and what became America Online (AOL) began to spring up so that individuals could join in. In 1990 the ARPANET was decommissioned, leaving the vast network-of-networks called the Internet. In 1991 the National Science Foundation lifted a restriction on commercial traffic on its NSFNET, the backbone of the Internet, opening it to commercial use. At that time, the number of Internet hosts exceeded three hundred thousand.

World Wide Web. In 1990 Tim Berners-Lee, a software engineer, invented The World Wide Web while working at CERN (*Conseil European pour la Recherché Nucleaire*), the European Organization for Nuclear Research, in Switzerland. It was based on a program he wrote for his own use in 1980 called "Enquire," and was a means for storing information using random associations that allowed him to move from one document to another through keyword links. In 1989 he proposed a global hypertext project, which he would call the World Wide Web. Building on his earlier "Enquire" software, he developed a way to more easily follow threads of knowledge within the information on the Internet by programming computers to store information in random associations. He wrote the HyperText Mark-Up Language (HTML), an easy-to-learn coding language that allowed others to create links in their documents and write their own web pages to connect into the World Wide Web. Berners-Lee also cre-

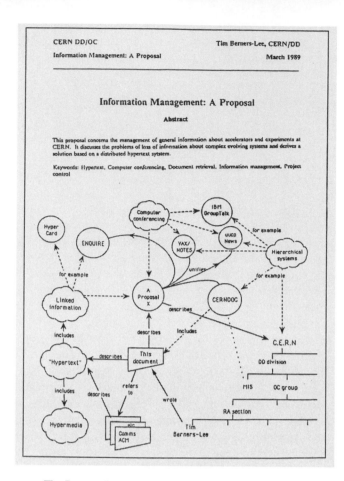

CERN DD/OC   Tim Berners-Lee, CERN/DD

Information Management: A Proposal   March 1989

Information Management: A Proposal

Abstract

This proposal concerns the management of general information about accelerators and experiments at CERN. It discusses the problems of loss of information about complex evolving systems and derives a solution based on a distributed hypertext system.

Keywords: Hypertext, Computer conferencing, Document retrieval, Information management, Project control

Tim Berners-Lee's proposal to Conseil European pour la Recherché Nucleaire (CERN) for creation of the World Wide Web (Image courtesy of the Computer Museum History Center)

ated an addressing system that gave each web page a unique location, or universal resource locator (URL), and a set of rules that allowed these documents to be linked together across the Internet. He called that set of rules HyperText Transfer Protocol (HTTP). With this addressing system nearly any Internet document, be it text, picture, sound, or video, could be retrieved and viewed on the World Wide Web. Berners-Lee also created the first World Wide Web browser, a text-based system that was able to read communications written in HTTP. The World Wide Web was released on the Internet in 1991. In the tradition of open-architecture, the World Wide Web allowed for maximum openness and flexibility. Web documents used a similar language to connect to each other, but there were no rules as to the content of these documents, and different types of browsers could be created to access them. While the World Wide Web would change the face of the Internet, it took another, easier-to-use Web browser to make it easily accessible to mainstream America.

Mosaic Browser and Netscape Navigator. Another development rocketed the Internet to nearly instantaneous acceptance by people worldwide. A new browser software for the World Wide Web was developed in 1993 by Marc Andreessen, a twenty-two-year-old student at the Univer-

sity of Illinois, along with a group of student programmers at the National Center for Supercomputing Applications (NCSA) located on the campus. Andreessen called it the Mosaic browser. While the first web browser developed by Berners-Lee was text-based, Mosaic was the first graphical Web browser, using a "point and click" interface. It encouraged users to load their own documents onto the net, including color photos, sound bites, video clips, and hypertext "links" to other documents. Mosaic incited a rush of excitement and commercial energy unprecedented in the history of the Internet. It turned the Internet into a graphically rich world, in which users could view text, use scroll bars, and move around the Web with the click of a mouse. In 1992 there were only fifty web pages on the Internet. In 1993, after Mosaic was released, the World Wide Web grew by 341,000 percent. Web browsers went commercial the next year when Andreessen cofounded Netscape Communications Corporation. Netscape released Netscape Navigator, its improved graphical browser in December 1994, and a communications revolution was on the way. That same year, Pizza Hut began accepting orders over the Internet. In 1995 Sun Microsystems released Java, an Internet programming language that radically altered the way that information could be retrieved, displayed, and used over the Internet. By the late 1990s, the Internet had become simpler to use, able to perform more complex tasks, and capable of carrying more types of information. In 1996 approximately forty million people in almost 150 countries were connected to the Internet. By 1999 there were more than eleven million domain names registered on the Web, with more than seventy million websites. In thirty years the Internet grew from a Cold War concept for communicating through the remains of a postnuclear society to an Information Superhighway that ushered in a social and economic revolution.

Sources:

Defense Advanced Research Projects Agency (DARPA) home page, Internet website.

Barry M. Leiner, Vernon G. Cerf, and others, "A Brief History of the Internet," revised edition, *Internet Society*, 14 April 2000, Internet website.

"PBS Life on the Internet: Net Timeline," *PBS Online*, Internet website.

Ben Segal, *A Short History of Internet Protocols at CERN*, CERN—European Organization for Nuclear Research (*Conseil European pour la Recherché Nucleaire*), April 1995, Internet website.

Robert H'obbes' Zakon, "Hobbes' Internet Timeline v5.0," *Internet Society*, Internet website.

INTERNET AND BIG BUSINESS

Microsoft Windows. In the 1980s Microsoft created the operating system (OS) known as Windows. Microsoft had made its name by creating DOS, the clunky OS that sat inside every IBM personal computer (PC). Windows was originally a graphical user interface (GUI) intended to run on top of DOS in order to make it easier to use. In other words, it was like a new and improved façade on top of an old building. A GUI used pictures rather than words, making the PC easy and intuitive. Computer researchers at Xerox Parc actually created the first GUI, using a mouse to point to information on the screen. Steve Jobs, cofounder of Apple Computers, saw a demonstration of the GUI at Xerox Parc and realized that it was the future of personal computers. Under his direction, Apple developed the wildly popular Macintosh with its GUI, which by 1987 was selling a million units a year, competing with the IBM PC. The Macintosh was so easy to use that it threatened the dominance of IBM, and hence, Microsoft's DOS, in the personal computing market. Microsoft answered with Windows, releasing version 1.0 in 1985. Compared to Macintosh, which had launched in 1984, Windows 1.0 was unstable and unattractive. But Microsoft continued to work on its new product. Windows 2.0 was introduced in 1987, featuring the use of icons (like the Mac), overlapping windows, and PIF files (instructions for Windows on how to run a DOS application). These additions made Windows a more attractive platform for developers, and it increased its application support and sales. Shortly after Windows 2.0 came Win/386, designed to take advantage of the Intel 80386, which could support a "virtual 86" mode and enabled Windows to run multiple DOS virtual machines with preemptive multitasking (each application is given a slice of the CPU's time). Windows 3.0, released in 1990, was a complete overhaul of the OS. It featured support for up to sixteen megabytes (MB) of random access memory (RAM) with 386 enhanced mode, increased color palette, program and file manager, multiple preemptive DOS session hierarchical menus, ini files and network support. Finally, Microsoft produced a graphical user interface (GUI) that made IBM PC's and all the PC clones as easy to use as Macintosh. Windows 3.0 sold close to 30 million copies in one year, consigning the Mac to a niche in the market. In April 1992 Windows 3.1 released a host of improvements, including the addition of True Type fonts, multimedia support, Object Linking and Embedding (OLE), and application reboot. Windows NT, introduced in July 1993, was the first version of Windows to support the thirty-two-bit programming model of the Intel 80386, 80486, and Pentium microprocessors. Windows NT also supported long file names, like those allowed by Unix systems. Windows 95, introduced on 24 August 1995 combined an operating system and graphical user interface into one package. It became the industry standard, supplanting DOS. Microsoft continued to improve its product, releasing Windows 98 on 25 June 1998, and Windows 98 Second Edition on 5 May 1999.

The Browser Wars. Microsoft CEO William Henry "Bill" Gates III built his fortune by cornering the market on PC operating systems. This was fine as long as PCs were stand-alone boxes on a desktop, but once they were connected to the Internet, a new type of software product was needed: the Internet browser. Realizing that the Internet was the future of computing, Microsoft created its own browser, Internet Explorer, to compete with Netscape Navigator, the first commercial graphical browser, developed by Marc Andreessen. Thus began the "browser wars" that led to an antitrust lawsuit against the software giant.

The base version Internet Explorer 1.0 was released in August 1995, included in the Windows 95 PLUS Pack. The original Internet Explorer 1.0 browser code was licensed from Spyglass (a commercial arm for the NCSA Mosaic browser), but the Microsoft team quickly made improvements to the original codebase. The first two product cycles occurred within a short amount of time—version 2.0 was released in November 1995 and version 3.0 in August 1996—allowing the browser to gain ground against its main rival, Netscape. Meanwhile, Netscape launched its ambitious 2.0 version, which introduced the browsing world to Javascript, frames, and plug-in technology. Internet Explorer 4.0, released in October 1997, was a big improvement over earlier versions of IE. Most importantly, IE 4.0 finally met most of the capabilities of Netscape Navigator. Internet Explorer browser soon had dominant market share, commanding at least 60 percent of the browser market with Netscape trailing at approximately 30 percent. However, Netscape alleged that Microsoft was using unfair business practices to edge Netscape out of the market. In 1998 Microsoft was charged by the U.S. Justice Department with using its monopoly on operating software—Windows—to coerce other companies to do its bidding in a broad array of business relationships.

Bundling. The case began with the claim that Microsoft was improperly "bundling" its Internet Explorer browser into its Windows software. Jim Barksdale, CEO of Netscape Communications Corporation (the former leader in the browser market), turned to the Justice Department for antitrust relief, charging Microsoft with using its dominance with Windows to put Netscape out of business, by forcing the public to buy the Microsoft Web browser, Internet Explorer, with every copy of Windows. He attacked the bundling tactic as an unfair, monopolistic practice that essentially crushed any competition. Because Windows was the number one operating system in the world, and because it came pre-installed (and therefore included in the price), bundling Internet Explorer with Windows almost guaranteed that a copy of the browser would make it to every desktop computer in America. Once the practice was started, Netscape lost most of its market share, and in 1998, the four-year-old company was bought by America Online for $4.2 billion. The case was still under consideration at the end of the decade, with U.S. District Judge Thomas Penfield Jackson presiding over the Microsoft antitrust trial. In a technological irony, both sides used e-mails written by the opposition to support their case.

IMac. Apple Computers released the iMac in August 1998. It was a computer with no floppy drive, geared toward home users. Omitting the floppy was a controversial move, but the iMac was the best-selling computer model in the months after its release.

AOL/Time Warner Merger. In early January 2000, a merger was announced between Internet Service Provider (ISP) America Online and cable company Time Warner. The companies saw themselves as positioned to speed development of the Internet and interactive content, according to a joint statement. Specifically, they would provide high-speed Internet access through broadband cable channels. Before the merger, AOL, along with the OpenNet Coalition, had been pressing for government intervention to open the broadband cable access industry, whereby people could gain Internet access through cable channels. Cable access was much faster and more reliable than the traditional "dial-up modem" system, which used telephone lines. Cable access also allowed Internet users to download much more data in less time than with a dial-up modem. Before the merger, the broadband cable market was dominated by AT&T, which had an exclusive contract with the ISP Excite@Home. AOL and other ISPs worried that, without government intervention, cable franchise owners would control Internet content and navigational services. The Federal Communications Commission (FCC) did not intervene, wanting to keep government regulation out of the emerging market. With the AOL–Time Warner merger, AOL could provide cable access to its clients. While some competitors feared that Time Warner, the second largest cable company in the United States, would only offer AOL over its broadband wires, AOL stressed that it would continue to support open access for the entire cable industry, as well as consumer choice of ISPs over all cable broadband networks. For Time Warner, the merger provided the media giant with a foothold in the Internet. Recognizing that the future of entertainment and information was digital, Time Warner through AOL positioned itself to be as big a player on the World Wide Web as it was in movies and television. The gradual shift toward broadband access meant a change in the way that websites were designed, promising an increase in media-rich content such as streaming video, better graphics, 3-D interactivity, and other data-intensive options. Still, since the majority of Internet users at the turn of the century used dial-up modems, an increase in multimedia content for them would mean delays in downloading information. Some companies put forth the idea of creating different sites for dial-up modems and broadband access.

LINUX. In 1991 Linus Torvalds, a student at the University of Helsinki, wrote the code for an alternative to the Microsoft and MacIntosh operating systems and called it Linux. He released it on the Internet for free, asking other programmers to help him develop the operating system (OS). Anyone could work on Linux, fixing bugs, adding features, and making it perfect. A more sophisticated version, Linux 1.0, was released in 1994. Linux developers kept improving the software, and by the end of the decade there were more than 140 different versions, or distributions, of Linux. All of these distributions were based on the original, free source code. Distributors could sell their versions of the OS, however, as long as developers were given proper credit and any changes to the source code were made public.

New Avenues. This approach to creating and distributing software was fundamentally different from that taken by mainstream OS manufacturers such as Microsoft and Apple. The source codes for Windows and Mac Operating Systems were closely guarded and strictly regulated. Apple and Microsoft maintained control over their share of the OS market, and reaped the revenues, but it also made for better compatibility between hardware and software, and between users. For example, most manufacturers built their products specifically for the Windows OS, so it was easy to buy software or hardware for Windows. It was also easier for users to exchange files, since 98 percent of PCs ran on Windows. Few hardware and software manufacturers made their products Linux compatible, and Linux users had a hard time sharing files with Windows and Mac users. Still, by 1999, with thousands of programmers around the world working on it, Linux was challenging the dominance of Microsoft in the OS market. A 1998 survey showed that 13 percent of companies used Linux on at least some of their computers and 17 percent of all servers ran on it. IBM, Dell, Intel, Oracle, and Compaq were all gearing up to support Linux at the end of the decade. As it got easier to install, Linux made more inroads into the consumer market. In 1999 Linux was coming to be embraced by the tech industry and the media. Its popularity stemmed from several factors. First, with the antitrust lawsuit against Microsoft well underway, the software giant's image as a monolithic, competition-squashing monopoly made it unpopular with many computer users. Open-source Linux emerged as an underdog by comparison. "Computer geeks" loved Linux for what it stood for. In addition, Linux was customizable, making it more reliable for niche applications than a one-size-fits-all OS like Windows. Linux was also more stable and less crash-prone than Windows NT. Plus, it was more cost-effective. For IBM to connect seventeen servers running on Linux, their total software cost was only $50. In comparison, ten client access licenses for one server running Windows 2000 would have cost $1,199.

Open Source. While Linux began to challenge Windows at the end of the decade, analysts predicted that Linux would not really take over the desktop market. Most computers came with Windows pre-installed, and Linux was not as user-friendly as the Microsoft product. Instead, experts guessed that Linux might become the OS of choice for portable, basic computing, and Internet-access devices (known as information appliances), because it was small, customizable, extremely Internet compatible, and free. Perhaps the most important contribution of Linux was the open-source model that it pioneered. This model, which hearkened back to the academic openness of the early Internet, spread to other projects, from computer games to Web browsers.

Y2K. At the turn of the millennium, people around the world worried about an impending computer-related disaster in the form of the so-called Y2K "bug." The bug was a computer glitch that was predicted to disrupt or shut down computer systems all over the world, including systems that were connected to essential services, such as water and electricity, beginning on 1 January 2000. Many nations and corporations took action costing in the billions of dollars to make sure that their computer systems were "Y2K compliant." The problem was that many old computer systems kept track of the date with a two-digit system, substituting 72 for 1972, for example. Analysts worried that as the clock rolled over to the new millennium, and these systems registered 00 instead of 2000, the computer would act as if it were the year 1900 instead of 2000. They suspected that this glitch would cause computer-assisted jets, nuclear-power plants, electricity-supply lines, and other essential services to shut down. The two-digit system became standard in 1960 with the development of the Common Business Oriented Language (COBOL), which was created by a team drawn from the Pentagon and several computer manufacturers. To save valuable memory space, years were abbreviated to two digits. Computer scientists, anticipating problems, urged companies to use the four-digit year. In 1967 the National Bureau of Standards was mandated by the White House to resolve the double-digit issue. The Bureau, under pressure from the Pentagon, stayed with the two-digit system. In 1979 one of the pioneers of COBOL, Robert William Bemer, warned in an article in the journal *Interface Age,* that the year 2000 could cause major problems. Still, there was little public worry. In 1993 Canadian Peter de Jager published an article prophetically titled "Doomsday 2000" in *Computerworld,* warning again about Y2K. The public began to take notice as the millennium loomed closer. The first U.S. Congressional hearing on the Y2K problem was held by the House Government Oversight and Reform Committee's Subcommittee on Government Management, Information, and Technology in 1996. The hearing focused on how federal agencies would convert their systems, predicting that the cost to the U.S. government would be $30 billion, with worldwide figures estimated at $600 billion. In 1998 the White House appointed John A. Koskinen as its Y2K czar. He was charged with coordinating the U.S. government effort to ensure that critical information technology systems operated smoothly through the year 2000. Even after the United States spent billions of dollars upgrading computer systems and making sure essential systems were ready for the end of the millennium, officials worried that other countries, such as China and Russia, would be crippled by the Y2K bug, and that this situation would in turn affect the United States. Many worried citizens began stockpiling food, water, and other emergency supplies in preparation for a disaster. Police, firefighters, and National Guardsmen spent New Years Eve 1999 waiting for the calendar to roll over and problems to begin. The moment passed smoothly, however, and few if any technical problems were reported.

Artificial Intelligence. The science of making machines think, artificial intelligence (AI), became a reality in the 1990s thanks to cheap microprocessors and new discoveries about how the human brain works. The study of modern AI began in the 1950s, after the invention of the digital computer. In 1950 mathematician Alan Turing published the first scientific article on AI, entitled, "Computer Machinery and Intelligence," which discussed the conditions that would determine the intelligence of a machine. Turing was widely regarded as the founder of both AI and computer science. In 1956, at Dartmouth College, a group of researchers conceived of programming a computer to model the way that humans think, and AI research was officially born. In 1960 Joseph Wiezenbaum of MIT developed a computer psychotherapist, nicknamed ELIZA, which was designed to simulate the dialogue a psychotherapist might have with a patient. The rudimentary language skills of ELIZA did not fool scientists or lay-testers into believing it was a human doctor, but the system laid the groundwork for a branch of AI called natural-language processing. Variations on natural-language processing were used in the late 1990s in Internet search engines such as *Ask Jeeves,* which allowed users to ask questions that would be answered by a computer-generated butler named Jeeves that was modeled after the Sir Pelham Grenville "P.G." Wodehouse character, and speech-recognition programs such as IBM ViaVoice Pro. Artificial intelligence was also used to create expert systems, or computers that were programmed to be experts in a specific area. The best known example of this form of AI was Deep Blue II, the supercomputer that beat World Chess Champion Gary Kasparov in 1997. Programmed to evaluate billions of possible moves, the computer essentially overwhelmed Kasparov with its sheer indefatigability. Although it was possible for scientists to create a computer whose computational abilities exceeded that of the human brain, they could not create a computer with human skills such as comprehension or the ability to set and achieve goals.

AI Advances. New knowledge about how the human brain worked was applied to AI research. After scientists discovered that the human brain was made up of a series of interconnected cells (neurons), researchers created artificial neural networks that imitated the structure of the brain. Scientists fed these neural networks genetic algorithms that combined and changed strings of symbols to evolve the most advantageous solution to a problem. Thus, they could evolve and adapt to solve new problems. These neural networks were then used to create "smart" prosthetic limbs that could adapt to changes in human muscles, and to develop more-complex artificial brains, some of which were being designed for use in robotic pets. Scientists predicted that by the year 2030, humans would be using AI-equipped technology to transcend the limits of our own brains and bodies.

Sources:

Kristina Blachere, "Thinking Machines: How Artificial Intelligence is Reshaping Technology," CNET, 18 January 2000, Internet website.

"Brief History of Microsoft Windows," Internet website.

Roger Chang, "The History of Windows," *ZDTV.com,* Internet website.

Adam Cohen, "Demonizing Gates," *Time,* 152 (2 November 1998): 58–61, 66.

Frank Condron, "Windows Timeline/History," *Frank's Windows Page,* Internet website.

"The Future of Linux," *CNET Linux Center,* June 1999, Internet website.

Jennifer Jones, "AOL Could Change Stance on Cable Access, FCC Official Says," *Infoworld*, on *CNN.com*, 13 January 2000, Internet website.

Tony Karon, "Welcome! Why You've Now Got AOL Time Warner," *Time Daily*, (10 January 2000) Internet website.

"Linus Torvalds," *Time Digital*, 27 September 1999, Internet website.

"Looking at the Y2K Bug," *CNN.com*, Internet website.

Joshua Quittner and Marc Andreessen, "The Rise and Fall of the Original Start-Up," *Time*, 152 (7 December 1998): 60.

Linda Rosencrance, "AOL/TW Deal May Change How Companies Design Web Sites," *Computerworld*, on *CNN.com*, 13 January 2000, Internet website.

Chris Taylor, "The Y2K Bug: Do We Still Have to Worry?" *Time*, 154 (29 November 1999): 64+.

"Thomas Penfield Jackson," *Time Digital*, 27 September 1999, Internet website.

Triumph of the Nerds: The Rise of Accidental Empires, television program transcripts, *PBS Online*, Internet website.

"The Twentieth Century: Artifact: Floppy Disk" *CNN.com*, Internet website.

"The Twentieth Century: Culture: Millennium Madness," *CNN.com*, Internet website.

Brian Wilson, "Internet Explorer (Microsoft®)" *Index DOT Html*, Internet website.

INTERNET AND DIGITAL CITIZENS

Who Was Connected? In September 1997 the *Wired Magazine*/Merrill Lynch Forum Digital Citizen Survey, conducted by Luntz Research Companies, polled 1,444 Americans to examine their views on technology and society. The results showed that a new technologically connected population was emerging. It divided those polled into four groups: the superconnected, who exchanged e-mail at least three times per week and used a cell phone, a beeper, a laptop, and a home computer; the connected, who exchanged e-mail at least three times per week and used three of the four technologies above; the semiconnected, who used at least one but not more than four of the target technologies; and the unconnected, who did not use any of the target technologies. Of those surveyed, 2 percent were superconnected, 7 percent were connected, 62 percent were semi-connected, and 29 percent were unconnected. The survey showed that "Digital Citizens"—connected and superconnected Americans—constituted 8.5 percent of the overall population. These Digital Citizens were young, but not as young as might be expected; there were more connected Americans in their forties than in their twenties, but only 11 percent older than fifty-five. By gender, they were almost evenly divided, at 52 percent male and 48 percent female. They were 87 percent white, 5 percent black and 4 percent Hispanic, and more than half lived in the suburbs. They were better educated than the population as a whole. More than half of the connected citizens had graduated from college, while only 16 percent of unconnected Americans had. The majority earned $30,000 to $79,000 per year, and 82 percent owned stocks, bonds, or mutual funds.

Citizens Revealed. What did the survey say about this group as citizens? It revealed that this distinct group of Digital Citizens was knowledgeable, tolerant, civic-minded, and radically committed to change. They were profoundly optimistic about the future, convinced that technology was a force for good, and that the free-market economy functioned as a powerful engine of progress. Whereas many in the media had portrayed highly connected citizens as isolated, geeky, and estranged from mainstream politics and social interactions, the poll revealed that Digital Citizens were actually highly participatory and viewed the existing political system positively, even patriotically, and that the on-line world encompassed many of the most informed citizens of the nation. These findings directly countered the common stereotypes of the Internet as a haven for alienated geeks and dangerous perverts, and the caricature of technology as a civic virus that bred disaffection from politics. In fact, the less connected people were, the more ignorant of and alienated from politics they were likely to be. The Digital Citizens stood out in their positive attitudes about the future and eagerness to embrace change. While Americans at the time were divided about whether technology was good or bad, with many intellectuals and journalistic leaders portraying technology as an out-of-control force that had an immoral impact on society, Digital Citizens viewed technology with caution, but rarely with fear. They saw technology as a powerful tool for individual expression, democratization, economic opportunity, community, and education. Furthermore, they were a socially tolerant group, embracing diversity as a healthy, positive aspect of American life, with 79 percent agreeing that a diverse workforce was more productive than one in which workers shared the same background, as opposed to the unconnected population, where only 49 percent favored a diverse workforce.

A Second Survey. A thousand days later, *Wired* repeated the survey, in February 2000, using a randomly selected sample of 815 American adults. Participants were asked to rank the importance of various technologies in their daily lives, and to rank their mastery of commonly used software programs. Based on their responses, researchers divided the sample into three groups: the "very wired" (31 percent), the "somewhat wired" (46 percent), and the "not wired" (23 percent). The "very wired" were defined as people who used four or more of the following technologies: the Internet, a cellular or wireless phone, a computer, fax, e-mail, on-line banking or investing, and on-line shopping. The "somewhat wired" used one of the targeted technologies, most often mobile phones, while the "not wired" did not identify any single piece of technology as playing an "important part" in their lives. The new survey indicated that the use of personal technology had dramatically increased since 1997. The distinction between the "connected" and the general public had become nearly meaningless, with 78 percent emerging as "very wired" or "somewhat wired." By the turn of the millennium, almost all Americans used cell phones, e-mail, or the Internet, or owned a personal computer. In addition, the attributes that were ascribed to the "superconnected" in 1997—optimism, belief in the power of markets, and social tolerance—had gone mainstream in a significant way.

Links. The findings showed a clear link among age, education level, and comfort with digital tools. Nearly everyone in the "very wired" category, 96 percent, said they used the Internet at home, work, or school, spending a median of five hours a week on-line, not counting e-mail. The majority of them, 62 percent, said they shopped on-line, 67 percent would vote on-line if they could, and 70 percent said they had a "more than basic understanding" of personal computer software. The "very wired" were the most highly educated group in the sample (45 percent were college graduates) and had the highest median household income, at $57,000. Their median age was thirty-eight. Among the "somewhat wired" group, 57 percent used the Internet, spending three hours a week on-line. Only about a quarter of them shopped on-line, and 42 percent said they would vote on-line if they could. Thirty-one percent were college graduates, and their median household income was $45,000. They were somewhat older than the "very wired" group, with a median age of forty-four. Of the "not wired" group, only about 20 percent used the Internet at home, work, or school, spending less than two hours per week on-line. Only 5 percent shopped on-line, and 26 percent said they would vote on-line if they could. They were less educated— only 17 percent were college graduates— and they earned far less than the other groups, with a median household income of $29,000. They were also much older, with a median age of fifty-six. Significantly, the results seemed to defy the conventional warnings about the digital divide. While it was true that low-income youth (who tended disproportionately to be nonwhite) had limited access to computers and the Internet, nonwhites on the whole were more optimistic than whites about the future benefits of technology. Nonwhites were more likely to use a computer either at work or school than whites, more likely to use the Internet either at home, work, or school than whites, and more likely to own a home computer or laptop. Pollsters speculated that technology was liberating for minorities, creating new differences in public opinion that transcended social differences such as race or party affiliation. The place where the digital divide did seem to exist was between generations. The chasm between the information haves and have-nots was first and foremost a function of age, with age being the most reliable indicator of attitudes about technology.

Fading Ambivalence. While Americans in 1997 were divided over whether technology was good or bad, the 2000 survey indicated that this ambivalence toward technology was fading, and a positive reaction was taking its place. Of those polled, 79 percent overall agreed that the technological advances of the 1990s had made their lives "much better" or "somewhat better." Among the "very wired" group, not surprisingly, 93 percent said technology had improved their lives. Yet, even among the "not wired," 61 percent said technology had made things better, and only 7 percent felt that it had made things worse. All three groups were again overwhelmingly positive when asked if technology had improved society at large. Still, they saw some prob-

Computer hacker Kevin Mitnick heads to court in Raleigh, North Carolina, on 17 February 1995 (Jim Bounds–News & Observer/SYGMA)

lems with technology, with privacy emerging as the single greatest concern. Only 4 percent of Internet users said they were "not worried" about the security of their personal information on the Internet. Nearly half said they were "somewhat concerned" about privacy, but that the benefits of going on-line outweighed the worry, while 47 percent said they were "very concerned" about the security of their data, so much so that they altered their on-line habits to protect themselves.

High Optimism. Overall, the survey found a high degree of social optimism about technology. American attitudes tended to focus on how to incorporate the benefits of technology into daily life while protecting citizens, especially children, from its detriments. Respondents to the 2000 poll looked more to the technological business leaders than the government to lead the way in both cases. More than 60 percent said the government should let the Internet develop on its own, only stepping in to correct problems when they arose, with nearly half indicating that they feared the government would try to overregulate the Internet. As the Digital Age progressed and citizens became more comfortable with new technological advances, it seemed that the nation as a whole became better educated, more tolerant, and more connected because of—and not in spite of—the convergence of the Internet and public life. Partisanship, religion, geography, race, gender, and other traditional political divisions were giving way to a new technological standard as an organizing principle for social and political attitudes.

Free Speech on the Internet. On 14 June 1995 the U.S. Senate passed the Communications Decency Act (CDA), by an eighty-four to sixteen vote. The CDA had its roots in a report about on-line pedophiles that aired in 1994 on the NBC show *Dateline*. Senator J. James Exon (D-Nebraska) used the program to launch a campaign to regulate on-line communication. The campaign failed on its own, but Exon's proposal, the CDA, survived as an amendment to an overhaul of the Telecommunications Reform Act of 1996. The amendment called for up to $100,000 in fines and two years in prison for putting "obscene, lewd, lascivious, filthy or indecent" language over the Internet, intended to annoy or harass, and content considered obscene by contemporary community standards. It put the Federal Communications Commission (FCC) in charge of Internet regulation and made on-line-service providers legally responsible for what their users posted. Proponents stressed that the aim of the CDA was to protect minors from "harmful" material. On 1 February 1996 both houses of Congress voted overwhelmingly to approve the Telecommunications Reform Act, including the CDA. President Bill Clinton signed the bill into law on 8 February. On the same day, the American Civil Liberties Union (ACLU) and nineteen other groups filed suit challenging its constitutionality. The ACLU charged that the definition offered by the CDA was unconstitutionally vague. It did not object to provisions banning obscene material, which it said had been defined satisfactorily for print and broadcast media for some time. It stressed, however, that "contemporary community standards" were quite different in various parts of the country. The ACLU also pointed out that the CDA would be virtually impossible to enforce against Internet users living outside the United States. Challenges to the CDA were also filed by the Citizens Internet Empowerment Coalition, led by the American Library Association (ALA), America Online, and the Center for Democracy and Technology. On 12 June 1996 a panel of U.S. District Judges issued a decision upholding a restraining order barring enforcement of the law, saying the act most likely violated the right to free speech. They stressed that, as the most participatory form of mass speech yet developed, the Internet deserved the highest protection from governmental intrusion. The case then went to the U.S. Supreme Court, where on 26 June 1997 the CDA was ruled unconstitutional. This decision was the first Supreme Court ruling on how the First Amendment and traditional free-speech principles applied to the Internet. The Supreme Court ruled that the act was too vague in its definitions and too broad in scope. The Court also pointed out that software that filtered out "indecent" material was available to parents as a means of protecting their children from obscenity on the Internet.

Web Filtering. In 1998 and 1999 debates and court cases raged over the use of Web-filtering devices in public libraries. The ACLU and other groups contended that their use constituted a violation of the First Amendment. In addition, critics charged that free information access was blocked to people who could not afford a home computer and instead relied on public libraries for Internet access, creating an unfair distribution of free information among the public. Because most censoring software looked for keywords in a website, more than just pornography and violence were often blocked. For example, when software was used to block any site that contained the word "breast," all information about breast cancer was also made unavailable. Those in favor of the Web filters argued that they were necessary to keep pornography and other undesirable material out of public libraries in order to protect children from harmful material. They claimed that adults could ask librarians to disable filtering software while they used the Internet.

A Public Forum? These battles were emblematic of the kinds of fears that free access and information sharing over the Internet sparked among U.S. citizens. While the Internet was lauded by some as the most-open public forum yet created, others worried that this freedom allowed dangerous material to be accessed by children, criminals, and others who might not deal with it responsibly. In addition to pornography on the Web, people worried about sites containing violence and hate speech, bigotry and racism, and sites containing information about how to create drugs and weapons. Many attempts were made to curtail this kind of information on the Web. Free speech advocates in the United States, however, fought fiercely to maintain open access. They worried that unnecessary regulation or censorship could cripple the growth and diversity of the Internet. Groups such as the ACLU feared that restricting free expression or enforcing ratings on websites would eventually lead to a homogenized Internet dominated by commercial interests. At the end of the decade, debates were still heated, and no real resolution was in sight. Yet, even the White House was becoming more reluctant to regulate technology, with Clinton saying in 2000 that he did not think it should be up to the president to mandate solutions, because "you don't want to kill the goose that laid the golden egg"; rather, the "technology whizzes" should devise better ways to protect the on-line privacy and security of ordinary citizens.

Hackers. By the early 1990s the Internet was being used as a tool for communication among government agencies, research institutions, and corporations. The ability to communicate freely, however, also brought concerns about privacy and security in the digital world. New words such as "hacker," "cracker," and "digital break-in" came to be part of the language; a hacker was defined as an expert at programming and solving problems with a computer, or more frequently, a person who illegally gained access to and sometimes tampered with information in a computer system. The openness of the Internet was a double-edged sword: the same technology that allowed for a free exchange of ideas and information in a cyberworld of global equality also gave rise to fears over privacy and security, not just at the individual level, but for society as a whole.

National Security. The U.S. government was especially worried about how to defend national security in an age of interconnectivity. In 1997 the Pentagon Defense Science Board urged Congress to spend $3 billion beefing up the U.S. military's defense system against information warfare. The most computer-dependent nation in the world, the United States, was uniquely vulnerable to cyberattack. The Pentagon believed that U.S. military computers were probed by outsiders close to one thousand times a day. Breaking into government computers required only smart hackers with Internet connections. These hackers could range from curious teenagers to malicious governments and individuals.

Cyber Cops. In August 1999 the Working Group was established under the leadership of Attorney General Janet Reno to address the issue of cybercrime. The group found that the Internet presented new and significant challenges for law enforcement at all levels. A report issued by the Group in March 2000 called "The Electronic Frontier: The Challenge of Unlawful Conduct Involving the Use of the Internet," recommended increased training for law enforcement officers, new investigative tools, and more legal authority on the Internet. The ACLU, however, found fault with the report. It argued that in the name of blocking Internet crime, the report contained dangerous recommendations that would strip away basic privacy, free speech, and free press protection. The Working Group's suggestion that anonymity on the Web should be abolished came under the most attack, with the ACLU arguing that anonymity is a basic constitutional right.

Infamous Hacker. One case in particular, that of Kevin Mitnick, highlighted the dilemmas that hackers brought to the American legal system. On 21 January 2000, Mitnick, age thirty-six, was released from prison after serving almost five years on charges of computer and wire fraud. He became an underground celebrity after leading the Federal Bureau of Investigation (FBI) on a three-year manhunt that ended in 1995 when investigators finally traced his electronic signals to an apartment in Raleigh, North Carolina He was the only computer hacker to make the FBI's ten most-wanted list. Mitnick, who began hacking when he was a teenager, was accused of causing millions of dollars of damage by hacking into the computers of such companies as Motorola, Novell, Nokia, and Sun Microsystems, as well as the University of California, and stealing software, product plans, and other data. Mitnick was sentenced to five years in prison in March 1999, after he pleaded guilty to five felony counts. He was given credit for about four years served while awaiting trial. In a case that highlighted the new challenges that Internet technology and security brought to the courts, Mitnick spent four years in jail after his arrest awaiting sentencing. High-tech crimes were often too complex for police and prosecutors to handle, a fact that led to unnecessary searches, arrests, and court delays. Often, the only person able to understand and explain the technical details of the alleged crime was the defendant. Lack of technical expertise by the prosecutors, and a lack of precedents in the courts contributed to delays. During the 1990s between 64 percent and 78 percent of federal computer-fraud cases were tossed out or sent to the states for prosecution. While government agencies tried to strengthen laws against cybercrimes and toughen up national defenses, many civil-rights groups argued that new laws violated individual and corporate privacy and enforced rules that were unnecessary. Some feared a threat to the decentralized, inclusive nature of the Internet if government agencies were allowed to monitor anyone's activity while in cyber-space. Another problem with prosecuting hackers was determining accurately what damages and costs had actually been incurred. In Mitnick's case, corporations were asked by the prosecutors to show the total amount of investment that went into the items (for example, software) allegedly stolen. Sun Microsystems claimed that the source code Mitnick allegedly stole was worth $80 million, even though Sun later sold copies of that same code to students and software developers for $100 each. Mitnick's lawyer argued that a distinction should be made between a recreational hacker and a thief or terrorist, since Mitnick did not destroy or erase the codes he accessed. He noted the similarity between joy riding and auto theft—two distinct crimes in California. Joy riding is a misdemeanor if the car is returned. If not, it is auto theft. The judge apparently agreed, charging Mitnick only $4,125 in damages, not the $300 million the government sought. After his release, Mitnick read a statement claiming that his crimes were exaggerated and that the prosecution and the media hindered his ability to present a legal defense. He said his crimes were simply those of trespass and curiosity. He claimed he did it for fun, never for profit. In a strange twist of events, at the turn of the century, he was advising a Senate panel on ways that hackers could infiltrate sensitive computer systems, and ways those systems could be made more secure. Mitnick counseled the panel to require agencies to assess what data is most important and to train employees to recognize an attack in progress. Mitnick boasted that, over a period of twenty years, he had hacked into every computer system he targeted except one. After his release, his lawyer stated that Mitnick planned to enroll in college and study computer technology. As part of Mitnick' s probation, however, he was prohibited for three years from using any electronic device that would give him access to the Internet.

Cyberslackers and Surveillance. Many employers worried about the time that e-mail and Internet surfing took away from worker productivity. A 1999 survey showed that people who surfed the Internet preferred to do it at work; 84 percent said they sent personal e-mail from work, 90 percent admitted to surfing recreational sites at work; and more than half "cyber-shopped" on company time. In response, there was a sharp increase in workplace surveillance as employers worried about lost productivity and possible lawsuits arising when workers viewed pornography at work. In 1999 more than two-thirds of U.S. companies engaged in electronic surveillance of their workers. There was an increase in so-called cybersnooping, made possible by newly developed software. Twenty-seven percent of companies were reviewing employee e-mail, up from 15 percent in 1997, and 21 percent were going over computer files, up from 13 percent. This new technology allowed bosses to see everywhere their employees had been on the Internet, everything they had read, and to read personal e-mails sent to and from work accounts. Xerox fired more than forty workers in 1999 for allegedly idling away up to eight hours a day on pornography websites, and downloading videos that choked the computer system, preventing other workers from sending or receiving e-mail. The company used new snooping software that allowed it to review every website its forty thousand computer users visited each day. Some companies used filtering software that barred access to adult websites. The majority of nonwork-related Web surfing happened not at pornographic sites, however, but at more benign sites such as the on-line-stock-trading site E*Trade. Many employers did not mind their workers using company time and computers for occasional personal use, as long as it did not interfere with work getting done, but some banned personal use altogether, angering workers who saw the bans as unreasonable. It was legal for a boss to fire a worker even for a five-minute visit to a recreational website, but some privacy experts challenged an employer's right to read personal e-mail, although the courts never ruled against it. Since copies of e-mails remained on a company's server, deleting them from a personal desktop computer did not protect a worker from company surveillance.

Sources:

Jay Branegan, and others, "Welcome to the Wired World," *Time*, 149 (3 February 1997).

Karen Breslau, "One Nation, Interconnected," *Wired*, 8 (5 May 2000), Internet website.

Ted Bridis, "Wanted: Hacker to Advise," *ABCNEWS.com*, 2 March 2000, Internet website.

John Katz, "The Netizen," *HotWired*, 12 December 1997, Internet website.

Michael Krantz, "Censor's Sensibilities: Are Web Filters Valuable Watchdogs or Just New Online Thought Police?" *Time*, 150 (11 August 1997): 48.

Michael J. Martinez, "A Non-Prosecution Complex," *ABCNEWS.com*, 13 August 1999, Internet website.

Ellen Messmer, "ACLU Asks Virginia Court to Ban Web-filtering by Libraries," *NetworkWorld Fusion News*, 9 February 1998, Internet website.

Keith Naughton, "Cyberslacking," *Newsweek* (29 November 1999): 62–65.

"Net Timeline," *PBS Life on the Internet, PBS Home*, Internet website.

David Noack, "Reno Attacks Anonymity on Internet," *APBnews.com*, 9 March 2000, Internet website.

Chris Oakes, "Internet Ratings Redux," *Wired News*, 9 September 1999, Internet website.

"Reno vs. ACLU: The Battle Over the Communications Decency Act," *CNN Interactive at CNN.com*, 1997, Internet website.

Michael White, "Mitnick Released From Prison," *ABCNEWS.com*, 21 January 2000, Internet website.

INTERNET AND SOCIETY

Society and the Internet. In the four years after Netscape Navigator was introduced to the public (between 1994 and 1998), the number of Americans using the Internet increased from five million to sixty-two million, with traffic on the Internet doubling every one hundred days. By 1999 there were more than eleven million domain names registered on the Web, with more than seventy million websites. "www," "@," and "dot com" had become new icons of the so-called Information Age. The Internet was only thirty years old. No other invention had grown so fast to reach so many people. The Internet was a revolution in communications. With e-mail, people could share ideas and information faster and cheaper than through telephones or letters. "Virtual communities" proliferated, with far-flung groups of people with shared interests connecting in chatrooms and newsgroups. Internet users had access to websites all over the world, and with the proliferation of commercial websites, they could shop for virtually anything on-line. By the end of the decade more e-mail was being exchanged than first-class letters delivered by the U.S. postal system. The Internet was responsible for one-third of the total U.S. economic growth in 1998, generating $301 billion in business. Yet, no one really controlled it.

Telepresence. One of the key social effects of the Internet was "telepresence," or the idea that people could communicate, work, shop, or find information all over the world just by logging onto the Internet. The Internet erased traditional barriers of space, time, and distance, and allowed for a whole new world of information and idea sharing. Telecommuting, whereby people could do their jobs over the Internet without having to go to a central office, became a widespread phenomenon. By 1999, for example, 29 percent of the management force of AT&T telecommuted. This translated into less reliance on cars and a decrease in the need for centralized office space. Many predicted that telecommuting would change the character of U.S. cities, as more and more people could choose where to live without concern for being close to a company office.

Decentralization. The new Internet technology decentralized power and allowed anyone to be a publisher or pundit, immediately sending information and ideas into a globally accessible forum. The idea that anyone with an Internet connection could publish information and have it immediately available to anyone else in the world was a major revolution that, some argued, rivaled the printing press in importance. One reporter noted that the symbol of the atomic age, which tended to centralize power, was a nucleus with electrons held in tight orbit; by contrast, the symbol of the digital age was the Web, with countless centers of power, all equally networked. Many saw the Internet as a sure foe to government censorship or totalitarianism, even in times of war.

The Dark Side. While the Internet was heralded as a tool for advancing the cause of freedom and democracy, many people feared the darker side of its instantaneous

Jewish Americans at the Kosher Cyber Café in New York (AP/Wide World Photos)

information sharing. The Internet, as an open, unregulated medium, had equal potential for good and evil. It could unite people across distances, but it was indifferent to whether they were chess-players, crusading environmentalists, or neo-Nazis. Parents feared that their children could access hate speech and pornography, especially when the generation gap between users meant that children were often much more Internet-savvy than their elders. Many also worried that the Internet was alienating, that people were plugged in to their computers, subordinated to the technology that was supposed to be liberating them, at the expense of real social interaction.

Spam. One unfortunate side effect of the global network was "spam," or Internet junk mail. As the Internet grew more sophisticated, and more people conducted business on-line, it was inevitable that the same kind of mass marketing and commercialism that infused life outside of the Web should make its way into the Web, filling e-mail boxes with offers from people or businesses the recipient might never have heard of, and colonizing websites with marketing "banners" that ran across the tops and bottoms of pages.

Sources:
Ivan Amato, "Can We Make Garbage Disappear?," *Time,* 154 (8 November 1999): 116+.

"Best of 1997," *Time,* 150 (29 December 1997).

Walter Isaacson, "The Passions of Andrea Grore," *Time,* 150 (29 December 1997): 46–53.

"Modern Marvels: The Internet: Behind the Web," television, *The History Channel,* 2000.

Stephen Segaller, *Nerds 2.0.1: A Brief History of the Internet* (New York: TV Books, 1998).

Robert Wright, "The Web We Weave," *Time,* 154 (31 December 1999): 197+.

MOBILE TELEPHONES

Wireless World. Mobile, or wireless, communications became a significant part of American life during the 1990s. At the turn of the century a *Wired* poll showed that the mobile phone was the most important technological development of the era, with a majority of respondents indicating that a mobile phone was the technology that they used most in their daily lives, more than a computer, e-mail, or the Internet. Mobile telephones became ever smaller and more portable, and could be carried inconspicuously. Lower costs and greater convenience gained millions of new customers for mobile-phone technology every year. By 1995 there were approximately eighty-five million users of cellular telephony worldwide, with thirty-two million in the United States alone. As of

June 1999 there were more than seventy-six million wireless communications subscribers in the United States, with 38 percent of these using digital wireless technology.

History of Mobile Communications. The walkie-talkie, developed in the late 1930s, was one of the first practical applications of mobile communications. Along with the first mobile telephone, invented in 1941, the walkie-talkie used radio waves to communicate. The first commercial wireless telephone service was actually available in 1946, but the equipment for it filled the trunk of a car, and only a handful of conversations could take place at any one time in the same city. To overcome these drawbacks, in the late 1940s, scientists at Bell Laboratories invented cellular technology, which allowed many mobile conversations to take place at once. With cellular technology a city was divided into small areas, called cells, each of which contained a large antenna, transmitter, receiver, and connection to the public telephone network. Another group of Bell scientists miniaturized the equipment used in mobile phones by inventing the transistor, forerunner of the microchip. Yet, in 1949, the Federal Communications Commission (FCC) restricted companies to creating very small systems that would only handle twenty-three simultaneous calls at once. Each company could only have a total of 250 customers, or subscribers, per city. As a result of the FCC ruling, even though the technology for cellular systems was available, they were not built. The growth of wireless communications did not begin until 1983, when the FCC repealed its restrictions. Bell Labs' Advance Mobile Phone System (AMPS) became a reality, and mobile phones began to be used throughout North America, mainly by business executives in their automobiles. During the 1980s and early 1990s, regions of the world such as Western Europe and Latin America also began to develop wireless communications. By the end of the decade, mobile phone use was widespread among the general population.

Signals. When a call was placed from a mobile phone, the caller's voice was converted into a radio signal and sent through a radio transceiver at the cell site to the Public Switch Telephone Network. The cellular system was able to maintain the call as the user moved from one geographical area to another, transferring the call from cell to cell in order to use the antenna that was closest to the user at any given time. This way the call was always handled by the cell with the strongest signal. Cellular phone systems could also be digital. With digital systems, the audio was converted to digitized samples, or numbers that represented the time-varying voltage levels at specific points in time, transmitted as ones and zeros. At the receiving end, the samples were converted back to voltage levels and smoothed out so that the listener heard nearly the same audio message. With digital transmission, the ones and zeros could not easily be confused or distorted during the transmission, and extra data was typically included in the transmission to help detect or correct any errors. This made the sound cleaner than analog, which tended to pick up interference such as radio frequency noise.

Sources:

Karen Breslau, "One Nation, Interconnected," *Wired*, 8 (5 May 2000), Internet website.

Roberto Diaz, "How Do Cell Phones Work?" *RobertoDiaz Homepage*, Illinois Institute of Technology, 20 January 2000, Internet website.

"The History of Wireless," *WOW-com*, Cellular Telecommunications Industry Association, 2000, Internet website.

"The Wireless Story," *Lucent Technologies*, 2000, Internet website.

MUSIC AND MOVIES

MP3. The Moving Picture Experts Group Level 3 (MP3) was a computer format that compressed tens of megabytes of a compact disc (CD)-quality audio file into just a few megabytes, making high-quality digital audio easily downloadable. Music industry executives were concerned about MP3, arguing that it was being used to steal intellectual property. Many websites offered songs without copyright permission, posing a major threat to record labels and performers. Record companies launched efforts in 1998 and 1999 to bring what they saw as bootlegging under control. Still, some recording artists felt that MP3 might be a good thing, introducing a new way to bring their music to the public. Many musicians saw MP3 as a way to sidestep the powerful music publishing business and use the Internet to distribute their songs. With the introduction of portable devices in 1998, MP3 became the most popular trend in consumer audio. The portable digital music players stored music files on tiny memory cards and played them back. They held about an hour's worth of music, which could be changed as often as the user wished, and could be carried anywhere. In 1998 record companies sued the makers of a portable MP3 player in an effort to keep them off the market, but lost the case.

DVD. Digital Versatile Disk (DVD) is a high-capacity multimedia data-storage medium, designed to accommodate a complete movie on a single disk, as well as content rich multimedia and high quality music-channel audio. DVD started in 1994 as two competing formats, Super Disc (SD) and Multimedia CD (MMCD). In 1995 developers agreed on a single format called DVD, and in 1997 it became publicly available in the United States. DVD-Video, the first widely used application in the United States, was embraced by the movie industry, which wanted a CD-like disk capable of holding a high-quality recording of a full-length feature with surround-sound audio. By the end of the 1990s DVD-ROM, the format for delivering data and multimedia content that could be played by computers equipped with DVD-ROM drives, was forecast to grow even faster than DVD-Video. With its capacity to hold the increasingly complex multimedia applications that were being developed, DVD-ROM was used widely in the computer industry and for new video games with better and more realistic video content. DVD-Audio was scheduled to be released at the end of the decade.

Poster for the first all-computer-animated movie, *Toy Story* (1995), produced by Pixar and Disney

Copyright Law. The Digital Millennium Copyright Act, signed into law by President Bill Clinton on 28 October 1998, prohibited "any technology, product, service, device, component, or part thereof, that . . . is primarily designed or produced for the purpose of circumventing protection afforded by a technological measure that effectively protects the rights of a copyright owner." The act was designed to protect the traditional rights of the music recording industry and the movie industry, which saw a loss of control over their copyrighted recordings with the advances in technology such as MP3 and DVD, and the dissemination of de-encryption information over the Web.

Prosecuting Thieves. Material on DVDs was encrypted to prevent unauthorized copying. In January 2000 two judges ruled that websites posting copies of DeCSS software, designed to circumvent the copy protection of DVDs, violated the Digital Millennium Copyright Act. DeCSS was originally created by Norwegian programmers who reverse-engineered the DVD Content Scrambling System (CSS) to give computers running the Linux operating system DVD playback capability. The San Francisco-based Electronic Frontier Foundation

(EFF) argued that the cases against DeCSS sought to censor free speech critical to science, education, and innovation. Reverse-engineering of DVD security systems, EFF contended, was important for system inter-operability, and for preserving individual rights in a democratic information age. Also, since the act only covered the United States, it could not guard against non-U.S. websites that posted de-encryption software. DeCSS was written outside of the United States, so it was not directly subject to U.S. law. Only U.S. based websites that carried the software could be prosecuted. The controversy over the Digital Millennium Copyright Act highlighted the difficulties that the U.S. government had in enforcing traditional rights of the music and movie industries over the Internet. These industries were in the midst of rapid changes that, at least in the short run, meant more power for the individual users and less control by big companies.

Toy Story. In 1995 Walt Disney Pictures released the huge hit, *Toy Story*, the first full-length animated feature to be created entirely by artists using computer tools and technology. The completely 3-D computer-generated movie took four years to make. To create the movie, Disney teamed up with Pixar Animation Studios, a pioneer in computer graphics and the first digital animation studio in the world. The movie contained a total of 77 minutes and 1,561 shots of computer-generated imagery. Using their own proprietary software, with computers as their tools, the moviemakers introduced a three-dimensional animation look, with qualities of texture, color, vibrant lighting, and details never before seen in traditional animated features.

Star Wars, Episode I: The Phantom Menace. George Lucas's long-awaited prequel to the *Star Wars* trilogy set a new benchmark for digital special effects. Of the 2,200 shots in the movie, 1,965 were digitally enhanced. Some of Lucas's fabrications were spectacular in an obvious way, such as the pod race; others were amazing because they were invisible. For example, if the director did not like an actor's facial expression in one scene, he would simply digitally replace it with a expression from another shot.

Sources:

Scott Bradner, "DVD and the Digital Copyright Act," *Network World Fusion,* on *CNN.com,* 4 February 2000, Internet website.

"DVD History," Disctronics Manufacturing (UK) Ltd. Homepage, 1999, Internet website.

"George Lucas," *Time Digital,* 27 September 1999, Internet website.

Ann Harrison, "Civil-Rights Group Blasts DVD Suit," *Network World Fusion,* on *CNN.com,* 19 January 2000, Internet website.

Rick Lockridge, "Downloading Music from the Internet: Theft or Democracy?" *CNN.com,* 3 March 1999.

Lockridge, "Music for the New Millennium is Bypassing Record Industry," *CNN.com,* 2 March 1999, Internet website.

"MP3 Revolutionizing Music Business," *CNN.com,* 2000, Internet website.

"Toy Story," *MOVIEWEB,* 1995, Internet website.

NANOTECHNOLOGY

Atom Level Manipulation. One of the most revolutionary technologies being explored during the 1990s was nanotechnology, which involved the manipulation of matter at the atomic level. Although it was still in the developmental stages by the end of the decade, important advances had been made toward mastering this extreme miniaturization of technology. Scientists speculated that nanotechnology would eventually have profound effects on information technology, medicine, national security, energy, and the environment, sparking the production of supercomputers that fit into the palm of a hand, or tiny devices to fight disease and repair injury from inside the human body. Nanotechnology dealt with matter in its most elemental forms: atoms and molecules. The basic measuring unit in nanotechnology, the nanometer, was the width of three atoms. Ten nanometers was one thousand times smaller than the diameter of a strand of human hair. Nanotechnology, scientists predicted, would make it possible to manufacture, replicate, or distribute any substance known to humans as easily as information could be replicated on a computer. By the end of the 1990s, extensive nanotechnology research was already underway in Japan, Europe, and the United States. In the United States at least eleven government agencies were funding molecular nanotechnology research, including the National Institutes of Health (NIH), National Aeronautics and Space Administration (NASA), Defense Advanced Research Projects Agency (DARPA), and the Departments of Energy and Defense. The White House had identified nanotechnology as a critical research area.

Negative Aspects? Despite the excitement about the potential benefits of nanotechnology, many scientists and ethicists worried that there could be major negative impacts with its development. Concerns ranged from what might happen if the technology fell into evil hands, to the fear that tiny robots, or nanobots, could mutate and swarm out of control. A nonprofit organization called The Foresight Institute dedicated itself to preparing society for the coming age of nanotechnology and making sure that it would be used for the good of humanity. In addition, many scientists stressed that by the time it was understood how to make nanotechnology a daily reality, society would better understand how to control it.

Applications. Nanofabrication, or the creation of tiny, nanoscale objects, was being practiced at the turn of the century. Computers proved essential to the nanofabrication process, from modeling to manufacturing. To turn a computer model into a real object, different processes were used. Molecular nanotechnologists use a process of trial and error, mixing the right chemical combinations in a beaker and hoping for success. Mechanical nanoscientists used more precise techniques involving lithography to carve specific structures into silicon wafers. With electron-beam lithography, which involved drawing on a silicon wafer with a focused beam of electrons, scientists could produce objects as small as twenty nanometers. To study these creations, the electron microscope was essential, the most important of which was the scanning tunnel microscope (STM). This was the first microscope that allowed scientists to see individual atoms. Its inventors, Gerd Binnig and Heinrich Rohrer, won the Nobel Prize in physics in 1986. Also crucial to the development of nanotechnology in the 1990s was the discovery of and research on fullerenes.

Fullerenes. In 1996 Richard E. Smalley and Robert F. Curl Jr., of Rice University, along with Harold W. Kroto of the University of Sussex in Brighton, England, were awarded the Nobel Prize in chemistry for their 1985 discovery and characterization of fullerenes, a family of soccer-ball-shaped carbon molecules that contributed to the field of nanotechnology. They made their discovery by zapping graphite with a laser beam and mixing the resulting carbon vapor with a stream of helium. When they examined the resulting low-density gas, they found a large number of molecules made of precisely sixty carbon atoms. Guessing that the structure of these molecules resembled the geodesic dome designed by architect/engineer R. Buckminster Fuller, they named them buckminsterfullerenes, later known simply as "buckyballs." The buckyball (C60) was a tiny hollow ball of carbon; the holes inside them measured just one billionth of a meter, or one nanometer.

Cowinners of the 1996 Nobel Prize in chemistry, Robert
F. Curl Jr. and Richard E. Smalley (on screen in
background). Curl holds a model of the fullerene,
a carbon molecule they discovered with Harold
W. Kroto (AP/Wide World Photos)

Fullerenes in Action. The researchers soon found that
the number of carbon atoms in the molecules could vary,
opening the way for the discovery of many new types of
fullerenes, as the family of molecules became known. At
first thought only to exist in the laboratory, fullerenes were
later discovered in nature, both in space and on Earth.
Although fullerenes were first discovered in 1985, it was
not until 1990 that other researchers found a way to make
large enough quantities of them to be useful for study.
Researchers soon created fullerenes that contained a single
metal atom, fullerenes layered inside each other, called
"buckyonions," and fullerenes that stretched into long tubes
capped with half of a buckyball or another fullerene at each
end. Some could hold atoms of other elements in their hollow interiors; others could conduct electricity. Given the
versatility of fullerenes, scientists predicted that they would
someday be used for, among other things, drug-delivery
systems, superfine electrical wires, and hairlike tubes of
unprecedented tensile strength.

Nanotubes. Researchers were also able to produce thin
tubes with closed ends, called nanotubes, arranged in the
same way as fullerenes. In May 1998, Smalley, who then
directed the Center for Nanoscale Science and Technology, and his coworkers announced a method for cutting
single-walled carbon nanotubes (SWNTs), or tubular
fullerenes, into fullerene pipes. Previously, SWNTs were
produced in the form of nearly endless, highly entangled
ropes of nanotubes, insoluble in organic solvents, making

it difficult to explore their chemistry and applications.
Nanotubes were one hundred times stronger than steel,
yet six times lighter. Nanotechnology researchers envisioned nanotubes as the connectors and cables in future
miniaturized electronics.

By 1999 organizations including IBM, Lucent, the
National Science Foundation and NASA were investigating the possibilities of nanotechnology. The science was
mostly experimental, carried out with computer models
and high-powered microscopes. By the turn of the century,
practical results included microscopic electronic components called micromachined electromechanical systems,
whose most common use was in car air bag sensors. Governments around the world were spending around $430
million annually in nanotech research.

Sources:

Robert Curl Jr., personal e-mail correspondence with author, 10 March
2000.

Ron Dagani, "Much Ado About Nanotubes," *Chemical & Engineering
News,* 77 (11 January 1999): 31–34.

"From Buckyballs to Used Cars," *Time,* 148 (21 October 1996): 52–53.

Alicia Neumann and Kristina Blachere, "How Nanotechnology Will
Change the World," *CNET,* 20 October 1999, Internet website.

Bruce Nichols and Alexandra Witze, "2 Rice Researchers are winners of
Nobel Prize in Chemistry," *Dallas Morning News,* 10 October 1996.

The Royal Swedish Academy of Sciences, "The 1996 Nobel Prize in
Chemistry," *The Nobel Foundation,* 9 October 1996, Internet website.

Stephen Schowengerdt, "$18.9 Billion Sought to Fuel Department of
Energy in 2001," *CNN.com,* 11 February 2000, Internet website.

Chris Stamper, "Science of the Very Small: Nanotech Visionaries Promise
Wonders," *ABCNEWS.com,* 1999, Internet website.

SPACE

NASA. Facing criticisms early in the decade that his
agency was wasting money, Daniel S. Goldin, director for
most of the 1990s of the National Aeronautics and Space
Administration, announced that NASA would find ways to
do more with less. His management mantra was "faster,
better, cheaper." NASA had great successes during the
decade, including the Mars Pathfinder Lander, built for a
tenth of the cost of its predecessors and hailed as a huge
success. In addition, NASA returned American hero John
Herschel Glenn Jr., the first American to orbit the Earth,
to space in 1998, to a surge of public approval. The space
agency, however, did suffer some humiliating losses during
the decade. The $194 million Mars Polar Lander, with the
Deep Space 2 Probe, was launched on 3 January 1999 and
lost on 3 December. Worse, perhaps, was the catastrophic
failure of the Mars Climate Orbiter, launched 11 December 1998 and lost in September 1999. The prime cause of
the failure was that the builder of the spacecraft, Lockheed
Martin Astronautics, provided one set of specifications in
old-fashioned English units, while its operators at the
NASA Jet Propulsion Laboratory were using the metric
system. The report on the failure also uncovered management problems that let the mistake go undiscovered,
including poor communication between mission teams,
insufficient training, and inadequate staffing. With the
"faster, better, cheaper" approach, the navigation team was

COMETS

On 22 July 1995 two men independently discovered a previously unknown comet at about the same time. Alan Hale, a professional astronomer, saw the comet from his home in southern New Mexico, while Tom Bopp, an amateur stargazer, saw it from the Arizona desert. Named after the two men, it was known as Comet Hale-Bopp. Scientists soon determined that the comet—a chunk of streaming ice, chemicals, and dust on a multi-millennial trip around the sun—was going to provide a great show for people on Earth. Estimated to have a nucleus twenty-five miles in diameter and a tail several million miles long, Hale-Bopp was thought to be the biggest and brightest comet to come near the Earth since 1811. Though it came no closer to Earth than 122 million miles, it was easily visible to the naked eye throughout much of 1997. It was not expected to return near Earth for more than two thousand years.

In 1994 Comet Shoemaker-Levy 9 provided the opening act for Hale-Bopp, when over the course of a week it crashed in fragments into Jupiter, the collisions visible to backyard astronomers on Earth. Shoemaker-Levy 9 provided scientists with their first opportunity to watch a comet collide with a planet, giving them an idea of what could happen if a comet were to crash into Earth.

Source: "The Twentieth Century: Innovations: Comets," *CNN.com*, Internet website.

---

seriously overworked trying to run three missions at once. Still, one of the advantages of the new streamlined management style was that when probes did fail, as some inevitably would, the loss was relatively small. Mars Observer, which was launched 25 September 1992, and vanished in August 1993 just before Goldin took office, cost the nation more than $1 billion, compared with the $125 million price for the Mars Climate Orbiter. More memorable than its failures were the great NASA successes that awed the nation during the decade.

The Hubble Space Telescope. In 1990 the space shuttle *Discovery* carried into orbit the Hubble Space Telescope (HST), one of the most significant NASA projects to date. The shuttle astronauts released the telescope into orbit about 370 miles above Earth. Because it did not have to look through the distorting prism of the atmosphere, it could view objects with greater brightness, clarity, and detail than any telescope on Earth. Hubble initially appeared to be a failure, as a flaw in the main mirror of the telescope meant that all images it sent to its operators were out of focus, but a shuttle repair mission in 1993 fixed the problem. The telescope then sent back spectacular, unprecedented photographs of planets, stars, and distant galaxies. It allowed scientists to look deeper into space than ever

before, providing evidence that supported the Big Bang theory, and indicating that the universe could be younger than previously thought. It also identified disks of dust around young stars that suggested an abundance of planets in the universe, which might mean a greater chance of life in outer space.

Life on Mars? In 1996 NASA officials called a news conference to announce that a meteorite from Mars found in Antarctica in 1984 was discovered to contain organic compounds, minerals, and "carbon globules"—all of which indicate the presence of bacterial life on Mars. They also speculated that wormlike structures seen by electron microscopes could be the fossil remains of Martian microorganisms born billions of years ago, when Mars was warmer and wetter. If the evidence was correctly interpreted, it could mean that life existed on Mars and might possibly be found on other planets as well. The announcement made banner headlines. The evidence presented by NASA, however, came under attack from many experts. A UCLA specialist on ancient bacteria said it was unlikely that the findings proved bacterial life. In 1998 three papers on meteors were published suggesting that the same features were found in lunar meteorites and that the Mars meteorite was forged at temperatures too high for the formation of bacteria. Even NASA admitted that the evidence was not conclusive.

Pathfinder. On 4 July 1997 two unmanned spacecraft landed on Mars, the Mars Pathfinder and a rover stowed aboard it called Sojourner. The Mars Pathfinder, cushioned by large air bags, crash-landed on Mars and almost immediately began to send back dazzling images from the surface of the planet. Sojourner, the first autonomous vehicle to travel on another planet, rolled out onto the surface to sample soil and rocks. Pathfinder continued its work for three months, sending back 2.6 billion bits of information and 16,000 images. Its last communication with Earth came on 7 October; an effort to hail the spacecraft on 1 November was unsuccessful. The Mars Global Surveyor orbiter also arrived at Mars in 1997, with the mission of circling the planet for two years to map its surface. NASA hoped that these maps would help find landing sites for future missions, planned for 2001, 2003, and 2005.

Living in Space? The International Space Station, a cooperative project involving the United States, Russia, Canada, Japan, and eleven members of the European Space Agency, was billed as a "city in space." It was first conceived by NASA in 1983, but went through many design changes and consumed large sums of money before the first piece was ever built. As envisioned in the 1990s, the station would eventually be the size of a football field and weigh 520 tons when completed, and it would serve as a platform for scientific experiments and space research. On 20 November 1998 a Russian Proton rocket blasted off from the Baikonur Cosmodrome in Kazahkstan, carrying the first piece of the station, the *Zarya* (Sunrise) module, providing the initial power, communications, and propulsion for the station. The second piece, the Unity connecting module, was brought into orbit a month later by a U.S.

The Hubble Space Telescope, launched 24 April 1990 (NASA—Johnson Space Center)

shuttle. At the end of the decade, the joint program was awaiting the launch of the Russian service module that would house hundreds of astronauts and cosmonauts over the life of the station. The key source of energy for the station was to be solar panels. Critics charged that the station was too expensive, with an overall initial cost of $40 to $60 billion, and an estimated $98 billion cost for the fifteen-year life of the project. Other detractors said the station had little real utility. It would be too expensive to manufacture anything aboard, and scientific experiments could be done more cheaply if the station were automated. Despite the criticisms, the International Space Station was being readied for its first three-member crew, scheduled to arrive in early 2000. Supporters of the project argued that it would allow for unprecedented scientific experiments in the near-zero gravity of space and serve as a platform for innovations in the next century.

Mir. The Mir space station was the culmination of the Soviet effort to maintain a long-term human presence in space. The permanently manned space station regularly hosted two to three cosmonauts, who performed scientific and technical experiments. At the end of the decade, Mir had been in orbit for thirteen years, having completed more than 79,300 trips around the Earth while hosting cosmonauts and astronauts from dozens of nations.

Through the 1990s, NASA sent nine shuttle missions to dock with Mir. These missions contributed to the creation of the International Space Station, as Mir's design was the inspiration for the international project. In addition, seven American astronauts spent time aboard Mir, including Shannon W. Lucid, whose six months aboard the Russian space station earned her the title of America's most experienced astronaut.

Sources:
Dan Cray, "Mars Reconsidered," *Time*, 154 (20 December 1999): 91.

Mark W. Curtiss, "Mir Space Station," *Maximov Online*, 2000, Internet website.

"Discovery-Mir dock in Space," *CNN.com*, 4 June 1998, Internet website.

"First Space Segment Orbiting Smoothly," *CNN.com*, 20 November 1998, Internet website.

"The Twentieth Century: Innovations," *CNN.com*, 1999, Internet website.

WARFARE

Battlefield Dominance. Technology played an important part in warfare in the 1990s, helping to make campaigns shorter and more precise, and ensuring U.S. military superiority through technology. During the Persian Gulf War (1991) the United Nations (UN) forces functioned with a computer-like war plan that devastated essential

Soldiers from the 24th Mechanized Infantry in chemical-weapons gear in Saudi Arabia, November 1990 (AP/Wide World Photos)

Iraqi command and control facilities. Superior weaponry and better information through technological resources helped UN forces to dominate the Iraqi military.

Chemical and Biological Weapons. Chemical and biological weapons were, unlike nuclear weapons, easy to produce, hide, and use. Biological warfare was the use of pathogens to harm or kill an adversary's military forces, population, food, or livestock. Any nation with a reasonably advanced pharmaceutical and medical industry had the capacity to mass-produce biological weapons, which were especially threatening because they could be self-replicating; simply infecting a few individuals could lead to a mass outbreak that could kill thousands. Yet, biological warfare was unpredictable. Biological agents could spread into unintended areas and were difficult to clean up. In the 1990s there was a general agreement among many countries that biological warfare was inhumane; however, many countries were suspected of harboring supplies of biological weapons, including the United States. Chemical weapons could be manufactured in a laboratory by any trained chemist with the right materials. Some of the most feared biological weapons included anthrax and botulinum toxin. Anthrax is an airborne bacteria that produces a toxin that could be fatal when inhaled; by the turn of the century, the U.S. military was routinely administering anthrax vaccines to its members. The bacteria botulinum toxin killed by

causing suffocation and respiratory failure, and could be fought with the injection of an antitoxin or by wearing a gas mask. Other possible chemical weapons included VX, a drop of which could kill by blocking the transmission of impulses along the nervous system; mustard gas, which caused painful blisters all over the body; and Sarin, a gas that, when absorbed through the respiratory tract or the skin, could cause death by suffocation. Desert Storm brought home to Americans the fear of chemical and biological weapons. Fortunately, no chemical weapons were used in the conflict, but the specter was raised, and for much of the decade, Americans were determined to rid other countries of these low-cost, highly dangerous agents. Beginning with this brief war, finding and destroying Iraqi biological and chemical weapons was a major preoccupation for the U.S. government and the UN throughout the decade. In March and April 1991 the UN voted that Iraq must disclose information on its weapons of mass destruction, and remove or destroy them. Yet, UN weapons inspectors were repeatedly thwarted in their efforts to find the Iraqi chemical and biological arsenal.

Sources:
Desert-Storm.com, Internet website.

Scott D. McCulloch, and others, "Biological Warfare and the Implications of Biotechnology," *Cal Poly CBW Page*, Spring 1996, Internet website.

"Strike on Iraq—Biological and Chemical Weapons: What they are and what they can do," *CNN.com*, 1998 Special Report, Internet website.

HEADLINE MAKERS

MARC ANDREESSEN

1971-

FATHER OF THE MOSAIC BROWSER AND NETSCAPE NAVIGATOR

Background. Born 9 July 1971, Marc Andreessen was often referred to as the "boy-wonder" of the new Information Age. The self-proclaimed "media junkie" helped to create a revolution in the way people accessed and shared information. In 1993 Andreessen was a student working at the National Center for Supercomputing Applications (NSCA) in Urbana-Champagne, Illinois, when he created an easy-to-use, point-and-click graphical interface browser for the Web, called Mosaic. (A Web browser is a computer program that retrieves and interprets documents on the World Wide Web.) That same year, he and his coworkers at NCSA released free versions of Mosaic for Windows and Macintosh. By the end of the year the browsers were being downloaded from the NCSA at an average rate of one thousand per day. While the invention of the World Wide Web made the Internet accessible to anyone, it was the invention of the Mosaic browser that permitted Web use to explode in popularity.

Commercial Ventures. After Mosaic was released to the public, companies wanting to commercialize the product began approaching Andreessen. In addition, users began to request improvements. Andreessen realized that Mosaic needed to continually evolve in order to meet the changing needs of the public. Along with Jim Clark, founder of Silicon Graphics, Andreessen set out to form his own company to commercialize the browser. The company, Netscape Communications, released its browser, Netscape Navigator 1.0, in 1994. It became an overnight success. Soon, however, the dominance of Netscape in the browser market was challenged. Software giant Microsoft came out with its own browser, Internet Explorer, and, critics claimed Microsoft used its monopoly in desktop computers to edge Netscape out of competition. The battle led to an antitrust lawsuit against Microsoft by the U.S. Justice Department. By the end of the decade, the lawsuit was still in progress, but a faltering Netscape was bought out by America Online (AOL) in 1998, just four years after Andreessen and his colleagues had created the company. Andreessen became the first technology officer of AOL in March 1999, but quit later that year, announcing that he would dedicate his time to nurturing start-up companies.

Sources:

Shannon Henry, "Discussion with Netscape Co-Founder Marc Andreessen," *Washingtonpost.com*, 16 September 1999, Internet website.

Henry, "New Mission for a Young Visionary," *Washington Post* (12 July 1999).

Joshua Quittner and Marc Andreessen, "The Rise and Fall of the Original Start-Up," *Time*, 152 (7 December 1998): 60.

TIM BERNERS-LEE

1955-

INVENTOR OF THE WORLD WIDE WEB

Background. Tim Berners-Lee created the World Wide Web, revolutionizing the Internet and making the vast sums of information it contained easily accessible to anyone with a computer. Born 8 June 1955, in London, Berners-Lee was encouraged to think creatively about science from an early age. He studied physics at Queen's College, Oxford, graduating in 1976, and once built a working computer out of spare parts and a TV set. After attending Oxford, he spent two years working for Plessey Telecommunications Ltd., a major British Telecom equipment manufacturer, and then at D. G. Nash Ltd. From June to December 1980 he consulted as a software engineer at CERN (*Conseil European pour la Recherché Nucleaire*) in Geneva.

Inventing the Web. While at CERN Berners-Lee wrote a program designed for storing information using random associations and called it "Enquire," short for *Enquire Within Upon Everything* (1856), a Victorian-era encyclopedia he remembered from his childhood. "Enquire" was never published, but it later became the basis for the development of the World Wide Web. The program was written, as he put it, to "keep track of all the random associations one comes across in real life and brains are supposed to be so good at remembering but mine wouldn't." Later, while working again at CERN, he proposed a global hypertext project, to be known as the World Wide Web, which would build on his earlier "Enquire" software. He could already link documents within his own computer, but he wanted to be able to link documents from one computer to another without having to manage a central database. He figured the easiest way to accomplish this task was to open his computer to others and allow them to link their documents with his. To this end, he wrote a relatively easy-to-learn coding system called HyperText Mark-Up Language (HTML), which allowed Internet users to add links into their text. Berners-Lee also designed an addressing scheme that gave each Web page a unique location, or universal resource locator (URL), and a set of rules that allowed these documents to be linked together on computers across the Internet. He called that set of rules HyperText Transfer Protocol (HTTP). With this new addressing system, nearly any Net document—text, picture, sound, or video—could be retrieved and viewed on the World Wide Web. Berners-Lee then created the first World Wide Web browser, which would allow users anywhere to view his creation on their computer screen. He proposed his project in 1989, began work in 1990, and the World Wide Web debuted on the Internet in 1991. From that point the Internet and World Wide Web grew as one.

WWW. The impact of his invention was enormous. He took a system whose difficulty to navigate limited its use to academic and scientific communities, and made it useful and available to the world. In five years the number of Internet users jumped from six hundred thousand to forty million. His approach allowed for maximum openness and flexibility. All World Wide Web documents are similar, but every browser can be different. Berners-Lee fought to keep the World Wide Web open, nonproprietary, and free. In 1994 he went to work at MIT, directing the W3 Consortium, the standard-setting body that helped software designers and other companies to agree on openly published protocols rather than holding one another back with proprietary technology. Five years later he became the first holder of the 3Com (Computer Communication Compatibility) Founders chair at the Laboratory for Computer Science at MIT.

Sources:

Joshua Quittner, "Network Designer: Tim Berners-Lee," *TIME.com*, Internet website.

"Tim Berners-Lee," *W3C (World Wide Web Consortium)*, Internet website.

EILEEN COLLINS

1956-
ASTRONAUT

Background. U.S. Air Force Lieutenant Colonel Eileen Marie Collins was the first woman ever selected to pilot, and later command a mission on a space shuttle. Born 19 November 1956, in Elmira, New York, Collins graduated from Syracuse University in 1978 and became one of the first women to go straight from college into Air Force pilot training. She was a T-38 instructor pilot and a C-141 aircraft commander, was chosen to join NASA in 1990, and became an astronaut in 1991. By 1999 she had flown more than five thousand hours in more than thirty different types of aircraft.

Shuttle Commander. On 5 March 1998, at the White House, Collins was officially named the first woman Space Shuttle commander. She led the crew of STS–93 on a five-day mission aboard space shuttle *Columbia* on 22–27 July 1999. The crew deployed one of the most precious cargoes ever taken into space: the $1.5 billion Chandra X-Ray Observatory, a huge, sophisticated telescope that would allow astronomers to see into deep space, observing black holes and quasars, in order to obtain more information about the origins of the universe.

Sources:

"Eileen Collins," *Sharing NASA: Women of NASA*, Internet website.

"Eileen Collins," *Space Physics and Aeronomy on the Web*, The Regents of the University of Michigan, 2000, Internet website.

Alain L. Sanders, "Beam Me Up, Eileen," *Time Daily*, 23 July 1999, Internet website.

JOHN GLENN

1921-
ASTRONAUT, POLITICIAN

Background. John Herschel Glenn Jr. was born 18 July 1921 in Cambridge, Ohio. He attended Muskingum College in New Concord, Ohio, and received a bachelor of science degree in Engineering. He received honorary doctoral degrees from nine colleges and universities. Glenn served as a naval aviator in World War II and the Korean War. He joined the ranks of legendary astronauts on 20 February 1962, when he climbed into the *Friendship 7* (Project Mercury) capsule and lifted off on an *Atlas-6*

rocket, becoming the first American to orbit the Earth. His orbital flight lasted four hours, fifty-five minutes, and twenty-three seconds, all but seven minutes being in weightlessness.

Politician in Space. On 16 January 1998 NASA announced that Glenn would return to orbit. From 29 October to 7 November 1998 he served as a Payload Specialist 2 on the STS-95 crew aboard the space shuttle *Discovery*. At age seventy-seven, Glenn was the oldest man ever to go into space. He was chosen for this space mission while serving as a four-term Democratic U.S. Senator from Ohio, a position he had held since 1974. Glenn had lobbied NASA to send him back into space in order to use him for research on aging. Space was a good place for geriatric study because of similarities between what happens to a body in zero gravity and what happens naturally over time on Earth. Glenn said he hoped to learn whether the "aging effect" of zero gravity, which included loss of bone density and muscle mass, manifested itself in different ways in people who had already been through the aging process. The 3.68 million-mile journey took the *Discovery* around the Earth 134 times. After the shuttle landed, Glenn underwent four hours of data collection for aging experiments.

Celebrity Mission. The nine-day mission included launching and recapturing a satellite and testing new hardware for the Hubble Space Telescope (HST), but Glenn's presence aboard the shuttle was clearly the focus for the media and the millions of people watching. NASA officials estimated that as many as one million spectators came to Cape Canaveral, Florida, to watch the liftoff in person. Among those present were President Bill Clinton and Hillary Rodham Clinton, many entertainers, and more than three thousand media representatives, as opposed to the mere hundreds who normally attended shuttle launches. Some critics argued that the mission was simply a public-relations stunt for NASA. By returning an American hero to space, the agency boosted its public image and garnered support for the high-budget projects, including the International Space Station, it had planned for the coming years. In response to these criticisms, NASA director Daniel S. Goldin announced simply that he was glad for the public interest that was generated by Glenn's return to space and that the goal of NASA was to open the space frontier so that every American could benefit. He also added that he hoped Glenn's mission would inspire older Americans to take on new adventures. On 1 March 1999 NASA renamed its Cleveland center the "John H. Glenn Research Center at Lewis Field."

Sources:

"Biographical Data," *Glenn Research Center*, NASA, Internet website.

David M. DeFelice, "John Glenn: Space Pioneer," *Glenn Research Center*, NASA, Internet website.

Lee Dye, "Glenn: Space is Our Destiny," *ABCNEWS.com*, 1998, Internet website.

"Glenn, Other Astronauts Get Down to Business," *CNN Interactive*, 29 October 1998, Internet website.

John Holliman, "It's Official: Glenn Will Return to Space," *CNN Interactive*, 16 January 1998, Internet website.

Holliman, "John Glenn Will Return to Space," *CNN Interactive*, 15 January 1998, Internet website.

"'I Feel Fine': Glenn Returns to Earth," *CNN Interactive*, 7 November 1998, Internet website.

SHANNON LUCID

1943-
ASTRONAUT

Backround. Shannon Matilda Wells Lucid was born on 14 January 1943, in Shanghai, China, but she grew up in Bethany, Oklahoma. She received a bachelor of science degree in chemistry from the University of Oklahoma in 1963, and master of science and doctor of philosophy degrees in biochemistry from the University of Oklahoma in 1970 and 1973, respectively. Selected by NASA in 1978, Lucid became an astronaut in August 1979. She married Michael F. Lucid of Indianapolis, Indiana, and has two daughters and one son.

NASA Record. Lucid was qualified for assignment as a mission specialist on space shuttle flight crews. Some of her technical assignments included the Shuttle Avionics Integration Laboratory (SAIL); the Flight Software Laboratory in Downey, California, working with the rendezvous and proximity operations group; Astronaut Office interface at Kennedy Space Center, Florida, participating in payload testing, shuttle testing, and launch countdowns; spacecraft communicator (CAPCOM) in the JCS Mission Control Center during many space shuttle missions; Chief of Mission Support; and Chief of Astronaut Appearances. A veteran of five space flights, Lucid had logged 5,354 hours (223 days) in space by 1999. She served as a mission specialist on STS–51G (17–24 June 1985), STS–34 (18–23 October 1989), STS–43 (2–11 August 1991), STS–58 (18 October to 1 November 1993), and served as a Board Engineer 2 on the Russian space station Mir (launching 22 March 1996 aboard STS–76 and returning 26 September 1996 aboard STS–79).

Honors. Lucid received many awards, including the Congressional Space Medal of Honor, awarded in 1996 by President Clinton. She was the first and only woman to have earned this award. She was also awarded the Order of Friendship Medal by Russian president Boris Yeltsin in 1997. This honor was one of the highest Russian civilian awards and the highest award that could be presented to a noncitizen. She held the U.S. single mission space flight endurance record, six months, on Mir. On that mission Lucid traveled 75.2 million miles in 188 days, 4 hours.

Mir. Part of Lucid's mission aboard Mir was to study how lengthy stays in space affect the human body. Bone mass is lost and muscles begin to atrophy when there is no gravity for them to work against. In addition, as fluids move from the lower body into the upper body, less blood is produced, and so astronauts may lose as much as a pint of blood a month, which can be a problem when they return to Earth. During her stay aboard Mir, Lucid exercised for two hours a day on stationary bicycles and a treadmill in an attempt to counteract bone and muscle loss, so NASA could learn how to prevent these problems in future flights. In addition, Lucid conducted biochemistry experiments with quail eggs and cultivated dwarf wheat to determine how things grow in microgravity and also to learn what supplies could be grown in space during long missions.

Sources:
Kathleen Adams, and others, "Notebook," *Time,* 194 (16 December 1996).

Jeffrey Kluger, "Marathon Woman," *Time,* 148 (30 September 1996): 63.

"Shannon Lucid," *Sharing NASA: Women of NASA,* Internet website.

"There's No Place Like Home, " PBS Online Newshour, transcript, 26 September 1996, Internet website.

NICHOLAS NEGROPONTE

1943-
COMPUTER PROGRAMMER, AUTHOR

Background. By envisioning the merger of newspapers, television, entertainment, and computers, Nicholas Negroponte became a prophet and visionary of the Digital Age. He grew up in Switzerland, London, and New York in a wealthy shipping family. Negroponte studied at MIT, where as a graduate student he specialized in the then-new field of computer design. He joined the faculty there in 1966 and for several years divided his teaching time between MIT and visiting professorships at Yale, University of Michigan, and the University of California at Berkeley.

Organizations. In 1968 Negroponte founded the pioneering Architecture Machine Group at MIT, a combination lab and think tank responsible for many radically new approaches to the computer-human interface. In 1980 he served as founding chair of the International Federation of Information Processing Societies' Computers in Everyday Life program. In 1982 he accepted the invitation of the French government to become the first executive director of the Paris-based World Center for Personal Computation and Human Development, an experimental project originally designed to explore the potential for computer technology in enhancing primary education in underdeveloped countries. Most famously, Negroponte was cofounder

and director of the MIT Media Laboratory, an interdisciplinary, multimillion-dollar research facility sponsored by nearly 170 corporations worldwide. Throughout the decade, the Media Lab led advances in digital video and multimedia technologies. At the end of the decade, researchers at the Media Lab were focusing on the problem of "how bits meet atoms," or how electronic information overlapped with the everyday world. He has served on the board of Motorola and provided start-up funds for more than twenty companies.

Author. Negroponte cofounded and was a columnist for *Wired,* a magazine covering computers, the Internet, and culture related to high technology. He authored the best-selling *Being Digital* (1995), which has been translated into more than forty languages. The book presents a visionary description of the digital future. Negroponte predicted in *Being Digital* that the Internet population would reach one billion by the year 2000 and observed that "bits know no borders." He was lauded for appreciating that digital technology was a medium of popular culture and that being digital was a fundamental cultural change, impacting absolutely everything in daily life.

Sources:
"About Nicholas Negroponte, the Author of *Being Digital,*" *Open Book Systems, Online Archive,* Internet website.

"Nicholas Negroponte," *The Media Lab,* MIT, Internet website.

"Nicholas Negroponte Biography," *TCP Online,* 13 April 1995, Internet website.

Nathaniel Wice, "The Billions and Trillions of Negroponte's Cyber Prophesies," *The Netly News,* 24 September 1998, Internet website.

CRAIG VENTER

1946-
GENETICIST

Background. Craig Venter graduated from high school in 1964, with the reputation of being a chronic discipline problem, and moved from San Francisco to Southern California to sail and surf. In 1967, when he was twenty-one, he went to Vietnam as a Navy hospital corpsman. Venter planned to become a doctor after the war and work in underdeveloped countries, but upon earning a Ph.D. in six years, he decided to go into in medical research. He married Claire Fraser, a molecular biologist, and the pair joined the National Institutes Health (NIH).

Research. In the 1980s Venter was studying genes at the NIH when he came up with a new, faster way to decode DNA by feeding messenger RNA (mRNA), copied into a more stable form known as cDNA, into an automated gene sequencer he had acquired for his laboratory. When Venter published his first paper based on this work, scientists had identified only about four thousand genes, each one representing years of painstaking labor. Venter's paper added 347 new genes to that list, and soon he was finding twenty-five per day. James Watson, director of the National Center for Human Genome Research (NCHGR) at the NIH, and codiscoverer of the structure of DNA, however, argued that Venter's findings were too abbreviated and incomplete, saying that if the NIH tried to patent his work, genetic research would be entangled in legal issues and slowed down. A battle ensued in the NIH, leading to the resignation of both Watson and Venter, along with Venter's wife.

A New Start. Venter then took an offer from a venture capitalist to head his own private research facility, which he named the Institute for Genomic Research (TIGR). In 1994 he teamed up with Nobel Prize winner Hamilton Smith of Johns Hopkins University, in order to map the entire genome of *Haemophilus influenzae,* a bacterium that caused ear infections and meningitis. The bacterium, which had 1.8 million genetic letters, was successfully decoded within a year using Venter's method. This was the first time the genetic secrets of an entire living organism had been exposed. By the end of the decade, a total of twenty genomes had been fully decoded worldwide, ten of them at TIGR. In 1998, Venter teamed up with Perkin-Elmer, the company that made the automated gene sequencer and had just come out with a gene-mapping computer fifty times as fast as older models, to form a new corporation called Celera (derived from the word "celerity," meaning swiftness). The company proposed to finish a map of the entire three-billion-letter human genome by 2001. Venter admitted that his "shotgunning" procedure would leave gaps in the sequence where segments could not be fitted perfectly, but he argued that those could be filled in later. Many scientists doubted whether he would actually be able to complete his work by 2001, but the threat of being beaten to the punch by Venter led the HGP to reevaluate its procedures and move forward its target date to 2003, with a "working draft" deadline of 2001.

Sources:

Jeffrey Kluger, "Who Owns Our Genes?" *Time,* 153 (11 January 1999): 51.

Michael D. Lemonick and Dick Thompson, "Racing to Map Our DNA," *Time,* 153 (11 January 1999): 44.

Dick Thompson, "Gene Maverick," *Time,* 153 (11 January 1999): 54.

PEOPLE IN THE NEWS

Texas billionaire **Edward P. Bass,** envisioning the eventual colonization of Mars, funded the creation of Biosphere II in 1991, in order to study how earthlings might survive in a totally enclosed, greenhouse-like environment that mimicked conditions on Earth. The experiment failed, and Biosphere II was turned into a research facility for Columbia University.

Commander **Curtis L. Brown,** pilot **Steven W. Lindsey,** flight engineer **Stephen K. Robinson,** mission specialists **Scott E. Parazynski** and **Pedro Duque** (of Spain), and payload specialist **Chiaki Mukai** (of Japan) were the six astronauts who accompanied former astronaut, U.S. senator, and senior citizen **John Herschel Glenn Jr.** on his return to space aboard the shuttle *Discovery* in October 1998.

In 1995 **R. Paul Butler** and **Geoffrey W. Marcy** helped develop a way to detect planets orbiting distant stars as far away as forty or fifty light years. On 18 October, **Michel Mayor** and **Didier Queloz** were the first astronomers to actually find a planet circling a distant star. Butler and Marcy did not actually see the planets, which would require technology even more sophisticated than the Hubble Telescope; instead, they inferred the existence of the planets by measuring their effects on distant suns. By April of 1996 they had discovered five planets outside of our solar system, two of which appeared to be the right distance from their suns to contain water, indicating that it might be possible to find life there.

Chairman, CEO, and cofounder of Intel, **Andrew S. Grove,** was named *Time* Man of the Year in 1997 as the person most responsible for the amazing growth and innovative potential of the microchip. Microchips, tiny wafers of silicon on which all of the information and entertainment of the world could be stored digitally, propelled the new digital and technological economy.

Donna Haraway, author and professor of the History of Consciousness at the University of California at Santa Cruz, in the late 1990s proclaimed herself a cyborg, or a fusion of animal and machine. She argued that most Americans were becoming cyborgs, pointing for example to people who had plastic surgery, artificial hip joints, and contact lenses, and people who were attached to their technology in various ways. She warned that technology was not neutral and that it mattered which direction technological advances took.

Calvin Crawford Johnson Jr. was freed in June 1999 after serving sixteen years in prison on rape charges when DNA evidence proved that he was innocent. Johnson was represented by lawyers **Peter J. Neufeld** and **Barry Scheck,** whose group the Innocence Project sought DNA testing for convicted rapists and murderers who insisted that they were innocent. The attorneys also represented O. J. Simpson during his murder trial. Johnson was the sixty-first inmate exonerated by DNA testing.

In 1998 the White House appointed **John A. Koskinen** as its Y2K Czar, as chairman of the President's Council on Year 2000 Conversion. He was charged with coordinating the U.S. government efforts to ensure critical information technology systems operated smoothly as the year 2000 rolled around.

In 1992 librarian and Internet enthusiast **Jean Armour Polly** coined the term "surfing the Internet." While writing an article about the Internet, she found inspiration for the phrase on her mousepad, which showed a picture of a surfer.

In January 1998 **Richard G. Seed** announced that he planned to use the same technology used to produce Dolly, the first mammal cloned from an adult cell, to attempt human cloning. The White House asked for government and private industry to comply with a ban on human cloning, and the U.S. Food and Drug Administration (FDA) announced its authority to regulate human cloning, making the process illegal. Seed declared that despite federal regulations he would attempt human cloning in the future.

In 1993 **Chris Sommerville,** director of plant biology at the Carnegie Institute of Washington, inserted a plastics-making gene into a mustard plant. The gene transformed the plant into a plastics factory.

Science Fiction novelist **Neal Stephenson,** with his best-selling hits *Snow Crash* (1991), *The Diamond Age* (1995), and *Cryptonomicon* (1999), was lauded as a genius for his ability to explain the new technology that swept through the United States during the 1990s, in a riveting, readable form.

During 1998 several hackers infiltrated Pentagon systems. Five teenagers were charged by the Federal Bureau of Investigation (FBI) for the crime, including alleged ring-leader **Ehud Tenenbaum,** a nineteen-year-old Israeli.

In 1994 *Ardipithecus ramidus,* a 4.4 million-year-old hominid, was found in Aramis, Ethiopia, by **Tim D. White, Gen Suwa,** and **Berhane Asfaw.** It was confirmed to be the oldest known member of the human family.

AWARDS

NOBEL PRIZES:

Physics:

1990: Jointly to **Jerome I. Freidman, Henry W. Kendall,** and Canadian **Richard E. Taylor** for their pioneering investigations concerning deep inelastic scattering of electrons on protons and bound neutrons, which have been of essential importance for the development of the quark model in particle physics.

1991: No American winner.

1992: No American winner.

1993: **Russell A. Hulse** and **Joseph H. Taylor Jr.** for the discovery of a new type of pulsar, a discovery that has opened up new possibilities for the study of gravitation.

1994: For pioneering contributions to the development of neutron scattering techniques for studies of condensed matter, Canadian **Bertram N. Brockhouse** for the development of neutron spectroscopy, and **Clifford G. Shull** for the development of the neutron diffraction technique.

1995: For pioneering experimental contributions to lepton physics, **Martin L. Perl** for the discovery of the tau lepton, and **Frederick Reines,** for the detection of the neutrino.

1996: **David M. Lee, Douglas D. Osheroff,** and **Robert C. Richardson** for their discovery of superfluidity in helium-3.

1997: Americans **Steven Chu** and **William D. Phillips,** and **Claude Cohen-Tannoudji** of France, for development of methods to cool and trap atoms with laser light.

1998: **Robert B. Laughlin, Daniel C. Tsui,** and German **Horst L. Störmer,** for their discovery of a new form of quantum fluid with fractionally charged excitations.

1999: No American winner.

Chemistry:

1990: **Elias James Corey** for development of the theory and methodology of organic synthesis.

1991: No American winner.

1992: **Rudolph A. Marcus** for his contributions to the theory of electron transfer reactions in chemical systems.

1993: For contributions to the developments of methods within DNA-based chemistry, **Kary B. Mullis** for his invention of the polymerase chain reaction (PCR) method, and Canadian **Michael Smith** for his fundamental contributions to the establishment of oligonucleiotide-based, site-directed mutagenisis and its development for protein studies.

1994: **George A. Olah** for his contribution to carbocation chemistry.

1995: Americans **Mario J. Molina** and **F. Sherwood Rowland,** and **Paul J. Crutzen** of the Netherlands, for their work in atmospheric chemistry, particularly concerning the formation and decomposition of ozone.

1996: Americans **Robert F. Curl Jr.** and **Richard E. Smalley,** and Sir **Harold W. Kroto** of Great Britain, for their discovery of fullerenes.

1997: Americans **Paul D. Boyer** and **John E. Walker,** of Great Britain, for their elucidation of the enzymatic mechanism underlying the synthesis of adenosine triphosphate (ATP), and **Jens C. Skou** of Denmark for the first discovery of an ion-transporting enzyme, Na+, K+-, ATPase.

1998: For pioneering contributions in developing methods that can be used for theoretical studies of the properties of molecules and the chemical processes in which they are involved, **Walter Kohn** for his development of the density-functional theory, and **John A. Pople,** of Great Britain, for his development of computational methods in quantum chemistry.

1999: **Ahmed H. Zewail** for his studies of the transition states of chemical reactions using femtosecond spectroscopy.

DEATHS

J. Franklin Hyde, 96, chemist, inventor of silicone—the stuff of breast implants—and other silicon compounds, 11 October 1999.

Henry W. Kendall, 72, physicist, cofounder of the Union of Concerned Scientists, winner of the Nobel Prize in physics in 1990, and professor of physics at MIT, 14 February 1999.

Joseph C. R. Licklider, 75, psychologist, Internet visionary, and advocate of computer science programs; as Director of the Information Processing Techniques Office of the Pentagon he established the intellectual framework from which the Internet would develop, 7 August 1990.

Linus Carl Pauling, 93, chemist, the only man in the world to have won two unshared Nobel Prizes, one in chemistry (1954) and one for peace (1962). Also considered the champion of Vitamin C and its curative powers, 19 August 1994.

Carl Edward Sagan, 62, astronomer and author, whose lifelong passion was searching for intelligent life in the cosmos, 20 December 1996.

Jonas Salk, 80, virologist, using killed virus discovered a vaccine for polio in the 1950s, 23 June 1995.

Alan Bartlett Shepard Jr., 74, astronaut, the first American in space and one of only twelve men to walk on the moon, 21 July 1998.

Eugene Shoemaker, 69, astronomer, helped to discover the giant Shoemaker-Levy 9 comet that slammed into the planet Jupiter in 1994, 18 July 1997.

PUBLICATIONS

Tim Berners-Lee and Mark Fischetti, *Weaving the Web: The Original Design and Ultimate Destiny of the World Wide Web by Its Inventor* (San Francisco: HarperSanFrancisco, 1999);

Jerry E. Bishop and Michael Waldholz, *Genome: The Story of the Most Astonishing Scientific Adventure of Our Time—The Attempt to Map All the Genes in the Human Body* (New York: Simon & Schuster, 1990);

Michael Crichton, *Jurassic Park: A Novel* (New York: Knopf, 1990);

Esther Dyson, *Release 2.0: A Design for Living in the Digital Age* (New York: Broadway Books, 1997);

Niles Eldredge, *Life in the Balance: Humanity and the Biodiversity Crisis* (Princeton: Princeton University Press, 1998);

Timothy Ferris, *The Whole Shebang: A State-of-the-Universe(s) Report* (New York: Simon & Schuster, 1997);

Bill Gates, with Nathan Myhrvold and Peter Rinearson, *The Road Ahead* (New York: Viking, 1995);

James Gleick, *Faster: The Acceleration of Just About Everything* (New York: Pantheon, 1999);

Thomas Gold, *The Deep Hot Biosphere* (New York: Copernicus, 1999);

Stephen Jay Gould, *Bully for Brontosaurus: Reflections in Natural History* (New York: Norton, 1991);

Gould, *Dinosaur in a Haystack: Reflections in Natural History* (New York: Harmony, 1995);

Gould, *Eight Little Piggies: Reflections in Natural History* (New York: Norton, 1993);

Gould, *Full House: the Spread of Excellence from Plato to Darwin* (New York: Harmony, 1996);

Gould, *Leonardo's Mountain of Clams and the Diet of Worms: Essays on Natural History* (New York: Harmony, 1998);

Stephen Hawking, *Black Holes and Baby Universes and Other Essays* (New York: Bantam, 1993);

John Horgan, *The End of Science: Facing the Limits of Knowledge in the Twilight of the Scientific Age* (Reading, Mass.: Addison-Wesley, 1996);

Stuart Kauffman, *At Home in the Universe: The Search for Laws of Self-Organization and Complexity* (New York: Oxford University Press, 1995);

Ray Kurzwiel, *The Age of Spiritual Machines: When Computers Exceed Human Intelligence* (New York: Viking, 1999);

Michael D. Lemonick, *Other Worlds: The Search for Life in the Universe* (New York: Simon & Schuster, 1998);

John Maddox, *What Remains to be Discovered: Mapping the Secrets of the Universe, the Origins of Life, and the Future of the Human Race* (New York: Martin Kessler, 1998);

Kary Mullis, *Dancing Naked in the Mind Field* (New York: Pantheon, 1998);

Nicholas Negroponte, *Being Digital* (New York: Knopf, 1995);

Richard Rhodes, *Dark Sun: The Making of the Hydrogen Bomb* (New York: Simon & Schuster, 1995);

Jeremy Rifkin, *The Biotech Century: Harnessing the Gene and Remaking the World* (New York: Jeremy P. Tarcher/Putnam, 1998);

Richard E. Smalley, "Great Balls of Carbon: The Story of the Buckminsterfullerene," *The Sciences,* (March/April 1991): 22–28 ;

Neal Stephenson, *Cryptonomicon* (New York: Avon, 1999);

Stephenson, *The Diamond Age, Or, Young Lady's Illustrated Primer* (New York: Bantam, 1995);

Stephenson, *Snow Crash* (New York: Bantam, 1992);

Clifford Stoll, *Silicon Snake Oil: Second Thoughts on the Information Highway* (New York: Doubleday, 1995);

Stephen L. Talbott, *The Future Does Not Compute: Transcending the Machines in Our Midst* (Sebastopol, Cal.: O'Reilly and Associates, 1995);

Sherry Turkle, *Life on the Screen: Identity in the Age of the Internet* (New York: Simon & Schuster, 1995).

American Scientist, periodical.

Discoverer, periodical.

Isis: An International Review Devoted to the History of Science and Its Cultural Influence, periodical.

Natural History, periodical.

Science, periodical.

The Sciences, periodical.

Scientific American, periodical.

SPORTS

by MARION ALDRIDGE

CONTENTS

Sidebars and tables are listed in italics.

1990

1 Jan. The University of Miami (Florida) Hurricanes claim the college football national championship with a 33 to 25 win over the University of Alabama Crimson Tide in the Sugar Bowl.

15 Jan. Joe Montana sets the National Football League (NFL) record for postseason touchdowns with numbers thirty and thirty-one, breaking Terry Bradshaw's record.

16 Feb. The NFL allows college juniors to become eligible for the draft by renouncing their remaining college eligibility.

10 June Jack Nicklaus wins the Seniors Professional Golfers' Association (PGA) tournament.

11 June Nolan Ryan, of the Texas Rangers, pitches his sixth no-hit game, a major league baseball record, against the Oakland Athletics.

17 July The Minnesota Twins become the first major league baseball team to record two triple plays in one game.

1 Aug. Ryan wins his three-hundredth game, beating the Milwaukee Brewers 11 to 3.

17 Aug. Carlton Fisk, of the Chicago White Sox, hits his 329th home run as a catcher, a major league baseball record. He ends his career in 1993 with 376 home runs.

25 Oct. Evander Holyfield knocks out James "Buster" Douglas in the third round to become the undisputed heavyweight boxing champion.

28 Oct. Fourteen-year-old Jennifer Capriati wins her first professional tennis tournament, the Puerto Rican Open.

1991

2 Feb. New York businessman Robert Tisch purchases a 50-percent interest in the New York Giants.

2 Mar. Del Ballard Jr. throws the most famous gutter ball in Professional Bowlers Association (PBA) history in the finals of the Fair Lanes Open. Needing only seven pins to win, Ballard hits the gutter instead, losing the $30,000 first prize.

21 Apr. Russell Maryland, a defensive lineman for the University of Miami (Florida), is selected by the Dallas Cowboys as the first player drafted into the NFL this season.

1 May Ryan pitches his seventh no-hitter, beating the Toronto Blue Jays 3 to 0.

15 July Sandhi Ortiz-DelValle becomes the first woman to officiate a men's professional basketball game.

28 July Dennis Martinez pitches a perfect game for the Montreal Expos against the Los Angeles Dodgers, winning 2 to 0.

16 Nov. The University of Miami (Florida) Hurricanes (#2) beat the Florida State Seminoles (#1) in college football, 17 to 16.

1992

18 Mar.   The use of instant replay in the NFL is not reapproved, stopping a six-year-old practice.

12 Apr.   Fred Couples wins The Masters golf tournament in Augusta, Georgia.

26 Apr.   Steve Emtman, a defensive lineman for the University of Washington, is chosen by the Indianapolis Colts, the first NFL draftee this year.

11 May   St. Louis businessman James Busch Orthwein purchases a controlling interest in the New England Patriots.

7 Sept.   Commissioner of Baseball Francis T. "Fay" Vincent resigns under pressure.

9 Sept.   Robin Yount, a shortstop with the Milwaukee Brewers, collects his three-thousandth baseball hit.

30 Sept.   George Brett, an infielder for the Kansas City Royals, bats four for four to reach three thousand career baseball hits.

29 Nov.   Jerry Rice, wide receiver for the San Francisco 49ers, catches his one-hundredth touchdown pass.

1993

1 Jan.   The University of Alabama Crimson Tide (#2) defeats the University of Miami (Florida) Hurricanes in college football, 34 to 13, in the Sugar Bowl to win the national championship.

14 Apr.   Sheryl Swoopes scores a National Collegiate Athletic Association (NCAA) record forty-seven points in leading Texas Tech University to victory in the Division I-A women's basketball tournament championship game.

25 Apr.   Drew Bledsoe, a quarterback for Washington State University, is the first NFL draft pick of the year, selected by the New England Patriots.

30 Apr.   Monica Seles, while playing in Hamburg, Germany, is stabbed by a rival's fan.

22 May   Roy Jones Jr. wins his first boxing title (middleweight) with a twelve-round victory over Bernard Hopkins.

16 Sept.   Dave Winfield, an outfielder with the Minnesota Twins, gets career baseball hit number three thousand.

22 Sept.   The Colorado Rockies complete their first home season with a major league baseball attendance record of 4,483,350 fans.

26 Oct.   The NFL awards the twenty-ninth franchise to the Carolina Panthers.

13 Nov.   The University of Notre Dame Fighting Irish (#2) beat the Florida State Seminoles (#1) in college football, 31 to 24.

14 Nov.   Don Shula breaks George Halas's career victory mark as an NFL coach with number 325.

30 Nov.   The NFL awards the thirtieth franchise to the Jacksonville Jaguars.

17 Dec.   The FOX Network outbids the Columbia Broadcasting System (CBS) for the rights to broadcast NFL games, ending a thirty-eight-year relationship.

23 Dec.   Dallas Cowboys quarterback Troy Aikman signs an eight-year deal worth $50 million, making him the highest-paid player in the NFL.

1994

1 Jan.   The Florida State Seminoles (#1) beat the University of Nebraska Cornhuskers (#2) in college football, 18 to 16, in the Orange Bowl for the national championship.

6 Jan.   Ice skater Nancy Kerrigan is assaulted while preparing for the U.S. figure-skating championships in Detroit.

7 Feb.   Michael Jordan, who retired from professional basketball the previous October after leading the Chicago Bulls to three consecutive NBA championships, signs with the Chicago White Sox as a baseball free agent.

14 Feb.   More than three hundred baseball players are awarded $59.5 million as baseball owners are penalized for "collusion."

18 Feb.   Dan Jansen wins the gold medal in the 1000-meter speed-skating event in the Winter Olympics.

19 Feb.   Bonnie Blair wins her third consecutive 500-meter speed-skating gold medal.

23 Feb.   Baylor University announces it will leave the Southwest Conference to join the Big 8. Before the week is out three other Texas schools (Texas A & M, Texas Tech, and the University of Texas) also announce their departure from the league.

23 Mar.   Wayne Gretzky, playing for the Los Angeles Kings, breaks Gordy Howe's career record (801) for National Hockey League (NHL) goals. He finishes his career in 1999 with 894 goals.

14 June   The New York Rangers win the NHL Stanley Cup for the first time since 1940.

22 June   The Houston Rockets win the first major-league title in the history of the city; Hakeem Olajuwon leads the National Basketball Association (NBA) franchise to victory.

   The U.S. team gets its first victory in World Cup soccer since 1950, defeating Colombia.

28 July   Kenny Rogers throws the first perfect game in the history of the Texas Rangers, against the California Angels.

4 Aug.   The Bowl Alliance is formed, with different sites to host the college football national championship game on a rotating basis.

12 Aug.   Major league baseball players go on strike at 12:45 A.M. to protest the owners' plan for a salary cap. The season is ended and the World Series is cancelled for the first time in ninety years.

15 Aug.   An NFL record 112,376 spectators watch the "American Bowl" in Mexico City between the Dallas Cowboys and Houston Oilers.

12 Sept.   The National Labor Relations Board (NLRB) awards NFL players $30 million in back pay from a lockout by owners at the end of a strike in 1987.

30 Sept.   The NHL announces the delay of the start of its regular season.

19 Oct.   The Duke University Blue Devils break the University of North Carolina Tar Heels 101-game unbeaten streak held by the women's soccer team.

31 Oct.   Because she was winning every junior tennis event she entered, Venus Williams, at age fourteen, turns professional.

1995

10 Mar. Michael Jordan retires from baseball and, nine days later, returns to professional basketball to play for the Chicago Bulls.

4 Apr. The America's Cup defense committee allows *Young America*, *Mighty Mary*, and *Stars & Stripes* to compete in an unprecedented three-boat, twelve-race event, starting 10 April.

22 Apr. Ki-Jana Carter, a running back from Pennsylvania State University, is selected by the Cincinnati Bengals as the first draft choice of the NFL.

6 May Long-shot Thunder Gulch wins the Kentucky Derby.

18 Aug. The new football stadium in Jacksonville, Florida, opens for a preseason game.

20 Aug. Jose Mesa, pitching for the Cleveland Indians, gets his 37th save in 37 opportunities, a major league baseball record.

6 Sept. Cal Ripken Jr., an infielder for the Baltimore Orioles, plays in his 2,131st consecutive major league baseball game, breaking Lou Gehrig's record.

1996

2 Jan. The University of Nebraska Cornhuskers (#1) defeat the University of Florida Gators (#2), 62 to 24, in college football in the Fiesta Bowl to win the national championship.

9 Feb. An agreement is reached that will allow Art Modell to move his NFL franchise from Cleveland to Baltimore with the promise that Cleveland will have a new Browns team no later than 1999. Modell's new team will be named the Ravens.

29 Feb. The Dallas Mavericks set an NBA record with eighteen three-pointers scored in a game and twelve in a half.

30 Apr. The transfer of the NFL Oilers from Houston to Nashville for the 1998 season is approved.

16 Aug. In the first major league baseball game ever played outside of the United States or Canada, the San Diego Padres beat the New York Mets in Monterrey, Mexico.

18 Sept. Roger Clemens, pitcher for the Boston Red Sox, ties his own major league record of twenty strikeouts in a nine-inning game.

23 Nov. With a victory over Marquette University, Pat Summitt wins her six-hundredth women's college basketball game while coaching the University of Tennessee Lady Volunteers.

30 Nov. The Florida State Seminoles (#2) beat the University of Florida Gators (#1) in college football, 24 to 21.

1997

9 Apr. Tiger Woods wins The Masters with a record eighteen-under-par 270.

12 Apr. Randy "Roadhouse" Spizer, age sixteen, wins the "Best Trick" category of the Professional In-Line Skating Challenge in Orlando, Florida.

19 Apr. Orlando Pace, an offensive tackle for Ohio State University, is the first selection in the NFL draft, chosen by the St. Louis Rams.

6 May	University of Kentucky men's college basketball coach Rick Pitino announces his resignation to lead a professional team, the Boston Celtics, for a ten-year, $70 million contract.
12 June	The San Francisco Giants beat the Texas Rangers in the first-ever regular season interleague game.
28 June	Evander Holyfield wins a heavyweight fight against Mike Tyson when Tyson is disqualified for biting his opponent's ear.
31 July	Mark McGwire, a first baseman, is traded from the Oakland A's to the St. Louis Cardinals.
14 Sept.	Jack Kent Cooke Stadium, the new home to the NFL Washington Redskins, opens in Maryland.
27 Sept.	Sportscaster Marv Albert goes on trial in Arlington, Virginia, on charges of sodomy and assault.
9 Oct.	After thirty-six years as basketball coach at the University of North Carolina, Dean Smith surprises fans by announcing his retirement.
25 Oct.	Kevin VanDam wins his fourth Bassmasters tournament, and second of the season, with a three-day total of fifteen bass weighing forty-one pounds, fifteen ounces in the Virginia Eastern Invitational on Kerr Reservoir out of South Hill, Virginia.
28 Oct.	The NBA announces the hiring of Dee Kantner and Violet Palmer as the first women to officiate in a major-league, all-male sport.
7 Dec.	The University of North Carolina women's soccer team beats the University of Connecticut for its fourteenth NCAA title in sixteen years.
31 Dec.	Future major leaguer Orlando Hernandez, half brother of Livan who plays for the Florida Marlins, defects from Cuba.

1998

6 Jan.	A split college football national title is announced, shared by the University of Michigan Wolverines (12–0) and the University of Nebraska Cornhuskers (13–0).
15 Jan.	Northwestern University athlete Dwight Brown admits to lying to the grand jury when he said he never placed bets on football and basketball games with a campus bookmaker. Brown played for Northwestern University from 1991 to 1994.
25 Jan.	The Denver Broncos and quarterback John Elway win their first Super Bowl, defeating the Green Bay Packers.
11 Feb.	Picabo Street wins the women's super giant slalom (Super G) skiing gold medal in the Winter Olympics.
20 Feb.	Tara Lipinski wins the women's figure skating gold medal.
1 Mar.	Venus Williams wins her first professional tennis singles title in the IGA Tennis Classic.
3 Mar.	Larry Doby, the first African American athlete to play in the American League, as an outfielder with the Cleveland Indians, is elected to the Baseball Hall of Fame.

8 Mar.	Kraig Welborn of DeRidder, Louisiana, catches a fourteen-pound, eleven-ounce largemouth bass near Anacoco, Louisiana, breaking the world record for that species by three ounces.
29 Mar.	The University of Tennessee Lady Volunteers win their third consecutive women's basketball championship.
30 Mar.	The University of Kentucky defeats the University of Utah to win the NCAA basketball tournament.
12 Apr.	Mark O'Meara wins The Masters.
18 Apr.	Peyton Manning, a quarterback for the University of Tennessee Volunteers, chosen by the Indianapolis Colts, is the first selection of the NFL draft.
6 May	Rookie Kerry Wood, a pitcher for the Chicago Cubs, strikes out twenty batters, tying a major league record, in a one-hitter against the Houston Astros.
17 May	David Wells pitches a perfect game, only the thirteenth in major league baseball history for the New York Yankees against the Minnesota Twins.
24 May	Eddie Cheever wins the Indianapolis 500.
25 May	Princeton University wins its fifth lacrosse title of the decade, 15 to 5, defeating the University of Maryland.
14 June	Jordan plays in his last NBA game as the Chicago Bulls beat the Utah Jazz to win the NBA championship.
9 July	Allan H. "Bud" Selig is elected to the permanent post as commissioner of major league baseball.
8 Sept.	Mark McGwire breaks Roger Maris's single-season home run record, hitting number sixty-two.
20 Sept.	Cal Ripken Jr. benches himself, concluding his streak of playing in 2,632 consecutive baseball games.
13 Oct.	The NBA cancels the first two weeks of regular season play, ultimately eliminating ninety-nine games from its schedule.
21 Oct.	The New York Yankees win the World Series, defeating the San Diego Padres in four games, after winning 114 during in the regular season.

1999

31 Jan.	The Denver Broncos and John Elway win their second consecutive Super Bowl, defeating the Atlanta Falcons, 34 to 19.
5 Feb.	The NBA schedule begins belatedly after the first work stoppage in its history.
14 Feb.	Jeff Gordon wins the Daytona 500.
17 Mar.	Reversing an earlier decision, NFL owners adopt a modified instant-replay system as an officiating aid for the 1999 season.
22 May	Mia Hamm becomes the all-time leading scorer in international soccer with her 108th goal.
27 June	During the Summer X Games, Tony Hawk completes the first "900" in the history of skateboarding competition.

10 July	Brandi Chastain's penalty kick leads the U.S. team to victory in the Women's World Cup.
25 July	Cyclist Lance Armstrong makes an amazing comeback after battling testicular cancer to win the Tour De France.
11 Sept.	Serena Williams, younger sister of Venus, wins the U.S. Open women's singles tennis championship.
26 Sept.	The Ryder Cup team, captained by Ben Crenshaw, makes the biggest comeback in the history of the competition to help the United States golf team defeat the European squad.
23 Oct.	In the first meeting between NCAA Division I-A football teams coached by a father and a son, Bobby Bowden's Florida State Seminoles are victorious over his son Tommy Bowden's Clemson Tigers, 17 to 14.
25 Oct.	Payne Stewart, winner of three major golf championships, dies with other passengers in a plane crash.
13 Nov.	Lennox Lewis defeats Evander Holyfield in Madison Square Garden in New York to win the first undisputed heavyweight boxing championship in nine years.
12 Dec.	The final World Wrestling Federation (WWF) event of the year, *Armageddon*, concludes with Chris Jericho defeating Chyna for the Intercontinental Title.
26 Dec.	Jordan is selected by the Entertainment and Sports Programming Network (ESPN) as the greatest North American athlete of the twentieth century. Babe Ruth is ranked second.
31 Dec.	Sherry Davis, the first female public-address announcer in major league baseball, is dismissed after seven years with the San Francisco Giants.

University of Nebraska football coach Tom Osborne being doused after his team beat the University of Florida 62 to 24 to capture the national title, in the Fiesta Bowl in Tempe, Arizona, on 2 January 1996 (AP/Wide World Photos)

OVERVIEW

Out of Bounds. Judging solely by media coverage, most of what was newsworthy in sports during the 1990s had little to do with the field of play. Athletics—professional, amateur, and casual—had become big business and news often occurred off the court. While ordinary men and women struggled to stay in shape at local fitness centers, sports entrepreneurs, media moguls, and lawyers came to represent the complex reality of modern sports more often than professional or college athletes. The annual *Sports Illustrated* swimsuit issue, which had nothing to do with athletics, was regularly the best-selling issue of the year.

Big Business. The business of athletics kept getting bigger, until the cliché "It's only a game" became meaningless. Big cities paid for huge stadiums to lure league franchises, hoping the economic benefits might somehow exceed the costs to taxpayers. Even smaller cities built new minorleague ballparks to promote the economic boom associated with sports. The collegiate bastion of amateurism, the National Collegiate Athletic Association (NCAA), charged the Columbia Broadcasting System (CBS) television network more than $6 billion for the rights to broadcast "March Madness," the annual men's college basketball championship tournament. Although the NCAA and participating colleges made money, and successful coaches garnered lavish contracts and earned millions of dollars through endorsements, the players continued to play for free. In the *Sporting News* annual report on the most powerful people in sports, people such as Rupert Murdoch (CEO of News Corp), Paul Tagliabue (commissioner of the National Football League [NFL]) and Michael Eisner (CEO of Disney), appeared far more often than athletes. The real competition seemed to be in the skyboxes rather than on the field. Not surprisingly, the most successful sports movie of the decade, *Jerry Maguire* (1996), was not about an athlete but a fictional sports agent. His client's motto spoke for the decade: "Show me the money!"

Scandals. On a different front, but also at the boundary of real sports, scandals reached unprecedented depths of sordidness. Former football star O. J. Simpson was tried for, but not convicted of, the murders of his wife Nicole Brown Simpson and her friend Ronald Goldman. Tonya Harding was implicated in an attack on her figure-skating competitor Nancy Kerrigan that was intended, but failed, to keep her out of Olympic competition. Even the Olympics, once a paragon of amateurism and civic virtue, suffered a black eye when evidence came to light that officials had become accustomed to soliciting and accepting bribes from cities seeking to host the Games. Boxer Mike Tyson was convicted of rape out of the ring and stained the sport by partially biting off an opponent's ear during a bout. Latrell Sprewell attacked and choked his basketball coach, P. J. Carlesimo. Drug abuse—especially of muscle-building steroids—and criminal behavior among athletes plagued sports at every level.

Cybersports. The Internet created an etherial world of sporting choices, from fantasy leagues in every major sport to chat rooms where one could brag on or gripe about favorite or least-liked teams. Unlimited amounts of information could be found about games (even in progress) or individual players. As Americans became increasingly flabby, sitting in front of their computers, they found that they could sign up for a week at a fitness spa or purchase sporting equipment through the Internet. More often they stayed at home and watched professional and college athletes perform on television. Cable television, already ubiquitous by the beginning of the decade, offered fans twenty-four-hour sports coverage on multiple channels. To fill the airwaves when nothing interesting was happening, broadcasters turned to increasingly obscure and nontraditional competitions.

Borderline Sports. Cheerleading, as the name implies, was once an activity during which noncompeting teams with lots of spirit roused the crowd and cheered on the athletes who were actually playing the game. In the 1990s an industry emerged with televised competitions among cheerleaders themselves, who now learned to be acrobats and gymnasts in order to compete against other pep squads, with routines that were part dance and part gymnastics. Ecotourism was a new twist on the oldest sport. Instead of hunting wild game with a bow or rifle, ecologically minded tourists pursued their quarry with binoculars and cameras. Often the goal was simply to experience the wilderness, unencumbered with modern conveniences. Ecotours in the United States ranged from dog sledding through the Alaskan tundra to rafting down the Colorado River to enjoying a shelling and snorkeling cruise on the coast of Florida. Professional wrestling, however tempting to ridicule, developed a devoted following that was impossible to ignore. Matches filled huge auditoriums with World Wrestling Federation (WWF) and World Championship Wrestling spectacles. Millions more watched WWF "Smackdown" fights on television. These performances might have been as carefully staged and choreographed as a Broadway musical, but they offered fans what they wanted: gratuitous violence. The sport featured good and bad guys, underdogs, and scantily clad leading ladies. Sports memorabilia auction sites on the Internet offered more wrestling autographs and photos for sale than traditional baseball cards. Nothing demonstrated the mainstream acceptance of wrestling more than the election of former professional wrestler Jesse "The Body" Ventura as governor of Minnesota in 1998.

Sports Memorabilia. Baby boomers collected baseball cards for the fun of it. When they grew up, they discovered that the cards they had thrown away decades earlier might have been worth thousands of dollars. Sports memorabilia became a growth industry. Millions of adults joined the hunt for sports-related materials; whether by buying autographed baseballs at a kiosk in the mall or bidding on a Wayne Gretzky jersey through an on-line auction, many Americans wanted to own a piece of the sports action. Sensing the market, managers of new stadiums incorporated sports museums and shops as part of the home-field attraction. Meanwhile, team logos and sports attire became a ubiquitous component of the wardrobe of the young American male. Teams regularly changed the styles and coloration of their uniforms and emblems to spur sales.

Movies and Television. It was a good decade for sports-related movies. Top revenue producers included *Days of Thunder* (stock car racing, 1990), *White Men Can't Jump* (basketball, 1992), *Space Jam* (space-age animated/real-life basketball movie featuring Bugs Bunny and Michael Jordan, 1996), *Cool Runnings* (bobsledding, 1993), *Tin Cup* (golf, 1996), *A River Runs Through It* (fly fishing, 1992), *The Mighty Ducks* (ice hockey, 1992), and *Jerry Maguire* (sports agenting, 1996). The short life of women's professional baseball during World War II provided the inspiration for *A League of Their Own* (1992). Other baseball movies included *Rookie of the Year* (1993) and *Angels in the Outfield* (1994). On television the best documentary on sports was the Public Broadcasting Service (PBS) production of Ken Burns's *Baseball*, a nine "inning" or installment history of the game that aired in September 1994. On Broadway, a 1995 revival of *Damn Yankees* (1955), starring at different times Jerry Lewis and Bebe Neuwirth, staged a successful run.

Physical Fitness and Health. Though most Americans were sedentary, a growing number got off the couch and started working out. The Young Men's Christian Association (YMCA) was on its deathbed, serving as the largest chain of fourth-class hotels in the world, when it was rejuvenated by millions of men and women who poured into their facilities to jog, lift weights, play pick-up basketball,

and take aerobics classes. Even churches built gymnasiums for their increasingly health-conscious members. Luxury spas provided similar, but more upscale, services including personal trainers, tanning and nail salons, mud wraps, and therapeutic massages. Investing far less money, many people walked or jogged in their own neighborhoods to promote their cardiovascular and mental health.

Extreme Sports. Also on the edge of the traditional world of athletics were the grassroots amusements that emerged in the competitive world as "extreme" sports or gravity games. Beginning in 1995 the Entertainment and Sports Programming Network (ESPN), the sports-only television network, hosted a biannual showcase for alternative sports, including non-Olympic and non-mainstream events in which participants attempted gravity-defying feats such as backflips on bicycles and tricks on skateboards. Promoted by such organizations as the Aggressive Skaters Association (ASA), participants toured Louisville, Milwaukee, and Richmond. In-line skating claimed to be the fastest-growing sport in the world with aggressive or trick-skating being the top-growth component within the genre. With designations such as Men's Verts and Women's Streets, and young winners with names unfamiliar to the public, such as Aaron Feinberg, eighteen, and Katie Brown, seventeen, it seemed possible that such cutting-edge competitions might eventually compete with football and baseball.

Women. Sports for women, outside of events in the Olympic Games, were once relegated to the middle pages of the newspaper sports section. Thanks to Title IX of the Federal Education Amendments (1972), a federal law requiring schools to fund women's sports on an equal basis with men's, some spectacularly capable athletes emerged into the national consciousness. Athletes such as Mia Hamm (soccer), Lindsay Davenport (tennis), Picabo Street (skiing), Brandi Chastain (soccer), Sheryl Swoopes (basketball), Bonnie Blair (ice skating), Betsy King (golf), Chamique Holdsclaw (basketball), Tara Lipinski (ice skating), Venus and Serena Williams (tennis), and Jackie Joyner-Kersee (track) became household names. Attendance at women's sporting events also shot up; for example, the Women's World Cup (soccer) was played before 90,185 fans on 10 July 1999. Like their male counterparts, women could misbehave spectacularly as well. Figure skater Harding's effort to eliminate her archrival, Kerrigan, from competition not only ended Harding's skating career, it sullied the otherwise etherial beauty of ice skating for many Americans.

Mainstream Sports. All of these new sports and attention on female athletics did not mean that baseball, football, basketball, golf, and hockey shut down for the decade. Baseball had some of its greatest moments ever thanks to Cal Ripken Jr., Mark McGwire, and Sammy Sosa. Michael Jordan, arguably the greatest player in the history of basketball (who also was voted by ESPN as the Athlete of the Century), was on the court for much of the decade and on the baseball diamond for one fascinating, if undistinguished, year. Football thrived at every level, from pee-wee to professional. Some players, such as Peyton Manning, were fun to watch as college players and continued to exhibit their mastery of the game at the professional level. The big debate in college football was whether to continue the tradition of bowl games—which came increasingly to bear the name of corporate sponsors—or to create a playoff system to determine a true national champion. Golf, in need of rejuvenation, welcomed a young man into its professional ranks after he had decimated amateur competition for three years running. Though he held extraordinary promise, Tiger Woods did not quite prove himself the greatest golfer of all time. Jack Nicklaus held onto that title throughout the decade and continued to play competitively as he approached age sixty. Ice hockey expanded into the Sun-belt states, becoming a truly national sport for the first time. Stock car racing enjoyed burgeoning popularity and moved into the cultural mainstream. Jeff Gordon, clean-cut and skilled at driving a race car, became a young counterpoint to the old guard of Richard Petty and Dale Earnhardt. Tennis, a thoroughly international sport, saw many Americans winning Grand Slam titles throughout the decade; Pete Sampras dominated the sport. Others who made their mark in tennis were Lindsay Davenport, sisters Venus and Serena Williams, and Andre Agassi. The Olympics were entertaining, with Summer and Winter Games being separated by a two-year span for the first time in 1992. Carl Lewis, Bonnie Blair, Kristi Yamaguchi, Dan Jansen, Shannon Miller, Michael Johnson, Picabo Street, and others headlined the list of gold-medal winners for the United States.

TOPICS IN THE NEWS

BASEBALL

Tale of Two Extremes. Major league baseball went from the depths of despair to the heights of joy, from disheartenment to jubilation, during the final decade of the twentieth century. Felipe Alou, coach of the Montreal Expos, said, "Sometimes, something has to almost die, like baseball did, for the miracle to take place." Greed and money nearly caused the downfall of the sport. Strikes and work stoppages were nothing new to professional sports, and baseball had experienced its share of both, befitting its rank as the eldest of major league athletic enterprises in the United States. But never before had a World Series been canceled, as it was in 1994 because of a 272-day strike by players that forced the cancellation of 920 games. The contest between owners and players focused on salary caps and revenue sharing. When baseball finally resumed, it did so amidst fan animosity directed at players, owners, and baseball in general.

New Iron Man. Salvation came, specifically, on 6 September 1995 at Camden Yards in Baltimore, Maryland, when Cal Ripken Jr., one of the most respected baseball veterans, broke Lou Gehrig's long-held, much-cherished record for consecutive games played. Everything came together to make his attempt to break the standard a media event of the first rank. Unlike a new record that pops up randomly (for example, six home runs hit in one game), Ripken's assault on the Iron Man's historic mark of 2,130 consecutive games played, which Gehrig had

Sammy Sosa hugging Mark McGwire after McGwire's sixty-second home run of the season on 8 September 1998 (AP/Wide World Photos)

Sports merchandising at the end of the century bore little resemblance to sporting-equipment sales in earlier decades. Hardware stores used to be the primary source for hunting and fishing gear. Department stores, such as Sears, sold footballs, baseballs, and four-wheeled roller skates. Baseball cards were bought, mostly for the gum in the packages, at local candy and corner stores. Golf equipment was purchased at the golf course Pro Shop and surfboards were found at shops near the beach. Coaches were responsible for obtaining team equipment, so helmets, pads, nets, and all the other accouterment of organized athletic enterprises were available only through a select group of sales representatives and catalogues with narrow professional circulation.

In the 1990s, however, locally owned shops and boutiques for specialty sports niches, from team clothing to exercise apparel, could be found in half the strip malls in the United States. Stores and products were also advertized in the Yellow Pages and on the Internet. An entire industry for sports memorabilia, ranging from traditional cards to figurines to autographs, tapped into the baby-boom interest in nostalgia. Sports bars, physical fitness centers, and sports medicine clinics proliferated. Of course, purchases of sports-related items could still be made at traditional department and discount stores.

In addition to the smaller specialty shops, a new institution arrived—the megastore, such as Sports Authority, Jumbo-Sports, and Sports Warehouse. In these cathedrals to athletic capitalism, entrepreneurial owners were utterly unconcerned with the traditional venues of sports: Fenway Park, Augusta National, Churchill Downs, and the Superdome. Instead of promoting the observation of sporting events in which only a few athletes were engaged, they made available a wide range of paraphernalia for hands-on sporting activity. University of Oklahoma coach Bud Wilkinson's quip that a football game is eighty thousand people desperately in need of exercise watching twenty-two athletes desperately in need of rest was finally being heard as a serious commentary. In response to his call for more exercise and athletic activity, Americans created an economic boom. In the cavernous warehouses of athletic obsession, one could purchase

almost anything related to sports: darts and yo-yos, bowling balls and badminton birdies, bicycle accessories, surfboards, skateboards and skis, hunting gear, toys, books, magazines, and videos. A treadmill might be available—at nearly $1,600. Packs of sports cards ranged in price from $1 to $10. Clothes with almost any conceivable relationship to sports could be purchased—camouflage shirts for hunting or merchandise advertising a favorite team—as well as hats, helmets, and goggles. In some of these giant stores customers could even participate in simulated sporting events such as rock climbing, skiing, and kayaking.

For those individuals disinclined to leave home, Internet shopping allowed consumers an even broader choice of products. On the Sports Authority website, for instance, the options were prodigious. One could purchase a wide range of apparel, shoes, exercise equipment, golf and tennis gear, games, and cycling accessories. Outdoor enthusiasts could find everything they needed for hunting, fishing, camping, hiking, boating, diving, and other activities (such as wake/knee boards and in-line skates). For those more interested in sports memorabilia, one could click on to an auction site and bid for treasures. A typical offer might be $13 for a "Peyton Manning Rookie Playoff Moment" card.

Sports-related items could also be found at the local convenience store. One could purchase mugs featuring stock car racers—even as one filled their gas tank with the "official fuel of NASCAR." Cups depicting favored wrestlers, baseball caps, and "high performance driving and sports eyewear" (with styles named "Aviator" and "Pit Stop") were prominently displayed on front counters. Along with milk and bread, a customer could pick up PowerAde or Gatorade drinks, as well as energy bars to keep themselves competitive. Sporting magazines, from *Baseball Weekly* to local recruiting reports, filled the racks formerly reserved for entertainment and tabloid publications. Under the cap of a favorite soda one might win a free trip to the NBA All-Star game or the Super Bowl. It seemed that at the turn of the millennium, one could not get away from sports merchandising; but that worked out well, since most Americans craved the paraphernalia of sports.

achieved during the 1925–1939 baseball seasons, created the perfect opportunity for a national countdown. For even more dramatic effect, the record was not actually bested when Ripken stepped on the field or when the umpire yelled, "Play ball." The game needed to be played for at least four and one-half innings in order to be official and recorded for posterity. Simply exiting the dugout and

doffing his cap after breaking the record would not pacify the fans, so Ripken trotted the circumference of the field, shaking hands and touching fans in the stadium for a half-hour while play was halted, and America rejoiced at this revalidation of its favorite pastime. The play-by-play announcers had the good sense to be silent and let the drama speak for itself. Parents called their children to the television set and Americans watched as one man—by sheer perseverance, goodwill, and charm—single-handedly revived a sport that had been deathly ill. He also hit a sixth-inning home run, to dispel any notion that his streak was an act of generosity or a public-relations ploy on the part of management. Ripken eventually played in 2,632 straight games, ending the streak only when he benched himself on 19 September 1998, during which a total of 266 players were utilized by the Baltimore Orioles. An American League starter in every All-Star game since 1984, Ripkin held the record for career home runs by a shortstop (402) at the end of the decade. He was voted league Most Valuable Player (MVP) in 1983 and 1991.

Home Run Derby. Ripken may have been a savior of baseball, but he got an assist from the Great Home Run Chase of 1998. Mark McGwire of the St. Louis Cardinals and Sammy Sosa of the Chicago Cubs lit up the scoreboards of the National League by each hitting more home runs in a single season than any other person in history. During the chase for the record, 70,589,505 fans attended games, many of them filling ballparks for the specific purpose of cheering McGwire and Sosa. People even came early to watch the two players, especially McGwire, in batting practice. McGwire did not just hit balls out of the field, he knocked them out of the ballpark—tape-measure feats that awed spectators. Tom Verducci, a senior writer for *Sports Illustrated,* conservatively estimated that the fans brought in by McGwire generated nearly $25 million in extra revenue at ballparks where he played. What McGwire and Sosa gave to the game in terms of goodwill is immeasurable. One of the most revered records in baseball was Babe Ruth's sixty home runs in 1927 and Roger Maris's sixty-one in 1961. The Babe's mark had seemed invincible, until Maris, in one of the most underappreciated displays of athletic prowess in sports history, topped it. Then, for thirty-seven years, Maris's mark stood; no one had even come close to breaking it. Willie Mays once hit fifty-two home runs (1965), as did George Foster (1977). Some people felt that Maris's record was a fluke, an aberration that would never be paralleled. Then, in 1997, McGwire and Ken Griffey Jr. gave fans a hint of the future. McGwire hit fifty-eight homers, while Griffey hit fifty-six. McGwire's figure was no fluke, as he had hit fifty-two home runs in 1995, powered by a six-foot-five-inch, 250-pound frame with arms sporting nineteen-inch biceps. He was the first player since Ruth to have back-to-back seasons with fifty homers. In 1998 the league expanded into two new markets, Tampa Bay and Arizona, and with long-ball friendly Coors Field in Colorado, the stage was set for a home-run derby. Such expansion inevitably dilutes the quality of pitching and McGwire, Griffey, Sosa, and Greg Vaughn took advantage of their opportunity. Sosa set a major league record in June 1998 by hitting twenty home runs, the most ever by a player in a single month. His eleven multiple home-run games tied the major league record. He led the majors in runs batted in (RBIs) and in total bases taken, and was

later honored as the MVP of the National League. During this amazing season, Sosa hit more home runs (sixty-six) than anyone else—except McGwire, who pelted the five-ounce sphere out of the ballpark a stupendous seventy times. The race heated up when McGwire set the new mark of sixty-two on 8 September 1998, with his shortest home run of the season. Sosa then became the first major league player to hit sixty-six homers in a season on 25 September, but he held that record for only forty-five minutes because McGwire hit five home runs in his last nineteen swings. Throughout the season both men displayed pure class, with Maris's family demonstrating equally amazing grace in the process of relinquishing their father's crown. McGwire did all the right things, acknowledging Maris and his family, hugging his own son, and basking in the glory that he had earned. Sosa showed remarkable poise as well, running in from the outfield, as the fates had him playing on the same field that magical day, to bear hug the man who had been his rival.

New Baseball Homes. Many people claimed that 1998 was the greatest baseball season ever. Baseball, the national pastime, had righted itself. The decade also brought a return to sanity in ballpark architecture. Rather than the generic, anonymous, symmetrical stadiums of the 1960s and 1970s, the opening of Camden Yards in 1992 introduced a delightful decade of interesting, fan-friendly venues for watching baseball. Other beautiful parks included the Ballpark at Arlington, Texas (Texas Rangers), Turner Field in Georgia (Atlanta Braves), the retractable-domed Bank One Ballpark in Phoenix (Arizona Diamondbacks), and Jacobs Field (Cleveland Indians).

The World Series. A half-dozen different teams claimed World Series titles during the decade, despite the series lost to the baseball strike. The New York Yankees won three championships (1996, 1998, and 1999); in 1998 they won more games (114) than any other team in baseball history. The Atlanta Braves also had a good decade, getting to the World Series five times, but winning only once (1995). The most unexpected championship season was provided by the Florida Marlins, the first and only team in major league history to win the World Series (1997) from a "wild card" berth. Immediately after the victory, owner Wayne Huizenga sold off the star players of his franchise, capitalizing on their high market value, and immediately watched his team drop from first to worst, from champs to last place in their division.

Rules of the Game. During the decade there were several substantive changes in the rules of the game. For the first time ever there was interleague play during the regular season. Unlike the designated hitter rule, this change met with almost unanimous approval as fans now had the opportunity to see teams that otherwise would never have competed in their home parks. Several structural changes took place, including the movement of the Milwaukee Brewers from the American to the National League in a first effort at realignment. A total of four new teams came into the major leagues, Colorado and Florida (1993) and

Arizona and Tampa Bay (1998). All but Tampa Bay joined the National League. A three-division format was introduced into each league, as was an extra tier of playoff games and a wild-card berth. Allan H. "Bud" Selig served as chair of the Major League Executive Council from September 1992 (when Fay Vincent resigned) until he was finally chosen as the ninth Commissioner of Baseball on 9 July 1998.

Sources:

MajorLeagueBaseball.com, Internet website.

Merrell Noden, *Home Run Heroes: Mark McGwire, Sammy Sosa and a Season for the Ages* (New York: Simon & Schuster, 1998).

BASKETBALL

Replay. As in previous eras in college basketball, many of the same teams stood at the forefront of the sport in the 1990s. National Collegiate Athletic Association (NCAA) championships were won by the all-time victory leader, Kentucky (1996 and 1998), as well as numbers two and four on the list, North Carolina (1993) and Duke (1991 and 1992). Only Kansas, third in all-time victories, did not win a championship, although they were runner-up in 1991. The University of California at Los Angeles (UCLA), a national power in the 1960s under John Wooden, returned to championship form with an undefeated romp through March Madness in 1995. In 1990 the University of Nevada at Las Vegas (UNLV), with the third-best winning percentage (.726) in NCAA history, behind Kentucky (.765) and North Carolina (.740), finally won a national crown. The universities of Arkansas (1994), Arizona (1997), and Connecticut (1999) won the other three Division I-A championships of the decade.

Women. The women's college basketball championships were almost equally predictable. Tennessee (with the highest all-time wins) took four titles (1991, 1996, 1997, and 1998; runner-up in 1995). Stanford won twice (1990 and 1992). Other NCAA Division I-A champions included Texas Tech (1993), North Carolina (1994), Connecticut (1995), and Purdue (1999). The University of Tennessee Lady Volunteers were dominant, winning every game in their 1997–1998 season and scoring an average 30.1 points more than their opponents, seventeen of which were top twenty-five teams. Most observers agreed they were the best women's college basketball team ever.

Domination? In NCAA I-A men's basketball, to say there was repetition of champions is not to say there was dominance by any team, league, or player. Duke had a down period following the surgery and recovery of Coach Mike Krzyzewski, who missed most of the 1994–1995 season with a back injury and stress-related exhaustion. Kentucky won its two championships under different coaches, Rick Pitino (who left to coach the Boston Celtics) and Tubby Smith, the first African American head basketball coach in the history of the college. Dean Smith, of North Carolina, surprised everyone by retiring after the 1997 season as the all-time winningest Division I-A coach with 879 victories, leaving his program in the hands of his

assistant, Bill Guthridge. As for league play, the Atlantic Coast Conference (ACC), Southeastern Conference (SEC), PAC 10, Big 10, and Big East could all make a case for their supremacy, but none made an unequivocal, indisputable statement for that designation. As for the player of the decade, Tim Duncan of Wake Forest could make as good a claim as anyone because he played a full four years with excellence, and was the best rebounder in the country in 1997 with 14.7 per game. He was awarded the Rupp Trophy and the Wooden and Naismith Awards and selected the Player of the Year; he was the first player taken in the 1997 National Basketball League (NBA) draft. In a new trend, many college players contributed to their team for a year or two and then declared themselves eligible for professional ball. Early departures from the college ranks included Shaquille O'Neal from Louisiana State University, Jason Kidd from the University of California at Berkeley, Allen Iverson from Georgetown University, Ron Mercer from Kentucky, Vince Carter and Antawn Jamison from North Carolina, Elton Brand from

Michael Jordan, guard for the Chicago Bulls, celebrating a win over the Utah Jazz in the NBA finals on 14 June 1998 (AP/World Wide Photos)

Duke, and dozens of others, many of whom never made it in the NBA.

Innovation. No innovations at the college level during the 1990s compared with the three radical changes introduced during the 1980s: a sixty-four-team field for the playoffs (1985), a shot clock to speed up the game (1986), and a three-point shot from the perimeter to increase outside scoring (1987). Instead, the most obvious alteration of the college game was that the NBA began to sign athletes right out of high school, thus allowing players who had little or no interest in academics to skip college basketball. Seven high school players entered the NBA, bypassing college, in the almost five decades from 1946 to 1994. In less than a half decade, from 1995 through 1998, another seven players made the high school-to-NBA leap. In addition to the dozens of early defections to the NBA and European teams, college basketball became less of a minor league system for the pros than it had been.

Popularity. Three of the top ten highest-rated televised college games were played during the decade, although all were in the first half of the decade, seeming to indicate a plateau in the popularity of the college game. The third highest-rated game was Duke versus Michigan on 6 April 1992; the fifth was North Carolina versus Michigan on 5 April 1993; and the sixth was Arkansas versus Duke on 4 April 1994. Any sense that college basketball was declining in popularity, however, was belied by the $6 billion price tag paid for the television rights to broadcast the end of season championship tournament, known as March Madness.

Bull Market. On the professional level, Michael Jordan was possibly the best athlete in the history of basketball. Other players did not necessarily look bad in comparison to him, but they certainly fell under his enormous shadow. Opponents could occasionally block his shots, or, in a given game, score more points, but the 1990s was his decade. Even during the labor dispute of 1998–1999, the first work stoppage in the history of the NBA, Billy Hunter, executive director of the players association, needed Jordan's considerable influence on their side to insure a favorable outcome for his constituency. Everyone understood that the game would not be the same when Jordan retired. It took no great marketing savvy to discern the significant difference in television ratings when Jordan and the Chicago Bulls were playing and when they were not. Jordan graciously delayed the announcement of his second retirement until the contract negotiations were concluded. The Bulls, largely because of Jordan, were the dominant team of the decade, even leading the league in merchandise sales. Other great players were a part of the mix at various times, including Horace Grant, Scottie Pippen, and Dennis Rodman. They also had an impressive coach in Phil Jackson. How these talented men might have succeeded without Jordan will never be known. For example, Jackson won six titles as Jordan's coach and none without him during the decade.

Other Stars. Jordan was not, however, the only story in the NBA. Other great players were a part of professional basketball, some of them of "all-century" caliber. Magic Johnson and Larry Bird ended their illustrious careers early, and Duncan began his career near the end of the decade. Charles Barkley, John Stockton, O'Neal, David Robinson, Hakeem Olajuwon, Clyde Drexler, and Karl Malone all played magnificently. These players helped formed two Dream Teams to represent the United States during the 1992 and 1996 Olympics, and they crushed their opponents to win two gold medals. The league seemed to become more competitive in Jordan's absence, as other "franchise" players had the opportunity to face off. Olajuwon, playing for the Houston Rockets, teamed with his former college teammate, Clyde Drexler, to defeat Stockton, Malone, and the Utah Jazz. Phoenix featured Barkley, while the San Antonio Spurs had league MVP Robinson. Orlando showcased the play of their star center, O'Neal. Even with such talented players, professional basketball was usually a delight to behold when Jordan was on the court. In addition to the grace with which he played the game, he had the charisma to keep the public fascinated and tuned in. Yet, none of the championship series in which the Bulls participated were blowouts. They always seemed vulnerable; there were enough subplots to keep the contests interesting and to make Jordan's heroics that much more amazing. In the 1996 finals against the Utah Jazz, Jordan faced Malone, who had won the MVP award that season. People wondered if the Malone/Stockton duo, after eleven years together, were good enough to overcome the Jordan/Pippen express. In the series Jordan averaged thirty-two points per game, hitting the buzzer-beater in the first game, scoring thirty-eight points in the fifth game despite being ill, scoring another thirty-nine points in the sixth and final game, and garnering MVP honors for the series. It took all of Jordan's magic to overcome the bad feelings of fans toward professional basketball on other fronts. Latrell Sprewell's choking of his Golden State Warriors coach P. J. Carlesimo on 1 December 1997, and his threats to kill Carlesimo, came across to the fans as typical of spoiled, rich athletes with whom spectators had little in common. It was impossible to retain the illusion that NBA stars were average men who had managed to succeed with hard work and talent. Clearly, such athletes were far from average. When a dispute between management and players threatened to halt play, it became hard for fans to contemplate paying $400 to attend a game while billionaire owners and millionaire athletes demanded a greater share of the spoils.

Women's Professional Basketball. Two women's professional basketball leagues were started during the decade, only one of which survived to the year 2000. The American Basketball League lasted from 1996 to 1998. The Women's National Basketball Association (WNBA) had sounder financial underpinnings, being sponsored by the NBA. It began in 1997 as a summer league, with eight teams, not in direct competition with the traditional basketball season. By 2000 the league had sixteen teams, double the original eight. The Houston Comets won all three league championships; Houston's Cynthia Cooper took two league MVP awards; Houston's Van Chancellor won Coach of the Year all three years. Attendance looked promising, and several female stars shined, including Cooper, Jennifer Azzi, Lisa Leslie, Rebecca Lobo, and Sheryl Swoopes.

Sources:
CBS.sportsline.com, Internet website.
NBA.com, Internet website.
Sports Illustrated 1999 Sports Almanac (Boston: Little, Brown, 1998).
WNBA.com, Internet website.

BOXING

Bothered and Bewildered. The sport of boxing, never tidy, was complicated and confusing during the 1990s. Much of what was not mystifying—for example, Mike Tyson biting off part of Evander Holyfield's ear during a 1997 bout—was deplorable. People began to compare professional boxing with professional wrestling, an image not helped when Tyson agreed to "referee" a wrestling match in Boston. The state of Washington broke another precedent when it sanctioned a boxing match between a man and woman—she won. It was a decade in which even boxing enthusiasts had a hard time finding positive things to say about their sport. Richard Hoffer, of *Sports Illustrated*, complained of the "forgettable seasons in boxing" and "unearned dollars for unexciting fights." In a fit of editorial pique, Hoffer wrote, "Holyfield zipped up to New York to meet Akinwande who had earned this title shot by . . . well, no one could say how." Tim Graham, writing for

Mike Tyson biting the ear of Evander Holyfield during the WBA Heavyweight match at the MGM Grand in Las Vegas on 28 June 1997 (AP/Wide World Photos)

ESPN.com, argued that the final year of the decade with regard to boxing was "an all-time low. . . . [It] was rife with larceny, tragedy, gluttony, stupidity. They're all ingrained aspects of the sport, but such heavy doses of them all were enough to choke a goat." Part of the problem, in 1999, was the indictment of International Boxing Federation (IBF) president Robert W. Lee Sr. and three others for accepting bribes and soliciting payments to alter rankings and arrange fights. It was hardly a decade to inspire confidence in fans of boxing.

Unclear Titles. Part of the confusion in boxing was the result of seventeen principal weight divisions (with fighters often moving back and forth among them) and three different sanctioning bodies. Producing a chart to show the current champions required fifty-two names. In addition to the IBF there was also the World Boxing Federation (WBF) and World Boxing Council (WBC). "Undisputed" titles were rare because getting the required matches arranged were difficult. Not only did both boxers have to be ready to fight at the same time in the same ring, their promoters had to have no conflicting engagements, commitments, or contracts, and the television sponsors needed to be in concert. If one boxer was signed exclusively with Home Box Office (HBO) and another was marketed through Showtime, then that became just one more obstacle to a title bout.

In the Ring. In spite of all these impediments, some good boxing did take place. At the start of the decade, Tyson, Holyfield, Canadian Lennox Lewis (all heavyweight fighters), Pernell Whitaker (a lightweight who moved up to welterweight), and Oscar de la Hoya (starting at lightweight, then a super lightweight and welterweight) all showed signs of having great potential, but the results were mixed. Tyson got in trouble with the law too often. De la Hoya could not decide whether to fight or run in the ring. Roy Jones Jr., however, became a fighting force; with a 14–1 record in championship fights, ranging from middleweight to light heavyweight, he was considered the best pound-for-pound boxer in the world. The decade ended with Holyfield as WBF and IBF heavyweight champion and Lewis as WBC champion in the same weight class. They fought to a draw on 13 March 1999 in Madison Square Garden, but Lennox won the undisputed championship in a rematch on 13 November, the first such unified champion since Riddick Bowe in 1992.

Sources:
ESPN.go.com, Internet website.
Sports Illustrated 1999 Sports Almanac (Boston: Little, Brown, 1998).

FOOTBALL: COLLEGE

Championship Confusion. The 1990s was an exciting decade for college football despite off-field distractions and a complex system that left much to be desired in determining which team was actually the best in the land. Eleven different teams claimed national championships, including three won by the University of Nebraska (1994, 1995, and a shared title in 1997 with

Grambling State University head coach Eddie Robinson speaking on the telephone with President Clinton on 7 October 1995, after his team's victory gave the coach his four-hundredth college football win (AP/Wide World Photos)

Michigan). Division I-A football was the only collegiate sport that had no officially sanctioned championship. Other champions included Alabama (1992), Florida State (1993 and 1999), Florida (1996), and Tennessee (1998). Such title confusion (for example, Colorado and Georgia Tech shared the 1990 title, and Miami and Washington shared it in 1991) led to the eventual establishment of the Bowl Championship Series (BCS). In 1998, though still without a playoff system, the National Collegiate Athletic Association (NCAA) organized an intentional end-of-the-season game between the two top-ranked teams (as determined by a complicated system of poll rankings, computer ratings, and losses). Beginning in 1995, prior to the BCS, a Bowl Alliance Championship Game was played, but this system failed to include the Rose Bowl, which matched the champions from the Big Ten and Pac-10 conferences. Even the BCS system, however, did not guarantee that the best two teams would play for the championship, but it was an improvement on the old system. Included in the BCS were the Fiesta, Orange, Sugar and Rose Bowls, which alternated as host of the "title" game.

League Realignments. Several conferences also adopted league Championship Games as a result of realignment and expansion, especially those conferences that increased from eight or ten teams to a maximum of twelve. The Southeastern Conference (SEC) began such a playoff between its two division winners with Alabama defeating Florida in its inaugural venture in 1992 at Legion Field in Birmingham. The Big 12 (formerly the Big 8) sponsored its first playoff game in 1996 with Texas defeating Nebraska. The conference had added, in 1995–1996, four teams from the defunct Southwest Conference (Baylor, Texas, Texas A&M, and Texas Tech). The SEC welcomed two new teams in 1990: Arkansas, from the Southwest Conference, and South Carolina, formerly an independent. The Atlantic Coast Conference (ACC) added Florida State in 1990 while the Big Ten picked up Penn State. The Big East Conference was founded in 1991 when its charter members gave up independent football status to form a league, which included such schools as Boston College, Miami (Florida), Pittsburgh, Rutgers, Syracuse, Temple, Virginia Tech, and West Virginia.

Parity on the Field. Some new teams emerged to challenge the dominance of traditional teams, while traditional powerhouses faltered. It was a decade of increasing parity in college football, in some ways, with teams such as Virginia Tech and Marshall rising to prominence while others, such as Notre Dame and Southern California, experienced less success than they were accustomed to achieving. At the same time, familiar names kept appearing atop the list of teams with the most wins, including Florida State, Nebraska, Florida, Tennessee, Penn State, and Miami. Marshall was one of two teams to dominate I-AA football, winning two national championships and being runner-up three times, before joining the I-A Mid-American Conference in 1995. They ended the final season of the decade undefeated. The other I-AA powerhouse was Youngstown State, which won four titles (1991, 1993, 1994, and 1996).

Coaches. Tom Osborne, after his Nebraska team won three national championships in four years, retired after the 1997 season. He had the highest winning percentage of any active coach (.836). Phillip Fulmer of Tennessee had the highest winning percentage of active I-A coaches, followed by Joe Paterno (Penn State), Steve Spurrier (Florida), and Bobby Bowden (Florida State). Eddie Robinson retired after fifty-five years at Grambling, a career that spanned eleven U.S. presidencies, as the most successful all-time college coach with 408 victories. Paterno and Bowden both approached Paul "Bear" Bryant's record of most wins by a I-A coach (323).

The Players. Some great players passed through the ranks of college football during the decade, despite many early defections to the professional ranks as National Football League (NFL) teams offered huge signing bonuses to the most skilled players. In the 1998 draft twenty different underclassmen were selected, including the number two pick, Ryan Leaf (quarterback) of Washington State by the San Diego Chargers and number four pick Charles Woodson (cornerback and Heisman Trophy winner) of Michigan by the Oakland Raiders. Nine underclassmen were selected in the first round. Notable top draft picks of the decade included Jeff George (Illinois quarterback), Drew Bledsoe (Washington State quarterback), Ki-Jana Carter (Penn State running back), Orlando Pace (Ohio State offensive tackle), Peyton Manning (Tennessee quarterback), and Steve Emtman (Washington defensive tackle). Heisman Trophy winners usually consisted of a totally different group of young men (for reasons only those casting the votes can explain), including Ty Detmer (Brigham Young, quarterback), Desmond Howard (Michigan wide receiver), Charlie Ward (Florida State, quarterback), Ricky Williams (Texas running back), and Eddie George (Ohio State running back). Other notable college players included Tommy Frazier (Nebraska quarterback), Randy Moss (Marshall wide receiver), Warren Sapp (Miami [Florida] defensive lineman), Marshall Faulk (San Diego State running back), Tony Boselli (Southern California offensive lineman) and Anthony Simmons (Clemson linebacker).

Sources:

The 1999 ESPN Information Please Sports Almanac (New York: Hyperion Press, 1998).

The Sports Illustrated 1999 Sports Almanac (Boston: Little, Brown, 1998).

FOOTBALL: PROFESSIONAL

Change for the Sunday Game. The 1990s was a decade of expansion and change for the National Football League (NFL). New franchises and stadiums, additional wild-card teams in the playoffs, expanding television coverage, and increased audiences and attendance all meant more money for the owners and players, but higher ticket prices for the fans. Several teams moved to new cities (for example, the Rams from Los Angeles to St. Louis; the Oilers from Houston to Nashville, now known as the Tennessee Titans) in search of better facilities, larger markets, and other financial incentives. The Jacksonville Jaguars and Carolina Panthers joined the league, and Cleveland was awarded a new team (although they kept their old name, the Browns) after the former franchise had moved to Baltimore (to become the Ravens). The expansion of the draft into the ranks of college underclassmen meant that good players often left school early to pursue large contracts. Multimillion-dollar salaries and bonuses for untested rookies became the norm.

On-and-Off-the-Field Problems. Many of the headaches for league officials came from off-the-field criminal activities, ranging from drug offenses to domestic abuse. There were ever-expanding fines against players for senseless fights away from the stadiums, as well as for shoving referees on the field. In July 1999 three members of the New York Jets were arrested following a bar fight. Current and former players were cited for possession of drugs, driving while intoxicated or vehicular offenses, and other violent actions; some NFL players even went to jail. Several players even attacked and wounded fellow teammates in practice sessions. Most seriously, at the end of the decade, Rae Carruth, a wide receiver for the Carolina Panthers, was on trial for the murder in a drive-by shooting of his wife, who was pregnant with their child, on 16 November 1999. Ray Lewis, a Baltimore linebacker, was for a short time also accused of murder, although the charges were eventually dropped. At the end of the decade the league instituted tougher penalties for players who committed serious offenses.

Super Powers. The decade began with perennial powers the San Francisco 49ers, New York Giants, Washington Redskins, and Dallas Cowboys winning Super Bowls. Dallas won three (1993, 1994, and 1996) and San Francisco two (1990 and 1995). The Giants (1991) and Redskins (1992) each won one, as did former "good ol' days" champions, the Green Bay Packers (1997), their first title in twenty-nine years. Their victory was widely hailed as a deserved reward for faithful fans and for three-time league MVP Brett Favre. Finally, a (relatively) new team won the championship when the Denver Broncos and John Elway finally took the title in 1998. No American Football Conference (AFC) team, inexplicably, had won a Super Bowl since 1984, until Denver won two in a row, the second in

1999 against the Atlanta Falcons. The final season of the decade ended with the St. Louis Rams and Tennessee Titans heading to Super Bowl XXXIV (which was played on 30 January 2000 and won by the Rams).

Trouble in Dallas. Once America's Team, the Dallas Cowboys seemed to be despised by many fans during the decade. Callers to radio sports-talk shows, and for that matter, sportswriters and commentators, could not show enough contempt for owner Jerry Jones and coach Barry Switzer. At the end of the 1980s Jones had brought in Jimmy Johnson from the University of Miami (Florida) Hurricanes to coach his team, and Johnson led the Cowboys to two consecutive championships. A series of off-the-field activities by his players, however, ranging from accusations of drug use to battery, some of which were later discovered to be false, stained the image of the team. Jones did not help himself either in the eyes of management, defying the NFL by signing sponsorship deals with Pepsi and Nike that broke the spirit and letter of league rules. Then, in a feud with Johnson, Jones fired his successful coach and hired renegade Oklahoma University coach Switzer, who had enough coaching skills and player talent to win one more Super Bowl, before he moved on from his own mutually disagreeable relationship with Jones. No wonder fans embraced Favre and the Packers in 1997–1998, and then Elway and the Broncos in 1998–1999.

Big Names. The fans cheered Joe Montana during his last years at the helm of the San Francisco 49ers dynasty that lasted into 1990, when he won another MVP award and the Super Bowl. Dan Marino, quarterback for the Miami Dolphins, eclipsed Fran Tarkenton (Minnesota Vikings and New York Giants, 1961–1978) in four passing categories—attempts, completions, yards, and touchdowns. Jerry Rice, wide receiver for the 49ers, established all-time records for receptions and reception yardage. Emmitt Smith, running back for the Cowboys, tallied twenty-five touchdowns in 1995, breaking the old standard. Barry Sanders, Terrell Davis, Steve Young, and Reggie White were other high-profile and popular players during the decade. Another enormously talented quarterback came on the professional football stage at the end of the decade; Peyton Manning led the previously hapless Indianapolis Colts into the playoffs in just his second year (from a 3–13 record to 13–3). A new crop of players were also poised to achieve stardom, including Randy Moss, Tim Couch, Kurt Warner, Edgerrin James, and Ricky Williams. Don Shula, longtime coach for both the Baltimore Colts (1963–1969) and Miami Dolphins (1970–1995), became the winningest coach in NFL history on 14 November 1993; when Shula retired after the 1995 season, he had led his teams to 347 victories.

Still Popular. In spite of its detractors, NFL football continued to be the most popular spectator sport in the country. It was so favored, in fact, that the league sold the rights to broadcast its games for an eight-year

---

SOUPER BOWL OF CARING

More than $7 million was raised for charity during the 1990s thanks to a creative response to a perennial problem by the youth minister of a South Carolina church. Brad Smith, associate pastor of the Spring Valley Presbyterian Church and founder of the Souper Bowl of Caring, came up with the simple plan in 1989 of having members of his youth group stand at the exits of the church with pots and pans on Super Bowl Sunday to collect $1 from each person. On a day of excess and extravagance, he reasoned, surely churchgoers could manage to give $1 each so that a hungry person could eat. The idea was so well received that it was shared with other churches in the area, then around the state, and then nationwide. The money was used in the village or city where it was collected. It was not sent "away" for someone else to distribute, but each church made the decision about which local charity should benefit. Sponsors were asked, however, to report the amount of the gifts received so that a nationwide tally could be kept. By the end of the decade even the National Football League (NFL) had joined the crusade, supporting the cause in a variety of ways. More than eleven thousand congregations participated in 1999, giving millions of dollars to local benevolence, an impressive amount for an organization and for an idea only ten years old.

Source: The Souper Bowl, Internet website.

---

period for $17.6 billion. No sport at any level capitalized on television as well as pro football. One example was the constant tweaking of instant replay. Banned after 1992 (after being in use for six years), it was reinstated in an altered fashion in 1999. Other evidence of television savvy was the addition of a additional wildcard level for the playoffs. Helping to keep the sport in the forefront was its remarkable level of parity during the decade, as many teams experienced disastrous declines or remarkable turnarounds in success. For instance, the participants in Super Bowl XXXIII, Denver and Atlanta, experienced the ignominy of having their records fall to 6–10 and 5–11 respectively, in the following season. Adding to the excitement for the fans, during the next-to-last weekend of the 1999 schedule every game played had playoff implications, an amazing result of parity and scheduling. Few fans cared that 8–8 teams made the playoffs. The goal was not to create a dynasty but to create fan interest. As a result, there was a per-game rise in average attendance at each game of about one thousand fans, up to 65,349. This figure represented an almost five-thousand-fan-per-game increase since 1996. Even expansion teams benefited from parity. In their second year of existence under head coach Dom Capers, the Carolina Panthers

Denver Broncos quarterback John Elway celebrating a touchdown scored against the Atlanta Falcons in the Super Bowl on 31 January 1999 (AP/Wide World Photos)

posted a 12–4 record and won the NFC West title. In the same year, 1996, the Jacksonville Jaguars, coached by Tom Coughlin, beat the Buffalo Bills and the Denver Broncos en route to the AFC championship game. What Aikman called a "watered-down league" became another term for exciting football. George Young, senior vice president for the NFL and former general manager of the New York Giants, asked, "Why should there be anointed teams and anointed cities? Wouldn't you get tired of that?" More to the point, Les Carpenter, a reporter for the *Seattle Times*, pointed out that "Parity equals profit."

Sources:

NFL.com, Internet website.

Official 1998 National Football League Record & Fact Book (New York: Workman, 1998).

Prosportspage.com, Internet website.

The Sports Illustrated 1999 Sports Almanac (Boston: Little, Brown, 1998).

GOLF

The Golden Bear. Any discussion of professional golf in the second half of the twentieth century has to pay attention to at least five things: the four major "Grand Slam" tournaments and Jack Nicklaus. Even in his sixth decade, Nicklaus dominated the news from the Professional Golfers Association (PGA) and the talk on golf courses everywhere. Though he did not win a "major" golf tournament during the 1990s, he kept things interesting

and exciting in a variety of ways. He was on every all-sports all-century list (ninth athlete overall on the ESPN list, the top golfer listed) that came out. In 1998 he made the Augusta National exciting with a Sunday charge that had him only two strokes off the lead on the front nine on the final day of the tournament. He ended up in sixth place, only four strokes more than the winner. He added an occasional visit to the Senior Tour to his regular participation in the major championships. He won two U.S. Senior Opens (1991 and 1993) and finally, after 146 consecutive appearances in the major championships, declined to participate in the U.S. Open, a streak unlikely to be broken.

A New Star. Yet, as Nicklaus's star began to dim, another player, Tiger Woods, seemed to challenge his status as the greatest golfer of the century. Indeed, no player other than Nicklaus had ever dominated the sport as Woods did toward the end of the 1990s. Woods's reign began as a teenager, when he won the U.S. Amateur for three consecutive years (1994–1996), as well as the National Collegiate Athletic Association (NCAA) championship in 1996. When he turned pro in September 1996, his first year was better than the lifetime careers of most players. He won the fifth event he entered, the Las Vegas Invitational, and six of twenty-five events, breaking the single-season money record. He won the 1997 Masters by shooting eighteen-under-par, twelve strokes better than

If anyone needed proof that real sporting events were merely the foundation for an industry that took on a life of its own, the media's pursuit of sports-related news—regardless of its relevance to actual athletic endeavors—provided all one needed in examining the sports section of the morning newspapers. Pick a day, any day. Toward the end of the millennium, a typical fall day, in the heart of college and pro football seasons, at the beginning of college and pro basketball seasons, the front page of the sports section of the popular national newspaper, *USA Today*, had five articles. Only one of these stories was about an athletic event: "Jazz Hand Blazers First Loss 92–87." The other articles, including the two leads, were mostly about politics and money. The self-proclaimed "Cover Story" was titled, "Entering the Political Arena: Ex-athletes, Sports People Get in the Game for Bradley," an article about the senator and former New York Knick who had entered the presidential campaign. The other lead story was, "Yankees' Payroll Surpasses $90M; Baseball's Average Pay Up to $1.57M." Other front-page stories were "NHL's Senators Suspend Yashin for Season" (about a contract dispute between a professional hockey franchise and a star player, or, more appropriately, a non-player), and "Smith Out; Aikman Uncertain" (about injuries sustained by two professional football players).

The front page of the *USA Today* sports section also had a "topbar" and a half-dozen "sidebar" stories, short blurbs about various sporting matters, or, in some instances, non-sporting items. One snippet reported that *Young America* (a yacht), though it had broken in two, still had a chance to qualify for the Louis Vuitton Cup if it could get its backup ready to sail. The top item in the sidebar directed readers to a "focus" article on page 3C about high school athletes choosing colleges at an earlier age: "Some say teenagers are being bullied into early decisions." The announcement of the American League "Top Rookie," Kansas City outfielder Carlos Beltran, was the next sidebar item, followed by an observation about an actual sporting story in process, jockey Laffit Pincay Jr.'s bid to overtake Bill Shoemaker's record of 8,833 victories. The next story was about the withdrawal of figure skater Nicole Bobek from an exhibition after she was taken to a hospital. Then came the announcement that prize money for the upcoming winter Goodwill Games would be $647,600. Finally, one sidebar announced that Fred Couples would substitute for Payne Stewart in the Skins Game. Stewart was killed in a 25 October 1999 plane crash.

USA Today also had the scores of pro basketball and pro hockey on the front page, and readers were directed to "coverage" further inside the paper. There was also a graph of the "NFL's All-time Career Points Scored Leaders." Front-page advertisements, as well, encouraged the reader to give a gift subscription to *USA Today*, purchase *Baseball Weekly* at a local newsstand, or fly KLM and/or Northwest Airlines. A framed block featuring a sports quiz asked: "Who is the youngest person ever to win a Wimbledon Match?" The reader had to turn the paper sideways to read the answer, "Jennifer Capriati, at 14 years, 89 days."

The front page featured four pictures, the largest of Bill Bradley with former NBA stars John Havlicek and Billy Cunningham. There are smaller pictures of an unnamed *Young America* crewmember preparing to abandon ship, of Rookie of the Year, Carlos Beltran, and of Michelle Munoz, a high school basketball player who had committed to play basketball at the University of Tennessee.

The entire sports section consisted of fourteen pages, and included stories on NASCAR, Tiger Woods, Ken Griffey, baseball payrolls, Emmitt Smith, domestic violence and the death of the wife of NFL defensive back Steve Muhammad, NFL standings, a full-page advertisement of Woods promoting American Express, NHL news including some game reviews and trade information, analysis and commentary on college basketball, field hockey, volleyball and cross country, female student managers, NBA "Team by Team Notes," an article on Michael Jordan dropping by "to see his former team," women's boxing, the new floor for the Boston Celtics, women's tennis (accompanied by a picture of Anna Kournikova–who was barely relevant to the story), betting lines, and a host of other lists, advertisements, and trivial bits of information. *USA Today*, like most other media at the turn of the century, was no longer merely a reporter of the news, but was part of the entertainment industry.

his nearest competitor. He suffered a "sophomore slump" in 1998, yet still compiled a record that many golfers would envy, winning three events. Then, in 1999, he dominated professional golf, setting another record in earnings, more than double any other golfer in history ($6,616,585).

Many Players Shine. Though Woods dominated the headlines, many professional golfers played well during the decade. Hale Irwin won the U.S. Open (1990), three PGA Senior Championships (1996–1998), the U.S. Senior Open (1998), and the Senior Players Championship (1999). Lee Janzen and Payne Stewart each won the U.S. Open twice. Stewart's death in a plane crash in 1999, however, cut short his brilliant career. Mark O'Meara had a good 1998, winning both the Masters and the British Open. John Daly won two majors, the PGA (1991) and

Justin Leonard after sinking his putt on the 17th hole at the Ryder Cup in Brookline, Massachusetts, on 26 September 1999 (AP/Wide World Photos)

Island, South Carolina, and in 1993 at the Belfry Golf Club in Sutton Coldfield, England. The Europeans evened the score with victories at Oak Hill Country Club at Rochester, New York, in 1995, and the Valderrama Golf Club in Sotogrande, Spain, in 1997. The 1999 contest, the tiebreaker for the decade, at The Country Club of Brookline, Massachusetts, began with the Europeans appearing to run away with the title. To overtake a talented squad led by nineteen-year-old Sergio Garcia, Paul Lawrie, Colin Montgomerie, and Jesper Parnevik, the Americans (led by Hal Sutton, Tom Lehman, Steve Pate, Jeff Maggert, and Phil Mickelson) required the greatest final day comeback in the history of the event. Beginning with an 8–4 deficit, the Americans tallied an 8½ to 3½ point margin on the final day for the victory. The excitement of Justin Leonard sinking a long putt on the seventeenth hole generated a premature celebration by the American team that was roundly condemned in the European press. The criticism was justified since the victory was not actually secured until after Jose Maria Olazabal missed his putt. Despite the flak, it was a great way for American golfers to end the decade.

Sources:

CNNSI.com, Internet website.

LPGA Tour, Internet website.

NandoSportserver.com, Internet website.

PGATOUR.com, Internet website.

The Sports Illustrated 1999 Sports Almanac (Boston: Little, Brown, 1998).

HOCKEY

Southern Exposure. Much to the consternation of Canadian fans, ice hockey moved south in the 1990s as six new National Hockey League (NHL) franchises played in the Sun Belt—the San Jose Sharks (1991), Tampa Bay Lightning (1992), Mighty Ducks of Anaheim (1993), Florida Panthers (1993), Nashville Predators (1998), and Atlanta Thrashers (1999). Only one traditional venue for hockey was added in the decade, the Ottawa Senators (1992). Having gained the Senators, Canada lost the Quebec Nordiques in 1995 when they became the Colorado Avalanche; at the same time the Winnipeg Jets moved to Arizona where they became the Phoenix Coyotes. Completing the southern migration of major league hockey was the relocation of the Hartford Whalers to Raleigh, North Carolina, to become the Carolina Hurricanes. In 1999 one of the southern teams even won the Stanley Cup, the symbol of league supremacy, when the Dallas Stars beat the Buffalo Sabres, four games to two. The southern orientation was the theme for minor league hockey as well. Delightfully named teams sprang up in surprising places where outdoor hockey was impossible: the Austin (Texas) Ice Bats, Waco (Texas) Wizards, Shreveport (Louisiana) Mudbugs, Monroe (Louisiana) Moccasins, Odessa (Texas) Jackalopes, San Antonio (Texas) Iguanas, and Louisiana Ice Gators. These "minor league" teams and arenas were not to be confused with the minor league baseball experience in many of these same Southern

British Open (1995), but toward the end of the decade seemed to be losing a battle with personal demons. Other players who won regularly and made big money included Davis Love III, Fred Couples, Tom Kite, and David Duval—each earning, by the end of the decade, more that $10 million apiece in their careers.

Ladies Professional Golf Association. Women's golf also had its bright lights. Betsy King began the 1990s as she concluded the 1980s, winning two U.S. Women's Opens (1989–1990) and three Dinah Shore Classics (1987, 1990, 1997) en route to becoming the all-time leading money winner on the women's tour with $6.3 million. Other multiple American winners in the major women's tournaments included Beth Daniel, Patty Sheehan, Meg Mallon, and Juli Inkster.

The Ryder Cup. One of the surprising golfing stories of the decade was the Ryder Cup. Traditionally, this event had been a match between the United States and Great Britain, annually dominated by the Americans. In 1977 other European golfers joined the British, and the result was some of the most exciting golf in the world. The United State won in 1991 at the Ocean Course at Kiawah

The nearly spontaneous emergence of "extreme sports" was a testimony to the competitive instincts of men and women. With roots often far outside traditional sporting pastimes, such as baseball and basketball, the development of competitions in these extreme sports had innocent enough origins. Indeed, these athletes were often the geeks and nerds who did not try out for "organized" team sports that required the systematic discipline of weight lifting and daily group calisthenics. These young men and women marched to their own drummer, did their own thing, even spoke their own language (for example, "fakies" and "grinds").

Originally, skateboarding was simply a preadolescent activity carried out in the neighborhoods and on the sidewalks of the strip malls while parents were shopping or having their hair done. Their presence was often unappreciated and scorned—what shopper with a pile of packages wanted to be knocked down by a pubescent boy with the social skills and graces of a young bull, and who cared that he was doing amazing things athletically on the skateboard? Signs were often posted that read: "No skateboarding or bicycling allowed." Skating therefore acquired somewhat of an outlaw and outsider image. Stickers on skateboards retaliated with the complaint "Skateboarding is not a crime." Yet, Saturday afternoon skating was hardly the stuff of Olympic endeavor.

Or was it? Competitive instincts ultimately kicked in as youths competed to see who could go fastest or whose trick was the most outlandish. Informal competition led from a casual contest in the emptied-out backyard swimming pool to more formal venues. Some communities even built special parks for skateboarders. As this new breed of athlete sought better competition and recognition for their sports, the Entertainment and Sports Programming Network (ESPN) stepped in to organize and televise the X Games (first held from 24 June to 1 July 1995 in Newport and Providence, Rhode Island, and Mt. Snow, Vermont). Promoted as a showcase for "alternative" sports, the X Games filled a sporting niche. The evolution is far from complete with new sports being added and "old" ones (such as bungee jumping) being dropped.

Four years later the 1999 X Games were more widely promoted. Resulting media coverage indicated that these activities were no longer considered part of the ghetto of athleticism. Although far from rivaling the Super Bowl or World Series, the X Games nonetheless attracted a national television audience. Soon other competitions, such as the Gravity Games and Big Air Invitational, not to mention the World Quarterpipe Championships, tapped into this burgeoning sports movement.

Athletes whose names were far from familiar in the average U.S. household, for example, Fabiola da Silva, Dave Mirra, and Tony Hawk, dominated the Extreme Games. In skateboarding, da Silva won the "Women's Vert" Gold from 1996 to 1998. In 1999 Hawk won the "Best Trick" contest by executing what many believe to be the ultimate skateboarding feat, a "900." Translated, he made two complete 360-degree rotations and another half rotation of 180 degrees, a total of 900 degrees or two and a half turns—coming out of a "half-pipe" in a vertical or "vert" jump. Indicative that there was something different about these games was the support Hawk received from his fellow competitors as he came closer to achieving what some have called the "Holy Grail" of skateboarding. Although the event was supposed to be completed within a specified time limit, as Hawk got closer and closer to achieving the 900 successfully, his rivals put down their own skateboards (figuratively speaking—in reality, they were banging their boards on the ramp) and watched him just miss on ten different attempts until, on his eleventh effort, he succeeded. The title, with their blessing, was his.

Mirra won the bicycle vertical (vert) jump gold medal for the third straight year in 1999. By the end of the decade he had a total of eight gold and two silver medals. Despite the doubters or athletic purists, who wondered at the difficulty of the skills involved, these athletes attempted and succeeded at remarkable feats, such as backflips on bicycles. Other extreme sports included (but are not limited to) Skysurfing, In-Line Skating, Barefoot Water-ski Jumping, Snowboarding, and Ice Climbing. Bowling and fresh water fishing may still be the most popular sports in the United States, but at the end of the decade in-line skating had more than thirty-two million participants, mountain biking eight million, skateboarding seven million, and snowboarding five million.

The language of these extreme or alternative games was as interesting as the sporting events themselves. Magazine articles mentioning "feeding the monkey" (the one that has been on your back while you have been waiting for the first snowfall of the winter), "gnarlier chutes," "a pillow of pow" (powered snow, soft to land on or in), and "straight-lining" dominate the genre. There were off-road skates, longboards, dirt bikes, gravity downhill skateboards, wakeboards, paraglides, snowmobiles, and all-terrain boards. There was no lack of merchandising possibilities in extreme sports, so there was no limit to corporate sponsorships in even the most alternative of these activities.

Sources: *Core Sports Magazine: The Magazine for Extreme Sports*
ESPN.com, Internet website.

Captain Tom Fitzgerald skates onto the ice at the inaugural game of the Nashville Predators hockey team on 10 October 1998 (AP/Wide World Photos).

towns, a laid-back gathering in the bright sunshine attended by a couple thousand baseball lovers and home-team supporters. There was nothing relaxing about the pace or enthusiasm with which these ice hockey teams were embraced by their hosts. Arenas that seated five thousand to twelve thousand people sold out regularly to fun-loving and occasionally rowdy fans, who loved their teams and the minor league prices ($5 per person, for example, with 25¢-hotdog nights).

New Players and Fans. League expansion did not increase the number of talented high school and college recruits to the professional ranks. The results were apparent on the scoreboard. During the 1997–1998 season, only 5.3 goals per game were scored, the lowest per-game average in forty-two years. Four consecutive years of four-game blowouts for the Stanley Cup title did nothing to help television ratings, which dropped 27 percent during the regular season and 22 percent during the playoffs. U.S. and Canadian talent often took a backseat to players from Russia, the Czech Republic, and Finland. In a move to increase public awareness of the sport in the United States, the NHL allowed a seventeen-day break from league play so players could participate in the Olympics in Nagano, Japan, in 1998, the first Olympics in which professional hockey players were allowed to participate. The ploy may have benefited hockey in other countries, with the Czech Republic beating Russia for the gold medal after beating Canada in the semifinals, but it did little for the sport in the United States. The team behaved badly off the ice, committing thousands of dollars worth of vandalism after a 4 to 1 loss to the Czechs. In marked contrast, the U.S. Women's Hockey Team won the gold at the same Olympiad.

Great Players and Coaches. Wayne Gretzky ("The Great One") retired, after a year as a free agent with the New York Rangers, in 1999 at age thirty-eight. Well past his prime, Gretzky still led the league in assists. In 1997–1998, he became the sixth player in NHL history to lead his team (the Rangers) in goals at age thirty-seven or older. Earlier in the decade, he led the league in assists from 1990 to 1992 and in 1994. He won the Art Ross Trophy (1990, 1991, and 1994) for most points scored, calculated by adding goals made and assists. Lemieux won the award four of the other seven years (1992, 1993, 1996, and 1997), and Jaromir Jagr won the award the other three years (1995, 1998, and 1999). Scotty Bowman, the all-time winningest coach in professional hockey, did not retire and kept on winning games and championships. With 1,300 career victories through the 1999 season, Bowman added three Stanley Cups to his resume (1992—with Pittsburgh, and 1997 and 1998—with Detroit, giving him a total of eight). No other coach, active or inactive, comes close. He had the highest winning percentage as well, at .651. Mike Keenan, whose New York Rangers team won the Stanley Cup in 1994, was second among active coaches in both categories with 597 wins and a .568 winning percentage.

Sources:
NHL.com, Internet website.

The 1999 ESPN Information Please Sports Almanac (New York: Hyperion Press, 1998).

The Sports Illustrated 1999 Sports Almanac (Boston: Little, Brown, 1998).

THE OLYMPICS

Albertville, France: (1992). The first Olympiad of the decade, and the first in the post-Cold War era, began with concern for the fragile alpine ecology of its venue. Competing athletes convened in Albertville, France, in 1992, only for the opening and closing ceremonies. Otherwise, they dispersed throughout the region for the games. That model, far less disruptive to the natural beauty of Winter Olympic venues, has been successfully adopted in each Olympiad since. The breakup of the Soviet Union and the dismantling of the Berlin Wall made an impact on the Olympics as countries such as Lithuania, Estonia, and Latvia competed under their own flags for the first time since prior to World War II. Germany fielded one team instead of two, and some former Soviet athletes competed under the Unified Team name, though the flags of their separate republics were raised as individual winners stood on the victory stand. In the actual competition the U.S. team as a whole turned in a fairly "typical" performance, placing fifth in the number of gold medals captured with five, behind Germany (ten), the Unified Team (nine), Norway (nine), and Austria (six). The most interesting medals won by the Americans were in the showcase event of women's figure skating, where Kristi Yamaguchi, the favorite, won the gold, and Nancy Kerrigan won the bronze. Kerrigan's rise to prominence was to be the ice skating story of the next two years as she won the U.S.

1992 Winter Olympics (Albertville, France)

Bonnie Blair, Women's Speed Skating, Long Track, 500 meter, Women's Speed Skating, Long Track, 1000 meter

Cathy Turner, Women's Speed Skating, Short Track, 500 meter

Donna Weinbrecht, Women's Moguls, Freestyle Skiing

Kristi Yamaguchi, Women's Figure Skating

Summer Olympics (Barcelona, Spain)

Mike Barrowman, Swimming, Men's 200-meter Breaststroke

Bruce Baumgartner, Freestyle Wrestling, Super-Heavyweight

Jennifer Capriati, Women's Tennis, Singles

Mike Conley, Track and Field, Men's Triple Jump

Oscar De La Hoya, Boxing, Lightweight

Gail Devers, Track and Field, Women's 100-meter

Nelson Diebel, Swimming, Men's 100-meter Breaststroke

Trent Dimas, Gymnastics, Men's Horizontal Bar

Janet Evans, Swimming, Women's 800–meter Freestyle

Gigi Fernandez and Mary Jo Fernandez, Women's Tennis, Doubles

Nicole Haislett, Swimming, Women's 200-meter Freestyle

Kevin Jackson, Freestyle Wrestling, Middleweight

Jackie Joyner-Kersee, Track and Field, Women's Heptathlon

Mike Lenzi, Men's Springboard Diving

Carl Lewis, Track and Field, Men's Long Jump

Mike Marsh, Track and Field, Men's 200-meter

Launi Meili, Women's Small Bore Rifle

Pablo Morales, Swimming, Men's 100-meter Butterfly

Summer Sanders, Swimming, Women's 200-meter Butterfly

John Smith, Freestyle Wrestling, Featherweight

Melvin Stewart, Swimming, Men's 200-meter Butterfly

Mike Stulce, Track and Field, Men's Shot Put

Gwen Torrence, Track and Field, Women's 200-meter

Quincy Watts, Track and Field, Men's 400 meter

Kevin Young, Track and Field, men's 400-meter Hurdles

1994 Winter Olympics (Lillehammer, Norway)

Bonnie Blair, Women's Long Track Speed Skating 500-meter, Women's Long Track Speed Skating 1000-meter

Dan Jansen, Men's Long Track Speed Skating 1000-meter

Tommy Moe, Men's Downhill, Alpine Skiing

Diann Roffe-Steinrotter, Women's Super G, Alpine Skiing

Cathy Turner, Women's Short Track Speed Skating 500 meter

1996 Summer Olympics (Atlanta)

Derrick Adkins, Track and Field, Men's 400-meter Hurdles

Andre Agassi, Men's Tennis, Singles

Kurt Angle, Freestyle Wrestling, Heavyweight

Charles Austin, Track and Field, Men's High Jump

Randy Barnes, Track and Field, Men's Shot Put

Brooke Bennett, Swimming, Women's 800-meter Freestyle

Beth Botsford, Swimming, Women's 100-meter Backstroke

Thomas Brands, Freestyle Wrestling, Featherweight

Brad Bridgewater, Swimming, Men's 200-meter Backstroke

Kendall Cross, Freestyle Wrestling, Bantamweight

Lindsay Davenport, Women's Tennis, Singles

Gail Devers, Track and Field, Women's 100-meter

Tom Dolan, Swimming, Men's 400-meter Individual Relay

Gigi Fernandez and Mary Joe Fernandez, Women's Tennis, Doubles

Kenny Harrison, Track and Field, Men's Triple Jump

Justin Huish, Men's Archery

Allen Johnson, Track and Field, Men's 110-meter Hurdles

Michael Johnson, Track and Field, Men's 200-meter, Track and Field, Men's 400-meter

Carl Lewis, Track and Field, Men's Long Jump

Shannon Miller, Gymnastics, Women's Balance Beam

Dan O'Brien, Track and Field, Men's Decathlon

David Reid, Boxing, Light Middleweight

Kim Rhode, Women's Double Trap Shooting

Jeff Rouse, Swimming, Men's 100-meter Backstroke

Amy Van Dyken, Swimming, Women's 50-meter Freestyle, Swimming, Women's 100-meter Butterfly

1998 Winter Olympics (Nagano, Japan)

Eric Bergourst, Men's Freestyle Skiing—Aerials

Tara Lipinski, Women's Figure Skating

Janny Mosely, Men's Freestyle Skiing—Moguls

Nikki Stone, Women's Freestyle Skiing—Aerials

Picabo Street, Women's Super G Alpine Skiing

Coach Bela Karolyi carrying injured U.S. gymnast Kerri Strug at the Atlanta Olympics on 23 July 1996 (AP/Wide World Photos)

women's championship in 1993 and then was assaulted on 6 January 1994 in an attempt by rival Tonya Harding to put a halt to Kerrigan's bid to go to the Olympics at Lillehammer. The other U.S. Olympic star in Albertville was Bonnie Blair, who won two gold medals in women's speed skating (five hundred meters and one thousand meters). No American men won gold medals in Albertville.

Barcelona, Spain: 1992. The star of these games may have been Barcelona itself, as beautiful a site and as accommodating a culture as has ever hosted the Olympics. Politics seemed to matter less than in previous years, as Cuba, North Korea, and Ethiopia ended their boycotts, each nation having missed two Olympic games. South Africa, which had been absent since 1960, also returned. Yugoslav citizens were allowed to compete, but the nation was banned from competition because of its military aggression against Croatia and Bosnia-Herzegovina. American athletes again performed "typically," which is to say with considerable distinction in many areas and below expectations in others. They managed only a fourth-place finish in baseball, a new Olympic sport, but the basketball Dream Team, made up of National Basketball Association (NBA) all-stars (the first time professionals were allowed to represent the United States in basketball) swept easily

to a gold medal. The U.S. team won thirty-seven gold medals, falling only behind the Unified Team. These wins were complemented by thirty-four silver and thirty-seven bronze medals. In track and field Carl Lewis continued to establish his claim during the 1980s and 1990s as the outstanding male Summer Olympic athlete of the century (the award was announced in December 1999), one of only two individuals ever to win nine gold medals in track and field. He was also one of two, Jesse Owens being the other, to win four gold medals in the same event. During the 1992 Olympics, affected by a virus, Lewis was still able to win the long jump, a feat he also achieved in 1984, 1988, and 1996. Jackie Joyner-Kersee was chosen the outstanding female Summer Olympian of the century. During the 1992 Olympics she followed up on her two track and field gold medals (heptathlon and long jump) in the previous Olympics by winning the gold in the women's heptathlon. The men's swim team won six golds out of nineteen events and the women's swim team won six out of twenty. Oscar de la Hoya was the sole U.S. victor in boxing, but three members of the freestyle wrestling team won gold medals. Jennifer Capriati won the women's singles tennis title, while Gigi and Mary Jo Fernandez won the women's doubles tennis gold.

Lillehammer, Norway: 1994. Like much else in sports, the decision to separate the Summer and Winter Olympics by a span of two years was driven by financial considerations. It made more sense to produce such a massive event, with television broadcasting rights and a host of other commercial interests at stake, every two years rather than both Games a few months apart every four years. The Americans performed as usual, winning but six gold medals at Lillehammer, placing fifth once again in total golds, in essentially the same events with the same cast of characters in the spotlight, but for different reasons. Figure skater Kerrigan, victim of the clubbing, valiantly trained and returned to the Olympics to give a silver-medal performance. Harding, who would later plead guilty to a charge of hindering the investigation, sued for the right to compete in the Olympic figure-skating competition, in which she placed eighth. The other repeat performer from the 1992 Winter Olympics was Blair, who was in her fourth Olympiad. Again she won the five-hundred- and one-thousand-meter women's long track speed skating gold medals, bringing her total number of Olympic victories to five. Dan Jansen, a sentimental favorite after having been thwarted in his previous attempts, won the men's long track one-thousand-meter speed skating race. He took an emotional lap with baby daughter Jane (named after his sister of whose death he had learned of immediately prior to his Olympic competition in 1988). Alaskan Tommy Moe won the men's downhill in Alpine skiing.

Atlanta, Georgia: 1996. The Summer Olympics came to Atlanta in July 1996, the first time the games had been hosted by a city in the southern United States. There was nothing typical about these Olympics. The very thing every host nation fears took place when tragedy struck, as a homemade bomb exploded on 27 July in the Olympic Centennial Park, killing one woman (a cameraman died of a heart attack later) and injuring 111. Following the precedent established by International Olympic Committee President Avery Brundage during the 1972 Olympics, when eleven Israeli athletes were taken hostage and later murdered by terrorists, the games continued. His rationale, which probably preserved the future of the games, was, "We have only the strength of a great ideal. I am sure that the public would agree that we cannot allow a handful of terrorists to destroy this nucleus of international cooperation and goodwill we have in the Olympic movement. . . . The Games must go on." Phillip Noel-Baker, an Olympian (1912) and Nobel Peace Prize winner (1959) agreed, concluding that sport may be humankind's "best hope." In the competition venues U.S. athletes shone, winning forty-four gold, thirty-two silver, and twenty-five bronze medals. Russia was the nearest competitor at twenty-six, twenty-one, and sixteen respectively. There was no lack of U.S. heroes during these games. Probably the most thrilling competitors were the tiny members of the women's gymnastics team. Shannon Miller won the

gold with her prowess on the beam, and the team won the gold medal with a gusty performance, especially by 4'9" eighteen-year-old Kerri Strug, who made her last vault landing on an already badly sprained ankle. Michael Johnson, ignoring criticism that the track and field schedule had been specifically altered so he could participate in both the two-hundred- and four-hundred-meter races, won both events. Gail Devers won her second consecutive gold medal in the women's one-hundred-meter race. The American women's swim team again dominated in the pool, winning seven of sixteen titles, along with five silvers and three bronzes. The men's swim team was not far behind with six golds, six silvers, and one bronze. The U.S. men's archery team was victorious, with Justin Huish winning the individual gold. Both Dream Teams won in basketball. Andre Agassi and Lindsay Davenport won singles victories in tennis, and Gigi and Mary Jo Fernandez repeated as doubles champions. The U.S. women's soccer team won their event, a prelude to winning the World Cup in 1999—both victories gave women's athletics a boost in the United States unlike anything since Title IX of the Federal Education Amendments (1972).

Nagano, Japan: 1998. From an American point of view, possibly the most notable thing about these Olympics was the fourteen-hour time-zone differential between Nagano and the East Coast. It was almost impossible for CBS Sports to sustain suspense about any event when the winner had already been announced to the world on CNN. By the time the tape of skier Picabo Street's gold-medal run in the women's Alpine super G was played for the first time in prime time, the result had already been announced by the Entertainment and Sports Programming Network (ESPN), and she had been interviewed on the CBS *Good Morning* show. Once again, the U.S. winter athletes put in an average performance, especially when compared to the success in the Summer Olympics. The U.S. team won six gold medals, three in the new "extreme" contests of freestyle skiing. With professional hockey players allowed in competition for the first time, the U.S. team disappointed on and off the ice, losing an important match to the Czech Republic four to one, then trashing three Olympic apartments in a sour display of unsportsmanlike conduct. The women's hockey team redeemed the sport by winning the gold. One delightful surprise was the gold medal performance of sixteen-year-old Tara Lipinski in women's figure skating.

An Olympic Scandal. The decade concluded with the exposure of a long-standing practice of old-fashioned bribery in the selection process of Olympic host cities. In many ways Americans were the most offended; much of the rest of the world did not understand the fuss about spending a relatively small amount of money to acquire something of so much worth. Not only were Americans the most offended, they were also the most guilty: Salt Lake City officials, who successfully bid to acquire the 2002 Winter Olympics, had spent at least $400,000 in "inappropriate material benefits" (cash payments, free housing, scholarships, and jobs) to secure the games. The International Olympic Committee (IOC), attempting to reverse this trend, asked six of its members to resign and accepted the resignations of three others who were implicated in the scandal. "Globally accepted guidelines and procedures" (IOC president Juan Antonio Samaranch's phrase), however, may be harder to determine off than on the field of play.

Sources:
Chronicle of the Olympics, 1896–2000 (New York: DK, 1998).

CNNSI.com, Internet website.

The Sports Illustrated 1999 Sports Almanac (Boston: Little, Brown, 1998).

David Wallechinsky, *Sports Illustrated Presents the Complete Book of the Summer Olympics* (Boston: Little, Brown, 1996).

TENNIS

Court Domination. Pete Sampras practically owned Wimbledon during the 1990s. Sampras not only won six Wimbledon trophies (1993–1995, 1997–1999), he also won the Australian Open (1994, 1997) and U.S. Open (1990, 1993, 1995, 1996). *Sports Illustrated* called him the best male tennis player of the century, edging out Bill Tilden, whose glory years were in the 1920s. At the end of the decade Sampras had won sixty-one career titles and spent more weeks as the top-ranked player

Venus Williams at the Acura Classic on 14 August 1996
(AP/Wide World Photos)

ECOTOURISM LINKS

Two trends of the 1990s were the increased use of the Internet and the desire to see the world in an environmentally friendly manner. Listed below are some websites and links that allowed one to see parts of the United States that most people did not usually have the opportunity to visit.

Action Whitewater Adventures—raft down the Salmon and Middle Fork rivers in Idaho: riverguide.com

Adventure Alaska Tours—wildlife viewing and wilderness travel in Alaska: AdvenAlaska.com

Austin's Alaska Adventure—dog-team trips and fishing from Golsovia River Lodge, Alaska: alaskaadventures.net

Calusa Coast Outfitters—excursions in Estero Bay, Florida: calusacoast.com

Desert Adventures—Jeep tours in the desert of Southern California: red-jeep.com

Hawaii Forest and Trail—full- and half-day nature adventures: hawaii-forest.com

Honey Island Swamp Tours, Inc.—tours of wetlands of Louisiana: honeyislandswamp.com

Kodiak-Katmai Outdoors, Inc.—Brown Bear viewing and wilderness camping in Alaska's Katmai National Park: kodiak-katmai.com

Off the Beaten Path—hiking, river rafting, Nordic skiing, horseback riding, nature tours, bear watching, and more from Alaska to the American Southwest: offbeatenpath.com

Orchids and Egrets—general interest and customized group tours into the ecosystem of the Everglades: naturetour.com

Walk Softly Tours—educational Jeep trips and ecotours of the Sonoran Desert of Arizona: walksoftlytours.com

than anyone in history. The fortunes of other Americans playing professional tennis were much more erratic.

Men's Tennis. In the men's tournaments, Andre Agassi was also up and down, winning five Grand Slam events—Wimbledon (1992), the U.S. Open (1994, 1999), the Australian Open (1995), and the French Open (1999). Other American men who had outstanding decades included Jim Courier and Michael Chang. Courier won twice in Australia (1992 and 1993) and twice in France (1991 and 1992). Chang is one of only three American men to earn more than $15 million in career winnings, along with Sampras ($35 million) and Agassi ($15 million). In the Davis Cup, the annual international team tennis competition, the U.S. men fared well during the decade, winning three times (1990, 1992, 1995) and placing second twice (1991, 1997).

Women's Tennis. Women's professional tennis provided at least as much entertainment in the form of competitive balance and glamour as the men's. Monica Seles, Lindsay Davenport, and the Williams sisters, Venus and Serena, all took center stage. Davenport won the titles in the 1996 Olympics, U.S. Open (1998), and Wimbledon (1999). Seles won nine Grand Slam events but had to endure time off the court at the peak of her career after being stabbed by a Steffi Graf fan in 1993. Having already won the Australian Open (1991–1993), the French Open (1990–1992), and the U.S. Open (1991–1992), Seles spent a significant portion of the next three years recovering. Remarkably, she returned to the Women's Tennis Association (WTA) Tour with a win at the Canadian Open (1995) and reclaimed the title in Australia (1996). Venus and Serena Williams were rising stars in popularity and ability, with Serena claiming her first U.S. Open title in 1999. Also at the conclusion of the decade, Martina Navratilova was recognized as possibly being the greatest tennis player, male or female, ever; ESPN ranked her the nineteenth best athlete in its Top 100 Athletes of the [Twentieth] Century.

Sources:

CNNSI.com, Internet website.

ESPN.go.com, Internet website.

The Sports Illustrated 1999 Sports Almanac (Boston: Little, Brown, 1998).

HEADLINE MAKERS

LANCE ARMSTRONG

1971–
CYCLIST

Comeback Kid. Lance Armstrong was born 18 September 1971 in Plano, Texas. He started competing at an early age: he won the Iron Kids Triathlon at thirteen and became a professional cyclist at age sixteen. Raised in a single-parent family by his mom, Linda, the young Texan achieved some significant athletic milestones before the age of twenty. Even prior to his graduation from high school, Armstrong qualified to train with the U.S. Olympic developmental team. His first great cycling achievement was winning the U.S. National Amateur Championship (1991). He competed in the 1992 Olympics in Barcelona as an amateur. His career continued to thrive and in 1993 he won ten titles, including U.S. Pro Champion and World Champion, as well as one stage of the Tour de France. At the 1996 Olympics Armstrong raced as a professional, when he was the highest-ranked cyclist in the world. Then Armstrong faced a foe more aggressive and deadly than any he would meet on a cycling course. In October 1996 he was diagnosed with testicular cancer, which had spread to his lungs and brain. He was given a fifty-fifty chance of survival. Following surgeries to remove a testicle and brain lesions, as well as undergoing aggressive chemotherapy treatments, Armstrong returned to training after only a five-month layoff. During his rehabilitation and return to cycling, Armstrong met (May 1997) and married (May 1998) fellow Texan Kristin Richard. They had their first child in October 1999, Luke David Armstrong.

Tour de France. Not only was his personal life improving, so was his cycling. In 1998 Armstrong won the Sprint 56K Criterium in Austin, Tour de Luxembourg, Rheinland-Pfalz Rundfarht in Germany, and Cascade Classic in Oregon. The comeback, however, was not complete until Armstrong won the Tour de France on 25 July 1999 with a lead of seven minutes and thirty-seven seconds. Only one other non-European had ever won the prestigious event. Greg LeMond, also an American, was a three-time winner whose last victory was in 1990. LeMond was supported by a European team, however, while Armstrong used an American team sponsored by the U.S. Postal Service. Mark Gorski, Armstrong's team manager, compared the victory to a contingent of French players winning the Super Bowl. According to Armstrong's agent, Bill Stapleton, the Tour de France victory would net Armstrong $2.5 million in prize money and bonuses from sponsors.

Sources:

Lance Armstrong On-line, Internet website.

Société du Tour de France, Internet website.

JEFF GORDON

1971-
RACE CAR DRIVER

King of the Track. Jeff Gordon was born 4 August 1971 in Vallejo, California. He was not an overnight phenomenon in the world of auto racing, but his direction, if not his destiny, was determined early. Young Gordon, encouraged by his stepfather John Bickford, raced go-carts and quarter-midgets as a five-year-old. A regular winner on the midget and open-wheel racing circuits as a teenager, Jeff made a natural transition at twenty to National Association for Stock Car Auto Racing (NASCAR) racing. By then, in 1986, he and his family had moved to Pittsboro, Indiana, to be near the center of the racing world. He had already become the youngest driver ever to obtain a United States Auto Club (USAC) license and had gained valuable experience by driving every kind of competitive vehicle from dirt cars in Indiana to sprint cars in Australia. In 1990 he became the youngest Midget Series champion in USAC history. After a stint in Buck Baker's Driving School in North Carolina, Gordon earned the Busch Grand National Rookie of the Year honors in 1991, winning the pole position eleven times. He did not remain in the minor leagues of motor sports for long. In 1992 he signed to drive a car for Hendricks Motorsports, and his introduction to the Winston Cup circuit began in the final event of the year, the Hooters 500, the same race in which Richard Petty's career ended.

Winston Cup and NASCAR. In 1993 Gordon finished fifth at Daytona and second in the Coca-Cola 600, along with capturing eight other top-ten finishes. He also won Rookie of the Year on the Winston Cup circuit. That year was just a foretaste of fame and fortune: he won his first NASCAR race, the Coca-Cola 600, and the inaugural Brickyard 400 at the Indianapolis Motor Speedway in 1994. He continued to finish first throughout the decade. He became the youngest driver to win the Daytona 500 and was the first ever to win three consecutive Southern 500s, winning his fourth straight in 1998. Gordon won the Winston point championship in 1995 (the youngest driver ever to do so), 1997, 1998, and was second in 1996. During a stretch through July and August of 1998 he tied the modern-era record with four straight wins, and he won eight out of ten races from June through September. NASCAR selected him as "Driver of the '90s," edging out Dale Earnhardt. Though the driver is clearly the crucial component of a driving team, the assistance of a good crew is vital to success. Gordon's Rainbow Warriors (so named because of the colors of Gordon's cars and the crew's competitive zeal)

made crucial decisions (for example, changing two tires during a pit stop instead of four) that contributed to Gordon's victories. Gordon concluded the decade with a relatively "down" year, winning a "mere" half-dozen races. Handsome, clean cut, with a beautiful wife (Brooke, a former Miss Winston), he was the driver some fans loved to hate, but he was the indisputable king of NASCAR during the last half of the 1990s.

Sources:
Frank Moriarity, *Jeff Gordan* (New York: Metro Books, 1999).
The Official Jeff Gordan Website, Internet website.

MIA HAMM

1972-
SOCCER PLAYER

An Early Star. Mariel Margaret "Mia" Hamm was born in Selma, Alabama, on 17 March 1972, one of six siblings. Although most people had not heard of her until the end of the 1990s, when Women's World Cup Soccer finally received media attention in the United States, she dominated women's soccer from the end of the 1980s. She made the U.S. National Team at age fifteen in 1987 and played for Notre Dame High School in Wichita Falls, Texas. As a three-time collegiate All-American and two-time winner of the prestigious Hermann Award as the best female college soccer player (1992 and 1993), while leading the University of North Carolina Tar Heels to four straight National Collegiate Athletic Association (NCAA) championships (1989–1993), Hamm was a familiar name and powerful force in women's soccer. She set the NCAA single-season record for points scored with ninety-seven goals. In 1994 UNC retired her number. She was honored as U.S. Soccer's Female Athlete of the Year each year from 1994 to 1998. On 17 December 1994 she married Christian Corey.

World-Class Athlete. Hamm's career peaked as she became a media darling whose face and form were instantly recognizable after the U.S. women's soccer team won an Olympic gold medal in 1996. In Athens, Georgia, she played in the Olympic finals in front of 78,481 fans and a national television audience. Three years later, during the final game of the World Cup at the sold-out Rose Bowl, Hamm and her teammates, who were collectively voted Associated Press Female Athletes of the Year (1999), played before a television audience of nearly forty million. Even her commercials with Michael Jordan became classics and she has endorsed products ranging from Gatorade to Pert Plus shampoo. After the World Cup Championship she shared the spotlight with other talented and recognizable women athletes from the world of soccer, such as Brandi Chastain, Michelle Akers, Julie Foudy, and Shannon McMillan. Hamm was, however, still the star. She became the all-time leading scorer in international soccer when she made her 108th goal on 22 May 1999.

Changing Times. The timing of Hamm's rise to national and international prominence was partly the result of factors beyond her control and a precursor of events to come. When President Richard M. Nixon signed Title IX of the Federal Education Amendments into law in 1972, mandating full equality for women's intercollegiate athletics, he helped move women's sports beyond the limitations of traditional activities such as tennis and ice skating to a far wider group of sports, including volleyball, basketball, golf, swimming, cross-country, and soccer. Without Title IX of the Federal Education Amendments (1972), Hamm might still have become the premier women's soccer player of the decade, but few would have noticed. In addition to the new law, the growing popularity of soccer as a participation sport provided her with an enthusiastic audience of knowledgeable fans, most of whom were not born when Title IX was signed. When Hamm said, "I owe a huge debt . . . to the girls who scream for us at every game. We play for you," she was not merely referring to their status as fans but as athletes.

Sources:

Amy's Mia Hamm Page, Internet website.

SoccerTimes, Internet website.

Women's Soccer World Online, Internet website.

MICHAEL JORDAN

1963-

BASKETBALL PLAYER, ENTREPRENEUR

Tar Heel Roots. Michael Jeffrey Jordan was born 17 February 1963 in Brooklyn, New York, but he attended high school in Wilmington, North Carolina. His high school coach did not recognize Jordan as a budding basketball star, however, and he was cut from the team as a sophomore. Despite this shaky start, he was recruited by the University of North Carolina, leading them to the national championship as a freshman in 1982. Two years later he was named College Player of the Year (1984), winning both the Naismith and Wooden awards. After his junior season, he was drafted by the Chicago Bulls, the third overall pick in 1984.

Air Jordan. There was something transcendent about Jordan's movements on the court, and he inspired commentary, even from jaded sports reporters, that bordered on adulation. After Jordan set a National Basketball Associa-

tion (NBA) playoff record for most points scored in a game (63), Boston Celtic forward Larry Bird said, "That was God disguised as Michael Jordan." Having conquered every challenge available on the basketball court, including NBA Rookie of the Year (1985), three MVP awards (1988, 1991, 1992), Olympic gold medals (1984 and 1992), and three NBA Championships (1991–1993), Jordan shocked the world by retiring from basketball on 6 October 1993, at the peak of his career. The death of Jordan's father, during a 1993 robbery attempt, may have helped push the basketball star to other pursuits. Success did not, however, always follow him off the court.

Basketball to Baseball, and Back Again. His venture into professional baseball was, in many ways, no different than that of thousands of other middle-age men in a mid-life crisis who paid good money to attend fantasy baseball camps for the opportunity to see how they might do in competition with former big leaguers. Because he was the most famous—and perhaps wealthiest—athlete of the decade, he got a chance not normally accorded men of his age. Playing with the Birmingham (Alabama) Barons in AA minor league ball, he batted .204, proof that he was mortal. When Jordan once again picked up a basketball, all questions about his incomparable domination of the sport were forgotten. One news report said that when speculation arose that Jordan would return to the Chicago Bulls after his year in baseball, the stocks of five companies whose products he endorsed climbed $2.3 billion dollars in three days. Returning on 19 March 1995, after a hiatus of one-and-a-half seasons, Jordan and the Bulls managed to reach only the second round of the playoffs, but then proceeded to win three more consecutive NBA titles (1996, 1997, and 1998). Jordan also captured MVP honors in 1996 and 1998. Each year the Bulls won the title, before and after his aborted retirement, Jordan won the MVP award for the Finals. He scored more points (5,987) than anyone else in the history of the NBA playoffs. His per-game average during the post season (179 games) was also the highest (33.4); Jordan was the only player, appearing in a minimum of twenty-five playoff contests, to top thirty points per game. His regular season stats were equally impressive. He averaged 31.5 points per game, 6.5 rebounds and 5.3 assists during his career. He led the league in scoring (1988–1993, 1996–1999). He was an NBA All-Star twelve times and Defensive Player of the Year in 1998. Jordan has been on the cover of *Sports Illustrated* forty-seven times, more than any other athlete. Jordan re-retired on 13 January 1999. Darryl Howerton, in a *Sport* magazine article, designating Jordan one of the five best athletes of the century, referred to Jordan as omnipresent. Even in other sports, people said of up-and-coming stars, "This could be the Michael Jordan of (fill in the blank)."

Business Interests. Basketball was not the only field in which Jordan excelled. He was featured in an animated movie feature, *Space Jam* (1996), with costar Bugs Bunny, a character hardly more ethereal than Jordan. In addition to his athletic prowess and entertainment appeal, Jordan had a strong influence in the business world. He opened a restaurant in Chicago, had a cologne named for him, and graced the cover of *Wheaties* cereal boxes. Jordan's "star" quality was clearly indicated by his endless television and media endorsements, for products ranging from basketball shoes to hamburgers to long-distance telephone services.

Sources:

Bob Greene, *Rebound: The Odyssey of Michael Jordan* (New York: Viking, 1995).

Darryl Howerton, "Michael Jordan," *Sport*, 90 (December 1999): 42–43.

NBA.com, Internet website.

GREG MADDUX

1966-

BASEBALL PITCHER

While the late 1990s may have been the era of the long ball, the personal domain of home-run kings such as Mark McGwire and Sammy Sosa, a quiet, humble, initially unimpressive pitcher became the dominant professional baseball player of the decade. His $57.5 million, five-year contract, begun in 1997, made him the highest- paid baseball player. Born 14 April 1966, in San Angelo, Texas, Gregory Allen Maddux began playing baseball when he was five years old. He attended high school in Las Vegas, Nevada, and was drafted by the Chicago Cubs in 1984. For two years he played in the minor leagues until he was called up by the parent club. Despite playing for the perennially cellar-dwelling club, in 1992 he won a Cy Young award, the symbol of the best pitcher in the National League (NL).

Strikeouts. When he signed as a free agent with the Atlanta Braves in 1993, he proceeded to secure three more consecutive Cy Young awards (1993, 1994, 1995), making him the only person in the history to win four in a row. In the years after receiving these honors, Maddux registered ERAs (earned run averages) of 2.72, 2.20, and 2.22. His worst performance was 3.57 in 1999. He won four ERA titles (1993–1995, 1998), and continued a streak of twelve consecutive seasons with at least fifteen wins and two hundred or more innings pitched. He had the best winning percentage in the NL in 1995 (19–2) and 1998 (19–4). Maddux was not a bad hitter either, for a pitcher, with a .178 lifetime average and a reputation as one of the best sacrifice bunters. He also helped his team in the field, winning ten Gold Glove Awards as the premier fielding pitcher in the league. His Atlanta Braves team won the World Series in 1995, during which he won the first game of the Series.

Precision Pitching. At 6 foot, 175 to 185 pounds, Maddux was not physically intimidating. San Diego first baseman Tim Hyers said, "I thought he was a god who came down from a mountain with Zeus. He's just a little guy who knows how to

throw." Maddux's self-analysis is similar, "I could probably throw harder if I wanted, but why? When they're in a jam, a lot of pitchers try to throw harder. Me, I try to locate better." Tony Gwynn, remarked, "He's like a meticulous surgeon out there. . . . He puts the ball where he wants to. You see a pitch inside and you wonder, 'Is it the fastball or the cutter?' That's where he's got you." Atlanta teammate John Smoltz agreed, "Every pitch has a purpose. Sometimes he knows what he's going to throw two pitches ahead. I swear, he makes it look like guys are swinging foam bats against him." Jeff Wetherby, a career minor leaguer who had the good fortune to make the majors briefly in 1989 and hit a home run off Maddux, recommended that batters, "Protect the plate and pray a lot."

Records. Because he was a crafty rather than an overpowering pitcher, Maddux held all sorts of odd records. On 29 April 1990 he set the Major League record for most putouts in a nine-inning game by a pitcher. Maddux's pitching style invited batters to hit grounders right back to the mound. In 1994–1995 he became the first major league pitcher to have an ERA of less than 1.80 in two consecutive seasons, since Walter "Big Train" Johnson accomplished that feat in 1918–1919 for the Washington Senators. In 1994 Maddux's 1.56 ERA was 2.65 below the league average, the greatest differential in modern baseball.

Sources:

Tim Crothers, "The Book on Maddux," *Sports Illustrated*, 89 (6 July 1998): 44–46.

"Players—#31, Greg Maddux, SP," *MajorLeagueBaseball.com*, Internet website.

I. J. Rosenberg, "On the Mound with Greg Maddux," *Baseball: A Timeless Tribute to America's Game* (Athlon Sports, 1996).

PAT SUMMITT

1952-

COACH

Tennessee Roots. Patricia Head was born 14 June 1952 in Henrietta, Tennessee, and raised in a farming family. Summitt played basketball for the University of Tennessee at Martin and earned her degree in 1974. Among her accomplishments, she played on a Pan-American Games team and helped the U.S. women's basketball team (on which she served as a co-captain) win an Olympic silver medal in 1976. Summitt began her coaching career with the University of Tennessee Volunteers in 1974 as a twenty-two-year-old graduate assistant (only one year older than several of her players), who accepted the head position when the senior coach suddenly left the team. Her first team posted a 16–8 record, and she never looked back. She coached the U.S. women to their first gold medal in the 1984 Olympics.

A League of Her Own. Arguably the best college basketball coach in history, male or female, Summitt led the Lady Vols to six National Collegiate Athletic Association (NCAA) championships—four during the 1990s (1991, 1996–1998). The three consecutive titles were a first for any women's basketball program. As 1999 concluded, her twenty-fifth season of creating a basketball dynasty at Tennessee, she had more than seven hundred victories, less than thirty shy of the all-time mark for a woman's coach, set by Jody Conradt of the University of Texas. Even in the years Summitt's team did not win the national championship, it still performed well, for example posting a 31–3 mark in 1998–1999 and making the round of eight in the playoffs. She led her team to the Final Four in fifteen of the past twenty-three years. Her teams won sixty-four of seventy-six NCAA tournament contests, more even than John Wooden, the revered men's coach of UCLA, who won forty-seven out of fifty-seven. Summitt became the first female coach to make the cover of *Sports Illustrated*. In the process of turning Tennessee into a perennial champion playing before sellout arenas in Knoxville, Summitt recruited and coached some of the most outstanding female athletes of the decade, including ten Olympians, sixteen All-Americans, and twenty-two future professional basketball players, among them Chamique Holdsclaw, Bridgette Gordon, and Daedra Charles.

Off the Court. Summitt was also a motivational speaker in high demand among big U.S. corporations. In 1997 she was recognized at the White House as one of the "25 Most Influential Working Mothers" as selected by *Working Mother* magazine. In October 1990 Summitt was enshrined in the Women's Sports Foundation Hall of Fame. On 24 May 2000 she was selected for enshrinement in the Naismith Memorial Hall of Fame, only the fourth woman to be so honored.

Sources
ESPN.com, Internet website.

The University of Tennessee Lady Volunteers, Internet website.

VENUS WILLIAMS
SERENA WILLIAMS

1980- AND 1981-
TENNIS WONDERS

Ghetto Cinderellas. In spite of her youth, only nineteen at the end of 1999, Venus Williams had been a high profile tennis player for several years. At six-feet-one-inch, 167 pounds, with 1,800 beads in her braided hair, she was physically stunning and hard to miss, even off the court. For at least half a decade, she was in the limelight of women's tennis, the topic of conversation and controversy, and the subject, with her father Richard and her sister Serena, of an award-winning article, "On Planet Venus," written by Linda Robertson in 1997. The glare on Venus shielded and shadowed younger sister Serena until, after winning the U.S. Open in 1999 at age seventeen, Serena, all of five-feet-ten-inches and 145 pounds, could no longer be hidden. The children of a hard-driving parent, Richard Williams, who had a master plan for the success of his daughters, the sisters were programmed for excellence since early childhood. Venus and Serena each began playing tennis with their father, who was first their coach and later their manager, on neighborhood courts near Los Angeles when they were four years old. They practiced tennis in the most difficult of circumstances, with "dead" tennis balls on cracked tennis courts strewn with broken glass. Drug deals, police helicopters, and drive-by shootings were a part of the immediate environment. They were home-schooled by their father from middle school. As part of their education, they put on tennis clinics for the underprivileged and spoke to inner-city schools. Their father said, "We're from the ghetto. Venus is a ghetto Cinderella."

Rise to Stardom. The hard work of father and children paid off. Venus had $12 million in endorsement contracts prior to winning her first professional match. After turning pro at age fourteen, Serena was allowed by her father to play in only one event that year, three the following year, and five the next. She won her first title at the IGA Tennis Classic in 1998 at age seventeen. By the end of the decade, she had won nine singles titles and more than $2 million in prize money. She claimed she did not want to play past age twenty-six. About the only thing that went wrong in this carefully scripted plan was that younger sister Serena won her first Grand Slam title, the U.S. Open (1999), before her older sister won one. Their mother, Oracene, said of Venus, "She thinks since she's the oldest, she should've been the first, that maybe she should've been tougher. That's something they've thought about all their lives: meeting in a final, two sisters. She feels she let everybody down." Maybe she let her father down, but everyone else who watched professional tennis was enthralled by the rise of these two young stars. In addition to their individual victories, Venus and Serena teamed up to win two Grand Slam doubles titles, the French Open (1999) and U.S. Open (1999). The number-one ranked female tennis player, Martina Hingis, eighteen, right between Venus and Serena in age, said of the competition in women's tennis at the end of the decade, "I don't think it can get any much better."

Sources:
Macontelegraph.com, Internet website.

Linda Robertson, "On Planet Venus," *The Best American Sports Writing, 1998* (Boston: Houghton Mifflin, 1998).

TIGER WOODS

1975-
PROFESSIONAL GOLFER

"Tyger! Tyger! Burning Bright." Even in his twenties, Tiger Woods promised to become the best golfer who ever played the game. His performance at times was stellar; however, great golfers have to prove themselves over decades of play and Woods had only begun his professional career in the late 1990s. He could not have demonstrated the prowess yet of great golfers such as Jack Nicklaus and Ben Hogan. Nicklaus, after all, tied for sixth in the 1998 Masters, at age fifty-eight, while Woods, in his golfing prime in the same tournament, tied for eighth. Still, what Woods did on the golf course was unprecedented and breathed far wider interest in a sport that was in danger of becoming staid. Born Eldrick Woods on 30 December 1975, to an African American father and Thai mother, Woods's early years were the stuff of legend. He appeared on the Mike Douglas television show to demonstrate his golfing prowess at age two and was featured in *Golf Digest* at age five. He won Optimist International Junior Tournaments six times (from age eight to fifteen). In an emotional speech, his father offered his Tiger as a gift to the world with portentous and ominous words, saying his son "will transcend this game . . . and bring to the world . . . a humanitarianism . . . which has never been known before. The world will be a better place to live in . . . by virtue of his existence . . . and his presence." Whether or not there is truth is that claim, Woods was surely the consummate golfer.

An Early Master. Woods was the first player ever to win three consecutive U.S. Amateur Championships (1994–1996) and was also the National Collegiate Athletic Association (NCAA) Men's Individual Champion in 1996, playing for Stanford University. As an amateur, he played impressively in the Grand Slam events, tying the British Open record for an amateur in 1996 as a twenty-year-old. In the history of golf, the professional debut of no other player had ever been more anticipated. He turned professional on 27 August 1996. In his forty-second week as a professional, at the age of twenty-one-years and twenty-four weeks, he became the youngest player ever to be ranked the number one golfer in the world by the Official World Ranking system. He also had the most rapid progression ever to achieve that ranking. He was the first player since 1990 to win two tour events in his first year as a pro and the first player since 1982 to record five straight top five finishes. At the turn of the century, he topped that record by winning five consecutive tournaments. For sheer audacity, no feat compares with his victory at the Augusta National in 1997. With a record score of 270, eighteen under par, Woods won by a record margin of twelve strokes. He was the first African American and/or Asian American to win the contest, as well as the youngest golfer ever to win the Green Jacket.

Pro Success. By the end of the decade, Woods, who turned twenty-four, had won twenty-four professional tournaments, fifteen on the Professional Golfers' Association (PGA) tour. In 1999 he was the first golfer to win four consecutive PGA events since Ben Hogan in 1953. He won another major championship in 1999, the PGA, and his tour earnings of $6,616,585 in the final year of the decade more than doubled the previous record total for one year. His career earnings in his few years as a professional totaled $13,989,832, not including endorsement contracts for millions more. Woods was selected by *Sports Illustrated* as the Sportsman of the Year in 1996, was the PGA Rookie of the Year (1996), Associated Press Male Athlete of the Year (1997 and 1999), and PGA Tour Player of the Year (1997 and 1999).

Sources:

Gary Smith, "The Chosen One," in *The Best American Sports Writing of the Century*, edited by David Halberstam (Boston: Houghton Mifflin, 1999), pp. 611–629.

Tiger Woods Official Golf Website, Internet website.

PEOPLE IN THE NEWS

Andre Agassi won two U.S. Opens (1994, 1999) and a total of five major championships in men's tennis, just the fifth man to win individual titles in all four majors during their career. He also won a gold medal at the 1996 Olympic Games.

Davey Allison won the Daytona 500 and Winston 500 in 1992. Allison drove to victory in eleven Winston Cup races from 1991 to 1993, before he died after a helicopter crash in 1993.

Bonnie Blair won two Olympic gold medals as a speed skater at Lillehammer, Norway, and was named Associated Press (AP) Woman Athlete of the Year in 1994. She also won two gold medals two years earlier in Albertville, France.

Barry Bonds was the National League (NL) Most Valuable Player (MVP) in 1990; he stole at least thirty bases and hit at least thirty home runs five times during the decade, matching his father's mark (Bobby Bonds, 1968–1981).

In 1994 **Ken Burns** wrote and produced the television program *Baseball,* for Public Broadcasting Service (PBS).

On 10 July 1999 **Brandi Chastain** was not the most famous member of the U.S. Women's World Cup soccer team—until she kicked the winning goal.

In 1997 **Roger Clemens** won his fourth American League Cy Young award.

Cynthia Cooper led the Houston Comets to three straight Women's National Basketball Association (WNBA) championships (1997–1999) to go with individual scoring titles and MVP awards.

Beth Daniel won the Ladies Professional Golf Association (LPGA) championship in 1990 and was named the AP Female Athlete of the Year. She earned seventeen LPGA Tour victories during the decade.

Lindsay Davenport was the gold-medal-winning singles tennis player at the 1996 Olympics and also won the U.S. Open in 1998 and Wimbledon in 1999.

Terrell Davis ran for 157 yards to lead the Denver Broncos in an upset Super Bowl win over the Green Bay Packers, 31 to 24, to end the thirteen-year losing streak of the American Football Conference (AFC) in the title game.

Oscar De La Hoya won the 1992 Olympic gold medal as a lightweight, the only American to win a boxing medal in Barcelona. In November 1992 he debuted as a professional, winning the World Boxing Organization (WBO) junior lightweight and lightweight titles in 1994. In 1995 he won the International Boxing Federation (IBF) junior lightweight belt, then the WBC super lightweight title in 1996. On 18 September 1999 he was defeated by Felix Trinidad for the welterweight title.

David Duval, at age twenty-seven, already the winner of eleven tournaments in his professional golfing career, was a member of the U.S. team in the 1999 Ryder Cup.

Dale Earnhardt, "The Intimidator," dominated National Association for Stock Car Auto Racing (NASCAR) in the early part of the decade as Winston Cup Champion (1990–1991 and 1993–1994).

Dennis Eckersley won the Cy Young and American League MVP awards in 1992.

John Elway, in spite of being the most sacked quarterback in National Football League (NFL) history (498 times), won two Super Bowls with the Denver Broncos (1998, 1999).

Brett Favre was NFL MVP three times (1995–1997) as quarterback for the Green Bay Packers.

In 1997 **Nomar Garciaparra,** playing shortstop for the Boston Red Sox, was named the AL Rookie of the Year.

On 18 April 1999 **Wayne Gretzky,** a Canadian who skated primarily for the Edmonton Oilers and Los Angeles Kings, retired as "The Greatest" hockey player in National Hockey League (NHL) history. He won the league MVP nine times (1980–1987, 1989).

Ken Griffey Jr., an outfielder for the Seattle Mariners, was the youngest current player to make a variety of all-century teams. In 1997 he led the AL in home runs, RBIs, and runs scored; he played on every AL all-star team during the decade.

Tony Gwynn, an outfielder with the San Diego Padres, won four consecutive NL batting titles (1994–1997) and led the major leagues in batting as he approached the age of forty in 1999. He was a member of the NL all-star team every year of the decade.

Chamique Holdsclaw was a dominant player for the University of Tennessee women's basketball team in 1998, leading the Lady Vols to their third straight National Collegiate Athletic Association (NCAA) title. She received the Naismith Trophy.

Evander Holyfield is reigning WBA heavyweight champion at the end of the decade with a record of 36–3–1 and twenty-five knockouts (KOs).

Dale Jarrett, NASCAR driver with twenty-two victories in the 1990s, won the Daytona 500 and Coca-Cola 600 in 1996. In 1999 he won the Winston Cup championship.

Michael Johnson was the AP Male Athlete of the Year in 1996, winning the 200- and 400-meter sprints at the 1996 Olympics.

Randy Johnson, the "Big Unit," pitching for the Seattle Mariners, struck out nineteen batters twice in 1997. He won the Cy Young Award twice during the decade (1995, 1999).

On 5 June 1999 **Roy Jones Jr.** defeated **Reggie Johnson** to become the undisputed light heavyweight champion (WBA, WBC, and IBF) with a record of 40–1–0 and 33 KOs.

Jackie Joyner-Kersee was named the Female Summer Olympian of the Century for track and field, for her feats accomplished in the 1980s and 1990s. She won the heptathlon in 1988 and 1992. *Sports Illustrated* named her the Greatest Female Athlete of the Twentieth Century.

Nancy Kerrigan won the silver medal in figure skating in the 1994 Winter Olympics after recovering from an attack in which a rival, **Tonya Harding,** was implicated.

Jimmy Key, pitching for the Toronto Blue Jays, New York Yankees, and Baltimore Orioles, had a dominant decade, at various times leading his league in wins or strikeouts, or by winning in crucial postseason games.

Betsy King was the all-time leading money winner on the women's professional golf tour with $6.3 million as of September 1999.

Mike Krzyzewski, coach of the Duke University Blue Devils men's basketball team, was named *Sporting News* Man of the Year in 1992.

Carl Lewis was voted as Male Summer Olympian of the Century for winning nine gold medals, including three in the 1990s; his final gold came in the long jump, which he won at the age of thirty-five.

Meg Mallon won the U.S. Women's Open and LPGA championship in 1991.

At the end of the 1999 season, following a crushing defeat by the Minnesota Vikings, rumors swirled that **Dan Marino,** quarterback for the Miami Dolphins, would retire; the speculation turned to reality on 14 March 2000. Marino held the record for most passes attempted in a career (4,967 completed passes in 8,358 attempts for 61,361 yards), most seasons leading the NFL in completions, most touchdown passes in a career (420), and a variety of other records.

On 15 September 1998 **Mark McGwire,** a first baseman for the St. Louis Cardinals, broke the most revered sports record in America, surpassing **Babe Ruth's** sixty and **Roger Maris's** sixty-one homers in a single season; he established a new benchmark on 27 September when he hit his seventieth home run.

In 1990 **Phil Mickelson** won the U.S. Amateur and NCAA Men's Individual Championship, then turned pro, joining the PGA tour in June 1992. He had thirteen tour victories in the decade and played on three Ryder Cup teams.

Dave Mirra won eight X Games gold medals from 1996 to 1999 doing bicycle stunts.

Tommy Moe won gold (downhill) and silver (Super G) medals in Alpine skiing in the 1994 Winter Olympics.

Joe Montana, quarterback of the San Francisco 49ers, was named AP Athlete of the Year in 1990. He led the 49ers to four Super Bowl victories, three in the 1980s and the final one in 1990, and retired from the game in 1994.

Eddie Murray, first baseman for the Los Angeles Dodgers, New York Mets, and Cleveland Indians during the decade, collected his three-thousandth hit on 30 June 1995 and 500th home run on 6 September 1996.

Jack Nicklaus, who was supposed to be past his prime, kept doing amazing things on golf courses during the 1990s, including winning with seven majors in six years on the Senior PGA tour.

Hakeem Olajuwon, center for the Houston Rockets, would arguably have been the best basketball player of the decade were it not for a player named **Michael Jordan.** Olajuwon won the NBA MVP in 1994 in Jordan's absence from the league.

Mike Piazza, who was picked behind more than 1,500 other players in the 1988 free-agent draft, played like a man headed to the Hall of Fame, beginning by winning Rookie of the Year honors in 1993 as a catcher for the Los Angeles Dodgers.

Scottie Pippen, a forward with the Chicago Bulls and member of the Olympic Dream Team, may be the best number two basketball player in history, always playing in the shadow of **Michael Jordan.**

Jerry Rice, wide receiver for the San Francisco 49ers, caught more passes (1,057) for more yards (16,455) than any other player in professional football history.

On 6 September 1995 **Cal Ripken Jr.,** an all-star infielder for the Baltimore Orioles, broke Lou Gehrig's consecutive game streak, eventually playing in 2,632 consecutive baseball games.

Pete Sampras began an impressive decade in tennis by winning the U.S. Open men's singles championship in

1990, along with ten other Grand Slam events during the 1990s.

Barry Sanders, the premier NFL running back of the decade, retired from the Detroit Lions after the 1998 season, despite closing in on **Walter Payton's** record for most yards gained in a career.

Deion Sanders played professional football (for the Atlanta Falcons, San Francisco 49ers, and Dallas Cowboys, as an All-Pro defensive back) and baseball (for various teams) during the decade.

On 9 July 1998 **Allan H. "Bud" Selig** was named the ninth Commissioner of Baseball.

During the 1995 season **Emmitt Smith,** running back for the Dallas Cowboys, rushed for one hundred or more yards in eleven consecutive games and set an all-time record by scoring twenty-five touchdowns.

In 1998 **Sammy Sosa** kept **Mark McGwire** company in the great Home Run Derby, hitting more home runs than any other major league player other than McGwire. He was voted the NL MVP for the season.

Sheryl Swoopes, a forward with Texas Tech, won the Naismith Trophy as the best female college basketball player in the nation in 1993 and was later named the AP Female Athlete of the Year. She was a member of the three-time champion Houston Comets of the WNBA.

Paul Tagliabue, an attorney, was commissioner of the NFL, having been elected in 1989. He helped usher in league expansion, a salary cap, and had to deal with increasing lawlessness of players and owners.

Amy Van Dyken swam for two gold medals in the 1996 Olympics and was further rewarded by being named AP Female Athlete of the Year.

Reggie White, defensive end for the Green Bay Packers, set the record for most sacks in a Super Bowl with three in 1997.

Steve Young, when he retired from the San Francisco 49ers in 1997, had the highest passing rate for a career in NFL history.

AWARDS

1990

Major League Baseball World Series—Cincinnati Reds (National League), 4 vs. Oakland Athletics (American League), 0

Super Bowl XXIV—San Francisco 49ers, 55 vs. Denver Broncos, 10

National Collegiate Athletic Association Football Champion—Georgia Tech and Colorado, cochampions

Heisman Trophy, Collegiate Football—Ty Detmer (BYU)

Indianapolis 500, Automobile Racing—Arie Luyendyk

Daytona 500, Automobile Racing—Derrike Cope

National Basketball Association Championship—Detroit Pistons, 4 vs. Portland Trailblazers, 1

National Collegiate Athletic Association Basketball Champion, Men—UNLV, 103 vs. Duke, 73

National Collegiate Athletic Association Basketball Champion, Women—Stanford, 88, vs. Auburn, 81

National Hockey League Stanley Cup—Edmonton Oilers, 4 vs. Boston Red Wings, 1

Kentucky Derby, Horse Racing—Unbridled (Craig Perret, jockey)

Ladies' Professional Golf Association Championship—Beth Daniel

U.S. Open Golf Championship—Hale Irwin

Masters Golf Tournament—Nick Faldo

U.S. Open Tennis Tournament—Pete Sampras and Gabriela Sabatini

Athletes of the Year—Joe Montana (football) and Beth Daniel (golf)

1991

Major League Baseball World Series— Minnesota Twins (American League), 4 vs. Atlanta Braves (National League), 3

Super Bowl XXV—New York Giants, 20 vs. Buffalo Bills, 19

National Collegiate Athletic Association Football Champion—Miami (Florida) and Washington, cochampions

Heisman Trophy, Collegiate Football—Desmond Howard, Michigan

Indianapolis 500, Automobile Racing—Rick Mears

Daytona 500, Automobile Racing—Ernie Irvan

National Basketball Association Championship—Chicago Bulls, 4 vs. Los Angeles Lakers, 1

National Collegiate Athletic Association Basketball Champion, Men—Duke, 72 vs. Kansas, 65

National Collegiate Athletic Association Basketball Champion, Women—Tennessee, 70 vs. Virginia, 67 (OT)

National Hockey League Stanley Cup—Pittsburgh Penguins, 4 vs. Minnesota North Stars, 2

Kentucky Derby, Horse Racing— Strike the Gold (Chris Antley, jockey)

Ladies Professional Golf Association Championship—Meg Mallon

U.S. Open Golf Championship—Payne Stewart

Masters Golf Tournament—Ian Woosnam

U.S. Open Tennis Tournament—Stefan Edberg and Monica Seles

Athletes of the Year—Michael Jordan (basketball) and Monica Seles (tennis)

1992

Major League Baseball World Series—Toronto Blue Jays (American League), 4 vs. Atlanta Braves (National League), 2

Super Bowl XXVI—Washington Redskins, 37 vs. Buffalo Bills, 24

National Collegiate Athletic Association Football Champion—Alabama

Heisman Trophy, Collegiate Football—Gino Toretta (Miami [Florida])

Indianapolis 500, Automobile Racing—Al Unser Jr.

Daytona 500, Automobile Racing—Davey Allison

National Basketball Association Championship—Chicago Bulls, 4 vs. Portland Trailblazers, 2

National Collegiate Athletic Association Basketball Champion, Men—Duke, 71 vs. Michigan, 51

National Collegiate Athletic Association Basketball Champion, Women—Stanford, 78 vs. Western Kentucky, 62

National Hockey League Stanley Cup—Pittsburgh Penguins, 4 vs. Chicago Blackhawks, 0

Kentucky Derby, Horse Racing—Lil E. Tee (Pat Day, jockey)

Ladies' Professional Golf Association Championship—Betsy King

U.S. Open Golf Championship—Tom Kite

Masters Golf Tournament—Fred Couples

U.S. Open Tennis Tournament—Stefan Edberg and Monica Seles

Athletes of the Year—Michael Jordan (basketball) and Monica Seles (tennis)

1993

Major League Baseball World Series—Toronto Blue Jays (American League), 4 vs. Philadelphia Phillies (National League), 2

Super Bowl XXVII—Dallas Cowboys, 52 vs. Buffalo Bills, 17

National Collegiate Athletic Association Football Champion—Florida State

Heisman Trophy, Collegiate Football—Charlie Ward (Florida State)

Indianapolis 500, Automobile Racing—Emerson Fittipaldi

Daytona 500, Automobile Racing—Dale Jarrett

National Basketball Association Championship—Chicago Bulls, 4 vs. Phoenix, 2

National Collegiate Athletic Association Basketball Champion, Men—North Carolina, 77 vs. Michigan, 71

National Collegiate Athletic Association Basketball Champion, Women—Texas Tech, 84 vs. Ohio State, 82

National Hockey League Stanley Cup—Montreal Canadiens, 4 vs. Los Angeles Kings, 1

Kentucky Derby, Horse Racing—Sea Hero (Jerry Bailey, jockey)

Ladies Professional Golf Association Championship—Patty Sheehan

U.S. Open Golf Championship—Lee Janzen

Masters Golf Tournament—Bernhard Langer

U.S. Open Tennis Tournament—Pete Sampras and Steffi Graf

Athletes of the Year—Michael Jordan (basketball) and Sheryl Swoopes (basketball)

1994

Major League Baseball World Series—not held

Super Bowl XXVIII—Dallas Cowboys, 30 vs. Buffalo Bills, 13

National Collegiate Athletic Association Football Champion—Nebraska

Heisman Trophy, Collegiate Football—Rashaan Salaam (Colorado)

Indianapolis 500, Automobile Racing—Al Unser Jr.

Daytona 500, Automobile Racing—Sterling Marlin

National Basketball Association Championship—Houston Rockets, 4 vs. New York Knicks, 3

National Collegiate Athletic Association Basketball Champion, Men—Arkansas, 76 vs. Duke, 74

National Collegiate Athletic Association Basketball Champion, Women—North Carolina, 60 vs. Louisiana Tech, 59

National Hockey League Stanley Cup—New York Rangers, 4 vs. Vancouver Canucks, 3

Kentucky Derby, Horse Racing—Go For Gin (Chris McCarron, jockey)

Ladies Professional Golf Association Championship—Laura Davies

U.S. Open Golf Championship—Ernie Els

Masters Golf Tournament—Jose Maria Olazabal

U.S. Open Tennis Tournament—Andre Agassi and Arantxa Sanchez-Vicario

Athletes of the Year—George Foreman (boxing) and Bonnie Blair (speed skating)

1995

Major League Baseball World Series—Atlanta Braves (National League), 4 vs. Cleveland Indians (American League), 2

Super Bowl XXIX—San Francisco 49ers, 49 vs. San Diego Chargers, 26

National Collegiate Athletic Association Football Champion—Nebraska

Heisman Trophy, Collegiate Football—Eddie George (Ohio State)

Indianapolis 500, Automobile Racing—Jacques Villeneuve

Daytona 500, Automobile Racing—Sterling Marlin

National Basketball Association Championship—Houston Rockets, 4 vs. Orlando Magic, 0

National Collegiate Athletic Association Basketball Champion, Men—UCLA, 89 vs. Arkansas, 78

National Collegiate Athletic Association Basketball Champion, Women—Connecticut, 70 vs. Tennessee, 64

National Hockey League Stanley Cup—New Jersey Devils, 4 vs. Detroit Red Wings, 0

Kentucky Derby, Horse Racing—Thunder Gulch (Gary Stevens, jockey)

Ladies' Professional Golf Association Championship—Kelly Robbins

U.S. Open Golf Championship—Corey Pavin

Masters Golf Tournament—Ben Crenshaw

U.S. Open Tennis Tournament—Pete Sampras and Steffi Graf

Athletes of the Year—Cal Ripken Jr. (baseball) and Rebecca Lobo (basketball)

1996

Major League Baseball World Series—New York Yankees (American League), 4 vs. Atlanta Braves (American League), 2

Super Bowl XXX—Dallas Cowboys, 27 vs. Pittsburgh Steelers, 17

National Collegiate Athletic Association Football Champion—Florida

Heisman Trophy, Collegiate Football—Danny Wuerffel (Florida)

Indianapolis 500, Automobile Racing—Buddy Lazier

Daytona 500, Automobile Racing—Dale Jarrett

National Basketball Association Championship—Chicago Bulls, 4 vs. Seattle Supersonics, 2

National Collegiate Athletic Association Basketball Champion, Men—Kentucky, 76 vs. Syracuse, 67

National Collegiate Athletic Association Basketball Champion, Women—Tennessee, 83 vs. Georgia, 65

National Hockey League Stanley Cup—Colorado Avalanche, 4 vs. Florida Panthers, 0

Kentucky Derby, Horse Racing—Grindstone (Jerry Bailey, jockey)

Ladies' Professional Golf Association Championship—Laura Davies

U.S. Open Golf Championship—Steve Jones

Masters Golf Tournament—Nick Faldo

U.S. Open Tennis Tournament—Pete Sampras and Steffi Graf

Athletes of the Year—Michael Johnson (track) and Amy Van Dyken (swimming)

1997

Major League Baseball World Series—Florida Marlins (National League), 4 vs. Cleveland Indians (American League), 3

Super Bowl XXXI—Green Bay Packers, 35 vs. New England Patriots, 21

National Collegiate Athletic Association Football Champion—Michigan and Nebraska, cochampions

Heisman Trophy, Collegiate Football—Charles Woodson (Michigan)

Indianapolis 500, Automobile Racing—Arie Luyendyk

Daytona 500, Automobile Racing—Jeff Gordon

National Basketball Association Championship—Chicago Bulls, 4 vs. Utah Jazz, 2

Women's National Basketball Association Championhsip Game—Houston Comets, 65 vs. New York Liberty, 51

National Collegiate Athletic Association Basketball Champion, Men—Arizona, 84 vs. Kentucky, 79 (OT)

National Collegiate Athletic Association Basketball Champion, Women—Tennessee, 68 vs. Old Dominion, 59

National Hockey League Stanley Cup—Detroit Red Wings, 4 vs. Philadelphia Flyers, 0

Kentucky Derby, Horse Racing—Silver Charm (Gary Stevens, jockey)

Ladies' Professional Golf Association Championship—Chris Johnson

U.S. Open Golf Championship—Ernie Els

Masters Golf Tournament—Tiger Woods

U.S. Open Tennis Tournament—Patrick Rafter and Martina Hingis

Athletes of the Year—Tiger Woods (golf) and Martina Hingis (tennis)

1998

Major League Baseball World Series—New York Yankees (American League), 4 vs. San Diego Padres (National League), 0

Super Bowl XXXII—Denver Broncos, 31 vs. Green Bay Packers, 24

National Collegiate Athletic Association Football Champion—Tennessee

Heisman Trophy, Collegiate Football—Ricky Williams (Texas)

Indianapolis 500, Automobile Racing—Eddie Cheever Jr.

Daytona 500, Automobile Racing—Dale Earnhardt

National Basketball Association Championship—Chicago Bulls, 4 vs. Utah Jazz, 2

Women's National Basketball Association Championship—Houston Comets, 2 vs. Phoenix Mercury, 1

National Collegiate Athletic Association Basketball Champion, Men—Kentucky, 78 vs. Utah, 69

National Collegiate Athletic Association Basketball Champion, Women—Tennessee, 93 vs. Louisiana Tech, 75

National Hockey League Stanley Cup—Detroit Red Wings, 4 vs. Washington Capitals, 0

Kentucky Derby, Horse Racing—Real Quiet (Kent Desormeaux, jockey)

Ladies' Professional Golf Association Championship—Se Ri Pak

U.S. Open Golf Championship—Lee Janzen

Masters Golf Tournament—Mark O'Meara

U.S. Open Tennis Tournament—Patrick Rafter and Lindsay Davenport

Athletes of the Year—Mark McGwire (baseball) and Se Ri Pak (golf)

1999

Major League Baseball World Series—New York Yankees (American League), 4 vs. Atlanta Braves (National League), 0

Super Bowl XXXIII—Denver Broncos, 34 vs. Atlanta Falcons, 19

National Collegiate Athletic Association Football Champion—Florida State

Heisman Trophy, Collegiate Football—Ron Dayne (Wisconsin)

Indianapolis 500, Automobile Racing—Kenny Brack

Daytona 500, Automobile Racing—Jeff Gordon

National Basketball Association Championship—San Antonio Spurs, 4 vs. New York Knicks, 1

Women's National Basketball Association Championship—Houston Comets, 2 vs. New York Liberty, 1

National Collegiate Athletic Association Basketball Champion, Men—Connecticut, 77 vs. Duke, 74

National Collegiate Athletic Association Basketball Champion, Women—Purdue, 62 vs. Duke, 45

National Hockey League Stanley Cup—Dallas Stars, 4 vs. Buffalo Sabres, 2

Kentucky Derby, Horse Racing—Charismatic (Chris Antley, jockey)

Ladies' Professional Golf Association Championship—Juli Inkster

U.S. Open Golf Championship—Payne Stewart

Masters Golf Tournament—J. M. Olazabal

U.S. Open Tennis Tournament—Andre Agassi and Serena Williams

Athletes of the Year—Tiger Woods (golf) and Team USA (soccer)

DEATHS

Joe Adcock, 71, first baseman for the Milwaukee Braves, established major league record for total bases (18) in a game with four home runs and a double (31 July 1954), 3 May 1999.

Lionel Aldridge, 56, defensive lineman and star (1963–1971) with three Green Bay Packers championship teams (1965–1967), advocate for those with psychiatric problems, 12 February 1998.

George Allen, 78, football coach for the Los Angeles Rams (1966–1970) and Washington Redskins (1971–1977), 31 December 1990.

Mel Allen, 83, "Voice of the Yankees"; he and Red Barber were the first two broadcasters inducted into baseball's Hall of Fame, 16 June 1996.

Davey Allison, 32, stock car racer, 13 July 1993.

Lyle Martin Alzado, 43, defensive lineman for the Denver Broncos, Cleveland Browns, and Oakland Raiders, 1977 NFL Defensive Player of the Year, 14 May 1992.

Andre the Giant (Andre Rousimoff), 46, professional wrestler, 29 January 1993.

Lucius B. "Luke" Appling Jr., 83, Hall of Fame shortstop with the Chicago White Sox, twice led the league in hitting (1936, 1943), 3 January 1991.

Eddie Arcaro, 81, only jockey to win the Triple Crown twice (1941, 1948), 14 November 1997.

Arthur Ashe, 49, first African American man to win Wimbledon (1975) and the U.S. Open (1968), a champion who rose above discrimination he faced; fought for public awareness of AIDS, which he contracted by a blood transfusion during a 1983 heart surgery; the new home of the U.S. Open is named Arthur Ashe Stadium, 6 February 1993.

Walter Lanier "Red" Barber, 84, play-by-play announcer, who worked for the Cincinnati Reds (1934–1939), Brooklyn Dodgers (1939–1953), and New York Yankees (1954–1966); elected in 1973 to the Baseball Hall of Fame, 22 October 1992.

Cliff Barker, 77, member of the 1948 NCAA basketball championship Kentucky Wildcats, 17 March 1998.

Laz Barrera, 66, horse trainer who won the 1976 Triple Crown with thoroughbred Affirmed, named outstanding trainer four years (1976–1979), 25 April 1991.

James "Cool Papa" Bell, 87, Hall of Fame baseball outfielder whose legendary career was limited to the Negro Leagues, 7 March 1991.

Phil Boggs, 40, Olympic gold-medal winning springboard diver (1976), three-time world champion (1973, 1975, 1978), and nine-time U.S. national title holder, 4 July 1990.

Paul E. Brown, 82, founder, owner, general manager, and coach of the Cleveland Browns and the Cincinnati Bengals, 5 August 1991.

Junius "Buck" Buchanan, 51, Hall of Fame defensive lineman with the Kansas City Chiefs, 16 July 1992.

Smokey Burgess (Forrest Harrill), 64, baseball catcher with 145 major league pinch hits, 15 September 1991.

Roy Campanella, 71, three-time MVP (1951, 1953, 1955) catcher for five pennant-winning (one World Series victory) Brooklyn Dodgers; one of the first African American major league players; severely injured in a 1958 auto wreck that left him in a wheelchair, 26 June 1993.

Harry Caray (Harry Christopher Carabina), 78, Chicago Cubs baseball announcer (1981–1997), known for his seventh-inning-stretch rendition of "Take Me Out to the Ball Game," 18 February 1998.

Wilton (Wilt) Chamberlain, 63, best remembered for scoring one hundred points in a basketball game (2 March 1962); all-time NBA leader in rebounds (23,924); only player to score four thousand points in a season (1961–1962), averaging 50.4 points per game, 12 October 1999.

Albert Benjamin "Happy" Chandler, 92, commissioner during the integration of baseball (1945–1951), following a political career in Kentucky as governor and U.S. senator, 15 June 1991.

Nat "Sweetwater" Clifton, 67, one of three African American basketball players to break the color line in professional sports in 1950; Harlem Globetrotters basketball star and forward for the New York Knicks (1950–1958), 31 August 1990.

Chuck Connors, 71, former pro baseball (Los Angeles Dodgers, Chicago Cubs) and basketball player (Boston Celtics) who later starred in *The Rifleman* on television, 10 November 1992.

Howard Cosell, 77, sportscaster, primarily for boxing and football, whose propensity for "telling it like it is" often made him controversial; helped make Monday Night Football a television staple, 23 April 1995.

Robert E. "Bob" Davies, 70, basketball Hall of Fame guard and coach, 22 April 1990.

Leon Day, 78, star pitcher in the Negro Leagues (1934–1950); elected to baseball's Hall of Fame six days before his death, 13 March 1995.

Joe DiMaggio, 84, "The Yankee Clipper" hit successfully in fifty-six consecutive baseball games; MVP winner in the American League in 1939, 1941, and 1947; an outfielder for the New York Yankees (1936–1942, 1946–1951), he led the team to nine World Series championships, 8 March 1999.

Don Drysdale, 56, Hall of Fame pitcher for the Los Angeles Dodgers (1956–1968) before becoming a sportscaster, 3 July 1993.

Leo Durocher, 86, baseball player and manager who won three National League pennants and the 1954 World Series, 7 October 1991.

Wilbur "Weeb" Eubank, 91, coach of the Baltimore Colts (1954–1962) and the New York Jets (1963–1973); in the biggest upset in Super Bowl history (1968), he led the Jets when they stunned the Colts (16 to 7) after his quarterback, Joe Namath, guaranteed a victory, 17 November 1998.

Rick Ferrell, 89, baseball Hall of Fame catcher for the St. Louis Browns, Boston Red Sox, and Washington Senators (1929–1945, 1947), 27 July 1995.

Charles O. "Chuck" Finley, 77, flamboyant owner of the Oakland A's; successfully introduced the designated hitter to baseball, 19 February 1996.

Curt Flood, 59, all-star center fielder for the St. Louis Cardinals, whose challenge to the reserve clause changed the economics of baseball, eventually allowing free agency, 20 January 1997.

William "Pops" Gates, 82, Hall of Fame player and coach of the Harlem Globetrotters, 2 December 1999.

Charlie Gehringer, 89, Hall of Fame second baseman with the Detroit Tigers; .320 lifetime batting average, 21 January 1993.

Isaac Grainger, 104, former president of the United States Golf Association (USGA) who helped unify the rules of golf, 11 October 1999.

Harold Edward "Red" Grange, 87, "the Galloping Ghost," football Hall of Fame running back primarily for the Chicago Bears, 28 January 1991.

Rocky Graziano (Thomas Rocco Barbella), 71, world middleweight boxing champion (1947–1948), 22 May 1990.

Tom Harmon, 70, 1940 Heisman Trophy winner at the University of Michigan, halfback for the Los Angeles Rams (1946–1947), and football broadcaster, 15 March 1990.

Billy Herman, 83, Hall of Fame second baseman primarily with the Chicago Cubs (1931–1941), coach, and manager of the Boston Red Sox (1964–1966), 5 September 1992.

Ben Hogan, 84, won nine major golf titles and sixty-three tournaments in his forty-two-year career (1929–1971), 25 July 1997.

William "Flash" Hollett, 88, first NHL defenseman to score twenty points in a season (1944–1945), with the Detroit Red Wings, 20 April 1999.

Chandler "Buss" Hovey Jr., 83, yachtsman, America's Cup competitor, 9 April 1998.

Frank James Howard, 86, colorful college Hall of Fame football coach at Clemson University (1941–1970), 26 January 1996.

Jim "Catfish" Hunter, 53, first big-money free agent in baseball (five years, $3.75 million beginning in 1975); Hall of Famer who won five World Series with the Oakland Athletics and the New York Yankees; won the Cy Young award in 1974, 9 September 1999.

Don Hutson, 84, wide receiver for the Green Bay Packers (1935–1945) and a charter member of the College and Pro Football Hall of Fame, 26 June 1997.

Henry Payne Iba, 88, basketball coach who won two national championships at Oklahoma State University (1945–1946) and two Olympic gold medals (1964, 1968), 15 January 1993.

Tommy Ivan, Hall of Fame coach and manager who won Stanley Cups with the Detroit Red Wings and Chicago Blackhawks, 24 June 1999.

Helen Hull Jacobs, 88, tennis player and author, won nine major championships in the 1930s, 2 June 1997.

"Badger" Bob Johnson, 60, hockey coach who led the Wisconsin Badgers to three NCAA championships (1973, 1977, 1981) and Pittsburgh Penguins to the 1991 Stanley Cup championship, 26 November 1991.

Florence Griffith "FloJo" Joyner, 38, three-time Olympic gold-medallist in track (1988), known for flashy and daring athletic wear, 21 September 1998.

Gene Klein, 69, former owner of the San Diego Chargers and of thoroughbred racehorses, 12 March 1990.

Jim Kropfeld, 58, hydroplane racer, won three national championships piloting *Miss Budweiser,* 3 January 1999.

Alan Kulwicki, 38, racecar driver, winner of the 1992 NASCAR Winston Cup championship, 1 April 1993.

Harry "Cookie" Lavagetto, 77, major league baseball infielder for the Pittsburgh Pirates and Brooklyn Dodgers; manager of the Washington Senators (1957–1961), 19 August 1990.

Walter "Buck" Leonard, 90, Hall of Fame first baseman for the Homestead Grays (1934–1950) of the Negro Leagues; made even more famous in retirement by his role in Ken Burns's televised documentary *Baseball* (1994), 27 November 1997.

Reggie Lewis, 27, basketball player for the Boston Celtics (1987–1993), 27 July 1993.

David Logan, 42, popular defensive lineman for the Tampa Bay Buccaneers (1979–1986) and sportscaster, 12 January 1999.

Ron Luciano, 57, major league umpire, known for his theatrics during games, 18 January 1995.

Sid Luckman, 81, Hall of Fame quarterback for the Chicago Bears (1939–1950), NFL MVP three times, and All-Pro seven times, 5 July 1998.

Horatio Lucy, 90, trainer of Kentucky Derby winners Decidedly (1962) and Northern Dancer (1964), 15 December 1991.

Mickey Mantle, 63, Hall of Fame baseball player for the New York Yankees (1951–1968), the most powerful switch-hitter in baseball history, with 536 career home runs, 13 August 1995.

Robert "Gorilla Monsoon" Marella, 62, popular villainous professional wrestler and television announcer, 6 October 1999.

Frank McGuire, 80, forty-one-year career as basketball coach at St. John's University, the University of North Carolina, and the University of South Carolina, as well as in the pros for the Philadelphia Warriors (1961–1962); led the undefeated UNC team to the 1957 national championship, 11 October 1994.

Louis Meyer, 91, first three-time winner of the Indianapolis 500 (1928, 1933, 1936), 7 October 1995.

Cary Middlecoff, 77, dentist who became a top pro golfer, won the Masters (1955) and two U.S. Opens (1949, 1956), 1 September 1998.

Johnny Mize, 80, Hall of Fame first baseman and slugger for the St. Louis Cardinals, New York Giants, and New York Yankees; won four home run titles, 2 June 1993.

Willie Mosconi, 80, world pocket-billiards champion thirteen times between 1941–1956, 16 September 1993.

Wally Moses, 80, outfielder with the Philadelphia A's, Chicago White Sox, and Boston Red Sox; coach with the A's; recorded 2,138 major league hits, 10 October 1990.

Marion Motley, 79, Hall of Fame running back for the Cleveland Browns (1946–1954) and Pittsburgh Steelers (1955), helped break the color line in professional football, 27 June 1999.

Bronko Nagurski, 81, running back and tackle for the Chicago Bears (1930–1937, 1943), 7 January 1990.

Lindsey Nelson, 76, sports broadcaster, voice of the New York Mets (1962–1978), 10 June 1995.

Ray Nitschke, 61, Hall of Fame middle linebacker with the Green Bay Packers (1958–1972), 8 March 1998.

Max "Clown Prince of Baseball" Patkin, 79, entertainer whose sideline and bleacher antics captivated baseball fans for more than thirty years, 30 October 1999.

Walter Payton, 45, "Sweetness," Hall of Fame running back for the Chicago Bears (1975–1987); rushed for more yards than anyone else in history (16,726); twice NFL MVP (1977, 1985), 1 November 1999.

Harvey Penick, 90, premier golf instructor and author of best-selling book on golf, 2 April 1995.

John Pennel, 53, first pole vaulter to clear seventeen feet, three-time world champion, 26 September 1993.

Kim Perrot, 32, guard for the WNBA champion Houston Comets (1997–1998), 19 August 1999.

Jim Pollard, 70, Hall of Fame forward with the Minneapolis Lakers (1946–1955), who played on five NBA championship teams; head coach at La Salle University (1955–1958) and the Lakers (1959–1960), 22 January 1993.

Shirley Povich, 92, sports columnist for *The Washington Post,* 4 June 1998.

Jerry Quarry, 53, contending heavyweight boxer who fought Muhammad Ali and Floyd Patterson, 3 January 1999.

Harold "Pee Wee" Reese, 81, Hall of Fame shortstop with the Dodgers (Brooklyn, 1940–1957; Los Angeles, 1958), provided team leadership in accepting Jackie Robinson during the first year of integration (1946) of major league baseball, 14 August 1999.

Roy "Wrong Way" Riegels, 84, football player for the University of California–Berkeley known for running sixty-nine yards in the wrong direction after picking up a fumble in the 1929 Rose Bowl, 26 March 1993.

Bobby Riggs, 77, professional tennis player, winner of U.S. Open (1939, 1941) and Wimbledon (1939), whose loss in the 1973 "Battle of the Sexes" match against Billie Jean King was helpful in creating awareness of potential and actual prowess of women in sports, 25 October 1995.

Bill Riordin, 71, tennis promoter who managed Jimmy Connors's early career, 20 January 1991.

Cal Ripken Sr., 63, player, coach, and manager for the Baltimore Orioles for thirty-six years, whose most famous role in latter years was as parent to Cal Jr., 25 March 1999.

Joe Robbie, 73, owner of the Miami Dolphins, 7 January 1990.

Leon "Red" Romo, 78, athletic trainer at the U.S. Naval Academy (1956–1997); worked with midshipmen such as Roger Staubach and David Robinson, 11 July 1999.

Alvin "Pete" Rozelle, 70, NFL commissioner from 1960–1989, presided over growth in the league from twelve to twenty-eight teams and the merger with the AFL; instrumental in creating the Super Bowl and Monday Night Football, 6 December 1996.

Wilma Rudolph, 54, conquered polio as a child and became, in 1960, the first woman to win three gold medals in track and field in one Olympiad; two-time AP Athlete of the Year (1960–1961), 12 November 1994.

Pete Runnels, 63, infielder (1951–1964) for the Washington Senators, Boston Red Sox, and Houston Astros; manager of the Red Sox (1966) for sixteen games; won two AL batting titles (1960, 1962), 20 May 1991.

Gene Sarazen, 97, made the most famous golf shot of the century, a double eagle on the fifteenth hole in the 1935 Masters; first golfer to win all four majors in a career; inventor of the sand wedge, 13 May 1999.

Helen St. Aubin, 69, female professional baseball player whose career inspired the movie *A League of Their Own* (1992), 8 December 1992.

Elizabeth Robinson Schwartz, 87, first woman to win an Olympic gold medal in track (1928), 18 May 1999.

Roland "Rollie" Schwartz, 85, manager and part-time coach of 1976 U.S. Olympic boxing team that won five gold medals; helped establish the rule that amateur boxers wear protective headgear, 7 April 1998.

Fred Shero, 65, hockey coach of the Philadelphia Flyers (1971–1977); won two Stanley Cups (1974–1975), 24 November 1990.

Jimmy "The Greek" Snyder, 76, oddsmaker and sports commentator, 21 April 1996.

Eddie "The Brat" Stanky, 83, second baseman for five NL teams (1943–1953); manager of three teams, 6 June 1999.

Payne Stewart, 42, winner of three major PGA titles, 25 October 1999.

Horace Stoneham, 86, owner and president of the New York/San Francisco Giants baseball team (1936–1976), 7 January 1990.

Carl E. Stotz, 82, founder of Little League baseball (1939), 4 June 1992.

George "Birdie" Tebbetts, 86, four-time all-star catcher for the Detroit Tigers (1936–1942, 1946–1947), better known as a manager of Cincinnati Reds, 24 March 1999.

Fred Trosco, 81, running back with Tom Harmon for the University of Michigan, and coach at Eastern Michigan University (1952–1964), 6 February 1999.

Jim Valvano, 47, inspirational basketball coach at North Carolina State (where he won the national championship in 1983); television commentator; the V Foundation for cancer research is named for him, 28 April 1993.

Johnny Vander Meer, 82, pitcher for the Cincinnati Reds (1937–1943, 1946–1949), Chicago Cubs (1950), and Cleveland Indians (1951); only major league ball player ever to throw no-hitters in two consecutive starts (11 and 15 June 1938), 6 October 1997.

"Jersey" Joe Walcott (Arnold Raymond Cream), 80, heavyweight boxing champ (1951–1952), 25 February 1994.

Helen Wallenda, 85, last of the original Flying Wallendas trapeze artists, 9 May 1996.

Rudolf "Minnesota Fats" Wanderone Jr., 82, pool hustler who was the model for Jackie Gleason's portrayal in *The Hustler* (1961), 18 January 1996.

Charlie Whittingham, 86, oldest trainer to saddle a winner at Kentucky Derby (1986) and Preakness (1989), 20 April 1999.

Bud Wilkinson, 77, University of Oklahoma football coach; won three national titles (1950, 1955–1956); won forty-seven straight games (1953–1957); also coached the St. Louis Cardinals (1978–1979), 9 February 1994.

Cleveland "Big Cat" Williams, 66, boxer who challenged Muhammad Ali in 1966 for the heavyweight title, 14 September 1999.

Alexander "The Great" Wojciechowicz, 76, center-linebacker for Fordham University, the Detroit Lions (1938–1946), and the Philadelphia Eagles (1946–1950); one of the "Seven Blocks of Granite"; inducted into both the college and pro football Halls of Fame, 13 July 1992.

Early Wynn, 79, Hall of Fame pitcher for the Washington Senators (1939–1948), Cleveland Indians (1949–1957, 1963), Chicago White Sox (1958–1962); won twenty victories five times and one Cy Young (1959); winner of three hundred games, 4 March 1999.

PUBLICATIONS

Hank Aaron with Lonnie Wheeler, *I Had a Hammer: The Hank Aaron Story* (New York: HarperCollins, 1991).

Jeff Benedict and Dan Yaeger, *Pros and Cons: The Criminals Who Play in the NFL* (New York: Warner, 1998).

Larry Bird with Jackie MacMullan, *Bird Watching: On Playing and Coaching the Game I Love* (New York: Warner, 1999).

Bill Bradley, *Values of the Game* (New York: Artisan, 1998).

John Feinstein, *A Good Walk Spoiled: Days and Nights on the PGA Tour* (Boston: Little, Brown, 1995).

Steve Fireovid and Mark Winegardner, *The 26th Man: One Minor League Pitcher's Pursuit of a Dream* (New York: Macmillan, 1996).

Doris Kearns Goodwin, *Wait Till Next Year: A Memoir* (New York: Simon & Schuster, 1997).

David Halberstam, *October 1964* (New York: Villard, 1994).

Scott Hamilton, *Landing It: My Life On And Off The Ice* (New York: Kensington, 1999).

Robert J. Higgs, *God in the Stadium: Sports & Religion in America* (Lexington: University of Kentucky Press, 1995).

Roger Kahn, *A Flame of Pure Fire: Jack Dempsey & the Roaring '20s* (New York: Harcourt Brace, 1999).

Ken Kesey with Ken Babbs, *Last Go Round: A Dime Western* (New York: Viking, 1994).

John Krakauer, *Into Thin Air: A Personal Account of the Mount Everest Disaster* (New York: Villard, 1997).

Spike Lee with Ralph Wiley, *Best Seat in the House: A Basketball Memoir* (New York: Crown, 1994).

David Maraniss, *When Pride Still Mattered: A Life of Vince Lombardi* (New York: Simon & Schuster, 1999).

Patrick F. McManus, *Into the Twilight, Endlessly Grousing* (New York: Simon & Schuster, 1997).

Marvin Miller, *A Whole Different Ball Game: The Inside Story of Baseball's New Deal* (Secaucus, N.J.: Carol, 1991).

Buck O'Neil with Steve Wulf and David Conrads, *I Was Right on Time* (New York: Simon & Schuster, 1996).

Harvey Penick with Bud Shrake, *Harvey Penick's Little Red Book: Lessons and Teachings from a Lifetime in Golf* (New York: Simon & Schuster, 1992).

Arnold Rampersad, *Jackie Robinson: A Biography* (New York: Knopf, 1997).

Glenn Stout, series editor, *The Best American Sports Writing* (Boston: Houghton Mifflin, 1991–1999).

Al Stump, *Cobb: A Biography* (Chapel Hill, N.C.: Algonquin, 1994).

Jim Valvano and Curry Kirkpatrick, *Valvano: They Gave Me a Lifetime Contract, and Then They Declared Me Dead* (New York: Pocket Books, 1991).

Geoffrey C. Ward, *Baseball: An Illustrated History* (New York: Knopf, 1994).

George F. Will, *Men at Work: The Craft of Baseball* (New York: Macmillan, 1990).

U.S. women's soccer player Brandi Chastain celebrating after scoring the winning goal in the World Cup championship match in Pasadena, California, on 10 July 1999 (AP/Wide World Photos)

GENERAL REFERENCES

GENERAL

Robert Bezilla, ed., *America's Youth in the 1990s* (Princeton, N.J.: Gallup International Institute, 1993).

Judith Condon, *The Nineties* (Austin, Tex.: Raintree Steck-Vaughn, 2000).

Congressional Districts in the 1990s: A Portrait of America (Washington, D.C.: Congressional Quarterly, 1993).

Philip John Davies and Fredric A. Waldstein, eds., *Political Issues in America Today: The 1990s Revisited* (Manchester, U.K. & New York: Manchester University Press, 1996).

Kenneth Dolbeare and Linda J. Medcalf, *American Ideologies Today: Shaping the New Politics of the 1990s* (New York: McGraw-Hill, 1993).

Reynolds Farley, ed., *State of the Union: America in the 1990s* (New York: Russell Sage Foundation, 1995).

Steven D. Gold and Sarah Ritchie, *State Spending Patterns in the 1990s* (Albany, N.Y.: Nelson A. Rockefeller Institute of Government, State University of New York, 1995).

David W. Haines, ed., *Case Studies in Diversity: Refugees in America in the 1990s* (Westport, Conn.: Praeger, 1997).

Daniel Heath and others, eds., *America in Perspective: Major Trends in the United States Through the 1990s* (Boston: Houghton Mifflin, 1986).

Stuart A. Kallen, ed., *The 1990s* (San Diego: Lucent, 1999).

Ann Kibbey and others, eds., *On Your Left: Historical Materialism in the 1990s* (New York: New York University Press, 1996).

Alexander P. Lamis, ed., *Southern Politics in the 1990s* (Baton Rouge: Louisiana State University Press, 1999).

Christopher Newfield and Ronald Strickland, eds., *After Political Correctness: The Humanities and Society in the 1990s* (Boulder, Colo.: Westview Press, 1995).

George Ochoa and Melinda Corey, *Facts About the 20th Century* (New York: Wilson, 2000).

Chaim I. Waxman, *Jewish Baby Boomers: A Communal Perspective* (Albany: State University of New York Press, 2000).

Herbert F. Weisberg and Samuel C. Patterson, eds., *Great Theatre: The American Congress in the 1990s* (Cambridge & New York: Cambridge University Press, 1998).

Bruce Yadle, ed., *Land Rights: The 1990s Property Rights Rebellion* (Lanham, Md.: Rowman & Littlefield, 1995).

ARTS

Russell Baker and others, *Inventing the Truth: The Art and Craft of Memoir,* revised edition, edited by William Zinsser (New York: Houghton Mifflin, 1998).

David Bayles and Ted Orland, *Art & Fear: Observations on the Perils (And Rewards) of Artmaking* (Santa Barbara, Cal.: Capra, 1994).

Harold Bloom, *The Western Canon: The Books and School of the Ages* (New York: Harcourt Brace, 1994).

James Lincoln Collier, *Jazz: The American Theme Song* (New York: Oxford University Press, 1993).

Louise Cowan and Os Guinness, eds., *Invitation to the Classics* (Grand Rapids, Mich.: Baker Book House, 1998).

Clifton Fadiman and John F. Majors, *The New Lifetime Reading Plan* (New York: HarperCollins, 1997).

Barbara Haskell, *The American Century: Art & Culture, 1900–1950* (New York: Whitney Museum of American Art in association with Norton, 1999).

Dave Hickey, *Air Guitar: Essays on Art & Democracy* (Los Angeles: Art Issues; New York: Distributed Art Publishers, 1997).

Steven D. Kendall, *New Jack Cinema: Hollywood's African-American Directors* (Silver Spring, Md.: J. L. Denser, 1994).

Michael Korda, *Another Life: A Memoir of Other People* (New York: Random House, 1999).

James Miller, *Flowers in the Dustbin: The Rise of Rock and Roll, 1947–1977* (New York: Simon & Schuster, 1999).

Ian Penman, *Vital Signs: Music, Movies and Other Manias* (London & New York: Serpent's Tail, 1998).

Henry Petroski, *The Book on the Bookshelf* (New York: Knopf, 1999).

Craig Werner, *A Change Is Gonna Come: Music, Race & the Soul of America* (New York: Plume, 1998).

Joseph Wesley Zeigler, *Arts in Crisis: The National Endowment for the Arts Versus America* (Pennington, N.J.: A Cappella, 1994).

BUSINESS

David Bach, *Smart Women Finish Rich: 7 Steps to Achieving Financial Security and Funding Your Dreams* (New York: Broadway, 1999).

Marcus Buckingham and Curt Coffman, *First, Break All the Rules: What the World's Greatest Managers Do Differently* (New York: Simon & Schuster, 1999).

James C. Collins and Jerry I. Porris, *Built to Last: Successful Habits of Visionary Companies* (New York: HarperBusiness, 1994).

Stephen R. Covey, *The 7 Habits of Highly Effective People: Restoring the Character Ethic* (New York: Simon & Schuster, 1989).

Diane Coyle, *The Weightless World: Strategies for Managing the Digital Economy* (Cambridge, Mass.: MIT Press, 1998).

Michael A. Cusumano and David B. Yoffie, *Competing on Internet Time: Lessons from Netscape and Its Battle with Microsoft* (New York: Free Press, 1998).

Bob Davis and David Wessel, *Prosperity: The Coming Twenty-Year Boom and What It Means to You* (New York: Times Business, 1998).

Samuel M. Ehrenhalt, *Profile of a Recession: The New York Experience in the Early 1990s* (Albany, N.Y.: Nelson A. Rockefeller Institute of Government, State University of New York, 1992).

Philip Evans and Thomas S. Wurster, *Blown to Bits: How the New Economics of Information Transforms Strategy* (Cambridge, Mass: Harvard Business School Press, 2000).

Bill Gates and Collins Hemingway, *Business @ the Speed of Thought: Using a Digital Nervous System* (New York: Warner, 1999).

Eliyahu M. Goldratt and Jeff Cox, *The Goal: A Process of Ongoing Improvement*, revised edition (Springfield, Mass.: North River, 1992).

Robert G. Hagstrome Jr., *The Warren Buffet Way: Investment Strategies of the World's Greatest Investor* (New York: Wiley, 1994).

Charles Handy, *The Age of Unreason* (Cambridge, Mass.: Harvard Business School Press, 1989).

Spencer Johnson, *Who Moved My Cheese?: An Amazing Way to Deal With Change in Your Work and in Your Life* (New York: Putnam, 1998).

Paul Krugman, *The Age of Diminished Expectations: U.S. Economic Policy in the 1990s* (Cambridge, Mass.: MIT Press, 1990).

Peter Lynch and John Rothchild, *Beating the Street* (New York: Simon & Schuster, 1993).

Bob Nelson, *1001 Ways to Reward Employees* (New York: Workman, 1994).

William J. O'Neil, *How to Make Money in Stocks: A Winning System in Good Times or Bad* (New York: McGraw-Hill, 1991).

Suze Orman, *The Courage to Be Rich: Creating a Life of Material and Spiritual Abundance* (New York: Riverhead, 1999).

Orman, *The 9 Steps to Financial Freedom* (New York: Crown, 1997).

Thomas Petzinger Jr., *The New Pioneers: The Men and Women Who Are Transforming the Workplace and the Marketplace* (New York: Simon & Schuster, 1999).

Peter M. Senge, *The Fifth Discipline: The Art and Practice of the Learning Organization* (New York: Doubleday/Currency, 1994).

Thomas J. Stanley and William D. Danko, *The Millionaire Next Door: The Surprising Secrets of America's Wealthy* (Atlanta, Ga.: Longstreet, 1996).

Kate White, *Why Good Girls Don't Get Ahead—But Gutsy Girls Do: Nine Secrets Every Career Woman Must Know* (New York: Warner, 1995).

Michael Wolff, *Burn Rate: How I Survived the Gold Rush Years on the Internet* (New York: Simon & Schuster, 1998).

EDUCATION

Mary Alampi and Peter M. Comeau, eds., *American Education Annual: Trends and Issues in the Educational Community* (Detroit: Gale, 1999).

Regis Bernhardt and others, eds., *Curriculum Leadership: Rethinking Schools for the 21st Century* (Cresskill, N.J.: Hampton, 1998).

Sari Knopp Biklen and Diane Pollard, eds., *Gender and Education* (Chicago: National Study of School Evaluation [NSSE], 1993).

Rita Chawla-Duggan and Christopher J. Pole, eds., *Reshaping Education in the 1990s: Perspectives on Primary Schooling* (London & Washington, D.C.: Falmer Press, 1996).

Lynne V. Cheney, *Telling the Truth: Why Our Culture and Our Country Have Stopped Making Sense, And What We Can Do About It* (New York: Simon & Schuster, 1995).

The College Board, *Higher Education's Landscape: Demographic Issues in the 1990s* (New York: College Board Publications, 1995).

Constance Ewing Cook, *Lobbying for Higher Education: How Colleges and Universities Influence Federal Policy* (Nashville: Vanderbilt University Press, 1998).

Marian Wright Edelman, *Lanterns: A Memoir of Mentors* (Boston: Beacon, 1999).

Edelman, *Stand for Children* (New York: Hyperion, 1998).

Samuel M. Ehrenhalt, *Public Education: A Major American Growth Industry in the 1990s* (Albany, N.Y.: Nelson A. Rockefeller Institute of Government, 2000).

Debbie Epstein, ed., *Challenging Lesbian and Gay Inequalities in Education* (Buckingham, U.K. & Philadelphia: Open University Press, 1994).

Roger Geiger, ed., *The American College in the Nineteenth Century* (Nashville: Vanderbilt University Press, 2000).

Clark Kerr, Marian L. Gade, and Maureen Kawaoka, *Troubled Times for American Higher Education: The 1990s and Beyond* (Albany: State University of New York Press, 1994).

Ronald E. Koetzsch, *The Parents' Guide to Alternatives in Education* (Boston: Shambhala, 1997).

Alan Charles Kors and Harvey A. Silvergate, *The Shadow University: The Betrayal of Liberty on America's Campuses* (New York: Free Press, 1998).

Helen F. Ladd, Rosemary Chalk, and Janet S. Hansen, eds., *Equity and Adequacy in Education Finance: Issues and Perspectives* (Washington, D.C.: Committee on Education Finance, Commission on Behavioral and Social Sciences and Education, National Research Council, National Academy Press, 1999).

David Levine and others, eds., *Rethinking Schools: An Agenda for Change* (New York: New Press, 1995).

Robert Lowe and Barbara Miner, eds., *False Choices: Why School Vouchers Threaten Our Children's Future* (Milwaukee, Wis.: Rethinking Schools, 1993).

Barbara Means, ed., *Technology and Education Reform: The Reality Behind the Promise* (San Francisco: Jossey-Bass, 1994).

Louis Menand, ed., *The Future of Academic Freedom* (Chicago: University of Chicago Press, 1996).

Roslyn Arlin Mickelson, ed., *Children on the Streets of the Americas: Homelessness, Education, and Globalization in the United States, Brazil, and Cuba* (London & New York: Routledge, 2000).

Christopher Newfield and Ronald Strickland, eds., *After Political Correctness: The Humanities and Society in the 1990s* (Boulder, Colo.: Westview Press, 1995).

Wendie C. Old, *Marian Wright Edelman: Fighting for Children's Rights* (Springfield, N.J.: Enslow, 1995).

Michael D. Parsons, *Power and Politics: Federal Higher Education Policy Making in the 1990s* (Albany: State University of New York Press, 1997).

Theresa Perry and Lisa Delpit, eds., *The Real Ebonics Debate: Power, Language, and the Education of African-American Children* (Boston: Beacon, 1998).

Diane Ravitch and Joseph P. Viteritti, eds., *New Schools for a New Century* (New Haven: Yale University Press, 1997).

Dolores A. Stegelin, ed., *Early Childhood Education: Policy Issues for the 1990s* (Norwood, N.J.: Ablex, 1992).

Sally Tomlinson and Maurice Craft, eds., *Ethnic Relations and Schooling: Policy and Practice in the 1990s* (London & Atlantic Highlands, N.J.: Athlone, 1995).

U.S. Department of Education, Office of Educational Research and Improvement, National Center for Education Statistics, *Digest of Education Statistics, 1999* (Washington, D.C.: U.S. Government Printing Office, 1999).

Donovan R. Walling, ed., *At the Threshold of the Millennium* (Bloomington, Ind.: Phi Delta Kappa Educational Foundation, 1995).

Grant Wiggins and Jay McTighe, *Understanding by Design* (Alexandria, Va.: Association for Supervision and Curriculum Development, 1998).

FASHION

Vilma Barr, *The Illustrated Room: 20th Century of Interior Design Rendering,* edited by Dani Antman (New York: McGraw-Hill, 1997).

The Fashion Book (London: Phaidon, 1998).

Philip Jodidio, *New Forms: Architecture in the 1990s* (Köln, Germany & New York: Taschen, 1997).

Richard Martin, ed., *Contemporary Fashion* (New York: St. James, 1995).

Kate Mulvey and Melissa Richards, *Decades of Beauty* (London: Hamlyn, 1998).

Anne Stegemeyer, *Who's Who in Fashion* (New York: Fairchild Publications, 1996).

GOVERNMENT AND POLITICS

Ryan J. Barrilleaux and Mary E. Stuckey, eds., *Leadership and the Bush Presidency: Prudence or Drift in an Era of Change?* (Westport, Conn.: Praeger, 1992).

W. Lance Bennett and David L. Paletz, eds., *Taken by Storm: The Media, Public Opinion, and the U.S. Foreign Policy in the Gulf War* (Chicago: University of Chicago Press, 1994).

George Bush and Brent Scowcroft, *A World Transformed* (New York: Knopf, 1998).

Dan T. Carter, *From George Wallace to Newt Gingrich: Race in the Conservative Counterrevolution 1963–1994* (Baton Rouge: Louisiana State University Press, 1996).

Elizabeth Drew, *On the Edge: The Clinton Presidency* (New York: Simon & Schuster, 1994).

Thomas L. Friedman, *The Lexus and the Olive Tree* (New York: Farrar, Straus & Giroux, 1999).

Ed Gillespie and Bob Schellhas, eds., *Contract with America: The Bold Plan by Rep. Newt Gingrich, Rep. Dick Armey and the House Republicans to Change the Nation* (New York: Times Books, 1994).

Martin L. Gross, *The Great Whitewater Fiasco: An American Tale of Money, Power, and Politics* (New York: Ballantine, 1994).

Mark Grossman, *Encyclopedia of the Persian Gulf War* (Santa Barbara, Cal.: ABC-CLIO, 1995).

Richard A. Posner, *An Affair of State: The Investigation, Impeachment and Trial of President Clinton* (Cambridge, Mass.: Harvard University Press, 1999).

Bernard D. Reams Jr., ed., *Health Care Reform, 1993–1994: The American Experience: Clinton and Congress—Law, Policy, and Economics: A Legislative History of the Health Security Act with Related materials* (Buffalo, N.Y.: Hein, 1996).

Stanley A. Renshon, *High Hopes: The Clinton Presidency and the Politics of Ambition* (New York: New York University Press, 1996).

Charles Tiefer, *The Semi-Sovereign Presidency: The Bush Administration's Strategy for Governing Without Congress* (Boulder, Colo.: Westview Press, 1994).

Jeffrey Toobin, *A Vast Conspiracy: The Real Story of the Sex Scandal That Nearly Brought Down a President* (New York: Random House, 2000).

Martin Walker, *The President We Deserve: Bill Clinton, His Rise, Falls, and Comebacks* (New York: Crown, 1996).

George F. Will, *The Leveling Wind: Politics, the Culture, and the Other News, 1990–1994* (New York: Viking, 1994).

Bob Woodward, *The Agenda: Inside the Clinton White House* (New York: Simon & Schuster, 1994).

LAW

Robert H. Bork, *Slouching Towards Gomorrah: Modern Liberalism and American Decline* (New York: Regan, 1996).

David I. Cahill, ed., *Modern Slavery: Organized Violence, Enslavement, and Trafficking in Humans in the 1990s* (Chicago: Cahill, 1994).

Ann H. Coulter, *High Crimes and Misdemeanors: The Case Against Bill Clinton* (Washington, D.C.: Regnery, 1998).

Alan M. Dershowitz, *Sexual McCarthyism: Clinton, Starr, and the Emerging Constitutional Crisis* (New York: Basic Books, 1998).

Steven J. Eagle, *Regulatory Takings* (Charlottesville, Va.: Michie, 1996).

Barry C. Feld, *Bad Kids: Race and the Transformation of the Juvenile Court* (New York: Oxford University Press, 1999).

Stanley H. Friedelbaum, *The Rehnquist Court: In Pursuit of Judicial Conservatism* (Westport, Conn: Greenwood Press, 1994).

Leslie Friedman Goldstein, ed., *Feminist Jurisprudence: The Difference Debate* (Lanham, Md.: Rowman & Littlefield, 1992).

Anita Hill, *Speaking Truth to Power* (New York: Doubleday, 1997).

Peter Irons, *Brennan vs. Rehnquist: The Battle for the Constitution* (New York: Knopf, 1994).

Alison Jamieson, ed., *Terrorism and Drug Trafficking in the 1990s* (Aldershot, U.K. & Brookfield, Vt.: Dartmouth, 1994).

Barbara Klier, Nancy R. Jacobs, and Jacquelyn Quiram, *Gun Control: Restricting Rights or Protecting People?* (Wylie, Tex: Information Plus, 1999).

John R. Lott Jr., *More Guns, Less Crime: Understanding Crime and Gun Control Laws* (Chicago: University of Chicago Press, 1998).

G. Steven Neeley, *The Constitutional Right to Suicide: A Legal and Philosophical Examination* (New York: Peter Lang, 1994).

Kathleen A. O'Shea, *Women and the Death Penalty in the United States, 1900–1998* (Westport, Conn.: Praeger Publishers, 1999).

Richard A. Posner, *An Affair of State: The Investigation, Impeachment, and Trial of President Clinton* (Cambridge, Mass.: Harvard University Press, 1999).

William H. Rehnquist, *Grand Inquests: The Historic Impeachments of Justice Samuel Chase and President Andrew Johnson* (New York: Morrow, 1992).

David A. J. Richards, *Women, Gays, and the Constitution: The Grounds for Feminism and Gay Rights in Culture and Law* (Chicago: University of Chicago Press, 1998).

David G. Savage, *Turning Right: The Making of the Rehnquist Supreme Court* (New York: Wiley, 1992).

James F. Simon, *The Center Holds: The Power Struggle Inside the Rehnquist Court* (New York: Simon & Schuster, 1995).

Christopher E. Smith, *The Rehnquist Court and Criminal Punishment* (New York: Garland, 1997).

Patricia Smith, *Feminist Jurisprudence* (New York: Oxford University Press, 1993).

Rickie Solinger, ed., *Abortion Wars: A Half Century of Struggle, 1950–2000* (Berkeley: University of California Press, 1998).

Gerry Spence, *Give Me Liberty!: Freeing Ourselves in the Twenty-first Century* (New York: St. Martin's Press, 1998.

Kenneth Starr, *The Starr Report: The Findings of Independent Counsel Kenneth W. Starr on President Clinton and the White House Scandals* (New York: Public Affairs, 1998).

D. F. B. Tucker, *The Rehnquist Court and Civil Rights* (Aldershot, U.K. & Brookfield, Vt.: Dartmouth, 1995).

Franklin E. Zimring, *American Youth Violence* (New York: Oxford University Press, 1998).

LIFESTYLES

Edward J. Blakely & Mary Gail Snyder, *Fortress America: Gated Communities in the United States* (Washington, D.C.: Brookings Institution, 1997).

Robert Bly, *Iron John: A Book About Men* (Reading, Mass.: Addison-Wesley, 1990).

Jill Wilson Brennan, *Gun Control in the 1990s: Gun Advocacy, the Gun Control Lobby, and the Militia* (Kettering, Ohio: PPI, 1997).

Farai Chideya, *The Color of Our Future* (New York: Morrow, 1999).

Deepak Chopra, *Ageless Body, Timeless Mind: The Quantum Alternative to Growing Old* (New York: Harmony, 1993).

Chopra, *Creating Affluence: Wealth Consciousness in the Field of All Possibilities* (San Rafael, Cal.: New World Publishing, 1993).

Hillary Rodham Clinton, *It Takes A Village and Other Lessons Children Teach Us* (New York: Simon & Schuster, 1996).

Stephen R. Covey, *The 7 Habits of Highly Effective Families: Building a Beautiful Family Culture in a Turbulent World* (New York: Golden, 1997).

Tom Diaz, *Making A Killing: The Business of Guns in America* (New York: New Press, 1999).

Susan Faludi, *Backlash: The Undeclared War Against American Women* (New York: Crown, 1991).

Faludi, *Stiffed: The Betrayal of the American Man* (New York: Morrow, 1999).

Elizabeth Fox-Genovese, *Feminism Is Not the Story of My Life: How Today's Feminist Elite Has Lost Touch With the Real Concerns of Women* (New York: Nan A. Talese, 1996).

Evan Gerstmann, *The Constitutional Underclass: Gays, Lesbians and the Failure of the Class-Based Equal Protection* (Chicago: University of Chicago Press, 1999).

Richard J. Herrnstein and Charles Murray, *The Bell Curve: Intelligence and Class Structure in American Life* (New York: Free Press, 1994).

Patricia Hersch, *A Tribe Apart: A Journey into the Heart of American Adolescence* (New York: Fawcett Columbine, 1998).

Jonathan Kozol, *Amazing Grace: The Lives of Children and the Conscience of a Nation* (New York: Crown, 1995).

Wayne R. LaPierre, *Guns, Crime, and Freedom* (Washington, D.C.: Regnery, 1994).

Michael Lerner, *The Politics of Meaning: Restoring Hope and Possibility in an Age of Cynicism* (New York: Addison-Wesley, 1996).

Judith Martin, *Miss Manners' Guide to Excruciatingly Correct Behavior* (New York: Warner, 1982).

Michael Nava and Robert Dawidoff, *Created Equal: Why Gay Rights Matter to America* (New York: St. Martin's Press, 1994).

Camille Paglia, *Sex, Art, and American Culture: Essays* (New York: Vintage, 1992).

Faith Popcorn, *The Popcorn Report: Faith Popcorn on the Future of Your Company, Your World, Your Life* (New York: Doubleday, 1991).

Dan Rather, *Deadlines and Datelines* (New York: Morrow, 1999).

Graham Scambler and Annette Scambler, eds., *Rethinking Prostitution: Purchasing Sex in the 1990s* (London & New York: Routledge, 1997).

Shelby Steele, *A Dream Deferred: The Second Betrayal of Black Freedom in America* (New York: HarperCollins, 1998).

Andrew Sullivan, *Virtually Normal: An Argument About Homosexuality* (New York: Knopf, 1995).

Steven A. Tuch and Jack K. Martin, eds., *Racial Attitudes in the 1990s: Continuity and Change* (New York: Praeger, 1997).

Naomi Wolf, *The Beauty Myth: How Images of Beauty Are Used Against Women* (New York: Morrow, 1991).

MEDIA

Beulah Ainley, *Black Journalists, White Media* (Stoke on Trent, U.K.: Trentham Books, 1998).

Robin Andersen, *Consumer Culture and TV Programming* (Boulder, Colo.: Westview Press, 1995).

Stephen Ansolabehere, Roy Behr, and Shanto Iyengar, *The Media Game: American Politics in the Television Age* (New York: Macmillan, 1993).

Joey Anuff and Ana Marie Cox, eds., *Suck: Worst-case Scenarios in Media, Culture, Advertising, and the Internet* (San Francisco: Wired, 1997).

Ben H. Bagdikian, *The Media Monopoly* (Boston: Beacon, 1983);

James Baughman, *The Republic of Mass Culture: Journalism, Filmmaking, and Broadcasting in America Since 1941* (Baltimore: Johns Hopkins University Press, 1992).

Margaret A. Blanchard, ed., *History of the Mass Media in the United States: An Encyclopedia* (Chicago: Fitzroy Dearborn, 1998).

Leo Bogart, *The American Media System and Its Commercial Culture* (New York: Gannett Foundation Media Center, Columbia University, 1991).

Charlotte Brunsdon, Julie D'Acci, and Lynn Spigel, *Film and Politics in America: A Social Tradition* (New York: Oxford University Press, 1997).

Lionel Chetwynd, *Life, Liberty and the Pursuit of Sleaze: Media and Politics,* video (Alexandria, Va.: PBS Home Video, 1999).

Lloyd Chiasson Jr., ed., *The Press in Times of Crisis* (Westport, Conn.: Greenwood Press, 1995).

Cynthia Crossen, *Tainted Truth: The Manipulation of Fact in America* (New York: Simon & Schuster, 1994).

David Croteau and William Hoynes, *By Invitation Only: How the Media Limit Political Debate* (Monroe, Me.: Common Courage, 1994).

Peter Dahlgren, *Television and the Public Sphere: Citizenship, Democracy and the Media* (London & Thousand Oaks, Cal.: Sage Publications, 1995).

Dahlgren and Colin Sparks, eds., *Journalism and Popular Culture* (London & Newbury Park, Cal.: Sage Publications, 1992).

John Dart and Jimmy Allen, *Bridging the Gap: Religion and the News Media* (Nashville, Tenn.: Freedom Forum First Amendment Center at Vanderbilt University, 1993).

Richard Davis, *The Press and American Politics: The New Mediator* (New York: Longman, 1992).

Linda Degh, *American Folklore and the Mass Media* (Bloomington: Indiana University Press, 1994).

Gail Dines and Jean M. Humez, *Gender, Race, and Class in Media: A Text-Reader* (Thousand Oaks, Cal.: Sage Publications, 1995).

C. K. Doreski, *Writing America Black: Race Rhetoric in the Public Sphere* (Cambridge & New York: Cambridge University Press, 1998).

Susan J. Douglas, *Where the Girls Are: Growing Up Female with the Mass Media* (New York: Times Books, 1994).

Bonnie J. Dow, *Prime-time Feminism: Television, Media Culture, and the Women's Movement Since 1970* (Philadelphia: University of Pennsylvania Press, 1996).

Susan J. Drucker and Robert S. Cathcart, *American Heroes in a Media Age* (Cresskill, N.J.: Hampton Press, 1994).

Bosah Ebo, ed., *Cyberghetto or Cybertopia: Race, Class, and Gender on the Internet* (Westport, Conn.: Praeger, 1998).

James S. Ettema and D. Charles Whitney, *Audiencemaking: How the Media Create the Audience* (Thousand Oaks, Cal.: Sage Publications, 1994).

James Fallows, *Breaking the News: How the Media Undermine American Democracy* (New York: Pantheon, 1996).

Robert Ferguson, *Representing "Race": Ideology, Identity and the Media* (London & New York: Arnold, 1998).

Martha A. Fineman and Martha T. McCluskey, eds., *Feminism, Media, and the Law* (New York: Oxford University Press, 1997).

Alec Foege, *The Empire God Built: Inside Pat Robertson's Media Machine* (New York: John Wiley, 1996).

Herbert N. Foerstel, *Banned in the Media: A Reference Guide to Censorship in the Press, Motion Pictures, Broadcasting, and the Internet* (Westport, Conn.: Greenwood Press, 1998).

Jean Folkerts and Dwight L. Teeter Jr., *Voices of a Nation: A History of Mass Media in the United States* (New York: Macmillan, 1994).

John Gabriel, *Whitewash: Racialized Politics and the Media* (London & New York: Routledge, 1998).

Glasgow University Media Group, *Getting the Message: News, Truth and Power,* edited by John Eldridge (London & New York: Routledge, 1993).

Philip Goldstein, ed., *Styles of Cultural Activism: From Theory and Pedagogy to Women, Indians, and Communism* (Newark: University of Delaware Press, 1994; London & Cranbury, N.J.: Associated University Presses, 1994).

Tim Graham, *Pattern of Deception: The Media's Role in the Clinton Presidency* (Alexandria, Va.: Media Research Center, 1996).

Marilyn Greenwald and Joseph Bernt, eds., *The Big Chill: Investigative Reporting in the Current Media Environment* (Ames: Iowa State University Press, 2000).

Jostein Gripsrud, *The Dynasty Years: Hollywood Television and Critical Media Studies* (London & New York: Routledge, 1995).

Larry Gross and James D. Woods, eds., *The Columbia Reader on Lesbians and Gay Men in Media, Society, and Politics* (New York: Columbia University Press, 1999).

Lawrence Grossberg, Ellen Wartella, and D. Charles Whitney, *Mediamaking: Mass Media in a Popular Culture* (Thousand Oaks, Cal.: Sage Publications, 1998).

Janice D. Hamlet, ed., *Afrocentric Visions: Studies in Culture and Communication* (Thousand Oaks, Cal.: Sage Publications, 1998).

John Hartley, *Popular Reality: Journalism, Modernity, Popular Culture* (London & New York: Arnold, 1996).

Darnell M. Hunt, *O. J. Simpson Facts and Fictions: News Rituals in the Construction of Reality* (Cambridge & New York: Cambridge University Press, 1999).

Earl Ofari Hutchinson, *Beyond O. J.: Race, Sex, and Class Lessons for America* (Los Angeles: Middle Passage, 1996).

Haynes Johnson and James M. Perry, *Contemporary Views of American Journalism* (Chestertown, Md.: Literary House Press at Washington College, 1993).

Alexandra Juhasz, *AIDS TV: Identity, Community, and Alternative Video* (Durham, N.C.: Duke University Press, 1995).

Yahya R. Kamalipour and Theresa Carilli, eds., *Cultural Diversity and the U.S. Media* (Albany: State University of New York Press, 1998).

Sara Kiesler, ed., *Culture of the Internet* (Mahwah, N.J.: Lawrence Erlbaum Associates, 1997).

Markos Kounalakis, Drew Banks, and Kim Daus, *Beyond Spin: The Power of Strategic Corporate Journalism* (San Francisco: Jossey-Bass, 1999).

Elisabeth Kraus and Carolin Auer, *Simulacrum America: The USA and the Popular Media* (Rochester, N.Y.: Camden House, 2000).

Howard Kurtz, *Media Circus: The Trouble with America's Newspapers* (New York: Times Books, 1993).

Paul Leslie, ed., *The Gulf War as Popular Entertainment: An Analysis of the Military-Industrial Media Complex* (Lewiston, N.Y.: Mellen, 1997).

Lisa A. Lewis, ed., *The Adoring Audience: Fan Culture and Popular Media* (London & New York: Routledge, 1992).

Peter Lewis, ed., *Alternative Media: Linking Global and Local* (Paris: UNESCO Publishing, 1993).

Jeremy Harris Lipschultz, *Free Expression in the Age of the Internet: Social and Legal Boundaries* (Boulder, Colo.: Westview Press, 2000).

James Lull and Stephen Hinerman, eds., *Media Scandals: Morality and Desire in the Popular Culture Marketplace* (New York: Columbia University Press, 1997).

Catharine Lumby, *Bad Girls: The Media, Sex and Feminism in the '90s* (St. Leonards, NSW, Australia: Allen & Unwin, 1997).

Maxwell McCombs, Edna Einsiedel, and David Weaver, *Contemporary Public Opinion: Issues and the News* (Hilldale, N.J.: L. Erlbaum, 1991).

Jonathan Mermin, *Debating War and Peace: Media Coverage of U.S. Intervention in the Post-Vietnam Era* (Princeton: Princeton University Press, 1999).

Susan D. Moeller, *Compassion Fatigue: How the Media Sell Disease, Famine, War, and Death* (New York: Routledge, 1999).

Wayne Munson, *All Talk: The Talkshow in Media Culture* (Philadelphia: Temple University Press, 1993).

Brigitte L. Nacos, *Terrorism and the Media: From the Iran Hostage Crisis to the World Trade Center Bombing* (New York: Columbia University Press, 1994).

Brian Neve, *Film and Politics in America: A Social Tradition* (London & New York: Routledge, 1992).

Scott Robert Olson, *Hollywood Planet: Global Media and the Competitive Advantage of Narrative Transparency* (Mahwah, N.J.: L. Erlbaum, 1999).

Richard Osborne and David Hewitt-Kidd, eds., *Crime and the Media: The Postmodern Spectacle* (London & East Haven, Conn.: Pluto Press, 1995).

David L. Paletz, *The Media in American Politics: Contents and Consequences* (New York: Longman, 1998).

John Pilger, *Hidden Agendas* (London: Vintage, 1998).

Jorge Quiroga, *Hispanic Voices: Is the Press Listening?* (Cambridge, Mass.: Joan Shorenstein Center, 1995).

M. L. Rantala, *O. J. Unmasked: The Trial, the Truth, and the Media* (Chicago: Catfeet, 1996).

Casey Ripley Jr., ed., *The Media & the Public* (New York: Wilson, 1994).

Clara E. Rodriguez, *Latin Looks: Images of Latinas and Latinos in the U.S. Media* (Boulder, Colo.: Westview Press, 1997).

Karen Ross, *Black and White Media: Black Images in Popular Film and Television* (Cambridge, Mass.: Polity, 1996).

Douglas Rushkoff, *Media Virus!: Hidden Agendas in Popular Culture* (New York: Ballantine, 1994).

Paddy Scannell, Philip Schlesinger, and Colin Sparks, *Culture and Power: A Media, Culture & Society Reader* (London & Newbury Park, Cal.: Sage Publications, 1992).

Janice Schuetz and Lin S. Lilley, eds., *The O. J. Simpson Trials: Rhetoric, Media, and the Law* (Carbondale: Southern Illinois University Press, 1999).

Martin H. Seiden, *Access to the American Mind: The Impact of the New Mass Media* (New York: Shapolsky Publishers, 1991).

William Shawcross, *Murdoch: The Making of a Media Empire,* revised edition (New York: Simon & Schuster, 1997).

Pamela J. Shoemaker, *Gatekeeping* (Newbury Park, Cal.: Sage Publications, 1991).

William David Sloan and Emily Erickson Hoff, eds., *Contemporary Media Issues* (Northport, Ala.: Vision Press, 1998).

Erna Smith, *Transmitting Race: The Los Angeles Riot in Television News* (Cambridge, Mass.: Harvard University Press, 1994).

Norman Solomon and Jeff Cohen, *Wizards of Media Oz: Behind the Curtain of Mainstream News* (Monroe, Me.: Common Courage Press, 1997).

C. John Sommerville, *How the News Makes Us Dumb: The Death of Wisdom in an Information Society* (Downers Grove, Ill.: InterVarsity Press, 1999).

A. M. Sperber, *Murrow, His Life and Times* (New York: Freundlich Press, 1986).

Sasha Torres, ed., *Living Color: Race and Television in the United States* (Durham, N.C.: Duke University Press, 1998).

Jeremy Tunstall and Michael Palmer, *Media Moguls* (London & New York: Routledge, 1991).

James B. Twitchell, *Carnival Culture: The Trashing of Taste in America* (New York: Columbia University Press, 1992).

Teun A. van Dijk, *Racism and the Press* (London & New York: Routledge, 1991).

Robert Venturi and Denise Scott Brown, *Two Responses to Some Immediate Issues* (Philadelphia: Institute of Contemporary Art, 1993).

Jim Willis, *The Age of Multimedia and Turbonews* (Westport, Conn.: Praeger, 1994).

James Winter, *Common Cents: Media Portrayal of the Gulf War and Other Events* (Montreal & New York: Black Rose, 1992).

Michelle A. Wolf and Alfred P. Kielwasser, eds., *Gay People, Sex, and the Media* (New York: Haworth, 1991).

Nancy J. Woodhull and Robert W. Snyder, *Media Mergers* (New Brunswick, N.J.: Transaction Publishers, 1998).

MEDICINE

Robert C. Atkins, *Dr. Atkins' New Diet Revolution* (New York: Evans, 1996).

John Duffy, *From Humors to Medical Science: A History of American Medicine* (Urbana: University of Illinois Press, 1993).

Michael Fumento, *The Myth of Heterosexual AIDS* (New York: Basic Books, 1990).

Edward S. Golub, *The Limits of Medicine: How Science Shapes Our Hope for the Cure* (New York: Times Books, 1994).

Elizabeth Haiken, *Venus Envy: A History of Cosmetic Surgery* (Baltimore: Johns Hopkins University Press, 1997).

Caroline Hannaway, Victoria A. Harden, and John Parascandola, eds. *AIDS and the Public Debate: Historical and Contemporary Perspectives* (Amsterdam & Washington, D.C.: IOS Press, 1995).

Joel D. Howell, *Technology in the Hospital: Transforming Patient Care in the Early Twentieth Century* (Baltimore: Johns Hopkins University Press, 1995).

Alan M. Kraut, *Silent Travelers: Germs, Genes, and the "Immigrant Menace"* (New York: BasicBooks, 1994).

Katherine Ott, *Fevered Lives: Tuberculosis in American Culture since 1870* (Cambridge, Mass.: Harvard University Press, 1996).

George Rosen, *A History of Public Health* (Baltimore: Johns Hopkins University Press, 1993).

Charles E. Rosenberg, *Explaining Epidemics and Other Studies in the History of Medicine* (Cambridge & New York: Cambridge University Press, 1992).

Rosenberg and Janet Golden, eds., *Framing Disease: Studies in Cultural History* (New Brunswick, N.J.: Rutgers University Press, 1992).

David J. Rothman, *Strangers at the Bedside: A History of How Law and Bioethics Transformed Medical Decision Making* (New York: BasicBooks, 1991).

Sheila M. Rothman, *Living in the Shadow of Death: Tuberculosis and the Social Experience of Illness in American History* (New York: BasicBooks, 1994).

John W. Rowe and Robert L. Kahn, *Successful Aging* (New York: Pantheon Books, 1998).

Nancy Tomes, *The Gospel of Germs: Men, Women, and the Microbe in American Life* (Cambridge, Mass.: Harvard University Press, 1998).

United States Presidential Advisory Committee on Gulf War Veterans' Illnesses, *Presidential Advisory Committee on Gulf War Veterans' Illnesses: Final Report* (Washington, D.C.: U.S.G.P.O., 1996).

RELIGION

Karen Armstrong, *A History of God: The 4000-Year Quest of Judaism, Christianity, and Islam* (New York: Knopf, 1993).

The Book of J, translated by David Rosenberg, interpreted by Harold Bloom (New York: Grove-Weidenfield, 1990).

Raymond E. Brown, *The Death of the Messiah: From Gethsemane to the Grave: A Commentary on the Passion Narratives in the Four Gospels* (New York: Doubleday, 1994).

The Dalai Lama, *Ethics for a New Millennium* (New York: Riverhead, 1999).

Donald J. Dietrich, *God and Humanity in Auschwitz: Jewish-Christian Relations and Sanctioned Murder* (New Brunswick, N.J.: Transaction Publishers, 1995).

Michael Drosnin, *The Bible Code* (New York: Simon & Schuster, 1997).

Richard T. Foltin, *Religious Liberty in the 1990s: The Religion Clauses under the Rehnquist Court: A Consultation* (New York: American Jewish Committee, 1994).

Richard Elliott Friedman, trans., *The Hidden Book in the Bible* (San Francisco: HarperSanFrancisco, 1998).

Robert W. Funk, Roy W. Hoover, and the Jesus Seminar, eds., *The Five Gospels: The Search for the Authentic Words of Jesus: New Translation and Commentary* (New York: Macmillan, 1993).

Dean R. Hoge and others, *Vanishing Boundaries: The Religion of Mainline Protestant Baby Boomers* (Louisville, Ky.: Westminster/John Knox Press, 1994).

Luke Timothy Johnson, *The Real Jesus: The Misguided Quest for the Historical Jesus and the Truth of the Traditional Gospels* (San Francisco: HarperSanFrancisco, 1996).

Mark Jurgensmeyer, *Terror in the Mind of God: The Global Rise of Religious Violence* (Berkeley: University of California Press, 2000).

Rodger Kamenetz, *Stalking Elijah: Adventures with Today's Jewish Mystical Masters* (San Francisco: HarperSanFrancisco, 1997).

Don Morreale, ed., *The Complete Guide to Buddhist America* (Boston: Shambhala Publishers, 1998).

Bill Moyers, *Genesis: A Living Conversation* (New York: Doubleday, 1996).

Sulayman S. Nayang, *Islam in the United States of America* (Chicago: Kazi Publishers, 1999).

Kathleen Norris, *Amazing Grace: A Vocabulary of Faith* (New York: Riverhead, 1998).

Bruce Perry, *Malcolm: The Life of a Man Who Changed Black America* (New York: Talman, 1991).

Ralph Reed, *Politically Incorrect: The Emerging Faith Factor in American Politics* (Dallas: Word Publishers, 1994).

Michael Warner, *American Sermons: The Pilgrims to Martin Luther King Jr.* (New York: Library of America, 1999).

Jack Wertheimer, *A People Divided: Judaism in Contemporary America* (New York: BasicBooks, 1993).

SCIENCE

Tim Berners-Lee and Mark Fischetti, *Weaving the Web: The Original Design and Ultimate Destiny of the World Wide Web by Its Inventor* (San Francisco: HarperSanFrancisco, 1999).

Jerry E. Bishop and Michael Waldholz, *Genome: The Story of the Most Astonishing Scientific Adventure of Our Time—The Attempt to Map All the Genes in the Human Body* (New York: Simon & Schuster, 1990).

Michael Crichton, *Jurassic Park: A Novel* (New York: Knopf, 1990).

Esther Dyson, *Release 2.0: A Design for Living in the Digital Age* (New York: Broadway Books, 1997).

Niles Eldredge, *Life in the Balance: Humanity and the Biodiversity Crisis* (Princeton: Princeton University Press, 1998).

Timothy Ferris, *The Whole Shebang: A State-of-the-Universe(s) Report* (New York: Simon & Schuster, 1997).

Bill Gates, with Nathan Myhrvold and Peter Rinearson, *The Road Ahead* (New York: Viking, 1995).

James Gleick, *Faster: The Acceleration of Just About Everything* (New York: Pantheon, 1999).

Thomas Gold, *The Deep Hot Biosphere* (New York: Copernicus, 1999).

Stephen Jay Gould, *Bully for Brontosaurus: Reflections in Natural History* (New York: Norton, 1991).

Gould, *Dinosaur in a Haystack: Reflections in Natural History* (New York: Harmony, 1995).

Gould, *Eight Little Piggies: Reflections in Natural History* (New York: Norton, 1993).

Gould, *Full House: The Spread of Excellence from Plato to Darwin* (New York: Harmony, 1996).

Gould, *Leonardo's Mountain of Clams and the Diet of Worms: Essays on Natural History* (New York: Harmony, 1998).

Stephen Hawking, *Black Holes and Baby Universes and Other Essays* (New York: Bantam, 1993).

John Horgan, *The End of Science: Facing the Limits of Knowledge in the Twilight of the Scientific Age* (Reading, Mass.: Addison-Wesley, 1996).

Michael S. Hyatt, *The Millennium Bug: How to Survive the Coming Chaos* (Washington, D.C.: Regnery, 1998).

Stuart Kauffman, *At Home in the Universe: The Search for Laws of Self-Organization and Complexity* (New York: Oxford University Press, 1995).

Ray Kurzwiel, *The Age of Spiritual Machines: When Computers Exceed Human Intelligence* (New York: Viking, 1999).

Michael D. Lemonick, *Other Worlds: The Search for Life in the Universe* (New York: Simon & Schuster, 1998).

John Maddox, *What Remains to Be Discovered: Mapping the Secrets of the Universe, the Origins of Life, and the Future of the Human Race* (New York: Martin Kessler, 1998).

Kary Mullis, *Dancing Naked in the Mind Field* (New York: Pantheon, 1998).

Nicholas Negroponte, *Being Digital* (New York: Knopf, 1995).

Richard Rhodes, *Dark Sun: The Making of the Hydrogen Bomb* (New York: Simon & Schuster, 1995).

Jeremy Rifkin, *The Biotech Century: Harnessing the Gene and Remaking the World* (New York: Jeremy P. Tarcher/Putnam, 1998).

Neal Stephenson, *Cryptonomicon* (New York: Avon, 1999).

Stephenson, *The Diamond Age, Or, A Young Lady's Illustrated Primer* (New York: Bantam, 1995).

Stephenson, *Snow Crash* (New York: Bantam, 1992).

Clifford Stoll, *Silicon Snake Oil: Second Thoughts on the Information Highway* (New York: Doubleday, 1995).

Stephen L. Talbott, *The Future Does Not Compute: Transcending the Machines in Our Midst* (Sebastopol, Cal.: O'Reilly & Associates, 1995).

Sherry Turkle, *Life on the Screen: Identity in the Age of the Internet* (New York: Simon & Schuster, 1995).

SPORTS

Hank Aaron and Lonnie Wheeler, *I Had a Hammer: The Hank Aaron Story* (New York: HarperCollins, 1991).

Jeff Benedict and Dan Yaeger, *Pros and Cons: The Criminals Who Play in the NFL* (New York: Warner, 1998).

Larry Bird and Jackie MacMullan, *Bird Watching: On Playing and Coaching the Game I Love* (New York: Warner, 1999).

Bill Bradley, *Values of the Game* (New York: Artisan, 1998).

John Feinstein, *A Good Walk Spoiled: Days and Nights on the PGA Tour* (Boston: Little, Brown, 1995).

Steve Fireovid and Mark Winegardner, *The 26th Man: One Minor League Pitcher's Pursuit of a Dream* (New York: Macmillan, 1996).

Doris Kearns Goodwin, *Wait Till Next Year: A Memoir* (New York: Simon & Schuster, 1997).

David Halberstam, *October 1964* (New York: Villard, 1994).

Scott Hamilton, *Landing It: My Life on and Off the Ice* (New York: Kensington, 1999).

Robert J. Higgs, *God in the Stadium: Sports & Religion in America* (Lexington: University of Kentucky Press, 1995).

Roger Kahn, *A Flame of Pure Fire: Jack Dempsey & the Roaring '20s* (New York: Harcourt Brace, 1999).

Ken Kesey and Ken Babbs, *Last Go Round: A Dime Western* (New York: Viking, 1994).

John Krakauer, *Into Thin Air: A Personal Account of the Mount Everest Disaster* (New York: Villiard, 1997).

Spike Lee and Ralph Wiley, *Best Seat in the House: A Basketball Memoir* (New York: Crown, 1994).

David Maraniss, *When Pride Still Mattered: A Life of Vince Lombardi* (New York: Simon & Schuster, 1999).

Patrick F. McManus, *Into the Twilight, Endlessly Grousing* (New York: Simon & Schuster, 1997)

Marvin Miller, *A Whole Different Ball Game: The Inside Story of Baseball's New Deal* (Secaucus, N.J.: Carol, 1991).

Buck O'Neil, Steve Wulf, and David Conrads, *I Was Right on Time* (New York: Simon & Schuster, 1996).

Harvey Penick and Bud Shrake, *Harvey Penick's Little Red Book: Lessons and Teachings from a Lifetime in Golf* (New York: Simon & Schuster, 1992).

Arnold Rampersad, *Jackie Robinson: A Biography* (New York: Knopf, 1997).

Glenn Stout, series editor, *The Best American Sports Writing* (Boston: Houghton Mifflin, 1991–1999).

Al Stump, *Cobb: A Biography* (Chapel Hill, N.C.: Algonquin, 1994).

Jim Valvano and Curry Kirkpatrick, *Valvano: They Gave Me a Lifetime Contract, and Then They Declared Me Dead* (New York: Pocket Books, 1991).

Geoffrey C. Ward, *Baseball: An Illustrated History* (New York: Knopf, 1994).

George F. Will, *Men at Work: The Craft of Baseball* (New York: Macmillan, 1990).

CONTRIBUTORS

WORLD EVENTS

ANTHONY J. SCOTTI JR.
Manly, Inc.
Columbia, South Carolina

ARTS

MEG GREENE
Midlothian, Virginia

MARK G. MALVASI
Randolph-Macon College
Ashland, Virginia

ROBERT MCCONNELL
Columbia, South Carolina

VERONICA B. MCCONNELL
Midlands Technical College
Columbia, South Carolina

BUSINESS AND THE ECONOMY

MEG GREENE
Midlothian, Virginia

MARK G. MALVASI
Randolph-Macon College
Ashland, Virginia

EDUCATION

LINDA HUSKEY
Middle States Commission on
Secondary Schools, Philadelphia, Pennsylvania

FASHION

MARY K. PRATT
Arlington, Massachusetts

GOVERNMENT AND POLITICS

RICHARD H. FOSTER
Idaho State University
Pocatello, Idaho

ANNE MCCULLOCH
Columbia College
Columbia, South Carolina

LAW AND JUSTICE

LISA S. MCLEOD
West Virginia Wesleyan College
Buckhannon, West Virginia

LIFESTYLES AND SOCIAL TRENDS	MEG GREENE
	Midlothian, Virginia
	MARK G. MALVASI
	Randolph-Macon College
	Ashland, Virginia
MEDIA	SUSAN M. SHAW
	Oregon State University
	Corvallis, Oregon
MEDICINE AND HEALTH	ROBERT J. WILENSKY
	Washington, D.C.
RELIGION	CAROL GRIZZARD
	Pikeville, Kentucky
	TANDY MCCONNELL
	Columbia College
	Columbia, South Carolina
SCIENCE AND TECHNOLOGY	HOPE CARGILL
	Asheville, North Carolina
SPORTS	MARION ALDRIDGE
	Columbia, South Carolina

INDEX OF PHOTOGRAPHS

General Index

Baltimore Sun 411
Baltimore Symphony 64
Balzac, Honoré 54
Banc One 97, 104
Bancroft, Tony 38
Banderas, Antonio 33, 35
Bangkok, Thailand 121
Bank America 97, 104
Bank mergers 104
Bank of China, Hong Kong 198
Bank of New York 110
Bank One Ballpark, Phoenix, Ariz. 561
Bankers Trust 105
Banking 104–106
Banks, Ken 364
Banks, Russell 30, 38
Baptist Faith and Message 472, 477
Baptist Joint Committee on Public Affairs 468
Barad, Jill Elikann 136
Barad, Thomas K. 136
Baran, Paul 522
Barbara Gladstone Gallery, New York 47
Barber, Walter Lanier "Red" 589
Barbie dolls 46, 136, 339
Barbieri, Paula 337
Barbour, Ian 500
Barcelona, Spain 574
Barings PLC 106
Barker, Cliff 589
Barking Man 51
Barkley, Charles 563
Barksdale, Jim 525
Barnard College 372
Barnes, Randy 573
Barnes & Noble 122, 347
Barnett, James H. 432, 444, 470
Barnett, Marguerite Ross 193
Barnett Banks 96
Barnevik, Percy 113
Barney, Matthew 41, 45, 47
Barney Miller 425
Barnicle, Mike 417
Baron-Phillips, Allie Terese 346
Barr, Bob 306
Barr, Roseanne 382, 403
Barrera, José 230
Barrera, Laz 589
Barrett, Andrea 38
Barrett, Kay 55
Barrie, Dennis 29, 42
Barron, Steve 28
Barrowman, Mike 573
Barry, Marion S., Jr. 284
Barrymore 84
Barth, John 30, 33

Barthelme, Frederick 28, 32, 34, 37
Bartlett, John 207, 230
Barton, Mark 354
Barton, Robert 390
Baseball 559–562
  rules changes 561
  team expansion 561
Baseball 558, 583, 591
Baseball Hall of Fame 554
Bashir, Omar Hassan al- 494
BASIC 141
Basic Instinct 30
Basie, Count 69
Basile 199
Basinger, Kim 36
Basketball 562–564
  professional 563
  rules changes 563
  women in 562–563
The Basketball Diaries 58, 164
Basquiat, Jean-Michel 44, 49
Bass, Edward P. 515, 545
Bass, Rick 34
Bassett, Angela 31, 34, 38–39
Bassmasters tournament 554
Bastard out of Carolina 31, 51
Bates, Daisy Lee 193, 277
Bates, Kathy 29, 38, 85
The Bath of Bathsheba 45
Batman (movie) 424–425
Batman and Robin 36
Batman Returns 30
Battle, Kathleen 64
Batts, Deborah A. 329
Bauer, Art 125
Bauer, Gary 356
Baumgartner, Bruce 573
Bausch, Richard 31–32, 35, 38
Bausch & Lomb 109
Bay, Michael 35
Baylor University 193, 552, 565
BBC America 405
Beachfront Management Act 299
Beanie Babies 333, 347
The Beans of Egypt, Maine 50
The Bear Went Over the Mountain 36
Beard, E. Lee 115
Beat Generation 87
Beatles Anthology I 35
Beattie, Ann 34, 49
Beatty, Ned 38
Beatty, Warren 28, 37, 56
"The Beautiful People" 68
Beauty and the Beast (movie) 29
Beauty and the Beast (musical) 73, 76
The Beauty Myth: How Images of Beauty Are Used Against Women 230

The Beauty Queen of Leenane 85
Beavis & Butt-head 387–388
Because It Is Bitter, And Because It Is My Heart 28
"Because You Loved Me" 36
Bech at Bay 38
Bechtel 117
Beck Center, Cleveland 82
Becker, Gary S. 145
Becker, Holly 137
Beckwith, Byron De La 336
Beckwith, Herbert L. 232
Bedelia, Bonnie 28
Bedtime Stories 71
Beech, Keyes 423
Beecroft, Vanessa 48
"Been Around The World" 38
Bega, Lou 71
Begley, Louis 33, 38
Being Digital 544
Being John Malkovich 39, 63
Belarus 246
Belfry Golf Club, Sutton Coldfield, U.K. 570
"Believe" 40
Bell, Bob 423
Bell, James "Cool Papa" 589
Bell, Madison Smartt 30, 32, 34–35, 50–51
Bell, Terrell H. 193, 277
Bell Atlantic Corporation 95, 97–98, 116, 128
Bell Biv Devoe 28, 72
The Bell Curve: Intelligence and Class Structure 149, 168
A Bell for Adano 87
Bell laboratories at Menlo Park, Cal. 122, 534
Bell Tower at Misono, Shiga, Japan 228
Belle, John 216
Belluschi, Pietro 232
Beloved (novel) 80, 416
Beloved (movie) 37
Bemer, Robert William 527
Ben and Jerry's Ice Cream 111
Bendheim, Fred 48
Ben-Dor, Gisele 64
Ben-Hur (movie) 89
Benigni, Roberto 85
Bening, Annette 28, 34, 58
Benjamin, Ben 49
Bennett, Brooke 573
Bennett, Robert S. 308
Bennett, Tony 86
Bennett, William J. 191, 363
Bennington College 150
Benny, Reginald 330

Benson, Ezra Taft 277
Benson, Stephen R. 421
Benton, Robert 33
Bentson, Lloyd Millard, Jr. 266
Benzinger, Theodore H. 462
Beresford, Bruce 39
Beretta U.S.A. 304
Bergalis, Kimberly Ann 462
Bergen, Candice 232
Bergen, Christopher C. 132
Berger, Thomas 33, 35, 40
Bergman, Andrew 30
Bergourst, Eric 573
Berkowitz, Daisy 68
Berkowitz, David 68
Berkshire Hathaway 138
Berlin, Irving 75
Berlin Wall 246, 250, 572
Berlind, Roger 84
Bermuda 514
Bernadin, Joseph Cardinal 470, 491, 501
Bernall, Cassie 473, 492, 501
Berners-Lee, Tim 523, 541
Bernstein, Leonard 86
Berry, Halle 35, 37
Berry, Shawn Allen 329, 383
Berry, Wendell 35
Bessette, Lauren 414
Bestsellers 379, 400
Bethel, Alaska, school shooting 309
Better Homes and Gardens 354
Betts, Doris 33, 37, 51
Betty Crocker 339, 423
Bewitched 424–426
Beyer Blinder Belle 216
Beyond Any Kind of God 456
Beyond Deserving 30
Bezos, Jeffrey P. 137, 358, 417
Bhagavad Gita 130
BHC Communications 419
Bianco, James A. 107
Bible, Geoffrey C. 138
Bible 474–475
    New Revised Standard Version 468, 476
Bickford, John 578
Biden, Joseph Robinette, Jr. 323
Big Air Invitational 571
Big Bang theory 538
The Big Country 87
Big East Conference 562, 565
The Big Knife 88
Big 10 562, 565
Big Ticket Television 391
Big 12 565
The Big Valley 425

Bigelow, Kathryn 29
Biggs, Jason 39
Bilingual education 160
Bilirakis, Michael 447
Bill and Melinda Gates Foundation 142
Bill Nye the Science Guy 189
Bill Nye the Science Guy's Big Blast of Science 189
Bill Nye the Science Guy's Big Blue Ocean 189
Billroth, Theodore 435
Billy the Kid (ballet) 87
The Bingo Palace 33
Binnig, Gerd 536
Binoche, Juliette 35
BioGenex 130
Biological weapons 540
Bioran Medical Laboratory 109
Biosphere II 506, 515, 545
Birch, L. Charles 500
Bird, Brad 39
Bird, Larry 563, 579
Bird, Rose Elizabeth 277
Bird on a Wire 28
Birinyi, Laszlo, Jr. 141
Birinyi Associates 141
Birkenstock 208
Birmingham Barons 579
Birmingham News 420
Birth control 433, 444, 470
Bishop, Katherine 115
Bishop College 150
Bishops Committee for Pro-Life Activities 492
Black and Blue 77
Black Betty 33
Black Crowes 66
Black Eyed Peas 69
Black Panthers 322
Black separatism 486
Black Star 69
Black Water 31
Black Zodiac 83
Blackmun, Harry Andrew 277, 301, 320, 331, 485
Blades, Ruben 76
Blaese, R. Michael 452
Blair, Bonnie 552, 558–559, 573–575, 583, 587
The Blair Witch Project 39–40, 63, 479
Blakey, Art 69, 79
Blanchard, Terrence 71
Blanchett, Cate 37
Blass, Bill 229
Blassie, Michael Joseph 457
"Blaze of Glory" 28

Bleach 66
Bledsoe, Drew 551, 566
Blige, Mary J. 66
Blinder, Alan 143
Blindspot website 49
Blizzard of One 84
Blobel, Günter 459
Blockbuster Entertainment Corporation 93, 396
Blond Ambition Tour 229
Blood Circus 66
Blood on the Fields 79, 83
Bloom, Allan 193
Bloomberg, Michael 158
Bloomberg L.P. 158
Bloomingdale's 122, 202
Blue 66
Blue Calhoun 31, 51
Blue-collar workers 100, 103, 135
Blue Light 37
Blue Sky 85
Blue Spruce 34
The Bluest Eye 80
Blumenthal, Sidney 308
Bluth, Don 36
Bly, Robert 485
Blythe, Bill 267
BMW 223–224, 371
Board of Education of Kiryas Joel Village School District v. *Louis Grumet* (1994) 470, 489
Board of Education v. *Mergens* (1990) 290
Bobbitt, John Wayne 285, 373
Bobbitt, Lorena 285, 373
Bob Jones University 324
Bob the Gambler 37
Bochco, Steven 413
Body & Soul 32
Body Count 483
The Bodyguard (movie) 30, 72
The Bodyguard (soundtrack) 86
Boe, Nils Andreas 331
Boeing 95, 117, 132, 134, 189, 290, 412
Boesch, Charles 417
Boggs, Phil 589
Bogus Pomp 82
La Bohème 77
Bohjalian, Chris 53
Bok, Derik 191
Bolick, Clint 366
Bolling v. *Sharp* (1954) 195
Bolt, Baranek and Newman 523
Bolton, Michael 65
Bombeck, Erma 374, 423
Bomber's Law 32
Bon Jovi, Jon 28

Cerf, Vinton Gray 523
Ceridian Corporation 369
CERN 507, 523, 541
A Certain Age 40
Cesar Pelli & Associates 202, 228
Chabot, Steve 306
Chafee, John Hubbard 277, 447
Chagall, Marc 36
Challenge Mission 511
Challenger, Gray & Christmas 134
The Chamber 33, 78
Chamberlain, Wilt 589
Champy, James 111, 145
Chancellor, John 423
Chancellor, Van 564
Chandler, Albert Benjamin "Happy" 589
Chandler, Raymond 51
Chandler v. *Florida* (1981) 389
Chandra X-Ray Observatory 542
Chanel 198, 200–202, 207, 209
Chang, Michael 576
A Change of Gravity 37
"Change the World" 72, 86
Channel One 150, 152, 172, 380
Channing, Stockard 32
Chapman, Brenda 38
Chappel, Tim 229
Chappell, Fred 35
Charismatic (racehorse) 588
Charismatic Association of Vineyard Churches 502
Charles, Prince of Wales 209, 398
Charles, Daedra 581
Charles F. Kettering Medal 461
Charles S. Mott Prize 461
Charleston, S.C. 253
Charming Billy 38, 55
Charter schools 170
Chase, Samuel 326
Chassler, Sey 423
Chastain, Brandi 556, 558, 579, 583
Chattanooga News-Free Press 424
Chattanooga Publishing Company 424
Chavez, César Estrada 146
Cheap Trick 71
Cheating Death: Catastrophes Caught on Tape 397
Cheb Mami 66
Chechnya 246
Cheerleading 557
Cheers 381, 419
Cheever, Eddie, Jr. 555, 588
Chemical weapons 540
Cheney, Dick 186, 236, 274
Cheney, Lynne 177, 186

Cher 40, 198
Cherry, Kelly 51
Chevron 116
Chevrolet 223, 231
Chiat/Day Main Street building 224
Chicago 75, 84
Chicago Bears 590–591
Chicago Blackhawks 586, 590
Chicago Bulls 552–553, 555, 563, 579, 584, 586–587
Chicago Cubs 555, 580, 589–590, 592
Chicago floods 335
Chicago Hope 413
Chicago Symphony 64
Chicago Tribune 421, 424–425, 487
Chicago v. *Beretta U.S.A. Corp.* 304
Chicago White Sox 550, 552, 589, 591–592
Chicken pox 432
Chick-fil-A 130, 363
Chico and the Man 424
Child Development Group of Mississippi 187
Child support 271
Children 341–346
    access to Internet pornography 391
    alcohol use 346
    buying power 72
    care of 351, 476
    crime 308–311
    drug use 309
    education 165–190, 344
    educational assessment 172–175
    full schedules 346
    gun safety 304
    in the justice system 288
    physical and sexual abuse 349
    premarital sex 346
    share of tax dollars 344
    violence 165
Children's Defense Fund 187, 344
Children's Health Insurance Program (CHIP) 448
Children's Scholarship Fund 162
Chiles, Lawton Mainor, Jr. 277
Chilly Scenes in Winter 49
China 57, 98, 420, 424
    agreement with General Motors 96
    avoids trade war with United States 94
    embassy in Belgrade bombed NATO 240
    lifting of U.S. trade sanctions 237
    President Clinton visits 240
    religious persecution 490

    revolution 244
    study of 186
    use of Internet 124
    Y2K problems 527
Chlamydia pneumoniae 435
Chloé 229
Choices 34, 51
Chopra, Deepak 130, 333, 342, 370
A Chorus Line 37, 75
Christian Broadcasting Network. *See* CBN.
Christian Century 181
Christian Coalition 294, 469, 471, 497
Christian Identity 295
Christian Knights of the Ku Klux Klan 323
Christian Reformed Church 471, 477
Christian right 356, 478, 497
Christian Science Monitor 171, 421
Christianity and Crisis 469
Christie's 44, 209
"The Christmas Song" 89
Chromosomes 517
Chronicle of Higher Education 162
Chrysler 94, 97, 103, 108, 145, 201 222, 231, 410
Chu, Steven 546
Chubb, John 172
Chung, Connie 381, 417
Church at Pierce Creek, N.Y. 470
Church burnings 294, 480
Church of Jesus Christ of Latter-Day Saints (Mormons) 277, 499, 501
Church of Lukumi Babalu Aye v. *Hialeah, Florida* (1993) 469, 489
Church of Satan 68
Church of Scientology 130
The Church of the Dead Girls 37
Churches of the Lutheran Federation 478
Churning (business fraud) 109
Chute, Carolyn 33, 40, 50
Chyna 556
Ciba Vision Corporation 109
The Cider House Rules (movie) 39, 63
Cigar Aficionado 347
Cigar Manufacturers Association 347
Cigarettes
    attack on 442
    use by juveniles 310
Cigars 347
Cimarron Rose 37
Cincinnati Bengals 553, 589
Cincinnati Enquirer 420
Cincinnati Reds 585, 589, 592
Circe 87

Coleman, Ornette 70
Coleman, Roger 350
Coll, Steven 418
Collector's Bedroom 48
College Board 150, 158, 161–163, 173
College Republican National Committee 497
Collegiate Times 383
Collier, James Lincoln 70, 80
Collins, Eileen M. 510, 542
Collins, Frank S. 517
Collins, John R. 220
Collins, Phil 28, 85
Colonial Williamsburg 232
Color Me Badd 30
The Color Purple (movie) 416
Colorado 557
   homosexual-rights policies 291, 337
   referendum on marijuana 294
Colorado Avalanche 570, 587
Colorado potato beetle 521
Colorado Rockies 551
Colorado University 565
Colson, Charles W. 500
Colt 304
Coltrane, John 70
Columbia Broadcasting System. *See* CBS.
Columbia Journalism Review 402
Columbia Records 71, 79
Columbia space shuttle 542
Columbia University 140, 143, 163, 194, 264, 372, 515, 545
   Law School 329
   Medical School 401
Columbine High School, Littleton, Colo. 58, 164, 308, 354, 401, 473–474, 492, 501
Columbus, Chris 28, 30, 33
Colvin, Shawn 86
Comanche Moon 37, 51
Comay, Sholom D. 501
Combs, Sean "Puffy" 69
Comcast Corporation 128, 395
Come Over to Me 66
Comedy Central 387
Comer, James P. 345
Comet, Catherine 64
Comets 538
   Hale-Bopp 471, 491, 510, 538
   Shoemaker-Levy 9 538, 547
Commager, Henry Steele 375
Comme des Garcons 200
Commission for Art Recovery 44
Commission for Racial Justice 501
Commission on Civil Rights 194

Commission on Sustainable Development 516
Common Application 155
Common Business Oriented Language. *See* COBOL.
Common Ground Project 492
Communications Decency Act 292, 382, 393, 509–510, 530
Community Newspaper Holdings. *See* CNHI newspapers.
Community Service 348
Community Television Inc. 424
Compact disc. *See* CD.
Compaq 97, 526
"Composer in the Classroom" series 64
Compuserve 523
Computers 114, 122, 449, 521–533
   in genetic research 517
   in schools 166
   used for crime 110
   viruses 506, 512
Computers in Everyday Life program 544
Computerworld 507
Con Air 36
Concentration 425
Concerto for Flute, Strings, and Percussion 65, 84
Condoms, distributed in New York schools 152
Cone, Steve 106
Confederate battle flag 152
Confederate Knights of America 329
Congo 242
Congregation for the Doctrine of the Faith 477
Conley, Frances 458
Conley, John J. 462
Conley, Mike 573
Connally, John Bowden, Jr. 278
Connecticut
   homosexual rights policies 357
   SAT testing 155
   teacher pay 154
Connerly, Ward 168
Connery, Sean 28, 32, 34–35
Connick, Harry, Jr. 38
Connolly, Norma 423
Connors, Chuck 590
Connors, Jimmy 591
Conradt, Jody 581
Conroy, Frank 32
Conservative Opportunity Society 270
Consortium on Productivity in the Schools 157
Conspiracy Theory 36

Consumer Reports 418
Consumers Union 105
Contact 36
Contemporary art 44
Contemporary Arts Center, Cincinnati 29, 42
Continental Airlines 335
Contraceptives 430
Contract with America 256, 271, 300, 408
"Contract with the American Family" 471, 488
"Country Roads" 87
Conversations With My Father 84
Converse College 187
Cook, Barry 38
Cook, Steven 470, 492
Cooke, Jack Kent 146
Cool Runnings 558
Coolidge, Calvin 99
Coolidge, Martha 32
Coolio 33–34
Cooper, Chris 39
Cooper, Cynthia 564, 583
Cooper, James Hayes Shofner 447
Cooper, John Sherman 278
Cooper, W. Kent 220
Cooperative Baptist Fellowship 468
Coors Field, Colo. 561
Coover, Robert 30, 35, 38
Cop Killer 483
Cope, Derrike 585
Copland, Aaron 87
Coppola, Francis Ford 28, 30, 35–36, 88
COPS 397
Copyright infringement 182
Copyright protection 160
Coraci, Frank 38
Corcoran College of Art and Design, Washington, D.C. 225
Corcoran Gallery of Art, Washington, D.C. 42, 225
Cord 232
Corea, Chick 70
CoreStates Bank 115
Corey, Christian 578
Corey, Elias James 547
Corgan, Billy 67
Corliss, Richard 57
Cornell University 80, 140, 145, 189, 326, 348, 369, 521
Corning, Inc. 109
Cornwell, Patricia 28
Corporate spiritualism 362
Corporate welfare 100, 117–119
Corporation for Public Broadcasting 411, 423

End of the Affair 39
"End of the Road" 31, 72
Endangered Species Act (1973) 289, 299
Endeavor space shuttle 506–507
Enderle, Rob 129
Endostatin 441
Enemy of the State 38
Engebretson, Milton B. 501
Engle, Howard A. 319
Engle, Paul 194
Engler, Paul 416
The English Patient (movie) 35, 85
Enquire 523, 542
Enquire Within Upon Everything 542
Enter the Wu Tang (36 Chambers) 69
Entered from the Sun 28
Enterprise Computing Solutions 123
Entertainment and Sports Programming Network. *See* ESPN.
Entertainment Weekly 416
EnterTech conference 512
Environment 289, 299, 507, 514–517
Environmental Protection Agency. *See* United States—Environmental Protection Agency.
Epcot Center 189
Ephron, Nora 32
Episcopal Church 471
   and ecumenism 478
   policy on same-sex marriages 481
Epitope, Inc. 161
EPMD 68
Eppen, Deborah 330
Eppen, Matthew 330
Eppen, Sunil 330
Equal Access Act (1984) 290
Equal Opportunity Commission. *See* United States—Equal Opportunity Commission.
ER 381, 420
Erdrich, Louise 33, 38
Eric Clapton Unplugged 86
Erlandson, Eric 67
Erotica 71
Escalante, Jaime 192
Escobedo v. *Illinois* (1964) 278
Esherick, Joseph 232
Eshoo, Anna Georges 394
ESPN 396, 409, 424, 556, 558, 571, 575
Espy, Albert Michael 287
Essence 171
Estes, Simon 64
Estes v. *Texas* (1965) 389
Estonia 572
Etheridge, Melissa 410

Ethics & Religious Liberty Commission, Southern Baptist Convention 482
Ethiopia 574
Ethnicity 343
Etiquette 361
eToys Inc. 122
E*Trade 123, 532
Eubank, Wilbur "Weeb" 590
Europe
   nanotechnology research 536
   need for oil 248
   post–World War II development 124
   use of Internet 124
European Community (EC) 191
European Organization for Nuclear Research (CERN) 507, 523, 541
European Space Agency 538
European Union (EU) 120, 521
Euthanasia 470, 492
Evangelical Christianity 342, 352, 541
Evangelical Church in America 477
Evangelical Covenant Church 501
Evangelical Lutheran Church in America 469–470, 477
   and ecumenism 472
   policy on homosexuality 482
Evangelista, Linda 198, 201
Evangelium Vitae 470
Evans, Bill 79
Evans, Faith 37, 40
Evans, Gil 70
Evans, Janet 573
Evans, Nicholas 35
Evans, Tony 487
Evening News with Walter Cronkite 424
The Evening Star 31, 51
The Everlasting Story of Nory 38
Evers, Medgar 336–337
Evers-Williams, Myrlie 337
Every Icon (software) 49
"(Everything I Do) I Do It For You" 30
Every Time You Say Goodbye 66
Evinrude 233
Evita (movie) 35, 58
Evolution 473, 483
Ewell, Tom 87
"Exhale (Shoop Shoop)" 36, 72
Excite@Home 395, 526
Executive Decision 35
Exner, Judith Campbell 375
Exodus International 356
Exon, J. James 530

Exosurf Intratracheal Suspension 430
Experience Music Project (EMP), Seattle 224
Expo 70, Osaka, Japan, 232
Export-Import Bank of the United States 117
Exposure 32
Extraterrestrial life 514
Extreme 30
Extreme sports 558, 571, 575
Exxon 98, 127
Exxon-Mobil 127
   value of 120
Exxon Valdez 420
Eyes Wide Shut 88
F. W. Olin Foundation 161
Fab Five Freddy 49
The Face of the Night, The Heart of the Dark 83
Face/Off 36
Face to Face with Connie Chung 417
Factor, Max, Jr. 146
Factor IX 520
Fads 347–349
Fagan, Garth 82
Fair Lanes Open 550
Fairbank, John King 194
Fairchild, Erika S. 331
Fairness and Accuracy in Reporting (FAIR) 401
FairTest 173
Fakeshop (website) 49
Falaise, Lucie de la 215
Falconer, Elizabeth 354
Faldo, Nick 585, 587
Fallen 38
The Fallen Man 35
Falletta, JoAnn 64
Falling Down 32
Falling Into You 86
Fallows, James 418
False Disparagement of Perishable Foods Products Law (Texas) 416
Faludi, Susan 352
Falwell, Jerry 340, 410, 473, 500
Familiar Heat 34
Families and Work Institute 367
Family Affair 424
Family and Medical Leave Act (1993) 285
Family Channel 497
Family Guy 388
Family law 350
Family life 349–350, 476
Family Pictures 28
Family Research Council 356
Fancy Free 86

Galati, Frank 84

Galaxy IV satellite 511

Gale, Douglas 106

Galileo spacecraft 509–510

Galinsky, Ellen 367

Gallagher, John 356

Galliano, John 202, 209

Gallina, Juliane 192

Gallo, Julio R. 146

Gallo, Robert C. 437, 455

Gallo Winery 146

Galotti, Ron 82

Gambling 348

Gambon, Michael 37

Gandy, Charles D. 231

Gang Starr 68

Gangs 346

Gangsta rap 68

"Gangsta's Paradise" 34

Gannett 385, 394

Gannett News Service 420, 426

The Gap 145, 212, 216

Garbus, Martin 60

Garcetti, Gil 329

Garcia, Andy 28

Garcia, Jerry 87

Garcia, Sergio 570

Garciaparra, Nomar 583

Garcinia cambogia 440

Gardiner, Lizzy 229

Gardner, Gayle 409

Gardner Museum, Boston 29

Garland, Diana 496

Garner, James 33

Garon, Jay 78

Garrett, George 28, 51–52

Garrett, Kenny 71

Garrison, Jim 56

Garrity, Wendall Arthur, Jr. 194

Garson, Greer 87

Gartner, Michael 422

Gass, William H. 34

Gastric lymphoma 435

Gated communities 355

Gates, Bill 96, 129, 141–142, 145, 157, 164, 313, 335, 414–415

Gates, Henry Louis 80, 493

Gates, William "Pops" 590

Gates Learning Foundation 142

Gathers, Hank 430

Gatorade 578

Gattaca 479

Gaul, Gilbert M. 420

Gaull, Gerald E. 463

Gaultier, Jean-Paul 206, 229

Gaylord, Frank C. 220

Gaylord Entertainment 133

Geffen, David 67, 208

Gehrig, Lou 553, 559

Gehringer, Charlie 590

Gehry, Frank O. 199–200, 203, 205, 215, 219, 224–225, 231

Geisel, Theodor Seuss 89

Gekas, George William 306

Geller, Abraham W. 232

Gellhorn, Martha 423

Gelsinger, Jesse 433, 451, 458

Gender gap 351

Gene therapy 458, 506

Geneen, Harold Sydney 146

General Accounting Office (GAO) 109

General Convention of the Episcopal Church 481

General Electric 97, 108, 113–114, 117, 120, 143–144

General Hospital 423

General Mills 409, 423

General Motors 93, 95–96, 103, 114, 119, 122, 145, 223, 272, 335, 418

General Motors Cancer Research Foundation Awards 461

The General's Daughter 39

Generation X 30, 211, 333, 350

Genesis 180

Genesis: A Living Conversation with Bill Moyers 471

Genetics 289

dog-tag program 506

engineering 505, 509, 519

"Genie In A Bottle" 40

Genome mapping 434, 506, 508, 510–511, 513–514, 517–519

Gensel, John Garcia 501

Gensler/HNTB 216

Genzyme Transgenics 510, 520

Geographies of Home 55

George, Eddie 566, 587

George, Jeff 566

George, William W. 130

George Foster Peabody Individual Achievement Award 413, 416

George magazine 414

George Washington University 140, 431, 507, 519

Georgetown University 160, 194, 264, 268, 562

School of Medicine 457

Georgia Baptist Convention 483

Georgia Institute of Technology 565, 585

Gephardt, Richard A. 192, 275

Gere, Richard 28, 32, 34–36

Gergen, David 487

Germany 44, 120, 244, 420, 572

Gershon, Nina 44

Gershwin, George 75, 84

Gershwin, Ira 75, 84

Get on the Bus 62

Get Shorty (movie) 34

Get Shorty (novel) 28

Geto Boys 183

Getty Center 203, 205, 220, 227

Getty Trust 220

Getz, Stan 69

GHM, Inc. 110

Ghost 28, 479

Ghost Town 38

Giamanco, Joseph 110

Giants Stadium, East Rutherford, N.J. 66

Gibbons, Kaye 416

Gibbons, Leeza 403

Gibson, Mel 28, 31, 33–36, 85

Gibson, William 52

Gibson, William F. 337

The Gift 33

Giga Information Group 129

Gilchrist, Ellen 31, 33, 37

Gillespie, Dizzy 69–70, 87

Gillette 139

Gilliam, Terry 38

Gilligan's Island 423, 425

Gilman, Alfred G. 459

Gilmore, Gary 47

The Gin Game 89

The Gingerbread Man 78

Gingrich, Newt 238, 242, 251, 255–257, 263, 270, 273, 278, 498

Ginkgo biloba 440

Ginsberg, Allen 87

Ginsburg, Ruth Bader 238, 285, 301, 320, 329

Girl Crazy 75

Girl, Interrupted 39

Girl Talk 423

The Girl Who Loved Tom Gordon 40

"Girl You Know It's True" 29

Girls 37

Gisele 215

Giuliani, Rudolph W. 40–41, 43, 178, 275, 382

Gladly the Cross-Eyed Bear 36

Glamour 419

Glaser, Elizabeth 463

Glaser, Paul Michael 463

Glaspie, April C. 247

Glass, Ira 411

Glass, Philip 65

Glass, Stephen 418

Glass 37

Glassboro State College 153

Gleason, Jackie 592

Gleason, Thomas W. 146

Grossman, Beth 359
Groundhog Day 32
Group of Seven (G7) 120
Grove, Andrew S. 145, 545
Grumpier Old Men 34
Grunge fashion 205, 211
Grunge rock 66–67
GTE 97, 128
Guadalcanal 57
Guarding Tess 33
Guare, John 73
Guess 201
Guggenheim Fellowship 47
Guggenheim Museum, Bilbao, Spain 203, 205–206, 219, 224
Guggenheim Museum, New York 39, 47, 199–200, 217, 219
Gugliotta, Tom 440
Guidelines on Religious Exercise and Religious Expression in the Federal Workplace 489
Guinness World Records: Primetime 397
Gulf War syndrome 442
Gumbel, Bryant 415, 417–418
Gun control 184, 302–305, 352–353
   mandatory waiting periods 305
   "right to carry" laws 303
Gun Control Act (1968) 352
Gun-Free School Zones Act (1990) 157
Gun shows 303
Gun use by juveniles 310
Gunn, David 444, 469, 484
Guns N' Roses 31
Gunsmoke 425
Gurganus, Allan 37
Guterson, David 32, 51
Guthridge, Bill 562
Gutman, Roy 421
Guys and Dolls 75, 84, 89
Gwathmey, Charles 218
Gwathmey Siegel & Associates 217
Gwinn, Mary Ann 420
Gwynn, Tony 580, 583
Gwynne, Fred 423
Gyllenhaal, Jake 39
Gypsy (ballet) 82
Gypsy (musical) 84, 89
H. Town 32
Habitat for Humanity 416
Hachette Filipacchi Magazines 414, 418
Hackford, Taylor 36
Hackman, Gene 31–32, 34, 36, 38
Hackney, Sheldon 155
Hadid, Zaha 215
Hadith 475

Haemophilus influenzae 508, 545
Haislett, Nicole 573
Haiti 236
Halas, George 551
Haldeman, H. R. 278
Hale, Alan 538
Hale, Alan, Jr. 423
Hale-Bopp comet 471, 491, 510, 538
Haley, Alex 87
Half a Look of Cain 33
Hall, Arsenio 381
Hall, Jerry 431
Hall, Robert 137
Hallinan, Paul J. 491
Hallmark Cards 341, 350
Hallström, Lasse 39
Halprin, Lawrence 220
Halston 232
Hamblin, Ken 400
Hamel, Gary 122
Hamilton, Jane 33
Hamlet 84
Hamm, Mia 555, 558, 578
Hammer (MC) 68
Hammer, Armand 29, 87, 375
Hammer, Michael 111, 145
Hammerstein, Oscar 75
Hammett, Dashiell 51
Hampton, Lionel 69
Handelsman, Walt 422
The Hand that Rocks the Cradle 30
Handy, Charles 112
Hanks, Tom 31–34, 38–39, 56–57, 60, 85, 438
Hanlon v. *Berger* (1999) 392
Hannah, John Alfred 194
Hansen, Chris 394
Hanson 37, 72
Hanson, Curtis 30, 33, 36
Haraway, Donna 545
Harbert, Ted 418
Hard Copy 400
The Hard to Catch Mercy 32
Hardin, Charles M. 331
Harding, Tonya 557–558, 574, 584
Hardison, Osborne Bennett, Jr. 194
Hardy, Arthur B. 463
Hardy, Harriet L. 194
Hare Krishna style 207
Hargrove, John R. 331
Hargrove, Roy 71
Haring, Keith 87
Harlan, John Marshall 326
Harlem, N.Y 80, 171
Harlem Globetrotters 589–590
Harley-Davidson 129, 233
Harlin, Renny 28
Harlot's Ghost 30

Harme, John 360
Harmon, James A. 117
Harmon, Tom 590, 592
Harper, Ralph 500
Harper's 411
HARPO Productions 416
Harrelson, Woody 31–33, 35, 39, 58
Harrington, Mark 415, 424
Harris, Ed 30, 36, 38
Harris, Eric 308, 354, 383, 492
Harris, Kevin 285, 295
Harris, Mark 33
Harris, Richard 31
Harris, Steve 216
Harrison, Don 424
Harrison, Donald 71
Harrison, George 370
Harrison, Giles 383
Harrison, Kathryn 32
Harrison, Kenny 573
Harry and Catherine 28
Harsanyi, John C. 145
Hart, Gary 262
Harter, Steve 132
Hartford Courant 422
Hartford Public School system 161
Hartford Whalers 570
Hartman, Phil 424
Hartmann, Patricia 215
Hartwell, Lee 460
Hartzler, Joseph H. 298
Haruf, Kent 51
Harvard University 80, 141, 155–157, 163–164, 190–191, 194, 224, 228, 326, 452
   Business School 122
   Center for Law and Education 187
   Divinity School 130
   Law School 125, 139, 326, 329
   Medical School 194, 345, 452, 455
   School of Public Health 156
      College Alcohol Study (1999) 445
Harvey 89
Hasidic Jews 207
Hastert, John Dennis 240, 257, 273
Hastings, Dwayne 482
Hatch, Orrin G. 302, 356
Hate crimes 357
Hate groups 294, 474
Hatfield, Mark O. 461
Hattori, Yoshihiro 335
Hawaii
   hit by hurricane 254
   legalization of same-sex marriage 289, 291, 338
   mangrove swamps 514

Society of Scholars Award 457
John's Wife 35
Johnson, Allen 573
Johnson, Andrew 260, 305, 326
Johnson, "Badger" Bob 590
Johnson, Calvin Crawford, Jr. 546
Johnson, Charles 28
Johnson, Chris 588
Johnson, Cookie 431
Johnson, Earvin II "Magic" 431, 458, 563
Johnson, Earvin III 431
Johnson, Elizabeth A. 500
Johnson, Lady Bird 233
Johnson, Lyndon B. 60, 194–195, 260, 277, 280
Johnson, Manuel H. 102
Johnson, Michael 559, 573, 575, 584, 587
Johnson, Mitchell 354
Johnson, Philip 219
Johnson, Randy 584
Johnson, Reggie 584
Johnson, Virginia Eshelman 458
Johnson, Walter "Big Train" 580
Johnson & Johnson Vision Products 109
Johnson Controls 319
Johnson Space Center, Houston 233
Johnston, J. Bennett 274
Johnston, Joe 39
Joint Chiefs of Staff 275
Joint Declaration on the Doctrine of Justification 478
Joker's Wild 425
Jolie, Angelina 39
Jones, Bob, Jr. 501
Jones, Cherry 84
Jones, E. Fay 231
Jones, Gayl 38
Jones, James 57
Jones, James Earl 28, 33
Jones, Jenny 384, 403
Jones, Jerry 567
Jones, Kadida 225
Jones, Madison 37
Jones, Paula Corbin 238, 243, 258, 260, 269, 275, 286, 305, 325, 399
Jones, Quincy 85, 225
Jones, Roy, Jr. 551, 564, 584
Jones, Stephen 298
Jones, Steve 587
Jones, Tommy Lee 29, 37, 39
Jonesboro, Ark., school shooting 162, 309
Jonze, Spike 39, 58
Jordache 225
Jordan 247

Jordan, Barbara Charline 279
Jordan, Louis 76
Jordan, Michael 552–553, 555–556, 558, 563, 579, 584, 586
Jordan, Montell 35
Jordan, Neil 30, 33, 39
Jordan, Vernon E., Jr. 275, 307, 325
Joshua Tree National Monument, Cal. 217
Jospin, Lionel 367
Journal of American History 177
Journal of the American Medical Association 440, 458, 463
Journal Register Company 395
Journey 71
The Joy of Painting 425
Joyner, Florence Griffith "FloJo" 590
Joyner-Kersee, Jackie 558, 573–574, 584
Judaism
    and hate groups 294
    and homosexuality 480
    roles of women 475
Judd, Ashley 39
Judeo-Christian values 474
Judge, Mike 387, 388
Judge Judy 384, 391, 405
Judicial Council of the United Methodist Church 481
Judicial emergencies 302
Juilliard School, New York 79
Jujamcyn Theaters 84
Julia, Raul 29, 88
Julian's House 51
"Jump Around" 31
Juneteenth 40, 51, 87
Jungle Brothers 68
Jungle Fever 62
Juniper Communications, Inc. 124
Jupiter 508, 547
Jurassic 5 69
Jurassic Park (movie) 32, 60
Jurassic Park (novel) 28
Juris Doctorate degrees 312
Juvenile courts 311
Juvenile crime 353
Juveniles in adult courts 310
K-Mart 372
Kabakov, Ilya 45
Kaczynski, David 295, 413
Kaczynski, Theodore John 286–288, 295, 379, 385, 412, 511
Kagan, Julia 418
Kahane, Meir 279
Kahn, Madeline 84, 88
Kahn, Robert E. 523
Kaiser, Robert G. 418
Kalifornia 58

Kaliski, John 229
Kalra, Krishan 130
Kan, Yuet Wai 460
Kander, John Fred 75
The Kandy-Kolored Tangerine-Flake Streamline Baby 54
Kane, Bob 375, 424
Kane, Carol 46
Kanin, Garson 88
Kanka, Maureen 329
Kanka, Megan 286, 329, 389
Kanka, Richard 329
Kansas 238
    State Board of Education 181, 473, 483
Kansas City, Mo. 350
Kansas City Chiefs 589
Kansas City Royals 401, 551
Kansas City Star 420
Kansas City Symphony 64
Kansas University 562, 586
Kantner, Dee 554
Kaplan, Paula 72
Kaplan, Richard 418
Kappner, Augusta F. 192
Kapur, Shekhar 37
Karan, Donna 199, 201–202, 206–207, 209, 226, 230
Karem, Brian 418
Karmazin, Mel 418
Karr & Hutchinson 324
Kasdan, Lawrence 29
Kasinga, Fauziya 458
Kasparov, Gary 510, 527
Kass, Carmen 215
Katen, Karen L. 145
Katz, Leanne 194
Katz Television Group 391
Katzenberg, Jeffrey 208
Katzman, Leonard 424
Kauff, Jerome B. 126
Kaufman, Philip 28, 32
Kawakubo, Rei 200
Kaye, Tony 37, 63
Kazakhstan 246
Kazin, Alfred 375
Kean, Thomas H. 192
Kearney, Michael 156
Keaton, Diane 28–29, 35
Keaton, Michael 30, 33
Keck Observatory, Mauna Kea, Hawaii 509
Keenan, Mike 572
Keene, John 34, 51
Keitel, Harvey 32
Keith, Brian 424
Keller, Catherine 477
Kelley, David E. 413

Kelly, Gene 88
Kelly, Kevin 360
Kelly, Michael 418
Kelly, R. 33, 40
Kelly, Wynton 70
Kemp, Jack 239, 256
Kemp, Tom 129
Kendall, David E. 306
Kendall, Henry W. 546–547
Kendle International Inc. 132
Kendrew, A. Edwin 232
Keneally, Thomas 57
Kennard, William E. 395, 407
Kennedy, Anthony M. 192
Kennedy, Edward M. 171, 344
Kennedy, George 29
Kennedy, Joey 420
Kennedy, John F. 56, 60, 87, 194, 195, 229, 233, 262, 268, 277, 280, 301, 463, 495
Kennedy, John F., Jr. 229, 338, 414–415
Kennedy, Marilyn Moats 134
Kennedy, Michael 375
Kennedy, Robert F. 187, 352
Kennedy, Rory Elizabeth Katherine 414
Kennedy, Rose Fitzgerald 375
Kennedy, William 31–32, 35
Kennedy Center, Washington, D.C. 84
The Kentucky Cycle 83
Kentucky Derby 553, 592
Kentucky Fried Chicken 336
Kenya 240
Keohane, Nan 191
Keppel, Francis 194
Kerkorian, Kirk 94
Kernis, Aaron Jay 65, 83
Kerr, Philip 52
Kerrigan, Daryl 230
Kerrigan, Nancy 552, 557–558, 572, 584
Kesey, Ken 31
Kety, Seymour S. 461
Kevorkian, Jack 290–291, 403, 430–433, 443, 456, 463
Key, Jimmy 584
Keyes, Leroy 327
KFBF radio 401
Kidd, Jason 562
Kidman, Nicole 28, 30
Kiley, Richard 88
Kilgore, Thomas, Jr. 501
Killing Mr. Watson 28, 50
Kilmer, Val 32
Kimball, Roger 45

Kimura, Doreen 152
Kincaid, Jamaica 36
Kind of Blue? 69
Kindt, John W. 348
King, Angus 192
King, Betsy 558, 570, 584, 586
King, Billie Jean 233, 591
King, Coretta Scott 337
King, John William 329
King, Martin Luther III 168, 373
King, Martin Luther, Jr. 220, 336–337, 502
    assassination of 352
    memorial 205
King, Rodney 284, 314, 317, 327, 329–330, 334, 365, 380, 483
King, Stephen 31, 33, 37–38, 40, 59, 78
The King and I 84, 89
King of the Hill 388
Kingburg Community Church 481
Kingburg United Methodist Church 481
Kingsley, Ben 31–32
Kingsley, Gregory 284, 329, 374
Kingsolver, Barbara 28, 32, 38
Kinkel, Kip 354
Kinsella, W. P. 31
Kinslow, Tom 229
Kirk, Grayson Louis 194
Kirkland, Lane 375
Kirsten, George 493
"Kiss From a Rose" 86
Kiss Me Kate 75
Kiss of the Spider Woman (movie) 88
Kiss of the Spider Woman: The Musical 84
Kiss on Wood 64
Kitagawa, Joseph 194
Kitchen, Deborah 304
The Kitchen God's Wife 30
Kitchen v. K-Mart 304
Kite, Tom 570, 586
Kitty Foyle 89
Klaas, Polly Hannah 330, 389
Klass, Marc 330
Klebold, Dylan 308, 354, 383, 492
Klein, Anne 202, 226, 230
Klein, Calvin 200–202, 204, 206, 209, 211, 214, 225–227, 230
Klein, Gene 590
Klein, Joe 35, 55
Klein, Joel I. 314, 330
Kleiser, Randal 29
Kleitman, Nathaniel 463
Kline, Kevin 29, 36
Kloor, Harry 156
Klose, Kevin 418

KMBZ 401
KMOL-TV 418
KMOV-TV 425
Knauss, Sarah 463
Knight, Gladys 72
Knight, James L. 424
Knight Ridder 385, 394
"Knockin' Da Boots" 32
Knudson, Alfred G., Jr. 460
Knudson, Tom 420
Kobayashi, George 159
Koch, Ed 391
Koch, Howard 88
Kohn, Walter 547
Komack, James 424
Komunyakaa, Yusef 83
Koolhaas, Rem 215
Koon, Stacey C. 314
Koons, Jeff 44
Koontz, Dean 31–32
Koplovitz, Kay 418
Koran 475
Korean War 52
Korean War Memorial, Washington, D.C. 202, 220
Koresh, David 295, 297, 327, 469, 474, 491, 494–495
Kors, Michael 198–199, 231
KORS line 198
Kortum, Samuel 124
Koshland, Daniel E., Jr. 461
Koskinen, John A. 527, 546
Kosovo 240, 242, 246, 269
Kotzwinkle, William 36
Kozol, Jonathan 171
Kraft Foods 424
Krall, Diana 71
Kramer, Larry 160, 437
Krauss, Alison 66
Krebs, Edwin G. 459
Kris Kross 31, 229
Kristof, Nicholas D. 420
Krizelman, Todd 145
Kropelnicki v. United States (1996) 304
Kropfeld, Jim 591
Kroto, Harold W. 536, 547
Krueger, Scott 161
Kruesi, Markus 346
Krugman, Stanley 369
Krzyzewski, Mike 562, 584
Ku Klux Klan 294–295, 323, 339
Kubrick, Stanley 88
Kuchel, Thomas Henry 279
Kuhn, Margaret E. 463
Kulwicki, Alan 591
Kundun 472, 479
Kuralt, Charles 381, 424

Kushner, Harold S. 499
Kushner, Rose 463
Kushner, Tony 74, 83–84, 438
Kuwait 236, 247, 267, 420
 aid from U.S. troops 236, 242
 invasion of 236, 242, 247
Kvaerner ASA 118
L.A. Confidential 36, 52
L.A. Law 413, 419
L.V. 34
La Face Records 72
La Salle University 591
Labor University of Mexico 120
LaChiusa, Michael John 77
Lacroix, Christian 198, 209
Ladder of Years 34, 51
Ladies Professional Golf Association
 (LPGA) 570, 583
The Lady Eve 89
Lafayette Industries, Inc. 134
Lagerfeld, Karl 198, 200, 209
Lake, Ricki 384, 403
Lamb, Wally 38, 416
Lamb's Chapel v. *Center Moriches
 Union Free School District* (1993)
 290, 469
Lambert, William G. 424
Lancaster, Burt 88
Land, Edwin Herbert 375
Landis, Frederick 331
Landmark Conference on the Future
 of Buddhist Meditative Practice
 in the West 471
Landon, Michael 424
Landscape with Smokestacks 45
Lane, Charles 418
Lane, Diane 35, 40
Lane, Mills 391
Lane, Nathan 84
Lane, Stewart F. 84
Lange, Jessica 85
Langer, Bernhard 586
Lansky, Aaron 82
Lantz, Walter 424
LaPaglia, Anthony 85
LaPierre, Wayne 352
Laramie, Wyoming 357
Larry King Live 93
Larson, April Ulring 469, 477
Larson, Gary 381
Larson, Jonathan 77, 83, 88, 438
Las Vegas, Nevada 580
Las Vegas Invitational 568
Lasch, Christopher 194
Lasher 32
Lasker, Mary 463
Lasker Foundation 463
Lasseter, John 34, 37, 40

Lassie 425
Last Action Hero 32
Last Night of Ballyhoo 74, 84
The Last of the Mohicans (movie) 31
The Last of the Savages 37
The Last Thing He Wanted 35
The Last Voyage of Somebody the Sailor
 30
Late Night with Conan O'Brien 415
Late Show with David Letterman
 415, 420
Latin America 265
Latvia 572
Laughlin, Robert B. 546
Lauren, Ralph 198, 211–212, 225,
 230, 372
Lavagetto, Harry "Cookie" 591
Law 288–332
Law and Order 380, 420
Law schools 311– 312
Lawrence, Margaret 52
The Lawrence Welk Show 425
Lawson, John 116
Lawyers 311–313
Lazier, Buddy 587
Leaders of the New School 68
Leaf, Ryan 566
A League of Their Own 31, 558, 592
Lear, Frances 424
Lear, Norman 74, 424
Lear Television 424
Lear's 424
Learn and Serve America 348
Leary, Timothy 375, 510
Leathers v. *Medlock* (1991) 392
Leaving Las Vegas 34, 85
Lebanon 237
Lecky, William P. 220
Ledeen, Barbara J. 127
Leder, Mimi 37
Lee, Ang 34, 36
Lee, David M. 546
Lee, Mark C. 507
Lee, Robert W., Sr. 564
Lee, Spike 31, 38, 40, 62
Lee v. *Weisman* (1992) 469, 489
Leeson, Nicholas 106
Legal issues 288–332
Legal Self-Help 379, 389
Legends of the Fall 208
Legion Field, Birmingham 565
Leguizamo, John 40
Lehman, Arnold 44
Lehman, Tom 570
Leibman, Ron 84
Leigh, Jennifer Jason 201
Leight, Warren 74, 85
Lekach, Illia 133

Lemieux, Mario 572
Lemmon, Jack 30, 34
Lemon, Ralph 82
LeMond, Greg 577
*Lenin's Tomb: The Last Days of the So-
 viet Empire* 419
Lennon, John 60
Lenox Hill Hospital, New York 454
Lenzi, Mike 573
Leonard, Elmore 28, 31–32, 36, 38,
 81
Leonard, Justin 570
Leonard, Walter "Buck" 591
Leoni, Tea 37
Leonid meteor shower 511
Leopold Foundation, Vienna 45
Lerner, Max 194
Les Miserables 38, 75
Lesbian rights 351
Lesbians on television 379, 408
Leslie, Lisa 409, 564
Lessing, Lawrence 125
A Lesson Before Dying 32, 51
Lethal Weapon 3 31
Letourneau, Mary Kay 162
Letter to the World 87
Lettice and Lovage 84
Levant, Brian 33
Lever House, New York 232–233
Levi Strauss 206
Leviathan 31
Levin, Martha 55
Levin, Morton L. 463
Levine, Lawrence 177
Levine, Philip 83
Levinson, Barry 33
Levitt, William J. 232, 375
Levittown, N.Y. 232
Levy, Jay 455
Lewinsky, Monica 55, 238–240, 243,
 258, 260, 269, 275, 287, 305, 307,
 325, 330, 382, 399, 496, 511, 520
Lewis, Carl 559, 573–574, 584
Lewis, Edward B. 459
Lewis, Jerry 88, 558
Lewis, Juliette 33, 58
Lewis, Lennox 556, 564
Lewis, Ray 566
Lewis, Reggie 591
Lewis, Shari 424
Lewis, Susie 388
Lexington (Ky.) *Herald-Leader* 421
Lexus 114, 223
Leyner, Mark 52
LFO 40
Liberation management 100–111
Liberty Group Publishing 385, 394
Libeskind, Daniel 215

Classical 63–65
Country 65
Grunge Rock 66
Heavy Metal 57–58
Hip-hop 68
Latino 71
Rap 68
Rhythm & Blues 72
women in 71
Music of the Heart 39
Musker, John 30
Muskie, Edmund 264, 279
Muskingum College 542
Muskogee High School, Oklahoma 159
Muslims 474
Mustard Gas 540
Mutual of New York 109
"My All" 38
My Cousin Vinny 31
My Cousin, My Gastroenterologist 52
My Darling Clementine(movie) 88
My Favorite Martian 424
My Heart Laid Bare 38
"My Heart Will Go On" 86
My Own Private Idaho 88
My People's Waltz 51
My Soul to Keep 51
My Three Sons 88, 424
"My Way" 38
Myers, Dee Dee 250, 275
Myers, Mike 31, 36
Myrick, Daniel 39, 63
Mystery Fiction 51
Mystery Theater 424
NAACP 193, 275, 279, 290, 331, 337, 500
Nabisco 98
Nabrit, James M., Jr. 195
Nader, Ralph 120
NAFTA. *See* North American Free Trade Agreement.
Nagano, Japan 572, 575
Nagurski, Bronko 591
Naismith Award 562, 579, 584–585
Naismith Memorial Hall of Fame 581
Najarian, John 458
Najimy, Kathy 31
Nakajima, Hiroshi 430
Nakashima, George 233
The Naked Gun 328
The Naked Gun 2 ½ 29
Nalder, Eric 420
Namath, Joe 590
A Name for Evil 88
Name That Tune 424
Nanocomputers 514

Nanofabrication 536
Nanotechnology 514, 536–537
Napalitano, Gabrielle U. 140
The Narcissistic '90s 341
Nas 69
NASA 151, 243, 509, 514, 523, 536–537, 543
Jet Propulsion Laboratory 537
NASA TV 405
NASCAR 578, 583–584
Nasdaq 96, 110, 134
Nash, David 44
Nash, Gary 176
Nash, John F., Jr. 145
Nash, Laura 130
Nashville 1864 37
Nashville Banner 383
Nashville Oilers 553, 566
Nashville Predators 570
Nashville Speedway USA 133
Nation of Islam 200, 274, 352, 486, 493, 500
National Abortion Federation 484
National Academy of Recording Arts & Sciences Awards (Grammy Awards) 85
National Academy of Sciences 511
National Academy of Television Arts and Science's Lifetime Achievement Award 416
National Aeronautics and Space Administration. *See* NASA.National and Community Service Trust Act (1993) 348
National Assessment of Educational Progress 150, 156, 158, 161, 194
National Association for Stock Car Auto Racing. *See* NASCAR.
National Association for the Advancement of Colored People. *See* NAACP.National Association of Broadcasters 407
National Association of Minorities in Cable 116
National Association of Sport and Physical Education (NASPE) 345
National Basketball Association (NBA) 552, 562, 574, 579
National Bioethics Advisory Commission 451
National Book Award 50
National Broadcasting Company. *See* NBC.
National Bureau of Standards 527
National Cable Television Association 407
National Cancer Institute 437, 442, 452, 455, 464, 507

National Cancer Institute Laboratory of Biochemistry 480
National Center for Construction Education and Research 135
National Center for Health Statistics 462
National Center for Supercomputing Applications 507, 524, 541
National Center on Addiction and Substance Abuse 163
National Center on Fair & Open Testing 193
National Coalition Against Censorship 194
National Collegiate Athletic Association (NCAA) 551, 557, 562, 565, 568, 578, 581–582, 584
National Commission on Teaching & America's Future 159
National Committee on Pay Equity 115
National Community Reinvestment Coalition 116
National Conference of Black Christians 501
National Conference of Catholic Bishops 471, 477, 491
National Conference of State Legislatures 443
National Constitution Center 417
National Council of Churches of Christ in the United States of America (NCC) 162, 474, 478, 480, 499, 502
National Education Association (NEA) 173, 182, 192, 323
National Education Commission on Time and Learning 192
National Education Goals Panel 175
National Endowment for the Arts (NEA) 29, 31, 42, 47, 63, 186, 192, 229, 243, 411, 498
National Endowment for the Humanities (NEH) 155, 176, 186
National Enquirer 385, 398
National Environmental Policy Act (1969) 299
National Football League (NFL) 327, 550, 557, 566, 583
National Gallery of Art, London 230
National Geographic 384, 397
National Governors' Association 175, 189
National Governors' Association Task Force on Readiness 189
National Health Security Act 447
National Historic Preservation Act 216

National Hockey League (NHL) 424, 552, 570, 572, 583
National Human Genome Project Institute (NHGPI) 517
National Industrial Conference Board (NICB) 143
National Institute of Biodiversity 506
National Institutes Health (NIH) 195, 430, 457, 480, 517, 521, 523, 536, 544
National Japanese American Memorial Foundation 220
National Labor Relations Board (NLRB) 552
National League Baseball 561, 580, 583
National Library of Medicine 462
National Medal of Arts 29
National Medical Enterprises 109
National Merit Scholarships 173
National Museum of American Art, Washington, D.C. 30
National Organization for Women (NOW) 155, 179, 187, 394, 401
National Practitioner Data Bank (NPDB) 430
National Public Radio (NPR) 380, 411, 418, 423
National Research Council 511
National Rifle Association (NRA) 303, 305, 343, 352
National Science Foundation 188–189, 523, 537
National Security Act (1947) 277
National Security Council (NSC) 264
National Study of School Evaluation (NSSE) 178
National Toxicology Program 464
National Urban League 487
National Yiddish Book Center 82
NationsBank 96, 97, 104
Native Americans
    ancient ruins 335
    display of symbols 159
    in business 115
    in novels 52
    influence on fashion 201
    on the federal bench 302
    punishment of youth 337
    religion 468–469, 489
Native Tongues 68
Natural Born Killers 33, 36, 58–60, 81, 183
Natural Selection 28
Naughton, James 84
Naughty Gear 212
Nauman, Bruce 45

Nautica 202
Navratilova, Martina 577
Navy Distinguished Public Service Award 457
Naylor, Gloria 31, 38, 51, 416
Nazi art thefts 44
Nazi death camps 219
Nazi Party 57
Nazis compared to homosexuals 485
NBC 146, 229, 328, 370, 380
NBC News 403, 415
NBC Nightly News 405, 411
Near Changes 83
Nebraska 238
Nederlander, James M. 84
Neeson, Liam 32, 38–39, 57
Negro Baseball Leagues 589–591
Negroponte, Nicholas 544
Nehru jackets 206
Neighborhood Design Center 231
Neill, Sam 28, 32
Nelson, Douglas 344
Nelson, Harriet Hilliard 425
Nelson, Judd 413
Nelson, Lindsey 591
Nelson, Louis 220
Nelson, Marilyn Carlson 130, 145
Nematode worm 518
Neon Vernacular 83
Nervión River 219
Nesmith, Jeff 422
Nestle, Marion 454
Net of Jewels 31
Nethercutt, George R., Jr. 274
NetIQ 129
Netmanage 134
Netomat 49
Netscape Communications 94, 98, 111, 129, 313, 339, 508, 524, 541
Netscape Navigator 129, 337, 338, 508, 524, 532, 541
Nettles, Bonnie Lu Trusdale 490
Network Television Association 380
Neufeld, Peter J. 546
Neuhaus, John Richard 500
Neumann, Peter G. 359
Neuwirth, Bebe 84, 558
Nevada referendum on marijuana 294
Nevermind 30, 67, 211
New Age bookstores 362
New Age movement 130, 342, 361–362
New American Schools Development Corporation 185
New Amsterdam Theater, New York 73
New Criterion 45

New England Journal of Medicine 294
New England Patriots 551, 587
New Jack City 29
New Jersey 169, 276
New Jersey Devils 587
New Mexico 118
New Orleans Symphony 63
New Orleans Times-Picayune 421
New Republic 358, 380, 414, 418
New Revised Standard Version of the Bible 468, 476
New York
    anti-abortion activity 444
    distribution of condoms 334
    incentives to business 119
    school-to-work initiative 167
New York City
    asbestos in schools 155
    distribution of condoms 152
    drop in gun dealers 305
New York Daily News 422, 424
New York Giants 550, 566–568, 585, 591–592
New York High School of Art and Design 226
New York Jets 566, 590
New York Knicks 396, 587–588, 590
New York Liberty 588
New York 415
New York Mets 553, 584, 591
New York Newsday 420
New York Philharmonic Orchestra 64, 86
New York Post 194, 418
New York Public Library 28
New York Rangers 396, 552, 572, 587
New York Stock Exchange (NYSE) 110, 140, 146
New York Theatre Workshop 84
New York Times 295, 305, 388, 405, 411–412, 418, 420–422, 453
New York University 106, 143, 150, 454
New York University Law School 414
New York Yankees 555, 561, 584, 587, 588–591
New Yorker 417, 425
New Zealand 273
Newhart 423
Newman, Paul 32–33
News America Digital Publishing 418
The News with Brian Williams 415
Newsday 388, 420–422
Newspaper mergers 394–395

Parks, Timothy 103
Parlux Fragrances Inc. 133
Parnevik, Jesper 570
Parnis, Mollie 233
Parson's School of Design 226
Parsons Technology 389
The Partner 37, 78
Pascal, Adam 77
Pasley-Stuart, Anne 368
Passenger 57 31
Passion (musical) 84
Pasteur Institute, Paris 437, 455
Pat and Mike 88
Patch Adams 38
Pate, Steve 570
Paterno, Joe 566
Paternot, Stephan 145
A Patchwork Planet 38, 51
Pathfinder spacecraft 510
Paths of Glory 88
Patil, Suhas 130
Patkin, Max 591
Patner, Josh 231
Patrimony: A True Story 30
Patriot Games 31
Patterson, Floyd 591
Patterson, Francine 82
Patterson, James 36
Patton 89
Pauley, Jane 418
Pauling, Linus Carl 464, 547
Pavin, Corey 587
Pavlick, Edward 230
Paxton, Bill 35
Paxton, Tom 34
Payne, Alexander 39
Payton, Nicholas 71
Payton, Walter 433, 585, 591
PBS 152, 189, 340, 381, 471, 558, 583
PDP-10 computer 522
Peabody Award 410–411
Peace Corps 502
Peale, Norman Vincent 502
Pearl Harbor 265
Pearl Jam 211
Pearl, Mississippi, school shooting 309
Pearson, Hutchinson 418
Pearson Education 385, 397
Pechter, Richard S. 84
Peck, M. Scott 130
Peddie School 185
Peery, Janet 36
Peet's Coffee & Tea 347
Pei, I. M. 35, 202, 218, 228
Pei & Partners 198
Pei Cobb Freed & Partners 219

The Pelican Brief (book) 31, 78
The Pelican Brief (movie) 33
Pell Grant 163
Pelli, Cesar 205, 216, 228, 231
Pellicer, Leonard 193
Penicillin 464
Penick, Harvey 591
Penn, Irving 232
Penn, Sean 34, 38, 57
Pennel, John 591
Penney, J. C. 410
Pennsylvania
    incentives to business 118
    preservation of farmland 420
Pennsyvania State University football 553, 565
Pentagon 339, 442
    computer hackers 531
    smoking banned 336
Pentagon Defense Science Board 531
Pentagon Papers 278, 417
Penthouse 412
Pentium processor 94
People 382, 414
People are Talking 416
People for the American Way 154
People of California v. *Orenthal James Simpson* 316
The People vs. Larry Flynt (movie) 35
The People's Court 391
People's Republic of China 241, 266
Peppard, George 88
Pepper Commission 447
Pepperdine University 276, 401
Pepsi 567
Pepsi Cola Building 232
Percy, Walker 88
Peretsky, Sara 52
Peretz, Martin 418
The Perfect Moment 29, 42
Performance art 48
Perkins, Anthony 88
Perkins, Elizabeth 33, 413
Perkins & Will Architects 216
Perl, Arnold 62
Perl, Martin L 546
Perlman, Lawrence 369
Perlman, Steve 405
Peron, Eva 58
Perot, H. Ross 56, 93, 242, 250–251, 256, 267–269, 272
Perot Systems 272
Perret, Craig 585
Perrot, Kim 591
Perry Ellis America 133
Perry Mason 423
Pershing High School, Detroit 160

Persian Gulf War (1991) 58, 143, 192, 246–248, 250, 266, 274–275, 380, 420, 442, 539
The Persian Robe 44
Pert Plus 578
Pesci, Joe 28, 30
PET (positron emission tomography) 449
Pet Safety and Protection Act 365
Peter, Lawrence Johnston 146, 375
Peter Pan 88–89
Peters, Bernadette 85
Peters, John 464
Peterson, Oscar 69
Peterson, Roger Tory 375
Peterson, Wayne 83
Peterson, Wolfgang 32, 36
Petrocelli, Daniel M. 328
Petronas Twin Towers, Kuala Lampur 202, 205, 228
Pets 111, 342, 363–365
PetsMart 364
Pettit, Mike 129
Petty, Richard 559, 578
Pew Research Center 365, 405
Peyton Place 89
Pfaff, Kristen 67
Pfeiffer, Michelle 30, 413
Pfizer Pharmaceuticals 145, 436,
PGA Senior Championship 569
Phagan, Mary 76
Phantom of the Opera 75
Phar Lap Software 359
Pharming 520
Phat Farm 212
Phelan, Mary 425
Phelps, Tom 485
Phencyclidine (PCP) 315
Phi Gamma Delta 161
Philadelphia (movie) 32, 85, 438
Philadelphia A's 591
Philadelphia Daily News 421
Philadelphia Eagles 592
Philadelphia Fire 28, 51
Philadelphia Flyers 588, 592
Philadelphia Inquirer 185, 411, 420
Philadelphia Naval Yard 118
Philadelphia Orchestra 63–64
Philadelphia Phillies 586
The Philadelphia Story 89
Philadelphia Warriors 591
Philip Morris 94, 138, 145, 318, 371, 381
Philippines 237
Phillips, Dale 51
Phillips, Jayne Anne 33
Phillips, Lou Diamond 35
Phillips, William D. 546

Riverdale (N.Y.) Press 422
Roach, Jay 36
Roach, Stephen 358, 369
The Road to Wellville 32
Roadwalkers 33
Robb, Candace 52
Robbie, Joe 592
Robbins, Jerome 86, 89
Robbins, John B. 460
Robbins, Kelly 587
Robbins, Tim 31, 33–34, 59
Robert Crews 33
Roberts, Julia 28, 29, 33, 36, 39
Roberts, Marcus 71
Roberts, Richard J. 459
Roberts, William 425
Robertson, Pat 68, 294, 356, 469–470, 472, 477, 485, 497
Robin Hood: Prince of Thieves 29
Robinson, David 563, 592
Robinson, Eddie 566
Robinson, Jackie 591
Robinson, Mary Lou 417
Robinson, Patrick 230
Robinson, Phil Alden 31
Robinson, Stephen K. 545
Roche, John Pearson 195
Roche, Kevin 231
Rochester, New York
    Xerox headquarters 129
The Rock 35
Rock and Roll Hall of Fame and Museum, Cleveland 35, 202, 219, 228
Rockefeller, John D., Sr. 127
Rockefeller University 457
"Rocky Mountain High" 87
Rodbell, Martin 459
Roddenberry, Gene 425, 510
Roden, Ben 495
Roden, George 295
Roden Crater, Arizona 82
Rodeo (ballet) 87
Rodgers, Richard 75
Rodman, Dennis 563
Rodriguez, Narciso 229–230
Roe v. Wade (1973) 277, 319, 326, 331, 484
Roffe-Steinrotter, Diann 573
Rogan, James E. 306
Roger Engermann & Associates Inc. 108
Rogers, Ginger 89
Rogers, Kenny 552
Rogers, Paul G. 461
Rogers, Roswell B. 425
Rogers, Roy 425
Rohde, David 421
Rohrer, Heinrich 536

Rohypnol 447
Rolle, Esther 425
The Rolling Stone Illustrated History of Rock & Roll 71
Rollins, Sonny 69
Roll-ups 132
Roman Catholic Church 68, 160, 470, 472, 474, 478
    accusation of blasphemy in art 44
    issues statement on Jews 469
    policies on homosexuals 480
    policies on women 477
Roman Catholic Commission for Religious Relations with the Jews 472
Roman Holiday 87
Romer v. Evans (1996) 291
Romero, Cesar 425
Romney, George Wilcken 280
Romo, Leon "Red" 592
Romper Room 423
Ronald W. Rosenberger v. Rector and Visitors of the University of Virginia (1994) 290, 471
Rookie of the Year 558
Room Temperature 28
Roosevelt, Franklin Delano 76, 220, 278
Roosevelt High School, Dallas, Tex. 155
Roosevelt Memorial 205, 220
Roosevelt University 345
Roots: The Saga of an American Family 87
Roper, William L. 442
Rosa, Emily 440
Rose, Frank Anthony 195
Rose Bowl 175, 327, 409, 565, 578, 591
Rose Law Firm 258
Roseanne 382
Rosen, Hilary 184
Rosenbaum, Ron 81
Rosenberg, Meredith 128
Rosenberg, Paul 45
Rosie O'Donnell Show 403
Roslin Institute 519–520
Ross, Bob 425
Ross, Gary 38
Ross, Steven J. 146
Ross, Virgil 425
Rossellini, Isabella 30
Roth, Christian Francis 230
Roth, Philip 28, 30, 32, 34, 37–38, 55, 83
Rouse, Christopher 83
Rouse, James W. 375
Rouse, Jeff 573

Roventini, Johnny 375
Rowan, Henry M. 153
Rowan, Roy 425
Rowan and Martin's Laugh-In 425
Rowan College of New Jersey 153
Rowland, F. Sherwood 547
Rowley, Cynthia 230
Rowley, Janet D. 460
Rowling, J.K. 345
Roxanne Slade 38
Roxette 28
The Roy Rogers and Dale Evans Show 425
The Roy Rogers Show 425
Royal Gold Medal 227
Royko, Mike 425
Rozelle, Pete 592
Rozsa, Miklos 89
RU-486 432, 434, 444
Ruben, Joseph 29
Ruby Ridge, Idaho 295, 491, 495
Rudin, Scott 84
Rudolph, Paul Marvin 233
Rudolph, Wilma 592
Rudolph the Red-Nosed Reindeer 422
Rue, Caroline 67
Ruff, Charles F. C. 306–307
Ruff Ryders 69
Ruga, Wayne 231
Rukeyser, Louis 141
Rum Punch 31
"Rump Shaker" 32
Run DMC 68
The Runaway Jury 35, 78
Runaway Soul 30
Runnels, Pete 592
Rupp Trophy 562
Rush, Geoffrey 35, 37, 85
Rush, Norman 30
Rusk, Dean 280
Russell, Charles 33
Russell, David O. 58
Russell, Donald 331
Russell, Kurt 29, 32, 35
Russell, Laura 116
Russia 246, 572, 575
    computer crime 110
    International Space Station 538
    Y2K problems 527
Russian Academy of Science 360
Russo, Rene 31–32, 34–35
Rutgers University 565
Rutgers University Law School 329
Ruth, Babe 556, 561, 584
Ruthless 72
Rwanda 242, 246, 421
Ryan, Arthur F. 109
Ryan, Meg 32, 35, 37–38, 58

Ryan, Nolan 550
Ryan, Richard M. 349
Ryan White AIDS Charity Foundation 434
Ryder, Winona 30, 39, 387
Ryder Cup 556, 570, 583–584
RZA 69
Sabatini, Gabriela 585
Sabato, Antonio, Jr. 227
Sabbath's Theater 34
Sabin, Albert Bruce 464
Sabrina 87
Sachar, Abram Leon 195
Sacramento Bee 420
Sacred Assembly of Men 486
Sacred Clowns 32
Sagan, Carl 189, 547
Sailor Song 31
St. Aubin, Helen 592
St. Florian, Frederick 220
St. John's University 591
St. John's Wort 440
St. Jude's Children's Hospital 425
Saint Laurent, Yves 207
St. Louis Art Museum 30
St. Louis Blues 86
St. Louis Browns 590
St. Louis Cardinals 554, 590–592
St. Louis Rams 553, 566
St. Louis Symphony 64
St. Mark's United Methodist Church, Sacramento 481
St. Mary's Seminary, Baltimore 491
Saint Maybe 30, 51
St. Patrick's Day Parade, New York 334
St. Patrick's Day Parade, South Boston 336
St. Paul's Episcopal Parish, Richmond 498
St. Petersburg Times 411, 421
Saito, Ryeoi 44
Saks Fifth Avenue 210
Salaam, Rashaan 587
Salameh, Mohammed 298
Saldivar, Yolanda 389
Salhany, Lucie 419
Salisbury, Harrison 425
Salk, Jonas 464, 547
Sally of the Star 426
Salomon Brothers 96
Salomon Smith Barney 137
Salonga, Lea 84
Salt Lake City 575
Salt Lake City International Airport 216
Salthouse, Chris 158
Salthouse, Courtney 158

Samaranch, Juan Antonio 576
Same-sex marriage 291, 357, 472, 480–481, 499
Sampras, Pete 559, 576, 584–85, 587
Samson and Delilah 88
Samuelson, Robert J. 107
San Angelo, Texas 580
San Antonio Iguanas 570
San Antonio Spurs 563, 588
San Diego Chargers 566, 587, 590
San Diego County Gun Rights Committee v. Janet Reno (1996) 304
San Diego Padres 553, 555, 588
San Diego State University 159, 566
San Francisco earthquake 254
San Francisco 49ers 328, 551, 566–567, 584–585, 587
San Francisco Giants 554, 556, 592
San Francisco Museum of Modern Art 49, 202, 219
San Francisco Opera Orchestra 63
San Francisco State University 194, 278
San Jose Mercury News 419–420
San Jose Sharks 570
Sanchez, Eduardo 39, 63
Sander, Jil 209
Sanders, Barry 567, 585
Sanders, Deion 585
Sanders, Dori 28, 32, 51
Sanders, E. P. 500
Sanders, Summer 573
Sandler, Adam 38
Sandra Nichols Found Dead 35
Sanford, Charles, Jr. 105
Sanford, Terrance 195, 280
Sanford & Son 423, 425
Sanger Center, Cambridge, U.K. 518
Sankt Anna Kirche, Augsburg, Germany 478
Santa Barbara Symphony 64
Santa Claus 388
Santana 86
Santeria 469
Santiago, Esmeralda 55
Sapp, Warren 566
Sarah Conley 37
Sarah Lawrence College 150
Sarajevo 421
Sarandon, Susan 29, 34, 39, 58, 85
Sarazen, Gene 592
Sargent, Dick 425
Sarin 442, 540
Sarnoff, Robert W. 146
SAT. *See* Scholastic Aptitude Test
Satanism 68, 485
Satcher, David 446, 458
Saturday Evening Post 425

Saturday Night 411
Saturday Night Live 67, 86, 225, 419, 423–424
Saudi Arabia 236, 242, 247–248, 266, 490
Saunders, Elizabeth 352
Savage, William 36, 60
Save Me, Joe Louis 32
Saving Grace 34, 51
Saving Private Ryan 38, 41, 57, 85, 479
Savio, Mario 195
SBC Communications 95, 97
Scalia, Antonin 188, 276, 299, 303, 320
Scanning tunnel microscope (STM) 536
The Scavenger Hotline 231
Scent of a Woman 31, 85
Schaeffer, Robert 193
Schafer, Natalie 425
Scheck, Barry 330, 546
Scheiber, Anne 156
Scheie, Harold Glendon 464
Scheie Eye Institute 464
Schenkkan, Robert 83
Schepisi, Fred 32
Schering-Plough Corporation 433
Schettino, Pascuale 110
Schiele, Egon 45
Schiffer, Claudia 198, 214
Schindler, Oskar 57
Schindler's List 32, 57, 85, 470, 479
Schirn, Janet 231
Schlessinger, Laura C. 372, 384, 401
Schmalz, Jeffrey 425, 464
Schmemann, Serge 420
Schmidt, Benno C., Jr. 172
Schmitz, Jonathan 403
Schnabel, Julien 214
Schneerson, Menachem Mendel 502
Schneerson, Rachael 460
Schneider, Peter 73
Schnurr, Valeen 493
Scholastic Aptitude Test (SAT) 150, 155, 161–163, 165, 172–173, 193
Scholastic Assessment Test (SAT) 155, 173
Scholes, Myron S. 145
Schonberg, Alan 134
Schonberg, Claude-Michel 75
Schoo, David 335
Schoo, Sharon 335
School violence 183–184, 308, 350, 354
   Conyers, Ga. (1999) 385
   Jonesboro, Ark. (1998) 385
   Littleton, Col. (1999) 385, 401

Stern, Daniel 28, 30
Stern, Howard 384, 401
Stern, Robert A. M. 230
Stern College for Women 156
Steroids 310, 557
Stevens, Brooks 233
Stevens, Gary 587–588
Stevens, John Paul 485
Stevenson, McLean 425
Stewart, Donald M. 193
Stewart, James 89
Stewart, Martha 146, 341, 361, 372, 419
Stewart, Melvin 573
Stewart, Patrick 33
Stewart, Payne 556, 569, 586, 588, 592
Stewart, Rod 33
Stigmata 479
Stiller, Ben 35, 38
Sting 33, 66
Stinson, Burke 127
Stir of Echoes 479
Stock car racing 559
Stock market 106–108
Stockton, John 563
Stolpa, James 374
Stolpa, Jennifer 374
Stone, Matt 388
Stone, Nikki 573
Stone, Oliver 29, 33–34, 36, 39, 56, 58–59, 81, 183
Stone, Peter 76
Stone, Sharon 28, 30, 201
The Stone Diaries 83
Stoneham, Horace 592
Stones from the River 416
Stones Throw 69
Stonewall Inn Riot 336
Stopfel, Barry 471
The Storm 38
Storm on the Sea of Galilee 29
Störmer, Horst L. 546
Storylines America 51
Stotz, Carl E. 592
Stowe, Madeleine 31, 39
Stowers, Freddie 374
Strand, Mark 84
"Strangers in the Night" 89
Strategic Defense Initiative (SDI, or "Star Wars") 507
Strategos 122
Strategy Lawsuit Against Public Participation suits 300
Stratocaster guitar 224
Strawberry, Darryl 330
Strax, Philip 464
Streep, Meryl 30, 33–34, 37–39

Street, Picabo 554, 558–559, 573, 575
Streets of Laredo 32, 51
The Street Lawyer 38, 78
Street News 418
A Streetcar Named Desire 89
Streisand, Barbara 198
Streptococcus-A 435
Strike the Gold (race horse) 586
String Quartet No. 2, Musica Instrumentalis 65, 83
Stringmusic (Gould) 83
Strominger, Jack L. 460
Strong Capital Management, Inc. 133
Strug, Kerri 575
Strumpf, Linda P. 141
Stuart, Jill 210
Stuart, Marty 66
Stuart Little 39
Studebaker 233
Student Right-to-Know and Campus Security Act 151
Stulce, Mike 573
Sub Pop Records 66
Sudan 490, 494
Sudden Infant Death Syndrome (SIDS) 431
Sugar Bowl 550–551, 565
Sui, Anna 199, 202, 230
Suicide 151
Suicide, assisted 290–291
Suicide Machine 443
Sula 80
Sullivan, Andrew 380
Sullivan, Kevin Rodney 38
Sullivan, Louis W. 442, 445, 458
"Summer Girls" 40
Summer of Sam 40
Summer Research Opportunities Program for Minority Students 188
Summer X Games 555
Summitt, Pat 553, 580
Sun Microsystems 129, 524, 531
Sunbeam Corporation 433
SundayTimes (London) 417
Sunday Morning 424
"Sunny Came Home" 86
Sunset Boulevard 84
Sunshine in the Courtroom Act 390
Suntory International Corp. 84
Super Bowls 388, 554–555, 567, 583
Super Disc (SD) 534
Superbad.com (website) 49
Supernatural 86
Surface 30

Surgeon General. *See* United States—Office of the Surgeon General.
Surgical Research Laboratories, Children's Hospital of Boston 441
Survivors of the Shoah Visual History Foundation 57
Suspects 35
Sutherland, Donald 29, 32–33, 38
Sutherland, Kiefer 28, 30
Sutherland, Thomas M. 237
Sutton, Hal 570
SUVs. *See* Sport utility vehicles.
Suwa, Gen 546
Sveda, Michael 464
Swallow 66
Swami Vivekananda 469
Swan Boats at Four 34
Swank, Hilary 85
Swartz, Jeffery B. 130
Swayze, Patrick 28–29
Swearer, Howard Robert 195
Sweat, Keith 36
Sweden
    economy 120
    Internet use 124
    workers 367
Sweet Charity 87
The Sweet Hereafter 30
Swing Era 70
Switzer, Barry 567
Swoopes, Sheryl 409, 551, 558, 564, 585–586
Sylvan Learning Centers 163
Symphony (Ran) 65, 83
Synanon 463
Syracuse University 542, 565, 587
Syria 237, 247
Syron, Richard F. 110
T-House, Wilton, New York 229
T. Rowe Price Associates Inc. 140
Taback, Gene 362
Taco Bell 129
TAD 66
Tadesse, Sinedu 157
Tag Team 32
Tagliabue, Paul 557, 585
Tailhook scandal 352
Tai-Pan 86
Taiwan 120
Taj Mahal 198
Take Our Daughters to Work Day 336
Takihyo Corporation 226
The Tale Maker 33
The Tale of the Body Thief 31
Tales of the South Pacific 88
Taliban 422
Taliesin Architects 217

Women's National Basketball Association (WNBA) 409, 563, 583

Women's Ordination Conference 477

Women's Rights Project 329

Women's Sports and Fitness 385

Women's Sports Foundation 408
Hall of Fame 581

Women's Tennis Association (WTA) 577

Women's Wire 381

Women's World Cup 556, 558, 578, 583

Wonderbra 201

Woo, John 36

Wood, Evelyn 376

Wood, Kerry 555

Wood, Percy A. 412

Wooden, John 562, 581

Wooden Award 562, 579

Woodham, Luke 354

Woodhull, Nancy Jane 426

Woodrow Wilson International Center for Scholars 264

Woods, James 39

Woods, Tiger 553, 559, 568–569, 582, 588

Woodson, Charles 566, 587

Woodstock '94 34

Woodstock '99 40

Woodward, Louise 330, 390

Woosnam, Ian 586

Workforce 99, 100, 134–136
aging of 116

Working Mother 581

Working-class consciousness 103

Work-Out 113, 144

Workplace discrimination 319

World AIDS Day 454

World Boxing Council (WBC) 564

World Boxing Federation (WBF) 564

World Boxing Organization (WBO) 583

World Center for Personal Computation and Human Development 544

World Championship Wrestling 558

World Conference of the Reorganized Church of Jesus Christ of Latter-Day Saints 472

World Council of Churches' Faith and Order Commission 502

World Cup 409, 552, 575

The World Doesn't End 83

World Economic Forum 120–121

World Financial Center, New York City 228

World Friendship Tour 494

World Health Organization (WHO) 430, 463

World Intellectual Property Organization (WIPO) 125

A World Lost 35

World News Tonight 418

World Quarterpipe Championships 571

World Series 552, 555, 559, 561, 580

World Trade Center bombing (1993) 237–238, 285, 288, 298, 385, 421

World Trade Organization (WTO) 120–121

World War II 44, 56–57, 70, 87, 244, 251, 257, 262, 264, 326, 464, 479, 558, 572

World War II Memorial 220

World Wide Web 99, 122, 182, 509, 513, 521, 523, 541

World Wrestling Federation 146, 556, 558

World's Deadliest Swarms 397

World's Deadliest Volcanoes 397

The World's Most Dangerous Animals 397–398

World's Scariest Police Shootouts 397–398

World's Wildest Police Videos 398

Worldcom Inc. 96, 339

Worm.Explore.Zip computer virus 512

Wreckz N Effect 32

Wrestling, professional 564

Wright, Charles 83

Wright, Frank Lloyd 203, 217

Wright, James 163

Wright, Robert 415

Wright, Susan Webber 258, 287, 325

WTVF-TV 416

Wu, Gordon Y.S. 158

Wu Tang Clan 69

Wuerffel, Danny 587

Wurst, Andrew 354

Wu-Wear 212

WVOL 416

WWJD (What Would Jesus Do) 492

Wyclef Jean 66

Wyeth, Andrew 29

Wyeth-Ayerst 432, 444

Wynder, Ernst 464

Wynette, Tammy 89

Wynn, Steve 44

Wynne, Benjamin 161, 445

Wynwood Press 78

The X-Files 381

X-cutioners 69

X Games 571

X-ray 442, 449

Xerox Corporation 129, 532

Y2K 358, 507, 526

Yahoo! Inc. 122

Yale University 47, 127, 151, 160, 265, 337, 412, 544

Yamaguchi, Kristi 559, 572, 573

Yamamoto, Yohji 198

Yankee Group 128

Yankelovich, Daniel 361

Yarborough, Ralph Webster 280

Yardeni, Edward 108

Year of the Woman 408

Yeltsin, Boris 507, 543

Yeshiva University 156

Yo 37

Yoder, Alma Kitchell 426

Yoga 440

Yogi, Maharishi Mahesh 370

Yokich, Stephen P. 146

York, Dick 425, 426

Yosemite Sam 423

"You Are Not Alone" 35

"You Make Me Wanna" 37

"You Oughta Know" 68

"You're Makin Me High/Let It Flow" 36

"You're Still The One" 38

You've Got Mail 38

Young America 553

Young, Andrew 478

Young, Coleman Alexander 280

Young, George 568

Young, Judith C. 345

Young, Kevin 573

Young, Robert 426

Young, Steve 567, 585

Young Frankenstein 88

The Young Lions 88

The Young Man from Atlanta 83

Young Men's Christian Association (YMCA) 558

Young Versace 214

Youngstown State University 566

Yount, Robin 551

Yousef, Ramzi Ahmed 238, 298

Youth Risk Behavior Survey 151

Yugoslavia 242, 246, 269, 574

Yun-Fat, Chow 39

Zaillian, Steven 37

Zaire 494

Zamani, Payam 129

Zamecnik, Paul C. 461

Zangara, Giuseppe 76